THE HUSTONS

THE
HUSTONS

LAWRENCE GROBEL

CHARLES SCRIBNER'S SONS
NEW YORK

Charles Scribner's Sons
Macmillan Publishing Company
866 Third Avenue, New York, NY 10022
Collier Macmillan Canada, Inc.

Library of Congress Cataloging-in-Publication Data

Grobel, Lawrence.
    The Hustons / Lawrence Grobel.
        p.   cm.
    Bibliography: p.
    Includes index.
    ISBN 0-684-19019-2
    1. Huston John, 1906–87.   2. Motion picture actors and
actresses—United States—Biography.   I. Title.
PN1998.3.H59G76   1989   89-10076   CIP
791.43'0233'092—dc19   [B]

Macmillan books are available at special discounts for bulk purchases
for sales promotions, premiums, fund-raising, or educational use.
For details, contact:

    Special Sales Director
    Macmillan Publishing Company
    866 Third Avenue
    New York, NY 10022

10 9 8 7 6 5 4 3 2 1

Design by Glenn M. Edelstein

Printed in the United States of America

for my mother and father

CONTENTS

PART SIX

PART SEVEN

PART EIGHT

PART NINE

". . . to knock around a bit . . . to see
foreign places, new faces, win fame . . ."

> —John Gore,
> John Huston's grandfather

"Oh, shut up!"

> —Adelia Gore,
> his wife

INTRODUCTION

I FIRST MET JOHN HUSTON ON MAY 2, 1984. HE WAS SITTING at a round table in a corner of his uncomplicated living room, listening to a Mexican worker telling him that if he didn't have some beams installed soon, his primitive concrete house could collapse at any time. His secretary had already warned me that because the rains had not come, there was no water out at Las Caletas, and she couldn't understand why Huston was staying there rather than in Puerto Vallarta, where he maintained a more civilized residence. To flush his toilets out there, she told me, he needed two buckets of water. To bathe, he had to swim in the sea. To communicate with her or anyone else on the mainland, he had to use his shortwave radio, which, like his plumbing, was on the blink. If the generator went or a sudden storm hit, he'd be stranded without electricity, water, or a means to communicate.

He might have been without water, but at least he had a washing machine. I knew that because I traveled in the open boat over the choppy waves with the appliance sliding from side to side in front of me. I must admit to having experienced a bit of panic at the time, when I realized the machine hadn't been secured in any fashion. In fact, I broke the ice with Huston by describing how I held on to the washing machine until my hands were numb with pain to keep it from falling back and crushing me. He listened with interest but didn't crack a smile—and I wondered, much later, after I knew more about him, if I'd been set up as a victim of one of his practical jokes.

I had flown down to Puerto Vallarta to interview the great man for *Playboy*. I knew he lived in this place he leased from the Indians called Las Caletas, but he had also lived in an Irish castle called St. Clerans, so I figured it couldn't be too bad. I just wasn't prepared for that harrowing half-hour boat ride. After telling the worker to go ahead and put up whatever beams he thought necessary to keep the roof from falling onto his head, Huston motioned me to sit down to begin our talk.

Over the next five days I'd repeat this scenario—taking the *panga* over from the Boca de Tomatlán—a fifteen-minute drive south of Puerto Vallarta, below Mismaloya Beach—and then spending a few hours interviewing Huston, in between his work with Janet Roach on the script of *Prizzi's Honor.* She was stuck on a hill in a house above Huston's, where she slaved in splendid isolation, uninterrupted by the petty annoyances writers usually suffer, like ringing phones or nearby taverns to sulk away unprofitable days.

After our third session John invited me to join him and Janet for lunch. Our conversation turned to why Ernest Hemingway seemed to be out of favor among readers. John said that it was because Hemingway wrote of courage and that wasn't in right now. When he asked Janet what she thought, she said, "I believe in gender when I read. I don't understand all that macho courage nonsense." John looked almost hurt. "That's why Hemingway's out of favor," he said, "because you don't believe in courage."

Huston wasn't on oxygen full-time then. He coughed a lot—but he was doing that for more than twenty years. His arms were scarecrow-thin, and he probably didn't weigh more than 140 pounds, but his face was magnificent: a monument of crags and pouches that indicated hard living and a slew of experience. His voice was as intoxicating as in his movies; in *The Bible* he mouthed an impressive Noah and a pretty fair God. When John Huston spoke, in that deep mellifluous grumble, you listened with abiding respect. It didn't matter if he was intoning about the snafu (situation normal, all fucked up), tarfu (things are really fucked up), or fubar (fucked up beyond any recognition) conditions at Las Caletas, or about the reason Humphrey Bogart may not have been as impressive in person as he was on the screen—whatever he had to say commanded your attention.

On my last day with him that May five years ago, he asked me what I was going to do with myself after I completed our interview. I mentioned the first draft of a novel I'd been working on. "You're writing a novel?" he asked, alert and curious. "You must send it to me immediately."

I thought he was kidding, but he wasn't. He insisted until I promised to send it. What could he possibly want with it, I wondered. He had just completed filming Malcolm Lowry's *Under the Volcano* and was knee-deep into Richard Condon's *Prizzi's Honor.*

Polite, I reasoned. He was being polite. So I sent the manuscript and tried to forget about it. Less than a month later I received a letter from him. It was full of praise, with only some slight suggestions to tone down a few scenes having to do with the rank behavior of a father toward his children. Then three weeks later he called to add one additional criticism. "In your novel," he said, and I could swear it really was the voice of Reason and Wisdom speaking, "you have a character who shakes his head yes. I think you do it twice. But you don't shake your head yes, Larry. You *nod*."

That was all he wanted to tell me, just that one detail. He hung up and I stared into the phone and first shook, then nodded my head. It told me more about him than anything he had said to me up to that time.

Two years later, when I was asked by Scribners if I would like to write a book about the Huston family, I was quick to say yes. But only if John agreed. We had maintained a correspondence and I had seen him a few times since our interview, but this would give me the opportunity to spend a lot more time with one of the more fascinating figures of the twentieth century. I wrote John a note and he wrote back to come see him the next time he was in Los Angeles. When we met he said he wanted me to think very hard about taking on such a project. "I've read your novel and your script" (yes, one of those, too), he said, "and this would be a completely different direction for you." He suggested that I meet with Anjelica, who had just won her Oscar for *Prizzi's Honor*, and with his son Tony, who was coming from England to work with him on the script for *The Dead*. "See if you like them," he said. He called Anjelica and two days later I was sitting at a table at Hymie's restaurant on Pico Boulevard, talking with her about writing a book that would undoubtedly be uncomfortable for her.

"Every family has a lot of twists and turns," she said, "and in my family there are probably more than in others and I'm not sure I'd like to see all the layers peeled." I told her I understood, but also that I knew that it would be my job to unpeel as many of those layers as I could and if she didn't want me to begin that process all she had to do was say so. She thought a moment and then said that since her father had already agreed she would also cooperate. It would be interesting, she felt, to learn more about her grandfather, Walter, who died before she was born. She told me how she once was in a remote area of Colorado where she recognized the name of a saloon—it was one in which Walter had once appeared as a vaudevillian—and she tried to imagine what a Gypsy-like existence it must have been for him.

Then I met Tony, who started to tell me things I wasn't expecting to hear, at least not in an introductory conversation. It was obvious that being John's first son had been a heavy burden on Tony and he was almost eager to relieve himself of what he'd been carrying with him all these years. I knew after that meeting that I'd be doing this book.

When I told John of my decision, he said he would cooperate in any way he could. All I had to do was tell him when I wanted to see him and he'd make himself available. He wanted nothing in return except for me to write the best book I could. He didn't want to see the manuscript when it was done and didn't think any member of his family should either.

I asked him for suggestions of people I should see, for his mother's writings, for leads into uncovering his parents' lives. He gave me three worn, leather-bound Smythson address books—one for Ireland and England, one for France, and one for the United States and Mexico—and instructed his secretary in Puerto Vallarta to send up his mother's papers and whatever boxes of photographs he still had that weren't already donated to the Academy of Motion Picture Arts and Sciences Library. He also gave me his correspondence and files since 1980 (the previous years were at the library) and sat for over a hundred hours of questions I put to him over the next sixteen months.

Always he was generous with his time when time was so precious to him. I'd see him in different borrowed homes in Malibu, Beverly Hills, West Hollywood, and his companion Maricela's small house on Spaulding Avenue, just a few miles from my own canyon house in the Hollywood Hills, where he once came to visit and laughed when my then three-year-old daughter put a string under her nose to mimic the plastic tubing that connected to the portable oxygen tank that enabled him to breathe without feeling as if he were choking. And I'd see him, more often than either of us liked, at Cedars-Sinai Hospital, where he'd talk to me between, and sometimes during, breathing treatments. One time I spoke to him on the phone and he told me he had had a bad night. "I was coughing blood," he said. "It's a damn nuisance." But no matter how poorly he might have felt, his mind was always clear and his memory sharp. Only once do I remember his health becoming so bad that we had to stop talking. He went into a spasm of coughing that lasted many minutes, and finally he said he couldn't go on. I stayed with him for a while anyway and felt that somehow we were forming a bond between us.

It was a bond of trust. He trusted that I would tell his family's story as honestly as I could, without glossing over the sensitive parts. I believed that after a television interviewer asked him off-camera, while I was there, what he had thought of the *Playboy* interview I had done with him. John had never said anything to me about it, but when he answered, "That's the reason Larry's here," I understood. John knew that a large part of his family's story had never been told and he himself had always shied away from discussing his private life. He wasn't about to turn our sessions into a confessional, but whenever I came to him with items about the more personal events in his life or his parents' lives, he didn't make any attempts to conceal them. Whenever I discovered a black hole, he would confide as truthfully as he could about it—be it his smuggling of pre-Columbian art in Mexico, his repulsive feelings toward Montgomery Clift, or his inability to love or stay with one woman at a time. When he knew I was seeing someone who didn't much care for him, he never tried to stop me or alter my thinking. And when people called him to ask him what they should tell me, he told them to tell the truth and not hold anything back. He even wrote a letter that enabled me to obtain interviews with people who usually don't talk to writers.

The only time John ever expressed concern over one of my interviews was right after I saw Nancy Reagan, when she was still the First Lady and her husband was the President. He called me that evening and asked if I'd talked about anything political with her. No, I said, mostly we talked about Walter . . . and about John's roguish ways. "Good, I didn't want you to talk politics," he said. Then I asked him what Mrs. Reagan had asked me to ask him: Did he think "Ronnie" was a better president than he expected him to be? And John answered as only he could. "Worse," he said. "Much worse."

My interviews continued, as did my visits with John on the set of *The Dead* and afterward, in the editing room. Once after sharply disagreeing with a certain cut his editor, Roberto Silvi, had made, he relieved the tension in the room by talking about the Sugar Ray Leonard/Marvin Hagler fight that Leonard had won two days before. Both John and Roberto had bet on Sugar Ray and Huston compared the beautiful way Leonard had fought with some other fighters he had seen. "Kid Chocolate, whom nobody here probably remembers," he said, "Sugar Ray Robinson, and Muhammad Ali. These fighters actually did float like a butterfly and sting like a bee. Beautiful fighters." Then Huston sighed before signaling Silvi to put up the next scene and said, "I would give a few thousand dollars to be transported back to the Harry Grebs/Gene Tunney fight."

Getting Huston to talk about the craft of moviemaking was often difficult—mainly because he believed that what he did was up there on the screen. But there were times when he would describe something like his use of close-ups to dramatize a scene when I found myself being pulled into his word frame, leaning closer to him as he set about explaining why he never liked to back out to a medium or long shot once he had brought the cameras in close on his actors' faces. "When you use the big head, it's to show something important," he explained. "If you pull back, everything becomes less important. Let's say I shoot you as you are in this kind of conversation with me. Now, you discover in what I'm telling you that I'm saying something false and you lean a bit closer and try to look into what's going on in my head. There's an importance there, an undercurrent in the scene taking place. I'll bring the camera in at this moment to you, when your mind and your suspicions become active. If I leave the close-up and come back to the shot I started with, it means that you no longer have any suspicions. But if the scene remains tense, then I remain in. And when I come around to shooting me, I'll make it this way, too. The moment I see you're suspicious, I become cautious. So we go into close-ups of me, unless I want to shoot it just from your point of view. Once you have tension, you don't want to leave it, because if you go back to shooting medium shots you're saying this is less important than what went on a minute ago. There are exceptions to this, of course, but generally I like to stay in there for what *is* interesting."

Even in our conversations, Huston managed to create a sense of drama between us, an occasional subtle tension that kept me on my toes and him from becoming bored. "If I'm threatened with boredom," he told me, "why I'll run like a hare."

Like Dick Diver in F. Scott Fitzgerald's *Tender Is the Night*, John was a disciplined, controlled man who had a layer of hardness about him, but also had the kind of charm that made you feel you were the center of his attention when you talked with him. He had a rare ability to focus on what you were saying, to actually listen, and when he spoke, as Fitzgerald described Diver, "his voice, with some faint Irish melody running through it, wooed the world."

I remember being with him at Maricela's house while she was having some renovations done and John was supervising the placing of bookshelves and the stripping of paint from the walls and floors. John would look at all the work being done and mutter, "It's been more trouble redoing this little house than it was doing St. Clerans." Then he would scratch the Rottweiler, Diego, under his mouth, making him growl angrily in what John swore was appreciation.

As he picked up a book about Africa, he said, "Look at the asses on these young Nubian girls. If I ever marry again, I'd like to marry one of them."

His smile lit the room and he enjoyed sharing a joke, a sports story, a comment about women or art or commerce. Sometimes he would call me to see if I knew the name of a 1930s labor leader, or the French expressionist painter of *Three Judges*, or the author of the 1912 Irish fantasy novel, *The Crock of Gold*, which he wanted his son Danny to read. The leader was David Dubinsky, the painter Georges Rouault, the novelist James Stephens. I didn't always know the answers, but I would always find out—either by research or from John, who would bring it up at a later date. One had the feeling that there was little John didn't know something about, and he always seemed eager to learn more. Life was an ongoing process, it didn't stop when the body began to crumble. There was always something new to discover, even if it had to come from pictures in books.

There was a bigness about John. He was a teacher for those who appreciated direction and he was a student as well. His favorite modern American painter was Mark Rothko, the directors he was most impressed with were D. W. Griffith, Charlie Chaplin, Akira Kurosawa, and Ingmar Bergman. The most important book of his time was Joyce's *Ulysses*, and after that he held in high regard the plays of Eugene O'Neill, Theodore Dreiser's *An American Tragedy* and *Sister Carrie*, the novels of Honoré de Balzac and Gustave Flaubert, the short stories of Guy de Maupassant and a few of Hemingway's, Tolstoy's *War and Peace*, Henri Troyat's biography of Tolstoy, most of Rudyard Kipling, Plato's *Dialogues*, François Villon's poetry, and the works of Rabelais, Melville, Dickens, and Mark Twain.

Once when we were driving somewhere I began to ask him about the cynicism of Lowry's *Under the Volcano*, and he said if I wanted to read a really cynical story I should pick up Mark Twain's *The Mysterious Stranger*. "Having read it you will say, 'Let them send off the fucking bomb, it doesn't matter.' " He laughed. "Twain was one of the direst men that America ever produced. He had a dark view of humanity, took a very dim view of human behavior." Then he said he could enjoy rereading it, so I stopped at a bookstore and bought two copies. He looked at the book as if it was a Cuban cigar or a rare vintage wine.

As I traveled throughout the United States, Mexico, and Europe interviewing people who knew John during different times of his life, the one thing that stood out was how everyone, without exception, was affected by him. They told me of his great charm, of his magical way of weaving a story, of the jokes he liked to play and the gifts he often bestowed. Some of the stories were so funny they brought tears to one's eyes. Some were equally poignant. When John heard of a former employee in Ireland who took sick, he wrote to the doctor and asked for all bills to be sent to him. When someone needed a house or a car or an opinion, John was always there. On the passing of a sculptor he met only once, he sent the largest bouquet of flowers the florist could deliver to the artist's widow.

What I came to realize as I listened to people talk about John was how much of a father figure he had become. Not only to his children but to the producers, writers, cameramen, sound men, editors, actors, production managers, assistant directors, and all the technicians who worked with him on his films, and his many friends of all ages who glowed in his presence. For John had the gift of being able to bring out the best in those who knew him. We all wanted to make him proud. We were all John's children.

For being so kind and gracious, for giving me as much time as I needed, for opening up his life and allowing me to peek into the dark corners, for writing a letter for me to send to all those I wanted to interview for this book asking them to cooperate fully with me, and for correcting my grammar and probing my intellect, I owe John Huston more than I could have ever returned to him.

I am also indebted to Tony, Anjelica, Danny, and Allegra Huston for giving of their time and memories.

So, too, am I grateful for the many people who not only invited me into their homes, but who spoke so openly and in such depth. I would like to thank: Pablo Huston Albarran, Marge Albarran, Valeria Alberti, Angela Allen, Ernest Anderson, Lauren Bacall, Albert Band, Sue Barton, Dirk Bogarde, Margaret Booth, Jeff Bridges, Richard Brooks, John Bryson, Joan Buck, Jules Buck, Jack Clayton, Joe Cohn, Jeff Corey, Maka Czernichew, Royal Dano, Desmond Davies, J. P. Donleavy, Brad Dourif, Philip Dunne, Doc Erickson, Rudi Fehr, José Ferrer, Lola Finkelstein, Frances FitzGerald, Michael Fitzgerald, Suzanne Flon, Guy Gallo, Ava Gardner, Lee Gershwin, Lillian Gish, Elliott Gould, William Graf, Stephen Grimes, William Hamilton, Carter De Haven, Olivia de Havilland, Katharine Hepburn, Maricela Hernandez, Irene Heyman, Walter Hill, Kelly Hodell, Celeste Huston, Margot Huston, Henry Hyde, Betty Jaffe, Dorothy Jeakins, Stacy Keach, Adrienne Kennedy, Evelyn Keyes, Howard Koch, Lupita Kohner, Pancho Kohner, Harry Lewis, Doris Lilly, Robert Littman, Leni Lynn, Eloise Hardt MacNamara, Ben Maddow, Lesley Black Marple, Ruth Marton, Bill

Mauldin, Donal McCann, Peter Menegas, John Milius, Arthur Miller, Justin Miller, Walter Mirisch, Robert Mitchum, Eva Monley, Inge Morath, Jess Morgan, Robert Morley, Oswald Morris, Paul Newman, Alex North, Edna O'Brien, Emily Paley, Billy Pearson, Roman Polanski, Victoria Principal, Jeremy Railton, Janet Roach, Nancy Reagan, Gottfried Reinhardt, William Richert, Lillian Ross, Zoe Sallis, Arturo Sarabia, Richard Sarafian, Eleanor F. Schmidt, Budd Schulberg, Wieland Schulz-Keil, Anne Selepegno, Tom Shaw, Lorrie Sherwood, Roberto Silvi, Jeanie Sims, Dorothy Soma, Philip and Avril Soma, Lizzie Spender, Ray Stark, Elaine Steinbeck, Gary Sugarman, Marietta Tree, Claire Trevor, Kathleen Turner, Bayard Veiller, Eli Wallach, Dennis Washington, Dale Wasserman, Susan and John Weitz, John and Katy Weld, Katherine Wellesley, Mary Wickes, Meta Wilde, Jilda Smith Williams, Sir John Woolf, Talli Wyler, Susannah York, Max Youngstein, Stephanie Zimbalist. I would also like to remember those who talked with me and have since passed away: Truman Capote, John Houseman, Paul Kohner, and Josh Logan.

During the many hours of talking to these and other people, it soon became clear that memories weren't always the same, that events witnessed by three or more people were often seen in three or more ways. I don't believe that anyone I talked with deliberately falsified his or her accounts of things past. Everyone told the truth as he or she saw or remembered it. But as a Ghanaian sculptor named Vincent Kofi once told me, truth is like the color turquoise—it varies under different light. This, then, is the turquoise truth. If at times stories contradict each other, that is the nature of a book attempting to be as detailed and comprehensive as this. In reconstructing events that go back into the last century I have tried my best to be faithful and accurate to all involved in this intriguing family saga.

Among the people I would like to express a special thanks to for their help and support are Larry Leamer, whose suggestion led to my doing this book; Marcia Meldal-Johnsen, who so diligently transcribed many of the tapes; Lynn Lemoyne, who brought me a trunk full of Walter Huston's scrapbook's; Frank Martin, who gave me access to transcripts of some of the people he interviewed for the John Huston documentary he directed; Roddy McDowall, who loaned me tapes of many Walter Huston films that aren't easily available; Sam Gill and his co-workers at the Academy of Motion Picture Library for their generous support; Diane Keaton, for her keen eye; Midori Firestone, Lloyd Fischel, and Zachary Intrater, who read the manuscript in its rough form and offered encouraging words; Enrique Cortés, who offered a perceptive critique of the manuscript; Carolyn Blakemore, who found a book in my pages; my editor, Robert Stewart, for his care and his late-night calls from New York that lasted hours, which made me wonder when he ever slept; and my agent, Peter Matson, who was always encouraging.

Finally, I would like to thank my two daughters, Maya and Hana, who, for a piece of candy or a stick of gum, allowed me to work in peace; and my wife, Hiromi, who has always been an inspiration, and without whom I could never have written this book.

PART ONE

1

"JUST GIVE 'EM HELL!"

THE SUN WARMED THE MEXICAN COAST ON CHRISTMAS day in 1986, but John Huston couldn't feel it. The chill in his bones began the night before and he knew, but would never admit, that his doctors had been right when they advised him not to make the trip. No one thought he should go—his children, his friends, those who were involved with his next picture all knew it was a bad idea to make such a journey in his condition.

It was madness to be so far away from Cedars-Sinai Hospital and the IVs and antibiotics that had become commonplace in his life. But once Huston had made up his mind to see Mexico for possibly the last time, no one was going to talk him out of it. The man was eighty years old and had been suffering from what one of his doctors called "the worst case of emphysema I've ever seen" for more than twenty years. He had been given up for dead at least three times. His lung had collapsed seventeen years before, in 1969, just as he was to begin *The Kremlin Letter* in Finland. Over the years he had suffered a gut operation, various bouts of pneumonia, gout, eye problems, and surgery for an aneurism—the same ailment that caused his father's death in 1950. Huston knew the risks involved in leaving Los Angeles, but he also

1

remembered that his father died at the Beverly Hills Hotel before the ambulance arrived. If John was going to die, then at least let it be the way he had lived his life: on his own terms. And even if his doctor had warned him about how severe his sickness was, the doctor had also told him that he'd probably live forever—an idea everybody who knew John Huston was beginning to believe.

Even Maricela, his companion, whom Huston said he had grown to love more than any of his wives, wasn't happy about going back to her native country for only a short time. She would have preferred to settle in, to see her mother and her family, to get into a routine. But with "that stubborn bull" there were no routines.

She was fifty years his junior. With her close-cropped hair and strong, stout body she resembled a young Gertrude Stein as Diego Rivera might have painted her. When she wasn't referring to Huston as an old bull, she called him "Papa Bear." He called her "Baby." Like many of the women in Huston's life, Maricela Hernandez was Eliza Doolittle—the only good thing to come out of his fifth marriage, he sometimes joked. When Cici, wife number five, threw him out one time too many, it was Maricela, Cici's maid, who came to him. Cici, he would later say, was a "crocodile." But Maricela was an angel—an illegal alien, totally devoted to taking care of him. "To this day," Huston observed, "her green card is more important to her than a doctor's diploma." Huston's first son, Tony, had come to believe she was a saint. "She's the only reason Dad is alive today." Huston had bought a house for her in Puerto Vallarta, and they went there for a week before Christmas.

Zoe Sallis, the forty-seven-year-old bronze-hued, attractive mother of Huston's other son, Danny, flew in from London, as was her custom, to be with them during the holidays. Zoe had been born in India, educated in England, was devoted to a guru, dedicated to her son Danny, protective of John, and not very fond of Maricela. Although they had never married, Huston had supported her most of her adult life.

John Hankins, Huston's longtime friend, who lived in Ajijic, near Guadalajara, had driven five hours to Puerto Vallarta to see him. They got to know each other in Africa, when Huston was making *The African Queen*. Hankins was his pilot. "The bravest man I ever knew," Huston would say. They became great friends. Now they played backgammon and reminisced about old times.

*   *   *

Both Tony, thirty-six, and Danny, who was not yet twenty-five, arrived three days before Christmas. Tony was tall, lean, and preppy, with a hawkish face, a smug smile, and a distinctive manner of speaking. All the psychological traumas of being the first son and growing up in the shadow of a great man had penetrated his soul. Danny had a rugby player's body and an innocent, congenial face. He resembled his grandfather, Walter Huston, as a young man. Since he had grown up seeing his father only on holidays, he didn't carry his elder half-brother's burden and was, subsequently, a delight to his father. Tony had brought a pound of caviar and Danny a book on Henry Moore to give to John.

Anjelica, Huston's daughter, wasn't going to make it; she was in Aspen with Jack Nicholson, but Allegra, Tony and Anjelica's half-sister, had flown in from London to be with her "father." Allegra, whose IQ was touted like a thoroughbred's lineage, was not Huston's by blood, but he considered her his daughter. When her mother, John's fourth wife, Ricki, died in a car accident in 1969, Allegra was only four. Although Ricki was still legally married to John, they had separated long before. Allegra's real father, an English Lord and travel writer named John Julius Norwich, never publicly acknowledged the child as his, and it was Huston who said he'd take her and give her his name. Now she was working for a publishing company. Her Christmas gift for John was a silver pen.

Once Huston decided to go to Mexico for two weeks at Christmas various friends planned to come down and visit him in Puerto Vallarta and at Las Caletas, the primitive home he had carved out of the jungle along the coast, which could only be reached by boat. The land belonged to the Chacala Indians and Huston had rented it for ten years, figuring they would be his last. But he survived the lease and had paid $10,000 for another year. It was a far cry from his huge Georgian manor in Galway, which he had filled with the art treasures he had collected over his life. There, dinners were formal affairs, guests were often celebrated, Tony had learned to raise falcons, Anjelica put on dog and pony shows, Huston became co-master of the Galway Blazers and rode to the hounds. At Las Caletas, Huston had decided to shed the material life. His only concessions to the outside world were a shortwave radio and a satellite dish, which brought him the sports he loved to watch. Despite the chill Huston felt the night before, he still insisted on taking the open boat there.

It was not an easy trip. Attached to plastic tubing that ran from his nose to an oxygen tank, he had limited mobility. From the car, a huge, heavy chair was brought for him to sit in and long poles were placed underneath to balance it. Huston, like an Ashanti chief in his palanquin, was lifted and gently placed on board the small boat. The ride over was choppy and took almost three-quarters of an hour. By the time they arrived he was looking gray, and Tony and Maricela were worried that they had made a mistake in letting him talk them into this trip. Tony was upset that his father wasn't showing appreciation at having his family with him. Zoe was upset with Tony's attitude, and Danny sided with his mother. Allegra never could bear Tony's arrogant behavior. And Maricela could do without them all; she was the one who would have to nurse John. And she was afraid that his pallor meant Tony better start calling Dr. Rea Schneider in Los Angeles.

When his other doctor, forty-five-year-old cardiologist Gary Sugarman, heard that Huston was in Mexico, he couldn't believe it. "Oh, shit. I specifically told that bastard he was not supposed to go. A cold or cough today, it's pneumonia in two days, and that's the easiest way to lose him."

The ordeal of caring for Huston was a heavy burden for Dr. Sugarman, who considered the grand old master not only "bigger than life," but also "the most singular, most interesting man I've ever met. Keeping him alive is a tremendous responsibility. I know he adores that place in Mexico, but he's got to give it up."

But try telling that to Huston, who had put so many things in his past—America, his U.S. citizenship, Ireland, fox hunting, big-game hunting, smoking, boxing, whoring, five wives, countless homes—all he had left was Mexico. "It's funny to think of my octogenarian father as being homeless," Anjelica observed, "but he is." No, he wasn't ready to put Mexico in his past.

Mexico was where, as a teenager, Huston first became fascinated by the "quest for adventure," where he saw generals driving long Pierce-Arrows, as their chauffeurs uncorked champagne bottles in the backseat, and theater ushers were shot dead for presenting an unacceptable seat to a self-important official. In the forties and fifties it was the place that brought out the pirate in him, as he explored jungle-covered ruins and smuggled out precious pre-Columbian art. And it was Mexico that was the site of some of his great film triumphs. It was where he directed his father in his only Oscar-winning performance in *The Treasure of the*

Sierra Madre, and brought home an Indian kid named Pablo to his unsuspecting third wife, Evelyn Keyes. Where he returned again in the sixties to sleepy Mismaloya Beach to make Night of the Iguana, bringing with him a cast of characters that had newspapers around the world sending correspondents to report the anticipated fireworks. And still again, in the eighties, to film Under the Volcano, Malcolm Lowry's classic study of drunkenness and despair in Cuernavaca.

Now he sat in his living room, with Tony and Maricela watching anxiously over each wheeze, with Zoe and Danny and Allegra hoping to get at least one swim in. Huston began to wonder whether it was worth making still another effort to ward off the inevitable. He'd been fighting for so many years—the chills, the colds, the fevers, the infections, the coughing and choking—perhaps it was time to live out his days in quiet, surrounded by his family. "I don't know," he said to his eldest son, his soulful eyes made deeper by the pouches below them, "whether I can face going back again. I don't know, sometimes, whether the battle is worth it."

For Tony, those were fighting words. He knew from experience that it was a dangerous sign when his dad stopped being grouchy. But Tony was also feeling something else. His father had come to Mexico to rest before he plunged into making The Dead. It wasn't a movie that could easily be taken over by another director. "The Dead," a short story written by James Joyce, was as delicate as a spider's web. Funds had been raised on Huston's name alone. It would probably be his last picture. With Huston directing, it could easily make back its low budget. But Tony's concern was what if his father was ready to forget about The Dead, what would happen to his chance? Tony Huston had written the screenplay for The Dead. It was his shot, at long last, to prove, not only to himself, but to his father as well, that he was capable of more than playing with falcons or casting a balanced rod.

At thirty-six, Tony's professional life was still waiting to get started. He had chances in the past: At twelve, his father cast him in The List of Adrian Messenger; at twenty, his father let him try his hand at rewriting The Last Run; at twenty-five, he attempted writing music for The Man Who Would Be King; at thirty, he was made a second assistant director, a gofer, on Wise Blood. Nothing had really worked. This time, with James Joyce to guide him and his father to direct, Tony felt he finally had a chance for an honestly earned credit. He needed his father to live long enough to let him have that chance.

On the shortwave to Dr. Schneider, Tony described his father's symptoms and she said he must be brought back to Cedars. Huston, who hadn't eaten for twenty-four hours, had finally consented to swallow some food when Tony burst in and said with as much conviction as he could muster, "Dad, we have to get you back." Huston put down his fork. Zoe, Danny, and Allegra were furious with Tony for not waiting until John had eaten, but Tony had Maricela on his side and just told them all to bugger off.

Danny almost came to blows with his half-brother. Zoe was beginning to sense a radical change in the family chemistry. Tony had always been put down by John, but John now was beginning to listen to him. Allied with Maricela, he could undermine everyone. Tony made arrangements for himself, John, and Maricela to catch a four P.M. flight from Puerto Vallarta to Los Angeles on December 26. Zoe, Danny, and Allegra would stay another day at Las Caletas.

Tony was pleased that he had taken charge. He was relieved to be away from the others, who weren't, really, he liked to think, the same kind of family as he was to his dad.

Still, it had been upsetting. "It was the first family brouhaha for a very long time," Tony said. "Zoe spent most of her time in Mexico telling everybody that they were hated by everybody else. . . . Telling Maricela that I detested her; telling me that Maricela hated me." Maricela, who was closest to John, had become the target because of a list of her alleged misdeeds that John Hankins had made and given to the family without John's knowledge. "It was ways that Maricela mistreated Dad," Danny recalled. "Like turning the generator off or saying it was broken and was sent to be fixed when in fact it had been sold. Or not giving him a breathing treatment when he wanted one. It was trivia like that and I thought this man was a little senile and thought he was seeing things that were not actually true." Nevertheless, the family met to discuss whether they should ignore it or mention it to John.

"Then Dad got ill," Danny continued, "and Tony blurted everything out to Maricela. Maricela blurted everything out to Dad, and it kind of got bigger than what it was supposed to have been."

Tony felt he had done nothing wrong, since he was siding with Maricela. "Actually," Tony said, "it's Allegra who looked down on Maricela, because she remembers her as Cici's maid. Allegra, in one sense, is very intelligent; in another sense, she's dumb. It's the dumbness of the supersmart. Allegra doesn't know that she hates Maricela, yet everything she does indicates it to somebody who can see. That's what it came down to: There was this tremendous jealousy of Maricela, who is one of the most remarkable people I've ever met. Nobody that I know has matured better than Maricela."

* * *

Five months earlier, in July, Tony had sat with his father in Burgess Meredith's Malibu home as Huston dissected his son's first draft screenplay of *The Dead*. It was a significant moment in Tony's life. "It was the first time that I've ever gotten on so well with Dad," Tony recalled. "And I learned something. Dad had the finest analytical mind I'd ever run in to. He was able to unravel something down to its basics. When he was criticizing my work, his mind was like a laser beam trying to get to the truth.

"But if you were not working with him on something, that laser frequently got turned on you. Particularly if you were his child. The very source of his writing ability could be extremely destructive in personal relationships. Because he could take one to bits."

The lesson Tony learned was a revelation: stay out of his father's way when there was no project to wedge between them. All those years of torment and abuse . . . if only Tony had known!

At that time, *The Dead* was only an idea without backing. Nevertheless, Huston had wanted to solve certain structural problems with the script before leaving for Europe to make a film of John Louis Carlino's *Haunted Summer*, about the summer Mary and Percy Bysshe Shelley spent in Italy with Lord Byron, when Mary Shelley conceived the idea for *Frankenstein*. Huston was excited about making the film. He had instructed the producer, Martin Poll, to hire his favorite art director and set designer, Stephen Grimes. He had discovered Grimes in 1954, when he was preparing *Moby Dick*. Over the next twenty-two years, Grimes was Huston's art director for fourteen pictures. They talked over details by phone between Italy and Malibu as Grimes got things ready for Huston's arrival in Rome in August.

Zoe and Danny were also awaiting Huston's arrival in London, where he had hoped to spend two weeks in final preparation for the film. Danny was especially excited because his father had asked him to assist him with the direction. But a week before he was to depart, Huston caught a chill, which turned into pneumonia. He was rushed to the intensive care unit at Cedars-Sinai—the ugliest, most depressing place in the world, as far as he was concerned—where they stuck needles into his bone-thin arms, intravenously fed him experimental antibiotics, and told him there was no way he could travel abroad to make a movie.

When Zoe and Danny heard that John was back in intensive care, they flew from London to be at his side. Tony was already there and so was Anjelica. "It was serious," Anjelica said, "but I'd seen him more critical than that. He was a terribly strong man, and his willpower was remarkable." His cardiologist instructed nurses to give Huston breath-ing treatments every hour all through the night, making sleep impossible.

The breathing treatments took twenty minutes each time and were vital to him, according to Dr. Sugarman, "because they improved the mechanical drainage and helped drain that junk out of there. Maricela literally churned him facedown on the bed and pounded on his back really hard to get all that junk out. It was a pain in the ass.

"With all the medication and breathing machines and treatments and oxygen, he was really put together with spit and glue," the doctor said. "He was a sick old man."

Still, when Huston was in intensive care and he hadn't had any sleep for two days and it required all of his strength just to sit up and suck on the oxygen hose, he never resisted, never said, as Sugarman put it, "Oh, fuck it, I can't do this anymore."

Huston fought his way out of intensive care that July, and Sugarman told him he could work, because not working was a waste. "We let him do whatever he wanted to do, except travel extensively and expose himself to the environment."

How little control Sugarman had over Huston's movements he soon discovered, but once Huston was out of intensive care, he recovered quickly. Within weeks he was living in the small house on Spaulding Avenue he had bought for Maricela so she'd have security in Los Angeles as well as Puerto Vallarta. The house was badly in need of remodeling and Huston began to supervise the changes there.

As his strength returned, old projects were revived and new ones considered. Wieland Schulz-Keil, a chain-smoking, balding, bearded man who had co-produced *Under the Volcano*, secured the rights to *The Dead* from the Joyce estate for $60,000, and was raising the $3.5 million it would take to make that film—though not in Ireland as Huston had hoped, but in Los Angeles. Huston and Tony were also revising another script, *Revenge*, based on Jim Harrison's novella, for producer Ray Stark. The family breathed a sigh of relief when he began to express interest in listening to new people, meeting other artists, or seeing an exhibit.

Photojournalist Peter Beard wanted him to add his voice to an ABC special about Beard's Africa. Oja Kodar, Orson Welles's last mistress, wanted Huston to consider putting the finishing touches on Welles's last epic, *The Other Side of the Wind*—a film about a decadent old director making a pornographic movie and starring . . . John Huston.

In October, Wieland Schulz-Keil made a call to Tom Shaw, who had been Huston's assistant director and production manager for nine films, beginning with *The Unforgiven* in 1959. The money for *The Dead* had been raised, the picture would begin in January, now it was up to Shaw to find a location.

Shaw, a pugnacious pit-bull of a man with the personality of a marine drill sergeant, had told Huston months before that since "the whole goddamn thing takes place in a house," *The Dead* could be shot anywhere. But at that time, Huston was loyal to his own Irishness, as well as to Joyce. "I don't want to ever make that movie unless it can be made in Ireland," he told Shaw.

But then he had no choice. Tommy found a warehouse in Valencia, two miles from the Magic Mountain Amusement Park, which had 18,000 square feet of floor space. Stephen Grimes, whom John had convinced to work on designing the set before *Haunted Summer* began, agreed that the warehouse could be transformed into a turn-of-the-century Dublin house and work began immediately.

During the first week of December, Grimes and his assistant, Dennis Washington, who was Huston's production designer for *Victory* and *Prizzi's Honor*, visited John at the house of a Beverly Hills businessman and art collector. They discussed the props they wanted to use, the lighting, and the cameraman, Fred Murphy. Huston wasn't familiar with him and Grimes had only talked with him over the phone.

"He sounded like an intelligent guy," Grimes said. "He asked the right questions." Then Grimes changed the subject.

"I must say, this Wieland Schulz-Keil is a cut above Martin Poll," he said of his new producer.

Huston told of Martin Poll's recent visit, while he was staying at Maricela's small house. "He thought it was beneath my dignity to be there. I love it. Said it to my agent, Paul Kohner, not to me. Oh, Christ."

"Poll's a pain in the ass," Grimes said.

"The point is," Huston joked, "he doesn't mean well."

Grimes walked over to a pre-Columbian stonework of a snake curled into itself. "Is this snake sucking itself off?" he asked in his soft, almost melancholy voice.

"It's an old practice," Huston said with a smile, "takes a while to learn."

Danny arrived as Grimes and Washington were leaving. John was on the phone with Oja Kodar. A newspaper had printed that Huston was going to complete Orson Welles's *The Other Side of the Wind*. Kodar was distraught. She had been secretly negotiating for years to get the negative of the film back from the Iranian producers who had it. Kodar's dysphoria was that if word of Huston's interest became known, the Iranians might hold out for more money, money Kodar didn't have. She wanted to know who had leaked Huston's involvement.

John denied it was anyone he knew. Then Danny made an admission that silenced the room. "I told a reporter about it, Dad. I didn't know it was a secret."

"Oh, Christ," Huston said. "You're going to have to learn about these things."

It was a delicate moment, but Huston used his snake-charmer's voice to soothe Kodar, saying there was no way he'd want any part of this to get out, especially since he had made no commitment. After he hung up, he looked at Danny, whose discomfort was obvious. It was a serious matter and he didn't want any "false air of conspiracy" about it. "Well," he said, "at least you owned up."

Tony then entered the room, bringing comic relief. He was wearing a sports coat with sleeves too short to cover his wrists.

"Who owned that jacket before you?" John asked, amused.

"I'm the original owner," Tony said defensively.

Huston's temporary secretary suggested a drink and John asked for a vodka and water. Tony wanted a 7-Up. "You're not having a proper drink?" Huston challenged. "Well, maybe I should have one, too, before I drink. One should always quench one's thirst *before* drinking. Then one should drink seriously."

As his life returned to some kind of grab-bag normalcy, Huston and Maricela began to take car trips the week before their trip to Mexico. They visited Knott's Berry Farm, where Maricela expected to fulfill her fantasy of swimming with dolphins. But when she put out her hand and the dolphins imitated her movement with jerks of their heads, she lost her nerve. "It's all right if you back down, isn't it, Pops?" she asked Huston.

Huston was the wrong person to ask about losing courage. He was a principled man who often judged others by their bravery under fire. But with Maricela he didn't force the issue. A younger John Huston would have insisted she make the plunge.

They drove down to the art museum in Laguna Beach to see a retrospective of Jan de Swart's sculpture. Excited by de Swart's remarkable craftsmanship, he and Maricela then drove to the Hollywood Hills to see a private showing of a Japanese fashion designer. He had to climb nineteen steps to get to the house—equivalent to a small mountain for

Huston, who took them slowly, stopped twice, sat once, lost his breath
. . . but made it. A sure sign, as far as he was concerned, that he was
ready to fly to Puerto Vallarta.

"It was quite nerve-racking," Zoe Sallis remembered, recalling the
Christmas night they all stayed up in Las Caletas trying to care for
John. "He didn't want to leave, but there was a sort of panic to get him
out."

"He had a bad night before he left Vallarta," Tony confirmed.
"Coming back in the boat from Caletas was scary."

They left John's jungle home before noon and by seven that evening
Huston was on the eighth floor of Cedars-Sinai in Los Angeles. He
didn't need intensive care.

"He was two days in hospital instead of two weeks—or a grimmer alternative," Tony said. "He soon became grumpy and that was a good sign."

Once out of the hospital, Huston took a room at the Bel Age Hotel.
Still concerned about John Hankins's allegations against Maricela, he
asked Danny for his opinion. "I just laid down all the facts in front of
him and Maricela," Danny said. "Maricela looked deeply hurt. When
she walked out of the room, Dad leaned forward and looked me in the
eye and said, 'Danny, do you think there could be any truth to this?' I
said, 'Of course not, it's crazy, absolutely not.' "

Satisfied that she was on his side after all, he instructed Maricela to
call Tommy Shaw and tell him that he wanted to see the set for *The
Dead* in Valencia.

When Shaw arrived at Huston's hotel room, he saw John sitting on
the edge of his bed. Shaw was struck by his old friend's outward show of
emotion and affection, which was unlike John. "He became more than
warm," Shaw said. But after they returned from the long drive to the
set, where Huston watched the carpenters and painters at work, Shaw
noticed how exhausted John seemed and wondered why he was going
ahead with the picture.

On the morning of January 5, 1987, Huston arrived with Maricela and
her sister, Jenny, at The Ranch House Inn to begin rehearsals for *The
Dead*. He wore a white, red, and black sweatshirt, white slacks and
socks, and brown leather moccasins. His days of Tauntz-designed tails,
Tattersall vests, and boots from Maxwell's had given way to whatever
clothing was the most comfortable.

There was a great deal of fluttering and bustling all around Huston, who sat calmly in his wheelchair in the center of the living room. They discussed what needed to be done during the week before shooting began; Shaw said that wardrobe was already fitting people and that he didn't know how long the hair would take. "The hair will take time," Huston said. "The hair was very elaborate in those days."

As they spoke, Anjelica walked through the sliding-glass-door entrance and greeted everyone in the room, leaning over to kiss her father. She wore a long gray wool skirt, a gold-and-black-patterned blouse, and a black wool zippered jacket with the word *witches* embroidered in black on the back. The bag she carried was a rainbow-colored cloth satchel. The Huston style had clearly been passed on to a new generation.

"I am not bemooned about Anjelica Huston only because she is among the most exotically beautiful women of our time," Richard Condon, author of the novel *Prizzi's Honor*, once commented, "but also because she is . . . endlessly entertaining, and wears clothes with the style that a work of art by Caravaggio wears paint."

With most of their father-daughter quarrels behind them, Anjelica was looking forward to working with Huston again on *The Dead*. She sat opposite her father and made inconsequential talk with Schulz-Keil, Shaw, and her brother Tony. Her face appeared to have been cast by a magician, the lines and angles changing her look from left to right and from light to shadow. Her distinctive features, which made her look either regal or common with a turn of her head, dazzled.

"Well," Huston said, not one for small talk when there was work to be done, "let's go."

Huston believed in the value of rehearsing, where he could hear the script come to life and actors could have an opportunity to "work things out." His genius as a director, it was often said, was in his casting—and Huston himself was usually the first to point that out, saying that he tried to direct as little as possible. "The more one directs, the more there is a tendency to monotony," he said. "If one is telling each person what to do, one ends up with a host of little replicas of oneself."

For *The Dead*, the actors were all Irish, with the exception of Anjelica, who qualified because she lived in Ireland until her teens. All were anxiously awaiting the experience of being directed by John Huston. They knew Huston wasn't about to offer insight into the craft of acting—they were hired because they presumably knew all that. He would be listening to lift Joyce's musical phrasing and keen observations of human behavior off the page and into his film, for *The Dead* was as subtle a piece of writing as one might ever expect to see made into a movie. As Huston himself had quipped, "The biggest piece of action is trying to pass the port."

It was John Huston's task to transform this literary piece of gossamer into a box-office success.

In the motel's conference room, Huston greeted the twenty-six actors and a documentary crew and introduced Tony and Anjelica. "Let's just read it through so I can start to associate the voices to the characters," he said. As the actors began finding their voices, Huston listened intently, "seeing" his film for the first time.

Anjelica's Irish accent seemed a bit thicker than the others and would have to be toned down. Huston scribbled a few notes, but then sat back in a revery when Frank Patterson, the tenor who had never acted before but was now engaged to play Bartell D'Arcy, began to sing "The Lass of Aughrim" in a sweet, lilting voice that, just as Joyce had described it, "faintly illuminated the cadence of the air with words expressing grief:

> O, the rain falls on my heavy locks
> And the dew wets my skin,
> My babe lies cold . . ."

For those moments, the old man in his wheelchair, tethered to his oxygen, remembered, like Gretta in Joyce's story, how his own life had been permanently altered in a Greenwich Village theater when he was just eighteen.

It was the fall of 1924, the first day of rehearsals for Eugene O'Neill's *Desire Under the Elms*. At the table on stage, under harsh electric light, sat the actors, including his father, Walter, who had turned forty in April and was on the verge of being recognized as a major new talent in the theater; the director, Robert Edmund Jones, who was the country's leading set designer; and O'Neill, brooding, handsome, soft-spoken, who listened carefully to each actor's run-through of the words he had written.

Those words had exploded like a bomb in John Huston's brain when his father had given him the play to read. O'Neill had captured the lives of this poor farming family and turned it into a Greek tragedy.

And each day, John got to sit in the theater and watch this tragedy come to life. Slowly, the actors gained an understanding of the depths of the play. O'Neill sat at the table with them for a week, listening, saying little; then he moved offstage, into the theater, where he watched Jones direct, and wrote notes suggesting ways in which the actors might say their lines more effectively. From its raw conception to the opening night, Huston witnessed a work of art develop, like a photographic print. Until that time he had wavered between following the paths of Jack Dempsey or Pablo Picasso. Now that changed. Words, acting, the theater could give him both the punch and the artistic satisfaction that warred within him.

On opening night, Huston went looking for O'Neill and found him sitting in a deserted dressing room of the Provincetown Theatre, blocks away from where his play was being performed. "Why aren't you at the Greenwich?" he asked the playwright.

"I'm frightened," O'Neill responded in a voice that had a jerky quality.

"It's the actors who should be frightened," Huston said, thinking of his father and what that evening meant for him.

"Ha," O'Neill shot back, "they're playing but one part apiece—I'm playing them all."

That was the moment when it hit John with the power of a Dempsey combination: That was what John wanted as well. He wanted to play them all. Not just act, like his father, but also write, like O'Neill; design sets, like Jones; find a way of combining the three.

". . . I used to go out walking with him when I was in Galway . . ."

The sound of Anjelica's voice brought Huston out of his revery. He looked at his daughter, then at Tony, and marveled how life really *did* imitate art. Ephraim Cabot, the patriarch in *Desire Under the Elms*, whom his father had played so convincingly, was now a figure he could identify with. Cabot brought home a young third wife, to the consternation of his grown sons, and promised her the land his youngest son believed was his birthright. Huston remembered the anguish he caused *his* children when he brought home to Galway his young fifth wife, who replaced their dead mother, and then sold his land a few years later, depriving them of what they considered to be their inheritance. Now he was working with both children on a film about Ireland. Time had healed some of the wounds. Work had brought them together.

It took ninety minutes to read through the script and the actors seemed pleased. They were given an hour's break and everyone left the room except Huston and Tony. John's secretary came and started to wheel him out of the conference room. "Where are we going?" Huston asked her.

"To your room," she said, concerned that he get some rest before resuming in the afternoon.

"Is there anyplace else?"

"The restaurant."

"Let's go there." There would be plenty of time to rest, he thought. A goddamn eternity to rest.

Tony was left alone in the room, writing notes. *The Dead* meant so much to him; he still hadn't gotten over the shock of hearing his wife tell him in September he wasn't welcome in their home anymore. In Joyce's story, Gabriel may have mourned the fact that Gretta held a secret passion, but at least they were still together. Tony lost everything— his wife, the children, his hawks and dog, his wonderful English gentry life—when he made the choice to be with his father and try to earn an honest living. Like Gabriel, Tony felt that "his own identity was fading out into a grey impalpable world." If Joyce's ending had seemed too dreary, Tony's own ending with Margot was much worse. The irony wasn't lost on him that, as he worked on a script about a man discovering that his wife never loved him passionately the way he would have liked, his own wife was telling him the same thing. Didn't his father once comment that Margot reminded him of Gretta in Joyce's story—years before they considered making the movie?

After Margot sent him that solicitor's letter and he learned she wanted him out of her life, Tony didn't know what to do. He called his father in Los Angeles. Should he fight it in any way?

"No," his father said, "just clear out."

It was not the advice he wanted to hear, but his father had far more experience with women than anyone he had ever known, and he thought it best to listen to him. "If a woman falls out of love with you, there's nothing you can do," he said sadly. "Just put your hands in your pockets and walk away."

On January 19, 1987, exactly two weeks after the first rehearsal, Huston was ready to begin filming *The Dead*. The dress rehearsal—with costumes, makeup, and hair—went smoothly. The actors walked through their positions, the cameramen steadied their cameras overhead, the sound man was ready with his Nagra. Huston was on the set in his wheelchair, breathing his oxygen. Tony was nearby.

Karen, the script supervisor, had never worked for anyone like John, who wanted to know every detail—costume, hair, placement. She was struck by how he noticed where the lapels on an actor's jacket were of a different material than the jacket itself. And he expected her to know the timing of every movement, something she had never been trusted to do before.

The first scene was complicated because it involved choreographing the movements of seven people, as guests came up the stairs and were greeted by Aunt Kate and Aunt Julia, played by Abbey Theatre veterans Helena Carroll and Cathleen Delany. Huston sat in the living room, away from the narrow hallway where the action was to occur, and stared at a large TV monitor. Over his head, a sound man held a boom mike—part of the documentary crew filming John as he prepared to direct. Thus, on this day, two films were being made: *The Dead* and *The Making of* The Dead. Tommy Shaw's gruff voice called for quiet for the final rehearsals before the cameras began to roll.

"Tony!" Huston suddenly called out, inviting his son to pick up the second set of headphones and listen to the actors. Huston's breathing was noticeably heavy, his heart was thumping vigorously in his chest, after forty films he still felt excitement. Making a movie still gave him a thrill, brought a rush of adrenaline through his body. There were very few things left in his life that made him feel so fully alive.

As they got ready to roll, the steadycam operator put on his Velcro vest and then attached the sixty-pound camera to it. Wieland Schulz-Keil mentioned to Huston how difficult it was to handle that camera, and how often it was the camera that stayed steady and swung the cameraman around. The image struck Tony as funny and he laughed.

By eleven-thirty, after the fifth rehearsal, Huston seemed satisfied that it wasn't going to get any better and said, "Very good, let's take a shot at it." The lighting was rechecked, floors were sprayed, waxed, mopped.

"Speed!" Tommy Shaw shouted from the hallway.

"Action," John said, his attention fully riveted on the television monitor.

The lighting man came to point out a minor problem and Huston told him, "If you want to change anything about the lighting, feel free · to."

After the second take, Tommy Shaw whispered to Huston that the documentary makers would like him to say "Action!" while they filmed him. "There's an extra charge for that," John joked, thinking what a shame Danny wasn't there with him. His younger son had planned to make the documentary; it would have felt right, having his three children together as professionals, but Danny had an even better offer: to direct a television movie for Disney. So while his old man was making *The Dead,* Danny was filming *Bigfoot.*

Huston spent the time waiting during rehearsals, between shots, and because of technical details to talk about things that interested him: art, Ireland, horses, his father, politics, literature, sports. Early one afternoon Tommy Shaw interrupted to say that stomachs were beginning to grumble and suggested an hour's break for lunch. Huston looked surprised. He had hoped to shoot straight through the day, but "I leave this to you, Tommy. I leave it to you entirely." Then he turned to look at the piano in the living room and said, "We need candles on the piano . . . to read the music. Lots of candles."

At three-fifteen, he returned from his trailer, watched another rehearsal, instructed one of the cameramen to lower his camera, and stated, "All right, let's iron away until it gets ironed out."

After thirteen tries, Huston asked for prints of takes six, eleven, and thirteen, then quipped, "This is not going to be like *Prizzi's Honor,* I can see that." Fifty percent of *Prizzi's* had been shot on the first take.

"There were fewer people," Schulz-Keil pointed out.

"Oh, I realize that," John said, telling the producer to sit down next to "Danny." Tony cringed but said nothing.

As he watched the monitor, Huston observed the frail Cathleen Delany in a scene and decided he wanted a backup shot of her. He called her in and said, "Aunt Julia, your eyes should be as bright as a little bird's." He took her hand and gently kissed it. As she walked back to the set he said softly, "Tell her she's a wren."

When asked if the film was proceeding at the pace he had anticipated, Huston replied, "This one is like lacework, compared to the forward direction of most films."

Anjelica worked on a scene where she took off her shoes in the bathroom. Huston wasn't satisfied with his cinematographer's work. "I don't like the pullback at all," he said gruffly. "Go in closer," he told Fred Murphy. "Get Aunt Julia right in there taking the other shoe from Anjelica. I don't want you to pull back at all."

"In order to hold Aunt Kate we have to pull back," Murphy protested, his ignorance of Huston's work now evident. Those who knew Huston's preferences were aware that he rarely let a camera pull back on a scene.

"I don't want pullbacks. Let me see it once."

Murphy aimed the camera down on Anjelica's foot, then came up to show her and Aunt Kate. Huston was pleased. "It works," he said. "You don't have to pull back. See." Then he told Anjelica to take the shoes out of the bag instead of going down for them, "So when she leans over we see the shoes."

Anjelica brought the shoes from the bag and held them to her face, mugging for the camera, making her father laugh. When the cameras rolled for another take, Huston noticed an awkward movement and yelled, "Cut! What the hell happened?"

"The camera is too jerky," Fred Murphy told him. "We need to go up slower. It may seem a little artificial, but . . ."

Huston cut him off. "It mustn't seem artificial."

The next time Anjelica pulled out the shoes too early and Huston heard Murphy instruct the steadycam operator, "Drift over . . ."

"No, you can't *drift*," John said. "When you come up with camera, you must hold tight."

Murphy tried to get technical on his director. "It's a one-eight-five problem," he said.

"Has to be graceful," Huston replied, ignoring the numbers. "Not drift up, *move* up." Fred Murphy was going to school whether he liked it or not. Huston wanted a fluid camera. He didn't want to be bothered with technical problems.

As the actors and crew broke for lunch John spotted Maricela. She was dressed in a white sweatshirt and white pants, with a pearl in each ear. "Will you have lunch with me . . . if you please?" he asked.

"Can I have anything I want? Including double dessert?" she responded playfully. Huston nodded. Then she asked, "Can anyone carry a gun here? I'd feel safer carrying my forty-five."

"You would, would you?" John coughed.

Maricela went down ahead of him and John turned to Wieland Schulz-Keil and said with a tinge of admiration, "Maricela wants to know if she can pack her revolver."

Over the next six weeks the sound man's Nagra blew a fuse, the prints of Anjelica removing her shoes were destroyed in the lab and had to be reshot, and Anjelica came down with mononucleosis. (Aware that her father's health was more fragile than her own, and that the picture couldn't risk a period of inactivity, she missed only a few days.) The bond company complained that not enough scenes were being shot each day but were told that Mr. Huston was a perfectionist and that he was getting his shots on schedule.

Huston was visited on the set by an old love, Marietta Tree, and numerous other friends, including Robert Mitchum. In the meantime, the cast began to appreciate their director's resilience and skill. When Donal Donnelly began overplaying his drunken character, Freddy Malins, Huston took him aside and said, "Freddy's on hooch, not cocaine." Donnelly understood immediately.

Tony compared his father to Eastern masters: "He was like the Zen teacher who gives his student a sharp tap with a cane, but doesn't embark on a great deal of explanation." When Tony used an arcane word like *bonif*, John would ask him what it meant. "Piglet," Tony replied. "Then say that," John said. "It's clearer."

Although the film was on schedule, John had trouble sleeping. His worrying emerged in conversations with Tony. Looking back on his life, he weighed all the things he had done wrong and wondered how it all balanced out. Tony said, "What is success anyway? A half dozen of your pictures will be remembered as long as pictures are remembered. You are working, you will never stop working, and that is more than most people can say. You have no reason to feel sorry for yourself."

It was good of Tony to keep the conversation on a professional level. Too often Tony agreed with his father about the wrongs he had committed in his personal life; now it just seemed pointless to open old wounds. Besides, Tony was beginning to feel thankful for the opportunity to work so closely, so importantly, with his father.

Unable to conceal his inner thoughts about what was happening to him, he confessed to feeling "liberated professionally" to a reporter. "I wonder—how much of it was planning and how much of it was fortuitous? Was Dad kind of keeping me on the back burner? Was he just waiting patiently until I'd done enough work by myself so that he could take me and I could learn from him, when I'd somehow got rid of the toxins of adolescence and could come to him to be finished, like a piece of furniture that he was able to do the final tooling on?"

Being on the set each day also gave Tony the chance to learn something firsthand about directing. "Not that I have any ambitions in that department," he hedged, "but it seems to me that writers either end up on Hollywood Boulevard picking up cigarettes out of the gutter, or they get fed up with what happens to their scripts and want more say about it, so it would be very foolish of me not to watch my father, the old master, at work."

What Tony hoped to learn was how his father told stories on film. Wieland Schulz-Keil, who first observed the process during *Under the Volcano*, believes that what made John such a specialist was that "he really knew what a story was, and in a very modern way. In a way that was commensurate with Joyce. Like Flaubert, who stood at the beginning of the tradition of realist writing in literature, John, amongst all filmmakers I know, was the one who most closely identified with that tradition."

"John," documentary maker Lilyan Sievernich asked on camera, "what *is The Dead* about?"

"The story is about a man being revealed to himself and we're being revealed to ourselves," Huston answered. "What we think we are and what we are are two different things . . . and the discovery of that can be pretty unsettling."

When the time came to shoot the last scene, between Gabriel and Gretta in a hotel room, Anjelica was feeling tense and apprehensive. It was the climax of the movie, the emotional unraveling of the story: Gretta's confession to her husband that young Michael Furey died for her. *"The night before I left . . . I heard gravel thrown up against the window . . . I ran downstairs . . . and there was the poor fellow at the end of the garden, shivering. I implored of him to go home at once and told him he would get his death in the rain. But he said he did not want to live. I can see his eyes as well as well! . . ."*

She was all too aware of how internal her role in *The Dead* was and how delicate the final scene had to play. Her father had told her and Donal McCann, as he had told his leading actors for close to fifty years, to work together on the scene without him. Still, she worried because she had to cry in the middle of the scene—and it was difficult to work up to it and then bring it down again in take after take. If they could shoot it in one take, she could go all out. But there had to be shots of her, shots of McCann, shots of the two of them. And who knew how many takes would be required because of technical problems?

"It's particularly difficult for me," Anjelica said, "not to start at the top of a scene with the full emotion but to get there quietly as the scene is going on."

When the scene came up, Anjelica felt that things went well. She would wind up "very, very upset" as she was supposed to, only to have to start again from the beginning. After a few such takes, her father called her over and asked, "Have you ridden your horse on Sunday?"

She smiled, knowing he was trying to keep her from "going over," bringing her down gently. Still, she was grateful. It had taken long, hard years for her to appreciate him. More than half her lifetime ago his slightest suggestion had brought tears to her eyes and anger in her heart. That was when he thought he was doing her a favor by starring her in a movie before she was ready to be an actress. She hadn't yet matured into the woman she would become. Now she adored her father. The resentments had faded.

"All the time I was growing up," she told a *New York Times* reporter while shooting *The Dead*, "I couldn't imagine him buying even a tube of toothpaste for himself. Taking care of him was a full-time job even before he was sick. Somewhere along the line he's become more human, more accessible. Now he is more emotionally generous than he ever was."

"I think Anjel and I are alike," John said, adding, "She has developed maturity . . . discovered self-confidence. She has had a chance to pull back and reassemble her forces."

After thirty-three days, *The Dead* was in the can, the actors were looking for their next job, the Hustons were beginning to talk to the press. It was time now to edit the 54,000 feet of film into an eighty-minute movie.

On April 1, Danny drove John to meet Jan de Swart, the seventy-nine-year-old artist whose work Huston first saw at the Laguna Art Museum before he began *The Dead*. Huston had invited Billy Pearson to join them, knowing how much Billy would appreciate de Swart's work. Pearson was an ex-jockey who rode John's horses in the late forties. They enjoyed each other's company and practical jokes and remained close throughout the years.

De Swart's house was filled with his complicated reliefs, intricate boxes, impossibly curved wooden columns, and he and Huston hit it off immediately. The Dutch-born sculptor had followed Huston's career and said, "That's some life you have lived, so many adventures, you must be three hundred years old."

"And you," John responded, his hand sweeping the room, "you must be Methuselah."

Before Huston left he bought a small box for $900, inquired about a $60,000 seven-foot-wide, aluminum-cast panel that he thought Anjelica's boyfriend, Jack Nicholson, should see, and was given a bench by de Swart as a gift.

As Huston began his ascent from de Swart's house to the street in a motorized chair, Billy Pearson came hopping up the garden steps saying, "Stop, John, I want to talk to you." But John's spirit was satisfied and he answered irritably, "I don't want to talk to you. Why don't you smoke another cigarette and run up the stairs?"

When Huston spoke like that, Pearson knew it was best to keep his distance. He couldn't help it if smoking hadn't debilitated him as it had John. He remembered once, some thirty years back, when they were in a hotel in Paris and he had a terrible coughing fit. "John, John," he said in alarm after coming out of the bathroom. "I've been coughing up blood." John looked at him oddly. "Doesn't everybody?" he said.

On the drive back, Huston and Danny talked about the movie Danny hoped to make of Thornton Wilder's last novel, *Theophilus North*, a lighthearted story about a young tutor who goes to Newport, Rhode Island, discovers that tiny electrical shocks emit from his fingers at strange moments, and changes the lives of the townspeople, who come to look upon him as either a saint or a healer. The idea had been pitched to Goldwyn and to Vista, but was turned down, Danny was certain, "because of Dad being an old, sick man and me being a first-time director." But Heritage Entertainment was willing to consider the project once Danny was able to get his father to meet with them and agree to act in the film and rewrite the script with *Prizzi's Honor* screenwriter Janet Roach. John had acted for Danny before in the hour-long production of *Mr. Corbett's Ghost*, but this was to be Danny's first feature, an important step in his career. Huston had helped solidify Anjelica's acting career with her Oscar-winning performance in *Prizzi's* and again in her subtle but powerful role as Gretta in *The Dead*, and allowed Tony full screenwriter's credit for the Joyce story so that his career could finally get off the ground. So he was pleased that Danny had also found a project that needed his help.

Danny was full of enthusiasm and confidence. He wasn't embarrassed to use his father's name to get work and bragged that he and his father "made a great team, hustling projects. One big hustler, one little hustler." If all went well, the Wilder script would be finished in May and the film would begin shooting in Rhode Island in early summer. Because John had agreed to do it, Anjelica and Lauren Bacall also signed on. At twenty-five, Danny was getting the kind of opportunities very few directors ever had.

•   •   •

On the sixth of April, Roberto Silvi, *The Dead*'s editor, was ready to show Huston a rough cut of the film on a big screen. Silvi, forty-three, had already edited three Huston films—*Wise Blood*, *Victory*, and *Under the Volcano*—and was an assistant editor on five others.

John was pleased with Silvi's cut but thought it needed fine tuning, so he made some suggestions and told Silvi that he would come to the editing room in Burbank in two days and go over it again with him.

Wieland Schulz-Keil was also there when Maricela drove John to Burbank, and the three men spent three hours making meticulous changes to keep the film, reduced now to seventy-eight minutes, flowing. Huston acknowledged that it had been "fine-tooth combed several times now," and Schulz-Keil joked that they were now using a "special dandruff comb."

Schulz-Keil said, "John looked at the movie as if he had never had anything to do with it."

As John watched Aunt Kate, he noticed what seemed to be an abrupt cut as she walked toward her guests. "How could you have made such a cut, Roberto?" he asked. "Do whatever you can to fix it, because it's just an awkward frame that you cut. Do away with her look-around. Just have them on the stair."

Huston was anxious to get to another scene he wanted changed. During the recital of a poem, Anjelica sat next to Mr. Browne, drifting dreamily off, only to be brought back to the party by the sound of applause. There were three cuts to Anjelica, far away in her thoughts, and twice it appeared that she was wakened from her revery. Huston didn't think that was necessary. "I just don't like the cut," he said. Anjelica looked too tragic at a point when the poem wasn't that compelling. "Change that to save the drama for the finish," Huston suggested. "She has no reason to look tragic at this moment. And we don't need that cut of her again, she does the same thing exactly. It's a bit of a bore."

"I need a cut there," Silvi argued.

"Then do something else. She shouldn't come out of the same trance, each time she's coming out of another world."

"I think it's wrong, John. They're applauding and she's still under."

"Better than waking up twice," Huston countered.

"Aw, she's not waking up," Silvi said, worried that the cut John wanted might be impossible to do because there wasn't material shot to cover it. But Huston knew what he wanted and when he saw that Roberto was being stubborn he said, "Can you do it now?" Huston wanted to make sure Silvi understood him. Silvi ran sections of film through the Moviola for Huston to see and together they made the necessary cuts.

For the rest of the afternoon, Huston was scrupulous in his requests: Chimes could ring before the singing began, Freddy Malins's whistle for a taxi should be "shriller," no effects were necessary during Gretta's speech at the end. "Stay with the drama, we don't need any effects there unless it contributes to the drama."

Before they finished, Schulz-Keil asked Huston about the opening credits. "After the last card, 'Directed by John Huston,' there will be another card in the right-hand corner, 'For Maricela.' Right?"

Huston nodded. It was the first time he had ever dedicated a film to anyone, and it was to be a surprise. It was his way of telling her what he felt, of thanking her for taking care of him.

With *The Dead* completed, Huston began thinking about directing *Revenge*, the script he had written with Tony for Ray Stark. John had made four pictures for Stark, who always treated him fairly. He considered Stark the most generous producer he had ever worked with and liked to joke that he could even forgive Ray for making more money than anyone else in California.

Stark had told John that he might be able to get *Revenge* off the ground at Columbia if Kevin Costner starred in it. Huston had seen a video of one of Costner's films and wasn't impressed. *Revenge* was a macho kind of picture about two men who battle each other and destroy a woman in the process. He was thinking more along the lines of an Anthony Quinn. But Stark asked Huston to come to his house to meet the actor. Huston wasn't pleased but agreed to stop by with Danny.

They drove up to Stark's impressive house in Danny's Volkswagen. Costner was waiting inside. After they shook hands, tea was served and Costner mentioned that he saw similarities between *Revenge* and certain stories of King Arthur. Huston looked at Costner, then turned his head and stared out at the Moore and Manzu sculptures in Ray Stark's garden and began to whistle. "There was the most awkward silence," Danny recalled. "Dad didn't answer the man's questions." The meeting was obviously over and Costner took his leave. When Stark returned to the room, John said, "I'm an ill man and I don't know how you could do this to me. I've been in this business fifty-odd years and you are telling me that I've got to work with this little guy?"

"He's important to Columbia," Stark said. "And he does have an attachment . . ."

"Well, Ray, just face it, you're a cocksucker." John then reminded him that Stark hadn't wanted Marlon Brando for Fat City and then they started to argue about The Man Who Would Be King. Danny was standing to the side watching—"No you didn't," "Yes I did"—and thinking that they had turned into children. Then his father turned to him and said, "Danny, this might come as a surprise . . ." And Danny thought, Oh, Christ, what's next? ". . . I would like to have Danny direct Revenge with me. Any kind of action that has to be shot, I want Danny to do it."

Stark looked at Danny and asked, "What have you done?"

"I've done an hour film in London, which really hasn't been shown anywhere." Danny smiled. "And I've just finished a Disney Sunday movie special."

Stark just stared at the boy. Huston had had enough. He picked up his oxygen tank and stormed out of the house, his son rushing behind him. Stark followed, and when he tried to embrace his old friend, Huston just patted him on the shoulder.

On the ride over to Heritage Entertainment, where they were to talk about Mr. North, John kept saying that he couldn't believe Ray could do that to him. "Kevin Costner would be good in the part of a man dying of AIDS," John said.

The meeting at Heritage was entirely different. The man in charge, Skip Steloff, scored points among his executives by the mere fact that John Huston had come to discuss a film. After listening to Huston talk about how quickly the script could be rewritten, Steloff said, "I'll put up the money. I haven't read the script but I feel that the elements are right. I want to do the picture with you guys."

"All this had happened in an hour and a half," Danny marveled. "Driving to Ray's, then to Heritage, both meetings . . . And back in the car, Dad chuckled over how proud this man was—'I haven't read this but I want to do it.' " Then Huston began thinking of who might best be cast for the lead in Mr. North and had an idea. "Look," he said to Danny, "you might think I'm totally mad, but what do you think of Kevin Costner?"

On April 25, Robert De Niro visited to discuss the next project John wanted to direct: Herman Melville's Benito Cereno. It was one of

Huston's favorite stories, and even though it would have to be shot on the high seas, John figured it could be done in the Caribbean after the hurricane season if the money was there. Exactly who might insure him for such a risky project was of no concern to the frail director. He had already rewritten Jonathan Hale's script and Robert Duvall had agreed to play the captain, after Paul Newman turned it down. De Niro had come to talk about playing Cereno.

Janet Roach had flown to Los Angeles from her home on Shelter Island at the tip of Long Island, New York, to work on *Mr. North*. Her work with John was intense. Sometimes she would write as many as eight or ten pages in a day and read them to him. "By then his eyes were no good," Roach said. "Sometimes you'd see that bony old hand flash out and he'd say, 'Oh, no, honey.' I'd die every time because I wanted so terribly to please him. He would say things like, 'We need a straight line here, honey, that's not a straight line.' Or, 'You have to dramatize this, honey, don't you know what that means?' I had the typewriter, he had the last word. It was only when I really screwed up that he would pick up a pencil and actually write something. He wanted what he wanted. He knew his time was limited and there was no margin to fool around."

Roach recalled how she and Huston had gone out for lunch. When they returned to his hotel, Huston sat down while waiting for the elevator, trying to catch his breath. "We'll have to make her see double, honey," he suddenly said. Roach looked at him and wondered what he was talking about. Then she realized it had to do with one of the characters in their script.

"He solved a problem that had been dogging us for ten days," she said. "My mind had been on lunch and on politics, but John's had been going over this problem we had failed to solve. And as soon as he said that it was clear what he meant. The body had betrayed him but his mind was still all there, and he used it and used it and used it."

By the end of May, after six weeks, the script was finished and plans were being made for John to fly to Rhode Island, where he would not only act but also executive produce *Mr. North*. Robert DeNiro had decided to turn down *Benito Cereno*, but Raul Julia had agreed to play the part, so that project was still going forward.

Danny Huston was having his own casting problems, trying to find

the right actor to play Theophilus North. When Timothy Hutton and
Tom Hanks weren't available, Danny settled on Anthony Edwards.
With a supporting cast of the two acting Hustons and Lauren Bacall, it
was a picture any young actor would be advised to take for the chance
to learn from such pros.

By June, Huston was staying at his old friend Burgess Meredith's
house. He had met with the organizers of the Santa Fe Film Festival
and had agreed to attend a press conference the following month
announcing the retrospective festival that was to be held in his honor.
On July 6, he was wheeled into the International Ballroom at the
Beverly Hilton Hotel in Beverly Hills and met with the press. He was
treated with respect and responded to all questions with both thoughtful and glib answers. Asked how he might attend the Come as Your
Favorite Huston Character Ball that was to be held in Santa Fe, he
answered, "I'd come as a horse."

Finally, John was asked if there was a most important quality that
went into the making of a good film.

"Yes: talent. And taste and ideas, intention. We can just go down
the list of all the fine qualities you can discover in human beings and
they all go to making a good picture."

As John talked, Maricela stood outside the ballroom watching. She
always stayed out of his limelight. Keeping him alive was her job.

"We're supposed to go next week to Rhode Island for six weeks," she
said, "but after he finishes his part he says he wants to stay and watch
Danny, see if he can help out. Then he wants to start *Benito Cereno*,
but so far there's no money. So maybe we'll go back to Mexico after
Rhode Island. But then it can all change if he gets sick."

A week after the press conference, Huston was in the hospital being
fed antibiotics intravenously. He wasn't well, but he was determined to
go to Rhode Island as scheduled to make Danny's movie. He had gotten
in touch with Robert Mitchum and asked if he would be available to fill
in if John was unable to complete his part. Mitchum joked with
Huston, saying he doubted anything would go wrong, but agreed to be
there if needed. Huston always liked Mitchum and considered him
among his few actor friends.

Another of those friends, Burgess Meredith, had surprised him with a
bill for $13,000 as the fee for Huston's stay in Meredith's home. John
had been telling people how generous Burgess was to let him stay there.
But Meredith's generosity didn't extend to the free use of his home.
John paid the bill but was disappointed that there *was* a bill to pay.

By mid-July, Huston and Maricela had arrived in Newport and settled in with the other cast and crew members at the Budget Motor Inn in Middletown. Everyone was excited to see him, especially Danny, who couldn't wait to begin his first feature film. The cast assembled on the veranda of a rented house in Newport for the first reading of the script. It went well and John told Harry Dean Stanton, "I called Bob Mitchum to have him stand by just in case I didn't feel well, but I feel great. How about that?" The following day they played poker and then, on the third day, there was another reading. This time John could barely stay awake and Danny had to nudge him when it was his turn. "Janet and I covered for Dad," Danny said. "If he dozed off or missed a line, either I or Janet would read it. That was the first time I thought that he might not be able to do it."

After a few days of rehearsal and shooting, it became apparent that the strength John had mustered when he directed *The Dead* was just not there. Working with Janet Roach on last-minute changes in the script, studying his lines, advising Danny . . . Huston had taken on more than he could handle. He hadn't sufficiently recovered from his last hospital stay and the excitement of a new project, coupled with the change in environment and climate, hit his fragile system hard. On the evening news on July 28 it was reported across the country that John Huston was in "grave condition" at the Charlton Memorial Hospital in Fall River, Massachusetts. The diagnosis was pneumonia.

Tony Huston was in Los Angeles when he heard the news. He had been finishing a first draft of a script about Alexander Hamilton and Aaron Burr for HBO. He called the hospital and found out that his father had turned purple a few days before and that his blood gases were "unbelievably low" when he entered the hospital, but his condition was beginning to stabilize. Maricela was with him, Anjelica was there, he was hanging in.

Danny met with his producers and crew and they decided that the movie would continue. It was obvious now that John could not act and Robert Mitchum was summoned. When Mitchum arrived, he went to visit Huston and joked, "You suckered me. You had no intention of acting in this thing." "Biggest hoax I ever pulled off, kid," John said. Like Huston, Mitchum dealt with the morbid by putting up a strong, defiant front.

So did Anjelica. "He's rallying like a bull elephant," she told reporters. But she knew differently. Her father was breathing through a resuscitator, practically choking at the same time. It was horrible to see him in such a vulnerable position.

"We were always scared, at Cedars-Sinai, for him to go on a lung machine," Danny said, "and he was on this lung machine and he couldn't talk. There was a tube in his mouth and more wires and tubes all around him. And the terror was he would never be able to get off the lung machine. We were extremely worried whether they were doing the right thing or not."

President Reagan sent a telegram, which gave Huston a sardonic chuckle, and Nancy Reagan tried to telephone but was told by a nurse that Huston wasn't receiving any calls. "Don't you know who I am?" the First Lady responded. "I don't care who you are," the nurse said. Apparently she really didn't know who was calling. John's hospitalization had shaken up the staff of Charlton Memorial; they had never had a patient of his stature before. The calls, mail, and media attention were overwhelming.

On the last day of July the hospital listed his condition as "serious but stable." The production company was saying that John was "fine." Plans were going ahead to celebrate his eighty-first birthday at the hospital on August 5. Allegra, who was to appear in a bit part in the movie, flew in from London. Tony came from Los Angeles. And when John turned eighty-one, he blew out one candle with the help of Allegra.

But it wasn't a time for celebration. Huston was troubled by family squabbles. Anjelica had broken up with Jack Nicholson again, and he felt she was wrong not to have married him. Tony had called Margot in London asking her to send the children with a nanny so his father could see the continuation of the Huston line, but Margot wanted to come as well; Tony didn't think it wise to bring her into the picture right now. Danny had found a young lady, but Huston knew it wasn't serious; Danny was sowing his oats. Zoe and Maricela were not on speaking terms and that bothered him greatly. When Zoe arrived to visit, Maricela would leave the room. Zoe felt so uncomfortable that she didn't come often and John would have to ask where she was. Danny was so busy with the movie that he could visit his father only rarely. And when the other children came, they always seemed in a rush. They stayed a half hour and then went off. It made him feel as if he was a burden to them all.

His spirits were considerably lifted when Marietta Tree came to visit. One of the great romantic loves of his life, Marietta had never married Huston, which was probably why they remained close. He had cast her years ago to act in a brief scene with Clark Gable in *The Misfits*, and she was asked to act again as a high-society lady in *Mr. North*. When she visited Huston in the hospital, the nurses noticed that the machines monitoring his heartbeat showed a rapid increase. He gallantly kissed her hand. They were two dear old friends with many memories, and John was able to put aside, however briefly, his discontent with his family and his situation.

By August 12 plans had been made to move him from the hospital to a rented house overlooking Newport Harbor. John was beginning to show signs of recovery and there was even talk of casting him in a cameo role in the movie. The resuscitator seemed to have worked. When Janet Roach visited him, he asked detailed questions about the film. He had read and approved of Tony's Hamilton/Burr script. Lauren Bacall had spent some time with him. And Zoe managed to stay a few nights as well.

"Before I came John couldn't speak, he was writing everything," Zoe said, "and the doctor was saying 'no family.' And he wrote ZOE in huge letters, question mark, FAMILY, FAMILY. He was so attached to me in the end. At least I knew that he really loved me. It had been a question mark for a long time, because he never showed what he thought. But in the end, I know he did. I think he asked for me more than anyone.

"Those two nights in the hospital were the only time I could get to be near him without drama. Maricela wanted to get out, so I was allowed my moment. John was beginning to think he was a burden on everybody. And he didn't want to be alone, ever. He was like a little, frightened, vulnerable child. All those tubes in him, it was so painful, he couldn't sleep. I think he was terribly happy because I let him sleep— he didn't have to call me more than once and I was there. I was doing everything for him and he felt comfortable. I didn't care if he peed, it didn't affect me. He wouldn't dare have done that in front of Marietta. But he didn't feel like his manhood was being threatened with me.

"Because he was sleeping so much I was scared he'd died. He wasn't moving. I put all the praying vibes I could possibly get into him. He had spent years criticizing my beliefs, but at the end he sort of realized that there must be something bigger than him. He asked me to get him tapes of Plato, Socrates, and Nietzsche to listen to. And he told me how dangerous ego was—so he got that in the end. When I said, 'Thank you for those beautiful nights,' he said to me, 'Well, you kept me alive.' "

Zoe was convinced that Maricela resented her because John kept asking for her. "I suppose when you've looked after somebody for that long and you see he keeps asking for someone else, I guess it must be irritating." Maricela, on the other hand, thought that Zoe was needlessly upsetting John by talking about how the family was all against her.

During the making of *The Dead*, Wieland Schulz-Keil observed the polarities between Zoe and Maricela and found Zoe to be "a vulgar and insensitive person who tries to organize other people's lives. The one thing about Zoe I dislike is that she dislikes Maricela so much and is constantly intriguing and spreading stupid rumors. If you follow Zoe's reading, Maricela is constantly mixing poison to somehow put herself in the position of the heiress. It's ridiculous."

On August 19, twenty-two days after he had entered the hospital, John was released. He was moved to the house overlooking the harbor and he began thinking about buying a house in Los Angeles; just one large room was all he wanted. He saw some of the rushes of *Mr. North* and seemed pleased. He also saw how on edge everyone was around him. The visits remained short.

Once settled in the house, Huston called old friends to let them know he was recovering. Marietta Tree had gone to Italy and John reached her there. He called Lillian Ross, who wrote a series of articles for *The New Yorker* in the early fifties about the making of *The Red Badge of Courage*, and remained dear to him for the rest of his life, and left a message on her answering machine, "I just want to reassure you that I'm quite all right. Goodnight, darling." On Janet Roach's last visit he read some changes she had written in the script and gave his approval. "Very good," he said. Those were the words she lived for when working with John.

But things weren't good at all when Anjelica came to visit and said she was planning to fly to Aspen for the weekend, and Tony, who was staying in the house with him, kept talking about going to the Venice Film Festival where *The Dead* was to premiere. It made John feel that he wasn't needed anymore, and he instructed Maricela to make arrangements for him to fly back to Los Angeles. Since no commercial airline would take him in his condition, he thought of who might help him—who was rich enough, powerful enough, and loved him enough to make it possible for him to get from Rhode Island to California. He tried calling Ray Stark, who had often told John that he could always count on him. But when Stark's secretary responded to the request for a private plane with information about how Huston could go about renting one, Huston became infuriated. The issue wasn't money—he could have easily paid for the plane—but rather of loyalty, love, friendship, all of which he felt Stark had betrayed. He scribbled a note to Stark in barely legible handwriting scolding Ray for not having helped his children, and now when he was desperate for help all Ray could talk about was money. He wanted nothing more to do with him, and he instructed Maricela to tell Ray exactly what he had written.

Then he gave Maricela the White House number he had and asked her to call Nancy Reagan, hoping that the president's plane might be available. But Maricela couldn't get through.

Without telling Maricela, John had arranged for her sister, Jenny, to come from Los Angeles and help them. He could see that Maricela was completely worn down. When Jenny arrived, Maricela was surprised. "What are you doing here?" she asked. "John called and told me to come," her sister answered.

On August 27 he was feeling weak, but when Danny and Zoe came, he boosted his young son's confidence, telling him, "Now just think, Danny, you've got only two weeks left. Can you imagine, Danny, two weeks?"

As they were leaving, Zoe smiled at John and felt chilled by the look on his face. When she got outside she began to cry and said to Danny, "That's it. I'm not going to see him again, because he just said, 'Good-bye.' "

"No," Danny protested, "he's done that look before. I've seen it countless times."

"He's never, ever done that," Zoe insisted.

When they returned to their hotel, Zoe knocked on Tommy Shaw's door and said, "He's not going to make it through the night."

At ten that evening, Tony shared a brandy with his father and John asked for a massage. But Tony found him to be "incredibly sensitive" and John complained that Tony was hurting him. "You're too grumpy, old man," Tony said, cutting the massage short, and when he left the room, he turned out the light, leaving his father in the dark.

That flick of a switch might just have been an insensitive gesture on Tony's part, but John felt it symbolically. He began to shudder. His face turned pale and tears filled his eyes. He shook the bell on his night table and Maricela came running. She found him crying, white, enraged. "Do you know what that sonofabitch did? He turned the lights out on an old man. He wants me dead," he said.

Maricela tried to calm him down, but he was so angry with Tony he kept saying, "I want you to tell the world what he has done to me." He complained about his children having no time for him, of making their own plans. "They're leaving me," he said. "I want to go home." Maricela felt his pulse and found it weak. She went to call the doctor, but John wanted no part of doctors. He wanted to talk.

He went on for hours as his pulse weakened and his rage against the one battle he would inevitably lose increased. He said he wanted her to destroy all his papers that had not already been donated to the Motion Picture Academy Library, including the letters from Buckminster Fuller and Nancy Reagan, the honorary degrees he had received, his business and personal correspondence, and especially his mother's self-revealing writings. If anyone wanted to know about him, let them read his book, which was a sanitized version of his life.

He worried aloud about Maricela and how she would get on when he was gone. He had provided for her in his will, had left her the houses in Puerto Vallarta and Los Angeles, but he knew that many of the people they knew would turn against her, and he told her that she was perfectly capable of supporting herself, of getting a job like everyone else.

At two that morning he grew weaker. Maricela cradled his head in her arms. She knew this was the end. "I'll call Tony," she said. Tony was the only family member staying in the house.

"He's the last person I want you to call," John said. "Call Tommy."

Tom Shaw would know what to do, Huston figured. You could always count on Tommy.

Maricela never questioned John's behavior that last day: the angry letter to Ray Stark; his belief that Tony wanted him dead, that his children were ungrateful; his asking her to burn his papers. It wasn't the behavior of a rational mind, especially not a mind so coolly analytical and precise as his had always been. Like King Lear, Huston felt betrayed, useless, trapped and was lashing out at friends and family. He was really angry about death itself.

He was angry with his brittle body, with its failing lungs, with his eyes that no longer focused and wouldn't allow him to read. He had fought off death for so many years . . . now he would go into the night with brandished sword and rifle cocked, but he wouldn't be returning to see the sun rise.

"John," Maricela asked, "what can I do?"

"Just take my hand," he said, looking into her eyes. "How many express rifles have we got?"

Without hesitating, she answered, "Thirty, John."

"How about ammunition?"

"Oh, we've got plenty of ammunition."

Then he squeezed her hand and raised it up over his head like a prizefighter. "Just give 'em hell," he said.

His hand dropped and Maricela held him tight. He had told her so many things, he had been so unhappy. Now he was dead and she didn't want to share him with anybody. She stayed in the room for hours, holding him for the last time.

Finally, at dawn, Maricela called Anjelica. "You'd better come," she said. She also called Tommy Shaw and Danny, who went into his mother's room at six-thirty to tell her. Before he could say a word, Zoe screamed.

"When did he die?" Tom Shaw asked Maricela when he arrived at the house.

"Around two o'clock," Maricela answered.

Shaw looked at his watch and said that they had better notify the police. "You do what has to be done," Maricela said. "John said you'd know what to do."

When a grief-stricken Tony entered the room, Maricela started to scream at him, blaming him for being so cruel to his father in the end. Tommy Shaw stepped in to calm her.

At first, Anjelica and Tommy had tried to revive John. The oxygen tank was still turned on. Maricela couldn't bring herself to shut it off. Danny and Zoe soon arrived, as did Steven Haft, the co-producer of *Mr. North*, who started making phone calls.

When the detectives arrived, they looked at the body and then asked who had been with him when he died. They went to Maricela's room to talk with her.

"Why didn't you call the doctor?" one detective asked her.

"Because he didn't want me to," she said. "I take full responsibility for my actions. I acted from my heart, not my logic."

The detectives didn't know what to make of Maricela. They only knew that a great man had died in his bed and no doctor had been called. He had been dead for four hours before anyone at all had been notified. Only this Mexican girl was with him in the end, and she seemed vague but defiant. So they did what police in America often do when confronted with a situation they don't understand: They put Maricela in handcuffs, placed her under arrest, and drove her to the police station.

Huston had been dead less than seven hours and the woman closest to him for more than a decade was now sitting under the harsh glare of a detective's lamp, being grilled about his death.

It was humiliating being there, under suspicion. It was not the place to grieve. When Steven Haft heard that Maricela had been taken in for questioning he went to the police station and told them exactly who she was. Maricela was released immediately.

"He had a very peaceful expression on his face," Zoe said when she viewed John's body. "Tony was sort of crying. We were all in a terrible state."

"I don't believe that Dad thought there were greener pastures than right here," Tony reflected. "He was incredibly attached to life, and to make his exit easier, it would be a psychological trick to make life actually distasteful. Certainly Ray Stark betrayed him. But he was also disappointed in Danny for something, disappointed in Anjelica, disappointed in me. He took my switching off the light totally out of proportion."

Huston's death almost didn't seem to register on Danny, who still had the responsibility of completing *Mr. North*. Zoe knew that it would hit him later, but the decision was made not to halt the production. Danny believed that his father wouldn't have approved of that.

John Huston's death was a major news story. Papers around the world ran his picture on their front page. National and local television news mourned his passing by showing clips from some of his forty-one films. *Daily Variety* covered his life over four pages, saying, "A flamboyant, prodigious and unpredictable artist, gambler, sportsman, traveler and connoisseur of painting, literature, food, liquor, horses and women, the rangy, craggy, enormously charming Huston gave the impression of having seen and done it all. His career was filled with great triumphs and colossal flops, and despite the cynicism and pessimism that runs throughout his work, no one seemed to relish life itself more than Huston. As he once acknowledged, 'My life has certainly been an occasion.'" *Variety* went on to quote actor Dennis Morgan's opinion that "John wrote his life as a script when he was very young, and has played it ever since."

The obituaries dwelled on his iconoclastic life-style, his affection for underdogs, hopeless causes, and the dark side of life. They covered his great love of women, his equally great love of gambling, and his practical jokes. They listed the major awards, pointed out how many of his films were based on literature, and noted how he was in the midst of a second renaissance. "Huston was a born storyteller whose ironic, tough-minded movies were an extension and reflection of his own rogue male personality," wrote Joseph Gelmis in *Newsday*.

Syndicated columnist Roger Ebert's salute read in part, "No one else made more great films over a longer time, films that stand up today as well as on the day they were premiered." Charles Champlin, in the *Los Angeles Times*, traced Huston's storytelling abilities to his "writer's passionate admiration for eloquent words" and his "filmmaker's sure command of the grammar, the vocabulary and the possibilities of the camera."

And Vincent Canby, in the *New York Times*, said, "John Huston's career was as long-lived and shapely as his movies—and as full of exuberant spirits. His most memorable films, even the autumnally sad ones, from *The Treasure of the Sierra Madre* (1947) to *Wise Blood* (1979), leave one experiencing the kind of exhilaration that only comes from being witness to craftsmanship in the service of an original, seriously amused mind."

Canby went on, "Huston's films are speculations on the ends to which a man can be led through his infinite capacity to delude himself. . . .

"Whatever its actual source, the characteristic Huston film appears to have had its origins in a tale told late in the evening, in a convivial, Conradian gathering of friends who want to be amused and astonished by some aspect of human experience that has never before occurred to them. More often than not, the people in Huston's films wind up losers."

Among the dozens of movie people quoted on John's passing, it was Robert Mitchum who seemed to best understand the larger-than-life qualities of the man. "All I can say," Mitchum cracked, "is they'd better drive a stake through his heart."

Huston's body was flown to Los Angeles on August 28, the day he died. He had told Maricela he wanted to be buried at Hollywood Memorial Park, in his mother's grave and beside his grandmother. Tony and Anjelica insisted that the funeral service be a private affair, which angered people like producers Ray Stark and John Foreman, who felt that John belonged to the people. The Directors Guild announced they would have a memorial service, but that didn't pacify a number of people who felt snubbed by Huston's children. When Billy Pearson was told he wasn't invited to the funeral, he told Tony that no one was going to keep him away.

On August 31, the service was held at the Chapel of the Psalms at Hollywood Memorial Park. John's body was on view in front of the twenty-five mourners, who were told that they were all welcome to stand and speak.

Zoe had dreaded seeing John's body, but when she did, she relaxed. "I had never seen anybody dead before, but that body had no person, it was like a house he'd lived in. I felt very happy for him. He was in his white track suit and I put a rose in there."

The person who seemed most devastated when he spoke was Billy Pearson, who stood before his best friend and cried, "Well, John, this is the only time you can't talk back to me. I've never seen you with so much makeup, John. You look awful with so much makeup. John, I know you're not dead. Any minute you're going to walk around the corner and say, 'Cut.' " Pearson went on, crying and rambling, remembering a flood of adventures they had shared.

"Nobody touched on what a humane human being he was," Zoe observed. "It was what a great filmmaker and how talented he was and that bravado thing that Billy Pearson was saying, 'Let's go and have a drink so that you can take off your makeup, John.' I hated it. That's the only side John ever showed anybody, but I saw the other side. He was just a sweet guy, just adorable. I remember walking out of there feeling relieved, that he was gone and was somewhere much better."

Anjelica was still numb from the shock of her father's death. Months later she would confide to a friend that as she watched her father's physical possibilities narrow because of his illness, "his mind expanded and he became more giving, more vulnerable, more creative, more of a father than he ever was before." Tony, too, was visibly upset, as were Danny and Allegra. Tony admitted to the press that it was difficult being Huston's first son and professed that it had been the "greatest joy of my adult life that I was able to collaborate with Dad in a creative way." Danny said that with Anjelica's acting, Tony's screenwriting, and his directing, "We will form a great mafioso within the film industry. My father encouraged it very much. It seemed to be what he wanted."

Maricela's only expressed feeling was that she felt as if she had been hit by a meat truck. Later that week she followed John's instructions and told Ray Stark what Huston had thought about him at the very end. "My God, Ray was absolutely stunned," Maricela said. "He said, 'I don't believe a word. John was my friend.' He sent a messenger over for the note and I gave it to him. Then Ray sent me a nasty note. I never answered it. What went wrong between them had nothing to do with me."

Eventually Stark's anger subsided and he sent Maricela flowers and gave her $5,000 to tide her over while John's will was still with the lawyers. Anjelica also loaned Maricela $15,000. His estate would be divided up among Maricela, Zoe, and the four children, but John, by his own estimate, was not a wealthy man. He once said he couldn't afford to buy a house in Beverly Hills, that he had less than $2 million.

Huston wasn't buried immediately. His cremation was private and the urn containing his ashes would be buried on September 13, the day after the memorial at the Directors Guild in West Hollywood.

Jack Nicholson and director Richard Brooks were the moderators of the memorial. Robert Mitchum, costume designer Dorothy Jeakins, Meta Wilde (the script supervisor on both *The Maltese Falcon* and *Prizzi's Honor*), producer Gottfried Reinhardt, Lauren Bacall, Jack Haley, Jr., Harry Dean Stanton, critic Charles Champlin, and Paul Kohner, Ray Stark, and Anjelica were all scheduled to share their thoughts. John Foreman had also been listed as a speaker, but he was still upset over not being invited to the private service and refused to attend.

Gilbert Cates, on behalf of the Directors Guild, welcomed the audience and listed some of Huston's major honors, the DGA's D. W. Griffith Award, the AFI's Lifetime Achievement Award, the Academy's Oscars. Before introducing the series of clips from many of Huston's films, he said, "If movies sometimes seem larger than life, John Huston always seemed larger than his movies."

And then the lights dimmed and there on the screen was John, slapping a peso into Humphrey Bogart's palm in that memorable scene near the beginning of *The Treasure of the Sierra Madre*. "This is the very last you get from me," Huston warns, "from now on, you'll have to make your way through life without my assistance." It was a fitting way to begin the tribute.

After the clips, Richard Brooks announced that President and Mrs. Ronald Reagan had sent a basket of flowers and then introduced Robert Mitchum, who told the story of how he got a nurse at the Charlton Memorial Hospital to pull up her skirt in front of John. Jack Nicholson then introduced Dorothy Jeakins, who read two short poems, one paraphrasing Elizabeth Barrett Browning, the other by W. H. Auden. Then Brooks read two telegrams from directors Fred Zinnemann and George Stevens, Jr., who put Huston among "the last vanishing breed of men who were great filmmakers and whose work illuminated the richness of their life experiences."

When Jack Nicholson began to speak, his voice cracked. "I got out of my shoebox this morning and threw the *I Ching*," he began, "that brilliant book which is always right. . . . All the strong lines were in the strong places and all the weak lines were in the weak places . . . and things were in order . . . and the only thing to avoid is decay and indifference, which is the root of all evil. Which is a bit pretentious for John." He then had to compose himself to tell a story John had once told him. "It seems that Jean-Paul Sartre was visiting and by mistake

Monsignor Ryan of Ireland chose this moment to come as well. Sartre was very stirred by his presence. He hadn't expected to debate philosophy on the weekend. John got them in the same room and Monsignor Ryan opened the conversation with a story about being on the Plains of Oblivion waiting for Judgment and a gentleman is standing there, lightning is going off . . . thousands of miles of murmurs rises and turns into cheers and great jubilation. Finally, the man standing in line taps the guy on the shoulder, muttering like John, 'What's going on? Why is everybody so happy?' And the man turns to him and says, 'They've just heard that fucking doesn't count.' "

When the laughter subsided, Nicholson finished by reading a list of what John disliked: "Any dish that contained chicken. Mawkish pop songs. Car metals in collision. Drunken women. Writing that tried too hard for effect. People with too much propriety who strain for social correctness and end only in pomposity and self-complacency."

Gottfried Reinhardt, who knew Huston for over half a century, spoke about John's tastes, talents, loyalties, and remarkable good luck. About working with him as producer of The Red Badge of Courage, he said, "We combined our efforts not only to reenact the Civil War . . . but we unleashed a civil war of our own at MGM. Louis B. Mayer was the first casualty."

Lauren Bacall, who accompanied Bogart to Mexico for Treasure and Africa for The African Queen, and acted with him in Huston's Key Largo, spoke of the "roughly forty years of visions" that flashed before her when she thought of John. "I see him in Mexico at the end of a work day, shooting pool, bowling . . . contests, always; fun, always. Teaching me to drink tequila. I see him carrying an antique cradle into Bogie and my firstborn's room. I see him in the Belgian Congo, riding to location in a broken-down car down a broken-down road lined with small African children, John in the rear, smiling and giving the royal wave. I hear him describe an elephant hunt—the danger, excitement—in that incredible Huston voice, making you feel that you could stand in the middle of a herd of elephants and survive."

Bacall concluded by speaking of Huston's bravery during his last weeks and how, even in his wheelchair, he "dwarfed everyone else in the room." Then Richard Brooks introduced Jack Haley, Jr., who directed Huston when he was a co-host of the 1970 Oscars and when he played Professor Moriarty for a TV movie, Sherlock Holmes in New York.

"Roger Moore was Sherlock Holmes," Haley reminisced, "and he screamed at me that John Huston was stealing every scene. . . . I once asked John why he agreed to do this show and he said, 'Well, Jack, I have the time, I can use the money . . . and Moriarty is a part I was *born* to play.' "

Jack Nicholson read a tribute Lillian Ross had sent describing her long and adventurous friendship with Huston, which began when she had come to Hollywood in 1948 to report on the effects on the film industry of the HUAC hearings. "For some mysterious reason," Ross wrote, "my image of him is always the same. . . . He looked to me exactly as he looked at the age of 42, when I first met him: 6'2", lean, rangy, with unruly thick black hair, a deeply creased weather-battered face, the high cheekbones and the bashed-in nose, his eyes narrowed against the smoke from the little cigar in the corner of his mouth. And his voice, too, was always the same. He could always deliver the most ordinary line and make it sound like music."

Meta Wilde followed Nicholson's reading with a soft-spoken memory of how she first met John on the set of *The Maltese Falcon.* Then Harry Dean Stanton, who acted in *Wise Blood* and became a poker-playing friend, told of playing in Huston's last poker game in Newport and how they both lost about $300. He then gave a spirited rendering, in Spanish, of a revolutionary war song called "El Revolucionario," which he dedicated to John and Maricela.

"Jesus," Jack Nicholson muttered when Stanton finished and he introduced Charles Champlin, who spoke of *Beat the Devil* as his favorite Huston film.

When Paul Kohner got up to speak, leaning on a cane and helped by his son Pancho, he received a gracious ovation. He had been John's agent for close to fifty years. Then it was Ray Stark's turn. "John was my oldest . . . and youngest friend," Stark began. "He was a combination of Puck and King Lear." He related a story having to do with *Night of the Iguana* but kept any private feelings to himself. Richard Brooks spoke a few words about how Huston had taught him "to challenge the lie until I found the truth" when they co-wrote *Key Largo.* Then he introduced Anjelica. She repeated what Maricela had told her of John's last words, thanked everyone for coming, and began to cry. On the curtain behind her, John's face appeared and Walter Huston's recording of "September Song" was played.

> . . . .And the wine dwindles down
> to a precious brew,
> September . . . November

As Walter so movingly sang, a great silent sadness filled the auditorium. John Huston was gone, his movies would never disappear, but what about the man himself? Why was so little said about the private Huston?

At the burial of his ashes the next day, at a spot overlooking the pond in Hollywood Memorial Park, Tony played Irish songs on the tin whistle and members of the family each spent a few private moments thinking of the man who had so profound an influence on them all. Only Maricela ever expected to be saying good-bye in the cemetery where they all now stood. The irony that he had wanted to be buried with his mother, whom he rarely talked about, and not his father, who was his great friend, was not lost on anyone.

PART TWO

2

MA, WHERE'S PA?

ON AUGUST 28, 1986, ONE YEAR TO THE DAY BEFORE HE died, John Huston made a curious confession. Although he had saved all of his mother's writings, *he had never read them.* "I really haven't got the nerve to look at them," he admitted. When she died in 1938 he had put the manuscripts of his mother's unpublished attempts at autobiography, fiction, and playwriting in a large brown folder and thought he might be ready to read them when he got older, but even at eighty he admitted to being reluctant. "I even shy a little from it now."

What power did his mother's words have over him that made Huston—a man who had hunted tigers and elephants, jumped horses, walked through mined fields, got into countless brawls, stood up to studio moguls, and reduced well-known writers to tears—so fearful of reading them? Was she the key, as so many women who knew him over the years have speculated, to understanding him?

"She was obviously extremely important, a central character in his whole growing up and in his whole psychology in the years that succeeded," Olivia de Havilland believes. Huston was the one great love of de Havilland's life, and even after forty-five years, her memories continue to create turmoil within her. "I always felt that John was

43

ridden by witches and that if I could only know the names of these witches or the name of this witch, perhaps I could help him. He seemed to be pursued by something destructive. If it wasn't his mother then I think it was his idea of his mother.

"He felt rejected by his mother. Lots of people thought that John was afraid of being bored by a woman. Well, that is something to fear and it's always a possibility! But his real fear was the other way around. It's because of his mom, who was an astoundingly original human being."

Director Willy Wyler's wife, Talli, felt that John "must not have had any respect for his mother. Something must have happened to him that he couldn't have a relationship for much more than three years. That he couldn't open himself up."

Huston had tried to share his life with Lesley Black, an Englishwoman he married in the late thirties, but like his other four marriages, it didn't work out. Lesley knew John's mother only briefly. "I had the feeling always that the grandmother and mother rather stifled him from a child on. Wherever John lived for any length of time, they always turned up. He was the center of their lives."

Tony Huston could understand that. His father was the center of almost all the lives he came in contact with, especially among family. And often that center was more a maelstrom than a calm. "When you get into Dad's Mum, he didn't say much," Tony readily acknowledges. "All he ever told me was that she was erratic. You wonder how people's relationships with their mother affect their subsequent relationships."

Jeanie Sims, who was Huston's secretary in the early fifties, speculates that Huston needed to destroy those who loved him, that "he had a compulsion to make people—especially women—love him, and then, once having secured their love, an equal compulsion to spurn them." Sims believes that "the key to this facet of his personality may well lie in his relationship with his mother. She has always been a shadowy figure about whom he has spoken little."

Zoe Sallis thought "his mother disappointed him in some way, so he never gave that trust to anyone else. Because she didn't give him love when he needed it, he rejected her in the end in retaliation—probably loathing her for liking him too late, when he didn't need it."

Huston's fifth wife, Cici, claims that he used to talk to her about his mother. "It was a pretty torrid thing—his relationship with his mother," she said, hinting as well at the similarities to her own relationship with John. "I reminded him of his mother a lot."

Huston's reluctance to talk about his mother bordered on painful.

"We're about to get into deeper water here," he said when the subject was first broached, "let's save her for another time."

Eventually the time had come.

"I have very mixed feelings about my mother. Great favor in one way . . . and, in another way, I thought she was suffocating. Not because she followed me from place to place, but she would adhere too closely. She wanted me to be an actor. I might have been one if it hadn't been for her. Our relationship was a very difficult one. She was a mass of contradictions. There was an element of desperation. She had extraordinary physical courage. Liked excitement. I admired her on the one hand, couldn't stand her on the other. She was alternately very true and very false. She could lie to herself as well as to others. She had the ability to deceive herself when it served her purpose. She believed what she wanted to believe.

"She was quite well read. No shape to her reading or her education. I'm not at all sure that she could multiply or do long division. She had no gifts along those lines whatever.

"She was better with animals than people. Complete trust in herself with animals, more than was justified. She wouldn't have hesitated to get into a cage of lions. In fact, she did one time, at a place where they were training lions. And she could train a horse. She told me she once crossed the Mississippi River on a horse, and she wasn't into exaggerations regarding herself. My first memory is being on a horse in front of my mother.

"Once she came home and there was a burglar in the place. She got her pistol and pulled it on him, put him in the car, and had him drive to the police station. He was thrown in the jug. Then she began to inquire about him. Next thing, she had an attorney for him. Then she paid his bail to get him out, didn't press charges. That was the sort of person she was.

"She was a very complicated woman. At one time she had a hysterical paralysis. In retrospect, I could see how she was a hysteric, in the Freudian sense. She was very nervous, tending toward the neurotic; very active, smoked. She had strong emotions but was not strong emotionally. Very chaste. Part of her raising was in a convent. She would have been a Catholic except that she had been divorced. Yet I never lived anywhere with my mother that she wasn't somehow involved in the Church. She would go to confession but not take communion. She pretended—or didn't, I don't know which—to subscribe to the myth of Christianity. Virgin birth, the whole thing. I made fun of it, which would make her cry. She could burst into tears anytime she wanted. And I'm not sure that her crying wasn't as false as what she was crying about.

"I tormented my mother with being an atheist. I wasn't really, but I could see it would get under her skin. And it got to be a game. I would press a button, she would cry. I did a caricature one time of Jesus as an absurd dramatic figure, and she burst into tears looking at this.

"She and my grandmother were very close, although I think my mother was more emotionally akin to her father than to my grand-mother. My grandmother and my mother used to have fearsome quarrels.

"She gave me a few beatings as a child. I forget the things that I did. She used a strap. I remember her saying, 'Say "I'm sorry, that you'll never do it again." ' And I would say, 'I'm sorry, I'll never do it again.' Submitting. Then she would stop."

Submission. Suffocation. Deceit. The patterns were set for Huston's later rebellion against how he had grown up. He felt on safer ground when he talked about the years before he was born, when he could elaborate on the stories he had heard about his grandparents and the settling of the Midwest.

"My mother was the daughter of Adelia Richardson and John Gore. She was born in Newcastle, Indiana [on November 28, 1881]. My grandmother was the daughter of William Richardson, who was a general in the Civil War and attorney-general of the state of Ohio. He lost his arm at Chancellorsville and our most treasured family possession was a sword given to him by the men of the 25th Ohio. A beautiful sword that I passed on to my son, Tony. When his London apartment was broken into the only thing they took was the sword. I was just devastated."

The sword, and Richardson's acceptance speech, made an indelible impression on Huston, who was able to quote from memory: " 'The value of this gift is immeasurably enhanced by the fact that it was given to me by men who have proven their valor in their country's cause on many a well-fought field. . . . Wealth, influence or favoritism might procure such a gift as this, but the esteem and confidence of brave men cannot be bought.' "

Bravery and valor remained part of Huston's personal code through-out his life. He was a man who welcomed being judged upon life's battlefields.

*   *   *

Huston's grandfather, John Gore, was a character who seemed to belong in a John Huston movie. As a young girl, Huston's mother "lived in terror of her father and his drunkenness," according to Huston. "Children are afraid of alcoholics and their behavior because they don't know what to make of it. So her fears, her terror, had substance."

Huston remembered going with his mother to Quincy, Illinois, to fetch his grandpa, who had been gone on a bat for some months. "We came to a white house sitting back on a lawn in the middle of which was a large tree," Huston recounted. "By the time we arrived, it was raining very hard. Grandpa was sitting on the front porch." His mother sat down on the porch swing next to her father as he asked about his wife, whom he called Deal. "Suddenly there was a blinding light and a tremendous crash. The air was full of ozone. My mother fell off the swing onto her knees.

" 'Is Deal in good health?' asked Grandpa.

"I stared at the tree in the front yard, seared down the middle and smoldering, and thought: 'This must be what it means to be drunk. . . . Grandpa doesn't even know when lightning strikes!' "

In the blood of my father runs a call of the wild so strong that he cannot resist the craving for excitement, Huston's mother, Rhea, wrote in her unpublished memoir. *To be content he must have some obstacle to overcome. He does not realize a life that is simply productive and dignified amounts to anything. He must run helter-skelter from one conflict to another more frequently than not creating havoc, not only for himself but for mother who is more gently inclined. His desires are at all times parent to his actions regardless of mother's advice. By nature he is a dreamer—by habit a showman, yet had any one suggested to him that he was either of these things he would have denied it.*

John Gore's running "helter-skelter" most assuredly did create havoc for his wife and child. He was a restless man who saw great opportunities in the settling of America in the late nineteenth century. According to Huston's grandmother, some of whose writings were also found in the envelope containing his mother's manuscripts, John Gore was "a tall slender man," who, at thirty-eight in 1881, was "prematurely gray" with a "long flowing mustache." John Gore had a "very pleasing manner and was well liked by everyone." People would later describe his grandson in similar terms.

In the spring of 1882 they went to Cincinnati on their way to Kansas and met a friend, who told them of the opportunities awaiting settlers in Florida. "To settle the matter we flipped pennies: Florida or Kansas. Kansas won." They went first to Wichita, where Adelia and eighteen-month-old Rhea found a place to stay. John Gore went on to Saratoga. Within a week he found a small house, set up a newspaper, and sent for his family. "When John left me he wore a neat dark blue suit and highly polished shoes and plug hat," wrote Adelia. "Now the man who said, 'Here I am,' wore a broad-brimmed gray hat, corduroy trousers stuffed in the tops of high-heeled boots, a gray flannel shirt, and a six-shooter." John Gore had become a cowboy.

Once settled in Saratoga, Adelia soon discovered that neither "one's religion nor politics cut any figure in this town, but woe be unto you if you were at all friendly with the inhabitants of the other town—Pratt Center—only 1½ miles from us." The reason for the unfriendliness was that both towns were vying for county seat; the town that won would eventually get the railroad and prosper, while the other town would most likely fold.

A few weeks before the legislature decided to give the county seat to Pratt Center, John and Adelia Gore had "seen the writing on the wall" and set out for Syracuse, Kansas, along the Colorado border. On the crowded train they met a woman named Kate Skidmore, who was on her way with her brother and his wife to Garden City to file a claim for 160 acres of land. John Gore listened with great interest.

Once in Syracuse, he and another man, Harry, started a newspaper, *The Democrat*. "Harry could set type and so could I," wrote Adelia. "John usually got what he went after, he was a good manager and promoter but he never did a real day's work in his life." Once the paper got rolling, John Gore went to Garden City and filed a claim twenty-two miles south of Syracuse.

Taking advantage of the Homestead Act passed by Congress in 1862, providing 160 acres of unoccupied public land to each homesteader who either lived there for five years or paid $1.25 per acre after six months' residence, he gathered his family and moved them to Stanton County in the southwest corner of Kansas, joining others who had done the same. Wrote Huston's mother, *Most of the men drawn West are from failures of yesterdays. Men who have failed to keep their hands off other men's property. Men who have failed to let live and men who have failed or been failed by their sweethearts and wives. Some are sleek and well groomed and fine of speech, while others look like ill-conditioned animals with stubby beards and large voices.*

These well-groomed men joined hands with the ill-conditioned animals to hammer and nail a house together in two days. To keep her young daughter occupied as the prairie was developed, Adelia Gore gave Rhea a container of salt and told her she could catch a bird by putting salt on its tail.

When the house is completed my father brings a load of truck containing bed and bedding, a table, a chair, a washboard and a tub. Then my father leaves us, saying he has other fish to fry.

John Gore went back to his newspaper in Syracuse. Adelia, Rhea, and Kate Skidmore, who couldn't afford the lumber to build her own house, lived together in this deserted country, five miles from the nearest watering hole.

When surveyors came to parcel out a claim adjoining theirs, Adelia discovered that their privy was not only on their new neighbors' land but in the next county. The outhouse had to be moved, so she hitched their bony horse and little gray mule to their wagon and set off to enlist the aid of other homesteaders, offering them the bread she baked in her cook-stove fueled by buffalo chips.

Life was difficult for these squatters: The land was rough, the insects murderous, the days hot, and the nights oppressively dark. Gunfights often settled quarrels, coyotes howled, and the occasional cyclone chased distant settlers together to huddle in an underground dugout. "It sounded like *Cimarron*," Huston once commented.

One morning, Adelia woke up and "as usual, opened the door and looked out toward the town of Edwin. Imagine my surprise when there was no Edwin. *Everything* gone but the post office. Gone to Richfield. While we claim holders slept and dreamed perhaps of the fortunes awaiting us, Richfield slipped in and moved our town away."

Undeterred, Adelia took Kate and Rhea on the stagecoach to the Land Office in Garden City in Finney County to "prove-up" their land. Adelia paid her money and became "absolute owner of a hundred and sixty acres of Kansas prairie." But instead of returning to the land, she and Kate decided to run the newspapers in Syracuse and Leoti, now owned by John Gore.

I can see mother sitting on a high stool before a slope-top desk picking little letters out of small boxes, placing them in a shallow metal trough she holds in her left hand. When the stick is full, she slides the type lines, without spilling, into a rack and runs a small inked roller over it then she covers it with a strip of white paper.

The paper recorded births, deaths, the filing of land claims, local news, and national politics. The big news at the time Adelia and John

Gore were running their newspapers was the election of Grover Cleveland as President of the United States in 1884. The scandal of that election was that Cleveland had an illegitimate child with a woman named Maria Halpin. The cowboys in Syracuse tied a red, white, and blue bow to young Rhea's hair and taught the child the latest ditty:

> Ma . . . Ma . . . Where is my Pa?
> Gone to the White House.
> Ha Ha Ha.

With Adelia living in a house on the outskirts of Syracuse, John Gore went to manage the paper in Garden City, where he became a leader of the temperance movement. *Editorials on Temperance take up much space in* The Democrat, Rhea Gore remembered. *Cowboys are now spoken of as "The Sons of Temperance." There hasn't been any gun play or a fist fight for more than a month.*

But it was a little too much for Adelia Gore to believe. She knew only too well that her husband was a periodical drinker who, when he drank, usually went on a spree that lasted from six to eight weeks. The end of the temperance movement came in the person of I Bar Johnson, who came into town and attended a meeting of the "Town Protectors."

"I Bar, have you been rummy enough to sign the pledge?" father asks.

"See here," says I Bar. "How long have I been comin' in and out of this here town?"

"Since before my time I reckon," father answers.

"And what's my reputation I'm askin' y'u?"

"Bang up," says my father.

"Such bein' the case," says I Bar, drawing himself up and hitching his belt a notch tighter, "do you fellows calculate that I tackled them five bank robbers single-handed, killin' one and dancin' the remainin' four to the calaboose without a posse on pink pop or sassafras tea? I'll 'low half of it was guts—but the other half was whiskey."

"All right gentlemen," says my father raising his hand for silence. "The signing of the pledge is hereby declared unconstitutional."

With arms around each other's shoulders all barriers of progress are burned away with firewater.

Adelia Gore would later write, reflecting upon her eighteen-year marriage, "I can truthfully say that I was a good wife and am sure I did not leave a stone unturned to help him overcome that terrible desire for liquor." As her grandson, who would inherit her love of words, would say, "My grandmother endured a hell of a lot."

Somehow I can feel my mother thinking—thinking things I intuitively know are heartbreaking. My father has taken the one drink that sets him off on another spree.

When Mother starts to cry I do the same. My father bangs the table so hard with his fist he skins his knuckles.

"Now see what you have done," he says, holding out his hand as though reaching for sympathy. Mother is aggravatingly silent. My father becomes pleased with himself, but his witless parlays do not bring a smile to her face. Father's mood changes gear—he is depressed and feels his aloneness.

"There is no point in me staying on here," he says, "life is just slipping away from me. It's too quiet and monotonous here for an alert man with ability. I'm going—right now."

"Going where?" asks my mother.

"Out into the wide world," says my father wistfully, "to knock around a bit . . . to see foreign places, new faces, win fame . . ."

"Oh, shut up," Mother says and walks slowly out of the room.

"That's enough," yells my father. "Many a woman loses her husband one way and another. Perhaps in your case it could have been avoided—you know I don't like petty squabbles. I'm going." With a hand on my shoulder he leans forward breathing whiskey on my face, then he reaches for his high hat and cane but he does not go because he cannot get his shoes on.

It all became a nightmare for Rhea, who sadly witnessed these fights and separations between her parents. Once he managed to get his shoes on, John Gore disappeared for months, knocking around in that wide, foreign world, reassuring himself, as his daughter would write, "that travel is a means of escape from a humdrum existence."

On one toot he sold off three of his newspapers—in Santa Fe, Garden City, and Saratoga. When Adelia heard of this, she wired everyone she knew in various parts of the country, telling them if they saw her husband to put him on a train and send him to her.

Eventually John Gore returned. On that particular occasion he brought home a fourteen-year-old orphan from Dodge City, named Henry. He had told the boy he was a rich sheep rancher and offered to adopt him. It was left to Adelia to set the boy straight.

She explains that every so often father does this sort of thing. At such times, she says, as his money and possessions diminish in reality, they increase in his fancy, sometimes reaching gigantic proportions. The nearer broke he becomes the greater is his imaginary wealth. When absolutely down and out, the truth then filters through his brain enough to prompt him to make a beeline for home.

Mother is very sorry for Henry as she takes his hand and leads him around the corner of the house. "There, son," says my mother, pointing to a few bedraggled chickens in an improvised coup, "are all of the rich rancher's sheep."

When my father is ready to sober up he tells my mother and together they prepare for the coming ordeal. "I am ready," he says, then he goes to bed to get up in another month if he is lucky.

John Huston was proud of his grandfather. He knew he was often compared to the wild old Gore who lived by his wits, couldn't stand being bored, and had a need to drink, gamble, and carouse. Huston's mother, as a young girl, couldn't understand why her father got so angry when she looked inside some of his private letters and smelled the perfumed sheets. Nor could she understand why that would make her mother cry when she told her about them. John Huston understood only too well. A man does what a man's got to do. Or, as his mother wrote, "When my father does not know what to do, he does as he pleases."

When he would sober up, decisions would be made. Where next? Together or separate? When a town called Jetmore, not far from Dodge City, secured the county seat in the mid-1880s, John Gore convinced Adelia to start a newspaper there.

There weren't many women who edited newspapers at that time, but Adelia Gore proved a tough and feisty editor of *The Jetmore Journal.* When a rival editor "with blood in his eye and a chip on his shoulder was ready to down me at any cost," Adelia uncovered his plot and fought back through the pages of her paper, devoting columns to undermine those who feared her competition. One Republican editor wrote an article calling her "the erudite masculine editor in female attire." But Adelia "lit into him. I told him things he did not think anyone knew. . . . I never saw . . . him again."

It proved to be an exciting eighteen months for Adelia, who became a popular figure in the town when she fought the Santa Fe railroad and saved Jetmore from becoming a ghost town. For John, it was just a place to dry out between his periodicals.

The Gore family, however, split up. Two things occurred to hasten their separation. One was an offer made to Adelia to buy *The Journal* at a substantial profit. The other was yet another row with John. With the sale of the paper, Adelia made a difficult but steadfast decision: She would travel farther west, to LaJara, Colorado, in the San Luis Valley—but only after taking Rhea by train to Indiana where her sister lived.

Mother explains that she will no longer be able to take me with her when she goes to work, that she will have to work for others to earn money to take care of me. She tells me I am to be placed in a convent to grow up.

On the morning they were to leave their home in Jetmore, Rhea remembered her mother being pensive and sad. *She remarks husbands are like styles—always changing but not for the better. My mother gently kisses my sleeping father and murmurs something about leaving him in a terrible predicament, adding to the horror of the situation. My mother's pale melancholy face oppresses me. I slip once more to my father and look at the pitiable spectacle of his condition.*

The child couldn't leave until she woke her father and asked him to sign her yellow autograph album. John Gore gripped the pencil his daughter placed in his hand and scribbled his name on an empty page. And then, beneath it, he wrote: *"A piece of God's carelessness."*

For Rhea Gore, who had already lived in numerous hotels and half a dozen homes in small towns, burgeoning cities, and desolate prairie, the separation from her parents and induction into convent life was, by far, the most formidable experience of her young life.

"The first thing I learn is that I shall henceforth be known by a number. Number forty-one." In defiance, she told a nun, "My father and my mother are separated. They are going to get a divorce so I am sent here that I may be out of the way while I study and grow up."

It was difficult to adjust to the monotony of her new life, doing "the same identical things we did yesterday and will do again tomorrow." She quickly learned: *A convent girl shall have no time to think for herself. It is a religious duty for her to have no will of her own, no thought for or of herself. Nothing changes but the length of a girl's hair and skirt.*

And in the world outside the convent, nothing seemed to change between Adelia and John Gore. In 1889, when Rhea was eight, the Oklahoma Territory was opened to settlement and John Gore was among the men who crossed the Kansas border by horseback to make a claim to land that had previously belonged to the Indians. Staking out a spot in what today is northern Oklahoma, they started up a town called Perry. The first two framed structures to go up were Big John's saloon and the courthouse. John Gore owned the saloon and became the town's magistrate. His life looked promising and he missed his family, so he wrote his wife and told her he would stop drinking if she would come and bring Rhea with her. Adelia had heard such promises before, but their life had developed into a pattern. She withdrew her daughter from the convent and put her on a train in the care of the conductor, sending her ahead to see her father. *Pinned on my frock front was a card with writing on it telling my name, my destination, and how to notify my mother if anything happened to me.*

It was an exciting moment for Rhea, the answer to her prayers that she be reunited with her mother and father. She couldn't wait to see her daddy. All the way there, she imagined what he'd be like: sober, in a new town, a judge! The trip took two weeks and when she arrived she was met by a stranger, who took her to the judge. "Sprawled in a nearby covered wagon lay my father," Rhea would never forget, "bleary-eyed and forgetful, strongly smelling of the cause of his condition." It was a crushing disappointment for Rhea, who had seen him like this numerous times but had never gotten used to the harsh reality of her father so destroyed by whiskey that he couldn't even recognize his little girl. She began to cry as she leaned over John Gore in that wagon, trying to make him understand that she had come by herself all that way to be with him, to live together again as a family. But Gore was in a half-dream land and a woman named Mrs. Fisher came and took Rhea home with her.

The next day, Mrs. Fisher brought Rhea to see her father in his role as town magistrate. At the courthouse, Rhea sat with Mrs. Fisher and watched her father "tottering on the bench, listening to all that was said for and against those brought before him." It was all so difficult for her to comprehend. Here was her father, larger than life, the voice of reason and justice in this newly settled town, yet so irresponsible that he couldn't even provide for his own family. But, she noticed, "When it came to rendering judgment my father each time reserved his decision and went on to the next case on the docket."

That was the last I saw of my father for many years, for when we got back to the tent home there was Mr. Fisher waiting with a letter from my mother. That night a tag was again pinned on the front of my frock and I was started on my long journey back to the convent.

Rhea Gore returned to the dormitory she had hoped she would never see again and "took to praying like a duck takes to water." Her prayers were usually for her wayward father; her thoughts often centered around death.

I hate the consecrated ground visible always from the dormitory windows. My last sight at night, my first in the morning. This graveyard hammers my subconsciousness morning and night, sending a convincing dread through my heart.

When she learned about the Immaculate Conception and the promised return of Christ, the idea that a virgin could bear a child was overpowering to her. *It left no doubt in my mind as to the awkward position I would be placed in if such an honor should foreshadow my destiny. My brain became haunted by the fear that I might be the next girl chosen and spiritually disciplined to give birth to a child without the aid of man. I strove to contaminate my purity and render myself unfit for so sacred a mission by writing such shocking words in my copybooks as scribbled in outhouses and on barn doors. The hubbub that followed their discovery left no doubt in my mind as to the accomplishment of my purpose.* She was reprimanded and threatened with expulsion.

As she matured, Rhea's dreams were of a worldly nature. She hoped to be a "gorgeous creature," wearing embroidered petticoats and dresses made of blue silk taffeta. She wanted to use the type of soap that would allow her to smell "like the soft brown earth after a rain." And, through her reading of the Book of Proverbs, she became convinced that she would become a mother herself one day. But gradually, during her years away from her mother and father, the rituals and beliefs of the Church began to have an effect on her. She was struck by the splendor of the priests' vestments, she participated in the convent's retreats, she learned the litanies of the saints and martyrs, she became enveloped by the sacrifice and teachings of Jesus Christ.

What stuck in Rhea's mind was "the fact that His father did not stick to Him," which made her feel that "Christ and I have something in common."

She began to believe that her family was dependent upon her. What she most wanted was to live with them again, but during one retreat decided she was prepared to make the ultimate sacrifice: She prayed to God to take her life so that her parents would be together. It became an obsession.

She bitterly resented being put in such a position, believing that "my father could save me if he would only quit drinking of his own accord." But she knew that would not happen and so she knelt in prayer:

Dear God, I put myself in your hands for you to tear me to smithereens— and after I am dead from dying, to send me to hell if you want to. I am shortening my life by many years that YOU may see fit, because of my sacrifice, to cause my father to keep sober that he and my mother may go back together and not get that divorce.

Once her prayer was offered, she began to dramatize her demise. *The girls will pass my bier with their eyes cast down in silent sorrow. And the sisters, with black beads sliding through their fingers, will choke and utter nothing save a sob. There will be a Requiem Mass in the chapel. I hope they will put some red stuff on my lips grown pale so they will not look dry but soft and fair in my repose.*

Lest there be any doubt about where John Huston got his sense of the dramatic, one need only to continue reading his mother's death fantasy, as she prepared herself to be lowered into the ground in a pine box. *I hope it won't rain. I don't want to lie in the sop—not the first night, for slimy nightworms to come out of the elements and squeeze through the cracks in the box to creep on my flesh and grow bloated on my lips. After rain weeds will sprout from my toes and the roots of the devil grass and dandelions will get tangled with my intestines. The fact that I shall not be conscious of it does not quiet my revulsion.*

When she awoke the following morning and realized that she was still alive she began to *howl at my Creator, screaming such four-letter words as I once wrote in my copybook. My unleashed emotions gush out in a torrent of hissing noises. I who recently offered my life reluctantly am now filled with fury because I exist. I who sincerely offered my life as a sacrifice, by no means easy, now believe I have been duped, tricked, and by God Himself made a target for His jokes.*

In her anger, Rhea barged in on the Abbess, "who is over all the nuns and novices including the Mother Superior in charge of the student girls." The Abbess was kind and listened to Rhea as she poured out her life story, ending with how she offered herself to God only to be betrayed and humiliated. Then the Abbess said, "It must have taken considerable egotism for you to look upon yourself as good enough to be so favored even if Jesus had been considering His return at this time." And she further chided her for her impudent anger at God's refusal to take her life, "Because you are unable to direct your own destiny you go into a tantrum like a three-year-old and rail out at Him in your doubt. Don't you see how truly ridiculous it is to give God your life and then dictate to Him in what manner He is to use it?"

When the Abbess has finished speaking I see more clearly. But somehow my religious ardor has considerably cooled.

When the time came for her to graduate and leave the convent in 1898, Rhea listened to one of the nuns lecture the graduating students about sex. "Those of you whose vocation it may be to marry, must be sure to choose fit men to be the fathers of your children," they were told. And with that advice, Rhea Gore was put on the train to

Cincinnati, where she would live with her mother and think about what it was she wanted to do with her life. It was only then that she realized "no part of a girl's education prepared her for any field of business."

Adelia, who was by then divorced from John Gore (he was living in Colorado, prospecting for gold when he wasn't running a saloon), had a friend who had made a fortune by opening a chain of drugstores, and Adelia thought the perfect job for her daughter would be as an apothecary apprentice. Rhea would have preferred being a nurse, but Adelia had the impression that nurses were not respectable. "Like ladies of the stage," remarked Rhea, "it is alleged they are prone to be seduced."

When Rhea suggested taking a business course, her mother again worried it might not be a proper vocation, since it would mean becoming a secretary and everyone knew that men took advantage of their secretaries. Frustrated and resentful at being treated like a child, Rhea snapped at her mother, "Do you think I'm an imbecile?"

But it wasn't her intelligence that was in question, it was her hormones. *I loathe these "advice to the innocent" lectures. It seems I must think of sex as something dirty.* Her mother warned her: "Once the good name of a girl is tarnished she can never live it down." *It throws me into tantrums of anger. I am going to do as I darn well please.*

On her own, Rhea got a job as a temporary receptionist in a doctor's office. Her mother immediately took sick. As soon as the position was filled by someone else, Adelia recovered. Although Rhea felt grown up, her "years of obeying set rules" prevented her from considering resistance. Ultimately, the conflict between mother and daughter made Rhea ill. She lost weight, her color paled.

Although Rhea had grown up away from her mother, Adelia still saw her as her little girl. Furthermore, the customs of the time didn't allow Rhea to do as she pleased. She was frustrated professionally, frustrated sexually, and her convent years hadn't left her spiritually satisfied. As she continued to become lean and sickly, her mother forced her to take health tonics and prepared food from magazine recipes. In a line that could have been written by John Huston about his mother, Rhea wrote about her own: "Aside from myself my mother seems to have no other interest in life. My welfare seems to be her sole aim in existing."

A doctor found nothing wrong with her, other than the fact she was "a bit nervous," and suggested Rhea be permitted to marry young. He then prescribed asafetida to be taken internally. The foul-smelling resin was probably considered the equivalent of a cold shower.

I have been made to wear a little sack of the horrid-smelling stuff hanging from a string around my neck. I think of it as worse than any possible disease it is presumed to ward off. I smell like something poisonous, molded, and rotten. It is utterly appalling—worse than garlic, worse than limburger cheese, worse than anything except asafetida.

The experience of being subjected to such a potent "cure" did result in giving direction to Rhea's life. *Under the stimulus of asafetida I conceive the idea of becoming a writer.* How smelling awful and deciding to become a writer coincide isn't exactly clear, but Rhea Gore credited this particular humiliation with stimulating her creativity. *It would be great to become a famous author and wherever I am to have people say, "Here she comes," and "There she goes."*

Where she went was to St. Louis. Her mother received a letter from John Gore in Colorado saying he was desperately ill and in need of her, so Adelia took Rhea to St. Louis, where she left her in the care of the manager of a family hotel, and continued on to help her former husband get over another of his periodicals.

It was to prove to be a most fateful move.

Attempting to write articles for the local newspapers, Rhea discovered that becoming a famous author wasn't easy. But there was one advantage in calling herself a free-lance writer: She was able to obtain free passes to all the plays and shows presented in the city under the pretense that she would write pieces about the performances. When a play called *The Sign of the Cross* came to town, she saw the show and then went backstage to interview the star, Wilson Barrett. She noticed one of the minor actors, an older man with a beard and carrying a staff, who had played a Christian, and felt uncomfortable at the way he eyed her—it was the look of a much younger rogue.

By then, Rhea was an attractive young woman who had already received one marriage proposal from the son of a shoe manufacturer. The proposal came in the mail and Rhea, who wasn't at all interested in marrying this man, sent the letter on to her mother in Colorado. Adelia wrote her a disheartening reply:

"The son of a nationally known shoe manufacturer should be able to provide for you well now and much better later. Willing as I am, I cannot take care of you always."

Her mother's suggestion that she consider marrying even though she felt no love made Rhea cry. She was alone and lonely and it was Thanksgiving when she entered the lobby of her hotel, where she noticed a young man wearing an outrageous pair of red crocheted slippers. She wasn't the only person who noticed—it seemed every guest in the hotel sneered and snickered at this man's flamboyance as he sat by the front window reading a newspaper, his silly red slippers in full view of those who passed by outside. Somehow this spectacle of the young man being ridiculed touched Rhea and made her heart roll over in sympathy.

When he caught her staring, he smiled and said, "I don't care a hump if they don't like me."

"It's your gay slippers which strike others as queer for a man to be wearing in public," Rhea said.

"I'm no fairy," the young man said defensively, explaining that his mother had crocheted them for him.

For some unknown reason my sympathies are aroused. I think it noble of the young man to defy the conventionalities and wear his red crocheted slippers when and where he darn well pleases. Then I really look at him for the first time. He stands arrogantly awkward as though holding onto a stepladder and afraid to let go. His face is thin and his hair no color at all. His mouth is extremely large and lids with long lashes drop over his eyes.

Since they were both alone and as it was Thanksgiving, the young man invited Rhea to join him for dinner, and because she felt sorry for him—especially after he mentioned that his father had recently died of a "tobacco heart"—she agreed. His name, he told her, was Walter Huston and he was an actor. In fact, he had a small part carrying a staff in *The Sign of the Cross*, only she probably wouldn't recognize him as he wore a false beard and was made up to appear much older.

Had it not been for a pair of red crocheted slippers, Rhea would later write, *things would undoubtedly not be what they are today. Their laces have tangled my life and knotted my heart strings in a way that cannot be undone.*

Over dinner that night and during subsequent dinners and dates to the World's Fair, which was the popular attraction in St. Louis in 1904, Walter Huston told Rhea Gore the story of his life—a life far removed from the one she had known. She was especially impressed by the young man's early independence and self-resolve, for he was just twenty when they met and she was twenty-three.

3

TO BE OR NOT TO BE

WALTER HUSTON WAS BORN IN TORONTO ON APRIL 6, 1884, the fourth child of Elizabeth McGibbon and Robert Houghston. His parents, who had married in Caledon, Ontario, on Christmas Day, 1872, when each was twenty-four, were of Scotch-Irish descent. Elizabeth's mother was a schoolteacher; Robert's father, Alexander, was a pioneer farmer who settled in the small town of Orangeville, a short distance from Toronto.

Robert Houghston had three brothers and none of them got along well with their father, who was like the character Eugene O'Neill created in Ephraim Cabot—a craggy, no-nonsense, individualist set in his ways and strict toward his sons. He once turned down an offer of decent grazing land because it wasn't rocky enough for him to get the satisfaction of making it work by the sweat of his own brow. When one of his boys brought home a violin, Alexander broke it into pieces because "it had the devil in it." When the old man died, the four boys divided his land evenly and sold their shares to finance other dreams. Two of them went to Detroit to open a furniture factory. Walter's father, an easygoing, good-natured man with a strong sense of humor and little ambition, became a contracting carpenter who specialized in cabinetry. None of the brothers had the hardened tenacity of their father and they weren't especially successful in their businesses.

As the youngest child, Walter grew up spoiled by his mother. His earliest memory was joyfully listening to the music played by the Salvation Army band outside his house. Music played an important role in their home, especially when it was discovered that Walter's sister Margaret was gifted with a remarkably beautiful voice and was encouraged to take singing lessons. Young Walter, not to be outdone, would return from church and convulse his family with his imitation of the preacher, singing nonsense hymns, and learning early that showing off would get him attention and applause.

Walter's best friend was Archie Christie, who shared his hatred of school and his love of adventure. Together the boys would play hooky and go off hunting, fishing, or ice-skating. On Saturdays, they sneaked into the variety shows at the Shea Theatre, where they sat in the balcony along with Walter's older cousin, Arthur, whose one ambition was to be a juggler, and watch the acrobats, dancers, yodelers, magicians, ventriloquists, rope climbers, animal trainers, and musicians perform. These shows were magical interludes for the boys and inspired them to imitate the acts they had seen and then to put on their own "pin shows" for the other children in their neighborhood, performed either in the basement of Walter's house or in Arthur's barn. The children who came to see Arthur juggle, Archie yodel, and Walter play the harmonica, jew's harp, and tin-can drum would each pay a fee of one straight pin. As acts improved, admission was upped to a safety pin, and finally the boys began to charge a penny.

The shows came to a crashing halt when Walter tried to create a professional-looking backdrop by swiping one of his mother's bed sheets and smearing it with green paint. She popped her head downstairs to see how the boys were faring, saw what her son had done, and charged down the steps screaming her favorite threat, "I'll put you to the stranger!" She grabbed Walter and ended his early theatrical career with a public beating. Pennies were refunded.

Undaunted, Walter and Archie continued to practice, in the woods, the acrobatics they saw at the Shea Theatre. His mother, hoping to encourage his musical side, tried teaching him the piano, admonishing him with another of her oft-repeated declarations, "I'll have no stupid children around me." Walter practiced for three years but the only lesson he learned was that he could not be *taught* anything—the same lesson he had come to learn in school as well.

In 1933, Walter talked to a reporter about his childhood. "When I was a boy, I knew that, by some weird freak of nature or the elements, I wanted to be an actor. I lived in a stern climate among practical, hard-working, hard-fisted men. To be an actor, in our family, was about as outlandish a notion as to be a gnome or a five-footed cow.

"I never read Shakespeare or poetry in those days. (I read very little now.) I never postured in front of mirrors. I wasn't unhappy or frustrated or any of those modern things, ever. I was best, in school, at such specific subjects as mathematics, history, and technical studies. During vacations my brother, Alec, and I worked on our father's building projects, and it didn't worry me for one minute to think that I was handling bricks and timbers instead of grease paint and scripts. I was about as far from the environment, the talk, the 'feel,' of an actor as any lad could be."

But Walter did have an early and memorable theater experience. The show was to be performed before the congregation of the Beverly Street Baptist Church and Walter was eight years old. When it came his turn to walk onstage, he balked and had to be pushed in front of the audience by his mother, who watched helplessly in the wings as Walter was stricken with such stage fright that he couldn't utter a word. It would be six years before anyone could persuade him to appear on a stage again.

His sister Nan boosted his ego when she convinced the musical director of St. Simon's Episcopal Church that her fourteen-year-old brother would be perfect performing in blackface for their minstrel show. Walter was still bringing home the acts he saw at the variety shows and entertaining his family, but he had strong doubts about playing before an audience of strangers. The musical director agreed to give him a chance to tell some jokes and to sing "My Linda Lee" at St. George's Hall. He was terrible in rehearsals, as he was for most of his career, but, according to Nan, her brother was the hit of the show and Walter discovered, to his everlasting relief, that instead of being dumbstruck, he was actually inspired by the audience.

The following week the minstrel show was repeated at an all-men's affair, called a "smoker" because of the tobacco smoke blown into the air. Walter performed confidently, and when it was over, he remembered taking his gloves from his pocket as he walked home and smelling the smoke. It was a significant, private moment for the teenager. The smell of those smoky gloves made him feel that he was no longer a boy. That night he had become a man.

*   *   *

Walter's sister Margaret was well on her way to becoming a serious opera singer. She, too, had performed before church groups, and when she turned eighteen a group of Toronto women made her their protégée and put on what was billed as the Margaret Huston Benefit Recital to help pay her way to Paris to study for several years. When she returned, she became a successful concert singer and was interviewed for the newspapers. The women who helped her on her way now accepted her as one of their own and her entrance into Toronto's High Society interested Walter. He remembered that his older sister had taped a little banner on her mirror that said, "I'm Going to Be a Millionaire." He decided if his sister could figure so prominently among the rich and snobbish, there was no reason he couldn't follow her example. He gave serious thought to becoming a singer, too, and spending a few years abroad, returning to the hurrahs of the high and mighty.

At the turn of the century, when they were sixteen and sophomores in high school, Walter and Archie tried out for a road show called *The White Heather* starring Rose Coghlan. They were hired to appear at a whopping fifty cents per show. Since the Wednesday matinee conflicted with school, they had to skip classes that day, but that meant they also had to contain their excitement and keep the news from their parents. As John would later write about his father, "From that moment acting became his life."

It took courage for Walter to approach his mother to talk with her about quitting school, knowing that his grandmother had been a teacher and how strongly his mother felt about education. But the experience of *The White Heather* had convinced him that he was not meant to spend another two years in high school. To his surprise, his mother agreed with him. He wasn't scholarly material, she admitted, but she'd be damned if she'd allow him to romp about with a lowly bunch of gypsy theater people who had to sing for their supper. If he didn't want to go to school then he'd have to go to work. The choice was his.

Walter's first job was as a timekeeper for an asphalt company. It didn't last. Next he was a clerk in a woolen store, then a clerk in the hardware department of Simpson's store. There he earned $5 a week and all he could steal, which was easy, since there were no cash registers then. But he hadn't lost sight of wanting to be an actor, and when he and Archie earned enough money they enrolled in the Shaw School of Acting. They had finally found a school to hold their interest.

At Shaw's they appeared in the story of Rigoletto called *The Fool's Revenge* and were discovered by a traveling tragedian named Edward d'Oize. D'Oize offered them $15 a week—money he didn't have—to join his repertory company. The attraction of being part of a company and "seeing the world" was too great an opportunity to turn down. They were seventeen and it was time to make it on their own.

Without telling their families, Walter and Archie joined up with d'Oize and became members of his road show. Walter made his first professional appearance as an old man of eighty in a play by d'Oize called *The Montebank*. On the same bill was a play called *David Garrick*, and Walter played another old man.

In *Garrick*, his character, Squire Chivey, was supposed to be drunk in the first scene. Since Walter didn't know how to *act* drunk he took his first swig of Scotch whiskey just before the performance and made his entrance genuinely drunk. The audience howled at his behavior onstage and Walter thought inebriation was just the way to approach the role. When the second act came, time had passed and the squire was supposed to be sober. As time moves faster in the imagination than within the human body, Walter could not play his character straight, so Squire Chivey was drunk again in the second act. An actor, Walter discovered, is someone who gives imitations of men who do things and is not a doer himself.

That first trip with d'Oize was to prove a severe test of his own desires. From Toronto, they traveled south and east, playing to near-empty houses in small theaters, rarely receiving their promised salary, yet having to come up with living expenses. Boardinghouses charged between seventy-five and ninety cents a day, to be paid in advance, since actors were considered, as Walter once put it, "weak, thieving, shiftless, drunken adventurers at best." It was a hard, dirty, and depressing life where hunger was a constant. Clothes had to be washed by hand but rarely got completely dry. The train rides were long and uncomfortable, the show houses dismal. Walter and Archie came to the same conclusion: They loved it!

"The old traveling shows made actors," Walter believed. "More of my illusions were destroyed on that trip with d'Oize than in all the balance of my life combined and still my determination to become an actor was not daunted in the slightest."

Not even when, on a bleak December day in Canandaigua, New York, not far from Rochester, the tour came to an end. There was no money to pay any bills and the company's trunks were confiscated, the actors stranded. For Walter and Archie it was an omen. The time had obviously come for them to pool the $3 they had between them and head for what was to them "Arabia, the peaks of the Himalayas, city of incalculable wonders," the Big Time: New York. They grasped hands and vowed to succeed.

They spent sixty cents for two train tickets to Rochester and then roamed the train yard looking for hoboes who could give them advice on how to bum their way to New York City. They opted for the boxcar on a freight train and spent a frozen night huddling together, swearing they'd never do such a foolish thing again. When morning arrived, they discovered they had hopped the wrong train and were in Lyons, forty miles from Rochester! They had to start all over. The next day it snowed, they froze again, but Walter and Archie made it to 125th Street in Manhattan. They figured the worst was now behind them.

Down to their last forty cents, they splurged it all on a decent breakfast. Then they walked along Broadway, staring at the marquees, dazzled by the very idea that they had actually made it. They told each other, "One of these days . . . soon."

With no money to rent a room and no one to call for a loan, Walter and Archie spent their first day in New York walking the streets, looking for temporary work. Walter spotted a sign in a restaurant window and got a job as a waiter. The money he earned enabled him to rent a small single room. Archie sneaked in each night and they shared the narrow bed.

As New York prepared for Christmas, Walter and Archie realized how miserable they were, away from their families, alone in a foreign city, one of them out of work and the other in a menial job. Their only joy was the theaters, where they hung around whenever they could. And then, one lucky day, Archie was hired for $25 a week to tour in a play called *Human Hearts*. He left immediately. Walter, while glad for his friend, was now alone in the city.

Then, two weeks later, Archie came through. He sent his friend $10 and Walter immediately quit his job. At last he could go to auditions, pound the streets, pursue the dream.

Walter was hired to play a juvenile in a touring company and for the next two months got a chance to act in the small towns of upstate New York. When he got back together with Archie they discovered they had saved $200 between them, enough to go on a spree at Saks and buy the loudest suits they could find, dandify themselves with canes and straw hats, and agree that they could now return to Toronto in style, having "conquered" New York.

"Where'd you get the money for that fool suit?" his father asked, refusing to believe anyone could earn enough from acting to buy such clothing.

It was not exactly a triumphant return. Archie heard about a troupe in Detroit and told Walter if it worked out, he would wire him. True to his word, when the lead in a play called *In Convict Stripes* called for a "big husky fellow, broad-shouldered, football hero type," Archie told the producer, B. C. Whitney, that he knew just the fellow to fill the bill.

"Big husky football type," Walter's mother scoffed. "Why, you're skinny as a rail beam." But since he had his heart set on leaving, his mother helped fatten him up by sewing padding into his jacket and into tights for his legs.

It was the hottest summer ever recorded in Detroit in 1902 when Walter arrived, wearing a quilted shirt under his padded suit. Archie thought he looked terrific, once he helped his friend pound the lumps in his shirt into what seemed like actual muscles. Walter auditioned for Mr. Whitney and was hired at $30 a week. The play was a one-dimensional melodrama where the mustachioed villain kidnaps the heroine's child only to be foiled by the hero.

In Convict Stripes toured from Detroit to the Far West. When it got to Rising Sun, Ohio, Helen Liese, the five-year-old child Walter rescued each night (who had taken over from Mary Pickford—then known by her real name, Gladys Smith) was replaced by another child, who was making her theater debut. She was known as Baby Niles, but her real name was Lillian Gish.

In Convict Stripes ended its tour in Toronto and Walter and Archie were then hired by the Toronto Stock Company to appear in various popular melodramas where the heroes were strong and brave, the villains cunning and weak, and the women either wanton or helpless. Acting, as Walter Huston would come to know it, with all its subtleties and shades, didn't yet exist in the time of these "10-20-30" shows (they cost ten, twenty, or thirty cents). What people came to see were the *Star Wars* battles of their day, with good triumphing over evil, black downed by white.

While he honed his talent, Walter was able to strut his stuff before his family and friends, convincing his mother that he was destined to be an actor, although his father still didn't believe it was a proper job for any son of his. "My mother never tried to prevent me doing what I wanted to do," Walter would remember. "She gave battle to anyone who tried to get me off that track. In the beginning my father firmly believed I was headed straight for hell, but after a while he became quite used to me as an actor, although his opinion of show business never changed."

In the fall, Walter returned to New York, this time without Archie, and took a job in a touring play called *The Runaway Match* by Mark Swann. It opened in New Jersey and then went west, where Swann ran out of money. Walter suggested to four of the actors who returned as broke as he that they share a room. It had one double bed that they took turns using, three in the bed, two on the floor. None of them had much luck and in November 1902 only Walter had work as an actor: for one night as a soldier extra in *Le Cid* at the Metropolitan Opera House. It paid $3, but Walter would have done it for nothing since it gave him the opportunity to hear the great Caruso in his second appearance in America. "He had a voice such as I had never heard," Walter recalled years later, "with a controlled volume that astounded my imagination."

Then Walter read for a bit part in the Richard Mansfield production of *Julius Caesar* at the Herald Square Theatre and was chosen over a hundred other hopefuls. He would receive the staggering, hunger-ending, rent-paying sum of $25 a week to say just four lines each evening.

Walter tossed all night on the floor, trying to memorize the four lines that would enable him to credit himself with being a Shakespearean actor. He tortured himself with the fear he would forget how to say:

> Prepare you, generals!
> The enemy comes in gallant show;
> Their bloody sign of battle is hung out,
> and something to be done immediately.

The next day he nervously attended his first rehearsal and managed to speak only the first two lines. The show was to open the following night, but he was told not to worry, to go home early and relax. After all, if he managed two lines in one day, then he only needed to remember two more and he'd have it.

But acting is a psychological endeavor, and making light of what had now become a serious mental block didn't help alleviate his fears. For the rest of that day he wasn't able to eat. Nor could he sleep. He paced the night away, repeating over and over again, "Prepare you, generals! The enemy comes. . . ."

All the next day, he repeated those lines. And then, as he was dressed in his armor and made up for his big moment, he read those lines as if they were a prayer, hoping beyond hope that repetition would eventually become memory. Finally, he was given the nod. He could barely move. Why, he kept asking himself, did he ever want to be an actor? What masochistic tendency led him to such a terrifying moment?

"Get out there, kid, you're on," someone yelled and his mind went completely blank. If someone had asked him his name he would have been unable to respond. Yet there he was, on the stage at the Herald Square, blinded by the green footlights, his lips unable to part and let the words out. "Faces seemed to swim through the darkness and into the light," he remembered vividly, the memory of the actor's nightmare etched permanently into his mind; "eyes, a million pairs of eyes, seemed to be fixed on me and pinning me to misery."

From somewhere deep inside, the first line came to him and he shouted it out in awkward triumph, *"Prepare you, generals!"* He looked up and saw Richard Mansfield, whose face had curled into a nasty snarl, and his mind closed down. No other words would come. "Get the hell out!" he heard Mansfield whisper, but he couldn't even do that. He was frozen to the spot. His body was so rigid he had to be lifted and carried from the stage, where he was unceremoniously stripped of his armor and clothing and thrown like a sack into the alley behind the theater.

"There has never been a point so low as that I reached in the alley of the Herald Square Theatre," he later recalled. "Shame now came to dominate my miseries."

His roommates had been in the balcony and witnessed that most ignoble performance and came to retrieve him. They did what friends were supposed to do, making light of what had happened, speaking only of the future. But for Walter, there was no way to excuse what had happened. Whatever his destiny might be, it certainly couldn't involve the theater, not after tonight. It was his turn to share the bed, his only solace was sleep, which he did—for twenty unconscious and dreamless hours.

When he finally read the review of the play in the *New York Times*, he was pleased to note that his own failure had been ignored, but Mansfield's Brutus was attacked as "a singularly colorless individual, vapid when he is not grotesque." That didn't deter him from quitting the theater, but it certainly helped him rationalize that Richard Mansfield caused his breakdown.

And breakdown it was for the eighteen-year-old Canadian who once thought he'd be following his sister Margaret's cultural path. She was appearing in concerts and receiving bouquets and standing ovations while he had to live with the memory of being removed from a New York stage during a performance. He would look for a job outside the theater and if he couldn't find one, he would return to Toronto. It almost didn't matter, for he had lost his ambition. He was a failure.

Walking the streets one day, wondering how much longer he could last without a job, he met an old friend from Toronto named George Harmon. They had played hockey together as kids and Harmon had gone on to play professionally for a team in Brooklyn called the Claremont Rink. Harmon said they were looking for a center that season. Walter went to Brooklyn, put on some skates, and was hired to play hockey for $20 a week. He played through the season, regaining his confidence and putting that night at the Herald Square Theatre in proper perspective. Could Richard Mansfield hit a puck past a goalie and into the net? Not likely. And sometimes, when that puck *became* Mansfield, Walter found himself hitting it extra hard.

Walter's return to the theater was gradual. He found he wasn't ready to audition to act, but he had a need to be around actors, so he got a job as an assistant stage manager for *The Bishop's Move*, which starred William H. Thompson. Walter discovered his personal hero in the sixty-five-year-old Thompson, who became fond of him and often invited him into his dressing room where they would talk. Thompson exuded a wisdom and kindness that struck Walter deeply. Later he would credit Thompson with giving him his "whole approach to acting."

"He was the first man I ever saw who stimulated in me the desire to be like him," Walter would say. "He was unlike any actor I had ever known: not petty or selfish; he never tried to hog the stage, never complained about his billing, his dressing room . . ." Thompson gave him the confidence he needed to join a touring company as an actor in a play called *The Sign of the Cross.*

As the company traveled through the South and the West, the players began to realize that there was something ill-fated about acting in a play where the character Nero cursed God. Two of the actors who played Nero before Walter joined the troupe had died. Then a third actor became Nero and he died as well. Walter took the part as a temporary replacement and played it cautiously, but when offered the role full time, he declined.

When the tour reached Missouri, two events occurred that would change his life. The first was news of his father's death, leaving him with regret that "I never got to know him very well." The second was meeting "a little girl, full of energy and interested in everything pertaining to the arts," who didn't laugh at his red crocheted slippers and who had lived a strange and adventurous life very different from his own.

4

GETTING MARRIED

ON THE LAST DAY OF THE YEAR 1904 AS THE GATES OF THE
St. Louis World's Fair are being permanently closed, Walter and I stand
together in an anti-room of the courthouse before Judge Bobby O'Carroll and
say, "YES."

They had known each other only a week, although Rhea invoked
poetic license to stretch it to a month; they were both lonely, away
from friends and family, believing that they could give each other the
companionship that was missing in their lives. Each needed someone to
talk to, to share dreams with. Rhea was spurred on by her mother's
letter urging her to marry someone she cared nothing for. Walter had
been up and down in his life more than he cared to admit, earning very
little money, suffering the hardships of the actor's life at the turn of the
century, wanting little more than some honest applause and a woman
to wake up to. It may have been foolhardy, but they preferred to call it
love.

It rained on their wedding day. Rhea wore a black veil and a
patterned dress that wasn't quite the way she wanted it. *During the brief*
ceremony I am careful to hold my vanity case in such a manner as to almost
hide the defect.

Water is constantly dripping from one of Walter's pockets where he tucked his pearl gray spats when he took them off dripping wet. Walter tells me later he could think of nothing but the cold trickle of water that ran down the flesh inside his trouser leg.

They agreed to keep their marriage a secret and to act *formal and circumspect in the hotel so that no suspicion may be aroused until we have formulated some plans for our future.* That evening, Walter took her to the theater where he was performing and she sat in the front row waiting to see her husband appear.

When Walter makes his entrance it is with a collapsed body intended to portray great grief. Lace falls from his sleeves over both clenched hands. He lifts his face as he straightens up and seems to be listening to a far-off melody. With a wide flourish he flings a portion of his long cape over one shoulder, as he dramatically strides across the stage. The calves of his stockinged legs bulge with heart-shaped muscles, made, he tells me afterward, by his mother out of padded iron-holders.

A few days after their secret marriage, the show closed and the company disbanded. Walter and Rhea occupied separate rooms in the hotel and it would be a few weeks before they got to know each other intimately. Rhea worried that the manager of the hotel would disapprove of their hasty wedding and write her mother about it.

"Getting married makes a fellow feel like he's done something wrong," Walter said to Rhea. "I think it would be easier to create something than to destroy." Rhea, those years in the convent and those lectures of perdition finally behind her, couldn't have agreed with him more.

But before they had much of a chance to do any creating on their own, a slick-talking promoter named Ned Nye appeared at their hotel and convinced the manager to invest in a musical called *The Man Behind.* Walter was offered the juvenile part and Rhea was persuaded to sing in the chorus. The night of the first performance, Rhea peeked through the peephole in the drop curtain and saw no women in the audience. *The house is full, full of men.* The printer had made a mistake with the poster and had advertised the show as *The Man's Behind.* The men had kept their wives and girlfriends at home and come expecting a rowdy good time.

Once the posters had been reprinted and sent ahead to St. Joseph, *The Man Behind* tried again. The villain of the show quit and Walter was asked to play both the villain and the juvenile. *The script has to be cut and scenes manipulated so that the villain and the juvenile will not appear on the stage at the same time. Walter has no time to memorize new lines but he says he knows the gist of the play and is confident he can improvise well enough to get by.*

According to Walter, he didn't have two parts to play but six and it resulted in "the only time in my life I ever actually fought with a man." Writing in a 1933 issue of *Picturegoer Weekly,* Walter reported, "I had grown pretty careless and cocky. The manager of the company decided to fire me. He wanted to make some changes in the six parts that I had. I went back to my hotel for them. When I arrived back at the theater, I found another young fellow rehearsing my parts!

"My temper took the grandest 'zoom' to the ceiling you ever saw."

Walter went backstage to retrieve his trunk. But the manager refused to give it to him until Walter handed over the six parts. So Walter returned to the hotel, told Rhea to go to the train station, and then took a wagon to the theater, where he proceeded to pull the manager off his trunk. When the manager attempted to hit him with his cane, Walter knocked him down the stairs.

"I ran from the theater, with the manager after me," Walter recalled. "A train was just leaving town and I boarded it, just in time. The manager arrived at the station as the rear end of the last coach pulled out. I stood at the end of that coach and did a good piece of melodramatic acting as I tore the six parts into small bits and let them drift like movie snow down the tracks toward my one-time boss.

"I felt fine for the first few miles out of town. I had given a great performance. I had shown that great big so-and-so who I was. But dark came on and with it a sober thought. 'Now, you fool, what have you really accomplished? You have made a manager angry. He'll broadcast your conduct everywhere.' "

When they reached Kansas City, Walter took Rhea to a first-class hotel, reasoning that such establishments didn't ask for money in advance. And since they barely had enough money for a room in a boardinghouse, Walter figured they might as well enjoy their "honeymoon" in style.

She wired her father for money and he wrote his mother in Toronto, asking her to send him $25—one of the few times he had asked for money since leaving home. They then enjoyed their stay at the classy hotel—out of work, down on their luck, with time on their hands for romance.

Knowing that they could not afford the evening ahead of them, they defied their poverty and splurged on dinner at the hotel. *We sat in a park-like garden surrounded by artificial rubber trees. Concealed lights play on the spray of a miniature fountain. Before a tastefully laid table I feel self-glorious yet timorous and bold if I so much as lift my eyes from my plate to meet the fond glance of Walter, whose foot stealthfully touches mine. Beneath the cloth my husband reaches and squeezes my knee and I know that he feels as I do.*

Both ate in keen anticipation of what was to follow. *Through half-closed lids Walter smiles a smile that denotes tender expectations. Little shivers race through my blood making my cheeks burn. My flesh has a pleasant odor. Death is completely absent from my thoughts. I am filled with the joy of living. I am happy—extremely happy—I have never before, in all my life, been quite so happy. I am glad that I am alive. Glad that I am going to live tonight.*

The following morning the newlyweds received $100 and two train tickets back to St. Louis, compliments of John Gore. Walter's mother mistakenly sent her contribution to Kansas City, Kansas, not Missouri, which Walter discovered when they got to St. Louis and read the letters that awaited them.

Walter's letter was from his sister Margaret, who wasn't pleased at her brother's decision to marry without consulting the family. Rhea's mother, Adelia, was equally upset. "Who is this boy I have never heard of before, that you have married upon a week's acquaintance? Where and how did you meet him and what pray tell do you know about him?

"After bringing you into this world and after all I have done for you, the instant my back is turned you do this outlandish thing. The young man may be all right but you should have consulted your mother who knows best, who made all the sacrifices to raise you.

"So my little girl is married. Well, now that you are a wife let me advise you: It will be very much better if you are not saddled with a baby, at least not for the first year or two."

Rhea and Walter properly ignored the castigations and went about the business of finding a one-room apartment and figuring out what to do to earn some money. Faced with the practicalities of daily survival, they both put aside their dreams of writing and acting.

Living together, getting to know each other, they spent long nights talking about their hopes and fears. Rhea told Walter that the only actual fear she had known was of her father going on another spree. Walter confessed to having a fear of physical pain. "As a little chap going to school," he told her, "the very idea of getting my body hurt terrified me. Even though I was strong and healthy, I would let a boy half my size cuff me around rather than fight back."

Rhea said that she had never given bodily fear a thought. If someone or something angered her, "I'd explode then and there, my anger bursting like a giant firecracker in the midst of other fireworks." She came to the conclusion that Walter had a more peaceful disposition than she, and told him, "You be careful not to hurt my feelings and I'll fight for you."

Rhea knew the formula for a beauty powder that offered promise, although she would reflect in hindsight, "It is incredible that two green youngsters should undertake without capital to manufacture a commodity of any sort."

While Walter considered himself incapable of finding anything outside of the theater that could capture his interest for any period of time, he discovered in his wife "a resourceful, capable woman. In those trying days she was a great help. As unlike me as a person could be, she was shrewd where I was foolish, unhesitating when I faltered, quick of thought in contrast to my slow mental processes."

They discussed their plans with a drugstore clerk, who thought the formula for the face powder was fine, although he suggested it might be improved by adding a small quantity of rosemary. They selected a name, Cupid Poudre, took the ingredients back to their apartment, and began to mix their concoction. Walter remembered that the clerk said the rosemary should be heated and, thinking two ounces a small quantity, poured the little bottle into a tin cup and heated it over a gas jet. The tin cup melted. *In an instant fire blazes from floor to ceiling. I scream. Walter yells at me to shut up. I step in the Cupid Poudre and the cracked bowl breaks. A white pool of paste spreads over the carpet. Walter yanks the curtains down from their rods and we are smothering out the last of the flame with bedquilts when the landlady bursts into the room.*

It was a scene presaging any of a number of silent film comedies, down to the angry landlady casting out the luckless couple and pitching their belongings through the window and onto the snow-laden street below.

Undaunted, they found another apartment, bought more ingredients, and created a facial powder that actually seemed to work. At least it had no bad side effects when applied. Once their product was jarred and labeled, Rhea went to see the owners of the Wolf and Wilson Drugstore, who agreed to allow her to demonstrate her Cupid Poudre in their store and sell it on a percentage basis. So, with Rhea selling and

Walter at home mixing the powder, filling the jars, and pasting on the labels, their venture began to thrive.

At the end of the first week I am called to the office and asked for the definite address of my [New York] firm so that the proceeds due them may be forwarded at once. I try to explain that my firm expects all settlements to be made with me direct but they will not listen. I have to wait until it is time to go home, to tell Walter of the predicament we are in.

The money owed them was $104, which was a significant amount for one week's sales. But how to get it? Since there was no New York firm they went to a printing company and inquired about ordering letterhead stationery. They couldn't afford large quantities, but the printers usually would make a few samples on different qualities of paper; they decided that would suffice for their purposes. The strategy worked: Samples of the fictitious New York letterhead were delivered to them. By the time their letter was written, authorizing all money to be paid to Rhea Huston directly, their earnings were up to $250. The envelope had to bear a New York postmark, so they sent it to Walter's old friend Archie, who was then managing a small hotel in New York. He received their forged business letter and sent it on to Wolf and Wilson.

Several weeks pass. Besides paying up all our bills and buying new clothes, we have what we call a hunk of money. But Walter is still stagestruck and wants to go to New York. I earnestly believe it unwise to cast aside something definitely good for an uncertainty.

Finally we agree that the smart thing to do is for him to take what money we have and go on to New York and for me to earn more money. It is understood that I am to join him as soon as he is established.

It was an especially sad time for Rhea, who soon discovered how much she missed her husband. And she had gotten pregnant, only she didn't know it. She thought her lack of appetite, weakened knees, and spells of nausea were symptoms of separation; what she was experiencing was morning sickness. Then, to add to her problems, she caught a heavy cold and got laryngitis. *Pains chase one another through my body. An invisible tight band about my head grows tighter causing me to want my mother more than anything else in the world. I send her a message saying on what train to expect me.*

Adelia was alarmed by her daughter's pallor and overall weakness and rushed her to a doctor, who tested her temperature and saw that it was dangerously high. When she began to miscarry he ordered her head shaved, hoping that might reduce her fever. Rhea blanked out and there was fear she might not pull through. When she finally opened her eyes, she saw her mother. Rhea put her hand to her head and was startled to feel it "bare as the cheek of a human buttocks."

"It will grow back," her mother whispered, gently explaining, "it had to be cut and shaved away because of a high fever when a little soul changed its mind about coming into this world."

Rhea was stunned. Walter wasn't even there, he never even knew. This lost child became her secret, one that she never told her son, John. "I knew she had her head shaved, but I thought it was because she had typhoid fever," John would say a few months before his death. "I never heard that she had a miscarriage. I never knew."

Rhea met Walter in New York, her head covered by a $10 wig. She hadn't wanted to spend any more money on it since her hair had begun to grow back and she knew it was only temporary. But she suffered an embarrassing moment when the wind from a passing subway train blew the wig off her head. Walter did his best not to laugh, but by the time they got to Bridgeport, Connecticut, where the troupe was performing, it had become a good enough story to make her feel at home among the other actors in the company.

The person who made Rhea feel unwelcome and out of place was her mother-in-law. Walter's sister Margaret had returned to Europe to further her musical studies in Berlin. Elizabeth, still grieving over the death of her husband and the marriage of her son without her permission, decided to visit Margaret. On her way home, she accepted Walter's invitation to come to Bridgeport, see him act, and meet his new wife. It was a meeting she wasn't looking forward to.

My husband's mother is of a majestic appearance that manifests a domineering spirit. When she walks it is with strong legs. . . . When she speaks it is of Mary Queen of Scots as an ancestor.

Rhea remembered her visit as a disturbing and often humiliating experience. *While Walter is at the theater, she closets herself in her room. Seeking her I am told through a locked door she does not wish to be disturbed. When Walter returns he is admitted and they have long chats.*

Near the end of the week, I insist upon speaking with her before she goes away. Reluctantly she listens to me while I beg of her to be friendly. I tell her how very much I love her son. . . . She turns from me in silent arrogance. My love for him is nothing more than she expects of every woman with whom he comes in contact. She makes me understand that I have intruded upon her rights. I hope my husband will defend me to a degree. Instead he offends me further by his indifference. He reminds me her visit is of short duration.

Her humiliation and hurt only increased when she discovered Walter was involved with another woman. She was told this by Minnie, the wife of another actor and friend of Walter's. The two men had decided to go to New York for a weekend, and Minnie had uncovered why the wives hadn't been invited. "The boys have no time for us because they are taking with them a couple of town tarts," she told Rhea. When Rhea refused to believe her, Minnie showed her a letter she had found. Rhea was reminded of the perfumed letters she discovered as a child among her father's papers.

She decided to fight back by using an old friendship to make Walter jealous. She had known another actor, Jack Warner Oland, before she had met Walter and learned that he was living in New Haven, Connecticut. She wrote to Oland, telling him she had gotten married and was in Bridgeport, and gave the letter to Walter to mail. Unsure whether he had or not, Rhea charred a piece of paper on the hearth. When Walter returned from the theater, Rhea told him she had heard from Jack. *Walter looks at me amused and calls my bluff, admitting he never mailed my letter.*

She told him that she had suspected as much and had written Oland again, mailing it herself. Oland had responded, saying he would come to visit them that weekend. Walter spotted the burned paper in the hearth and, just as Rhea had hoped, grew suspicious. "Your boat leaves about half an hour before Jack gets in," she baited her husband. "Too bad you won't get to meet him."

Walter took the bait. "He ever kiss you?"

"Only a couple of times," she responded.

"Well, at least you're honest about it," Walter mumbled.

When the weekend came, Walter complained of stomach pains and doubled over in agony. She offered to put a very strong mustard plaster on his abdomen and was surprised that he let her. *He prefers the torturous mustard on his flesh to leaving me alone with another man who may admire me. When the steamer blows its last whistle and we each know, unknown to the other, the girls have sailed alone—his recovery is rapid.*

Walter took the mustard plaster from his scorched stomach and jumped into a bath to prepare for their visitor. Rhea came clean. "I know all about the town tarts you and Howard were going to take with you to New York. I won't share you with another—not that way. If you would rather have someone else, come right out and say so. But if you cheat and deceive me, I'll make you sorry."

"Come Bug," said Walter, embracing her, "don't let it get to you. It won't happen again. You're the only one I've ever loved."

When the summer was over, so was Walter's job, and they went to New York in the fall of 1905. While Rhea deplored the mediocre hotel where they stayed, she was fascinated by the city. Walter was back pounding the streets, going from one audition to the next. Rhea began to notice that his suit was too loose, his felt hat too cheap. What made this time even more depressing was the news that Walter's best friend, Archie, had died of tuberculosis.

Once again, Rhea found herself writing to her father for money. John Gore responded by sending them a check and making them an offer to come to Nevada, Missouri, where, according to Huston family legend, he had won a large chunk of the town in a poker game.

Oddly, the thought of leaving the cold, hard city and joining John Gore appealed to them both. *My father said my husband could begin at the bottom and work up. To Walter, discouraged by his unsuccessful stage pursuits, this looked like an oasis in a desert. Like a speckled hen, I cackled at the thought of nesting.*

They took the long train ride west and were met at the station by the new proprietor of the public utilities. John Gore was happy to see his daughter, who had been removed from his life for all her grown years, and hugged her heartily. When she introduced her husband, Gore grasped his hand and eyed his new engineer steadily. The opportunities he painted for the young couple made their future and the future of Nevada seem gloriously intertwined.

"Being twenty-one and standing on the threshold of life," Walter remembered, "I decided to grasp the opportunity so graciously offered and give up once and for all my childish fancy for the theater."

Once settled in their new home, "the finest house in town," as John Gore had promised, they talked into the night, eventually getting around to Adelia who, Gore felt, "never should have gotten that divorce." Rhea saw a tear in his eye but didn't press the subject. She, more than anyone, knew the suffering her father had caused her mother.

Walter and John Gore seemed to hit it off immediately. *To ascertain the true value of my actor husband's worth my father has started him, as he said he would, at the bottom by sending him out with a tin lunch bucket to dig ditches for a new sewer.*

"I knew my little girl wouldn't marry a mollycoddle or a work-shirker," John Gore said. "Tomorrow morning you take over the job of General Superintendent of the Public Utilities. Boss of the entire works," Gore told him. It was all a bit sudden for Walter, who knew nothing about taking over such a responsibility.

But Gore wouldn't let a minor thing like inexperience stand in his way, especially since he had no intentions himself of learning how everything worked. "If my little girl can marry you in one week," he said, "her dad can promote you in two days if he sees fit."

Walter protested, "I would gum the works in short order. I'd make an ass of myself and you, too."

No one would dare complain, Gore laughed, since he had the power to "turn off the gas and light and shut off the water when and wherever I want."

Walter saw in John Gore that "rare combination of an illusionist and an honest man. He never failed to keep his word, no matter how romantically he painted the future." Taking Gore's advice, Walter went to inspect the gas plant and saw that it was in bad shape. He went to the library and learned how to get it up to near full capacity, which convinced John Gore his instincts were correct and that his son-in-law was a genius who had finally found his calling.

It didn't take long for resentments to divide the chief engineer and the new superintendent, who, no matter how many books he read, was still only twenty-one and wet behind the ears. When Walter found out that the engine at the light plant was also in need of repair, he ordered the chief engineer to oversee the job. But the chief engineer refused and Walter had little choice but to fire the man he knew he most needed to keep everything from falling apart.

The ex–chief engineer immediately appeared before the town council and aired his grievances. "The light plant is being run by an incompetent youth," he told its members. "The engine is in danger of blowing. The entire water system is a carrier of disease."

The council was alarmed and ordered an investigation. It was just the kind of showdown John Gore relished. With his back to the wall, he behaved like an alley cat. When members of the council appeared at the light plant for an inspection, Gore stood before them and refused to allow them onto his property. When one of the committee members drew his gun, Gore met the challenge by drawing his own. Walter, who stood by his father-in-law up until that point, figured there was no sense getting blown to pieces over a local town matter and ducked behind a boiler. All hell broke loose in Nevada that day.

The dispute lasted for weeks, until John Gore decided to get things back to the way they were in frontier fashion: He paid off the town council to leave him the hell alone.

On August 5, 1906, Rhea Gore gave her daddy the best present he ever received when she gave birth to a son, whom she and Walter decided to name after him. Walter was managing to keep the public utilities running fairly smoothly now, so John Gore, becoming a grandpa for the first time, figured the time was right for him to go to St. Louis with a case of whiskey and have himself a spree. He gave Walter the address of the hotel where he would be and told him to come get him in exactly three weeks and not a day sooner.

With Gore gone, Walter decided to drain the reservoir so that it could be cleaned. It was his duty to make sure no health problems might arise. It took a few days to empty the reservoir and Walter remained there day and night, making sure everything was done properly. By the time the job was completed, Walter was exhausted. But at eleven-thirty that evening, a fire broke out and Walter was awakened by a call from the fire chief demanding water to put out the blaze. Realizing that the reservoir was empty, Walter saddled his horse and rode to the water-works, where he ordered that the pumps start filling the reservoir. He cursed as he turned up the water pressure and gave the fire department everything he could.

But it wasn't enough. The fire chief demanded more. Not wanting to be lynched because he refused to cooperate, Walter increased the pressure by another ten pounds and ran like hell. There was an explosive bang as the earth opened under the waterworks. The main water line had burst.

Walter ran back in and shut off the pumps. "But," he vividly recalled, "something told me my engineering career had come to an end."

The next day the town council convened and without John Gore there to threaten them with pistols they voted against extending the franchise with Gore Utilities. The council had effectively forced John Gore into bankruptcy.

When Walter told Rhea the result of the meeting, she looked from him to their baby and wondered what was to become of them. It was obvious that the townspeople weren't going to let them continue to live there in peace. He hitched some horses to their wagon, threw in their belongings, and headed for St. Louis to tell John Gore that his dream was over.

Walter realized it wasn't yet three weeks and Gore might not take such news easily. But the old man surprised him. "There's nothing to go back to," Walter told him.

Gore looked at him through hazy eyes. And then he laughed. "Goddamn serves the bastards right. Now wipe the worry off your face and pour yourself a drink."

In St. Louis, Walter decided to go to school to study steam engineering. The theater still interested him, but he had a family to support now and he knew that would be impossible playing the 10-20-30 circuit. With his recent experience and the books he had read in the Nevada library, it didn't take him long to pass the state exam and get a license.

He took a job with the Union Electric Power Company and within a year had helped build a power plant on St. Charles Street, where he was made operating engineer. By the summer of 1908, at the age of twenty-four, Walter was earning a respectable $200 a month.

He had only one problem: He had proven himself capable, but he wasn't happy. He was playing the part of the dutiful husband and father, but he was tiring of the role. He missed the theater, the lights, the squabbles, the traveling, the applause.

By the spring of 1909, he agreed to move to Weatherford, Texas, on the advice of Rhea's doctor, who told him she needed to live in a warmer climate. He accepted $250 a month to run the town's electric light and power plant.

"My first memories are of Weatherford," John Huston wrote, "being in the saddle in front of my mother at night, mesmerized by the sound of the horse's hooves striking cobblestones."

If it was a happy time for three-year-old John, it was not for his parents, who were beginning to drift apart. "We had never been what might be termed ecstatic mates," Walter confessed, "but now we approached the end."

Walter's sister Margaret had returned from a concert tour in Europe and suggested he meet her in New York. She had always believed in her younger brother's talent and felt she could help him. Certainly, she said, the life he was living was really no life at all.

Rhea knew Walter was tempted to take Margaret up on her offer to help him turn his life around. One night, Walter told Rhea that if it wasn't for John, he'd have left long ago. Rhea's response was to pack her belongings and take John with her to live with her mother in Dallas. Her whole nature, she would write, finally revolted at her husband's "petty cowardices."

Their marriage had lasted almost five years. Now they were free to do what each really wanted to do—with a vengeance.

PART THREE

5

THE HEART OF A TROUPER

"YOUR FATHER IS AN ACTOR, THAT'S WHY HE'S GONE AWAY"
was all John Huston was told when his parents split up. After Rhea left,
Walter had also gone to Dallas. A talent agency there found a traveling
troupe for him to join in Okmulgee, Oklahoma, and Walter was back
on the road, playing in what he called "rep, tent and tab" in open-air
theaters. Walter was offered $25 a week and accepted happily. "To be
trouping again—to be putting up with as many discomforts as civiliza-
tion offers and to be bawled out, called down, and derided—that was
my rhythm."

After admitting to her mother that she might have made a mistake
marrying Walter, Rhea began to look for work as a journalist. Adelia
looked after John, who, at an early age, showed signs of being gifted.
"My grandmother was, in many ways, more a mother to me than my
mother," Huston recalled. "Gram" would spend hours reading to him
and John would absorb the stories he heard, memorizing those that
most interested him. Once, when his grandmother couldn't find her
glasses to read one of his favorites, a forty-eight-verse piece of doggerel

called "Yankee Doodle Dandy," John picked up the book and, making believe he could read, recited the whole thing from memory. Adelia didn't live with John Gore all those years without some of his show-manship rubbing off, and she saw in her three-and-a-half-year-old grandson the kind of talent that could bring in a paying audience. "The next thing I knew," Huston remembered, "I was on a stage in Dallas, reciting those verses in an Uncle Sam suit."

John's stage career didn't last very long, as he soon grew tired of being hauled around Texas as some kind of boy wonder. The precocious child began to turn inward. He described himself then as having big feet, skinny legs, and big ears and thought of himself as being clumsy. What he most wanted was a pet he could sleep with at night, but his mother didn't want to deal with an animal in the house. John found a box, in which he put some torn newspapers and waited for it to be filled with a pet on his fourth birthday. When the day came and the box remained empty, he refused to believe his mother and grandmother could be so cruel, so he invented a pet that only he could see and called it The Hopadeen. "I don't know where I heard the word," Huston later mused. "How could a kid make up that word?"

"I can't remember seeing The Hopadeen," Huston later said, "but I wanted everybody else to believe in it. I remember once a waitress being fresh, and she asked me what The Hopadeen would have."

The Hopadeen gave John a playmate. If he became scared, The Hopadeen was there to comfort him. And The Hopadeen became a useful companion for his mother and Gram, who would tell it to keep an eye on John and not let him wander onto the road. They encour-aged The Hopadeen to make sure John put his toys away and washed behind his ears. The Hopadeen was also there while John was learning to read and write. Naturally, John did all these things because by obeying The Hopadeen, he would be proving it was real.

Walter, meanwhile, probably wished he had The Hopadeen to watch over him as he returned to playing heroes and villains in the same uninspired melodramas he had given up when his son was born. But gradually, the thrill of being back with his fellow troupers wore thin, and by the end of the summer Walter headed for New York to see if his sister Margaret could help him break into the legitimate theater. He was twenty-six and feeling that his life was going nowhere. He remem-bered this time as "a period of self-disgust, a period during which the mere thought of myself nauseated me; my life seemed to have been nothing but a series of misdeeds and mistakes."

*   *   *

John was also going through a period of discontent—not having his father around, not seeing his mother often enough. He started first grade while living with his great-aunt and uncle in Greensburg, Indiana, then was shuffled off to first one and then another boarding school. He was not happy in either of them, even with The Hopadeen sleeping under his bed. When his mother finally landed a job as a journalist, she and Adelia took him out of school altogether and between them taught him what they thought he needed to know.

This period of John's life was one of traveling from city to city, state to state, as his mother worked for the *St. Louis Star*, the *Cincinnati Enquirer*, the *Niagara Falls Gazette*, and the *Minneapolis Tribune*. "I never tired of traveling from town to town with Mother," he wrote. "I've always loved trains. I remember so well the smell, look, taste of soot; the sounds of passing over trestles and bridges; walking through the cars, feet braced and struggling for balance."

He remembered his mother being very good at scoop reporting: "people who would get to a story before anybody else. She was something of a sob sister, very well regarded by other women reporters. Maybe that's putting her down a little bit, worse than she deserves. But I remember reading things of hers and there was a quick, short stabbing quality that her writing had."

Because Rhea was often following a story, Gram took care of John. Sometimes, though, Adelia had her own things to do and a nursemaid would be hired to watch over him. One of those nursemaids introduced him to feelings he hadn't known existed, when he found himself in bed with her. "Somehow her dresses got up and her behind was bare," Huston fondly relived. "I fiddled with her behind and laid my cheek against it and thought this was marvelous." When his mother returned, five-year-old John instinctively knew that he best not mention what had happened. "But from that time on I was trying to get little girls to show me their genitals."

And for the rest of his life, girls did. Huston exuded a magnetism and charm that made sexual conquests almost elementary. It also led to ambivalence toward women. Perhaps it's too great an assumption to see in this youthful incident the beginnings of a pattern in Huston's relationships, but throughout his life, each time he experienced moments of intimacy and love, those feelings would be cut off and either he or the woman would disappear, just as both his father and his mother had disappeared with such regularity during his childhood.

He was still too young to be told about sex, but even later, according to John, the discussion never did take place. "Boys didn't have affairs in school; girls were supposed to be virgins. However, there was a shady area. Young men sowed wild oats. I think she had the good sense to understand that one should first hear about sex in the gutter," Huston laughed. "Advice about sex, along with admonitions, is one of the dullest things a parent can contrive to do to a child."

One day his mother and Gram thought it would be a good idea to take John to visit his grandfather, who had returned to the newspaper business. But just before they set out on their journey, John fell from a balcony of a house and landed on his head. He was unconscious for two days and his mother thought she might lose him. When he came to, they treated his return to consciousness as a miracle.

Walter arrived in New York with $2 in his pocket and Margaret waiting to turn him into something he wasn't. He moved into her apartment on the northeast corner of Sixth Avenue and 57th Street and dutifully attended her concerts at Town Hall or the Plaza. The audiences were a far cry from the ones he was used to. They were sophisticated, cultured, polite. Nobody threw things or shouted opinions, there were no humiliating signs like those he had seen in small Western towns saying: No Dogs or Actors Allowed. And the people who came to visit Margaret were musicians, composers, writers. "Circulating with all those rich and famous people properly impressed me," Walter remembered. "Still, I could never imagine myself living as they lived."

What didn't impress him were the clothes these people wore—too dull and gray for his taste, quite unlike the loud clothes he preferred and which his sister tried desperately to make him change. Nor was he impressed by their manicured nails, their snobbish manners, or their delicate foods.

To overcome his feeling of awkwardness around these people, especially since Margaret kept telling him how important they could be for his career, Walter used his talent as an entertainer. He told stories about himself, about John Gore, about things he had heard from other troupers on the road, and jokes he read in books. He had a way of telling a story that could hold an audience, even one as cosmopolitan and snobbish as Margaret's friends. His voice had a mesmerizing quality, his inflections were on the mark, his laughter was infectious. His acceptance among these people pleased him but worried Margaret, especially when he was encouraged to turn his stories into an act and try his luck as a vaudevillian. Walter, who had had no luck finding work in the legitimate theater, took such encouragement seriously. Margaret, who was the first woman to sing Debussy in America, felt vaudeville was beneath her brother's true talents. It was certainly beneath hers.

Vaudeville was a rogue's gallery of eclectic acts that had its roots in the variety shows made popular in the middle of the nineteenth century. Those jugglers, acrobats, and yodelers that so enthralled Walter as a boy in Toronto were part of the great vaudevillian tradition, which started as a means to keep men drinking in saloons and bars in towns large and small across the United States and Canada. These simple, unsophisticated, often vulgar and naive shows sometimes went on until the last drunken man fell facedown off his bar stool. If there wasn't room in the local beerhall to set up a stage when a traveling troupe came into a town, then other buildings, including churches, livery stables, barns, and warehouses, were transformed. They used stock sets, crude makeup, and music was usually provided by a piano, coronet, and drums. Gambling and the sale of whiskey brought in more money than the price of admission to these shows and, like the troupes Walter had traveled with, the vaudevillians were often left stranded with IOUs and empty bellies.

After Walter Huston tried out his stories, jokes, and songs for the Packard Agency, they were able to book him into small-town honky-tonks for $35 a week. They also introduced him to an actress seven years his senior named Bayonne Whipple, who was performing an act she called "Harmony Discord." It wasn't working and she was looking for a partner to make it click. Walter didn't think he could add anything to what she was doing, but he had another thought. The idea involved a prop that he and his brother, Alec, perfected when they were kids. They painted a face on a stretch of rubber; it became animated when moved. Walter convinced Bayonne that if he wrote a skit around this prop, they might have something people would pay to see. The skit Walter wrote was called "Spooks." It took eighteen minutes to perform and Whipple and Huston made their living from it for the next five years!

In it, Walter sang a song originally called "I'm the Guy," but he changed the title after a few weeks to one that, he would lament, was to brand him "as certainly as if I had been tattooed across the forehead." It was called "I Haven't Got the Do-Re-Mi," and Walter became known as "the guy who sings that Do-Re-Mi song." He would strut the length of the stage with a hat cocked over one eye, twirling a cane between his fingers, as he sang, *"When you get yourself a wife, you're taking chances on your life,/If you haven't got the do-re-mi."*

Not only did they do this silly bit for five years, but they did it three to five times a day. "Hardly a life one would choose if one had a choice," John Huston would say. "I marvel that this was the same man who later became a close friend of people like Bernard Baruch, George C. Marshall, Arturo Toscanini, and Franklin D. Roosevelt. If ever there was a caterpillar who became a butterfly, it was my old man."

Yet John acknowledged that his father "was very much the vaudevillian. He had great respect for it always. He never thought himself above it."

Some of the tedium was eased by having a partner of the opposite sex to travel with him. Groucho Marx once recalled being on the same train with Walter. "You were fucking a girl in the lower berth," Groucho teased Huston years later, when they were both starring on Broadway, "and I was dropping coat hangers on you from the upper."

Walter handled the business end of Whipple and Huston, making sure they got proper billing, decent dressing rooms, and paid on time. But even when they started playing the Keith-Albee-Orpheum circuit, which was the big time as far as vaudeville was concerned, they still had to pay their agent and hand out "bits" to the musicians and various technicians. And then there were hotel bills, traveling expenses, and tips before they could see any money for themselves.

In 1912, when John was six, Walter and Rhea were officially divorced. Within three years, they were both remarried—Walter to Bayonne in Little Rock, Arkansas; Rhea to Howard Eveleth Stevens, a senior engineer of the Nothern Pacific Railroad, in St. Paul, Minnesota—although neither thought of themselves as being truly in love the second time around.

By 1915 the constant battle over billing and boredom with the act had begun to take its toll on Walter and Bayonne. John Gore had come upon what he considered to be the grandest get-rich-quick scheme of his career, and when he wired Walter to bring his new wife and join him in Texas, they were receptive.

The invitation infuriated Rhea, because Walter remained in her father's good graces. Her anger didn't abate when she heard that Walter and Bayonne had decided to give up vaudeville and accept Gore's offer. John Gore had discovered that the liquid waste drained from gas pipes, which was currently junked, could be used to make explosives. To Walter, this sounded just like something the wild old man could successfully exploit.

When they arrived in Texas, Gore took Walter and Bayonne to his house, where he had installed a still. The distilled waste from the gas, he insisted, could be sold for sixty cents a gallon. Since the gas companies weren't using the stuff, Gore could collect it for pennies. Then he took them outside and set off an explosion that duly impressed them. But before they went ahead they decided to have the distilled chemical analyzed by the Dupont de Nemours Chemical Company in Delaware. Within weeks of sending off their sample, they got back not just a confirmation but an order to buy all the stuff they could ship! The champagne could be uncorked, the end of the rainbow had been discovered.

Further tests proved that what they had was not only good for explosives but, as distilled gas, more than doubled a car's miles per gallon, from twelve with regular gas to twenty-six with theirs. Walter and Bayonne would go to Toronto to visit the gas companies there and make tests of that city's drippings. Meanwhile, Gore would take the money he had collected from two eager investors and get a factory going.

But most important of all, John Gore realized, he must secure contracts with all the gas companies to ensure their unlimited supply of the waste product. He went to St. Louis first, then to New Orleans, before joining Walter and Bayonne in Toronto. In each city he was hit in the gut with the same news: Contracts had already been signed with someone else. They were too late.

John Gore never found out who had beaten him out of what was the surest shot at true wealth he had ever had, but he always suspected the Delaware chemical company. His spirit broken, he headed back to Waco, Texas, where he would die in a cheap hotel on the edge of town. When John Huston's mother went to claim his body she found an empty bottle of whiskey by his head and two suitcases of raincoats that he had been selling door to door.

.   .   .

In her never-completed memoir, Rhea Gore Huston Stevens stopped
writing in the first person around the time John was born. She didn't
pick up the narrative again until years later, when she had given up
journalism and married Stevens. By then, she was writing in the third
person, trying to gain a better perspective of her life's story:

*When she married Stevens, it was with maturity's full realization of what
she was doing. It was not like the blind passionate eagerness that swept her off
her feet when she met and married Walter, before her hair was up and her
skirts down. She had just walked out on Wally because eventually her whole
nature revolted at his petty cowardices. . . . With her decision to marry again
came the determination to make a go of it and to remain with him until death
did them part.*

John Huston liked his mother's new husband, thought he was a "nice
guy," although he never felt that his mother particularly loved him. His
own life "came into a regularity that I didn't have before. St. Paul was
the only place I ever felt any connection with as a child." Stevens was
a widower who had two children of his own, a son Howard Jr. and a
daughter Dorothy, both of them a few years younger than John. He was
also a wealthy man. "Anybody who had a fine house and servants was
rich then," Huston said. "And I got whatever I wanted that money
could buy."

Huston's memories of Howard Stevens were all positive. "He liked
me and was very decent to me as a kid. He was a conservative in habit,
but along with that formal front he had a kind of New England
up-country vulgarity, where they like to hear their farts in the morning.

"There was something a little peculiar about his walk, one heel
dragged slightly, and I imitated it once. Instead of giving me a smack
on the mouth, my mother and grandmother [who had come to St. Paul
to live with them] thought it was very funny.

"Howard and Dorothy, his children, I swear to God, were not all
there. Howard was a year or two younger and didn't respond to sympathy, so nobody gave him any. Least of all me. I did something awful to
Howard one time. He was with his pants down on the end of a log,
which was sticking out into the river. And a turd was hanging half out
of him. I couldn't resist the impulse. I turned the log. What a dirty little
sonofabitch would do a thing like that! I'm appalled at the wickedness."

One day a maid took sick at their house and the doctor came. It
would prove to be a housecall that would change their lives.

Huston was standing by the door of the maid's room and the doctor was struck by the unusual fleshy pouches under his eyes, which John had had since he was an infant. "Come here, son," the doctor said. When John approached, the doctor turned to his mother for permission to examine him. Then he unbuttoned John's shirt, took out his stethoscope, and listened to the ten-year-old's heartbeat.

"There's a murmur in his heart," the doctor said—words that would ring in Huston's ears all his life. "I don't mean to alarm you," he told Rhea, "but I'd have the boy checked by a specialist."

Up until this time, Huston had led the life of a normal boy. He played games, got into fights, was wicked to his stepbrother, rode his horse, traveled with his mother, spent summers with his father on the vaudeville circuit, thought life was pretty grand. Suddenly everything changed. His mother took him to a heart specialist in St. Paul who pronounced that her son had an enlarged heart. Albumen was discovered in his urine and a kidney specialist was consulted. After the two doctors conferred, Rhea was told that John was seriously ill. "Not only does he have an enlarged heart," the doctor said, "but he's got chronic nephritis, which is a disease of the kidneys known as Bright's disease."

"How serious is serious?" Rhea asked.

"It could be terminal."

The specialists agreed that John's only chance for survival was to be completely bedridden. He shouldn't exercise, he should be taken out of school, he should go on a vegetarian diet—eliminating eggs, salt, spices—and he should avoid the rigors of a Minnesota winter.

"It was just a thoroughly bad diagnosis," Huston said with disgust nearly three-quarters of a century later. "I didn't have an enlarged heart, just a big heart. And the nephritis, which was mild, was inherited."

To his mother's credit, John was taken to other specialists, where the diagnosis was the same. Then she and Stevens agreed that he shouldn't remain in Minnesota. Gram would stay on with Stevens, taking care of Howard and Dorothy, and Rhea and John would go first to New Orleans for further tests, then to Texas, to visit John Gore's grave, and finally to Los Angeles. It was to be the end of her marriage to Stevens and John always suspected his mother welcomed their escape, for she had found life in the St. Paul suburb of Miriam Park dull.

Over the next two years, John lived under the "Shadow of Death." Doctors in five different states had concurred in their analysis. If he exercised, he would die. If he ate red meat, he would die. If he shivered in a snowstorm, he would die. Even if he whistled, one doctor told him, the strain of forcing air from his lungs might kill him. For a boy who loved Kipling, the only adventures he was permitted to have were those that took place inside his head. Books became for him an important alternative life.

In Los Angeles they stayed at the Alexandria Hotel, at 5th and Spring streets, where motion picture actors, visiting royalty, and presidents often stayed. The Alexandria opened its doors in 1906 and became the focal point for business and social gatherings almost immediately. Rudolph Valentino was discovered there in 1918. Jack Warner lived there. Gloria Swanson met her husband, restaurateur Herbert Somborn, in the hotel's dining room.

One day the phone rang and one of John's mythic heroes was calling, asking if he could visit. Charlie Chaplin had heard there was a very sick boy at the hotel, and when he appeared, John's heart beat so hard he thought it might burst. Chaplin had come to the States in 1910 as part of a troupe of performing actors, appearing before live audiences the same year Walter Huston was teaming with Bayonne Whipple. Now there was no brighter star in the world of entertainment.

Chaplin told Rhea he'd like to be alone with the boy, and she left the apartment for an hour. While she was gone the actor-writer-director entertained Huston with pantomime, hand puppetry, and explanations of how moving pictures could be slowed down, speeded up, or reversed to create the various illusions that sometimes baffled and always enthralled moviegoers. "To be an audience of one for my idol," Huston wrote, "was beyond words wonderful."

Chaplin's visit was the only highlight of those sick years for Huston, until he discovered on his own that he could defy death and experience an exhilaration that would also be "beyond words wonderful."

The almost complete disintegration of his body led Huston to seek out a hazardous adventure when he was under strict instructions not to exert himself. He was taken to Phoenix because it was thought the heat would make him sweat out the albumen from his kidneys. On top of that, he was given sweat baths twice a day. Those baths and his meagre diet began to drain the very life from him. He grew weaker, thinner, sadder. His hair fell out. He was, his mother was convinced, dying.

Since he was going to die anyway, he harbored a secret wish. There was a canal only a block away and on the few times he was taken out of the house he would see kids swimming there. Oh, how he wanted to be normal once again, so he could go for a swim before he joined his grandfather under the ground. He thought a great deal about it and one evening, when everyone else was asleep, he decided that before he died he was going to swim in that canal. He dragged his weakened body from the bed and sneaked out a window. The night air was refreshing as he walked to the canal, stripped off his clothes, and entered the water. Floating happily on his back, he became a kid again, not just some object of pity. "It just became an obsession with me," he said.

He came back a few nights later, entered the canal, and swam close to the bridge, where large watergates regulated the water that entered the canal. That night the gates were open and Huston was swept under the water, through the locks, and out the other side. For a while he thought he was going to drown, the force of the water was like riding a rapids and then going over a small waterfall, but when he emerged and caught his breath he was elated. He couldn't remember ever experiencing anything as thrilling as that. The next time, he rode the waterfall intentionally. He wasn't going to take death lying down.

When still another doctor came to check his condition, he was alarmed to see how thin the boy was, how strange that he was bald. "You're killing him," he scolded Rhea. "The boy is suffering from malnutrition. Feed him, for God's sake!"

With considerable trepidation, Rhea started to feed him eggs, then some meat. She watched as John gobbled it all up and asked for more. When the doctor came and saw his improvement, he instructed Rhea to allow him to start exercising, suggesting swimming as a good place to begin. John was in heaven. Real food and the chance to show off his daredevil waterfall ride! "I was a sensation!" he happily remembered. "*Nobody* had ever gone over the waterfall until then, but from that time on, it was the thing to do."

The news of his son's recovery lifted Walter Huston's spirits considerably as he and Bayonne began to break in their new act, after working on it for six months. The fiasco with John Gore had brought them up short and the idea of returning to the same "Spooks" act depressed them further. So Walter structured an act around a shoe store. Walter would play the role of a shoe clerk, Bayonne a customer.

They called the act, not surprisingly, "Shoes" and opened it in Toledo, Ohio. Fellow vaudevillian Jack Haley, who would later go on to fame as the Tin Man in *The Wizard of Oz*, saw Whipple and Huston perform this comedy sketch and thought it worked because of Walter. "There was funny dialogue, he got the laughs. He did a song and dance. After the curtain dropped, they came back again and did more song and dance."

When they were ready to take the act to New York, they took out an ad in *Variety*, which had come into existence in 1905 and was the show business bible. Bookers and agents came to see them and the act generated enough interest for them to be offered $450 a week and a date at the Palace. "The Palace," Walter acknowledged, "was to vaude-villians what the Court of St. James' was to debutantes."

But Walter's crowning moment was marred by the death of his mother in 1917. Whipple and Huston had to be temporarily removed from the marquee as Walter journeyed to Toronto, arriving the day after Elizabeth Huston died. She had believed in Walter's success ever since he went on in blackface at fourteen and had only faltered when he had married Rhea and given up his dream. But with him back onstage and with Margaret to look after him, Elizabeth knew she wouldn't have to worry about her youngest son. On her deathbed, she had told her daughter Nan, "Don't worry about Wally—there won't be a country in the world but'll know his name."

John and his mother and grandmother were still in Arizona when World War I ended, but left soon after for Los Angeles. Walter and Bayonne were still performing "Shoes," although they had changed the act's name to "Boots." And Margaret Huston married William Carrington and finally became the millionaire she always knew she would be.

Carrington, who made his money as a grain merchant, was also from Toronto and had heard Margaret sing in concert halls there. Attracted to the arts, he offered his fortune to furthering opera in America, serving as president and financial backer of the American Opera Company. He treated his new wife like a princess, providing luxurious homes for her in Italy; Santa Barbara, California; outside Greenwich, Connecticut; and a Park Avenue apartment at 72nd Street in New York.

But tragedy struck both Carringtons soon after their marriage. William was thrown from a horse and severely damaged his hip, leaving him confined to a wheelchair for the rest of his life. Margaret swallowed a fish bone that scraped her vocal cords and destroyed her beautiful voice and singing career. It was a considerable loss to the world of music, as Margaret was truly one of the leading singers and interpreters of the music of her time. Robert Edmund Jones, the foremost scenic designer in America and a close friend of both Carringtons, once described Margaret's voice as "majestic. I never heard a sound like it."

Margaret, who was autocratic and arrogant, suffered her loss with dignity. No longer able to perform herself, she perfected a system of teaching phonetics and took on, without pay, a carefully selected number of professionals who came to her seeking improvement. Over the years, she trained the voices of John Barrymore, Alfred Lunt, Orson Welles, Lillian Gish, and her brother Walter. Her studies in London, Paris, and Berlin gave her an understanding of how the voice projected and she devised what she called a "litany of vowels" to work the muscles that were usually ignored by most voice teachers. The nonsense sentence she came up with that contained all the vowels a singer or actor needed to repeat was: "Who knows aught of art must learn and then take his ease." Robert Edmund Jones said of her theories, "She had come to believe that it was possible to free the speaking voice to such an extent that she could hear, not the speaker's intention or his personality, but his inner essence. Only a child or a saint or a genius could hold such a belief and Mrs. Carrington was all of these."

If Margaret could have heard the screams of joy that came from the mouth of her thirteen-year-old nephew after he and his delinquent friend Sherman blew up a condemned pier at Anaheim Landing with a homemade bomb, she would have forced upon him more than a sentence full of vowels. It was the beginning of John Huston's wild and experimental period, when he was willing to take any risk. This devilish side of Huston would last throughout his life, tempered and refined by puckish pranks and elaborate practical jokes. Sherman, who was a few years older than he, was just the "diabolic influence" he needed to counter those wretched, helpless, demeaning years spent at the mercy of ignorant doctors and a mother who never questioned his treatment.

"Sherman was a gifted young scientist," Huston remembered with a grin, "a young Edison gone rotten. We stole some dynamite from a building site and then cooked it to get nitroglycerin, which was dangerous, but we handled it carefully. Then we made our own gunpowder, which was easy to make, and put it together to make some pretty good bombs."

Whenever Sherman's parents took a trip, John was invited to go along. At Lake Arrowhead, one of their bombs blew up a hotel's toolshed. In a railroad yard, they once derailed a train parked on a steep slope by releasing the car's brakes. And they were arrested in Los Angeles after torching a condemned building that was part of Occidental College. Sherman was booked at the city jail; Huston was taken to the Juvenile Detention Hall. When Rhea got her son home, she went for the strap and beat him soundly. "You've gone too far," she screamed as the leather whistled through the air.

Huston's days as "a sorcerer's apprentice" were over. If he wasn't going to die from a kidney ailment, she sure as hell wasn't going to let him die from a bomb or a blaze of his own making. And if he wouldn't listen to her, then perhaps the time had come for some military discipline. He and Sherman were not allowed to see each other again and Rhea's threat of punishment became a reality when she enrolled John in the San Diego Army and Military Academy.

If lives are molded by one's childhood experiences, then the patterns had been set for Huston's adventurous, rebellious, independent life: on horseback at two, onstage at three, an imaginary companion at four, falling on his head at five, separated from his father, read real literature by his grandmother, never having a permanent home, crisscrossing the country by train to watch his father on the vaudeville circuit or his mother chasing after a story, pronounced deathly ill, visited by Chaplin, braving a roller-coaster waterfall in the dead of night, beaten to submission by his mother.

The military academy might have kept him from winding up in reform school, but it was far too dull to keep him there for more than a semester. He proved himself an able student by getting good grades and made sure he wrote his mother regularly. One of his letters still exists among his papers.

> Dear Mother,
> Just a line to tell you how well I feel and all that, how is Gram? Be sure and get my money to me by Friday if you have to wire me because I can go to a dance this week.
> If you give me your consent I am going to get another pair of pants, because it is very hard to get along with only one pair. I need no coat as now we do not have to wear one in class and at drill.
> Well old dear I was perfect in all my studies today did you get a report card from the Major if so send it I would like to see it.
> With much love
> John

Perfect in his studies and marching to drills—Aunt Margaret would have approved. By 1920 she had become a major in her own right, putting the likes of one of the theater's principal luminaries, John

Barrymore, through a routine set of drills of her own making. She was by no means an easy taskmaster.

John Barrymore made his stage debut in 1903 and his first silent film in 1913. The youngest of the "Fabulous Barrymores," he became a matinee heartthrob and a heavy drinker long before he reached the peak of his career when he did *Richard III* and *Hamlet* under the careful guidance of Margaret Carrington, who trained his voice; Robert Edmund Jones, who designed his sets and costumes; and Robert Hopkins, who produced and directed him. Barrymore had a good, strong voice but when he decided to play the evil, hunchbacked King Richard III, he had doubts about how to deal with Shakespeare's pentameters. Margaret was called in to guide the thirty-seven-year-old actor in his most demanding role to date.

Margaret coached Barrymore five hours a day for six weeks in her Park Avenue apartment. It was, she would write, "like playing on a harp with a thousand strings. He worked as he walked in the streets, prolonging his vowel sounds until he acquired the muscular control required to read through to the end of a sentence on one breath."

Credit for the success of *Richard III* was not just Margaret's coaching of Barrymore, but also of Robert Edmund Jones's remarkable sets. Jones was to play an important role in influencing both Walter and John. He was also in love with Margaret and married her when William Carrington died in 1930. Jones had studied at Harvard and then in Europe, where he sat in on the repertory of Max Reinhardt's Deutsches Theater in Berlin in 1913 and became aware of what was then known as "the new stagecraft": the fusion of acting, lighting, and setting into a dramatic whole. When he returned to New York in 1915, he successfully designed the set and costumes for a play called *The Man Who Married a Dumb Wife*, beginning a career that would make him what John Huston once called "the Gordon Craig of America."

Jones was considered to be a prophet, a visionary of the theater. He was also a practical craftsman who sought to integrate all the elements that go into a theatrical production: lighting, sound, costumes, props, set design, the playwright's words, the actor's interpretation, and the director's vision. "Each element has its own particular relation to the drama and plays its own part in the drama," he wrote in his now classic book, *The Dramatic Imagination*. "And each element— the word, the actor, the costume—has the exact significance of a note in a symphony."

In considering these "notes," Jones formulated his theories about the staging of drama. Lighting wasn't merely an inanimate beam sent down to spotlight an actor, but was just as alive as the player on the stage. "We use light as we use words," he wrote, "to elucidate ideas and emotions. Light becomes a tool, an instrument of expression, like a paintbrush, or a sculptor's chisel, or a phrase of music."

Costuming was another of the elements that brought out Jones's genius. "Costuming is not dressmaking," Jones believed. "The problem of costume is the problem of the man who wears it and of what he is trying to do and say in it."

Jones was the first American set designer who worked as an equal with a play's producer and director. He knew that a stage designer must be a "jack-of-all-trades," and he worked diligently to be just that. "He understands architecture, but is not an architect," he wrote in an essay, "To a Young Stage Designer." "Can paint a portrait, but is not a painter; create costumes, but is not a couturier. . . . These talents are only the tools of his trade. His real calling is something quite different. He is *an artist of occasions.*"

Two years after *Richard III*, Margaret, Jones, and Hopkins would again join forces to mold John Barrymore into one of the century's most effective Hamlets.

"I suggested that we put the books away and find out for ourselves what the play was about," Margaret Carrington wrote, recounting the summer of 1922 when Barrymore came to Denby, her Greenwich, Connecticut, estate. Margaret and Barrymore would spend eight hours each day working out the role in the garden, the woods, the house, studying the play as if it were a "modern script that had never been performed."

Barrymore's performance, with the brilliantly inspired sets of Robert Edmund Jones, brought raves from the critics. Writing in the *New Republic*, Stark Young said Barrymore "seemed to gather in himself all the Hamlets of his generation . . . his Hamlet was the most satisfying I have ever seen." (Young would also later write about Margaret Carrington, that she was among the "half dozen most distinguished and brilliant figures of the last two decades.")

Margaret was almost ready for her greatest—and most personal—achievement as a teacher: the transformation of her brother from a song-and-dance man, a lighthearted melodramatic vaudevillian, into a subtle, refined actor of the highest stature, the favorite of two of the most critical and skeptical artists of the theater, Eugene O'Neill and George M. Cohan.

*   *   *

With Whipple and Huston on the road during the time of Margaret's involvement with the Bard and Barrymore, John Huston was learning some tricks of his own that would whet his appetite as a lover and fighter. After proving himself at the military academy for six months, he was allowed to return to public school in Los Angeles. One day he met a girl in the park and, stirred by the memory of rubbing his cheek on his nursemaid's buttocks when he was a child, decided he was old enough to do what the boys at school were always talking about. Knowing that his mother was not going to be home until evening, he invited the girl to his house, took her up to his bedroom, and pulled down the shade. The girl didn't resist and John gladly lost his virginity that afternoon.

"When I stopped being an 'invalid,' " Huston said, "physical things attracted me very much. My secret life was boxing. My mother didn't know about it until very late on. If she had known she would have done everything she could have to stop me."

Huston had an older friend named Harold Hansen, who introduced him to the sport. Hansen knew about an old fighter, a Mr. Lott, who was an instructor at a city playground. For a dollar and a half each, Mr. Lott agreed to teach the two boys how to box. "He had us punching through an imaginary circle, learning how to lock the wrist and turn the arm as the punch is thrown," Huston recalled. Lott stressed the finer points of the sport—timing, footwork, precision—and after six months he felt Hansen was ready to try out at the Los Angeles Athletic Club. Huston went down with his friend but because he was only fifteen he was told by the club's coach, George Blake, that he shouldn't hang around. Huston would never forget Blake's dismissal and, later, refused all fights at the club.

Even though Lincoln Heights High School was an hour's streetcar ride from his house, Huston transferred there because of the boxing program. Almost six feet tall and weighing only 140 pounds, Huston quickly established himself as a lightweight. His city park training gave him an edge over the other young boxers and he won his new school's division championship. After school he would go to the Hollywood Athletic Club and box some more.

Huston loved this time of his life, even though he was "so damned skinny I'd feel a beating for several days afterward." Because of his height and reach advantage, he was able to keep his opponents at a distance and he remembers several bouts where he broke his adversary's ribs, as well as getting his own nose broken on his way to a 23–2 amateur lightweight record.

*   *   *

By the summer of 1923, Huston knew that he would not finish high school, and he nurtured visions of putting on some pounds and one day becoming welterweight champion of the world—a vision that was enhanced when he traveled east to spend the summer with his father and Aunt Margaret in Connecticut.

"Life at Denby was formal and different from anything I had ever known," he recalled. There were afternoon teas on the lawn, Sunday morning services at the Episcopal church, formal dress, polite manners, butlers and servants, trips into New York to attend concerts at Carnegie Hall and theater matinees, dinners with the very wealthy, cultured conversations, and the uncomfortable feeling that his father was at a crossroads in his life.

Walter, by then, was at the end of his rope. From the time his mother died until his son's summer visit, he and Bayonne had continued performing "Boots" and then changed their act for a third time at the suggestion of Eddie Darling, the chief booker at the New York Palace. Darling proposed that Walter and Bayonne put together a jazz band, and that was what they did, investing their life savings of $8,000 into an elaborate show they called *Time*. Darling was able to book them into the Bushwick Theatre in Brooklyn, then they moved into Manhattan, playing in an uptown Loew circuit theater. Walter played character parts, told stories, danced, and sang. Bayonne was at his side. The band was exciting. The problem was money.

It was a bad time for performers, who never banded together into a union. The business of vaudeville had consolidated among the big-time circuit owners and the United Booking Office. The booking agents organized and the managers of the circuits were able to cut out the little independent theaters. The high salaries of vaudeville's golden age tumbled. The movies, radio, and the legitimate theaters began to lure audiences.

Walter Huston may not have seen it coming, but he sure felt it. To get the price he thought they deserved, he would have to leave the Loew circuit and join up with the Shuberts, who, in 1907, accepted a buy-out and agreed to stay out of vaudeville for ten years. Now the Shuberts were back, battling for the big acts, willing to pay more money but unable to guarantee anyone that they were in for the long haul. It was the most difficult decision of Walter Huston's career, to abandon the Loew circuit and take the Shuberts' offer of $1,800 a week for a guaranteed eighteen weeks. He knew there'd be no turning back. But the Shuberts had ten theaters and were willing to pay what Walter felt he and Bayonne and their jazz band were worth. They'd take the $1,800 and their chances.

Over the next ten weeks, *Time* played in all ten Shubert theaters and then repeated, but the Shuberts couldn't meet the payroll the last few weeks and their circuit folded. The Loew circuit wouldn't think of taking them back—at any price. Walter and Bayonne were effectively blacklisted from vaudeville.

It was the spring of 1923. Walter Huston was thirty-nine. His son would be coming to spend the summer with him. He was very depressed. "I was the longest of long shots: nearly forty, expelled from my one sure means of livelihood, with no education to speak of, with no 'trade,' no money, an ugly geezer who had never stayed in one place long enough to have influential friends. Big boy, what now?"

"He was always a very simple man," John Huston said of his father. "He wasn't well read, he wasn't well educated, but he was very thoughtful and he had an innate wisdom. I liked him very much. He lived the life of a vaudevillian for, God, about fifteen years, doing just three or four acts that he wrote. I didn't see a great deal of my father until I was seventeen years old. I suppose it was because I saw him so infrequently that he would put himself out, so it was always a very pleasant relationship. Because he hadn't performed as a father, he never assumed that role with me. We were more like brothers or good friends. That summer I visited him, he took me to the Dempsey-Firpo fight."

Jack Dempsey was "a god" to Huston. "Nobody in my lifetime has ever had such glory about him. He walked in a nimbus." Dempsey had become the heavyweight champion in 1919 when he knocked out Jess Willard in the third round after knocking him down seven times in the first. Huston was thirteen then and had followed Dempsey ever since that fight, but the battle against the Argentinian Luis Firpo in the Polo Grounds was to be the first time he ever saw the Manassa Mauler fight. No other athlete, with the possible exception of Babe Ruth, had captured the imagination of the public as did Jack Dempsey. He had come out of small mining towns determined from the time he was just a kid to be a fighter. By 1921 he was fighting in boxing's first million-dollar gate. It was publicized as the "Battle of the Century," but

Dempsey knocked out his opponent, George Carpentier, in the fourth round. He was a devastating brawler with the fastest hands ever seen in a heavyweight and an absolutely lethal left hook.

When Walter and John entered the Polo Grounds, they sensed the electricity in the crowd. Their seats were in the first tier of elevated seats and they had a good view of the ring. Firpo entered first wearing a brown robe. He was huge, almost frightening to look at. Dempsey, Huston would remark, looked like a kid next to him and never stopped moving once he entered the ring. As soon as the bell rang for the first round, Dempsey came shooting across the ring and knocked the Goliath Firpo off his feet. Firpo got up and Dempsey flattened him again. The roar of the crowd was deafening. Again Firpo got up, again Dempsey swarmed all over him, knocking him down. But Firpo was strong, he had to be to keep getting up, and though Dempsey knocked him down seven times that round, Firpo sent the crowd into delirium when he hit Dempsey with a right hand that landed so squarely it sent the champ through the ropes and clear out of the ring. Nobody who saw it could believe it. There was Jack Dempsey, sprawled out among the sportswriters he had landed on. There was no way Dempsey would have been able to get back into the ring on his own before the count of ten, but the writers loved Dempsey as much as the public and they lifted him up and pushed him back between the ropes. Firpo came at him, exhausted, thinking he was going to become the new heavyweight champ. He threw wild punches in his effort to end the fight in the first round, but Dempsey ducked, slipped, and blocked the bigger man's punches until the bell rang.

Dempsey had that all-important minute to clear his head before the second round. When the bell sounded, he did exactly what he did in the first round, crossed the ring and knocked Firpo down. The crowd continued to go crazy as Firpo got back on his feet, but this time Dempsey knew he had to end it. He put everything he had into the punch that sent Firpo down and kept him down.

Huston, like everyone else in the stadium, couldn't believe what he had just seen. What could be more dramatic, who could be more courageous, what performance could ever top such a fight for sheer, raw guts and determination? All the way home, he and his father couldn't stop talking about the fight, a fight that would be immortalized on canvas by George Bellows.

And it would take something as intriguing as painting to make John Huston aware there were other avenues in life to pursue besides boxing. An article about "Futurism" in the Hearst Sunday Supplement so intrigued him that he made an effort to further explore the artists being put down in the Hearst paper. The artists singled out were Picasso, Matisse, and Duchamp, and the "Futurism" being ridiculed was really Cubism. Where the writer of the article saw humor, Huston saw mystery. The work illustrated there began to haunt him. "I'd had a certain gift for drawing from the time I could hold a pencil," he wrote, "but before I stumbled upon this article, art per se had never entered my consciousness. Now I caught fire."

Back in Los Angeles he told his mother he wanted to enroll in art school and she didn't stand in his way. But after a few dreary months outlining and then shading nude models "frozen into position" at the Smith School of Art, he heard about the Art Students League, a more informal but far more exciting group of artists who met three times a week in a small studio on Main Street. It was a derelict-ridden slum area, but when his mother took her seventeen-year-old son there, he knew he had found his place. He also found a mentor, a tall, thin man in his thirties with a fancy mustache and a high forehead who had studied in Paris and spoke French, Spanish, Italian, German, and Chinese. His name was Stanton MacDonald-Wright and Huston credited him with furnishing "the foundation of whatever education I have." He taught Huston about the great Italian quattrocento artists; about Michelangelo's *contrapposto* principles of drawing; Cézanne's understanding of color. He brought him to French literature. "Although I had been exposed to music, opera, and ballet, he introduced me to Scriabin, Alban Berg, and other experimentalists."

MacDonald-Wright "had an extraordinary turn of mind and tongue," which impressed Huston. "I remember how he described a fat woman he'd seen on the street as looking, below her waist, like two young boys wrestling."

Those years, when Huston was sixteen and seventeen, were fulfilling, formative ones where he had seriously considered two widely different arenas as potential vocations: boxing and painting. He managed to capture the pull between the two when he painted a self-portrait at the time. The face and a bandage show him as a fighter, the paintbrush as an artist, and the portrait is of a tough young wounded artist, a figure not looking for any favors but not expecting to be messed with.

He left Los Angeles in 1924, at eighteen, to live in New York, fell under the influence of his father, and discovered yet another profession to pursue.

By then, Walter Huston had made some significant changes of his own. In 1923 he gave up his Canadian citizenship and became an American. "I had been living in the United States the greater part of my life, since 1902. I felt I owed to the U.S. a greater debt than I owed to Canada."

He also gave up vaudeville—he had to, since the major circuits had crossed him off their lists. "Where could I turn? There was but one answer: the legitimate theater."

But he was looked upon as an entertainer, not a serious actor. Unless he could finance a play himself, no theater was willing to give him a chance. It would have been hopeless if it hadn't been for Margaret. With her belief, and her husband's checkbook, Walter Huston got his chance.

The play was *Mr. Pitt*, written by Zona Gale and produced by Brock Pemberton. It told the story of a kindhearted but tactless traveling salesman, subjected to the cruelty and disdain of others and, though aware of his faults, unable to change, thus becoming isolated and lonely. It was almost a reflection of Walter's position. Producers saw him as a broad-ranging, overly theatrical performer who couldn't cross that subtle bridge to the refined legitimate stage.

Walter knew the part was right for him and when Brock Pemberton asked William Carrington to consider financing it, Carrington agreed, on one condition: His wife's brother must play the title role. Put that way, Pemberton did what most producers would do, he cashed the check and signed Walter Huston to a $500-a-week contract.

It was left to Margaret Carrington to do for her brother what she had done for John Barrymore. She had watched Walter perform since childhood and knew he had a tendency to exaggerate. She wanted to strip him of such habits for Broadway. As she had told Barrymore, she now told Walter to forget everything he thought he knew about acting. She had him practicing her nonsense sentences, teaching him to deepen his voice, to breathe through his vowels, elongating them with downward inflections. She urged him to speed through his long opening speech in a single breath. She wanted to help Walter find his sound, "the basic sound you have never spoken." And Walter didn't resist. He knew he was lucky to have her.

*   *   *

On January 23, 1924, Mr. *Pitt* opened at the 39th Street Theatre in New York and Walter Huston was singled out in the reviews, discovered, at long last, as a remarkable new talent. Margaret's suggestion that he open the play with an attention-getting rapid-fire speech was applauded instantly by the audience, allowing Walter to relax for the rest of the show.

"Nobody in the house, apparently, had the least idea as to the identity or past performances of Walter Huston, whose name was on the program in black type," E. W. Osborn wrote in the *New York Times*. "After the first act everybody wanted to know who and what was this Huston, who, for one thing, had proved himself to be Marshall Pitt to the life." A Brooklyn critic wrote, "Walter Huston, until last night an obscure vaudeville actor, stepped forth in the role of Mister Pitt as one of the biggest finds of the present season. Not since David Warfield opened in *The Music Master* 20 years ago has a better character actor than this man appeared."

The reviewer at the *Washington Herald* was familiar with Walter: "Those of us who have seen Walter Huston in the past have not realized his infinite possibilities. Here is a man whom we have seen as a vaudeville comedian, an amusing fellow with a jazz band—a man who had an individuality, to be sure, but we didn't know he could act. And now we see him in a characterization that may well make stage history."

The play ran for three months and before it closed Walter knew two things: that he had only just begun to act, and that his marriage to Bayonne Whipple was about to end.

It had been tough on Bayonne, used to working each day with her husband, to suddenly find herself excluded from his rehearsals and performances. Walter realized it and even managed to get Brock Pemberton to offer her a small part in the play, but she was too proud to be so reduced. "She had been a star before I joined her in vaudeville," Walter said. "It was only natural that she should suffer the pangs of loneliness, if not jealousy."

By the time John Huston arrived in New York, Mr. *Pitt* had closed but his father was in another play at the same theater, *The Easy Mark*, a more stylized and formula-type play that attempted to cash in on Mr. *Pitt*'s success but which, according to John, was "vulgar in conception and dialogue." John stayed with his father and Bayonne and observed the disintegration of their marriage, which didn't disturb the young man in the slightest.

"I remember secretly thinking: My God, how could my father bear to have this tagging along?" Huston said. "She was just dull, narrow. A vaudevillian trying to be a lady. She was full of pretenses. But I must say, the Hustons were extraordinary with her: They treated her as though she was possible. And she wasn't."

Walter, too, recognized this. "With our one common interest—work—thrown entirely on my side, the scales did not balance."

Although John Huston never acknowledged it, he made his professional debut as an actor in *The Easy Mark*. He had seen the play five times when one of the supporting actors had to leave the show. The director had one day to find a substitute. Walter suggested John, who thought it might be a lark, and then spent Sunday coaching his son so that he would be ready to rehearse with the company on Monday. By Monday evening, John was ready to make his father proud.

"John had a feeling for acting even then," Walter would say years later. "Three nights later, Jack Dempsey and Estelle Taylor came backstage and Jack said, 'Watch out, Walter, that new youngster in the cast will steal the show from you. Who is he?' John's name was not on the program. I was pleased because all my rehearsing with him would have accomplished nothing without his own native ability."

"My father taught me a lot without ever telling me anything," John Huston once said. "The best learning experience I ever had was watching the rehearsals of Eugene O'Neill's *Desire Under the Elms.*"

It was this play that would mark a turning point in not only John Huston's life, but also in Walter's and in Eugene O'Neill's. John got to see a major work of art come to life, got to understand how words written by a master playwright could effect change, see how action could be created by dialogue alone. It would change his mind about boxing and painting and turn his attentions to writing and the theater. For Walter, it would establish once and for all his ability to make a character his own, would give him the credibility he sought as a genuine actor on the legitimate stage, instill in him the confidence that there was nothing he couldn't do if the character was well drawn. And for O'Neill, it solidified his reputation as America's leading new force in the theater. And for all three, the controversy the play stirred up was a further lesson in the power and excitement of the theater.

Eugene O'Neill wrote *Desire Under the Elms* in just five weeks. He told Walter Huston that the idea had come to him in a dream. He had already written twenty-seven plays between 1916 and 1924, and had won a Pulitzer Prize in 1920 for his first Broadway play, *Beyond the*

Horizon. He had been a member of the Provincetown Players and it was through this group that he got to know Robert Edmund Jones. When the Players decided to put on *Desire Under the Elms* in Greenwich Village, Jones was chosen to design the sets and direct. Jones suggested Walter for the part of the cantankerous seventy-five-year-old patriarch, Ephraim Cabot.

O'Neill wasn't sure. He knew about Huston's performances in *Mr. Pitt* and *The Easy Mark* and both characters were weak figures. The actor he was looking for had to be able to play the tough old geezer he had created, a man who would outdance, outstrut, outbrag, and out-fight any of his sons and neighbors half his age.

But O'Neill knew how close Robert Edmund Jones was to Walter Huston's sister Margaret, and he was aware of what she and Jones had done for John Barrymore in *Hamlet*—a performance that inspired the playwright to write a note of praise to the actor, saying, "Your Hamlet was the very finest thing I have known in the theater—an inspiring experience for me!"

If Margaret Carrington and Robert Edmund Jones could turn John Barrymore into the finest thing he had known in the theater, then perhaps she and Jones could pull off their magic and make the forty-year-old Huston into a curmudgeonly seventy-five-year-old tyrannical New England farmer. It was a chance O'Neill was willing to take and one he would never regret.

Desire Under the Elms dealt with such themes as lust, incest, adultery, sin, and infanticide. Its central conflict was between Ephraim Cabot and one of his three sons. When O'Neill first jotted down notes from the dream he had of the play, he summarized the plot in his notebook:

> Play of New England—locate on farm in 1850, time of California gold rush—make N.E. farmhouse and elm trees almost characters in play—elms overhanging house—father, hard iron type, killed off wives (2) with work, 3 sons—all hate him—his possessive pride in farm—loves earth to be as hard—in old age in a moment of unusual weakness & longing marries young woman, brings her back to farm, her arrival brings on drama, youngest son falls for her.

Right from the very first descriptive paragraph of the elms, Walter knew he was encountering something altogether different from anything he had ever known. And the character of Ephraim sounded just like his grandfather, who wore his sons down with his hardass ways. Walter knew what the play was about, it was in his bones. And when he gave it to his son to read, John Huston agreed with his father. "I think it's one of the greatest things I've ever read," he said.

It was time to go see Margaret.

Margaret Huston Carrington's dominance cannot be overestimated. After both parents died, she became the indisputable head of the Huston family. "There was about her a great sense of power," John would write of his aunt, whom he respected but never really liked, "a forcefulness (amounting almost to ferocity), disciplined but all the more formidable for being so self-contained." When Walter showed her O'Neill's play, she immediately recognized the poetry in the writing and the ruthlessness of the character Walter would have to master. Walter wasn't worried—all he had to do was think of Margaret and the character was his.

John went with his father to meet with Eugene O'Neill and Robert Edmund Jones at the Greenwich Village Theatre. O'Neill asked Walter to read Ephraim's long speech about his past and liked the way Walter did it. Walter never told him about his grandfather.

When the play went into rehearsals, John attended every day, sitting in the back rows of the theater, totally absorbed. And each day, as Huston watched his father and the other actors grow, he found himself changing as well. The lines of the play had become a part of him, he knew them all by heart—"the rhythm and cadence and flow of the play had got into my bloodstream. I hadn't gone there seeking anything in the theater. I had only gone to see my father, but what I learned there during those weeks of rehearsal would serve me for the rest of my life."

It probably took Walter longer to "get" Ephraim Cabot than it did John to memorize the entire play. John remembered that it was a "slow transformation" for his father, who "never read well when he sat down to read a part."

Desire Under the Elms opened on the evening of November 11, 1924, to a shocked and scandalized audience. "What made it a success," John Huston recalled, "was that people thought it was dirty. Can you imagine? This Greek tragedy. And it was excoriated by the critics, which brought people to see it. My God, there were a bad bunch of critics, although they thought Walter and Mary Morris were fine."

The *American*, the *Post*, and *Time* magazine were among those "bad bunch of critics," as they denounced the play as "cantankerous cancerous proceedings," with "hideous characters." It was called a "tale of almost unrelieved sordidness." *Time* felt that "that existence could not possibly be so brutal."

The *New York Herald Tribune*, however, thought the play inspirational, and Stark Young, writing in the *New York Times*, also liked it and especially Walter's performance. "What Walter Huston does in *Desire Under the Elms*," he wrote, "is an interesting illustration of the problem that the actor has to struggle with in most of Eugene O'Neill's plays. . . . He might have acted [Ephraim Cabot] to the life. . . . He might have acted close as a microscope to nature. . . . Mr. Huston might delight us with all the pleasures of recognition, make the piece of acting an impersonation. . . . He might, in the usual meaning of the term, give us a character. He does none of this. What he does is give us the idea of the part, its underlying quality, its poetry. . . ."

What made these critics uncomfortable was the underlying sexual tension of the language. When Abbie attempts to seduce a resisting Eben, she says: "Hain't the sun strong an' hot? Ye kin feel it burnin' into the earth—Nature—makin' thin's grow—bigger 'n' bigger—burnin' inside ye—makin' ye want t' grow—into somethin' else—till ye're jined with it—an' it's your'n—but it owns ye, too—an' makes ye grow bigger . . ."

And when old Ephraim Cabot declared himself to his new wife, he brought snickers from the audience when he said, "Yew air my Rose o' Sharon! Behold, yew air fair; . . . yer two breasts air like two fawns; . . . yer belly be like a heap o' wheat . . ."

But it was the passion between Eben and Abbie that brought out the protests and cries of immorality and obscenity from certain critics. With such raw emotion being presented on the stage, coupled with incest and the murder of an infant, moralists began an organized protest to close the play, which, of course, brought more and more people to the theater. On January 12, 1925, the play was moved from Sheridan Square to the Earl Carroll Theatre on Broadway, where *more* people could see it for themselves. The move not only increased the controversy but also, finally, put Walter in the do-re-mi, since his salary was raised to $500 a week *plus* ten percent of the gross receipts over $10,000.

The strength and power of *Desire Under the Elms* was Ephraim Cabot as Walter Huston played him. The old man was a true life force, God and Nature and unvanquished Man rolled into one heel-kicking performance the likes of which had never been seen before on an American stage. Ephraim Cabot symbolized the ruthless Almighty of the Old Testament, as elemental as the elms over his roof, an evil, self-righteous, materialistic, destructive bastard—and yet still human, with a stubborn prideful frailty that bordered on the heroic.

The question of whether *Desire Under the Elms* was obscene or not moved to the front pages of the newspapers and the district attorney of New York, Joab Banton, tried to make a name for himself by moving to close the play. The mayor, James A. Walker, appointed a committee to judge for the city whether or not to allow the play to continue. After the committee was announced, the box office began taking in $18,000 a week!

Once the committee attended a performance, they brought the mayor their verdict: The play was a work of art, the playwright an artist. The show would have a run of 208 performances, but Eugene O'Neill was greatly disturbed by the fact that his work was a success for all the wrong reasons. Years later, though, he would say, "There have been only three actors in my plays who managed to realize the characters as I originally saw them," naming Charles Gilpin who played *The Emperor Jones,* Louis Wolheim as Yank Smith in *The Hairy Ape,* and Walter Huston as Ephraim Cabot in *Desire Under the Elms.* "Only those three live up to the conceptions I had as I wrote."

O'Neill had conjured the character of Ephraim Cabot, Huston had brought him to life, and Margaret Carrington was the midwife. And as important as Margaret was to Walter's career as a serious actor, Walter would be to his son's. Family tradition and support had begun among the Hustons.

6

RISING STARS

WHILE WALTER WAS BUSY COMPARING MARY MORRIS'S breasts and belly to two fawns and a heap o' wheat six nights a week at the Earl Carroll, John was finding success of his own as an actor in the Provincetown Playhouse Theatre in the Village. Kenneth Macgowan asked him to read with the Players and offered him "a great part, the star part" in Sherwood Anderson's one-act play, *The Triumph of the Egg.* John had moved into his own one-room apartment on MacDougal Street by then and his father had encouraged him to see how he liked it when the lights shone on him. Huston was more interested in writing than in acting but listened to the advice of Eugene O'Neill, relayed through Walter: "If he wants to write for the theater, the best way is for him to be around the theater."

There was irony in the part John was asked to play—a failed chicken farmer—because chicken was one food that Huston never ate. He had seen their behavior in a barnyard as a young boy and decided they were not "models of delicacy."

When the play closed, he appeared in another, called *Ruint* by Hatcher Hughes. There he played the part of a wealthy young liberal on his way to Palm Beach whose eyes are opened by the dismal poverty and the superstitions of a rural Southern mountain town. The play had some success, "But even then," he realized, "I thought this isn't for me, not to be an actor." The best thing about it was that he made a lifelong friend with one of the other actors, Sam Jaffe.

Jaffe was fifteen years older than John and engaged to be married. He shared Huston's interests in writing, painting, and boxing and was also a gifted musician and mathematician. "Sam said that the first moment he met him, he knew that John was very special," recalled Jaffe's second wife, Betty, who married the actor in 1956. "He said there was a largeness about his whole being—his gestures, his voice, his intense desire to learn more and more. He and Sam would spar together, go to museums together." They lived in the same apartment building, which had a honky-tonk dance hall on the first floor, where bootleg liquor was sold under the counter and hid in Huston's hall storeroom. Huston had worked out a convenient arrangement with the proprietor. "Every so often I got a bottle of gin as a payoff."

For John's nineteenth birthday, Jaffe asked him what he wanted as a gift. Huston said a horse. So Sam went and found "the oldest, saddest, most worn-out gray mare" in the city and tried to sneak it into Huston's room. As he was pushing the horse up the stairs, the manager heard the commotion and came running and screaming, "Are you crazy! Stop this immediately!" John came out and saw the old mare and couldn't stop laughing. "It was the best birthday present I ever had," he said.

John received other presents, including an expensive sweater from his Aunt Margaret. Soon after his birthday, John and Sam went to visit his aunt, who, in her imposing manner, made a disparaging remark about Jews. "Sam reprimanded her in very sharp terms," Huston remembered. "She then made the mistake of saying, 'Some of my best friends are Jews.' And we both walked out. She called us back and apologized." But her apology wasn't enough. John wrapped up the sweater, brought it to his aunt's door, rang the bell, and left.

After nearly eight months, *Desire Under the Elms* completed its run and O'Neill was encouraged to dust off a play he had written earlier, *The Fountain*. It was about Ponce de León and the dream of eternal youth. Walter auditioned for the part, and although O'Neill found him "Not inspiring," Walter convinced him he could pull it off. The play opened on December 10, 1925, and lasted for just twenty-four performances.

Drama critic Stark Young wrote in the *New Republic* that it was "dull" and said that while Walter had "no hint of the actor ass," he "lacked distinct style and rhythm. . . . Even when he is bad he could always be bad in so much worse a way."

"Young picked my work apart as a surgeon operates with his scalpel," Huston said after the critic visited him backstage. "He told me exactly and without mincing words just where I was off key. I boiled inside. It was difficult to be even polite to him as we said good-bye." When Walter's anger cooled, he reflected on the actor's need for praise: "We resent criticism . . . because we won't be honest with ourselves. It is too painful to face our own shortcomings. We can't escape the consequences of our own stupidities, so why try?"

It was about this time, while Walter was beginning to forget "the hard lessons I had learned in my youth," that John came down with an earache that developed into a mastoid infection. As there were no antibiotics to prescribe, he had surgery. The memories of his childhood illness came back to him during the two weeks he spent in the hospital, and when his father suggested he might want to recuperate in a warmer climate, John jumped at the opportunity to have an adventure. He decided to go to Mexico.

Walter gave him $500 plus a ticket to sail on the *American Banker*. John left New York and cruised into Veracruz, where he caught his first glimpse of true poverty before taking a train to Mexico City. He was on his own, in a strange and wild land, determined to touch and taste everything that was made available. In 1964, Huston wrote a prologue to a revised edition of *Little Mexico* by William Spratling, a character Huston had known. In it, he described the Mexico City of his youth.

"It was a perilous city then, after nightfall. There was a 10:30 P.M. curfew and, after it sounded, you walked the streets in double jeopardy: stickup men and cops. It was simply a question of who got to you first. Getting robbed or being fined, it was for all you had on you. Outside Mexico City, you only traveled by day. Bandidos still ranged the countryside—leftovers from the Revolution. . . ."

For the next year Huston lived at the Hotel Genova, where he became friendly with its manager, a Mrs. Porter. She introduced him to Hattie Weldon, who was a "squarish German woman in her sixties," and one of the finest horsewomen in Mexico. John visited her stable, and when he demonstrated his ability to ride she introduced him to Colonel

José Olimbrada, who taught dressage at Hattie Weldon's *ménage* in his
free time. The colonel agreed to take Huston on as a private pupil.
When John's money ran out, Olimbrada offered to continue his lessons
for nothing, but John was too proud to accept. So Olimbrada got him
an honorary commission in the Mexican army that included free meals, a
free bunk in the barracks, a temporary rank of lieutenant, and a choice
of horses. Huston jumped at the opportunity to join the wildest bunch
of men in Mexico.

"The whole scene was pretty abandoned," Huston reflected. "I became sort of a mascot for the other officers. It was a crazy country,
much more so than it is now. There were poker games in whorehouses,
loaded pistols thrown into the air, a swimming pool filled with whores
without any clothes on—that was at the home of José Avellaneda, who
became secretary of the treasury and printed his mistress's face on the
currency. Life was a constant revel then."

Rhea wasn't happy that Walter had allowed John to go by himself to
Mexico. She had received letters from John and began to worry that he
didn't seem to have any direction. What was he doing down in Mexico
for so many months? She decided to pay him a visit and find out.

What she saw disturbed her. Her boy had turned into an irresponsible
gringo soldier: drinking, smoking, whoring, gambling, jumping horses,
going to parties and bullfights, living the hedonist's life. When John was
challenged to a gunfight, the time had come for her to put the brakes
on his year of craziness.

"That duel was an absurd thing," Huston remembered. "The man's
name was Count Alphonse de Vanderburg, at least that's what he
called himself. He was in hot pursuit of the wife of an American I got
to know and she was afraid to tell her husband about it. She wanted
him warned off, so I undertook to do it. I got a message to meet him at
a corner of the Paseo de la Reforma where he would kill me in a duel.
Well before the stroke of the hour I took up my position behind a
tree. I was going to shoot him as he turned the corner, so there
would be no question of the outcome of it all. I waited and he didn't
turn the corner. . . . my mother did. She came and disarmed me.
'Behave,' she said. 'Don't be a damn fool.' And that was the end
of that."

It was also the end of his first sojourn in Mexico. It had been a great
adventure, John wrote Walter when he got to Los Angeles. Now he was
thinking about getting married and settling down. Dorothy Harvey, the
girl he had in mind, had gone to the same school he had before he
dropped out. She was two years older and beautiful, with "a heart-

shaped face and wide-set gray eyes." She was in college, majoring in philosophy, when Huston set out to find her.

Walter, who was still married to Bayonne but was seeing actress Nan Sunderland, wasn't one to give advice when it came to women. So he refrained from telling John what to do. Instead, he told him about the "cheap piece of melodrama" he had been appearing in called *Kongo* by Chester Devon. He suffered through it until *The Barker* came along.

Written by Kenyon Nicholson, it told the story of a traveling carnival that, in the words of one Boston critic, "has no more resemblance to a circus than a wheel burlesque show has to grand opera." Walter played Nifty Miller in the title role, the fast-talking barker whose words drew the curious into paying their money to see the sideshow inside the tent. Using his sister's technique of breath control, Walter mesmerized the audience with his first spiel. It was so effective that reporters approached him afterward to ask him how he did it.

Walter was satisfied with the success of *The Barker* and with the additional income he made endorsing Lucky Strike cigarettes. In full-page newspaper ads, Walter revealed "how he protects his voice." "In the first and last acts of *The Barker*, I am called on to give a real carnival 'ballyhoo.' This taxes the utmost strength of my voice. I have always been a confirmed Lucky Strike smoker and I am happy to say that besides the pleasure I get from them, Lucky Strikes always leave my voice clear and fresh for my work on the stage." Just top-quality Virginian tar and nicotine to smooth a trouper's tired throat. He was glad for the commercial work, happy to go from one play into another, but he was also becoming aware of other horizons—namely, the movies.

The movies were still in their infancy and the idea of "talkies" had only been introduced in 1926, when John Barrymore appeared in *Don Juan*, his voice played on a record accompanying the picture on the screen. But even in such a crude form, the producers of movies saw the future and knew that an actor's voice would be as important as his ability to act and take direction.

Then, in 1927, Al Jolson sang "Mammy" in blackface and his voice and ad-libs were in synchronization with his image. *The Jazz Singer* created a whole new excitement for the movies. The talkies were born and new actors were needed, actors who could speak as well as act.

Walter Huston could do both. When MGM offered to give him a screen test, he figured he had nothing to lose and a new audience to gain. At their New York studio, Huston played a dramatic scene before a movie camera for the first time and really threw himself into it. He moved about the set grandly, chewing whatever scenery there was, playing to the last row of his imaginary audience. When he was through, he was told that the movies already had one Lon Chaney and that he should stick to the theater. Disappointed, he asked if he could see his test. What he saw so shocked and depressed him, he couldn't face himself in the mirror for days. But he had learned an important lesson: For the camera, you didn't need to exaggerate as you did on the stage. If anything, you needed to downplay your scenes.

The experience disturbed Walter enough to send him reeling backward, to vaudeville, where he signed as a headliner for ten weeks. Coming from the legitimate theater, Walter was treated differently than he had ever been on the circuit before. He was now a celebrity.

Walter met George M. Cohan for the first time on the road, at the Hollis Theatre in Boston. Cohan was appearing in *The Merry Malones* at the Colonial Theatre and Walter went backstage one evening to pay him a visit. Cohan invited him for dinner and asked Walter if he'd be interested in taking a look at a new play Ring Lardner had written that Cohan was going to produce. It just happened to be about an egotistic baseball pitcher, a hick named Elmer. Sure, Walter said, I'm interested. After that disastrous MGM screen test, he was ready to sign on for a George M. Cohan production without even *looking* at the play.

Back in New York, Huston met with Lardner at Cohan's apartment, where they drank champagne and talked through the night, exchanging stories of the crazy early days of vaudeville, the state of the theater, and the emergence of the movies. As the sun began to shed fresh light into Cohan's apartment, Cohan told Walter, "You're the greatest actor in the world." And Walter told Cohan there had never been anyone like him in the theater. Ring Lardner, who was extremely shy, didn't know whom to praise, so he remembered that he had promised to see his children off to school and took his leave.

"You a college man?" Cohan asked Walter.

"Nope," Huston answered.

"Shake hands," Cohan said, relieved to find another fellow self-educated like himself. Walter would later say of Cohan, "George had a secret respect and outward contempt for an educated man. He was one of the most interesting and entertaining men I have ever known."

At eight that morning, both men tipsy from champagne, Walter got up to go. "See you at the Astor in four hours," he said.

"Sure," Cohan responded, "we'll talk business."

"Why don't we do that now?" Walter suggested.

"All right," Cohan agreed. "How much do you want to play *Elmer the Great?*"

"I got $750 for *The Barker*," Walter told him.

"Then I'll give you a thousand a week," Cohan said, "plus ten percent of the gross over ten thousand, and you can write your own ticket on the billing."

"Shake hands," Walter said.

While Walter was grasping Cohan's hand, John was more passionately attempting to win the hand of his first true love. "I don't want to marry you now," Dorothy Harvey resisted. "Wait until I finish college, then we'll see."

But Huston was never one for waiting. "I wanted complete surrender or nothing," he would write. Spurned by her unwillingness to act spontaneously, Huston decided to go back to Mexico, where spontaneity was a way of life.

It was a short and dangerous trip. The boat ride to Acapulco was uneventful, but the seventeen days as part of a mule train to Mexico City gave him second thoughts. First, he was attacked by fleas, which nearly drove him crazy, settling in the warmth of his crotch. Each night he rubbed himself with alcohol to relieve the itching, but as soon as he fell asleep the fleas started biting again. Then, about six days into their journey, three rough-looking, armed Mexicans came into their camp on horseback and asked for food and cigarettes. The chief of the mule train complied. But when they asked for ammunition, the chief refused and kicked them out of the camp. That night a rifleshot echoed in the darkness and a bullet struck their campfire. Everyone scattered, shots were fired, and then one of the bandits shouted out, demanding that goods and ammunition be left behind when they started out the next morning. The chief refused and that day the mule train moved on slowly, without incident but with great concern. Again, that evening, a bullet was discharged into the campfire. Huston rolled for cover along with the others. He was scared. He knew a bullet could just as easily hit him as the fire, but there was nothing any of them could do but wait until morning and prepare an ambush.

The next day four men stayed behind as the mule train moved on. In the afternoon, the four men caught up with the train. They had captured one of the bandits. Another had been wounded but escaped with the third man. Their prisoner was turned over to the *rurales* in the town of Chilpancingo where he would be executed.

It was an adventure he would use years later when he made *The Treasure of the Sierra Madre*, but at the time there was nothing remotely romantic about it. The only romance in his life was back in Los Angeles. After a few lonesome days in Mexico City he faced up to the fact that he was in love and got on a train back to California.

Dorothy had also had a change of heart. She found herself unable to concentrate on her studies. There was something about John that was different. He was more advanced than any of the boys she had known; he had a sense of humor, a certain charm and confidence, an eclectic intellect, an interesting family, a sense of destiny. It would be fun, she concluded, to be married to him. Philosophy could wait.

Without telling anyone, Dorothy and John found a justice of the peace and had a private ceremony. They spent their first married night at a hotel and then went the next day to tell Dorothy's parents and then John's mother and grandmother. The reaction from both sides was the same: first shock, then fury. How could two supposedly intelligent young people do something so impetuous? How were they going to live?

"It was a thoroughly depressing reception," Huston said and laughed. Once again, his mother was calling him a damn fool. And his grandmother was even more upset than his mother. "Gram turned on the girl. She didn't turn on me because I couldn't do any wrong." They didn't even know this Harvey girl. Who was she? And could she possibly be good enough for their John? "Just like you, Rhea," Adelia said. "Just like you."

Looking for someone to congratulate them, John called his father in New York, but not even Walter was actor enough to fake exuberance. "How much do you have?" he asked his twenty-year-old son. "The usual," John replied. Walter understood and told him he'd send a $500 check as his wedding gift. John would spend it on a chandelier and Walter would later say that he "hadn't worried about him much since then."

"The seriousness of what we'd done hit us," John wrote after they settled temporarily in a small cottage owned by Dorothy's parents. With the sad, exasperated faces of their in-laws as a harsh awakening to their giddy union, their love became confused with hate and they thought of getting an annulment, then thought of getting away and seeing how they really felt without parental gloom around them. They moved to a shack on the beach in Malibu and discovered that they had been right all along. "We were both happier than we'd ever been," John wrote, "perhaps happier than we'd ever be again."

With John happily sketching nude pictures of his new wife as she read her favorite philosophers to him, Rhea and Adelia decided to go their own ways as well. Adelia went to Greensburg, Indiana, to stay with her sister and Rhea decided to let her anger simmer by going to Europe. As a railroad vice-president, her estranged husband, Howard Stevens, was able to provide her with free or reduced passage on trains and boats, and Rhea was to travel extensively over the years.

In 1927, stories from Europe were very much in the news. Stalin had consolidated his power in Russia and Trotsky was expelled from the Communist party. T. S. Eliot had renounced his American heritage and become a British citizen. Color television was being demonstrated in England. And a twenty-five-year-old pilot named Charles Lindbergh had soloed across the Atlantic Ocean from Roosevelt Field on Long Island, New York, to a hero's welcome at Le Bourget airfield in Paris, where 25,000 people nearly tore him and his plane, *The Spirit of St. Louis*, apart. But most significant for John Huston was the copy of James Joyce's banned *Ulysses* that Rhea had smuggled back into the country from her trip abroad. No other book would affect him in quite the same way. As he said after reading it, "doors fell open."

In New York, Ring Lardner and George M. Cohan thrashed out the problems of *Elmer the Great* at Lardner's Great Neck, New York, home. Lardner had finally shuffled his three drafts to satisfy Cohan, who was busy impressing Walter as "the greatest stage director I have ever worked with." What Cohan gave to Walter was a sense of timing and the importance of pausing for effect. During rehearsals, Cohan had asked Lardner to write a new scene that the actors dutifully learned. Then Cohan cut the scene but told the actors to take the same amount of time *thinking* the scene instead of saying the dialogue. The idea was to get the actors to pause, not rush from speech to speech but to convey real life by holding onto silence. Walter, who had learned to talk rapidly without pausing from Margaret, was now being told by Cohan to slow down, the part of a hick pitcher was anything but a slick vaudevillian. "That was one of the best acting lessons I ever learned,"

Walter would say, "the value of long pauses for certain effects." He would go on to credit George M. Cohan for giving him "certain gestures I use as part of my own personality which I copied from him."

Cohan would return the compliment, saying that Walter was "a great actor . . . one of the best." But Cohan also noted that Walter took direction only when he agreed with it. "I insisted that Walter change a certain character around a bit. Huston listened carefully to everything I said. 'Sure, George,' Walter said. 'I'll try it that way.' And he did. That very night. But the next night, darned if he didn't go right back to playing it the way he saw was true. That's Huston."

Huston, his co-star, Kay Francis, and his lover, Nan Sunderland, opened the play in 1928 at the Lyceum Theatre in New York, where they appeared in eight performances each week. *New York Times* critic J. Brooks Atkinson credited Walter for making the play work. "The more one reflects upon the satiric contradictions in the character of *Elmer the Great*, who is Ring Lardner's baseball bonehead, the more remarkable Walter Huston's acting of the part appears to be." Atkinson outlined the problems as he saw them and then returned to his appraisal of Walter's performance: "Somehow Mr. Huston manages to resolve the several moods of the play into a strong, forthright characterization. Elmer the braggart, Elmer the trencherman, hold their own with Elmer the pathetic victim of bunco men and Elmer the bashful swain."

After Broadway, the show went on the road, playing in Worchester and Boston, Massachusetts, and Chicago, Illinois, where Edith Luckett Robbins, an actress who had appeared in a play once with Nan Sunderland, joined the troupe. Edith and Walter became friends and she introduced him to the man she was going to marry, Dr. Loyal Davis, a surgeon. Edith's young daughter, Nancy, the future First Lady Nancy Reagan, would grow up calling Walter "Uncle Wally."

Nancy remembers that "Uncle Walter and Nan stood up with my mother and father when they were secretly married in New York in October. Then when the play ended, they were remarried in May, in Chicago, and I was the flower girl. I was about six."

Walter felt close enough to Loyal Davis to make him a member of the Crovenay Society—a unique and elite club aimed at pricking bombast whenever and wherever it appeared. Over the years, other members included Margaret Carrington, Robert Edmund Jones, George M. Cohan, Sinclair Lewis, José Iturbi, Ty Cobb, Max Baer, Willy Wyler, Max Gordon, Brian Aherne, and Myron Selznick.

Walter was its founder. Back in 1916, while Walter was on the road, he and another vaudevillian, Harry Norwood, were waiting for a train in northern Minnesota. Sitting on a bench was a derelict who had a mangy-looking dog. For lack of anything better to do, Walter and Norwood play-acted an argument over the dog's breed. "I'm telling ya," Walter said with an actor's air of authority, "that there dog's a Crovenay."

"Like hell it is," Norwood said. "I'll bet you five bucks that dog's no Crovenay."

"Say, buster," Walter asked the derelict, "that dog of yours, it's a Crovenay, isn't it?"

The confused hobo lifted his shoulders and said, "This here un ain't, but his ma was."

And thus began a running gag, based on a nonsense word, that would last a lifetime. When the train arrived, Walter and Norwood continued to test what would become a theory about human nature. Spotting a flock of birds in the distance, they argued over whether they were Crovenays or not. The conductor came by to settle the dispute. "No, they're not, but you get Crovenays up around the Great Lakes." Stopping by a fruit stand, Walter picked up a melon and asked the shopkeeper if it was a Crovenay. "No, that one has a thicker rind."

"A Crovenay is a hoax," Walter would declare, "a gag, a trick aimed at that great weakness in human nature that refuses to acknowledge ignorance. Stuffed shirts of every kidney have fallen in the trap from the drawing rooms of London to the barbecue-pitted patios of Hollywood."

During the run of *Elmer the Great*, Walter agreed to make his first movie. Paramount believed he would be perfect for the part of a journalist, fallen into the throes of dishonest publicity and then re-formed, in *Gentlemen of the Press*. It had been a play by Ward Morehouse, who adapted it for the screen. Charlie Ruggles was hired to play a drunken reporter. Huston suggested his *Elmer* co-star, Kay Francis, as the leading lady for the four-week shoot. She was hired and Walter signed a contract for $10,000, more money than he had ever received in his life.

It wasn't a memorable film, but Walter got firsthand experience about what the movies were all about. He didn't particularly like it—waiting for the harsh lights that were hard on the eyes, for the endless camera changes, and the dozens of details to be synchronized before the actors could perform—but the money was worth the waiting.

*   *   *

Walter was seriously involved with Nan Sunderland, who appeared as his girlfriend in *Elmer the Great,* and wanted to marry her. But he couldn't convince Bayonne to give him a divorce. At one point, she paid a visit backstage to Nan and accused her of "living with my husband." "I certainly am," Nan replied, infuriating Bayonne. Stubborn and proud, she differed from Walter's first wife, Rhea, in that she refused to accept that his ambition as an actor could split up their marriage.

Rhea, upon her return from Europe and a visit with her son in California, decided to settle in New York, where she became friends with a rising young writer named Thomas Wolfe. She landed a job as a reporter on the *New York Daily Graphic,* the first illustrated newspaper, which John described as "the worst possible scandal sheet, a model for all bad newspapers."

With his mother writing, his father on the verge of becoming a movie star, and Joyce's interior monologues spinning in his head, John told Dorothy he was going to put aside his dream of painting and take a stab at writing. He didn't need his wife's encouragement, for she was already harboring dreams of writing herself. And she had seen what John's one attempt at earning some money with his fists had done to him. Huston, who hadn't boxed in three years, picked up a fight at the Lyceum in Los Angeles. His opponent beat him up so badly he could hardly see and barely breathe. With his nose broken a second time and his ego as badly battered as his body, John conceded that his boxing days were over.

Knowing that his son was uncomfortable taking money from him, Walter worked out an agreement to support John's writing efforts in return for half the money he made if he sold anything. "John was not a boy to be goaded or even guided with light rein," his father said of him. "He could be reasoned with but not forced. John wanted to work out his own destiny the hard way. I let him do it."

Gram, missing him in Indiana, also made an offer: John and Dorothy could live with her in Greensburg, where they could save on food and rent and concentrate on their writing without any distractions. Since the biggest distraction in Malibu was the beach, which they loved, they decided Greensburg might be just the place to get some work done before making an assault on New York.

Victor Du Lara was a young Italian. He had the shape of head you often see on clever boys. You would call it conical. . . . He was short with a strong back, so he could hold like a vise and pound in the clinches. He was a slugger with a lot of native speed. Like a nail he made his own openings, and he followed up fast, hammering like a carpenter.

The story was called "Fool," and John was wisely following the writer's dictum to write about what he knew. The story was about his teenage boxing years. The unnamed narrator was closely modeled on himself: *I was tall with long arms, and I knew how to keep them out. I was naturally a straight hitter, right from the start when I had my fights at grammar school. I developed a short jab in my left that was almost automatic.*

The narrator, with the long arms and the short jab, hero-worshiped Victor Du Lara, who had gone to Lincoln Heights High School like himself and who had turned professional at sixteen. One night Victor's opponent doesn't show, and in order for Victor to get his $20 he has to fight someone. So his friend agrees "to pull a fake." Knowing that Victor is stronger, he figures he'll just clinch, throw light punches, and dance the rounds away. But then, *My left went out automatically, and chopped him right on the nose. I knew what I had done and I climbed into a clinch where I apologized. Victor, as a welter, could have killed me. . . . I didn't know whether he was angry or just keeping up the bluff.*

It was a mature, Hemingwayesque story, and when Huston finished it he sent it off to his father. Walter thought it was good enough to show to his friend Ring Lardner, who wrote about sports better than any writer he knew. Lardner passed it on to H. L. Mencken, the editor of the *American Mercury* and one of the most influential journalists of his day. Mencken decided to publish it.

"This was the high moment in my life," Huston said. "The *American Mercury* was a kind of gospel to people of my time. I can't begin to describe the importance Mencken had in my young manhood. He was the most prestigious figure in this country, as far as I was concerned, the arbiter of taste and judgment, the editor of the finest magazine. And when I got a letter of acceptance signed 'H. L. Mencken,' why, I suppose, that was the biggest moment I've ever experienced. I was really writing to make money and the idea of being published in the *Mercury* was so remote as to be inconceivable. I'd written several things and sent them to other magazines but they had all been rejected. I didn't even know my father had passed on that story to Ring Lardner."

Along with Mencken's letter was a check for $200, the first money Huston ever received for something he had written. He couldn't wait to cash it and send half, plus a dollar, to his patron, along with a letter:

Dear Dad,
  Enclosed you will find a check for half the amount given by the
Mercury. I am sending along a little extra for you to buy some
playthings. Get hold of some good bond and salt it away, keep it and
it will keep you. Naturally, I am anxious to hear about your work. I
am very much interested and believe you have the stuff, but I would
like to see anyway two or three close-ups.

John's letter went on to talk about how Mencken had made the
Mercury "the only magazine in the United States worthy of an intelli-
gent person's attention." And he expressed a desire to one day meet
Mencken.
  Walter was busy making movies for Paramount when John and Doro-
thy arrived in New York. "I was naturally curious to meet Dorothy,"
Walter told a *Picture Play* reporter, "but when John brought her East my
faith in his taste and judgment was fully confirmed."

In 1929 a South African named Ryall wrote a book, *Twelve Against
the Gods*, under the name William Bolitho. "It wasn't very well written,
the phrasing was somewhat archaic, but it had an enormous effect on
my life," John Huston said, "especially the introduction, which was all
about what an adventurer really was."
  Of the twelve adventurers Bolitho wrote about, the one who had the
most immediate impact on Huston was Casanova, gambler and lover,
who "shirked constancy" and whose adventure was "the forbidden
country of women."
  The self-educated budding writer hungrily devoured Bolitho's belief
when writing of Casanova that the "only education that makes a man
interesting" was "an omnivorous autodidacticism." Huston could find a
connection to Casanova, who, "before he was out of his teens, had the
elements of the best talker in Europe (save Voltaire)." And he could
identify, too, with Casanova's love for gambling. Casanova once "lost
every penny and every shirt" playing cards with a one-eyed monk. By
the time Casanova was thirty, "His adventures with women become
more complicated, even more numerous; . . . Never once does he sink
to a mere lady-killer, or a mere libertine; not one of his loves is a
repetition, and hardly one is without a human, almost artistic charm. . . .
He had so many selves."
  So many selves—that was *exactly* how John felt about himself. He
was capable of going off at any time, in any direction. In New York,

with Dorothy, waiting for the *Mercury* to confirm him as a writer, going with Sam and Lillian Jaffe to parties at George Gershwin's apartment off Riverside Drive, getting to know Ring Lardner and Sinclair Lewis through his father, listening to his mother talk about Thomas Wolfe and his first novel, *Look Homeward, Angel*, taking in the museums, the theater, the nightclubs of Harlem, the fights, the six-day bike races—he was absorbing it all. "There were so many levels of existence in New York," he recognized. The social, the sporting, the literary, the artistic. "Each one had its own followers, but I drifted from one to the other and so my life was never wanting in variety."

And when the March 1929 issue of the *American Mercury* finally appeared, there was "Fool" on pages 347 to 351, in the same issue as Margaret Mead's "Americanization in Samoa." For just fifty cents, the reader could be introduced to Huston's rough-and-tumble world of young punk Los Angeles boxers and read what Mencken thought about Calvin Coolidge, a man of "shadowy ethical ideas" and "rudimentary tastes."

At the time, Huston's secret fantasy was to one day edit the *Police Gazette*. "New York then had the gangs, the whole thing was a scam," he said. "Madison Square Garden was going full blast. They were just dramatizing wrestling matches. Before that, wrestling was as straight as boxing. Everything was crooked. Gambling, floating crap games, horse racing. All those things brought together, I thought, would be fascinating. I would have liked to have edited that."

It was a fancy notion for a young man whose first story was appearing on the newsstands. Huston knew that before he could become an editor, he would have to first learn something about being a reporter. His only contact with the newspaper world was his mother, who was writing under the name Rhea Jaure and was considered, along with Walter Winchell, to be among the *Graphic*'s top reporters. She managed to get him a job on the paper. It was a humbling experience.

Huston had neither the patience nor the temperament to be a good reporter, and he found himself in a constant state of tension trying to please two city editors. The day editor, Bill Plumber, liked him; the night editor, named Scheinmark, did not. Every time Huston got his facts mixed up and blew a story, Scheinmark would fire him. Plumber would then rehire him the next day and send him out to cover something uneventful and less trying. "I was hired and fired three or four times," Huston admitted without any trace of embarrassment, "and all my sympathies were with the night editor. I had no talent as a journalist whatever."

* * *

Sunday was visiting day in New York, and John's crowd usually congregated at Lou and Emily Paley's small house in Greenwich Village, where "the usual geniuses of New York would be in attendance," among them S. N. Behrman, Lillian Hellman, George and Ira Gershwin, Emily's sister Lenore, who married Ira Gershwin in 1926, the same year Lou Paley gave George a copy of DuBose Heyward's novel, *Porgy,* which inspired George to adapt it into the opera *Porgy and Bess.*

"That was a whole world and society then," Huston said, recalling the games of wordplay, the musical performances, the literary conversations. He once did a caricature of George Gershwin, highlighting his "sweeping eyebrows, curling lip, wide, sloping shoulders and jaw." The composer had it printed as a Christmas card. "At that time, I didn't know where I belonged, but they were marvelously kind to me. Lou Paley was one of the most modern, decent, and truly free men I've ever known. Very learned. He was a grade school teacher who also wrote lyrics for George Gershwin."

Emily Paley remembers how John would bring Dorothy to their house for dinner and how he and her husband would talk into the night. "They were such a nice couple, so alive, so interested in everything," Emily Paley says. "They had the whole world before them."

Another man whose knowledge Huston soaked up was the bacteriologist and writer Paul de Kruif, whom he met through his Aunt Margaret. De Kruif had just written a book called *Hunger Fighters* when John met him and found him "a fascinating, interesting man. He was very like Hemingway, even in appearance. Strongly built. He and Hemingway met very late in his life and they recognized each other. I had great evenings with Paul. Dorothy and I used to go out and stay in their condominium in Forest Hills. Many of the good things in life, Paul introduced me to.

"He didn't like modern art. But he was fascinated by my position, what I thought. Paul did not like Shakespeare. He didn't like poetry, saw no reason for it. Someone told me that he would rather talk literature with me than with anyone he knew. He didn't share my enthusiasm for Joyce at all, so I tried to win him over. In defending *Ulysses,* I read to him the first page, where Buck Mulligan has a Latin phrase—he comes upstairs carrying his shaving mug—and says '*Introibo ad altare Dei.*'

" 'What does that mean?' Paul challenged. And I couldn't tell him. I had the feeling I knew—God on high something—but I couldn't translate the Latin. I remember Paul leveled his gaze at me because I

professed to appreciate something hugely and then was unable to inter-
pret it correctly. I never made the same mistake again."

Next to Stanton MacDonald-Wright, Huston considered de Kruif
"the most important formative influence in my life." It was de Kruif
who urged Huston to write and who "read my writing and criticized it,
praised it, faulted it." Among the writings he praised was a play for
puppets John wrote for a woman named Ruth Squires, who made
marionettes and gave shows with them. It was based on the folk legend,
Frankie and Johnny, and there were passages that clearly revealed his
sense of rhythm and dialect.

FRANKIE
I wisht we could love like the flowers does, without toil an' sweat.
Sometimes I get a feelin', Johnny,—I get a-scairt. What if somepin
should happen to come between us?

JOHNNY
You're allus sittin' on a egg.

FRANKIE
It's nowise impossible. I ain't the first ye've knowed.

JOHNNY
I've chanctes enough if I'd a mind to— Well,—they's allus somepin
handy.

"The avant-garde of that day said it was revolutionary," wrote screenwriter Allen Rivkin about Huston's play, which had obviously been
influenced by O'Neill. Another writer, John Weld, who would become
friends with both John and Walter Huston in the mid-thirties, had
another, more cynical view of John's efforts. "He took *Frankie and
Johnny*, which is a classic, and wrote his name on it. Marvelous! I wish
I'd have been able to get by with it."

When Huston decided that the story might make a good play for
marionettes, he did some research, found early versions, and adapted
them into his play, to which he added some original characters. As a
puppet show, with his friend Sam Jaffe's improvised background music,
it met with surprising success. "The damned thing went over like a
house afire," Huston wrote.

It was such a novel idea that George Gershwin gave an exclusive
party, where it was performed with Gershwin himself at the piano

playing the incidental music. "It was remarkable," Huston remembered. "George's music was simply great. And he said he would like to think of it as a musical, it was good material."

But with Gershwin preoccupied with *Show Girl, The Dybbuk, Strike Up the Band,* and *Girl Crazy* around that time, it wasn't exactly a priority. Billy Rose, on the other hand, was very interested. Rose, who married the original Funny Girl, Fanny Brice, was producing his first musical then, *Crazy Quilt,* and he wanted *Frankie and Johnny* as part of that show. He even gave Huston a $300 advance and told him that Fanny Brice would play Frankie.

With a real chance of his simple play being produced by Rose and starring Brice, Huston used what he had learned by watching Robert Edmund Jones to sketch some designs for his play. "My drawings for the sets were pretty good."

Billy Rose was impressed and told him, "It's much better to do these than to turn it over to a scene designer. I'm going to get you put in the union."

John knew that "it was one of the hardest unions to get into, but I was going to get it, there was no question, because anyone under the aegis of Robert Edmund Jones—who was like a god at the time—and Billy Rose would have no trouble. I was very excited by the prospect of doing stage designing."

The only thing that stood in the way of the production and his becoming a union set designer was the approval of Rose's *Crazy Quilt* director, Jed Harris. "Jed Harris at that time was the hottest thing that ever came down the pike," Huston knew. Moss Hart, in his autobiography, *Act One,* wrote that "Harris could do no wrong. Production after production, whatever play he turned his hand to, was catapulted into immediate success, and his vagaries, his flaring tempers, his incisive way with a script were already a legend and fast becoming Broadway folklore. I do not think it too great a stretch of either logic or imagination to say that every aspiring playwright's prayer in those days probably went exactly along the same lines, to wit: 'Please, God, let Jed Harris do my play!' "

Now it was Huston's chance. Only he didn't have to go through the agony of submitting his play to an agent and then waiting anxiously for weeks or months. He had Jed Harris's producer who *wanted* to do his play. He had Billy Rose's brightest star, Fanny Brice, who had agreed to be Frankie. Billy Rose was going with him to Jed Harris's hotel room. All he had to do was charm Harris. And everyone knew that John Huston could charm the skin off an onion.

When they met, "He was in a brown bathrobe," Huston remembered, "and my impression was he didn't have anything on underneath. He was very Jewish-looking, but in a good, handsome way. So racial it was striking. Long, sharp features. Thin. He had kind of a vanity and disdain, a general air of superiority, not unfounded. He was a decidedly unpleasant piece of work, very subdued, very full of himself. I didn't like him at all at the time. And we didn't get on all that well. And the next thing I know, *Frankie and Johnny* wasn't going to be. I got a letter from Billy. Harris had disliked me as much as I had him, which usually is the case. I sent Billy back his advance. I couldn't afford to do it, it was just a gesture."

It is interesting to speculate on how different Huston's life would have been had the chemistry been more agreeable between the young writer/designer and the powerful stage director. Huston himself believed that he would never have made the movies he went on to make, acknowledging that Harris's rejection of both him and his play marked a career turning point. "Certainly, my path took another direction," Huston admitted.

All was not lost with *Frankie and Johnny,* however. Albert & Charles Boni decided to publish it, along with the twenty earlier versions and John's commentary about them. They paid Huston a $500 advance for what Huston considered "a kind of bastard sort of book" and hired one of the leading illustrators of the day, Miguel Covarrubias, to design and illustrate it.

Huston took the $500 to Saratoga to bet it all on a friend's horse. But before the race began, he fell into a crap game and "began rolling naturals. I let it all ride, and ran my $500 up to $11,000!" He forgot about his friend's horse, which lost its race, and thought instead about the time he went to the track in Lexington, Kentucky, with his mother when he was a boy. She had a hunch on a hundred-to-one long shot named Corncracker that didn't disappoint her. Gambling was in her blood, as it would be in her son's.

Everyone was excited about the forthcoming publication of Huston's play. His mother hoped that it would give him some direction, after his failure as a reporter. His father anticipated that he'd soon be able to support himself and not depend on the $150 a month Walter gave him. Margaret fancied that the boy might just become a playwright. And Dorothy looked in vain for the $11,000 he told her he had won, which had been diminished considerably by other less lucky bets. But in spite of the fiascoes with Jed Harris and the *Daily Graphic*, life was still looking good for John and Dorothy in the summer of 1929. "Those first two years of my marriage to Dorothy were wonderful," Huston said, "on the strength of them I would recommend early marriages because it's a lovely experience."

By this time Walter had completed three feature films and three shorts for Paramount and experienced what it felt like to be recognized and pursued by adoring movie fans, very different from the demure stage audiences. Walter had slipped into the theater to see the preview of his first film, *Gentlemen of the Press,* in Yonkers, New York, and sweat out what was, in effect, an opening night. He got to see himself as part of the audience, but when the film was over and the lights came on, a woman looked at him and began to shriek as if she had seen a ghost, then realized the actor on the screen was among them and started to chase him. The next thing he knew, a crowd of people were in pursuit, tearing at his clothes and begging for his autograph. It was an upsetting moment for Walter, who suddenly grasped what torture real public heroes had to endure.

Walter had dreamed of his name in lights, of pleasing an audience, of hearing their applause, of seeing his picture in the papers, but this crazy adulation, these looks and leers gave him pause. When Paramount offered him $1,700 a week to make movies exclusively for them, he hesitated. The money was extraordinary and devilishly tempting, but was that what he really wanted?

Walter finally agreed to do three short films for Paramount and a second feature, a smart comedy of New York life called *The Lady Lies,* in which Claudette Colbert became a star as widower Huston's showgirl-mistress. "*The Lady Lies* practically clinches Walter Huston's title as the stage star who has gone farthest and done most in talking pictures," wrote the *Evening World.* Commented Florence Fisher Parry in the *Pittsburgh Press,* "For the first time since talkies cast their ominous shadow upon the theater, I am driven to the admission that the stage has a serious rival."

Huston was paid $15,000 for the movie and had to retake a kiss with Colbert twenty-nine times, which some on the set considered a shrewd maneuver on his part. He also received $3,000 for each short; one of them, *The Carnival Man,* was based on some of his vaudeville skits from *Time.* When he saw the results, he was angry with himself for putting on the screen an act he could have lived on in bad times for at least five years. This mistake, along with the screaming fans at the Yonkers preview, marked the beginning of Walter's resentment of the movies.

The other two shorts were *The Bishop's Candlesticks* and *Two Americans*, the second notable because John made his film debut—he spoke all of eight lines. The two Americans, Abraham Lincoln and Ulysses S. Grant, were both played by Walter—Lincoln erect, Grant crouched and smoking a cigar. "It was a tour de force," John observed, "unabashed in its theatricality."

In the spring of 1929 Walter was offered $20,000 to go to Hollywood for four weeks and play a bad guy opposite Gary Cooper in *The Virginian*, directed by Victor Fleming. Four weeks, twenty grand, Hollywood: Walter found himself earning more money than he had ever thought possible and was being offered a free trip out West to see what all the fuss was about.

The train stopped in Pasadena, where publicity people for the movie had a makeup artist waiting to transform him into the mustached villain Trampas. Mary Brian, the leading lady, was also on hand, and as soon as Walter was made up, they posed for the press and then returned to the train for the ride to Sonora, where the film was being shot. Gary Cooper and Richard Arlen, the other stars, weren't impressed with this New York actor. If Walter wanted to be accepted, he would have to prove himself.

The first question director Fleming asked Walter was, "Can you ride a horse?"

"How long I got to learn?" Walter answered, not possessing the skill of his son or first wife.

"We shoot in an hour," Fleming told him, giving him a copy of the script so he could begin to learn his lines, and assigning a trainer to teach him how to ride.

The trainer got him onto the horse and pointed him toward a stream, where Walter dismounted, picked up his script, and began his process of getting into character. His mood, however, was interrupted by the hiss of a rattlesnake that caused his horse to rear. With no one around to shoot the snake, Walter swallowed his fear, picked up a rock, and struck the rattler dead with one blow. So this is Hollywood, he thought.

Had anyone seen his act of bravery, he would have been accepted immediately, but it took another near-disaster in front of the crew to gain their respect. In his first scene he had to ride his horse to the top of a hill, singing and smoking a cigarette. Once he reached the top, he was to turn his horse sharply and continue singing. He made it up the hill, but he turned too abruptly and the horse went down with him in the saddle. The horse could have fallen on top of him, but Walter played it like the saddlebum cowboy he was being paid $20,000 to be. With the cameras rolling, Walter went down with the horse, remained in the saddle, continued with his song and his cigarette, and managed to get the horse back on its feet.

"How come you kept singing?" Victor Fleming marveled, the shot in the can. "Why didn't you fall off?"

"Why, a fellow like Trampas wouldn't have done it any other way," Walter said, now no longer a "New York actor" but one of the boys.

The Virginian was a classic Hollywood western, one of the first. Early in the film Walter got to mouth his best line, after Cooper stuck a gun in his stomach and told him to "smile when you say that." "With a gun against my belly, I always smile," Huston retorted.

Later on, when Trampas is feeling his oats, he says to the Virginian, "You're a lyin', white-livered skunk. Get out by sundown or I'll shoot you on sight." It's the kind of line a thousand bad guys would repeat in a thousand westerns to come, but when Walter said it, it hadn't yet become a cliché.

When the film came out at the end of the year, the *New York Times* credited "the intelligent acting of Mr. Huston and Mr. Cooper" as being "believable characters brought to life from the days of half a century ago."

By the time that review had appeared, Walter was already disillusioned with the movie business. His restless nature would continue to pull him from and then draw him to the movies. What soured him in this instance was his meeting with B. P. "Budd" Schulberg at Paramount after learning that the studio had bought the rights to *Elmer the Great* and had hired Jack Oakie to play the role Walter had created on Broadway.

"How can you do that?" Walter challenged Schulberg. "I was born to play Elmer. Cohan, Lardner, and I developed that character."

"You sign a contract with us?" Schulberg asked.

"No, I did not," Walter said.

"Well, Jack Oakie has. Long term. He's playing Elmer."

"The way I see it," Walter said, "there are just two kinds of people in Hollywood: those trying to get contracts and those trying to get out of them."

"And where does that put you?"

"Back in New York where I belong."

Walter left California "homesick for Broadway, where people had some sense. I hated the movies. I hated Hollywood." The money he had made "did not compensate for the nonsense and boredom."

He returned to New York to appear in a play, *The Commodore Marries,* about an eccentric New England romantic who believed his house was a ship and his servants sailors until marriage changed him. But even with Arthur Hopkins producing and Robert Edmund Jones designing the sets, Kate Parson's satire was treated as a farce and it lasted only six weeks.

In the fall of 1929 farce took a backseat to tragedy. On October 24, Black Thursday, the stock market fell . . . and fell . . . and fell. The Hustons did not share the country's woes. They were climbing steps, not descending them. Just as John had narrowly missed becoming a stage designer, he also missed, by choice, becoming a stage director that year. Sam Jaffe had become friends with a producer, Herman Shumlin, who was looking for someone to direct *Grand Hotel.* Jaffe told Shumlin about *Frankie and Johnny.* Jaffe was so convincing that Shumlin sent the play to Huston along with an offer to direct it. After John read it he told Shumlin, "It's a very commercial property, but not a great work of art," and suggested that the producer direct it himself.

Shumlin did. "And he did a beautiful job," Huston later said with a smile, not regretting for a moment that, when he was only twenty-three, he had missed the opportunity to direct the biggest hit of the 1930–31 season.

Walter, after vowing to stay in New York and on the stage where he belonged, was lured back to the movies by a role and a director he wouldn't dare refuse. D. W. Griffith had decided to make his first talkie, and he chose as his subject Abraham Lincoln. When it was suggested to him that Walter Huston would make a great Lincoln, Griffith, who had considered fifty actors for the part, went to see George M. Cohan to ask what he thought about Huston. "That guy could play Grover Cleveland," Cohan replied.

Griffith had had his share of problems over the years, going from an independent producer in total control of his pictures to being a studio employee in 1924 at Paramount, where he made three uninspired films over the next two years before returning to United Artists in 1927. So when he agreed to return to Hollywood for the first time since 1919, it was understandable that he felt he was in "a nightmare of the mind and nerves."

Walter, too, looked upon this project as more than just another film. He had read Lincoln's letters and speeches and had felt "we were engaged in the creation of something immortal, something which would never be outmoded, something as enduring as the plays of Shakespeare."

His best clue to the man came from a letter Lincoln had written to his shiftless brother, who had begged a loan of $40. Instead of saying yes or no, Lincoln advised his brother to find a job, and Lincoln would match every dollar he earned. In that way, his brother would become an asset to his family and community and make more than the $40 he requested. Huston admired Lincoln's "clear, simple logic, the product of a mind that has the interests of the individual and the community at heart."

To get into character, he told a reporter, "I didn't try to walk like Lincoln. I tried to *think* like Lincoln, knowing that if I captured the secret of the man's mental processes the rest would follow. I approached it the way I would approach any characterization. I said to myself, 'What kind of man is this? How would he act in this situation?' "

Griffith's film was a success and Huston's performance was hailed. But seeing it now, one notices that the sweep and scope of Griffith's vision has been reduced to just a few battle scenes and then mostly talking heads making serious proclamations. To capture Lincoln as a young man, the forty-five-year-old Huston was heavily made-up with rouged cheeks and lipstick, which made him appear effeminate and clownish. But as Lincoln aged, Walter began to look remarkably like the portraits. Lest one forget what it was Lincoln should be best remembered for, Griffith and screenwriter Stephen Vincent Benét hammered home his belief in the preservation of the Union in seven scenes, turning a courageous and inspired stance into a platitude. After freeing the slaves with the stroke of a quill-tipped pen, he paces like a Shakespearean figure in a large empty room, worrying whether the country would hold together. "Did we ever . . . sleep?" he asks his wife, Mary.

The story has been told more times and in more ways than any other president's and Griffith didn't shed any new light on Lincoln. In hindsight, Walter was disappointed with the film. A noble effort, but not an immortal one.

•   •   •

From the grandeur of Lincoln, Walter was next cast as the suave Mexican bandit Pancho Lopez in Warner's *The Bad Man* and as a Russian general in Paramount's melodramatic *The Virtuous Sin*. *The Bad Man* had been made as a silent film by First National in 1923 and would be made again by that company in 1937, striking out all three times. To get into the head of the Mexican outlaw, Huston convinced himself that everyone would like to take the law into their own hands if they had the nerve.

"Pancho Lopez was not a bad man in his own estimation. He was just naively unmoral. He is an elemental character, and, for this reason, I found him one of the hardest to essay. During the time the picture was under production, I lived the life of Pancho Lopez. I kept very much to myself after working hours for fear that I might forget myself in company; and I did not want to undo my work by slipping back into being just Walter Huston."

In New York, Margaret Carrington's invalid husband died, which greatly saddened Walter. "He left the greatest imprint upon my life," Walter told Jack Austin in *Picture Play*. "He made no attempt to influence me. But I admired him and wanted to be like him." William Carrington's death did not surprise Margaret, who had watched his health deteriorate over the years. To help take her mind off his passing, she and Robert Edmund Jones began to make plans to stage *Camille* in Central City, Denver's old gold mining town.

Lillian Gish remembers the time Margaret called her about it. "It was eleven o'clock at night when Mrs. Carrington called and said, 'How would you like to go to Colorado and reopen the oldest theater in America with *Camille*? You will get a thousand dollars a week for your rehearsals and more than that when you play. On opening night, the people will come in stagecoaches and covered wagons, wearing costumes to match the play's period, and they will pay a hundred dollars for a seat.' When I hung up I said to mother, 'I didn't know Mrs. Carrington drank.' But it all came true. And all the governors from the surrounding states did come in costumes and in carriages of that period, paying a hundred dollars a ticket. I wore real diamonds and jewelry donated by the people of Denver and they had to get someone to sit in the entrance and watch me because I was full of this fortune. Robert Edmund Jones directed it, and did the scenery, the costumes. It was a success beyond belief."

It was while living in a hotel in Central City, where most of the women in the troupe stayed, that Gish overheard poor Jones's anguish. "The rooms were divided and the ceilings didn't go all the way up, you could hear everybody. I used to listen to Bobby Jones cry at night. I thought it was because I was so bad as Camille. Finally, I was told he was in love with Mrs. Carrington and she wouldn't marry him. She finally married him to console him and he was a happy man from that time on."

Walter, who wasn't happy about his last two films, agreed to play a tough district attorney and prison warden in *The Criminal Code*, directed by Howard Hawks. Boris Karloff signed on to re-create his stage role as the prisoner Galloway. Before he had started the film, Richard Arlen complained to Walter during a round of golf that his D.A.'s role had entered into his private life. "For God's sake, Huston, quit barking at me. You're not a district attorney yet."

But in Huston's mind, he already was.

As Warden Brady, Walter was convincing: strong, concise, upright, decent. When his ex-wife Rhea saw the film, she couldn't help thinking how ironic it was for Walter to play such self-assured characters. In her memoir, she noted, *Funny when you thought of it how the very thing that made her go away and leave Wally later made him famous. This, his nerve lacking inhibition, being his most valuable asset when his big chance came and he could act the part of the man he wanted to, but could not be. In his success he could even see himself as others saw him—on the silver screen, leisurely smoking a big cigar as he strolled through a courtyard of cowering convicts hired to look like bad men.*

She had seen the film in Europe, where she had gone soon after the publication of her son's first book, with its dedication not to her but to his wife, Dorothy. "No matter what part of the world [I] roamed," Rhea wrote about Walter, "[I] was almost sure to see his name in electric lights."

Although her divorce from Stevens had come through in 1928, she continued to take advantage of the free passes she got from him as she roamed the world, seeking work in foreign lands.

While Walter was filming *The Criminal Code* John and Dorothy arrived in Hollywood, where Herman Shumlin had talked Samuel Goldwyn into offering John a job as a contract writer at the Goldwyn studio.

Walter left First National studio early to meet them at the train station, handing John the keys to a new Buick. Walter was proud of his boy, whom he called "a highbrow with his feet on the ground." With a book out, some proven talent as an actor, and now a contract to work as a screenwriter, Walter bragged to a reporter, "He knows much more about what he wants and how he's going to get it than I do."

7

DREADFUL
MELODRAMAS

"JOHN HAD BEEN ABSOLUTELY SPOILED BY HIS MOTHER, there's no question about that. When I first met her in Paris, she was rather plain-looking, nobody of any charm or attractiveness. She wasn't pretty and she wasn't dressed particularly smartly, but she *was* very talkative. And *all* about John. She just thought the sun rose and set in this boy. God almighty!"

John Weld was a reporter for the *Paris Herald* and Rhea, who had turned fifty in 1931, had come to him with a letter of introduction from a mutual friend in New York. Weld was the same age as John and had worked as a stuntman in Hollywood, where he doubled for John Barrymore and Tom Mix. Then he became a journalist for the *New York American*, where he worked for two years before setting sail for Europe during the time when the most exciting writing was being done abroad.

In a book Weld wrote, *Young Man in Paris*, he described how Rhea Gore Huston had come to Paris looking for a newspaper job, was unsuccessful, and after a brief time returned to New York. In the three days he tried to help her she "bored" him "to distraction" as she "talked incessantly about her son, John, and his father, an actor named Walter Huston, of whom I had never heard."

"I had never heard a doting parent brag so shamelessly," Weld wrote. "She felt that writing was only one of John's talents; she was confident he would make a strong mark in the world."

Weld, who was a handsome young man with a healthy ego and literary ambitions of his own, found it a bit overbearing. "I certainly did not believe that anyone—with the possible exception of myself—could be as lavishly talented as Rhea Huston insisted her son was."

Around the time Rhea was in Europe, Nan Sunderland had also taken a trip overseas, encouraged by Walter to travel until his divorce from Bayonne was final. She met up with "Petey" Ostrer, wife of Mark Ostrer who, with his brother, owned Gaumont-British Film Company. Soon after Walter completed *The Criminal Code*, he began to miss Nan. He had never been to Europe and he was not very happy with his last three films. "I tried to tell myself that it was better to be seen by millions than thousands," he rationalized, "but that fall, feeling guilty as hell, I packed my bags and hopped a train [for New York]." What was making him feel guilty was the amount of money he was earning at a time when able-bodied men were standing in breadlines and begging for spare change.

Nan and Petey were there when he arrived in France by boat and promised to cheer him up. They went to Paris, Cannes, Nice, Monte Carlo, the Italian Riviera, Milan, Berlin. They gambled, went to museums, saw the great cathedrals, the operas, and the Folies-Bergère. Walter wasn't impressed. He had a romantic's vision of Europe and was disappointed by the inefficiency, the uncleanliness, the unfriendliness, and the language barriers. But he had plenty of money and spent it freely, if not elatedly, and managed to enjoy himself.

When Walter returned to Hollywood to play another district attorney in *Star Witness* for Warner Bros., he told Nan to stay in Paris until his divorce with Bayonne was settled. He feared Bayonne would demand an outrageous sum of money if she knew of Walter's plan to marry Nan as soon as he legally could. He had already agreed to pay Bayonne $100,000. "I wanted complete disentanglement," he said. "Long since I had found a lady whose companionship I craved; I wanted to marry her."

What Walter never found out was that while Nan was waiting for his telegram she met and had an affair with John Weld. Weld wrote about it in his book, which wasn't published until 1985, long after it could have hurt anyone. "Nan Sunderland was a beautiful woman," according to Weld. "She was tall—about five feet nine—with auburn hair, brown eyes, and a sprinkling of freckles on her nose." They had met at a dinner party at the home of the European head of United Artists and talked about Walter Huston's first wife.

"I've never encountered so much maternal idolatry in my life," Weld said about Rhea. "I don't believe anybody could be as gifted as she says John is. Do you know him?"

"I've met him," Nan answered. "He's charming. But you're right. His mother really lays it on thick."

Weld saw her home that night, and to his surprise she kissed him. "I was nonplussed, elated, aroused and emboldened," Weld wrote, telling Nan he couldn't fly on one kiss and getting a second. She had told him about her engagement to Walter, but "she was far away from her fiancé, and our relationship cast no reflection on her betrothal. She had had other sexual encounters. She had not promised to be chaste. . . . Thus we had a rare and wonderful opportunity to enjoy a brief fling. . . . I don't think Nan ever felt any guilt."

They went to restaurants, galleries, and the theater, saw each other almost every day. Weld took her to Sylvia Beach's bookstore, Shakespeare and Co., and one day they met Eugene O'Neill along the Champs Elysées, and he told them about his next play, *Ah, Wilderness*, and about how he wished he had written *Mourning Becomes Electra* as a novel. Then it all came to an end, and Nan met Weld at the Deux Magots to say good-bye. She had heard from Walter. Bayonne had gone to Reno. "Coast is clear," cabled Walter on October 15, 1931.

Weld ordered drinks and put on a happy face. The next morning he saw her off at the train station. "We hugged clumsily and kissed for the last time. We were lovers no longer . . . she belonged to someone else."

As Nan sailed across the Atlantic on the *President Garfield*, Walter was finishing *A House Divided*, a Universal film directed by William Wyler. He had made three other pictures that year: *Star Witness*, about the intimidation of a family after they had witnessed a gang-war killing; *The Ruling Voice*, in which he played a food racketeer; and *A Woman from Monte Carlo*, in which he starred as the commander of a French battle cruiser whose unfaithful wife (German actress Lil Dagover in her American debut) confesses to her adultery and saves him from being court-martialed. He didn't think much of any of them but was more interested in *A House Divided* because he was able to get John his first screen credit as a dialogue writer. Universal was initially reluctant to give him the job until Walter brought them a copy of *Frankie and Johnny* along with some of John's magazine stories.

"Although I recommended him," Walter said, "I didn't push the matter. His own work sold him, as I felt certain it would." Walter didn't *have* to push; *his* work had made him enough of a draw that the studios would have gone out of their way to please him.

John was lucky his father was around to get him the job, since on his own, his dealings with Sam Goldwyn had come "to absolutely nothing." John never forgot the first time he met with Goldwyn, who sat behind his desk and never moved when Huston entered. "He wasn't very friendly. . . . He and Shumlin didn't get along. I don't think Sam got along well with anybody, that wasn't his approach to life. He went at everything as though he was the antagonist."

By this time Huston's second story had appeared in the May 1931 issue of *American Mercury*—a series of six short sketches called "Figures of Fighting Men." The monthly had doubled in price, to a dollar, by then and the feature story was "Hair" by William Faulkner. Huston's piece ran only three pages, but his writing was sharp and pungent as he told about six fighters at different stages of their careers.

The sketches demonstrated Huston's talent for writing both tough and tender, ironically and sensitively. In an autobiographical note printed in that issue, he drew a self-portrait of his gangly face with tight lips and a boxer's nose, and wrote that he was at work on two books, "one a novel, the other to be called 'The Gambler's Rose,' and to be made up of stories of artists, composers, etc., whose names have been forgotten, or were never known—mainly fly-by-nights, who had much to do with the culture of this country and who now rest in shallow graves."

Walter was impressed with John's knowledge, but he never lost the slight competitive edge between them. "My son knows so much more about books and literature than I do, I sometimes feel ashamed," he told a journalist. "Most of what I know about human nature, I have learned from people. Perhaps in this way I have found out a lot of things that son John doesn't know."

John may have felt the truth in his father's remarks, for he soon abandoned the two books he had been working on and looked to Hollywood to fill whatever void in human nature he felt he might be missing. He found the movies more suitable to his personality. Books were a solitary form of expression, the movies were more collaborative and John Huston never really enjoyed working alone.

* * *

At Universal, John was given an office to share with other writers, and he worked on two pictures for his father. The first, *A House Divided*, wasn't very good and Walter felt that John could punch up the dialogue. It was loosely based on O'Neill's *Desire Under the Elms*. "This plot," wrote John, "in hands other than O'Neill's, had become bad melodrama. I saw how the script could be improved by bringing the dialogue down to an absolute minimum, making the characters inarticulate. This would give the picture both a certain starkness and a distinguishing style."

Willy Wyler approved of John's work, as did Universal's boss, Carl Laemmle, Jr., and the film's associate producer, Paul Kohner. Kohner said he took an immediate liking to John because of his "enthusiasm and confidence." It was to be the beginning of a lifelong friendship between Wyler, Kohner, and Huston.

Although the *New York Times's* Mordaunt Hall considered the film to be "dour" and "sometimes strained," calling Huston's acting "a little too stern," the critical majority were more along the lines of the *Hollywood Reporter*: "It presents Walter Huston at his best, giving the portrait of a rugged, calloused seaman, with ice water for blood and a lump of concrete for a heart." And *The New Yorker* singled out John's writing, noting that "those pictures where the speech is most satisfactory are invariably those wherein it is least noticeable. . . . It is due . . . to this terseness of the spoken word that *A House Divided* seems unusually honest and stirring, seeming plausible though it is in fact quite overwrought melodrama."

After *A House Divided*, John was put under contract at Universal, where he next worked on another of his father's films, *Law and Order*, based on W. R. Burnett's *Saint Johnson*, about Wyatt Earp and the gunfight at the OK Corral. Burnett was the kind of writer John championed, where he would "close the book and have to walk around the block." The film was directed by Edward Cahn and the credited screenwriter was Tom Reed, although John, as with *A House Divided*, wrote the words the actors spoke.

"There were screenplay writers and dialogue writers then," Huston noted, "it was a false distinction. The screenplay writer was thought to have the older, wiser head, the practical mind. Whereas the dialogue writer was thought to be more artistic and creative."

John thought the final script read better than it played and soon after it was finished, he and his father went their separate ways: Walter to marry and film another Burnett story, John to write dialogue for an Edgar Allan Poe story and then sink into a quagmire of bad luck.

Walter and Nan married in Walter's attorney's office on November 11, 1931, putting to rest the gossip columnists' speculation that Walter was seriously involved with his *Lincoln* co-star, Una Merkel. The very next day Walter began *The Beast of the City*, having finally capitulated to the studio system by signing a five-year contract with MGM. He had fought to maintain his independence as a free-lance actor but came to realize that the best parts were passing him by. MGM had promised him good pictures.

The Beast of the City was a cop/gangster picture, with Walter playing an overzealous police captain, Jean Harlow a gang moll, and Jean Hersholt a Capone-style gang leader. An Englishman, Charles Brabin, directed it and John Lee Mahin wrote the script from W. R. Burnett's story. Walter plays his role with conviction but it's a two-dimensional portrait, his character never changes.

A review in the *Fort Worth Star-Telegram* said, "The story has some power, but it is Huston's acting that raises this picture out of the class of a mediocre melodrama. . . . There are so few actors in Hollywood who give the impression they are persons in real life." W. R. Burnett thought "everything about it was wrong—making an American hoodlum picture and giving it to an Englishman who'd go to sleep right in your face during a story conference." Still, Burnett acknowledged that the end result was "one of the best crime pictures of all. Hersholt was a greasy, offensive Capone. Really good."

Everything about John's next job, writing additional dialogue for Robert Florey's *Murders in the Rue Morgue*, was also wrong . . . and stayed that way. Tom Reed from *Law and Order* and Dale Van Every from *A House Divided* were credited with the screenplay, about a mad doctor (played by Bela Lugosi) who tries to mate a woman with a gorilla; but John's attempt at remaining faithful to Poe was not appreciated. "I tried to bring Poe's prose style into the dialogue," Huston wrote, "but the director thought it sounded stilted, so he and his assistant rewrote scenes on the set. As a result, the picture was an odd mixture of nineteenth-century grammarian's prose and modern colloquialisms."

During this time at Universal, John was running wild. He liked to drink until drunk, ride horses, gamble, and see other women. His behavior was already becoming the subject of stories told at Hollywood parties. One had to do with a Cadillac he had traded in his Buick for. The car was a lemon and had given him trouble from the moment he drove it out of the showroom. One day Huston was driving this hated status symbol over the unpaved Cahuenga Pass on his way to Universal when "the goddamn thing started making this sound through the cylinders. The sound got bigger and bigger and the car stopped." Huston slammed the door, unscrewed the gas cap, found some matches, and began to do a strange tai chi–like dance around the Cadillac, striking the matches and throwing them at the gas tank. He wanted to blow it up. Instead, he left the car at the top of the Cahuenga Pass and never returned for it.

Dorothy heard these stories and didn't know what to do. Her husband had changed since they returned to Los Angeles and they were growing apart. He was always out with the boys, working on movie ideas at the studio, going for drinks afterward, coming home late after gambling along Sunset Strip at the exclusive Clover Club, the Garden Club, or La Boheme. She, too, had aspirations and worked on stories. But she didn't get the feedback he did, and she never completed her stories. "She would write things up to a certain point and then they'd dwindle out, go unfinished," John said with some sorrow. "She wrote very well, but there was something in her that couldn't finish anything, even a short story. Then, when I started going out to work, she just stopped. That's when she began to drink."

Huston wasn't much help to Dorothy because he was always trying to finish stories of his own. In February 1932 he put together a treatment for a film he wanted to call *Black Rust*, based on the writings of Paul de Kruif about Mark Alfred Carleton who, born in Ohio in 1866, figured out how to cure a deadly wheat fungus.

In April he wrote *Steel Man*, a treatment about a woman tease and the men in a steel mill. In June he reworked *U-Boat*, the German submarine story, and wrote a treatment for the *Invisible Man*. In August his mind was in the Cameroons, the story, *Nagana*, about a bacteriologist who loses his girl and commits suicide. In September he worked on an idea called *The Hero* about a department store floorwalker who resembled a gangster and winds up shooting the five most notorious gangsters in the country, landing on the front page, getting the girl he loved and a New York parade. In October it was *Jack of Diamonds*, about a big-time gambler who finds a bum who resembles the Jack of Diamonds and feels he can't lose a bet as long as he's got his "Jack."

With nothing happening on any of these treatments, John began work on two stories with Willy Wyler. He had read the Pulitzer Prize–winning book *Laughing Boy* by Oliver La Farge. The title was ironic as it was a harsh story about the plight of the American Indian, dealing with prostitution, interracial sex, and the struggles that existed between Indians and whites. Huston gave the book to Wyler, who passed it on to Universal.

Huston wrote a full-length script but Universal wasn't interested because they couldn't find the right actor to play the lead. Then Wyler suggested they consider making a film having to do with the depression. So the two of them, with ten cents in their pockets, went off to L.A.'s skid row, where they talked to bums, shared cheap wine, ate a free meal at a mission, and slept in a shelter. They then embarked on a script based on Daniel Ahearn's story *The Wild Boys of the Road*. It had to do with children whose parents were victims of the depression. The kids rode the trains, many of them dying in boxcars. Huston and Wyler traveled throughout California talking to these children, as well as to railroad workers and hoboes. The script ended with a boy standing over his dying friend, pointing a gun into the camera, and shouting, "You killed him!"

According to Huston, the picture was never made because Roosevelt became president in January 1933 and these kids were soon off the roads and working in reforestation programs. "Overnight it seemed there was a new spirit in the air, a feeling of high confidence."

Hollywood, at the time, was enjoying a carefree sort of recklessness during the last years of Prohibition. Glamour, not depression, was the key word, and the public ate up the press accounts of what Gloria Swanson and Norma Talmadge were wearing, who Jean Harlow and Ruby Keeler were dancing with, how much jewelry Marion Davies displayed, what Mary Pickford, Carole Lombard, Marlene Dietrich, Lupe Velez, and Kay Francis were up to. The nightclubs were booming, as were the gambling establishments on land and at sea.

While John was out on the town, Dorothy continued to drink at home and for a long time John wasn't aware that she had a problem.

He just knew she could mix a damn good martini, complemented by little pearl onions rather than olives, and that she seemed to settle into a somewhat conformable "Hollywood wife" life: tennis lessons, long gossipy lunches with the other industry wives, weekly dates with the hairdresser, swimming in their apartment pool on Wilton Place, and leaving the business of housecleaning to their maid. Although there were times when they would go out together, more often than not, John would wind up at some Hollywood nightspot on his own or in the company of friends, including other women. He had become involved with a beautiful Hungarian-born actress named Zita Johann, who had appeared in D. W. Griffith's last film, *The Struggle,* and was married to but separated from playwright-director John Houseman.

One drunken night, on his way to the Clover Club, Huston crashed into a parked car and wound up spending the night in jail once the police took a whiff of his breath. "This was not an uncommon experience in the crowd that we moved with," Huston acknowledged.

In February of 1933, Huston was again drunk behind the wheel. Zita Johann went flying into the windshield when their car struck a palm tree in the Hollywood Hills. John Houseman was on his way home from the theater in New York when he found out about the accident. He couldn't miss it. The *Daily News* ran a front-page photo of her and a banner: BEAUTY MARRED. She rated the headline because she was currently appearing in movie theaters as the reincarnated Egyptian princess pursued by Boris Karloff in *The Mummy.* John was merely "the son of actor Walter Huston." Dorothy was the little woman fuming in the background.

"I was not emotionally involved then," John Houseman recalled, "but seeing that headline was a shock. I called her the next day and it was not nearly as serious as it sounded. It *sounded* like she was completely disfigured, but she wasn't." Johann did get cut up and also broke a tooth in the accident; Huston was booked for drunken driving and had to pay a fine.

And then John really blew it: He allowed Dorothy to find him in a compromising position with another woman, forever shattering whatever illusions she might have had. "Our marriage had become conventional," John confessed, "extending even to the point of conventional misbehavior on the part of the male animal. I began having affairs. There were so many pretty girls. It was completely inconsequential, never serious—until Dorothy entered a room at the wrong moment."

They never talked about it, there was no confrontation, but Dorothy's life altered permanently the moment she saw her husband making love to another woman. She knew he was wild, got drunk, smashed into cars and trees, put an actress through a windshield, but he always came home to her and she never probed too deeply. But this was irrefutable evidence of the deterioration of their marriage.

"It was my mother who first told me that Dorothy was drinking," Huston said. Rhea had returned from Europe and gone to Los Angeles to see how John and his wife were getting along. What she saw disturbed her. John was out working and Dorothy was home drinking. She recognized the symptoms immediately, having grown up living in fear and loathing of her father's "periodicals." When she told her son about it, John "couldn't believe it. She told me that she was drinking martinis in the afternoon while I was away at the studio. I thought it was my mother interfering again with my wife. We had a standup quarrel." Rhea had found out about John's infidelities and blamed him openly for what was happening to Dorothy. "She felt that I was responsible for Dorothy's drinking," Huston said defensively. "But I can't accept that wholly. It may have been the thing that set her off, but it was a real addiction, no question."

Rhea and John fought so bitterly over this—she demanding that he change his ways, he insisting that she get out of his life—that Rhea found her own nerves almost shattered and fled, once again, to Europe. She and John would have no communication for an entire year.

Rhea reflected about this time: *She thought of her son's childwife and of how his success went to his head by the cocktail route in Hollywood. She wished there had been something she could do to straighten things out, but these children believed themselves wise and refused to benefit from the experiences of those who had gone before.*

With his mother gone, Huston hoped that he could patch up his marriage, but he soon began to see that his mother had been right. "I thought a few times Dorothy's behavior was queer," he said. "And the next thing I knew, she was openly drunk. We made an attempt to get back on rails again, going down to Malibu and staying there. No drinking for either of us. I thought for a while that something very strange and psychopathological had happened, that late in the afternoon her vision began to get blurred, her speech slurred and her step unsure. Dorothy would try and make beautiful gestures when she was in her cups. So beautiful that she would always end up by knocking the glass over. I thought, Christ, this was the hour when she used to get drunk. It's penetrated that deeply. Then I discovered she had bottles hidden in places you wouldn't dream of, like shoes. A laundryman was bringing her bottles. And when I confronted her, she denied it. She had become a liar. She had totally changed. In her eyes I saw flashes of resentment, even hatred. Living so isolated out there I had become her jailer."

Huston took her to doctors but they didn't know what to do. "There was no regular treatment for alcoholics at that time, no such thing as AA." And so, for the next few months, John tried to do what he could to help his wife, but he knew deep in his soul that it was too late.

While Dorothy sank into alcoholism and John wrecked cars and women's lives, Walter was busier than he had ever been making movies, buying Morgan Russell paintings, and building a house in Running Springs, near Lake Arrowhead in the San Bernadino mountains, a hundred miles away from the madness of Hollywood. Walter and Nan couldn't resist buying the four acres of land in the area known as the Rim o'the World with its giant pines and panoramic view of the valley. Walter had planned on building a small mountain cabin himself out of rough-hewn logs, but Nan talked him into doubling the size of what Walter had designed as a "love nest for two." She also convinced him to add a guest room, a tennis court, a gymnasium, and a swimming pool. "Anybody now can have those logs who'll take the trouble to haul them away," Walter wrote in a column that appeared in the *Cincinnati Post*. "It's no longer my house—it's my wife's."

He did feel, though, that of all the things he had done in his life, building his own house gave him the most satisfaction. "I've never had a home before, or the feel of my own earth under my feet, my own woods and bricks and storm windows and trees." A polished bronze chandelier hung from one of the beams above the forty-five-foot-high living room. In front of the stone fireplace and massive chimney, Walter built a sunken semicircular couch that could sit twenty people on cushions of chenille velvet. The stairway leading to the bedrooms was made of hand-hewn white pine and the double bathroom was tiled in cobalt blue and had a ceiling of silver leaf.

On why he wanted to live so far away from where he worked, Walter told reporter Arthur Kempner, "If you are too close to your work, and to the people with whom you work, you lose all perspective. You shut yourself up in a little world inadequately small. By living away from it I can see Hollywood in a clearer light." He looked forward to inviting friends up to Running Springs for "three to four days at a stretch," anticipating the "good talk and good food and good sleep."

Once he agreed to expand the house, he remembered his engineering days and the disastrous fire in Nevada, Missouri, and took precautions to protect his new home. He had high pressure pumps installed that could utilize the forty thousand gallons of water in the swimming pool and spray it two hundred feet if necessary. He equipped the house with its own diesel electric plant that switched on if there was a power failure. He also had a large food storeroom in the basement, in case they were ever snowed in.

To pay for this idyllic retreat, Walter made movies—eleven of them in two years—until he couldn't look at himself in the mirror and see an actor looking back. MGM had not fulfilled its promise of putting him in only top-notch, stimulating pictures. The contract system had turned him into just another acting cog in the movie-grinding wheel.

In *Film Weekly* he complained of being "fed up with the kind of parts I had been asked to play. . . . I was getting into a rut. . . . Whenever people saw my name outside the cinema, they knew just what to expect: Walter Huston, the hard and heartless man of iron."

In *The Wet Parade*, based on muckracker Upton Sinclair's anti-Prohibition novel, Huston's challenge was to personify the evils of bad bootlegged booze that turned him into a wife killer. Writers had a field day describing his character as a "vainglorious weak-willed dipsomaniac" and a "moronic old roué." Walter said he played him as a "poor, besotted weakling." But it was a character he considered among his favorite parts. "That poor fellow was real," he said. "That's the kind of thing I like to do best of all."

The Wet Parade led to a colorful episode in Huston's life when Aimee Semple McPherson, the nation's most flamboyant evangelist, agreed to "debate" him about Prohibition on a nationwide radio hookup to be broadcast from her Angelus Temple. The idea was hatched in the publicity department at MGM and McPherson agreed only on the condition that since it *was* the law, her pro-Prohibition position would have to "win." She also insisted on meeting with Huston beforehand to hear what he was going to say in defense of drinking. Walter was amused by the whole thing and found her "startling, magnetic, gracious." He also found it bizarre when he entered the Angelus Temple on April 11, 1932, to a packed audience and had to escort Aimee, in her flowing white gown, carrying a large bouquet of lilies, down a ramp to the stage. "I have been in some strange places in my day and done some odd things," he said, "but coming down that ramp with Aimee on my arm exuding hallelujah is one of the weirdest things that ever happened to me."

As for the "debate," "It all was very silly. I, the champion of liquor, was hissed and booed, and Aimee, the crusader of temperance, lifted up her vibrant voice and hypnotized her hearers."

John was in the audience watching his father, finding it hard not to laugh. "It was a publicist's stunt, part of the coloration of California." The actual vote was 19,741 in favor of Prohibition and 14,563 against.

After playing a corrupt judge in what he considered "simply a bad picture" called *Night Court*, Walter was loaned to Columbia for "a good picture made by a first-class director, Frank Capra, to run in second-class theaters." The film was *American Madness* and it was quintessential Capra, a contemporary social melodrama about a decent banker trying to save his bank from a run by frightened depositors. His conservative board of directors don't like his liberal tendencies but Walter (as Tom Dixon) defends his loan policies, saying that the people are his friends who need an institution like the bank to help them through the hard times. "Character: it's the only thing you can bank on; and it's the only thing that will pull this country out of the doldrums." He's got a lot of convincing to do, but eventually Dixon prevails.

For his part, Walter felt that the banker he played most closely resembled his own self-image. "I figure I'm quite a bit the type of man he was, wanting from life the same things he wanted, with pretty much the same set of values and beliefs. He didn't demand too much of life. Neither do I. He believed in people and expected the best of them. So do I. He didn't worry about things he couldn't help. Neither do I. He was roused to action when there was vital and imminent need—and I would be likewise. He wouldn't have given a thought to mistakes that are done and past. I wouldn't, either. He wouldn't have worried about what is to come when this life is ended. I don't. I am content to leave such matters to those who have control of them. I haven't."

He certainly didn't have any control over the "dreadful melodrama, class-B bust" of *Kongo*, his next film, or of the histrionics of Joan Crawford in *Rain*, the adaptation of Somerset Maugham's story "Miss Sadie Thompson." In *Kongo*, he got the chance he didn't get with *Elmer the Great*—to put on the screen the character he created for the stage—though the film was more graphically violent than the play. Huston's crippled ivory trader, Deadlegs Flint, was made up like a voodoo witch doctor, evil to the core and deserving of his horrible end.

In his book *Hollywood in the Thirties*, John Baxter singled out *Kongo* for its relentless sadism: "The cruelty is not, however, without a sick humour. Dragging himself out of his wheelchair, the crippled, unshaven Huston thrusts his scarred face into that of [his mistress] and demands, 'Have you ever of all the men you have known seen such an Adonis?' " But the picture was a mess and served only to further alienate Walter, who felt that "although I was being worked like a truck-horse, I had not been given a chance to show that I could act."

His feelings didn't change much when he came up against Joan Crawford, even though he clearly demonstrated his talent. United Artists wanted Crawford for the part of the fallen, irredeemable Sadie Thompson, and Walter was borrowed from MGM to play the self-righteous and unforgiving soul-saver Mr. Davidson (toned down from Maugham's preacher because the Production Code wouldn't allow ministers to be ridiculed or shown as villains). The part of a "hypocritical, thoroughly nasty and lustful" reformer might seem one that Huston should have relished, but the actor felt slighted by the attention paid to Crawford. "When the weight of such a box-office star as Miss Crawford is plunked on a play, no matter how good, it becomes a lop-sided affair—a series of scenes showing the lady's face in varying close-ups as she runs the gamut of emotions."

Actually, Huston managed to hold his own against the leading lady and was convincingly terrifying as a disturbed and fanatical bigot attempting to lead Miss Crawford from her sinful ways only to succumb himself to the weakness of the flesh.

Back at MGM, a World War I movie was waiting for him. *Hell Below* featured Robert Montgomery, Jimmy Durante, Robert Young, and Madge Evans. Walter played the tough commander of a submarine. The screen was filled with sailors fighting, Durante boxing a kangaroo, ships sinking, depth bombs exploding, planes attacking, and the submarine and its crew trapped on the ocean floor. Huston's opinion of this one? "A star-studded box-office behemoth, a two-dimensional piece which had about as much relation to life as the Tom Swift stories."

His frustration carried over to his private life. He felt stuck, "plugging up pictures that were bad, substituting for other actors when they refused to do a part, being subjected to the whims and caprices of stars, shunted into the background by cutters and cinematographers. In other words, playing the goat."

Nan, who often helped him prepare for a role at home, was bitter about MGM's not making better use of her husband and told Walter to tell the studio to "go to hell!" But Walter's option wasn't coming up until November and he knew his hands were tied. His only hope was that a picture with a meaty part would come along.

Gabriel Over the White House was such a picture and when Walter Wanger was put on it as producer, he wanted Huston to play the part of a crooked politician who becomes president, is injured in a car accident, and turns into a decisive leader willing to take on the problems facing the nation and the world and actually solving them. Wanger was a trusted old friend and Walter felt comfortable with him. He also liked the script. The country was still in the throes of the depression, although the new president, Franklin Roosevelt, was promising the people a "New Deal." The troubles facing the world were frighteningly real, economically, politically, socially. And here was a movie that showed how one man could come to the rescue and bring about peace and prosperity that everyone wanted but no one expected. Reviewers were unanimous in their praise, calling the film "electric," "galvanizing," "epic," "intrigu-ing." The best review of all, however, came from Walter's sister Margaret, who sent a telegram: "Thrilled with your acting appearance and marvelous impersonation. Am sure there will be a nationwide Huston for President campaign. It is by far the best thing you have done."

Gabriel allowed Walter a temporary respite from his contract anxieties, but two of his next three films—*Storm at Daybreak* and *Ann Vickers*—only reinforced them. The third, *The Prizefighter and the Lady*, was an enjoyable lark.

Storm at Daybreak opened with an exciting re-creation of the 1914 assassination of Archduke Francis Ferdinand in Sarajevo, which precipitated World War I. But it went downhill from there, focusing on Kay Francis's infidelity to her Hungarian husband, played by Huston.

In *Ann Vickers*, Walter played a corrupt state supreme court judge who, in the midst of disgrace, was sustained by the loyalty and love of Ann, played by Irene Dunne. Huston was lent to RKO for the film and felt that it "didn't develop dramatically."

Walter had fifth billing for *The Prizefighter and the Lady*, but that didn't matter because he got to play a boozy fight manager and pal around with the two leading heavyweights of the day, Max Baer and Primo Carnera. Carnera was the heavyweight champion at the time and Baer the number-one contender, and they were scheduled to fight for the title. Before that, however, they would have a chance to assess each other in a choreographed fight for the movie. Myrna Loy also starred as a nightclub entertainer and Otto Kruger a racketeer. The film bout between Baer and Carnera was refereed by Jack Dempsey, and other fighters were brought in for cameo roles during the fight sequences.

"Fight fans won't believe the incredible world's heavyweight championship fight in this picture," Ed Sullivan observed in his *Daily News* column, "but they will believe Huston's rich portrayal of the Professor, the veteran fight manager. . . . After seeing him . . . I'm convinced that Walter Huston comes pretty close to being the No. 1 character actor of North America."

Walter wasn't the only one who looked forward to each day's work. When John heard about the fighters on the set, he came around, too. His work may not have been appreciated and his private life may have been in shambles, but he could forget all that during the days he got to watch the antics between the giant Carnera and the wily Maxie Baer.

"They were always afraid during the shooting that Maxie and Carnera would start trading punches," John recalled. "Every blow for the film was measured and timed, everything was premeditated, by design. Still, there was this concern that one or the other would let go and the championship would be decided on the backlot of MGM."

John was feeling guilt and responsibility for Dorothy's descent into alcoholism, and he finally made the decision to "cut and run." He just didn't know how he could help her. When he got back from work she would be floating in a martini haze. She couldn't keep off the stuff and he didn't like playing the watchdog. Finally, they decided to get a divorce, with Dorothy filing and asking for nothing from him. A friend of hers, a Scandinavian actress named Greta Nissen, was going to make a movie in England and invited Dorothy to join her, to help her get away from the misery in which she was drowning in Malibu. John felt relieved when she agreed to go.

Freed from the burden of having to deal with a drunken wife who resented him for his irresponsible ways, Huston tried to immerse himself in work. His contract with Universal had expired and wasn't renewed, but Darryl Zanuck had called him in to see if he would be interested in writing a treatment for a movie for Wallace Beery about P. T. Barnum. Zanuck had left his position as studio head of Warner Bros. and had started a new company, Twentieth Century Pictures, the forerunner of 20th Century-Fox. Huston described Zanuck as a small man with prominent front teeth who spoke "in a voice several decibels too loud for the size of the room."

Huston read everything he could about P. T. Barnum and enthusiastically came to the conclusion that Barnum was "the shrewdest man alive, an exemplification of the nineteenth-century American dream of conquest and Manifest Destiny." On June 17, 1933, he wrote to Zanuck: "If you were to be asked what are the ten most common qualities the American people have in general, your list would pretty nearly sum up the character of P. T. Barnum." He went on, pitching the man who had already been sold on the idea, and concluded, "Reflecting the American spirit as he does and as Barnum will be played by Beery, he will certainly reach the hearts of audiences because they will see so much of themselves in it."

Huston's letter was fine, but his script wasn't. "Zanuck read my script and shook his head," John said with a laugh. But he didn't laugh when Zanuck thought the script needed a whole new approach and took John off the project. The movie was eventually made a year later but John didn't think much of it: "It didn't hold a candle to the one I'd written."

Walter was upset by John's personal and professional problems but didn't have the time to try to be of any help. He also didn't think much of the RKO film he began in August, a story about a soldier who befriends a horse called *Keep 'em Rolling*. It was just another of those ridiculous movies that were beginning to drive him crazy.

What Walter wanted was a good play. And during the filming of *Keep 'em Rolling* he found one. It came in the form of a telegram from Sinclair Lewis and Sidney Howard, who were collaborating on an adaptation of Lewis's novel *Dodsworth*, with Max Gordon producing. Was Walter interested in playing it on Broadway?

Was he ever! Even without seeing the play, Walter's instinct told him it had to be better than the scripts he was doing in Hollywood. Huston told Lewis, Howard, and Gordon that he would gladly meet them in Washington, D.C., where he was going to be on location in Fort Myer. His only concern was that MGM wouldn't release him from his contract, which was due for renegotiation in two months. "My professional life was in bondage," Huston knew. The question was, How to escape?

Walter and Nan went to Washington and read the play. Max Gordon thought Walter would be the perfect Dodsworth, a man who travels to Europe with his wife, loses her to a European romance, meets and falls in love with another woman, and then is torn between doing what he thinks proper or following the dictates of his heart. Walter said that he very much wanted to do it, but, again, he couldn't be sure the studio would release him. The two men discussed strategies. Walter was being paid $2,500 a week by MGM. The upcoming option was for $3,000. But the studio often tried to save that extra $500 per week by pointing out that times were still bad and citing the gross receipts of the pictures the star had made. In Walter's case, there hadn't been any blockbusters and more than likely they would try to get away with not increasing his salary. If they gave him that opening, Gordon suggested, tear up the contract and walk out of there before anyone has a chance to change his mind.

What also interested Huston about *Dodsworth* was the part of Mrs. Cortright, the woman Dodsworth falls in love with. It was, he believed, perfect for Nan. She had given up her acting career after they had married, but she missed it terribly and Walter felt this was the right vehicle for her. It would also bring them together in rehearsal and onstage.

In print, Walter painted a rosy picture of their marriage, saying, "I am perfectly and completely happy in my third marriage, which will go on for as long as we both shall live. At 48, love wears a slightly different face to a man than the face it wore when he was 20. No less lovely, but sex attraction is not the single thing it then was. At 48, one demands more of love than that alone. There must be grace of living, and charm and kindred tastes and a communion of thought and taste that make argument impossible."

It sounded pretty good, but Walter also had a reputation as a woman-izer. Unlike his son, however, he preferred one-night stands to the entanglements of love. He had no intention of ever leaving Nan.

"Walter was very much a ladies man," observed John Weld, who returned to the States some months after Nan had. He worked as a scriptwriter for a while and had gotten to know Huston through Nan. They became friends and Weld suggested he ghostwrite Walter's autobiography. Huston agreed to let him try. So Weld began to consider Walter's ways—not just the public image but the private man as well. And he quickly discovered that Walter had an eye for the ladies. "He'd put a girl in bed just as soon as he could get her there," Weld noticed, "and that never stopped all his life. They were fly-by-night for the most part and he was kind, considerate, generous. But he was never one to be serious. It was just a sexual thing."

Nan liked the idea of appearing in *Dodsworth*. She knew that she would play both Mrs. Dodsworth and Mrs. Cortright in their home, as Walter rehearsed his part, and she hoped that Max Gordon might consider her. But they decided not to say anything yet. Not until Walter knew what his situation with MGM was going to be.

By mid-September, both Walter and Nan were sweating out the November contract meeting. Production manager J. J. Cohn would not let an actor out of his contract if it could be avoided. "In those days," Cohn recalls, "you invested money in these people and you took a chance with some of them. So why should you spend money establishing them and then let someone else have the fruits of your labor?"

The logic was understandable. The forced labor and the lousy pictures were not. As Walter wrote in a movie magazine, "The fun of winning one's spurs is over for me. All I want is the chance to give as good a performance as possible with the best possible material." And that material was not coming from the writers at MGM.

John, at this time, was also sweating things out. When Zanuck took him off the Barnum picture, he began to lose faith in the movie business. He had worked on a dozen projects as a writer, had outlined a number of film ideas, written treatments for some, full-length scripts for others, but nothing had come of any of them. Herman Shumlin was back in New York, Willy Wyler had rebounded from their failures with *Laughing Boy* and *The Wild Boys of the Road* by making other films. Walter was busy with his house and his plans to return to the stage as soon as he could. Dorothy was a ruined lush somewhere in London. His own reputation was that of a wild, immature, self-serving boy who used his father's name shamelessly to get ahead and to get out of the bad publicity he received for his two drunken car accidents. Things couldn't get much worse. But just as he thought he had reached the bottom, he sank even deeper.

It was late in the evening of September 25, 1933, when Huston was driving the car he had borrowed from Greta Nissen, who was in England with Dorothy, and picked up a hitchhiker on Sunset Boulevard. A poor driver who admitted that "my attention strays," he never saw the woman who stepped off the curb between parked cars at Sunset and Gardner just as he approached that corner. In a flash, the body jumped from his hood to his windshield with a sickening thud and then flew forward thirty-six feet. Huston's foot slammed onto the brake pedal in time to prevent his car from running over the stricken body but the damage was already done. She lay motionless in the street, her body crumpled, her head crunched.

Huston, who swore that on this occasion he had not been drinking, was devastated. "There was just nothing that I could have done, absolutely nothing," he said, defensive and sensitive more than fifty years later. "I was sober. There was a flow of traffic and she simply stepped out in front of another moving car into my headlights. I was going about thirty-five miles per hour. The whole thing was so fleeting. Only the people coming in the other direction saw it happen. Practically the only witnesses were this man that I had picked up and a fruit vendor on the corner. I was completely occupied with getting her to the hospital and praying to Christ that she would recover."

While he waited to hear about her condition, a detective came and questioned him. "I might well have been to blame," Huston said, "but in this instance, I wasn't." Then he asked someone at the hospital to call his father, who had been at a party. Walter and Nan came immediately, but before they arrived the woman died. "She never regained consciousness," Huston said with remorse. "I was the instrument of someone getting killed."

The woman's name was Tosca Roulien. She was a dancer and the wife of Brazil's "Valentino," Raoul Roulien, who had been starring in Spanish-speaking films in Hollywood. That made it an international incident and the press was quick to jump at the story: the twenty-seven-year-old playboy son of a famous Hollywood actor, previously arrested and fined for two drunken car accidents within the past six months, now the cause of the death of a Brazilian star's wife.

John was in shock. His father and Nan took him back to their house on Camden Drive, where he spent an uncomfortable night replaying the accident and fighting the demons that had begun to take possession of his mind. "The experience seemed to bring my whole miserable existence to a head. My marriage had broken up, I was writing not to any particular point or advantage, then this came on top of it. I felt as though I had run into a streak of bad luck and I felt like getting the hell away from that scene, the Hollywood scene, which I had no great liking for anyway."

The story hit the newspapers the next morning and a grand jury was to investigate whether or not John was guilty of murder. The gossip columnists started calling and Walter sensed that his son's career was in jeopardy. He went to see Louis B. Mayer at MGM. Louella Parsons was one of the two reigning gossip queens who, along with her rival, Hedda Hopper, could cause serious damage to a fledgling writer like John if she smelled blood. Parsons wrote for the Hearst papers and Mayer had a connection with William Randolph Hearst. Since 1924, MGM, through Mayer, financed all of Hearst's Cosmopolitan films, paying Hearst's mistress, Marion Davies, $10,000 a week and giving Hearst a share in the profits. Walter asked Mayer to do what he could to keep Parsons from making too much out of his son's streak of bad luck. Then Walter went to see Marion Davies, to see if she could help keep a lid on the sensational nature of John's troubles. Walter was calling in all the chips he had.

"Everybody was talking about it at the time," Meta Wilde remembers. Wilde was a scriptgirl for Warner Bros. then and would be assigned to work for John seven years later on *The Maltese Falcon.* "People spoke about John as being a bad boy. The scuttlebutt at Warner's was that Walter, Warner's, and MGM came to his rescue to help quiet the whole thing. The hearsay was that the studios had put up about $400,000 to keep it quiet and get him out of the problem. I heard that he had to leave the country."

Producer Gottfried Reinhardt, who had come to Hollywood that year, remembers John as a "very flamboyant character" and Walter as "more equalized, less eccentric, not as brash, more conventional." Reinhardt would later produce *The Red Badge of Courage* for John. During the battles they were to have later over *Red Badge,* Reinhardt found himself with John in L. B. Mayer's office, arguing over the commerciality of the project. It was then, according to Reinhardt, that Mayer shouted that he had saved John's ass when Walter had come to see him about John's accident and Mayer made a deal with the D.A., who, Reinhardt recalled, "had the reputation of being corrupt. And the deal was that John would have to leave the country and he could never drive again."

The grand jury exonerated Huston. It was shown that the traffic signal was in his favor, that Mrs. Roulien had carelessly stepped into the street, and that John wasn't speeding and had not been drinking. But it was the lowest point of John Huston's life. And in spite of Walter's maneuverings, Hearst's *Examiner* went after John in a bold and accusatory editorial under the headline: "WHY SHOULD AUTO MURDERERS GO FREE?"

"An automobile in the hands of an incompetent or reckless or drunken driver is about as dangerous as a machine gun in the hands of a gangster," the *Examiner* stated, and then examined the case of "young Mr. Huston." It brought up his earlier accident with Zita Johann and went on to call him "a menace to the community" and demanded "that the prosecuting attorney disregard the verdict of the Coroner's jury and proceed against Mr. Huston as a dangerous auto killer."

The State ignored the *Examiner*'s demand, but it wasn't the last John would hear of it. Raoul Roulien sued him for $250,525 for damages and funeral expenses. For Roulien, it was a matter of honor. The suit would take two obsessive years for Roulien and in the end he would be awarded a $5,000 judgment, which Huston had to pay.

It was, ironically, Dorothy who helped John get away from Hollywood. She had read about his troubles and went to see Mark Ostrer, Walter's friend at Gaumont-British in London. She pleaded with him to help John out and Ostrer agreed to offer John a three-month contract at $300 a week, three times the standard salary for English writers. Dorothy called John in Hollywood. It didn't take much to convince him to accept Ostrer's offer. John wanted to get away, even though his father was against his going to London and being near Dorothy. Walter felt that their relationship had run its course, their divorce had come through, and it wouldn't be good for either of them to be close to one another again. But John's mind was made up and he went to New York and caught the first ship to London.

With John gone, Walter went back to negotiate with Louis B. Mayer, only this time for himself. Mayer figured with what he had just done for Walter's son, keeping the actor at $2,500 a week should be no problem. Walter pointed out that the contract specifically called for a $500-a-week raise, but Mayer said that was just a detail and $2,500 a week was a *lot* of money. Then you don't want to exercise your option? Walter asked, hanging on the answer. We want you to work here, he was told, but we want to keep you at your current salary. Walter took out his contract, tore it in half, and thanked them for the years he had worked with them. A shocked Mayer muttered, "You know you're always welcome here." Walter said he was glad for that and walked out a free man with only one thing on his mind: a play bound for Broadway called *Dodsworth.*

John made it to London, where Dorothy was waiting for him. "She didn't look well," Huston noted, "and her hands were shaking. I soon discovered that if there had been any change it was for the worse." Her friend Greta had given up on her. And John's reappearance just sent her back to the bottle.

"Dorothy was lovely, but she was drinking too much," Katherine Wellesley recalled. "Kay" was a close friend of Huston's while they were both at Universal. Then she met an Englishman named Gordon Wellesley Wong, quit her job, and moved to England with him. Wong dropped his last name and became the head writer at Associated Talking Pictures, Ltd., a forerunner of the Ealing Studios. Kay also began to write and, with John's help, became a prolific and successful screenwriter.

John told Kay and Gordon what had happened to bring him to London. "John took it very hard, that he had killed a girl," Kay Wellesley remembered, "it was very much on his mind. His father was getting a lot of unfavorable publicity and that also bothered him. He was just in a bad mental state."

To help him out of that state, he spent his first paychecks on an MG sports car in which, said Kay, "he ran around in the company of one or more young ladies staying at the Dorchester Hotel who were in an American troupe of dancers known as 'Les Girls.' John was very taken with them. His time was divided in three ways. He went to the studio occasionally. He was looking after Dorothy, who was a hopeless alcoholic. And he ran around with those young ladies in his MG."

At Gaumont-British his high salary was resented by the other writers as well as by the Balcon brothers, who were actually running the studio. Trying to prove himself worthy, he suggested three ideas for stories. One was about the founding of Oxford University, another was about the playwright who wrote *School for Scandal*, Richard Sheridan. The third occurred to him while visiting at Dorothy's flat, where someone was selling Irish Sweepstakes tickets. John and a few others purchased some and signed the tickets "Burmese"—he had just bought a small Burmese figurine at a country curio shop. It gave him an idea for a movie about three strangers who are united by a single Sweepstakes ticket, which they sign with the name of a goddess. By the time of the lottery, the three have followed their own sordid paths, which eventually leads to one of them killing another. When their ticket wins the Sweepstakes, it presents a dilemma—for it also links one of the surviving two with the murder.

The head of the story department liked *Three Strangers* and brought Huston to meet a young director named Alfred Hitchcock. "I had never heard of him," said Huston, "but I told him the story. He listened and expressed interest and that was the last I heard."

Apparently the Balcon brothers didn't care for it. They were fed up with this young American writer who couldn't fit into the English way of doing things. He was too wild, and he wasn't spending enough time at the studio to justify the money he was being paid. So, when John "pulled a bluff" on Michael Balcon, threatening to quit unless Gaumont-British started to take his ideas more seriously, they took him up on his threat and let him go.

He and Dorothy were living together in Chelsea, on Grebe Place, because of her self-destructive condition. When she was living by herself, he found her unconscious on the bed, the ash from a cigarette burned into her chest. John had her admitted to a hospital where she underwent a radical treatment for alcoholism that involved taking small doses of strychnine.

When he visited her in the hospital, Dorothy told him she was dying. "And I knew she was," John said. "She was shaking convulsively. Her complexion had gone green, and her lips and the area around her mouth were deathly white." The poison was killing her. Huston became angry when told that her doctor wasn't available to order the treatment stopped. He kicked down the door to her room, threatening "to kick my way through every door in the hospital unless something was done for her at once." His tantrum brought results: Her doctor appeared and she was saved.

When she was released, Huston brought her to the house he rented in Chelsea. Once again, he tried to take care of her, but she continued to drink when he wasn't there and once even threw a crystal inkwell at him. He now had no work permit and couldn't legally get another job. Dorothy needed care and he had no money. Yet he was too proud to wire his father for some. All his life he lived with a dream that always brought him to consciousness in a sweat. "I dream that I'm broke someplace and I have to ask my father for money and I don't like that dream. It's close to a nightmare."

He finally got Dorothy off his hands, allowing him to sink further into his own misery. One of those Irish Sweepstakes tickets he had signed "Burmese" came in and he won a hundred pounds. It wasn't a huge sum but it was enough to pay for Dorothy's passage to Los Angeles, where her parents could care for her. His own passage was still "steps down," into the gutter.

"John should have gone home," Kay Wellesley believed, "but he stayed on. Of course, he never saved any money and soon he had none."

"It was a bad time," Huston understated. "I owed a lot of money, so I skipped out of Chelsea and ended up in a dreadful joint run by a fairy in a brown bathrobe called Mr. Charles. He used to read my letters; realizing I was on the lam from my creditors, he began blackmailing me. I was destitute. I could have asked my father for help. Or my mother. In fact, my father tried to find me. I didn't write to him but he tried to locate me to find out how I was and what the hell was going on. I just didn't write because I didn't want to lie about it. At the time I only thought of myself as unlucky—under a dark cloud—but that fuming dark cloud undoubtedly emanated from my own spirit. I don't believe in God, but I do believe in luck. You just have to reduce the bets and keep rolling. My scruples might not have been quite so strong if it had been the winter, but fortunately it was summertime and I could afford to take that stance."

His mother did manage to find him on her way back to the States and took him to lunch at Simpson's In The Strand. It was the first food John had eaten in days but he tried not to show it as they discussed an interview John had given to *Film Weekly* when he first arrived in England. It was published in the May 11 issue and entitled "My Father." Walter was a popular star in England and people wanted to read about why he had given up Hollywood. John gave them his opinion.

"There was nothing sensational, no disagreement, or unpleasantness about his departure," John said. "Dad is a vaudeville actor by instinct. He belongs in a world of stage managers, curtain calls, and grease paint. So he was never really happy in Hollywood. Professionally he got, I suppose, a better deal than anyone else in the place. The variety of the parts they gave him was amazing. But even that was not enough for him.

"I never think of him as an *actor* of character parts for the simple reason that he draws his characters straight from life. . . . Lionel Barrymore and Wallace Beery, great actors both, in their way, speak another language to him. They are what I call character actors, and not in spite of, but because of, their personality. If you met Beery in the street, you would know exactly what to expect. If you met my father, I don't think you would."

Rhea never told John what she really thought of his father—that he was weak, inhibited, a pretender. But she didn't hesitate to tell him what she thought of what had happened to Dorothy. Rhea wanted him to go back to his wife. He tried to explain that he had done all he could. Mother and son had not seen or talked to each other for nearly a year; now they were enjoying a reconciliation over lunch before her ship sailed for New York. She looked at her grown son and thought of him when he was a sickly child who wasn't expected to live. *She was grateful that God had heard her supplications and spared the life of her small son now grown to young manhood. And such a young man he was, such a son, so blithe, so gay, so gallantly devoted to his mother. During all the tough intervening years they had been wonderful pals. To her he came with all his confidences, just as he had done as a little boy. It was a comfort to know that she had never failed him.*

John would have shaken his head in wonder had he known what his mother was thinking. Blithe? Gay? He had never been so depressed in his life. And he had hardly gone to her with all his confidences. Indeed, he never confided that he was getting married, never told her about the other women after he was married, never told her much of anything. And he didn't tell her now how down and out he was, how broke and in debt. She may have believed she had never failed him, but he believed that she had nearly suffocated him. All those quarrels, all that yelling. If he had problems relating to women for any length of time, it was as much because of her overbearing personality as anything else. Her heart may have dilated with pride when she thought of him, but his was torn between love and hate for her.

As he drove her to the harbor they spoke of the accident that had sent him to England. He kept his gambler's feelings about riding out his bad-luck streak to himself. He didn't want to ask her for anything. And when his MG broke down on his way back to London, he barely cursed the gods of misfortune. Instead, he left the car—like the Cadillac rusting along the Cahuenga Pass—where it stopped running and hitched back to his rundown flat where the gay proprietor in a brown robe was blackmailing him over his unpaid bills.

That's when Eddie Cahn showed up. Cahn had directed Walter in *Law and Order* and John had worked on the dialogue of that picture. The two men ran into each other in a sleazy London dive. Cahn had come over to work on a picture but, according to John, "before he ever had a chance to start the film that he'd been hired for, his company was defunct. There were all kinds of wildcat companies that were making use of whatever advantages the government had to offer. They were putting pictures together and doing con jobs on suckers. They'd make a film and fold up. When it happened to Eddie, who was not a very good director but a nice guy, he was *completely* out, like Chaplin in *City*

Lights—his shirt was coming through the hole in his pants. And me, too."

Mr. Charles now had two American louts to deal with and, sensing that he wasn't going to get his rent money from either of them, he confiscated John's passport "as a sort of ransom." The situation was so bad that Huston and Cahn left their belongings in their apartments and became street bums.

"We hung around Hyde Park and slept on the Embankment at night," Huston said, describing how they were reduced to rolling bums for spare change. "I had finally hit *really* rock bottom. I played the harmonica a little, very little, and Eddie and I would sing cowboy songs. People would give us six pences and we'd go into a pub and have a hard-boiled egg. We learned how to ride buses without paying the fare."

His life had begun to parallel what he had read about the life of Casanova in Bolitho's *Twelve Against the Gods*, when, having returned to Venice after a mysterious stay in Constantinople, Casanova was "penniless, hopelessly down and out . . . reduced to playing the violin" for money and "no longer" feeling worthy to " 'set foot in the good society I had frequented before I fell so low.' " Casanova's analysis of his situation could just as easily have come from Huston's lips: "If I was worthless, I was not altogether conquered, not having in the least renounced the cult of Chance. For I was still young, and that fickle goddess does not desert youth."

When they were desperate for a meal or a place to wash, Huston and Cahn went to Gordon and Kay Wellesley's apartment. "They were really in a bad way," Kay Wellesley said. "They spent a lot of time at our flat. We didn't have enough room to put them up, but my husband was very generous and tactful with them. Then my husband met a chap who was interested in motor racing and wanted to make a film about it. He knew nothing about movies and went to Ealing Studios asking for a writer and a director. Gordon recommended Huston and Cahn and set up an interview. Our maid washed their shirts and pressed their clothes and made them look reasonably decent."

The interview went well. John bluffed his way through a spur-of-the-moment story and said he could write a treatment in less than two weeks, which he did—"on pages of magazines, just over the print." Gordon Wellesley had it typed and Eddie Cahn delivered it to the automobile people. John waited anxiously at the Wellesleys' apartment for Cahn to return with their decision. When he showed up, he kept his hat on. "How did it go?" Huston asked.

"Quite well," Cahn answered, lifting his hat and letting the £5 notes he had stuffed inside float gloriously to the floor. Then he pulled out his handkerchief from his breast pocket and more notes fluttered out. They had finally nailed a sucker with money and immediately moved from Hyde Park to the Dorchester Hotel, which was only proper for two American filmmakers.

The picture was called *Death Drives Through* and the two of them made just enough money on it to pay their bills. Cahn returned to the States, but John decided to see Paris before crossing the Atlantic. The American consulate had issued him another passport and he crossed the English Channel to spend a few months feasting on the great paintings in the museums and the experienced streetwalkers on both sides of the Seine. "I was tempted to forget about writing and the movies and be a painter again," he said, but his money soon ran out and he knew the time had come to take on the industry that had treated him with indifference and left him destitute in the streets and parks of London and Paris.

8

FATHER AND SON: CENTER STAGE

JOHN'S SELF-IMPOSED EXILE MADE HIM MISS THE 1934 OPEN-
ing nights of two of his father's most important stage roles, Dodsworth
and Othello, although he would get a chance to see them both over the
next two years. *Dodsworth* was Walter's longest-running play and the
Shubert Theatre was always packed for each of his 1,238 performances.
Producer Max Gordon had pawned his life insurance policy and flirted
with bankruptcy before the play opened out of town, in Philadelphia.
Gordon took his first easy breath in months after the curtain came
down on that first performance and the audience beat their hands red
with applause. "Let me tell you something," he predicted to his star,
"you may never get back to the movies. You'll be playing this in Texas
two years from now."

The veteran stage actress Fay Bainter had recently completed her first
film, *This Side of Heaven,* before taking on the role of the frivolous Fran
Dodsworth. As the more balanced and rational Edith Cortright, Nan
Sunderland had held her own and Walter was proud of her. He admitted that he didn't want to be seen as a temperamental actor who foisted
his wife upon the production. His relief after that first performance was
as much for her as it was for himself. Nan, too, claimed in an inter-

view, with Walter there, "I admit I was worried when *Dodsworth* opened. I wanted so much for you to be all right not because I am married to you, but because I wanted Walter Huston to be a success because it was his play and he was the star and I was just another player in the cast."

Nan knew only too well how important the play was for him. If he failed, he would have had to "crawl back into motion pictures with my tail between my legs." Hollywood exhausted him, the theater rejuvenated him. It was the place where he hoped to recapture "the zest which the movies sap from you." He always felt that he could have given better performances in his films if he only had the time to study his parts the way he was able to for the stage. And even after four or five weeks of rehearsals, he knew that with each performance he would learn more about his character. "By the time you've played the part a few weeks, you've been able to round the character, touching it up and making it really live," he believed.

"Yet there's something to be said for the film. I'd always been told that a good actor stood the best chance of making a screen success. I was certainly a better actor after my five years in Hollywood. I had learned to be natural—never to exaggerate. I found I could act on the stage in just the same way as I acted in a studio: using my ordinary voice, eliminating gestures, keeping everything extremely simple. The studio technique of acting forced on one by the camera lens that never misses the smallest thing was, I discovered, also the best technique for the stage."

Samuel Dodsworth was an automobile maker who sold his business after twenty years so he and his wife could take a trip to Europe and start enjoying life. It was Walter's ability to keep this complex business-man simple, almost innocent, that allowed audiences to identify with the struggles he faced trying to keep his wife happy and his marriage intact. Sidney Howard had captured the flavor of Sinclair Lewis's book and written a touching and searing portrait of a man who wanted to enjoy the fruits of his labor and a woman who refused to age gracefully.

Walter never had any doubt that the play worked on many levels and had a universal theme that would keep audiences sympathetic not only to Sam Dodsworth but also to his frivolous wife and to the "other" woman, Mrs. Cortright. "Everybody knows Sam Dodsworth and his wife. We recognize them among our friends and neighbors—the earnest, plodding chap who has devoted himself to business so unrelentingly that he has forgotten all about play and romance, and his pathetic wife, bored with the mere spending of money, who craves the things that quicken and color life before the fires of youth are gone forever."

The play that would most pique Walter's interest, however, was one he had never considered for himself: Shakespeare's *Othello*. It was Robert Edmund Jones's idea. He was still in charge of the summer theater festival in Central City, Colorado (the one in which Lillian Gish played *Camille*). Watching his brother-in-law in *Dodsworth* made him think of a dream he had ever since *Desire Under the Elms*: to direct Walter as the passionate, jealous, misguided Moor in *Othello*.

"You must be kidding, Bobby," Walter reacted. "I can't play Shakespeare." Even the thought of it sent shudders of humiliation through him, as Richard Mansfield's angry face loomed over him and the line that followed "Prepare you, generals" was once again forgotten.

"Have you ever read the play?" Jones asked.

"I don't need to," Walter answered.

"Just read it," Jones urged. "And think of Nan for Desdemona."

"What does Margaret think?"

"She thinks you can do it, that's what she thinks. And so do I, or I wouldn't be asking."

So Walter promised to read *Othello* and after he did, he read it again, aloud, with Nan. The music of the lines knocked him out.

"There is nothing one-dimensional about Othello," he told John Weld. "He is a great soldier, a brave and honorable man, but he also is dull-witted and tyrannical; an aristocratic Moor in Venice, yet he is quick to manifest inferiority; the greatest general of the state, he grows petty in his narrow jealousy, and, hero that he is, commits a murder in cold blood without investigating charges which prompt him to kill. What cannot an actor do with a character like that? He is tender and brutal, passionate and cold, strong and weak, hero and villain."

Walter's excitement was so infectious he managed to convince Max Gordon to close *Dodsworth* for six weeks during the summer of 1934 so he could rehearse *Othello* and then play it for the two weeks of the festival. Gordon wasn't thrilled with the idea of shutting down the most successful play on Broadway, but he struck a deal with Huston and Jones. If Walter ever decided to bring *Othello* to Broadway, Gordon would produce it.

And so, while Walter and Nan appeared in *Dodsworth* every night, they spent their days rehearsing *Othello*. Robert Jones had hired Kenneth McKenna to play Iago and Helen Freeman as Emelia. Walter became so involved with the part that he started to talk about trying *King Lear* next and then to do both *Lear* and *Othello* as films. "I think Shakespeare can be made understandable," he said. "We've all had so much of him crammed down our throats at school that we *expect* to be bored."

No one yawned during the two weeks *Othello* played in Central City, and the United Press's syndicated review said that the production "proved that when the Shakespearean tragedy is turned into a pageant of color it is not too heavy for the most critical summer audience."

Walter felt that they had just begun to scratch at the nuances of the play. "I had contracted a disease," he said, "that taste of Shakespeare was alive with microbes; it generated in me the desire to do the job right."

To do it right meant to take it to Broadway, which he and Jones agreed to do as soon as Walter was finished with his other commitments: *Dodsworth* into the next year, and then a film about Cecil Rhodes for his friend Mark Ostrer at Gaumont-British in London.

It had been a wonderful summer. He and Nan had a chance to go from an American industrialist and a world-wise American expatriate to a fiery Moor and an innocent but doomed wife and back again, working together in harmony, resting between roles at their home on a mountaintop surrounded by pine trees. For all appearances, Walter seemed a satisfied and happy man.

Rhea was neither happy nor satisfied as she returned to the States after lunching with John in London. John had put up a good front, but instinct told her that he was a troubled young man. She knew about his accidents and was thinking about them when she had an accident of her own, one that put her in casts of plaster and steel for eighteen months.

She tripped over some rope at the entrance to the telegraph room on board ship. It was dusk and the deck lights had not yet been turned on when Rhea came up against the *huge coils of slimy deck hose carelessly left leaning in the darkness against the rear of the radio shack.*

Her leg was broken. When the ship landed in New York, she was in a foul mood, *detained aboard ship for many hours after landing, to be man-handled and mauled in a loathsome examination by a port doctor.* The ship company was not liable to passengers for any accidents that occurred during sailing and refused to help her get to a hospital. Angered, Rhea immediately called her former husband, Howard Stevens.

As a big shot in the transportation business himself, Stevens would surely be able to do something for her.

He was, initially, incensed at the way the ship company had treated her and encouraged her to sue them.

Then the ship company opened a correspondence with the president of the railroad calling attention to the harm that could be done to all brotherhood transportations using similar waivers on the backs of their tickets if such a suit was permitted to go on.

Stevens's boss met with him and they realized that a lawsuit could be detrimental to the railroad. Stevens thought the matter would be settled long before legal arguments would be heard.

As Rhea wrote: *Without hurting his own prestige Stevens wanted to swoop down upon and bag as much money as he could in as short a time as possible. He told the president he, too, saw the precariousness of the situation and thought the smart thing to do was to let the steam ship company stew in its own fat until the very last day. He expected that meanwhile its officials would volunteer to at least pay her hospital bill. It was finally agreed upon between the president and the vice-president of the R.R. that things should just drag along until the last moment and then if nothing had been accomplished by this coggery to just let the matter drop by failing to appear.*

Rhea, of course, couldn't have known this for certain, but she believed her speculations to be true and she was bitter. She was also afraid.

Her mother, Adelia, had come from Indiana to be with her and the two women stayed in an apartment in New York. Unable to walk without crutches, she went through three lawyers before getting one to try her case in court. By this time she was convinced Stevens was not on her side.

Before her lawsuit reached the courts, Stevens traveled to New York to see her. She had seen little of him over the years, although she received a semiannual allowance from him that she considered "meagre." As far as she was concerned, she was "the discarded wife of a prominent man."

There was an attempt at civility, but Rhea was suffering from what John had later described as a "hysterical paralysis," and Stevens's visit just made her overly self-conscious of her condition.

He had asked her what the doctors had to say and she had told him that it took time, that they always were wanting to operate and always she demurred. She recollected how he seemed to look upon her instead of at her. His calculating eyes told her plainer than words that her face was over-white and her lips too pale.

She told him that the doctors charged her less when they didn't know he was paying the bills, so she suggested that he consider sending her "a couple of hundred dollars" directly so she could pay her own bills. But *he became obsessed with the idea that she could easily obtain money from him in this way to use for other purposes. He told her that if he received a bill either directly from the doctor or through her he would publicize her in the newspaper informing the world that he refused to be responsible for her debts.*

He also said that he wouldn't compensate her lawyer, who had agreed to work on a contingency basis, and he also informed her lawyer that he would no longer be responsible for any of her bills. When she finally had her day in court, she lost her case and was left "head over heels in debt." To pay her way out, she "sacrificed all of her little personal belongings"—her collection of Wedgwood china and her first editions.

John returned from Europe in early 1935 while his mother was engaged in her lawsuit against the steamship company and felt very strongly that she was wrong to sue and wrong about Stevens. "I'm entirely against her in all this and expressed myself so at the time," he later said. "Stevens had gotten her passes on every railroad, ship, and boat in the world, so she was a freeloader on the boat and had this accident and saw it as a way of collecting some money. I did everything I could to dissuade her. Stevens had treated her marvelously, he was ever so decent to her, but she went ahead with the suit. And lost it."

Once again, mother and son were at odds. Rhea felt betrayed. Even her own son had turned against her when she was at her most vulnerable: broken boned, in a cast, "incurably afraid," dragged down by "spasmodic pangs of pain" and "nagging discomfiture." But John was still young, he had made so many mistakes of his own, had become so close to his father, how could she expect him to sympathize with her?

Instead, she chose to ignore his insensitivity to her plight and beamed with pride when he came to tell her about the job he had taken at a new magazine called *Mid-Week Pictorial.*

This boy he was a great one, she wrote about John, *the desire of a mother's heart fulfilled she could now learn things from him. Before her loomed the presence of her son, his caressing voice and the beaconing light of his personality. How could she complain of mere physical suffering and domestic tilts when God had been so lavish in His gifts?*

The *Mid-Week Pictorial* was originally a part of the *New York Times,* but when *Life* magazine was announced, the *Times* decided to sell the *Pictorial* rather than compete. It was bought by a man named Monte

Bourjaily, who was confident that he could give *Life* a run for its money. Unfortunately, money was what Bourjaily lacked—at least the kind of money needed to launch a picture feature magazine. Bourjaily met John and the two men connected. Bourjaily was impressed with John's experience, his early magazine credits, his published book, his last name. He couldn't offer much money, but he agreed to share in the profits once the magazine took off. For Huston, it was a chance to fulfill a youthful dream. If *Mid-Week Pictorial* wasn't exactly the *Police Gazette*, it was a legitimate magazine with a huge potential to tell in words and pictures the kinds of stories that interested him. John also saw it as an opportunity to get himself back on his feet.

By this time, Walter and Nan had finished their eighteen-month run of *Dodsworth* and had returned for a much-needed rest to Running Springs. He read the script Mark Ostrer sent him about Cecil Rhodes, which he didn't like, and admitted to missing the letters he had regularly received from his film fans "especially from England, where character acting is appreciated more than anywhere else."

Still ambivalent about returning to films, he sent John the Rhodes script and asked if he might punch it up a bit. Nan returned to Central City that summer and Walter stopped in New York to see John, who had rewritten the Rhodes script, which Walter thought was an improvement.

In London, the Rhodes picture was delayed. While waiting for Nan to arrive and *Rhodes of Africa* to begin, Walter accepted a small "special portrayal" part as an American president (again) in a futuristic melodrama Gaumont-British was doing called *Trans-Atlantic Tunnel*. *Films in Review* described it as a well-made and highly imaginative picture. Walter described it as something-to-do.

When Nan arrived, they stayed at the sumptuous home of Mark and Petey Ostrer, with their nineteen servants. Walter let his hair grow long and grew a mustache for his portrayal of Cecil Rhodes, a man he saw as "more a legend than a human being."

In reading about Rhodes and meeting with John Hays Hammond, who was Rhodes's chief engineer, he began to understand that it would be "easy to show him as a ruthless conqueror, crushing everything that interfered with his ambitions. But that would not be a true picture. As I see him, Rhodes was an idealist who was forced into the strife of statesmanship by his ideals. His vision was of a South Africa, rich and fertile, governed by the Anglo-Saxon race."

Walter's views regarding his defense of Rhodes and the colonialization of South Africa seem parochial and naive. But to an American reporter he said, "he was a hard, cold man and I have played him that way. Many more persons feared and hated him than ever loved him."

But *Rhodes of Africa* never came together. As John said, "He was a strange, fascinating, and rather terrible man, but the picture they did about him then wouldn't be the one they'd do about him today."

Walter was out of the country when *Mid-Week Pictorial* made its debut, and he never got a chance to buy a copy off the newsstand. It lasted only a few months before a slick-looking *Life* appeared and showed the way a pictorial magazine could look if it had enough money and a large staff. "By comparison, we looked pretty tacky," John said.

With *Rhodes* and *Trans-Atlantic Tunnel* behind him, Walter and Nan returned to the States, where they eagerly began their tour of *Dodsworth*. Their schedule was hectic, crossing the country from Washington, D.C., to Los Angeles, even stopping at Toronto along the way. It had been ten years since Walter toured a play.

The highlight of the tour was when they played the nation's capital with the president in attendance. Franklin Roosevelt was a fan of Huston's and the two men had first met when Walter was working on *Keep 'em Rolling*. Roosevelt told him then how much he had enjoyed *Gabriel Over the White House* and this time he invited Walter, Nan, and Fay Bainter to join him for drinks at the White House. A car was sent to pick them up in front of the National Theatre. The two women fretted over the short notice of the invitation but Walter took it in stride.

Roosevelt was waiting for them in his study, along with his cousin, Assistant Secretary of the Navy Henry Roosevelt, and his wife. The president's personal secretary, Missy Le Hand, was also there, but it was Roosevelt himself who waved them in and served the drinks. Nan was completely taken by FDR's charm, especially after he said to them, "What a thrill you gave us tonight." He offered Walter a cigarette and lit it for him, which astounded Nan, who soon found herself sitting next to the president and asking him about the upcoming election.

Three days later, Nan recorded the excitement of their late-night evening at the White House when she wrote a long detailed letter to her mother, beginning, "This is a 'Believe It or Not' letter," and ending, "Your girl who talks with presidents." She said the meeting "topped all our previous thrills. . . . For two days after we couldn't think of anything else and that night we didn't sleep much. A combination of the honor, the informality, the wonderfully satisfying conversation, *and his charm* have floored us." She admitted that "for the first five minutes I couldn't open my mouth. Fay and Walter were easy and gabby from the start," and enthused that "following Huston is like being a big elephant in a triumphant parade."

When the tour hit Chicago, Walter and Nan stayed with Dr. Loyal and Edith Davis. According to John Weld, Edith was the ambitious one. Through her friendship with Walter, she made her apartment a stopping-off place for actors on their way to either coast. "The only way to get across the country at that time was on the Super Chief. You always had to change trains in Chicago. Edie, whose nickname was 'Lucky,' got to know everybody in Hollywood through Walter. He's the one who opened the doors to Hollywood to the Davises and that's how Nancy came in. Edie was *very* ambitious about Nancy, about getting her in the movies. And Nancy was ambitious, like her mother."

Lillian Gish was one of those people whom Edith Davis met at the station. "When I'd get in the car and come down Michigan Avenue with her, all the people would stop and ask her to do something for them. The police, too; she practically ran Chicago."

Katy Weld, who married John Weld in 1937, observed this as well: "Edie Davis was the power behind her husband, behind the *whole* thing. She ran their lives. Loyal Davis was a famous surgeon, very high up in his profession, but she pushed him up in society also. Edie was always behind everything. And they were very, very fond of Walter."

The *Dodsworth* tour ended in March 1936 at the Taft Theatre in Cincinnati, where the reviews were as effusive as they were throughout the country. "Huston's feelings for the character of Sam is sure and masterly," wrote Edward Carberry in the *Cincinnati Post*. "His Dodsworth—simple, fine, appealing—slowly gathers the audience's sympathy." Another critic, Joseph Sagmaster, wrote that Walter "proves himself one of the most competent actors on the American stage. His is a character-study of restrained power. Though his face, voice, bearing seem to change hardly at all, he manages to suggest a subtle but continuous growth in character."

Praise was also forthcoming for Nan, who left her role as Edith Cortright to play Dodsworth's flighty wife Fran when Fay Bainter became ill. Commented Sagmaster, "In hands less gifted than those of

Nan Sunderland, Fran Dodsworth would seem a scatter-brained and unfeeling woman, who deserved all she got. With rare skill, Miss Sunderland makes her, for the most part, sympathetic and everywhere understandable." Carberry noted of her Fran: "shallow, vain, selfish, yet so lovely that she makes Sam's subservience to her completely credible."

Walter alone knew of Nan's desperation, as the show came to an end and preparations for the movie were under way. Samuel Goldwyn had bought the rights to the play for $160,000 after it opened in 1934—at that time one of the highest amounts ever paid.

There was never any question about who would play Sam Dodsworth, although Walter had it written into his play contract that if anyone else was chosen for the film, he would collect ten percent of the money paid for the screen rights. Willy Wyler was hired as the director and Ruth Chatterton was chosen over Fay Bainter for the role of Fran. Edith Cortright hadn't been cast yet, although Geraldine Fitzgerald and Mary Astor were under consideration when Wyler came to see the play in Cincinnati. This might have been the reason Nan decided to switch to playing Dodsworth's wife, not knowing the role had been cast. She was attempting to hedge her bets.

Nan learned that Mary Astor, who had made nineteen dreary, forgettable films since *Red Dust* with Clark Gable in 1932, had been chosen to play Edith Cortright. It was hard for her to accept; the part was something she very much had wanted. Although she would go on to play Desdemona again on Broadway, this rejection changed Nan. Like Bayonne Whipple, who watched from the sidelines as Walter's career advanced to the legitimate theater, Nan, too, was now cast to one side as Walter continued to move forward.

John Weld, who was by then living at the Hustons' house and taking care of Walter's correspondence, believes that "Nan was always quite a problem for Walter. John and Walter had a similar weakness: They didn't have very much judgment about women. Walter married John's mother and he really didn't want to. Bayonne Whipple was older than he was and she was the star of their vaudeville act and he needed a job. And Nan was not the girl for him at all. She was schizophrenic. She got into fits of depression and was very jealous of him and very jealous of the fact that she wasn't getting further in her acting career."

Katy Weld remembered Nan as being "quite rational" most of the time, "but she was very demanding. Very possessive. She almost pushed Walter into other women's arms because she was so cruel to him. She would rant and scold him in front of people."

"But he wouldn't combat her at all," John Weld said.

Combat, during the making of *Dodsworth,* was left to Wyler and Ruth Chatterton, whom he didn't like, and the press and Mary Astor, who was the subject of a full-blown scandal the likes of which Hollywood hadn't seen since the early twenties.

Chatterton, according to Wyler, "played Fran like a heavy and we had momentous fights every day." David Niven, who played a small part in the film, described Wyler's "Jekyll and Hyde character" and witnessed Ruth Chatterton's anger when she slapped Wyler's face and locked herself in her dressing room. In her book, *A Life on Film,* Mary Astor wrote that "Ruth Chatterton hated Wyler. She disagreed with his direction of every scene, and he was stubborn and smiling and it drove her to furious outburst. She didn't like the role of the wife of Sam Dodsworth, because the character was that of a woman who is trying to hang onto her youth—which was exactly what Ruth herself was doing. But she gave a beautiful performance in spite of herself."

Astor had no such troubles, since most of her scenes were with Walter, whom she considered "warm and easygoing." At that time, her turmoil was happening off the set, in full view of the American public, who avidly followed her courtroom battles with her husband over the custody of their daughter. It was an embarrassing, titillating drama highlighted by the public airing of the actress's diary, which covered the years 1929–34, including: her first husband's death in a plane crash in 1930; her romance and marriage to her doctor, Franklyn Thorpe; the birth of their daughter Marilyn; and her passionate love affair with the playwright George S. Kaufman, which was described in graphic detail. Juicy portions of her diary were leaked to the press by the actress's husband and the story made headlines.

"It was all pretty hairy," wrote Astor, who avoided reporters by moving into a dressing-room apartment at the studio. "I had achieved the reputation of being the greatest nympho-courtesan since Pompadour. It was absurd, and I made jokes along with everybody else—but it was never very funny to me, really, because it just wasn't true."

One studio head came to her defense after hearing her side: Sam Goldwyn, her current boss. According to Arthur Marx, the other executives insisted that Goldwyn invoke the "morals clause" and fire Mary Astor from *Dodsworth.* "Instead of yielding to the hypocritical demands of the other executives," Marx wrote, "Sam finessed the situation with a simple declaration. 'A mother fighting for her child,' he mused in a tone calculated to give a heart-tug to even the most calloused. 'That's good.' . . . Sam showed the kind of class that made him Sam Goldwyn and not Harry Cohn."

The court never allowed the diary to be admitted as evidence and the judge decided that both parents should share custody of their daughter. The sensational diary was impounded and, with Mary Astor's permission, incinerated. "I wasn't 'smart' or 'clever,' " recalled Astor, "but I was completely rattleproof, thanks to Edith Cortright. Without her, without the craft I had been so long in learning, I would have been shattered emotionally by the ugliness of that trial."

Goldwyn liked Wyler's cut of *Dodsworth*. He hoped that the Mary Astor scandal might remain in the public's mind so they would go see the movie out of curiosity, and when reporters began writing about *Dodsworth*, they focused on Mary Astor. Journalist Kate Cameron wrote: "Her future in films depends greatly on the reception she receives from the public in *Dodsworth*." Edward Carberry wrote: "How would an audience react to her? Would they remember the glimpse into her private life they had been given and snicker? Would they go moral and hiss? They did neither. As one man, they wildly applauded her."

Carberry went on: "*Dodsworth* is all anyone could ask. Cast with meticulous care, directed with taste and skill, acted with fine understanding, it is so far above the common run of films that it is likely to make anyone who sees it impatient with the ordinary cinema product for months after."

Walter was named the year's Best Actor by the New York Critics and was nominated for his first Academy Award, one of seven nominations *Dodsworth* received. The only Oscar it won was for Art Direction, and the box office was disappointing, considering all the publicity surrounding it, the critical praise, and the Academy nominations.

In his book *Hollywood*, Garson Kanin relates how he once wanted to write a film about a mother and daughter who fell in love with the same man. He took it to Sam Goldwyn, who told him it wouldn't work because "You can't sell a middle-age love story." When Kanin pointed out that Goldwyn had made *Dodsworth*, Goldwyn responded: "*Dodsworth*—f'Chrissake. Don't talk to me about *Dodsworth*. I lost my goddamn shirt. I'm not saying it wasn't a fine picture. It was a *great* picture, but nobody wanted to see it. In *droves.*"

A few months after this conversation Kanin reported meeting up with Goldwyn and Wyler as they were trying to cast a small but crucial part for an upcoming film. " 'Listen!' Goldwyn shouted suddenly. 'I got it! I'll call him up and ask him to do it for me. I'll ask him as a personal favor.'

" 'Who are you talking about, Sam?' asked Willy Wyler.

" 'Why, Walter Huston,' said Goldwyn.

" 'He'd be great," said Willy, 'but I thought you wanted someone with more box office.'

" 'Who's got more box office f'Chrissake than Walter Huston?' shouted Goldwyn. 'Didn't I have him here in *Dodsworth*? You should remember *Dodsworth*, f'Chrissake. You *directed* it. One of the biggest hits I ever had. It made a *fortune!*' "

With the movie behind him, Walter returned to Running Springs to work with Nan on *Othello*, hoping that by returning to the stage she would forget about *Dodsworth*. John, who had been on the set of *Dodsworth* watching his father and Wyler work, was back in New York, trying to write some short stories and visiting his mother and grandmother. Rhea, during her recuperation, banged out versions of her autobiography on a typewriter as well as stories that had filled her imagination. She enjoyed writing about oddball characters who were usually gamblers of one sort or another.

She also tried to patch up the relationship between her son and his alcoholic ex-wife. When she was back on her feet, she found Dorothy and invited her to New York. "Long after we had broken up, Dorothy came and stayed with them," John recalled.

But John was not one to go back. Kay Wellesley believed that "Dorothy never stopped loving John. And John was fond of her. She was a hopeless case. But he helped her financially until she remarried. He once told me, he was so gracious, 'It was my privilege to look after her financially.' "

Dorothy never got over her alcoholism, although she finally stopped drinking in 1974 when her body couldn't take it any longer. John kept in distant touch with her until her death in 1983.

A face-slapping dose of reality was in store for Walter Huston, who had invested a good deal of money and a career's worth of pride in his *Othello*, which was to bomb at the New Amsterdam Theatre on Broadway in January 1937. It wasn't merely a failure, it was a complete and utter disaster. And until the critics had their say, Walter thought it was as good a performance as he had ever given.

Feeling it was a sure thing, Walter wanted to invest his own money in the play and split the production costs fifty-fifty with Max Gordon, who felt the same way. They were both so confident that they didn't spare any expenses. Bobby Jones had gone to Venice to capture the flavor of the Italian settings. They decided on ten settings, elaborate costumes, and Margaret to coach the entire cast so that "there might be no discordant notes in the symphony we intended playing."

Robert Keith was cast as Iago and Natalie Hall as Emelia, but although the reviews were positive when they previewed the play in Hartford, Gordon thought Keith wasn't a strong enough Iago. Walter agonized over the thought of having to fire him, but he had to agree with his producer: Iago needed an actor whose reputation was equal to Walter's. When Bobby Jones got Brian Aherne to agree to do it, Walter was left with telling Keith. "It was the hardest thing I ever did," Walter admitted, but with Aherne coming on, they felt the play would be strengthened.

Aherne had gone to Scotland to appear in a play only to discover when he arrived that Laurence Olivier was already playing the part. The embarrassed producer paid Aherne £500 for his error and that's when Bobby Jones's call reached him. Angry over how he had been treated, Aherne laid down a few conditions that proved to be disastrous. First, he insisted on playing Iago the way he wanted without any directorial interference; second, he wanted a ten-week guarantee at $1,000 a week, or four weeks with the privilege of giving two weeks' notice regardless of the play's run.

The previews continued in New Haven, Boston, Providence, Springfield, Albany, Rochester, Washington, D.C., and Philadelphia before they brought it to Broadway. By then, the mismatched Aherne and the rest of the cast were doing two styles of acting. Aherne's Iago was a "swashbuckling villain, a colorful, personable fellow with gestures and overtones, blatantly obvious." But the other actors had agreed with Walter, and were playing their roles in a low-key manner. "I determined to underplay him all the way," Walter said, "so that the more dramatic scenes would have their proper breadth and power. As it turned out, Brian, handsome, flashy, shimmered across the stage and completely threw the production out of kilter."

John traveled to Philadelphia to see the production prior to its Broadway opening and was made "uneasy by what I saw. Jones's sets were superb, as were the costumes. Every scene was a delight to the eye. You couldn't fault the production. Indeed, its very magnificence was one of the things that disturbed me; it seemed to diminish the performances. One came away with a sense more of spectacle rather than drama. The magic that had happened when I had seen the play in hotel rooms and rehearsal halls, close up, just wasn't there in this large theater."

Opening night Walter felt supremely confident. So did Nan, Max, Jones, and the rest of the cast and crew. "We had it in the palms of our hands," Walter said. "I never felt better on any stage than I did that night. My performance, it seemed to me, had never been so keen." And the audience responded with shouts of "Bravo!" and "Encore!" Mary Wickes, who was a twenty-one-year-old actress at the time, thought it was "one of the most breathtakingly beautiful productions ever done. And Jones's costumes! Nan Sunderland was absolutely stunning!" After repeated curtain calls, the shouts continued, calling for Robert Edmund Jones to take a bow as well. "I have never known an audience to act as that one did," Walter beamed at the cast party. To Nan, he said, "When a thing is good there's no mistaking it."

By three that morning, the elated, exhausted, proud couple finally got to sleep. Four hours later, Walter unfolded the New York papers expecting to read of his glorious triumph. What he read at first confused him. The *News*'s Burns Mantle gave the play a tepid two and a half stars. The *Times*'s Brooks Atkinson was just as bad. Other critics were worse. Huston, they said, had blown it. The power of the play was too much for this particular cast. Aherne was playing a passionate, rowdy Shakespeare; Huston a subdued and subtle one.

Stunned, shocked, depressed, he howled in his own defense, "Did they not know that I had studied the role longer, had given it more thought than any other role I had ever played?" And then, when the force of the negative reviews really set in, he sat on his bed, with the papers sprawled about him, and he began to laugh. Not a casual or a sarcastic or a defensive laugh, but a riotous, volcanic roar of laughter that brought home the absurdity of ever believing in a "sure thing."

His laughter filled the apartment at the Waldorf Towers and filtered out into the hallway. John had spent a sleepless night waiting to read the reviews himself and had brought the bad news with him to break it as gently as he could to his father. "I knew this meant more to my father than anything he had ever done," John later wrote. "Just as I was about to knock, I heard laughter from inside. 'Well,' I thought, 'he won't be laughing when he sees these!' . . . As I entered, I saw the papers strewn over the floor. He was laughing at himself! All those years of work and planning that had gone into his *Othello* . . . down the drain! The joke was on him. Pretty soon he had me laughing, too."

When he caught his breath, Walter had time to reflect. "Not since *The Easy Mark* had I received anything but plaudits, from critics, from the public, from friends and relatives. I had come to believe that I was that impossibility—an actor-who-can-do-no-wrong."

Aherne thought Huston was to blame for the critics' lack of enthusiasm. "The trouble was Walter was too gentle and kind a man to play *Othello*. He was incapable of arousing the intense emotions the part demanded."

By that evening Walter had also concluded that he wasn't ferocious enough, that he didn't "rant and rave sufficiently." He decided to throw himself into the part using every cheap dramatic trick in the book, raving like a madman, doing away with every nuance and subtlety he had so carefully rehearsed. And the audience loved it! But he didn't. "It was 10-20-30 melodrama of the very lowest sort," he said.

After two weeks, the gross receipts were only $2,300. With sixty-eight people to pay, they were losing $6,000 a week. Then Walter was asked to do the Kate Smith radio show, seven minutes for $2,000, and he laughed at the irony of it. *Othello* ran for a third week before it closed. Robert Edmund Jones's imaginative and elaborate sets were taken to Fort Lee, New Jersey, and burned, and Walter and Nan returned to their mountain retreat.

The following month, on February 21, 1937, Bayonne Whipple died of heart disease. She was sixty years old and never forgave Walter for leaving her behind.

Now it was John's turn to put himself center stage. It happened accidentally, when he ran into Robert Milton, a balding, pink-haired theatrical director he once knew at the Provincetown Players and had seen again when they were both in London. Milton had a play, written by a young playwright named Howard Koch, called *The Lonely Man* that reincarnated Abraham Lincoln as a contemporary college professor in the coal country trying to free the industrial workers as he had once freed the slaves. He asked Huston to read it. It came at a time when John was between things. Specifically, he was between borrowing money from his father again or cleaning up his harmonica for a few street verses of "Bury Me Not on the Lone Prairie."

"The main problem we faced was to find a young actor with the authority to play the Lincoln character," wrote Howard Koch in his memoir, *As Time Goes By*. He and Milton just couldn't come up with the right actor. Then, during a torrential New York rain, John Huston knocked at Koch's apartment door. "This tall man came in dripping with rain. It was as though he had been driven by the wind and I knew in five minutes that Robert Milton was right, this was the man. I didn't know whether he was an actor, but I knew he was a personality."

Koch was liberal-minded: *The Lonely Man* was his attempt to "extend the concept of freedom to all races and all segments of our society." When an offer came from the federally funded WPA Theatre in Chicago to produce the play, he and Milton called Huston and the three men left New York to reincarnate Lincoln in the city infamous for its gangsters.

Walter was also eager to see how John fared in *The Lonely Man*, amused that the boy was following in his acting steps, tackling that most noble of American heroes. He had been concerned about John and hoped that playing Lincoln might help set him straight.

"Walter regarded John as a ne'er-do-well," Howard Koch believed. "That he was trying everything and hadn't found himself. *The Lonely Man* and John's performance changed Walter's mind."

"When Walter went to Chicago to see John, he became very, very pleased with him and admired how he was playing Abraham Lincoln," John Weld said.

"Best Lincoln I've ever seen," was Walter's assessment.

Koch is convinced that the Blackstone Theatre was packed during the run of the play solely because of John's compelling performance. "He came over with such intensity that people came from all over just to see him. It wasn't a great play, it was just a great performance. He *was* young Lincoln. His voice, his mannerisms, everything was just right." Koch wrote: "He used none of the usual makeup—no beard, no stovepipe hat, no drawl. He *thought* Lincoln with a brooding intensity that came over the footlights with such conviction that the audiences were mesmerized into accepting the story's fantastic premise."

During the run of *The Lonely Man*, Koch and John found they had what Koch called "a social and political affinity. I was peace-oriented, antiwar, and even though John's life wouldn't be called a peaceful life, he did have feelings that this world could be a better world. I started talking to him about an idea I had about Woodrow Wilson." John was interested, but their collaboration didn't materialize for a few more years.

As Koch got to know Huston, he came to see that "when he gave you his attention, it was total. You alone existed for him, but only as long as he could draw out of you what of immediate interest you had to give; then, in movie terms, fade out and fade in to whatever next claimed his probing concentration. Once you understood this and accepted him on his own terms, you could remain his friend. However, with women . . . well, proceed at your own risk. Many were drawn into the magnetic field of his sexuality, few escaped without some scars."

One whose spell John magically fell under was an Irish-born, English-raised young woman named Lesley Black, recently divorced and on an American holiday. "Lesley was right out of the Arthurian legends," wrote John, "a Lily Maid. I spent every moment I could with her."

But he didn't have much time, for she was only in Chicago for four days in mid-June. She was a friend of Robert Milton's and had gone to see *The Lonely Man* as his guest. She didn't find the play as memorable as the main player, whose modern Lincoln she thought "very good." That first evening Milton introduced them and John "fell head over heels, promptly—as well I should." He boldly told her he'd like to marry her and she looked at him curiously.

"I thought it was very strange," Lesley recalled. "I thought Americans were funny people." She didn't take John's interest seriously but continued to see him "quite a bit" until the time came to travel west. She had New Mexico, Nevada, Hollywood, and San Francisco in which to think about the tall, gangly actor who had told her about his adventurous and iconoclastic life. If she had seemed to him something out of the Arthurian legends, he must have seemed to her like a character Mark Twain might have concocted. When she returned to Chicago on her way to Montreal, from where she was to sail back to England, John proposed again. "Without a sou, asked her to marry me. Absurd," John knew, believing that he "had no more business marrying Lesley than I had had marrying Dorothy."

"There was a quality in Lesley that he respected," Howard Koch recalled. "She was a very high-brow English lady. He valued her. She was not a girl you could pick up. Lesley would have to be courted and won over, which, of course, he did."

Perhaps it was precisely the absurdity of it that made her answer in kind. Yes, she told him, she would marry him. But not until she returned to England and the South of France, where her mother and sister were staying, to tell them the news and bring them back for the ceremony.

Stunned by the quickness of her decision, John knew that the time had come to figure out a way to make some money. It certainly wasn't continuing in *The Lonely Man*, where he was earning just enough "to pay my bar bills." Jack Warner had sent him a telegram that he had read aloud to Lesley at the Medina Club in Chicago—it was an invitation to return to Hollywood for some interviews—and John responded by dusting off *Three Strangers*, which had been conceived in England. As Howard Koch put it, "The play ran as long as John stayed with it. Then he got a Hollywood offer, they grabbed him."

Koch, who was also to be grabbed by John Houseman and Orson Welles to write radio plays for their "Mercury Theatre on the Air," figured John only had to wire his father to advance him some money until he got to Hollywood, but John still lived with the nightmare of doing just that. "I rewrote the treatment and called Willy Wyler collect, an SOS. He sent me five hundred bucks and I went to Hollywood and stayed with him. Willy was shooting a picture at Warner Bros. and I went over there to see him. I took a copy of my treatment." Wyler took him to Warner's to see a producer who read the script. He took it to the head of the writing department. "And they bought it."

It would take another nine years before Warner's actually made *Three Strangers*, but the $5,000 John received for the treatment, along with a contract to write the screenplay, enabled him to wire Lesley and say that he would meet her in New York in September. And, best of all, he wouldn't have to borrow a nickel from anyone to pay for it.

When John wasn't writing, he often went up to Running Springs to visit his father, who was spending a lot of his time in his workshop making furniture for the house.

"Dad was a great companion," John said fondly. "I never laughed with anyone so much as I did with him. We had this game we played, sometimes with other people, often just the two of us. The game was to try and make the other person laugh. If you failed, you always had to come back and it was very hard to get the other one to laugh the next time, so it kept getting grimmer and grimmer. I remember once he couldn't make me laugh and on the fourth occasion he disappeared, as one always did, and when he reappeared he was nude and had on six neckties: one at his throat, one on each wrist and ankle, and one around his cock. Well, I broke down. There was no attempt to top that one."

John Weld, who had become Walter's companion, also participated in these games. Along with taking care of the actor's correspondence, Weld played tennis, swam, and rode horses with Huston. "They had such fun together," Katy Weld said with pride. "They did all kinds of silly, crazy things. They'd go skiing or they'd go into Walter's workshop and make furniture or they'd play cards or they'd rehearse. Walter at that time was doing a lot of radio shows for RCA."

Weld remembers Walter once bragging, "At fifty-three, I can play several sets of tennis, swim, walk five miles, chop a quarter of a cord of wood, and cook a steak dinner for a dozen persons—all in one day without feeling fatigue."

Being as close as he was with Walter, Weld said that "Walter didn't see himself in John at all, it was almost as though John didn't belong to him. John wasn't at all like Walter. John was a remarkably complex guy who had three marvelous weaknesses. One was money, he had absolutely no sense or respect for it; another was he had no sense or respect for time; the third was that when it interrupted anything that he wanted to do, he had no sense of others. Walter was exactly the opposite in all three of those categories."

The Welds were in Running Springs that summer of 1937 when the Davises visited. Loyal Davis, who certainly had a sense for money, found himself thinking one evening about how Walter could get $75,000 for acting in the film of Dodsworth while he earned 1/150th of that for slicing open a person's brain. "I had more education than he," Davis wrote in A Surgeon's Odyssey. "I could read aloud better than he. I convinced myself that by applying myself, given the opportunity, I could be Sam Dodsworth just as effectively as Walter had been and demand the same salary. I found myself looking at him critically, watching him to see what he had that I didn't.

"Suddenly, Walter said, 'I've got a machine over there that we can make a record on and play it back. I'll be the announcer, and you and Nancy play the parts. It'll be sponsored by the Crovenay Bear Rug Company and star Nancy Pantsy Davis.' I leaped at the invitation. Here was my chance to show how well I could act."

Davis remembered how he used to wait in the wings and watch Walter and Nan play the last scenes in Dodsworth when they were in Chicago, and suggested that they try that. Walter recorded them and was full of praise when they finished. Then he suggested they try something from *Othello*. Nancy would be Desdemona, Davis Iago, Walter the Moor.

"I read with assurance against Nancy's young, childish voice," Loyal Davis described. "Suddenly Othello spoke. I looked up, and there Walter was in a pair of tennis shoes, swimming trunks, and a T-shirt sitting in a chair. As I listened, his hair became darker and curly; his face became black, and I could see the earrings in his ears. There before me was Othello in the flesh. I was late in picking up my cue, and as I read on I became worse and worse. I was trying to match that expressive voice and face. I failed miserably and knew it, but true to his personality, Walter made Nancy and me feel that we had done a good job. . . .

"The next evening after supper we sat about the fireplace, and Walter announced his surprise and played the *Dodsworth* segment. Edith and Nan congratulated Nancy but were effusive in their praise of my performance." Then came *Othello*. "Edith looked at me in surprise and disbelief. Nan shook her head. When it had finished, Edith said she couldn't believe that I could have read it so badly after having heard the *Dodsworth* record.

"Several days later Walter and I were sitting at the edge of the pool looking over the mountains at peace and without the necessity for conversation. Suddenly, he put his hand on my knee and said, 'Kid, the first time I sat in the stands and saw you operate, I thought I could do it, too.' "

"Uncle Walter had been aware all the time of what Father had been thinking, but never let him know it," Nancy Reagan observed. "When he did, he did so with great gentleness."

Sitting on a couch in her ninth-floor suite at the Beverly-Wilshire in Beverly Hills, the First Lady reminisced about her teenage years, when she and her family would spend summers with the Hustons in their mountaintop home, where the only other neighbors were agent Myron Selznick and actor Reginald Denny. "Uncle Walter was a very special, happy man. Nan was tall, redheaded, a little more complicated than Uncle Walter. Nan could get thrown by things. He was very, very even-tempered. We had great times. We'd walk up the hill from the house where he had a barbecue and a telescope; we'd look at the stars. Or sometimes his friend Jack Smith would come and have us all out there exercising: swimming, playing tennis. Then there were evenings when it would just be us and we would sit in front of the fire and Uncle Walter would read to us. He'd read Shakespeare, poetry. I sat mesmerized."

One memorable day for Nancy was when Walter suggested they make a home movie, with all the Davises in front of the camera and Walter directing. "We shot it on the tennis court," Nancy said with a smile. "Nobody ever took it terribly seriously, it was just a way of filling your days."

Nancy Reagan often compared Walter with Spencer Tracy. But to John Huston, Walter was not to be measured against any other actor. "Spencer Tracy was always Spencer Tracy," John pointed out. "Walter was never just Walter. Someone made an interesting observation: that if Dad had been a European actor, he would have been known as the greatest actor alive. Stanislavski thought he was the greatest American actor."

In September 1937, John got on a train and traveled to New York to meet Lesley, her mother, and her sister when they disembarked from their ship. "We were married three days after we got to New York," Lesley said. The wedding wasn't fancy and the reception was at Barney Gallant's in the Village.

For the second time, John didn't tell his mother or grandmother that he was getting married until after he had done it. Lesley doesn't remember where Rhea or Gram were at the time, but before leaving for Hollywood she did meet Aunt Margaret and Bobby Jones at their New York apartment. "Margaret was an astounding woman, very impressive," Lesley observed, "but she wasn't somebody you really would care for. I remember one evening Bobby asked her if she would read some Shakespeare and it was absolutely riveting. She was sort of heavyish and she didn't have any kind of particular good looks, but this *thing* that came out of her when she was reading Shakespeare—one could understand how she was sought after as a coach."

Margaret and Bobby were in Santa Barbara when John and Lesley were in Hollywood, and Lesley remembers visiting them in their home up the coast. John was driving again—at first it was a $500 Ford convertible, but as soon as his salary at Warner's was raised, he traded it in for another Cadillac.

John Houseman paid a visit to the Joneses in Santa Barbara and found Margaret very ill. Mary Wickes, who in 1946 would act opposite Walter in the Broadway play *Apple of His Eye*, also visited Margaret and Bobby Jones, where she entertained them with her monologues. Wickes had once done some secretarial work for Margaret, when she was eighteen and looking for work in the theater. At that time "Mrs. Jones looked like the pictures you see of Sarah Bernhardt—she had that sandy-red hair, and a lot of it. She was an imposing figure, not terribly tall, with rather heavy features, like Walter. She dressed well. She wanted someone who would do some social secretarial work for her and I had the temerity to say I could only do it in the mornings because in the afternoons I had to look around for jobs. She said okay."

"I got a telephone call from Margaret at her Villa Reposa in Santa Barbara," John said. "It was a beautiful place—it had a music pavilion, quartets, summer entertainment. The best people of Santa Barbara came to these functions." But this time Margaret was not calling for social reasons. She'd taken ill and asked John to drive up immediately. She was in the hospital when John arrived.

"John," she said to her nephew, "I don't know what's wrong with me. I know something is wrong, but I don't want to think about it. I don't want to concern myself. I'd like to put that burden on somebody else. I don't want Wally to be the one, he's always an optimist, he always sees the good side, the hopeful side. Nan is a goose. Robert is useless in such matters. I'm turning to you, but I want you to think about it. It's a lot of responsibility and you may not want to assume it. Go back and call me and tell me what your thoughts are."

When John conferred with the doctors, he learned that Margaret had cirrhosis of the liver. He called Loyal Davis, who recommended a diagnostician in Los Angeles. John brought this doctor up to examine her and he said she had no more than a year to eighteen months to live, depending on how active she tried to be. John never told her what these doctors said, he just agreed to oversee her requests.

"I place everything in your hands," she said. "Tell me what to do." And from then on, whenever Margaret wanted to do something, she'd call John and ask him if she could.

Margaret's benediction of trust, Lesley's faith in setting up life with a man she barely knew, and Willy Wyler's insistence that John could breathe life into a script that hadn't quite jelled, all combined to force John to take himself more seriously than he had in the past, to settle down and get on with this new phase of his life: his emergence as a filmmaker.

"Willy ran into a snag on his picture *Jezebel*," John said shortly after his association with Warner Bros. had started. "The writers wanted to do a whole sequence in Paris with Bette Davis, and Hal Wallis at the studio didn't want to do that. Willy asked me to read it and see if I had any ideas. So I did and had a suggestion. And they all thought it was marvelous. It really didn't amount to a hell of a lot, but it did away with the expense of building Maxime's and the Eiffel Tower. Willy thought it was fine for the picture, so I wrote it."

That suggestion gave Wyler an idea. In a letter dated October 28, 1937, Hal Wallis wrote to Henry Blanke, his co-producer: "Wyler came up to talk to me and explain that he wanted John Huston to sort of represent him in preparing the last half of the script in collaboration with the writers and yourself. . . . He apparently knows Huston and will see him at night, and he maintains that Huston knows exactly his feelings and thoughts about the script. . . . He explains that he himself cannot devote the time to consult with the writers, and Huston apparently will be a sort of go-between operating between the writers, and you, and himself. In order to keep Wyler happy on the picture, and to get a script out as quickly as possible, I have agreed to put Huston on the picture. . . ."

Jezebel was Jack Warner's answer to David Selznick's *Gone With the Wind.* Selznick had expressed an interest in Bette Davis for Scarlett O'Hara, but Jack Warner refused to loan her out. So instead, Davis played a spoiled and tormented pre–Civil War Southern belle opposite Henry Fonda—and walked off with her second Oscar. In her autobiography, *Mother Goddamn,* Davis said that it was "All Wyler. I had known all the horrors of no direction and bad direction. I now knew what a great director was and what he could mean to an actress."

Wyler also meant a great deal to John Huston, who, Lesley immediately discovered, was "a very good, very close friend." John Weld credits Wyler for sparking John's career. "It was *all* because of Willy Wyler. Wyler was the one who got him in there. Without Willy, I don't know that John would *ever* have made it."

There is no doubt that Willy Wyler was important for John. He answered Huston's distress signal and loaned him the $500, put him on *A House Divided,* worked with him on two scripts, went with him to sleep among L.A.'s skid row homeless, gambled with him across the border. But there were others who influenced his career at the time, two of whom, Hal Wallis and Henry Blanke, produced *Jezebel.*

"Something had happened to Hollywood," John said about his return. "People who worked in studios were expert, all the departments were good in all the studios. They all knew what they were doing—the special effects, the production, the decorators, set designers, all excellent people. And the level of taste had risen: Two or three pictures and two or three innovators had made their mark. And Warner's reflected their imagination. Zanuck had just come to the studio, and Hal Wallis, a man of fine taste and excellent judgment, was there. He was prepared to take risks. And Henry Blanke, who was probably the finest producer I ever worked with. It was a very sympathetic atmosphere."

Yet Blanke had told James Agee that John, prior to his marrying Lesley and coming to Warner Bros., was "Just a drunken boy; hopelessly immature. You'd see him at every party, wearing bangs, with a monkey on his shoulder. Charming. Very talented but without an ounce of discipline in his makeup."

Budd Schulberg once overheard Walter Huston say about his son, "Nothing would surprise me about John, nothing. If he wound up in jail or won the Pulitzer Prize. I don't know which way he's going to go, but I know he's going somewhere."

Compared to Walter, Schulberg found John to be a more flashing personality. "John was much more like an actor—flamboyant. Walter seemed kind of solid. There was a show-off side to John and a serious artist. It was almost like he was ashamed to expose that serious side."

Henry Blanke credited Lesley with bringing out the serious artist in John. "When we got married," Lesley said, "he was ready, for the time being, to settle down. He wanted to make a life and work, and the opportunity just happened to be there."

"Lesley meant settling," according to Howard Koch. "He had been wandering from one job to another, one place to another, he wanted a little regularity. He'd had everything else. When they were together, it was a relationship of mutual respect. It was not sentimental; it was a real understanding. A number of factors converged to change John's life: the fact that he was a success in *The Lonely Man*; that Walter wanted him out there; and that Lesley came into the picture. There was no doubt Walter liked Lesley, too."

Katy Weld agreed: "Walter *adored* Lesley." And Lesley found Walter to be "one of the most extraordinary people I've ever met. There was nothing small about him. I never heard him be petty or mean about anything. I loved him very much. We saw quite a lot of him, we used to go up to the mountain house. And Nan and I got on very well, too. And Walter and John had a marvelous relationship. I think they were happier together than they were with anyone else."

Lesley didn't feel quite the same about John's mother, whom she finally met a few months after they had moved to Los Angeles. "They got to know each other, but never very well," John said. "They liked each other. After Lesley and I came to Hollywood, my mother followed. Another instance of her doing that. She and grandmother got an apartment."

Rhea was impressed that Warner's had picked up John's option and his salary was raised from $500 to $750 a week. She also approved of their deciding to build their own house on some undeveloped land in the San Fernando Valley. John had borrowed $25,000 to get the house under way, but that didn't worry his mother, who had always been a gambler by nature. What did begin to worry her was the constant headaches she was having. Sometimes they would last two hours and bring tears to her eyes. But with John working diligently on his screenwriting, she didn't want to bother him about it.

The Amazing Dr. Clitterhouse was the next project John was assigned to co-write with John Wexley. It was a gangster picture, a genre that was a Warner's staple, and it was to be a vehicle for Edward G. Robinson. At the time, Warner's had a lineup of actors who comprised what was known as Murderer's Row: Robinson, Paul Muni, James Cagney, George Raft, and John Garfield. When a good crime story came up, one of these was chosen for the lead and then the secondary characters were cast. *Clitterhouse* also featured Claire Trevor and Humphrey Bogart. This trio—Robinson, Bogart, and Trevor—would reunite a decade later for John Huston's *Key Largo*, but for *Clitterhouse*, John was in the same position as the actors: All assignments came from the producers.

The material Huston and Wexley had to work with for *The Amazing Dr. Clitterhouse* was based on a play by Barré Lyndon, about a psychiatrist (Robinson) who, in order to study the criminal mind, becomes a criminal himself. He gets involved with a gang whose leader is Rocks Valentine (Bogart)—until Clitterhouse proves his superior intellect and takes over. The gang steals jewels, silver, and furs and sells them to Claire Trevor. Clitterhouse carefully documents the criminals' physiological and psychological behavior. When Rocks attempts to blackmail him, Clitterhouse sees that he was missing his ultimate chapter: homicide. He kills Rocks.

Writer John McCarty points out, "One can't help notice how much the title character has in common with many future Huston protagonists. Clitterhouse starts out a winner (a respected doctor), but winds up a loser—a master criminal defeated by his own delusions of grandeur."

After the success of *Clitterhouse* Henry Blanke asked John if he'd like to work on a screenplay about Benito Juarez, the "father" of the Mexican Republic. John couldn't have asked for a better assignment. But the joy of researching and writing about the conflicts that tore Mexico apart would result in enormous frustration. Their efforts were compromised by the inflated ego of one of the studio's biggest stars. It was to become a significant lesson, so insufferable that Huston vowed that as soon as he could, he would never again lose control of his work. He would direct films himself.

"Paul Muni really ruined *Juarez*," Huston lamented. "I depended a great deal on that picture at the time. Two other men worked with me for almost a year on the script and contributed just as much as I did—Wolfgang Reinhardt and Aeneas MacKenzie." The story presented the conflict between ideologies: between royalty and democracy, between an imposed foreign emperor and a deposed peasant president. Maximilian was sent from France to rule Mexico, but the Mexican people wanted Benito Juarez to return as their leader. Maximilian in the end was executed, and his wife, Carlotta, went mad.

Huston, Reinhardt, and MacKenzie worked in complete harmony. "Wolfgang had a scholar's knowledge of Europe during the period of Napoleon III and the Hapsburgs; I was a Jeffersonian Democrat espousing ideas similar to those of Benito Juarez; and MacKenzie believed in the monarchical system. . . . Thus the actual writing was by way of being dialectic."

When the script was turned in Hal Wallis said it was the best script he had ever read. That's when Paul Muni took over and what Huston considered "a very fine script" became butchered.

"The original script was written so Juarez would just come into the story at vital, special moments," Huston said, "and what he said, every word counted. This was in contrast to the grace and eloquence of Maximilian. Well, the first thing Muni wanted was more dialogue, more pages. He was a very fine actor but he had a huge ego and was a humorless man who was vastly impressed with himself. It was heavy going around Muni."

The director, William Dieterle, had made two biographical pictures with Muni: *The Story of Louis Pasteur*, for which the actor had won an Oscar; and *The Life of Emile Zola*, which received an Oscar for Best Picture. But Dieterle and Muni didn't agree with how Juarez should be played, and Muni threatened to walk out if he didn't get his way. With the aid of the Mexican government, Muni, Dieterle, Hal Wallis, and Henry Blanke spent six weeks in Mexico following Juarez's footsteps, and then Muni's brother-in-law was brought in to rework the script.

"His changes did the picture irreparable damage," said Huston. But "the studio had lent itself to the creation of Muni's ponderous prestige; now it had to pay the consequences."

When they were finally ready to shoot the picture, Dieterle's wife,

Charlotte, convinced her husband that he shouldn't yell "Camera" or "Action" when he wanted the cameras to roll because, according to her numerologist, six letters were lucky and she wanted to save all the luck for the six-letter title, and so Dieterle dutifully began each shot with the words "Here . . . we . . . go!"

If this was how pictures got made, with spoiled stars bringing in their in-laws to doctor scripts and directors' wives consulting their numerologists, was it any wonder that Huston wanted to take a film from idea to the screen all by himself?

The only way to do that, Paul Kohner said, was to have it in writing, which is what Kohner did for Huston as soon as the producer-turned-agent took on the writer-who-wanted-to-be-a-director as one of his first clients. He had written into Huston's contract that if Warner's wanted to take up his next option, Huston would be allowed to direct a movie. There were still a few years to go before that option came up, so Warner's took a wait-and-see attitude and agreed.

Paul Kohner had come to America from Germany to work, along with Willy Wyler, in Universal's shipping department in New York. By 1925 he was a production assistant and then a producer of two-reelers. He had a falling-out with his boss and moved first to Columbia and then to MGM as a producer.

Excluded from MGM's inner circle, he sat idly in his office waiting for a picture to produce when he decided that he'd rather be working for himself. On a whim, he rented an office and thought he'd try being an agent, since there weren't many agents in Hollywood in 1938. "My European friends said they'd be my clients and each sent me a check for $5,000, even though they all had agents already. I only knew Universal, so I went to see Joe Pasternak there, and he said, 'Why don't you find me a story for Deanna Durbin?' He invited me to lunch and said I should tell him a story then. I walked out and met a writer named Konrad Bercovici and asked him if he had a story for Deanna Durbin. He told me he had a wonderful story about a Gypsy girl. Then I went to have lunch with Joe and told him the story. He loved it and asked how much it was going to cost. 'Joe,' I said, 'other studios want this story, too. You'll have to pay at least $25,000.' He said he'd be glad to pay it. And I said, 'And another $25,000 for the writer.' So he made a call and said to me, I've got a deal. Then I went and asked Bercovici if he had an agent. He said no. I said 'Yes, I am your agent. How much you want for the story?' He said, 'Maybe $5,000?' I said, 'I got you $25,000 for the story and $25,000 to write the script— $50,000.' Tears started rolling down his face. So the first day I had already made a $5,000 commission. And I thought, this is a wonderful business!"

By the time John Huston was involved with *Juarez*, he knew he needed someone to represent him. Since Kohner had believed in his talent from the time they had worked together on *A House Divided*, it seemed natural for John to go with him. And after Kohner got a clause into the Warner contract for John to eventually direct, Walter decided to change agents, too.

"One day, my secretary came in and said, 'Mr. Walter Huston is here to see you,' " Kohner proudly related. "Walter came in and said, 'My son says you're a good agent. Since he's so enthusiastic about you, would you like to represent me?'

" 'Mr. Huston, I'd be honored,' I said. So I called my secretary and asked her to prepare agency contracts for Mr. Huston. He looked at it and said, 'I want you to know something. This is the same kind of contract I refused to sign with Charlie Feldman. If you are willing to take my handshake, I may stay with you for a long time.' My father had once said to me he'd always rather take a man's handshake than a contract, so I tore up the contract, we shook hands, and he stayed with me until the day he died."

Kohner remembered once discussing John with Walter, who expressed concern that he might not fulfill his potential. "I told him that I felt that John's talent and his genius, his brilliance, would eventually blossom. I was convinced that John would make it big."

While John was establishing himself as one of Warner's more valued screenwriters, Walter managed to put behind him the disaster of *Othello*, as well as put some distance between himself and his understandably depressed wife, by starring in *Of Human Hearts* for MGM. Based on a sentimental story by Honoré Morrow about a young doctor and his father, a country minister, facing the hardships of moving to a village along the Ohio River during the Civil War, it was considered by some critics to be one of the best films of the thirties and the best film Clarence Brown (who directed seven Garbo pictures) ever directed. Walter played the stern, sarcastic, at times fanatical circuit-riding preacher with dignity and understanding; Beulah Bondi played his wife, James Stewart his ambitious doctor son.

The role was different enough from Dodsworth and Othello to make it a challenge for Walter, and he was pleased with both the film and his performance. Frank S. Nugent wrote in the *New York Times* that Huston's preacher was "as much a part of the American scene as Plymouth Rock."

Better news than any good review, though, was the welcome surprise that Lesley was pregnant and Walter was going to be a grandfather early the following year. John knew that she had desperately wanted a child and noticed how happy and radiant she was when she found out she had conceived. John, too, was ecstatic. The house was under way, the work was steady, the money was coming in, a baby was just what was needed to complete the family picture.

The only shadow cast upon the family in the early summer of 1938 was Rhea's continuing headaches. They had become intolerable, and when she finally turned to John for help, he immediately called Loyal Davis, who was teaching surgery at Northwestern University. Davis told him that his family was planning to spend the summer at Walter's house in Running Springs and he would look in on Rhea when they came out, but suggested he take her to another doctor in the meantime. This doctor left the door to his examining room opened and John could hear his mother's responses.

"At first her answers were intelligent and to the point. Then, in responding to a query about her everyday activities, she began to talk in a random, illogical fashion, describing a life-style that existed only in her imagination: friends, parties, joyous occasions."

Neither John nor the doctor knew what to make of it. "She didn't make any sense," John said, "and then she had a strange tantrum. The doctor thought it could have been psychosis."

When Loyal Davis came, he, too, believed she was suffering from a psychosis, "and he was the greatest neurological surgeon at the time," said John. Davis felt Rhea needed to be kept under observation and John found a nursing home. When he talked to her about it, she would speak in a garbled tongue. "The syllables were interchanged, it was like pig latin."

He told his father about it, but Rhea was a distant memory. "There was not much to talk about. I wouldn't go to him for emotional aid."

Walter, that summer, was entertaining an offer from Josh Logan to return to Broadway in a satirical musical about Peter Stuyvesant, the seventeenth-century peg-legged dictatorial governor of New Amsterdam, written by Maxwell Anderson. Logan had come, with his friend Jimmy Stewart, to Running Springs to pitch the idea in person.

When Logan had first been approached to direct *Knickerbocker Holiday*, he recognized that in Anderson's plot, which was based on Washington Irving's stories, "the old fat Dutch burghers were pure Weber and Fields and the boy and girl were pure coy. It wasn't until peg-legged Peter Stuyvesant entered, flashing his silver-encrusted stump of a leg, that things began to crackle. He was obviously a dictator and, less obviously, a satire of Roosevelt. . . . We knew that we needed a great star for Stuyvesant, and also that it was a comparatively small part which made attracting a big star difficult."

Kurt Weill, the play's composer, pushed Logan to call Walter Huston. "Walter was the best American actor on the stage, no question about it," Logan said in his New York apartment, a frail, sick man with a barely audible voice. He had had two Broadway hits, *On Borrowed Time* and the musical *I Married an Angel*, when he agreed to direct *Knickerbocker Holiday*. "The part of Peter Stuyvesant didn't come on until the end of the first act, but I made it the strongest part of the play. I flew out to California and then I rented a car and drove to Lake Arrowhead, where Walter lived. He had visitors staying with him: a young girl named Nancy Davis and her mother and father. They arranged immediately for me to read them the play aloud. So I put on a big show. And Nancy Davis sat there and howled and laughed, she was the best audience I ever had."

Walter, with some reservations, was intrigued by the chance to return to a vaudevillian-type part and told Logan, "He's such an old sonofabitch, I can't stand him, but I'll play him if I have one chance to be charming and I can make love to the young girl. Just so that she can consider him for a fraction of a second when she hears his song."

"What song?" Logan asked.

"Something nice I can sing to her, a moment for the old scoundrel to be charming."

"I'll get you a song, I promise you that," Logan said.

"No, no," Walter responded, "I'm smarter than that. I want to *hear* the song. Over the phone if necessary."

Logan flew back to New York and told Weill and Anderson to write him a song. Within two hours they came up with the poignant "September Song."

"We called Walter immediately," said Logan, "and Kurt said, 'I want to sing him the song.' But I said, 'You have a thick German accent, he won't be able to hear the lyrics.' He said, 'I'm going to sing the song.' So he sang the song to Walter over the telephone. Walter said he couldn't understand what the song was all about, 'Let Josh sing it.' He'd heard me sing all the other songs. I didn't know it very well, but I sang it: *When I was a young man courting the girls/I played me a waiting game . . .*"

"Play the tune again," Walter said when Logan finished. And what followed, neither Logan nor Weill could believe. Walter sang it back to them! Logan was dumbfounded. "I never met an actor as good as Walter Huston in my life," he exclaimed.

As Walter began to practice the melancholy song about the days growing short when you reach September, Rhea was struggling to make it through August. Her scrambled babbling had ceased and she had retreated into silence. It was no mere psychosis from which she was suffering but a brain tumor. Her only chance was surgery to remove it.

Lesley and John visited with her in the hospital before the operation. Lesley had told Rhea that she was carrying John's baby, but she couldn't tell whether Rhea understood. Before her surgery, John whispered to her, "Mother, they know what's wrong with you. They're going to fix it now."

Her eyes were closed when he spoke to her and she hadn't spoken a word for weeks, but suddenly, with clarity, she turned to her son and asked in a ghostly voice, "Can they fix it, John?"

"Yes, they can fix it, Mother."

The doctors operated and then Rhea was brought back, alive but unconscious, to her room. There was nothing anyone could do for her, and after a while John and Lesley left.

With Rhea hanging on, John and Lesley went to dinner at John and Katy Weld's home in Encino on August 15. "We had invited these people to entertain us," John Weld recounted, "a man and his wife who had been in vaudeville for a number of years; one was playing the piano and the other was telling jokes and singing. We were all very cheerful, having a good time. And then the telephone rang. His mother had died. John just crumbled. He didn't cry, but he was extremely depressed. I never saw him feel so strongly about anybody as he felt about his mother. He was very, very down. Greatly moved. He and Lesley picked up and left right away."

A great sob of sorrow swept through him as they drove to the hospital in Hollywood. She wasn't even fifty-seven, hadn't fulfilled herself in either her personal or professional life. As his mother she had been dominating, demeaning, hysterical, overbearing, proud, protective. She was an adventuress, a gambler, a horsewoman, hardened by convent training, embittered by an alcoholic father, unlucky in love, frustrated in her dream of being more than a sob-sister feature writer for newspapers. She worked hard on her plays and stories, which were never published, and on her autobiography, which she endlessly rewrote; she longed for the success she had seen come to her friend Thomas Wolfe, and to Walter.

Like Joyce's Stephen Dedalus, who refused to kneel and pray for his dying mother, John wasn't sentimental enough to have told his mother that he had loved her. He was left now with his memories and her papers, which he tied together in a brown folder and never could bring himself to read.

His father was his friend—had taken him to fights, given him money, gotten him jobs, saved his ass, made him laugh; but his mother was his parent—taught him to ride, made him appreciate the written word, stood up to his shenanigans, followed him from coast to coast and country to country, slugged him when he needed slugging, smothered him. He made his father proud; he made his mother cry. Walter called him wild, she called him a fool. But she loved him so dearly and completely that she eliminated in her imaginings any difficulties between them.

Now she was gone and he felt an emotional tangle that wouldn't be resolved until he was on his own deathbed, when he would tell Maricela that it was his mother, not his father, with whom he wanted to be buried. In the end, she deserved his respect.

PART FOUR

9

"THE STUFF THAT DREAMS ARE MADE OF"

IN THE FALL OF 1938, NEW LIFE AND NEW PROJECTS KEPT Rhea's death from occupying John's thoughts. Lesley was starting to show; Lupita Kohner, Paul's wife, was carrying a basketball she would call Pancho inside her; Walter was off previewing *Knickerbocker Holiday*; and Willy Wyler asked John to put some finishing touches on his next film, *Wuthering Heights*. Wyler also confided to his friend that he had met a twenty-four-year-old secretary-turned-actress named Margaret Tallichet and was going to marry her. John suggested they use his father's place in Running Springs, and agreed to keep it a secret.

Wuthering Heights, Emily Brontë's romantic Victorian novel, had been whittled down to movie size by Ben Hecht and Charles MacArthur, who had previously collaborated on *The Front Page* and *Twentieth Century*. "That was a famous team," John remarked. "They had written a beautiful screenplay but it was almost in treatment form, so I put it into a screenplay. I didn't want any credit. For me to have intruded my name would have been vulgar."

The thirty-six-year-old Wyler had known Talli for only five weeks when they drove up to Running Springs on Friday, October 21, to spend the weekend with John and Lesley, Paul and Lupita Kohner,

201

lawyer Mark Cohen, and Willy's parents and brother. Only John and Lesley knew about the Saturday wedding. Lesley had prepared a cake and decorated it with flowers from Walter and Nan's garden.

Talli remembers that "Lesley made all the arrangements. It was a moment when everybody was having children. John and Lesley were tremendously excited anticipating the arrival of their child." Soon after she married, Talli also became pregnant.

Although Walter's work kept him from being at the wedding, he was in their conversation as his picture appeared in *Time* magazine that week. The accompanying story had to do with the fact that President Roosevelt had gone to the theater for only the second time since entering the White House—to see his old friend Walter in *Knickerbocker Holiday*. The president's first play was *Dodsworth* in 1935.

"The President tossed his head and roared," *Time* reported in their National Affairs section, "when among seven ridiculously fat New Amsterdam councilmen one answered meekly to the name of Roosevelt. Peter Stuyvesant, one of Franklin Roosevelt's predecessors as Governor of New York, was represented as a tyrant who eventually capitulates to Democracy. Line with most visible effect on Franklin Roosevelt's funny bone: 'Democracy is when you're governed by amateurs.' "

Roosevelt had gone to see the show the week before it opened in New York, and Josh Logan recalled how the theater was "crawling with Secret Service. It was a historic time, not long before Hitler's invasion of Czechoslovakia and just after Roosevelt's letter to Hitler—the famous Munich letter. Anderson had satirized this by having one old Dutchman named Roosevelt say (about a war threat from Connecticut), 'Maybe ve send dem a letter—maybe dy go vay.' "

Roosevelt once again invited Walter and some others back to the White House after the play. The president played the perfect host, asking what everyone was drinking, then he critiqued the play. He had greatly enjoyed it, with one exception. As Josh Logan remembered, the president said, "That 'letter' thing wasn't funny. In the first place, it was a *telegram* I sent to Hitler and I sent it personally. The important thing was the fact that that bastard's secretary didn't throw it into a wastebasket. If it hadn't come from a *powerful* United States it would never even have gotten onto that desk. We've simply *got* to stay powerful enough to stay out of the wastebasket."

Walter took Roosevelt's words to heart and during the run of the show he called upon his fellow actors to join with him in boycotting German-made products.

Josh Logan credits Walter for the success of the play. "He made *Knickerbocker Holiday*. He knew everything there was to know." All through rehearsals Walter never let Logan see how he was going to walk with a peg-leg. He had figured out a way to cushion his bent knee and made a cloth sling and wooden braces to relieve his bent leg from any strain that might cramp his muscles or tighten his tendons. Finally, at the dress rehearsal, Walter performed using the silver-incrested wooden leg that he had modeled after the one John Barrymore had used in *The Sea Beast*, wearing a bulky cloak that covered the sling and braces and a sword that stuck out behind the bent leg, preventing the audience from seeing the apparatus. Logan stopped worrying. "I knew we had a hit."

"He taught me one of the most important things I learned in my life about direction," Logan said. It had to do with what Walter had learned from George M. Cohan about pausing. To demonstrate, Walter used two examples from Shakespeare: Hamlet's "To be or not to be . . ." and Macbeth's "Tomorrow and tomorrow . . ."

" 'To be,' if you pause there, the audience has no idea what you're pausing for. 'To be or not to be': that's fair, it means you're thinking about something. But if you pause after: 'To be or not to be, that is the question,' you can pause forever and the audience won't care, because they know that you're thinking and they're thinking, too. Never pause until you come to a full stop, a full thought.

" 'Tomorrow and tomorrow . . . till the last syllable of recorded time.' Don't pause before that, then the audience will know that you're really in trouble and you're thinking about it."

When *Knickerbocker Holiday* opened at the Ethel Barrymore Theatre on W. 47th Street on October 19, 1938, Logan was pleased with the ovations from the audience but worried about the critics. "It got terrible reviews," Logan remembered, but "the play became a smash hit because of Walter singing 'September Song.' "

Lloyd Lewis was the first critic to review the play around the song: "the boastful plea of a middle-aged war chief for a 20-year-old girl to marry him and know the delights that a callow young husband could never provide. . . . His voice was very quiet, just audible above the low flutes of a distinguished orchestral performance . . . pausing with beautiful artistry now and then, resting with a great actor's gift for nuance, building a song to lyric heights without ever singing it at all."

Josh Logan was so impressed with Walter that he said he found only one other actor during his stage and film career who came even close—and that was Marlon Brando, whom Logan directed in *Sayo-*

nara. "Walter Huston didn't mind losing sympathy and neither did Brando. Brando was brilliant that way, but Walter was a more honest person than Brando, who kept his talent to himself.

"Walter was an actor in the same tradition as Laurence Olivier. He acted only on the stage, only when he played the part. Walter was a far greater actor than his son was a director, which is a terrible thing to say, I know, from another director. But I was never jealous of John Huston. I was jealous of Walter, because he was my ideal of greatness. He never made a false step."

One of the reasons Walter liked appearing in New York was that he could carry on discreet affairs with women when Nan wasn't there. One woman, John Weld remembered, had written him a note and Walter invited her backstage. "She was kind of like a whoring sort," Weld said, "and he would see her whenever he was in New York for a number of years. But only just to have one lay. She was the only one that I knew of that he kept. He corresponded with her and called her whenever he got to town."

The thrill of being singled out by the president, playing an old rogue, singing a hit song, and enjoying other women came to an abrupt halt with the death of his sister Margaret in November. No one had ever meant as much to him.

Soon after Rhea's death, Margaret had decided that she didn't want to be in Santa Barbara in the fall. She wanted to return to Connecticut to see the seasons change. She called John about making such a move and John asked to think about it. He then called her doctor, who said that it would be taking months off her life. John called Margaret and asked her how important returning to Denby was to her and she said very. "Go on then, Margaret."

Bobby Jones described Margaret's last months as an enchanted period. At night, she would get out of bed and the two of them would go down and walk in the garden or sit on the veranda. They would drink champagne and talk. She told Jones, "I should have lived my whole life like this." Jones told John, "It was Margaret at her best."

Two months later, in January 1939, there was another death. Lesley had gone into labor a month early and had given birth to a girl. But the child was still-born. Within five months, John had lost his mother, his aunt, and now his first child. It took him weeks to get over the loss, but Lesley never fully recovered. John described her reaction as "extreme" and said that an "atmosphere of unrelieved grief enveloped the house." He sought refuge in his work and in other relationships. Her mother came to stay with them. Their relationship changed.

Walter Huston (1884–1950).

Adelia Gore, JH's grandmother, Rhea's mother. A pioneer woman, married to John Gore for eighteen years.

General William P. Richardson. JH's great-grandfather, Adelia's father. (Courtesy of Tony Huston)

Rhea Gore Huston, JH's mother. Born in Newcastle, Indiana, in 1881, she was married to Walter from 1904 to 1909. (Courtesy of The Academy of Motion Picture Arts and Sciences)

John Huston, age three years and seven months.

Walter, forty, as seventy-five-year-old Ephraim Cabot in Eugene O'Neill's *Desire Under the Elms,* 1924.

JH self-portrait, age seventeen. (Photo by Lawrence Grobel)

Walter's sister, Margaret, photographed in Paris in 1895.

Walter (left) meeting John's first wife, Dorothy, and John.

Bayonne Whipple, age fifty-four, Walter's vaudeville partner and second wife.

John and second wife, Lesley Black, on a hunting trip in Idaho in the late 1930s.

Walter (left) and John, early 1930s.

Scene from *The Prizefighter and the Lady*, 1933. Walter (second from right) played a boozy fight manager. Primo Carnera (second from left) was then the heavyweight champion. Max Baer (right) was the number one contender. Jack Dempsey (third from right) played a referee. (© 1933 Metro-Goldwyn-Mayer Corporation; renewed 1960 Metro-Goldwyn-Mayer, Inc.)

Walter and wife Nan Sunderland on Broadway in *Dodsworth*, 1934. (Courtesy of Nan Sunderland estate)

Walter as Peter Stuyvesant,
Knickerbocker Holiday, 1938.
(Courtesy of Nan Sunderland
estate)

Marietta FitzGerald, mid-1940s, who
married Ronald Tree after John married
Evelyn Keyes. (Photo by Louise Dahl-
Wolfe. Courtesy of Marietta Tree)

Olivia de Havilland and John, August
1943. (Photo © Jules Buck)

From left: Col. Frank
Capra, Capt. John Huston,
Col. Anatole Litvak, Lt.
Col. William Wyler. At
Olivia de Havilland's house,
Los Angeles, August 1943.
(Photo © Jules Buck)

From left: James Cagney, Jeanne Cagney, Rosemary DeCamp,
Walter in *Yankee Doodle Dandy*, 1942. (Photo by Mack Elliott; © 1943
Warner Bros. Pictures, Inc.; renewed 1970 United Artists Television, Inc.)

From left: Charlie Grayson, Daye Eliot, John, Doris Lilly. The Onyx Club, New
York, 1945. (Courtesy of Doris Lilly)

From left: Anatole Litvak, Evelyn Keyes
Huston, Billy Wilder, John. Late 1940s.
(Courtesy of John Huston)

John, Claire Trevor, Walter in 1949. All
won Oscars: John for writing and directi[ng]
The Treasure of the Sierra Madre, Trevor f[or]
Best Supporting Actress in *Key Largo,*
Walter for Best Supporting Actor in
Treasure.

John, Pablo, Evelyn Keyes. Pablo's portra[it]
was painted by John. Late 1940s. (Photo [©]
Jules Buck)

Lupita Kohner was in the hospital, having delivered her son by cesarean, when Lesley was brought in. "Losing that child played a big part in their lives," she said. "I always wonder what would have happened if that baby had lived, whether they would have stayed together, because it was a very happy, congenial marriage."

"It was just tragic when the baby didn't live," Talli Wyler said. "It seemed to be more important to Lesley than to John. She was so eager to have another one, but she was never able to get pregnant again."

Today, fifty years since she lost the child, Lesley can't bring herself to talk about it. All she will say is, "That's private."

The disintegration of John and Lesley's marriage was not rowdy but internal. John would stay out all night. When he returned, no questions were asked.

In March, Howard Koch made his first trip to Hollywood. John had convinced Henry Blanke at Warner Bros. that Koch had the potential to write movies. Blanke hired Koch. John met his friend at Union Station and brought him to the Chateau Elysee in Hollywood. "This is where I stayed when I started," John told Koch, "it's a lucky place." Koch later discovered that, among the movie people, the hotel was known as the "Easy-Lay" and thought he better understood the kind of luck John was talking about.

Coming from the cold of Manhattan, Koch was impressed with the California weather, with the "seductive fragrance of the yellow-blooming acacia trees." He was equally impressed with John and Lesley's house high up in Outpost with its view of the valley below, its swimming pool, and the French Impressionist paintings on the walls.

Koch had put together a draft of the play he and Huston had discussed when they were in Chicago, *In Time to Come*, about the tragedy of Woodrow Wilson and the failure of the League of Nations. He showed it to John, who made some suggestions. "Now Howard, try this," he would say and Koch would write down Huston's thoughts.

"He was a man of ideas," Koch said. "He had a sharp critical sense. He let me do most of the actual writing." Koch put together another draft, but they put the project aside when film assignments came up for both men.

At John's instigation, Henry Blanke offered Koch a plum assignment: a projected Errol Flynn film, *The Sea Hawk*. Koch shocked the producer by turning it down because the story was historically incorrect. When Blanke told him to make it correct, Koch changed his mind and became a screenwriter.

Wolfgang Reinhardt asked John to take a look at a script Norman

Burnside had written based on an idea Heinz Herald had about the life of Paul Ehrlich, the bacteriologist who pioneered the use of dyes in isolating disease-causing microbes, discovered a "magic bullet," Salvarsan, for the treatment of syphilis, and shared a Nobel Prize in physiology in 1908. Having some knowledge about bacteriology from his friendship with Paul de Kruif, Huston was anxious to read what Burnside had written but was thoroughly disappointed in it. "It was shit," Huston said.

John wanted to do something daring: He wanted to eliminate any love story, eliminate the cliché of a scientist's travails. He wanted "a really straight, true rendering of the Wassermann story. It was different than anything anyone had ever tackled for the screen. My approach was scientific." The drama, for Huston, was in the experiments themselves, not in Ehrlich's life.

When Reinhardt gave him the go-ahead, they worked on the rewrite. Heinz Herald was also included because it was his idea, but, according to John, "he couldn't write." When they finished and turned in their version of the bug-meets-dye story, Huston was convinced Warner's "would think me insane. I thought they might throw me out of the studio." Instead, they assigned it to their biography director, William Dieterle.

Then Burnside challenged Huston's contribution. "When the scripts were turned in to the Writers Guild," Huston recalled, "I put my name on it last. Burnside objected to my name being on the script at all. There was arbitration. What I'd written was underscored in one color ink and what he'd written in another. He hadn't written anything. Maybe a few lines of dialogue. The Writers Guild wanted to take his name off the script. And *he* had made the protest! I insisted that his name be kept on. But it was put on last then. He came to me afterward, the poor devil, and apologized that he'd been foolish."

The idea of tackling a subject that had at its core the conquering of a sexually transmitted disease was cause for concern at the studio. Nervous letters were exchanged between Will Hays, the president of the Motion Picture Producers and Distributors of America, and Joseph Breen, the director of the Production Code Administration. Hal Wallis assured both men that they would not exploit the sexual aspects of the movie in any way. "We will work over the script immediately and reduce references to venereal diseases to a minimum."

Huston wasn't happy with what Dieterle did with *Dr. Ehrlich's Magic Bullet*, feeling "it was a bit fucked up. Dieterle tried to dramatize things that didn't need to be dramatized in a heavy-handed way. "

The script was nominated for an Oscar (Huston's first nomination) and Edward G. Robinson considered it to be "one of the most distinguished performances I've ever given. Among all my plays and films, I'm proudest of my role in *Dr. Ehrlich's Magic Bullet.*"

Huston agreed that Robinson did "the best acting of his career. Eddie Robinson was always longing to be respectable and to play men with great minds and high ideals and souls. He thought this was great."

In 1939, after touring with *Knickerbocker Holiday*, Walter Huston managed to squeeze in a supporting role in William A. Wellman's *The Light That Failed* for Paramount. The Kipling tragedy about a man slowly going blind starred Ronald Colman and Ida Lupino. In November, Walter and Nan joined Orson Welles in the Campbell Playhouse radio version of *The Magnificent Ambersons*. Nan liked doing radio and Walter encouraged her. Another radio play became a full-length Broadway drama. It was originally broadcast on "Mercury Theatre," the John Houseman–Orson Welles show. *A Passenger to Bali*, written by Ellis St. Joseph and produced by Montgomery Ford, was sent to Walter right after he had turned down *Life With Father*, a play that would become an enormous success. John Weld remembers reading St. Joseph's play to Walter and Nan. "We were all kind of mystified about it, so we discussed it and then I said, 'Maybe if we read it again we'll find out what it's all about.' It was supposed to be about a man who controlled all of the evil in the world and it seemed to Walter that the part of this stranger who comes aboard this ship was a great part for him—a great acting role—and that pleased him. But still, it was a little vague about what the hell it was all about. If he controlled all the evil, what did he do with it?

" 'Well, I'll tell you,' Walter said, 'I could do this if we could get the producer to let John direct it.' "

Just as William Carrington agreed to finance *Mr. Pitt* on the condition that Walter star, Walter saw an opportunity to give John a shot at directing. John had been assigned to rewrite a script, but Warner's released him from the assignment after two weeks so he could direct his father on Broadway.

If Weld and Walter were mystified by it, John seemed to have a clear idea about the meaning of *A Passenger to Bali*. He saw it as a contest between a demagogue and a man of conscience. The demagogue (Walter) was a fake clergyman who joins a steamer crossing the China Seas. The captain attempts to get rid of this troublemaker, but no port will take him and the reverend proceeds to undermine the captain's authority until finally the ship hits the rocks and goes down in a storm. "The question propounded by the play," John said, "was: Should the captain have put the passenger adrift in an open boat some time beforehand and saved his ship, or was he right in having acted according to the law even at the cost of his ship?"

In New York and New Haven, John Weld worked on the play with both Hustons but felt that "we still couldn't get the theme." Walter then remembered John Houseman's involvement with the radio version and asked him to see what he thought of their New Haven preview. "I spent two days in New Haven to see if I had any ideas," Houseman said. "There was nothing very much that anyone could do to make the show work in Broadway terms. A *Passenger to Bali* was a short story made into a play. It was *The Flying Dutchman* all over again, with a more rational explanation. We were able to swing it as a fifty-minute radio show. But it didn't really work. I don't know why Walter did it, except that he wanted to work with John."

The fact that John was directing his father generated a lot of publicity before the play opened at the Ethel Barrymore Theatre in mid-March 1940. In his *New York Herald Tribune* newspaper column "Stage Asides," Lucius Beebe wrote about sons who follow in their father's footsteps, pointing out that it was "more common among businessmen, soldiers, and flagpole sitters than in the theater. . . . But John Huston, the son of the great Walter, is no mere chip off the old block; he is a whole slab or joist, and while acting as a particularized form of expression isn't his stuff, the theater from almost every other angle very definitely is."

Beebe quoted John as saying he had no difficulty handling his father on the stage, needling Walter as "having the makings of a very fair actor in him."

To another reporter, Walter said he always had faith in his son. "John was born to the theater and since he was seventeen he's been his own man and not my son. He and I and Miss Sunderland have never gone in for a royal family act and don't like ourselves billed as 'The Stage Family Huston.' We just happen now and then to be implicated in the same stage crimes, but they are seldom premeditated."

To Beebe, John said, "Until recently I had thought that writing for the theater and the films was the most advantageous means of dramatic expression. Now I am convinced that direction and production are equally important and I believe the shortest route to film direction lies through Broadway."

There could no longer be any doubt about John's ambition. Writing could only bring an idea so far, directing completed the vision. Beebe wrote: "Here is no posturing dilettante trading off his father's prestige for a living." Directing a play was just the next step, a warm-up, to becoming a film director. And when questioned about his relative youth and inexperience, John responded: "There isn't any longer any necessity for a director in the films to worry about camera, technique, lighting, costuming, and the production details which once were an important part of his function. These have been so perfected and so competent a generation of specialists in these fields has grown up that the sole concern of the director today is the handling and conduct of the actors involved."

It was a belief he would carry throughout his long career: to hire the best and let them do what they do.

Unfortunately the play bombed. The critics praised Walter, acknowledged John, and agreed with Weld. They just didn't know what the hell it all meant.

John considered his first effort as a director "an honorable failure." Even though the play closed after just four performances, "It confirmed me in my desire to become a director."

As the lights went out on A Passenger to Bali, Nan's voice could be heard on CBS radio as she played Katherine in the Columbia Workshop musical comedy version of Shakespeare's Taming of the Shrew. Walter took on another play, William Saroyan's Love's Old Sweet Song, which brought him back to familiar territory, playing a medicine pitchman similar to his role as Nifty Miller in The Barker. The play was a hodgepodge of surrealistic ideas and, like A Passenger to Bali, was clobbered by the critics. "As muddled a mess of pretentious words as ever befogged a first-nighter," remarked Donald Kirkley.

John hadn't stayed to see his father churned through the critics' wordgrinder a second time. When Hal Wallis sent him a book to read, he knew it was time to return to Hollywood to take on another writing assignment.

"I just finished High Sierra," John wrote Wallis four days after A Passenger to Bali closed. "I must admit to being a pushover for W. R. Burnett's stuff.

"It would be very easy for this to be made into the conventional gangster picture, which is exactly what it should not be. With the exception of Little Caesar, all of Burnett has suffered sadly in screen translation . . . if it's gone at with the seriousness Burnett deserves, it could be made into a fine and outstanding picture."

A week later John wrote Wallis again, this time explaining that he wasn't writing a treatment of Burnett's story, since he considered the book itself "a very complete treatment," but was already well along in the actual screenplay. Warner Bros. had wanted George Raft for *High Sierra*, but Raft was supposedly sick and tired of playing gangsters who got killed in the end. "They had to get the script to him by a certain date," Huston recalled, "and if he didn't do it, they didn't have to pay. So it was important from Jack Warner's vantage to get the script to him."

Mark Hellinger, who was producing the film, although his title was associate producer under Hal Wallis, was under great pressure from Jack Warner to get Huston to complete the script. He would call Huston and say, "Jack Warner's on me, he's driving me nuts."

"Tell him to go fuck himself," Huston responded.

A few hours later Hellinger called again. "John, I don't know what I'm going to do, Warner's going to be on the goddamn intercom in another minute."

"Tell him to go fuck himself," Huston again responded, hearing the buzz of Hellinger's intercom in the background and then Jack Warner's voice asking about the script.

"GO FUCK YOURSELF!" he heard Mark Hellinger scream.

John couldn't believe it. Neither could Warner, who got rid of Hellinger as soon as his contract expired at the end of that year.

After Raft, Warner Bros. hoped Paul Muni would play Roy "Mad Dog" Earle, the Dillinger-based main character in Burnett's novel, who gets out of prison to prepare a hotel robbery but is assisted by two novices who bring along a girl and thereby violate the criminal's code of professionalism by which Earle lived. Whatever can go wrong, does, and Earle gets killed in the end.

Muni had a code of professionalism of his own. Not only did he dislike the idea of dying in a movie, he distinctly disliked being asked to do a film George Raft had already turned down. When John met him at a party he was drunk enough to let Muni know exactly what he thought of him. Huston had never been able to forgive Muni for ruining *Juarez*, and when he was through telling Muni off, Muni told Jack Warner that he wouldn't do anything Huston wrote, which meant he was pulling out of *High Sierra*. Jack Warner then told Huston to bring in W. R. Burnett as a collaborator, so if Muni continued his objection, they could counter by saying, "For chrissakes, what do you want? We got the author on it."

High Sierra was becoming more trouble than it seemed to be worth to Jack Warner, but Hal Wallis believed in it, believed in Huston, and felt confident that once Burnett got involved, the final script would soon follow.

"I never had so much fun in my life, John and I working together," Burnett said in an interview before he died in 1982. "We laughed most of the time; we could hardly get any work done. I work fast on the typewriter and he dictates. He likes to sit down and completely talk out a scene, which would take a day and wear me out. Anyway, we got a fine script and gave it to Muni, and Muni turned it down again. You know what happened? Warner fired him. I thought the studio was going to collapse that day. Everybody went around saying, 'For chrissakes, they fired *Muni*. He's getting five thousand a week. You can't fire the star.'"

With Muni out, the studio offered the part to James Cagney, who didn't want to be third-fiddle to Raft and Muni, then to Eddie Robinson, who didn't like the idea of following behind Cagney, and to John Garfield. With their "A"-list of gangster types depleted, Warner's turned to Humphrey Bogart, who had told Hal Wallis in a note in April that he was interested in the part.

In May, Hal Wallis declared the Huston-Burnett script a final draft. Burnett remembered fighting with the Motion Picture Code officials, who were on the set practically every day asking for changes. "We had twenty-seven pages of objections from the Johnston office," Burnett said. "We had to rewrite the script and send it to them. But we got most of 'em through. We had a girl living with two guys and we got away with it . . . in 1940!"

That girl was Ida Lupino, who was the subject of a Hal Wallis memo to Jack Warner in September. "Don't you think we ought to reverse the billing on *High Sierra*, and instead of billing Bogart first, bill Lupino first?

"Lupino has had a great deal of publicity on the strength of *They Drive by Night*, whereas Bogart has been playing the leads in a lot of 'B' pictures, and this fact might mitigate against the success of *High Sierra*."

The billing was reversed, Lupino was first . . . but it was Bogart who was mobbed by adoring fans after the film was released.

"*High Sierra* marked a turning point in his career," Huston said. "It established him."

We'd seen bad guys, hundreds, maybe thousands of them, before, but the bad guy Bogart played was a decent man. He had a sense of loyalty, a code of ethics. He could feel sorry for a neglected dog or a crippled girl and go out of his way to help them. He was essentially a loner, a man up against a system, and even though he knew how to use a machine gun and was on the wrong side of the law, he was likable. The way Bogart played him, you couldn't help rooting for Roy Earle. In the end, when he got shot and Ida Lupino mumbled he was free, you hoped through your tears that she was right.

Raft, Robinson, Muni, and all the others would have to take a step back—a new kind of tough guy had appeared on the screen. As Otto Friedrich pointed out in his *City of Nets*, "Bogart must have instinctively realized, as he was shot down over and over again during the late 1930's, . . . [that] every snarling death [was] just another snarling death, until, in *High Sierra*, he saw his first chance at playing a fugitive convict who could become a romantic hero."

All Bogart needed to cross over into the hearts of moviegoers was to take that tough, no-nonsense fugitive with a heart of gold and put him on the right side of the law. Make him, for instance, a private detective. And support him with a cast of actors trained on the stage and polished to perfection.

"My standing at Warner's was quite high as a writer," Huston said. His option had come up and that clause Paul Kohner had inserted into his contract about his being allowed to direct a film was now an issue. "They didn't want me to direct, particularly, and I didn't think they'd take up my option, because it was so difficult for a writer to become a director. Preston Sturges had just directed his first picture. It had never happened before. But then Henry Blanke said, 'What would you like to direct?'

" 'The Maltese Falcon,' I said."

Written by Dashiell Hammett in 1930, *The Maltese Falcon* is about some shifty characters trying to find a statue of a bird they believe to be worth a fortune. The hero of the story is a private investigator named Sam Spade who is hired by a mysterious woman, a psychopathic liar named Brigid O'Shaughnessy, to help her out of a tight situation. Warner Bros. paid Hammett's publisher, Alfred Knopf, $8,500 for all movie rights and made two films based on the novel, one in 1931 and one in 1936.

"They were such wretched screenplays," Huston said of both pictures, "no understanding, just assholes, idiots, of what Dashiell Hammett had done."

The first was renamed *Woman of the World* and then changed to *Dangerous Female*, starring Ricardo Cortez as private eye Sam Spade and Bebe Daniels as Brigid O'Shaughnessy. The second was released as *Satan Met a Lady*. Sam Spade became a laywer named Ted Shayne, played by Warren Williams, Brigid became Valerie Purvis, played by Bette Davis. Davis considered it "one of the worst turkeys I ever made." It was directed by William Dieterle, whom John had little respect for and felt sure that he could do better if given the chance.

"Blanke backed me up in my wanting to direct this," Huston said, "and Wallis and Jack Warner were astonished and delighted because they owned it. It had been made badly twice before and it makes sense to remake a bad picture."

Warner, Wallis, and Blanke "acted out of friendship toward me," John said, "out of goodwill. They agreed to give me a shot at it and, if it didn't come off all that well, they wouldn't be too disappointed as it was to be a very small picture."

But before John could get that shot, there was one more picture they wanted him to work on as a writer. It was considered a big movie having to do with an extremely timely subject: becoming a soldier and fighting for your country.

The war in Europe was accelerating. Hitler was on a rampage as German troops invaded Norway, Denmark, Belgium, the Netherlands, Luxembourg, and France. It was a grim, gloomy period and Americans were becoming convinced that they, too, would soon be at war. Warner's wanted Huston to work on a story about World War I; the hero: Sergeant Alvin York, the Tennessee farm boy who single-handedly captured a whole German company at Meuse-Argonne in 1918 and became a symbol of the American patriot, the most publicized hero of the war. Producer Jesse Lasky had pursued York for six months, finally landing the rights to his story. He hired Harry Chandler and Abem Finkel to write a first draft. Huston and Howard Koch were then put on it to make the projected million-dollar picture work.

"I took that picture over," John said proudly. "I worked alone on it. It was one of those things, everything was right."

Howard Koch remembered it slightly differently. John may have thought he was alone, but Koch was also in the room, talking about the story as John drew his portrait. "If some idea of mine struck John as useful," said Koch, "he would stop his sketching and often improvise the action for a whole scene."

John met with York a couple of times while they were writing the script and again on the set. York had made three requests: He wanted

Gary Cooper to portray him; he didn't want a sexy Hollywood star to play his wife; and he wanted the film to be truthful. "Everyone stood in proper awe of this foremost of living American heroes," Huston remembered.

Warner's had to let Sam Goldwyn have Bette Davis for *Little Foxes* to get Cooper, Joan Leslie (the club-footed girl in *High Sierra*) played the girl York would marry, and the spirit if not the facts of York's life was kept true enough to keep York from making any protests. It became the most successful picture Warner Bros. had in years and earned Huston and his co-writers an Oscar nomination for Best Original Screenplay.

When they finished writing *Sergeant York*, Huston's thoughts were elsewhere. He was preparing a draft of *The Maltese Falcon* and the house he had designed in Tarzana was ready for him and Lesley and her mother to move into.

"We had no architect," Lesley said. "John made a sketch of the house, simply, and talked to an architect and drew up plans for the builder. It was a beautiful house, based on John's sketch."

John had hired the same contractor who had built Walter's house. As John described it, "The land was some seven acres at the foot of a high hill, and it had two small knolls on it. The house was built on those two knolls with a bridge between them to serve as a gallery. A pool came out from beneath the bridge, and you could dive into it from the rear veranda. The valley was quite hot, so I designed a small attic space with louvers running the length of the roof."

Huston was very proud of the house, with the spacious ceilings, and when his contractor asked if he could bring the renowned architect Frank Lloyd Wright to see it, John and Lesley welcomed him like visiting royalty.

"He arrived with his pupils behind him, like a sort of Jesus and his disciples," Lesley said. "And he looked like a shepherd, with a sort of shepherd's crook, and he had flowing white hair and a cape. When he got to the front door there was a threshold, a slight step into the hall, and he said, 'Oh, that . . . of course, I don't believe in that at all.' The living room was a big room with a big open wood ceiling; high, very high. He looked up at that and said, 'Don't like that at all.' He was very much for low ceilings at that time. And John said, 'I'm very tall, I like space. All my life I've had to go under things.' And he looked at John and said, 'Oh, yes, any man over five-foot-seven is a weed!'

"We were amused. We went out in the back and he said, 'Oh, so beautiful! It's wonderful! I *dread* to turn and look at the house!' He finally left and the next day we heard from a friend of his that Wright had said about our house, 'Not bad . . . not bad at all. Of course, only I could have given those young people what they really wanted.' "

The only person who could have given John what he really wanted was Jack Warner, who did, when he made *The Maltese Falcon* a "go" project. And the person John most wanted to tell the good news to was his father, who had completed two films since returning from New York and was committed to do four others.

William Dieterle had left Warner Bros. to form his own company and had cast Walter as the devil, Mr. Scratch, in Stephen Vincent Benét's *The Devil and Daniel Webster*. (The movie was originally called *A Certain Mr. Scratch* and finally released as *The Devil and Daniel Webster*.) Edward Arnold was hired as Daniel Webster and James Craig as Jebez Stone, the poor New Hampshire farmer so down on his luck that he summons up old Scratch when he curses his fate as being "enough to sell a man's soul to the devil—and I would for two cents." Walter, sporting a jacket and a hat, wearing a goatee, with thick eyebrows and a puckish manner, all smiles and shrewdness, full of cunning and charm, is so riveting he helped turn the movie into an American classic, one still frequently shown on television today.

It was a performance so rich and delightful, it earned Walter another Best Actor nomination. "He was so great in that part, it was like a revelation," remembered Jeff Corey, who had a small part in the picture. "It was one of the great performances of all time. If you liked acting, you had to like him."

Corey remembers that "it was a succès d'estime, but it didn't make any money. And the version they have now on TV has been atrociously cut because they had to fit in commercials. I was told that the only full copy of it is in the Soviet Union."

While he still had his devil's goatee, Walter went with Nan to visit her brother, who lived on a ranch in Porterville, in the middle of California. Walter claimed to have no interest in the area, but when his brother-in-law told him about a three-thousand-acre piece of property that was for sale nearby, Walter went to see it and decided to buy the land, along with three hundred head of cattle. He had a small cabin built and, at the age of fifty-seven, decided to become a cowboy.

When he and Nan moved into their new cabin, Walter began to attend Farm Administration meetings and visited the county seats of several nearby counties in his attempt to become a learned rancher. "The ranch is just far enough away from Hollywood," he told a reporter, "that being an actor means nothing at all."

Walter got into the role of being a cowboy by agreeing to play one for Howard Hughes. Ben Hecht had written a script about Billy the Kid. Hughes bought it and hired Howard Hawks to direct. It told the story of the young gunslinger Billy and his developing friendship with Doc Holliday as they fought off Sheriff Pat Garrett and fought for the affections of a beautiful young girl. An unknown actor named Jack Beutel was hired to play Billy; an unknown chiropodist's receptionist named Jane Russell was turned into a $150-a-week actress and played the sexy, spunky love interest; Thomas Mitchell was cast as the sheriff; and Walter was Doc Holliday. The movie was shot in Arizona, but when Hughes looked at the early rushes and didn't see any clouds in the sky, he wired Hawks that he should take his time and wait until there were some clouds worth photographing. Hawks responded by suggesting Hughes take over the direction himself, that way he could shoot it exactly the way he wanted it. And that's what Hughes did. He resumed shooting at his own pace, which often included filming throughout the night.

The Outlaw made Jane Russell an overnight star after George Hurrell's photograph of her lying languidly in a haystack appeared on the cover of *Life*. Walter was upstaged by Jane Russell's jugs, which so fascinated Hughes that he designed a seamless brassiere to better display them. His design was never used, however, as Russell found it "uncomfortable and ridiculous."

For Walter it was a solid performance in an amateurish movie, but he had come a long way since *The Virginian*, his bad guy wasn't really bad, his confidence around horses and guns was evident, and he kept his opinions of his eccentric director to himself.

Then, as John was preparing to direct his first feature, Walter took a supporting role (although he had star billing) as a Southerner wronged by an unfaithful wife in Jean Renoir's first American film, *Swamp Water*, shot on location in Georgia's Okefenokee swamp. He was earning $6,000 a week for such roles and figured he could put the money into cattle. He also told John that he wanted to appear in *The Maltese Falcon*, for good luck.

"I made drawings of every setup," Huston said, describing how he meticulously sketched each scene as he envisioned it. Alfred Hitchcock would use this method throughout his career, but Huston abandoned it after his first picture. While Huston drew, Paul Kohner worked diligently on his client's behalf, negotiating Huston's new contract with Warner Bros. The previous year John had written four scripts for Warner's and received $56,000—an average of $14,000 per script. On May 26, 1941, Huston signed a 68⅓-week contract which stipulated that he would receive $1,250 per week for the first 16⅓ weeks and $1,500 per week for the next fifty-two. The contract also included the studio's option to pick up Huston's services through September 15, 1946, with an increase of $250 per week each year.

With Huston taken care of, Warner's tried to convince George Raft and Geraldine Fitzgerald, two of their contract players, to star in the film. By mid-May Henry Blanke wrote a note to Hal Wallis saying that he had met with Mary Astor and given her the script of The Maltese Falcon, in case Fitzgerald turned it down. Wallis, in turn, wrote to casting director Steve Trilling to give his approval of Astor if Fitzgerald said no. (Fitzgerald did bow out and Astor was engaged.) George Raft was expected to play Sam Spade until four days before the picture was scheduled to begin. On June 6 he wrote directly to Jack Warner, saying, "As you know, I strongly feel that The Maltese Falcon, which you want me to do, is not an important picture and, in this connection, I must remind you again, before I signed the new contract with you, you promised me that you would not require me to perform in anything but important pictures."

Raft neglected to write that he didn't think much of Huston and certainly didn't want to be directed by a first-time director. Huston wasn't a fan of Raft's either. "He fancied himself an actor, but he was not really a good actor."

With Raft out and the picture ready to shoot, Warner's decided to take Humphrey Bogart off suspension (he refused to appear in Bad Men of Missouri) and stick him in this low-budget gangster flick. When Huston was told who his leading man was to be, "I thanked God. It was a blessing!"

It also proved a blessing that the studio allowed Huston to use his artist's eye when it came to casting Sydney Greenstreet and Peter Lorre as the bad guys who would stop at nothing to lay their hands on the black bird. Greenstreet, sixty-one years old and 285 pounds, had made his living as a stage actor and had never been in a film before, but he was the perfect Fat Man, Casper Gutman, as Dashiell Hammett described him: "Flabbily fat with bulbous pink cheeks and lips and chin and neck, with a great soft egg of a belly that was all his torso . . ." The German

Lorre, who had so chillingly played a child-murderer in Fritz Lang's M, was memorably cast as the perverse perfumed Joel Cairo. Huston considered him "one of the finest and most subtle actors I have ever worked with. Beneath that air of innocence he used to such effect, one sensed a Faustian worldliness."

Huston's own worldliness impressed Mary Astor, as the two of them worked together privately on the characterization of the "amoral Brigid O'Shaughnessy." As Huston rehearsed her tremulous, pleading, hesitant voice, with her lying eyes full of candor, she became his perfect notion of the "enchanting murderess." And as she fell under his hypnotic spell, he was captivated by her beauty and ability. He was a first-time director; she was his leading lady with a checkered past. His marriage had reached a nadir, and his wife showed no signs of coming out of her depression.

They were about to embark on something more than just another "B" movie. And so, when they entered into a liaison that would never make the gossip columns, it was with a sense of lightness and joy. Except for John's closest friends, like Willy Wyler, no one was the wiser. But Wyler's wife, Talli, was upset. "It was the first time that I was aware of John's infidelities," she said, "the first time that I was aware that his marriage had a crack in it."

"It was Huston's picture, Huston's script," Mary Astor wrote in *A Life on Film*. "He'd had the wit to keep Hammett's book intact. His shooting script was a precise map of what went on. Every shot, camera move, entrance, exit was down on paper, leaving nothing to chance, inspiration or invention."

With his sketches drawn, Huston showed them to Willy Wyler, who made some important suggestions that Huston incorporated. Then he went to see Henry Blanke, who gave him the single most important piece of advice he would ever receive as a director: "Shoot each scene as if it was the most important scene in the film."

The Maltese Falcon was shot with Blanke's advice in mind, as Huston faithfully transposed Hammett's characters to the screen. The hero—or, in more modern terms, the antihero—Sam Spade, is a cold-hearted, selfish, cynical manipulator; a greedy gambler, attracted to evil, able to coolly pull off an affair with his partner's wife and just as coolly drop her when his partner is killed.

Morally ambiguous, he is able to tell the woman who killed his partner but whom he may have fallen in love with: "If you're a good girl, you'll be out in twenty years. I'll be waiting for you. If they hang you, I'll always remember you." It's a complex portrait of a special kind of private eye, a portrait Huston felt at home with.

"The story was a dramatization of myself, of how I felt about things," Huston said. "Hammett's mentality and philosophy were quite congenial to me, and I implicitly accepted Hammett's writing. He was one of the great American writers. I attempted to transpose his highly individual style into camera terms with sharp photography, geographically exact camera movements, and striking but not shocking setups. The book was told entirely from the standpoint of Sam Spade, so also was the picture. There could not be a scene in which Sam did not appear. The audience was to know nothing Sam didn't know. And they meet the other characters only when Sam does. There was just one exception when Sam doesn't appear in a scene. That's where his partner, Archer, is shot. You only see the gun come onto the screen and don't know who fired it. The studio wanted that. I didn't. I reconciled myself by saying, 'That's really not a part of my picture.' "

The district attorney questioned Spade about two murders. If he has nothing to conceal, he has nothing to fear, the D.A. says. "Everybody has something to conceal," Spade answers. As Colin McArthur wrote in *Underworld USA*, "This remark could stand as a text for *The Maltese Falcon*, in which nothing is as it seems: personal identities are shifting and uncertain, relationships are characterized by duplicity and even objects prove false."

When Elisha Cook, Jr., reported for work as the lackey who did the dirty work for the Fat Man, he hadn't seen the script. "I never met John until I walked on the set," the pugnacious actor recalled. "I didn't know any of the other actors. It was a job, meat and potatoes." And forever after, *The Maltese Falcon* would leave its mark upon Cook, as he was continuously called upon to play "pimps, informers, cocksuckers."

But for Bogart and Huston, the movies would never be what they had been before the *Falcon*. "Bogart was a second-class star," Huston remarked, "who then became a big star." Released from his gangster roles, he showed that he could win over audiences by playing a tough, no-nonsense good guy antihero. As Otto Friedrich noted, "*The Maltese Falcon* was the movie in which he created the persona that not only made him famous for the rest of his life but gradually became his own permanent identity." As for Huston, it established him as a major talent. He no longer agonized over whether he should be a writer, a painter, a set designer. He was a director. He could be them all.

What often is noted about *The Maltese Falcon* is the way each camera shot is so carefully framed, how the lighting sets the mood, how the low camera angles make Gutman even broader and more menacing. "By the time I got around to making motion pictures," Huston said, "the great painters were so much a part of me. I was certainly aware of how Seurat framed his pictures. And Toulouse-Lautrec framed marvelously. He made a great point of it."

"The *Falcon* was a jigsaw puzzle," Mary Astor observed, "and each scene related to what had happened before and what was to happen—precisely." It all had to be orchestrated and Huston's personal intensity was infectious; he excited his actors and crew, and when the day came to begin shooting, they were all prepared and the work went fast.

"There was something in John's personality that everybody wanted to do the best job they could," Meta Wilde, the script supervisor, recalled. "He was such a gentleman, courteous to everybody, he made it easy to want to go to work."

"Mary dear, hold my hand, tell me I won't make an ass of meself!" begged Sydney Greenstreet of Mary Astor just before he was to appear in his first movie scene—where he had to give a long monologue telling the history of the Black Bird as he waited for the knockout drops he had put in Sam Spade's drink to take effect. As Greenstreet so perfectly spoke his lines, Huston found himself holding his breath, a subconscious practice he continued throughout his career.

Another scene between Greenstreet and Bogart was the most technically complex in the film, a scene that Huston and his cinematographer, Arthur Edeson, devised between them so that the camera could follow twenty-two uninterrupted moves. "It was an incredible camera setup, we rehearsed two days," Meta Wilde said. "The camera followed Greenstreet and Bogart from one room into another, then down a long hallway, and finally into a living room; there the camera moved up and down in what is referred to as a boom-up and boom-down shot, then panned from left to right and back to Bogart's drunken face; the next pan shot was to Greenstreet's massive stomach from Bogart's point of view. The choreography of it was exacting and exciting. One miss and we had to begin all over again. But there was the understanding that we were attempting something purely cinematic, never tried before, and everyone—stars, camera operators, and cablemen—worked industriously to bring it off. . . . After a nerve-racking seven minutes or so, Huston shouted, 'Cut' and 'PRINT IT!' A shout went up and crew members heartily applauded Bogart, Greenstreet, and Edeson and his camera specialists."

Huston was so impressed with Arthur Edeson's work that in an article for *The American Cinematographer* in December 1941 he confessed that "Not so long ago, my concept of cameramen was that they were nice fellows who concentrated their efforts on turning out pretty compositions and making the leading lady look glamorous.

"But that was before a change from writing scripts to directing them put me out on the set actually to work with these men of the camera. Practical experience very quickly forced me to revise my ideas, and convinced me that the industry's cinematographers are, as a class, perhaps the most invaluable and yet generally underrated men in Hollywood."

Walter came to play his "good luck" cameo as the wounded ship captain who staggers into Spade's office with the falcon, mutters something about the bird, and then falls dead. It was a brief, simple scene, but John couldn't let his father off easily. He shot it over and over again, holding back his laughter as Walter kept dying and complaining, "Didn't expect to have to put in a day's *work.*"

"Sorry, Dad, you missed your mark," Huston would say. Or, "This time, try it without staggering so much." By the time Walter left the set, he was in a foul mood, but John wasn't finished with him. The next day he had Mary Astor call Walter, pretending to be John's secretary.

"Mr. Huston is sorry," she said, "but something happened to the film in the lab and we'll have to retake your sequence this afternoon. Could you be ready to shoot at one o'clock?"

"You tell my son to get another actor or go to hell!" Walter screamed as Astor held the receiver out so everyone could hear. "He made me take twenty falls, and I'm sore all over, and I'm not about to take twenty more."

Even though it was his first picture and he was being watched by the Warner executives, Huston felt comfortable enough on the set to break for long lunches with his actors at the nearby Lakeside Golf Club and plan elaborate practical jokes on unwanted visitors. "We had an odd, childlike territorial imperative about our set," Mary Astor said. "It was hard work, and we didn't want anyone looking over our shoulder. Also, we had a sneaky feeling that we were doing something different and exciting, and we didn't want to show it to anyone until it was finished."

When the publicity department brought a group of priests to the set they watched as Mary Astor sat in Spade's office and elaborately crossed her knees. Before the scene was shot, Astor looked down and said, "Hold it a minute, I've got a goddamn run in my stocking." The PR man turned pale and quickly ushered out the priests and the crew hollered their delight. She had inadvertently found a way to get on-lookers off the set.

Astor was impressed with Bogart's "brilliant" technical skill. "His precision timing was no accident. He kept other actors on their toes because he *listened* to them, he *watched* them, he *looked* at them." She described his smile as "a mistake that he tried to keep from happening." And she felt that he "related to people as though they had no clothes on. If they grabbed at their various little hypocrisies for protective cover, his laugh was a particularly unpleasant chortle."

Bogart was generous when it came to praising his director, whom he thought was "just a mite teched with genius. You have to be a mite teched to be a genius." He went on to say, "One reason Huston is so good is he makes the book. He doesn't write in new characters or themes. That's what he did with *The Maltese Falcon.*"

Huston actually did make some changes, but they were meant to clarify not to obstruct. In the book, Casper Gutman gets shot by his own man at the end, but Huston liked the Fat Man too much to do him in. Also, when the detective asks Spade what the falcon is, he replies, "The stuff that dreams are made of." It's the last and most quoted line of the film and it wasn't in the book. For forty-eight years the line has been attributed to Huston. "This would be in the way of a revelation," Huston confessed toward the end of his life. "It's never come up, but that last line in the *Falcon* . . . it was Bogie's idea. It's been quoted a number of times, but this is the first opportunity I've had to tell where the credit for it lies. Before we shot that scene Bogie said to me, 'John, don't you think it would be a good idea, this line? Be a good ending?' And it certainly was."

Huston was visiting his father on the United Artists' set of *The Shanghai Gesture,* directed by Josef von Sternberg, when the trade reviews came out, raving about *The Maltese Falcon.* "My father met me when I went over to the set; he had read the trades, and he said, 'My God, this is terrific, John.' And von Sternberg congratulated me. I didn't really know how terrific it was."

He found out soon enough; the movie was released on October 3, 1941, and was generously praised by the major critics. John was in New York at the time, working again with Howard Koch on their Woodrow Wilson play, when he read what the New York papers had to say. "*The Maltese Falcon* . . . only turns out to be the best mystery thriller of the year, and young Huston gives promise of becoming one of the smartest directors in the field," said the *New York Times*. The *New York Herald Tribune* called it ". . . a classic in its field. It is hard to say whether Huston the adapter or Huston the fledgling director is most responsible for this triumph. In any case, it is a knockout job of cinematic melodrama."

In years to come the French would credit the movie with starting a new genre called *film noir*—dark, urban, brutal, disturbing, misogynistic stories focusing on private eyes. James Agee and Pauline Kael would continue to praise it as "The best private-eye melodrama ever made" and "The most high-style thriller ever made in America." And director Richard Brooks, who co-wrote *Key Largo* with Huston in 1947–48, would observe that all the elements of what he considered a recognizable Huston style were there at the beginning, in the *Falcon*.

John's involvement with Koch and their play about Wilson lasted only a few weeks before he got the call from Warner Bros. to take on *In This Our Life*, a major, star-studded picture. As Koch had written the script, he didn't mind that John returned to Hollywood while he remained behind to work with John Houseman, who came on as a writer for *In Time to Come*. Otto Preminger, who wanted to direct it, optioned the play for $500.

"I felt rather ashamed of the way I got into *In This Our Life*," Huston told film historian Gerald Pratley. "[Director/producer] Bryan Foy said, 'You don't really rate as a director until you've worked with the stars and show how you make out with them!' With *In This Our Life*, ambition stepped in. It was laid out on a silver platter—the biggest stars in Warner Bros. all together: Bette Davis, Olivia de Havilland, George Brent, Dennis Morgan, Charles Coburn. I thought, Oh, boy, I've arrived!"

Then he studied the script, which he later told de Havilland he never understood. "It was really not my kind of picture at all. More of a soap opera. But here was a chance to work in the 'Big Time.' So I did it. Because it was good for my career. Balls! One should never do anything that's good for one's career. Every time I've done that, I've fallen right on my ass."

The film, based on a Pulitzer Prize–winning novel by Ellen Glasgow, was a story about the modern South and dealt with jealousy, deceit, suicide, bigotry, and self-destruction. Bette Davis got the role of the spoiled, mean-spirited, older sister, Stanley, who steals her younger, decent, and kindhearted sister's husband away, then torments him until he kills himself. She wreaks havoc on everybody's life, implicating a black law student in a crime she commits and finally killing herself in a car crash.

The only thing about the film that interested Huston was the way it presented the law student. "It was the first time that a black man had ever been treated other than as comedy relief or as a faithful servant. He was a character in his own right."

Off the set John became strongly attracted to de Havilland. Second picture, second star . . . but this time it was more serious. At twenty-five, Olivia de Havilland had become known to the public acting opposite Errol Flynn in such films as *Captain Blood* and *The Adventures of Robin Hood*, and had achieved stardom as Melanie in *Gone With the Wind*. She had been linked with Flynn, Howard Hughes, and Jimmy Stewart—tall, lanky men, built like Huston but lacking his intellect and passion. She had also a strong rivalry with her younger sister, Joan Fontaine, which made certain aspects of *In This Our Life* seem almost autobiographical.

On the first day of shooting certain players from *The Maltese Falcon* turned up to make uncredited cameo appearances. When the script called for a shadow of a man on an office door, Humphrey Bogart cast his. Walter appeared as a bartender who shows his disgust at Bette Davis's behavior. When Olivia saw the congenial way John behaved with his father and the look that passed between them, she began to feel there was something special and tender about him. When she and John realized their mutual attraction, they became entangled in a romance that wasn't kept out of the press, as his affair with Mary Astor had been.

"I knew very little about Olivia," Lupita Kohner recalled, "but we were very good friends with Lesley, and that affair is what broke their marriage."

Lesley was more discreet: "John just didn't have the constitution to stay settled. He always needed to have a challenge arise and something new coming up. Things happened when he made his second picture, but that's private."

It may have been a private matter to Lesley, but it was a very public affair, as articles were written about "Livvy's New Love" and how she expected to marry Huston as soon as he could free himself. Even forty-five years later the actress told writer Dotson Rader, "There was a man, someone I felt very, very deeply about after my long-term crush on Errol Flynn. He was a man I wanted to marry, and knowing him was a powerful experience, one I thought I would never get over. I watched him bring great destruction into the lives of other women. Maybe he was the great love of my life. Yes, he probably was."

"Olivia wanted to get married," Huston acknowledged, "but it was just impossible for me to get married at that time. She really was a wonderful, marvelous person."

When Howard Koch returned to Los Angeles he saw John looking "as troubled as I ever remembered him. He put his problem bluntly": He still loved Lesley but he was *in* love with Olivia—"and they were having an affair."

"Olivia was not an easy woman to win over," Howard Koch recalled. "She was very attractive and she wasn't out to get another woman's husband. John had to do the leading there because she was a rather serious person. She had some of the qualities that were in Lesley. She was not an easy pickup. And with John, it was partly a game: Here was a beautiful woman, could he win her?"

"She was crazy about John," Talli Wyler said about de Havilland. "Women *were* crazy about John. And Olivia just always comes on very emotionally. It's typical of her character to come on at a very high pitch about almost everything."

De Havilland first met John in the thirties, during Max Reinhardt's radio broadcast of *The Miracle*. "Miriam Hopkins and I played the two women characters and John played the male character," she recalled. "I didn't see him again until *In This Our Life*. He had just done *The Maltese Falcon*, which was not an 'A' film, although, of course, he made it one."

It was Olivia's hope that their relationship would also be recognized— not just by a titillating press, but legally. "The idea was that as soon as he could get a divorce, we would get married, but so many destructive things happened. It was a very difficult situation. He had not been formally separated from his wife, but the marriage had been in difficulty for about a year. I had very strict ideas about a relationship and I didn't want to be destructive. He assured me I didn't have to worry about that. We tried awfully hard not to make anything evident. Only the close friends knew."

Once John showed his interest, she found him to be romantic and vulnerable. "I remember his desire for children was quite strong and he was afraid that he couldn't have them. He knew that I was a person who would want children and he was afraid that he couldn't give them to me.

"John had a largeness of spirit that was wonderful. I loved his conversations. He was always full of ideas and reactions. And he was very articulate. He knew a great deal about all the things I cared about. He knew a lot about painting, he had read a great deal. All of that to me was immensely exciting. It was a powerful coming together of two people when our relationship began in November and December of 1941, when we shot *In This Our Life*."

During the making of the film neither Hal Wallis nor Jack Warner was happy with the way Huston was allowing Bette Davis to chew up the scenery. Nor did they like the way Huston was favoring de Havilland with camera angles and close-ups. When Wallis first saw the rushes, he exclaimed, "My God, John, hold Bette Davis down."

"She's doing what I want her to do," Huston replied.

"You're wrong," Wallis said. "She's just going wild with this picture."

"That's the way it should be," Huston said.

When Jack Warner saw the way the picture was going, "he was even more convinced than Hal Wallis that Bette Davis was tearing the picture to pieces," Huston said. When Warner challenged Huston's direction, John brashly told him. "This is the only way I see to do it. If you don't agree with it, find another director."

Huston saw "something elemental" in Bette Davis, as if she had "a demon within her which threatens to break out and eat everybody. The studio confused it with overacting. Over their objections, I let the demon go."

Warner invited both Bette Davis and de Havilland to the projection room to show Davis "how Huston's manly pulse, beating for Olivia, had ruined her big scenes." At first Davis didn't protest, but then Warner baited her by saying he wouldn't go to the preview. Then Davis got angry. "She used all the four-letter words, and some that were new to me," Warner wrote in his autobiography. "She came close to tearing out every seat in Projection Room No. 5, and she would have given everyone a punch in the nose if I hadn't interfered.

"The next day Huston reshot many scenes he had taken from Bette Davis and it turned into quite an important film. Bette later made her peace with Olivia, but after that she wouldn't have Huston around driving a truck."

Olivia herself was on the verge of collapse during the making of *In This Our Life*, having made two pictures back-to-back—*They Died With Their Boots On* and *The Male Animal*—before getting involved physically with this film and emotionally with its director. She had also coveted Bette Davis's part, as she was tired of playing the good sister. But de Havilland claimed that she and Bette Davis "became friends on that film and have remained friends ever since. She was absolutely stunning! She thought of nothing but the development of the role when she was working."

Halfway through *In This Our Life* Huston began making plans with Willy Wyler and director Anatole Litvak to go to China. "I'd never been to the Far East," he said, "nor had Willy or Tola. We were all right in our prime. We could just shove off and support each other." On December 7, Litvak had arranged for a travel agent to come to his house in Malibu and Huston and Wyler agreed to meet there to go over the route. While they were at Wyler's house, Paul Kohner called and told Talli that the Japanese had bombed Pearl Harbor.

"Everyone immediately started talking about how fast they could get into the army," Talli Wyler remembered. "There was no way, with their natures, that they could sit out this war."

Soon after Pearl Harbor John informed Warner Bros. that he had volunteered for the Signal Corps, where he would be given an officer's commission. Willy Wyler had enlisted in the air force. It would take four months before Huston's orders came through, and during that time he continued working at the studio.

"There was a scare here where there had been no reason for one," Huston remembered. "Apparently, the Japanese had surfaced a submarine and fired a few rounds at some oil wells along the coast. It was a comedy—the sky was full of searchlights in Los Angeles. Even guns were fired." And the next day Harry Warner called a meeting of all the departments at Warner's to talk about gearing their pictures to help fight the enemy.

With the country at war, and while waiting for his orders, Huston completed *In This Our Life* as Howard Koch returned to New York to make final preparations for their Wilson play, which suddenly seemed badly timed. "The play was quite starved," Huston said, "it needed fleshing out. Howard would send an act to me and I would put a couple of licks in and then neglect it." John Houseman was also working on the play.

Houseman, who resented Huston for that drunken car accident with his former wife, Zita Johann, found himself in a strange position, since at the time Huston was involved with Olivia, he was "the lover of her sister. That's a snakepit right there. The whole thing was extremely difficult and fairly unpleasant. That was a very strange relationship he had [with Olivia]. I got into a situation with John where people were repeating things about us, so that for years there was a kind of shadow between us.

"I got involved in that play he and Howard wrote about Woodrow Wilson. It was the wrong time, of course. We finally got a production in New York, but there were too many names on it, so I never put mine on."

The play opened at the Mansfield Theatre on W. 47th Street on December 28 to decent reviews but to an uninterested audience. John Anderson, in the *Journal American*, called it a "Genuinely exciting evening in the theater." Richard Cooke in the *Wall Street Journal* believed, "There can hardly be anyone who has seen or will see *In Time to Come* who will not feel that the course of his own life is affected by what the play has to say." Brooks Atkinson wrote in the *New York Times*: "What makes *In Time to Come* a moving and memorable experience is the central portrait of a man broken by a faith that is not shared by the politicians with whom he is dealing. His ordeal is a cruel one. To have an exalted idea on a magnificent scale [the League of Nations] and then to have it pared down, subordinated to a destructive peace and finally repudiated by his own people is to endure great pain."

Despite many positive reviews, the play ran only until the end of January and would have been forgotten except that when Darryl Zanuck decided to make a movie about Woodrow Wilson two years later, he borrowed some of *In Time to Come*. "Zanuck used, by far, our best scene, between Wilson and Henry Cabot Lodge," John Houseman said, "which became the best scene in the picture."

Because of his commitment to his second picture, John remained in Los Angeles and never saw the play performed. On Christmas Eve, four days before the play opened in New York, Henry Blanke had a party to which John and Lesley were invited. John told Lesley that he would meet her there after making the rounds at the various office parties at the studio. But John never showed up. People at Blanke's house felt sorry for Lesley as she tried to make excuses for him. They all knew that the studio festivities had long been over and that John was probably with Olivia.

In February, Jack Warner wired his New York story editor, Jacob Wilk, to ask if there was any chance they could get Dashiell Hammett to write a sequel to *The Maltese Falcon*, but got angry a month later when he heard that Hammett actually wanted to be paid decent money to do it. He fired off another wire to Wilk saying, "Won't give Hammett over $5,000 guarantee for *Falcon* sequel. If he hasn't confidence in his ability to write an acceptable story, let's forget it."

Warner's decided to go ahead and make another picture using most of *The Maltese Falcon* cast and crew, hoping to repeat the magic. The picture they decided on was *Across the Pacific*, written by Robert Macaulay and based on a *Saturday Evening Post* serial, "Aloha Means Goodbye," by Robert Carson. The script, which had to do with a Japanese plot to destroy Pearl Harbor, was written before December 7, and so had to be reconstructed.

While the script was being rewritten, Hollywood was focused on the Academy Awards for 1941. Both *The Maltese Falcon* and *Sergeant York* had been nominated for Best Picture, along with eight others, including Orson Welles's first film, *Citizen Kane*; *Here Comes Mr. Jordan*; *The Little Foxes*; *Suspicion*; and *How Green Was My Valley*. Walter Huston was up for Best Actor for *The Devil and Daniel Webster*, competing against Welles, Gary Cooper (*Sergeant York*), Robert Montgomery (*Here Comes Mr. Jordan*), and Cary Grant (*Penny Serenade*). Both Sydney Greenstreet and Walter Brennan were nominated for Best Supporting Actor for *The Maltese Falcon* and *Sergeant York*. And Mary Astor and Margaret Wycherly were up for Best Supporting Actress, Wycherly for *Sergeant York*, but Astor, surprisingly, for *The Great Lie* and not for *Falcon*. Huston was passed over for Best Director (the Oscar would go to John Ford for *How Green Was My Valley*, which also won Best Picture), but he was nominated for Best Screenplay (*The Maltese Falcon*) and Best Original Screenplay (along with Harry Chandler, Abem Finkel, and Howard Koch for *Sergeant York*).

But what made the Oscars memorable that year was that Olivia de Havilland and Joan Fontaine were competing against each other (and against Bette Davis, Greer Garson, and Barbara Stanwyck) for Best Actress. De Havilland was up for *Hold Back the Dawn* and Fontaine for *Suspicion*. All of Hollywood knew that there was no love lost between the sisters, and Joan Fontaine, who won that year, would later say that her older sister disliked her from the day she was born: "My mother told me that Olivia would not even look into the crib after I arrived."

Talli Wyler remembered that Oscar ceremony, where she and Willy shared a table with John and Lesley. "Olivia was sitting across the dance floor and it was uncomfortably obvious that John was blowing kisses at Olivia."

It had been an uncomfortable evening for Olivia: seeing John across the floor with Lesley; having to endure Ginger Rogers's announcing Joan as the Best Actress of 1941; having to deal with the press afterward. But Olivia was a pro and she managed to act her way through the evening.

Walter lost out to Gary Cooper, which came as no surprise, since *Sergeant York* was one of the biggest hits of the year, and John lost his two writing nominations to Orson Welles and Herman J. Mankiewicz for *Citizen Kane* and to Sidney Buchman and Seton I. Miller for *Here Comes Mr. Jordan*. Sydney Greenstreet didn't get an Oscar either, but Mary Astor did. Later, Astor would write, "I would have preferred getting my Oscar for Brigid rather than for Sandra [in *The Great Lie*]."

If the evening was awkward for Olivia de Havilland, it was also strange for Mary Astor, who was still fond of John. As for John, who was there with his wife, blowing kisses at Olivia and beaming his gracious smile at Mary, it was all part of the Hollywood circus that he could thoroughly enjoy, knowing that soon he would be called to serve and would be far away from all the glamour and tension of musical romances.

Patriotism was very much a part of Hollywood in the early forties, as each studio did its best to contribute to the war effort. The most patriotic movie of all turned out to be about Walter Huston's old friend and director, George M. Cohan. Cohan had led the kind of life that seemed suitable for a musical biography, and writer Robert Buckner got to know the showman, convincing him that the story of his life would make a good film.

Buckner outlined a story only to be thwarted by Cohan when he saw that Buckner wanted to fictionalize his life. James Cagney's brother, William, got involved because he wanted his brother to star as Cohan. Cagney had been falsely named as a member of the Communist party, and even after he had appeared before a congressional committee to clear his name, the smear still worried him. A film about such a staunchly pro-American figure as the man who wrote and performed "Over There" and "Yankee Doodle Dandy" would go far to change the public's attitude.

It took Buckner and William Cagney six months to convince Cohan that altering his life story for dramatic effect would only make the movie better. They promised Cohan to stick to the spirit if not the facts of his life, and Cohan finally came around to seeing it their way. Cohan was pleased that Walter Huston was cast as George's father, as his scenes would mostly revolve around the vaudevillian acts of the Four Cohans. For Walter it was a trip down memory lane, a chance to do a little theatrical hoofing, and a way of paying back Cohan for the confidence he had shown in him.

The story was told by flashback, with Cohan going to the White House to see President Roosevelt and then retelling the story of his life.

Cagney pulled out all the stops in a tour de force Oscar-winning performance (Walter also would be nominated for Best Supporting Actor) that made *Yankee Doodle Dandy* one of the most successful pictures Warner Bros. ever made.

With the picture in the can, Walter told a journalist that he was beginning to change his mind about Hollywood. "I think motion pictures are getting better all the time. Scripts are sounder and more intelligent now than they were five years ago. Direction is keener. Actors are both more direct and more imaginative. We're making an increasing number of films which aren't about love."

When he finished with *Yankee Doodle*, Walter agreed to do another film, *Always in My Heart*, where he got to work with an old acting partner, Kay Francis. Walter played the part of an innocent man who, after spending thirteen years in prison, returns to the fishing village where he and his family had lived. He finds his children are grown and his wife is being courted by another man; rather than interfere, he keeps his distance, until his two daughters create complications that bring him back to the family.

It was exactly the kind of film that made Walter long for substance, and he found that his son, who was involved with *Across the Pacific*, was thinking along the same lines. The two men talked about doing four films together as soon as the war ended: Dostoyevski's *The Gambler*; Theodore Dreiser's *Sister Carrie*; the life of Tolstoy, whom Walter felt he physically resembled; and *Moby Dick*. John even had a writer friend, Charlie Grayson, begin work on a treatment of Melville's great epic. But when their talk wasn't about the future, it turned to the past, and they would find themselves stirring old memories and laughing to the bemusement of the surrounding crew.

On March 6, 1942, the Signal Corps sent John an order to report to Washington, D.C., on March 20. But Huston got a sixty-day deferment, which enabled him to make *Across the Pacific*.

So, by mid-March, the cameras began to roll on Huston's third film. Bogart played an undercover agent named Rick who joins a Japanese boat going through the Panama Canal in order to keep an eye on a Japanese sympathizer played by Sydney Greenstreet. Rick discovers the Japanese plan to bomb the canal, but he manages to foil the attack in a somewhat ludicrous ending, where he destroys the bomber in a hail of machine-gun fire.

Mary Astor marveled at the "remarkable reproduction" of the boat the studio had constructed. "We had several genuine cases of seasickness." And she was delighted with the joke John played on Sydney Greenstreet when Peter Lorre visited the set.

"One afternoon Lorre donned a white coat and walked through a scene in which Sydney, Bogie, and I were being served breakfast on the ship. We didn't know John had made the switch with the actor who was playing the waiter. He was behind us, so we couldn't see him, and Peter served us, making tiny mistakes—holding a platter a bit too far away, just touching Sydney's arm as he lifted a cup of coffee. Finally he leaned down and kissed me on the back of the neck and we all broke up. We could always have fun, even though the subtle sense of success was not a part of this picture."

Huston also involved Bogart in a more elaborate practical joke that he played on Charlie Grayson, who would visit John on the set to discuss his progress with the *Moby Dick* treatment. "One day I got a call from some Jewish Relief organization," Huston recalled, "asking me if I could write something for them. I said yes. Then I said to Charlie, 'Would you do it for me?' He put everything he had into it and I called him and said, 'Charlie, they think it's marvelous and they want me to expand on it.' 'Sure,' Charlie said. Well, I kept it up. It became so good, I told Charlie that I told them who it was who was writing this and they wanted to know if Charlie would consider making a speech at the Roosevelt Hotel. Charlie was flattered. A few days later I said a group of rabbis saw the event as much more important than what they originally planned and they wanted to take it to the Hollywood Bowl.

"As this was unfolding, I got a secretary of Hal Wallis's calling for additional pages on *Moby Dick*. This is all me, of course, nothing was really happening. So Charlie was burning the midnight oil, writing this speech for the Jewish Relief and writing dialogue for *Moby Dick* during studio hours. Now, Bogart had a wonderful Jewish accent, real Bronx-comedy Jewish. And Bogart became Rabbi so-and-so, the spokesman for this event. He made a luncheon date with Charlie. On the appointed day, we coached a secretary to call Charlie and tell him that there would be two dozen rabbis coming for lunch. Then Bogart got on the phone as the rabbi and talked to Charlie, who was twenty-five feet away from him on the other phone. Charlie couldn't have twenty-five rabbis in the studio dining room and he broke down entirely. He was going crazy. And that's when I told him the whole thing was a setup."

With the film winding down Huston got to play one last joke. He had received his orders from the Signal Corps but threw away the list of military names, thinking it was junk mail. Then, while on the set, he received a call for "Lieutenant Huston" directing him to report to Washington in four days. Huston needed a few more days to finish the film, but he did not want to resign his commission and so he had no choice.

He had shot to where Bogart was being held prisoner. He decided to "make things as difficult as possible for my successor. I had Bogie tied to a chair, and installed about three times as many Japanese soldiers as were needed to keep him prisoner. There were guards at every window brandishing machine guns. There was no way in God's green world that Bogart could logically escape. I shot the scene, then called Jack Warner and said, 'Jack, I'm on my way. I'm in the army. Bogie will know how to get out.' "

Bogie, naturally, did not. Neither did Vincent Sherman, the director assigned to complete the picture. So Sherman went backward rather than forward, took the ropes off Bogart and had only one guard in the room. Bogart easily disarmed him before going about his last-minute heroics.

Lesley was saddened by John's leaving; she knew him well enough to understand that he wouldn't be coming back to her. Walter was proud that John was going in as a lieutenant and wished he was younger so that he, too, could enlist and thereby make a clean break from Nan, who had become a burden to him. Olivia didn't know what to think since John had not yet divorced Lesley. She could only wait for him to come back in one piece so they could begin a new life together.

10

WOMEN AND WAR

FOUR DAYS AFTER JOHN LEFT FOR WASHINGTON, OLIVIA
followed. She had joined the Hollywood Victory Caravan, a group of
stars touring cross-country to help the war effort by selling war bonds.
Along with Olivia, such names as Bing Crosby, Cary Grant, Bob
Hope, James Cagney, Desi Arnaz, Charles Boyer, Claudette Colbert,
Bert Lahr, Laurel and Hardy, and Groucho Marx were part of the
Caravan.

Huston somehow managed to join them in Washington. But when
the Caravan moved on, he remained behind, suffering through the slow
pace of regimented military life. The Signal Corps didn't know quite
what to do with him. "No idea. They were nice guys, but nothing in
the way of brilliant."

What the corps came up with was to have Huston make his first
documentary, in Los Angeles. "It was about a B-25 and the compo-
nents that go to make a B-25. It was what amounted to a propaganda
film. It was to make people give their services to go and make airplanes,
and to keep their spirits up, to let them know that what they were
doing was a great thing. You see in the film how the B-25 was put
together—so you who helped make the bomb sight, your polished nails,

Madam, actually sank a Japanese submarine. It wasn't instructional and I didn't get any credit. Nobody got credit of any kind. My name isn't on any of the films I made during the war."

When John completed the film he returned to Washington. It was midsummer. "Jesus Christ, was it hot," he remembered. "We all had those woolen jackets. You weren't allowed to go in shirtsleeves. I remember being on the verge of tears, complaining bitterly to Tola Litvak about having nothing to do. They had me studying army charts, army protocol. And I thought it was important that I learn this. Then I realized they only had me do this to keep me occupied.

"Then Darryl Zanuck went on a trip to the Aleutians, which was the only theater in which we were active. And just as I was about to start sobbing about my situation in Washington, the bomb bays opened and there was Kiska."

John was ordered to the Aleutian Islands to lead a five-man crew in the making of a documentary about building an air base and about the air combat over the Japanese-held islands Attu and Kiska. Near the end of August John stopped off in California to see Olivia and to attend a series of meetings at Warner's. He had almost completed a screenplay of Eric Ambler's novel, *Background to Danger*, and negotiations had finally been completed with the illusive B. Traven for Huston to make a movie of his novel, *The Treasure of the Sierra Madre*. The Traven project would be put on hold. The Ambler thriller had been written for George Raft, who insisted that his part as a government agent be made more powerful. Raft's pompous insistence provided Huston with an exit line. "Gentlemen," he said, "I am going to the Aleutians." He signed over the rights to the Ambler script and left the power struggles of Hollywood for the desolation of the Aleutian Islands, where, over the next four months, he would be struck by the barrenness of the mountainous islands, "without a tree or anything like a tree for 1,500 miles."

Olivia de Havilland remembered "when he went off to the Aleutians in September of '42, it was a very difficult separation. And painful. When he was making *Across the Pacific* I didn't live with him, but he was a guest in my house, off and on, for more than two years. When he went to the Aleutians he was in great danger up there."

It was his introduction to war. He and his crew were given the opportunity to watch how soldiers prepared for battle. If it seemed dull, with men washing themselves out of their helmets and playing sad tunes on guitars and harmonicas, it picked up considerably when the Japanese flew over Adak and became aware of their presence. His two cameramen were Rey Scott and Jules Buck. Scott "was a man who had no regard for appearances, and no particular regard for authority," Huston said with admiration, "a bloody, no-good rogue and a lovely fellow." Buck "was my one-man army through the war," Huston said in an interview eighteen years later, before they had a major falling-out.

Making this film brought him up against his own fears. On his first flight in a B-24 the brakes froze as they came in for a landing at Adak and the plane skidded down the rain-soaked runway shearing off the wings of two other B-24s. When the plane finally came to a halt, someone screamed to get out fast, before the bombs went off. Huston grabbed a camera hoping to film the rescue team working to save the unconscious pilot and co-pilot under the threat of a sudden explosion. "I remember trying to get a shot, and saying to myself, 'Good man, Huston. Nerves of steel.' But just as I was congratulating myself I began to shake uncontrollably. I put the camera down and ran. The bombs didn't go off."

On another mission the cameras didn't work properly because of a simple technical mistake Huston had made—the film came out blank because he had forgotten to run out the leader in any of the cameras. It became the shot he never got and it would haunt him throughout his film career. It taught him the importance of understanding his equipment or, at least, making sure he worked with the best people he could find.

The realities of war made Huston see things differently. He became determined to capture what it was *really* like in the Aleutians, to record not just the occasional air battles but also the times in between, the long stretches when the weather became as much a factor as the enemy—the fog banks, the hurricane gales, the rain.

On his second flight to Kiska, the Japanese pilots attacked and Huston attempted to photograph the air battle over the shoulder of the waist gunner, who was killed in the action. "The belly gunner motioned me to take over his gun while he took the waist gun. . . . We were quite thoroughly shot up, but managed to limp back to Adak."

At night, by the light of a Coleman lantern, Huston wrote his impressions, reflecting on the poetic vision of the B-24s as they took off into a rainbow. His film, which the *New York Times* would call "one of the war's outstanding records of what our men are doing," would show these men at work and at play, as they tussled amongst themselves, played music, buried their dead. The words he wrote would eventually be narrated by his father. "The thunder of engines makes the earth tremble and the ravens rise . . . soon the earth below will blaze with hatred."

While his son was capturing these scenes of hell and survival, Walter was appearing in a Warner Bros. war movie, *Edge of Darkness*, starring Errol Flynn, Ann Sheridan, Judith Anderson, and Ruth Gordon. Walter played a doctor in a Norwegian fishing village which revolted against the Nazis. There were many delays due to fog along the Monterey coast, where some of the film was shot, so by the time they returned to the studio in Hollywood everyone was anxious to get on with their lives. Tired of all the waiting around, Walter would occasionally start singing "September Song" for the other actors and proposed to Judith Anderson and Ruth Gordon that the three of them hire the Biltmore Theatre for a day, put on some costumes, and act up a storm. "We may have to hire it for two days," Judith Anderson said. "We've got so much acting we want to do. And it's going to be loud acting, with no director around."

Walter was eager to hear John's stories when John stopped in Los Angeles on his way to New York, where he would work at the Astoria Studios on Long Island. Walter also confided to his son that Nan's depressions were getting worse and he didn't know what he could do about her. "Their marriage got to be very rough," John said, "which was hard on my father. Nan would go into hospital with depressions. Loyal Davis recommended a psychiatrist whom she saw. I think Nan was very jealous of my father and his popularity. She wanted to be a star. He took her up to the ranch which her brother was running, and they saw nobody for months. But her behavior became worse and worse until she really went off the deep end."

With his son at war and his wife having a breakdown, Walter kept himself together by accepting parts in movies like *Edge of Darkness*, *The North Star*, *Mission to Moscow*, and *Dragon Seed*. He also did broadcasts for the Office of Facts and Figures, narrated ten wartime documentaries, and headed the motion picture division of the Treasury Department's $1 billion bond drive.

John was promoted to captain while he was in New York working on his *Report from the Aleutians* and met a woman whom he would love for the rest of his life. Her name was Marietta FitzGerald and she was married to a Wall Street lawyer who was serving as an officer in the Far East. They had a child named Frances, who would grow up to become a Pulitzer Prize–winning writer. To John, "she was the most beautiful and desirable woman I had ever known." Thoughts of Olivia, of Lesley, seemed to fade when he looked at Marietta, at "the slope of her neck from shoulder to ear; the angle of her jaw, as though drawn by Piero della Francesca." And she, too, was taken by him.

*   *   *

"I met him at the end of 1942, when he just got back from the Aleutians," Marietta remembered in the living room of her Sutton Place apartment in New York. "Sidney Kingsley, the playwright, and his wife, Madge, asked me to dine at '21' and they introduced me to this very long, gangly fellow with a big smile called John Huston. I had never heard of him before and couldn't think of anything to say, so I said, 'Are you any relation to Sam Houston?' He thought for a bit. 'Who's Sam Houston?'

"That first evening I thought he was extremely attractive and interesting. It was a very romantic period and he had knockout charm. To get to know him was like entering another universe for me, because of his unique vision of the world." Her life was quite unlike John's. Her father was a minister who later became a bishop, and she was brought up in a world of the Church, among aristocrats from the Northeast.

"John's outlook was so arresting and exciting," she recalled, "everything he said was an astonishment and of intense interest. It was all seamless: his personality, character, point of view. I was enthralled by his way of looking at art, history, making films. It was like going to another planet. I was overwhelmed by his knowledge, which was amazing from a man who really didn't have much of a formal education. There was nothing thin or superficial about him, no chinks or soft spaces anywhere. He surely was a genius.

"John and I didn't talk about marriage and it never entered my head. I was very young and imbued with the idea of being faithful to my husband on the front. But all my life, the people who have attracted me are very articulate and witty. I can't say I was in love with him the very first few years I knew him, but I was enthralled by him. He was probably the greatest storyteller that I've ever met in my life. John was a perfect storyteller . . . dragging it out a little bit, keeping you in suspense. And his stories were not about Hollywood or how he made a film."

Their first dinner date at "21" became an embarrassment she would never forget. "That day I felt perfectly awful and had taken two pills. We had bourbon on the rocks and then wine with dinner. I saw people looking at me and I took out a mirror and saw great big purple welts all over my face. I said, 'John, I'm getting chicken pox or measles and I must go this very moment.' He said, 'We'll have a brandy and then I'll take you home.' I got up and then I fainted, pulling at a tablecloth. When I came to there was a circle of faces over me. John was nowhere to be seen. I thought, how shaming, how shaming. I was helped downstairs by the headwaiter. Then John appeared from nowhere and took me home. I was a little bit sad that he wasn't more protective of me. I called the doctor the next day and he said there should have been a warning on the pill bottle never to take a drink with it. I never discussed it with John from that day to this. In any case, he disappeared, he wasn't any gallant gentleman."

"Not true," Huston countered when told this story. "I was very much there. I remember her fainting very well. We put a cold compress on her. I was very concerned. She got up and one of the first things she said was, 'I'm not drunk.' "

John's budding romance with Marietta was interrupted by his army duties. He had to complete his Aleutians film; to do so he had to travel out to the Astoria Studios, which, he came to believe, "deserved a picture in itself. It was a marvelous place, funny as hell. Everybody there was doing something else while being a soldier. It was run by old army officers who had no idea how to handle such talent. Junior Laemmle was a private, Gottfried Reinhardt was a corporal, Irwin Shaw was a private, and Bill Saroyan was there. So was Burgess Meredith. They were assigned to writing and producing training films. Litvak, Wyler, and myself were officers, we would be there only briefly."

When his film was completed Huston took it first to Washington and then to California, where his father did the narration. Frank Capra had asked Huston for some help with one of the films in his *Why We Fight* series, but while they were working on that, President Roosevelt had asked the Signal Corps to show him whatever footage had been made of the invasion in North Africa. Unfortunately, what Tola Litvak and his crew had shot had been lost when the ship carrying the film was sunk. "The brass was acutely embarrassed," Huston said, "and the president was not to know that only one man and his crew had been assigned to the landings." Their solution was to summon Capra and Huston to Washington, ordering them to "manufacture" a North African film. Capra was put in charge of this bit of fakery and Huston was his assistant. They flew out to an army training base in the Mojave Desert, which they hoped would resemble Tunisia, and staged a mock invasion, complete with P-39 fighter planes bombing and blasting away for the cameras. "It was a big forgery and not very convincing," Huston said.

But working on *Tunisian Victory* gave John the opportunity to see Marietta again, which balanced out the distasteful assignment of having to fake an invasion to fool the president.

•   •   •

"I was twenty-three then," said Marietta, "doing research for the editor of *Life*. It was the most marvelous education and was quite a different life from this romantic Irish world of John's. I was working hard and my life was full, but whenever he came everything seemed to stand still. He was just this extraordinary domineering figure. I used to go out with him night after night after night, where he would just tell me stories. In those days, Third Avenue had about two Irish bars a block and we'd start out at, say, P. J. Clarke's and go to bar after bar. He drank a great deal. Sometimes he would just tell me a fictional story. He'd tell me the whole story of *Sierra Madre* and it might have taken four hours. It was part of himself, this story. And he'd tell me what his mother was like—a remarkable woman who encouraged him to be a writer. Writing was important, it was a way that she could support them. And being Irish herself, she brought a great deal of romantic notion to him. He was a very romantic person. At least one side of him. The other side was very antiromantic."

Huston was staying at the St. Regis in New York while working on the Tunisian "mockumentary" when he met an attractive American Indian woman named Rose Winston at a cocktail party. Huston was in uniform. After they had talked for a while, she said, "My husband and I have an apartment at 270 Park Avenue and we're moving out to the country, feel free to come and stay there. The servants are there, it's better for someone to be there. If you'll tell the St. Regis it's all right, I'll go and pack for you."

Huston didn't believe the woman, but when he returned to the hotel, he discovered that his things had been sent to the apartment. So he and Frank Capra went to the Park Avenue address where both the doorman and the elevator operator addressed him as "Captain Huston." When he entered the apartment, he lost his breath. There were paintings by Matisse, Picasso, Dufy, Braque; Modigliani sculptures; a fully stocked bar; four servants. "I just couldn't believe this," Huston said, and he settled in for "one of the best times I ever had."

Four days later he received a call from the woman's husband, Norman Winston. "I'm calling you about a very special brandy which I have there," Winston said.

"Oh, Mr. Winston, I wouldn't dream of touching your brandy."

"Oh, no, I particularly want you to open this crate." He also instructed Huston to call his warehouse cold room to order steaks whenever he felt like entertaining. John couldn't believe his good fortune. The best brandy, the best meat, the most incredible apartment, all during the wartime shortage. It was too good to last and after three glorious weeks it came quickly to an end as Huston, Capra, and writer Anthony Veiller were ordered to Washington because someone had the bright idea of combining the phony footage they had shot with real footage the British had captured.

"They sent us to England on the first plane," Huston grumbled, "to induce the English to throw their picture in with Frank's. I didn't even have time to buy a razor. Everything in the army was always done in a rush. Same psychology prevails as the movies."

In London, Capra and Huston stayed at Claridges and met with their British counterparts. They discovered that the British "had a good deal of very fine material. I must say I didn't have much heart for any of this. They had a picture quite ready to show, and it was delayed for us."

While they worked at putting together some kind of joint effort that wouldn't prove too embarrassing, John resumed his old friendships with Kay Wellesley and department store heiress Connie de Pinna, both married, and met another young woman who managed to make him forget, for the time, the women back home. Her name was Leni Lynn.

"I met John at a party at the Wellesleys'," Lynn reminisced. "I had just turned eighteen and was doing my second film at Elstree Studios, singing 'Caro Nome' from *Rigoletto*. Before I married an Englishman and moved to London, I was at MGM in Hollywood from 1939 until 1943. Once I met John we were inseparable when he wasn't busy. We would meet for dinner, mostly at Grosvenor House."

Their first dinner alone John showed her a picture of Olivia de Havilland. "At that time he seemed unhappy over the situation," Lynn recalled. "He tried to tell me that it was over. I got the feeling it was something I shouldn't know and didn't want to know.

"He was married at the time and I said, 'John, if this is what you do, why do you get married?'

" 'Women need to be married,' he said. 'Women need the respect and the commitment of marriage. And frankly, if I am married to that woman, I will be committed and she will have the best of me and the best I can offer in life. And the same with my relationships.' "

Lynn's attraction to John wasn't the same as his was to her. "Although John and I got to feel a love for each other," she said, "I had no intention of being engulfed by him. I wanted to keep it platonic because my English husband was in the RAF and I felt very strongly about marriage. I had no idea that John would feel any other way. So this became a problem.

"We were very friendly with Emerson Baimbridge and his wife, Connie de Pinna. They lived in the Arlington House in London. Emerson was a Lord and had a castle in Scotland and John used to go there for weekends. I could never go because I was always working on a film. But I overheard Kay warning him one day that she would never forgive him if he took me there. So I kind of got the idea that there were goings-on at the castle that were not for me. Like *La Dolce Vita* going on there. And Kay knew that John could be cruel. His pattern, when he broke up with anybody, sometimes he would just walk into the bedroom and say, 'Meet my girlfriend.' Kay told me he had done that.

"Anyway, Connie de Pinna was a fascinating, extremely exotic character, a book in herself. She had the most incredibly exotic body and look of any person I've ever seen in my life. And she talked in a very wry, exotic voice. And Emerson was a very quiet, reserved Englishman. He and I used to disappear in the corner of a room when we got tired of talking to people and he would say how he wished he could get away from the crowds. But Connie, forget it! Her life was entertaining. When Connie's child was being christened, Johnny and I were in the car with her and Emerson. She had half a dozen godfathers. I said to her in front of John and Emerson, 'How come you have all these godfathers?' And she said, 'Well, darling, I don't remember which one was the father.' Now, I'm quite sure that John didn't remain celibate all the time we were going out together. And I know he spent a lot of time at their castle. The child could have been John's!"

Around this time John met a Canadian journalist, "a tall, stately looking gal," whom he found attractive enough to invite to the Baimbridges' castle in Scotland "to shoot a stag." Before going, he invited her to dinner at the Ritz with the Baimbridges and another couple. "There was no involvement," Huston said, "but it was about to become an involvement. We were talking about the ceiling of the dining room of the Ritz, one of the most beautiful ceilings in any hotel anywhere. It was a French design. And this brought her around to Napoleon, whom she felt was a great man. In fact, there were many similarities between Napoleon and Hitler. Then there was a justification of Hitler's hatred for the Jews. He certainly carried it to extremes, she thought, but perhaps for the good of the world it would be just as well if they were all herded into an enclosure and blown up.

"I listened to this with growing horror. I was appalled and then it got worse than that. At this point she'd run her course and I said, 'You, Madame, are the blackest bitch I've ever encountered.' And I elaborated briefly on that.

"She stood up and had a fur over the chair. Her chair fell over and no one at our table went to pick her coat up. She got down, took her coat, and that was the last time I ever saw her."

But it wasn't the end of the incident. The woman lodged a protest against Huston with the American ambassador, claiming to have been insulted by an American officer. "He was almost thrown in the hoosegow by counterintelligence," Jules Buck recalled, also remembering that there must have been *some* involvement because the woman had given John "a bad case of the clap." The American ambassador began an investigation of his own and came to the conclusion that the woman was very probably a Nazi agent. Huston was left alone . . . to continue his final pursuit of Leni Lynn.

"What was disturbing to me was how it ended," Lynn said sadly. "One day John invited me to a private party at his apartment, which was not too far from mine. I arrived and found it was *really* private, there was nobody else there and no one expected. John was all excited. He had out the hors d'oeuvres and the champagne. I knew I was in trouble. John was a wonderful teacher. He listened to you; he made you feel that you were the most important person at the moment that you were with him. He brought out a book on Impressionism and shared it with me, tried to teach me what it was all about. He was always doing that. John loved to direct! But I realized that he was getting kind of excited in a way that I couldn't handle. I also realized that I was terrified to be with John alone. Apart from his size, he had a great deal of fire and energy, he was all-enveloping. Had I been single even, I don't think I would have allowed myself to fall in love.

"He went into the kitchen for ice and I wrote him a note. I literally ran away. Running through the streets for a while before I got a cab. I was crying. I knew I had to end it."

At the studio the next morning there were messages from John, "and the usual flowers, fruits, and battery of gifts, which I wouldn't touch." He finally reached her by phone at her apartment. "He was begging me to come out one night to Scotland. He must have been planning to leave the country, because the phone calls got kind of wild at different times of the day and night. He told me, too, that he could arrange to get me out of the country, that he wanted to see me safe. And somehow I couldn't get across to him that I was married. That was a side of John . . . when he wanted something, he had blinders on.

"John once said you can't love someone honestly and fall out of love with them, no matter what they do or what you do. Love is a part of growth, it changes, but it's still there.

"Then he disappeared. A couple of weeks after he'd gone, I got a little package and there was a diamond bow, clusters of diamonds. It represented a knot of some kind. It was telling me that there was a tie.

"I was sorry that I left him the way I did because I never saw him again, but I was grateful and happy for the time we spent together, it was one of the most beautiful years of my life."

For Olivia de Havilland, 1943 was a year of stress. Being separated from John was difficult for her, and hearing secondhand stories about him only increased her insecurities. "Someone had seen him in London," she said, "and told me, 'I ran into John and he'd start talking about you and he'd say, "I can't live without this woman!" And at four o'clock in the morning I'd see him dead drunk and in the arms of some odd lady.' "

Such reports led her to find solace in the arms of another soldier, a Major Joseph McKeon, for a brief intrigue. And when the major was ordered to China, she decided to turn down a part in a Warner Bros. picture, *The Animal Kingdom*, to spend time with him. The studio suspended her for the sixth time. It was one time too many. De Havilland was sick and tired of being treated like chattel, enslaved to a studio system that added suspension time on to the end of the contract "and that meant it could really go on forever." She found a lawyer who told her that under California law she wasn't bound to this extended servitude, but since no actor had ever challenged the system, it would take a courageous court battle to free her—and all the other actors working under the contract system in Hollywood.

Olivia decided to fight. She was unhappy with the pictures Jack Warner kept putting her in, even her body rebelled when she made such films, with her legs swelling, her weight fluctuating, her temper exploding. "You had to fight very hard," she said. "It was as important to say no to something as it was to say yes. I read the law and it was very simple. The crux of the matter was: Did the law that limited the right of an employer to enforce a contract against an employee to seven years mean seven calendar years or seven years of work? It seemed to me rather clear it was calendar years."

The battle would take her into the spring of the following year and Jack Warner had her barred from making any films until a decision was reached; but when the smoke cleared, de Havilland emerged the victor. The California Supreme Court declined to review the favorable decisions of two lower courts, and the Hollywood studio system was dealt a fatal blow.

De Havilland's gutsy stand was cheered by Walter Huston, who had rebelled against the contract system a decade earlier but hadn't thought of challenging it through the courts. Walter was involved in a different kind of controversy for portraying U.S. Ambassador to Russia Joseph Davies in a pro-Soviet, pro-Stalin film, *Mission to Moscow*.

In his book *As Time Goes By*, Howard Koch described how both Harry and Jack Warner talked him into writing the script based on Davies's book. Koch had just finished co-writing his most famous picture, *Casablanca*, and didn't see *Mission to Moscow* as a plum and turned it down. He was called into Harry Warner's office. "I was baffled," wrote Koch. "As president of the company, he ran its financial affairs but had little contact with its artists." Harry Warner was at his desk; his brother Jack stood behind him. They started to talk about the importance of the Davies project and after Koch listed his reasons why he didn't feel qualified to write about Soviet affairs Jack Warner said, "Look, Koch, you can't turn this down." Koch was surprised by Warner's vehemence. "Well, Russia's our ally, whether we like it or not."

"This isn't just a studio matter," Harry Warner added. "We're doing the picture because our government wants it done."

Jack Warner had been invited to dinner at the White House. Ambassador Davies was there and Roosevelt suggested to Warner that he should make a film of Davies's book. Americans knew so little about the Soviet Union; if they were going to fight the war together a better understanding was needed to counter the anti-Soviet sentiments that were prevalent in the country. Warner was flattered that the president thought he could make a difference and agreed to the project without even reading the book.

Koch realized he was backed into a corner. "How could I refuse to work on a project which the President of the United States considered important to the war effort?"

That was exactly how Walter Huston felt when he was approached to play the ambassador. Roosevelt was delighted that his favorite actor had agreed to star, but Joseph Davies wasn't. "Mr. Huston doesn't look like me," Davies complained to the director, Michael Curtiz.

Koch believed that the Warners wouldn't have minded dropping the picture, since "they were beginning to have capitalistic qualms about portraying the Soviet Union in a favorable light." But they had "trapped themselves into making a film with which they were not entirely in sympathy," and when they reached a compromise with Davies, allowing him to appear on the screen as himself at the opening of the picture, the impasse was resolved.

Koch was appalled with the idea of starting with a prologue, but Jack Warner told Koch that Davies probably wanted to be president and hoped to use the film as a way of projecting himself into the limelight.

"Walter wasn't as politically aware as John was," Koch observed. "I don't think he had a particular interest in doing this picture."

On the set one morning Walter became despondent when he couldn't remember his lines. A concerned Michael Curtiz called Paul Kohner and told him something was wrong with Walter. Kohner came immediately and found his distraught client in his dressing room. "I cannot remember lines," Walter mumbled. "It's nothing to worry about," Kohner said, "these are things that come and go with old age. Lie down for an hour, it'll be all right." At fifty-eight, Walter didn't exactly feel like an old man, but he listened to Kohner and an hour later his memory returned.

Mission to Moscow began with Davies—whose selection as ambassador Saul Bellow once called "one of the most disgraceful appointments in diplomatic history"—saying about Russia: "How they keep their house doesn't matter to me, only one thing matters, how good a neighbor they'll be in case of a fire." He is shown visiting steel plants, looking at the tractors and tanks, the oil fields, coal mines, machine shops, cooperative farms. The idea was to impress upon the moviegoer how bold and imaginative Russia was. When the ambassador is told that the embassy might be bugged, he doesn't consider it a problem, since he wouldn't say anything there he wouldn't say directly to the Soviet leaders. The Soviet purge of the Trotskyites is defended, based on the volumes of annotated transcripts Davies had given to Koch of the controversial Moscow trials of 1938. There are plenty of yawn-provoking, long-winded toasts and speeches as this distorted picture of the avuncular Joseph Stalin emerges. And when this dreadful picture finally comes to an end, we are treated to a chorus singing, "You are, yes you are, your brother's keeper. Amen."

"When the film was released," said Howard Koch, "we expected some controversy, but I doubt if any of us were prepared for the violence of the reactions, both pro and con. . . . No doubt some of the criticism was justified. We had weighted the picture heavily on the positive side of Soviet accomplishments, since in our opinion the negative aspects had been amply publicized in our press ever since the revolution. . . . Whether we should have given more footage to the shortcomings of the Soviet system is an open question. We were venturing into new territory for feature films with no precedent to guide us."

Bosley Crowther, writing in the *New York Times*, called it "The most outspoken picture of a political subject an American studio ever made." It was advertised as "The Story About Who Stopped Hitler!" and "The Story of Two Guys Named Joe!": Davies and Stalin. Pictures of both men were used (with Walter as the ambassador).

Ambassador Davies was so taken with the film that he brought a print to Russia and showed it to Stalin, Molotov, and other members of the Presidium. The Soviet leaders were pleased and the Society of Soviet Artists of Moscow invited Walter to attend the film's premiere there, which Walter was unable to do. Not surprisingly, the movie became enormously popular in postwar Russia.

Walter wrote to Jack and Harry Warner praising their "courage of high order to tackle such a controversial subject and to resist the pressures brought to bear upon you." He considered the film "a milestone in film history," and felt it opened "new horizons of public service for Hollywood." He also thanked them for the privilege of portraying Ambassador Davies, who had become a friend.

"One very nice thing that came out of *Mission to Moscow*," he said after the war, "was getting to know Joe Davies. Mrs. Huston and I usually visit him and Mrs. Davies during the summer at their home in the Adirondacks." Walter admitted that he was rankled by the considerable criticism he received for appearing in the film.

Four years after the film was released, Jack Warner appeared at a hearing before the House Un-American Activities Committee, which, among other things, was investigating Communist infiltration of the motion picture industry. Before being questioned, he read a statement that included comments about *Mission to Moscow*: "That picture was made when our country was fighting for its existence, with Russia as one of our allies. It was made to fulfill the same wartime purpose for which we made other pictures.

"If making *Mission to Moscow* in 1942 was subversive activity, then the American Liberty ships which carried food and guns to Russian allies and the American naval vessels which convoyed them were likewise engaged in subversive activities. This picture was made only to help a desperate war effort and not for posterity."

Following *Mission to Moscow*, Walter Huston portrayed a sympathetic Russian village doctor for Sam Goldwyn's *The North Star*, directed by Lewis Milestone and written by Lillian Hellman (and, though uncredited, Edward Chodorov). Once again, it was President Roosevelt who wanted the picture made, in his efforts to show Russia in a positive light.

The film takes place in 1941 as German planes bomb Russian peasants and German troops occupy Russian villages. While the village men are hiding in the mountains as guerrillas, the German doctors take blood from the Russian children to augment their plasma supply. Eventually there is an uprising, and Walter kills two Fascist officers. Typical of the war films put out by the studios at this time, the last line was intended to be uplifting and inspirational. In *The North Star* the tag is delivered by Anne Baxter: "The earth belongs to us, the people, if we fight for it. And we *will* fight for it."

Lillian Hellman felt Goldwyn and Milestone made her story "a sentimental, badly directed, badly acted mess." Originally, Willy Wyler was to direct, but when he was called into the army he was replaced by Milestone, who was coming off *All Quiet on the Western Front*. Hellman wanted a gritty, realistic, documentary look to the film, which she had meticulously researched. Instead, it became a backlot picture of innocent peasants set upon by the big bad Germans. Milestone came to believe that Hellman "knew *nothing* about Russia—especially the village," and he requested fifty pages of script changes, which an insulted Hellman refused to make. She went to see Goldwyn, who sided with his director. Hellman was so angry that she ended her eight-year association with Goldwyn and paid $30,000 to buy out her contract.

The North Star received surprisingly good reviews (although Mary McCarthy called it "a tissue of falsehoods woven of every variety of untruth") and would garner five Oscar nominations, including Best Original Screenplay. When it was released for television in 1957, it was renamed *Armored Attack* and given a new narration, which altered the pro-Russian sentiments to an anti-Russian feeling in keeping with the negative spirit of the Cold War.

As Walter was doing his part to show the Russian leadership and its people worthy of our sympathy and support, John received orders to leave behind his room at Claridges, his dinners at the Ritz, his Dionysian weekends in Scotland, his frustrated attempts at seducing Leni Lynn. He was to go to Italy and make a film of the Allies' triumphant march into Rome.

It didn't seem like much of an assignment at the time, but it was an opportunity to return to filmmaking, and Huston was aware that the Germans had made some effective films about their triumphs in France and other parts of Europe. As it was to be a joint Anglo-American venture, John asked the English novelist Eric Ambler, whose *Background to Danger* he had worked on adapting before entering the army, if he'd like to join him in Italy and write the script of whatever came out of their adventure. In October 1943, the two men flew to Marrakech in Morocco in a U.S. Air Force transport plane, where they were met by Jules Buck, whom Huston described to Ambler as his "fixer." Ambler wasn't impressed with Huston, considering him a bit pretentious for wearing, as he did, the dark sunglasses that had been given to him in the Aleutians, but he did see that the director was earnest in wanting to get to Italy and make a film. It wasn't easy to get from Marrakech to Rome, but they finally managed to get a plane to Naples.

There John made friends with the photographer Robert Capa, whose work he had admired. Capa was a kindred spirit, a courageous man who had a vision and presented it to the world through his photographs. At the end of 1938, after he had spent two years covering the wars in Spain and China, *Picture Post*, a British publication, ran eleven pages of his work and called him, "The greatest war photographer in the world." His first published story was of a 1932 speech Leon Trotsky delivered in Copenhagen on the history of the Russian Revolution. Capa caught the bespectacled Trotsky in full dramatic power, the fingers of both hands curled toward his face, his mouth opened in a shout. Capa's photographs told stories. They were pictures of strength, defiance, nobility, and tragedy. Huston knew his work, was impressed with his dedication, his courage, and his ability to be at the right place at the right time. Capa captured the lives of men at war in a way that was instructive to Huston. His images would pass into Huston's own as he worked on his Italian documentary.

And Capa was a friend of men Huston admired, men like Picasso and Hemingway. They also shared a love of gambling, and so the two could not only trade stories of war and peace, but they could also play cards, a favorite way to pass the time between assignments.

When Huston and Ambler left Naples, they proceeded to Caserta, where they joined Colonel Gillette, the commander of the Signal Corps photographic section, who was staying in a modern house next door to a palace that had long reflecting pools and housed the army troops. Neither of them was very impressed with Gillette. "His job," wrote Ambler, "was to indent for photographic supplies, distribute it to the trained personnel under his command . . . and get the results back for processing, censorship, and distribution. . . . Thanks to an eight-week guided tour of Hollywood studios to prepare him for this mission, he knew all about moviemaking. You just set your camera up, pointed it at what you wanted to see, and pressed the button or pulled the trigger. . . . He knew nothing about Captain Huston except that he made good movies."

Huston tried to make the colonel understand the importance of good filmmaking and the need to get some cameras appropriated as quickly as possible. Then, word came down that General Mark Clark considered the joining of the Goums, a regiment of French colonial troops from North Africa, with the Fifth Army an important public relations story. Anxious to please the general, Colonel Gillette struck a deal with Huston: cover the Goums story and he'd provide him with the cameras, crew, and film stock to make his documentary.

"John accepted," said Ambler. "We spent a day or two with the Goums and then made ready to do our duty to Psychological Warfare. We had by then agreed that our best plan would be to move into a small town immediately after the enemy had left, and then make a film of what happened next to its inhabitants."

They chose San Pietro, at the entrance to the Liri Valley, forty miles southeast of Rome. "From San Pietro," observed Ambler, "it was possible for a few German troops, well dug in and with plenty of fire power, to hold off indefinitely frontal assaults from superior Allied forces."

And that's what the Germans did, as they held their position and bloodied the valley with the dead bodies of American, British, and French soldiers. The Germans had mined the entrance to the valley, crisscrossed the area with barbed wire and booby traps, and held off three Allied frontal assaults. Then the 143rd Infantry Regiment sent in sixteen tanks to take San Pietro. Twelve were destroyed. It became, noted Huston, "one of the most fiercely contested landmarks of the Italian campaign. . . . We could see the tanks burning and exploding, and men running and trying to hide. After it was over we crept forward and photographed the disastrous results."

Buck photographed parts of bodies that had been gruesomely scattered along the road and in the fields—a leg, a torso. Some of these bodies were men from a company of Texas Rangers who had earlier asked Buck to film them for the newsreels back home. Huston used shots of these men talking and smiling with shots of them dead, their bodies being bagged and zipped for shipment home. But these powerful shots were eventually cut when the film was reduced from five reels to three.

"After one of these firefights," Jules Buck remembered, "John did a terrible thing. One soldier, who was a real hero, hadn't gotten decorated. We were having coffee when John said to this young soldier, 'Christ, I've got wonderful news. You're getting the Silver Star.' The kid couldn't believe it. And it wasn't true. I said, 'John, you sonofabitch, why'd you do that?' And he said, 'Oh, having some fun.' Fun? It was the shittiest thing I ever heard!"

By mid-December the Germans began their retreat and army intelligence told Huston and his crew that San Pietro had been evacuated. "I made for the town immediately," Huston said, "we wanted to be on hand as soon as our occupation began so we could film the entire proceedings."

But intelligence was soon proved wrong. Huston led his six-man crew past the fields of dead until they reached the outskirts of the town. At this juncture John noticed that half his crew was missing. They had decided that it was too dangerous to be the first to enter the town and left Huston, Buck, and Ambler on their own. Suddenly, machine-gun fire rained bullets down upon them and they realized that the Germans were still there. They dropped to the ground and then the Germans sent in mortar bombs, which created enough dust to block the view of the machine gunner and allowed them to run to safety.

The next day, intelligence claimed that the road into San Pietro had been repaired and it was safe to enter the town. Once again, Buck, Ambler, and Huston made their way, by jeep this time, to the mounds of rubble that was once a village. As Buck switched on his camera, three planes flew by overhead and then came another sound, of incoming howitzer shells. The three men ran for cover in a nearby cave. "The Germans thought the Americans had come in," Huston said, "and the Americans thought the Germans were still there!"

Once the heavy shelling ceased, Huston, Ambler, and Buck ran to their jeep and Buck drove them out of San Pietro. In front of them, another jeep was blown up by an .88 shell and Buck took his eyes off the road just as they were crossing a metal bridge constructed of two "I" beams spanning a gully. Their jeep's wheels got stalled in the "I" beam and Huston panicked. He was sure another .88 would get them, too. "I just knew we'd had it," he recalled. "The Germans had that road zeroed in so they could hit a dime."

According to Ambler, John leaned forward to Jules Buck and said, softly, "Now then, you filthy little shit, keep absolutely calm. Just back off, you bastard sonofabitch, and keep calm." Ambler was shocked at the "stream of abuse" that followed. "It touched on Jules's religion, his

parents, and his personal habits." Buck somehow managed to keep his
head and get them back safely, and later that day he accepted John's
apology, but he never forgot that John had called him a dirty Jew
bastard.

Huston spent the rest of that day composing a letter to Colonel
Frank Capra in Washington, asking advice about whether to pull out of
San Pietro or to remain and try to complete his film. He, Buck, and
Ambler then drove to an American airfield near Naples where John
gave his letter to a friend who got it to Capra. John also wanted to go
to Naples because he heard that Humphrey and Mayo Bogart were
there visiting troops. John hadn't seen Bogie since he left him tied to a
chair surrounded by Japanese at the climax of *Across the Pacific*, and the
two held a welcomed reunion as they drank themselves drunk through
the night.

Then Ambler received orders to return to London. Huston and Buck
returned to San Pietro to record the faces of the people as they emerged
from the rubble to greet the American soldiers. They had captured
enough of what really happened to put together a film that John would
write and narrate himself, a film that cartoonist/journalist Bill Mauldin
would call, "The best documentary easily that anybody ever did on the
war."

The 143rd Regiment needed eleven hundred new soldiers after San
Pietro. John was there as the troops were crossing the Rapido River at
night. A steel cable had been stretched across the river, which the
company used to get from one side to the other. The Germans,
however, had a position and mowed down these soldiers like flies. A
major, whose hand had been blown off, stood waist-deep in the water,
dead bodies floating all around him, and saluted each soldier with his
stump as they began to cross the river.

Years later Huston broke down and cried as he retold this incident to
producer Michael Fitzgerald. "That was what it was all about to him,"
Fitzgerald said. "And it was because of that sort of thing that all the
bullshit of the movie business was so relative to him. John knew honor
and courage when he saw it, and that vision haunted him all his life."

Huston also witnessed the Allied bombing of the fourteen-hundred-
year-old Benedictine monastery at Monte Cassino, which served as an
observation post for the Germans, but it only sickened him as "the
rubble gave the defenders greater protection than had the building

itself." Repeatedly, the Germans turned back the Allies and all the bombing and killing began to get to Huston. When he returned to Caserta, the whine of a jeep turning a corner sounded like an .88 shell coming in and he fell to the ground. He knew it was time to get out of Italy when a second jeep turned the same corner and he hit the dirt again.

Before Monte Cassino finally fell to Polish Resistance troops in May 1944, Huston had received orders to return to the United States and put together his San Pietro documentary.

"When he returned from Italy he was always out in that place on Long Island where these war films were being processed," Marietta remembered. "All his friends were with him, they were all directors and writers and were a perfectly brilliant group of men. They used to collect every night in a certain corner of the downstairs room at '21,' it was like a club. Burgess Meredith was there. Tola Litvak was John's closest friend. Sitting beside us was Humphrey Bogart and his then wife, Mayo. He would get terribly drunk and they would have terrible brawls. Mary Astor would come and she was still very beautiful, but a little alcoholic. Willy Wyler was John's hero, he admired him more than any other director for his skill and enormous intellectual discipline. John identified more with the writers than the directors. He felt the writers were the brightest.

"Then there was Jules Buck, who was sort of John's spiritual lieutenant, the head of his entourage. It was like Don Quixote and Sancho Panza. 'John, is there anything I can do for you? Can I get you something?' He would do anything just to be in the presence of the divine one. That was the only irritating part of knowing John—this entourage around him wooing, which he encouraged."

While John was smitten with Marietta, she, like Leni Lynn, was more infatuated than involved. "I didn't become emotionally involved with John until much later," she said. "Or perhaps I was without realizing it. It was a growing thing. He would come back from Italy and we'd have ten more days of him telling me stories. I'd say, 'Yes, and then what?' That's all I'd say all night long. My education, in a sense, started with John. He was the most wonderful teacher. He introduced me to all these painters and told me how to look at them."

Although she was aware that John had a roving eye, it wasn't a subject either of them broached. "I had known about his relationship with Olivia de Havilland, but he was very gallant about women, he didn't talk about them. I gathered from others that that was a thing of the past. I know many, many women have felt suicidal about John and

I was quite aware of this side of him, but I think that was part of my charm to him: that I wasn't just head-over-heels about him."

Perhaps it was Marietta's ability to keep her head that drove John to so many other women during this time. In spite of what Marietta was led to believe, Olivia still assumed that she and John would marry as soon as he and Lesley were divorced. Then there was Harry Warner's daughter, Doris. "She was nuts about him," Jules Buck said. "Doris virtually offered him the studio." Buck also remembered John having an affair with "the wife of a congressman from the South." There was also a Russian princess. And a young woman named Doris Lilly, who thought she wanted to be an actress and wound up a gossip columnist, writer, and one of the inspirations for Truman Capote's Holly Golightly in *Breakfast at Tiffany's*.

"I was seventeen when I met John," Doris Lilly said with a broad smile. "It was at the St. Regis Hotel in New York. I graduated from Santa Monica High School when I was sixteen and I was in the movies—I had a teensy part in one picture. But I decided I didn't want to be an actress. I wanted to go to New York and become a writer.

"My girlfriend Pam and I got an apartment in New York and I got a job as assistant beauty editor at *Town & Country* magazine. I was going out every night. With everybody. I was the toast of New York. Pam knew this guy called Charlie Grayson and he invited us to a cocktail party. That's all we ever did, go to parties, stay out all night. He said John Huston was going to be there. I said, 'John Huston . . . that sounds familiar.' He had a romance with Olivia de Havilland. So I decided to go, because of Olivia de Havilland. I wanted to get what she got.

"I was very attracted to John. He was in a uniform and he had Italian mud on his boots. The idea that there was Italian mud on his boots was just absolutely devastating, it was so divine. I sat on the bed and eventually I took my shoes off. John was admiring my feet. He had a thing about feet. He used to draw pictures of feet all the time when he doodled."

John talked about San Pietro, and how he had followed soldiers into battle. He described one scene where soldiers were darting behind trees and he said, "I found myself following one man and hoping that he would be shot, because then I would have a good shot."

"Golly!" Doris gulped.

War talk led to seduction, and Lilly was ready. "I'd been out with a lot of guys before John, but he was the first man in my life. It happened that first night I met him. Even to a man as thoughtless and unfeeling as John that still had to mean a lot. I just wanted to have fun; I didn't care about sex. But John seduced me. And then I used to seduce him. John was probably the most prolific man sexually I ever knew. Oh, he was a rascal, John."

Lilly was completely taken in by John's success and magnetic charm. "You felt you were hitching your wagon to a star. And nobody ever said no to him, he got anything he ever wanted from anybody. And he never overtly asked you to do anything for him. One characteristic of his was he didn't give a damn about money. Never had a money clip or a wallet in his life. He used to put his hand in his pocket and bring out little balls of money.

"We once went to Tony Soma's restaurant on 52nd Street. Tony used to entertain everybody by standing on his head. And his daughter, Ricki, was there and John was introduced to the daughter. She was studying ballet and John said, 'Sometime I'll take you to the ballet.' He filed that one."

John was as active as ever, but was suffering from what he called "anxiety neurosis." He often woke up in the middle of the night and left the St. Regis to walk in Central Park. The newspapers reported an unusual outbreak of muggings in the park and John found himself packing a .45 pistol, "secretly hopeful that some hapless bastard would try to jump me." He realized that "emotionally I was still in Italy in a combat zone. I couldn't sleep because there were no guns going."

It was in this state that he worked on his documentary at Astoria, where Rey Scott, one of his cameramen from the Aleutians, was getting himself into trouble. Scott had also been in Italy and Huston remembered seeing him on New Year's Eve at a bar in Caserta. "Rey had been living in a cellar near the big monastery, he was right in the middle of the bombardment all the time. Some colonel was complaining that night that he'd been six years in the army and never saw any action. Rey said, 'Would you like to see some action, Colonel?' And he whisked him off to his digs. Three hours later they came back. The colonel was wounded; he had bandages all over him.

"When Rey's orders were up he was sent back to Astoria, where he was made officer of the guard. Had to go around the installation and check to see that all was well. Rey had a bottle and proceeded to get drunk. At midnight he called up Colonel Barret at his home and said,

'Colonel Barret, twelve o'clock and alllll is well.' Barret hung up confounded, first time that's ever happened to him. At two A.M. he called again, 'Colonel Barret, Officer of the Guard Captain Rey Scott, two o'clock and allll's well.' Then he called him at four A.M. and did it again, and began shooting his pistol. They had to arrest him.

"Out of sympathy, they sent him not to the brig but to Mason General Hospital for psychiatric examination. I received a letter from Rey—they were going to do electroshock therapy. I interceded, saying, if anything, he should be released from the army. Because he was a little bomb-happy."

Huston wrote a number of letters to various officers until one was able to respond, saving Scott from having his brain fried. Huston even went to the hospital in Brentwood, Long Island, to visit Rey, who wept when he saw John.

When Tola Litvak was sent overseas on assignment, he suggested that Huston might want to use his secretary, Anne Selepegno. Huston was glad to have someone so competent while he worked on *The Battle of San Pietro* and she became a lifelong friend. "Cut out that captain shit, will you?" was the first thing Huston said to her when they were introduced and Selepegno liked him immediately. When Huston and Jules Buck left New York to complete their film in Hollywood, Anne went with him and wound up helping John run his Tarzana home with its stable of horses. There she met another young woman, Eloise Hardt, whom people called Cherokee. She, too, helped run John's home.

Eloise's mother was a Cherokee Indian, her father a stern German electrical engineer who had been crippled by lightning. They were Okies. After a failed suicide attempt her father moved to Texas, leaving Cherokee, her mother, and her six brothers to fend for themselves.

Her two older brothers went to California and eventually sent for the others. In her early teens Cherokee worked as a model, married, and landed a one-year movie contract with Howard Hawks. After Pearl Harbor her husband went overseas and she worked at the Hollywood Canteen, where she fell in love with a flyer who was killed in action, leaving her heartbroken. She got divorced and found a job with photographer Tom Kelley, who brought her to Huston's house in 1944.

"There were people there who were much older than me, like Charlie Chaplin and Sir Charles Mendl, and they would all come out to his house on Sundays," Cherokee recalled. "John went to get a horse from his stables to show him off, but there was a mare in the back in heat and the stud didn't want to go with John. I said to myself, 'That fool is going to kill himself.' He hadn't gone more than ten feet when the stud reared up and brought John down to his knees. I ran and got the horse and took him back to the stable. After that, John said, 'Do you know anything about horses?' I said, 'I'm from a farm in Oklahoma and we rode them to school three miles.' And he said, 'Would you like to exercise mine?' I said, 'Oh, God, I'd like to do anything if I could stay out here; there are about eleven people in one room at home.' So that was the beginning of a long relationship of trying to educate me."

She already had considerable life experience, but Huston's world was light-years away from anything she knew. "He gave me full run of the house, gave my brothers clothes, showed me art books. I remember the greatest conversation we had, walking up in the hills, about how babies were made, in a purely clinical way. How you get certain genes.

"He wasn't married when I met him, and he was playing the field. One night Ava Gardner would come. All the glamour girls of Holly-wood came. John wasn't a macho guy, but he was put in macho positions with women. Women were so available and John was so weak, he couldn't say no to a woman. And he always ended up in bed with them. And these were the years when I was not involved with him personally."

In contrast to his wildness, Cherokee also saw a "very tender, graceful side of John. When he was alone he was just like an Okie. I could sleep next to him and he wouldn't touch me. I trusted him totally. I could never associate him with the person on Sundays who would get drunk. His personality changed when these people got around. He became very theatrical; the intellectual games started. The jokes. He was Irish, so I guess it went with the territory. But he did get falling down drunk at times.

"One Sunday he said to me, 'Come into the house.' I went in and people were laughing at me, at things John would ask me. He was putting me on. I was really a sideshow. He really exploited me."

If John sometimes reminded Cherokee of her cruel father, she found Walter friendlier. "His father, when he'd come to the ranch, never took John's girls seriously. He was always very nice to me and would pat me on the head. Walter liked John, but he didn't have much time for him. There was enormous competition between them, but in a nice way, because his father expected miracles out of John. Walter had a lot of class, a lot of character. John had it, too. Because deep down John was a man of great value and that was why I always loved and cared for him."

*   *   *

Walter may not have had much time for John because he was either busy working or a couple of hundred miles away on his ranch in Porterville. In March 1944, Walter was approached by backers of the Democratic party to see if he had any interest in running for Congress for the seat vacated by Will Rogers, Jr. He didn't. Walter's voice was also much in demand for radio broadcasts and he had agreed to be the master of ceremonies for NBC's upcoming "Cavalcade of America," which would feature dramas, comedies, and real-life exploits. Walter also appeared on another NBC broadcast, "Everyman's Theatre."

In the movies Walter could be seen as a Chinese peasant farmer in MGM's adaptation of Pearl Buck's novel *Dragon Seed*, which was about the effects of the Japanese invasion on a Chinese farming community and starred Katharine Hepburn as Walter's daughter.

During the six months it took to make *Dragon Seed*, Walter grew particularly fond of a young actress, Jacqueline de Wit, who also played his daughter. She would remain an intimate friend. And there were others. Anne Selepegno was present at one of John's parties. "There was one dame who wouldn't let John alone," she recalled. "Walter was there and John said, 'Dad, will you do me a favor and take that dame off my back.' Walter did and she was very happy."

Olivia, at this time, wasn't happy with John. She had done her tour of duty while he was away and done battle with the studio contract system on the homefront. She had also taken care of John's grandmother, Adelia, when Huston was in Italy. "She was very sick then," Jules Buck recalled. "She needed nursing care."

"The day I left Seattle for the Aleutians to visit the soldiers in hospitals there, John came back from Italy. Isn't that astounding!" de Havilland exclaimed. "And he tried to find out where I was from New York. He wanted them to stop the plane! That was John."

John was also a man with a strongly embedded double standard, which Olivia did not appreciate. "John couldn't take the suggestion of any kind of rejection without desperately going off and comforting himself with some female conquest. He was always imagining rejection or infidelity on the part of the other person. And he certainly expected fidelity, it was very important to him. He was always nervous about the other person being attracted to somebody else or straying off."

Gradually, de Havilland began to see John as self-destructive. "I suppose Richard Burton had some of the same characteristics," she said. "He was paranoid. And I saw Barrymore in John. I once said to John,

'You must be very careful because you don't want to end up just like John Barrymore.' "

During the war she once went with him to his vacant house in Tarzana. "He was very eager to sell the house because that would be helpful in his arrangements with Lesley, he wanted to settle some money on her. But it was difficult to sell the house during the war because of gas rationing. Houses that were out of the way were difficult to sell.

"When John moved away from that house, Lesley had a nervous breakdown. Doctors said to him, 'the best thing for her is if you would move back into the house.' I said, 'There is no question about what you should do, you must move back.' And so he did. All of that was very painful for me. He kept telling me that I shouldn't blame myself in any way. But you feel the other person's pain, you can't help that. And at the same time, you feel the pain of your own situation."

Some years later, when Olivia and Mary Astor were making *Hush, Hush, Sweet Charlotte*, Astor told her they had something in common and spoke openly of her relationship with John during *The Maltese Falcon*. "Then she saw him with me one day and she said, 'I think I better dismiss this from my mind, as painful though it is,' " Olivia recalled. "She told me this herself! She was adorable when she brought this up, but she stunned me.

"But that was John. I'd pick up the newspapers in Los Angeles and read about his adventure with some other lady in New York. He was in the newspapers all the time with Doris Lilly. He had no self-discipline. And he didn't have much taste either—although there were some splendid women, like Marietta, for whom I have the greatest regard. I had heard about that romance. We met at a dinner party and she was very straightforward about her adventure with John. She told me how he pursued her, everything! I said, 'When did this take place?' She said, 'When your relationship with him was over.' That isn't quite the case. It was collateral.

"I must say that when I met Marietta, I thought, 'You are the one.' That would have been an absolutely wonderful union. But she's had an awfully good life without him. She said this charming thing about her passage with him which sort of sums it up. She said, 'He taught me one thing: that I was not Miss Boston, I was, instead, Miss World.' Isn't that delightful?

"She also asked me, 'Do you have fantasies about him? I have the fantasy that he's old, sick, poverty-stricken, and he turns to me.' I said, 'Mine is the deathbed. He's on his deathbed and he calls for me!' That was in 1976."

* * *

The kinds of things John did to undermine his relationship with Olivia were often very public. He sent for Doris Lilly and took her to parties at Sam Spiegel's. Spiegel had managed to produce a film, *Tales of Manhattan*, in 1942 and within a few years had established a reputation for good taste and even better parties. "I used to go there all the time," Huston said. "Sam's house became a gathering spot, a source for a certain side of Hollywood. There was always someone interesting to talk to." Huston was one of a contingent of people who had helped Spiegel out when he first came to California in the early forties. "All the people who had connections with Germany knew Sam," John said. "He came to the States from Mexico, where he had put together a musical and got in trouble for writing bad checks. Sam was not a stranger to material difficulties. When he wound up in Hollywood, all of us who knew him and were now in better circumstances chipped in and kept him afloat. It was an act of friendship and a recognition of an actual ability on Sam's part."

Doris Lilly remembers seeing more of John in California than she had in New York. "He paid for everything. I had to quit my job at *Town & Country* and I stayed at a boardinghouse on DeLongpre. Things weren't so sophisticated that I would stay with John, but I would go there. And he was always taking me to Sam Spiegel's house. Sam hated to see me there because I was this young, unsophisticated, badly dressed nobody and he liked glamorous women. But he didn't dare say no to John. Sam needed John. And John greased life for people that he cared about—but you paid for it with your dignity."

One night when John stood her up and went out with another woman, Doris got so angry that she went to John's house in Coldwater Canyon and, in a drunken rage, began to throw rocks through his windows. Then she took a knife, cut through a screen, and entered the house. "There was glass all over . . . and no John. I felt terrible, but I was so drunk I thought the only thing to do was to go to sleep. So I laid down on the bed and fell sound asleep. Then lights came on and John came in and saw the mess and saw me. He got rid of the girl.

"The next day he said, 'Well, honey, I think you'd better get the Yellow Pages and have a man come to fix the windows.' He never got mad. You could never make him mad, no matter what you did. It infuriated me. So I started going out with Errol Flynn. I was maybe eighteen then."

*   *   *

On July 20, with Huston close to finishing his cut of *San Pietro*, Gram died. She was eighty-nine and the cause of her death was listed as heart failure and senility. She had lived a rich, eventful life: had helped settle the Kansas prairie; baked bread over a buffalo-chip stove fire; stopped a lynch mob; fought a railroad; saved a town; typeset, edited, and published Midwestern newspapers; stayed married for eighteen turbulent years; and was alive to see what her daughter never did—the success of her grandson as a major film director.

Jules Buck accompanied John to Hollywood Memorial Park to assist in the arrangements. At the funeral home, Buck recalled, "John was dark attired, his hands rubbing together. The director of the home didn't know who he was. 'We'll see that she has a good send-off,' he said. John looked at me, we didn't know what the fuck he was talking about." Then he showed John some elegant caskets.

"It's not what I had in mind," Huston said.

"What did you have in mind?" the funeral director asked.

"Something not quite as ostentatious. She wouldn't want it that way. She was from the plains. She came from deep, deep country." He spotted a plain wooden box behind a curtain and asked about it.

"Oh," the director protested, "that's for Orthodox Jews, that's not for your grandmother."

"How much is it?" John asked

"Ninety-nine dollars and ninety-nine cents."

"My grandmother was the most Orthodox Jewess who ever lived in Indiana," John said.

"She doesn't look Jewish," the surprised director said.

"I'm a Jew, too," Huston said, then pointed to Buck, and said, "he's not."

11

PSYCHIC
LANDSCAPES

BY AUGUST 1944 *THE BATTLE OF SAN PIETRO* WAS READY
and John set up a screening for some of the army's top brass. It was
the uncut, five-reel version that showed the futility of war, the failure
of the frontal assault on the village, the field of bodies that had been
blown apart, the dead faces of soldiers laid out in a row on their
bedrolls, their voices talking about how the world was going to be a
better place after the war. It was too much for the generals.

"The room where it was shown," Huston said, "was full of three-star,
two-star, and one-star generals and their entourages. I was sitting in the
projection room and the highest-ranking officer present got up and left.
Then a two-star general left, and then a one-star general. They withdrew by rank. The reaction was strongly against the picture being
shown; they felt it would dishearten any young soldier who had never
been in combat and I was called in to General Surrold's office. One of
the generals there said, 'This could be interpreted as an anti-war film.'

" 'Gentlemen,' I said, 'if I ever make anything other than an
anti-war film, I hope you take me out and shoot me.' "

The generals decided that the film should not be released. And it
wouldn't have been if General George C. Marshall hadn't heard about

it and asked to see it. Marshall was greatly moved and felt that not only should it be released, but it should also be used as a training film for every soldier going into combat. Marshall suggested that some of the more brutal ironies, such as the voices over the dead soldiers, be cut in deference to those soldiers' families, but with his approval, "the whole atmosphere changed," Huston said. He was given a medal and promoted to the rank of major and came away feeling enormous respect for General Marshall.

Novelist Herbert Gold was one of those teenage soldiers who saw *The Battle of San Pietro* when it was first released. "I had not yet acquired the notion of my possible mortality," he recalled. "I was itching to be dropped behind the German lines." What so overwhelmed Gold was how Huston and his crew were able to bring home the reality of war, to show innocent grunts like himself just what he was about to get into. "The reason that this film about war has an immediacy not to be found in any other," Gold would write, "is that John Huston and the others were there, no shit, really right there under fire while the men were dying . . . and the faces of the cameramen were brother to the faces of the men who lay broken-skulled, destroyed, with pants stained. . . . Even cut and distorted, the film is a masterpiece of experienced immediate horror."

When it was released to the public the following year, it was cited as the best film of 1945 by *The Nation*'s critic James Agee, in spite of the fact that the edited version had been reduced to a mere thirty minutes and an unnecessary introduction by General Mark Clark, written by Huston, was included, along with the Mormon Tabernacle Choir singing over the faces of the children of San Pietro as they emerged from the rubble of what was once their homes. Agee called it "As good a war film as I have seen; in some ways it is the best. . . . It is clear that Huston understood what he was recording . . . as a soldier and an artist and a man."

Film historian Arthur Knight considered Huston's film, along with two others made at the same time—Willy Wyler's *Memphis Belle* and John Ford's *Battle of Midway*—"masterpieces of on-the-spot war reporting. . . . They never suggested that war was a heroic, glamorous business. It was always a means . . . to a vital end—the preservation of democracy. The democracy that they extolled was implicit in the films themselves, ingrained in the spirit of the men who made them."

The success of *San Pietro* helped lift John's spirits following the death of his grandmother and the dissolution of his once-torrid affair with

Olivia de Havilland. He agreed to work on a script for Mark Hellinger based on Ernest Hemingway's short story "The Killers." And for Sam Spiegel, he discussed writing *The Stranger*, a script about a Nazi war criminal hiding out in a Connecticut town, where he commits a murder and attempts to cover it up. The Hellinger film was for Universal and the Spiegel one for RKO, but since Huston was still under contract with Warner's, he knew he wouldn't be able to take screen credit for either of them, although he had hoped to work out an arrangement so he could direct *The Stranger*. He also felt that since he was still in uniform, it wouldn't be right to take credit for civilian work. On both scripts he would work with Anthony Veiller, who would be out of the army and uncommitted to any studio, and thus could take the credits.

Another of John's scripts, *Three Strangers*, the one he had outlined when he was down-and-out in London, had been polished by Howard Koch and was finally being made at Warner's with Jean Negulesco directing.

With two movies to write and *The Treasure of the Sierra Madre* to plan while waiting for his next assignment from the Signal Corps, Huston was enjoying his stay in California. In November he spent a week at Walter's ranch in Porterville, writing to Doris Lilly in New York, "Outside are some thousand head of cattle mooing near and far. I do miss you ever so much, dear . . . write me a line and miss a guy a *little bit*." When Doris didn't immediately respond, John wrote her again. "Don't you like me anymore? Am I no longer your favorite man in the universe? Is your life not desolate without me?" Doris replied, and on December 20, John wrote to her again from Hollywood. "Doris Darling," he began. "Your letters are ever so dear and I can't tell you how much they mean to me out here in this place I like least of anywhere. The sun shines all the time and everybody has beautiful tans and it's all simply terrible. I called you several times but you are always out being unfaithful. Are you pretty as ever? And your feet? And your bottom? I don't think I'll be out here too much longer. You may be sure I'm making every effort in the direction of New York. And Darling Darling Doris, who's my very best girl, even if she doesn't come home nights, damn her. I love you Darling."

On March 25, 1945, Walter Huston accepted an invitation to appear at the Civic Auditorium in San Francisco to deliver a speech to the San Francisco Council of Civic Unity. It was written for him by H. S. Kraft and was so stunning that pamphlets of it were published by the council because of the large number of requests from people "who felt it was one of the great experiences of their lives." It was a long, moving oration that Walter delivered with all the nuances, pauses, and emotion he had learned from his sister and from George M. Cohan. "I consider this trip and this meeting important to the war effort because unity isn't just a word," Walter began. "Unity is a weapon of war." He praised the courage of Paul Robeson, who had gone to Russia and Spain and "came back and told us the truth." He chastised the "America Firsters," who didn't condemn Mussolini, Hitler, and "the Japs." He came out on the side of Roosevelt, Churchill, and Stalin as well as Henry Wallace. And he came out against the "weapon of the lie. The lie, in the last twenty years, is responsible for more deaths and devastation than bombs or guns." He was particularly stirring against "the most vicious" lie of all: "the lie that's responsible for anti-Semitism. It's the most vicious because it's the easiest. . . . You know the old carnival trick, while the belly dancer is shaking a mean hula-hula, the sharpie picks the farmer's pocket. Cry 'Jew' and the people forget the real causes and the real issues. . . .

"I hate baiters of every kind. Because I know a Jew baiter is a labor baiter and a labor baiter is a Negro baiter and a Negro baiter is an American hater. I'm not here to speak in defense of the Jews, or in defense of any minority. I'm here to speak in defense of people and the welfare of people in a democracy. I'm speaking in defense of myself because, as sure as the day follows the night, the honest Christian will follow the Jew to the grave, or the burning pit, or the concentration camp, if bigotry ever takes root in this country."

The speech brought the audience to its feet over a far more serious issue than the Prohibition debate he once staged with Aimee Semple McPherson. The only people it left frustrated were the New Dealers, who would have liked to have made a political candidate out of the gentle actor.

John applauded his father's oration, although he had anything but unity on his mind before he left for New York for the opening of *The Battle of San Pietro*. Lesley had told him that she wanted to make their break final. On April 6, 1945, she appeared as the plaintiff before the judicial district court in Clark County, Nevada. She wasn't alone, she discovered. "Mayo Bogart was also there, because Bogart was going to marry Bacall."

With John free, one might assume that Olivia de Havilland was shopping for wedding bands, but it was too late for them as well. "John was a gambler, gambled about everything," she said. "He certainly gambled with relationships that meant something to him, and I think ours did mean a great deal to him. But he gambled with it and he lost."

"Olivia de Havilland always was a very outgoing and aggressive and positive person, an 'I want' kind of dame," Cherokee observed. "She had claimed John during their life together and never could understand why it wasn't the greatest love affair in history. But John had such disrespect for himself that if you liked him then he knew there was something wrong. That was in the female department. In every other department, he had enormous respect for himself. But with women, I think it was because he didn't think he could feel. He felt that love had to be something big and overwhelming and, of course, real love isn't. So he kind of faked it by making a lot of noise.

"John was everybody's lover because he let you fulfill your fantasy. He gave nothing of himself and the girls gave everything, they wrote their own story and he helped them fill in the blanks. He slowly saw that women were not pure and sweet and angelic, but more and more he needed their adulation. But the more you loved him, the less respect he had for you."

By then, Cherokee was finding out about sex and romance with such actors as Gilbert Roland and Jimmy Stewart, whom she found to be "like a dial tone, I didn't consider him at all attractive because he was slow, he had hair growing out of his ears and nose and he was dull. And at the time John was courting me, I didn't consider him handsome either, his feet were too big, his arms were like a monkey. He never was attractive to me and that used to drive him nuts! Then I brought home Gilbert Roland and he said, 'And that's attractive?' I said, 'Well, I like his style of romancing a person.' "

Cherokee went to Mexico to work on a picture with Roland and when she returned John surprised her. "No, no, no, you don't do that," he said in his kitchen on a Sunday, as they waited for fifty guests to arrive. Then he added, "I suppose we ought to get married." "That's the only time we ever discussed it," Cherokee said. "We weren't sleeping together or living together, we were living with everybody else. In those days, when I wanted my romantic fill and my idea of a man to sleep with, it was not John. I truly loved John, but I was not in love physically.

"He was my brother, he was my father, and he became my lover, but it was not a successful relationship. I loved cuddling and being with him and I loved everything he represented, but I didn't particularly like the sex. He filled every other bill, except he wasn't romantic. We could love each other without sexual love very easily, because he was a bad lover. He didn't love the physical part of you. I loved him until he would start to love me and then I knew that wasn't real. I know what it is but he didn't."

On April 29, John was at a party at David Selznick's house when Errol Flynn said something "wretched" about one of Huston's women that so angered John he felt compelled to challenge Flynn to a fight to protect the lady's honor. Like Huston, Flynn was an experienced fighter and the two men went into Selznick's garden to duke it out. The actor outweighed the director by twenty-five pounds and his athletic ability gave him a definite advantage. Flynn knocked Huston down almost immediately, but John got up. Flynn knocked him down again, and again John got up. By this time Flynn had managed to sober up his drunken opponent and John started landing some punches of his own. The savage fight lasted nearly an hour and Flynn cut up John's face, breaking his nose with one of his blows.

"I remember that the language on both our parts, although not heated, was about as vile as it could get," Huston said. "Errol started it, but I went right along with it. And those were the days when 'motherfucker' was not a term of endearment." Sure that Flynn would kick him when he was down, Huston was impressed with Flynn's fighting according to Queensberry. "Neither of us committed any fouls, and there was nothing we could complain about afterward."

Huston and Flynn went to separate hospitals to avoid publicity, but the fight made the newspapers and was the talk of the town. When he spoke with John on the phone, Flynn reported that he had two broken ribs; John told him that he had thoroughly enjoyed their fight and hoped they could do it again sometime.

"On the Saturday night he had that fight with Errol Flynn, I was called to come and get him," Cherokee said. "I met him in front of a hillside house and was appalled! He was all bloody. Those were his drunken Saturday nights. John was a professional boxer but he never came out ahead because he was drunk. He fought like an Irish barroom fighter. It was just expected on Saturday night that you were going to go out and get drunk and show whose girl was whose. But with John, he didn't fight over any woman. He was fighting over his standing with the guy. John didn't give a shit about any woman. The only woman he really cared for was Marietta—and that became a fantasy of what a woman should be."

* * *

Anne Selepegno had gone by boat to Balboa with a friend and when she returned, she heard the newsboys yelling the headline: "Mussolini has been assassinated." But when she bought the paper all she saw was John's face on the front page. "What the hell did he do now?" she wondered. When she reached him by phone he said, "You ought to see the other guy."

Walter told her that John had got beaten up badly but that it wasn't a fair fight because Flynn had been wearing a ring on his finger and it cut up John's face. "If they could have a return bout at the Hollywood Bowl and have the proceeds go to charity, I'll bet you that Johnny could beat the shit out of him," Walter said.

John never told anyone whose honor he was defending, although most people believe it had to do with Olivia. "That surprised me very much," Olivia said. "I don't know what the remark was, but Errol might have tried to provoke John. It happened quite some time after I decided that I better somehow separate my feelings from John."

Doris Lilly was sure the fight was over her, even though Huston specifically denied it. "Errol told me John said to him, 'I hear you are having a good time at my expense,' " Doris recalled. "Errol thought he meant Olivia because Olivia was mad about him. And John said, 'Doris Lilly.' Errol said, 'Go fuck yourself.' John hit him and they had a big fight. It was over me, because Errol told me. Errol and I were pals."

That their fight made the front page was an indication that the war was winding down. But the very next day the Huston-Flynn battle was old news as rumors that Adolf Hitler had killed himself began circulating. And then on May 8, 1945, came V-E Day, signaling the end of the war in Europe. What remained was Japan, which was cruelly hit with two atomic bombs on August 6 and 9. The world had changed and there was less to cheer about on August 14, when World War II officially came to an end.

"The atom bomb changed my thinking," Huston told an interviewer. "I think it is all right for soldiers to go out and get killed—even if they don't want to—but when it gets to the point that weapons are so devastating that they threaten existence itself—not just the life of a soldier, but human existence—then you'd better start thinking in other terms."

As the country welcomed their soldiers home, Paul Kohner got Walter Huston $40,000 for five days' work as a revivalist preacher in

David Selznick's *Duel in the Sun*, which Selznick hoped would be a western *Gone With the Wind*. He had hired a star-studded cast, with Jennifer Jones, Gregory Peck, and Joseph Cotten starring and supported by Huston, Lionel Barrymore, Lillian Gish, Charles Bickford, Harry Carey, Otto Kruger, Herbert Marshall, and Sidney Blackmer. King Vidor was hired to direct and when he couldn't take the producer's over-the-shoulder involvement, William Dieterle took over. Selznick exercised his option of keeping Walter available for ten weeks at $4,000 a week and then paid him more to remain overtime.

Before Huston worked on *Duel in the Sun* he had completed two other films. The first, *And Then There Were None*, based on Agatha Christie's novel, gave him the opportunity to play a suspect/victim in a series of murders involving ten strangers invited to a strange house with the host missing. The second was *Dragonwyck*, also based on a novel, by Anya Seton, and also involving mystery and murder in a dark mansion on the Hudson River. It was produced by Ernst Lubitsch, directed by Joseph Mankiewicz, and starred Gene Tierney, who had worked with Walter in *Shanghai Gesture* and was "thrilled" to be in his company.

The money Walter made from these pictures went for purchasing more land and more cattle as he became comfortable in his role as rancher. He even took home movies of his workers as they castrated the calves.

John was never as interested in cattle as he was in horses, and he enjoyed spending as much time as he could at his home in Tarzana with his four horses. He had given up the idea of selling the house after his divorce from Lesley and stayed there while waiting for the Signal Corps to give him his next assignment.

He was asked to make a film about soldiers who had survived the war but were psychologically disturbed and in need of psychiatric treatment at Mason General Hospital, where he had visited Rey Scott. Huston felt he was being given a chance to look at the aftereffects of war in a way no filmmaker had ever done before. It was a privileged opportunity, to bring his cameras directly into the mental ward of an army hospital and record the treatment of soldiers under hypnosis and trance-inducing drugs.

While he worked out the details for making *Let There Be Light*, John took Marietta to meet his old friend and mentor, Paul de Kruif. John proceeded to get drunk and de Kruif assumed the posture of teacher as he told his successful friend that they had both sold out. It was a distressing, disappointing evening for Huston, quite unlike the night a few years earlier when H. L. Mencken chastised him at a restaurant. Huston explained that he had become a director and Mencken told him, "You'll get over that" and said he should have remained a writer. John enjoyed telling the Mencken story, but with de Kruif, who was such an important formative influence, his cynicism was devastating.

"It was just really too much for me," Huston said. "De Kruif asked Marietta if she wasn't a society girl. Very heavy-handed. He then said to me, in a way of it being a confession, that neither of us lived up to expectations. We had settled for money instead of the things we believed in. It was shocking to hear this from de Kruif, who, my God, had—I always thought—lived true and straight. I thought I would be better at directing films than I would be at writing books. I had a more natural expression that way."

Just as John was sure he had chosen the right profession, he was also sure that he had found the right woman and tried to convince Marietta to marry him. Marietta, though, was worried about what her husband, Desmond, would think when he returned from his tour of duty. "She wished to tell him about us in her own time," Huston would later write. "I didn't hear from her for three days after Desmond arrived, then she came to my hotel. I could see that she'd been through an ordeal: her face was drawn and her eyes swollen. Desmond had agreed to give her a divorce but only on condition that she see an analyst and undergo therapy before starting proceedings. I protested that that might take years."

When Marietta refused to let John talk to Desmond, he painfully agreed to stay out of her life until she called him. He resumed his relationship with Doris Lilly, but his heart was with Marietta.

"The only woman that John ever was in love with that he couldn't get was Marietta," Doris acknowledged. "Everybody who knew John then says the same thing. He would have married her like that, but he couldn't get her. She would not have it. And, of course, the more he couldn't get her, the more he wanted her."

Yet according to Doris, Marietta wasn't the only woman Huston considered marrying. "John had never discussed marriage with me, but he cared for me a lot," Doris said, "and couldn't stay away. It was a great physical attraction. Had to be, for him. Because there were so many women and they were all after him. He was charming, cruel, and that's what they liked, those women. One time he told me, 'I'm incapable of loving anyone. What I've done to my ex-wives, I'm ashamed. But I personally can never be in love, ever, with anybody.'

"Then he said, 'Look, this is what we'll do. I want you to go to this doctor with me and if you get pregnant, I will marry you.' Can you imagine! I nearly died! So I said no. And then he really let me have it.

He was half drunk and called me all kinds of names. He called me a tart. I wasn't a tart.

"He was just the world's number-one womanizer. And John's conquests were fabulous women. Warren Beatty's got broads, but John, he was screwing everybody in New York. He didn't miss anybody, he had every movie star you can think of. No lines were ever drawn. Including people who worked for him—maids, cooks. I once caught him and his secretary, Anne Selepegno, in the shower together."

Anne Selepegno also remembered this incident, but it wasn't what Doris thought it was. "John would do anything to make anybody mad," Selepegno said. "I was taking a shower at Tarzana . . . Doris Lilly was there for the weekend and he deliberately jumped in the shower with me. 'John! Get out of here!' I said. Now, he did that to get on Doris's nerves. And she had a fit about it."

Doris was convinced that "John had a thing about women that was really cruel. It wasn't that he used women. I mean, they used him as much as he used them. But I really believe that John didn't like women very much. I can't help but think that. I hate to even say it, but he might have had homosexual feelings. It might have been something that happened to him when he was very young. It couldn't have been his father, because Walter screwed around like mad.

"But there was something lurking underneath John. That's why he could direct Bogart the way he did. That's why he was such a good director—and you have to give genius credit: His films just stand up like rocks. But if you look at his pictures, you'll find something in every single one of them where he humiliates a woman in some way. Look at Claire Trevor in *Key Largo* when he had her mascara smeared. And in *The List of Adrian Messenger* John had that bag of dead animals in the last scene. Every damn picture he made he had something cruel in it. I was afraid of him. He wasn't physical, I don't mean that. He just could be so mean.

"One night he was working on a script with Peter Viertel and he asked me to come in. Then he read me some dialogue and wanted my opinion. So I fainted. I was so scared because I didn't have an opinion. After that, every time I wanted to get out of a situation, I'd just faint."

For three emotionally exhausting, yet exhilarating months, Huston submerged himself in the mental disorders of the patients at Mason General; it became the closest thing he ever had to a religious experience. Each week the hospital admitted two groups of seventy-five patients in various conditions of emotional distress. "Some had tics, some were paralyzed, one in ten was psychotic," Huston observed. He decided to make his film by following one group through their eight weeks of therapy. Cameras were set up in the receiving room as patients arrived, in the rooms where doctors worked with patients, and wherever Huston felt he wanted to put a camera to capture the experience. He observed the different methods used to break through to these patients, from simple hypnosis to violent shock therapy, and he was given a passkey to enter any section of the hospital. As his cameras recorded thousands of feet of film, he began to see what appeared to be miracles taking place: Men who couldn't walk were walking, men who couldn't talk were talking, men who always cried stopped crying.

He even picked up the technique of hypnotizing patients and was occasionally asked to do so when the chief hypnotist, Colonel Simon, was not available. With Charlie Kaufman, Huston wrote a script as the picture was shot, beginning with a narrator commenting on a troopship as it enters a harbor: "The guns are quiet now, the papers of peace have been signed, and the oceans of the earth are filled with ships coming home." As nurses wheel patients down a gangplank we hear: "Here is human salvage, the final result of all that metal and fire could do to violate mortal flesh." We see another gangplank, soldiers walking unaided, then an ambulance arriving at a hospital, a receiving room for patients who show no bodily wounds. "These are the casualties of the spirit, the troubled mind, men who are damaged emotionally. Born and bred in peace, educated to hate war, they were overnight plunged into sudden and terrible situations. Every man has his breaking point; and these, in the fulfillment of their duties as soldiers, were forced beyond the limit of human endurance." After the patients are briefed by an officer the interrogation between doctors and patients begins, and we follow the progress of this particular group of men as their blocked memories are unblocked and they relive their fears and guilts.

By the end of the eight weeks we begin to see a return to normal life as the patients are shown reading bulletin boards, eating ice cream, working with their hands. The narrator explains, "And now the days begin to seem long. There's the old healthy sound of bellyaching in the air. 'Spinach? Spinach again?' And 'How about a *good* movie for a change?' No longer is a man shut up within the lonely recesses of himself. He's breaking out of his prison into life. . . ."

We see the men playing baseball now, running and sliding into bases. Then, by means of a flashback, we see them as they were when they first entered the hospital. A true transformation has occurred. It's a documentary of hope and renewal.

John asked his father to narrate *Let There Be Light*. Walter was impressed with how John had managed to capture the various stages of war in his three films. But the army was disturbed by John's often shocking penetration into the treatment of mental disorders—it was too unsettling, it opened a whole Pandora's box of the evils of war and the effects on not only the vanquished but also the victors. When Huston got permission to screen it for an invited audience of friends at the Museum of Modern Art, the MPs arrived moments before the screening room darkened and the film was confiscated. As far as the army was concerned, John Huston had made a Top Secret film.

In the May 11, 1946, issue of *The Nation*, James Agee expressed his outrage. "John Huston's *Let There Be Light*, a fine, terrible, valuable non-fiction film about psychoneurotic soldiers, has been forbidden civilian circulation by the War Department. I don't know what is necessary to reverse this disgraceful decision, but if dynamite is required, then dynamite is indicated."

Huston thought the film wasn't released because "wounds that you can see—heroes without legs or arms—are acceptable, because it shows a love of country and patriotism and the right stuff; but with men who were emotionally injured, who'd been destroyed in their spirits, that's a different question.

"The authorities wanted to maintain the 'warrior' myth, which said that our American soldiers went to war and came back all the stronger for the experience. Only a few weaklings fell by the wayside."

In December 1980, after some powerful lobbying by Jack Valenti, president of the Motion Picture Association of America, producer Ray Stark, and others, *Let There Be Light* was finally released for public viewing, on the orders of Vice-President Walter Mondale.

When screened together, Huston's war documentaries make a compelling trilogy as he so precisely captured the preparations for war, the actual gritty fighting, and the lingering aftereffects. On February 13, 1946, Huston was discharged from the Signal Corps and a chapter of his life as a documentary filmmaker came to an end. His work was powerful, widely praised, and highly controversial. *Report from the Aleutians* was nominated for an Oscar in 1943; *The Battle of San Pietro* earned him the Legion of Merit and was called "the most humane, most moving, most nearly perfect of war pictures"; and *Let There Be Light* was considered so disturbing that it took a vice-president to get it released thirty-five years after it was made and it was *still* touted as one of the most insightful and moving documentaries ever filmed.

This period altered the way Huston would make his future films. "It gave me a sense of the reality of human behavior," he distinguished, "as against the conventions that the Hollywood screen rather cannibalistically had come to accept as behavior. It also inculcated in me a vast desire to work away from studios. I found a freedom and an inspiration from a location that the barren walls of the studio didn't give me."

Opting for freedom and inspiration after appearing in a dozen films and narrating twelve others since the United States entered the war, Walter Huston decided to return to the stage, to play an Indiana farmer in "a light little comedy about an old guy who falls in love with a young girl. The neighbors and relatives raise hell but he wins out in the end." It was called *Apple of His Eye*. Walter decided to star as well as to co-produce. Kenyon Nicholson, author of *The Barker*, wrote the play with Charles Robinson. Jed Harris was to direct it and be Walter's partner.

John was in New York finishing *Let There Be Light* and visited the rehearsals. "I met Jed again and he was another person entirely," John recalled. "Delightful. I liked him enormously. My father did, too, and thought he was a hell of a director, which he was. I was just getting out of the army at that time. Jed had a place on Fire Island and he'd come into town. Rooms were terribly hard to get in New York and I was forever ending up with Jed in the other bed. But he was a marvelous companion. He was very thoughtful, very observant of the passing parade."

Mary Wickes, who had worked for Walter's sister Margaret, was cast as Walter's daughter-in-law in the play and thought Jed Harris was "a damn good director," although "very eccentric." Wickes was also impressed with Walter, whom she considered "Olympian. 'Gimme the part, where's the stage? And what are we playing?' He loved the stage, he hankered for it. But he didn't fraternize with us at all. In fact, there were things going on in the company, things were getting a little out of kilter, and Walter did not choose to know anything about it. He stayed aloof. He was a straight-on, businesslike kind of actor."

"The fact that these folks happen to live on a farm is unimportant," Walter told a reporter. "In any community you can find tragedy and comedy in the situation of an older man falling painfully in love with a young girl. I played the same role as Peter Stuyvesant in *Knickerbocker Holiday* and liked it so much that this play appealed to me."

They previewed the play for two weeks in Philadelphia before opening at the Biltmore Theatre on Broadway on February 5, 1946, six years after Walter's last appearance on the Great White Way in *Love's Old Sweet Song*. "It's so much easier for me, the stage is," Walter told reporter Seymour Peck, "the pressure is so much less than the movies." *Born Yesterday* with Judy Holliday had opened the previous night and Mary Wickes believed that the raves over Holliday's performance cut into their play. "We got all right notices," Wickes said, "it wasn't embarrassing, but it wasn't a big hit."

Four days after the play opened Walter wrote to Paul Kohner, "The New York critics were not as kind to the play as the out-of-town reviewers. They seemed to like me, but they went out of their way, we thought, to be a little mean."

John enjoyed watching his father playing what he knew to be a fairly accurate portrait of a man with a roving eye. But with his own heart's desire unwilling to see him until she sorted out her affairs, John decided to return to civilian life in California, where he waited for Marietta's phone calls. "I lived from one call to another," he said. "Sometimes she'd be late calling and I'd sweat blood, waiting. It was a time of frustration for me. Never was there any reassurance from her. . . . The weeks became months. I became more and more certain that it was all over between us."

He expressed his anxieties to his father over the phone. Curious about what kind of woman could hold such power over John, he decided to pay Marietta a visit.

"I was in bed with the flu, streaming red nose, lank hair, and the doorbell rang," Marietta related. "Meg came and said, 'There's a man at the door who wants to see you, Mr. Huston.' I said, 'You must have gotten that wrong because he's not in New York. Just tell whoever it is that I have the flu.' A few minutes later, into my bedroom came Walter Huston! He was a terribly attractive man. I was horrified thinking that I would give him a bad bug, and perhaps paramount was the fact that I looked so terrible and I wanted him to see me at my best.

" 'I see you are feeling awful and I sympathize,' he said. 'Don't talk. I'll just talk to you. I hear you know my son.' I said, 'Yes.' 'No more talk about him. Now, what would you like me to do?' I had seen him in *Knickerbocker Holiday* and I said., 'I'd like you to sing "September

Song." ' So he stood in front of the window and sang 'September Song.' It was the most marvelous, marvelous occasion.

"Then he sat down on my bed and said, 'You don't mind my telephoning, do you darling?' I was not brought up in a world where everybody called you 'darling.' I remember John calling an operator 'dear.' Calling the operator 'dear'? You can't imagine the different worlds we came from. In any case, Walter telephoned one lady and asked her out that night. She couldn't make it so he made a second call to Gilda Gray, the shimmy artist. 'Gilda! How wonderful!' And then a great explosion of happiness. 'We haven't seen each other for at least seven years, how would you like to come and dine with me tonight?' With this mission accomplished, he put down the phone and said, 'Well, I'll be going now. I'm very glad to have met you; I've heard a lot about you.' "

Walter would hear even more when John told him how seriously in love he was with Marietta and that he wanted to marry her. For Marietta, it was a difficult time. "When John wanted to marry me, it was all very mixed up. I'd rather not talk about that time, it was a painful period, which lasted about two years. He just wasn't what you'd call marriage material and I was never really seriously thinking that I would marry him. I was certainly in love with him, he was the most attractive man possible and he changed my whole world around, but nobody should have married him. He was certainly a very restless person and that's why he shouldn't have married anybody. We remained so close because one knew that it really wasn't possible. It didn't have anything to do with smartness on my part but with survival. Or just native instincts."

PART FIVE

12

KEYES TO A TREASURE

"I MUST SAY I FELT HATRED FOR JOHN FOR A LONG TIME," Olivia de Havilland confessed more than four decades later, her memories still fresh, still bitter. "He saw me at a party when I was about to do *To Each His Own* in 1946 and he began his pursuit again. But I had simply been through too much. I didn't really trust him anymore."

Still hoping that Marietta would come around, John enjoyed himself back in California after his discharge, going frog hunting in Bakersfield, to the races at Santa Anita, playing cards with his friends. Tola Litvak, Sam Spiegel, David Selznick, and Willy Wyler used to invite him to play gin with them, but Huston preferred poker. "I wasn't a good gin player," he said, "and they all played gin for big stakes. Gin requires great immediate concentration on numbers, percentages, remembering cards that had been played. It wasn't my idea of a fun game."

At a dinner party at Sir Charles Mendl's in Beverly Hills John found himself sitting next to a twenty-six-year-old actress named Evelyn Keyes, who had been recently divorced from director Charles Vidor. She had been a nightclub chorus dancer before starting her film career in 1938 and had appeared in twenty-two pictures, including *Gone With the Wind*, *Here Comes Mr. Jordan*, and *The Jolson Story*. Errol Flynn sat on

Keyes's left, and both men vied for her attention, ignoring each other but behaving in a civilized manner. Keyes found Flynn to be "more beautiful than ever, absolutely in his prime," and yet she was more attracted to Huston, who was "not beautiful at all, if anything almost ugly. Handsome eyes though. . . . Deep pouches underneath gave them a sad look. Generous mouth, good teeth. Weird posture. The long back curved forward, a bit hunched over. A really queer nose . . . And he had a way of talking, leaning in, wrapping his melted caramel voice around you, in appealing pied-piper fashion."

She attempted to get him to notice her after dinner, but John was too absorbed in other people. When she was ready to go she made sure he saw that she was leaving alone and walked out slowly to her car. Then she heard footsteps clicking behind her and a voice calling her name. She turned, her heart pumping wildly, as John caught up with her. "He seemed to be pondering some momentous decision," she would later write in her book, Scarlett O'Hara's Younger Sister, "a characteristic of his over even the smallest consideration." Then he invited her to have a nightcap. It was two-thirty in the morning and the bars on Sunset Strip were closed. John proposed "an adventure." Evelyn "shivered with excitement" as he took her over the canyons to his Tarzana home, where he showed her his horses, dogs, cats, cows, goat, and then his house, with its huge living room and fireplace built of fieldstone. She was taken by the things he had collected but she felt the living room to be "rather barnlike and impersonal," too much indirect lighting, "devoid of actual life. There were no flowers. No green things growing." When he suggested she spend the night, she suspected a seduction scene, but John was "stylish" and showed her to a guest room. "I was smitten," wrote Keyes.

It didn't take long for Gentleman John and Smitten Keyes to consummate their love affair. She found his lovemaking to be "sure, with authority, and cool." They began to see each other regularly, whenever they weren't working, she at Columbia, he writing The Treasure of the Sierra Madre. "How good we all were with the beginnings," she reflected. "How beautifully we played the courtship parts, the romancing business—we all had so much practice."

In August 1946, John took Evelyn and her mother to a preview of The Killers, which starred Burt Lancaster, Edmund O'Brien, and Ava Gardner. Only Tony Veiller was credited with the screenplay, but it was fully acknowledged that John had written it as well. Huston liked the picture and was attracted to Gardner, who, at twenty-four, had already been divorced from Mickey Rooney, pursued by Howard Hughes, and was in the throes of a bad marriage to band leader Artie Shaw. She was a woman of near-perfect proportions, with a classically beautiful face and an impetuous spirit that drove men wild. She had been cast more for her looks than her talent. *The Killers* showed that she could act as well and she credited producer Mark Hellinger for seeing her as an actress and not just a sexpot. Jules Buck was assistant producer of *The Killers*, and on the Sunday after the screening he and his wife, Joyce, brought Ava to John's house in the valley for dinner. John also invited Evelyn, but she felt jealous and wouldn't come. "I wasn't going to get caught in a dumb trap like that," she thought, "competing with Ava Gardner."

Ava remembered the evening very well, how they all "got a little sloshed" and went night swimming in John's pool. "I was diving off the balcony," she said with a laugh. "We had a chasing match, he chased me around out in the bushes behind his house. It was a big joke. Oh, funny, funny. And God knows what time it was, it was so late and we had a long, long drive back to town. 'Why not spend the night?' John said. 'No, I want to go home,' I said. So we left at dawn with John standing in the doorway, waving good-bye, and Jules and Joyce saying, 'Oh, poor John.' And later that day he went off to Las Vegas with Evelyn."

John thought it was a few days later, but Ava's memory coincides with Evelyn's. He had called Keyes on the set that day and they made a date for dinner at Romanoff's in Beverly Hills. They drank vodka, ate butterfly steaks, held hands, and John whispered to her, "I missed my darling so much."

"I missed you, too, John," she whispered back.

"I don't want to be without my girl, ever again," he said.

"Then why don't we get married," Evelyn heard herself saying.

John looked at her for a long, silent time. He had struck out with Ava the night before, he was tired of waiting for Marietta . . . here was a woman who wanted him, who was bold and brassy enough to take the initiative. It was so crazy, so unexpected, it seemed right. "Why not?" he replied.

"Tonight," Evelyn said recklessly. "Now. Las Vegas."

Humphrey Bogart and Lauren Bacall walked into the restaurant and noticed them sitting in a booth. "Both of them sloshed," Bacall noticed. "And that's how they went to Vegas to get married."

"It was spur of the moment the night we went off and got married," Evelyn recalled with a slight sense of bewilderment some forty years later. "We didn't have a ring, of course, so we called Mike Romanoff over and said, 'We're going to Las Vegas to get married but we don't have a ring.' He said, 'I have one at the bottom of my swimming pool.' At that point I was looking for the prince and the happy-ever-after. What a fool I was. You get it all wrong if you think people go around falling in love, although John was a good lover, very thoughtful, and he made it fun, made it pleasurable.

"We went to Las Vegas and got married and I didn't sleep all night. I went to work the next morning, I was doing *Johnny O'Clock*, and then we started working at night. I hardly saw John at all. That's when I called John and said he could come and get his new bride. It was three in the morning and he was asleep. 'Who is this?' he said."

David Selznick threw them a wedding party, which gave Evelyn an early clue as to what she had to look forward to. "We're the bride and groom and I never saw John much. To me, he was supposed to be at his bride's side."

She moved into his Tarzana house, which she found "marvelous," with its huge fireplace, long couches, and matching chairs. "I was so grateful the whole thing was there," she said. "I didn't have to furnish it; I didn't have to hire the help or tell them what to do. I just did whatever he wanted me to. He'd call up and say ten people were coming to dinner. Then they'd come, and he'd forget to come. But there was plenty of help and it was nice having company. I didn't have to do any of the work. I didn't know how to cook; I didn't know anything. I hardly knew what the kitchen looked like. Whatever women were supposed to do then, I didn't do. But it wasn't expected of me. John didn't want that, he wanted me to ride horses and go hunting and fishing and do that kind of stuff. Unfortunately I'm allergic to horses and always sneeze when I'm around them. It was a bitter blow for him. He'd start hugging and kissing me after being with his horses and I'd start sneezing."

His friends all laughed when they heard John got married. "Nobody took it seriously," Evelyn said. "His father, Walter, laughed loudest. I remember one night soon after we were married I woke up and heard Walter and John talking about his love, Marietta. Who was Marietta? I found out that John was with Marietta when he met me, and I'd gotten the impression that he just got pissed off at her because she hadn't gotten the goddamn divorce from her husband. It was like, 'I'll show you.' After I heard him talking about her to Walter, I became wary of John. I knew that ours wasn't going to be the happy-ever-after, 'perfect' marriage."

Evelyn soon found that John's girlfriends didn't take his getting married seriously either, and they continued to call and send him notes. Doris Lilly had read about the event in the newspaper and called. "What gives you the right to call me at a moment like this?" John shouted in anger at her. She heard Evelyn in the background and hung up quickly.

"Scared the hell out of me," Doris said. "I'm not trying to say that I was the love of his life. I wasn't. But for many years I think he felt more for me than he did for maybe even Evelyn. Because, don't forget, he was the first man in my life."

Eloise Hardt didn't think his marriage to Evelyn was funny in the least. "It wasn't that I minded him marrying her but I minded the way he did it. He went on a dinner date and didn't come home and married Evelyn, who he thoroughly disliked! John started changing in my mind then and I started writing him off, because I, too, grew up and became a woman who was having affairs.

"After Evelyn he started going downhill as far as morals and as far as I was concerned. I lost enormous respect for John. After that I gave up my career and married Hans Habe and went to live in Germany for eight years. Hans was brilliant, as brilliant as John. Actually he was far more real in that intellectual thing than John pretended to be. He said, 'I don't think you ought to be an actress, you ought to come and live with me and we'll get married.' Hans didn't drink, he was so stable, I thought he was everything I liked. But I hated losing John. That was the first time I realized that I was possessed totally."

Anne Selepegno found out about John's marriage from Walter the next morning when he called to tell her. "I don't think Evelyn liked me very much," Selepegno said, recalling an evening soon after the marriage when she and John were playing backgammon and Evelyn appeared, looked at them, then threw her handbag at John. "John," Anne said, "I think I'd better not play anymore."

"It's your move, dear," John said, sipping his drink, "go ahead and move."

Olivia de Havilland was convinced that she had overcome her own possession with John and she proved it by marrying a Texas novelist, Marcus Aurelius Goodrich, the same month that John married Evelyn.

And what about Marietta? How did she take the news? The day after he had married Evelyn John remembered sitting in a taxi on the way to the studio. "Only then did the utter damned absurdity of what I had done flood over me," he recalled. "How could I have done such a thing to Marietta?" He thought of getting an annulment, but then decided to try and make a go of it. Pauline Potter, who was a great friend of his and Marietta's, called to ask him if it was true and he told her it was. And then a few weeks later Marietta finished with her analyst and decided to get her divorce. She, too, had found someone else.

"When I finally decided to get a divorce, it was the most traumatic period in my life," Marietta said sadly. "For a bishop's daughter to get a divorce was sort of reducing everything he stood for. I felt like I was murdering my family in a way. At the same time, I felt that my husband's life and mine were leading nowhere and we were both making each other . . . not miserable, it was just a kind of dead end. It was just poisoning our whole lives.

"But I also knew I wouldn't divorce unless I could marry a man that I could not only love but feel he'd be a good father to Frankie, who would be dependable as well as delightful.

"In those days you had to go to Nevada for six weeks to get a divorce. I rented a pretty house out on the shores of Lake Tahoe. While I was there Walter called me one day and said, 'Say, you're getting a divorce and you're going to marry Ronald Tree. Do you love him?' I said I did. 'Do you really love him?' I said, 'I think we are going to be very happy together.' 'Well,' he said, 'I'm sure you and John will meet in the third act.'

"Isn't that marvelous? I don't know if John asked him to call. I have a feeling that John had too much pride to do that. Walter must have felt that he would have liked him to call."

Walter was still appearing in *Apple of His Eye* and singing "September Song" as an encore, "for the tax" he told his audiences. He was also appearing in magazine and newspaper ads for Williams Shaving Cream and Nescafé coffee. He had turned down an offer to play Kit Carson in a film of William Saroyan's called *The Time of Your Life* and an RKO offer to do Eugene O'Neill's *Mourning Becomes Electra*, but he took time off in the summer to play the father in *Summer Holiday*, an MGM musical made from Eugene O'Neill's only comedy, *Ah, Wilderness*. The film starred Mickey Rooney and wasn't very good, but Walter was to be paid $6,250 a week for a minimum of eight weeks. When the film wrapped he returned to *Apple of His Eye*, taking it on tour. He also looked forward to playing the old prospector, Howard, in *The Treasure of the Sierra Madre*.

By the time he turned forty on August 5, 1946, John had completed his script of B. Traven's novel and had sent it off to the reclusive author. To celebrate, he entered an amateur steeplechase soon after his marriage, where he was almost killed when his horse crashed through a fence. He cracked some ribs and one of them had scratched his lung, which caused him to spit up blood. But, as Evelyn wryly put it, "if you want to be a legend in your time, those are the breaks."

While he recovered, John told Evelyn that he would like to have a baby. "If he wanted me to have his baby, didn't that mean that maybe he . . . cared?" she wondered. She had felt so insecure. At night he would wander through the rooms, unable to sleep. He would whisper Marietta's name to his father when they talked on the phone. He behaved in every way like a bachelor. And yet he wanted a child and Evelyn felt that it might change everything. She went to the doctor for an exam and was told she was in excellent shape. Then the doctor asked her to obtain some sperm samples from John so that he could check them. "It turned out that his sperm count was low," Evelyn reported, "so I was to give him shots in his ass three times a week. We did that, but I was irregular. Of course we were all smoking—he was smoking like crazy—and drinking. He wasn't taking care of his health to improve anything. He even blamed his cough on his horse accident instead of his smoking."

In September, John and Evelyn went to New York, where John was to direct Jean-Paul Sartre's play *Huis Clos* (*No Exit*). Dorothy Parker had introduced John to Ruth Ford, an actress who had been cast in one of the three parts. She brought the play to him. He obtained permission (again) from Warner Bros. to do it. The producer, Oliver Smith, had seen *The Maltese Falcon* and was convinced that Huston was the right man to handle the existential drama about a man and two women trapped in a hotel room for eternity—Sartre's vision of hell. "I had read a little existentialism and I thought it was a chance to slip something in before coming back to films after the war," John said. "Kind of a cushion." Paul Bowles had been hired to translate and adapt the play into English.

There were lines of dialogue and situations in Bowles's translation that intrigued John. Garcin, the male character who would be played by the French actor Claude Dauphin, was stuck in hell because he treated his wife "abominably." "Night after night I came home blind drunk, stinking of wine and women. . . ." He boasts that "she admired me too much." He wonders whether he was a coward and talks about the price of evil. "A man is what he wills himself to be," he says, sounding very much like Huston. "I didn't give a damn for wealth, or for love. I aimed at being a real man . . . I staked everything on the same horse."

When Ruth Ford's character, Estelle, whose "husband was old enough to be my father," says to him, "I'll take you as you are. And perhaps I shall change you," Garcin replies, "I doubt it." And then he tells her, "I shan't love you; I know you too well."

And earlier, Inez, played by the French actress Annabella, says to them both, "We've had our hour of pleasure, haven't we? There have been people who burned their lives out for our sakes—and we chuckled over it. So now we have to pay the reckoning."

Is it any wonder that such material appealed to Huston, who could identify strongly with each of the characters?

The English title for the play was found after John, Bowles, and Smith all had searched through Dante, Eliot, Milton, Poe, and the Bible. Nothing suitable to Sartre's *Huis Clos* was found. Bowles hit upon *No Exit* when he was going through a subway turnstile.

When he wasn't working on the play, Huston was introducing Evelyn to the textures of New York life. "One late night we went into some bar," she recalled. "There were a lot of tough-looking guys in there and John had been drinking quite a bit before we got there. I told John I wanted to go home and John said, 'Usually I fight my way out of these places.' When we left, we walked past St. Patrick's Cathedral and John unzipped himself and peed right on the corner of the cathedral."

When he wasn't pissing freely in the streets, he was relieving himself in the homes of the social-register crowd. "John was sort of a pet of upper-class New York society," Evelyn soon discovered. "They adored him. They were well-born, moneyed, intellectually and artistically inclined, and he was their artist."

At parties he would disappear with one of his friends, like Hattie Carnegie's head designer Pauline Potter, who would eventually marry Baron Philippe de Rothschild, or Marietta. "John never promised *not* to have a mistress," Evelyn said. "He was a big giver of himself, and if it was women he was giving of himself to, then he could wind up in bed. He just wouldn't stop because he had a wife at home.

"I met Marietta when we were at a party and he disappeared into a room with her. They left discreetly, I just happened to be watching."

Marietta also remembered that party, which she had gone to after marrying English member of Parliament Ronald Tree. "I went," she said, "very happy that I was the new bride of Ronnie Tree, although he didn't go. I wanted to see John and when I saw him he took me aside and said, 'Won't you lunch tomorrow?' Of course I accepted. We had a very nice talk, nothing tremendously personal, and suddenly he said to me, 'Well, one doesn't have to be proud about everything one does, does one?' "

Paul Bowles wasn't proud of his adaptation of Sartre's play, which opened on November 26, 1946, and he was surprised that it ran as long as it did and that it received the New York Drama Critics Circle Award for the best foreign play of the year.

John was asked to direct Eugene O'Neill's new play, A Moon for the Misbegotten, but Warner's thought he should return to making movies, so they refused to give him permission. Jack Warner's refusal to let him do it was one of the reasons John would opt to leave Warner Bros. as soon as his contract was up. Evelyn was in the room when John called O'Neill and she noticed how "John's voice changed when he talked to O'Neill, it was quite emotional. He really wanted to do that play."

On December 16, John went back to work for Warner's. He had received a long letter from B. Traven commenting in detail on his script for The Treasure of the Sierra Madre and praising John's work. "I am delighted over your script," Traven wrote. "It goes as close alongside the book as a picture ever will allow." He was glad that John hadn't "sugar-coated" it and even liked the scene where Curtin saves Dobbs's life after the cave-in at the mine—a scene that was not in his book. He also approved of another addition. "In the book I left both survivors a little bit of money. . . . You cut even that little bit and leave them not one single ounce. By so doing you drive the message clear cut home." Traven concluded his letter by again complimenting Huston's "super excellent writing," saying, "I don't know anybody or can imagine anybody who could have written a script better liked by me than the one you wrote."

Huston responded to Traven's letter with appreciation, listing the actors he hoped to cast (his father as the old man, Bogart as Dobbs, Ronald Reagan for Curtin, Zachary Scott for Lacaud—or Cody, as he renamed him) and tried to flush out the secretive author by suggesting that perhaps they could meet to discuss the matter when Huston flew

down to Mexico in early January to scout locations. Traven's reclusiveness
had heightened his popularity around the world. No one claimed to
have seen him, no one even knew his nationality. It was speculated
that he was really Jack London or Ambrose Bierce or the illegitimate
son of Kaiser Wilhelm II. Not even Paul Kohner, who acted as Traven's
movie agent, had ever met his client. And Kohner piqued Huston's
interest when he related the difficulties he had securing the rights to
Traven's work by first going to see his publisher in Switzerland and then
traveling to Mexico with his wife, Lupita, whom Traven had loved
from a distance before she married, when she was a well-known Mexican
actress. Traven had followed Lupita Tovar's career, had saved clippings
about her, had even, he claimed, once danced with her in Guadalajara
in 1930.

Traven agreed to meet with the Kohners at the Reforma Hotel in
Mexico City, and on the appointed hour there was a knock at their door.
A bellhop delivered a box of candy with an orchid on top, along with a
note saying that Traven had been kidnapped. "My husband called the
police," Lupita related. "Then we got a note, he had been in front of the
hotel and he described what I was wearing. I thought it was ridiculous!"

On another occasion Traven agreed to meet Lupita on a beach in
Acapulco. Again Traven didn't show and again a note was later sent to
her saying that he had been in the water watching her.

So when Huston heard from Traven saying that he would meet him
in Mexico City, John felt that he was about to unravel a mystery.
Traven had also written that he approved of Bogart as Dobbs but didn't
think Walter Huston would work for the old man, Howard. "You know
as well as I do that Howard, not Dobbs, is the heart and soul of the
picture," Traven wrote, concerned that Walter was "too robust and
looks too young for the part. My idea would have been somebody like
Lewis Stone, really old, stocky, looking sickly somehow." Traven wanted
John to make Walter look "over seventy" and it was this concern that
most likely convinced John to have his father play the part without his
dentures.

When Huston went down to Mexico City, he stayed at the Hotel
Bamer on Avenida Juarez. On the day Traven was to meet him there
he didn't show up. A week later, though, Huston, who never locked
his door, awoke to find a strange man standing by his bed. His card
read "Hal Croves, Translator." Then he produced a letter from B.
Traven. It said that Traven was ill but Croves was authorized to act on
his behalf. Huston arranged to meet Croves later that day, where they
discussed the script in detail. "Croves had a slight accent," Huston

observed. "It didn't sound German to me, but certainly European. I thought he might very well be Traven, but out of delicacy I didn't ask. On the other hand, Croves gave an impression quite unlike the one I had formed of Traven from reading his scripts and correspondence. Croves was very tight and guarded in his manner of speaking. He was nothing at all as I had imagined Traven, and after two meetings I decided that this surely was not he."

John had more pressing things on his mind than solving the mystery of B. Traven. *Treasure* was one of the first American films to be shot entirely on location outside the United States. And after scouring the Mexican countryside for eight thousand miles, the perfect spot was found in the mountains surrounding the village of Jungapeo, near San José Purua, in the state of Michoacán.

On February 17, 1947, Huston took a small crew down to Tampico for preproduction background material, but they ran into trouble their first week when a local newspaper complained that Huston wasn't going to portray Mexico in a favorable way. It became an issue and Huston was forced to close down the production until the matter was straightened out. Luckily, Huston had friends in the right places—two of Mexico's leading artists, Miguel Covarrubias, who had illustrated *Frankie and Johnny*, and muralist Diego Rivera, went to see the president of Mexico, who ordered a government investigation into the matter. It took two months, but by April the cast and crew arrived in San José Purua, along with an "alternate" crew to satisfy the government. Huston signed up a bargaining agent to deal with the hiring of extras, paying 10 pesos for those on foot and 15 pesos on horseback. When he asked how much for an extra who falls from a horse, the agent said 25 pesos. Huston offered to double it and the agent said, "For 50 pesos, señor, you can shoot them in the arms and legs. But mind you, no killing."

The two-month delay caused scheduling problems, but it came as a relief for Walter. His activities—the play, the MGM film, the radio broadcasts, the preparation for his Mexican adventure with John—only served to put Nan in a deeper and deeper funk, and in February she entered Passavant Hospital in Chicago. Paul Kohner tried to make light of her situation in a letter he wrote to her. But Walter was only too aware that her instability was severe, and when the doctors strongly recommended she begin a series of electroshock treatments to help bring her around, he sadly consented.

She had changed so. She was no longer the person he had gazed upon so fondly, as she smiled coquettishly back when they played in *Elmer the Great* and he knew he was really in love. Or as Desdemona, when she looked at him as Othello, her enraged and jealous husband, in bewildered innocence and trust. Or as Edith Cortright in *Dodsworth*, so decent and charming and pure. They were all memories now. It had been years since he had had those kinds of feelings for her. She had turned inward, had become the grand dame without a stage—a tragic figure. And as her husband was getting ready to depart for what would be his greatest triumph, she prepared for the shock treatments that would send electricity surging through her brain as she lay helplessly strapped to a table with a rubber bit in her mouth.

Walter was with her at the hospital and then back in their apartment in New York until April, when he was expected on the set of *Treasure*. It was a sad and difficult two months, but by the time he departed he could see that she was improving somewhat and that with the help he hired she had the best of care.

Most of the original cast was there when Walter arrived, with two exceptions. Bruce Bennett rather than Zachary Scott had been cast as Cody and Tim Holt, not Ronald Reagan, got Huston's approval to play Curtin. "The studio wanted me to have Reagan," John said. "I'm not sure he wanted to do it or not. But actors like to be pursued and coaxed and in that particular instance I didn't pursue it because I saw another person for the part. Reagan turned it down. It wasn't as though he'd have spoiled the picture, he could have played it, but when he said no, why, I was just as well pleased."

According to Reagan, *Treasure* was a picture he wanted to do and he did not turn the part down. Warner Bros. made the decision, insisting that he star in *The Voice of the Turtle*, which was a Broadway play they wanted to make into a movie at the same time Huston was shooting *Treasure*. Reagan expressed regret that he lost the opportunity to work with Huston.

John discussed with his father what he expected from him. "John said he saw my part as an old man who talked fast and throws away his lines," Walter said; "a hard-bitten old prospector used to spending weeks and months in solitude. I told John that was the way I envisaged the old coot, too."

Bacall described Walter and John as being "like a couple of kids together—they made each other laugh, they enjoyed and understood each other's wickedness." Bacall found the elder Huston to be "a wildly attractive man. And he had incredible charm. Younger, he would have killed women. I had the same feeling about Walter that I always had about John, he was a man you couldn't pin down. Walter was a devil, with his white hair and his white beard, always taking his teeth out. And physically, he moved so well, better than John."

"Walter didn't treat John like a son in any way," said Evelyn Keyes, who was one of only three women on location when the picture began. "You could see that John was the child of this man, something about the mouth and the jaw and the manners. There was something in the nature of the sound of the voice, the honest extraordinary charm, the winningness of John that came from Walter."

One night Walter and John smoked marijuana for the first time. Walter found it amusing, but John became rigid after smoking two joints. When Evelyn asked if he was all right, John said, "No," and she got the company doctor, who gave him something "to balance things out" and put John to bed. He never smoked grass again.

Bogart didn't participate in their drug adventure. He preferred drinking beer. "The only two Spanish words he thought worth learning," Evelyn said, were "Dos Equis." Bogart was suffering from a vitamin deficiency that caused his hair to fall out in chunks and had to have three wigs of varying lengths to wear for the film. He knew he was in for a rough time when his plane had to be diverted to Veracruz because of fog the first time he and Bacall flew down. "The pilot tried to land four times before the plane almost ran out of gas, and Bogart was agitated. It was an annoying way to start our location work."

The locations Huston had found only made Bogart more miserable. "John wanted everything perfect," the actor said. "I have to admire him for that but it was plenty rough on our troupe. If we could get to a location site without fording a couple of streams and walking through rattlesnake-infested areas in the scorching sun, then it wasn't quite right. We got to calling him 'Hard-Way Huston.' "

Bogart was concerned about being fed decently. "We had what was supposed to be a Viennese chef, but after a few samples of what he served us, we almost took up a collection to send him back to Vienna. The menu got so monotonous that finally Lauren got to making regular trips to the kitchen to whip up ham and eggs and other plain but mighty tasty American food."

Bacall remembered the food as a disaster before she took over. "A whole fish with bulging eyes that looked raw, or a rubber turkey." But her contribution only made it harder on Evelyn. Bacall felt Evelyn was treated in a humiliating fashion by John and came to believe he had disdain for women. "Poor Evelyn would say something and John would say, 'What? What was that, Evelyn? Now wait a minute—I want everyone to hear this' and Evelyn was on the block. Any casual, innocent, occasionally thoughtless remark was magnified and she was made to look like a fool. He'd say, 'Here's Betty seeing to our dinners . . . and all you can do is complain.' I didn't envy her, married to John. He was brilliant, he was fascinating, he was fun . . . but stay a friend. Better still, a friend's wife."

In her book Evelyn described an incident where she wore a Mexican print skirt and a separate top that was "not much more than a glorified bra." John didn't approve of her breasts bouncing into view whenever she leaned forward and told her not to wear it. But a few nights later she put it on again. When John came back from work, "He didn't say hello, didn't smile. He didn't even frown. All he did was reach out, take hold of the brief top, and rip it in two. 'Put something on, honey,' he said, 'and let's go to dinner.' " Not long after that Evelyn returned to Hollywood to start a comedy, *The Mating of Millie*, with Glenn Ford.

During one scene Bogie was supposed to stick his hand under a rock looking for hidden gold, but he hesitated when Tim Holt told him that a poisonous Gila monster had crawled in there. Challenged, Bogart withdrew his hand and then the beaded lizard came out. The close-up for this scene had to be done back in the States and that gave Huston plenty of time to cook up a way of scaring his friend. "I got a camera clamp," he said, "and I climbed underneath the set, which was made of that material which rocks are composed of in studios, and when Bogart put his hand in I put on the clamp while the cameras were running and he screamed, thought he had a Gila monster on his hand."

But when it came to cruelty, Hal Croves, B. Traven's alter ego, suffered the most from John. Huston had offered B. Traven $1,000 a week as a technical adviser, but for Hal Croves, the offer was considerably less, $150 a week. Determined to separate himself from Traven, Croves accepted the smaller amount, even though almost everyone was convinced that Croves was Traven. Evelyn said he gave himself away by often saying "I" when it should have been "he" and by using phrases similar to ones he wrote in letters to Huston. But John doubted that he was "the one and only B. Traven." Lupita Kohner felt John "treated him like a nincompoop." Although the Kohners—Paul, Lupita, and Pancho— would all come to the conclusion that Croves was definitely Traven— even getting Croves to *admit* he was the author just before he died in

1969—Huston held to the belief that Croves *became* Traven after Traven died, or that Traven was actually two men who worked in collaboration. "B. Traven, in his writing, was expansive," John observed, "there was a bigness, a magnitude about him. And Croves was quite the opposite."

Huston may have had his doubts about Croves, but he had no doubts about B. Traven as a writer, "a combination of Conrad and Dreiser, if you can imagine such a thing." Aside from eliminating the political class struggle in the novel, John remained faithful to *The Treasure of the Sierra Madre*. The opening shot of Bogart as Dobbs looking at the lottery results and then tearing up his ticket established Dobbs as a loser. And Bogart's mean-spirited, greed-obsessed character would only fall farther into paranoia and madness as the film progressed.

The opening of the film also gave Huston a chance to act in a movie for the first time. He played a white-suited, cigar-smoking rich man who thrice gives a peso to a begging Dobbs. Over the years, as critics began to recognize that Bogart's best work was under Huston's direction, this small scene would become a classic clip at occasions honoring either man.

After Dobbs meets Curtin on a park bench, both men land a job working on an oil rig for $8 American a day, but after three weeks of backbreaking labor, they don't get paid and wind up on cheap cots at the El Oso Negro. It's there they first hear Howard, the old prospector, talking about gold. Like much of the dialogue in the film, it's edited from Traven's book: "Gold is a very devilish sort of thing," Howard says. ". . . It changes your character completely. . . . The more you have, the more you want to add."

Dobbs interjects that wouldn't happen with him. Howard says, "I know what gold does to men's souls," and outlines a litany of partnerships gone afoul and murders occurring, all from the lure of gold.

Once they decide to include the old man and prospect for gold, chance plays its part, as Dobbs finds he's holding one-twentieth of a share of a winning lottery ticket. Just enough to cover the cost of burros and equipment. But after a long journey of climbing steep hills under the torturous sun, the two novices are exhausted and ready to quit.

At this point old Howard, who has been sifting dirt through his hand, cackles and responds: "Well tell my old grandmother! I got two very elegant bedfellers who kick at the first drop of rain and hide in the closet when thunder rumbles. My, my, my, what great prospectors!" He begins to laugh maniacally.

"Shut your trap," Dobbs yells, picking up a rock, "shut up or I'll smash your head flat."

Curtin attempts to calm Dobbs. "Aw, leave him alone, can't you see the old man's nuts?"

But Howard's not nuts, he's just discovered what they've been looking for. "Nuts? Nuts am I? Let me tell you something my two fine bedfellers, you're so dumb there's nothin' to compare you with." Again, the wicked, crazy laugh, which John had first heard after the Broadway opening of *Othello*. "Ah ha ha ha," he burst, like a dam overflowing. "You're so dumb you don't even see the riches yer treading on with your own feet. Ahh haaaa haaaaa," he began to dance the jig he learned from Eugene O'Neill's description of Ephraim Cabot's vigorous dancing.

O'Neill had taught him the jig, *Othello* the laugh, and in *Treasure* Walter had a chance to put it all together in his most startling and memorable performance. Before they shot the scene, Walter had told John not to cut at the end of it but to let the cameras roll. The idea for the dance was all Walter's and he wanted to surprise John with it. John was definitely surprised.

"When he does that dance of triumph," John wrote, "the gooseflesh comes out and my hair stands up: a tribute to greatness that has happened, with me, in the presence of Chaliapin, the Italian thoroughbred Ribot, Jack Dempsey in his prime, and Manolete. It was certainly the finest performance in any picture I ever made." Bogart stared in wonder as he watched Walter steal not only that scene, but the entire movie. "One Huston is bad enough," he mumbled, "but two are murder."

Two weeks before shooting completed in Mexico John took an interest in one of the boys who had been used as an extra and was running errands for the crew. His name was Pablo Albarran, and Lauren Bacall noted that he was always hanging around the location. "John suddenly liked this boy and made him a gofer—made him go and get water or coffee or whatever. And then he became like a little pet. He was very cute and John decided he was this perfect little mascot."

Pablo's father, a farmer, had died of malaria in 1946 and his mother died of a brain tumor the following year. The thirteen-year-old boy went to live with his older married sister. But he was unhappy there and often found odd jobs in Jungapeo.

One evening after Evelyn had departed, Huston was dining with Bogart and Bacall when he spotted Pablo and called him over. "How would you like to go to the States, boy?" Huston asked. "You could come and live with me, I've got horses you can ride, you can go to school and have your own room." Pablo didn't speak any English and needed someone to translate. He wanted to think it over. Then Huston took him to the club where he tried to teach him how to bowl and play shuffleboard. It all seemed peculiar to the Bogarts and when John told them he was going to adopt the boy, a stunned Humphrey Bogart said he thought that was ridiculous.

"What kind of a crazy idea is this?" Bogart said. "The kid's great in Mexico, but you're going to take him to California and he's not going to be happy." But, as Bacall noted, when Huston got an idea, "that's it, try and stop him. It was another fantasy of John's: I will take him away from all this and he will become Albert Schweitzer."

That night Huston followed the boy back to the old station wagon where he slept. He then motioned with his hand for Pablo to come with him. "He grabbed me by the hand," Pablo recalled, "and he took me to his room where he took one boxspring off his bed and put it on the floor. He gave me a toothbrush and toothpaste, got me in the shower and I bathed. From then on he wouldn't let me out of his sight. He said he'd be my father and I would live like his son."

Pablo didn't know what to make of Huston, but he knew an opportunity when he saw one. "I was looking for affection and I had what I wanted and my stomach was full." Huston was offering him an education, and a chance to escape.

John thought Pablo was five years younger than he was and didn't know about Pablo's sister. He thought he was an orphan. "He attached himself to me," Huston said, "and when it came time to leave, I thought, why not? I didn't tell Evelyn anything about it. I inquired how difficult it would be to bring him to the States and they said not difficult at all."

Jack Warner had been reluctant to put close to $3 million in a film shot away from the studio, with no one but Henry Blanke to oversee it. And when he began to see the rushes he expressed contempt over the way Huston was portraying his stars. Bogart looked like an unshaven bum, Walter was toothless and hardly recognizable, there were no women, no sex, the Mexican bandits were speaking in *Spanish!*

If Jack Warner was anxious about Huston's independent ways, Bogart was getting more and more testy as it became apparent that John wasn't going to finish shooting by the end of June. "Out to make a fuckin' masterpiece, right, John?" he began to nag, becoming like his paranoid character. One night he took it too far. "For chrissakes, John, just how long is this miserable picture going to take?" Huston leaned forward, grabbed Bogart's nose between his index and middle fingers, and twisted hard, bringing tears to Bogart's eyes. Bogart stopped complaining after that, even when he was told that they'd have to shoot for a few more weeks in California, after they left Mexico.

With John still in Mexico because of Pablo, Walter spent the next few weeks at his son's Tarzana house, getting to know Evelyn, and seeing Linda Christian, a twenty-four-year-old actress he met in Mexico. She had appeared in a movie called *Holiday in Mexico* in 1946 and *Green Dolphin Street* in 1947. Walter was attracted to her beauty and brought her back to Hollywood. Their affair was discreet, although fan magazines often reported her other affairs before she married Tyrone Power in 1949.

Coming off one of the best parts he ever played in the movies; being with a young, ambitious starlet; entertaining Evelyn; and learning that Nan was feeling better, Walter felt rejuvenated. One night he and Evelyn listened to an album Walter had made with other stars for the war effort and Evelyn noted that Walter's contribution was the best. He spent an hour explaining what his sister Margaret and George M. Cohan had taught him about phrasing. When John called to tell her he was bringing home a surprise, Walter, who knew about Pablo, weighed John's surprise against Evelyn's possible reaction and thought it might be best if he prepared her.

"My heart sank with a thud, then rose in outrage," Evelyn wrote after Walter told her that John was bringing home a Mexican boy for them to raise as their son. "What a lunatic move! I wasn't ready for a baby, much less a practically grown boy. He might have asked me how I felt."

But then she calmed down and realized that her husband was behaving in an extremely benevolent manner. She did her best to exclaim her delight to Walter, but deep down she began to think her marriage wasn't going to last.

13

WHEEL OF FORTUNE

"THIS WAS ONE OF THE CARELESS THINGS JOHN DID," EVE-lyn stated. "You don't bring a kid home when you're married without asking your wife. But I talked myself into liking the idea. If that was what he wanted to do, what difference did it make? We had lots of help, I wouldn't be stuck with baby-sitting. By the time John and the kid got off the plane, I was saying, 'Wow.' "

America was a new world for Pablo. When he saw Evelyn he thought that "deep in her mind it was a shock that she was a mother. But she went along with the situation. And to me also it was strange, her being so young and so beautiful."

The first thing Evelyn did was ask him if he wanted something to drink and Pablo asked for *café*. "No," Evelyn told him, "you're going to drink milk. *Leche*."

"He was a primitive kid," she recalled. "I had to show him how to flush the toilet. He'd never had shoes on before. I bought him a bed. I took him to buy clothes. I was working all the time so I brought him to the studio. Then I had to find a school for him. You couldn't take him to a public school because they weren't bilingual then. I knew very little Spanish and John knew none. 'Mother' was the first word he learned in English.

"Pablo was like a kind of toy. Maybe we all were. John did an oil portrait of him with a guitar. After he got used to me he used to twiddle my breast. He knew what he was doing, of course he did. But then I didn't know what his jokes were. He came from not only a different culture, but from a different culture within the culture. People in Mexico City wouldn't know what he was about.

"When I think back, we didn't handle it very well. I don't know what John wanted with Pablo, really, except that he wanted a child."

John left Pablo with Evelyn for two weeks to continue with the movie. Jack Warner was sounding off that the film was behind schedule, but Huston knew what he had and didn't want to spoil it because of a projected deadline. While they were in northern California John confessed to Bogie that he had a problem: "You seem to have your life so together," he told Bogie. "You're a successful star, you've got a wife, children, you're happy, and you still do your own thing. How do you manage to do all that and not get bored? The trouble with me is that I am forever and eternally bored."

When Bogart told Lauren Bacall what John had said, she thought it was "a sad and revealing remark, diagramming the internal war raging within him."

On July 22, twenty-nine days behind schedule, *Treasure* was finished and John made the mistake of inviting Walter to see the first cut. "I brought my father to see his best picture. He had a sense that we were getting something extraordinary. Then he saw this rough cut—a bad print, no music—and he was disappointed. I tried to explain to him that everything would be different when he saw it finally, but I could see that he had doubts. There had been some talk of Walter becoming a director, but after *Treasure* he wanted no part of directing."

Three days later Warner Bros. bought the rights to Maxwell Anderson's play *Key Largo*, written in blank verse. Jerry Wald was assigned to produce the movie and John was asked to direct and write it with Richard Brooks, a young writer who had done the research on *The Killers*. Huston didn't care for the play, which had starred Paul Muni as a Spanish Civil War veteran who returned, disillusioned, to the Florida Keys to see the family of his friend who died in Spain. There he finds a gambler and his cohorts have taken over the family's small hotel. The vet doesn't want to get involved, but eventually he does, aware that he will probably lose his life.

John met with Wald, Brooks, and Bogart, whom Warner's wanted to star in the film, at the Lakeside Country Club and after lunch he and Brooks drove back to the house in Tarzana. Brooks was eager to work with Huston, but Huston told him, "I don't want to do this." Brooks tried to convince him but couldn't find the right argument. "You come up with a story on this thing that makes some sense and I'll think about it," John said. "Otherwise, the way the play is now, I can't see myself doing it."

Brooks came up with the idea of throwing out the Spanish Civil War background and changing the gambler to a mobster. When he told Huston how he saw *Key Largo*—as *Little Caesar* from Cuba—John thought it might work and the two began to collaborate on a treatment.

By this time Jack Warner had seen a cut of *Treasure* with the music by Max Steiner; he cabled his general sales manager in New York:

"THIS IS THE FIRST TIME I HAVE EVER DONE THIS BUT LAST NIGHT I RAN . . . THE TREASURE OF THE SIERRA MADRE. I WANT YOU AND THOSE ASSEMBLED TO KNOW THIS IS DEFINITELY THE GREATEST MOTION PICTURE WE HAVE EVER MADE. . . . A FEW YEARS BACK THIS ONE PICTURE WOULD VIRTUALLY PUT OVER A WHOLE SEA-SON'S PRODUCT."

Soon after Jack Warner's enthusiastic response, John and Evelyn decided to celebrate their first anniversary in a properly abandoned fashion at Keyston Ranch, a large area of land they had bought in Calabasas. A list of the two hundred guests was printed in the newspaper and Evelyn called it "the best goddamn party I ever went to." Freddy Karger assembled a group of musicians and formed a band for the all-night event, which featured John Garfield's energetic rumba, Danny Kaye's samba, Edgar Bergen's waltz, and Henry Blanke's Russian danc-ing. Betty Grable sang songs from *Call Me Mister*; Georgia Gibbs sang for Lana Turner, Tyrone Power, Charlie Grayson, and the Louis Calherns; and Sono Osato stirred things up with a sexy burlesque ballet. Judy Garland and Frank Sinatra also sang, Oscar Levant joked, Robert Mitchum smoked dope, girlfriends fought with their lovers' wives, couples fell into the pool clothed or unclothed, and nobody called the police. "Our town, at play," observed Evelyn.

The behavior of these adults was confusing to Pablo, who was taking in a life-style far removed from the way people lived in Jungapeo. He saw that women followed John "like honey. It wasn't as much that he wanted to have them, but they followed him. I knew about a dozen. I think he was seeing Paulette Goddard."

Evelyn was aware of her husband's meanderings. "My presence and Pablo's in John's life hadn't made much change in the way John conducted himself," she observed. "He continued to live like a bachelor."

But it wasn't just the master of the house who was carrying on, Pablo said. Evelyn would occasionally introduce him to "a gentleman and I could see it was more than professional business. One time it was her agent, another time it was Dick Powell, then there were other actors."

Pablo was slow in learning English and he didn't take to horses the way John had wanted him to. John had once told him about his own childhood and how he had overcome illness and an enlarged heart to accomplish what he had wanted to do. But he didn't know if he was getting through to the boy, and one day he brought Pablo to the Kohners' house and asked Lupita to explain to him that he was too lazy and wasn't making an effort to adjust. Lupita translated John's words and Pablo told Lupita it wasn't that he was lazy but he had a bad heart. He had misinterpreted what John had told him and thought the talk about a bad heart concerned him.

"That time . . . I'll never forget it," Pablo said with sadness. "Made me feel so bad, so bad. I think that I soaked the carpet in tears. He didn't say only that I was lazy, the words were more harder, like I was abusing the situation. John could have told me things man to man. I didn't like the idea that he took me to somebody else to talk to me."

In September he was sent to Ojai to go to school, which he found very difficult at first, but he studied public speaking and learned Shakespeare, memorizing whole passages from *Othello*. John wrote to Walter in New York telling him about Pablo, how pleased he was with *Treasure*, and his progress working with Brooks on *Key Largo*. Walter wrote back: "Dear Jonnie,

"Yours was a swell letter and full of such good things to read. Isn't it wonderful that the picture has turned out so well. I cannot possibly tell you how happy that makes me to know you are so well satisfied. . . .

"I can't say that I have much enthusiasm for doing just another picture. I would like the idea of doing just one a year with you and let it go at that. . . .

"I am gradually becoming an expert in the kitchen. Our meals are something to look forward and back on. Glad to hear you have put Pablo in such a good school. I hope he makes the grade."

In late September Walter and Nan returned to their home in Running Springs and Nan wrote a note to Paul Kohner, thanking him for sending on reviews of a bit part she did in a play. She also thanked Kohner for visiting her when she was in the hospital and wrote, "Walter told me you too had experienced depressions. We are said to be the 'favored' ones—well, we have already had our hell in our journey to heaven. Yes?"

While Walter cared for his wife, cooking extravagant meals and making furniture in his shop high in the San Bernadino mountains, a dark cloud from the East began to hover over Hollywood. On September 27, 1947, the House Un-American Activities Committee (HUAC) subpoenaed forty-three witnesses to appear at their hearings in Washington, D.C., the following month. To John, Willy Wyler, and their friends, it seemed like Pearl Harbor all over again, only this time the enemy was from within.

In the 1946 elections the Republicans had wrested control of the House of Representatives from the Democrats; those who had opposed Roosevelt's New Deal were now out to expose the liberals and left-wingers who still believed they lived in a country that, under the Bill of Rights, protected them from being persecuted for speaking freely and joining whatever organizations they wanted to. HUAC, under the chairmanship of J. Parnell Thomas, correctly figured that by going after the Communists in Hollywood they would catch the attention of the media and boost their own images in the eyes of the public. The movie industry influenced large segments of the American public, the committee figured, and pro-Russian films like Mission to Moscow and The North Star were now seen as propaganda for the wrong side.

"In the Second World War I had as high hopes as anybody," John said with a heavy heart. "It looked to me as if we were on our way to some kind of understanding of life. Then came the Communist witch-hunt and the whole idea of the America of the Founding Fathers was lost. And then one wondered, was it all an illusion?"

For the nineteen writers, actors, directors, and producers who became known as the "Unfriendly Nineteen," life soon became a nightmare. Before the committee was through, hundreds of people in the movie industry would find their names on hidden blacklists, and some of the most talented people in the industry were forced to go underground, write under new names, go abroad to find work, or never work again because they had attended a Communist meeting, joined the Communist party, or were named as having Communist connections even if it wasn't true.

Among the writers who were subpoenaed were John Howard Lawson, one of the founders and first president of the Screen Writers Guild; Dalton Trumbo; Ring Lardner, Jr.; Samuel Ornitz; Alvah Bessie; Lester Cole; Albert Maltz; Richard Collins; Gordon Kahn; Bertolt Brecht; Waldo Salt; and Howard Koch. "Besides Howard Koch," Huston said, "they were mostly all Communists. They were, for the most part, well-intentioned boobs, men mostly from poor backgrounds, and out in Hollywood they sort of felt guilt at living the good life. Most of these men's social conscience was more acute than the next fellow's."

When the subpoenas arrived, Huston, then vice-president of the Screen Directors Guild, met with Willy Wyler and Philip Dunne, who wrote *How Green Was My Valley*. Together they joined in the creation of Hollywood Fights Back, which would soon became the Committee for the First Amendment (CFA). As they saw it, the issue wasn't whether or not any of the subpoenaed men were Communists. They organized because they felt their basic rights—freedom of speech, freedom of assembly—were being challenged. "Communism was as nothing compared to the evil done by the witch-hunters," Huston wrote. "They were the real enemies of this country."

One of the CFA's first meetings, held at Ira Gershwin's home, was packed with stars of varying magnitude. The Bogarts were there, Judy Garland, Eddie Robinson, Burt Lancaster, Danny Kaye, Gene Kelly, Billy Wilder. A formal petition was drawn up that expressed their "disgust" and "outrage" by HUAC's attempt to "smear the Motion Picture Industry." Five hundred people signed the petition and the press soon picked up the protest.

John was aware that the signatures of some studio executives were needed on the petition, so it wouldn't look as if only the liberals in Hollywood were involved. John wanted to get David Selznick and MGM vice-president Eddie Mannix to sign. Selznick insisted on adding that those who were signing were not members of the Communist party. The changes were made and Selznick and Mannix signed it.

At Willy Wyler's home there was a telephone setup where some of the "Unfriendly Witnesses" could report back to the group and keep them up to date on what was happening in Washington. "It was a cry for help," Lauren Bacall remembered. "They wanted a group of us to come to Washington to give them moral support. . . . There was no talk of communism—communism had nothing to do with it. It had to do with the Hitlerian tactics being employed."

Huston and Dunne agreed to act as the official spokesmen for the group as they began to make a list of who would go to Washington.

Gershwin, Kaye, Kelly, Garfield, Paul Henreid, June Havoc, Evelyn Keyes, Jane Wyatt, Sterling Hayden, Larry Adler, the Bogarts, volunteered. Howard Hughes offered to provide a plane.

The next day they all flew off on Hughes's plane to make their presence known in Washington. (Wyler wasn't able to make the trip because he had become deaf in one ear during the war and his doctor forbade him to fly.) The plane stopped along the way and there were crowds at every airport hoping to catch a glimpse of some of the stars. It took a long time for the plane to reach Washington and Dunne recalled that there were a lot of card games as well as some heavy drinking aboard. "Everyone was getting just a little smashed," he said. "There was a certain amount of camaraderie and bravado. John and I were the spokesmen and the rule was no one else was to say a word. But we had a lot of maniacs. It was scary as hell."

"Oh, we were so naive, it was ridiculous," Bacall said in retrospect. "We were all there for the news conference where John said we had not come to attack anybody, nor to defend the unfriendly witnesses, just to fight the growing censorship in Hollywood. Afterward, when the press started to talk to us all and ask us questions, they had a field day. We were all such idiots, it was unbelievable. But it was a great experience."

Dunne felt that "it was important that we were trying to protect our people from too close association directly with the Hollywood Ten. We kept saying, 'We support nobody, we attack nobody, we defend nobody. But we do defend the right of anybody to be free of political persecution, blacklist, and censorship.' "

According to Dunne, the CFA had two specific goals besides their defense of those principles. "We timed our flight to Washington to support the testimony of Eric Johnston, spokesman for the Producers Association, who had publicly declared that the motion picture companies would never impose a blacklist nor submit to censorship. And we intended to confront Richard Nixon, the congressman on the House committee from our home state, and request that he either call off the hearings or insist on a reformation of its procedures."

But when they arrived, they found out that Tricky Dick Nixon had flown back to California. Dunne called Willy Wyler to get their petition to Nixon at his home, but the congressman wasn't to be found. "Somehow," Dunne observed, "he had managed to disappear into thin air—or behind a stone wall, even then."

At the press conference Dunne admitted he was "scared shitless. People in the press were saying, 'Ah, come on, you're either for the

Commies or against them.' My answer was, 'You're either for the Constitution or you're against it.'

"We got all the decent newspapers on our side," Dunne said, including the *New York Times* and *Herald Tribune,* the *Washington Post, Detroit Free Press,* and *Miami Herald.* "The right-wing press—Hearst, the *L.A. Times*—was very much against us. Public opinion polls were about fifty-fifty on the House Un-American Activities Committee, which was amazing when you consider with all their weight, half the nation still opposed them."

Before the CFA arrived in Washington, HUAC had heard from fourteen "friendly" witnesses beginning with Jack Warner. Some of those Warner fingered, like his *Casablanca* writers Howard Koch and Julius and Philip Epstein, had never been Communists, and some, like Sheridan Gibney and Emmet Lavery, were ardent anti-Communists.

Warner was later embarrassed by his testimony, and when he had a chance to talk to Huston about it, Huston reported having "an extraordinary conversation" with his boss. "That makes me a squealer, doesn't it?" Warner asked. "Yes," Huston answered, "it does."

Louis B. Mayer followed Warner and director Sam Wood and told on three "cracked" writers: Lester Cole, Dalton Trumbo, and Donald Ogden Stewart. Novelist Ayn Rand next criticized the movies that portrayed Russia in a positive way. Actor Adolphe Menjou had dozens of names to report. And after Howard Hughes's uncle, Rupert, had his say, other "name" actors appeared: Robert Taylor, Ronald Reagan, Robert Montgomery, George Murphy, Gary Cooper. Reagan said he detested and abhorred the Communist philosophy and their dishonest tactics, and Cooper said, "I don't know the basis of communism . . . [but] from what I hear, I don't like it because it isn't on the level." Lela Rogers and Walt Disney completed the testimony of the friendly witnesses and the stage was set for the real show to begin.

Huston and Dunne met privately with the unfriendly witnesses and their lawyers on the eve of the appearances. The CFA had agreed to a simple declaration if asked the only question HUAC was interested in having answered: Are you now or have you ever been a member of the Communist party? Their response would be: "I must respectfully decline to answer that question on the grounds that the information is privileged under the First Amendment to the Constitution." They would then call a press conference, ask Supreme Court Justice Felix Frankfurter to put them under oath, and answer all questions reporters might ask. "The strategy would underline our basic premise," Dunne believed, "that any *official* inquiry into political beliefs and affiliations was unconstitutional."

When Huston suggested that the nineteen consider the same strategy, "it was greeted by stony silence." They had decided that the best way to fight was to read prepared individual statements before being questioned and then beat the inquisitors at their own game, by refusing to answer incriminating questions, but to answer around them, rather than to plead the First or Fifth Amendment. They wanted to give the appearance that they were cooperating and at the same time that they wouldn't be bullied. "They'd come up with this cockamamie idea," said Dunne, "of saying 'I'm trying to answer the question in my own words' and then delivering a diatribe against the committee."

Huston was troubled by their attitude and felt uneasy. "John knew what the committee was up to, that they wanted to stop dissent," Howard Koch said. "It became clear from the outset that this was no impartial investigation, but an inquisition, designed to vilify the political and social beliefs of those who dissented from the now-established Cold War policies."

His concern for Koch led John to speculate what he would do if he was called before the committee. "I didn't know what I would do," he said. "Whether I'd be a squealer and the one to break the whole thing or take the line the others did."

The morning of the hearings, Huston, Dunne, and the other representatives of the CFA took their seats in the back row, there to lend support to Eric Johnston, who was scheduled to be the first witness. But J. Parnell Thomas cleverly switched the order of appearances and called first the most avowed and recognized Communist of the nineteen, John Howard Lawson. It became a fiasco.

Asked if he had ever been a member of the Communist party, Lawson responded defiantly, "The question of communism is in no way related to this inquiry, which is an attempt to get control of the screen and to invade the basic rights of American citizens in all fields." The pounding of J. Parnell Thomas's gavel echoed throughout the chamber as he cited Lawson for contempt and ordered him to be forcibly removed from the hearing. It was a disturbing sight and it was repeated when the next witness, Dalton Trumbo, was called. Trumbo also refused to answer yes or no to the two questions posed, and as he was held in the clutches of the police he shouted, "This is the beginning of the American concentration camp!"

"One after another they were knocked down," Huston noted. "It was a sorry performance. You felt your skin crawl and your stomach turn. I disapproved of what was being done to the Ten, but I also disapproved of their response. They had lost a chance to defend a most important principle. It struck me as a case of thoroughly bad generalship."

It was a disastrous day for Huston, Dunne, and their Committee for the First Amendment. The witnesses had behaved like belligerent buffoons, the spokesman for the producers didn't rally against a blacklist but, instead, invited the committee to root out the Communists, and the right-wing newspapers began to link their support of such hostile and obviously guilty-as-charged witnesses with the fact that the CFA must be a front for a Communist organization.

When columnist George Sokolsky challenged Humphrey Bogart in print to tell the world who put him up to defending Communists, Dunne wrote a letter to him that Huston signed taking full responsibility for the CFA's Washington sojourn. Sokolsky then publicly asked, "Who are Huston and Dunne? What is their connection with the Communist party?"

Frank Coniff, a Hearst columnist, wrote that "There is very good evidence that John Huston is the brains of the Communist party in the West!"

"He was an idiot," Huston said of Coniff. "It did nothing to me and my career because my nose was completely clean, I had no Communist inclination. I would have been delighted if they had subpoenaed me."

But it never came to that. Of the nineteen, eleven were called before pressure from the liberal press challenged the proceedings and the hearings were suspended. Those unfriendly witnesses who appeared before the committee were all cited for contempt of Congress and became known as the Hollywood Ten (the eleventh, Brecht, left the country).

The Committee for the First Amendment sponsored two national radio broadcasts condemning HUAC, and they also ran ads containing the signatures of hundreds of stars in the trade papers. Even such figures as Albert Einstein, Thomas Mann, and Helen Keller, among many others, issued statements of support. It appeared that the good guys had won, they had stopped—or at least put on hold—the threat of government interference in the movie business. But the studios themselves banded together to rid Hollywood of the stigma of communism.

The executives, led by Eric Johnston, declared their own war against communism, vowing to "discharge or suspend without compensation those in our employ and we will not reemploy any of the ten until such time as he is acquitted or has purged himself of contempt and declares under oath that he is not a Communist." The despicable blacklist had begun.

"It was a sorry time in our history," Evelyn Keyes wrote. "It didn't matter that Mr. J. Parnell Thomas went to jail himself for defrauding his government, or that the HUAC member who made it to the Oval Office was forced to resign some twenty-five years later. Lives, careers, and families had been destroyed. And it left a permanent scar on all of us."

When their plane left Washington for a stopover in New York, the representatives of the CFA felt they had been through a battle and had come through bloodied but unbowed. They decided to celebrate at "21," where Danny Kaye entertained and John, swore Bacall, "was hysterically funny." But if he was in high spirits that evening, the overall effect of the hearings hit Huston some days later when he flew to Key West in November 1947, to work on *Key Largo* with Richard Brooks.

"I was waiting for him in the bar where Tennessee Williams used to hang out," Brooks said. "He was in a foul mood because of this Washington fiasco. They didn't know what the hell they'd run into. "

"Is there any such place as Key Largo?" Huston asked. Brooks said there was and John said, "Well, let's go see it."

"There's only one hotel there, and it's not open," Brooks said, "but the owner is an Irishman and he's coming here."

Both men's wives, Evelyn and Harriet, were there when the owner of the Hotel Largo showed up. Huston convinced him to open his hotel and they all drove to Key Largo in the owner's car. Huston's mood was still sullen and he was thinking how much he disliked Maxwell Anderson's play when they arrived. "What do you do around here when you've got a storm?" he asked the owner. "Where's the storm basement?"

"There are no basements here, Mr. Huston. You dig down two feet and you're in the ocean."

Huston turned to Brooks and said, "I told you the guy who wrote the thing about the storm cellar is a phony. Let's go home."

Panicked, Brooks tried to reason with John. "It's not in our story. What the hell's the difference if there is a storm cellar or isn't?"

The hotel owner showed them to their rooms, brought in a cook, and gave them the run of the place. "Jesus, it was hot," Brooks remembered. "And it was humid. But John never perspired. He wore turtleneck sweaters. The routine was: John would go out on the pier and fish, then come in, read what I had written, take a little nap, wake up, go to the end of the pier and smoke."

John wanted to cast Charles Boyer as Johnny Rocco, the boss gangster, but Jack Warner vetoed that idea. Then Huston came up with

Edward G. Robinson. "Let's get the best," he said. "He's Little Caesar. Just look at him, you know who he is."

Rocco's first appearance was coming down the stairs of the hotel, which John thought was boring. Neither Brooks nor Huston could figure out a satisfactory solution until Huston walked in on Brooks when he was taking a bath with a fan blowing on him, trying to beat the heat. "That's not bad," John said. "That's Rocco. Give him a cigar." It would become the most memorable scene in the movie and Huston would later describe Robinson in the bathtub as looking "like a crustacean with its shell off."

Toward the end of the film Bogart was supposed to take the gangsters to Cuba in a boat and disarm the gunman. After Brooks wrote the scene John challenged the character's motives—or lack of them. "Why does he do it? Whatever they wanted him to do before, he does. If they want him to shut up, he shuts up. They slap the girl around, he doesn't do anything. The only thing he does to defy them is bring the girl a drink after she sings. Why suddenly does he do this? I've got to know why."

For the rest of the night Brooks struggled to come up with something and the next day he told John: The high swells of the sea could cause the gunman at the stern to get seasick and Bogart could see that if he got rid of the gunman he has a chance.

"That makes sense," Huston thought. "Write it."

Brooks didn't resent Huston's constant probing, it forced him to be the best he could. "John was clinical most of the time. He'd force me to find the truth according to the nature of the characters. It was the finding of the solution that excited him."

What also excited him, Brooks discovered, was gambling. After a week the hotel owner realized his guests were going to be there for a while, and he had some gaming tables brought in—for craps, roulette, and cards.

"Thank God," John said. Now, after working during the day, he had something to do each night. But as Brooks recalled, "No matter how we played, we'd lose. Consistently, beyond belief."

Brooks was worried that he was losing the entire $8,000 he was getting to write *Key Largo*. The fact that neither man had been paid by the studio made it even worse, as they had to sign IOUs to the hotel owner each night.

"The number of lost dollars kept climbing as the liquor supply diminished," said Evelyn, who didn't find it amusing. Brooks's wife was becoming extremely nervous about their gambling and Evelyn suggested they go to Nassau. "I don't think our mates ever noticed our departure," she said.

By the end of their stay credit was cut off and they had lost their salaries. John was down $40,000, Brooks $8,000. And then, from Cuba, Sam Spiegel, Tola Litvak, and Charlie Grayson showed up. Evelyn and Harriet returned from Nassau and Evelyn surprised John by bringing him a baby capuchin monkey. They were in high spirits and the atmosphere was convivial, even though Brooks felt "devastated." There was a storm and the group stayed for dinner. During their conversation John asked, "Anybody here know what the Immaculate Conception is?"

"I don't care what it is," Evelyn answered.

"Probably has something to do with the birth of Christ," Spiegel guessed.

There was a gleam in John's eye as he said, "What about the Irishman who owns this hotel. Get him over here."

Brooks called him over and John asked, "You know what the Immaculate Conception is?"

"Of course," the man answered. "Christ was born without sin."

John turned to Brooks and asked, "How much are you stuck?" John added it to his debt and devilishly asked the owner, as the sound of the storm against the windows added to the drama, "You want to bet forty-eight thousand dollars?"

"Not that much," the Irishman said, mumbling a trifling three-figure number under his breath.

"Hey," Brooks piped in, his anxiety running high. "How are we going to prove this?"

"We could call Monsignor Perry in Miami," the owner suggested. He went to the windup phone and managed to get through. "Monsignor," the man said, "I want to introduce you to a fellow here, we are having a discussion about the Immaculate Conception."

"The Immaculate Conception is that Mary was born without sin," the Monsignor said.

Brooks thanked him and returned to the dining room and said, "Well, we don't know from shit." They all looked at John, who smiled as he turned over the piece of paper where he had written, "Mary born without sin."

"Well," John said to the hotel owner. "Come up with the forty-eight thousand."

The owner balked. "First of all, Mr. Huston, we didn't bet forty-eight thousand. Second of all, you haven't given me any money yet, all you're doing is signing things."

"Well, what did we bet?"

"A hundred dollars."

Without a moment's pause, John said, "Well, let's have it." But instead of money, they took chips.

"John," Brooks chirped, "this is religious money, we could win some of what we lost back."

"Of course we'll win it back," Huston intoned. "But I've lost a lot more than you, so I should have the majority of the chips. And don't play at the table I'm playing at."

With his wife and friends there to cheer him on, Huston's luck changed and he won back almost his entire debt. Brooks also won about $3,000 and thanked the Virgin Mary for being without sin. John preferred to give his thanks to Lady Luck.

Three days before the holiday season officially got under way with the Bogarts' annual Christmas Eve party, Mark Hellinger died. He was only forty-one, the same age as John.

John took Hellinger's death in proper Irish fashion: He spent the holidays mostly inebriated. On the day before Christmas, Evelyn delivered presents to their friends as John prepared for Bogie's party by first getting drunk at Charlie Grayson's house. When Evelyn stopped by to see how he was doing she saw John and Charlie dancing in chorus-line fashion with two young girls. "John had unzipped his fly and poked his finger through the opening, with this absurd grin on his face, looking for all the world like the proud possessor of the world's smallest penis."

It began to rain and Evelyn had a minor car accident when her brakes didn't hold; by the time she made it to the Bogarts', John was already there, still drunk, on the floor tweaking his host's dog's balls. There were more than seventy guests at the party and after they all toasted Mark Hellinger, John, according to Evelyn, stuck his hand under Bacall's skirt and shouted, "I'm going up the Amazon!" To which Bogie shouted, "Oh, no you're not!" and jumped on the man he had already nicknamed "The Monster."

Evelyn and Jules Buck managed to get John out the front door, but as Evelyn walked toward the car, John made his move. "He came at me full speed from the rear," Evelyn recalled, "and tackled me like a football player. We skidded along this slippery, dewy grass. I was wearing a new pale blue suit and I couldn't wear the suit again."

John made up to Evelyn by making love with her in the car after they had driven home, and they spent the next day exchanging presents and taking Pablo to a party. John's present to Evelyn took her by surprise. It was a small box with a gold key inside. John told her to look outside, where she saw a yellow Cadillac convertible with red leather upholstery. She burst into tears.

When the Hustons gave a small dinner party for the Bogarts, Ida Lupino, and producer Collier Young, it turned into another drunken memory. "John and Bogie were like children," Evelyn observed. "Bogie is the one who said, 'I wouldn't trust anybody who didn't drink.' That explained Bogie: that to be open, he felt the need to drink. But with John it was a social thing to do. They began to play football with a Chinese Ming vase and Collier dropped it. Then Bogie stepped on the pieces with his bare feet, cutting himself as Betty scolded him."

The next day, as John nursed his hangover, Ronald Reagan and his wife, Jane Wyman, came by. John served Bloody Marys and then they decided to go to Olivera Street for Mexican food. John and Jane drank beer there and Reagan wasn't pleased with their behavior. "They got a little sloshed," Evelyn said, "and Ronnie was very strait-laced. He took over the driving. I sat beside him and the two gigglers were in the back. He said, 'Evelyn, let's be the policemen.' "

On New Year's Eve, the best-known stars in Hollywood could be found at Sam Spiegel's party, which Huston ranked "along with the Rose Bowl. It became an institution." John invited Richard Brooks, who was knocked out by all the fur coats on the bed. "All the stars of the world were there," Brooks said.

Brooks didn't think Huston liked Spiegel. "He knew Sam was very bright, erudite, spoke four languages, knew about painting. But even though he had the old-world mannerisms, Sam was half an inch away from hysteria most of the time and hysteria bothered John. He didn't like to handle it and he didn't want to be around it."

"There's something in that," Huston agreed when told of Brooks's assessment. "But with his back to the wall, Sam would not be close to hysteria, he would suddenly cool down and become as good a man as I knew. He was the sort of person who, if you woke up in a hotel and there was a woman in your bed with a knife in her chest and there was an empty whiskey bottle and you had no recollection about what had happened . . . what do you do? Billy Wilder said he'd call Sam Spiegel. And that's what I'd have done, too."

Evelyn's favorite Spiegel story centered around the time he came to their house for dinner and the monkey she had given John was loose. Hearing Spiegel's car door slam, the startled monkey peed into a bowl of nuts just as Sam got to the door. When he entered, he grabbed a handful of the nuts and popped them into his mouth, asking the maid, "Is that ape ever allowed in the kitchen?" When told the small monkey was, Spiegel replied, "In that case, I think I'll just stick to these nuts."

In January 1948, as John prepared to direct *Key Largo*, *Treasure* was released, to overwhelming critical praise. *Time* called it "one of the best things Hollywood has done since it learned to talk; and the movie can take a place, without blushing, among the best ever made." *The Nation* was even more effusive: "Huston, next only to Chaplin, is the most talented man working in American pictures, and . . . *The Treasure* is one of the very few movies made since 1927 which I am sure will stand up in the memory and esteem of qualified people alongside the best of the silent movies. . . . This is one of the most visually alive and beautiful movies I have ever seen."

Time called Walter's performance "his best job in a lifetime of good acting." *The Nation* elaborated: "Huston has for a long time been one of the best actors in the world and he is easily the most likable; on both counts this performance crowns a lifetime. . . . This man who has credibly played Lincoln looks small and stocky here, and is as gaily vivacious as a water bug. . . . In spite of the enormous amount of other talent at large in the picture, Huston carries the whole show as deftly and easily as he handles his comedy lines."

That both these reviews were written by one man, James Agee, wasn't lost on John, who sent him a warm letter thanking the writer for his perceptions. John's letter awoke in Agee a vision of being something more than a critic. "On receiving word from the director," Agee's biographer Laurence Bergreen wrote, "Agee began to seethe with schemes for self-advancement. He would meet Huston. He would write a profile of the director for one of the Luce publications, even *Life*. . . . Huston would ask him to write a screenplay. With the proceeds, Agee would be able to quit *Time* for good and, supported by the easy money from the screenplay, complete his two novels before the year was out." Eventually Agee's talent matched his scheme.

While Agee dreamed of one day working with Huston, Hal Croves, and apparently B. Traven, wanted nothing more to do with him. In a letter published in *Life* in March 1948, Croves responded to *Life*'s review in which they claimed that Croves and Traven were one. "Never again will Mr. John Huston have an opportunity to direct a picture based on any other of Traven's fourteen books. . . . A writer of books like the ones Traven created . . . will be read, loved and admired, or, yes, perhaps severely criticized still when nobody any longer can remember a movie director who, once upon a time, long, long ago, did a picture based on a story by said writer. . . ."

B. Traven's books are still in print and widely read, but as a prophet, H. Croves came closer to fulfilling Huston's own opinion: that he was a ridiculous and petulant little man who may have disguised himself because the writer B. Traven had long ago lost his talent.

Agee concluded his review in *The Nation* by making an insightful comment about the effect of the House Un-American Activities Committee's hearings, which had created a pall over the movie industry. *The Treasure of the Sierra Madre*, Agee believed, "is what it was possible to do in Hollywood, if you were talented enough, had standing enough, and were a good enough fighter, during the very hopeful period before the November Freeze. God knows what can be done now. But if anybody can hope to do anything, I count on Huston. . . ."

Agee didn't have long to wait. *Key Largo*, he declared, demonstrated Huston's abilities "even more impressively than *The Treasure of the Sierra Madre*." Before that film began on the Warner Bros. lot in Burbank, California, John put his actors through an intensive three-week rehearsal. He had gathered together an extraordinary ensemble: Bogart, Robinson, Lionel Barrymore, Claire Trevor, Lauren Bacall. And Richard Brooks was on hand for last-minute rewrites. Writers were usually barred from the set, but Huston knew that Brooks had ambitions to direct and had even encouraged him.

Claire Trevor was a screen veteran with forty-four pictures under her belt in the fifteen years she had been in movies. Although she appeared in a few "A" films, such as *Dead End* and *The Amazing Dr. Clitterhouse*, where Huston first became aware of her, she was mostly cast as the cynical gun moll, the floozy-with-the-heart-of-gold. And in *Key Largo* she played that role to perfection, Johnny Rocco's broken-down girlfriend, desperate for booze and bored with life.

"People always say, 'Didn't you have fun making that picture?' " Trevor remarked. "Well, you *don't* have fun. It's not a party. It's hard work. But *Key Largo was* fun. And I *adored* John. I was just enchanted by him."

Trevor was able to appreciate the way Huston directed without seeming to intrude on an actor's sense of space and movement. Huston's talent, she felt, was rare: He never overarticulated what he wanted. "The director who does that," she said, "kills a lot of ideas that an actor has. I don't remember John saying anything of an analytical nature. He'd make a gesture, or there would be a look on his face; he'd say, 'She's a little bit . . . like *that*. . . .' And it would say worlds. He'd like take a key and open a door to a whole warehouse full of emotions and pictures."

Huston was taken with Trevor's talent and her ability to grasp a scene, although there was one specific scene where she felt she needed coaching. It was when Rocco refuses to give her a drink but finally says if she'll sing for it, he'll give her one. So she sings "Moanin' Low" and when she finishes, Rocco says she's lousy and still won't give her the drink. "I knew I had to sing a song," Trevor related. "The character had been a nightclub singer of sorts and dreamed about becoming a big star, but she got caught up with this gangster. They picked 'Moanin' Low,' which is a difficult song, it goes up and down, and I'm the world's worst singer. I was after John all the time to rehearse this song and he'd always say, 'Plenty of time.' Then we came back from lunch one day and he said, 'We're going to shoot the song.' I said, 'WHAT!?' I was furious. I was totally unprepared. And he stood me up in the middle of the room. The piano offstage hit one note. He said, 'Go.' And that's how I sang it. He knew what he was doing. I was embarrassed. I was *supposed* to be embarrassed. I thought that day would never end. That was torture. But that's what got the effect."

Harry Lewis, who played one of Rocco's lackeys, Toots, watched wide-eyed as Claire Trevor sang that song and whispered to Tom Gomez, who played another henchman, Curly, "She's going to win the Academy Award for that song alone." And then they all broke into applause.

Lewis, according to Trevor, became Huston's whipping boy. "He wasn't a very good actor and Huston sort of lit into him. And Harry Lewis was one of those actors who would have given his *soul* to become a good actor. He played the young gangster with the white hat. John scared a good performance out of him. But after that he couldn't get work. So he opened a little hamburger stand on Sunset. And he married a girl who was very prudent. They worked very hard, it became a restaurant, and you know what it is now? Hamburger Hamlet!"

Before Lewis sold his chain of twenty-four restaurants for $33 million in December 1987, he recalled how Huston worked with him to get the character of the young maniacal killer in *Key Largo*. "He would sit down on his knees in front of me and say, 'When you are reading the comic strips, you've got to come up with this high-pitched laugh.' And the way he dressed me was exceptional. It was his idea to do the big trousers, the white hat, the suspenders, the coat, the whole look was something that he dreamed up. No other director ever worked with me like that."

When his agent told Eddie Robinson that he was being asked to take second billing to Bogart, "I didn't even argue," Robinson recalled. "At fifty-three I was lucky to get any billing at all. Let me tell you something about Bogie. On that set he gave it all to me. Second billing or no, I got the star treatment because he insisted upon it. When asked to come on the set, he would ask: 'Is Mr. Robinson ready?' He'd come to my trailer dressing room to get me." As for Lionel Barrymore, "We both gave *him* the deference he deserved. Certainly we were all very conscious of Claire Trevor's position and dignity, but if you really want to know who got the A-one eighteen-carat bowing, it was Lauren Bacall . . . in the middle of romance, and that gets the highest priority always."

Trevor felt a little sorry for Lauren Bacall, who was playing "a dull girl, stuck in this little town with her father, who falls in love with this soldier. She was supposed to be an ordinary girl. And it's hard for Bacall to be ordinary. Also, as an actress, she was insecure."

Bogart often tried to help her on the set. "The audience is always a little ahead of you," Bogart said to her before one scene. "If a guy points a gun at you, the audience knows you're afraid. You don't have to make faces."

Bacall said that when Huston wanted to make a suggestion to her, he would walk her to one side. "He would never embarrass me in front of another actor."

Her insecurities surfaced in the scene where Rocco whispered something in her ear and she responded by spitting in his face. "I had written out all the obscenities," Richard Brooks said. "And John said, 'That's terrific, that's just what he would say. But he can't do that in the movie.' So he said, 'Suppose we didn't hear what he said?' "

The audience would understand by Bacall's reaction, but spitting in Edward G. Robinson's face wasn't easy for the young actress. "The actual mechanics of doing that made me very nervous," she said. "John helped me by explaining what was going on, and he said, 'You just do it straightforwardly.' He was hypnotic. He could convince you to commit murder."

Bacall remembered how delighted Huston was when Lionel Barry-more's character had to defend Franklin D. Roosevelt, whose politics he personally disliked. Another time Huston noticed that Barrymore had fallen asleep while he was still in a scene, and he said to Richard Brooks, "Take a look. This is the only time in your life you will ever see a movie star sound asleep during his close-up."

John would often talk to Brooks about how he framed things, sug-gesting that he learn to compose by studying the French painters like Cézanne, Monet, Seurat. Brooks, whom Eddie Robinson called "as feisty, individual, unpredictable, and honest as any man I've ever known," looked at the paintings John suggested and found "it was true, the way they filled the canvas, the use of space was something really to learn. That's all frames of movies are: pictures, paintings."

"His way of directing was quite different from others," said Rudi Fehr, the film's editor, "and his way of editing was somewhat different, too. Every director has his own idea how editing should be done. He was the easiest man I've ever worked with and he didn't print a lot of takes. He moved the camera a great deal. There was one key scene where they were all in the room—Lionel, Bacall, Bogart, Robinson—and he shot that beautifully. And each night he'd bring the cast up to watch the rushes. After I put something together and showed it to them, to my amazement there was applause at the end."

Key Largo was Huston's way of fictionalizing his documentary experi-ences of the war. His hero, Frank McCloud, lost his friend at the battle of San Pietro. Since his return, McCloud is apathetic, like some of the psychologically scarred soldiers Huston saw at Mason General Hospital. He comes up against an evil force in Johnny Rocco and, for a while, he doesn't seem to care. But he is spurred out of his isolationist attitude to take a stand.

It would have been easy for Bogart to fall into one of his past roles to play McCloud, but Lauren Bacall felt that John was able to keep him fresh. "They communicated so incredibly well," she said. "He got Bogie to do things that he would never have done. Bogie wasn't one to analyze parts, but John certainly knew what he wanted and would make that clear."

He may have controlled his actors, but Huston had a harder time getting his wife to follow instructions. One of John's horses, a filly named Lady Bruce, which he co-owned with actress Virginia Bruce, was entered to run in a six-furlong race at Santa Anita. Huston was confident that she would win. Unable to get to the track because of the movie, he withdrew whatever money he had from his bank account, borrowed $4,000 from Willy Wyler and Anatole Litvak, and asked Evelyn to beg, borrow, and steal every dollar she could get her hands on to bet on Lady Bruce. He was so sure, he told everyone on the set to bet on the horse.

The heavy favorite for that race was a horse named Dry, owned by a South American named Luro. According to Billy Pearson, Evelyn got a ride to the track with Luro, who convinced her that Lady Bruce didn't stand a chance of beating Dry. She also conferred with John's trainer, who agreed with Luro. So, of the $8,000 she had collected, she placed only $100 on the filly to win.

On the *Key Largo* set, everyone had gathered around a radio to listen to the results and when Lady Bruce was declared the winner, there was great excitement, especially after it was announced that she paid $26.80 on a $2 bet. John quickly calculated that his winnings were in the six figures and he could hardly contain himself. "This was perhaps the greatest news I'd ever received. One minute I'd been scraping the bottom of the barrel, and the next minute—thanks to this marvelous animal—I was rolling in dough."

He already knew what he was going to do with the money. He had a number of debts to repay, chief among them the $75,000 he wanted to give Lesley, which she had put into their Tarzana house. She had never asked for the money, but it was a point of honor with John.

A celebration was called for and Huston chose Chasen's to meet Evelyn and Billy and some of his other close friends. But then John received a phone call and was told that Evelyn hadn't bet the money. She had been afraid to call John herself. An hour into the evening Evelyn called and talked to John. He tried to be magnanimous about it, but she rambled on and on until he lost it. "You bitch!" he hissed into the phone. "You dismal, wretched, silly bitch!"

His explosion should have been warning enough for her to stay away, but Evelyn figured she had deserved it and that once he had gotten it out of his system, it would be safe to make an appearance. She was wrong. "I walked in," she said, "and they were at the first table. John stood up in front of this star-studded crowd and grabbed me by the hair and took me out and *whack!* slapped me. He was in a fury. I don't think he came home for days."

"I'd a killed her," Billy Pearson said. By then John was too drunk to care. Instead, he went out and killed a horse. It was an accident. "Let's go jumping," he proposed to Billy at midnight. They got two horses saddled and John said, "Now just follow me, kid." Billy hadn't mounted his horse when he saw John take off "like a sonofabitch. And then *wham!* Someone had closed the gate and he ran into it full blast at thirty miles an hour. Killed the horse! And then he stumbled back, moaning, torn, bloody. Jesus."

Billy Pearson was an adult version of Huston's boyhood friend Sherman, the one he used to get in trouble with until their parents separated them. He knew horses; had a passion for pre-Columbian art; liked to gamble, smoke, drink; loved to laugh; and told a good story. John once described him as being "one of the most entertaining persons alive. He has a gift of being able to go beyond the limits of acceptable behavior and yet never loses his membership in polite society."

Pearson saw John as an "old-fashioned guy. The fisherman, hunter, drinkin', playin' poker all night kind of guy. Women are not too much into that world. Unless you're very ballsy, like Betty Bacall. She was wonderful around those kind of guys 'cause she was kinda like a guy."

"They were Mutt and Jeff," Lauren Bacall said of the two of them. "There was this giant of a man and this tiny little jockey. What they had in common was horses."

After the last shot was taken and *Key Largo* was finished, Huston, Richard Brooks, and the cameraman, Karl Freund, participated in a ritual that Rudi Fehr witnessed and said he had never seen before or since. "They all peed on the floor of the set. I didn't understand that. I was shocked."

James Agee, knowing that Huston would be reading his *Key Largo* review, flatly stated that John was "the most vigorous and germinal talent working in movies today." The *New York Times* noted the tension achieved in the film but criticized the script as being "too full of words and highly cross-purposed implications to give the action full chance. Talk—endless talk—about courage and the way the world goes sums it up."

To get away from the endless talk that often follows the release of a movie, Huston and Billy Pearson went on a dove-shoot in Antelope Valley. Instead of doves, Pearson shot a half-dozen yellow thrushes, which he put in John's bag, exchanging them for the doves John had shot. At the end of the day, when the birds were counted, John was mortified when the thrushes were discovered. "He thought he was losing his eyesight, that he couldn't tell color between a gray dove and a yellow thrush." Pearson laughed. "He wound up giving all his bird guns away."

Pearson knew that he could get away with things that other people who knew John wouldn't dare attempt. "I was the only guy that was totally outside the movie business. So I could say to him, 'Aw, that's shit,' and no one else dared say that because they were in it. Like Spiegel, who was just a goddamn thief, which I said to John, but John would defend him."

Initially, Huston had good reason to defend Sam Spiegel, who produced pictures under the name S. P. Eagle (he had a trail of bounced checks, unpaid loans, and nights in jail and couldn't work under his real name). Spiegel knew that *Key Largo* was John's last contracted picture for Warner Bros. and that Huston wanted to leave the studio. He also knew that after Evelyn blew his big gambling score John had asked for a loan of $50,000 from the studio and was turned down.

Spiegel was looking for a partner to start an independent production company and figured Huston was ripe to approach. At a party at screenwriter Salka Viertel's house, he ran into Huston, who said he had a picture in mind based on a story called *Rough Sketch* by Robert Sylvester, having to do with corruption in Cuba and an attempt to overthrow the government. John had already begun working on a script with Salka's son, Peter, and John Garfield had expressed interest in playing the lead. Spiegel made his move: He would loan Huston the money needed *and* produce his next picture *if* Huston would agree to be his partner in a production company.

Huston knew only too well the temper of the times. The studios were already giving in to the worst elements of government pressure. Blacklisting had begun. Television was eroding the monopoly movies had on visual entertainment. It seemed clear to Huston that the studio system had had its day and that the future would be in independent productions. So Huston accepted Spiegel's offer and they formed Horizon Pictures, which they referred to as Shit Creek Productions.

"Sam came up with the amount and we became one of the first directing-producing partnerships independent and free of studios," Huston said, at last able to pay back Lesley. "And then we did *We Were Strangers*." Huston would never forget a performance of Sam's that left him in admiration decades after their partnership had dissolved.

"MGM had just instituted a new wrinkle," Huston recalled. "All their department heads—casting, art, so on—would meet once a week and whatever new ideas were forthcoming would be put on the table. This was when L.B. [Mayer] was the kingpin. Well, the whole thing sounded rather awful. How do you get up and tell the casting director how you're going to make a motion picture? But our being invited to do this was quite something, because MGM was the holiest of the cathedrals then.

"The night before our meeting, I went to a party at Bogart's and got as drunk as I've ever been in my life. *Really* drunk. I telephoned Anne Selepegno and asked if I could sleep on her sofa. Anne, who was what they called at the racetrack a 'lady regular,' woke me the next morning with Sam on the phone. Like a fine detective, he found me and said, 'Good God, John, do you realize what time it is?'

" 'I don't realize anything except that I'm blind, have a cleft palate, and stink abominably.'

" 'Get Anne to bring you to my place as quickly as you can.'

"Sam gave me one of his shirts and a sports jacket that was too short, but it was the best we could do. Then we went out to MGM, where I met these people for the first time. I'd met L. B. Mayer once before at a party. I had said, 'Sam, I have trouble remembering my name, there's no possibility of me telling this story.'

"Finally, the rest of their business was done and Sam and I were introduced. Sam held forth for about fifteen minutes and I sat there in wonder. Sam had no idea of a story, but the words *glamour, exotic, excitement, suspense* kept reappearing.

"Now there was a good deal of feeling about Sam at that time in Hollywood. He was not a popular figure. The deal didn't go through with MGM on this picture—they thought they were several cuts above the likes of Sam Spiegel. It was generally thought that I'd done a rather foolish thing. For money. But the gates of MGM were open to me at any time—in fact, I made a deal with MGM, which accounted for my being able to pay off the rest of my debts. Those several years in the army had cost me! I wasn't betraying Sam in doing this. We did *We Were Strangers* at Columbia."

Walter, according to John, "wasn't keen on Sam." Spiegel had visited with Walter in March 1948 to try and talk him into playing a part in *Command Decision,* which John was considering as well. It was Spiegel's hope that if Walter agreed, then John would direct it. But at that time, Walter was concerned about Nan, who was still in poor health, and he wrote to Paul Kohner, "I have done such a good job so far I wouldn't want to do anything until I know she is okay. A year later would be all right but not now."

Walter had already turned down an offer to do a weekly half-hour dramatic radio show, but he wanted to bring *Apple of His Eye* to the screen. Paul Kohner wanted to produce it, with Jed Harris directing and Ginger Rogers co-starring. The movie business, though, was slow the first few months of 1948, even after the rave notices for *Treasure*. Walter responded to an agent's praise of that film by saying, "That may be a good performance, but John Huston certainly ruined my sex appeal with no teeth and long underwear." Kohner wrote to his client, "There hasn't been any worthwhile proposal for any really good part to report to you. We shall simply have to wait for the right role."

To keep busy Walter fixed up their New York apartment at 406 E. 50th Street, requesting Kohner to track down photographs from all his plays and movies. "I have a little bar room here in the apartment and in my spare time, which is plenty, I have been framing and putting up photos of characters I have done on the stage and screen. I have now about 25 on the wall. The only thing wrong with it is it makes me realize how old I am." He especially wanted his agent to send him the picture of himself with President Roosevelt and General George C. Marshall.

In March, Walter had written to Kohner asking for advice concerning Henry Wallace's attempt to wrest the Democratic presidential nomination away from Harry Truman. "They are putting the pressure on me here to go out for Henry Wallace. He certainly makes more sense than any one else. What do you think? I know what the reaction to this will be. And it's quite a problem. He certainly needs support at this time."

Kohner advised Walter to follow his brain, not his heart. "My advice would be to stay away from all politics this year and not come out for anyone. There are times when the wiser course is to keep your mouth shut—and that is what I propose to do."

John asked Philip Dunne for advice on the same matter: organizing a Wallace for President Committee. "I listed my objections to the Wallace candidacy," Dunne said. "But he did take it on and the most prominent members of it were the Hollywood Ten."

Soon after, Sam Spiegel called Dunne and wanted to know why he had persuaded John to come out for Wallace. "You've ruined me, that's what you've done!" Spiegel shouted. "Sam's anger," Dunne said, "was inspired by the fear that John's political faux pas would cost him financial backing for the picture they were making."

*   *   *

John's research trip to Cuba at the end of April 1948 was a welcome relief from the troubles of the Hollywood Ten, the clandestine naming of names that was going on throughout the movie industry, and the political maneuverings of Harry Truman, Henry Wallace, and Thomas Dewey for the presidential nominations. He and Evelyn went down to Havana with Peter Viertel, his co-writer on *We Were Strangers*, and Viertel's wife, Gige. John had known Peter as a boy; his father, Berthold, had directed *Rhodes of Africa*, which John had polished for Walter, and his mother, Salka, was a prominent figure in the Hollywood community, a collaborator on a number of Greta Garbo films. Viertel had gotten to know Ernest Hemingway in what John observed was "close to a father-son relationship," and Peter brought the two men together. "That first meeting was anything but easy," Huston said, but once Hemingway decided Huston passed his shit-detector test, he invited them all out on his boat, the *Pilar*.

John was a great admirer of Hemingway's work, especially the short stories, which influenced his work as a director. "The best that I can get out of a scene," he once observed, "is when it stops being something that you're looking at and becomes an experience. In literature this happens rarely, but when it does it's extraordinary. Certain American writers have a penchant for this, a peculiar ability to re-create, to make you feel that you are actually present in something. If Hemingway had anything, he had that."

Hemingway also had a mouth like a sewer, which Evelyn felt was directed mostly at her. "Papa, as they called him, had this big, big hole in his shirt. I had this chartreuse silk jersey which just clung. At the sight of me, I don't know if he talked that way all the time, but Hemingway never stopped saying, 'fuck,' 'shit,' 'cocksucker.' I felt it was for my benefit, because of my dress. He wasn't well, but he did all the talking."

One of the things Hemingway said about the troubles of the Hollywood Ten struck John. Hemingway hadn't spoken out against HUAC at that time, but he was of the opinion that some of the best things that had been written had been done in jail and, remembered John, "he hoped that these writers would see this opportunity to make the most of their incarceration."

During their fishing excursion they spotted an iguana on a rock and, depending on who was telling the story, either John or Hemingway took a shot at it. Huston's version was that Hemingway wounded the animal, then spent hours in the water tracking it down in order to kill it. Evelyn said it was John who had wounded the iguana and Hemingway who insisted it be found. John and Viertel went to look for it but gave up and then Hemingway jumped in. "Peter and John, like chastised children, followed after him." But Huston and Viertel again tired of the game and returned to the boat, leaving Hemingway alone in the blazing sun. It took him two hours but he found the iguana "quite dead," said Evelyn; alive and hissing, said John, who was impressed. "I have never seen such persistence and determination," he said. "All macho business," said Evelyn.

The macho business started again a few days later when Huston noticed a few pairs of boxing gloves at Hemingway's *finca vigia* and suggested they go a few rounds. "I just want to see what your style is," he said, but the thought of actually boxing with Ernest Hemingway was what really propelled him. Hemingway sized him up and said, "You've got longer arms and you're supposed to be a good boxer, you wouldn't stay out there and jab my nose, would you?" "No, I wouldn't do anything like that," John replied. So Hemingway went into the other room with Peter Viertel and said, "I'm going to cool the sonofabitch." But Mary, his wife, who, remembered Evelyn, "cleaned her toenails with a long knife and cut the bread with it afterward," told John that Hemingway had been having trouble with his heart. "No one is supposed to know this," she said, "but please don't box." So Huston never got the chance to add this story to his collection of experiences. Aware that Hemingway had a big punch, he thought "perhaps it was just as well."

When he wasn't trying to out-macho Papa, John was out gambling or checking out the whorehouses of Havana. "Cuba was just a little place that the U.S. had fucked up," he found. "Batista was running the show, but it was owned and operated by the United Fruit Company. Everything was a payoff. But I do remember the street of whorehouses in Havana."

So did Evelyn. "I didn't like it," she said. "He talked about how the whores picked up coins and cigarettes with their twats. Is that attractive? I wanted him to be better than that. It just diminished him. Things like that take a little chip off, bits and pieces."

When they returned from Cuba, Evelyn had just about had it with their marriage. "I had a one-night stand with David Niven once, but I never told John," she said. "After that I went into analysis, because I didn't understand what I was doing anymore. Those of us who felt we weren't coming out right went into analysis, trying to find out about ourselves, but John didn't need that. It seems to me he had the life he wanted."

For his forty-second birthday she hoped to surprise him with a saddle horse, but the night before all her resentments came to a head when, on their way to a party at Sonja Henie's, John crashed her yellow Cadillac into a parked car. "You crazy . . . *lunatic!*" Evelyn shouted in a blind rage. "Why didn't you look?"

John, who abhorred the sound of cars in collision—a sound he had become only too familiar with—grabbed her arm and twisted hard. "Shut . . . up," he snarled.

That night they went their separate ways. But in the morning she remembered the horse she had ordered and rushed back to their ranch. When John arrived, she gave it to him and he went for a ride. When he returned, she said, "I realize it's over between us and . . . I'm sorry." John took her to bed, but the smell of horse was all over him and she sneezed all night.

Soon after she packed her bags and found an apartment in the same building as Paulette and Burgess Meredith, who were also having marital problems. "When I realized we weren't working out, I decided to move into town by myself. He went to Cuba again to shoot exteriors, and when he returned he asked me to pick him up at the airport. He said, 'Where do you live, honey?' So I showed him and he just moved in."

By this time Walter and Nan had returned to Running Springs in spite of his not wanting to bring her back for a year. They had come in June and had been greeted by a freak snowstorm and a swimming pool "only good for polar bears." A month later Paul Kohner found a part for Walter as Captain Bearing Joy in *Down to the Sea in Ships,* to be directed by Henry Hathaway for 20th Century-Fox. "I know that after you have read it," Kohner wrote to Walter, "you will agree with my recommendation that you should accept this part." Walter met Hathaway in August and agreed to do the picture, but Fox balked at Kohner's insistence on $75,000 for a ten-week guarantee and signed Lionel Barrymore for less. Losing that deal made Kohner reassess their asking price for Walter's services and wrote to his client that he would "very much like, the next time you come to town, to take up the question of our salary demands for pictures. I find definite resistance everywhere to salary increases at this time. . . .

"I would like to know from you how you feel about it and if you would be willing to accept an assignment at the same salary you have had before, meaning $50,000 for a maximum of 8 weeks."

Walter apparently thought he was worth more because his contract for *The Great Sinner* was for $7,500 a week for a five-week minimum, $1,250 a week more than he made for *The Treasure of the Sierra Madre*.

John's own finances were still a shambles and he was beginning to have doubts about the movie he and Spiegel were making for their company. "It was one of those pictures that didn't come together," he felt. "The script wasn't very good. Instead of having a natural climax, it went cliché. The hero became a cardboard hero."

The whole picture didn't ring true. Jennifer Jones and John Garfield were supposed to be Cubans, which they weren't. They spoke in unaccented English. "The very fact it was in contemporary Cuba and they weren't speaking Spanish led, right off, to a false start," he said.

One film historian, Scott Hammen, didn't agree with Huston's assessment and felt that *We Were Strangers* was a brave and courageous movie for Huston to have made at a time when so many of his colleagues had been "intimidated into avoiding political subjects. . . . Huston had dared to suggest that elected representatives might choose spiritless acquiescence in the face of a demagogue's attack on liberty, and he did so not long before an uncannily similar phenomenon occurred between Senator Joseph McCarthy and the United States Congress."

Jennifer Jones devised an elaborate joke to get even with John for placing a fake arm in a Cuban cemetery where Jones was digging during filming. At the wrap party, Jones, who had left a stormy marriage with actor Robert Walker and was involved with producer David Selznick, had a surprise for John.

"It was a big monkey," Evelyn said, her memory still vivid. "And it had fallen for John. The monkey with its raggedy arms was wrapped around John and she wouldn't get off him. It was the drinking again, everybody was feeling no pain. So the chimp person followed us with the cage to my apartment and I couldn't stand it, so I called Paulette Goddard, who lived upstairs, in the middle of the night and said, 'We've got a chimpanzee down here, can I come up?' The next morning I came back and there wasn't anything that the chimp hadn't destroyed;

it was chaos. At first I was mad. I shook John, who was still sleeping. He looked around and started to laugh. Well, it *was* funny. So we cracked up; we laughed so much it hurt. Then the chimp would look at me and start to lick my hand and then she'd bite me. Just enough to scare me. John went in to shower and the chimp started banging on the door. I opened it and she went in and started washing, too."

But Evelyn said the chimp couldn't stay at the apartment and John told her, "She can't be separated from me, so I'm going to have to stay out at the ranch with her." At that point, according to John, Evelyn gave him a choice. John chose the monkey.

It wasn't over between them yet. There was still another animal adventure awaiting them. After *We Were Strangers* was completed in January 1949, John felt the need to get far away and spend a few weeks hunting deer. He chose a place in the Bitterroot Mountains in Idaho, "so remote and so hard to get to," Huston said, "that no other plane ever ventured in."

It sounded just perfect for Huston, who took Evelyn, Gilbert Roland, who had acted in *We Were Strangers*, and James Agee, who was writing his *Life* profile of Huston and hoped to get in his good graces.

Throughout his life Huston attracted good journalists and welcomed them to probe his public life and work, giving them the same considerable attention he gave to directors, producers, light and sound men, boxers, jockeys, women, and panhandlers. His attention was seductive, he acted as if that person was the most interesting person he had ever encountered. And with Agee he found a similar trait. "I felt he often gave people credit for being more interesting and intelligent than they really were because of his way of reading deep meanings into commonplace remarks."

They traveled first by car and then by plane. "The hunting lodge nestled in a miniature valley," wrote Evelyn, "in the heart of giant masses of earth and rock. . . . Our cabins were the same sub-zero temperature as outside. So was the toilet."

Their first day John taught Evelyn how to shoot a 30–30 rifle. Then they all got on horses and rode along the steep slopes and ridges. Evelyn found John very happy to be doing "the rugged stuff." When John spotted a deer, he jumped from his horse and threw himself to the ground, bagging it with one shot. Roland was impressed, but Evelyn and Agee were not. Agee refused to kill anything, wouldn't even carry a gun.

During this two-week outing Agee confessed to Huston that what he really wanted to do was write a script for him. John wasn't surprised. Most writers he knew, other than Hemingway, wanted to write for the movies. But John recognized Agee's talent and, without committing himself, indicated that he understood.

On their last day, after John and Roland had shot their quota, John went out with Evelyn, encouraging her to get at least one deer. They finally spotted one and Evelyn reluctantly fired her rifle. "I hit the damn thing and he was kind of proud of me," she said. But then John told her to find the deer, to make sure it was dead and not just wounded. "I was alone in this vast wilderness, in sub-zero weather," she recalled, wondering if John had the gall to just leave her there. But she found the deer, John did return, and the head wound up on a wall at their ranch, next to one of the bucks that John had shot. "John later said that that hunting trip was the best part of our life together," Evelyn said. "Go figure that."

At a party at their ranch soon after their return, a young stage director who was about to direct his first feature film asked Huston how he should handle his actors. Huston replied, "Talk to them about things they don't know. Try to give them an inferiority complex. If the actress is beautiful, screw her. If she isn't, present her with a valuable painting she will not understand. If they insist on being boring, kick their asses or twist their noses. And that's about all there is to it."

Jean Negulesco, along with the other directors and writers at the party, applauded Huston's drunken but sound advice as John happily puffed one of his Cuban cigars. He had been speaking from experience, having had his way with Mary Astor and Olivia de Havilland and having twisted Bogart's nose. But when he talked about actors, there was always one exception to any rule: Walter. After all, it was Walter, not John, who played golf with George C. Marshall, had the respect of Eugene O'Neill, and hung autographed pictures of Franklin D. Roosevelt on the wall.

Walter had completed his small role as a charming, roguish general who used his daughter's beauty to obtain gambling money in *The Great Sinner*. The movie starred Ava Gardner, who, during the making of the film, told a reporter, "Deep down, I'm pretty superficial," and Gregory Peck, who played the writer obsessed with gambling. Walter's part was an amusing sidelight to their story and he mouthed such lines, co-written by Christopher Isherwood, as "Love is a pastime for the middle class."

Nan didn't care much for *The Great Sinner,* just as she hadn't liked *Summer Holiday,* which she felt "didn't come off and that is putting it very kindly." She thought highly of *Treasure* and enjoyed *Key Largo,* telling Paul Kohner that John was still her favorite director. Nan had stayed in touch with Lesley. "I think she is fine now," Nan wrote Kohner. "She *never* refers to the past. She looks and sounds so beautiful."

Kohner, the month before the Academy Awards ceremony, had been doing everything he could to get the academy members to vote for his two Huston clients. John was up for Best Screenplay and Best Director, Walter for Best Supporting Actor. Kohner was so confident, he was already figuring in the thank-yous before the awards were given.

Walter was back in New York on March 1 when Kohner sent him the first draft of *The Furies,* which Hal Wallis expected to produce in September. Barbara Stanwyck had consented to star and Walter was being offered the part of her father, a prosperous and forceful land-owner. Kohner hoped Walter would like the script and stressed that they were "anxious to know whether you would be interested."

Walter was. He was even more interested in finding out whether he would win his first Oscar at the Academy Award Theatre in Hollywood on March 24, 1949. His competition was Charles Bickford in *Johnny Belinda,* José Ferrer in *Joan of Arc,* Oscar Homolka in *I Remember Mama,* and Cecil Kellaway in *The Luck of the Irish.* All good actors, but Walter was the odds-on favorite for what many critics called the performance of a lifetime.

The competition for Best Picture was stiff. *Treasure,* which hadn't done well at the box office, was up against *Johnny Belinda, The Red Shoes, The Snake Pit,* which starred Best Actress nominee Olivia de Havilland in a tour de force performance, and Laurence Olivier's *Hamlet.* Olivier was also nominated for Best Actor and for Best Direc-tor. The three other directors nominated were Fred Zinnemann for *The Search* and two of John's close friends, Anatole Litvak for *The Snake Pit* and Jean Negulesco for *Johnny Belinda.* It came as a surprise that Humphrey Bogart was not nominated for his performance in *Treasure* and no surprise at all that Claire Trevor was for *Key Largo.*

Springtime in Los Angeles is usually tanning weather, but on the day of the Awards it snowed. The weather didn't affect the Hustons' night, however, as Walter won his Oscar, John won two, and Claire Trevor took Best Supporting Actress. John didn't say anything when Deborah

Kerr announced his name for Best Screenplay, he just lifted the Oscar over his head and smiled. When director Frank Borzage called him up for Best Director, he looked at the statue, then at his producer, and said, "If this were hollow and had a drink in it, I'd toast Henry Blanke." Walter acknowledged his son: "Many years ago," he said, "many, many years ago, I raised a son and I said to him, 'If you ever become a writer or a director, please find a good part for your old man.'" And Claire Trevor, picking up on Walter's comment, told the audience, "I have three boys and I hope they grow up to be directors so they can give their old lady a job."

It was a night to celebrate even though Nan had remained in New York and Olivier's *Hamlet* was named Best Picture. After the ceremonies, Walter picked up Jacqueline de Wit and joined John and Evelyn at the Macambo, where Jack and Harry Warner congratulated their winners. John was as pleased about his father's award as he was about his own and the two men happily posed for photographers' pictures. The celebration continued into the morning, but what John had most to be thankful for had nothing to do with the awards he had won. He had luckily stayed away from Olivia de Havilland, who had lost the Oscar that night to Jane Wyman for *Johnny Belinda*. Olivia had gone to the ceremony with her husband, Marcus Goodrich, who had heard so much about the way John had done Olivia wrong that he planned his own sweet revenge if Huston so much as looked at Olivia or upset her in any way. John would later confide to Doris Lilly that Marcus Goodrich had arrived at the Oscars wearing a cape. "I was told he had a gun inside the cape," John said. "He wanted to shoot me that night."

14

"THERE'LL NEVER BE ANOTHER LIKE ME"

WITH HIS OSCARS IN HAND, JOHN WAS IN A POSITION TO have helped Evelyn's career, steering her toward interesting projects, developing something that Horizon could have produced, advising her on scripts, considering her for one of his films. But for one exception he never did, and Evelyn never took advantage of being married to her two-Oscar husband.

"It never occurred to me to get John to find something for me to be in," she said, "which was so stupid, because I needed that one thing to get me higher up. Once I did ask him to help with a script which wasn't coming out right. *Mrs. Mike.* Dick Powell was the producer and I said, 'I've got this guy at home who won an Academy Award, would you like to talk to him?' John read the script and said, 'Your problem is you're using three tragedies in the script. You can't have that many.' But that was the only time I ever asked him to read a script. If I would have said, 'John, I want to be a big star, let's get a part for me,' he probably would have done it."

But Evelyn had enough problems playing the role of wife, a part she never particularly got the hang of. With John and his animals at the ranch in the valley and she at her apartment in West Hollywood, they saw each other mostly on social occasions.

At one of David Selznick's parties, John was introduced to a beautiful girl named Ricki Soma, one of Selznick's protégées. Selznick had seen her on the cover of the June 9, 1947, *Life*, looking like a modern Mona Lisa, and had offered her a seven-year contract, which her stepmother Dorothy had to initial because she was underage. At sixteen she had been the youngest member of Ballet Theatre, the best ballet company in America, according to the article in *Life*, and her landing on the cover of that magazine two years later was a stroke of luck, of being in the right place at the right time. Photographer Philippe Halsman spotted her in a dance line. He was struck by her classic beauty and thought he could make her resemble not only da Vinci's enigmatic Lisa but also Degas's ballerinas.

John didn't remember the *Life* cover, but he felt sure he knew her. Ricki teased him, saying that he had once stood her up on a date; then it all came back to him. She was Tony Soma's daughter, the one he had promised to take to the ballet during the war. How could he forget? The little girl who, along with her brother Philip, had greeted the diners at her father's restaurant as if they were houseguests had grown into a ravishing young woman, provoking Evelyn to reflect, "Is there something appealing about a girl-child growing up to a fuckable age under your nose? Probably. Particularly if the girl-child has no hesitancy in using her newfound wiles." Before the night was over their behavior embarrassed and angered Evelyn.

"He was all over her," Evelyn bitterly recalled. "They were embracing with all these people around. I remember sitting down by William and Mrs. Wellman. John had flipped out and was necking in public. She said, 'Who's that with John?' And Wellman said, 'I guess it's his wife.' And I said, 'No, I'm his wife.' "

John had done it again. Ricki was young, innocent, attractive, in need of learning. A refreshing jolt to his worldly, jaded demeanor. He promised he would see her again, and it didn't take long for Ricki to find an excuse for not seeing Robert Walker, the actor she had occasionally dated, or Gian Carlo Menotti. According to Lizzie Spender, daughter of the poet Stephen Spender and a friend of Menotti's, the composer was driving with Ricki, discussing Laurence Olivier, when Menotti said he found the actor a bit of a ham. "Stop the car," Ricki supposedly said. "Mr. Menotti, you've been very kind to me, but I just can't take that from anyone." And that was the last time he ever saw her.

• • •

On April 27, 1949, John was accused of being a Communist in the *Hollywood Reporter*, or at least that was the implication from their review of *We Were Strangers*. The reviewer blasted "its blatant propaganda content. It is the heaviest dish of Red theory ever served to an audience outside the Soviet Union." Huston found the review "absurd" and laughed when, the following week, the *Daily Worker* said the film was "capitalist propaganda." "I'm proud and delighted to have both of these lunatic ends converging on me," he said.

But it wasn't something he could easily ignore. Louella Parsons came to his defense, but Hedda Hopper was his "avowed avenging angel." Jerry Wald tried to get Hopper off John's case, but John told Wald, "Shit, I want nothing to do with her."

Columbia's Harry Cohn was so enraged by the *Hollywood Reporter*'s review that he barred the trade paper from his lot and withdrew his studio's ads from the publication for six years.

Other reviews of the film were mixed. Robert Hotch in the *New Republic* wrote that "Huston is building himself a reputation as the strongest, most assured director in Hollywood and *We Were Strangers* is a notably disciplined picture." *Theatre Arts* thought it was "even better than *Sierra Madre*." *Time*, on the other hand, while calling it "above average" but "not a Grade A Huston," said that "coming from the man who made *The Treasure of the Sierra Madre*, it is a disappointment."

The commercial failure of *We Were Strangers* put Huston in a deep financial hole and Paul Kohner managed to arrange a $150,000 loan from MGM. Since John had agreed to do two pictures for them, it was considered good-faith money.

It was time to make some money and so John agreed to take on *Quo Vadis*, a picture dear to L. B. Mayer's heart. Arthur Hornblow, Jr., was the assigned producer, a man who John thought "had style. His words were well chosen. He didn't indulge in colloquialisms. Or if he did, it was with amusement." But when Huston told Hornblow that he didn't like the pages he had been given, the producer strongly disagreed. To settle their disagreement they went to see the studio chief, Dore Schary. "I made derisive remarks about the script and about one particular scene which Arthur thought was quite marvelous and I thought was utterly foolish," Huston said. "And Dore sided with me. And I went about writing the script myself with a classics scholar named Hugh Gray. It was quite a defeat for Arthur. He stood for it, however."

Huston thought highly of *Quo Vadis* as a book and hoped to capture "the evil of Nero," rather than focusing on the hero, to be played by Gregory Peck, and the more religious aspects of the story. "They wanted a spiritual, uplifting experience, a C. B. DeMille picture. I wasn't interested in that. The delineation of Nero really plumbed into a depth of evil. That was what interested me." He saw a parallel between Nero's fanatical determination to eliminate the Christians and Hitler's attempt to eradicate the Jews two thousand years later.

After completing half the script, Huston and Gray's pages wound up on L. B. Mayer's desk. Mayer didn't like what he read—MGM was, after all, the studio of glamour, of musicals, of romance—and asked Huston to come to his house on a Sunday. "I had no respect for Mayer whatever," Huston said, "but great admiration and a sneaking liking. One of the greatest fools I've ever known. But a heroic fool." Mayer began to describe the kind of warm, emotional, family-oriented picture he wanted. "He described to me the way he had once hired Jeanette MacDonald against everybody's advice," Huston related. "Everyone said MacDonald pissed ice water—I'm quoting L. B.—but he knew that she had heart, and he sang her a Jewish song, 'Eli, Eli,' which brought tears to her eyes. She went on and sang 'Ah, Sweet Mystery of Life' in that picture and it was an experience that no one ever forgot. He wanted me to make *Quo Vadis* that kind of picture and he sang 'Eli, Eli' to me! Then he said if I could do that, he would get down on his knees and kiss my hand, and then he proceeded to do exactly that. I kept thinking to myself, 'This is not happening to me.' "

John left the house "in a cold sweat" and went immediately to see Arthur Hornblow, convinced they should forget about making *Quo Vadis*. But Hornblow talked him into continuing. By this time John had grown to like Hornblow and they went to Paris for casting. The picture was due to begin filming in Rome in July 1949, but Gregory Peck developed an eye infection and the film was postponed. Arthur Hornblow then resigned and when he did, so did Huston. "Arthur was surprised," John said. "That I could be against him one minute and stand behind him the next. That made us very good friends."

Mayer assigned Sam Zimbalist to produce it and Mervyn LeRoy to direct and got the story he wanted. Hornblow and Huston asked for, and got, *The Asphalt Jungle*.

Dore Schary had bought the film rights to W. R. Burnett's novel and gave it to Hornblow, which Burnett thought an unusual choice, since the producer "had built his reputation with a far different type of picture." But when he heard that Huston was to direct, he was pleased. They had worked well together on *High Sierra* and Burnett felt that

Huston was "adept at putting a property on the screen—how to dramatize its essence. And this he did very successfully with *The Asphalt Jungle*. He stayed close to the characters, the action, and the atmosphere." Burnett had begun his detailed examination of a robbery and its aftermath with the "horrific news of the nightly toll of crime coming in over the Commissioner's radio, the voice of the asphalt jungle, as the Commissioner delivers a needed lesson to the newsmen." But Huston didn't think the frame Burnett had mounted was necessary; he wanted to plunge right into the story of how criminals come together to pull off a crime.

Huston brought in Ben Maddow, who had written *Intruder in the Dust*, to work on the screenplay with him. When Huston spoke highly about Burnett's talents as a novelist, Maddow kept his thoughts to himself. He found Huston fascinating, a man with "fourteen different sides to him." But he also found that he had "this tremendous respect for certain people like Burnett, which was a sign, to me, of an intellectual amateur. He didn't think that Faulkner was a giant, but rather would think that a writer of a small detective novel was. Maybe it was a certain form of reverse snobbery."

Huston had rented Tola Litvak's house in Malibu to work on the script and Maddow recalled how their long conversations led to a lot of "wasted time." Once Maddow went home for dinner and then returned only to find John sitting at a table with his father and a young woman. "She was Walter's girl," Maddow said, "a big, handsome woman." Maddow had come into their conversation, which was about hypnosis. John was saying that his success as a director was due to his ability to hypnotize his actresses. "Walter Huston was rather doubting it," Maddow remembered.

But John persisted, wanting to prove his point by hypnotizing the girl. She refused. "How about you, Ben?" John asked his collaborator. Maddow agreed.

"You have to realize my point of view," Maddow said. "I'm trying to get this script going. He had me stand up and he took off his wristwatch and dangled it in the light in front of me. My eyes were closed."

"You are feeling sleepy," John intoned. "Your arms are rising without your help." And Maddow's arms rose. "I'm going to pinch you and you won't feel it." John did and Maddow didn't respond. "I'm going to give you a post-hypnotic suggestion," John said. "I'm going to snap you out of it and when I offer you a glass of brandy, you will taste it and say, 'This is the finest drink I've ever had in my life.' " John snapped his fingers, Maddow opened his eyes, John offered him a brandy, and everyone watched as he drank it. Then they waited in silence. "Well," John said impatiently, "how does it taste?"

"Fair," Maddow said.

John stopped talking about hypnosis and they buckled down to work on the script. Each would write a different scene and then give it to the other to work on. "My versions were usually too long and he would cut them," Maddow said. In this movie John came up with what would become his favorite line of dialogue, when Louis Calhern as the corrupt lawyer, who attempts to outswindle the crooks he is backing, expresses to his wife the theme and tone of the film by saying, "Crime is only a left-handed form of human endeavor."

When it came time to begin casting *The Asphalt Jungle*, Huston decided he wanted fresh, fantastic faces that hadn't been seen before. "So the first one he cast was Marc Lawrence, as Cobby, a small-time crook," said Albert Band, Huston's production assistant, with a laugh. "Marc was probably the most famous criminal face in the movies at that time. So that was kind of a shock. But after that he decided to test people for the main roles."

One day Huston told Band he had a great idea for the lead, Doc Riedenschneider, the master criminal who is looking to organize a small band of hoods to crack open a safe full of jewels. "Who?" Band asked. Ludwig Bemelmans, Huston said. "We'll bring him out from New York and test him." Band thought that, physically, Bemelmans, a writer and artist, was perfect: short, bald, with expensive taste and big cigars. For Emmerich, the attorney, Huston suggested a "tall, seedy" writer friend of his, Tom Reed. Both men came for their test, which Band described as "the worst crap you've ever seen in your life. Bemelmans was shaking he was so nervous. It was just a disaster."

While Huston was testing his nonacting friends, Arthur Hornblow was testing real actors. After John ran the results of Reed and Bemelmans, no one said a word. Then Hornblow instructed the projectionist to put on his reel. It was of John's old friend, Sam Jaffe, with his hair standing straight up, playing a mad scientist. "Wouldn't Sam be great for Doc?" Hornblow asked. "Oh, Sam can do anything," said a delighted Huston. The studio also suggested Louis Calhern for the corrupt attorney. But it was John who cast Sterling Hayden as Dix Handley, the hood with a dream.

Hayden hadn't worked in a long time. Paramount had fired him, he was seeing an analyst because his marriage wasn't working, he froze before the camera and didn't know why. "Shit!" he complained in his autobiography, *Wanderer*. "I went through the war. I jumped out of bombers. I played kick-the-can with E-boats . . . Yet whenever I get a close-up in a nice warm studio I curl up and die. Why?"

Huston couldn't give him an answer, but he could make him relax and feel wanted when Hayden went to see him on the MGM lot. "The moment John sees you," Hayden observed, "he swings to his feet and cleaves the room with his eyes on you alone." Hayden reflected on how seldom one found a face like Huston's in an office. "It's one that belongs on the road, in a boxcar doorway, in a mine, or in a Left Bank garret."

Huston admitted that the studio wanted a star but that he was holding out for Hayden. He then described how he saw the character. "Dix is a loner who hails from a Southern farm who can't fit into the groove. . . . So he does the only thing a man with his limitations can do: He becomes a hood." It was enough for Hayden to understand the character, and when he tested the following day he overcame his psychological problem and got the part.

Huston also cast Marilyn Monroe as Louis Calhern's dumb blonde girlfriend, Angela. W. R. Burnett had described her as having "flaming red hair," "slenderly but voluptuously made; and there was something about her walk—something lazy, careless and insolently assured—that was impossible to ignore." To Emmerich, she was "a doll—no doubt about it . . . but on close acquaintance, a lazy, ignorant, mercenary trollop."

Johnny Hyde, her agent, brought the twenty-three-year-old Monroe to the Thalberg Building to read for Huston. Hyde was in love with her and determined to make her a star. Hyde "was the first kind man I ever met in my whole life," Monroe told Garson Kanin, complaining that she had been "knocking around, and I mean knocking around, for about six years" before *The Asphalt Jungle* came along. She was on the verge of giving up her ambitions of being an actress to settle for being a negative cutter like her mother had been when "Johnny Hyde happened."

Hyde had come to see Huston first, asking John to read her "as a courtesy," Albert Band remembered. When Monroe walked in, she was shy and nervous. Huston gave her a scene to read and told her to go into the back room to rehearse it with Band. A half hour later she returned and began. "John started to doodle," Band said, "and when he doodled it was the kiss of death." Monroe knew she had not done the scene well, even though Huston had smiled and said it was just fine.

"That was terrible, Mr. Huston," she said. "Let me do it again." It was the first time an actress had done that to Huston and he said, "Well, sure, honey, sure."

Her second attempt was as bad as her first, thought Band, but this time Huston wasn't doodling, he was looking at her, impressed with her nerve. When she finished he said, "Well, honey, that was terrific, thank you darling, thank you. I'll let you know."

"Arthur Hornblow went bananas," Band said. "He could see that John was interested in the girl who couldn't act."

"She's got a lot of spunk," Huston said, drawing the blind and looking out the ground-floor window. When Monroe left the building he noticed the wiggle in her walk and said, "Look at the ass on that little girl." It was Angela's walk all right, just as Burnett had described it, "careless and insolently assured—impossible to ignore."

"That's how she got the part," Band said. "And she was exactly that way as a person, coy and manipulative, but not cerebral."

Huston had no idea when he cast her that she was going to become "America's sex queen." "You felt that she was vulnerable and might get hurt—and she damn well did. She moved women as much as she did men, it wasn't just a sex thing, that was no more than half of her attraction."

Ben Maddow was impressed with the cast. The New York actors created a "friendly rivalry" amongst themselves that "raised the level of their performances to where it was like a Broadway play. There was no star, nobody prominent in it."

Huston was in his element making The Asphalt Jungle, a dark, at times claustrophobic film with not a ray of sunshine filtering through. He was glad to have been relieved of Quo Vadis, enjoying his relationship with Ricki, and still friendly with his wife. Albert Band remembered having to pick John up at Evelyn's apartment. He was nursing a hangover "like you never saw before. He turned to me and said, 'What scene are we shooting today, kid?' I'll never forget it. We got on that set and he composed a shot in which ten elements were working all at the same time. Took half a day to do it, but it was fantastic. He knew exactly how to shoot a picture. His shots were all painted on the spot. And he had a genius for doing shots that were difficult to fuck up. He had a great eye and he never lost his sense of composition."

The studio had hoped that John would make the picture in thirty days but allowed him a ten-day leeway. It took forty-nine days, "primarily," said Band, "because he was pulling a lot of jokes on everybody and losing a lot of time. And some of them were very cruel. He enjoyed himself a lot seeing how far he could push people."

Band should know—he was the victim of one of Huston's crueler practical jokes, one that Huston still found amusing in the retelling. "I sent Albert out to look for locations in downtown Los Angeles," he said. "Then these detectives, who were friends of mine, picked him up and threw him in the can. For vagrancy. Suspicious behavior. He was in a cell with a colored man and they heard them talking. Albert told him what had happened and the colored man commiserated and offered to be his legal counsel.

"When Albert was finally restored to freedom a few days later and brought back to the set, he said, 'You have no idea what happened.' And I listened to this whole thing. He told me every bit of the story, except his conversation with the colored man. . . . And then I told *him* that.

"He was utterly astounded!"

Huston was satisfied with the film when it was completed. "I thought it was a hell of a picture," he said. "With beautiful perform- ances. It was easy to make because the people were so good. Every- thing was fine-tuned." Most people who saw the film agreed, some considering it the finest film Huston ever made. Louis B. Mayer, however, wasn't one of them. He called it "full of nasty, ugly people doing nasty, ugly things. I won't walk across the room to see a thing like that." But Mayer called John and told him it was marvelous, simply marvelous.

W. R. Burnett thought it was "without a doubt one of the best films of its genre," although he lamented that MGM "had no experience in marketing such a picture, and they bungled it. . . . It should have been a blockbuster."

Marilyn Monroe's career was launched with the picture and she called Huston the first genius she'd ever met. He was interested in her acting, she said. "He not only watched it, he was part of it. And even though my part was a minor one, I felt as if I were the most important performer in the picture—when I was before the camera. This was because everything I did was important to the director."

"In a part practically without lines, she had nevertheless made a definite impact," Arthur Miller observed. "She had seemed more a prop than an actress, a nearly mute satirical comment on Calhern's spurious propriety and official power, the quintessential dumb blonde on the arm of the worldly and corrupt representative of society."

The movie was touted as a classic *film noir*, with its elements of alienation and despair. Huston was faithful to Burnett's novel. "The story of the good doctor, who was the brains of the gang, unable to tear himself away from the sight of this little girl's wiggling ass and thereby causing his downfall, had a lovely classic shape to it," he felt. He was praised for giving each character a human dimension and for, once again, initiating a genre, this time the caper film.

In his personal life John had pulled off a caper of another order. Unable to impregnate a woman since Lesley more than a decade before, he was to discover that there was still life in his sluggish, stubborn sperm. Ricki had gotten pregnant. "Are you sure it's yours, John?" Evelyn asked him when he told her. "It doesn't matter," John answered, making Evelyn realize that she hadn't understood him for the last three years.

"A light bulb went off in my head," she said. "He wanted progeny any way he could get them. That was why he had brought back Pablo."

Paulette Goddard found it amusing and told Evelyn that the shots she had given John got him ready for Ricki. But Evelyn wasn't laughing. At another party, with Ricki and Evelyn both there, John found himself pouring on the charm to some blonde who had sat on his lap. Evelyn marched over, lifted her by her long blonde hair and said, "I'm his wife, that's his mistress, and you're one too many!" John smiled through it all.

Eventually Walter Winchell got wind of the situation and announced the official split between John and Evelyn on his Sunday night radio broadcast. The next day John called Evelyn and asked if it was true.

Walter Huston was also concerned and went to see Evelyn to find out what had gone wrong. The good outweighed the bad, she said, taking part of the blame for not knowing how to live with a man

Ricki, meanwhile, was living with John in Malibu. In August, while John was still working on The Asphalt Jungle, Ricki's younger brother Philip, eighteen, had come from New York to see her. "It was something that I had never run into before," Philip said, "that an unmarried woman would be living with a married man." That the unmarried woman was also pregnant and happened to be his sister made it all the more difficult for him to accept. Still, he found her life with John exciting. He met Marilyn Monroe and thought she was "a fantastic girl," and dreamed of going out with her. And he took two trips with John and Ricki. They drove in a Cadillac limousine to Walter's ranch in Porterville and then on through Yosemite, Philip wide-eyed at John's driving at seventy-five miles an hour most of the time. Then they flew to the California/Oregon border to hunt deer and visit a ranch that was for sale. Driving fast, flying, hunting, fishing, racing horses, owning acres of land where deer and mountain lions roamed, making movies— John's life seemed like something out of an adventure book, Philip thought, so completely different from the life he and his sister had known growing up in New York.

Ricki was born on May 9, 1929, Philip two and a half years later. In March 1932, five months after Philip's birth, their mother, Angelica, died of pneumonia. She was in her early thirties and had been a professional singer. Her death had a traumatic effect on the family. Tony Soma was devastated, believing he had lost the perfect wife, and partially blamed his infant son, Philip, for her death.

Although Tony would remarry two years later, he could never forget his first wife and lived into his eighties with her ashes on the mantel-piece. He also could not forgive his wife's sister Charlotte, who wanted to raise Angelica's children.

Tony Soma was in the speakeasy business, operating a successful restaurant on W. 52nd Street in Manhattan and later another on E. 55th Street. He spoke four languages and had been a waiter, a busboy, and a fabric salesman in Europe before immigrating to the United States with his brother in the early 1920s, when he started his restau-rant, "catering to the greats and near-greats of Broadway at that time," Philip remembered, ticking off names like Robert Benchley, critic Ward Morehouse, Dorothy Parker, Edmund O'Brien, Mario Lanza. Tony's dream was to be an opera singer and he was an early health and yoga fanatic, drinking hot juices for breakfast, doing forty-five minutes of breathing exercises, and standing on his head each day. He insisted that his children also stand on their heads and in the *Life* article they are all seen upside down.

Ricki and Philip were raised by nurses and governesses even after their father met Dorothy at a singing studio and married her in 1934. It wasn't easy for Dorothy—the children never fully accepted her and Tony too often lived with past memories. "My stepmother was under a lot of pressure," said Philip. "She had to put up with the constant argument that Angelica was perfect and she was not, and that damn sure colored her thinking and her feelings toward me and Ricki."

"Ricki accepted me rather cautiously, although she never listened to me," says Dorothy Soma. "Philip never accepted me as his mother. And his father treated him so badly. I fought all of Philip's battles for him. Tony could be a real bastard. I remember once when Philip was about eight and he was five minutes late coming home from the park. His father hit him so hard on the side of the head it knocked him to the floor. And he grew up with that, feeling that there were two sides to everything: Ricki's side and the wrong side."

Philip remembers his father's favorite story, when Ricki came to him crying that Philip had pulled out a lock of her hair. His father was furious and demanded to know why the boy had done such a thing. "Because she hit me in the head with a hammer," Philip answered.

Dorothy and Tony had three other children, but Ricki was always Tony's favorite. "He singled her out," Dorothy said. "He filled her full of such hogwash. He told her that in any given situation, she was to consider herself first." It was Dorothy, though, who enrolled Ricki in ballet classes at the age of seven. "She was such a stiff, ungraceful child," Dorothy remembered, "that I said to myself, she is going to be taught how to bend if it's the last thing I do. It's been said that she went into ballet because she was so graceful. Nothing could be farther from the truth."

In 1937, Ricki was enrolled in the Gardner School on E. 70th Street because it was close to her ballet classes. There she met Ellie Frohnmaier and the two girls became close friends, enacting fantasies in Central Park, swimming at the Hotel Barbizon, and playing tennis at the York Street courts. Ellie remembers that the more demanding Ricki's dance classes became, the more she was absent from school. "She lived with such an intensity to *shine* that about once every two months she was allowed to take off from school and dance class for two or three days of bed rest." When the two girls played together, it was "not run-of-the-mill little girl playtime— she hated all my dolls—we were angels and devils, the poorest peasants in European history, prisoners in dark and terrible places, people tortured by oppressive kings, and always she succeeded in becoming the world's greatest ballerina."

Ricki had an early love of the theater, which seemed "more real than real" to her, and she often participated in school plays. But as she got older, "more and more of her time was diverted to her dance classes and the ambition to become a great dancer." Ellie remembers how Ricki wore out her ballet shoes. "Her toes often bled and the shoes were worn clear through from practice."

As long as Ellie knew Ricki, "there was no thought in her head that she would consider Dorothy her mother." Dorothy went to all of Ricki's ballet classes, but she was critical. "She improved, but she didn't want to apply herself. The old man had given her the idea that because she was so beautiful everything was going to be handed to her on a silver platter."

When she decided to drop out of the public school system at fifteen, she received a letter from New York's Mayor LaGuardia, who said she was underage and couldn't do it. "She wrote a letter to him," Philip said, "and said that ballet was her chosen field and she could do it. She was quite upset. The mayor shouldn't have worried because she was very clever." Philip didn't think his sister would ever have become a prima ballerina because at nearly five foot six she was too tall and at 120 pounds too heavy. "But she was adequate for the chorus and made several treks to Cuba before Batista left, and then to London." Before she entered the Ballet Theatre, Ricki studied with George Balanchine and had danced with the Ballet Russe de Monte Carlo. When she was sixteen she had also begun modeling and had appeared on the cover of *Seventeen.* Then came the *Life* cover, the Selznick offer, and Hollywood.

For Christmas 1948, Ricki returned to New York on a visit and took Philip to the Metropolitan Opera. "She wore a green velvet strapless evening gown and she was glowing," Philip remembered. He felt sad when he walked her to the train station a few days later. She suggested he come out to visit her in Los Angeles the following year. By the time he arrived, she had met John Huston and was carrying his baby. John introduced him to Pablo, who was back from school and staying with Evelyn.

"Pablo was very outgoing, excitable," Philip remembered. "He acted like a big man, John Huston's son, although he wasn't living with John and Ricki in Malibu. In September I moved out of their house and Pablo and I moved to a ranch in the valley where we took care of some horses before he went back to school. Pablo was essentially a peon. He was brought into this great wealth, and he may have been a little like a fish out of water. I got along well with him, but Ricki thought he expected too much of John."

John's split with Evelyn had greatly disturbed Pablo. "He took that pretty hard," Huston said. "As if he'd been our child. He wept. I tried to explain that we just didn't get along. Evelyn was no longer all that sympathetic toward him either."

In the winter of 1949, John took Ricki and Billy Pearson and his wife on a skiing trip near his father's house in Running Springs. Neither of the women skied, nor did the men, although that didn't stop them. "We pulled up to this ski lift in a limousine," Pearson recalled. "We got on the lift and went up the mountain, only we didn't get off where everyone else did, we went up to this thing called The Wall, which was just a sheer ice wall.

"We stood at the edge and John said to me, 'Now what do I do?' I said, 'I thought you knew how to ski!' He said, 'I thought *you* knew how to ski!' There was nobody else up there except a blizzard and from below they watched us with telescopes, two idiots falling, falling, falling. I lost John after the first couple of hundred feet. I came in about an hour ahead of him. John lost all his shit: clothes, poles, hat, gloves. Blood was coming from his ear, he had run into a high tension wire, nearly killed himself. I was laughing when he came in. He didn't say anything, just shook his head and pointed to the car. We drove back to his dad's house where we thawed out and got drunk."

Ricki wasn't very fond of Pearson and perhaps was jealous of his closeness to John. "Ricki said Billy was like a little playboy," Philip Soma related. "It was very unnerving to her. When she and John would be in bed with nothing on, Billy would plop himself down on their bed and start his conversation with John for the day."

While John was entertaining at Running Springs, Walter was in Tucson making *The Furies*, his forty-eighth film, with Barbara Stanwyck. Walter was especially taken with Stanwyck, who had agreed to do the picture only if Walter played her ruthless, cattle baron father. The forty-two-year-old actress who began as a chorus girl with the Ziegfeld Follies and had appeared in such critically acclaimed films as *The Lady Eve*, *Meet John Doe*, and *Double Indemnity*, was a strong admirer of Walter, whom she considered "perfection in every sense of the word"—unselfish, giving, caring. "Our profession is a team effort," Stanwyck believed, "but sad to say, many in the business do not feel that way. Walter did."

Walter was equally full of praise for his co-star. "Barbara has guts and intelligence," he told the *Daily News*. "She gets what she wants. In this instance she wanted to surround herself with the best possible actors because she knows they will make her look even better." To another reporter he confessed that he "never saw anybody like that girl; wants to work all the time."

When asked how often he'd like to continue making pictures, Walter answered, "One picture a year will just about do me from now on." In the summer before he started *The Furies*, Walter and Nan stayed in Running Springs, where he made cabinets, fiddled with photography using a 3-D Stereo-Realist camera, cooked a different meal every day for a month before repeating himself, and kept discreetly in touch with some of the women who contacted him through Paul Kohner's office. "Walter was very careful," Anne Selepegno observed, "but he always had a mistress. Always."

He also always had a job—or at least a lot of offers, most of which he turned down. In September his agent sent him *The Three Wishes of Jamie McRuin*, a play by Charles O'Neal. Paul Kohner found it "rather charming," but Walter passed, just as he had the role of Willy Loman in Arthur Miller's *Death of a Salesman*. According to John Weld, Walter "hated it." But to a reporter Walter said, "When they sent me the play script of *Death of a Salesman*, I figured, 'Not for me! This is gonna be a hit.' When you get into a hit play you're sunk; runs on and on. . . . Personally, I think I'm about through with the stage unless something of great interest comes along. I'm 65. Age offers a lot of good things, and the most satisfying of all are the ones you don't *have* to do."

In December 1949, after completing *The Furies*, Walter was paid $75 to record "September Song" for Paramount. He had previously recorded *Rip Van Winkle*, an album for Decca. He and Nan brought in the New Year in California and made plans to go to New York in January.

With Ricki in her seventh month, John did what he had to do to make the baby legitimately his. On February 10, 1950, he went to La Paz, Mexico, and divorced Evelyn. The next day he married Ricki. "It was at one of those marriage joints that they have in Mexico," John said, "at a justice of the peace."

"I've seen the wedding pictures," Dorothy Soma exclaimed. "That whole wedding party should have been lined up against the wall and shot! The way they looked." Her husband, Tony, though, was delighted. "Because that all worked into his plan. She was gonna become this great actress. The world just opened up for her and he was gonna live his life through her."

Ricki had called them to let them know she was pregnant and her father bragged, "The man was supposed to be impotent—that proves the dominance of the Italian race!" Ricki's brother said that their father remembered John as a drunk and a gambler. But Tony Soma had seen *The Treasure of the Sierra Madre* with Philip and knew that John was smart and made good movies. "It was something my father felt John could do for his daughter," Philip said, "put her into movies. 'That must have been the reason she married him,' he said."

When Doris Lilly read of John's marriage and Ricki's pregnancy she sent him a telegram: "Congratulations on the Immaculate Conception." John wasn't amused. "He called me up and called me a few names and hung up on me," Doris said. "I was always picking on him. I never would allow him to forget me. Never."

Walter had mixed emotions about John's divorce and marriage. He had liked all of his son's wives and many of his girlfriends, but wondered whether, with his disposition, John should marry at all. Walter understood temptation. But with Walter it was purely extracurricular, like playing golf or making a record. If he occasionally wandered, it was never far and never destructive to his relationship with his wife. With Nan he shared his life . . . up to a point.

A week after his son's fourth marriage, Walter was offered the lead in *Old 880*, a movie Darryl Zanuck was going to produce for 20th Century-Fox. It was based on a series of articles that had appeared in *The New Yorker* about a forger known by that moniker because that was the number of his government file. The man forged only one-dollar bills in small quantities and for years the government was unable to find him. Paul Kohner thought it was a "natural" for Walter, "too good a thing not to snap up." It would only take five or six weeks to make, which wouldn't interfere with Walter's summer vacation. "It is one of those things that only comes along once in a great while and I believe you should do it."

Walter read *Old 880*, written by Robert Riskin, and liked it. He received instructions from the studio that the picture would begin shooting on April 10, 1950, and that he was expected to report on April 3 for tests and fittings. But then his friend, composer Kurt Weill, who had written "September Song" for him, died, and so did producer Arthur Hopkins. Walter's thoughts turned to his own mortality. He told Walter Winchell, "Since they died, I haven't been able to sleep." He went to a bar and after a few drinks told the bar's owner, "I ought to have a checkup." The owner recommended a doctor who would be thrilled to examine the great actor and Walter made an appointment. The doctor noted that he might have a few problems and instructed him to watch his diet and stay away from spicy foods.

On Friday, March 31, a woman named Helen Parkhurst brought Walter the record of a half-hour documentary he had narrated on foster children. Miss Parkhurst had interviewed youngsters from the Children's Center in New York at the request of the State Charities Aid–State Placement & Adoption Society. Walter had listened to these interviews and had been very moved, agreeing to do the narration. He was struck by the children's wisdom and told Miss Parkhurst that he might like to make a film with them. He also spoke to her with pride of Pablo, his adopted grandson, and said, "Some day we'll use him."

It had taken him twelve hours to complete the narration, but he was concerned enough to want to get it right. When Miss Parkhurst asked him if he was a perfectionist Walter said he wasn't. "It has always seemed to me that your work gave evidence to that," Helen Parkhurst countered. "Well, there you've got me," Walter said with a twinkle in his eye. "In my work, no one knows how perfect I want that to be." She complimented him on his ability to make words laugh and Walter was surprised at her perception. "Words laugh . . . they do," he told her, "well, I always thought so but no one ever agreed with me before."

On April 4, Walter flew to the West Coast by himself; Nan decided to remain in New York to comfort Lotte Lenya, Kurt Weill's widow. It was a day after Fox expected him and on the fifth he was fitted and tested for *Old 880*. Then he saw Jacqueline de Wit and her mother, who was born on the same day as Walter, April 6. For the last decade they always tried to celebrate together. Jacqueline was appearing in a play in Pasadena and when they talked, Walter told her he had been to see a doctor, who wanted him to stay off spicy foods, which de Wit thought amusing since Walter didn't like spicy foods. But she joked with him, "You're not going to die, are you?" "Oh, no, no," Walter said. Later Jacqueline's mother asked her how Walter was feeling. "He seemed quite restless," she noticed.

On Thursday, his sixty-sixth birthday, Walter had lunch at the Beverly Hills Hotel, where he was staying, with Charles Kern, a musician who was also caretaker of Walter's home in Running Springs; Robert Gordon, a TV producer; Paul Kohner; and Kohner's thirteen-year-old daughter, Susan. Then he talked to Jacqueline and made arrangements to pick her up in his new Jaguar at eight the following morning for a drive to Santa Barbara to visit Walter's sister, Nan.

John had arranged a birthday celebration for Walter at Romanoff's with Jed Harris, Spencer Tracy, Sam Spiegel, Charlie Grayson, Charles Kern, and Benny Burt, an old vaudevillian whom John had cast as a stool pigeon in *The Asphalt Jungle*. But in the early evening Walter felt some sharp, mysterious pains in his back and thought it prudent to skip the party. "You go ahead," he told his son. "Don't worry about me, I'll be fine." John joined the others at the restaurant, reported his father's discomfort, and after they toasted Walter, John excused himself to return to the hotel, where he took a room across from Walter's and called Dr. Loyal Davis in Chicago, who suggested he contact Dr. Verne Mason. Mason came and thought Walter was suffering from a kidney stone. Walter mentioned that he had seen a doctor in New York who had taken some X-rays. They called him at once. "He said something about an aneurysm," John recalled, "but I'd never heard of an aneurysm. The idea was that he just stay in bed that night and go to the hospital the next morning for examinations. So he did. I stayed with him until it was time for him to go to sleep."

By then Charlie Kern had also returned from Romanoff's. He relieved John, who went across the hall to his room. Walter had a terribly hard time trying to sleep. The pains grew sharper and he kept getting up to go to the bathroom as his abdomen filled with blood, which pressed on his bladder. Kern had to help him as the pain increased. Then Walter passed out and Kern ran across the hall to get John. "Your father's unconscious," Kern told him.

John immediately called Dr. Mason and then went to be with his father and sat holding his hand until the doctor arrived. Mason no longer thought it was a kidney stone. Walter was bleeding internally. There was nothing he could do. Walter's breathing became heavy and as John held his hand, he knew that his father was dying. He said no prayers, made no bargains, just sat by Walter's side until his breathing stopped at eight that morning. There were no last words, no good-byes between them. He had never regained consciousness.

"He died peacefully and without struggle," John would say in a statement released to the press that morning. "I have never seen so quiet a death. He died as modestly as he had lived. . . . He was too good a man to get sick. When the time came, he just died."

Walter's picture appeared on the front pages of newspapers throughout the country and his death, which hit Hollywood with "stunning suddenness," was announced in large-type headlines. His credits, wrote *Variety*, "over a 48-year stage, screen and vaude career read like a rollcall of top vehicles in the history of American show business." The *Evening Herald & Express* wrote that "no figure in the movie town was more beloved by his fellow workers," and went on to say, "Whereas his heartwarming roles in his later years were those portraying lovable old rogues, on the stage on Broadway he was famous as a polished leading man." And in another report, Walter was quoted as claiming to have played every role in the repertoire of American stock companies, "except the cake of ice in *Uncle Tom's Cabin*."

Walter's first wife was not mentioned in the majority of obituaries, which erroneously reported Bayonne Whipple as John's mother.

News of his death traveled fast, and over the next few days many who knew him sat down to write notes of condolence to both Nan and John. "What a perfect final exit for him," wrote Lillian Gish. "No long-drawn-out illness and, I hope, no pain. Just the reward for a good life." The governor of California, Earl Warren, wrote, "His great portrayals have added to our culture and perhaps even more important—endeared him to people all over the world." James Agee observed, "He was so much of everything a *man* ought to be and that so damned few are. . . . There can't be many sons as lucky as their fathers. . . ." Writer Irwin Shaw said, "Ever since the first time I saw him on the stage, and long before I met him, I admired him without qualification. He was so simple and honest and real that he seemed to come right across the footlights and join you as a friend. And, with it all, he was an absolute original. There was no one at all like him and he cannot be replaced."

John couldn't help thinking of Walter's death scene in *The Furies*, when he said, "There'll never be another like me." They were his final words on film.

Katharine Hepburn wrote to John, "You have been ever in my mind since Spence called to tell me about Walter—what a waste for him to die at only sixty-six—I always felt that he would just go on forever always making everyone he came in contact with feel better—He had such an enthusiasm for life—and you certainly were a big part of it—He just really seemed to like you tremendously and to be proud of you and he seemed to get a most enormous toot out of your being his—and the wonderful performance in *Sierra Madre*—how wonderful that you could do that together—I hope you know how rare it is for a son to make his father happy—this is usually left to daughters—and that you are getting warmth and joy out of this even now."

But the letters that touched John the most were the ones that remembered Walter as an engineer or when he was first getting started. Harry Woodworth, who was superintendent of the Union Electric Power Company in St. Louis when Walter worked there, wrote to say, "He had many friends among stationery engineers and here in St. Louis we all loved him." Willie Gladstone, "a pal from the old attic days," recalled, "Your father was my first roommate and oldest friend in show biz. . . . He and I lived in a little attic room for weeks in N.Y. in 1904." Joe Shriner wrote, "It has been years since I saw you and that was one day on Broadway, you still going to school, and your dad as proud as hell, walking alongside of you. . . . Wally and I were friends when he was doing a tour on the old Sullivan & Considine circuit . . . you were a little shaver then." And Arthur Kober remembered "when I first saw him on the stage, as the male half of Whipple & Huston, wearing a red fez and singing a song."

It was the laughter John would miss most. No one had ever made him laugh the way his father had. And he would never laugh that way again.

Dr. Loyal Davis, who had flown out the day Walter died and was at the Pierce Brothers Mortuary in Beverly Hills for the autopsy, performed on Sunday, April 9, 1950, by Dr. A. R. Camero, sent John the report "so that you may read it and get a completely accurate description." The external examination described a "robust, muscular, well-preserved white man 66 years of age." The internal examination reported a liver "slightly softer than normal" and kidneys "somewhat firmer than normal." The principal diagnosis was: "massive left retroperitoneal hemorrhage from ruptured arteriosclerotic aneurysm of abdominal aorta."

Davis and Ben Burt accompanied John to the airport, where he met Nan and her companion, Mary Daniels, and took them to the Beverly Hills Hotel. Davis did his best to comfort her, fully aware of what she had been through in the last three years. But what got to her the most was when John introduced her to Pablo and asked the boy to recite Othello's last passage. Pablo didn't know who Nan was. "I met her under very strange circumstances," he remembered. "She wore a black veil, very handsome. All John said was 'Meet Nan,' and then asked me to recite what I knew of *Othello*. I got up there and I recited."

> *Soft you; a word or two before you go.*
> *I have done the state some service, and they know't;*
> *No more of that. I pray you, in your letters,*
> *When you shall these unlucky deeds relate,*
> *Speak of me as I am; nothing extenuate,*
> *Nor set down aught in malice: then must you speak*
> *Of one that lov'd not wisely, but too well . . .*

When Pablo finished everyone applauded and Nan embraced him. "Tears were coming down her face." Then John told him that Nan had played Desdemona on Broadway. "I couldn't find a place to crawl," Pablo said.

But when Nan remembered *Othello* she thought not of the Moor's last words, but of his wretchedness after realizing how he had wronged his wife. "Whip me, ye devils,/ From the possession of this heavenly sight!" he cried. "Blow me about in winds! roast me in sulphur!/ Wash me in steepd-won gulfs of liquid fire!/ O Desdemon! dead, Desdemon! dead! O!"

On Tuesday, April 11, at 11:45 A.M., a memorial service was held for Walter at the Academy Theatre on Melrose Avenue, the same theater where Walter and John had received their Oscars the year before. The lobby was filled with flowers and sprays sent by dozens of people and organizations. Six hundred people attended the memorial, where they saw a bust of the actor done by Max Adel on the stage, along with Western brush and acorns that had been gathered from Walter's ranch. An organ played two of his favorite songs, "September Song" and "When You Walk in the Room." Among the honorary ushers were Humphrey Bogart, Edward G. Robinson, Brian Aherne, Walter Brennan, Michael Curtiz, Hal Wallis, Jack Smith, Lewis Milestone, John Garfield, Paul Kohner, Sam Spiegel, Charles Kern, Anthony Mann, Jack Fife, Henry Blanke, and Spencer Tracy. John was there with Ricki, Pablo, Nan, and Walter's sister Nan. Evelyn Keyes had received permission from Joe Losey, the director of her current picture, *The Prowler*, to take the day off so she, too, could attend. Lupita Kohner was also there, deeply grieved.

The Academy president, Charles Brackett, spoke first. "Walter Huston died last Friday," he said, "and if you could have listened as the news went out over the wires and the airwaves, you would have heard America catch a long and painful breath at the loss of a beloved friend."

Then Spencer Tracy delivered the tribute, written by two Writers Guild members who had helped organize the service. "Professionally he's easy to rate," Tracy said. "He was the best. . . . Two Americans have won the Nobel Prize for literature. It's no accident that when you mention Sinclair Lewis or Eugene O'Neill you think of Walter Huston. He helped them tell their stories better than anyone else. He gave more color to their lines, he gave more drive to their action. He turned guts into a good word. He filled in with forty-five years of the best playing you'll ever see. It was the works—singing, dancing, Shakespeare. Call your shot. Huston could do it.

"For all the days we knew him, Walter Huston had a gentle mind and he had the only thing that makes such a virtue endurable. He had the strength to quietly oppose the things that were wrong. He had a unique copyright on kindness. There was a gentleness in Walter Huston. Certainly he gave to this craft some splendor it did not have before."

Tracy spoke of how Walter was a lucky man, adding, "He had one other piece of good luck. There is almost a pathological desire in most big men to see their sons held in some kind of good estimate . . . Walter Huston was lucky in this, too. One night, a year ago, he stood thirty feet from here and watched this theater rock with applause. And it was the best applause of all, because it was for the Hustons."

Tracy then asked the audience and the entire motion picture industry to pause for two minutes of silence, after which he concluded the service by reading the Ninety-first Psalm. "There was a moment about halfway through," Lauren Bacall remembered, "when a deep, half-muffled sob emanated from John. A chilling sound. I thought of him differently from then on."

At Pierce Brothers Mortuary, Walter's body was cremated and his ashes put in a Mesopotamian jar. More than twenty years later John discovered his father's ashes on a shelf in a downtown funeral parlor. He brought the ashes to Walter's ranch in Porterville and gave them a proper burial. But that would not be his final resting place. After Nan died in 1973, John returned to the ranch to accompany Walter's ashes to Fresno, where they would be buried in the Sunderland family plot next to Nan.

On April 16, nine days after Walter's death, Ricki went into labor. Her brother Philip was with her in the apartment she and John had taken on Alta Loma, just below the Sunset Strip. Philip drove her to the hospital at a cautious fifteen miles an hour and Ricki told him, "I'm not an egg, I won't break." John was with Albert Band working on preparations for his next film, *The Red Badge of Courage*, but made it to the hospital in time for the birth of his son, whom they named Walter Anthony after both grandparents. The next day, Ricki called John and asked if he wanted the boy circumcised. John said no, "for aesthetic reasons."

He was forty-three years old. His mother was dead; Gram was gone; his father . . . He had lost his first child at birth, had three failed marriages, and wasn't sure if he loved his latest wife. But she had given him a son, his name had been passed to another generation. The climate of the country was changing. Joe McCarthy and the House Un-American Activities Committee were beginning to push into a higher gear. The all-powerful studios no longer possessed their stranglehold on the creative community. His own company was proof that pictures could get financed and made independently.

"You couldn't really make pictures here," Evelyn Keyes observed. "They were making light, fluffy pictures, no hint of anything political. It was as though everyone was scared. All the good guys had left. They just weren't in town anymore." Huston had one more picture to make, one last attempt to test the Hollywood waters, and when that turned into a political battle within the studio he knew that he, too, would be leaving, heading across the Atlantic to begin a new chapter of his already speckled life. As his former wife remarked, "The world was opening up to the John Hustons."

PART SIX

15

RED BADGE AND
THE QUEEN

JOHN WAS NEVER ONE TO SHOW EMOTION, AND AFTER Walter's death he kept busy with his new family and preparations for his next picture. Yet there were moments when melancholy and sadness overcame him and he would go to see Evelyn Keyes for comfort.

"He came to see me a lot then," she recalled. "Always to talk about Walter. He'd sit and cry once in a while. In a way, it's like the end of your own life."

Letters from all over the country continued to remind John of Walter's passing. Most were sincere expressions of condolence, but some were simply inane. A lawyer wrote saying that he looked like Walter and would gladly play minor roles in John's movies. The director of the 3rd Street Gallery in Los Angeles wrote to ask about Walter's abstract and contemporary art collection—she wanted to show it at the gallery and was willing to take it if John wanted to dispose of it.

But most curious of all was Spencer Tracy, who was insulted that John hadn't thanked him for delivering the eulogy. "I don't think you write a letter thanking somebody for a thing like that," John said. "It makes Spencer a complete fool. When I was told that he was disappointed that he hadn't received a letter from me, I thought, My

God, are actors that bad? They expect a round of applause to read a eulogy?"

Walter left the bulk of his estate to Nan. His sister in Santa Barbara was left a $20,000 trust fund, and John received a $30,000 trust fund and Walter's watch.

Two weeks after Walter's death Richard Watts, Jr., wrote a column, "Notes on the Late Walter Huston," for the *New York Post* which ignored the fact that Walter had been born in Canada and claimed him as "a very American figure. . . . There was something especially engaging about his rugged masculinity, something that seemed to symbolize the sort of virile pioneer virtues that we like to think of . . . as peculiarly national. Americans are the most gregarious and yet the most lonely of men, and in that, too, he seemed a kind of symbol." Watts singled out Walter's roles in *Dodsworth* and *Desire Under the Elms*, and then attempted to make a case that Walter wasn't really a character actor but a star who always played himself "whatever the part may be." Watts was dead wrong in his assessment: Walter may have been a star, but he was most definitely a character actor who rarely played himself.

A more fitting tribute came from Albert Maltz, one of the Hollywood Ten. "Last year," he wrote John, "when I learned that Walter Huston wanted to play a character that I had written I felt that I was about to be given one of those rare gifts that few writers enjoy—a visual creation of a character in which the quality of the actor would make the author's work classically unforgettable, not so much because of the character as written but by the creative force of the actor who took command of it. And so in my own way I felt a personal loss that will never be made up because there will never be an artist of your father's quality." That same April the U.S. Supreme Court refused to review the contempt of Congress citations issued by HUAC against the Hollywood Ten, and they were all sentenced to a year in prison.

The infringement of personal freedoms and the defiant stand taken by the accused writers and directors made John feel that his adaptation of Stephen Crane's *The Red Badge of Courage* was all the more timely. The issue of courage under fire had concerned him since the war. In Crane's story the hero is a Civil War soldier who turns and runs when faced with the possibility of dying in battle and then must come to grips with his fears.

The idea of making a film of the novel was Gottfried Reinhardt's. Louis B. Mayer opposed it, but Dore Schary, vice-president in charge of production, talked him into giving his okay. But then Mayer had second thoughts and met with Huston and Reinhardt, convincing them to forget about making the picture. Schary, who loved the book, told them they were "cowards" and that he intended to make the picture with or without them. The battle lines were drawn as Schary dictated a memo to his boss.

"I cannot guarantee that *The Red Badge of Courage* will be a highly successful picture," he wrote Mayer. "I can only tell you that . . . I believe it has a chance of becoming a highly important motion picture that will bring honor to the studio, plus every reasonable chance of ultimately making money . . . it is possible that it will be a classic. . . . In the hands of as brilliant a talent as Huston's, all these things are possible."

The next day Schary received a note from Huston that said, "I felt like a complete shit yesterday. . . . L.B. had Gottfried and me in to see him today and as a result of your letter, which he allowed me to read, he has withdrawn all pressures against the making of the film. . . . The honesty and courage of your letter hit him right where it should. . . . And I tell you again, honey, I'm going to break my ass."

During that second meeting with Mayer, John realized there was a power struggle going on between Mayer and Schary that brought in Nicholas Schenck, the president of Loew's, Inc., who had final say at MGM. "I didn't want to be the cause of broken careers," Huston said. "So I said to L.B., 'If you don't want this picture made, I'll just pull out.' And he said, 'Huston, do you yourself want to make this picture?' I said yes. 'Then fight for it.' " So Huston waited until final word came down from Schenck, who sided with Schary. Just as Mayer had once toppled Irving Thalberg, now it was Mayer who was out.

Both Huston and Reinhardt wanted Norman Mailer to write the script, but when he wasn't available Dore Schary told John he should do it himself. "That was the first mistake," Gottfried Reinhardt reflected. "Because he didn't write it. We finally shot, more or less, the book."

Albert Band, Huston's production assistant, claims that *he* wrote the script. "John had written his version and I'd written my version," Band says. "All I did was follow the book. When John read mine he was so in love with it that he took his version and literally threw it in the wastepaper basket in my house." Huston had no recollection of throwing away his script but acknowledged that Band did work on it.

Dore Schary had a problem with the central theme of *Red Badge*. He couldn't see the hero of the movie running away from battle. "Dore minimized the plot," Reinhardt said. "I just couldn't stomach the man. He was weak. Whatever the others at MGM were, they were strong.

Mayer was a dreadful demon, but he was strong." Production manager J. J. Cohn agreed with Reinhardt, adding that "Mayer had a much, much bigger mind than Schary."

Mayer, Schary, Cohn, and Reinhardt agreed that the casting of The Young Soldier was the key to the film and all wanted an experienced, commercially accepted actor. But Huston wasn't interested in professional actors. He had something else in mind. He thought Audie Murphy, the most decorated soldier in World War II, would make a perfect youth who had to come face-to-face with his own cowardice.

Gottfried Reinhardt was opposed to casting Murphy, whom he thought was "empty," and made it an issue with Huston. "We even looked for arbitration between us," he said. "John chose as his arbiter Willy Wyler and I chose [director turned producer] Sidney Franklin. Willy, while not agreeing with John, said to me, 'If you want to make a picture with John, do it his way.' Which was a mistake. I knew from the first rushes it was not going to work."

As he had in *The Asphalt Jungle*, John looked to nonactor friends to complete his cast. For The Tall Soldier he chose John Dierkes, whom he had met in London during the war. For The Tattered Soldier he was struck by a nervous inexperienced actor named Royal Dano, who had come for an interview while John was in New York.

"I was twenty-seven and pounding the streets when I heard there was going to be interviews at the MGM offices," Dano recalled. "I had never been in any big, executive rooms before and it was damned impressive. So I was nervous and fumbled around a bit when they asked me to read. Then this voice came from the corner and said, 'That's a hell of a thing to ask somebody to do at this time of the morning. Take it easy, kid.' I had seen them all as the enemy, but this was a warm, reassuring voice. It was Huston of course. So I did this little scene and he liked it."

John called *Stars and Stripes* cartoonist Bill Mauldin and said, "I'm going to prove I can make a movie without actors," and asked if he wanted to be The Loud Soldier. "I'm typecasting it," he joked.

Huston had hoped to shoot the film in Virginia, but when that proved to be too costly he settled for his own backyard. Literally. The film was mostly shot at the Calabasas property he and Evelyn had owned.

A two-week rehearsal schedule was set for the beginning of August and actual shooting for August 25, 1950. That month Walter Huston's last picture, *The Furies*, was released and Walter was singled out for a bravura performance. Kay Proctor in the *Los Angeles Examiner* described how the audience broke out in cheers: "It happened, long and loud, not once but several times. . . . The cheers were for the performance of one man, no mistake, and that man was the late Walter Huston. . . . How fitting and fine that his farewell role was such a lusty, flamboyant one."

James Agee's *Life* magazine profile on John also appeared, entitled "Undirectable Director." Helped by the astute background analysis of Huston's work by Jules Buck's wife, Joyce, it was the first major article to turn John's diverse life into popular myth. "There is nobody under fifty at work in movies, here or abroad, who can excel Huston in talent, inventiveness, intransigence, achievement or promise," wrote Agee. "Huston has done more to extend, invigorate and purify the essential idiom of American movies . . . than anyone since the prime of D. W. Griffith."

In describing Huston's appearance Agee observed that "He roughly suggests a jerked-venison version of his father, or a highly intelligent cowboy. . . . The forehead is monkeyishly puckered, the ears look as clipped as a show dog's; the eyes, too, are curiously animal, an opaque red-brown. The nose was broken in the prize ring. The mouth is large, mobile and gap-toothed. The voice which comes out of this leatheriness is surprisingly rich, gentle and cultivated. The vocabulary ranges with the careless ease of a mountain goat between words of eight syllables and of four letters."

Agee wasn't the only one writing about Huston at the time. A *New Yorker* writer named Lillian Ross had asked for and received permission to write about the making of *The Red Badge of Courage*. Initially it was going to focus on Huston, but once Ross talked to all the principals and attended various meetings she realized she was on to something bigger than a magazine profile and extended it into a book called *Picture*, which was published in four installments in *The New Yorker*.

Huston was fond of Ross, respected her as a reporter, and liked her as a friend. "She cut any number of 'famous' people down to size—including me," he noted.

"If anybody was telling a story," Bill Mauldin said, "we quickly learned to shut up when Lillian came around." Mauldin learned his lesson when he told a *Time* reporter that "she was a royal pain in the ass," which was quoted back to her. "And she was," Mauldin insists. "I didn't like her at all. She never misquoted anybody, but she also could kill you with her accuracy. I got pissed off at her for treating Reinhardt so shabbily in that book."

Albert Band thought Gottfried "came out the best," but also thought that Ross's account was "rather vicious. People do the things that she wrote about, but they didn't say them as she wrote them. I thought it was kind of shoddy. But Gottfried and John came out well; it's the other people around who came out like shit. Even Schary had her standing behind him to see how he ran the studio for one day—fuckin' idiot!"

Gottfried Reinhardt said that Ross "had this talent—people made complete jackasses of themselves, they pranced for her." He felt that she was "infatuated with John" and that Huston "didn't give a damn" how she portrayed him "as long as he was colorful."

"As a journalist," Huston would later say, "I've never known anyone to be her equal. Her reporting is uncannily correct."

Like Agee, Ross commented on John's leathery face, reddish-brown eyes, and bashed-in nose. She also noted that "his eyes look watchful, and yet strangely empty of all feeling, in weird contrast to the heartiness of his manner."

When John and Audie Murphy sat together she quoted Murphy saying, " 'Seems as though nothing can get me excited anymore. . . . Before the war I'd get excited and enthused about a lot of things, but not anymore.'

" 'I feel the same way, kid,' said Huston."

But as the picture got under way, Bill Mauldin observed how Murphy always managed to search out excitement. "He was a scrappy little sonofabitch," Mauldin noted. "He would get into bare-knuckle fistfights just for fun with stuntmen. He was five foot four and he'd beat these guys up. They were tangling with a wildcat. That's why Huston really liked him."

Huston knew soldiers who had fought with Murphy and believed him to be an authentic hero. "It was as though he was one of those people who became an angel," he said. "He did things human beings aren't expected to do. Even heroes."

Was it any wonder, then, that Audie Murphy, warrior hero, had a hard time admitting his cowardice to Bill Mauldin, wartime cartoonist, in a scene for *The Red Badge of Courage?* "He couldn't hack it," Mauldin remembered. "After about twenty-seven takes I suggested to Huston, in front of Audie, 'I think Audie is having trouble confessing to a *Stars and Stripes* cartoonist that he ran from battle.' And Audie said, 'You got it, Mauldin.' I said, 'Well, why don't you have me confess that I ran away first?' Huston agreed and there was no trouble at all."

Albert Band would often get exasperated when the script got changed by the actors. "We would spend an entire night on a page," he said. "John would take a bath, I'd follow him into the bathroom and rub his back, trying to think of a line. It drove me crazy. He'd get on the set and rehearse the actors and they'd say the line and then one schmuck would come up and say, 'Mr. Huston, instead of saying that line, could I say . . . ?' 'Sure, kid.' He'd let 'em."

John Dierkes began to take himself seriously as an actor and started asking why he wasn't given a private dressing room like Murphy and Mauldin. Huston had his name put outside one of the chemical portable toilets. Before he entered Dierkes was impressed—a whole trailer to himself!

Gottfried Reinhardt considered both Mauldin and Dierkes "raving dilettantes." Mauldin was "charming and nice, but he wasn't very good. He wasn't an actor."

"He called me a goddamn dilettante?" Mauldin barked. Before he heard Reinhardt's remark, Mauldin thought him "a great guy." He had even felt sorry for him as he watched Huston take him in poker. "Huston was marvelous as a poker player simply because he didn't give a shit. He'd throw his last seven hundred dollars in to make a point. He was a powerful bluffer and he had Reinhardt pretty heavily in debt to him. I felt so sorry for Reinhardt that I got him a copy of Jacoby's book on poker. And in no time at all he had turned the tables and had Huston about fifteen thousand in debt to him. And he calls me a dilettante? That sonofabitch!"

Huston told his cameraman, Harold Rosson, the look he wanted for *Red Badge* was that of Mathew Brady's Civil War photographs. "I tried to reproduce the feel of the photographs with a kind of bleached effect," he said. "I wanted the blond fields, the bright skies and foregrounds, contrasted with the explosive quality of the black-and-white. This was the first time that I had been able to bring into filming my interest in photography and art. The organization of subject and people within the frame is something which I learned to feel from looking at paintings within their frames. I don't believe there's been another film about the Civil War which looked like *The Red Badge of Courage*."

Huston even managed to work in the Civil War sword of Colonel William P. Richardson, his great-grandfather. Douglas Dick, who played The Lieutenant, used it to lead a charge. Bill Mauldin considered him a "classic jerk, a kind of knucklehead," and still laughed at the memory of Dick "sticking the saber through his foot. I shouldn't laugh, but we all thought it was funny. Douglas was jamming it into the ground and *wham!* put it right through his foot! John worked it in some way, in the sequence where the last we see of Dick he's limping ferociously."

The best scene in the movie never made it through the final cut. It was The Tattered Man's death scene. It followed the death of The Tall Man and everyone who saw it felt they had witnessed one of those rare times in an actor's life when he moved men to tears and stunned silence by his ability to capture a moment perfectly.

Mauldin noted that "Huston, with his great talent for turning actors loose, said to Dano, 'We're going to walk you for a quarter mile. Murphy will be by your side. You know you are dying, but try to talk yourself out of it.' That's all the direction Huston gave him. And Dano went into this real shit-kicker act, with the whole thing silhouetted against the sun. I still remember it. He's walking along, stumbling, losing blood, leaning on Murphy from time to time. Murphy doesn't want any part of him; he's had enough of this shit. As a matter of fact, it was Murphy's best performance, too. They gutted the movie when they took Dano out. He really got screwed, it would have made him as an actor."

Dano knew what he had done and knew what he had lost when Dore Schary said that the hero couldn't run away from a dying man and ordered the scene cut. "By removing it they removed the turning point of the story," Dano said. "It was like removing the baby and leaving the afterbirth."

John was as impressed with Dano's acting as Dano was with John's directing, and they paid each other the highest compliments. "He's a great actor," Huston told Lillian Ross. "I don't have to tell him a goddamn thing. The only other actor I've known who had that was Dad."

"Everybody adored John," said Dano. "If he'd've been a broad I would have fucked him!"

It took forty-nine days to shoot *The Red Badge of Courage*, and on Saturdays John often went to the track to watch Billy Pearson ride his horses. One time he got to the track and Pearson was on a horse John wasn't familiar with. As Pearson paraded by he nodded at his friend and Huston took it as a signal. He rushed to bet $5,000 on the horse and when it came in last, he sat in his box, tearing up his stubs. When Billy came by and saw the pile and the look on Huston's face, he asked him why he had bet on such a lousy horse. "Because you gave me the nod," John said. "Hell," Pearson said, "I was only saying hello."

On Sundays, when Pearson didn't ride, they would sometimes go to the bullfights in Tijuana. Once John brought a new girlfriend along who started to throw up when the bull was killed. When she began to cry as well, John told her to go to Caesar's Restaurant and he'd meet her there. "Of course we headed right off in the opposite direction," Pearson recalled, "to a place below Rosarita Beach." They walked into a small cantina where six Mexican soldiers sat. Then a drunk general wearing "a solid mass of medals" on his chest entered, took out his .45, and placed it on a table. He looked at Huston and Pearson and started saying nasty things in Spanish. "John was wonderful in those kinds of spots," Pearson said. "Because he always did the wrong thing. If a guy with a lot of medals and a big gun started talking to you bad in a language you didn't understand, John was going to talk to him bad."

"Look at that big fat pig," Huston said, staring at the general. "That's the reason there was a revolution, to kill those shit faces."

The other soldiers watched as the confrontation between the tall drunken gringo and the shit-faced general mounted. Abruptly, the general picked up his gun, cocked it, and pointed it at Huston's chest. John stuck his little finger into the gun barrel and said, "Go fuck yourself." The general pulled back and John stretched forward. His finger was stuck in the barrel!

"John had the Mexican general's arms through his legs," Pearson said, "and the gun barrel was up his ass." The bartender told them to go to the kitchen to get some soap and Pearson fled to the Rosarita Beach Hotel, not believing he survived the night. "I'm not asleep an hour when in came the general and Huston, asshole buddies, arm in arm, singing old songs. John was even wearing one of his medals!"

Bill Mauldin didn't think very much of John's friendship with Pearson. "John was not the world's greatest judge of human character," he said. "Pearson always struck me as essentially a hanger-on type. And I had the same opinion of Pearson that I had of Pablo." Pablo, who was then enrolled in high school in Santa Monica, was frequently at the ranch location and once even doubled for Tim Durant (The General) on horseback. Mauldin thought he was "a smartass teenager. A not very bright Mexican boy. I didn't like him."

Ricki also came to visit, developing a friendship with Lillian Ross and Bill Mauldin's wife, Natalie. "Natalie was a good-looking woman in her twenties," said Mauldin. "Ricki was like twenty-one, a raving beauty, and Lillian couldn't have been much over thirty, kind of drab-looking. At some point Lillian must have bugged John to the point that he decided to chivalry her a little bit. He got one of the crew, a prop man, whom he knew well, to romance her. Lillian was not the kind of girl who got much romance. The next thing we knew they were going around holding hands. Natalie was outraged. She confronted Huston, saying, 'This is a cruel thing to do.' Huston told her to mind her own business. So Natalie said to me, 'You've got to tell Lillian what Huston is doing to her.' 'You tell her,' I said. Well, Lillian's face just froze up. She instantly realized that it was true. Nothing was ever said about it. Lillian just dropped the guy. It was a nasty thing for Huston to do to her."

Perhaps this incident spurred Ross to use a comment Gottfried Reinhardt made to her about Huston. "John is like a racehorse," Reinhardt said. "You must keep him in a good mood all the time. John is a charmer, you know, but he is really very forlorn. . . . He is out of touch with human emotions."

Mauldin also saw this in the way John behaved with Ricki. "He was pretty gruff with her," Mauldin noticed. "One night we went fishing and she wanted to go along. John told her to get lost. He treated her in some ways more like a gruff father than a husband. I don't think he liked women very much. He tended to be mean to them. He was sort of a man's man."

When Mauldin and Natalie visited Ricki in Malibu, they found her unhappy and "somewhat disillusioned with John because he was so horribly in debt. She showed Natalie a typewritten list of their debts, which added up to hundreds of thousands of dollars. 'Here I am married to a guy making all these films, this famous man, and we've got process servers, we have to run in to hide all the time. When we park the car, we never know if it's going to be missing and somebody's going to repossess it.' She had grown up rather rapidly in that situation and she came down to earth with a thud. She was pissed at John for being irresponsible."

Gottfried Reinhardt, who had known Ricki when she was fifteen and appeared in the corps de ballet of a 1944 Broadway show, *Helen Goes to Troy*, wasn't too fond of her and never felt that "there was a real warmth between them." The producer also thought that John behaved irresponsibly when he refused to look at rushes. "Like John Ford, Huston showed a coolness toward his product."

When Reinhardt felt one particular scene should be reshot, John said to him, "You tell me what's wrong and I'll do it over." But the producer insisted he see for himself, so Huston did and the next day he reshot the scene—*exactly* the way he had shot it before.

By mid-October the picture was in the can ready to be edited. As usual John hadn't used a lot of film shooting different angles. Royal

Dano had even questioned him about it. "Why aren't you coming around the other way to get another shot of this?" he once asked. "I don't want to give them two ways to play the scene," Huston responded. Nonetheless, as Dano remarked, "they screwed him anyway." Albert Band said that he made the first cut of *Red Badge* with the editor, Ben Lewis. Gottfried Reinhardt said, "I cut the entire picture,' blaming Huston for not having the "*zitsflasche*" to sit in the editing room to work on it himself.

In any event, while the movie was being shaped, Huston got involved in a political battle at the Screen Directors Guild. The president of the guild, Joseph Mankiewicz, had opposed a loyalty oath for guild members. Cecil B. DeMille, a member of the board and a strong anti-Communist, favored the oath and maneuvered to oust Mankiewicz. In August he had convened an emergency board meeting to approve the oath while Mankiewicz was in Europe. Soon after, DeMille attempted to recall Mankiewicz as president. Huston joined the Mankiewicz forces and chaired an October 13 strategy meeting at Chasen's; on October 22, 1950, five hundred guild members met at the Beverly Hills Hotel for the showdown between DeMille and Mankiewicz.

Huston disliked DeMille intensely both as a person and as a director. "He was a thoroughly bad director. A dreadful showoff. Terrible. To diseased proportions," he said.

DeMille was the leader of those guild members who, according to Huston, "wanted to discover and segregate, if not execute, the left-minded. It was a very carefully worked out plot." When the motion of whether members should take a loyalty oath was introduced and passed, a second one followed concerning whether it should be by a show of hands or by a secret ballot. Huston was strongly against a show of hands and was the only person to raise his own hand against it. Then Billy Wilder, who was sitting next to him, followed Huston's lead. "No one else did," Huston recalled, adding, "It was certainly the bravest thing Billy Wilder ever did. There were boos from the floor. A real row of anger at us." The reason he had opposed an open vote was because he felt "it was a way of marking out who was against taking the loyalty oath and who was for it. Of course, any real Communist would have lied, so it had no other purpose than to single out these assholes who would say they were against the loyalty oath, whom I was defending."

The meeting began at 7:30 P.M. and lasted seven hours. "That night was the climax," Huston said. "It was part of the blacklist thing and I was very much involved." He delivered an impassioned speech that helped sway the guild members to support Mankiewicz and force DeMille and fourteen other board members to resign.

Deeply involved with the politics of moviemaking and Red-baiting, John paid scant attention to his own family. Ricki had been acting in small theaters and Nan Huston was back in New York, trying to overcome her grief by seeing old friends. But John didn't think much of Ricki as an actress and preferred she concern herself with young Walter Anthony. Nan wrote to Paul Kohner in November asking how the baby was, since she had "had no word from John or Ricki." She told Kohner she was doing "quite well considering. New York City is helpful with its many diversions and our friendships here." Kohner wrote back that the baby was fine and added this news: "There has been a rumor that Ricki is expecting another baby but we haven't heard anything about it from the principals involved." John, his agent added, was "very busy" working on his next picture for Horizon Productions, *The African Queen.*

The rumor was true, Ricki was again pregnant. It was also true that John had put *Red Badge* out of mind and was working with James Agee on adapting C. S. Forester's 1935 novel about two very different people—a hard-drinking, uncouth, riverboat pilot named Charlie Allnutt and Rose, a pious, virginal woman, sister of a missionary—brought together in the Congo during World War I after the death of the missionary and the threat of approaching German soldiers. Together they attempt an uncharted trip down a Congo river, where they eventually and comically fall in love just before being captured by a German gunboat. After Sam Spiegel bought the rights to the book, Huston finally gave James Agee the opportunity he had been hoping for: to collaborate on a script with the director he most admired.

By December a considerable amount of the story had been outlined. Humphrey Bogart had agreed to play Allnutt, Katharine Hepburn the prim and proper Rose. Spiegel had told each that the other had already agreed before either actually had and by so doing landed them both. Agee, who liked to think in literary terms, envisioned the trip they would be taking down the river as symbolizing the act of love. When he told that to Huston in front of Lillian Ross, Huston replied, as Ross took notes, "Oh, Christ, Jim. Tell me something I can understand. This is a screenplay. You've got to demonstrate everything, Jim. People on the screen are gods and goddesses. We know all about them. But we can't touch them. They're not real. They stand for something rather than being something. They're symbols. You can't have symbolism within symbolism, Jim."

In early January Agee and Huston went to Santa Barbara to work on the story without interruptions. John wanted to combine their work with a regimen of tennis and relaxation but discovered that Agee didn't know how to relax. Both men liked to drink, but Agee also stayed up most of the night working, and Huston soon found that writing alternate scenes wasn't working because Agee wrote so much faster than he did.

Agee told a former *Time* colleague that working with Huston was "exciting and fascinating, and so is watching that particular intelligence and instinct work. And so is learning from him—any number of basic things a day, which had only vaguely occurred to me before, about good craftsmanship and taste and imagination." Agee's biographer, Laurence Bergreen, noted that Agee "poured a considerable amount of his own personality into the character of Allnutt and a considerable amount of his mother's into Rose. Like Agee, Allnutt was a hard-drinking loner who sought freedom but usually found oblivion, and like Agee's mother, Rose was a repressed, self-righteous, Bible-thumping woman. . . . Allnutt and Rose were sinner and saint, heroic scalawag and pious biddy. In the movie, if not in life, they made a splendid couple."

On January 15, Huston flew up to San Francisco to look at some pre-Columbian pieces Billy Pearson had told him about, and while he was gone Agee had a heart attack. He was in critical condition when Huston returned. Agee apologized for the trouble he had caused and was feeling guilty because they hadn't found an ending for *The African Queen.* They then talked about other things, like smoking against doctors' orders and whether Agee should divorce his wife to marry a young woman he had fallen in love with. "We arrived at the same ringing affirmation of the minimal, irreducible right of a man," Agee later wrote: "That he has the right, even the obligation, to write and to fuck as much as he can and in the ways he prefers to, even if doing so shortens his life or kills him on the spot."

On February 1, 1951, Gottfried Reinhardt's two-hour-and-fifteen-minute cut of *The Red Badge of Courage* was previewed before a general movie audience. Reinhardt thought "it looked marvelous. I didn't think we pulled it off, but I must say I didn't expect those previews."

"Disastrous," was Schary's one-word summary. "The audience began to file out toward the end of the first hour, the pace of exodus increasing as the second hour wore on." What surprised Reinhardt was that "people laughed at everything." Huston was in the audience and was stunned by the reaction. "The audience hated it," John said. "During the best moment in the picture, where The Tall Soldier dies and then The Tattered Soldier dies, people began to walk out. I never saw such an exodus!" When the preview cards were returned Schary found them painful to read: "slow," "lousy," "stinks," "burn it."

Huston wondered what went wrong. "At the time there was the Korean War," he said, "and maybe that had something to do with it, maybe it was a bit close to the bone, it was not a story of heroism per se." Huston considered that preview "one of life's darker moments." He told Schary, "I'll talk tomorrow . . . I have to go somewhere and get a *drink—get a lot of drinks.*"

But the next day, when Reinhardt showed up at Schary's office to discuss what they might do to save the picture, Huston wasn't there. "He was disgusted with it," Reinhardt said. Huston was aware that there was a time to fight and a time to cut and run. He phoned Dore Schary. "He said he had received a call from London offering him an important assignment. He asked me to take over the film, assuring me that I could fix it. . . . I guessed he had found a usable raft but that we were to go down with the ship."

John's raft, of course, was *The African Queen*. The "important assignment" came from Horizon, his own production company. Sam Spiegel had found a source to cover the pounds sterling they would need to use in the Congo, and Huston certainly didn't want to preside over the agony of reducing what he considered a masterpiece to just another war story. "I thought *The Red Badge* was safe," he told an interviewer, "since I left it with two men who had championed it all along, Gottfried Reinhardt and Dore Schary. But the studio decided the audience hadn't been sufficiently aware that they were watching a masterpiece. They had to be told. So they changed my opening. They had the picture open with a copy of the book, with the title and 'By Stephen Crane,' so that the audience would appreciate that something serious, *important*, was coming up. And they added a narration, too, that I hadn't wanted."

Gottfried Reinhardt never held it against John that he left. "He wouldn't have helped if he had stayed. Dore could only work with ass-kissers and John wasn't one." What Schary and Reinhardt proceeded to do was cut out everything that had gotten a laugh at the preview.

"We made a hodgepodge of it," Reinhardt admitted. Albert Band said that Schary was the one who cut the picture down to sixty-one minutes. "Whole chunks were taken out. Four major battle scenes were reduced to two. The whole concept of the picture changed when it got into Schary's hands."

Years later Huston told Reinhardt that he had never seen the final cut of the movie, but that wasn't true. "I did finally see it," he admitted. "It was very bad. I don't agree with what happened, but I sympathize and understand their doing it. They were trying to save the picture and were doing what they thought was best."

When the film was finally released John noted that "it got beautiful reviews but nobody went to it, not a soul. And then some critic in London had seen the picture at a suburban theater where it was running on a double bill and said this is a masterpiece and why haven't we been allowed to see this great picture? So he had a showing with all the London critics. Metro took an ad out with all the critics signing it and it opened on the West End . . . and nobody came."

The original cut of *The Red Badge of Courage* no longer exists. John made a 16mm version of most of the movie, but it was lost. And Reinhardt told Royal Dano that MGM burned the scenes that had been cut. "To make sure nobody would know what a horrible mistake they made," Dano said. "It's like going in to take out the wrong kidney."

Leaving his pregnant wife and year-old son behind, John could hardly have known that his departure to make *The African Queen* was the beginning of a new life. The Belgian Congo was the first of ten countries he would traverse to make his next eight films, before returning to the States ten years later for *The Misfits*.

"At the time there were the Communist scares in Hollywood," English producer Sir John Woolf recalled. "A lot of stars were starting to rebel against the studio system and the end result was that a number of them were only too willing to come over to England to make pictures; directors, too." Woolf and his brother, James, founded Romulus Films in 1949. "My brother and I had the idea to try to get the British film industry out of its doldrums," Woolf said. "I had the idea of making Anglo-American films to bring over important stars and directors." James Woolf was in California when he met Sam Spiegel and a deal was made.

"Romulus Films would provide the financing in England and Africa, the total production cost. And Spiegel's Horizon Pictures would provide the money to pay for Huston, Bogart, Hepburn, and Spiegel. It came to about a quarter of a million pounds for each side."

The actual breakdown for the talent was that Huston would receive $87,000 to direct; Bogart, a deferred payment of $125,000 and a thirty percent interest in the film's profits; and Hepburn $65,000 in cash, a like amount in deferred payments, and ten percent of the profits. It cost Spiegel $50,000 to buy the story from Warner Bros., which had hoped to make the film in 1938 with Bette Davis and David Niven until Davis backed out. And six percent interest in the profits was also promised John Collier, who wrote a draft of the screenplay before Agee was brought in.

When Katharine Hepburn arrived in London she learned that there was still no final script for her to read, which, along with her suspicions that Spiegel really didn't have the money to make the picture, put her into a "total frenzy." The first thing she did was to call her father, asking him to put $10,000 in a London bank so that she wouldn't wind up stuck in Africa if everything fell through. Then she met with Spiegel, the Woolf brothers, and Huston, who was the only one she noticed. "Because when Huston is present," she observed, "everyone focuses on him, exactly as when there is a small child in the room." When she later visited John in his room, two days before he left for Africa, he avoided talk of the script, instead showing her his riding boots, "all of them. His pink coat—his britches—his vests—his socks— his silk hat—in fact, he put them on . . . His funny little face and scrawny neck took on a country-squire look." Hepburn wasn't amused. "I was frothing at the mouth with disgust at the whole lackadaisical atmosphere," she said. "And I felt exactly as though I were conducting the last desperate moments of an extremely unsatisfactory love affair with Mr. Huston. Verging on the actively unpleasant."

"The arrangement," Sir John Woolf said, "was that Spiegel would be in Africa and my brother and I would be in London. And all rushes would be sent back to London. We'd let them know how the thing was looking."

Before there were any rushes to look at, before Huston left for East Africa to scout locations, there were money problems between John and Sam. Spiegel was to have taken care of the hotel bill in Santa Barbara where Huston and Agee had worked, but he never did. "Sam did not pay bills," Huston said. "He was so used to sidestepping that anything he didn't have to pay, he avoided. And God, that bothered me! Owing a penny disturbs me deeply. It's like the devil has a piece of my soul if I owe somebody money. And Sam . . . he felt like a fool whenever he paid a bill." In England Spiegel had assured Huston that Ricki would receive a certain amount of money every week, but after a month she hadn't received anything. On the eve of his departure to Africa John threatened his partner, "If she's not paid tomorrow, I don't go."

"John, I haven't got it," Spiegel said. "I'll have it by next week, I swear to you."

Huston's instincts told him to stay until Spiegel came through with the money, since he knew Ricki was hounded with unpaid bills, but the pull of Africa overcame the more responsible position. He had elephants on his mind.

Guy Hamilton, the assistant director, first met Huston at Claridge's Hotel, where his room looked like an armory. "There were people who were selling him crocodile guns and elephant guns," Hamilton recalled. "John wanted to shoot an elephant. That was really what the whole picture was about as far as he was concerned."

Peter Viertel, who accompanied Huston to Africa to work on the ending that John and Agee never finished, wound up chronicling Huston's obsession in a thinly disguised novel he later wrote called White Hunter, Black Heart.

When Huston, Viertel, and Guy Hamilton finally left for Nairobi, John's new guns were promptly confiscated by the authorities because, Hamilton was pleased to note, one wasn't allowed to shoot defenseless animals in Kenya. But then Hamilton didn't see Huston for several days "because he was off in a little light plane and discovered the Belgian Congo where you could shoot defenseless animals, and he also discovered a location for the film. John literally dropped a white handkerchief out of the plane and said, 'I found a location.' The art director and I wandered around the Belgian Congo and actually found this handkerchief."

John had also found another gun. Actually he won it in a poker game from Alex Nill, one of his two pilots. Nill didn't want to give it up because it was his favorite. "Well, you lost it, you know," Huston said, and took the gun.

As his actors traveled from London to Rome to Leopoldville to Stanleyville on the Congo River, Huston worked with Viertel on the script and spent most of his time hunting and dreaming about elephants. An hour before Bogart and Hepburn arrived in Stanleyville, Huston departed for Biondo, the village where they were to begin shooting, on the Ruiki River, which infuriated Hepburn. "It was an utterly piggish thing to do and it makes me mad to think of it even now—goddamn—goddamn. . . ."

When they finally arrived he was waiting for them in a bar in Biondo and Hepburn couldn't hold back. "What about the script?" she demanded, reflecting later on her "old fusspot" behavior. John just smiled broadly and talked about the anticipated joys of shooting an elephant. "You must only remember to stay downwind of them," he told Lauren Bacall, who had accompanied Bogart on location. Bacall was enthralled by Huston's enthusiasm but Bogart laid down the law. "You're not going anywhere with John with a gun," he warned her.

In Biondo John met the film's script girl for the first time; she was a twenty-two-year-old named Angela Allen who had previously worked on the Woolf brothers' *Pandora and the Flying Dutchman*. Sam Spiegel had hired her in London. Before she had a chance to meet the man who would so affect her life, Lauren Bacall told her, "John needs a woman and you're the available one." Allen didn't know what to make of Bacall's remark, but she knew what she had been hired for and that was all she expected to do. When Huston made his inevitable pass at her she cried, and he wisely left her alone. She was too valuable as a script girl to tamper with her innocence.

It was overcast the first day of shooting, and when John was informed that a herd of elephants had rampaged a nearby village, he took his sound man, Kevin McClory, and quietly left Biondo to do what he had wanted to do since arriving in Africa: track and kill his first elephant. "They said there was a big tusker among these elephants," Huston related, "and one of the things I wanted to do was get a very good trophy, nothing less than a hundred kilos. I knew practically everything there was to know about African game through having read a book called *Big Game and Big Game Rifles*. I wanted a photographer along to photograph the game, but none was available so McClory volunteered. He's a very plucky bird who had a wild stammer."

"We got into a pirogue and went down the river," McClory remembered. "We came to a village that was absolutely flattened, as if a hurricane had hit it. John pointed down and said, 'See that? Elephant spoor.' I said, 'Are you sure it's not a m-m-mammoth?' "

They walked in single file, Huston between the two native trackers, McClory in the rear. "How often have you been elephant hunting, John?" McClory asked.

"This is actually my first time," Huston answered. "But don't worry about a thing. Just be careful of the red buffalo. It's very quick, charges without warning, and usually goes after the last man."

"I'm the f-fellow at the back," McClory stammered nervously.

"Yes, that's why you should be careful," John said, observing that from that point on McClory walked backwards.

Viertel left after the filming began but not before Huston had gotten to him. He had subjected the writer to his big-game hunting obsession, had taken him on scary plane rides looking for elephants, and had paid scant attention to the ending of the script Viertel had been brought along to write.

In the beginning John left Katharine Hepburn in varying states of "fury, insecurity and indecision." Bacall noted that Hepburn seemed nervous and talked compulsively. John saw that she was skeptical of him. "Katie was born suspicious," he said, "and she had great reservations regarding me that she was in no pains to conceal. She knew that both Bogart and I were wastrels, but Katie has a weakness for wastrels— Spencer Tracy was also one. So we put it on for her. We pretended to be even bigger wastrels than we were, doing childish things that shocked her, like writing dirty things on her mirror in soap."

Initially Hepburn felt terribly out of place: unsatisfied with the lack of toilet facilities; envious of Bacall's youth, complexion, and good nature; "stuck with two over-male men"; slightly appalled at Huston's "childish worship with the hunting set"; and annoyed with Bogart, who never seemed to know his lines as quickly as she did. She resented her discomfort, seeing how Huston seemed to fit right into the jungle life. But gradually she calmed down; even abandoned her "Queen's Throne," the nickname the natives gave the chemical lavatory that had been placed on a raft for her private use.

What brought her around, and what made her appreciate Huston, was her finally understanding how to play Rose. John discovered he was directing a comedy only after seeing the strange, humorous chemistry between his two stars. It made Hepburn's dour seriousness seem wrong and he had an idea. He went to see Hepburn in her hut and said, "Have you ever seen Mrs. Roosevelt visit the soldiers in the hospitals?" Hepburn nodded and John said, "Did you notice that she always smiled?" Hepburn looked at him for a moment and he continued. "Your face is very thin and your mouth goes down, Katie. When you're serious-looking it looks heavy. Mrs. Roosevelt, who felt she was ugly, always put on her society smile. . . ."

Hepburn didn't have to hear anything more. "That was the goddamnedest best piece of direction I have ever heard," she said.

"He told me exactly how to play the part. I was his from there on in."

She was so impressed, she was willing to forgive him his lack of common sense and irresponsible behavior. "He ain't where he is for no reason," she concluded.

Huston felt closer to Hepburn than to anyone else on the set. "Not in a romantic way; there was no room in her life for anybody but Spence," he said. "But I took more joy working with Katie and getting to know her than I ever did with any other actress."

Lauren Bacall made herself useful by preparing the food, as she had in Mexico during the filming of *The Treasure of the Sierra Madre*. Because she wore shorts and a scarf around her top, the natives called her Mamsahib Mbila Bgua—"Lady with a two-piece." While most of the crew drank bottled water, Huston and Bogart stuck to Jack Daniel's. Bragged Bogie, "Nothing bites me. A solid wall of whiskey keeps insects at bay." Added John, "Anything that bites me soon drops dead, so I'm safe."

Huston would have liked to have taken a bite out of Sam Spiegel's hide when he and his stars learned that no money was going into their London accounts. "The American bank Spiegel had used to raise money hadn't gotten a guarantee of completion," Sir John Woolf revealed, "and they wouldn't accept Spiegel's. The upshot was that I personally guaranteed the completion of the film. I must say with some trepidation."

Woolf's trepidation stemmed from his being warned against the whole project by no less a luminary than Alexander Korda, who had been a friend of Woolf's father. "He called me and said, 'I heard that you are making a film about two old people going up and down a river in Africa. It will be a disaster. I beg you not to do it. Huston's last film was a terrible failure. You'll find him unreliable. The film will be awful.' "

But the Woolf brothers were too far into the project to back down. And John Woolf didn't agree with Korda's assessment of Huston. "He was highly reliable," Woolf said. "And so different from the British directors that we'd worked with. He had enormous charm and efficiency."

One morning Guy Hamilton came running to Huston in a panic to tell him that the *African Queen* had sunk. Huston was having coffee with Bogart and Bacall and he looked at Hamilton and said, "I can't believe my ears, would you say that again?" The natives had been told to watch the boat—and that's exactly what they had done: They watched it sink! Huston ordered Hamilton to get fifty men and raise the

Queen and then took advantage of the delay to spend the rest of the day hunting.

After the boat was raised and repaired the crew began to grumble about the necessity of shooting in Africa. "Some of the more cynical members of the unit claim that parts of the jungle look remarkably like Epping, and that places on the Nile could be mistaken for Maidenhead—if it weren't for the crocodiles that line the banks," reported David Lewin in the *Daily Express*. Huston was aware of the crew's feelings and ordered them to make the set look "more African." So, Guy Hamilton said, "We made flowers out of Kleenex. John was quite interested in this and he'd look through the camera and say, 'Make some more flowers, over there.' So the unit would pop over with their Kleenexes and make marvelous orchids."

Both Hepburn and Bogart defended the decision to make the film in Africa. "It would have been a terrible mistake to do that kind of an adventure story unless you were really there," commented Hepburn. "Otherwise it wouldn't ring all that true." Said Bogie, "You have to fight the jungle all the time, and that gets into your performance. Out here you don't need to have sweat sprayed on your forehead to show it's hot. It's damn hot."

It wasn't the heat that finally got to the actors but the armies of red ants. "I came home from work one day," Hepburn chillingly recalled, "and I was undressing in my room and I felt sort of itches. I looked down and there was a wide column deep with ants coming right up my legs. They were all over me. Up my front and down my back. I was bitten, bitten, bitten." As she ran out screaming she almost ran into Bogart, who was also running out of his hut screaming. "The floor of our bungalow was thick with ants," Bacall remembered. "The natives put the feet of our beds in kerosene so the ants couldn't crawl up them. That's when we knew we had to get out and go to the next location."

Before they left the Congo for Uganda Huston became aware of another troubling situation: When he had first arrived in Biondo, the food was supplied by one Congolese in charge of hunting game for the pot. It turned out that game was scarce, the fellow's rifle was old, and he couldn't shoot very well. When soldiers turned up to arrest the man Huston discovered what had happened. "Villagers had been missing," he said. "And this was why. He was furnishing meat for the pot, but it was mixed with deer and monkey and so on and we who shared in the pot didn't know." As Bacall later said about the food in general in Africa, "It was not advisable to ask what we were eating . . . we didn't want to know." They had been sharing in an ancient Third

World custom not known to be practiced anywhere in Africa today: cannibalism.

No one was sad about leaving the Belgian Congo and the Ruiki River to complete their work in Uganda. After three weeks the company was given a day off in Entebbe, where Bogart was invited by the British who lived there to play a game of cricket on the pitch overlooking Lake Victoria. Bogart didn't know the sport, but he was game, and was cheered for his efforts, even though his team lost by 105 runs.

In Butiaba Huston came within inches of killing Hepburn. It began when she chastised John about his hunting obsession. "It just doesn't go with the rest of your character," she said. "You're not a murderer, and yet you shoot these beautiful animals." "Katie," Huston responded, "you can't really understand unless you come with me and experience it." Humphrey Bogart was horrified, warning her that John couldn't hit "the broad side of a barn." But Hepburn wanted to better understand her director. She also figured, "We'll probably never be here again. I know it's cuckoo, but you can't always be cautious."

At first they hunted antelope and waterbuck, and Huston watched as Hepburn became "a veritable Diana of the hunt. She would wake me before dawn to get in an hour of shooting before we started work. One morning there were elephant signs. We were in a very heavy forest and we worked carefully downwind." Hepburn heard their trumpeting and was told by a tracker that the elephants sensed their presence. They walked in a circle and saw a herd of twenty elephants on a hill. "Then someone shot," Hepburn said, "and they disappeared into a low forest."

"Well, let's go in after them," Huston said.

"You have to be the silliest man that ever was born," Hepburn admonished. "That's very dangerous!" Nonetheless, when Huston ignored her, she followed, not wanting to be left alone in the jungle.

Suddenly they heard a very loud growl. It was the sound of the elephants' stomachs digesting their food. They were a rifle's length away! "We froze, of course," Huston related, "and the elephants didn't know we were there. But then the breeze changed and hell broke loose! There were elephants going by like train engines. You must not run under those circumstances, because that only confuses the elephants, which are trying to get away from you. And if they're confused, they're likely to pick you up and throw you away for good. I turned and looked at Katie, who had my light rifle up to her shoulder. She was going to go down like the heroine she is."

"They came as close to me as you are," Hepburn said, sitting comfortably in her New York town house, recalling one of the great adventures of her life. "Knocking down trees. We were just bloody lucky."

"I breathed very deeply and wiped the sweat off my brow," Huston said. "Katie wasn't shaken by the experience. I was *profoundly* shaken. It was a hell of a note, my submitting my star to that sort of thing."

Then, as they regained their composure and started back, John saw Hepburn fifty yards ahead of him photographing "the biggest forest pig I've ever seen, a huge boar with long tusks, ready to charge." He lifted his rifle slowly, knowing from the books he had read that even with a bullet in the boar's heart, it could still charge forward and probably kill her. "Kate!" he whispered. "Kate! Come back! Stop!" Hepburn noticed the firmness in John's voice and took a few steps back. The boar's family passed in the background and the boar turned away.

"My God, Katie," John said, "you don't know how close you were to it."

"Oh, he knew I wouldn't hurt him," she said.

Before they left the jungle they shot a deer, which Hepburn then tried to bleed by cutting its throat. "But I couldn't," she said, "nobody had a knife really sharp enough. So we dragged the poor deer. We were very hard up for any meat to eat."

Butiaba was the location for burning down the missionary outpost. The facades of huts had been built, which confused the natives who had agreed to appear as villagers in the movie. When none of them showed up, Huston had to trek twelve miles to talk to the local king to find out why. "They are afraid you are going to eat them," the king said through a translator. "Oh, no," Huston promised, wondering if they had heard about the incident in the Congo, "we would not dream of doing anything like that." The king called for volunteers and two villagers came forward. Huston brought them back, wined and dined them, and had them returned to their village the next day. The rest of the villagers appeared the following morning.

Sam Spiegel also arrived, although John said that he wasn't "keen about Africa, and showed up there as little as possible." On this occasion he'd got bitten by a tarantula and developed a boil on his neck. "He was the most out of place human being you've ever seen in those surroundings," said Lauren Bacall. When he started to complain about Huston being behind schedule and about the food, which Bacall had prepared, John began to foam.

"Don't you talk to Betty like that!" he screamed. "And we're not shooting one more second until there is bottled water here for everyone to drink!"

"He was a little frightening to watch," Bacall said. "A knock-down-drag-out fight ensued. Sam was unnerved but calmed down eventually; he'd been in London and had no idea what everyone was going through."

Jeanie Sims, John's secretary, who worked out of the Romulus offices, was aware of the troubles between Huston and Spiegel. "They were constantly fighting," she said, "although I really think they were enjoying it. But nobody could have got that picture through but Spiegel. When everything was bogged down and the road was impassable, somehow Sam would get the truck through."

When they returned to work Huston decided that he wanted a steeple with a cross built onto the missionary church. Hepburn told him that since they were supposed to be Methodists, a steeple would be inappropriate. "Well," John said, "*this* Methodist is going to have a steeple!"

"He wanted it because he wanted to pan from the tops of the trees down to a cross," Hepburn said. "So we had to sit and wait while they built a steeple."

During this time many of the crew began to get sick from malaria and amoebic dysentery. They discovered the bottled water they had been drinking was contaminated. Huston and Bogart, who stuck to whiskey and never drank the water, weren't affected, but Hepburn got a bad case of the runs. During one scene where she was supposed to play the organ as the natives sang, she had a terrible attack and ran to the outhouse, almost losing control when a black mamba snake came slithering out of the toilet!

Huston did his best to console her, giving her back rubs in the evening, closing down the set for a few days. To production assistant Eva Monley he said, "Katie will eventually get dysentery, then she will understand what the part is about." When a telex was sent to Spiegel that she was ill, he wired back: "Keep her sick for 56 hours." Spiegel wanted to make sure the delay would be covered by their insurance policy.

"It was very debilitating," Hepburn said. "I couldn't take the remedies at all and function. I couldn't eat anything hot. I'd throw it up, terrible. I lost about twenty pounds."

"John swore that she actually knew how to look like a person who had been beat up by Africa after she had gotten sick," Monley said.

At one point, when a long shot was needed of Hepburn on the river, Angela Allen doubled for her. "I was the only female," she said. "I was meant to be on the tiller and a boy was doubling Bogart as the lookout. We had to go around this terrifying place with all those crocodiles lying on the bank. But I got to direct those pickup shots for two days."

Huston liked his script girl's spunk and professionalism. Over the years John would try to catch her in an error, but rarely succeeded.

On July 9, 1951, Huston received word that Ricki had given birth to a little angel she named Anjelica, after her mother. Champagne was brought in, toasts were made, John was very happy. First a son, now a daughter. He sent Ricki a cable, said he hoped he would be back in England the following week and would call from there.

Their time in Africa was almost finished. They had stayed in huts and on a paddle steamer, survived mosquito and wasp attacks, ant invasions, dysentery, elephant charges, tarantula and jigger flea bites, parasitic river worms, flared tempers, drenching rains and scorching heat, the sinking of the *African Queen*, news of the deaths of Hepburn's close friend, Fanny Brice, and Bogart's ex-wife, Mayo, and the birth of Huston's daughter. At Murchison Falls, with only two days left, Bogart was counting the hours when Huston decided they'd need a third day. "He got *so* angry with him," Bacall said of Bogie. "John didn't care, he would stay away for ten years, just didn't give a damn. But after eight weeks Bogie thought it was about time to leave."

Shooting wrapped on July 17 and resumed at the Shepperton Studios and at Worton Hall in London for the next six weeks. The early scenes with Robert Morley as Rose's missionary brother were shot then. Morley, who considered himself an actor of the theater and didn't take films all that seriously, embarrassed himself his first day on the set because he hadn't learned his lines. He had been appearing in a play called *The Little Hut* and thought he'd have more time to ease into his role, but he found Bogart and Hepburn "very professional," and felt himself an amateur when it came to films. "But I liked working with Huston, he did know the grammar of making pictures."

After Morley's screen death Hepburn had to cry over her brother. Hepburn turned on her emotions, weeping, grunting, groaning . . . waiting for John to yell, "Cut!" But John didn't, leaving her to emote for what seemed a cruel and endless time. "So bloody stupid," Hepburn felt. "That fool John. Funny as a baby's open grave." A few weeks later he sent her a present: a record he had cut of her grunts and groans, with a note saying it was the sound track of the movie and a suggestion that she listen to it at the sound department at MGM.

Jeanie Sims recalled another "terrible thing he did" to Hepburn. It was the scene right after Charlie and Rose made love in the boat. Allnutt went ashore to get wood for the boiler and she remained, pumping out the water. John had liked an earlier thing Hepburn had done when she poured coffee without realizing she was missing the cup and told her to do something like that. "I just want to know that you're thinking about him." So Hepburn began to fondle the pump handle as she brought it up and down, quite unaware of how it appeared. "Katie," John interrupted, "that's very nice, but just look at what you're doing!" When it dawned on her, she turned scarlet, jumped to her feet, and shouted at Sims, "Willy Wyler's in town, get him on the phone right now! I'm not working with this man anymore!" As the crew stifled their laughter, Sims observed, "She was furious. She's shockable, old Kate."

The incident provided Huston with a perfect going-away present for his star, which he gave to her all wrapped up the day she was leaving: the pump handle, with a slightly altered quote from the film inscribed on a gold band: "Nature, Miss Hepburn, is what we are put in this world to rise above."

The biggest problem John had with Bogart was shooting the scene where he emerges from the water with leeches all over his body. Bogie absolutely refused to allow real leeches to be used. John, honing in on his friend's squeamishness, just as absolutely insisted that the leeches couldn't be faked. He went so far as to tell John Woolf that he had to call Bogie and threaten to sue him if he didn't listen to his director. Woolf made the call but Bogart didn't back down. "I'm not going to do the leeches."

A man who bred leeches brought a tank of the suckers to the studio. Huston played on Bogart's terror right to the end, when he finally capitulated. He made a close-up of a real leech attached to the chest of the breeder, then used rubber ones on Bogart. "They certainly looked real," Hepburn said, "although we had a terrible time getting them to stick to Bogie, he was so skinny."

During the shooting of the leeches scene Peter Ustinov visited the set. John noticed that he was standing underneath the rain machine and turned it on, drenching the actor. John thought that was hilarious. A week later, asleep in his room at Claridge's, Huston received a midnight call from a hospital. "You are Mr. Huston?" the operator asked. "We have a man here who says he knows you, been involved in a serious accident. Says he won't be able to come to work tomorrow."

"Who is he?" John asked.

"Says his name is Bo something. Bogie?"

"Put me on to the matron!" John demanded. The matron came on and said the same thing, then a doctor, and another doctor. Nobody could tell him how badly Bogart had been injured, but it was suggested that John come out to the hospital. John talked with eight different people, all of them played by Peter Ustinov, who figured a lost night's sleep and high anxiety was at least equal to a public drenching!

There was one further near disaster when a huge tank, to be used for the underwater shots of Bogie attempting to pull the *African Queen* out of the mud, burst. The scene was scheduled for Monday and the tank fell apart on Sunday. "Isn't that amazing!" Katharine Hepburn marveled. "We could've been in it! Boy! Bogie and I would have been demolished!"

But there was still no ending for *The African Queen*. It had been a problem right from the start, with John wavering between an improbable but upbeat ending where the sunken *African Queen* blows up the German gunboat, and a more realistic but pessimistic one where Charlie and Rose take their wedding vows and then are hung by their captors. For a change Huston had opted for the lighter, happier ending. "I don't know what else we could have done with it," he said. "I don't dislike the ending. Maybe it gets a little broad."

Angela Allen, who would eventually be the script person on fourteen Huston films, believed that John was "bent on self-destruction. So frequently in his pictures he made a wonderful film, but when it came to the end he did something that kind of blew it. And he knew that he was doing it."

Acknowledging her admiration for Huston, Katharine Hepburn said fondly, "That's the great self-indulgence, isn't it? To do what interests you?" But she didn't particularly like what he did with the ending of *The African Queen*. "He got too bored to think up a good end. It wasn't on a par with the rest of the film. It's a wonderful picture," she said, "but the end is a bore."

There was no critical indication at the time that *The African Queen* would become one of the most beloved movies ever made. Bosley

Crowther in the *New York Times* considered it "a slick job of movie hoodwinking with a thoroughly implausible romance." *Variety* thought Bogart "has never been seen to better advantage. Nor has he ever had a more . . . talented film partner than Miss Hepburn." The British Film Institute's *Monthly Film Bulletin* singled out Hepburn's "beautifully pitched" performance, ignored Bogart completely, and judged the movie "a misfire."

But Huston knew what the public wanted—and knew he had succeeded. In a letter to Hepburn he ignored the *Monthly Film Bulletin* and wrote, "You've probably seen the English reviews which are, without exception, positively lyrical. It's as though one critic was trying to outdo the other in his praise. I am told it's the very first time that a picture has made the headlines."

Hepburn, who kept a diary of her time in Africa, would eventually publish her first book about the making of *The African Queen*. But what she didn't say in her book, and never told Huston or Bogart or Bacall, was that she never saw the completed film. "One is self-conscious about oneself," she admitted. "I don't think it's ever a source of great joy."

Lauren Bacall refused to believe that Hepburn hadn't seen one of her greatest screen performances. But not even such surprising news could dampen Huston's own feelings about making *The African Queen*. "I never made a picture under more fascinating circumstances. It was one of the few experiences in life I could well live over again."

16

WILD IN PARIS

WHILE JOHN WAS IN AFRICA DOROTHY SOMA TRAVELED
to Los Angeles to be with Ricki during her last weeks of pregnancy.
A few days before Ricki went into labor Dorothy told her, "Wouldn't it
be nice if you had a girl, now that you have Tony?" "I don't really
care," Ricki replied, shocking her stepmother. "I don't like competition."

After Anjelica was born Ricki went into a severe postpartum depression. Dorothy told Ricki that since the delivery went well, she was
going to return to New York. "Ricki started to cry and she never let up.
So on the airplane back I thought, I have to think up something to do
with this girl. And I came up with this brilliant idea." Ricki would drop
off Tony and Anjelica with Dorothy on Long Island and go to see John
in London. Ricki was thankful for the opportunity to make the trip and
watch John finish his work with Hepburn and Bogart. Dorothy, though,
was stunned when she saw the condition the baby was in.

"She got off the plane with Tony still in diapers and Anjelica six
weeks old and covered with a rash from the top of her head to the tips
of her toes. 'What is going on?' I asked. Ricki didn't know. An hour
after a feeding Anjelica would start to cry, and cried until the next
feeding. So she had taken her to a pediatrician who prescribed this

green medicine and that took care of the crying. Ricki stayed a few days and then took off. I didn't do anything while she was there." But the minute Ricki left Dorothy called her old pediatrician and showed him the green medicine. He told her it was phenobarbital. "The child was being *doped!* No wonder she didn't cry! And that's what had caused the rash. So I poured it down the john."

Determined to nurse Anjelica back to health, Dorothy bought enough formula to feed her "until it came out of her ears. She took a whole bottle the first feeding, and half the next. She slept right through to the next feeding." For the next three months Dorothy took her own children out of school in the city and stayed on the Island, taking care of Ricki's babies, turning Anjelica into "the most beautiful pink and white, plump baby you've ever seen in your life!"

John and Ricki set up house in a flat in Grosvenor Square, and while *The African Queen* was being edited John Woolf gave Huston a copy of Pierre La Mure's *Moulin Rouge*, a romanticized novel about Toulouse-Lautrec, to read. It told the story of the last ten years of the artist's life, the last decade of nineteenth-century Paris. Lautrec's legs stopped growing when, as a boy, he broke them in a fall. Called an "ugly little monster" by his first love, he moved to Paris to become a painter. He fell in love with a prostitute, who also rejected him, considered suicide, but instead began to capture the can-can world of the Moulin Rouge in his paintings and posters. When a model fell in love with him he couldn't accept it. He then drank himself into oblivion and died in an accident.

The Woolf brothers thought it would make a wonderful movie but Huston didn't agree and didn't want to make it. The Woolfs, however, persisted, convincing Huston that he would be just the one to pull it off. "Eventually," Woolf said, "we talked him into it."

What changed Huston's mind, apparently, was a vision of the ending, where he imagined Lautrec on his deathbed, hallucinating his past, as apparitions from the Moulin Rouge came to say good-bye.

Considering John's own life, his interest in painting and studies in Paris, his love of whores, the dwarf Lautrec's failures with women and his down-and-out alcoholic artist's existence, it was too tempting to turn down. His only stipulation was that he didn't want Sam Spiegel involved. When Spiegel came through with the money he owed everyone, John would consider including him on some project. But at that time, as Angela Allen attested, "Sam was in financial difficulties. He was virtually bankrupt. Before *The African Queen* came out he did not have a penny. I know, because I was working for him and his check bounced."

When they discovered that José Ferrer, who had won an Oscar for his *Cyrano de Bergerac* two years before, owned the rights to the novel and intended to turn it into a play, Huston and Woolf flew to New York to meet with the actor. Ferrer was a big fan of John's, having sat through *The Asphalt Jungle* four times without leaving the theater, and was even more in awe of Walter, whom he had once met. He told John about it: "To me, Walter was a giant, 110-feet tall, a man who walked through walls, the power of his artistry was incredible." Ferrer had seen Walter onstage in *The Barker, Dodsworth, Othello,* and felt that "the things he did on screen didn't even scratch what he was capable of."

John appreciated Ferrer's homage to Walter and asked him how he thought he might play Toulouse-Lautrec. "He's an aristocrat and he shouldn't whimper," Ferrer responded. "That's fine," Huston said. He had his star . . . and the rights to the novel as well.

Romulus was providing the pounds sterling, but an American company was needed to provide the dollars. After shopping it around to little enthusiasm—a period picture about a degenerate *dwarf* artist who preferred the company of *prostitutes?*—it wound up at Allied Artists. "I was excited by it," said Walter Mirisch, who discussed it with the company's president and with his brother Harold, who supervised distribution. "We all agreed that this film would be most prestigious and showed great promise of being commercially successful. We agreed to finance the American end, about $300,000, mainly to be paid to John and Joe Ferrer." But Ferrer wasn't satisfied with Allied Artists and their offer was rejected. The Mirisch brothers decided to put up the money themselves, arranging distribution with United Artists. "It was the first investment I'd made in a picture," Mirisch said, "and it really came from a tremendous belief in the material and John."

After Huston returned to London he flew to France to find suitable living quarters to work on the script with Tony Veiller, who had collaborated with him on *The Killers.* He found a small villa in Chantilly and was soon joined by Ricki. He wrote to Billy Pearson, encouraging him to consider racing in Europe. It was an almost idyllic time—*almost,* because he still hadn't received any money from Spiegel, and because his children were still on Long Island with the Somas.

"Everything I was being paid for *Moulin Rouge* over and above our living expenses went toward back alimony and other indebtedness," he said.

When *The African Queen* was ready for release in England Huston flew in for the press screening. John Woolf prepared a reception and he and John got drunk from the flow of booze and the strong praise from the British press. "Every one of them came up and said, 'It was one of the greatest British films that had ever been made,' " Woolf recalled. He and John "went dancing up Old Compton Street afterward." And when the picture was released, "it was the only film I've ever known that didn't get one poor review. All raves."

In America, however, there was concern about it before it was released. Max Youngstein, who was then a vice-president and director of advertising and publicity at United Artists, remembered that "Everybody expected Bogart with a gun, knock-you-on-your-ass macho. Here he was playing a grizzly, lackadaisical guy. And there was no action. Katie Hepburn had been voted a couple of years before as number-one box-office poison. The combination wasn't exciting." But Youngstein was convinced the picture could be sold and managed to calm his company's fears.

Back in Chantilly, John and Veiller continued working on their script. In December Huston heard from Dorothy Soma, who told him to send Ricki back to pick up her children. "I hated to do it," Dorothy said, "because I knew Anjelica would get messed up again. But Ricki had the idea that those children were going to turn John around and make him a devoted father and husband. Didn't happen." When Robert Capa returned from Paris to New York for Christmas, Dorothy recalled that "He'd come *roaring* through the restaurant. He'd just been with Ricki and John. 'Now tell me, honestly, what's going on with those two?' And he thought for a minute and said, 'I would say that John and Ricki are having a horribly wonderful time.' "

During the filming of *The African Queen* Huston had shown Humphrey Bogart a novel called *Beat the Devil*, written by Claud Cockburn using the pseudonym James Helvick. Huston recognized something of *The Maltese Falcon* in the off-beat story about an English couple's misadventures with a group of ludicrous thieves. The thieves were incorrigible misfits stranded in the South of France awaiting passage to the Belgian Congo, where they hoped to claim rights to land rich in uranium deposits. He had come across the book during his first visit to Ireland, where both he and Cockburn stayed as the guests of Lady Oonagh Oranmore and Browne, one of the three Guinness sisters. Bogart was interested enough to buy the rights to the book for his Santana production company and Cockburn was paid $7,500 to write a script. The Woolf brothers and Roberto Haggiag in Italy would also come in as partners. At the same time Huston and Katharine Hepburn discussed working together on another project, *Miss Hargreaves*, which would follow *Moulin Rouge*. But in early January 1952, Bogart began getting anxious about *Beat the Devil* and wanted Huston to commit to *his* picture. Huston was reluctant to ask Hepburn to relieve him of his commitment to her, although, he wrote to Bogie's business manager, Morgan Maree, he would "infinitely prefer" to do *Beat the Devil* first. "The only suggestion I have is that you and Bogie go to Katie and acquaint her with the benefits to be derived by me from making such a switch. Take her completely into your confidence," Huston wrote in a four-page letter. He was referring to his own obligations to MGM, which would be satisfied. "The point is that the choice does not lie with me, but with her. And because of our friendship, I feel a profound moral obligation to her," he said, admitting that he did not "wish to face the embarrassment of going to her myself and making a plea on personal grounds."

Before Hepburn agreed to relieve Huston of his commitment, David Selznick also wrote to him wanting to know if there was any part for Jennifer Jones in his upcoming films. John wrote back that neither of the two women's parts in *Moulin Rouge* offered "sufficient scope for Jennifer's talents." But, he thought, there might be something for her in *Beat the Devil*, "although, I'm afraid, not a great deal . . . Let's put it like this: I think the picture would be more fortunate in getting her than she would be in getting it." Then he gallantly added, "Jennifer can play anything she pleases in any picture I make. If she'd like to put on a beard and play Toulouse-Lautrec, I'll gladly have negotiations stop with Ferrer."

In late January Billy Pearson wrote John from Pasadena asking if he'd found a "good stable that would be interested in me," and signed his letter "Wyatt Earp." John wired back that he had arranged several rides and signed off "Doc Holliday." In February Pearson kissed his wife, Queta, good-bye and went to France. "For "Holliday" and "Earp" it proved to be wilder than even they could have imagined.

"I lived with John out in Chantilly," Pearson said. "He had this great château that had belonged to La Rochefoucauld. John and I were usually playing backgammon waiting for the mail each day because he was expecting a check from Sam Spiegel. We'd read in the trades that

African Queen was the biggest smash that had ever been in England and
we were starving to death! And no check from Sam ever arrived. Jeanie
Sims would start to cry the minute John and I would break open a
bottle and start playing backgammon and betting."

"How can you stand it!" Sims would shout. "We don't have fifteen
francs for lunch and you're betting five hundred dollars!"

"Of course, it was all bullshit, IOU stuff," Pearson said.

Pearson was convinced that what John really wanted to be in life was a
jockey. "He was absolutely horse-crazy; he didn't know any normal fears
and was a natural-born rider," he said. Huston introduced Pearson to
the best-known French jockeys. They liked him, but it took a month
before he was given a horse to race. Before his race he and John moved
to the Hotel Lancaster on the rue de Berri, "so that he could be near
me when I was riding at Longchamp," Pearson said.

Pearson quickly learned that he was not a welcome addition to
French racing. In his first race, as soon as the horses were out of sight of
the grandstand, the French jockeys shoved him and hit him with their
whips. When he told John what happened Huston said he needed a
sponsor, and to get one he had to show some style. "I don't need style,"
Pearson said. "I need a winning horse." "In this old cheese of a
country," Huston said, "style is everything. Die as you live, kid.
Beyond your means."

Pearson, who had been around a lot of big spenders—"Texas oil
hoodlums, New Yorkers with decaying family real estate, people like
Nick the Greek, the Aly Khan, King Farouk"—considered them all
amateurs compared to John when it came to "tossing it away." "I've
been with him at night in Paris with a herd of millionaires, and he
would outspend them. For every franc they spent he would spend a
dollar whether he had it or not."

In Paris John saw Cherokee, whose marriage to the German novelist
Hans Habe was not working out and she had decided to take their small
daughter and sneak away to Paris, where she found work as a model.
"John was staying at the Lancaster and he very rarely went to
Chantilly," she recalled. "Ricki would have to go into town to try and
get some money for her kids. I saw the pain Ricki was in. I realized one
thing, that Ricki was married, he wasn't.

"To this day Tony breaks my heart when I'm with him because I can
still see him crawling on the floor in Chantilly. Those kids had no love
at all. Ricki was spending all her time chasing John and John couldn't

care. It was a horrible marriage, a classic example of kids caught in a crossfire between two people who were so involved with themselves."

Over the next few weeks Pearson rode in other races but always with the same results: The French jockeys conspired to make sure he never won. John told him he should ride one more race, to "get even with all those jocks." So one drunken evening at Fouquet's, Huston and the American contingent in Paris—including Art Buchwald, John Steinbeck, and Anatole Litvak—outlined a plan for Pearson's farewell to French racing. John code-named their plan "Suppository" because, he said, "what we are going to do is inject into the Frenchman's society something he wouldn't like—but it's good for him."

It was a horse race run like no other. Pearson came out shouting every American battle cliché ever spoken: "Remember the Alamo!" "Damn the torpedoes! Full steam ahead!" "Don't give up the ship!" "Geronimo!" Twelve jockeys started the race, six finished, with Pearson in front. Pearson threw others from their mounts, leg-locked some, grabbed the bridle of others. "I was Paul Revere on a racehorse!" Pearson said. Said Huston proudly, "Billy committed every foul in the book and others never seen before in the history of French racing." To no one's surprise he was disqualified. To everyone's surprise he was only given a fine, a few days' suspension, and allowed to ride again. "It was said," noted the jockey, "that night was the only time since the war when American tourists in Paris were treated with respect and their bills not padded."

Pearson went on to win the French Oaks and he and John actually had some money, about $3,000, and they decided to celebrate. They got drunk and by three A.M. wound up in Montmartre, where they picked up some whores and decided to sneak them into the Lancaster. "John would talk to the night clerks and security people," said Pearson, "while I'd sneak up the back stairs with the girls. Once we got 'em up to our suite of rooms, we realized there were six of 'em. Once you're naked you can't just hold the $3,000 in your hands while you're trying to fuck them. So John said he'd hide the money where they wouldn't find it. And he hid it so well *we* never found it! The ladies never got paid. We had to give them things from the room—desk sets, furnishings—and then smuggle them back out with the stuff." The money was never found, although Huston claimed it was Billy, not he, who lost it.

Ricki and the children had gone to Deauville on the northern coast of France and were staying at a farmhouse while John was at the Lancaster with Pearson. They decided to pay her a visit and attend the races and casinos. Walking around the harbor John noticed a small gallery and they wandered in. "The owner asked us if we wanted to see some more paintings from her own collection. We went up with her into a small room. But my God! She began to take things out from under the bed—paintings by Van Gogh, from his *Potato Eater* series. A beautiful painting of Monet's *Sunflowers*. Another of his *Nymphias*."

Every painting was a masterpiece. The woman was one of the biggest art dealers in Paris and had brought down a number of her favorite paintings while she was in Deauville visiting her son. John walked into another room and stopped short before a painting that covered the wall from floor to ceiling. It was one of Monet's *Waterlilies*. He called Pearson in to look at what he thought was one of the finest paintings he'd ever seen, then asked the woman how much she wanted for it. She told him $10,000. John could hardly believe the price, but even so cheap, he couldn't afford it. "I was broke," he said.

They had about $800 between them to last through the week. That night they went to the casinos and John sat down to play chemin de fer. He lost all his money and asked to sign a voucher, but the proprietor said no, since he didn't have any credit. "Mike Todd was there," Huston recalled, "and he said he'd be good for it. I took a thousand dollars." He put down a $600 bet as Billy wandered off. "A little bit later," Pearson said, "the bartender said to me, 'Your friend, looks like he's hit a roll.' John had won his first bet, which gave him $1,200, and let it go. He won four more times by the time I got over there, which was $19,200, and people were going, 'Yeaaaah.' Then he won again, and the next one. He looked up at me and nodded. At $153,600 he was going for $307,200! Ten times! I was saying, 'John! John!' By then the casino was having trouble covering it and everybody was around the table. Of course, they were all betting against him. At last it was covered, he dealt . . . and he won! They were considering closing the table. Other people began to realize that, at eleven, they *had* to bet against him, the odds were too great. And they began to bet."

"I was having one helluva time," John said. He let the money ride . . . and lost it all on the next deal.

"Monsieur, *s'il vous plaît*," the dealer said as he pushed a small stack of chips over to Huston with his paddle. It was what the house couldn't cover. Just over $10,000. John turned to Billy and smiled.

"Well, kid," he said, "we won the Monet."

The painting wasn't the only thing they won. For over a month they had been placing bets on a French horse called Thunderhead II for the Two Thousand Guineas race in London. Pearson was assured by the horse's jockey that Thunderhead II was going to win, even though the odds were 30–1 against him. "The English bookmakers have a wonderful system," Pearson noted. "You don't have to have any money to bet on horses. We'd get drunk and call up England." Each time they'd bet £200 or more. The week of the race John and Ricki flew to London. Billy met them there. "That day," Pearson said, "was one of those days among horse players that *never* happen. I had won four thousand dollars when John and Ricki arrived. John said he liked some horse in the third race and we bet on that and won. Then came the big race. Along with our future book we put down all the money we had just won on Thunderhead II." When the race began the three of them shared binoculars, trying to find their horse, but they never saw him until the finish, when they realized that he had jumped off to such a fast start that he was *eight* lengths *ahead* throughout the race! With the money they collected from the track they sat down on a blanket, bought bottles of champagne, and got giddily drunk.

Since it was illegal then to take more than £10 out of the country, the only thing they could do with all that money was enjoy it there. "We took over the whole sixth floor of Claridge's!" Pearson said. "We had parties for every American in London. We brought up the string quartet from the lobby—six old ladies with two harps and violins." They ran up quite a tailor's bill at Maxwell's and Tautz, bought some African bronzes, and paid the old ladies to play their sweet music until the money ran out.

Pearson returned to Los Angeles and Huston began to assemble his crew for *Moulin Rouge*. But first he had to take care of some nasty business with Sam Spiegel.

When no payments had been made, even after the *The African Queen*'s strong box-office success, Huston called Bogart in California to see if he'd been paid. He hadn't and was preparing to sue Horizon. "There was a meeting between Morgan Maree, Sam, and Bogie," Huston related. "Quite a sum had to be accounted for. It was discovered that Sam's expenses for himself were very liberal. And afterward, when I was getting along all right, but not by any means on the back of the pig, Sam was living it up at Les Ambassadeurs for lunch every day, parties, and so on. I came to find out that Sam was paying a salary of four percent of the gross to the producer's agent, who went around to check the box offices to see that the accounts were correct. Four percent! An unheard-of sum! Sam was taking a kickback. And in the presence of everyone Sam turned to his attorney and said, 'I told you we'd never get away with that.' "

John called Paul Kohner and said, "Get me out of Horizon." He wanted to distance himself from anything that might "kick back" at him, where he might wind up "in the same cell as Sam."

"Either I was paid twenty-five thousand or I paid twenty-five thousand. I just wanted out. It was my last communication with Sam; I never had another serious conversation with him for the rest of his life. And it was one of the silliest things I ever did. Sam had allowed me to screw myself. I gave up all profits to *The African Queen*, which would have been in the millions. But since I had a talent for spending as much as I had, I don't know if it would have changed my life radically!" But it changed Spiegel's life. "It wasn't until after *The African Queen* that Sam had any kind of a purchase on life," John said with a touch of irony.

Intrigued by the idea of doing *Moulin Rouge* like a Toulouse-Lautrec poster, Huston hired *Life* photographer Eliot Elisofon as a color consultant for the film. He then began interviewing cinematographers, settling on a thirty-seven-year-old Englishman who had been a camera operator before the war and had four films, only one in color, to his credit. His name was Oswald Morris, and he would go on to work for directors as diverse as David Lean, Sidney Lumet, and Sir Carol Reed. But his name would be forever linked with Huston's, for whom he would photograph eight movies.

"When I went to see John in his suite at Claridge's I was absolutely in fear," Ossie Morris recalled. "He was sitting down, totally relaxed, sketching at a table. He started to ask me about Toulouse-Lautrec, but I didn't know much about him. Then he showed me what he'd been sketching—he'd done a beautiful portrait of me. I thought, how can this man possibly listen to what I'm saying and concentrate on his drawing? I left not knowing whether I had the job."

Huston said that he knew right away that Morris "was someone out of the ordinary—sensitive, intelligent, and with the attitude of a creative man. He was never guilty of the slightest exaggeration. Everything he said was *exactly* right. He was a man of precision."

Morris arranged to meet Huston again to talk about the look of the film. "I want it to look as though Toulouse-Lautrec had directed it," was the only instruction Huston gave Morris. John told him to take a second unit down to Albi, to the museum in the town where Lautrec was born, to see the painter's works. "Kid, everything you want, you must have," John said, knocking some of the wind out of Morris, who wasn't used to moving so quickly. "With Huston it was all there, but it had to be right," he said.

Morris and his crew went to Albi while Elisofon researched Lautrec's colors. When Ossie and Eliot met they didn't like each other, but Morris credits him with coming up with the idea of using different colored gels when photographing the main characters: blue-green for Lautrec, delicate pink for the model Myriamme, purple for the prostitute Marie.

"In those days," Morris said, "Technicolor was harsh and garish, but that was the way they sold their product. Strong, hard, powerful colors, which John didn't like. 'We've got to change this,' he would say. So I came up with the idea, and it was *my* idea, not Eliot's, of putting a lot of fog and mist into the set, and also some very strong fog filters on the camera. We did some tests and I showed them to Huston and he became very excited."

"One of the things I look for in a colored film is the palette," Huston said. "What palette do I use? Just as a painter, when he approaches a subject, decides what colors and tonalities. With *Moulin Rouge* that played a role in my decision to make it."

But tampering with Technicolor's colors soon became a major problem. "I had a deputation from the Technicolor people," Morris recalled. "It was a franchise system: They loaned you the cameras, you never bought the cameras, it was their trademark. I was killing their line, their crispness, their definition by desaturating their colors." Dr. Herbert T. Kalmus, who owned Technicolor, sent his wife to see the tests Morris was shooting and she told him, "We cannot accept this color." Morris told John about it and Huston said, "What do you think, kid?" "I think we're onto something," Morris said. "I'm very excited about it." "So am I, kid, so *fuck* her!"

The color tests continued in London while John met with actors and with Jack Clayton, who was under contract to Romulus as an associate producer. Clayton was a tough, headstrong man who wasn't afraid to stand up to Huston. When John told him he'd like to shoot *Moulin Rouge* in continuity, Clayton said it was impossible, given their budget and the limited number of stages available to them. When Huston insisted Clayton walked out. He went to a small cafe, downed three brandies, and then Huston appeared. "Kid," he said, "you do have a temper, don't you?" He told Clayton he wanted him to stay on the film and left him with these words: "Incidentally, kid, don't get mad, don't argue until you become a director." From that moment on, said Clayton, "it was a love affair."

One of the great love affairs of Huston's life began soon after he cast Suzanne Flon as Myriamme. She first met John when she auditioned for a part in *Quo Vadis*. He noticed her then, but took a far greater interest in the twenty-nine-year-old actress when he had a chance to spend more time with her. He was captivated by her charm and intelligence, her sensitivity, and her "unselfish outlook on life."

Most of the crew thought Huston would go after Colette Marchand, who played the prostitute Marie, but right from the start John zeroed in on Suzanne. It was because of this passion that he didn't want Ricki on the set. In his script Huston had Lautrec say what he believed: "Marriage is like a dull meal with the dessert at the beginning." Ricki had hoped that he would cast her in the picture—she had her heart set on playing the dancer/singer Jane Avril, but Jimmy Woolf had promised that part to Zsa Zsa Gabor. John wasn't pleased with Gabor, but even if he had his choice it wouldn't have been Ricki.

"John didn't want to have Ricki too close to him," Philip Soma observed. "He wanted her to just look after his two children." Angela Allen, who thought Ricki was "the most stunningly beautiful gal I'd ever seen," saw that John "treated her poorly after he met Suzanne. He didn't want her around. He gave Ricki a very, very hard time."

"She found out I didn't take bedrooms all that seriously," John said. "I didn't take *marriage* all that seriously." He said it never occurred to him to cast Ricki in any of his films. Dorothy Soma once asked him about it and John told her he would never use Ricki, "because Ricki cannot see anything in life outside of herself."

Jeanie Sims remembered that Ricki never came on the set. "She sort of adapted," Sims said. "She knew what John was like, that he was capable of playing around. He was immensely attractive to women. She couldn't believe her luck in having married him. And, of course, she had given him the children and that made her very important in his life. But she was nervous. She was always a little bit on the defensive. But she adored him."

Sims thought that John "tested his love for people and theirs for him to such an extent that it could break. He had to be cruel to see whether you were going to come through that and still be fond of him. And he was continually doing that to people."

Huston's cruelty was tempered by his understanding of his actors' sensibilities. He instructed Sims, "Whenever an actor comes up to see me, always be nice, always know their names. Because an actor is one of the few people in the world who has only himself to sell." Yet when he needed a performance and wasn't getting it, he wasn't always so nice. When Colette Marchand complained of her corset being too tight during a scene in a restaurant with Ferrer, Huston made her go over it again and again. "She was in tears," Sims said, "she kept complaining, 'I can't breathe.' And John was shouting at her. That's when he said to me, 'Go and get a bottle of champagne and a dozen red roses.' " Angela Allen said that was the only time she ever saw Huston try to get his actress to the point of tears. "To get her to the pitch, he really drove her very hard. But it was for a purpose," Sims added. "And he got the scene out of her. Then he went over and embraced her, gave her the champagne and sent the flowers."

Their problems with Technicolor still hadn't been resolved. When the last series of color tests were printed, the company arranged a screening. "John, as usual, was late," Morris said. "All the higher-ups at Technicolor were there. When John arrived we ran the film. John was very pleased. Then one of the Technicolor people said, 'We cannot accept any responsibility for what you are doing. I'm pleading with you to change your style. You are ruining the name of Technicolor.' "

Once again Huston asked Morris what he thought, then he asked Jack Clayton. When they both stood behind him John expressed directly the same feelings he had toward Dr. Kalmus's wife when she tried to interfere. "Gentlemen," he told the men from Technicolor, "I'm prepared to shoot the film as it is and I don't care about the result. So *fuck* you!" He stormed out of the screening room, leaving Ossie to take the letter from Technicolor disclaiming any responsibility for the look of the film.

"He's the only director in the world that I know who would have stood up to that pressure," Morris commented. Ossie also found that Huston was the first director he'd worked with "who really cared about sound. He wanted direct sound." Since much of their shooting was done in the streets, it took a long time to get everyone quiet. "But he didn't care if it took all night," Morris said. "He wasn't a fast director and he wanted perfection."

One Sunday they got permission to shoot at Maxim's, one of the major restaurants of Paris. "We brought in our arc lights, which gave off lots of carbon dust, and we put in more smoke—the Maxim's people were horrified. But John wanted it and he was very happy to sit outside, reading the galleys to Peter Viertel's novel about him, saying, 'Give me a call when you're ready, kid.' "

It must have taken considerable courage for Viertel to give the galleys of *White Hunter, Black Heart* to Huston to read, but John was a good sport about the book, which presented a rather unflattering portrait of him. He not only read and commented on Viertel's effort, but he offered him, at Bogart's suggestion, another screenwriting assignment. Claud Cockburn's script for *Beat the Devil* hadn't measured up and Huston put both Tony Veiller and Peter Viertel on it.

When school let out in California John sent for Pablo, who traveled to Paris by boat and train. He was met at the station by Jeanie Sims. It didn't take him long to observe that "she loved John so bad . . . you could see it. And she tried every trick." With Huston in love with Suzanne Flon and his secretary apparently in love with him, Ricki's anxiety brought her to the point of asking Pablo to spy on John. "Ricki tried things to get me to check on John's extracurricular activities," Pablo recalled. "But I covered for him."

According to Angela Allen, Pablo, who was almost seventeen, had eyes only for one thing. "Most of the crew had to spend their time pulling him out of brothels," she said, "because he was well underage." Pablo denied going to brothels but said, instead, that he went to bistros. "I picked up girls. In Paris I picked up an air hostess. Afterward she fell in love with me. And then John also got me a woman. She was a hairdresser who wore a blouse that when she bent down you could see everything. One day John saw me and said, 'Why don't you go to my room with the girl whose throat you keep looking down?' "

Pablo was also briefly reunited with his "mother," Evelyn Keyes, who had fallen in love with an Argentine diplomat in Paris, but John talked her out of marrying him. Huston also tried to talk Evelyn out of her half of their forty-piece pre-Columbian art collection. They had been drinking at Alexandre's one night, joined by the Peter Viertels, the Irwin Shaws, Bob Capa, and Tola Litvak, when John said to her, "Honey, I've always thought it a pity that that collection of ours should be separated. . . ." Evelyn agreed and suggested he send her his pieces. He wasn't amused and came up with a more interesting solution: They should flip a coin. Evelyn didn't want to do it but Huston wouldn't let up until she agreed.

"He made a fine ceremony of it," she said. "He got out a coin. He jiggled it. He moved it back and forth between his fingers. 'Heads or tails, honey?' he asked." She called heads and the fate of the collection was decided. Evelyn got them all.

With Suzanne Flon, John came close to losing his life. "On Bastille Day," he recalled. "I had been with Aly Khan, Zsa Zsa Gabor, José

Ferrer, and Suzanne. Afterward I took Suzanne home in a taxi, and when the taxi door opened somebody came in and belted me—hit me two or three times before I knew what was happening. I got out of the cab and followed the man. He came down some steps with a pistol, which he pointed at me. I went toward him and he pulled the trigger. I heard the pistol click and decided it wasn't loaded. The taxi driver and a bystander got between us, and Suzanne kept begging me to leave, so I did. But he had bruised me around the eyes and I had to put on some dark glasses. He was in love with her; he was jealous and had been waiting to see who was taking her home.

"Well, I found out where he lived, and I had a kind of goon in the company who I asked to come with me, since I knew he had a gun. I knocked on his door and he opened it, and I hit the door hard enough to knock him back, then proceeded to kick the shit out of him. He tried to kick me in the balls, so I gave him a little extra punishment for that. Then he began to beg, saying he had loved her for so many years, and there was a knock at the door: the gendarmes. We said it was just a friendly scuffle—he was bleeding from his nose and mouth. I said, 'Let me see your gun,' it was only a .22, but you can kill somebody with a .22. I took the clip out of the gun and, sonofabitch, the round had misfired!"

"I was scared to death," Suzanne Flon said of the unpleasant memory. "When you see somebody with a gun, it is always terrifying."

"John arrived on the set with the biggest black eye you've ever seen," Ossie Morris said. "Imagine, all this is going on and he's trying to make a film!"

Jeanie Sims remembered that there would be times during the shooting when John would go for three or four days with only an hour's sleep, "because we were shooting nights and working days." Along with the gambling, drinking, and fighting John was also committing some of his most creative practical jokes. His target was the pompous Eliot Elisofon, whose egocentricity became more and more unbearable as the filming progressed. He even insisted on having a chair with his name on the back, so Huston had one made that said, "Elisofon Go Home."

Huston managed to obtain some stationery of the Royal family because his assistant director's brother worked at Buckingham Palace. "John concocted a letter to Eliot summoning him to the palace to photograph the Royal family," Ossie remembered. "It terrified the life out of me when he did this. Eliot could not contain himself. 'Well, now, Eliot,' John would say, 'how are you going to dress for the occasion? Protocol is very important, you know. You can't just go looking like a goddamn Yankee.' " Huston convinced Elisofon that he needed a tailor, then he convinced him that he couldn't be driven in a car but should, instead, hire a horse-drawn carriage to take him to the palace. The gag went on for weeks. It wasn't until Elisofon canceled another *Life* assignment in preparation for his exclusive date at Buckingham Palace that he was told to forget about his fancy tailoring and horse-drawn carriage.

One would think that by this time Elisofon would have caught on, but Huston made him a victim of an even crueler joke after that. Eliot had taken an interest in a young actress and had shown her some pictures in his darkroom. Huston heard about it and got José Ferrer to write a letter to Eliot from the girl's "mother," accusing him of making indecent advances to her underaged daughter. The letter was addressed to the Manager of the Studio, and the next day the chief of security called Elisofon to his office. Once again everyone was in on the prank. Eliot swore that nothing had happened between him and the girl, but the joke became more complicated when the Home Office was informed that Elisofon intended to leave for New York with his wife and child before the matter was settled. He was told he couldn't go. Unnerved, he went to see Jack Clayton, who said he must talk with John, but Huston was always too busy to talk with him. His boat was leaving in a few days, his wife didn't know what the delay was about, and Eliot was on the verge of a nervous breakdown. Finally, after picking up a head-shaking tic, he managed to pin down Huston, who asked him in all seriousness, "What *did* happen in the darkroom?" Elisofon got down on his knees and swore on the life of his family that *nothing* had happened. At that point John could no longer contain himself. "If I'd been just a little better person, compassion would have flooded through me rather than mirth," he confessed. "But I wasn't, and it didn't. I began to laugh." Finally it dawned on Elisofon that it had all been another of Huston's damn jokes! But he was so relieved that instead of getting angry, he offered to buy drinks for everyone. "I wished he had punched me instead!" Huston said.

While he was able to release certain hostilities through practical jokes, there was nothing he could do about Zsa Zsa Gabor, whose talent could barely fill a thimble. "He wanted to replace her," Sir John Woolf said. "But we decided to keep her because we were dubbing her singing voice, anyway." Ossie Morris said, "She moved like a tank, so he got Colette Marchand to show her how to move." Gabor was intimidated by Huston. "He was the kind of dour, listening man who makes me feel that he thinks everything I say to him is a lie," she wrote in her autobiography. One time Huston threatened her, "If you go dead again on the end of a line, I'll shoot you!" She felt "utterly humiliated." Yet when it was all over she credited Huston for making her a "star."

Gabor wasn't the only one who had problems. During filming John Woolf began to worry about the budget and thought that perhaps José Ferrer could be talked into taking a cut in salary. Afraid to broach the subject himself, Woolf asked Huston to talk to Ferrer about it. Ferrer at first agreed but wanted to know who else was taking a cut. When they wouldn't tell him he got angry and said he wouldn't do it. "They accused me of breaking my word," Ferrer said. "How could Woolf accuse me of reneging when he wasn't there and never spoke to me in the first place? Was I the only one expected to take a cut?"

Ernie Anderson, Ferrer's publicist, said that Ferrer and Huston didn't get along because Ferrer's "ambition cursed him. He was an ugly man who couldn't accept that he was a character actor. He said things about John behind his back and John's friends told him and John called him on it. And that was the end of their friendship."

"I really have no idea how John felt about me," Ferrer said years later. "I didn't think he particularly liked me. He belonged to a reckless breed that I admire and intellectually envy. I don't have his physical courage at all. But I loved being with him and found him an illuminating conversationalist and a stimulating guy. He looked through the viewfinder and saw pictures that nobody else saw. Between his artistry and his public and private personalities, half angel, half devil, he added up to a mythological figure."

When told that Huston felt *Moulin Rouge* would have been a much better film had it dealt more honestly with the gritty world Lautrec inhabited, Ferrer defended the picture. "I've always felt suggestion is every bit as good as statement and that picture makes explicit what was going on. It didn't avoid or sidestep anything. John took a book about a man who fell in love with a woman who said, 'Get away, you're ugly and weird,' and who then hung around with prostitutes because he could buy their love. John *did* make it explicit. It *was* a whorehouse; he *was* an alcoholic. If the ending was sentimental, John was very proud of it. I don't know what truth was avoided."

"If I were to do that picture again," Huston said, "it would be entirely different. At that time censorship wouldn't have permitted the telling of the real story. Lautrec was an individual who looked at life clinically. He had a heart like an icebox and was not himself a romantic in any sense. It would be interesting to do another version."

On September 3, 1952, Billy Pearson sent John two cans of peanut butter and a note that said, "I sure do miss you. In my whole life I never had such a great time as that which I spent with you." On the fourteenth John wrote back thanking him for the peanut butter: "In order to keep my wife and children from getting to it, I'm living out at the studio." He mentioned that he saw a white marble sculpture of a horse's head from the Acropolis that was "the finest thing I've ever seen outside a museum." But the price was $3,000. "Oh, sweet Jesus, for another winner like Thunderhead!"

In October Humphrey Bogart wrote to Huston regarding *Beat the Devil*. Jennifer Jones had already agreed to play the consummate liar and flirtatious tease, Gwendolen Chelm, after Jean Simmons, Audrey Hepburn, Ingrid Bergman, and Lauren Bacall were considered. Huston had written to Bacall about it, and Bogart wrote back: "Dear Fly in the Ointment,

"Because I always open my wife's mail, I read your insidious and immoral proposals to my wife. It is perfectly safe to promise Miss Bacall a leading part in our picture as soon as you are perfectly sure that she is knocked up—by me, that is. I have therefore instructed Miss Bacall to disregard your blandishments and as your employer may I request you not to further fuck up my home."

Then Bogart got down to serious business: He was convinced that Huston was making a mistake wanting to shoot *Beat the Devil* in black and white. "Within a very few years there will be practically no black and white pictures exhibited," Bogart wrote, and "with an eye to the future residuals of this epoch [sic]," color should be considered. "This is entirely up to you," he added, "and since I've won the Oscar I have tremendous respect for your opinions, drunk or sober." Thinking of the film as a return to his earlier works like *The Maltese Falcon, Key Largo,* and *The Asphalt Jungle,* John thought that color wasn't necessary.

Not above sharing some gossip, Bogie told Huston about Sam Spiegel suing his wife for divorce, Lana Turner's breakup with her latest paramour, "and the papers are full . . . of your amoral and immoral escapades, including black eyes."

In November John wrote that he didn't think the picture would be improved by using color but left the final decision to Bogart. "It all comes down to this: would its sale, in time to come, to television, be made so much more attractive by employing color as to warrant the extra expenditure at this time? This is a question that I, a lowly craftsman, am less able to answer than you big corporation guys. Whatever you and Morgan decide is fine with me." He noted that he wasn't delighted with Veiller and Viertel's rewrite of Cockburn's script, and wondered whether it was "a drama, a comedy or an action picture." Regarding Bogart's wardrobe as Billy Dannreuther, "I'd like to see you a very continental type of fellow. An extreme figure in a homburg, shoulders unpadded, French cuffs, Regency trousers, fancy waistcoats, and a walking stick. The eyepatch is debatable."

On November 26, Bogart replied, "As regards your brilliant conception of my wardrobe, may I just say that I think you're full of shit. May I suggest that *you* wear the costume that you describe and that I go around in old tweeds. May I also suggest that you rig up some kind of a contrivance that will permit you forever to walk on your knees in this costume. As regards the cane, I don't have to tell you what you can do with *that*!"

Before he could concentrate on fixing the script problems of *Beat the Devil*, Huston backed José Ferrer in his unsuccessful efforts to be included in United Artists' advertising campaign for *Moulin Rouge*. Max Youngstein had hired an artist to create an ad that would be "every American's dream of what his first trip to Paris would be like." The drawing included the monuments, the dancing girls, the hookers . . . but not Toulouse-Lautrec. Ferrer was furious and John went to see Youngstein in New York. When he insisted that Lautrec be included, Youngstein shouted he was within his legal rights not to. "We got into a very violent argument," Youngstein recalled, "and Huston threw a punch at me. While I was sitting down! I got so goddamn angry I was ready to kill him. I don't take that kind of shit from anybody. So I swung my chair around and *kicked him right in the balls* as hard as I could! He went down hard. I lifted him into the chair and he sat there, gasping. Gave him a shot of whiskey, he came to . . . and walked out. I didn't hear from him again for years."

The rush to release *Moulin Rouge* in time to be considered for the 1952 Oscars was similar to what happened the year before with *The African Queen*, when Sam Spiegel personally carried the film cans through customs and managed to have it released on the last day of eligibility. That strategy had paid off—*The African Queen* received four nominations—for Bogart, Hepburn, and Huston for directing and co-writing with Agee. Only Bogart won an Oscar, but José Ferrer was hoping to get his second for *Moulin Rouge.*

Huston worried that the censors might object to the can-can at the beginning of the film, but the Johnston Office cleared it. *Variety* was critical of Huston's rush to qualify the movie for Oscar consideration, saying that it left the film "without the polish and finish it should have to make the most of its undeniable quality." *Moulin Rouge* would go on to garner seven nominations and two Oscars (for Art Direction and Editing), although it got off to a rocky start before its West Coast premiere on December 23, when members of the American Legion Un-American Committee protested the Communist leanings of its star and director.

"I went to the theater on opening night," Huston said, "and here were American Legion members carrying pickets. They were actually a splinter group. They did it without the consent of the authorities of the Legion. It was more anti–Joe Ferrer, who had the reputation for being Communist. Which he wasn't."

Ferrer said that he and Huston had been warned about the pickets and had spent a few days dealing with their leaders to keep it from being blown out of proportion and damaging both the film and their careers.

Huston much preferred the film's reception at the Venice Film Festival, where the festival's president and his countess wife threw a party at their palazzo on the Grand Canal. John Woolf smiled at the memory of the procession of boats, with "flunkies in white wigs and such marvelous costumes and jewelry."

The reviews of the film were mixed, leaning more toward the negative, like *Newsweek*'s, "Pretty heavy going . . . reeks of sentimentalized invention." The British Film Institute's *Monthly Film Bulletin* considered it "long and pretentious . . . slick and passionless," having "no evidence of Huston's virtues . . . it highlights his faults—facility, superficiality, lack of feeling." But the review in *Cue* called it "one of the great films of this, or any year." The *Hollywood Reporter* thought it was "flawlessly directed." And columnist Louella Parsons, whom Walter Huston had once feared might ruin John in print after he accidentally ran over Tosca Roulien in 1933, put John "in a class by himself" after seeing *Moulin Rouge.* "This is a very great picture about a very great artist as done by a very great artist, John Huston," she wrote.

José Ferrer remembered only his notices, "which were universally bad. I thought I was in a masterpiece! And it was all the creation of one man: the color, the concept, the casting—it was all John Huston."

The experiment with color, however, paid off handsomely, as the *New York Times* noted, "The eyes are played upon with colors and forms and compositions in a pattern as calculated as a musical score." Ossie Morris felt vindicated. "Visually it got stunning notices," he said. "John and I got two letters from Technicolor, which said how proud they were to have been associated with such a magnificent, breakthrough color film!"

In January 1953, John received a fan letter from the science fiction writer Ray Bradbury. "I have rarely experienced a 'bouquet' in a film theater," he wrote, "and yet that seems about the best way to explain the way you have molded an atmosphere in this picture. The film, for me, seemed *distilled* rather than manufactured with camera, crew and actors. . . . I left the theater exhilarated, which happens less and less as I get older." More brash, but no less ambitious than Agee, Bradbury was blunt about the *real* reason for his letter: "I also laugh at the very certain feeling that someday, somehow, in some way, I want to work with you. I *must* work with you on a picture. I have never been more sincere and I have never spoken more urgently in my life. . . . I will wait patiently and I will wait a good, long time. . . . But in the end, I know and feel in myself that we were meant to try something together."

Another letter came in mid-February from Dean Rusk, then president of the Rockefeller Foundation. Rusk wrote of his "appreciation and admiration for the artistry and skill which you and your associates put into *Moulin Rouge*, particularly its composition, color and musical score. Although I am a complete amateur in such matters, I have the feeling that this production represents a notable advance in the use of the capabilities of a motion picture, and suggests the promise of a brighter future for that medium than it is fashionable in some quarters at the present time to accord to it."

But what made Huston smile most, considering his financial and back-tax problems, was the box-office figures, which at last managed to get him out of debt. He was especially pleased with his association with the Woolf brothers, who were "unscrupulously honest. Instead of trying to conceal profits, they took pleasure in giving one his dues." And Huston's dues as co-producer made *Moulin Rouge* his biggest commercial success. He could now afford to live wherever he wanted and, not surprisingly, he knew where that was.

17

THE DEVIL AND THE
DEEP-BLUE SEA

"MY FIRST NIGHT IN IRELAND," HUSTON WOULD FOREVER
remember, "was spent at Lugalla, in the mountains of Wicklow. We
arrived by night and I was aware of evergreen trees on a precipitous,
narrow road. We had to stop the car because of a stag who stood in the
middle of the road in the glare of our headlights. I went to bed late that
night, but awakened early the next morning, went to the window and
looked out. It was a sight I shall never forget. Beyond the wildflowers
was a white sandy beach and a lake of black water and on the opposite
side, rising out of it, was a great black rock of granite with purple
heather on its side falling like a shawl over a piano.

"Ireland had me!"

With enough money coming in to be able to afford a place to live,
Huston returned to Ireland with his family to settle in a rented house
called Courtown near Kilcock, in County Kildare. It was a large house
on three hundred acres of land and came with a staff of servants. John
had fallen in love with not only the land but also the Irish character.
He felt at home with men who loved to tell their stories over a glass of
whiskey and who judged time by the lives of their horses. In certain
ways Ireland reminded him of his early years in Mexico: It didn't cost

400

much to live there and there was a certain wild abandonment that was appealing. In Mexico, when he wanted to jump a horse, it was often over the hood of a car. In Ireland it was over stone walls and wooden fences, and usually in pursuit of a fox. "This was a revelation," Huston said about fox hunting. "It was something I had never experienced before and it was just great, the best in the world."

Ricki, too, wanted to learn to ride to hounds, but John was "dead set against it. She had no aptitude as a rider." But when she insisted John unsuccessfully attempted to tutor her. "God, Ricki would fall!" he said. It would take her some time, but eventually, with another, more patient instructor, Ricki managed to stay on her mount, although she took so many falls that she broke a front tooth and had a few bumps on her head that never went away. "Once," John observed, "when her horse refused at a fence and I saw her go flying head over heels, I said to myself, 'That was the mother of my children.' "

One of Anjelica's earliest memories was of a magical night when her parents woke her and Tony and carried them downstairs to the front porch, where "the sky was just alive with meteors. I remember lying in my mother's arms watching the stars fall. And she told us we had to make a wish and it would come true. I remember wishes falling through the sky! It was just extraordinary."

While he found it enormous fun getting properly outfitted to ride with the Kildare Hounds and watching meteor showers light up the Irish sky, Huston also had to focus his attention on getting *Beat the Devil* into shootable shape so he could earn the $175,000 Bogart's company was paying him to direct. In early January 1953 he submitted the Veiller/Viertel final draft to the Breen office for censorship approval. On February 13, ten days before the start of the picture, with Huston and Bogart already in Rome, Joseph Breen handed down his decision. The script was unacceptable under the provisions of the Production Code. First because it didn't treat as wrong the adulterous relationship between Dannreuther, Bogart's role, and Gwendolen, the part to be played by Jennifer Jones. And second because Bogart's character was a "glamorization of a criminal. . . . This story would seem to indicate that a man of this kind is a very dashing character. . . . He should be thoroughly denounced by someone in the story."

Going Breen one step further, Huston denounced the whole script. "It just wasn't good," he said. "Both Tony and Peter didn't want to work on it any longer. I was pissed off." Not wanting Bogart to lose any more than he already had, Huston suggested they drop the picture altogether, but Bogie talked him out of it. "It's only money," he said.

When David Selznick heard of their dilemma he cabled a suggestion to John. Truman Capote happened to be in Rome at the time and Selznick, who had hired him to do a polish on a film of his, *Indiscretions of an American Wife*, which starred Jennifer Jones and Montgomery Clift, considered the twenty-eight-year-old writer "one of the freshest and most original writing talents of our time." Capote was small, strange, high-voiced, sharp-tongued, unashamedly homosexual, and startlingly smart. Huston, who often felt uncomfortable around homosexuals, had nothing but respect for Capote, whom he called "an extraordinary little man who had the courage and the determination of a lion."

Huston gave Capote the book to read, offered him a salary of $1,500 a week, and told him he'd meet him in Ravello, where the picture was to be shot. He then hired a driver to take him and Bogart to Naples and almost lost his leading man. "At a fork in the road," he said, "the driver couldn't make up his mind and went straight ahead through a stone wall. Bogie was asleep in the backseat. Knocked his teeth out. He had bitten through his tongue. We got him to the hospital and had to wait ten days for his bridge to be duplicated and sent over."

"He was probably hoping they'd never arrive so he wouldn't have to go through with the picture," Bogart said.

"Bogie was minus his front tooth and John thought it was hilarious," Ossie Morris remembered. It was only his second film with Huston, but Morris, by then, was beginning to understand how Huston's devilish mind worked.

Gina Lollobrigida was cast as Bogart's wife. While a star in Italy, it was her first American picture and the company had a problem with her billing. It was finally settled that she would be billed above the title in Europe and below in America. At first Bogart described her as making Marilyn Monroe look like Shirley Temple, and Huston said she was built like an apartment house with balconies, but they soon settled for calling her Lola Frigidaire. Robert Morley, Peter Lorre, Ivor Barnard, and Marco Tulli made up the merry band of desperate characters trying to get to Africa with Bogart to stake out the uranium-enriched land. Edward Underdown played Jennifer Jones's crusty English husband, Harry Chelm, who heads for Africa to take over a coffee plantation.

On Friday, three days before the picture began, Huston told Morris he wanted to throw a party. "And the centerpiece of the party was . . . tearing up the script!" Morris said. Then Huston told everyone Capote was arriving the next morning and there would be pages by Monday. Somehow there actually *were* pages before the cameras began to roll, but after two days, it became necessary for Huston to think up ways to delay production to allow Capote time to write more pages. What he usually did was look at a camera setup that Ossie Morris had spent the morning preparing and then suggest a different angle, which would take up the rest of the day. Or sometimes someone would suggest a new routine—Robert Morley being unable to close his luggage was one—and Huston would agree and order a special track built so the cameras could dolly out in a certain way. He would do whatever he could to stall, as Capote sat in his loft room in the suite he shared with John trying to catch up.

Although Capote and Huston shared the screenwriting credit, Capote claimed that he alone wrote the script. "He never wrote a word," Capote insisted. "He was like Irving Berlin, who had the little nigger boy in the trunk writing all his songs! While I was working he was playing cards and drinking." Huston smiled when he heard Capote's allegations and said, "We wrote together." In fact they were both right. Capote was the one who actually set pen to paper, but Huston was there making suggestions and altering lines, along with everyone else on the set. Jeanie Sims, who was assigned to work with Capote, verified that "there was a big input from John. Truman and I would work during the day and in the evening we would sit with John and go through what we had done. Bogie would put on a white coat and mix martinis for us."

"Sometimes scenes that were just about to be shot were written right on the set," Capote said. "The cast was completely bewildered . . . sometimes even Huston didn't seem to know what was going on. It was totally mad, but it was meant to be. I was always just one day ahead, sometimes I was down there in the morning distributing the script to the cameramen and the poor actors."

"Everybody respected and loved Truman," Sims said. "We used to tease him a bit, but it was affectionate teasing. Once we were having a drink in Naples and Truman called out an order to the barman. And the barman said, 'Yes, signora.' I laughed. So did Truman."

"Everybody thought Huston and I were having an affair since we were living in the same rooms," Capote said, "including Humphrey Bogart, who spread it everywhere—the sounds that he could hear in the room at night between me and Huston, Huston had finally gone that way. . . .

And Huston played straight into it because he thought it was funny. Half the crew were barely speaking to him, they were so appalled. I enjoyed it. I didn't mind a bit." Nor did Capote mind Huston's character, which he perceived as a "classic seducer," his "ungentle" eyes "bored as sunbathing lizards." He considered Huston "a man of obsessions rather than passions, . . . a romantic cynic" who believed "that all endeavor, virtuous or evil or simply plodding, receives the same honorarium: a check in the amount of zero."

Robert Morley quickly spotted the level of absurdity they were working at when Capote disappeared for a few days because his raven refused to speak to him over the phone and he had to go back to Rome to find out what was wrong.

Angela Allen remembered how everyone kept changing their lines on the set. "Every scene just took on its own life," she said. "Morley was very inventive, Peter Lorre was, too. Robert used to write his own witty lines and the others would put in their penny's worth. We would fall about laughing because they were so funny."

Morley didn't think much of Bogart's attempts at dialogue. "It was very strongly Bogie," he noted. "A nice man but not much brain, really." And he didn't at all care for Peter Lorre, "who I always thought was a rather unpleasant character, an unlovely man in every way." When Lorre first arrived John thought it would be funny to describe his character as having blond hair. Then he instructed Jeanie Sims to just keep staring at Lorre's hair whenever she saw him. "Eventually it was leaked to him that he should have blond hair," Sims said. "It was supposed to be a gag, but Lorre went to this gay hairdresser and got his hair dyed. It turned out to be successful because it looked unusual."

Ossie Morris thought Jennifer Jones was a bit neurotic and believed that around this time she started to report to David Selznick, who was in Morocco, how disorganized things were. The infamous Selznick memos began to arrive. "They were all about Jennifer, nothing else mattered," Morris said. "So Huston and Bogart came up with a wonderful idea for a gag. They decided to concoct a long, long cable, which didn't *quite* make sense anywhere. David wouldn't be able to understand it and would ask for a recheck; it would keep David quiet for possibly a week. John had the pages of the cable numbered 1, 3, 4, 5, skipping page 2. Then, whenever he communicated with Selznick, he kept referring to that nonexistent page which, Huston learned, "drove him right up the wall."

But Selznick's memos worked against Jennifer Jones, because John decided to take out his frustrations on her as well. In one scene she was expected to be in the background high up on the boat's mast, exercising. John thought it would be great fun if she stood on her head. "He made her climb the rigging, which was rather ridiculous," Robert Morley said. "He bullied her. She came down shaking." Jack Clayton was radioed to bring the motorboat and take her away. "She was in tears," Clayton said. "That was part of John's cruel side. By the time we got to shore I had persuaded Jennifer to go through with the shot. When I told John that I had brought her back, he said, 'Why did you do that, kid? I wouldn't shoot her tonight, anyway.' "

Clayton felt that John treated him like a son. He would often call Jack to join him for a nightcap when he was unable to sleep. "In Ravello," Clayton said, "he would telephone about two A.M. 'Are you asleep, kid?' 'I was, John.' 'Come over and have a drink.' I knew that all I would have to do to send him to sleep was to get him drunk. Fortunately, in those days, I was able to drink him under the table. I would bring a bottle of whiskey and a bottle of brandy and for about three or four hours he used to tell me all about his life. I've always had a sad feeling about John. He numbered amongst the ten best directors of our era, but I was very sad, because my feeling was that he really didn't care very much about film directing. I think he should have been a painter. He had an unbelievably wonderful pictorial eye."

What impressed Clayton was how Huston would always come up with a different camera angle than the one Clayton had set up. "I had not yet learned to be original; I was thinking in what would be a normal way of shooting a scene. John, at his best, never shot in a normal way. But the most important thing I learned from him was the meaning of courage, which was to always stick by your guns and never compromise, regardless of producers or money. And I loved the fact that he wouldn't stand anything that wasn't perfect."

One morning John was late and Ossie Morris went to his room. "I could smell burning wood," Morris said. "All his bedroom was in darkness and his door was ajar. You had to be very careful if you woke him up, in case you scared the life out of him. I crept through the door and there was a three-kilowatt electric fire going full onto the door; the bottom was red ash. Obviously he'd had a lot to drink the previous night, staggered into bed, and kicked this heater by the door. I went over to him and said, 'John . . . John . . . it's Ossie.' 'How are ya, kid?' 'I'm fine, John. Your bedroom door is alight. It's on fire.' 'Oh, how I love the smell of burning wood,' he said and went back to sleep."

•   •   •

As the movie progressed Ossie saw that John never protested about any of Gina Lollobrigida's "crazy cockeyed costumes," or any of the suggestions from his actors. "I thought, this can't be right," Morris said, "but of course, in the end, he was making a shaggy dog film." It took a while for Robert Morley, who looked thoroughly confused throughout the filming, to realize that Huston had decided "to send the whole thing up a bit. It became the first high-camp movie."

Ossie felt sorry for Angela Allen, who was trying desperately to keep the story together in spite of all the changes. At one point, when they were shooting on the boat, John decided to test her breaking point. "Angie, dear," he said, "we've just done this shot where Bob Morley and Peter Lorre have walked one way, where the sea is going right to left. Now they're coming down another way, and the sea is going left to right in the background. Won't that make it look as though the boat's going backwards?"

Allen said she'd try to work it out. "It was ridiculous," Morris said, "but Angie fell for it. And she couldn't make it work. And he rode her and rode her and in the end, she screamed. She ran up the deck, onto the bridge, threw her script, which is her Bible, into the air, and passed out cold. John didn't bat an eyelid. They got a tot of brandy and brought her around. She wouldn't speak to him or any of us, and he turned and said, 'Well, Os, that's one way of getting a brandy, isn't it?' "

"He'd sort of driven me mad," Angela Allen concurred, "trying to confuse me quite deliberately. I was so naive in those days." Morley, who was not naive, and whom John considered one of the wittiest men alive, was pushed by Huston during the scene where the car he and Bogart were in was stalled along a mountain road. "That was the only time I ever really slightly stepped up with him," Morley recalled. "We got to the top of the hill and Bogie and I were supposed to push the car. Huston said, 'Now Bob, we have someone in the car lying down just out of sight of the camera, he'll put the brake on just as you get to the edge of the cliff, so there's no danger. Start pushing the car and then jump in and Bogie will get in the other side.' So we started pushing and, of course, it gathered speed quite quickly and I was left behind. Bogie jumped in and saw that there was nobody in there and he immediately jumped out again and the car went over the hill. I was a bit outraged. I said, 'Really, John, that was not very carefully planned, was it?' 'Well, you weren't in it, were you, Bob?' "

The car had damaged a number of houses on its way down, and throughout the rest of that day people came up from below to claim damages, which John dealt with happily. "Huston was a sort of child of the party," Morley observed. "Having the most fun of anyone. And you didn't want to break up his dream."

"I wouldn't say that I had fun directing *Beat the Devil*," John said. "I was so harassed always trying to get ahead by a scene. No, it wasn't fun."

Still, when visitors like Ingrid Bergman, Roberto Rossellini, Orson Welles, Bob Capa, and George Sanders came to visit, Huston made sure *they* all had fun. A young Stephen Sondheim also visited the set with his rich friend, John Barry Ryan, and Angela Allen said that Sondheim used to "tinker on the piano, but John never noticed him because he wasn't a rich boy."

Capote, on the other hand, noticed *everybody*. Jeanie Sims said he was always looking out the window, identifying new arrivals. And when someone of his sexual persuasion was said to be around, "he always looked so hopeful." Bogart took to calling him "Caposy" and once challenged him to an arm wrestling match. To his surprise Capote won. Bogart asked for a rematch and Capote bet him $50 he'd win again, and he did. Then he beat him a third time. When Jeanie Sims cheered, Bogart needled her and Capote said, "You can't speak of a member of the script department, and my friend, that way. Come outside." Bogart couldn't stop laughing as he followed Truman out. Then Truman stuck one foot behind Bogie, punched him first, then pushed him down, and sat on him. "Bogie was still laughing as Truman got him by the ears and starting banging his head," Sims said. "There was no way that Bogie was going to hit Truman. The next day we had to put special makeup on him because he'd cut his lip."

"John loved the fact that Capote and Bogie had a fight," Jeanie Sims said. "He put Bogie on his ass," Huston said, laughing. "He was a little bull." But what most impressed John was when Capote's face swelled up because of an impacted wisdom tooth and he had to be taken to a hospital. "That night," John said, "six pages came back to me that he had written in the hospital. That was typical of Truman."

Then Huston suffered a back injury and had to be carried down the steps to see a doctor. "I was right in the middle of bragging to Bogie that I was as good a man as when I was eighteen," he recalled, "and I leaned over to pick up a box of matches on the floor and my hipbone severed a vein in the back and it began to swell, a big blood blister came up. Jesus Christ, did it hurt! I couldn't walk and the doctor had to draw the blood out."

Toward the end of the picture John was getting anxious to leave so he could meet Suzanne Flon in Paris. Jack Clayton said that he got the last page of the script on the last day of shooting. "He did rush to finish," Angela Allen noted. "He was always like that, but on this one, we said, 'That doesn't make any sense what we are doing at the end.' Didn't matter; he just wanted to finish it." "He shot five days on the last day in a flurry of activity," Robert Morley said. "Then at four o'clock he got in his car and went back to Paris and Suzanne."

Most of the people who knew John believed, like Jeanie Sims, that Suzanne was "the love of his life, the only one who never irritated him." "He really was very much in love with her," Ossie Morris said. "He bought her a lot of very valuable paintings. I thought he was crazy, because Ricki was a super girl." Jack Clayton, also, was partial to Ricki, who he felt had that "very natural American charm. Within one minute of meeting you, you felt at home. They should really have never got married." John felt closer to Suzanne Flon "than to anyone on this earth," and acknowledged that he never felt that way about Ricki. "We were not good friends. We were always well-behaved. But it was impossible with Ricki."

What made it impossible was John's inability to stay faithful to one woman. The pattern of his relationships had been set from the time his mother would leave him to follow a story and continued through every marriage and every affair. "I regret that lack within myself that enables a man to pour all his affections into one individual," he candidly admitted.

Thinking that Suzanne might be the woman he would like to spend the rest of his life with, John told her that he would try to free himself from his marriage. "A divorce was contemplated," he said.

Ricki, in Courtown, had her hands full trying to raise two small children and deal with Pablo, whom she warned, "You know how John is, one day he is going to dump you." Pablo was "shocked" and "didn't pay much attention," because he felt that Ricki never liked him. Later he realized that "she was trying to protect me, to wise me up as to what would be my outcome."

Ricki's warning had come after she received his progress report from the principal of Rosse College in Dublin, a business school where Pablo had been enrolled. Before Huston had left to make *Beat the Devil*, his lawyer, Mark Cohen, informed him that a petition of adoption had been prepared for Pablo and that Pablo "must return to the U.S. in

May because his re-entry permit expires at that time. Also, in June, he will be 18 and will be required to register for the draft." John never officially adopted Pablo and delayed sending him back until he completed his schooling. He had arranged for him to study with two tutors and at Rosse. But Pablo wasn't a good student and Ricki knew, when she read the principal's report, that John would not be pleased.

It's doubtful that Ricki forwarded this report to John, who, two months later, on May 30, wrote about Pablo to Walter's widow, Nan, from his office at the British Lion Studios. "Pablo has been over here just a year," he wrote, "and in this time he has been with two tutors . . . and in a business school in Ireland for a short course. He knows the Greek classics—philosophers, playwrights and poets—far better than do most American University graduates . . . I must say that I am wonderfully well pleased with Pablo's development. He is as straight and honest as anybody can be. I'd stake my neck on it that he wouldn't tell a lie in his own interests and, by the same token, he is quite incapable of an underhanded action. He is extraordinarily good and open-hearted. . . . The main thing I can say against Pablo is that he is a terrible Good Time Charlie. I suppose this is largely due to the fact that, throughout his early childhood, he knew only deprivation and sorrow. . . . He thinks, and I think, too, that he should go into some agricultural pursuit, with a view finally to returning to Mexico and owning his own ranch." John would soon send Pablo back to California to attend Pierce College, an agricultural school, for a year.

When the cast and crew of *Beat the Devil* returned to London, Robert Morley cabled John Woolf: "We have now returned to our capital and we hope that yours will return to you. But we doubt it." The actors weren't sure what they had on film. Huston thought it was funny but none of the producers were laughing. Woolf fretted over how badly overbudget they had gone and couldn't understand, "to this day, why we didn't make it in color, except we may have been short of money." Huston, too, came around to believe that "it might have been a better picture in color." And David Selznick was *convinced* that his wife would have benefited. He told Huston, "She is far more beautiful in color and also looks younger." But it was too late to consider what might have been. The film in the can was in black and white.

At Shepperton, John left most of the editing to Jack Clayton. "He used to come in for a few days," Clayton said, "but he was bored. I don't think he ever *lost* interest—you can't be a genius like he was and not have an editor's mind—but John was a visual director and not an editing director. He was, in no way, the kind of director who sought his film in the cutting room. He either got it on the screen or he didn't."

One of John's diversions while in London was renewing—or trying to renew—his old passion for Olivia de Havilland, who was passing through the city on her way back from the Cannes Film Festival. She had had a child, been through a divorce, and no longer felt hatred for John. "I just felt irrational," she said. "There was simply no possibility of this relationship growing. Old passions were stirred, certainly, but the situation was impossible again because he had married again, and had two children. There was no room for me."

Another woman from his past, Doris Lilly, had discovered Europe and John found the accounts of her exploits amusing. "John knew I was getting around a lot and I wasn't really interested in him, quite frankly. See, when he should have gotten me was before I knew what it was all about. But I knew that he was screwing all his secretaries, that he had a big thing with Suzanne Flon, that Ricki hated him, that he demolished people. He was definitely the most unforgettable and striking character I've ever known, but he still scared me. It's like an angel with a gun in his pocket. As rotten as John was, he knew how to make converts. You either loved him or you hated him, but there was no one remotely like him, except, maybe, Lucifer."

In June John received a letter from Bogart asking if *Beat the Devil* had any chance of making back its cost. "It's more difficult for me to come to any opinion about it than any picture I've ever done," John wrote back. "It wasn't at all the kind of picture it started out to be. Veiller and Viertel conceived it as melodrama, but the finished article is comedy—and rather broad comedy at that. . . . However, if the humor comes off, as I pray it will, I believe it will make some very tidy sums. . . . On the other hand, if the jokes should fall flat, well, God help us."

Viertel and Veiller read the final Capote/Huston draft and waived any claim for screen credit.

John returned to Ireland to spend time with his children and see what Ricki thought about a divorce. According to Pablo, Ricki had begun establishing a life of her own. "She was seeing Sadrik Khan, the brother of Aly Khan," he said, but it wasn't serious enough for her to jump at John's offer. "She was upset about Suzanne Flon," Dorothy Soma observed. "That was the beginning of the end." Although they had been separated for three months John and Ricki agreed to spend the summer apart—she in Portofino, he in Paris and then meeting Billy Pearson in Rome—to give her some time to think.

Before they parted, however, they experienced a frightening moment that forced them to look beyond themselves. Tony narrowly escaped death when he fell off his pony and his foot got caught in the stirrup. "His scalp was practically torn off," Anjelica remembered, as she watched in horror with her nanny as her three-year-old brother came trotting out of the woods, the groom by his side, when the pony bolted. "He was dragged all the way up the driveway to the front door where the pony stopped, shivering. My father and mother came out of the house immediately. It was serious stuff. Tony was taken to the hospital and came back with a white bandage wrapped around his head."

At Courtown Anjelica had had her share of accidents as well. Once she fell over Rosie, the dog, and scarred herself. Another time she stuck her finger in a lawn mower and had a piece of it chopped off. There was also a clothes wringer, where she experimented with a washcloth and screamed in pain when her arm got caught up to the shoulder in the wringer.

Anjelica's other memories of that time are of her father "striding up and down in a meeting," of helping her mother "button up the back of her dress as she was going downstairs to a party," and of "a very large, intricate doll's house belonging to the owner's daughter, which I wasn't allowed to touch." But what she remembered most was the loneliness of not having many preschool playmates. "There weren't a lot of other children. You just didn't drop over to someone's house. It was an expedition."

Jeanie Sims observed that when the children were young John seemed to favor Tony, although Tony recalled that his father found children boring and never knew how to play with them. "Once he did try to spend the whole day with me," Tony said. "He was making a model airplane and said, 'I wonder if it will ever get off the ground.' Well, by the end of the day I'd asked him that at least a hundred times. Then we went up to the top of the house and he flew the airplane and it went straight down. Never got off the ground!"

The house John rented in Paris was near where Willy and Talli Wyler were staying, and Huston invited his old friend to see a rough cut of *Beat the Devil.* "John," Wyler said, "I think you better make another film."

Bogart became worried after he screened the film for a select audience of friends. They all "felt confused after the first ten minutes," he wired Huston. "Could not tell whether straight melodrama or comedy. We all think picture needs something to set mood. Have you any suggestions?"

Bogart's concern and Wyler's remark planted strong doubts about the chances the film would have when released, and John told a reporter for the *Empire News* in England that he wanted his name removed from the film. "Don't get me wrong," he said, "I like the film, but it's not my usual style and may be misleading to the public. It's not for one moment intended to be taken seriously."

His remarks were taken *very* seriously by John Woolf, who wrote Huston a note: "The papers pick up pretty well everything you say. If you would be kind enough not to give them any ammunition which they would be likely to use to the effect that you yourself do not think too highly of the film, I would be much obliged, as we all have so much at stake."

John obviously didn't feel he had as much at stake as the producers, especially since the money was coming in from *Moulin Rouge* and he'd made a bundle from directing and co-writing *Beat the Devil*. When he ran into Bill Mauldin in Paris and Mauldin asked him if he'd gotten himself out of debt, John answered, "I've not only got all my debts paid, I don't have to worry the rest of my life. I've got a million dollars, free and clear. I don't even have to work again." They were on their way to the races when he gave this exaggerated accounting and Mauldin asked him how much money he had in his pocket. John told him ten thousand dollars. "You're going to take that to the races?" Mauldin asked. "Do you have any idea what the income from a million dollars is? If you invested carefully, it might be twenty-five thousand a year; if you invested wisely, you might get fifty thousand. You blow that *in a week* sometimes!" When it dawned on John that he couldn't live his life-style on the interest of a million dollars he mumbled, "Oh, shit." And then went and pissed away the money he had at the races.

Huston left Paris to meet Billy Pearson in Rome. They planned to head off into the Umbrian hills, traveling to Orvieto, Assisi, then into Tuscany, to Siena, and up to Florence. They had talked about such a trip, feasting on the great works of Italian art and architecture, for five years. Pearson had a surprisingly devoted interest in art, and a photographic memory for the names and dates of the most obscure paintings.

In Rome, Pearson had just over $15,000 with him and spent it all on a
Ferrari before John arrived. Huston was impressed when he saw the car,
and they hired a cab to lead them to the autostrada and point them in
the direction of Orvieto. Two hours outside of Rome they stopped for
lunch. "We got into the wine," Pearson remembered, "then got back
into the car and John asked, 'What if you had your choice of any three
art objects, what would you take?' " Before Billy could answer John
decided they should flip a coin to decide who got first choice. John won
and chose the *Pieta of Avignon* in the Louvre. "I fucking near drove the
car right off the road," Pearson exclaimed. "I said, 'Jesus Christ, John!
You *know* that the *Pieta* is my favorite art object in the world.' " To
retaliate Pearson chose what he knew was John's favorite: Rembrandt's
Nightwatch. "You fucker!" John said. "When you saw that painting you
didn't like it. It's *mine*!" Pearson just smiled and John said, "Well, fuck
you. I take the *Assyrian Lion Hunt* in the British Museum." Billy
slammed on the brakes. "He knew that was my second greatest thing in
the world. I threw his bag out of the car and yelled, 'This is *my* fucking
car, get out, sonofabitch!' And I left him standing on the road with his
bag. Didn't see him again for almost a year. When I asked him why he
had taken the Avignon *Pieta* as his first choice he said, 'Well, my
thought was that you were going to come up with some great thing and
that I could use it for a trade.' He was gonna *trade* it!"

While John was left stranded on an Italian road two hundred miles
north of Rome, Bill Mauldin was visiting Ricki and the children in
Portofino. Tony had recovered from his pony accident but then had
another one. "We were on a boat," he remembered, "and I leaned over
the side. Everyone kept telling me not to do that and I fell in. It was
sort of pleasant, I didn't mind. I was fished out by my mother."
Mauldin said Ricki treated him "like a long lost friend. She was really
mad then. She said, 'The only thing I can think of to fix the sonofabitch:
I won't give him a divorce!' "

John had said it was her decision, and she had made up her mind.
Although her father thought she *should* divorce John, keep his name,
and go on to become a great star in her own right, her brother believed
that Ricki thought "she was better off being the separated wife of John
Huston instead of the divorced wife of John Huston." It didn't matter
to Dorothy Soma that John fooled around, "husbands *do* that! I don't
know how any woman could say that marriage to John Huston was a
mistake."

After Ricki made her decision John began to realize that it was the right one. Ricki now knew where she stood, they didn't have to play any games, they could be free to go their own way and still maintain the appearance of a marriage for the children's sake. But coming to accept their relationship put him in a vulnerable position. He began to worry that Ricki might change her mind. In the fall he was briefly in New York and he visited Dorothy. "What's the matter with you?" she asked. "I'm afraid Ricki is going to divorce me and take the children," John answered. Dorothy asked if he wanted her to go over to talk with Ricki. John said he'd buy her a ticket. Dorothy needed a week to get ready.

"He never wanted a divorce," Dorothy said. "He wanted the protection of marriage, like a lot of men do. And that would give him freedom to play around." When Dorothy arrived in Ireland she found Ricki "restless and unhappy. She lived in a world of expectations. She was a greedy girl. Not for money but for attention. She wanted everything. I tried to talk to her about John's always being with other women. 'If you were smart,' I said, 'you'd never let any of them back you into a corner!' "

"Oh, Ma," Ricki answered, "you've never had these experiences. You don't know anything about it."

What was there to know? Dorothy wondered. "John liked women if they did their job of being women, otherwise he didn't have much use for them. Huston was a free soul. He had to be allowed to soar. I was all for him. I could never understand all those women who tried to change him. If you choose to marry a man who has a history of other women, and you have any intelligence at all, you know you are *not* going to change him. You can adapt to him. And if you've got any sense that's what you *do!* Or you don't marry him!"

What kept John and Ricki together for the next seven years was the discovery of a run-down, three-story estate in Galway that Ricki visited when she went out to attend a race meeting. It was made of stone and was surrounded by 110 acres of land. The roof leaked, the floors were gone, there were ruins on the property, along with a trout stream, stables, and smaller cottages. It was called St. Clerans and was owned by the Land Commission. Ricki told John about it and they decided to buy it at an auction for £10,000. It was a huge undertaking that would take two years to restore, but it allowed them to focus their combined energies on creating what would become one of the more intriguing houses in Ireland.

It was an exciting prospect and the purchase allowed Huston to look toward the future just when the box office closed down on his latest release. The reviews of *Beat the Devil* were surprisingly positive. The newspapers in England called it an "unadulterated joy . . . one of those pictures you want to see again." "John Huston's worst film—but it is still ten times more diverting than the conveyor-belt pieces turned out by lesser directors." *Time* magazine thought it was "as elaborate a shaggy-dog story as has ever been told . . . A sort of screwball classic." *The New Yorker* praised it as "a hugely entertaining work . . . a satire on melodramas dealing with international intrigue. . . . The whole affair is marked by an easy spontaneity, and every now and then it flashes with a kind of bright lunacy that used to be a conspicuous virtue of Evelyn Waugh. Logic is hardly a requirement of a picture as carefree as this one."

Film historian Eugene Archer considered the movie "a parody within a parody, a private joke, amusing to the initiated, incomprehensible to the uninformed. . . . It is a film for connoisseurs, who treasure it highly—most highly, perhaps, because it is valueless for the layman."

Thirty-four years after its release, *Los Angeles Times* critic Charles Champlin would call *Beat the Devil* his favorite Huston film, claiming to have seen it thirty times and quoting that "lovely speech of Peter Lorre's: 'Time, time, what is it? The Swiss manufacture it, the French hoard it, Italians want it, Americans say it's money, Hindus say it does not exist. You know what I say? I say time is a crook.' " Champlin felt that "In its rather quirky way it's about loyalty, and loyalty is a major theme that runs through so much of Huston's work, from *The Maltese Falcon* forward. It is also a celebration of rascals, lowlifes, underdogs and born losers who didn't always lose more eloquently and fondly than John Huston did." Champlin said that he had once met Jennifer Jones and told her his favorite among all of her roles was the crazy blonde in *Beat the Devil* and, "She smiled thinly and said, 'When Johnny was persuading me to do it, he said, "Jennifer, they'll remember you longer for *Beat the Devil* than for *The Song of Bernadette*." I think the SOB was right.' "

By the time Champlin made his observations *Beat the Devil* had been securely ensconced in the category of cult classic, but at its release audiences weren't prepared for an irrational, tongue-in-cheek comedy by John Huston. Letters from irate moviegoers began pouring in. "If I may speak frankly," one said, "it is pictures like this which is ruining the industry." Another wrote, "My wife and I, my mother and my cousin, went in to see *Beat the Devil*. It should have been called *Beat the Customer*. What a lemon! So incoherent! So lousy! We were in there exactly thirty minutes and walked out disgusted." From the Bronx: "You could have used a gun just as well to take our money." From a theater manager: "What an awful show . . . couldn't understand how Huston directed such a picture and Capote wrote it and Bogart played in it. It should go down as a freak picture in the Museum of Modern Art."

Huston regretted that Bogart never lived to see how the picture became one of the first "underground" films. When it first appeared he was all too aware "it was generally conceded to be a minor disaster, frivolous, self-indulgent, at a time when such qualities were not accepted."

From frivolity and high-camp Huston next turned to the most difficult story he ever attempted to put on film, the picture he had most wanted to make when he first considered becoming a director: *Moby Dick.* The story of one man's obsession to destroy a force larger than himself. John was sixteen when he first read Herman Melville's epic and believed it to be, alongside Mark Twain's *Huckleberry Finn,* America's greatest novel. It was a picture he and his father had often talked about doing, with Walter as Captain Ahab. Warner Bros. agreed to put up some money in return for worldwide distribution rights. The Mirisch brothers went into partnership with Warner's and poured their profits from *Moulin Rouge* into completing the financing of *Moby Dick.*

Over the years Huston had writers attempt a script, but each time they failed to achieve the grace and poetry of the book. Tony Veiller had been the last to try, but after his failure with *Beat the Devil* John never even read the seventy-five pages Veiller wrote.

"My mother said that that broke my father's heart," said Veiller's son, Bayard. "John was a living presence in our house; we talked about him all the time. But when it came to *Moby Dick* John replaced my father with Ray Bradbury. I don't know why."

Bradbury turned out to be a mystery to Huston. The writer had written him fan letters, sent him copies of his books, asked to work with him. John had liked his stories and remembered the poetry of his writing, saw "something of Melville's elusive quality in his work." He decided to give Bradbury a chance and invited him to Ireland; Bradbury, who had a fear of flying, crossed the Atlantic by ship. On his way over he read *Moby Dick* and wrote an opening scene. He saw Ahab as "the most American character in all our literature, who says, 'I will deal with the universe on the terms which it presents to me—death, annihilation, mystery, afflictions, paradoxes, evil. I would strike against it.'

He works against nature to survive." He would read the book eight more times, write thirty outlines and twelve hundred pages over seven months before he produced his final draft, and by then his opinion of the director he had so admired had altered radically, as had Huston's of him.

"Ray is the best argument I know of for those who believe that Hal Croves was B. Traven," Huston noted. "He's a mass of contradictions. Sending someone to Vega or to other constellations is a commonplace with Ray, but when I knew him he didn't want to get on an airplane, wouldn't ride in a fast car. He's a gifted man but a bore beyond description. There's also a monster there, too. I remember Ray talking about his love for his children and what he'd do to anyone who kidnapped them, how he would tear them to pieces. And he began to enjoy it, defending his children. He's that kind of a monster."

Evelyn Keyes was told that Bradbury had "worshiped" John, and that when he was first with him "he couldn't move, he was so awestruck." Of course, said Keyes, the minute you did that "John would let you have it." When he managed to compose himself, Bradbury asked Huston, "What kind of script do you want? Are you a Freudian? A Jungian? A Melville Society man?" John swallowed his drink and motioned away such nonsense. "I want Ray Bradbury's *Moby Dick*," he said.

Bradbury's problem was that he still didn't know what Huston wanted and for months he would agonize over it, bringing pages for John to read, feeling deflated when John kept poking holes in his logic. "I saw in Huston the same confusion I suffered," he said. "We were way out over our heads. He didn't know where we wanted to go. We were both children, hoping somehow to blunder through."

"He would try to get Huston's attention," Ernie Anderson remembered, "always asking him to please look at his stuff. John would be standing at the bar in the foyer of his house making a dry martini. He would ask him why Ahab would say what Bradbury had written. 'There's got to be some reason *why* he said that, it can't just be something you made up to put in there. It's got to grow. See you later, Ray.' I don't think Huston was cruel; he was trying to prompt him. Every writer who ever worked with Huston got the same treatment."

Jeanie Sims, who was now John's production assistant because Huston had brought over a new secretary named Lorrie Sherwood, felt that Bradbury and Huston "were chalk and cheese. Bradbury's a sweet man with the most marvelous imagination, but he's very naive. He is basically a small-town American. And John was one of the great eccentrics, the last of the swashbucklers. Ray was exactly the opposite.

It was very easy to prick the bubble of his pride. He has such a big ego, you had to keep pumping it up to work with him. And John wasn't about to do that. He was the one with the needle."

Lorrie Sherwood, who had once worked for Howard Hawks, was there as John's secretary during the whole time Bradbury worked on the script. At first, she said, "they worked together beautifully." But after Bradbury refused to fly with him to Paris, John's attitude changed. "When John found a weakness," Sherwood said, "baby, you were in trouble, because he'd rub your nose in it. But I blame nobody but John for what happened." John had found a way to goad Bradbury and took full advantage of it. He and Betty O'Kelly, a great horsewoman who became Huston's estate manager, were in the car with Bradbury while Sherwood was driving. John was sitting up front and suggested that Lorrie not drive so fast. She was only going thirty-five miles an hour, but O'Kelly picked up on it and began telling her to slow down. Believing she was speeding, Bradbury began to panic. "Lorrie," he stammered, "please don't . . . Lorrie!" Finally Sherwood stopped the car and shouted at John, "You know damn well I'm not doing it." By then Bradbury was a bundle of nerves and John was delighted that Betty had gone along with him. "I found their treatment of Ray so stupid," Sherwood said. "So the man's afraid of going fifty miles an hour, what's wrong with that?"

The Bradbury-baiting continued until the writer's confidence was badly shaken. At one point, when Ray was blocked, Huston told him that Jack Warner wanted to include a love interest for Ahab, sex the script up a bit. Of course it was a joke, but Bradbury wasn't laughing any longer. It did serve to help snap him out of his blockage and one morning, while he was in London, he got out of bed, looked in the mirror, and said, "I am Herman Melville!" And over the next eight hours he rewrote the last third of the script. "The ghost of Melville was in me," he said. "I ran across London to Huston's hotel and I threw the script at him. 'There! I think that's it!' And he read it and said, 'Jesus Christ, Ray! This is it. This is the way we'll shoot the ending.'

"My inspiration was to have Moby Dick take Ahab down and wind him in the coiled ropes and bring him up among the harpoons on this great white bier, this great cortege, this funeral at sea. Then we see, 'My God, these two should be together forever through eternity, shouldn't they—Ahab and the white whale?' It's not in the book, but I do believe that Melville would have approved."

With the script finally finished, as far as he was concerned anyway, Bradbury was ready to take his family back to the States. Before he left, though, Huston so upset him that he was never able to bring himself to talk about the man he once so admired. Ray attended a dinner John gave at the White Elephant Restaurant, along with twenty other people, many from *Beat the Devil*—Truman Capote, Humphrey Bogart and Lauren Bacall, Gina Lollobrigida and her husband. Jeanie Sims and Jack Clayton were also there, and so was John's *Key Largo* writer, Richard Brooks. "John was in one of those moods," Brooks recalled. "He started to pick on everybody at the table, one at a time, like a gunman taking them on. Number one was Ray Bradbury. 'You're the fellow who writes about going to Mars, but you don't fly. How do you write that shit? Don't you find it inconsistent?'

"This went on until he had Ray in tears. Peter Viertel had to take him outside. Then John started on Bogie and Betty and their politics. Then Lollobrigida with her phony doctor husband and 'with all your beauty you're probably a lousy lay.' Everything was personal and he knew something about each one which was not so much a weakness as a soft spot. He got everybody, including Capote, and most of them were weeping. It was a rough evening; he was brutal. He started on me, I was the man who wasn't going to have a foreign car or a swimming pool or wear a suit, and, of course, I had them all by then. But I was one of the few who wasn't crying, which Capote never forgot. Then, like Beethoven's 'Sixth,' the storm blew over. Suddenly it was all peaceful. It was like a devil was inside him and he had to get it out of the dark recesses of his brain."

Outside the restaurant, when Huston was sitting in his limousine with Lorrie Sherwood, Bradbury returned. "John said something to him," Sherwood related, "and Bradbury leaned in and hit him! It was just a culmination of things and, finally, the man hit back. John was rather proud of Ray for doing it. If Ray had kicked him in the balls three months earlier, their relationship might have been different!"

When asked to reflect upon this time Bradbury demurred. Acknowledging that he was "deeply grateful to him for changing my life, only for the good forever, by giving me the job of writing *Moby Dick*," Bradbury still couldn't put aside the humiliations he suffered. "I can't see how I can talk about Huston," he said. "Any personal discussion might turn into sour grapes . . . so I had best not even get started."

Perhaps Bradbury thought he took some of the acid out of those grapes when he wrote about Huston in a half-hour cable TV drama for his "Ray Bradbury's Theatre." Called "Banshee," Bradbury told a radio interviewer, "A lot of the dialogue is right out of John Huston's mouth." The story was about a writer like himself, who had rewritten a script for a cynical, diabolical, practical joke–playing director who lived in a stone mansion in the Irish countryside. The director, whose name is John and whose initials are J.H., was played by Huston's friend and former Irish neighbor, Peter O'Toole. He greets the writer by the door with a drink in hand, saying, "Get this in ya, kid." Then he condescendingly takes the script and drops the pages one by one to the floor as he reads. Then, just as Huston apparently reacted when Bradbury gave him the last third of the script, he says, "Damn you to hell, I think I hate you. It's good."

With that pronouncement there is a howling outside. The writer imagines it's the wind but the director knows better. It's the banshee: "Spirits of women who roam the woods the night someone is to die." He then proceeds to make the writer as uncomfortable as he can, asking him, "Ever wonder how many women I've had? Hundreds." He reads a review of the writer's work, adding nasty comments, and when the writer tries to see for himself, the director throws the paper into the fire.

"John, for God's sake, what's wrong with you?" the writer asks. (How many times must Bradbury have wanted to pose that question?) "I did it to get your goat," John says. The wind howls again and the director challenges the writer to go outside. "Are you coward, kid?"

The writer takes up the challenge and goes out. The director closes and bolts the door, then shouts from a window, "Don't be yellow, kid." Out in the woods the writer sees a beautiful woman dressed in white. She's from a nearby cemetery and has been waiting for her "Willy" all these years. Her Willy is also her Johnny. "He wipes his hand on flesh, girls are his napkins, women his midnight feast," she says, asking the writer to send her Willy/Johnny out, so she can lie with him and never get up.

The writer returns to the house and tells his story. The director then goes out, even though the writer warns him that he will probably meet his death. The writer waits, listens. He hears someone coming back, there is a knocking, then a pounding on the door. But the writer is too scared to open it. He moves away and listens until the pounding ceases.

The scene immediately switches to Bradbury, sitting at his typewriter. "That's enough for today," he says. And then he laughs—a hollow, wicked, self-satisfied last laugh. Bradbury, who was subjected to Huston's jokes, called a coward for his phobias, finally found his revenge: leaving J.H. to the mercy of the spirits of women who were once his midnight feast!

*   *   *

While in Ireland, Bradbury was obviously aware of the intricate web of relationships that entwined Huston's life. Married to Ricki, off on weekends to Paris to be with Suzanne, out riding with Betty O'Kelly, locked up in his study with Jeanie Sims or Lorrie Sherwood—one didn't need the fertile imagination Bradbury possessed to get an idea of the bacchanalian life Huston was living. Jeanie Sims, who had to share a room with Sherwood on location for Moby Dick, didn't think much of John's new secretary. "I didn't like her from the beginning. She was very pushy and tried to edge me out."

That's what others thought about Sherwood, which didn't surprise her, because there was a "tremendous amount of jealousy" going on. Sims remembered a story about Lorrie and John that appeared in Confidential magazine, which Sims felt sure Sherwood herself had planted, "since there was only one person it could have come from, because journalists liked John and didn't print stories of his little flirts, and they also liked Ricki and didn't want to hurt her." As Sherwood asserted herself, Sims began to feel that John had outgrown his need for her and she began working for Ernie Anderson, doing publicity.

Even after he began filming Moby Dick John would still fly to Paris to see Suzanne whenever there was a few days' delay. During the last week of May 1954 he and Suzanne had dinner with Anne Selepegno and Tola Litvak, whom she was working for. Robert Capa had also joined them. He had been in the Orient, first in Japan, then in Laos and French Indochina, where he was returning to cover the war between the French and the Viet Minh forces. Huston was always eager to hear Capa's war stories, enjoying his company as they drank and played poker into the night. Selepegno remembers that later, on their way to Switzerland, she and Litvak stopped in Milan, where they saw Huston, who was "white as a sheet," talking to someone. "Don't talk to me now," he said when she approached. And then he told her that Bob Capa had been killed after stepping on a mine along the road to Thaibinh in Indochina. It wasn't a death he took lightly, and he was thankful he had Moby Dick to occupy his thoughts and cover his grief.

After Bradbury departed John employed two other writers: Roald Dahl and John Godley, Lord Kilbracken. Dahl worked on the script for three weeks "to work on the problem of how to make Ahab appear to be satanic to the crew at first, before he wins them over," Huston said.

"He wrote something and gave it to me, but it didn't come to anything. It was one of the key scenes, the very heart of the story, where Starbuck goes to Ahab and explains why the crew thinks it's an unholy quest. God, I worked on this! Ray Bradbury didn't have an answer. Neither did Dahl. But it had to be there. That the crew thought it was devilish in its intent. Finally, one day in Ireland, driving in the car, it hit me: The crew were mostly Quakers. What was oil for? To furnish light to the dark places of the earth, where people could read scripture after the day's work. It was bringing God to the world. And to leave a pod of whales and pursue one whale out of vengeance, was a sacrilege. It was this idea that made the scene. I wrote it myself. It's a good scene, too. It's not in Melville at all."

John Godley first met Huston at Lugalla in 1952 and found it "difficult not to be aware of him," as he was dressed in a black riding jacket, canary waistcoat, tan breeches, riding boots, and top hat. At a Christmas party Godley heard Huston sing a traditional Irish song "in a high authentic Irish accent . . . his head cocked to one side and his eyes either tightly closed or fixed on the ceiling." On that occasion John wore a green velvet tuxedo and slippers embroidered with gold foxes. Originally Godley was asked to read for the part of Ishmael, but after Richard Basehart was chosen, he was asked to work on the screenplay under the condition that he would receive no screen credit.

In his memoir, *Living Like a Lord,* Godley wrote that "Huston, to work with, is the epitome of quixotry, unpredictability, inconsistency, and volatility. He is one of those men of fantastic personal magnetism and charm who can behave completely outrageously, and then, with a smile and a gesture, make one again instantly devoted to him. He is also a man of real genius . . . responsible for all that matters in every single department of every movie he directs. In his moments of inspiration, one stands aghast at his virtuosity. Yet, at times, he makes errors of judgment, of taste, of understanding, so gross that one feels it cannot be the same man."

Godley worked during the last third of the film and described frustrating days of trying to get to see Huston, who was always too busy to give him much time. Huston became, for him, "the image of Moby Dick."

Ernie Anderson said that after working with John for nearly ten weeks Godley finally couldn't take it anymore. "He saw the *Pequod* coming back to port and he ran down to the railroad station, got on a train, and that was the last we saw of him. The rest of it, Huston wrote."

The writing credits for *Moby Dick* listed Bradbury and Huston. Bradbury felt John's name didn't belong on *his* script and took Huston to arbitration by the Writers Guild. Lorrie Sherwood had kept copies of every version of the various scripts and was able to help prove that Huston's contribution was worthy of credit. "John always worked with his writers," Sherwood said. "He rewrote *Moby Dick* as we went along." Ernie Anderson went so far as to question Bradbury's final contribution. "His name really shouldn't be on it," he felt.

Huston's fascination with *Moby Dick* had to do with its multiple levels of ambiguity. On the surface it was a hell of an adventure story, depicting one ship's attempt to track down the largest, most terrifying creature on earth. On another level it had to do with the obsession of the ship's captain, seeking to revenge himself against the creature that took his leg in a previous battle. As with *The Maltese Falcon*, *The Treasure of the Sierra Madre*, *The Asphalt Jungle*, and *Beat the Devil*, it was a tale of a motley group of characters engaged in a quest destined to fail. But then, in the realm of symbolism and psychology, *Moby Dick* took on deeper meanings. Some saw the white whale as an all-powerful God and Ahab as a satanic force attempting to destroy it. Others saw just the opposite, that the whale was the devil and Ahab the God who wanted to rid the world of such evil. This is what Huston believed. He noted that no critic of his film ever recognized that the work was "a blasphemy. The message of *Moby Dick* was hate. The whale is the mask of a malignant deity. Melville doesn't choose to call the power Satan, but God."

John saw *Moby Dick* as another opportunity to experiment with color. The look he wanted was the harsh, masculine tones based on the steel engravings of nineteenth-century sailing ships. "We tried to get a black outline, like an etching effect, onto the film," Ossie Morris said. "We gave it to Technicolor to try—of course, now we were the blue-eyed boys—but they couldn't get what we wanted. We were within forty-eight hours of making the film and we hadn't gotten a color process. I had an idea to desaturate the color and then add a gray image to it, which was really a marriage of color and black and white. I asked John what he thought and he said, 'Anything you say, kid. Do what you want.' That was his way of getting the best out of me. He just sat back and relaxed."

Because whale models of various sizes had to be made, John looked for a sketch artist who could draw the kinds of scenes he wanted to capture—from harpooning whales to chasing Moby Dick, where Ahab meets his death. The drawings would be useful in determining which scenes would be shot on the open sea and which in studio-built tanks. Stephen Grimes was painting mat shots for Technicolor in London when John happened to visit the laboratory. He had found the artist he was looking for.

"I did a whole lot of watercolor sketches of the first whale hunt and took them, with some trepidation, to John. He looked and said, 'Yeah, fine, fine, fine.' I discovered later that that was *exactly* what he wanted. He said, 'Don't worry about how anybody is going to get the shots, just do them as you see them.' Grimes was eventually put in charge of the second unit, working with the whale models at the studio.

"We had this huge whale head on a rocker which went up and down in the tank," he said. "It had eyes that actually moved. When you saw the eye it got you into the evil. Quite a good effect. Then we had a huge rubber tail made that was supposed to flap up and down, but we didn't have enough time to make it work very well. We had that pulled by a tug in the open sea, which was hell because the Irish Sea can be very rough." Grimes was also involved in the building of the top half of a ninety-foot whale. It cost $30,000 and was lost in a storm after only two shots. A second whale was built on a barge, but they lost that one, too.

"It became a question of rescuing the men in the boats or the whale," Huston said and laughed. "We allowed sentiment to overcome our better judgment and we saved the men. The picture had to stop while they built a third whale. That winter off the coast of England was one of the worst in history. Lifeboats capsized, the *Pequod* was dismasted three times."

The ship they converted into the *Pequod* had been located, after an extensive search, at Scarborough on the Yorkshire coast, where it was being used as a tourist attraction. It was a hundred-year-old, 104-foot-long, wooden-hulled three-master that Huston modified at an English shipyard. Engines and generators were added, but their sound caused problems during production.

Huston was roundly criticized for casting Gregory Peck as Ahab. Bradbury thought it should have been Laurence Olivier, who had the quality of madness he felt was needed. Stephen Grimes thought it should have been someone like George C. Scott. But Warner's had insisted on Peck, and Huston always defended the choice. "Ahab is anything but the ranting figure he's thought to be by people who haven't read the book," John said. "The figure in the book, and the one I wanted on the screen, was one of great dignity and a marvelous power of expression that's almost biblical. The criticism of Peck was that he looked too much like Lincoln."

Walter Mirisch felt that the comparisons of Peck to Lincoln became a "terrible joke. It was difficult to cast off that image." He thought that Peck was too young to have played Ahab. "I always thought about how really marvelous Walter Huston would have been: his power, age, the weight that he had." Jeanie Sims felt that John was trying to make Peck into Walter. "But Walter was dead," she said, "so John should have been Ahab." Angela Allen agreed: "All the actors responded to him as Captain Ahab. And he was! Gregory Peck would get up there and, for me, it was like watching suet pudding after watching a soufflé." Even Peck himself thought that John would have made a better Ahab than he did. In fact, when Huston had first approached him, Peck figured it was for the role of Starbuck, which would have more suited him. "Later I learned he needed me to finance the production. John wove his spell and convinced me I'd be the ticket as Ahab. . . . But Huston was more Ahab himself than any actor could be. His intense desire to make this picture without any compromise was certainly comparable to Ahab's relentless quest to kill the whale."

When Gottfried Reinhardt visited the set Peck complained to him that John didn't rehearse enough. "Huston was not that great an actor's director," Peck told one writer. "When people were perfectly cast, like Bogart and Lorre and Greenstreet, he was great with them. But he was not very good at helping actors to find a performance. I think that John really didn't have that much respect for the craft of acting. Writers and directors were the people who made the movies, and actors were the people to be dealt with." To another reporter he criticized what little direction Huston gave him: "I remember one scene on which all he said was: 'Feel the camera on your face.' And in the important scene in which I had a long speech beginning, 'If there is a God there must be a malevolent God,' I was told: 'Kid, if you ever deliver the goods this has got to be the time.' Is that direction?"

Ossie Morris didn't think much of Peck as an actor. "He's very slow thinking. If you told Greg a story he would have no reaction. Then, fifteen seconds later, he would suddenly begin to laugh. On one occasion Greg became very difficult, and John did the famous screwing-Gregory-Peck-into-the-ground. Most directors don't like actors to see the rushes because they're so self-centered. John couldn't care less.

Greg came and said, 'John, I'm not very happy with that scene. I would like to reshoot it.' John took no notice. A couple of days later Greg said, 'John, you won't forget about reshooting that scene, will you?' This went on and on and he got under Huston's skin. John finally snapped, 'Greg, not only are you bad in that scene, you're bad in the whole of that sequence. I think we'll reshoot it all.' Greg protested but we reshot five days of material, which cost a fortune. And it wasn't any better; Greg's a very limited actor. But John didn't care."

Orson Welles was cast as Father Mapple and was to deliver a five-minute sermon from the poop-deck pulpit of his church. Lorrie Sherwood noticed how Welles and Huston got along—"like a couple of old con men." Angela Allen was impressed with how Welles was "word perfect." Ossie Morris remembered that "Orson was engaged for two days at a fee of six thousand pounds, which was a horrendously high fee in those days. And he did the whole scene in one day. He told John he'd rewritten the scene, which wasn't exactly the thing you said to Huston when Huston had obviously written the scene. Most directors would have argued with Orson and there'd've been a terrible bust-up. But not Huston. He let Orson do his version, which we shot. Then John said, 'Now, Orson, that was great. Just give me another one. Do it the way it's written in the script.' So he did the other version and, of course, that's the one that's in the film."

For the cannibal Queequeg, John hired Friedrich Ledebur, an old friend, an Austrian count who he knew was a bit down on his luck. But Ossie Morris pointed out, "he didn't tell Friedrich he had to be completely shaved and have all this tattoo stuff put on him. John told him, 'Now Friedrich, I don't want you to be worried, but we're just going to do a little thing to your hair.' And they shaved him completely bald! He had long, lovely flowing locks of hair. He wasn't even allowed to protest. This is what people did for Huston."

The movie was budgeted at $3 million for six months. It took nine months and cost $4.5 million. Walter Mirisch said that *Moby Dick* became "a financial nightmare which consumed all of the profits of *Moulin Rouge.*" The film was shot off the coasts of Ireland, Wales, Portugal, and the Canary Islands, and at each location the weather became a major disturbance. The harbor scenes were shot at Youghal, in the south of Ireland. The harbor was transformed to look like a New

Bedford whaling town and the town was so pleased with their new façade that they made Huston an honorary Freeman. "John could do no wrong," said Kevin McClory, who worked as Huston's assistant. "He strode like a Colossus into Youghal."

For the bit part of the half-crazed soothsayer who prophesied, "You see land where there be no land. . . . And on that day all, all save one, will go down . . . ," John brought over his Tattered Man, Royal Dano. "We were living in what we called a temperance hotel, The Metropol, where you couldn't get a drink," Dano recalled. "A hell of a place to put a company like ours! So we worked it out with the waiters, who'd bring you tea loaded with whiskey."

For the scenes involving the white whale the company moved to Fishguard in Wales. "That's when the real trouble began," Huston noted. What Lorrie Sherwood most remembered was that it got so cold on the sea "you could freeze your *tochis* off." John Godley said that in Fishguard "everything somehow became chaotic." Out on the *Pequod* "there was no semblance of comfort; we *were* at sea in an early nineteenth-century whaler." On good days they were able to shoot about forty *seconds* of film. Gregory Peck told a *Newsweek* reporter that *Moby Dick* was "an impossible picture to make. A ship at sea with scenes on its deck! It was technically impossible—but we did it."

The rough seas and the worsening weather and the need to build a third whale forced the production indoors, where it was decided to spend the next two months doing studio work. But since both Huston and Peck had visa problems and could only work for ninety days in England, it was necessary for them to fly over to Paris every Friday night and return on Monday mornings. "So you couldn't have Greg on a Monday until about twelve o'clock," Morris said, "because he had to be made up. Huston was always buggering off to Paris to see Suzanne. And all that time I was shooting the models. There were these full-scale sections of whale to be built, the mechanics had to be figured out to work the big jaw, and it all had to be planned ahead of time. What was needed was a plan director. But with Huston, that was just a joke, he wasn't organized at all.

"When we finally finished in the studio we had to find somewhere to complete the film. It was mid-winter now and the nearest warm water was in the Canary Islands. So we had to all go down there, where we shot that famous scene where Ahab is roped to the whale and beckons. And the final scene with Richard Basehart on the coffin. Simply because we couldn't do it in England. We'd run out of summer."

·   ·   ·

The waters may have been warmer off the Canary Islands, but the sea was rough and, for a third time, the cable of the metal, wood, and latex whale broke and it almost doomed the picture. It was New Year's Eve 1955, and John knew that "nobody anywhere ever again was going to come up with another white whale." He didn't want to bring in the new year on such an ominous note, so he grabbed a bottle of Scotch, climbed into the whale, and shouted, "Lose this whale and you lose me!" As the rest of the crew looked on in amazement, Kevin McClory and another strong swimmer grabbed the cable and dove down beneath the whale, attempting to connect the cable to a metal ring. "They were at considerable risk," Huston said, "as tons of whale could come down, *wham!* But they did it—saved the whale, saved the picture, saved me!"

To strap Peck to Moby Dick was a complex and risky venture. "We built a side section of the whale on a swivel," Stephen Grimes recalled. The idea was that it could rotate completely in the water like a giant drum. There was a hole in the whale where Peck could put his foot and it was tested by Kevin McClory, who had bravely volunteered "to be the guinea pig," Grimes said. "There was an element of hazard in it," Huston admitted. "It was a shot that a stuntman would usually do, but Greg wanted to do it himself, and it was better for the picture because we could get close-ups." John instructed Peck to keep his eyes wide open when he emerged from the water, with his dead hand beckoning his men to follow him.

"They tied me on and rotated me under the water," Peck said. Huston had saved this scene for last, just in case anything went wrong and Peck accidentally drowned. "The danger was that the contraption might get stuck while he was underwater," John said. "The model was twenty feet in diameter, so Greg was underwater for a good long time each revolution. I got the shot to my satisfaction but Greg said, 'Let's do it again.' I said we didn't need to but he insisted. So we did it again."

Ernie Anderson had no trouble getting press for *Moby Dick*. The media was fascinated with John and expectations were high. *Life* ran three different stories. *Newsweek* had a four-page special report on January 9, 1956, while the film was in the last stages of editing, and said, "If Huston has lived up to his material and his reputation, *Moby Dick* should be one of the great pictures of the decade, if not the century." But before its release, Anderson complained, there was "a big panic going on at Warner Bros., which had just changed hands. The new management thought the picture was a mistake, which is a typical

John, directing *The Asphalt Jungle*, 1949. (© 1950 Loew's Inc.; renewed 1977
Metro-Goldwyn-Mayer, Inc.)

Humphrey Bogart, John, Lauren Bacall on set of *Key Largo*, 1948. (Courtesy of The Academy of Motion Picture Arts and Sciences)

John, Gladys Hill, John Garfield, Jennifer Jones. *We Were Strangers*, 1948. (Photo © Jules Buck)

From left: Cinematographer Russell Metty, John, John Garfield, Peter Viertel, Sam Spiegel (seated), Jules Buck. *We Were Strangers*, 1948. (Courtesy of Jules Buck)

Humphrey Bogart, Katharine Hepburn in *The African Queen*, 1951.

Ricki Soma, eighteen. (Photo by Philippe Halsman.
Life Magazine © Time Inc.)

Suzanne Flon, 1953. (Photo by Studio
Lipnitzki, Paris; courtesy of Suzanne
Flon)

From left: Kevin McClory, John, Truman Capote. *Beat the Devil*, Ravello, Italy, 1953.

John with Angela Allen, his scriptgirl on fourteen pictures. (Courtesy of The Academy of Motion Picture Arts and Sciences)

St. Clerans, near Galway, Ireland, where John lived from the late 1950s to the mid-1970s.

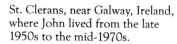

John, Anjelica, Tony. St. Clerans. (Courtesy of John Huston)

From left: Tony, Anjelica, Joan Buck, Marina Habe, Christmas 1959. (Photo © Jules Buck)

Ricki, John, Betty O'Kelly. St. Clerans. (Photo © Jules Buck)

Maka Czernichew and John. They met in Mexico during the making of *The Unforgiven*, 1959. (Courtesy of Maka Czernichew)

Lord John Julius Norwich, father of Ricki's daughter, Allegra. (Times Newspapers Ltd.)

Clark Gable, John. *The Misfits*, 1960. (Photo by Inge Morath, Magnum)

Tony and John. (Photo by Louis Goldman. Courtesy of The Academy of
Motion Picture Arts and Sciences)

John and Tennessee Williams on the set
of *The Night of the Iguana*, Mismaloya
Beach, Puerto Vallarta, 1963. (© 1964
Metro-Goldwyn-Mayer Corporation)

John, Paul Kohner, 1965. Kohner was John's
agent for nearly fifty years, the longest agent/
client relationship in Hollywood history.
(Photo by Frank Shugrue. Courtesy of Paul Kohner
Agency)

Anjelica, John, Tony. (Courtesy of Phillip Soma)

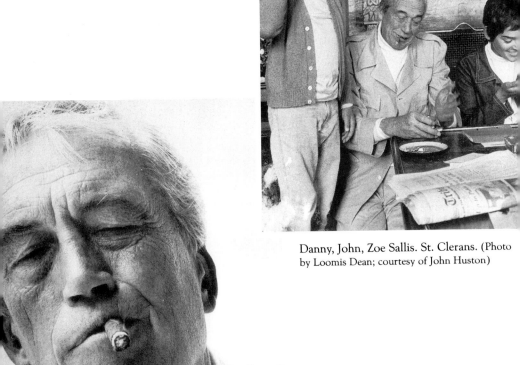

Danny, John, Zoe Sallis. St. Clerans. (Photo by Loomis Dean; courtesy of John Huston)

Hollywood situation. They wanted to squelch the picture. Any artistic stuff . . . get rid of it. They only wanted to see Gregory Peck and pretty girls. The bill posters showed him grinning, without the beard. They had painted it out."

Lorrie Sherwood, who considered the Moby Dick years the best of her life, said that everyone was "devastated at the reception. John was very hurt. He wasn't too well thought of in the Hollywood community, more for his way of life than for his pictures. It was a real back-breaker."

"I thought it would have a big audience," John said. "And one hopes for a film to be universally admired. Not to be considered just an art film. It got the New York Critics Award, but the fact that there wasn't a multitude clambering to see Moby Dick was a great disappointment."

Three decades later John watched the film again on television. "I seldom look at anything of my own a second time," he said. "But I'm unbudged regarding the performance of Peck. There was a kind of massive dignity that he had. That speech where he says to Starbuck, 'It's a vile, vile day.' My God, the voice is just right." After having seen Steven Spielberg's Jaws, Huston recognized where he had gone wrong. "If you made Moby Dick today," he said, "you would take that whale and do things with it that would terrify the audience. I wasn't imaginative to dream of doing what Spielberg and Lucas and those guys do today. All the scenes with the whale should have been far more dramatized. You could hardly see the teeth of our whale. In Jaws you couldn't help seeing anything but the shark's teeth. It was gory, and if you could have had some of that gore and action in Moby Dick, it would have made the film work better. But I settled for literature. It was my failure not seeing it." When it was pointed out to him that the technology didn't exist to create the special effects that appeared in Jaws, Huston waved his hand and said, "It wasn't there because no one invented it. There wasn't a need yet for it. I should have invented it. If I could have another shot at some of my films, I'd like to make the ending of Moby Dick more powerful."

18

UP TO THEIR HEADS

IN 1955, WHILE JOHN WAS STILL EDITING *MOBY DICK*, HE was approached by Harold Mirisch about joining Willy Wyler and Billy Wilder in making films for Allied Artists. It was the company's hope that by hiring notable directors they could compete with the major studios. Wyler had agreed to make *Friendly Persuasion*; Wilder, *Love in the Afternoon*. Huston told Mirisch he had two projects he wanted to develop: *The Man Who Would Be King*, an adventure story by Rudyard Kipling (which Peter Viertel had tried to turn into a screenplay in 1954), and another Melville story, *Typee*. John felt the Kipling story, about two rogues out to seek their fortunes in India and Afghanistan, would make a perfect buddy-buddy vehicle for Humphrey Bogart and Clark Gable. For the Melville tale of a young man's experiences among a primitive tribe on one of the islands of the Marquesas, Huston wanted to cast Gregory Peck again. Allied acquired the rights from the Kipling estate and hired John's *Juarez* collaborator, Aeneas MacKenzie, to write another script. For *Typee* they put on an English writer, Nigel Balchin.

As soon as he was through with *Moby Dick* Huston accepted an invitation from an English friend, Felix Fenston, to go tiger hunting in India, justifying it as location research for the Kipling film. Fenston, who had lost a leg during the war, was "the Donald Trump of real estate in London," John said. "A marvelous, piratical little man who had nothing but contempt for his fellow businessmen. He was also a big-game hunter, which, at that time, wasn't a disgrace."

During preproduction for *Moby Dick* John had gone whale hunting off the Portuguese coast of Madeira. "It was thrilling," he said, "but not as fraught with peril as one might think." While he was there he witnessed salesmen demonstrating the very latest in whale killing: the mechanical harpoon. Huston was to change his mind about the killing of the very beasts he had found so thrilling to shoot or harpoon in a more innocent era. "The next development, of course, was a harpoon that not only fired, but that exploded in the body of the whale. And that's why there are hardly any whales left. I wouldn't kill a whale now any more than I'd kill a tiger."

But in 1955, Huston had no such qualms about sitting in a howdah on top of an elephant, firing a bullet into the heart and brain of an eight-foot female tiger running a hundred yards away from him. The hunt, organized by the Maharaja of Cooch Behar, was an event that thrilled Huston's sense of drama. Five domestic buffalo were used as bait over a twelve-square-mile area. When a tiger killed one, thirty elephants were assembled to lead the way into the jungle as Huston, Fenston, and one other hunter tried to still their beating hearts so their aim would be steady. Huston kept a journal of the hunt in which he described his first glimpse of a tiger as "yellow-and-black flashes against the green backdrop of the jungle." As the beaters pounded the ground and the elephants trumpeted when they picked up the scent, Huston wrote that "for sheer suspense and spectacle, I've never seen or heard anything like it."

After the hunt Huston toured India, from the splendor of the Maharaja of Jaipur's palace to the squalor of Calcutta and the mosquito-infested city of Cochin. He then went to Nepal and Afghanistan before returning to Ireland with old bronzes, exotic fabrics, and new stories to tell his children. Anjelica's memory of her father at this time was that he always smelled of tobacco. "I loved the smell of cigarettes growing up. I remember his height and how I always held onto his legs below his knees. And his voice . . . laying my ear against his chest, listening to him sing. There was a warmth about him."

They lived in what they called the Little House, which was like an English country house. Anjelica and Tony shared one of the three upstairs bedrooms; downstairs was a living room, guardian room, and a general washing area. It was only little in comparison to the Big House, which was still being restored. Inside, where limestone was discovered under the white plaster, rooms that had been subdivided were returned to their former grandeur. "It was a particularly dreadful time in Galway," Ernie Anderson said, "and about the only work there was that house. He had about forty people working on it."

Along with the Kipling and Melville projects Huston was also thinking of making a film with Suzanne Flon about Joan of Arc, called *The Lark*, and another with Marilyn Monroe and Laurence Olivier, *The Sleeping Prince*. He even had an idea to direct four ninety-minute live television shows, among them Aristophanes's *Lysistrata* and a version of one of his father's more memorable movies, *The Devil and Daniel Webster*. But when it looked as if *Typee* might be ready before any of these others, John convinced Allied Artists that a location trip to Tahiti was in order.

Stephen Grimes was working as a sketch artist for Disney in London when John called and offered him the job of art director. Ossie Morris was to be the cinematographer; Gus Lohman, who worked on *Moby Dick*, was the special effects man, and a man named Harry Templeton, who knew of Huston by reputation, was made the American production manager. "At the mere mention of the words 'Working for Huston,' Templeton hit the bottle," Morris recalled. "Then another strange man appeared, named Don Beach. We found out he was Don the Beachcomber, who owned all these restaurants. John was taking him out to Tahiti with us. I asked Harry Templeton, in between bouts of inebriation, why Beach was coming along. 'Oh, he's going to set up the catering for John.' Now that had to be a joke, because John wouldn't bother about catering."

Before John left he stopped in Los Angeles to visit Humphrey Bogart, who was in the hospital recuperating from the removal of a malignant esophagus. Lauren Bacall had arranged with a nurse to take Bogart for a walk, so that John could sneak into his bed. "When Bogie came back," she said, "there was Huston. It was a great thing for John to do. It made Bogie laugh." It was a tough time for the two men who had had such a profound effect on each other's careers, but John told Bogart that he was counting on him to get well so that after he finished with *Typee* they could get started on *The Man Who Would Be King*.

It took four days for Huston and his crew to reach Tahiti. As soon as they arrived Ossie Morris said the location wouldn't work. "If there's only one flying boat a week, that didn't sound good for a film. Particularly with Huston, who was liable to ask for some strange thing over-night. Then it became obvious that we were going to be out there in the middle of the monsoons. John didn't even know what a monsoon was, let alone worry about it. So I told Harry Templeton about these problems and he told John, blaming me, and John got ahold of me and said, 'Os, what's this, kid? You're worried about this location? Greg Peck's already committed.' "

Morris was faced with a dilemma: If he didn't say anything to Allied Artists about the problems he foresaw, a lot of people's time and money would be invested in attempting a film that would be impossible to shoot. On the other hand, since Huston seemed set on wanting to go ahead with it, it would be disloyal to ruin his fun. It was decided that Ossie and Templeton and Don the Beachcomber should return to California while Huston, Grimes, and Lohman stayed in Tahiti. Huston instructed Morris to see Paul Kohner before talking with Harold Mirisch. Kohner met him at the airport and Ossie told him the problems they faced. "Paul understood perfectly," Morris said, "because he knew John even better than I did. He said he'd talk to Mirisch, and then Mirisch saw me. He thanked me for bringing this to his notice and, to make a long story short, they didn't make the film. They had to pay Greg Peck off. And I don't know to this day whether John was cross with me, but I felt I had to do it."

John always thought it was Templeton, not Ossie, who killed *Typee*. "From the time we left Los Angeles until the day he returned," Huston said of Templeton, "he didn't draw a sober breath. And he made the recommendation that we not do the picture, that it would lead to a catastrophe. He was never sober, never saw the goddamn island! We were all prepared to go through with it, would have made a fine picture, but they pulled out."

Walter Mirisch blamed the costs of Wyler and Wilder's movies, both of which went way over budget, for aborting Allied Artists' attempt to become a major film company and so "the plan to produce *Typee* was discarded. The problem was really the failure of the other two pictures." Walter and his brother Harold then left Allied and started the Mirisch Company with United Artists.

Besides Huston, the person most disappointed when *Typee* was canceled was Billy Pearson, who was going to make his acting debut opposite Peck. "I wudda loved to have done it," he said. *His* version of why it never happened was "some little nothing Mexican outfit decided to shoot the same story, because it was in the public domain, and it would have been out first, and that was more than the company would gamble against."

But Pearson's luck took a dramatic turn when he was suddenly catapulted into national prominence after appearing on a TV quiz program that was all the rage in 1956, before it was hit by scandal when it was discovered that some of the contestants had been given the answers. The show was called "The $64,000 Question" and contestants were allowed to choose their category and then answer questions. It began with $64, which multiplied quickly to $4,000, and up to $64,000 in five weeks. Pearson chose "Great Art and Artists." His first question was to identify the artist who painted George Washington on the dollar bill. By the end of the first show he had won $256. The following week he ran that up to $8,000, then doubled that. He heard from Huston, who was following the show from Ireland. "Pick up the chips and go home," John advised. But Pearson was a gambler and made it to $32,000 the next week. Huston then sent him a long telegram: "My tax accountant has figured it up, and on the next $32,000, you'll get to keep about $4,000. So you're risking $32,000 to win $4,000. Don't be a horse's ass." But just as Huston believed that crime was "a left-handed form of human endeavor," Pearson felt that if he quit without going for it all, "it was kind of a left-handed way of being a winner." So with $64,000 at stake, Billy was shown six reproductions of six portraits by Holbein, Velásquez, Renoir, Van Dyck, Sargent, and Goya and asked to name the artist, the subject of each portrait, and a master under whom each of the artists studied. With Huston sweating out the show by telephone, he heard his friend answer correctly. It was a great moment, which Pearson extended by partying with Burl Ives and Ernie Anderson through the night. Pearson had captured the public's imagination and Simon and Schuster offered to publish his autobiography. Huston wrote the introduction, which included this warning to the Uffizi Gallery: "Billy covets the Cimabue *Christus*. Go ahead and laugh, but Billy, to quote himself, would steal a hot stove and come back for the smoke."

Pearson's sudden wealth made John think about his own luck. He had a slew of projects but found himself not knowing what he would be doing next. He asked Paul Kohner to find the right deal and Kohner came up with a three-picture offer from 20th Century-Fox. Buddy Adler, Fox's executive head of production, whom John had known since the Signal Corps, sent him a script by John Lee Mahin called *Heaven*

Knows, Mr. Allison. John was aware of the novel by Charles Shaw, which had "exploited all of the obvious sexual implications of a marine and a nun cast together on a South Pacific island." But he thought Mahin had "laundered the story tastefully." Mahin was an old pro who knew John from their days together with the Provincetown Players, and had written four of Walter's movies in the early thirties. He agreed with John that it had been a "very dirty book." When the co-producer, Eugene Frenke, read the script, his only comment was that it wasn't sexy enough. When Adler, Frenke, and Mahin met with Huston to discuss it, John suggested he and Mahin go down to Ensenada for three weeks to work on it. "Tell you what it needs, Mr. Huston," Frenke said. "She's gotta have an itchy cunt." John never had a chance to respond—Adler threw Frenke out of his office.

Before they left John paid a visit to Evelyn Keyes, who still had a Juan Gris painting Lesley Black had given him, and John wanted to get it back to hang at St. Clerans. Evelyn was then involved with Mike Todd, who became very jealous when he heard that John was with her and that they had been drinking together. John had to call Todd on the phone and convince him that he was only looking out for his own interests.

One of the reasons Huston wanted to work on the script with Mahin was that he had run into Marlon Brando at Lew Wasserman's MCA office, when Wasserman was still an agent. Brando was John's first choice for the marine in *Heaven Knows, Mr. Allison,* and when he mentioned the script, Brando told him he had read it and didn't think it was all that good. "I didn't want to run down the writer, who was a friend of mine," John said, "so I just let it go at that." It was John's hope that after he had a chance to work on the rewrite, he might be able to rekindle Brando's interest.

John had tried once before, in 1953, to convince Brando to appear in Shakespeare's *Richard III.* The two men exchanged letters about it, with Brando listing his reasons why he didn't believe Shakespeare should be done on film, which was curious, as he had just played Mark Antony in *Julius Caesar.* "I countered each of his reasons," Huston said, "negating his arguments. But I never heard from him."

While John was down in Ensenada he celebrated his fiftieth birthday on August 5, 1956. Certain special friends—his lawyer, Mark Cohen; agent, Paul Kohner; secretary, Lorrie Sherwood; recent thoroughbred investment partner, Gregory Peck, and his wife, Veronique; Billy Pearson; and Suzanne Flon, who had flown in from Paris—were among the honored guests. Kohner had brought down the cake, decorated with small replicas denoting something from each of John's films, but it had been turned upside down in the delivery and when it was opened, it was impossible to cut, so people just reached in and grabbed hunks. Sherwood recalled that Gregory Peck managed to get the *Pequod.* Suzanne Flon wrapped herself in a sheet and did a takeoff on *Heaven Knows, Mr. Allison.* And John proceeded to get so drunk that he was shocked to find out the next day that he had walked stark naked through the lobby and restaurant of the hotel where they were staying. He would later deny it had happened, saying he was the victim of one of Pearson's practical jokes and the real person who had walked naked that night was a dentist. But John Lee Mahin and his wife clearly remembered that it was John. "God, it was awful," Mahin said. "He didn't know where he was. And he was a bad drinker, always wanted to fight. People surrounded him, they rushed the publicity department down from the studio, and they covered it up. They said it wasn't Huston, that it was a tourist named John Hamilton; and he was kicked out of the hotel. My wife gave him a big sombrero, with big lettering knitted across it: 'Heaven Only Knows, Mr. Hamilton.' He had to laugh."

Around this time John and Gregory Peck had a falling-out that would never be resolved. John wasn't sure what he had done to so offend Peck, but he suspected that it had something to do with Veronique. He remembered going to give her a friendly kiss, but she pulled away in a "queer, clumsy piece of behavior . . . and from then on Greg avoided me." He asked Lorrie Sherwood if Veronique ever said anything to her, but she hadn't. Peck's avoidance bothered John, and he felt insulted because he couldn't figure out the reason for it. When, some years later, Peck saw Huston on a studio lot and acted friendly, John turned away. "It was far too late to start over."

Before going to Tobago to film *Heaven Knows*, John and Sherwood had cholera shots. It knocked Sherwood out for eighteen hours, but John ignored the potential aftereffects and went deep-sea fishing with Pearson and Mahin. The next day John had such a severe reaction to his cholera shot that a doctor had to be flown down from Los Angeles to treat him. After he recovered, he and Sherwood went to Mazatlán, where John was stricken with gout, an acid condition that so swelled his foot he was unable to stand. "It was painful as hell," Huston said and he suffered "on and off for years" after he turned fifty.

When the pain subsided John flew to Mexico City to see Pablo, who, he was told, had taken a rented car out of California and had sold it in Mexico. Since John had been making the payments on the car, he wanted to find Pablo and get to the bottom of it. Pablo had spent a year at Pierce College before returning to Mexico to become a sportswriter for a local newspaper. John had given him $200 when he left Pierce and was sending him $35 a month. "He gave me another sermon," Pablo said resentfully about their meeting. "I got mad. I said, 'The car, I didn't sell it. I tried to take it back, but I wasn't allowed to cross the border, so I sent it back with a friend. And how do you expect me to live on thirty-five dollars a month?' " "Well," John said, "that's your problem, isn't it?" Pablo then took out a newspaper and showed him his byline. "You wrote that?" John asked, reading. And then, Pablo remembered, John began to cry. He had wrongly accused Pablo, had considered him worthless, and was feeling guilty for misjudging him. Then Pablo told him that he had fallen in love with an Irish girl named Olga and wanted to go to Dublin to ask her to marry him. John didn't approve. "He thought it was best keeping me in Mexico," Pablo said. But Pablo was in love and eventually went to Ireland to see her. Olga wasn't sure he meant it, but she soon went to the States, where she worked in a photography shop and Pablo began sending her flowers. They were married in Mexico and she immediately got pregnant; she had a boy they named John. When Pablo decided to become a "cheesecake and marriage ceremony" photographer, Huston bought him the cameras. But the future didn't look bright for Pablo.

Whenever Huston was asked whether he thought he had a specific style, he would often answer that he wasn't aware of one and that he usually looked to make his next picture as different as possible from his last, so that he would always be interested in uncovering something new within himself. After the physical hardships and long delays encountered by the numbing weather and the loss of two model whales during *Moby Dick*, going off to the West Indies to make a small, two-person film like *Heaven Knows, Mr. Allison*, became a lighthearted and joyous experience for Huston.

Deborah Kerr was set to play the nun marooned on an island before having taken her vows. A veteran of two dozen films, she was best known for her Oscar-nominated performances in *From Here to Eternity* and *The King and I*. Huston was still hoping that Brando would agree to star opposite her—they had appeared together in *Julius Caesar*. In John's mind Brando was the best actor of his generation and it was a great disappointment when he again turned the film down. "Fox had a two-picture deal with Robert Mitchum," Ossie Morris recalled, "and they insisted that he do this part, which didn't exactly please Bob. He was pissed off at being second fiddle to Brando, and then when he found out it was to be shot on Tobago, the shit really hit the fan! He'd been there for his last picture and didn't want to go back. So he flatly refused to come onto the island to start the movie."

If Mitchum wasn't thrilled about the assignment, neither was Huston about Mitchum. "But it turned out magnificently," Lorrie Sherwood observed, "because they really hit it off." John went to talk to Mitchum when they were both in London. Mitchum also remembers a visit by Ossie Morris, who appeared while he was still finishing *Fire Down Below*. Ossie wanted to do some wardrobe tests and Mitchum "didn't know who he was or what he was talking about." Ossie apologized and introduced himself as John Huston's cameraman. "I knew nothing about it," Mitchum said, "but all I needed to know was John Huston and Deborah." So he allowed himself to be fitted for a marine's uniform, and soon found himself back on Tobago for what turned out to be one of the most physically challenging films of his career.

It took a while before Mitchum eased himself into being back there again. Stephen Grimes remembered him drinking vodka as if it was tea or coffee. At the opening of the picture he was to get washed ashore in a rubber raft. "While we got ready for this," Ossie Morris said, "Bob was in his hut, drinking vodka in the morning. The assistant director, Adrian Pryce-Jones, was sent to get him and he returned, saying Mitchum didn't want to do the scene. Huston sent him back to tell Mitchum they were ready. Adrian went again, stayed for a much longer time, and when he came out he was staggering. John thought it was a great joke and sent Adrian for a third time. When he returned, according to Morris, he was flat-out drunk. So then John went to Mitchum's hut and said, 'Bob, we're ready.' Bob came out, good as gold, got into the raft, and John told him to row out. It was very hot and he must have been feeling awful having got through most of the bottle of vodka by ten A.M. And John left him out there for a couple of hours. It was John, getting his own back, you see. There was no need for Bob to be in the raft, it could've been a double."

When he saw what he was up against Mitchum decided to get through all the rough stuff first. So they pushed ahead the scene where he was to take possession of the island by swimming through the coral waters, then crawling through the underbrush. A washtub had been dropped into the water and dragged across the reef to see how rough it might be. When it was torn to pieces Mitchum had a clear idea of what might happen to him if he got caught down there. John also saw the shredded tub and looked at Mitchum and asked, "Think it'll kill ya, kid?" "We'll find out," Mitchum responded.

Mitchum also had to crawl through a gully that no one had cleared beforehand. "It was filled with dried, broken coconut shells and old bedsprings, like razor blades," Mitchum discovered. "So I screeched to a halt, came back, and said, 'Did anybody check out that path? There's a ditch down there full of razor blades and the goddamn thing is forty feet deep.' 'No shit, kid,' Huston said, 'how wide?' "

After an acceptable first take John looked at Mitchum and asked him, "How was that?" "Too Jewish?" replied Mitchum, giving Huston his standard flip remark about a first take. When Huston didn't respond, Mitchum said, "John, I've been on this island before, it's no big thrill to me. You tell me if you like it. If you do, print it. If not, tell me what you want and we'll do it again." "It was swell, kid, but I think even more." And that was the extent of Huston's directorial advice to Mitchum throughout the shooting.

Mitchum came to appreciate John's talents, not only as someone who understood the nature of actors but also as a designer. "He had probably the greatest sense of rhythm and punctuation in dramatic flow of any director I've known," Mitchum said. "And he was best left on his own. Who was going to design sets for John? He had a better eye than anyone."

During one scene where Mitchum and Kerr were on a boat chasing a turtle, Kerr had to row hard to keep up with the turtle. Once Mitchum grabbed its tail, he was pulled overboard, leaving Kerr calling out to him. "Row faster, Deborah," John kept shouting as her hands became blistered. When the oar broke she leaned back and shouted, "That'll tell you how fucking fast I'm rowing!" John was amused, but the local nuns who happened to have been visiting the set that day were not.

"The biggest problem we had was getting giant turtles," Ossie Morris said. "John wanted a turtle as big as a table. No director but Huston would have sent a man through the West Indies looking for giant turtles."

Then there was a scene where Kerr had to run through a swamp. "It was horrible," Kerr recalled. "There were leeches all over, the stench, I was covered in alligator excrescence from head to foot. The shot was over, John said, 'Fine, cut. We don't need to do that again.' And I went up to him—he was in his white pants and white shirt—and I flung my arms around his neck, pressed my body against his, and all this filth went all over his jacket, shirt, and slacks."

Because of the delicate nature of the subject—a rough marine and an innocent nun alone together—the studio thought it might be a good idea to have a censor from the Legion of Decency visit the location, just to make sure the film didn't offend a Christian audience. The man who came was named Vizzard, which the company quickly rhymed with buzzard, and, naturally, Huston thought the visitor should be treated with all due consideration. So he carefully considered the situation and discussed it with Mitchum and Kerr.

"Jack Vizzard used to see salacious things in things that nobody else did," recalled Jilda Smith, who worked as a production secretary on the film. "He got on everybody's nerves and was a pain in the neck. So they decided to play a joke on Jack Vizzard. Mitchum came over to Deborah and put one hand down the front of her dress and the other up her skirt. She kneed him and Jack said, 'You can't do that!' And Huston said, 'I don't see why not.' "

Vizzard didn't know that Ossie Morris hadn't put any film in the camera. Mitchum thought it was great fun. "I was groping and grabbing Deborah and she was huffing and puffing," he said. "And John told him this was the revised scene, that the one before was unusable. Vizzard was absolutely speechless."

Jilda Smith's first dealings with John almost caused her to have a minor breakdown. Ossie had "put the fear of God" in her when they were still in London, warning her not to do or say anything silly in front of Huston. Her first encounter was at the hotel in Tobago. John was staying elsewhere and was going out to dinner that night. He instructed Jilda to get him a room so he could change without having to return to his hotel. "I was alone in the office when in walked Huston, this tall figure with the black cigarette and terrible cough," she said. "He asked me to show him where he was to change and then he said, 'I'm going to take a shower, honey, and this is the loneliest time in a man's day, so I want you to come and talk to me.' I was terrified! But I sat outside the bathroom door and he said, 'Well, talk, Jilda.' 'Have you had a good day, Mr. Huston?' 'Not bad, honey, not bad. Carry on talking.' I've never been so scared in my entire life!"

Huston had brought Ricki and the children to Tobago and set them up in a house away from the set. Jilda never spoke with Ricki but remembered her "sitting on a beach, looking in a mirror and plucking her eyebrows. She was beautiful." Mitchum recalled a bizarre moment on the terrace of the Blue Haven Hotel when Ricki arrived. John had been talking to Mitchum's wife, Dorothy, and Ricki sat down on the stool next to him. "John looked at us and smiled," Mitchum said, "and you had the feeling he hadn't a clue as to who she was. When the kids walked in, it all came to him."

Anjelica was five then and has fond memories of Tobago. "I remember a costume party and a tutu my mother made me of pink and yellow layers. I remember my mother leaving out coconut on our bedside table. And there was a crab stew on Saturday night. Everyone would come and play the steel band outside the house. And the girls would limbo. And there was a beautiful beach, like paradise. I remember swimming in the rain with my father and brother and mother, and coming out and picking up this perfect cowrie shell about six inches across, the kind deep-sea divers look for. And of going onto the coral reef and looking through a glass tray at all the colored fishes. We weren't on the set too much, but we knew he was making a movie. I liked to be around Deborah Kerr, who I called Mrs. Boogum. I thought she was beautiful. And there was the big beautiful black guy who took care of my brother."

His name was Irwin Allen, and from the moment John saw him he had visions of making him the heavyweight champion of the world. It didn't matter that he couldn't box, that would come with training. He had been hired to watch after Tony, to be a companion. "John decided he looked like a gladiator," Mitchum said. "He asked me to put the gloves on with him. I didn't feel like it, but John said, 'Go on, go on.' So I did. I just stuck my left hand out and he fell down."

Allen's lack of fighting skills didn't deter John from sponsoring the young man. But Mitchum's reputation as a fighter was enhanced when he took on a handful of American sailors who approached him at the bar of the Blue Haven Hotel. "The reason they came to the hotel was to get me," Mitchum recalled. "It was a great evening. I was like Errol Flynn, fighting them off. I hit one guy and he went down the stairs. Then I hit the biggest one, and his eyes crossed. Then another one said, 'I'd like to have a shot at you.' I said, 'Go ahead.' So he took a shot. I turned away and he belted me again. I grabbed him, had him over the edge, there was a child's wading pool down below. I thought I could spot him right into that pool, but just as I was getting ready to fling him down there somebody was attacking me from the back. I turned around and it was my wife with the heel of her shoe. 'Wait a minute,' I said. 'You're supposed to be on *my* side.' And she said, 'You're beginning to enjoy it.' "

Mitchum came to believe that he was safer fighting off drunken sailors than facing the challenges Huston set up for him. The underwater coral ripped open his chest, as did the broken bits of coconut shell, and during one scene he twisted his ankle and had to be taken to Trinidad for X-rays. "That sonofabitch is trying to kill me!" he complained to Jilda Smith. "He tries to kill all his leading men. Look what he did to Gregory Peck when he strapped him to that whale!"

It was a mosquito, not Huston, however, that was responsible for bringing down both Mitchum and Kerr when they caught dengue fever, which causes intense joint and muscle pain. Mitchum actually passed out and Kerr had to be hospitalized for a few days. During her absence John and Mitchum played poker, often through the night.

During these interludes John would talk to Mitchum about *The Man Who Would Be King*. "Ever hear of Bhutan?" John asked. "Yeah," Mitchum replied, "you can't get in or out of there. How are *you* going to do it?" "Parachute," John answered. "Oh, yeah? And how will you get out?" "Well," Huston said, convincing Mitchum that he surely had a touch of madness, "I figure that after we are there for a while, they'll be happy to see us leave."

Although Mitchum would later call John the "most comfortable" director he'd ever worked with, a man of great humor and no pretensions, he wasn't so complimentary when a reporter asked him how he liked working with Huston. "Well," Mitchum replied, "he's taller than Mervyn LeRoy."

Toward the end of the film, according to Jilda Smith, Huston, out of boredom, began to wonder what he could ask his crew to get that they'd never be able to find. There was a scene when the marines landed and Mitchum had to be carried off. They were to cross a small stream and John came up with the perfect request: a Bailey bridge, an assembled floating bridge that was used in wartime. So while John played poker over the weekend, his production manager was instructed to find such a bridge, which would have to be erected and then painted before the shot on Monday. It was an impossible request, but Mitchum knew a guy who worked for Gulf Oil in Trinidad and he made a call. The Bailey bridge was put on the company's plane and flown into Tobago. Generators had to be rigged so the bridge could be assembled overnight. On Monday John was informed that the bridge was in place. Without missing a beat John looked up and said, "Bailey bridge? Didn't I tell you about that? That scene doesn't work at all."

Another scene, involving explosives, almost worked too well. The Japanese on the island were being bombed by American planes and the stunt coordinator was in charge of setting off a string of explosives as the soldiers ran away. A forty-foot platform was built two hundred feet away for the cameras to capture the action. There was a master switch that would set off the explosives, but it had rained the night before and when it was thrown, John noticed smoke coming out of the ground. "Jesus Christ," the stunt coordinator muttered in horror. "I knew instantly what was happening," Huston recalled. "I didn't say 'Camera' or anything like that. I just shouted, '*Action!*' and the Japanese ran. And as the last man ran out of range, the whole bloody thing went up! Not like a string of bombs, but a great explosion that blinded and deafened us all. Every last one of them, over fifty men, could have been killed. Who would have anticipated a short in the wires simply because it had rained?"

Other directors might have looked for somebody to blame, but Huston rarely got angry over production mishaps. When something went wrong he would wait until it could be righted. But when he felt slighted on a personal level he wasn't so benign. During their time on Tobago Lorrie Sherwood got involved with Stephen Grimes. Even though Ricki was also on the island, Huston wouldn't tolerate letting anyone else fool around with his secretary. "We had our first falling-out over Lorrie," Grimes remembered. "He'd been treating her rather badly and I felt sorry for her. She was miserable and I'd taken her out. John got all upset about this. If I had thought they were together I wouldn't have dreamt of it. There was nothing ever direct, but I was definitely way out of favor. After that the sets were never right. It was very easy for John to find fault when he wanted to." It took Huston nearly nine months before he could forgive his art director for trespassing on what he considered his territory.

Jilda Smith also said that John treated Angela Allen dreadfully and came to believe that he was "a very sadistic sonofabitch." Ossie Morris never forgot the "awful thing" John once did to Angie when he noticed her wearing a bathing suit "a bit brief at the crotch, where you could see a certain amount of pubic hair showing. John was sitting in his chair, in his shorts, with an enormous pair of testicles hanging down half his leg, which you could see. He called to Angela, 'C'mere, kid.' She went over and stood by his side with her script. 'You really must do something about this,' he said, pulling at her hairs."

On October 25, 1956, David Selznick cabled John in Tobago regarding Hemingway's *A Farewell to Arms*, which Selznick wanted Huston to direct from a Ben Hecht script. John was interested but should have been warned what he was in for when he read the cable, which asked if he would be willing to concentrate "wholly" on *Farewell* "until completion photography, after which believe you would feel safe leaving post-production, including editing, entirely my hands?" Selznick admitted to being worried that John might resist and resent his functioning solely as director and not as producer/director, but made it clear that the credits would make it a Selznick and not a Huston production. Knowing that he would be free right after *Heaven Knows*, John agreed to Selznick's offer before reading what Hecht and Selznick had done to Hemingway's novel.

Before John crossed the Atlantic he went to see Humphrey Bogart for what would be the last time. It was Lauren Bacall's decision not to tell Bogie what everyone knew: that he was dying. John went to visit with Billy Pearson, who remembered how shocked they were when the dumbwaiter came down from upstairs with Bogart curled up inside. "Betty asked me to help get him out," the diminutive jockey said. "I reached in and picked him right up! He must have weighed eighty pounds. Imagine what he *looked* like." Pearson placed Bogart in a wheelchair and John started telling him how good he looked. "He was bullshitting about how they were gonna make *The Man Who Would Be King* and how he never looked better," Pearson said.

"Bogie's treatment was very severe," John recalled. "Chemotherapy makes you sick as a dog. We all knew he wasn't going to live, but he was still having those goddamn treatments. They wouldn't give up the ghost. We had a drink and Bogie said, 'Look, fellas, come clean. Am I gonna make it or not? Tell me the truth.' And Morgan Maree said, 'Of course you are, Bogie. We're not kidding you.' Lying through his teeth. Which was all right. Bogie looked relieved and prepared to go on with it. When I saw that, I said, sure. He didn't want to know. And Betty didn't want him to read in the paper that he was going to die, so everyone who knew him put the best face on they could. And she defended him that way like a lioness."

Bogart died on January 14, 1957. Bacall asked Spencer Tracy to deliver the eulogy, but Tracy felt he wouldn't be able to maintain his composure, and she then asked John. The words he spoke about Bogart would, thirty years later, be spoken about him as well. After describing Bogart's illness he concluded: "No one who sat in his presence during those final weeks will ever forget. It was a unique display of sheer animal courage . . . one quickened to the grandeur of it, expanded and felt strangely elated, proud to be there, proud to be his friend, the friend of such a brave man. . . . We have no reason to feel any sorrow for him—only for ourselves for having lost him."

Bacall was greatly moved by John's words. She believed that, besides John's father, Bogart was the only man who had a deep, emotional effect on his life.

When John returned to England he brought his West Indian discovery, Irwin Allen, with him, found him a trainer, and watched his workouts. "He hit a bag harder than any fighter I ever saw," John said. "But he wasn't very good at hitting people. He had three fights, all disappointing. He won them all, but they were setups, and he didn't look good."

Huston was being generous. Allen may have "won" the fights John fixed, but he didn't make it through the second round of his first legitimate bout. "He tried to crawl out of the ring," Robert Mitchum heard. "He got the shit kicked out of him." In the car after the fight Allen said, "I didn't do very well, did I, Mr. Huston?" "No, you didn't, Irwin," John replied. "Did I do *anything* right, Mr. Huston?" "Not a thing, kid."

Jilda Smith said that a few months later Allen called her looking for John, who was out of the country. He had no money, his rent was overdue, and he didn't know what to do. When she managed to track Huston down he said he had no idea Allen was in such a bad state. "But he *did* know," Jilda said. "And I never heard any more about it."

Beginning in 1957 and continuing over the next seven years, Huston's career would parallel his perceptions about Irwin Allen: He would get involved with pictures that, on the surface, seemed sound, looked promising, had potential; but when they appeared before the public they bombed badly. Even the critics, who so often championed John, would turn away and wonder whether the best Huston could deliver wasn't already in his past.

The first blow was, perhaps, the most ominous, for it would result in Huston's leaving a picture for the first time and dropping the $250,000 director's fee. And it happened over a film he truly wanted to make: Hemingway's *A Farewell to Arms*. After reading the fifth draft of the script that Ben Hecht and David Selznick had written, John immediately realized that Hecht had compromised his talent to give Selznick what he wanted: a love story for Jennifer Jones. Selznick had no intention of being faithful to Hemingway's story, which was a war story with a love interest as background. Huston, conversely, prided himself on his fidelity to the books he transposed to film. Selznick's former production manager, Ray Klune, had warned the producer that it would be a great mistake to hire Huston in the first place, fearing the two men might kill each other.

"David Selznick genuinely believed that the producer was more important on a film than the director," said Ossie Morris, who pointed out that anyone who challenged Selznick on that would be asked to name the director of *Gone With the Wind.* "Nine out of ten people couldn't tell him," Morris said, "and then he'd ask who produced it, and they'd all say David Selznick. That was his set piece."

Huston always found Selznick amusing and enjoyed his company, but when he saw that Hemingway's book was being destroyed in the best interests of Jennifer Jones, he just couldn't be a part of that destruction. On location in the Dolomite mountains in Italy, with five thousand troops from the Italian army dressed in World War I gear, and Rock Hudson and Jennifer Jones as the stars, Selznick insisted on rehearsals. "One thing John didn't like to do was to rehearse ahead of time," Morris said. "But David wanted them, so John said yes. David said eleven A.M. tomorrow with Rock and Jennifer and at eleven there was no sign of John. They waited an hour and then it would all be abandoned. Obviously John was taking no notice of what David was saying."

Angela Allen worked for the first, and last, time as John's secretary in Italy, but she found it far more grueling than being his script girl. "I realized then that I could never have been his secretary because he was so possessive. You were on duty twenty-four hours a day. I didn't have any life of my own." Lorrie Sherwood was also there, taking care of John's personal life, setting up his living quarters. John had forgiven Stephen Grimes about his indiscretions with Lorrie and Grimes was off "looking at locations in the Alps," as Huston set up the first part of the picture. And then, just two days before filming was to commence, the shit hit the fan in the form of a sixteen-page memo Selznick sent to John, itemizing his complaints over the way John worked. "I should be less than candid with you if I didn't tell you that I am most desperately unhappy about the way things are going," it began. "It is an experience completely unique in my very long career."

Huston could feel his stomach churn as he continued to read. By the third paragraph, when Selznick wrote that it was unthinkable that any changes Huston wanted to make should even be contemplated, John had to catch his breath. "We are making a motion picture, we are not

photographing Hemingway's book like slaves," Selznick lectured, bringing up the fact that Huston had not achieved fidelity with *Moby Dick*
and that "lectures given at Harvard repeatedly attacked the complete
failure to realize Melville in the film."

The memo only got worse. Selznick attacked Huston's "strange phobia against short scenes" and of "telling things en route to a scene." He
criticized him for his self-indulgence, for not telling the production
department what he had in mind on various locations, and for his
"habits of procrastination or of creating things on the spur of the
moment." He said if he lost John he would be "up against an even more
serious situation than when Cukor left *Gone With the Wind.*" But he
made it very clear that he was in charge and that if Huston couldn't
stand to be under his thumb, then he would prefer that John resigned.

John never finished reading the memo. He said he got about halfway
through it when the first mention of resignation came up and he called
out to Sherwood to start packing. "He was ready to go hit the old
man," Sherwood said. "It was a pretty nasty note." It was Sherwood's
contention that Selznick had used John to help finance the film and
then wanted to get rid of him because he couldn't control him. Huston
instructed Paul Kohner to meet him in Rome and he, Sherwood, and
Angela Allen quit the picture that afternoon. They took a train to
Venice, got into a gondola in the middle of the night, and caught
another train to Rome, where reporters were waiting. Huston did his
best to keep up appearances, saying nothing against Selznick, blaming it
all on a difference of opinion. Selznick had already gone on the record,
saying, "In Mr. Huston, I asked for a first violinist and instead got a
soloist." Sherwood said it was the most unhappy time she ever had with
John. "It was pretty rough to have someone that he thought was his
friend use him in that way. It was really unforgivable. John played it
down considerably," but he was clearly hurt by Selznick's actions.

Before he departed John told Ossie and Grimes he didn't think they
should quit. "He was aware that people need to work," Grimes said.
Ossie felt that John was "absolutely right to do as he did." Both men
decided to stay on but neither would finish the picture. Ossie saw what
they were in for when Charles Vidor arrived to replace Huston. "He
was a very nervous man," Morris said. "Bit his nails, twiddled his
fingers. He told me they had given him a great party when he left
California and his friends were going to give him another one in three
weeks, after he'd been fired from this movie. I thought, well, that's

good for a start. He was terrified of the actors, of David, of the memos by the mile. He became a total nervous wreck, but he did a lot of what Selznick wanted." Ossie stuck it out for fifteen weeks before Selznick's memos "began to drive me up the wall. In the end I got one accusing me of deliberately sacrificing Jennifer's look for the sake of Rock Hudson. You could take so much but that was it." Soon after, Grimes got fed up with trying to cope with the production designer and also left.

A Farewell to Arms failed for many of the reasons John had foreseen and he came to believe that Selznick never made a worthwhile picture after he married Jennifer.

From Rome, John went to Paris to see Suzanne and to meet with Darryl Zanuck, who wanted John to direct Romaine Gary's *The Roots of Heaven*, a novel dealing with the conservation of elephants in Africa. Elephants, Africa . . . the idea appealed to Huston. Gary was hired to write a script and Zanuck sent people down to what was then French Equatorial Africa to scout locations. In the meantime John found another script, written by his old friend Charlie Grayson, to keep him occupied. Called *The Townsend Harris Story*, it was about America's first diplomat to Japan in 1856. Huston promised Zanuck he would make *The Roots of Heaven* after he returned from Japan. Then he left for California to meet with Grayson and producer Eugene Frenke for his second picture with 20th Century-Fox.

Huston, Grayson, and Lorrie Sherwood went down to San Miguel Allende in Mexico to work on the script. As a foreign resident Huston managed to avoid paying American taxes as long as he didn't work in the United States, so he was constantly heading down to Baja to develop scripts. When they had finished, Huston, Grayson, and Jack Smith, the art director, flew to Tokyo to look for locations and for Japanese actors. John Wayne was going to play Townsend Harris, a role quite unlike anything he had ever done before. Wayne's wife, Pilar, said that the picture would require a real stretch for Wayne, and "he counted on Huston to help him turn in a creditable performance." Huston believed that John Wayne was "a better actor than he knew," and felt that "his massive frame, bluff innocence and rough edges would be an interesting contrast to the small, highly cultivated Japanese; that the physical comparison would help serve to emphasize their dissimilar viewpoints and cultures."

The effect this first American in Japan had on the Oriental culture interested Huston, who knew enough about the Japanese to know that they had "different souls" and different conceptions of life. Townsend

Harris was not welcomed with open arms when he arrived in Japan, nor was it accepted when the Japanese woman the governor sent to spy on him fell in love with the American. To find someone to play the crucial role of Wayne's love interest, Huston visited geisha houses. He enjoyed the search but didn't find his actress until a few days before he returned to California. A tall, long-legged woman named Eiko Ando from Hokkaido was presented to him and Huston was immediately attracted. She wasn't a classic beauty by Japanese standards, but she certainly was by his.

John didn't meet with John Wayne, who was being paid a record $700,000, until he returned to Japan in December 1957 for the start of the film. The first thing Wayne did was to give Huston a thirteen-page memo presenting his views on how the picture should be made. Wayne's tact and timing couldn't have been worse, even though he could not have known about the Selznick memos that had driven Huston off his last picture. John took the memo but never read it, not even the first page.

A few days after his arrival in Japan Wayne wrote his wife that he had been "unable to establish any rapport with Huston," and that he "couldn't get a handle on Huston's character." He soon began to feel lost. "Duke wasn't used to working in a totally unstructured atmosphere," Pilar Wayne observed. "He'd learned his craft from directors like Ford and Hathaway, men who wouldn't dream of letting an actor loose in a single scene, let alone throughout the course of an entire production." When Pilar arrived in Japan just before Christmas she found her husband full of hostility. "I ask him what's on tomorrow's shooting schedule," Wayne griped, "and he'll tell me to spend more time absorbing the beauty of the scenery and less time worrying about my part. When I tell him I can't memorize the script unless I know what we'll be shooting, the bastard says 'Don't worry, we'll improvise.'" Wayne went on to say that John "hated my guts." And the feeling was obviously mutual. "The sonofabitch can't make a good movie without his father or Bogart to carry him," he told his wife.

"John Wayne loathed him," Angela Allen said, calling the actor "a terrible coward. He used to say, 'I'm gonna kill him!' I said, 'I'll fix up the appointment, what time do you want to come?' But he didn't want to be left alone with Huston. He was very regimented and could only go in one way. Very professional, but he wasn't that bright. So they had nothing in common."

Wayne would get upset because the script kept changing, because Huston was always late in the mornings, because Huston got more press coverage than he did, and because his co-star, who wasn't a professional actress, happened to be sleeping with the director. "It was a physical thing with Huston," Lorrie Sherwood said, "and that certainly didn't help him much with his work. Also, people weren't too respectful of him, if you know what I mean. It was 1957; you didn't just go into the hay and swallow each other's tongues for all to see."

Lorrie's jealousy eventually brought her to leave Japan before the picture was completed. "I *had* it on that one, thank you very much!" she said with sadness. Betty Jaffe saw that "Lorrie was very bright, very attractive, and mad about John. I could tell by her look how she felt about him. And John was in love with Suzanne then and sent her a beautiful Christmas gift. As for Eiko, she was beautiful and charming and when you work on a picture, relationships, almost in spite of themselves, become rather intimate. It's like being in war together."

Betty was in Japan because her husband, Sam, had been cast by John to play the part of John Wayne's translator. Lorrie Sherwood observed that John treated his old friend with great respect, more like his mentor. Jaffe had suffered from being blacklisted, and John fought for him to work on this film. Jaffe had told his young wife all about his early years with John, but she had never met him until Japan. "John was not happy with some of the props and sets," Betty remembered, "and so we went shopping with him. John bought so many beautiful things, which he said he would buy back from the studio, so it was really an experience going with him. A friend had asked me if I could get her a Noh mask. I asked John if he knew where I might find one. The next morning there was a note from John that said we won't shoot today, let's meet for lunch. And John came in with a package which he put in front of me. He had taken the day off to buy these three antique masks. I was overwhelmed!"

Huston's delight with Japan and his relationship with Eiko helped offset the problems he had with his star, his cameraman, and even some of the people in the small fishing village of Ito, where a scene they shot almost resulted in the village burning down. In the movie, after an outbreak of cholera, Townsend Harris comes up with a way to keep the disease from spreading throughout the country. All the dead are gathered onto boats, then taken out to sea, where they are burned. A forty-foot barge was constructed with a cable attached to one end. At night the barge was to be set on fire and pushed down rollers into the sea. But when it came time to shoot the scene the cable snapped and the winds blew the barge back toward the village, where power fishing boats were anchored in the cove. For a while it appeared as if the entire cove would catch on fire and destroy the nearby homes, which were all made of wood and rice paper. "We worried that the whole bloody town would go up in flames," Huston said, "and God knows what the cost in life would have been." As they watched in horror, a Japanese fisherman in his rowboat jumped into the water, grabbed the cable, and brought it to the pier. The barge was secured as the villagers came out to help extinguish the boats that had caught on fire. "Then a chain of riots started that went on into the night," Huston said. "Boy, you talk about samurai violence! There it was, plus! The people went crazy, attacking the Japanese connected with the film company. Many were clubbed unconscious." Still, Huston understood their reaction. "It could have been the worst disaster of any of my movies," he acknowledged.

By the end of February, three and a half months after they began, Huston finished his version of the picture, whose title had been changed by Fox to *The Barbarian and the Geisha*, which John particularly abhorred. Because Darryl Zanuck had completed preproduction work on *The Roots of Heaven* and everyone was assembled and waiting for him in Africa, John left directly to begin his next picture. He wasn't involved in either the editing or the changes, and when he finally saw it, he found they had turned what he had thought was a pretty good picture into one that was dreadfully bad.

"It was really a fucked-up proposition," he said. "I would have had my name taken off the picture except the head of the studio, Buddy Adler, was a friend of mine and he was dying of a brain tumor and I didn't want him to have a further complication. It was an entirely different story with *Red Badge of Courage*. I didn't agree with what happened to that, but I sympathized and understood their doing it. In this case, after I left for Africa, John Wayne began making demands and Buddy succumbed."

"Duke said if it wasn't redone he wouldn't work for Fox again," Lorrie Sherwood said. "It's not a horrible picture, but it sure wasn't the one John shot."

The critics were less harsh with the movie than Huston was. The *Saturday Review* called it "an unusually beautiful film, directed with spirit and remarkable taste." The *New York Times* praised it as "just about as lovely to look at as any we have ever seen." The *New Republic* agreed that "the scenery and the clothes are beautiful," then said, "But what a reason for commending a Huston film!" As for John: "I'd like to forget *The Barbarian and the Geisha*."

*   *   *

He would feel the same way about *The Roots of Heaven* only for different reasons. John wasn't willing to take the blame for the Wayne disaster, but he felt fully responsible for botching his second African venture. Darryl Zanuck had assembled an impressive cast: Trevor Howard, Errol Flynn, Eddie Albert, Orson Welles, Paul Lucas, Herbert Lom. He had also insisted that the female lead be played by the woman he had fallen in love with, Juliette Greco, a nightclub singer with some acting ability. Stephen Grimes, Ossie Morris, and Angela Allen were there, as well as Eva Monley, who had worked in the production office on *The African Queen* and knew Africa well enough to be of assistance once again. When Huston arrived, two days before filming was to start, he was surprised to find how arid it was. "I saw this as a jungle picture," he said, and Monley was dispatched to find some jungle.

Besides his dissatisfaction with the "bone-dry desert," John was also unhappy with the script and had a friend of his, a travel writer named Patrick Leigh-Fermor, brought in to rewrite it. Stephen Grimes thought that Romaine Gary's script was very good but John turned against it when he learned that Gary had once had what Grimes called "a little fling" with Eiko Ando. Gary supposedly told John about it as a way of sharing a common experience and Huston reacted by calling for another writer.

"John had no period of adjustment," Eva Monley said. "He was in a sort of limbo between Japan and reality. He was still full of love for Japanese ladies walking up and down his back. Suddenly he was in the middle of no place. We lived in huts; there was no hotel. And we had a trilingual crew: Italian, French, and English. The climate was appalling. It was the toughest movie I've ever worked on in my life—and I spent two years on *Lawrence of Arabia*, which couldn't touch what we went through on *The Roots of Heaven*."

The 130-degree weather, which got down to 100 degrees in the evenings, made the experience of *The African Queen* seem like Tahiti. During the six months they were on location there were 960 logged sick calls. The local girls passed on virulent forms of gonorrhea, mosquitoes brought malaria, and those who didn't stick to the pink cans of Evian water that were flown in from Paris came down with amoebic dysentery. "We spent months under the worst conditions perhaps any picture has ever been shot except, maybe, in combat," Huston said. "People fell down and only got up to be sent home. Some actually went out of their minds, becoming deranged."

Among the actors, Eddie Albert, who played a photographer covering the story of Trevor Howard's rebellion against the slaughter of elephants, was most affected by the sun. "He just went cuckoo," Angela Allen remembered. "He went climbing a hill in the midday sun and came back thinking he could deal with witch doctors. He couldn't walk, he was totally nuts. Then we had an American cameraman who disappeared. The last time any of us saw him he was stark naked. And there was a local Frenchman who became totally, screaming mad and had to be shipped out in a straitjacket."

Trevor Howard kept his sanity by drinking heavily, as did Errol Flynn, who consumed quantities of vodka *and* morphine pills. "Flynn was using the local hospital as his drug supply," Grimes said. "He discovered a cooperative French doctor who also sent young girls meowing like cats outside his hut at night." He would quickly let them in and, in his drugged state, soar even higher on what would be the last movie he would ever make.

Ossie Morris lamented that Flynn, who played a mercenary, was "hopeless, he could never remember a word. Eddie Albert had gone bananas. Zanuck spent every night keeping the whole camp up trying to chase Greco, who didn't want to have anything to do with him. And John was going through his Japanese period, in the middle of French Equatorial Africa, wearing his white, full-length kimonos. It was obvious from about day two that John was doing it purely and simply for the money."

Just as John had given Angela Allen a chance to direct a second unit during *The African Queen*, he let her do some pickup shots again, to save himself a three-hour trip to a distant location. She took a small crew and when she couldn't find someone to double for Eddie Albert— "you couldn't put a black man in for a white man, and I didn't have any white men with me"—she decided to do it herself. "But you've got a female bottom," the French cameraman protested. "Well, it's too bad, isn't it, dear?" she smiled. Eva Monley always felt that Allen was a "strange, frustrated director." Ossie Morris and Stephen Grimes used to joke that what Allen most needed was to lose her virginity. But what none of them knew was that *The Roots of Heaven* had a special meaning for Angie. "I think I fell in love on the film," she said coyly. "John never knew."

Stephen Grimes was also enjoying himself. According to Ernie Anderson, "Zanuck was trying to have his big fling with Juliette Greco, who was having *her* big fling with Stephen Grimes." Huston once told Eva Monley his theory on how the soft-spoken, mild-mannered Grimes managed to do so well with women. "It's because nobody can hear him. He'd talk to a pretty girl and she would lean in closer and closer to hear what he was saying and, pretty soon, they'd be in bed."

Because he was in Africa John also fell in love, but not with any woman. First it was with a mongoose that Juliette Greco had given to him. But someone left the animal's cage in the sun while they were away on location and it died. "I hated everybody for days," John said. He got over the mongoose when he acquired an eight-foot python. He kept that one for months before letting it go in the forest. By then he had found a young elephant named Albert who was so playful that he wired Betty O'Kelly in Ireland about bringing him back to St. Clerans. "She took a very dim view of putting an African elephant in with our thoroughbreds." And finally there was a giraffe that used to steal his hat and then drop it to the ground.

Although he was making a movie about one man's crusade to stop elephants from being hunted and killed, Huston was still obsessed with hunting. He had given up the idea, though, of bagging an elephant, and when he had a few free days between moves from Fort Archambault to Bangui he, Friedrich Ledebur, whom he had again cast to keep him company, and Errol Flynn went on long treks looking for game. "I shall never forget it," Flynn wrote in his autobiography. "We saw everything: great surges of elephants; the African fauna with their strange names; the very rare giant eland; . . . the water buffalo. Huston got one of the largest pairs of horns for a trophy. He was obviously very good in the jungle. I thought I was pretty good, on foot, but this fellow Huston, no youngster, leaped along like a big spider swinging through the trees."

"It was a hard safari," Huston remarked, "we'd walk as many as twenty-five miles in a day. When the whole thing was over Errol said, 'I'll never forget this, it's been the best time I've ever had.' He did not have a drink or a pill that whole period."

When they finished in Bangui the cast and most of the crew flew to Paris, where the picture would be completed in the studio. But Huston and Ossie and a skeleton crew remained behind, traveling to Gangia Nobodio in the northern Belgian Congo on the Sudan border, where they were told they would find enough elephants to shoot the stampede they needed. "It was an elephant farm," Ossie said, "quite a lovely spot. We did a bogus sort of stampede with a few of these elephants. It was quite hairy, really. They just let us set the camera up and they pushed these elephants through the jungle. They could have torn into us. John was standing safely back in his Land Rover and left me out there with the crew."

When he returned to Paris to edit *The Roots of Heaven* Huston was forced to face the glaring weaknesses of what had been shot. "Clumsy," cried the *New Republic* when the picture opened. "The Huston who did *Sierra Madre* would have lighted his cigar with this script." Commented Arlene Croce on both *The Barbarian and the Geisha* and *The Roots of Heaven* in *Film Quarterly:* "It is saddening to think that the director of *The Asphalt Jungle* . . . has gained professional freedom and international celebrity in order to become, at 51, yet another taskmaster who goes out in the midday sun."

"The depths of the novel were not touched," Huston sighed. "It became, in our hands, a kind of adventure story, a shoot-up. It could have been a very fine picture . . . but the fact remains, it wasn't."

19

SHOOTING IN MEXICO

JOHN HAD BEEN AWAY FROM HIS FAMILY FOR A LONG time, and when he arrived in Paris Ricki brought the children to the airport to meet him when he landed. They were excited to see him, even more to see what he had brought back from his travels. "I was not disappointed by his gifts," Anjelica remembered. "He brought beautiful things back. He had a gray parrot with a red head from Africa. Coco. It was in with all these hampers of gifts—kimonos and beautiful porcelain Japanese dolls with long, perfect hair. Semiprecious stones from Mexico. A Spanish dancing dress with blue polka dots for me."

Because his father was more often away than he was home, Tony's image of him was that of a benign Santa Claus who came into their lives bearing presents and then left for some distant country to make movies. "In any particular era," Tony reflected, "there's one art form that is *the* art form. At the turn of the century it was opera. In the fifties you had jet-setting for the first time. Up until then, if you went to Paris, you went like Hemingway or Fitzgerald, by boat. But this was the first time you had lots of people to-ing and fro-ing, with films being made on location. It was a very heady atmosphere for people who were making it big in the film business."

There were times, though, when John attempted to act like a father and discipline his children, but those times were often awkward and erratic and didn't result in pleasant memories. Tony had a pig he was fond of. It was, said Tony, "the runt of the litter, fed it bottled milk, it played with the dogs. I hadn't seen Dad for a while and he came back and one day he asked me if I had cleaned out the pig's sty. What I'd done was what anybody in Ireland would do: I'd put some fresh straw on top of the old stuff instead of cleaning it out. I was about eight and when Dad discovered my handwork, the pig was immediately taken away from me. It was very extreme, always. It was like, at that moment, I would no longer be George Washington because I'd actually told a lie. It was of that magnitude. The pig was given to my sister, who didn't care much about it, and shortly after it was made into bacon. It was traumatic at the time."

Ricki and the children were still living in the Little House. John moved into a room above the stables, where he could be close to his horses, paint, and direct changes he wanted to make in the Big House, still being renovated. He had bought a Japanese bath that he wanted installed, and sacks of sand and wrapped white rocks for a Zen garden. When one of his Irish workers suggested that he didn't need to go all the way to Japan for rocks, there were plenty in Ireland, John got the message and abandoned that bit of landscaping.

Ben Maddow, who had collaborated with him on *The Asphalt Jungle*, remembered visiting John in the fall of 1958 to discuss a script he had written based on a novel by Alan LeMay called *The Unforgiven*. "John had a castle, but it wasn't lived in because it had no electricity or plumbing and they were chiseling into the walls trying to find channels for it. So I would be driven out there from my hotel in Galway and meet with John in this stone house above the stables. He would appear in his long robe and white slippers, a very elegant man. And the place was crowded with stuff that he'd collected. Huge bolts of beautiful silk brocade, a marble head from Greece that he'd smuggled in."

The two men, along with James Hill, part of the independent production team Hecht-Hill-Lancaster that owned *The Unforgiven*, would go over Maddow's script and discuss ideas for the movie, which was to be shot in Durango, Mexico. The film had already been cast, with Burt Lancaster, Audie Murphy, and Doug McClure playing brothers; Lillian Gish as their mother; and Audrey Hepburn as their half-sister. Hill was there to see if Huston was interested in directing. *The Unforgiven* was about an Indian girl raised in a white family. None of her brothers knew she was an Indian, and when they found out their reactions propelled the story to its fateful conclusion. One brother, which Murphy would play, hated Indians and left the house. The oldest brother, Lancaster's part, had more than brotherly feelings toward Rachel (Audrey Hepburn) and protected her, even when attacked by the Kiowas in their attempt to get her back. The youngest brother gets wounded, their mother killed, and their home burned, but they manage to drive away the Indians and face whatever the future holds.

"Maddow's script was better than he knew," John said. "The film had the potential to be a western about racial intolerance, but that wasn't what the producers wanted. They saw it as another larger-than-life cowboy movie."

Maddow also saw it as a different type of western, but not the kind of story that Huston could put his mark on. He thought that Huston was very good at *his* story, "which is the story of fate overtaking good intentions."

Maddow looked at Huston as a "Renaissance prince. He would indulge himself in any possible way, whose consequences on other people's lives he observed with great interest, but no compassion." Maddow quickly sized up the estrangement between John and Ricki. One evening John walked over to the Little House and invited Ricki to join them for dinner. "God, you really must be lonely," Ricki said, refusing his company. Instead, John invited Maddow into her house, where they sat before the fireplace and John read aloud "the entire Ecclesiastes. 'Vanity of vanities . . . all is vanity.' It was a terrific performance, corny, but very effective. Ecclesiastes represented the way he would like to think, it expressed his point of view."

It also included a passage very close to Huston's own life at the time he quoted it to Maddow—about being great and making great works, building a house, planting a garden, hiring maids and servants, and gathering all the "peculiar treasures of kings. . . . Then I looked on all the works that my hands had wrought, and on the labor that I had labored to do; and behold, all was vanity and vexation of spirit, and there was no profit under the sun."

It may have expressed his personal outlook, but it surely didn't restrain his collecting. Aside from the money he was being offered to direct *The Unforgiven*, the reason John was taking on the project had nothing to do with making a film but rather with acquiring more pre-Columbian vanities. It had become an obsession with him. Since *Moby Dick*, John had gone into partnership with Billy Pearson. Pearson had opened a primitive art gallery with the money he had won on "The $64,000 Question" and had mastered the art of smuggling pre-Columbian figures out of Mexico by hiding them in coffins, lining false bottoms of boats, or bribing border guards. Business had been so good that they planned to invest in a hotel in Cuernavaca to use as a front for their smuggling operation. With his house in Ireland almost ready to show off his collection, Huston thought the timing was right for a trip to Mexico. He could go up in a plane, locate an undiscovered tomb, and send Pablo and a crew of Mexican Indians to excavate it under Billy's supervision. *The Unforgiven* would serve as a front for such activities.

In October, Maddow's second draft arrived and John suggested further changes, which didn't please Burt Lancaster. Jilda Smith, who had worked for John, was now with Lancaster's company and told her new boss stories about Huston that made Lancaster think he might have made a mistake in hiring him. "Whatever contract they had with John was pretty watertight and they couldn't fire him," Jilda recalled, "but they rather hoped he might resign. I can remember phone calls when John was still in Ireland, which they would record, hoping John might say something that would enable them to say that he was in breach of contract. It was all a bit sinister."

"I don't think John ever knew quite how near he was to being fired on that," Angela Allen confirmed. "John was changing the script, messing about a bit, and they were quite tough boys. Burt Lancaster felt that John had tremendous talent which he, at times, dissipated." Allen agreed. "It often upset me that he didn't always use his gifts," she said. "I know what he *could* have done, and I know that he was capable of so much more. In John's early days he was very, very fussy visually about his setups, his framing. With age he became less involved. He let the cameraman do things that he used to be much tougher about. He just became lazy."

The cinematographer for *The Unforgiven* was Franz Planer because Ossie Morris was tied up with another picture. When John couldn't get Ossie he'd often get angry. "I was expected to be available every minute of the day of the year," Morris said. "If I wasn't available, I was ostracized."

In December, John left Ireland for Los Angeles after receiving Maddow's final draft. Lorrie Sherwood, who wasn't sure her nerves were up to working on another film with John, remained behind. When John saw Jilda at the Hecht-Hill-Lancaster offices, he requested that she work for him while he was at the Beverly Hills Hotel. They agreed, and Jilda would often just sit in John's room all day, sometimes until midnight, "with nothing to do, just because either he was being mean," she said, "or because he wanted somebody there." Billy Pearson would come by and update him on his latest findings, which always got John's complete attention. Especially when Billy described how he had bribed some Mexican official.

Billy had hired a man named Jim Gabriel to work with him. Together they would bring the pre-Columbian pieces they would uncover or buy from Indians to Mazatlán, where they would crate them and put them on shrimp boats bound for Ensenada. "Once you got pre-Columbian into Baja, California, it was safe," he said, "because no one ever heard of such stuff."

When John told Billy that Pablo had gotten married and was living in Cuernavaca, Pearson found it ironical. "The bastard couldn't come in out of the rain," he said. "So I said to John, 'Let's go meet the wife.' " They went down to Mexico for Christmas, where Pablo and Olga were going to throw a party for them. When they got there Billy looked at Olga and thought she had "about the same mentality as Pablo. One of those Irish girls, right out of a sod hut, from that freezing weather where they ate those goddamn rotten potatoes for twenty generations. That was the kind of girl that Pablo married."

There were a lot of people at the party and John said to Jilda Smith, "Isn't it wonderful, honey, that they've got all these marvelous friends?" And Jilda thought, "If it wasn't *you* going to be here and if his last name wasn't Huston, then nobody would give him the time of day. Because Pablo, who clearly worshiped John and thought the sun shone out of him, was a total failure, poor little devil." But John saw that Pablo's photography business was struggling and sent Jilda out to buy him new equipment. Then he took Pablo aside and told him about the ruins he wanted him to plunder.

On a visit to the Hotel Colonial, which he had bought, John saw that the place that was to be "a good center for our activities" was, in reality, "no use whatsoever. I was the only one who put money into it and I lost everything."

From Cuernavaca John went to Mexico City, where he met a taxi driver outside the Hotel Bamer who would become his best friend in Mexico and "one of the finest men I've ever known." His name was Arturo Sarabia.

"I met Mr. Huston at this hotel," Sarabia, now an independent tourist guide, said. "The doorman told me he needed a driver. Mr. Huston said, 'Well, you look like a good man, would you like to work for me?' He asked me if I spoke English and when he found out I had been a fighter, I always had to tell him how I started to fight." "I knew him by reputation," John said. "He was going to be welterweight champion of the world, but then he almost killed a man in the ring and put down his gloves in 1949." "From that time," said Sarabia, "wherever Mr. Huston went, he would tell me to come with him, like family. I was from a little village. I had no father and when I found him, that was the father I wanted to have."

Sarabia became not only John's driver in Mexico but also his valet. When Huston asked him what he most desired, Sarabia replied, his own car. So John bought him a 1955 Chrysler, which freed him to work for himself.

The open space surrounding Durango, about six hundred miles northwest of Mexico City, is often used as a setting for Hollywood westerns. Robert Mitchum made a number of pictures there and considered it "bad territory. That's where the best *pistoleros* came from. Every time I worked there we never once came back with a complete crew. Somebody always turned up missing. I once talked with a guy in the local Chamber of Commerce and he said, 'I don't understand why we don't have more tourists in Durango; it's on the Pan-American highway, at the beginning of the big Sierra, we have hotels. . . .' And all the time he was talking his conversation was punctuated by gunfire outside, they were blowing each other away."

Ben Maddow saw the city as a large, industrial town. But on Mission Sunday he caught a glimpse of what a strange place it was. It was a day set aside for the Catholic missions to collect money. There was a parade of floats, some filled with Mexican children in blackface or made up as Orientals, others presenting religious scenes. On one, a man was tied to a cross, and blaring from a microphone all along the route came a voice shouting, "Christ on the Cross, courtesy of Coca-Cola."

Maddow stayed long enough to see that John rarely told Franz Planer where to put his camera and left "of my own volition" after the actors began to complain to him that Huston wasn't giving them any direction. He found Burt Lancaster to be bright and shrewd, James Hill in "a complete state of panic, afraid to drink the water," and Lillian Gish, on her first day of shooting, still stuck in the era of silent films. "She came out with pancake-white makeup, made her look like a clown. It took quite a while to get her to peel off that stuff." The casting, on the whole, he found "weird." Especially the attempt to pass off Audrey Hepburn as an Indian girl.

Tom Shaw, who would begin his long association with Huston as first assistant director on this film, recalled how his first days on the set were ones that tried his soul but which demonstrated to John that he had found another valuable addition to his team. Stephen Grimes had built his set in the side of a hill, with the top of the hill becoming the roof of the house where Gish and her family lived. "The first day of the picture," Shaw said, "we started with the camera on the roof. We pulled back and dropped down to where the door opened and Audrey Hepburn walked out to the river, fifteen yards from the house. She bent down, got some water, and then went back to the house. I guess I had to prove to John how fuckin' smart I was, so I hollered, 'While we're in the long shot, let's do the exit of Audrey.' And he didn't even turn around to look at me. He just said, 'I don't make movies like that. While we're in the *close-up* of her we'll do her exit.' For the rest of the day, when he'd look at me, it was like fuckin' death. I can't tell you how depressed I was."

Privately, over the next few days, Shaw began to curse Huston and the movie business, desperately looking for an opportunity to prove himself. One scene called for a big sandstorm. Although the wind often blew outside Durango, it couldn't be counted on to blow on cue. Giving the problem some thought Shaw came up with a solution. "I remembered there was an airport run by an American, Bill Pickens. So I got him to fly me out to the location and asked if he could land another plane out there as well. With two planes I figured I could make this sonofabitch *blow!* Just by turning the asses of the planes around to act like wind machines. It was only five hundred yards from the original location, and with the sand and the Joshua trees and the cactus all over the place, it wouldn't make a difference in a sandstorm." Shaw showed John the new location, but Huston objected. "It doesn't match," he said, "doesn't look anything like what we've already shot." "It looks *exactly* the same," Shaw protested, "and what the hell difference does it make if the goddamn wind is blowing? You can't see the shit anyway. Sand looks the same!" Huston felt Shaw's hostility and said, "I don't want to talk about it anymore."

Back in the car James Hill sided with John and Shaw turned on both of them. "I was so fuckin' mad I was gonna quit," he recalled. "Then John turned around from the front seat and looked at Hill and said, 'You know, Jim, we're both full of shit.' He looked at me and said, 'Tom, when d'you want to do what you want to do?' This was the *first* time he called me Tom. From that moment on it didn't make any difference what I told him, he never questioned it. That was really the beginning of our relationship."

Lorrie Sherwood attempted to assert herself by showing up unexpectedly in Durango and John suddenly had to deal with *that*. John had asked a budding screenwriter, Johnny Melson, to act as his temporary secretary and had also invited Jilda Smith to stay with him in his house. But once Lorrie appeared it became uncomfortable for Jilda. At dinner John made it a point to ignore Sherwood and pay attention to Smith. "How was your day, today, Jilda?" he would ask. "Tell me everything you did." Jilda finally felt too uncomfortable to remain in the house and packed her bag. But John insisted that she stay, which she did, until Lorrie, according to Jilda, threatened her. "I'm here with my Johnny," Lorrie apparently said, "and I love my Johnny and he loves me and I don't want you here. If you don't leave I'm going to kill you now and then kill him later." Jilda didn't know if Sherwood was bluffing, but she told Burt Lancaster that she was moving out of Huston's house. At dinner that night Jilda sat between Lancaster and John when Lancaster shouted, "Have you told John that you're leaving yet?" Jilda could feel John's rising anger and he refused to speak to her for the rest of the movie. She also suspected that John would have liked a better end to the conflict. "He probably would have preferred that Lorrie had killed me," Smith said, "so then people could have asked him, 'What happened to the other one?' and he could have answered, 'She died in the electric chair.'"

"Jilda was doing *my* job and living in *his* house when I got there," Lorrie Sherwood confirmed. "But she wasn't living there *after* I got there!"

Tensions off the set led to tensions on, as well. Dorothy Jeakins, an Oscar-winning costume designer who worked for Huston for the first time on *The Unforgiven*, remembered noticing how "John would not watch the actors during a take, he would listen to their voices. If the dialogue sounded right he'd look at Angela Allen, who would wink if it looked right. And he'd say, 'Print that.' John was more concerned with how an actor sounded than how he looked."

His apparent lack of direction to actors who were doing what he expected them to do made Audie Murphy nervous. "He used to complain bitterly that John never said anything to him," Jilda Smith said. "He wanted the reassurance, he *wanted* to be directed."

John remembered having "a bit of a time" with Murphy. "He was the next thing to being unstable. I suppose he hadn't caught up with the things that had happened to him. There were thoughts of suicide. He said, 'I feel like getting in my airplane and riding into a mountain.' My Christ! That's the way he got it a year and a half later, although he wasn't piloting the plane."

While Huston could rationalize Murphy's problems as psychological, he didn't know what to make of Lancaster, except that he didn't like him. During the first week of shooting Stephen Grimes said that Lancaster started to tell John where the camera should be. John listened, nodded, and said, "I don't do that, the camera should be where I put it." Lancaster didn't argue, but when it came to a scene with Lancaster, Hepburn, and John Saxon, Lancaster refused to back down. The scene, which never appeared, was essential to the story, according to Tom Shaw. It involved a confrontation between Lancaster and Saxon over whether or not Saxon had slept with Hepburn. It demonstrated the emotional unrest and jealousy of Lancaster's character. "What it boiled down to," Shaw said, "was that Burt didn't want to believe that she could fuck somebody else. It was strictly a big ego thing. And John and Burt roamed around the goddamn desert *arguing* this scene for two days! Finally John just got tired and gave in. It was a mistake, because it was one of the key scenes."

It was Shaw's belief that Lancaster ruined the movie. Robert Mitchum knew Lancaster to be arrogant and figured the film had little chance, since "John didn't admire an attitude of arrogance." Lancaster told Jilda Smith that he would never work with Huston again. And John told Lorrie Sherwood that if anyone ever made a movie of Peter Viertel's *White Hunter, Black Heart* the one actor he *didn't* want to play him was Burt Lancaster. When Lancaster was asked to comment on Huston he curtly answered, "There's nothing I can say about him. I just don't want to talk about it!" Ernie Anderson wasn't at all surprised by Lancaster's behavior. "He's a pain in the ass, like John Wayne was," Anderson said. "His attitude was, 'It's either your picture or my picture.'"

The other actor Tom Shaw felt helped ruin the movie was Lillian Gish, whom he called "a terrible actress. She might have been good in 1912, but boy, she was absolutely fucking awful!" Jilda Smith recalled Gish's long scene where she told how she came to adopt the child. "She said that she had a baby of her own and it had died after birth and then she heard this crying and found this Indian baby and she had to say the line: 'And my breasts were hurting with all that milk and I took the Indian baby and fed it.' She's a very fastidious lady and John knew she didn't like the line and he'd say, 'Very good, Lillian, not too heavy on the breasts, honey.' And he made her do that take God knows how many times. It was agonizing."

"We did that scene *all day long!*" Tom Shaw exclaimed. "Every time we did it he would say to her, 'Absolutely wonderful, but we're just going to do it once more.' That was his method, of just breaking the woman down, where she had no energy at all. She was just fuckin' *whipped!* And so was I! He got her so worn out she wasn't looking for D. W. Griffith anymore. That's what she constantly did: 'D.W. wouldn't do it that way.' "

"I'd been with Griffith for years," Lillian Gish said, defending herself. "I knew more about pictures and been with more successes than John had ever had. So we got along beautifully, although he got along with the men better and spent more time with them. The men were all amazed that I was a better shot than any of them. They didn't expect that!" Besides feeling that John didn't pay enough attention to his actresses she was critical of how he handled Audrey Hepburn. "Audrey had great talent, and he never used it."

One thing Hepburn didn't have much talent for was riding horses, but she understood it would be impossible to shoot anything in close-up if a double was used. The horse she was given to ride, Diablo, was a white stallion who once belonged to President Batista of Cuba.

Hepburn was riding and Jilda Smith felt that "there was no necessity whatsoever to do the shot the way John had it done. But it was devised so that she cantered up to the camera and got off in one shot. She did it a couple of times and it wasn't right. On the third time they tried to stop her from coming any farther and the horse changed its gait from a canter to a trot." Someone jumped in front of the horse and waved his arms, which spooked Diablo and made him buck. Dorothy Jeakins saw Audrey go "flying through the air." When she landed she didn't move. John rushed over, saw she was in great pain, and called for Arturo Sarabia. "He wanted me to massage her spine," Sarabia said. "Because when I was fighting I used to give massages and I would often give Mr. Huston a massage for his legs and his back. But I didn't want to do it because it could be damaged. I said not to touch her." Hepburn was pregnant at the time and worried about losing the baby. "She also worried about her husband, Mel Ferrer," Lillian Gish said. "She didn't want him to hear about it from anyone else."

She was taken to a hospital in Durango and the next day Ferrer and her doctor flew down from Los Angeles. "He was obviously furious," Angela Allen said of Ferrer. "He thought it was all John's fault, that she shouldn't have been riding." She had four fractured vertebrae, but no surgery was required. Hepburn was flown home in an ambulance plane to Beverly Hills to recuperate and the rest of the company had an unexpected vacation until she returned.

During her absence John suffered another attack of gout and had to fly to Mazatlán to be treated. But before he left he had a terrible row with Lorrie Sherwood when, according to both Jilda Smith and Dorothy Jeakins, she went after him with a knife. It was later reported in a newspaper with Lorrie mentioned only as his "secretary-mistress" who tried to cut him up because she was "outraged at his alleged infidelity." Said Jeakins, "She was in a psychotic condition and they had to get her out of there."

Sherwood said that she went to Mazatlán with John, "because he couldn't take the shots for his gout in that high altitude of Durango. And that's when I left. He had told me to come to Mexico and everything would be fine. I did and it wasn't . . . and I went back to Ireland." All John wanted to say about the whole matter was that *The Unforgiven* was the last picture Lorrie ever worked on with him. "I don't think I ever saw her again after that."

In Mexico City John met a woman named Maka Czernichew, a talented and beautiful artist who could sing, dance, paint, write, and ride horses. Her mother was Spanish-Mexican, her father a Russian count who became a refugee in Germany. After the war they moved to Mexico. She had been married and divorced at least twice by the time she met John.

They met at a party; John was amusing a group of people with the story of how a chimpanzee broke up his marriage to Evelyn Keyes. "I know that story," she interrupted him. "That's impossible," John said. Maka proceeded to tell him that she had just come from Los Angeles and was at a party where Evelyn Keyes was telling the same story. John appreciated the coincidence. A few days later they both appeared at a party at the French embassy. The ambassador asked Maka to sing and as she did, John sat in front of her, dressed in his safari suit, smoking his Cuban cigar, looking her straight in the eyes. "I thought, God, what is this? Something very strange and tumultuous," said Maka. "There is some other transcendental substance mixed into her flesh," John would later say of her. "Look at her mouth when she smiles: it is the Olmec jaguar's mouth. Her eyes are too shiny. She is undoubtedly a *bruja*."

*   *   *

While John and Maka were getting to know each other Pablo gave John some exciting news. The site in Jalapa that Huston had located by plane had begun to pay off. Pablo had hired a number of local people to help him dig and they uncovered enough artifact fragments to indicate a major discovery. John was so pleased to hear this that he told Rosa Covarrubias, widow of the artist who had illustrated *Frankie and Johnny*. What John didn't realize was that she was connected with the museum of anthropology and, said Pablo, "she opened her mouth and shot everything down the drain." When Pablo got back to the site he read in the newspapers that the director of that museum had taken credit for discovering the ruins and that Pablo Huston was involved in sacking them. "An expedition of soldiers were sent to capture me," Pablo said. He called John to ask him what he should do, but John was too heartsick about the loss of such a discovery to give him any advice. When he hung up the phone all he could say was, "He can't even rob graves!"

Pablo fled to Mexico City, where he stayed with John. "Pablo got out by the skin of his teeth," Huston said. "Next thing I know, I opened the paper and it said one of Mexico's leading archeologists had discovered it and it was one of the country's greatest finds."

The treasures that might have been theirs wound up in the anthropological museum in Mexico City, where they belonged. But getting so close only whetted Huston's appetite, and he and Billy sent Pablo to Veracruz, south of Jalapa, to try again. "We had as many as seventy men digging in Veracruz, under the direction of his idiot adopted son, Pablo," Pearson said. "His supervising consisted of sitting under a tree in the shade, reading comic books. And every time they dug up something, they didn't hand it to Pablo, they stole it! Pablo was just payin' them. When I got down there and saw what was going on, I moved them to another area at a place called Tierra Blanca."

By the time Billy reached Tierra Blanca, Audrey Hepburn had returned to Mexico and *The Unforgiven* resumed. John sent Arturo Sarabia to pick up Maka at four A.M. and bring her up to Durango. The hour was far too early for her and she resisted, but Sarabia was patient, and when she arrived John had yet another diversion to keep him from thinking too seriously about all the compromises he had already made regarding the movie. "At the beginning," Maka said, "we had a very tender relationship, but then it became a challenge, mixed up with a lot of love. If you were weak in front of John, you were through. I am not the type to become weak. With John, you had no time to go to pieces, to reason. He would talk beautifully in front of people, but in private it was more difficult. We lived around the bed or in the bed, eating sandwiches, playing dominoes. I asked him why he became a director and he said that once he was on a picture, it came so easily that he decided he would never pick up something else that he would have to study."

Maka soon discovered, as all of his women eventually did, that "John had a very man's life. Men were men and women were something else. He kind of despised women, despised anything that would be weaker than he was. He was an adventurer. He admired Hemingway, Errol Flynn, Orson Welles, Humphrey Bogart. And Katharine Hepburn, because she was brave when the elephants came on them. He admired strength, and everything that would resist him."

Maka found John to be jealous and possessive. "I couldn't even talk to Burt Lancaster, because I was not supposed to get close. They weren't pals. Lancaster was living alone in a house and would never go out. And there were some rules with Audie Murphy, whom he liked very much. But Audie was a crazy man; he was the only one John could never step on. In public I couldn't even approach Audie, but Audie helped me and protected me in many circumstances. He would always have his plane ready for me in case I wanted to leave. One time I was so mad at John that I had my revenge. I wanted to go and John sent Johnny Melson to say I had to stay. So I left with Audie for the airfield. We got in his plane and he saw John from the air and came down just to his hairs! Audie was mad! I said, 'Audie, he's going to throw you off the picture.' 'Oh, I don't give a damn,' he said." Maka was pleased with her revenge because it was "a public humiliation." But when Murphy's plane began to sputter and he was forced to land, she suddenly became afraid of what John might do to her.

"I crossed the door to come back and he was sitting on the edge of his bed and asked me for a drink. He controlled himself. 'You know, baby,' he said, looking at me, 'it was miscast. You took my part.' 'Yes, I know,' I said. 'I'm leaving tomorrow.' The next morning I was sitting with my luggage waiting to leave and John came in—he had stopped shooting— and asked me to stay. 'I didn't calculate on sentiments,' he said. That was the only thing he said. And then he went to pieces in that moment. So I stayed."

Maka's *bruja* powers not only brought Huston to tears, but the reclusive Audie Murphy felt close enough to tell her about his dreams, how he was always reliving the war, shooting Germans over and over. "He couldn't sleep," she said. "And once we had to call the doctor because he couldn't breathe. He was put in a tent of oxygen. It was all anguish."

One early evening photographer Inge Morath, who had come to cover the picture, saw through her telescopic lens that Murphy was in trouble out on the lake where he had gone to shoot wild ducks. He had fallen out of the boat and, in a state of panic because he couldn't swim, was resisting any help from an exhausted Bill Pickens. She stripped down to her bra and panties and dove into the water. When she reached them she got Murphy to lie on her back, as he held onto her bra strap. "He was pretty groggy," Morath said. "I said, 'If you move, you drown me.' I got him back to shore, barely." It was a humbling experience for World War II's most decorated hero, and afterward Murphy gave Morath the watch he had worn throughout the war. After Huston heard about the rescue Morath joined Katharine Hepburn as one of the bravest women he was proud to know.

Soon after this excitement John received an emergency phone call from Billy Pearson, who was holed up in a penthouse suite in Mexico City. There was a car full of some of the greatest pieces of pre-Columbian art he'd ever seen parked in the garage, and a bunch of bandits who wanted to kill him and take it were staking out the building. "You've got to get me out of this!" Pearson demanded. So John sent Arturo to the rescue.

"We hit a big, big cache of stuff at Tierra Blanca," Pearson explained. Some local Indians uncovered the pieces and then sold them to the highest bidder. Billy had the money but not the manpower to get the goods safely away from his competitors. He loaded one truck and filled a car with the pre-Columbian figures, but by the time he made it to Mexico City he had lost the truck to hijackers. The best pieces were in the car, with him, and he managed to elude the thieves and make it to the apartment building where Ted Finlay and his wife lived. "They were very rich," Pearson said, "owned two things in Mexico: the franchise for Caterpillar tractors, and Pepsi-Cola. They also owned a big stable of horses and I rode for them. I holed up in their apartment house because it was well guarded. They owned the two top floors. I couldn't dare go out or those hijackers would have kidnapped me and held me ransom for the pre-Columbian."

Sarabia helped Pearson pack the three life-size Veracruz figures in large baskets. These were the pieces that so excited Pearson that he had filmed their excavation. He figured they were at least a thousand years old and they were in perfect condition. When Sarabia's Chrysler was packed with the goods, Billy crawled inside so he couldn't be seen and the metal garage doors were opened for their getaway. "Of course, within a minute, there was a carload of guys after us," Pearson said. "Arturo took out two .45 automatics from the glove compartment and handed me one and put the other on the car seat. 'If they catch up,' he said. I said, 'For chrissake, it's only pre-Columbian art; there's no sense to start shooting each other! We'll give them the fucking art!' " Sarabia recalled how he had to "drive back and forth to lose them. When I saw the highway there was another car after us. But we lost them."

When they finally got to Durango John was on location, so they planned a surprise for him. They prepared a party with two of the three Veracruz pieces as the centerpiece. Billy covered them with a sheet. That evening, Maka remembered, "They took off the piece of cloth and the two pieces appeared. John was happy as hell." The figures were Huston's, to cover the debt Billy owed him for their investment. The third figure, of the king, Pearson held back to give to a Texas wildcatter named Ted, who would help them smuggle the art into the States.

"Ted drilled oil wells," Pearson said, "and wherever he drilled they made temporary landing fields. The idea was for him to keep one of these fields lit all night so that we could fly a plane in from Durango and unload it." They wanted to borrow Audie Murphy's plane, but Huston was afraid that if they got caught Murphy could be implicated. So they decided not to get Murphy involved. They would *steal* his plane!

They arranged for someone else to fly the plane. It was John's job to get into a poker game with Murphy while Pearson and the pilot loaded the plane and flew to Texas. "We tiptoed out and got into Murphy's plane and took off," Billy said. "We flew about a hundred miles, when I'm not feeling good. I was on the floor in the cabin, my head wedged underneath the foot pedals, in convulsions. The pilot turned the plane around. The next thing I knew I was in a hospital bed with long needles in my stomach. The next day John came and said, 'Well, it's all been delivered.' Everything was perfect! Audie didn't know that we'd stolen his plane. And those pieces ended up at St. Clerans with John."

While Pearson was in the hospital Burt Lancaster and Audie Murphy agreed to play in a local golf tournament. That gave John an idea for one of his capers. He sent Sarabia to buy two thousand Ping-Pong balls and had them brought to Billy's hospital room, where they spent hours inscribing them. "We wrote every dirty thing you could think of," Pearson said. " 'Burt Lancaster sucks!' 'Yankee sons of bitches, go home!' All this stuff. Then we got Bill Pickens to fly Audie's plane over the golf course. Now Audie was playing in the tournament—he looked up, saw his plane dumping all those goddamn balls!"

"It was a triumph," Huston said, laughing. "The tournament was canceled and everybody was furious—especially Burt Lancaster, who took his golf quite seriously."

Somehow, through all this, the movie got made. Paul P. Kennedy, a *New York Times* reporter, wrote a story about how relaxed Huston seemed. "Even during tense moments he is likely to be sauntering among the spectators or gossiping with the crew." When it came time for Lillian Gish to die, Huston worried that she might overact and Jilda Smith said he did "a terrible thing to her. He never shot her death scene. She died after she was wounded, without realizing she had died." For another scene, where the Indians had to cross the river to attack the house, he saw that the river was too low and that the crossing would be too easy, so he ordered Johnny Melson to send workers out in the middle of the night to fill the river with big rocks. "The next day," Maka observed, "all the Indians on their horses went straight to the river and the horses started falling in. John was thrilled. I don't know how many got hurt, but he would do any goddamn thing to get his scene. He was a dangerous man. He always had to live, privately or publicly, on the verge of the limit. He had to be thrilled all the time."

He also, apparently, enjoyed torturing Maka. The worst time was when they went on a turkey shoot soon after she discovered she was pregnant. "I started to feel bad," Maka recalled. "I went back to my room . . . and I had a miscarriage. God, I felt like hell!" The next morning they were scheduled to fly with Audie Murphy to a location, but when Murphy looked at Maka he suggested that she be taken immediately back to Mexico City to see a doctor. Whether John knew of her condition isn't clear, but he refused to let her go with Murphy. "Instead," Maka said, "John called Arturo, who took me back home." Sarabia drove her to Mexico City, and Maka never understood why John behaved the way he did. "It was his character," she shrugged. "He didn't care. Much later, after knowing John for years and years, then he would take care of me whatever I would need. He could be very cruel, and he had a very tough character, but I had, too. That's the way we could survive for almost thirty years. It was a very long relationship. We must really have liked each other quite a lot."

Inge Morath had no idea how right she was when she observed that John was so preoccupied during the making of *The Unforgiven* that "half the time his head was not in directing the movie. You had the feeling that he wasn't really there. A certain amount of disjointedness took place on account of that." And no wonder! With all that went on behind the scenes—between the smuggling and his tempestuous relationships with Lorrie Sherwood and Maka, plus his actors' accidents and the practical jokes—had he turned the cameras on his own life at the time it would have made a far more remarkable film!

When Huston returned to Los Angeles to work on the movie, Paul Kohner introduced him to Doc Erickson, who had been Alfred Hitchcock's production manager for five pictures. It was his job to "ride herd on the art and prop departments, supply the assistant directors with all the logistical things that are needed, deal with payrolls, budgets, and general organization." Doc was thirty-five and hoping to work with John on a television series about painters. But that project fell through; instead they talked about potential locations for *The Man Who Would Be King*. To Erickson it was just idle talk because John went back to cutting *The Unforgiven*, then sent for Maka to join him for the preview. "He was very nervous about it," Maka said. "And after, there was a party in the lobby, but he didn't wait, he grabbed me by the hand and walked into a terrible, dark bar. He started drinking and wouldn't say a word. We went back to the Beverly Hills Hotel and I stayed with him for five days."

When Huston returned to Ireland in the summer of 1959 the Big House was finally ready for him. At last he had a home for the sculptures, paintings, and furniture that he had been collecting all his life. He found just the right walls for his Gris, his Utrillo, his Monet. But his greatest prize, the pieces he was most proud of, were the Veracruz figures that had arrived from Texas. They were so important to him that he got in touch with the wildcatter, Ted, and said that he thought the three pieces belonged together and offered to buy the one that Billy had given him. Ted was reluctant, but when John asked him to name his price, he said $20,000. "It was as much as I could afford to pay," Huston said. Then Ted's attorney wrote to John saying his client had decided to keep the figure. John wrote back that a deal was a deal, but if Ted didn't want to sell his figure for $20,000, then he would have to buy the other two for $40,000. John got his king.

Over the next fifteen years those three figures sat in a place of honor in Huston's house until he sold St. Clerans and most of the works he had collected. The Veracruz pieces went to a collector, John Wise, for $225,000. Two years later, in 1976, Wise donated them to the Dallas Museum of Art, where they were displayed until the spring of 1987, when *Connoisseur* magazine published an article claiming that a forty-five-year-old art restorer named Brigido Lara had forged thousands of clay works that were currently in the collections of some of the most esteemed private collectors and in a number of major museums as well, including the Metropolitan Museum of Art, the St. Louis Art Museum, and the Dallas Museum of Art. It was a major art scandal and, on April 26, 1987, the *Los Angeles Herald-Examiner* wrote, in a front-page story, that "Dallas museum officials announced . . . that three of their most prominent pre-Columbian artifacts were not 1,000 years old, but instead were thought to have been made in a Jalapa, Mexico, workshop in the 1950s.

"The three ceramic sculptures are all lifesize sitting figures made in the manner of figures dating from A.D. 600 to 900 in what experts call the Veracruz style. Laboratory tests confirmed the newness of the figures."

"I think the pieces are good," John would say, refusing to believe that he had lived with fakes all those years. "I think this fellow Lara said he did them as a way of getting out of jail." Huston was right about that. In 1974, Lara was arrested near Veracruz for looting a priceless artifact from a tomb. He was convicted and sent to prison although he protested that he wasn't a looter but a forger. When authorities brought clay and tools to his cell he proceeded to make a duplicate of the piece that he had been arrested for looting. Lara was released from prison and eventually was hired by the government as a restorer and replica maker.

"This guy Lara," Huston said skeptically, "would have been twelve years old when he made those pieces. So that tells you."

Actually, Lara was seventeen in 1959. When Billy Pearson pointed out that he had witnessed the pieces being dug up and had even filmed it,

Carol Robbins, the acting curator of new-world cultures at the Dallas Museum of Art, told the *New York Times* that Pearson was probably the victim of staged excavation. "It's not unlikely that people in Mexico would go to such lengths to give the appearance this was a burial." But Pearson countered that by questioning the motive of such an elaborately staged trick. "It doesn't make any sense," Pearson said. "Who would benefit? Where was the payoff? In those days you couldn't give pre-Columbian art away." Billy, of course, knew differently, but even so, would he have been chased by bandits had they known the pieces were fake?

Pearson had called Huston when the story broke and informed him that someone had already committed suicide as a result of the disclosure. Huston was faced with a dilemma: The thought had to cross his mind that his old and trusted friend had cheated him. If that was true, then their friendship was phony . . . and that was something even more damaging than the Veracruz pieces.

"I really don't want to go into a lot of this," Billy Pearson said when challenged about the authenticity of the figures. "It does me no good, it does John no good; I'd like to see it all blow away. There's no feathers in anybody's cap."

Even though the Dallas museum had removed them from display, Huston sided with Billy. "I think they're good," he said, unwilling to admit that his treasures of the Tierra Blanca were, in fact, his Maltese falcons.

PART SEVEN

20

THE PHILOSOPHER, THE KING, AND THE GODDESS

IN THE SPRING AND SUMMER OF 1958, WHILE HUSTON WAS in Paris completing *The Roots of Heaven*, he put into motion two projects that would become his twentieth and twenty-first films. On May 31, 1958, he met with French existential philosopher Jean-Paul Sartre to discuss writing a screenplay about Sigmund Freud, the founder of psychoanalysis. In July he heard from American playwright Arthur Miller, who had written a script called *The Misfits*, based on a short story he had published in *Esquire* about existential cowboys who no longer fit into modern society. Sartre was considered France's leading intellectual; Miller, one of America's two leading playwrights. Given Huston's penchant for working with the best, he had high hopes for bringing in the sixties with style and force.

His interest in Freud began while he was at Mason General Hospital on Long Island, New York, filming *Let There Be Light*. His own interest in hypnosis had also whetted his appetite for the way the mind was open to suggestion. But Freud had gone beyond hypnosis when he came upon his theories of psychoanalysis at the turn of the century, and Huston had always thought that in Freud's discoveries was the basis for a film that would make a good mystery thriller. He even had his collaborator on *Let There Be Light*, Charles Kaufman, draft a treatment for such a movie, but the idea was shelved for years, until Wolfgang Reinhardt renewed his interest. Reinhardt had worked with John on *Juarez* and had since become, like his brother Gottfried, a producer. He was a serious student of Freud and agreed with John that Sartre would bring the right intellectual weight to such a complex subject. It was their intention to focus on his moment of epiphany, when he abandoned hypnosis, defined the Oedipus complex, and laid open the field of psychoanalysis.

Sartre was a daring choice; he hadn't studied Freud and was considered to be anti-Freudian. But Huston, who had directed Sartre's play *No Exit*, felt he would bring "an objective and logical approach," and he asked Suzanne Flon to make the introductions and act as translator in Paris. Huston offered Sartre $25,000 to write the script, which may not have seemed like a great deal of money for a screenplay, but to Sartre, who had recently borrowed money from his mother to pay his taxes, it was a very large sum indeed. Huston also promised that the picture would be done regardless of censorship, which Sartre misinterpreted as meaning there would be no restrictions as to the length of the story. By December 15, Sartre sent Huston a ninety-five-page treatment, which John approved. Ten months later he delivered his first draft, over three hundred pages long. Huston invited Sartre to St. Clerans in October 1959 to discuss the script. Sartre arrived with his young mistress, Arlette El Kaim, whom he would later adopt as his daughter. John mistook her for Sartre's secretary.

Sartre and Huston didn't hit it off at all. Physically, John thought he was the ugliest man he'd ever seen: "One eye going in one direction, and the eye itself wasn't very beautiful, like an omelet. And he had a pitted face." Intellectually, he found him boorish, a man so in love with his own words that he was constantly writing down what he'd said and never allowed anyone else to speak until he had finished, which never happened. "He couldn't stop talking," John observed, blaming it on the stimulants he took.

Sartre's impressions were recorded in a letter to Simone de Beauvoir: "Through this immensity of identical rooms, a great Romantic, melancholic and lonely, aimlessly roams. Our friend Huston is absent, aged, and literally unable to speak to his guests." Since they weren't communicating, Sartre concluded that "The man has emigrated. I don't know where. He's not even sad: he's *empty*, except in moments of childish vanity, when he puts on a red dinner jacket or rides a horse (not very well) or counts his paintings or tells workmen what to do. Impossible to hold his attention for five minutes: he can no longer work, he runs away from thinking . . . because it saddens him."

Not to be out-observed, Huston noticed that his guest "wore a cheap, ill-fitting, three-piece suit with the same necktie, and although his shirts looked laundered, it was always as though he had the same clothes on." John found Sartre to be the most "obstinate and categorical" man he'd ever worked with. Sartre considered Huston's "interior landscape . . . the last stop before the moon. . . . His emptiness is purer than death."

If nothing about Huston impressed Sartre, Sartre's lack of vanity certainly caught John's attention. When Sartre developed a toothache Huston sent him to a dentist, who pulled the tooth. "One tooth more or less was of no consequence to Sartre. The physical universe did not exist for him. Only the mind mattered."

After ten days Sartre understood that scenes had to be cut from his script and he returned to Paris and cut some. Unfortunately he also added scenes, doubling the size of the screenplay, making it impossible to turn it into a two-, even a three-hour movie. What Sartre had written would take eight hours to film. Rather than try to get him to reduce it by seventy-five percent, John had Universal hire Charlie Kaufman to attempt a rewrite. The result, however, was banal, and John saw that he would have to work with Wolfgang to get a shooting script. But Wolfgang was involved in the production of *The Sound of Music*, so *Freud* was put on hold as John turned his attention to *The Misfits*.

Arthur Miller's introductory letter to Huston described the story, set in the backcountry of Nevada, as one which "concerns two cowboys, a bush pilot, a girl and the last of the Mustangs up in the mountains," and indicated that his wife, Marilyn Monroe, was available for the girl. He was aware that Huston didn't want to work in the United States, but thought that perhaps if he liked the story enough he might change his mind. Or, "having seen so much of the earth, perhaps you'll know of a foreign locale equivalent." Huston wrote back, "It's true that for various reasons I prefer to do pictures outside the United States for the present time, but making a good picture is much more important. There are, however, parts of Mexico that are identical to northern Nevada."

Once John read Miller's script he sent him a one-word cable: "Magnificent." Miller wrote back that "Not since [*Death of a*] *Salesman* have

I felt such eagerness to see something of mine performed. . . . I have a sense that we are all moving into one of those rare productions when everything touched becomes alive."

Miller had stumbled upon his story when he had gone to Reno to obtain a divorce from his first wife. The cowboys he met would go into the mountains and round up mustangs, which they'd sell to be made into dog food. Huston read the script and immediately thought of Robert Mitchum for one of the cowboys. Mitchum was in Ireland making *The Night Fighters*, and John brought him the script. He also showed Mitchum a letter he had written to Arthur Miller saying that the script was perfect as written and that he wouldn't presume to offer any suggestions. "I read the script," Mitchum said, "and made absolutely no sense from it. So I hid from John. I said, 'If John Huston calls, tell him I died.' "

While John was hoping for Mitchum, agent Lew Wasserman thought that the script might interest Clark Gable. But Gable, also, didn't know what to make of it. It wasn't a real western; it didn't have a standard plot. Miller was asked to meet with him. "We got along pretty well," Miller recalled, "but he didn't understand how you could do a picture that was in western costume and in a western setting where the audience would expect certain things to happen, and they weren't gonna happen. He was going by the old signposts. The way I saw it, the picture was gonna deal with a place associated with straight-forward, uncomplicated action. Which had now become introspective and full of trouble. This script was about the trouble in paradise." Finally Miller told Gable, "It's sort of an Eastern western. It's about our lives' meaninglessness and maybe how we got to where we are." Gable laughed and promised to read the script again. The next day he agreed to do it.

Huston began to think about locations, not only for *The Misfits* but also for *The Man Who Would Be King*, which he couldn't get out of his mind. He arranged, with Stephen Grimes, Johnny Melson, and Doc Erickson, for a Middle East, Near East, and Far East location trip.

In London to obtain the necessary visas, John ran into Robert Mitchum, a meeting Mitchum would never forget because John had an unusual monkey at the bar with him. "John was sitting there playing with the monkey's dick," Mitchum said. "The monkey had a very strange red-white-and-blue dick like a barber's pole. I said, 'John, what are you doing?' He said, 'He likes it, kid.'"

After Mitchum sat down John said, "I'm a little disappointed in you, kid."

"Why?" Mitchum asked.

"Script," Huston said.

"John, I read that script and it made absolutely no sense to me."

John tried to tell Mitchum that the script could have been changed, but Mitchum reminded him that he had seen John's letter to Miller saying he wouldn't change a thing. "Did I show you that?" John asked. "How stupid of me!" Then John told Mitchum that Gable was going to do it.

"I know," Mitchum said, "you're going to kill him. I had lunch with him a few weeks ago and he's got the trembles. He's drinking two quarts of whiskey a day and they say he's grouchy. He's had two or three heart warnings. You get him at the end of a rope, fighting those horses, and that's going to be the end of him."

The Asian tour was a whirlwind and relatively uneventful, with no locations agreed upon. In early December 1959, John flew to Nevada for two days and approved the Reno location for *The Misfits*. Then he returned to Ireland, found an unsolicited script among the mail with a friendly note from the producer's temporary secretary, and instantly made one of the most important decisions of his life, which was to hire that secretary.

Since Lorrie Sherwood's departure John had no one to make order of his chaotic life. The woman who jotted the note was Gladys Hill. She had been Sam Spiegel's secretary until she married in 1952 and went to live in Mexico. When John was writing *The Stranger*, Spiegel had loaned her to him and he remembered her competence. She was recently divorced and John invited her to "Come to Ireland and work for me forever and ever." She accepted, and when she arrived he gave her the loft above the stables where he had lived, and she organized his life the way no other woman—wife, secretary, mistress—had ever done before. "I never had to make decisions with Gladys around," John said. "And she kept certain people informed about me and arrived at a personal relationship with them, carrying on a sizable correspondence."

"She was his goddamn right arm," Billy Pearson said of her. "John never remembered to carry money or keys in his pockets, his brain was somewhere else. But Gladys was always there. Betty O'Kelly controlled the house and the horses, and Gladys controlled the studio stuff, the movies. It took someone with an obsession to take care of him. And there was no question that both Gladys and Betty were in love with him." Dorothy Jeakins saw Gladys as a plain woman who was "a bank of keeping-his-life-together deposits." Inge Morath thought Gladys was "a kind of latter-day saint. She was terribly nice but rather a pain, because whatever John did, she did."

Anjelica remembered Gladys as being "very mild, upstanding, kind, solemn. She had her wild side, too, but she was very West Virginian. She would laugh, but she was controlled. A good-hearted woman. Not ebullient, but she had personal pride. When she and my father worked, doors were closed." Tony said that she was "a Puritan. With an open mind as far as Dad was concerned. But her morality was absolutely rigid and, in a funny way, she was also a maternal figure for Dad. The only reason Gladys could last so long was because she was not involved with any of his affairs, she was able to keep her distance. She was always the bridesmaid . . . and had quite a lonely life. Early on—I only heard my mother say this—Gladys would disappear for weekends somewhere and she'd be ragged a bit when she came back, and so that stopped. Then she just managed everything that had to do with Dad."

Tony barely remembered the time Jean-Paul Sartre visited St. Clerans, because "we were all sort of segregated: We were with my mother in the Little House and Dad had his court up at the Big House, and the only time we all got together was for lunch. *If* that. It was very much two households separated by half a mile." The children were just beginning to understand that all was not well between their parents.

"Anjelica and I were surprisingly naive," Tony said. "It was one of the great shocks to me that neither of us had an inkling of anything. Clearly there was an awful lot going on on both sides, but one was sort of shielded from it."

Anjelica thought of her parents as "sophisticated" and "quite eclectic. I love them both very much, for their own separate personalities. They stood on their own. They were sort of two stars in the heavens when I was growing up."

An expanded imagination was the key to growing up at St. Clerans. John, of course, was already a fantasy figure, who swept dramatically in and out of their lives. The only children Anjelica and Tony saw on any regular basis were Paddy Lynch's six kids. Paddy Lynch was the groom, who taught them how to ride and to care for their ponies. But Tony was aware from the beginning that these children were not his social equals. "Until I was ten I didn't go to school. I had French tutors and I never met any children of my own social background. It was isolated."

"One found one's own pursuits," Anjelica recalled. "One didn't really *miss* companionship, because there never were a lot of children in the house." Being only a year and a half apart in age, a good deal of their growing up consisted of battling each other.

Both children were watched over by Nurse, Kathleen Shine, who became part of the family. "She was a saint, a rare breed," Anjelica remembered. "She looked like Katharine Hepburn. She had a great, wry sense of humor. A good eye. And very kind. She commanded a good deal of respect. I loved her." Often they would take long walks together, or play with Anjelica's dog, Mindy, or go riding. Sometimes they would listen to Betty O'Kelly's stories about Daly, the ghost of St. Clerans, who was lynched two hundred years ago and whose spirit remained to haunt the house. "Fantasy ran rampant," Anjelica said.

Her fantasies ran from being an actress and a ballet dancer to a bride and a nun. "Anything that walked and wore a veil was extremely attractive to me," she said. "I loved to dress up and I loved pretty things. There was a glamour to actresses that I had met or seen that I thought was enviable and beautiful." She had fallen in love with Dorothy Jeakins's teenage son, Steven, who was twice her age, when he came to visit and built her a tree house, where she would put offerings for the fairies. "I married Steven," she said with a laugh. "It was a solo wedding on the front lawn. I wore the dress and carried some flowers." Going to a convent school, she thought that becoming a nun was attractive, because it was so pure. "The nuns liked me because my father was a local hero, so they never gave me a hard time. I bought a lot of black babies. You could pay two and six pence and give your name to a black child in Africa, so I adopted eight black babies and gave them all different names." When she told her father she wanted to become a nun he said, "That's great, when are you going to start?"

Before Tony was enrolled at the Christian Brothers School in Loughrea, he suffered through a number of tutors. "They usually didn't last long," he said. "I remember playing practical jokes on them, stink bombs and stuff like that. Dad was always on the side of the anarchist, so it was rather difficult for the teacher, because if ever I did anything wrong Dad would conceal me."

With the ghosts, fairies, pets, and ponies, their memories of those early years in western Ireland are cheerful, although Tony usually found John's gifts too lavish. "As a small child I remember being given an amazing toy that did everything, but what I wanted was a pop gun. When I was ten he gave me a boat the size of a room. My only feeling was, I'll never be able to use it. And I never did. He very rarely gave you the present that you actually wanted."

While they had no television, they often saw John's films projected in 16mm onto a wall. "We saw *Treasure* a lot," Anjelica said. "And *African Queen.*" John said that when Anjelica was a child she would often do imitations of his guests, and he regretted that he never filmed her, because she was very perceptive. "I just liked pretending to be other people, it was a form of play," she said. She had an awareness of Greta Garbo because people often said that Ricki resembled her, but Anjelica was far more interested in Sandra Dee and Hayley Mills.

When Jules and Joyce Buck brought their daughter, Joan, and Cherokee Hardt brought her daughter, Marina, for a Christmas visit in 1959, Ricki left such a positive impression on the girls that they wished that she was their mother. To eleven-year-old Joan, Ricki appeared wearing a peasant shirt of Irish wool, looking like "the most astoundingly beautiful woman" she'd ever seen. Behind her stood eight-year-old Anjelica, "with a little weasel face, very pointy, playing with her braids."

From the hall an "august figure with a booming voice" appeared. "Hello, honey," John said, and Joan was introduced to her godfather. He seemed so "godlike," so different from her father, who was short, unsettled, unathletic. "I always felt terribly sorry for my father at St. Clerans," she recalled. "I didn't know why. Dad, Mum, everybody had a little nervousness in their throats before opening their mouths to talk to John. He was a hero. People would come fawning with scripts and projects. And the Irish would come fawning because he was famous. Journalists were there to write about him. Everybody always tried to be clever and witty and heavy when they spoke with him."

Peter O'Toole was also there that first Christmas. O'Toole was Jules Buck's discovery. After working with John during the war and as an assistant producer for him and Mark Hellinger, Buck had gone to England, where he saw O'Toole in a play, recognized his talent, and produced *The Day They Robbed the Bank of England* with him as star. Buck and O'Toole then formed a company, Keep Films, Ltd. Joan Buck remembered how proud Jules was, standing between O'Toole and Huston, the catalyst of their meeting. "He was probably uncomfortable, seeing how well they got along. O'Toole wasn't waiting for John's approval. They were the same height, had the same charisma, talent." Joan began to see that there were people with talent, like Huston and O'Toole, and people like her father, who "exploit, guide, direct the talent."

Anjelica thought the Bucks were glamorous because they were Americans. "Jules was small and dark and smoked cigars. Joyce was very stylish, she looked like something out of the twenties, short haircut, wore Chanel suits, very dashing and personable. Joan was very pale, with long dark hair. I was about her height, so I didn't feel all that intimidated when I met her. She was carrying a green purse that had a medallion on it that I liked a lot. And *Little Lulu* comics, which I liked even more. She wanted to stay up in the Big House with her mother and not in the Little House with me, which didn't disturb me because basically I wanted her comics, which I managed to get."

Joan remembered that Ricki had said to her, "You're going to stay down at the Little House with me and Anjelica and you'll like it." And all Joan could think was, "Who are these horrible, mad people? I had never before known anybody where the wife lived in a different house." But gradually Joan became more comfortable with Anjelica and Ricki and began to observe how life at St. Clerans was lived.

Joyce Buck's first reaction to St. Clerans was, "Oh! A mirage and a barn." And once past the four white granite columns that stood at the entrance to the Big House, one couldn't help but be impressed with the first hall of black marble and a giant pair of brass scales. The second hall had the stairway, the bar, the Christmas tree. In the window by the stairs was the marble horse's head that John had once written to Billy Pearson about. In the study, done in Prussian blue, was where John displayed his pre-Columbian and African art; "heavy statements," Joan Buck recollected, "primitive blood stuff everywhere." In the gun room John's pedigree guns stood in a rack, with the heads of the tiger and a water buffalo he had shot mounted on opposite walls. Upstairs were rooms with names like Napoleon, Lavender, Bhutan, each decorated accordingly.

The Big House was intimidating, where children like Joan sensed a lot of "weird stuff" went on between grown-ups, "and that was really what life was all about." In contrast the Little House was "very down to earth, totally unpretentious, a place where you curled up around the peat fire" to read, look through scrapbooks, play games, talk. Ricki kept a green velvet album filled with articles she clipped about the strangeness of Ireland, like "Tipperary House Collapses in Rain." Joan appreciated her sense of absurdity, "coupled with an astounding taste and aestheticism. She taught us how to wash glasses, bake bread. Once, in the laundry, we were talking about clothes. Ricki had a black suede Chanel suit and she said something about elegance being just for whores."

An image Joan never forgot was of Ricki holding Anjelica on her knees, something Joan had stopped doing with her mother years ago. "I found it somewhat shocking that there was that amount of affection," she said. "It was Ricki's warmth, Ricki's earthiness." As Joan settled in she saw that a rivalry developed between her mother and Ricki, "because I just decided I wanted Ricki to be my mother."

On that first Christmas the Buckses gave John and Ricki a leather ice bucket, which Ricki used as a planter for the guest bathroom. John gave Jules an Epstein drawing of a nude woman, which, Joan noted, "even at eleven I saw it as a real special gift." All the women were given saris, and Anjelica, Joan, and Marina were given tin boxes with oysters in them. Inside each oyster was a pearl. Anjelica also got a canary diamond, Joan an opal.

Joan thought Tony was very competitive, boisterous, "sort of impossible." Cherokee remembered how he and Anjelica "hit and spit and hurt each other. They used to tie Marina up and I'd go get them and beat the shit out of them. They didn't mean it, but they were so jealous. John adored Marina because she was a blue-eyed blonde little girl. That ticked the kids off, too. Ricki was decent with them and reared them properly and played fair with them, whereas John didn't even show up."

Marietta Tree, when she visited St. Clerans, saw it differently. She thought John was wonderful with his children. "He did everything he could to make Tony enjoy nature, be a good fisherman, man the hounds, be an Irish gentleman. Of course, when he turned out like an Irish gentleman John was disgusted. But that was how he brought him up to be."

John wasn't aggravated about Tony's becoming a gentleman; it had more to do with his disappointment that Tony wasn't showing any ambitions to be anything *more*. John, of course, thought he did everything he could to live the Irish gentleman's life: the formal dinners, the embracing of the outdoors, the tall, colorful tales told around a fire over a few pints. He even consented, with considerable pleasure, to be Joint Master of the Galway Blazers—"ten of the best years of my life," he said. Tony said that John was named Joint Master because he put up enough money to support the hunting club. It also put him in a position of being an arbiter over local disputes. "Dad was very good whenever there were irate farmers. He was able to bring objectivity to bear and resolve the problems, which usually had to do with sheep being chased by the hounds or walls falling down from the hunt. Dad was an expert at diplomacy, which meant the farmers wouldn't put in for damages."

While his guests complimented Huston on the grandeur of his home, it was really Ricki who deserved the credit for overseeing its completion. "It was agony getting anything done in Ireland," Dorothy Jeakins said, "and Ricki did the entire supervision. John was the collector, but it was Ricki's touches, and she handled the whole thing." Inge Morath believed Ricki never found where she would be happy. "There was some lamentation of her own on not achieving something. That was the undertone in her life."

Cherokee felt that John stayed married to Ricki because she didn't suffocate him. "But that was a guise. He kept saying, 'love, love, love,' but what he actually meant was, 'God, I hate women because this woman ate me up.' "

Cherokee had a hard time dealing with John's Irish life-style. "He was sleeping with Betty O'Kelly and he could have three mistresses in the same house, and I would say, 'John, how can you do that?' He said, 'I don't do anything, that's what they want.' I mean, he was a whore!

"And there were always such hysterics in that house. It was either Betty who ran away with hurt feelings or Gladys who was crying in her room. He treated her like shit. She had no life other than John and she was rapidly becoming a drunk. Gladys eventually learned not to show any emotion. I imagine he slept with her earlier, because he slept with every female who was in his life. He thought they expected it and maybe they did, because they fell in love and he obliged them.

"Everybody had their little episode at St. Clerans. He had to forever have some intrigue and romance going on. The more intriguing and involved and black Irish it got, the better he liked it. He liked putting all those people together, stirring up the pot, and then watching it. He was a true theatrical person. John had one motto: never apologize and never make excuses."

Marietta Tree found the drama surrounding St. Clerans more amusing. "There was something like eight women living in the house—a real harem—and he was blissfully happy. That was the way he should have lived, with eight different women. There was Gladys, of course, who ran everything and who loved him in such an unselfish way. And there was Betty, who took care of his horse side. Then there was another one who took care of the fishing side. And an Italian mistress who couldn't speak English, she would sit next to him at every meal and was perfectly mute.

"John was terribly Irish. He mixed his sense of paradox and irony with a streak of black humor. He could be sadistic. Very often the person wasn't realizing he was being flayed alive. I was very lucky that he wasn't sadistic to me."

Like John, Billy Pearson enjoyed his share of black humor and when he was again in Cuernavaca he saw Pablo, who showed him the kind of pictures he was taking to earn his living. "He photographed dead people!" Pearson laughed. "To put on the mantels, framed pictures of grandmother, that sort of thing. Godawful, horrible photographs. I got a couple of them and mailed 'em to John, to show him the great work that Pablo was doing."

The pictures disturbed John, who sent Pablo $2,000 soon after he saw them so that Pablo could get out of the photography business and open a bookshop. Pablo said the shop was part of a hotel and the books he sold were mainly tourist guides in English. Billy Pearson said it wasn't really a store, but a corner newsstand where Pablo sold mostly used comic books for three years.

In the spring Arthur Miller came to St. Clerans to work on *The Misfits* with John. The movie had been delayed because of Marilyn Monroe's commitments, but was scheduled to begin in July, when the temperature in Reno could be brutal. Before Miller arrived John broke his left leg when his horse threw him as he attempted to jump a five-foot-high wall.

John made light of his hobbled condition as he played host to Miller. When Miller commented that Ireland seemed to be staying out of the twentieth century, John told him, "Ireland is the reverse of every country in the world. That's why I live here." As talk turned to the movie John summed it up as its being about people who weren't willing to sell themselves out. "They will sell their work, but they won't sell their lives, and for that reason they're misfits." Miller smiled and said, "Now I know what it's all about."

For Miller, the making of *The Misfits* would turn out to be his most exhausting collaboration. "More than anything before or since," he said. "I was in a peculiar position. I was married to the star. It was my film. I just felt I had to do everything I could to make it happen. It went on for months. And we were working in hundred-degree heat a lot of the time. And then, that uncertainty as to whether we were gonna get any shooting done that day."

The uncertainty had to do with Monroe. She was coming off a picture, *Let's Make Love*, in which she had gotten emotionally involved with her co-star, Yves Montand. Her relationship with Miller was falling apart. She was insecure about working with Clark Gable, whom she used to fantasize as her father when she lived in an orphanage as a girl. She respected Huston but felt he might have resented her when he wasn't chosen to direct *The Prince and the Showgirl*. She was full of anxieties about acting in a serious dramatic movie and insisted that her acting coach, Paula Strasberg, be hired at $3,000 a week for support. She couldn't sleep without pills, couldn't stay awake without more pills. She was thirty-four years old and had made quite a journey from the bit-part bimbo in *The Asphalt Jungle* to becoming the biggest sex symbol in the American cinema, internationally adored, internally a basket case. Like Clark Gable, Monroe would never complete another picture. *The Misfits* would be their last.

The media, of course, was fascinated. Monroe was always interesting copy. But the movie also brought together some of Hollywood's brightest stars: Clark Gable, "The King," as her love interest; Montgomery Clift as her soul mate; Eli Wallach and Thelma Ritter as her friends. Filming in the only state that legalized gambling, and putting it under the direction of a legendary gambler like Huston, who was returning to make his first picture in the States since *The Red Badge of Courage*, was also cause for editorial celebration. One writer, James Goode, came to write a book about it. One photo agency, Magnum, was given the exclusive picture rights so as to keep the distraction of photographers to a minimum. *The Misfits* had all the elements of a three-ring circus, but what was missing was the laughter, the fun. The movie became grueling. As photographer Ernst Haas put it, "It was like being at your own funeral."

Because of the stark nature of the film, John decided that it should be shot in black and white, a decision that Arthur Miller backed. "The whole damn picture was basically about waste," Miller said, "and you get more waste in black and white." That the film's overbudget cost would be $4 million, making it the most expensive black-and-white movie ever made up to that time, was of little consequence to John, as were the reviews for *The Unforgiven*, which appeared the month before he started *The Misfits*.

Those reviews called his latest work "A hodgepodge of crudely stitched sententiousness," and "A work of profound phoniness." "Can this be the man who gave us *The Maltese Falcon* and *Beat the Devil?*" asked critic Dwight Macdonald. It could; it was—but even the harshest critic wasn't as hard on that film as John was himself. While he may not have cared for some of his films, *The Unforgiven* was the only one he truly disliked.

If he was the sort who felt he had anything to prove, after the disasters of *The Barbarian and the Geisha*, *The Roots of Heaven*, and *The Unforgiven*—three turkeys that would have sunk most directors—then *The Misfits* was his chance to show what he was capable of creating. Instead, he was lucky to have come out of it with a picture at all.

"I was amazed how good the end result was," he would say, "because it was really an ordeal." Huston and Miller both suspected that Montgomery Clift would be the problem. After his disfiguring car accident Clift was an emotional wreck. "He was a mess," John said. "Clark Gable had a bad back, a slipped disc; Monty would slap him on purpose. Gable didn't have much use for him. But it wasn't Clift who made filming *The Misfits* an ordeal; it was Marilyn Monroe. She was always trying to wake up or go to sleep."

"Monty tried to be troublesome," Doc Erickson remembered, "but Marilyn was such a problem that nobody paid him any attention. We knew she was on pills—uppers, downers. She had a great fear of going to the set. Seemed to just terrorize her."

"She acted like she was never, ever late," Tom Shaw said. "She was *never* on time." Angela Allen said that there were special calls on that film. "Eleven o'clock for Marilyn. Well, you might be lucky if she showed up at three. And she gave you half an hour's work. Then she'd say it was a hard day, that we overworked her! One day we asked Marilyn to come in at nine A.M. It was Gable's scene and we wanted to shoot it with a certain light. Ten o'clock comes, eleven, twelve! There Clark sat. Finally she appeared, with her entourage of about fourteen people. I watched Clark's hands wringing. I went over to John and said, 'You'd better tell her to apologize.' John did and Clark was a gentleman, but he was fuming. And rightly so."

"By the start of *The Misfits*," Arthur Miller wrote, "it was no longer possible to deny that if there was a key to Marilyn's despair I did not possess it." John hadn't realized that Miller and Monroe were at odds until well into the picture. "I was impertinent enough to say to Arthur that to allow her to take drugs of any kind was criminal and utterly irresponsible," John said. "Shortly after that I realized that she wouldn't listen to Arthur at all; he had no say over her actions."

The person who seemed to have the most influence with her was Paula Strasberg, wife and disciple of the high priest of method acting, Lee Strasberg. "She was a strange figure in black, loose-robed taffeta," said photographer Eve Arnold, "a costume completed with a conical-shaped hat like the dunce cap of old. She kept saying that she wanted to be invisible, but her get-up was a very strong silhouette against the stark desert sandscape." Tom Shaw named her "Black Bart," which stuck. He couldn't stand the way she would always be by Marilyn's side, even during shooting, just out of camera range. Angela Allen noticed that Marilyn always looked at Paula after a scene, never at John. If John liked a scene but Strasberg didn't, Monroe would want to do it again. Strasberg also wrote notes on Monroe's script, which Allen happened to see one day. At one place it said, "You are a tree," at another, "You are a bird flying." Allen was fascinated.

Often John would call Tom Shaw over and point to Black Bart. "He got the biggest fucking kick out of it," Shaw said. Arthur Miller observed that John's way of dealing with Paula was to offer her "absurdly elaborate congratulations—on her wearing a black dress in this terrible heat, for example—and by listening to everything she had to tell him with a seriousness so profound as to be ludicrous. It took her a while to catch on."

But as the weeks wore on Marilyn's behavior and her dependence on Strasberg began to get to him. Miller realized that "it made John's job impossible, because it was like working through a translator." He began to spend his nights at the gambling tables. His desire to gamble was enhanced when he received an account from Morgan Maree of exactly how much the renovations of St. Clerans had cost him: a million dollars! Considering how little he had paid for the house, it was a sobering figure. It would take more than three *Misfits* to earn back that money. Hell of a lot easier to do it with a good run of the dice.

His early bad luck set him back $25,000, money he didn't immediately have. So John called Paul Kohner and instructed him to finalize his deal with Universal for *Freud*. Then he secretly left Reno with Doc Erickson to fly to San Francisco, sign the deal, and pick up an advance for $25,000. "John made his deal," Erickson said, "got his money, and we flew back and he paid off his debt. He told Paul Kohner, 'I learned my lesson, I'll never get involved with craps again, you can trust me.' It wasn't even five hours after we got back, there was John at the crap table."

Another photographer, John Bryson, caught John's attention at the casino in the Mapes Hotel. "I really got hot with the dice," Bryson said, "and at the other end of the table was Huston. Where I was betting twenty-dollar chips, he was betting thousands. He stayed on me, and, by God, we both made a killing." Arthur Miller remembered seeing John in his crisply pressed bush jacket, playing craps and drinking Scotch. And when he got up the next morning John was still at the table. "His bush jacket looked as neat as it had before," said Miller. "Just thinking about standing up all night exhausted me."

Marilyn had physically moved away from Miller and into Strasberg's apartment. "Paula had finally won our long undeclared war," he admitted. "I was only going through the motions of caring about the rest of the picture. It now seemed a hateful thing that had cost me too much."

In spite of the indignities and humiliations he suffered, his loyalty to Marilyn had him coming to her defense at a cost of what was precious to him: the truth. Angela Allen gave Miller the latest version of his script, which he was to give to Marilyn for the next day's shoot. But the next morning Marilyn denied ever getting it, and Miller backed her up. "She never had it," he said. "Oh, yes, she did," Angela Allen said. And John believed her. "Don't you ever do that again, Arthur," he said. Allen was disappointed with Miller. "He was still so besotted with her," she said, "he just let her do whatever she wanted. He had no control whatsoever."

The Misfits was made during the 1960 presidential campaign between John F. Kennedy and Richard M. Nixon. Marietta Tree, who was a friend of Adlai Stevenson's, had attended the Democratic convention. When it was over she flew to Reno to visit John. He introduced her to Clark Gable, who said, "I choose you," and she gave him a puzzled look. John explained that Gable was in the process of selecting the woman who was to play a small part in the film, at the very beginning, where he was saying good-bye to a girlfriend at the train station. Her only line was, "And remember, I have the second biggest laundry in St. Louis." Marietta had never acted before and she lost her breath when Clark Gable looked into her eyes and said she was to play this woman.

She rehearsed her line over and over and after she had been on the set for three days the scene was shot. "I terribly enjoyed that," she said. If it hadn't been for Marilyn Monroe's terrible behavior, she would have come away believing that making movies was actually fun.

"Marilyn was wicked to Arthur Miller in front of the whole set," she said. "After a scene was over, which she always had to do twenty-seven times, she would walk off into a waiting car with Mrs. Strasberg. They would both get in with Arthur right behind them, and they'd close the door in his face. Everybody saw it as public humiliation."

Soon after Marietta left, Suzanne Flon arrived for two weeks. "They just barely missed each other," Inge Morath remembered. "I was wondering what kind of juggling was going on in John's life," Doc Erickson said. "But these visits were scheduled properly." When Marilyn admired a necklace Suzanne was wearing Suzanne gave it to her. "It had no value at all, but she liked it." Marilyn gave Suzanne a diamond ring the next day. Flon sensed Monroe's anxiety, as she had Montgomery Clift's. "You could feel he was walking near his shoes, as we say in French. He was very touching."

Frank Taylor, the film's producer, considered Clift and Monroe "psychic twins. They were on the same wavelength. They recognized disaster in each other's faces and giggled about it." Tom Shaw said Clift wasn't his kind of guy, but Arthur Miller was more understanding. "I happened to like Monty a lot," Miller said. "I thought that he was just a tortured soul. But he was such a marvelous actor, you forgave him everything. Monty had a culture behind him. He could read; he could think. It doesn't hurt for an actor, who wants to attempt more and more things, to have a brain in his head. He could have done the great roles."

John also thought highly of Clift as an actor and believed, with his sensitive, searching face, that he could play Freud. And in spite of all the difficulties with Marilyn, he seriously considered her for the part of the composite woman whom Freud would analyze. But thoughts of *Freud* had to be set aside in the Nevada desert, as mustangs were rounded up, and Ernie Anderson planned a surprise fifty-fourth birthday party for John.

Billy Pearson flew in from San Francisco, Burl Ives from Kansas City, Mort Sahl from Chicago, Friedrich Ledebur and his wife, Iris Tree, also came, and a ninety-five-year-old Paiute Indian chief gave John a new name: Long Shadow. John told the chief he was proud to be a Paiute.

A few days later John received a letter from Marietta Tree, who had gone on to the West Indies for a vacation. "I've always been aware of

your genius," she wrote, "but to see you in action—at a story conference or working with actors and technicians, knitting a huge, disparate
group together, your long blue denim back gliding in and out of the
cameras, every molecule alert to every detail. All this combined with
your kindness and delicacy and appreciation of each individual was a
revelation!" Two week later John found time to write back: "Everything
continues swimmingly . . . Marilyn was actually on time three days last
week—well, almost on time—which is some kind of record. Clift has a
drink or two but doesn't ever get drunk and he's giving a splendid
account of himself. The odds against him were staggering."

All, however, was not going swimmingly when, on August 27, the
picture came to a sudden halt when Marilyn Monroe took an overdose
of sleeping pills and had to have her stomach pumped. "We were
dealing with a helpless woman," Arthur Miller sadly said. "Marilyn had
no control over what she was doing. She just stopped functioning."

During the break Miller and Gable went to Los Angeles, Clift to
New York, but Huston stayed in Reno to work with Tom Shaw's
second unit as they got shots of the wild mustangs and to participate
in a wild camel race against Billy Pearson on Labor Day in Virginia
City. The race was a good way to blow out some of the tensions of the
last two months. It was to be a four-camel affair, with two riders from
Indio, California, also entered, but John knew his only competition
would be Pearson, so he prepared a faultless strategy. A few days before
the race he had the one-mile course changed from an area outside of
town to one that began on the main street and finished at the barn
where the camels were kept. John arranged to have his camel, a
five-year-old Bactrian, or two-humped camel, taken out to the starting
line and then led back to the barn and fed. He had the keeper do that
twice each day before the race. There was a champagne breakfast in
Reno on the day of the race, then an antique car ride to Virginia City.
By the time they got there, "everyone in the entire town was rollicking
drunk." Billy, who was dressed in his racing silks, complained that his
camel only had one hump. John, wearing English jodhpurs, a mauve
shirt, and a Faubus-for-President button, told him not to complain,
since neither of them had ever ridden a camel before anyway. When the
gun went off the two other riders went in the wrong direction. Billy's
camel, according to John, "started off at an angle, scattering the crowd,
jumped onto the bed of a pickup truck, cleared a Thunderbird, and
finally, going full tilt, disappeared into Piper's Opera House, with Billy
hanging on for dear life." John's camel, sufficiently programmed, ran
straight to the barn.

Interviewed on radio after the race John was asked what he thought of Pearson's ride. "Billy Pearson is an obvious disgrace to the camel-riding profession," John proclaimed. "He rode over parked cars, windows, orphans . . . in fact, there are camel-stunned babies scattered all over these historic hillsides. It is a scene of carnage owing to Pearson's shocking disregard for life, liberty, and the pursuit of happiness. He just doesn't belong up there on the hump of a camel."

On September 6, Monroe returned to Reno. "There was a remarkable physical change in her," Doc Erickson noticed. There seemed to be a change with everyone else as well. The tensions that had turned the production into a pressure cooker had been relieved. It was almost like starting fresh. During a scene where Monroe and Clift were dancing, as Gable and Eli Wallach got drunk watching, Wallach was having some problems, which Huston resolved in much the same way he had when, during the filming of The African Queen, he told Katharine Hepburn to think about Eleanor Roosevelt. "Eli," John said, "yesterday in Virginia City I was deeply drunk. So drunk it didn't show." It was all the direction Wallach needed to play the scene. "He directed me by indirection," Wallach noted. "People said he left you alone, but actually he didn't. He understood actors."

The Catholic Church made an attempt to weaken the picture when a monsignor and a priest attended a screening, but Arthur Miller wouldn't allow their censorship. "They objected to some language," Miller said, "but the big scene that they simply wouldn't swallow was the one where Marilyn walks out of the house and she embraces a tree. She's fully dressed. Her shoes were off. What's the problem? Well, it's obviously masturbation. I said, 'The scene's gonna stay. If you want that out, I'm gonna write a little article to the New York Times about how this scene represented masturbation to the Catholic Church." Huston's comment regarding censorship was the same thing he said after watching one of the Nixon-Kennedy debates: "Who do they think we are?"

When the time came to shoot Gable, Clift, and Wallach rounding up the mustangs, each actor had a stunt double, but there were some shots that were impossible to do that way. Gable, who was fifty-nine and about to become a father, had "a virility complex," according to publicist Harry Mines. "No man, no understudy, no stand-in could do anything he couldn't do." But Tom Shaw, who was in charge of directing those scenes, knew the horses could be tough and swore that Gable "had absolutely nothing to do with anything physical. He never got anywhere near a wild horse on that movie. Most of the time it was me on the end of the fucking rope, and four other guys."

There *were* scenes, though, in which Gable was dragged across the desert, that were shot from the back of a truck. "He was padded for that," Doc Erickson said. "All he had to do was hold on." Arthur Miller remembered that day "when Gable was being dragged on a piece of leather, holding onto a rope, a few hundred yards. Then they'd do it again. That was about it. Of course, if you've got a bad heart, which I didn't know he did have, I suppose that could do you in. But the script called for that kind of stuff." "Clark was a big enough boy to understand that as well," said Erickson. "He was nobody's fool."

When Gable's wife, Kay, saw his bruised and bloodied body that evening, she asked what had happened. "He said he was dragged on a rope 'by accident.' I told him he was out of his mind."

James Goode, in his eyewitness account, reported that on September 13 no stunt doubles were used as Gable, Clift, and Wallach tried to throw a mustang. "The mare dragged Gable and Wallach around the lake floor, and Clift was in a particularly bad situation. For some reason he had not been wearing gloves when the sequences began and could not put them on now. . . . He was forced to throw the mare bare-handed with his single rope. . . . His hands were lacerated and bleeding, but there was nothing anyone could do about it."

"Monty did his own thing and is one bloody young man," Gable told his wife, "but he's self-destructive like Marilyn. They don't care if they live or die. What surprised me is that no one gave a damn if *I* got killed or not. We were never allowed to take chances when the studio had us under contract. I was curious if Huston would try to stop me. Hell, no. He was delighted!"

The Misfits was Gable's seventy-second feature. He, more than any actor of his time, was the movies' great heartthrob. He could be rough, but he was all man, and women responded much the way Marilyn Monroe and her mother did, by pasting his picture to their walls and dreaming about him at night. He was among the highest paid actors in the business, but he never received more than he got for *The Misfits*: $750,000—more than Huston and Monroe's combined salary—plus ten percent of the profits and $48,000 a week for overtime. It was his participation, more than Huston's direction or Miller's script, that convinced Marilyn Monroe to make the movie.

In their one bedroom love scene, Marilyn was nude under the covers when Gable came in—it was the morning after for them—and kissed her. "I was so thrilled when his lips touched mine, I wanted to do it over and over," she said. During the scene Marilyn let the bedsheet fall, exposing her breast. It wasn't a slip—this was *her* moment with Gable and she wanted to give it everything she had. "Let's get the people away from the television sets," she would say in defense of using that particular take. "I love to do things the censors wouldn't pass."

Tom Shaw was more interested in Arthur Miller's reaction than in Marilyn's sudden exposure. "Movie crews are a different kind of breed," he said. "They don't give a shit; they're not even looking at Marilyn Monroe's breast. I happened to look at Miller—and this is why I hate him. And I have never told this to anybody. He almost looked evil to me. It was like he was thinking, 'Look at that. She's mine, and I'm fucking her, nobody else is.' Maybe he wasn't thinking that at all, but that was the impression I got. From that day on I've never liked him."

Huston's reaction to Marilyn's daring was a gruff, "I've seen 'em." Later he would say, "I've always known that girls have breasts." But not in his pictures. As Norman Mailer observed, Huston "will not want the aesthetic slant of his film to be nudged by her competitive tit." John admitted to being uneasy with intimate embraces on the screen. "They bore the hell out of me," he said. "Makes me uncomfortable. It's the same reaction I have when someone's telling me a long, pointless joke."

Miller, by that time, felt he was "worse than useless" to Monroe, "a bag of nails thrown in her face." He believed that Marilyn had felt too insecure to give herself over to Gable. "I don't know that any director could have overcome that."

Marilyn spoke highly of Huston as the picture drew to a close. "John has meant a great deal in my life," she said. "Nobody would have heard of me if it hadn't been for him. Working with John ten years later is very good. He's a different kind of director than the people I've been working with. He's an artist with a camera—he sees it like a painter."

"Monroe was in a daze," John said. "One of the things that still needs to be said about her is that everybody wanted her for one reason or another. Mostly from the time she became a star. People either wanted to get her to do a part and cash in on her as a star, or they wanted to sleep with her."

Marilyn wasn't the cause of *all* the delays on *The Misfits*. John had to take two days off when he came down with bronchitis, which, added to his emphysema and his refusal to stop smoking, gave him a hacking cough. "I thought John was gonna collapse," Arthur Miller said. "He'd start coughing and he'd never stop coughing." The telltale sign that he was feeling better was his return to the casino, where, by October, he was down $50,000. One night Marilyn joined him at the crap table. When the dice came to her she rattled them in her hand and said, "What should I ask the dice for, John?" John never took his eyes off the table. "Don't think, honey, just throw. That's the story of your life. Don't think, do it."

Since the film was shot in sequence, the unresolved problems about the ending created new friction between Huston and Miller. John preferred something more cynical than the happy ending Miller had devised, with Marilyn going off in the truck with Gable. Even Monroe had told him that she thought they should break up in the end. But Miller was fighting his own demons; he didn't want *his* marriage to Marilyn to end. The movie had become an extension of his psyche. "Aware of the hopefulness with which I had conceived the story and my uncertainty about my future now," he wrote, "I still could not concede that the ending had to be what I considered nihilistic, people simply walking away from one another."

Montgomery Clift thought that his character and not Gable's should have wound up with Marilyn. "Arthur was doing some wish-fulfillment," he said. "He identified with the character played by Gable. Arthur wanted him to keep Marilyn because he wants to himself. But their marriage is over, and he might as well face it. My character represented something new, the future—Marilyn's future. Maybe Marilyn and I would have gotten together one day if we weren't so much alike. As it is, it's too much like brother and sister getting together. That's what's wrong with Gable going off with her. It's like a girl going with her father. . . . All idols fall eventually."

Miller said that John became impatient with him toward the end and believed it was because of his commitment to a happy ending. "I don't think that the picture had earned a tragic ending," he said. "Although, God knows, one didn't have the feeling they were gonna last very long. But I felt it would be milking it to break them up and have a sad parting, with him riding off into the sunset."

Miller didn't blame John. "It was my fault," he said. "I didn't want it to be as concrete as it turned out to be. See, the movies are very strange; it's the director's medium, not the writer's. The camera makes everything concrete; whereas words can make things real by making them less concrete. I remember thinking, jeez, this isn't the way I saw it at all. I would have thought that he would have shot more material that showed man against that big, vast backdrop of waste. We lost the context of this group of people wandering around in this waste. One didn't get that right off."

As was her practice, Angela Allen reached her threshold as the picture wound down, threw up her script in exasperation, and announced that she was quitting. "They baited her a lot," Arthur Miller observed. "She usually was right. I don't know how anybody makes a picture without Angela Allen."

Marilyn Monroe had suspected that Allen and Arthur Miller might have been doing more than making changes in his script and had said mean things about them. Marilyn's suspicions that Miller might have eyes for someone else would prove correct—only it wasn't Angela Allen he became involved with, it was Inge Morath, who had only been on the picture early on. Morath said she hardly saw Miller when she was there, because he was always with Marilyn in their hotel room, before she moved out. "The only thing that intrigued me," she said, speaking like a professional, "I could never get a photograph of the two of them together. So I took a famous picture of everybody looking in a different direction." It wasn't until the movie was completed and Miller came to Magnum's offices in New York looking for photographs that he invited Morath to lunch. "I thought, Oh, God, he's a very serious man," she said. "But after a while I became aware he's very funny, too. I fell in love, I suppose."

On October 17, while still in Nevada, John threw a birthday party for Miller and Montgomery Clift. Many of the cast and crew attended, including Marilyn. Nan Huston was also there. John was always polite and respectful around his stepmother, who had withdrawn considerably since Walter's death. Although John paid most of her bills, she had complained to their lawyer, Mark Cohen, that she was "living in a state of constant worry about money," and resented "very much having to relate to anybody" her personal affairs. She desired to live her "own life again." And she didn't like the arrangement of John's paying her accounts. Nan had become a Christian Scientist and her only link to her theatrical past was to make recordings for the blind. She had also

become a friend and confidante of Montgomery Clift, and they exchanged an intimate and sexual correspondence, which her niece burned
out of embarrassment when it was discovered years later, after Nan's
death.

On November 3, the day before shooting ended at the studio, Ricki
visited John. He treated her like a friend, perhaps puzzled by her
appearance. She watched with some interest as Gable cut the rope,
freeing the mustang whose capture had caused such anguish for Marilyn's
character. Ricki had had a lot of time alone in Ireland to think
about her own loss of freedom and had decided to make a bold move of
her own by taking an apartment in London. She thought it was
something worth discussing with John, since she wanted to take the
children with her. John preferred talking about it when they were back
at St. Clerans.

On the very last day of filming, November 4, Marilyn Monroe told
John that she had decided against doing *Freud,* even though he had
told her that Sartre considered her among the best actresses in America.
"I can't do it because Anna Freud didn't want a picture made," she
said. "My analyst told me this." Before John could say anything that
might get her to reconsider, she turned and left. "She first wanted very
much to do it," John said, "and then her analyst advised her against it.
Really fitting."

Her behavior, at least, was consistent. Marilyn had been a thorn in
his side from the very beginning. That he would have *wanted* her in his
next movie seemed almost masochistic on his part. He must have
realized that as he sat in the editing room with Doc Erickson. "Never
say never," he muttered, "but Jesus, I would have to be starving to
death before I'd ever want to do this again."

Because Huston edited *The Misfits* as it was shot, Clark Gable was
able to see enough of the film to consider it the best thing he'd ever
done. Arthur Miller saw a "certain heroism" in Gable's performance,
which, he thought, "had a lot of John in it." Norman Mailer would say
that "never has Gable been more real. . . . Finally we have an idea of
what Gable is really like. He is not bad!"

Gable missed the "wrap" party on Friday because he was feeling
some pain. On Sunday he suffered a heart attack and ten days later
he was gone. John Kennedy had brought in Camelot with his

election as president, but the news around the world was that The King was dead.

Blame immediately was cast upon two people: Marilyn, for making him wait long hours in the hot desert sun, and John, who worked him too hard when he should have used stuntmen. Kay Gable told the press, "It wasn't the physical exertion that did it. It was the horrible tension, that eternal waiting, waiting, waiting. He waited around forever, for everybody. He'd get so angry waiting that he'd just go ahead and do anything to keep occupied. That's why he did those awful horse scenes where they dragged him behind a truck. . . . I told him he was crazy, but he wouldn't listen."

Robert Mitchum said columnist Hedda Hopper called him and said, "Your friend John Huston, you know he killed Gable. He's a murderer." "Yeah," Mitchum answered, "how many times do you think he tried to kill me, for chrissake?" Tom Shaw jumped to John's defense. "I read that old bitch's column," he said, "making John out like he was a murderer. We didn't do *anything* that could ever have killed him. The only aggravating thing was Gable and myself in the middle of the desert, waiting three and a half hours for Marilyn Monroe."

"Let's not forget something," Arthur Miller said. "Gable smoked the end of one cigarette onto the beginning of another one. He *never* stopped smoking. We know now that that kind of smoking can kill you. And I have a feeling that he would have gotten it anyway."

Five days before Gable died Marilyn Monroe announced her separation from Miller. After Gable's death she was so despondent that she locked herself in her New York apartment for days. At one point, when she thought she might have been the cause, she considering jumping out the window and was stopped by her maid. "I felt guilty when he died," she told a writer, "in case I'd put too much strain on him. But that was stupid. He had a bad heart. . . . I wept all night. I'd have gone to his funeral, but I was afraid of breaking down."

"Clark was one of the few holdovers from the days of the champs," said Huston. "His career in pictures had the same sweep and color as Dempsey's in the ring. Put his name on the list with the Babes, the Galloping Ghosts, the Flying Finns. He is the only screen actor I can think of who rated the sobriquet, The King. His throne, I fear, will remain empty for some time to come."

Because of Gable's death there was pressure to get *The Misfits* released within the month, to qualify it, and especially his performance, for

Oscar consideration. However, the score for the film hadn't been composed. Aaron Copland was the first considered, but he wanted $55,000, which Frank Taylor thought was too much. Alex North, who had written the music for *Death of a Salesman* and *A Streetcar Named Desire,* was hired and shown the picture for the first time on December 1. "They wanted me to write the score in time for the nominations and John interceded," North said. " 'You can't treat an artist that way,' he said. John was aware of what it meant to put notes down on paper. So I was given several more weeks to write that score. He told me that he had infinite trust in my judgment. This is a reflection of Huston as a decent human being and an artist."

Both Doc Erickson and Tom Shaw believed *The Misfits* was ahead of its time. It was reported that when Arthur Miller screened the completed film, he cried. He said it was from immense relief. Although he regretted the year and a half of his life he spent on it, "It certainly turned out better than I dared hope. First of all, I wasn't sure Marilyn was ever gonna be able to complete the picture. Second, I just had the feeling that we were not getting the soul of it. It's good, but it's wanting in some ultimate connection. Maybe it should have ended more tragically with the breakup of everybody, going back into the hills. But I kind of respect the picture. It's quirky. A picture of that sort will endure because it has an individuality. You certainly can't mix it up with anything else. And maybe that's all you can ask."

21

CIVILIZATION AND ITS DISCONTENTS

IN THE SPRING OF 1961 A NAIVE, AMBITIOUS TWENTY-ONE-year-old Indian girl named Zoe Ismail read a story in a London newspaper about John Huston preparing for his next picture, *Freud*. Against her father's wishes she had dreams of being an actress and received a scholarship to attend an acting school. Her father said that only prostitutes were actresses, but she was determined to show him that a good girl could become a famous actress without disgracing her family's name. She had appeared in minor parts in the theater and on television when she read about Huston's movie and decided that *he* might be kind enough to give her a break if she could only get to see him. She knew she didn't have the credits to go through an agent, so she boldly picked up the telephone and called St. Clerans, where she spoke with Ricki. Mr. Huston was in Paris, Ricki said. With Sartre.

Such obstacles become challenges to young actresses who believe in karma, and when Zoe was able to get Sartre's address, she went to Paris in search of Huston. When the philosopher appeared at his door Zoe went into the best acting she would ever do. "I'm here to see Mr. Huston," she said in carefully broken French. "I was supposed to meet him. I just arrived, there was no one to meet me,

501

he gave me this address, I don't know where else to go." Tears filled her eyes.

Sartre gave her John's number, which Zoe took nonchalantly, thanking him as she slowly turned. When Sartre bid her au revoir and closed the door she ran down the stairs as fast as she could, found a telephone in a nearby tavern, and made the call. Gladys Hill answered and Zoe began to stumble, trying to come up with the right lies to get to John. But it wasn't necessary, Gladys was used to women calling and passed him the phone. "I've just spoken to Sartre," Zoe began. "I spoke to your wife in Ireland and she told me you were here." The name-dropping worked. John invited her to his suite at the Lancaster.

When she finally got her audience the first question John asked was, "How do you know Ricki?" Zoe smiled shyly, nervously, and said, "I don't." "How did you get here?" John asked. "By train, boat, bus," she answered. Huston appeared flattered. He appreciated her effort and asked what it was she wanted. "I've read about your film and I just wanted to know if there's a chance for me. If there is, fine; if not, just say so and I won't bother you anymore." She was an attractive girl, John thought. Brash, direct, illogical.

"Sit down," he said in his gracious manner, sensing her insecurity and putting her at ease. "Tell me about yourself." For the next hour Zoe entertained him with stories of growing up in a wealthy Muslim family in India, of having to leave everything behind when the partition with Pakistan brought massacres, escaping to London, seeing her father start over.

John told her she must come to see him in Ireland, to meet the film's producer, Wolfgang Reinhardt, and to read the script. He made no promises. Gladys Hill, observing her youth and innocence, looked at them both but said nothing.

Huston's meetings with Sartre were just as frustrating in Paris as they were in Galway. Sartre was a thinker not a filmmaker. "The fault is partly mine, and partly Freud's," Sartre later told critic Kenneth Tynan. "My scenario would have been impossible to shoot; it would have lasted seven or eight hours. One can make a film four hours long if it has to do with Ben Hur, but a Texas audience won't sit through four hours of complexes."

John hadn't been pleased with Charlie Kaufman's attempts at revisions, nor with Reinhardt's, who became part of the problem rather than contributing to some solution. "Not a single line of Charlie's ended up in the picture," John said. "I liked him very much, but I didn't like what he had written. I would have broken it to him easily, but Wolfgang told Charlie that I didn't like what he'd done and I wanted him off the picture. I never heard from Charlie Kaufman after that."

John's relationship with Reinhardt became one worthy of Freudian study itself. "Wolfgang had read Freud deeply, much deeper than I had," John noted. "I had read a half dozen books, especially the early part of his life, which brought him on to the Oedipus complex. Wolfgang had gone much farther than that, he read manuscripts written at the time of Freud's death."

How to make something like repression work on the screen was the kind of problem Huston had to deal with, and he soon found out that "Wolfgang couldn't write at all. He tried . . . and it was terrible. So I wrote the script, out of all those pages that Sartre had written."

It took John months to do, and it was an agonizing chore. He didn't think much of Freudian therapy but considered Freud's theories as a way into the mind "extraordinary." While preparing for this film John made a significant breakthrough in understanding the patterns of his mother's behavior. How she reacted to his teasing drawings of Christ. Her conduct after she had her shipboard accident. How she slowly began to disintegrate.

Stephen Grimes came during the summer to discuss the sets. Zoe Ismail also came to read the script, although Grimes immediately sensed more than that was going on. With Gladys, Betty, Wolfgang, and Doc Erickson, the Huston circus was in full swing. "Because there were so many people," Grimes said, "I was put in the Little House with Ricki and the children. One evening at dinner we traipsed to the Big House. It was the first time he had the concubine with the housewife still there. Ricki appeared to be fairly amused by it. I suppose it had gotten beyond that stage. After dinner we all went back to the Little House. She had some new records and some very good brandy. Zoe was dead against going there. I don't blame her. You could see there was much game-playing between the ladies. But Zoe came, and John also edged into the spirit of the game. About eleven-thirty I suddenly found myself in the curious position of standing on the doorstep with Mrs. Huston saying goodnight to Mr. Huston. Doc Erickson made it worse by saying to Ricki, 'Goodnight, Mrs. Grimes, thank you very much for the lovely evening.' Which John heard. And Ricki and I, after closing the door, fell on the floor, laughing."

"They were separated," Zoe said of her first visit to St. Clerans, "and on the verge of divorce. He had other people—she knew about it; it was all quite open. She had her role clearly defined. She had the two children, she had whoever she wanted to have, he had whoever he wanted to have, and he kept her and looked after her. He never shirked his responsibilities."

St. Clerans was overwhelming for Zoe. "Everything in there, every piece of furniture, every work of art, was just perfect," she said. "He had amazing taste. And he was a talented artist."

Zoe was also happy that John thought enough of her to offer her a part in the picture, and then to make her pregnant. It happened in August, after John had begun seeing her during his frequent trips to London.

"I began to find him fascinating," Zoe recalled. "To me it was his mind and the fact that he was so much older. He was like a master figure; he had all this knowledge. And he had such a curious mind, grasping everything. I used to look at all the people my age that I was going out with and they seemed so insipid in comparison. My only regret was that I wasn't old enough to really appreciate all the things that he was. He had an uncanny knack for seeing things, a wonderful eye for art. He was also a great-looking guy who got better with age, like Hemingway. And he loved dressing well—very chic, not flashy. A lot of tweed jackets, well-cut suits, beautiful shirts, handmade shoes. To me he was the most attractive person I ever saw in my life. The moon, the sun, the stars shone from his direction."

But she also felt something tragic about John. "Superficially, you couldn't possibly have thought that—with his secretary following him and his great conversations, he had everything and he looked perfectly happy. But to me he was just a tragic, tragic personality. I remember him getting drunk and I felt so sorry for him. Here was a person who was sad and lonely and having these idiotic relationships. And when he told me about his earlier days I'd think, 'Oh, gosh, how sad'; he'd say, 'No, it wasn't.' And he'd never admit it was. But look at how it was: alone in London, without money, sleeping in Hyde Park, having an alcoholic wife, having other affairs, doing a painting of himself with no face and an opened hand. I just cannot see all that as a very happy, carefree time. I didn't find it amusing, it touched me very deeply."

Her maternal feelings for him were not what he might have expected. "I had a tremendous feeling of protection for him. I believe that we have all been different things to each other in our past lives. We've rotated roles until we've paid off certain karma to each other and the score is settled. I feel that I might have been John's mother."

Her pregnancy created a kind of desperation in John. It was not something he could dismiss or take lightly. Zoe was a very young woman, almost the same age as Ricki was when she was pregnant with Tony. She had her whole life before her. Having the child would also complicate his life even more than it already was. Her parents were furious when they heard about it, and John cautioned her to think very carefully before deciding to keep the baby. He even went so far as to get in touch with Maka, in Mexico, to ask if she might consider taking it. But Maka had children of her own and didn't want anything to do with the results of John's dalliances. The decision was Zoe's.

"I've always been an extremely idealistic person," she said. "I thought if ever I made love to anybody—because I never had—the person you made love to was the person you loved. You wait until the great love of your life comes, because people didn't go to bed with everybody in those days. If you love somebody and he's everything to you and then you get pregnant, you obviously have the child. It's created out of all this love."

Love wasn't exactly what John had on his mind by the end of that summer. Ricki would have to be told, and that would undoubtedly send her to London. He would no longer be able to keep her isolated in Ireland, as the children's caretaker. His children performed for him on his fifty-fifth birthday, and as he watched, he thought that he'd probably only see them at St. Clerans on holidays and summer vacations. But then he realized that that was the only time he *ever* saw them anyway. The important thing was the work. All else, as he once emphasized to Ben Maddow, was vanity.

When Wolfgang returned from Rome, where he had gone to see Sartre, he told John that Sartre had refused to read the truncated script, which was now 150 pages. "I was pissed off at this," John said. "Sartre had been rather well treated. Then I got a letter from him telling me, correctly, that I'd better listen to Reinhardt as he knew more about Freud than I or he did. Which was true. But this indicated to me that Wolfgang had sided with Sartre. And I never felt the same about Wolfgang after that."

Montgomery Clift came to St. Clerans to discuss *Freud,* and soon after his arrival John would never feel the same about him again either. His work on *The Misfits* had shown John that in spite of his accident and his drinking and drug problems, Clift was still capable of putting memorable performances on the screen. Katharine Hepburn, who had worked with Elizabeth Taylor and Clift in *Suddenly Last Summer*, warned John that Clift couldn't remember his lines and he should probably consider another actor. "I told him so in no uncertain terms," Hepburn said. "So John *did* know. Monty was absolutely brilliant, but he couldn't remember anything."

On Clift's first night at St. Clerans a reporter came to interview him. John joined them for a while, then excused himself and went to bed. The next morning he awoke to discover what everyone else in the business had known for years, that Clift was a homosexual. The reporter had spent the night and came out of Clift's room just as John walked by. It shattered any feelings John had for Clift as an actor. It was all right to be an alcoholic, a pill head, a gambler, a womanizer. But unless you were obvious like Truman Capote, it was unforgivable to be a homosexual, and especially to indulge in the home of your host. *That* was a flagrant violation of Huston's hospitality.

"It was the first time I had my nose rubbed in it," John said with some distaste. To Clift's biographer, Patricia Bosworth, John said, "The incident seemed trashy—I felt Monty had insulted me. I wish he'd considered my family and how I felt about it. I can't say I'm able to deal with homosexuals."

When he related this incident to Angela Allen, he said, "I never knew" about Clift's sexual preferences. "At that time," said Zoe, "John loathed homosexuals." From that moment on John had it in for Clift. Freud be damned! *Freud* was damned.

"Then a doctor from London, a neurologist and psychiatrist, David Stafford-Clark, came over to advise me on technical points," John remembered. "Clift wanted to be present, and was, and would interrupt our conversations constantly. The more he drank the more interruptions, until I threw him out of the room. I had to lock the door to keep him out. He stayed outside the door and cried. I swear to God, it was something! Stafford-Clark just shook his head. He was only astounded that this was our selection to play Sigmund Freud, in his eyes the greatest figure of the century."

John realized he had made a mistake when Clift arrived in Munich in September to start the picture. "He had to be restrained on the airplane," Huston said. "He wouldn't fasten his seat belt. He drank. They had to hold him down in his seat." Ernie Anderson remembered Clift being "blind drunk. He got off the plane and fell right on the floor. And we had half the press of Germany there—to photograph Freud's return. From then on it was just one catastrophe after another."

Doc Erickson said that "there was a thought of replacing him before we started. John discussed it with me very seriously. About his drinking, drugs, and his being absolutely incorrigible. 'What do you think we should do?' I said, 'It's up to you, John, you're the man. From my point of view there is nobody more right for the part than Monty.' "

"He had no idea of what the picture was about," John said. "No idea of the character, of how to say the lines. Jesus Christ, I wanted to walk away. In *The Misfits* his speech was of colloquialisms, and he was at home with that kind of talk. But this was a new language. The cadences of the turn of the century, as well as the scientific talk. It was so painful. And his behavior was simply revolting. He had a plastic bottle filled with grapefruit juice and vodka. I never took a drink out of it, I didn't want to touch *anything* that his lips were near."

John's revulsion was so great that everything about Monty offended him. He complained that "there was an odor that came out. He belched and he farted. It was terrible, terrible, just repelled one. But he didn't do this to women. All females felt protective toward Monty. It was a strange thing. They became moist over him. Particularly if they were a few years older. But he was in his last stages. There was brain damage there and he couldn't remember a line. He was revolting. It was a combination of drugs, drink, his being a homosexual, the whole thing became a soup that was gag-making."

What John didn't know, and was never told, was that Clift was suffering from a hypothyroid condition that made him lose his balance, caused muscle spasms, memory loss, and premature cataracts. It was a rare metabolic disorder that, when diagnosed, was treated with vitamin D and extra calcium, but according to Monty's physician, "he never really returned to normal."

Ricki had come to Munich with the children, having first stopped in Paris, where Ernie Anderson introduced her to Louis Armstrong, who was there making a film, *Paris Blues*. "I want you to meet Mrs. John Huston," Anderson said. "Hey, Lucille," Armstrong called to his wife, "come and meet one of John Huston's girlfriends." Armstrong didn't mean any harm, Anderson said, but Ricki didn't like it. Nor did she like the fact that Zoe was also in Munich, two months pregnant, and no longer cast as Freud's wife. "That was my choice," Zoe said. "John had given me the part, but I gave it up. I already had quite a part for me!"

Angela Allen once noticed twelve-year-old Tony looking despondent and went over to him. "I hate to visit," he said, "there's always a different woman." John saw them whispering to each other and demanded to know what was being said. "We're talking about airplanes," Angie snapped.

"The poor kid," she said, "he was absolutely trembling. He was quite nervous around his father. Tony was bitterly resentful. It was normal that a child should hate somebody who has supplanted his mother."

Tony was put in a U.S. Army school while in Munich and experienced severe culture shock. Some of the older boys began to give him a rough time and when John saw how afraid Tony was to go to school, he gave him his first boxing lessons. Tony returned to the school, had another confrontation, and put up his fists. "I got properly knocked out," he said. "But it worked. I was taken to the principal's office with the other boy and he was told to lay off me. I never even touched the guy."

When Paul Kohner's children, Susan and Pancho, were hired to work on *Freud*, the picture began to seem like a family affair. The part of Martha Freud was given to Susan Kohner, who had coveted the more substantial role of Cecily, the patient Freud analyzed. Uncovering Cecily's repressed guilt-ridden sexual feelings toward her father leads Freud to his breakthrough of understanding the significance of the unconscious. "I wanted that part in the worst way," Susan Kohner said. "I even typed up something to John, saying I had a Cecily complex. I pasted a picture of myself on it and sent it to a 'Dr. Freud,' explaining why I really should play that role. John probably had a good laugh out of it." Her action took considerable courage, since John had been such a strong presence throughout her life.

Susannah York, who had acted in only two films, was asked to play Cecily. She credited John with having the foresight to go beyond the typecasting she was beginning to feel so early in her career. "I always gave him a lot of points for that," she said. "People were already casting me as the English Rose. John had the imagination and sheer old-fashioned nose to see something different." It proved to be a difficult picture for York, who said she didn't know what psychoanalysis was before the film but was interpreting her dreams once it began. "John kept coming in odd phallic dreams and nightmares during that time," she said. "I always dreamt of this magnificent Corinthian column, going up and up, wonderful great big thing, with countless leaves coming out of the top; decoration, scrolls, swirls . . . and absolutely hollow inside. That's what he seemed to me. But now I know I must have been wrong."

York's confusion about John was a direct result of his treatment of Clift. "They were at odds from day one," Doc Erickson said. "John would not comment on any script suggestions from Monty, wouldn't even discuss things with him." Susan Kohner, in her early scenes with Clift, thought him "a dear, sweet man to be protected and pitied." Susannah York found him "constantly searching for the truth. I felt so close to him. I loved his digging. I spent just about every evening with Monty; we'd have dinner and then go back to his hotel where we would work until three in the morning, just learning our lines, working out how we would want to do a scene."

The problem, she and Clift soon realized, was that the script often changed by the time they were ready to shoot, so what they had learned had to be relearned. "Blue pages replaced yellow pages," York said. "We'd reshoot the scene, and three days later we'd be given pink pages to reshoot the blue/yellow scene. Some scenes were rewritten and reshot four times. John kept rewriting it. And we would rewrite on John's rewrites. Finally I just rebelled."

One scene, where Freud was to lecture a few hundred students, was rewritten so often it began to shake Clift's confidence. "As an actor," York said, "it's hard enough having to learn a speech on a particular subject in one way, but it is *unbelievably* hard to relearn it. It leads to distrust. And the more distrusting you are of what you're saying, the more it seems farther from the truth. It was no longer what you thought you were playing." Because of these changes, Clift kept looking down at his notes, as he thought a lecturer would do anyway. But John didn't want him to use notes or glance down—it disturbed the camera shot—and he insisted that Clift do it from memory. "It was a long, complicated speech," said Angela Allen, "and he just couldn't learn the lines." Stephen Grimes noticed that when John would tell Clift to "Go again," he would never give him any suggestions, as he sometimes did with other actors. "We all felt sorry for him," Grimes said.

Desmond Davies, who had been a clapper boy on *The African Queen* and worked as a camera operator under cinematographer Douglas Slocombe on *Freud*, was responsible for setting up some of the difficult shots John envisioned. "You really had to be sure that you understood what he was saying," Davies remembered. "He used to work through the viewfinder and put chalk marks on the floor, then go off the set and say, 'Call me when you're ready.' Douglas Slocombe would light it, I would line it up, we'd run the shot until it worked right, and then he would come back. You had to be really skilled at your job—whether it was cameraman, sound recordist, camera operator—because if you said you've made it work, it *had* to work. He was ruthless in that way. He wanted the best. And when he got a take he'd print it. He never covered himself. His genius was he really understood cinema. He knew exactly how a camera views a scene."

A key scene in the movie was Freud's discovery of Cecily's problem regarding her father's death. She had told Freud that doctors brought her to the hospital, where nurses then took her to her dead father. But under hypnosis the story changed. The truth was that he had not died in a hospital but in a brothel, and it wasn't doctors but the police who had come for her. Susannah York asked John to hypnotize her so she could know what it was like, but it didn't work. "I remember him waving this pencil," she said, "and I just fell about." A hypnotist, Dr. Stephen Black, was brought in to advise her. He never hypnotized York either, but he brought several patients to the set whom he put under. Dr. Black also became friendly with Clift, joining him for lunch on several occasions, and once unsuccessfully attempting to hypnotize him. Clift began to believe that Black had actually been hired to observe him, and when he confronted Huston John waved him off, saying, "You're paranoid, boy."

If he was, then it would have been just another symptom Clift had to cope with. Inge Morath, who had come once again to photograph a Huston movie, stayed only long enough to get her pictures, because "it was all so terrible. John really had it in for Monty at that point," she said, "and it's always uncomfortable to work if there is great tension between the director and one of the lead actors. Monty was desperate, a tortured creature, and John had the instinct of a hunter. Monty was incredibly sensitive and had a very poetic side to him, but I don't think John particularly cared for that. You could spend an hour with him talking about Rilke, and the next hour he'd go to a restaurant, climb on the table, and bark at ladies' legs. Then he would invariably order a steak that was barely cooked, which he would send back five times. It just got boring!"

Six weeks into the film the company was behind schedule and overbudget. Not only was John having problems with Clift, but also with his costume designer, the formidable Doris Langley Moore. Her costume collection filled a museum in Bath and, as Angela Allen noted, "she could look at a seam and say it was made in 1862 and not 1863 because of the way it was turned." Desmond Davies observed some of the arguments over the costumes. "Sometimes John would want fifty more extras, who all had to be dressed. Or he would agree on a costume, then the actor would walk on and he'd want it changed. There was a huge argument at the Munich railway station one night. He didn't like the way the extras were dressed and she had to change them all. Doris was quite a tough in-fighter herself and, of course, that made John fight even harder."

"I'm an old woman," Langley Moore said when asked her thoughts about this time, "and I prefer not to have to spend my time talking about unpleasant subjects. My contribution toward John would not be in the vein of rapture and admiration." John's feeling was mutual. Recalled Angela Allen: "If I ever mentioned Doris to him he'd get very nasty and say, 'That bitch.' I'd never known him to be like that."

John's most upsetting battle, though, was with Susannah York, who kept coming to him with her own last-minute changes in the script. "She had the courage of foolhardiness," Desmond Davies said. "Their arguments were about the way the scenes were done." Angela Allen saw that "Susannah was not a timid creature. She was an accomplished actress and they fought quite a bit about the interpretation of her part." Their worst fight came after John refused to accept some of her revisions. "But John," York protested, "these words are terrible and I can't say them. I can't get them out." It wasn't very tactful, since John had written those words.

"It was a really bad fight," she said, "and I was in a storm of tears. And *he* stormed out of the room and slammed the door!" Two hours later, when York returned to her hotel room, she could barely open the door because of all the flowers John had sent. "There were red roses everywhere. I went fighting my way through them, sitting down on the bed, and crying all over again. And thinking, 'Why couldn't he just have sent me half a dozen roses or a bunch of violets?' I would have liked it much, much better."

Susannah's anger turned to shock when she saw how John wouldn't allow Clift to protect himself physically during a dream sequence where he was to pull himself up a mountain with a rope. "Part of his costume was white gloves," York said, "and John said, 'No, no, I don't want gloves.' And Doris got really heated and said, 'John, he could not be without gloves.' Men wore gloves in those days. 'Monty's not wearing gloves,' John said."

The scene was carefully constructed to make it visually separate from the rest of the film and had to be shot in nine takes. "Because Monty was not well coordinated," Angela Allen said, "his hands were all torn to pieces. I had to say to John, 'You've got to look at his hands. He can't go on like this.' " But, said York, "John made him re-do and re-do. In some ways Monty was a masochist, but John was behaving undoubtedly sadistic." Clift would later tell his doctor that it was on this scene that Huston "earned his reputation as the laughing sadist." Desmond Davies agreed: "There was a sadistic streak in John. Seeing an actor tear his hands to pieces." "I've met careless directors, shallow directors, ill-prepared directors," York said. "But John was the first grown-up bully that I met in my professional life."

In his own defense John said, "I was never kinder to anybody than I was to Clift. Sometimes I spoke harshly to him, but it was an attempt to make him come to his senses." For the rope-climbing dream scene, he pointed out, mattresses were placed below him for his safety. At the end of each take, all Clift had to do was drop the rope and fall the few feet to the mattresses, but instead he held tightly and slid down, burning the palms of his hands. This disturbed Huston, who had seen Monty bloody his hands during *The Misfits*, and he conjectured that perhaps Clift was desensitized by drugs and didn't feel the pain. To those who blamed him for cruelty, John had two words: "Unthinkable nonsense!" As far as he was concerned, "Monty, for his own reasons, was beating himself up."

By the time Dr. David Stafford-Clark arrived as a consultant on the film, sides had been drawn and cliques formed between those who thought Huston was being unbearably cruel to Clift and those who felt John was only doing what he had to do in order to get any sort of performance at all out of an actor who had lost his ability to act. "There were very strong divisions of loyalties," Stephen Grimes said. "Monty's people and John's people. I stayed strictly neutral." Susannah York considered it "the nature of the way John worked on that film, to divide." Doc Erickson noted that York, Davies, and Doris Langley Moore were all "anti-John. And probably correctly so, from their point of view. His behavior was bad. But he was the director, and he had the right to demand what he wanted to make the movie."

Stafford-Clark stayed long enough to hear the grievances, to spend some time talking with both Huston and Clift, and to form his own theories about what was going on between them. Patricia Bosworth, in her Clift biography, noted that Stafford-Clark felt that Huston had developed a love/hate relationship to Monty. He loved him as a son when he played a vulnerable cowboy in *The Misfits* but hated him as the genius Freud who no longer had any need for his advice. Stafford-Clark himself didn't feel he could discuss his observations because Huston and Clift had spoken to him in professional confidence. But if Stafford-Clark was reluctant to offer his professional analysis, there was no lack of amateurs whispering in the wings.

"Everyone had a pocketbook of Freud in their back pocket," said Pancho Kohner, who was twenty-two when he was hired as a $100-a-week gofer on the picture. Desmond Davies said that everyone was "turning into amateur psychologists. Sexuality, homosexuality, Oedipus complexes. All of us, the whole crew, were muttering about John—who really had a dislike of homosexuals because it was against his whole Hemingwayesque world—'I bet he's a repressed homosexual.' And when John got to hear of this he would laugh about it. He said, 'I know you all think I'm a repressed fucking fag.' He thought it very funny."

Angela Allen heard John's comment and didn't think it funny at all. "I thought it was a remarkable remark to come out with about himself," she said, believing there was some truth to it. She felt John's repression had more to do with his "certain amount of hatred of women" than the way he treated Clift. "He didn't like women," Susannah York believed. "He may have adored them. He could lunch them and flower them, but he didn't truly like women." York found John's being such an "extremely macho man" and his "repugnance of things gay" to be "very deep-seated. I would be very interested in John's relationship with his mother," she said.

Zoe Ismail, whose pregnancy became increasingly visible as the months went by, saw John through the eyes of a young lover. To her, there was no room for cynicism . . . or for Freud. "John and I had great fun," she said. "I was on the set quite a lot. I never thought of him in terms of a lover. There was something much deeper in my relationship with him than that. He was a noble soul. He was something superior than the normal person. Lover, to me, undermines what he really was. That's such a side element. He had his faults, but the good outweighed the bad."

What Zoe didn't see, or refused to see, was the fault that had bothered all of John's wives except Evelyn Keyes: his absolute weakness when it came to other women. On *Freud* it happened soon after a school friend of Susan Kohner's visited the set. "She was a bohemian type," Susan recalled. "John was trying to find people who could be hypnotized easily, and she was sure she could. An affair ensued. And afterward she had nothing but lovely things to say about him. There must have been hundreds of these kinds of relationships in his life."

During the time the production moved to Vienna for a few weeks, Montgomery Clift had an accident that caused still more friction between him and Huston. There was a scene that never appeared in the film, where an extra knocked off Freud's hat and called him a "dirty Jew." During one take the extra inadvertently hit the hat into Clift's eye. He complained that he couldn't see and insisted on taking time off to be checked by his doctor in London. The delay angered John until he received word that Clift's vision was, indeed, blurred, due to his cataracts, and he would have to undergo an operation as soon as the picture was finished. Susannah York had not been there when the incident occurred and on the following Monday when she saw John and Doc Erickson laughing together, she approached them and asked to be let in on the joke. "I think it's a little localized," Erickson cautioned. "No," John said with a smile, "Susannah's a big girl now, she can hear it." "Oh, do tell me," York said. "We've just decided we'll get a club together to get a Seeing Eye dog for Monty for Christmas," John told her and laughed.

His laughter stopped, however, when Susannah reacted in a most unexpected manner. She curled her hands into fists and attacked him. "I absolutely went for John, beating him on the chest," she recalled. "He crashed back against the wall. He was so astonished, and so was I. Doc Erickson, all of us, we were just completely surprised. It all happened so quickly, and then I just ran. From that moment I was *deeply* angry with him. I just couldn't forgive him for that."

John saw Susannah as spoiled, "the personification of the uninformed arrogance of youth." York agreed that she was uninformed *and* arrogant, but not spoiled. "I would say *willful.*" She also thought the same was true about Clift. "Monty was like steel," she said, "and for a long time he would bend and bend and bend and you couldn't break him." In the end, though, "he did break. And I felt that I must be there to help pick up the pieces."

Ernie Anderson remembered the only time he ever saw John lose his temper. "I remember a take forty-seven," he said. "And Huston called for a little recess. Then he strolled off the set, walked to his office, punched his fist through the wall, and turned over his desk." John himself devised a strategy to *scare* Clift into a performance. As Desmond Davies knew, Clift "was very female, very timid, easily frightened, like a little mouse. In spite of being such a big star. And John frightened the hell out of him."

Huston admitted to getting rough with Clift, even once entering his dressing room and slamming the door so hard that a mirror fell and shattered. John wanted to shake Clift up to get a performance out of him, but instead Monty just looked at him blankly and asked Huston if he was going to kill him. John glared at him and said he was seriously considering it.

With word of the polarities that had been drawn on the set, along with the costly delays and expenditures, Universal became so concerned that they sent accountants and insurance people to audit the picture. What they were hoping for was that either Clift would quit and be replaced by Eli Wallach, or that he would file an insurance claim because of his cataract problem, which would save the studio a million dollars. Clift, concerned about his future career, refused to do either.

"They were trying to get him to resign," Angela Allen said, "because if they fired him they'd have to pay him. One day, by accident, I went into the theater looking for the editor and stumbled upon a doctor the studio had sent over from London. He was looking at all the outtakes so he could certify that Monty was brain-damaged—just on the basis of what he could see on this film. This was the game they were trying to play. It got so bad in the end that there was literally a spy thing going on. Our phones were tapped; we were being followed. It was all presumably to do with trying to get Monty off the picture, to salvage what they knew was going to be a disaster. I'm sure John didn't know everything, but he must have known something."

Clift's inability to remember his lines led Angela Allen to ask him if he would like to read from cue cards, a practice she knew John abhorred. He agreed. John also consented, "out of desperation," Angie said, and Monty's lines were written on boards, on bottle labels, in door frames, wherever he turned.

* * *

By mid-December the shoot had just gone on too long and John "got very bored," according to Stephen Grimes. "We all did." Some relief came with the Christmas holidays, as John returned to Ireland to play host to John and Elaine Steinbeck; Afdera Fonda, who was separated from Henry Fonda; and many of the friends and neighbors that made St. Clerans such a special place on such occasions. In her memoir *Never Before Noon,* Afdera Fonda recalled how she and Huston "had a long-standing, if uneasy, attraction and I thought, well, why not: let's take the plunge!"

Once again a woman made the decision to go after John, and once again John complied. Only this time it didn't work out. "The setting was ideal," Afdera wrote. "A fairy castle in the middle of rolling green hills and woodlands, the clean rain and, below ground in the cellars, the most amazing Japanese garden, big plants, a sauna, a swimming pool where everyone swam naked. It was all very erotic. John had decided that, finally, this was the time but, when it came to it, I couldn't. I felt a mental chemistry, but not a physical one. Everything about John was too long: his arms, his legs, his prehistoric monkey face—everything! It was most embarrassing—in fact, I had to tell him a little lie—that I had a strange illness. He didn't believe me, but he had to pretend to."

With all that he had been through on *Freud,* Afdera's teasing flirtations most likely didn't break John's stride. Especially not after receiving a note from Marietta Tree, who was in Barbados: "Have dreamt of you every night for the last three," she wrote. "Are you alright? I *evidently* miss you. Hope the picture is going well. . . . Much, much love."

When filming resumed in Munich after the new year, Ricki took the children to London, where she enrolled them in separate schools. Anjelica was put in the Lycée Français, where she was expected to converse in French, and Tony was put in a cramming school called Davies, where he would learn Latin and be properly prepared to pass the entry exam for Westminster, a privileged public school. John, initially, was against the children being educated in England and had tried to convince Ricki that Switzerland might be better for them. But once he agreed to London he said to Tony, "If you go there, you'll be able to go to the theater." It was a stormy Irish day and Tony looked out the window and said, "There's my theater, out there." Tony loved

Ireland and didn't want to leave. It had been a happy Christmas for both children, as Tony got the 8mm movie camera and projector he had wanted, and Anjelica a yellow diamond from Boucheron's in Paris. "It was very, very different living in London," Tony recalled.

Shooting finally ended on February 10, 1962, and no crew was ever happier to leave a production than this one. Susannah York left believing John's cardinal sin was, "basically, inhumanity," but felt she would "never have the experience wiped off my slate." She was "learning about life and people's relationships to each other in a way I didn't really understand at the time." Montgomery Clift flew to New York for a hernia operation and saw Nan Huston, telling her all about his troubles with John. Desmond Davies received an engraved viewfinder from Huston, which he has used on every film he has made since becoming a director.

Wolfgang Reinhardt and Charles Kaufman received credit for writing *Freud* even though the finished picture contained none of their work. John would have liked the credit to read "By Jean-Paul Sartre and John Huston," but Sartre wanted nothing to do with the film and John didn't file early enough to get any credit. "As the director, you had to declare yourself the screenwriter at some date before starting it and I hadn't known of it. That was the sole reason."

Ernie Anderson began the publicity campaign but found that Universal itself was divided over the film's release. "The head of advertising and publicity said, 'This picture will never be shown, so there is to be no publicity,' " Anderson recalled. "The reason was that almost half of the board didn't want the picture to be made."

There was publicity, of course. And Universal attempted to spice it up by adding *The Secret Passion* to the title. The posters advertised the picture this way: "Alone, He Fought Against His Own Dark Passions . . . Against the Taboos of an Outraged World . . . Knowing That the Shocking Truth Could Ruin His Career . . . Destroy His Marriage! . . . He Dared to Search Beyond the Flesh!"

The campaign failed to draw an audience, although Anderson said, "I've never seen Huston prouder of a picture." "I was amazed how good the end result was," said John, "because it was really an ordeal. And in spite of the difficulties, Monty gave an extraordinary performance. His genius showed through. I was surprised it didn't have an audience— and it certainly didn't. I would have thought that there would have been enough people curious about the work of the man, that name."

The reviews were mixed, from *Time*'s praise as "a taut, intellectual thriller . . . directed with dominating intelligence," and the *New York Times*'s calling it, "as daring and dramatic as the probing of a dark, mysterious crime . . . An excellent, tasteful picture," to *Film Quarterly*'s pan: "What John Huston has produced is a feature-length classroom film, even down to arty 'think' titles, an intoning narrator, and the awkward mouthing of lines . . . written to be read."

The narration, spoken by Huston, particularly disturbed Susannah York. "The thing that I find horrific about the final version is John's commentary," she said. "Because it was told in the 'I' person and the voice is so terribly different from Monty's. It was the act of a supreme egoist to use his own voice."

Stephen Grimes thought John's idea of making a detective story out of *Freud* was a good one, but he didn't think it came through after the final cut. John agreed with him, angry once again with what the studio did to another picture of his. Scenes he thought were essential were "literally mutilated" and there was nothing he could do about it.

"*Freud* must have been exceptionally difficult for John," Susannah York finally understood. "Anyone who worked in that film didn't come out unscathed. It was a very dangerous six months."

22

"I HAVE A NEW BROTHER"

IT WAS ZOE'S DECISION TO MOVE TO ROME TO HAVE THE baby and live in a city where she wouldn't have to compete for John's family loyalties. "Let Ricki have England; I'd have my own country," she felt. "I didn't see why I should cramp her style. She seemed not to want to acknowledge this whole thing. She was furious about our relationship." In the late spring, after delivering *Freud* to Universal, John joined her. "It was just a beautiful time," Zoe remembered. "John was doing this painting of me pregnant and he was terrified that he wouldn't finish it in time and that he'd lose his model. He was in a terribly good mood. We had so many laughs together. Other times it was making films, pressures, people were around, but that time it was just very calm and quiet. We went to lovely restaurants. Gladys was in and out all the time."

They had talked about marriage, but it didn't work out because Ricki wouldn't give him a divorce. "She was being very difficult," Zoe said. "It would have happened beyond a doubt; therefore, to me, I was married to him." "I would certainly have married her," John agreed, "except that I didn't want to contest a divorce, with two kids. And Ricki didn't get one because she would have to pay taxes, so it wouldn't have been to her advantage."

John was with Zoe when Danny was born in May 1962. "He stayed with me in the hospital," Zoe recalled. "He slept there that night. In fact, he thought *he* was giving birth. He was very sweet and very supportive. Then, after a week, he had to get back to Ireland and I stayed in Rome. My sister was there, so I had somebody with me, but I was very depressed. I didn't think he should have left; he should have waited another two or three weeks until I got over that."

John gave Danny his last name. To his surprise Zoe took part of Huston's middle name, Marcellus, and made it her own. "I changed Ismail to Sallis, because Ismail typed me. And the way I look I could play Italian, French, Spanish."

But it was the role of mother that seemed to suit Zoe best, as she settled into her new life: a single parent, raising a baby son in a foreign country, away from her family, friends, and lover. John would visit her whenever he could and she would spend the holidays at St. Clerans, but other than the financial support she received from him, Zoe and Danny were on their own.

"I have a new brother," Anjelica whispered to Joan Buck in the kitchen of the poet Stephen Spender's London house, which had been lent to Ricki while she looked for a flat to rent. Neither Tony nor Anjelica had been told about the situation with Zoe by either of their parents. News of Danny's birth reached Anjelica when a friend of a friend of Zoe's first heard about it. Anjelica was only eleven and Joan said it was "an awful trauma" for her. Tony was told by his best friend Tim, Stephen Grimes's son, "who had heard that Danny existed and had just let this sort of slip out." They weren't absolutely *sure* Zoe had had a baby, and they didn't ask Ricki about it, so the event hovered like an enigma for a few years.

Joan remembered how Anjelica would sometimes cry over the separation of her parents. "This is because your parents are really extraordinary people," Joan would tell her, "and that's why it's all complicated and peculiar. My parents are really dull people, they're never going to divorce or have any problems and that's the advantage, but the disadvantage is that they're really, really dull."

With his children now in London and Rome, John still didn't forget about Pablo and his family in Cuernavaca. He *might* have forgotten, had Pablo and Olga not kept writing to him, keeping him up to date on

Pablo's failing bookstore, on the slowness of the real estate business, and of the difficulties they had making ends meet. In May, Pablo complained to John, "I know you are very busy, but I do wish that sometimes you would drop us a line." He then said that his eldest son, Johnny, four, and their younger boy, David, both had typhoid and they were worried that their new baby girl, Linda, might also get it. He asked for $200 to pay for their medical bills. A month later Olga wrote thanking him.

Back in Ireland John began to make final preparations for a light mystery thriller he had agreed to do for Universal. He had originally planned to make *The Lonely Passion of Judith Hearne* with Katharine Hepburn next, followed by *The Man Who Would Be King* and *Montezuma*. But Allied Artists wanted Rosalind Russell instead of Hepburn. "I don't think Katie knows to this day what happened," he said. "Her star had set temporarily at that time and they wanted Russell, who was the big star. I wouldn't do it." The Kipling story still wasn't ready, and although Dalton Trumbo's script for *Montezuma* was, the estimated $15 million needed was prohibitive. So John settled for *The List of Adrian Messenger*, based on a novel by Philip MacDonald.

The book was set mostly in London, but John thought of transposing it to Ireland and centering it around fox hunting. "That's why he wanted to make it," Stephen Grimes said, "so he could get in a bit of fox hunting and work at the same time."

The "List" of the title is discovered by a Scotland Yard detective, played by George C. Scott, after a plane crash that killed Adrian Messenger. On the list are eleven names, all previous victims of a murderer who needs to kill just two more to inherit an English title and large estate. What made the picture interesting and irreverent was the idea the producer, Ed Lewis, had of disguising not only the murderer, played by Kirk Douglas, but also many of the other people in the film so that the audience would be trying to guess which characters were being played by Burt Lancaster, Robert Mitchum, Tony Curtis, and Frank Sinatra. "It was a trick to get names on the marquee," Huston said. Definitely a distracting idea . . . but there was something to be said about the nature of identity and disguise, especially when dealing with stars who were always attempting to conceal their real selves from public scrutiny.

Cherokee gave John the clue as to who should write *Adrian Messenger*. She was living in West Hollywood in the spring of 1962 when John visited her and complained that he didn't know of any writer he could turn to. She suggested that "the best writer in town is living across the street." "Who's that?" John asked. "Tony Veiller," she said. Veiller's writing career had foundered and he and his wife had opened an antique store. John's disappointment with Veiller for dropping out of *Beat the Devil* had subsided, and Cherokee threw a party to reunite them. "Tony's hair had turned white in those intervening years," John recalled. "And his wife was a kind of troublemaker who had given him the idea that he was being taken advantage of. But Tony and I talked for a while and immediately the old sympathy was reestablished."

Tony Veiller agreed to write the movie, and for the next six weeks he would meet with John at his bungalow at the Beverly Hills Hotel. As he was being paid by the week, Veiller told his thirteen-year-old son Bayard, "If I start printing, I think I can stretch this out to seven weeks."

Bayard's first recollection of John was when he came to the antique store. "I didn't know who he was, until I saw the 'JH' on his shirt. John was the single most charming man on the face of the earth. I fell prey to his lure as easily as anyone else. He took a liking to me and asked if I'd like to come to Ireland for two weeks in August and visit his son, who was a year younger than I. So I did that."

"When I heard 'Tony Veiller,' I laughed," Ricki wrote to John from London, remembering his anger with Veiller eight years before. "It feels as though wheels come full circle in their own lopsided way after all." It was easier for John to take a little ribbing from Ricki than it was for him to read her request for $10,000, to match the $10,000 her father had sent her to remodel the house at 31 Maida Avenue that she had found. She insisted that after living like a nomad, moving from place to place with the children until finding what she felt was the perfect house, it was important to make it as comfortable as possible for the kids. Financial matters between them were handled by John's business manager, Morgan Maree. Ricki often felt frustrated by that arrangement and this time she demanded that John deal with it directly.

On August 5, 1962, Huston's fifty-sixth birthday, news of Marilyn Monroe's alleged suicide shocked the world. John heard about it with sadness. "Here was a child, scarcely educated, her upbringing a pretty scattered proposition, ill-prepared for the role she was to play, that of sex symbol," he said. "It takes background and character to stand the assault on that kind of career. She had no mental preparation for what was to come, just a great innocence, a childishness; the kind of faith that was very often betrayed, too, because people began to exploit her. It's almost like an allegory in which innocence has attracted evil. Her innocence failed to recognize evil, and the evil then destroyed her."

Angela Allen was more cynical. She wrote a letter to John in which she expressed doubt that Marilyn had committed suicide. "Just the usual overdose, but that time with no one around to haul her off to the stomach pump."

Robert Mitchum, who was about to act again for Huston, now had regrets that he didn't do *The Misfits*. Not only because Clark Gable might still be alive but also because of Marilyn. "She would have been up and out like *that*," he said, snapping his fingers, "on time, all the time, if I'd been there. She trusted me. Anything I told her, she believed and she'd do it." When he considered her life, he thought that "she burlesqued herself. She didn't have any sex. She thought she wasn't very pretty. She had a lot of problems, physical problems. Every time a director called 'Action!' she began to menstruate. She'd turn blue. You'd have to throw her down and massage her. She was a funny girl and had an incredible sense of loyalty"—Mitchum sighed—"although to the wrong people."

Bayard Veiller arrived at St. Clerans soon after Marilyn's death. Joan Buck was also there, visiting Anjelica and Ricki, who had returned for the summer. Bayard got along better with the girls than he did with Tony, whom he found obnoxious. By then Tony had become a decent fisherman and horseback rider and had even been blooded on a fox hunt. "When you're there at the end of a good hunt," Tony recalled proudly, "the master dips the tail in the fox's blood and bloods you. That's your initiation ceremony." Bayard admitted to feeling "awkward, being in a world I knew nothing about."

Bayard considered himself "a precocious child who knew no intellectual fear, which John really liked because he could talk to me. I don't think he could deal with his own children on the same level. I was a short adult in that sense, so Tony felt awkward about that and we really didn't hit it off." Tony, for his part, doesn't even remember Bayard's visit, but Anjelica does.

"It was fun when people came," she recalled. "Then we'd have big games of Sardines—like hide-and-seek, only instead of finding the person, you got into the hiding place with the person. We had a trampoline and we all jumped on it forever." Anjelica and Joan Buck would spend afternoons in John's loft using his paints as makeup for their dolls. Or they'd go into his study in the Big House and draw on pads with felt-tipped pens. They'd play in the ruins of the Norman castle on the property, sometimes uncovering cannonballs covered with lead. They'd put on pony shows and, when no one was looking, they'd sneak into the loft above the stables and watch the horses mate.

"Anjel and I loved the loft because we could watch the horses fuck," Joan recalled. "John was breeding Connemara ponies, so the mares would be brought out and this stallion would mount one mare after the other. Anjelica and I thought this was the way it went."

Their new friend was Stephen Spender's blonde daughter, Lizzie, whom Joan described as "this big, uncomplicated English beauty. We would be terribly jealous of each other because we were Anjelica's two best friends. She could ride better but I spoke French." She and Anjelica became close, Lizzie said, because they "were very alike. We were very lonely children whose parents were away a great deal. And we both had black poodles. We had great plans to start a poodle parlor. Then we realized there weren't any other poodles in Galway." Instead they came up with the idea of putting on dog shows. Although Lizzie's childhood included meeting some of the best English writers of the day, such as W. H. Auden, T. S. Eliot, and Christopher Isherwood, as well as various cabinet and prime ministers, none of them, she said, "had the charisma of John. He was like an old-fashioned king or sultan. The whole world revolved around him." Her famous poet father "seemed very small-fry in comparison with being a movie director. And my parents seemed incredibly low-key in comparison with John and Ricki. St. Clerans was like a big movie."

But life at St. Clerans wasn't always easy for the children. "My father was more inclined toward what was adult in children than what was childish in children," Anjelica said. "Because of his intellect he didn't suffer fools gladly. Once, at the dinner table, the subject of Van Gogh came up. I said somewhat flippantly that I didn't like Van Gogh. He said, 'You don't like Van Gogh? Then name six of his paintings and tell me *why* you don't like Van Gogh.' I couldn't, of course. And he said, 'Leave the room, and until you know what you're talking about, don't come back with your opinions to the dinner table.' "

*   *   *

Tony also suffered John's put-downs whenever he expressed an opinion he couldn't support, but when it came time for John to cast the twelve-year-old boy who could ride in *Adrian Messenger*, John asked Tony if he wanted to do it. "Yes," Tony answered very matter-of-fact. But he wasn't so cool about it with Anjelica or Lizzie. "Oh, God!" Lizzie Spender exclaimed. "He used to drive us *mad* in the morning, going over his lines at breakfast. He was just impossible then, so full of himself. His favorite way of waking us up in the morning was to run into the bedroom and throw a glass of water in our faces. Tony's the only person I've ever tried to kill in my life. I literally, seriously, tried to kill him with my bare hands. I guess it was worse for him than for Anjelica, growing up. She always had a girlfriend. He didn't have many friends."

While Ricki recognized the wonderful opportunity for Tony to work with John, she was also concerned about his taking a two-month leave of absence from school. She wrote to John saying that the decision should be Tony's, not theirs. John had no problem with that, since he knew how much Tony loved to ride.

Anjelica remembers being "incredibly jealous" of Tony's acting debut, getting to ride "a huge great horse, carry a crop and wear a pink coat, which you didn't get to wear on a hunt unless you were an adult. I thought it was pretty glamorous." She didn't, however, find it so glamorous the following year when she was blooded on her first cub hunt. "I wasn't wild about having guts spread on my face," she said, "but it was really a big compliment."

John found Tony's work in *Adrian Messenger* to be "very good. He did exactly what I told him to do. He said his lines reasonably and sensibly. He wasn't being an actor or anything. There was one thing I was quite proud of. He was to jump a horse over a gate. There was a stuntman who fell twice with his horse. Tony wasn't at all spooked by that. I knew his pony was good and that Tony was good, or I wouldn't have let him do it. And he did it beautifully, without turning a hair."

To Stephen Grimes, *The List of Adrian Messenger* was "a throwaway sort of film." Angela Allen thought it was one of those John did for the money. Robert Mitchum remembered it mostly for all the time he spent in makeup. He had been talked into the film when John saw him at the Beverly Hills Hotel and said, "I've got a gimmick picture, kid." Mitchum said, "If you've got an old lady, I'll play that."

John smiled and said, "As a matter of fact I do." Of course, Mitchum laughed, "Burt Lancaster did that."

Mitchum, like the other actors, had agreed to work for a set fee of $75,000, although John had offered to pay him with a Paul Klee painting instead. "Which I should have done," Mitchum now regrets, complaining that while he actually had to act in the film, Frank Sinatra "never worked one day. All he did was take the mask off at the end." John thought that audiences turned against the picture because of the gimmick of using well-known actors in disguise, even though he admitted that it was basically only Mitchum who actually did any acting among the cameo appearances. "The rest of them," he said, "had a mask made of the actor who played them and then they'd peel it off at the end. It wasn't grand theft, but it was pretty close to it. Burt Lancaster was scarcely in the picture, don't think he said a word. And Sinatra. Mitchum, though, was marvelous. The picture was pretty slick and well-constructed. But the fact that the audience was used that way got their backs up, which backfired."

Newsweek called the film "clever"; the *New York Times*, "mediocre." Critic John Russell Taylor thought it "a small joke of a film," but compared it favorably with *Beat the Devil* for its "great charm," both having been "clearly made in cheery disregard of their audiences. The director doesn't give a damn—he will amuse himself." He concluded that both films were misunderstood, "largely because nobody thought that Huston of all people would be so casual and dilatory as to play games on film."

The film had a more personal meaning for Tony, who could "never remember being in Dad's arms. He never was a physical father in any way. It just didn't come naturally to him. But," he said, "I can remember sitting in his lap when we were making *The List of Adrian Messenger*." Not, perhaps, an all-embracing hug of approval, but a significant gesture all the same.

John also rewarded Tony with a trip to Mazatlán, where they went deep-sea fishing in November. Pablo had hoped that they would visit him and his family. Things had gotten so bad that he had to close the bookstore and had begun to sell car insurance. But time was short, since Tony had to get back to school, and the fish were biting.

*   *   *

Anjelica still wasn't sure why her mother had left Ireland to put them in such dreadful English schools. "We were going to school in London, but we didn't really know why," she said. "I was too surprised a lot of the time that I didn't know what hit me."

She didn't like the Lycée Français because her teachers were mean, and she had to repeat her first year because she was bad in math and couldn't write French as well as the other children, who were all French. "Although I could speak French and I had a very nice accent," she said, "I was considered stupid by most of the other children. So I had to repeat the same year twice, and if you ever had to do that, you hate the school."

She begged Ricki to take her out of the school, "but she made me stay for the second year. I remember wishing that my mother had more money so I could come to school in a limo like the other little girls. I didn't like taking the underground one bit. I never liked to talk about money, I still don't, but after we got to London there was talk of money, which I never heard talk of until then. I was embarrassed by it."

She finally got out of the Lycée when Ricki saw the careless disregard shown when Anjelica had an accident in the schoolyard. "Someone pushed me over another kid," Anjelica remembered. "I went to ask the nurse if I could sit in her office, which was a trick most of the kids used because it got so cold in the yard you used to go in just to warm up, and she wouldn't let me stay. That afternoon I started to get hazy and they wouldn't let me go home. Finally I was hurting. A joint had been broken at the top of my spine and I was in a plaster cast from my neck down for a few months."

In 1962, John received a call from Otto Preminger, who wanted him to be in a movie he was producing and directing called *The Cardinal*. Other than the two plays he did in the twenties for the Provincetown Players and *The Lonely Man* in Chicago, John had confined his acting to bit parts in his father's or his own pictures. He had often taken the position that one great actor in the family was enough, but Preminger was persuasive, offering him a chance to play not simply a priest but a savvy Boston cardinal, a member of the Church's royalty, who cunningly aids a young, idealistic priest as he maneuvers his way through the Church's echelons.

Preminger had produced and directed John's and Howard Koch's play *In Time to Come* in 1941–42, had successfully acted as a Nazi in plays and films, had challenged Hollywood's censorship, and was the first director to hire one of the Hollywood Ten after they had served their time in prison. John considered him "a bit of a one-man revolution, the Henry Miller of the cinema." The role had originally been offered to Orson Welles, who didn't quite grasp it, according to Eva Monley, the production manager for the film, and it was Preminger's brother, Ingo, who thought of Huston. When John said he would do it, but only if he could be paid in two Jack Yeats paintings, Preminger readily agreed, and Huston suddenly found himself with an opportunity to begin a new career.

"I didn't want to use any of the established character actors," Preminger said, "because they would bring too much of their familiar image to the role. I wanted someone new but also impressive." Huston was both, Eva Monley noted, as he managed to steal "every frame he was in. *Every* frame."

He was so convincing that, while the critics panned the movie, they praised John's acting. "The film's outstanding performance," wrote Judith Crist, "is that outstanding director, John Huston, who brings throbbing vitality and sophistication to the role of Cardinal Glennon." The *New York Times*'s Bosley Crowther wrote: "It is this old boy, played by John Huston, who arrests and fascinates me. He's the one who reveals in just a few scenes toughness, authority, political acumen, compassion, and a fine philosophical turn of mind." The Motion Picture Academy agreed and Huston received a 1963 Best Supporting Actor nomination, losing out to Melvyn Douglas in *Hud* but establishing himself as a forceful screen presence.

John's own feeling about the movie was that it was a cliché, but he had to chuckle over the way Preminger worked with actors. "Otto didn't realize how he could upset people," he said. Tom Tryon, who would give up acting soon after starring as the young priest and become a best-selling author, "was so nervous and high-strung," recalled Huston, "that he was visibly shaking. I told Otto to take it easy on him, that he'd get a better performance that way. So on the next scene Otto walked behind Tryon and shouted at him, '*Relax!*' Which nearly gave Tryon a nervous breakdown right there!"

John's only request when the picture was finished was for his cardinal's costume to be sent to him in St. Clerans. Preminger thought the role had gone to John's head and asked him if he was going to wear the vestments around his house. John told him no, but he thought it would be fun to dress up and visit the seminary in a nearby town, letting everybody wonder who the new cardinal was.

After she saw the picture Nan Huston described John's voice as "soft as pussywillows." Lorrie Sherwood "damned near flipped. I always thought John would make a great fucking priest, but a *cardinal!*" Dorothy Soma requested an autographed picture with John in his cardinal robes. Both Cherokee and Talli Wyler thought the role affected John's behavior for a while, that his pontifications made him difficult to be around.

While John would continue to act for the rest of his life, he looked upon it as a lark, an easy way to pick up some decent cash. "Whether the pictures were good or bad or indifferent was of no consequence," he would say, "as I don't take that part of my life seriously. Always and forever, I'm a director."

The picture he directed after acting in *The Cardinal* was *The Night of the Iguana*, based on Tennessee Williams's play, which would bring together some of the biggest stars and most of the entertainment media to the small yet undiscovered Mexican coastal town of Puerto Vallarta.

Ray Stark brought the project to Huston. Stark had been a literary and talent agent who formed the Seven Arts Productions company with Eliot Hyman in 1957. He had made one movie, *The World of Suzie Wong*, before *The Night of the Iguana*. "I thought it would make a wonderful picture, especially in Mexico," Stark recalled in his office off Sunset Boulevard, a few buildings from the Kohner agency. "John, of course, was the guru of Mexico. I just got him at a lucky time when he wanted to go back there." Stark found John to be "the best read and the most knowledgeable man I've ever met, or that's ever been connected with the film industry. He was a Renaissance man, and everything he did was bigger than life."

John found Ray to be "adept at throwing people off balance," and though he swung "from bonhomie to a fierce enjoyment of an open row," John noted in Stark "a steady, calculating intellect."

The story of *Iguana* had to do with the decline of a defrocked minister, T. Laurence Shannon, who had sunk so low as to have become a tour guide for matronly American women traveling the coast of Mexico. Trouble comes when a teenaged seductress who left her chaperone one night is found in his bedroom. In his attempt to patch things up with the group, he winds up taking them to a crumbling hotel run by a lusty, no-nonsense old friend of his, Maxine. In the surrounding absurdity there is a symbol of goodness in the person of a sketch artist and her poet grandfather. But Shannon's bout with booze and the various women make him feel trapped, like the chained iguana being fattened for slaughter, until he manages to see inside himself before it's too late.

When Stark went to see John they agreed that the casting was the key to the film. John favored Marlon Brando as Williams's debauched ex-minister, but Stark thought Richard Harris or William Holden might be better. They tossed around some other names, but then flew to Switzerland and convinced Richard Burton he was their first and only choice. Coming off of *Becket*, Burton agreed, and Stark and Huston went to London to see Deborah Kerr, who had married Peter Viertel. She was willing to take on the role of the sketch artist. For Maxine, John wanted Ava Gardner, who had been in *The Killers* and who had once turned down his advances before he went off and married Evelyn Keyes. Gardner had already been through three marriages, with Mickey Rooney, Artie Shaw, and Frank Sinatra, and was considered to be among the most beautiful, untamed women in the world. She had a carefree, hedonistic reputation; drinking, smoking, and dancing into the wee hours, and not giving much of a damn about her career as an actress. They went to see her in Madrid.

"I knew damn well that Ava was going to do it," John said. "She did, too—but she wanted to be courted. So we went out with my beloved Ava two or three nights running. She lived a very rigorous existence, I must say. We'd meet late in the afternoon, have drinks, then go to dinner around ten o'clock. After dining, it was the clubs and the dancing, and this would go on all night. Ray was made of stronger stuff than I—not quite of the metal and fiber of Ava, who was quite capable of going on through that night and through the next day and the next night and the next! I presently dropped out and Ray went on as her escort for several nights until we left Madrid."

"What a night it was!" Ava Gardner laughed. "I took them to flamenco joints and we stayed up all night long, drinking rotten brandy and not talking about the picture at all. In fact, I almost talked Huston out of it. I'm sure if Ray Stark had appeared on his own I would have said, 'Okay, let's go out and get drunk and see a flamenco,' and that would have been the end of it. But with Huston it was hard to say no. He didn't sit and say, 'You must do this, this is good for you'—none of that crap. He never mentioned anything. Which was the same way he directed."

Even though Ava agreed, Stark put out some feelers to find out if Melina Mercouri was available in case Gardner backed out.

John thought the Gavin Lambert script Stark had commissioned had too much sex and missed the real issue: "Of a man, desperate and full of despair, at the end of his rope." He asked Tony Veiller to work with him on a new script, and together they flew to Key West, Florida, to talk to Tennessee Williams about it. Like Truman Capote, Williams was upfront about his sexual leanings and, like Capote, a genius. But Williams was a strange, temperamental character who could fly off in anger at the slightest insult, and who managed to put Huston off-balance when he took him deep-sea fishing. "He tried to entertain me," John said. "I don't think he had ever been deep-sea fishing in his life. He had along with him a young man who he claimed had a great talent as a poet and was his newest lover. We dived overboard for a swim and Tennessee's golden lad swam around the boat and suddenly panicked. It became a travesty. He had to be rescued. I pulled him in and Tennessee gave him artificial respiration while the captain looked on in disbelief."

From Key West John went to Los Angeles where he cast Sue Lyon, who had just finished *Lolita*, for the young girl who seduces Burton. For the part of "the world's oldest poet," Deborah Kerr's grandfather, Nonno, John wanted Carl Sandburg, but Sandburg was in poor health. He finally settled on Cyril Delevanti, an actor in his eighties who considered it his most important role. He met with a Mexican architect, Guillermo Wulff, who told him that he had a lease on Mismaloya, a peninsula just south of Puerto Vallarta, which might prove perfect as a setting for *Iguana*. Huston decided to go down and have a look.

The barrenness, the inaccessibility, the lack of housing, the surrounding jungle would have made most directors drop any idea that a picture could be made in such a location. But aware of the commotion such high livers as Burton and Ava Gardner could cause in any normal setting, Mismaloya seemed ideal.

Wulff, who owned the only small hotel in the area, was contracted to build the set, under Stephen Grimes's instruction. "I decided the way to keep John interested in the picture," Ray Stark said, "was to let him build a house. It would be a relaxation for him, since his mind always had to work on something." Grimes said that Ray and John also hired Wulff to build housing that they would eventually turn into a profitable resort. But when Grimes saw that Wulff was using the sand by the beach to make cement, he told him not to do that for the set, since the beach sand had too much salt, which would weaken the cement. They argued about it and Wulff wound up using the beach sand for the housing project, and less salty sand for the set.

•   •   •

With the construction under way John returned to Ireland for his fifty-seventh birthday. Ricki and the children weren't there when Tony Veiller joined him to finish the script. Veiller brought his family, and they stayed in the Little House. Bayard Veiller was fourteen then and remembered how John would cross the bridge from the Big House to join them for dinner. "Either he was lonely or bored or he saw that we had a family life and he wanted to be included," Bayard said. He noticed that John drank a great deal, but he never saw him drunk. "In Ireland the only two things to do were hunt and drink." He also saw that his father was entranced by John.

"My father wanted to be John in a lot of ways," he said, echoing what Joan Buck said of her father. "My father was a short, plump, ordinary man who had a marriage, children, a mortgage, responsibilities. He didn't go out and have adventures. John was this blithe spirit who did what he damned well pleased, and got away with it. All the time."

Suzanne Flon came to St. Clerans while the Veillers were there and they couldn't help comparing her relationship with John and Ricki's relationship with him, which they witnessed the year before. "There was a politeness between John and Ricki that was almost through clenched teeth," Bayard observed. "Underneath they would spar. We would be at lunch and Ricki would say something about Matisse and John would look at her and say, 'Oh, do you *really* think so, *dear?*' But you could damn well see beneath those words what he meant: 'You're an idiot to think that. Didn't you learn *anything* when I talked to you about modern art?' But on the surface I never heard an argument. Those passions had been spent."

The warmth and respect Bayard witnessed between John and Suzanne Flon was completely different. "One evening we were sitting downstairs playing bridge," Bayard said. "Suzanne was watching and at ten o'clock she said, 'I think I'll go to bed now. Goodnight everybody, goodnight John.' And she trailed her arm across the back of his shoulders as she walked behind him. Later on we went back down to the Little House and Mother and Dad were talking about how they seemed like an old married couple. That wasn't something you'd ever think about John, but they were."

Before the filming of *The Night of the Iguana* in September, John was already agreeing to his next picture. He had read a well-written script of *The Bible* by Christopher Fry and liked it. The Italian producer Dino De

Laurentiis came up with the idea of making the greatest movie ever, based on the greatest story ever told. He hired the English poet and playwright Fry to shape a script based on the entire Book of Genesis and planned to have five segments directed by different directors: Robert Bresson for the Creation and the Garden of Eden; Orson Welles for Abraham, Jacob, and Esau; Luchino Visconti for Joseph and his Brethren; Federico Fellini for an undetermined segment; and Huston as the artistic overseer of the project, as well as a segment director.

On August 29, 1963, John cabled Paul Kohner: *"Bible* script magnificent Will Do Yes repeat Yes." Excited by the news, De Laurentiis flew immediately to Puerto Vallarta to see Huston. "After one hour," he told *The New Yorker's* Lillian Ross, "it was as though John and I had been talking about this picture for a year."

John would call De Laurentiis his "Italian Ray Stark," and for a while it seemed as if the two producers were in competition for his talents. Stark had sent Huston *Reflections in a Golden Eye*, Carson McCullers's strange and disturbing novel about sexual aberration and latent homosexuality on a U.S. Army base in the South. John found it an "important" book whose theme fascinated him. He was also impressed with how well McCullers understood the people she wrote about, without hatred or moral evaluation. "There's something *lasting* about her prose, considered and deep," he felt.

But before he could consider translating such a story into a movie, he and Stark had to deal with the strange and wonderful mind of Tennessee Williams and how best to open up his successful play for the screen. As late as July and August, Stark was suggesting writers like Peter Schaffer, Paddy Chayefsky, or Ben Hecht to come in and doctor the script. As for himself, Huston was satisfied with what he and Veiller had done, although he agreed that Tennessee Williams would be good to have around if they needed him.

Huston and Stark's first disagreement was over whether the film should be shot in color or black and white, which was what John had previously done for *The Unforgiven, The Misfits, Freud,* and *The List of Adrian Messenger.* Initially Stark worried that color might be too costly, and that "the lush green quality [of the] rain forest . . . would photograph just about as phony as blood does." But knowing how successfully Huston had handled color in *Moulin Rouge* and *Moby Dick,* he came around to feeling color would be best. John, on the other hand, agreed with Stark's first instinct. Stark was still a novice as a producer, and since he considered Huston "one of the three or four great geniuses of film," he conceded the color issue and didn't regret it. John, on the other hand, came to believe that he had made a mistake and that Ray should have *insisted* it be shot in color.

One of the first things John did before shooting began was to assemble his five stars—Burton, Lyon, Gardner, Kerr, and Skip Ward—along with Elizabeth Taylor, who came with Richard Burton. Their relationship caused a sensation ever since she left Eddie Fisher for Burton during the filming of *Cleopatra*. For his own amusement John had six gold-plated derringers made, along with five bullets engraved with the names of each of the other actors.

"The opportunity for shoot-outs was even greater than those names might indicate," John said. "Peter Viertel, Deborah Kerr's husband, had had, before his marriage, a romantic encounter with Ava. Liz's number-two husband, Michael Wilding, made sporadic appearances as Burton's agent. Tennessee Williams was there with his current lover, and Sue Lyon's intended, a tall, pale youth ravaged by love, haunted the surrounding flora. Word got about that he was murderously inclined toward both Burton and Skip Ward, who had love scenes with Sue." Deborah Kerr joked that she "was the only one who wasn't having an affair with anybody." John had also hired as his assistant director Emilio Fernandez, his friend and fellow wild man who had worked with him on *The Unforgiven*.

Ava Gardner thought John's little gift was funny. "He fueled the publicity fires by giving us all pistols," she said. "When we arrived in Puerto Vallarta it was a fishbowl. And John was having a ball with it, enjoying the whole thing. There was no getting away from them, day and night. Elizabeth Taylor was marvelous because she's very good with the press, she's fearless. So she did a lot of that which would have fallen on my shoulders. I've never been very good with the press because I'm frightened of them."

Ray Stark admitted that he didn't do anything to prevent important press from coming down. "I may have screwed John up a bit by exploiting the picture. It was one of the most publicized pictures of its time." And despite Ava Gardner's belief that she wasn't good with the press, Stark saw that she generated wonderful publicity. "She was the most popular single lady in that part of Mexico at the time. Every eligible Mexican was after her."

"The press gathered down there," John said, "expecting something to happen with all these volatile personalities being there. They felt the lid would blow off and there would be fireworks. When there weren't any, they were reduced to writing about Puerto Vallarta. And, I'm afraid, that was the beginning of its popularity, which was a mixed blessing.

The beaches became lined by big hotels and condominiums. The natives have become waiters, chambermaids, or cops. There are traffic jams, burglaries, muggings. Most of the shops are tourist-oriented. But the water is potable. Nobody's face is pitted from smallpox anymore. Typhoid and typhus have almost ceased to exist. Children have as good a chance to be born alive as anywhere in the States. And there are schools now."

With so much attention aimed at the stars, John was able to bring Zoe and eighteen-month-old Danny to Puerto Vallarta without any publicity at all. "John was on an island and I was on the shore," Zoe remembered, "so I didn't see him very much. I used to get lonely and sad at times." He also hired Pablo as a messenger, again avoiding any mention in the press.

It was Pablo's wife, Olga, who asked John to give him a job. Their three children were healthy, but their own relationship wasn't good. "We were short of funds," Pablo said, "so we were fighting. Olga was bitter because she thought that she was going to get the benefit of John's wealth. Then she told me she had met this doctor who said she had beautiful eyes and was madly in love with her and wanted to marry her, buy her a house." When John made him a messenger Pablo was insulted that he wasn't assigned as a photographer. "I was angry with my work, running errands," he said. "I thought I was treated like a slave."

One American tourist named Marge saw Pablo attempting to deal with the press on the beach and wondered who such an arrogant young man was. She and a friend then attempted to visit the set and Pablo came running, "all hyper about how we got over there." A few days later she was at a restaurant when Pablo came in and asked her to dance. She told him to get lost. "I stayed a while and then I left," Pablo said. "The following day we became friends."

Their friendship would lead to the breakup of his marriage, leaving his children, a complete break with John, and a continuation of the hard-luck life that seemed to be his fate even before John had pulled him out of the jungle of Jungapeo seventeen years earlier.

Just as Tom Shaw found fault with Arthur Miller, he felt even more critical of Tennessee Williams. "I hated that mean sonofabitch," Shaw said in his typical bulldog manner. "I was having a drink at the bar before we went to the dailies and he was berating the shit out of this poor Mexican bartender! I didn't even know who he was. I said to myself, 'Who is this asshole?' He was a vicious kind of faggot."

Even though Angela Allen thought John also had "a personal thing going against Tennessee because he was a well-known gay," and that "whatever he wrote, John was going to say 'No,' " it didn't stop John from turning to Williams whenever he got stuck with a scene. Once, when an intimate encounter between Richard Burton and Sue Lyon didn't seem to have the kind of edge John felt it must have, he asked Williams to try to come up with something. "The situation was good," John noted, "but the dialogue didn't work. Burton was in his hotel room and she comes to see him surreptitiously. She wants him to make love to her and he resists. He's shaving, and there's a whiskey bottle on a shelf."

The next day Williams returned with new pages that so impressed John he often used the incident as an example of how a writer of genius could turn a scene that wasn't working into the best scene in the picture. "When she comes in," John said, describing Williams's changes, "instead of dialogue, her very appearance startles him and he bumps against the shelf and the whiskey bottle falls off and breaks on the floor. He's barefoot. He begins to tell her why they must not make love and, in talking, he walks up and down, the broken glass cutting his feet. She watches him become a kind of martyr with fascination, then she takes off her shoes and joins him in his martyrdom, cutting her own feet as their dialogue is played over that. It just lifted the scene on to another sphere."

The ending, however, was something John and Tennessee were never able to resolve. Williams had a far more cynical attitude toward his characters than John wanted to give them, especially at the end. Williams saw the Reverend Shannon as a broken man, destroyed finally by Maxine. But John saw the Ava Gardner character as providing Shannon with his salvation. It seemed more fitting and uplifting.

Apparently Ray Stark had the first crack at the rewrite. "That's the worst piece of shit I've ever read," Tom Shaw told John. Then Ray Stark appeared and John asked Shaw to repeat what he had said about the pages. Shaw did. "I then found out that Ray Stark wrote it," Shaw said. "My relationship with Stark has never been good since. But I also think that Stark was envious and jealous of my position with John."

Stark remembered staying up all night with John, Gladys Hill, Richard Burton, and Tennessee, arguing about the ending. "John was very fixed in his ideas and he really didn't want to change it," Stark said. "I felt that it wasn't quite right." Williams, at Ray Stark's request, attempted to rewrite the ending, changing it from what he had written in his play but keeping it consistent with his outlook. Angela Allen worked as his secretary, typing the pages.

"What do you think?" Williams often asked Allen.

"I can't wait to get to the next page," she said enthusiastically. Unlike Tom Shaw, she considered the playwright a "very gentle man."

"What do you think John's going to think?"

"He's bound to say no," Allen answered.

When Ray Stark read Williams's new ending he thought it was brilliant, but John wouldn't have it. "There were quite a few arguments between them," Allen remembered. "Ray even asked me if I could persuade John to take it. I tried, but he would not take the ending. Poor Tennessee went back very discouraged."

John defended his rejection of Williams's ending because he felt it was wrong. "The most amusing character in the play was the one played by Ava Gardner, who had the most penetrating remarks," he said. "Yet in the end, Williams wanted her to be a female spider. He himself had written her sympathetically, and it seemed to me he was pulling back his sympathy at the end. He resisted the finish as we had written it for the screen, but couldn't come up with anything as good. Finally I said, 'Tennessee, I think you've got it in for women; you don't want to see a man and a woman in a love relationship, and that's at the bottom of it.' He didn't contest that; he just thought about it and stopped arguing. Yet years later, at a luncheon party in London, the last thing he ever said to me was, 'John, I still don't agree with you about the finish.' "

Tom Shaw convinced John that rather than break for lunch, they should begin shooting at 7:30 A.M. and quit by one. "When you go to lunch," he said, "there's a big fucking letdown after and by the time you get organized again, you've blown two hours. Particularly if you've got a lot of women in the goddamn cast, where you've got to re-do the makeup." John told him to do whatever he wanted, and Shaw assembled the cast and made them a deal: If they'd be ready to shoot early, they'd be finished by one, so they could enjoy the beach and have the afternoons to themselves. What Shaw never anticipated was that Richard Burton would begin *his* good time a half hour *before* they started shooting.

"It used to amaze me," Shaw said, "seeing Burton at seven in the morning drinking beer. And he'd drink beer all morning long. By the time we finished he would have had a case of beer. And *then* he'd shift into high gear! He started into that tequila, and *man*, you'd never've known he'd had a drink! He was a big-league drinker. There was *nobody* in that league."

It wasn't only Burton who drank. "They were all into the tequila," Zoe Sallis said. "Burton and Elizabeth had a lot of rows. John barred Sue Lyon's boyfriend from the set because he didn't like their necking in front of him. He didn't like massive smooches. Steve Grimes was with some weird German who kept dancing on the tables nude. Emilio Fernandez was ferocious. I thought he was going to shoot anyone who didn't do exactly what he said."

Ava Gardner had her own experiences with the stoned and drunken beach boys who were instructed to dance around her in the movie, and who continued to dance around her off the set as well. "They never walked in the movie," Tom Shaw said. "I used to watch John dancing to show them what he wanted them to do." Ava remembered how she would find these boys "dead drunk" on her patio in the morning. "I had a house with no roof," she said, "and a twenty-foot wall on the outside. They could scale it like monkeys, and you never knew in the morning when you woke up who would be lying out there, next to the bedroom. And to get them to work, oh, boy. They were high on pot, or this cactus booze called *raicilla,* which kind of twists your mind."

When Ray Stark was concerned that an important scene between Burton and Deborah Kerr wasn't working, he pointed it out to John. John saw that Kerr had "shaped her performance for a theater audience." He gently got her to modulate it for the cameras.

With Ava Gardner, though, it took more than a suggestion. She was a genuinely insecure actress who was always putting herself down. Her self-doubts led her to turn down lead roles in such films as *Sweet Bird of Youth, Love Me or Leave Me,* and *The Graduate,* all of which she later regretted. "I'm sure I'd have been sorry not to have done *Night of the Iguana,*" she said. "Especially because of Huston, because he created a whole atmosphere, not just for the actors but for the whole set. I've worked with some damn good directors, but John was unique. I relied completely on him. It was sheer magic. John put you in the mood, got you to feel you could do the right thing, and then let you go.

"When I get frightened I completely close up and I don't know what to do, because I'm basically very shy. There was one scene I had to do with the two beach boys . . . God knows what hanky-panky was supposed to be going on. And I was to wear this bikini bathing suit and go out in the water with them. But I had this mental thing about it. I said, 'John, I can't do it in the daytime. If it were night it wouldn't be so difficult.' So he had lights brought in from Mexico City, he went to God knows what sort of trouble, I'm sure we lost a whole day's work, and he literally turned the day scene into a night scene. But I was still frightened. He said, 'Forget the bikini, go in with the same old rag you've been wearing.' He said it was more plausible anyway, she wouldn't have stopped to undress and put on a bathing suit. So he waded into the water with me and he stayed there, holding my hand. Without any words. Then he said, 'You all right, kid?' I said, 'Yes, I'm fine.' And we did the scene. One take, boom boom boom."

Dorothy Jeakins, who won an Oscar for her costume designs for the film, found Ava "sort of a lost soul. An unhappy woman. She was difficult to harness, like a wild horse—fractious and bucking and stomping. It didn't matter too much what she wore as long as it looked raffish and makeshift, attractive but sexy."

Budd Schulberg, who had been living in Mexico since 1959, stopped by the location for five days before going to New York with a script for a musical he had written. It was slightly uncomfortable for him when he saw Peter Viertel, because they had a troubled past: Schulberg's first wife divorced him and married Viertel. Also, he was angry with Ray Stark, who had bought the rights to his novel *The Disenchanted* three years before and had wanted to turn it into a love story with a happy ending. But on the *Iguana* set it just added to the cat's cradle of connections each person seemed to have with the others.

A few days later San Francisco columnist Herb Caen appeared to record his impressions of what was going on south of the border. Ray Stark recalled sitting one evening, having drinks with Taylor and Burton, Kerr and Viertel, Ava and John, when Herb Caen posed the question: "If you had one choice in your life as a way of life, what would you want?" Stark, who had had a narrow escape from sharks that afternoon when he had gone waterskiing against John's advice, immediately said "Peace." Upon further reflection he realized, "That was something I never in my life would have said, except for the sharks, because I know if I had peace, I would die." Richard Burton answered: "Adventure." Elizabeth Taylor: "Wealth." Ava Gardner: "Health." Deborah Kerr: "Happiness." Peter Viertel: "Success."

"All clichés," Stark said. "Then John, in his usual way, bobbed his head and in his deep voice said, 'That's a difficult question. I believe the answer would be *interest*.' " For Stark it became "a guiding point. If you have interest in life, you can be broke, but you can survive. You can have a terminal illness, but if you have interest it keeps you going."

* * *

John's interest in his family was piqued when he received a four-page letter from Ricki in mid-November. She had just returned from a trip to Morocco and was pleased to report that Anjelica was doing well in German and the history of ancient Egypt at her new school, St. Mary's Town & Country. "She doesn't complain of Maths," wrote Ricki, "does her homework the moment she gets home, has sketched hieroglyphics into her history notebook and recites Wordsworth—whom she despises! not to mention the fact that . . . she is to be Scrooge's sister in *A Christmas Carol* given Dec 9th at Rudolf Steiner Hall, Baker Street."

News of Tony centered around his preparation for the entrance exam to Westminster public school. After being tutored by a friend, Leslie Waddington, who had first tutored both children at St. Clerans in 1955, Ricki reported that "Tony went off as relaxed as it is possible for so highly strung a child as he is." Tony failed on his first attempt to get in and Ricki's own anxiety was high over whether he would make it this time. She told John that she bought him a Berber rifle, which she would give to him for Christmas.

On November 15, Ricki was relieved to hear from the Headmaster of Westminster: "Although we thought Anthony was still a bit of a marginal case, I am sure he is an intelligent boy and that we can safely admit him." She immediately cabled John: "LET JOY BE UNREFINED HE MADE IT."

There was no joy in Mismaloya the following week when Tom Shaw was nearly killed in a freak accident. It happened after the first night work, when Shaw realized that Ava Gardner's big dramatic moment wasn't going to be captured that evening. She had been so terrified that she had been drinking before the shooting began. "The more we'd go on, the more Ava would drink," Shaw said, "and we weren't getting what John wanted. At exactly two-fourteen A.M. I said, 'John, we're wasting our time.' He said, 'Do whatever you think best.' So I just said, 'That's it, goodnight everybody.' And I went to my room. Then I walked out onto the balcony, which was eighteen feet up in the air, and sat down. Next door I saw my assistant, Terry Morris, and told him to come over so we could go over what we needed for the next night. He sat down next to me and when he did, the goddamn balcony went out."

The salty sand from the beach that was used to make the concrete had cause a terrifying accident. The balcony gave way as if there had been an earthquake, and Shaw and Morris fell amidst the rubble to the ground below. Morris landed on top of Shaw and was able to walk away with only minor injuries. But Shaw's back had been broken in two places. At the moment it happened, Deborah Kerr was walking down the hill, and the horror of the accident brought her close to fainting. Elizabeth Taylor was also nearby and she acted immediately, rushing to nurse Shaw until others came to his rescue.

"It was exciting," Ray Stark recalled, "with John and all these Mexicans carrying Tommy Shaw on their shoulders, their mouths were really deep in water, taking him out to the boat."

"We got a plane and had him flown out that same morning," John said. "It was touch-and-go for some time whether he would live or not."

The accident put an end to Stark's and Huston's dream of using the hotel and houses Guillermo Wulff had constructed for a resort area after the film was completed. As Stark noted, "We had a sixty-day schedule and half the bungalows started to fall apart after sixty days." In the end, the only thing left standing was the set, which Grimes had insisted be made with different sand. "A nice twist," Grimes would say. "Looks much better now than when we shot it. Aged beautifully."

On November 22, 1963, three days after the accident, President Kennedy was killed by an assassin's bullet in Dallas. The news reached the set during a break in the morning's shooting. "We were sitting at a table in the middle of the day," John remembered. "The company manager came out of his office and said, 'Our president is dead.' We were just shocked." Stephen Grimes said that John made a short, moving speech. The cast and crew were already glum over what happened to Tommy Shaw, now the news of Kennedy's assassination cast a pall over everyone. "There was certainly a pause," Grimes said. "We broke for lunch. But the feeling was there was nothing we could do. So we went on shooting."

When it came time to shoot the disputed ending, Ray Stark implored John to do it twice, hoping that he would agree to make some of the changes Williams had come up with. But Stark soon learned the same lesson Gottfried Reinhardt had when he pleaded with John to reshoot a scene during *The Red Badge of Courage*. "He finally did the scene over," Stark said, "and he did it exactly the same way as he had shot it in the beginning. John was very fixed in his ideas. John's pictures are John's pictures. And he must have been right, because the ending turned out rather well."

At the "wrap" party the celebration went on into the morning. Gladys Hill was doubly pleased because she had made her acting debut, as one of the women on the tour bus. Tony Veiller was already back at work, writing *The Man Who Would Be King*. John was so delighted with Richard Burton, he now thought to cast him and Peter O'Toole in that movie. And Pablo was beginning to fall in love with Marge, the American tourist he had met.

"She wanted to be in the center of the happenings," Pablo said, and so he invited her to the party. "There was a full moon," Marge remembered. "It was romantic. I didn't meet any stars though. I didn't have the nerve." She did, however, agree to write to Pablo after she returned to San Francisco.

While in Puerto Vallarta, Huston was visited by Cherokee, who remembered it because John told her he had decided to give up his American citizenship. Just as his father had left Canada to become an American, John was ready to become Irish. "John," Cherokee wept, "if you are running because of what is going on in America, it's *your* America, why don't you change it?" They argued, but John had made up his mind, under the advice of his accountants, who told him it would be to his tax advantage. "For money you give up your citizenship?" Cherokee challenged.

It was true that his tax situation always left him in debt to the government, but money wasn't the only reason. John had grown disgusted with America during the HUAC hearings. After the Hollywood Ten were imprisoned he had little desire to return from Europe. He also expressed a genuine desire to get to the roots of his ancestors. After Kennedy was murdered, what little glimmer of political optimism he had abruptly faded. If he was ashamed of his country of birth, he was definitely proud to be considered an Irishman.

Before returning to Ireland to make his nationalization official, John stopped in Los Angeles to visit Tommy Shaw, who had been fitted with a special brace for his back. Shaw's young children were running about when John arrived with his attorney, Mark Cohen. "What would it take you to get along now?" John asked his assistant director. Shaw told him he could get by on $500 a week. John turned to Cohen and instructed him to make sure Shaw got the money. When Shaw protested that he didn't know how he would be able to repay Huston, John said, "Nobody asked you to pay me back." But Shaw was too proud to take John's money. He told him he'd manage, and by the first week in January he was back working on a film in Stockton, California.

Loaded down with Christmas gifts, including a $1,500 Florentine crossbow for Tony, John returned to St. Clerans to tell of his adventure making *The Night of the Iguana* and to see his children. He didn't expect the news he got from Ricki: She had fallen in love with a married English Lord and was carrying his child.

23

"AND THE CHILDREN STRUGGLED TOGETHER"

RICKI BECAME PREGNANT IN DECEMBER OF 1963. SHE HAD met an attractive, titled man named John Julius Norwich, who had served in the foreign service and had ambitions to be a travel writer and a historian. At thirty-four he had begun his first book on the medieval Norman kingdom in Sicily. Norwich came from an illustrious family. His father was Duff Cooper, who was named First Lord of the Admiralty in 1937, then raised to the peerage and appointed British ambassador to France after the war. His mother was Lady Diana Cooper, one of the world's great beauties, who made her mark as a stage actress in Max Reinhardt's *The Miracle*, then served as a hostess for the politicians and artists she and Duff Cooper entertained. Her three-volume autobiography—*The Rainbow Comes and Goes, The Light of Common Day*, and *Trumpets from the Steep*, written between 1958 and 1960— captivated her countrymen. John Julius became the 2nd Viscount Norwich.

Ricki saw him as a charming, reserved man who often dressed in bow ties and velvet suits. He lived on Warrick Avenue, just across the canal from where she lived on Maida. She had fallen in love with him and thought he felt the same way about her. Ricki knew she could get a divorce from John at any time. But for Norwich it was more difficult. He and his wife were not on the best of terms, and he had two children, a son and a daughter close to the ages of Tony and Anjelica. He wasn't the kind of man who welcomed the publicity leaving his family for John Huston's wife would generate.

In Ricki, John Julius had found a perfect mistress. She was exciting, attractive, creative, had her own life, and didn't interfere in his. Friends of Ricki's remember how he always used to come around. Polite, interesting, dedicated to conservation causes, but always on the run. And it was always he who came to her. Ricki was under the illusion that he was going to dedicate his first book to her, that he would leave his wife and marry her. Especially once she had their baby. But Norwich had no such thoughts. He saw no need to cause a scandal, embarrass his mother or his wife.

"John Julius came from that sort of conventional English upper crust: You have the kid and work it out later," said Zoe. "Ricki had been so angry about us, she went right out and did the same thing." When Cherokee heard about it she felt that Ricki's pregnancy was "her slap in the face back at John. It was right for Ricki, because she had her fantasies, too, or she wouldn't have ended up with John. She didn't want an ordinary world. And she was trying very hard to get some-body with a bigger name to put John in his place. She wanted to marry the Aga Kahn because that would be her one-upmanship against John. It was part of the horrendous game that went on during that period."

Tony Soma reacted positively to Ricki's pregnancy. He thought John Julius was "a wonderful choice," according to Ricki's brother, Philip, "because he was a writer, a brilliant man. She didn't have to marry him." Philip felt differently. "My reaction was, 'Any dog can have pups.' That wasn't my sister." Dorothy said, "Ricki thought that she was gonna enter the Royal family by the back door. It didn't work. She was intelligent but not very smart."

Philip Soma said that John was furious when he found out that Ricki was pregnant. Ricki told John by letter, the tone of which deeply angered him. It wasn't so much the news of the baby; there were other things that caused his fury—things best left unsaid between them; things that made him see her differently. For the children's sake he would keep up a pleasant front whenever they were together, but he no longer liked Ricki.

Although she had said nothing to her children about being pregnant, Ricki did tell Tony that she would like to have a baby. "I didn't take great joy in the news," Tony said. He saw it "initially as a competitive thing against Dad."

Tony was fourteen at the time and suffering through his first year at Westminster. "I came from the most unorthodox childhood to the most conventional English public school," he remembered. "Boys would ask where I lived and I'd describe St. Clerans. Of course, this would make you instant enemies. An English public school is designed to fill the city with clones. The boys who went to Westminster were very much children of upper-middle-class professional people. Anything that smacked of difference didn't go down very well.

"The first night I was there my pajamas were filled with glass wool. And then I was given cold baths. I became a day boy as soon as I could, instead of boarding there. I was certainly one of the least popular people at Westminster. I did not have what it took to be a successful English public school boy."

Living in another country created a psychic distance between John and his children. "Here he was," said Tony, "pursuing his career, paying for everything, and his children were becoming strangers to him, becoming apprehensive of him, and he found it very difficult." "I didn't spend time with them," said John. "There wasn't a 'father's hour' when they were in Ireland. Ricki was a very good mother, but she led her own life."

For a brief while Ricki had worked as a TV news reader. She thought of going into the antique business. She decorated her house in an eclectic manner that became fashionable when it was featured in a book called *English Style.* She encouraged Tony's poetry, took Anjelica to the theater, and began to have Sunday brunches that brought together artists, actors, and writers. Actor and writer Dirk Bogarde remembers how he first met Ricki: James Fox, another actor, had brought her to visit on Christmas Eve, saying, "This is my gift to you. I *know* you'll like it." Bogarde was struck by her appearance. "She was still under the influence of a heavy 'Oirish' brogue," he recalled, "and dressed, that evening, in an enormous fisherwoman's cloak, which she shed, revealing a stunning gown, black with a wild floral design, which had stockings to match. *Exactly.* I'd never seen *that* before!

"She was a radiantly beautiful woman, and with her fun, her avid desire for any form of intellectual feeding, her wide range of friends, and her utter composure and relaxation, we became friends instantly."

Another of her close friends was Leslie Waddington, owner of the Waddington Galleries in London, who first met Ricki at his father's gallery in Dublin in 1955. He was a student in France then and she had hired him to tutor Tony and Anjelica. Waddington thought Ricki to be "the most intelligent member of the family, but she was unable to channel her energies." Tony he found to be "a very strange, interesting boy. He would attach himself to someone, to the detriment of everything else. I believed he was very lonely." As for Anjelica, she was, "from the start, a manipulator. She was probably the most narcissistic female I have yet met."

Dirk Bogarde observed that Ricki and Anjelica "were more like sisters than ever like 'Mum and daughter.' " For Anjelica, however, Ricki was very definitely her mother. "It was confusing in terms of relationships after my parents split up and we were living in England with my mother," Anjelica recalled, "because I don't remember anything being clarified at the time. I didn't ask a lot of questions."

Through Lizzie and her father, Stephen Spender, Anjelica got to meet W. H. Auden, David Hockney, Laurence Van der Post, and Henry Moore. "We went to Henry Moore's house in the country," she recalled, "and walked around his gardens and looked at his sculpture. He was very sweet and we stayed and had tea."

John, also, was enjoying the company of artists at this time. The Japanese sculptor, Isamu Noguchi, visited him at St. Clerans in January 1964, and they spent much of their time discussing the revolutionary architectural ideas of R. Buckminster Fuller, who was a friend of John's. The Italian sculptor, Giacomo Manzu, was also a friend whom John greatly admired, and before he began *The Bible*, he asked Manzu to make earth sculptures of the creation of man. Manzu put aside the bronze doors he was creating for St. Peter's and agreed to work for John for no pay.

Dino De Laurentiis had changed his mind about using five directors to work on *The Bible* and asked John to take over the entire project. John consented to presenting the first twenty-two chapters of Genesis, from the Creation through to Abraham's willingness to sacrifice his son to God, and wanted to change the title to *The Bible . . . In the Beginning*. But De Laurentiis had already put up a block-long billboard on Broadway in New York, promoting Huston's involvement in *The Bible,* and didn't want to reduce its scope.

Before John left for Rome he heard from Richard Condon, who had a movie idea called *The Righteous Are Bold.* The idea didn't appeal to Huston, but his contact with Condon would continue and finally culminate twenty-one years later with *Prizzi's Honor.* He also received from Ray Stark a draft of *Reflections in a Golden Eye,* written by a young writer named Francis Ford Coppola. John felt it needed work and the novelist Christopher Isherwood was hired to see if he could bring his homosexual sympathies to get closer to what Carson McCullers had written. Then John turned his attention to the challenges of putting on screen the most widely read book in the English language.

"That picture took about a year to put together," Zoe recalled. "We went to Egypt, Sicily, all over." Dino De Laurentiis gave John a free hand and promised not to interfere, which was a refreshing change from dealing with the Hollywood studios. "I do not ask him in advance what he is going to do," De Laurentiis told Lillian Ross. "It is like giving an artist paints and brushes."

Huston said to Ross: "I can't begin to describe the exquisite deference that Dino shows me. He is the only intelligent and creative man actually running his own studio. Zanuck spends most of his time abroad, and so does Jack Warner. There is no one man at the head of Metro, Columbia, Universal, or Paramount. Most of the decisions made these days are made by boards of directors."

The Bible was a stimulating challenge for Huston, who considered himself an atheist. "I'm not an orthodoxly religious person, and I don't profess any beliefs," he said. "The mystery of life is too great, too wide, to do more than wonder at. On occasion I envy those people who have it all down pat." He saw the Bible as the first adventure story, the first love story, the first murder story, the first suspense, and the first story of faith. He told the French critic Robert Benayoun, "I am interested in the Bible as a universal myth and support the idea of multiple legends. The Bible was a collective creation of man destined to temporarily resolve, in the form of a fable, a certain number of very troubling mysteries to the mind in an unscientific era. To me the Creation is something permanent."

To capture that permanence Huston sent photographer Ernst Haas around the world to film natural phenomena. Haas went in search of primordial nature: the flow of lava from a volcano, torrential waters, bubbling mud, steaming gases. From these images, which would occupy four minutes on the screen, the creation of life would emerge.

A private park an hour outside of Rome, owned by Prince Odescalchi, was chosen for the Garden of Eden. The Tower of Babel, which supposedly reached unto the heavens, was to be constructed in both Egypt and Rome; Noah's ark would be two hundred feet long and sixty feet high, built on the backlot of De Laurentiis's studio. De Laurentiis had his own crew: Giuseppe Rotunno, who worked with Visconti, as cinematographer; Mario Chiari as art director; two Italian assistant directors. But John felt comfortable with his own people. Neither Ossie Morris nor Angela Allen was available, but he asked Tommy Shaw, who had fully recovered from his *Iguana* accident, if he would come over for the Noah's ark sequence, and Stephen Grimes, who agreed to work as a set adviser.

What remained was for Huston and De Laurentiis to agree on the actors. It was decided that unknowns would be best for Adam and Eve. A television actor named Michael Parks was selected to play Adam. A nineteen-year-old Swedish college student named Ulla Bergryd was discovered at the Göteborg Museum of Art and, after being tested without her clothes, was declared "as genuine as a fingerprint" by Huston, who was looking for someone who would *not* project sex, since it was the world's only time of innocence before the serpent slithered into their lives.

Richard Harris was cast as Cain, who slew his brother Abel, to be played by Franco Nero. Instead of casting Laurence Olivier as God, which was De Laurentiis's idea, John came up with using Peter O'Toole as all three angels, "because what do angels look like if not alike?" For Abraham and Sarah, John wanted George C. Scott and Ava Gardner, although De Laurentiis preferred Maria Callas as the Mother of the Jews. For Sarah's handmaiden, Hagar, John cast Zoe, hoping to give her the acting break she had so desperately wanted. And for Noah, John's first choice was Charlie Chaplin, but Chaplin couldn't bring himself to be directed by anyone other than himself. Orson Welles and Alec Guinness were both tied up with other projects, so John decided to grow a beard.

Before shooting began in May, Huston received a telegram from Paul Kohner informing him that he had been selected by the Writers Guild for their sixteenth annual Laurel Award, honoring his many contributions to the literature of films. Kohner strongly urged him to attend the dinner. John flew ten thousand miles to accept the award, and when he spilled some champagne, he held up his glass and told the audience: "An overflowing toast out of an overflowing heart."

The following month John returned to Los Angeles to attend the Academy Awards ceremonies, where he was in contention for Best Supporting Actor for his role in *The Cardinal. Tom Jones, Hud, Cleopatra,* and 8½ were the big winners that night, but Huston seemed to take it all in stride.

When John ran into Lauren Bacall during one of his visits back to Los Angeles, she was eager to introduce him to Jason Robards, Jr., whom she had married in 1961. Robards had distinguished himself in Eugene O'Neill's *The Iceman Cometh* and *Long Day's Journey into Night,* and his father had acted with Walter in D. W. Griffith's *Abraham Lincoln.* But John couldn't help feeling that Bacall had betrayed Bogart by marrying again, and he wasn't friendly. "John was ice cold," Bacall said. "He never said anything, but his allegiance to Bogie was so strong. It was quite clear."

In London, as a six months' pregnant Ricki turned thirty-five, she decided it was time to talk to Anjelica about her condition. "Can't you make this easier for me?" Ricki asked. "Don't you know that I'm pregnant?"

Anjelica, not yet a teenager, didn't know what to say, so kept quiet. "I thought she was putting on weight," she reflected. The shock of her mother about to have a baby was difficult enough for Anjelica, but she was soon slapped with another dose of reality when she and Tony flew to Rome to see John before school started. John had decided it was time for them to meet their two-year-old half-brother, Danny.

"He told us to sit down," Anjelica remembered, "and then he told us very matter-of-factly that we had a little brother." Even though she had known about it, it had never been confirmed, and seeing Danny with Zoe was still unnerving for her. "Anjelica was bitterly upset when we were told that Danny existed officially," Tony said. "Danny spent most of the time under the table pretending to be a dog. And Dad would say, 'That's a good little dog.' And Danny would go, 'Yap yap yap yap yap.' And that was our first meeting with Danny."

Zoe recalled that Tony and Anjelica "weren't very keen on the idea of Danny and me. Tony hated the whole situation. Anjelica absolutely went into a crying fit and left the room."

Dino De Laurentiis also wasn't happy about their situation and wanted to keep it out of the press. "Our relationship was kept hushed up," Zoe said, "because Dino didn't like the image of John playing Noah and my playing Hagar and there was all this hanky-panky going on. Had I stayed in films it would have all come out, but I never found anything that fit into Danny's schedule, so I led a quiet life."

Anjelica said she didn't resent Zoe, whom she liked and thought very beautiful. "She was my companion in Ireland," she said. "I used to hang out with her and we'd go for walks when she visited. Try on her makeup. She was fun." John didn't approve of her wearing makeup as a young girl, but dressing up and making up were a way for Anjelica to enter into a fantasy world, a world she often preferred, because she could have some control over how things appeared.

With her family life changing almost as rapidly as her body was maturing, Anjelica's emotional life went through episodic states. She could be ecstatic over a pair of high heels and bummed out over the color of the carpet her mother chose for her bedroom. She could shout songs in the back of a car with her new friend Emily, then think about her parents and feel depressed. The most difficult thing she had to deal with at that time was the death of her poodle, Mindy, who had kidney failure and had to be put to sleep while Anjelica was away. "It was horrible. An animal death is almost worse than a human death."

Her mother did her best to console her. The swinging London sixties were just getting under way and one of Ricki's friends was the head of Atlantic Records, who would send her the latest albums. "I remember sitting there with my mother listening to Dylan singing 'Tambourine Man.' Changed my life," Anjelica said. "I brought it to school the next day. That album changed *everyone's* life. It was just incredible!" The times were definitely changing. Anjelica first heard the Beatles with Lizzie Spender. She walked down Carnaby Street and Kings Road and knew that a revolution was taking place. At thirteen she was "a bit too young to have appreciated it fully, but I was definitely a child of the sixties."

Dirk Bogarde recalled how Ricki did her best to keep up with the changing times. "She was extremely caring about young people, and she kept as close to them as she could, knowing all their 'fads,' their music, their taste in clothes, their 'new' freedom. She was firmly determined to share the youth of her children, and did so brilliantly."

Tony also listened to the music, but he had become enamored with a hunting sport of another century. In a secondhand bookshop he had discovered the perfect passion for his isolated nature. "I found a book about what boys could do in the Victorian era," he said. "And one of the things you could do was take a young hawk and train it. So I immediately remembered one visit, when I was six, to a man called Ronald Stevens, who lived about an hour and a half away from us in the west of Ireland. He was a great falconer and a friend of my mother's came over and wanted to see this spectacle and he took me along. I didn't think about it at all until I found this book, and I've been sunk ever since. It is *the* most exciting thing I know, apart from sex."

That summer of 1964, Tony returned to St. Clerans to go hawk hunting. Anjelica was in school, Ricki was in her last months of pregnancy, and John was directing *The Bible* and having to deal with disturbing news from Pablo and Olga in Mexico and Tony Veiller in California.

On May 30, Olga wrote to John: "Pablo has left me and the children and wants a divorce." She apologized for involving John, but she was obviously distraught. "Don't blame Pablo for everything," she said. "I would rather not get a divorce, but it is up to Pablo right now."

Three days later she wrote again. Pablo told her she could keep John's monthly check, but she needed John to have it sent in her name. On June 18, John wired Pablo: "Write immediately all particulars regarding yourself and Olga. No further checks will be sent either of you until I have your explanation situation." The very next day Pablo responded.

"Dear Father," he wrote, explaining that things were tough financially. "The tighter things got the more she nagged. . . . Within the last six months, she has told me about 15 times to get out of the house, that I'm not good enough for her as a man and as a provider. . . . I think that Olga believes that you should support us in luxury for the rest of our lives. . . . You have already done enough for me by giving me my education, plus things I couldn't have learned in books, in addition to helping me financially. . . . Now I have reached my limit of all the guff that she has handed out, and I'm asking for a divorce. . . . I am sorry I have failed you and caused you lots of headaches. . . . I hope that you won't think too badly of me."

That same day Pablo also wrote to Olga, angry that she wrote John without telling him. The next day Olga wrote to John again, enclosing Pablo's letter to her. She again said she did not want a divorce, but added, "I am told he has a girlfriend." She appealed to John "as a mother. I think Pablo should think of the children first instead of himself or me." Depressed, she indicated that she had "an offer that someone wants to adopt my David."

Reading Pablo's belittling letter to her so angered John that he wrote first to Olga, informing her that he would continue to send monthly checks to her, insisting that she "use this money exclusively on yourself and the children. Do not give Pablo *any* of it." Then he wrote to Pablo exactly what he thought about their situation: "The idea of your getting a divorce before you're even able to support your children is as absurd a thing as I have ever heard. . . . You must be able to provide for them— and provide for them well—before contemplating such a thing. . . . Just what the hell is in your mind?"

On July 10, Pablo answered John's letter. The facts, according to Pablo, were that he had no intention of deserting his children, that he didn't love Olga and she didn't love him, and "a home without love is no home to begin with and is detrimental to Olga, the children, as well as me."

By then Pablo could have saved the money he spent on postage: John's Pygmalion experiment had failed. Pablo was a wash. "He left his wife and three kids for some other dame," John said. "It was the kind of irresponsibility that I can't tolerate. It's all right to leave a wife, but you don't leave a wife and children. That was the end of Pablo."

What Olga never wrote John, but which she hinted at by saying she suspected her husband had a girlfriend, was that she had opened five letters that Marge had sent to Pablo. "I was very angry," Pablo said. "Olga begged me to go back with her. I just proceeded with the divorce."

Olga moved with the children to Guadalajara and Pablo met Marge in Veracruz. Within two years they would marry. Pablo would continue to dabble in real estate, then try selling insurance to tourist guides in Mexico City. Marge suspected that he had "a *casa chica*," and complained that while she worked to support them, "He just sat around the Zona Rosa watching the girls go by." Marge had Pablo's son six years after they were married.

Pablo would divorce Marge and marry again. His third wife died of cancer in 1977, leaving him $60,000 in debt. None of his four children have had any communication with him. Pablo had no desire to contact either woman and felt that his children would probably want nothing to do with him. He was surprised to know that his oldest son had become a doctor, and that he was a grandfather. He was working as a caretaker of a small farm sixty miles north of Mexico City, and considered a fourth marriage if he could raise enough money to get out of debt. He respected John enough not to contact him after he left Olga. "I think he would have felt better if I had," Pablo said, "but he taught me never to crawl. And that is the best lesson anybody could teach you."

* * *

While dealing with the problems between Pablo and Olga, John received a letter from Tony Veiller describing how he had lost half his esophagus and half his stomach to cancer, but that the operation had been a success because he was still alive and thinking about *The Man Who Would Be King*. John knew that picture was still some years away and wondered if Veiller would be around to see it through.

In July he also received Christopher Isherwood's script of *Reflections in a Golden Eye*, and while he had respect for Isherwood as a writer, he had to tell Ray Stark that the problems had not been solved and another writer was needed. He thought of a Scottish writer named Chapman Mortimer, whose novels were "shadowy, hypnotic, surrealistic," and Stark agreed. He convinced Mortimer to attempt his first screenplay.

By August, Ricki forwarded Anjelica's summer term report to John, who was pleased to read that she was doing well. But he was concerned when told: "Her work would show even better results if she could be persuaded to set aside the fantasies she is so apt to concentrate upon. These only serve to withdraw her from her group socially and absorb her intellectually."

John could understand how Anjelica might be withdrawn. She had gone from private tutors to Irish nuns to a French lycée and now this English school, and she was only just beginning her teenage years; she had to come to grips with the fact that her parents would never get back together, that her father had a child with another woman, and that her mother was about to have a baby with a man whose identity she suspected but didn't want to know.

Ricki gave birth to a girl at the end of August. The child was named Allegra and on her birth certificate the father was listed as "Unknown." "Everybody knew who it was," Dorothy Soma said. "But John Julius was caught between a rock and a hard place. He was married and his wife had all the money. I think she had a nervous breakdown. They were subsequently divorced. As far as I know he never contributed a penny to Allegra's expenses until she was grown up."

News of Allegra's birth reached John in his suite at the Grand Hotel in Rome. Jules Buck was visiting and described John's face as ashen, his anguish real, as he cursed Ricki and shouted, "She didn't have to do it to me!" Though he might have wondered what Tony and Anjelica must have thought about it, he never discussed it with them. It was, after all, just another diversion, and he was forced to concentrate on larger matters. Like the Creation of the world. The first murder of a brother. A forty-day rain that came close to destroying all life. *"The Bible* was like doing several pictures," he ruminated. "Each picture presented a whole new set of problems."

The beautiful garden of Prince Odescalchi had changed drastically after John asked for an artificial lake to be constructed. "Everything for a hundred yards around was knocked to hell!" He laughed. "They brought in earth-movers and diggers to make the lake. It was my idea of Hell, not Eden. Mud up to the hips. I called Prince Odescalchi and when he saw it, he went off his rocker! It's a wonder he didn't sue everybody! It was utterly hopeless, so we moved the whole operation into the middle of Rome, where there was a zoological garden. It was a wild place with thickets, trees, bushes, everything we needed."

Once Adam and Eve lost their innocence and were banished from the Garden of Eden, the company moved to the south of Italy to shoot the Cain and Abel sequence. Then they returned to Rome for what had to be one of the trickiest scenes Huston ever directed: getting the elephants, hippos, giraffes, zebras, bears, tigers, and all the other animals to follow him into the ark, two by two.

"Nobody, except me, thought it could be done," John said. But Huston found a German circus owner who suggested that a road be built with a ditch on either side, leading to a false front of the ark. "The entrance led right out on the other side to a road, so that it was all a circle," John said. He had each pair of animals trained to walk the road through the ark. "Some animals picked up habits very quickly; I had bridles made for other animals, and the men who led them walked in the ditch! Finally the great day came. And we got it the first shot! But nobody ever commented on it. Everyone assumed that if animals went in two by two, they *should* go in two by two. It was what was expected of them!"

With his love and understanding of the animals, Huston's Noah is far more tender than the harsh and cynical characters he more often played. As writer Scott Hammen observed, the Huston/Noah story "seems to mockingly echo the theme that critics have been most eager to define as the central one of his career: that of the eccentric engaged in an impossible quest. Besides the figure of his father as the jovially obsessed prospector seeking fabulous wealth, there is John Garfield seeking to overthrow a government, gangster Sterling Hayden seeking to acquire a horse farm, river rat Humphrey Bogart seeking to defeat the kaiser in Africa, and Gregory Peck seeking the death of a giant whale. Noah, with his harebrained scheme for saving every species on earth from extinction, is the ultimate Huston eccentric striving toward the most impossible goal."

John considered the designing of the Tower of Babel "a triumph of ingenuity. It was a combination of locations, models, and glass shots. The base was in Italy and the top, the peak of the tower, was in Egypt poised on a precipitous incline, rising above the desert." Negotiations had been worked out with the Egyptian government to provide six thousand extras to shoot the building of the Tower and for the Battle of Sheva scene. These extras were rounded up in the streets and were treated badly—given only bread to eat and not provided with water. When John protested he was told that they would not be expecting anything more, since they were the outcasts of Egyptian society. The corruption appalled Huston, and when these outcasts finally rebelled a riot broke out. "Stones were flying in all directions," Huston recalled. "I saw 'Abraham's soldiers' charging down the hill to do battle. I couldn't believe it! I raised my arms and shouted for them to stop. Because they took orders from the director—and for no other reason— they came to a halt." The riot was quelled, but Egypt became an experience he wanted to forget.

By the time he went to Sicily to film the Sodom and Gomorrah sequence, Tommy Shaw noticed that John seemed more interested in doing crossword puzzles than directing actors. "There must have been five hundred people on this set," Shaw said, "and they were all waiting for John. He got out of the car and sat down with his puzzle. Everybody was just standing around, nobody was doing anything. I couldn't stand it! So I asked, 'Why the hell doesn't somebody do something?' And they said, 'Well . . . John . . . signor Huston . . .' I said, 'Bullshit! This is ridiculous!' After about an hour and a half I walked over to the camera and said, 'Put me on this goddamn crane.' It was the first time the audience sees the city. So I go up and it wasn't a bad-looking shot. I came down and walked over to John and said, 'Why don't you get on the crane and we'll do this and we'll do that.' 'Fine,' he said. He didn't like what I did, but it made him think of something better. He couldn't care less about *The Bible*. He was really at his best when he was working with small numbers."

When it came to working with George C. Scott and Ava Gardner for the Abraham and Sarah scenes, John's best consisted of keeping them from destroying each other. As actors he had no complaints. Scott was a consummate professional who brought "a magic quality, a true mysticism" to his role, and Ava gave what he considered a beautiful performance, although, as in *Iguana*, it had to be coaxed out of her. But when Scott fell crazy in love with her their romance got completely out of hand. At one point, when a drunken Scott went to strike her, John "was on his back and stopped him, with six other people." John didn't like Scott after that, but reasoned that "a man drunk and in love behaves with a degree of madness sometimes."

Stephen Grimes remembered John coming to see him one morning to find out whether he had taken Ava out the night before. Grimes had been involved with Gardner "before George got ahold of her," but told Huston that Scott had eased him out. "They had a big love affair," Grimes said, "which got a bit rough. Ashtrays being thrown and finding their mark. Scott was screwing up the film and things got a little tense." Tony Huston, who visited the set, remembered how Peter O'Toole and his bodyguard wanted to go beat up Scott after Scott had belted Ava.

When things got to the point where it was affecting Gardner's performance, John had to do what he could to calm her. In her dressing room, when she asked him to come talk to her, he held her hand and didn't say a word. "It was like a vibration, just sitting there with him," Gardner said. "Finally I said, 'Okay, it's all right now, I can do it.' He just sat with me for a few minutes, quietly. That was the magic of the man when he was directing."

Zoe Sallis, who played Ava's handmaiden and went on to become her friend, felt that "Ava had an infatuation with John" when George made his move on her. "Ava's got a sort of madness and she attracts mad situations, drama, passion. George was crazy about her and she seemed like she was crazy about him, then she'd turn off."

Tom Shaw found himself more involved with Scott and Gardner than with helping John. "I was always separating them," he said. "I mean, two people drunk don't make for a good love affair. I'm almost convinced he never fucked her. I don't know why. But I've been in that position where you're loaded . . . and it was going on constantly." Ava's former husband, Frank Sinatra, once called Shaw at three A.M. "He wanted to know if it was true what he heard: that George Scott beat the shit out of Ava." No, Shaw lied, not wanting to get crushed between Scott and Sinatra.

Ava Gardner said it was impossible to keep Scott sober and that to get him off the booze he had to be sedated and then locked up in a "nuthouse with bars on the windows." After a few days John would instruct Ava to go see if he had calmed down. Ava brought him back to the set, and it would start all over again. "When George is sober," she said, "he's highly intelligent and, God knows, a wonderful actor. But when he drinks he goes absolutely crazy." Crazy enough to get physically violent, which deeply disturbed Gardner. But throughout the filming she continued this mad relationship because she felt sorry for him. It wasn't until after the film was done and he followed her to the Savoy Hotel in London, where he broke down a door to get at her and was locked up overnight, that she realized how dangerous Scott could be. When he later went out of control at the Beverly Hills Hotel, she finally decided to stop feeling sorry for him and accepted Sinatra's offer of protection from Scott's destructive passion.

Scott denied Huston's allegation that he "damn near broke her nose," admitting that it "was a very low point in my life" and cutting off any interrogation by saying, "I *never* talk about Ava. Don't ask me *anything* about her."

John found romance of his own during *The Bible*. Her name was Valeria Alberti and she was a countess. Although Zoe was there, her relationship with John had run its course. Three years was about as long as Huston could remain interested in any one woman. "We stayed great friends, but our relationship was over," Zoe said. "I had gone on. You were always part of an entourage and I was a bit fed up with that. I think I just grew up. I wanted to be important to one person. John wasn't incapable of that, it just never happened."

By her own admission Zoe would never get over John. Nor, she believed, did any of the women who had fallen for him over the years. "I think Ricki was still very hung up on John," she said. "All his women were. He had a massive amount of women who just clung. Ricki, Evelyn Keyes, Suzanne Flon. Suzanne was deeply in love with him. But he didn't marry her because he met me. And there was Marietta Tree— if he was so in love with her, why did he marry Evelyn Keyes? Who was his great love? I would really like to know that one. I know he was terribly fond of me, but he also felt tremendously for Suzanne Flon and for Marietta. And Lesley . . . there was something very deep there."

Valeria was different from the other women in John's life because she didn't speak English, and so their verbal communication was minimal.

"She was a good girl," John said. "I liked her very much. She was a friend of someone who worked for me on *The Bible*, that's how I met her. She wasn't rich, but she was independent and had a lovely apartment. She lived with her mother and brother."

Valeria was a painter and knew a number of the artists who worked on *The Bible*, like the painter Giulio Turcato; the sculptor Mirko, who produced the sets for Sodom; and Corrado Cagli, who designed the Tower of Babel and the Tree of the Knowledge of Good and Evil. She had seen *The Night of the Iguana* before visiting the set and felt that John had "an extraordinary understanding of the human spirit." She was taken by his ability to charm the animals, who followed him everywhere. As a director, she watched as he calmed down high-strung actors by just talking with them. "John appeared to be a wise man," she thought. "He understood the human spirit like the great writers and the great artists." They fell into a mutual attraction and, "even though we spoke very little, we were in tune," she said. "It was a fairy-tale love story."

Both Valeria and Zoe joined John in Ireland for the holidays. Valeria called Zoe "a marvelous girl, beautiful and sensitive, but it was a kind of Oriental sensitivity, borne out of politeness and passiveness." Zoe returned the compliments: "She's a very nice, gentle woman of the old Italian school of charm, great taste; an artist. I didn't get to know her at the time, because she thought I was still involved with John and was perhaps a little jealous. But we did get to know each other later, when things had died down, and I liked her very much. There was nothing neurotic about her."

Valeria was less kind about Gladys, whom she called "a perfect secretary, maybe too perfect. She actually identified herself in John. In some way she gave me the impression that she thought she *was* John Huston. Or, at least, his spirit. But John was a man blessed with great individuality: He let Gladys play 'John Huston's Spirit,' but only when he felt like it."

With his neighbors coming around, the Bucks and Peter O'Toole arriving, and the John Steinbecks on their way, Huston embraced his role as host with zest. In the mornings he put on his fox-hunting tails and top hat and joined his beloved Galway Blazers as they galloped over stone walls and through wet forests. Neither Peter O'Toole nor Valeria had any desire to join them, Valeria noted, "so Peter and I would go on a pub crawl, and when they would return, so would we; but we clearly couldn't have been in harmony: They had too much hunting, and we too many pubs."

John Steinbeck was thoroughly taken with all the women surrounding John during the holidays. He would gleam at his wife, Elaine, while looking at Valeria, Zoe, Gladys, Betty O'Kelly, and other visiting women who would come to St. Clerans to spend a few days. "Isn't it wonderful how everybody gets along marvelously?" he would say to Elaine. "You're the only one here who's not in love with him. I hope!" His wife would laugh and say, "No, but I'm close to it!"

Elaine Steinbeck thought that Huston, whom she called Sean, to distinguish him from her John, was at his "very best when Steinbeck was around because he valued him so. Sean would have at those house parties a mishmash of ex-wives and girlfriends, and it was a rather chaotic household." The one woman she couldn't figure out, and whom she had "no sympatico feelings with," was Valeria. "She was always there but didn't participate. I had a feeling she was very jealous of him. I really could not see what he saw in her. She didn't have the humor that everyone else around her had. She probably had a good mind."

At St. Clerans Huston and Steinbeck would often sit in the Japanese bath together, talking for hours about politics, the theater, and literature. "My John was very enamored of Lyndon Johnson, and Sean disagreed with him," Elaine Steinbeck said. "But other than that they agreed about most everything. My John was very stage and movie struck. They shared a sort of mysticism. Huston said St. Clerans was haunted and my John felt it deeply. He felt there was a spirit in the house. He said he saw it upstairs in the hall. He was going to write a short novel that could be turned into a screenplay."

In a letter Steinbeck wrote to Huston after they had talked about Daly, the ghost of St. Clerans, he said: "I think often of Daly . . . I have the feeling that in this story are all the beauties and all the truths including the aching lustful ones. And so I'll write the little tale as well as I can and we will see whether the sound and color of it will translate to the visual." But when a visiting priest heard of their interest he discouraged them from going any further with it, since Daly's hanging was still too fresh to exploit. Two hundred years, to the Irish clergy, was still recent history.

"There was a lot of scaring people with ghost stories," Joan Buck remembered. "A *lot!* John would do it. Betty would do it. Anjel and I would do it. We'd walk up from the Little House in the middle of the night to go hide in the linen cupboard and wail like banshees. Then we'd go into guest's rooms and get very upset because we were always finding the wrong people in bed. We never went into John's room, but couples who had arrived separately would be in bed and sort of run out."

Elaine Steinbeck was taken with Anjelica but hesitated about Tony, who "had a way of being a know-it-all. He was just learning falconry and he often had a falcon on his wrist. He could tell you all about it and he already knew more than his instructor. And this was annoying to his father, although a part of Tony's attitude was to get his father's approval: If he showed him how much he knew, Sean would love him more. Anjelica really wasn't that way. She wasn't a smartass. Very often we would play charades or other games after dinner. In the great hall there was a big chest which had a lot of costumes. She'd run to that chest and start pulling out things. She'd put on a hat with a big plume. You could see her mind just working. Then she'd find a shirt or blouse and then a skirt and wrap it around herself and come in and do her bit, as if she were going out on the stage to play a great part."

The costume-filled trunk was a great place for Anjelica and her friends to fantasize. Once, with Ricki along, Anjelica, Joan Buck, and Lizzie Spender decided to dress up as the four seasons. Joan and Lizzie still talk about that day, trying to remember who wore what. As Spring, Joan said, Lizzie wore a pink nylon nightie with jade beads over one shoulder. Ricki put on her white tutu to be Winter. And because Anjelica was born in the summer, she got to put on a blue bathing suit with sweet peas sewn on. "Joan was a great Autumn," Anjelica said, "with a maroon kimono and an eighteenth-century hat full of berries from the garden." When they showed John their costumes he would invent things for them to do. Joan remembered when he told one of them, "You're a bottle of wine that's just been uncorked." Not an easy thing to be, but they all made an attempt because "everybody wanted to be loved by John."

John recognized Lizzie Spender's beauty and he once smacked Tony when he didn't stand up when she walked into the room. He used to chide Tony, "Son, if you don't flirt with Lizzie within sixty days I don't know what I'll do." Tony responded by saying, "In other words, if you were fifteen you'd marry her?" "If I was twelve I'd marry her!" John countered.

Yet when Elaine Steinbeck noticed Lizzie and said to John, "Isn't she the prettiest young girl you ever saw?" he answered, "No, Marietta Tree is."

*   *   *

On Boxing Day, the day after Christmas Day, Gladys and John decided that John Steinbeck should play Santa Claus for all the children. Elaine Steinbeck said her husband, "the shyest man in the world," was amazed that anyone could convince him to be Father Christmas. "Gladys and Betty made him a cap and a beard," she said, "and Huston was having a ball, directing him. I heard one little Irish kid say to another, 'I don't know who it is, but it ain't Miss O'Kelly.' "

On New Year's Day Huston gathered the Steinbecks, Gladys, and Peter O'Toole and announced that they were going to go to Connemara for a picnic. "It was the wildest country you've ever seen," Elaine Steinbeck remembered, "rocky, beautiful, by the raging Irish sea. We had the most elaborate picnic lunch, with pâté, beautiful cheeses, champagne. And we would all laugh. The tears would freeze on our cheeks, it was so cold. Huston knew all the neighboring farmers, all the craftsmen, and all the fishermen."

When the holidays ended Gladys asked Elaine to deliver a box she had brought from Egypt to a Midlands' bank vault in London. When Elaine asked what was in it, Gladys answered, "I can't tell you. Just say you were doing it for me." When Steinbeck saw the package on the plane he became disturbed. "You should have more sense than that," he told his wife. "It's from somebody they know in Cairo," Elaine said. "Oh, my God!" Steinbeck moaned.

The package contained an ancient Egyptian figure and nearly $500,000 worth of jewels that Gladys had smuggled out of Cairo as a favor for an aristocratic family she had befriended while they were shooting *The Bible*. Had she been caught by customs, Huston said, she would have "undoubtedly spent the rest of her life in an Egyptian dungeon." Now she had passed on the responsibility to the Steinbecks.

"When we got out of the airport," Elaine Steinbeck related, "John took it from me and put it in his arms. He knew that we had to get it through. The customs man said, 'Hello, Mr. Steinbeck, how are you?' and stamped his passport. Then John turned to me and said, 'Don't ever do that again!' But when we got to the hotel he decided that it was the most fun he'd ever had in his life."

On January 6, 1965, after Steinbeck delivered the package under a veil of great secrecy and high drama, he wrote to Gladys: "Your mission was carried out in a manner that would have made you proud. James Bond may be dead but I became 007⅜ for the afternoon."

• • •

Gladys found an apartment at Via Bevagna 114 in Rome for John, where he spent the first three months of 1965 completing and editing *The Bible*. It had been the longest schedule of Huston's career, and when it came time to do the narration, which included the voice of God, John, as he had with *San Pietro* and *Freud*, used his own voice. Initially he was reluctant to do it, because there was a scene where Noah talks to God, and he felt it might seem awkward to be having a conversation with himself. He tested a few actors, but found their voices too recognizable. Considering the timbre and texture of his voice, it was hardly anonymous, but it certainly was effective. If God *had* a voice, it would probably sound like Huston's.

The Bible wound up costing $18 million, and when it was finished Dino De Laurentiis said, "John Huston has made my dream come true. Working with John has been an experience of always perfect harmony." He compared Huston to Federico Fellini in charm and understanding of audiences. "John and Federico know how to create art that gets across to humble people as well as to intellectuals," he said. "Both are geniuses of a contemporary art."

For his part, John wasn't disappointed with the film, although he felt that certain parts "were a little long," and that it was wrong to call it *The Bible*. "It was successful largely because it was called *The Bible* and had the kind of audience that its name and subject matter would attract," he conceded. "But it also repelled many people for the same reason. Cultured people saw it with a prejudiced eye."

Critic Pauline Kael thought he tried to do too much, but gave him credit for the effort. "Huston's triumph," she wrote, "is that despite the insanity of the attempt and the grandiosity of the project, the technology doesn't dominate the material: when you respond to the beauty of such scenes . . . as the dispersal of the animals after the landing of the ark, it is not merely the beauty of photography but the beauty of conception."

Rex Reed, however, saw absolutely nothing to praise. "Christians, Jews, or Zoroastrians," he began his review, "there should be something to offend just about everyone in *The Bible*." To the vitriolic Reed, the movie was campy and ludicrous. "What happened to the economy of talent that turned out *The Maltese Falcon*? Or the poet who made *The Misfits* ten years ahead of its time?" He then proceeded to flay each sequence of the film. The Creation was "a pretentious ballet"; the Garden of Eden "looks like a garden party in Bel Air"; Noah's ark, "a multilingual *Titanic*." In Huston's hands, he concluded, "*The Bible* looks like the Hebrew's answer to Greek mythology."

*   *   *

With *The Bible* behind him Huston became involved with a number of projects that would keep him busy over the next few years. For Jules Buck he agreed to make a picture called *Will Adams*, which Dalton Trumbo, one of Hollywood's blacklisted writers, would write, and which would star Peter O'Toole. Like *The Barbarian and the Geisha*, the story involved a Caucasian in Japan during the shogun period. This one was about an English navigator for a Dutch combine in the seventeenth century whose ship survived a storm and whose life was spared by the shogun because of his knowledge of navigation, ship-building, and weaponry. Also, Dino De Laurentiis had asked Huston to direct *Waterloo*, a $20 million film about Napoleon, which would also star O'Toole. Ray Stark was still planning on doing *Reflections in a Golden Eye* once the script was done to everyone's satisfaction. There was a story about a brash, young, nineteenth-century Scottish soldier defector called *Sinful Davey* that Walter Mirisch wanted to produce. It interested Huston because it could be done in Ireland. Charlie Feldman was putting together *Casino Royale*, a spoof of the James Bond movies, for Columbia and wanted John to act and direct one segment. And as an intriguing diversion, Huston was offered an opera, *The Mines of Sulfur*, to direct for a premiere at La Scala in Milan. No matter what some critics might say of his work, he never worried about future offers. They just kept coming.

In the summer of 1965, John received a telegram from Paramount producer Eugene Frenke regarding *Will Adams*. "Combination of circumstances make your services this project imperative and irreplaceable. Therefore you can write your own ticket with Paramount." Jules Buck was especially excited about being involved with *Will Adams*, bringing together Huston and O'Toole, and working with John, rather than for him, as he had during the war and for many years after that. Buck had finally come into his own. His and O'Toole's Keep Films, Ltd., had produced both *Becket* and *Lord Jim*, and Buck figured to extend that success with the *Adams* project.

Lizzie Spender recalled how she and Anjelica and Joan Buck used to fetch drinks for the three men during summer parties at St. Clerans. Jules would be behind the bar and ask whom the drink was for. If it was for O'Toole, he'd say, "Half water, half vodka, he won't notice." For Huston: "Give him water, he won't notice." Lizzie said they used to serve the drinks "really scared, in case we got into trouble."

Tony's pranks contributed to that feeling of madness and fantasy that was so much a part of their growing up at St. Clerans. Lizzie recalled a time when Tony pretended the IRA had taken all of John's guns. "He took all the guns out of the gun room and made it look like the rack had been broken and that they had surrounded the house. I was really scared."

Joan Buck remembered how Tony was always singing Irish Republican songs and writing epic poems, "stuff about men in arms, fighting each other." Joan used to wonder about Tony and Anjelica's future. "It was open-ended as to what moment of history we were living," she said. "And the demands on Tony about what was he going to grow into. I think Anjelica's options looked like princess."

"They were given such extreme achievement images," Lizzie Spender agreed. "And I believe your life is wrestling with the images from your childhood. But Tony and Anjelica were brought up as if they were gods. What has been hard for them is just having to become ordinary human beings."

Lizzie never dared tell Anjelica that she harbored a secret ambition to be an actress when she was thirteen. "I kept absolutely dead quiet," she said. "Anjelica is very competitive and always has been. It was already competitive enough that I existed on this planet. And that John Huston paid me compliments." Joan Buck also had an ambition, not to act but to direct, only she was bold enough to tell Anjelica during one of their nightly walks in the rain. "We'd only walk in the rain because it was good for our complexions," she said. "On one of those walks I said I wanted to be a director. I sensed that this was something not to have said to her, because it was like wanting to be John."

With her friends honing in on *her* domain, it was no surprise that Anjelica once dreamt of destroying them both. "She had an extraordinary dream one night," Lizzie related, "in which she killed us all. She was running around the bedroom in the middle of the night, screaming her head off, dancing with shirts at the end of the bed, shouting, 'You're dead!' If you're Anjelica, you grow up quite deeply involved in fantasy on all different levels."

These levels often extended into reality, especially when John was there to encourage it. Among Huston's neighbors who always looked forward to being invited over for dinner were Lord Peter Patrick and Lady Ann Hemphill. "It was a great thrill to go there," recalled Lady

Ann, who admitted that for a long while she was "absolutely terrified of John." Lord Hemphill remembered how John "shocked all the neighbors by having this very, very, extremely modern art such as had never been seen or heard of in the west of Ireland. But in the middle of all that he had the most beautiful Monet, and some Gris. And he fell completely for Jack Yeats.

"If he found there was a feud between two households, nothing would amuse John more than to insist upon having them to dinner so he could observe them. He would love to push on their feud a little further."

The Hemphills observed Tony and Anjelica as they grew up. Anjelica, they said, enjoyed riding and hunting but not as much as Tony did. "Tony was a terrible show-off," Lord Hemphill said. "Anjelica wasn't." Lady Hemphill agreed: "Tony used to get rather annoying at times. He was always a problem—difficult, very wild."

The naughtiness of both children, and of their friends, was never better demonstrated than when they conspired, with John, to pull off a fantasy dinner with the Hemphills and other neighbors, Derek and Pat Trench, as guests. "It was a very creative evening," Anjelica remembered. "We were just running amuck. We felt ourselves old enough to participate in an adult dinner, but we hadn't been invited, so that was what spurred us on." The evening started with all the children—Tony, Anjelica, Joan Buck, Lizzie Spender, and Tim Grimes—wearing masks. Then Grimes "lit up some empty gun cartridges on the windowsill, so we had a flare-up."

Their best moments were saved for the dinner. Earlier in the day Tony and Tim had shot some pigeons and caught some trout. They were given to the cook, Mrs. Creagh, to prepare. When the first course of fish was served, one of the children complained from their separate table that it seemed a bit rancid. "Well, Tim," John said, "why don't you go and find some decent trout in the river." Tim left the room and returned in his bathing suit and flippers, carrying a spear. He walked past the guests, jumped into the river, and returned two minutes later with the trout on the spear. Within minutes Mrs. Creagh brought out the other half of their catch, delicately cooked and ready to eat.

When the second course was served the children once again complained. John suggested to Tony that he get his Florentine crossbow and shoot some pigeons. Anjelica and Joan ran upstairs to the room above the portico, where they had stashed the pigeons that had been shot earlier. Tony down below was shouting to the guests to come out and see what was happening. When they appeared Tony shot his arrows into the air and the girls threw down two of the pigeons. The birds were brought to the kitchen where Mrs. Creagh had secretly prepared a pigeon pie, and ten minutes later she brought it out.

"It was just a series of events we put on to entertain them and certainly to entertain ourselves," Anjelica said. "Also, it was daring because people had come to dinner and had never seen this behavior before." But the Hemphills and Trenches didn't think it was funny, Joan Buck recalled. "They thought it was rather annoying."

Frivolities turned to sadness when, on his fifty-ninth birthday, John went to London to attend Tony Veiller's funeral. Though Veiller had died in Los Angeles in June, he had wanted to be buried in England. His son, Bayard, remembered how John and Jules Buck came in a rented Rolls-Royce, and John insisted on holding Veiller's ashes on the ride to the cemetery. "John and my mother, brother, and I sat in the back, Jules in front with the driver," said Bayard. "Everyone was talking, there was no dead silence. It was a gloomy, rainy day. After my father's ashes were interred we went to a local hotel and everybody had drinks and told stories and John took me aside and said, 'I'll be your old man from now on.' Then he invited us all to St. Clerans.

"He was quite hurt by my father's loss. All during that day John never said it was his birthday. And I've never forgotten his holding my father's ashes in his lap. Wouldn't let go. Didn't make a big thing out of it. It would have been nice if he were the sort of man who could have indicated that feeling when my father was alive. But it's certainly something that's meant a lot to me over the years."

24

REFLECTIONS

AFTER TONY VEILLER'S FUNERAL JOHN MET WITH DALTON
Trumbo and Jules Buck at St. Clerans to discuss *Will Adams*. Trumbo
had been encouraged to go there by Joseph Levine and Eugene Frenke,
the American producers of the project. There were problems with the
last half of the story and Huston came up with the idea that Adams
embrace Buddhism "with the same fervor that had colored his
Protestantism." Huston invited Trumbo to stay in the Little House, but
Trumbo was determined to go to London and work by himself. By
mid-September Joe Levine had concluded his deal with John's "hatchet
men," Mark Cohen and Paul Kohner, and wired John: "My head is
bloody but unbowed but I am very happy. Ditto for Jules Buck." John
received a sizable advance and the picture was put on Paramount's
schedule for the summer of 1966. But when Trumbo returned in
October, Huston discovered that "nothing whatever had been accomplished in the interim. He now wished to begin on page one and discuss
the first half scene by scene, then rewrite it into final form before
embarking on the latter half." Trumbo had a reputation of being a fast
writer, but Huston was beginning to worry that he was having difficulties with the material.

* * *

By December things had decidedly cooled between Huston and Buck over the lack of progress with *Will Adams*. The Bucks didn't come to St. Clerans during the holidays. Evelyn Keyes, who had been invited to spend Christmas with Huston, was a friend of the Bucks, and deduced from their absence that "something was going on." Keyes suspected that "underneath, what happened is that John was the daddy and Jules was the child. Jules was learning from him and improving his career, and then he became a producer on his own, so he didn't want to be treated like the child anymore."

If Keyes's analysis sounded psychological it was because she was undergoing psychoanalysis herself. When she told John his reaction was, "Oh, honey, we'll get you out of that." Evelyn looked at John and wondered, "Who was this white-haired gentleman in the flowing Oriental robe? Apparently everybody but me knows you can't go home again."

She was struck by how tall and sophisticated Anjelica seemed, but was disappointed with how harsh John was with Tony. Once, when John snatched a magazine from him, she wondered what he wanted of his son.

Valeria Alberti and Nan Huston were also visiting while Keyes was there. Evelyn liked Valeria, and they communicated in Spanish. She chuckled at the memory of hearing John and Valeria in the bathtub together, "so I knew they were more than just friends." Nan, though, seemed "slightly spooked." She had heard of Nan's shock treatments and saw how John protected her.

"After my father died," John said, "she turned to me. Whatever she did, she asked my permission. When she'd be ill, wherever she was, she'd find Christian Scientists to say prayers for her. She was fast in it. God Almighty, to me it's savage."

Just as John saw how Nan continued to deteriorate after Walter's death, Jules Buck believed that John had become a different person without Walter's governing influence. "I learned tremendously from John," Buck said, "but the greatness that he had burned out when Walter died."

By the end of December John's judgment concerning *Will Adams* was confirmed by a reader he trusted who thought it was too long, lacked humor, had awful dialogue, and ended badly. Other than that, he enjoyed it.

On January 16, John received a memo from Dalton Trumbo regarding *Will Adams* that convinced him "we were beating a dead horse."

Trumbo had failed to make the story dramatic. The script lacked tension and spark. Will Adams's character was oversimplified. Trumbo had missed the point entirely regarding Will's conversion to Buddhism. Trumbo's plans for the last half of the script, John thought, "lacked any essential idea that would make it more than an assortment of ill-related episodes."

The next day John told Jules Buck that without a script there could be no movie. Behind John's back Buck began to blame him for the collapse of *Will Adams.* He told Eugene Frenke that John had sent Trumbo off to work on his own; that he didn't make himself available to them; that he was only marking time at Paramount's expense while the *Waterloo* script was in preparation; that once it was decided *Will Adams* would have to be postponed, Huston didn't want to consider doing another picture in its place until a *Waterloo* date was decided.

When Frenke called Huston to tell him what Buck had said, John refused to believe him. Buck was one of his closest friends, and it was unthinkable and preposterous that he would have said any of those things. But then Paul Kohner called John and repeated what Frenke had said. John discovered that Buck had written "to various people who had money in the film, as though he had been betrayed by me." Shocked at such falsehoods John sat down and wrote Buck one of the longest letters he had ever written, an eight-page single-spaced typewritten letter of anger and disappointment.

He listed each of Buck's "lies" and explained the truth, as he saw it, in detail. And when he finished responding to Buck's charges, he spent five paragraphs addressing Jules himself—questioning his spirit and calling him things Buck was never able to forget. John demanded that Buck cable a retraction to everyone he talked to, threatening to send out copies of this letter if he refused.

Buck's response to Huston's "vicious, nasty" letter was a letter of his own. "To save you the postage," he wrote, "I am having copies made to all concerned. Your hysterical ravings speak for themselves."

The break between the two men was final. Years later Buck could only call John "an unmitigated shit of the highest order. I arranged for him to get thirty thousand dollars a month for *Will Adams,* and he was sabotaging the whole bloody thing. The reason he was so bothered was because I *fired* him from that picture. I have a total contempt for him. I detest him beyond belief."

John refused to give Buck a second chance. "Buck's behavior was shocking," he said. "He was scared shitless and thought by shedding the blame he could survive. He had been practically a body servant to me, a slave. And I didn't abuse him because it's not my nature to abuse someone I thought was a faithful, decent man. And he turned out to be a low sonofabitch. A born sycophant."

Having written Buck out of his life, Huston returned to the matter at hand: the opera, *The Mines of Sulfur*. The music was written by a London composer, Richard Rodney Bennett. The libretto was by Beverly Cross. The set designer was the artist Corrado Cagli. The conductor was Nino Sanzogno. Huston was invited to direct because La Scala "wanted to create a deeper harmony between acting and singing. They wanted a better synthesis," John said.

The grim, three-act play took place in a country house in eighteenth-century England. It dealt with the murder of the old owner by his young mistress's lover. After the murder a troupe of actors came asking for shelter. They put on a play that parallels the terrible deed just done in the house. When the actors discover the truth they are all threatened with death. They manage to escape, except for one, who brings down the old man's murderer.

The Metropolitan had once asked John to direct an opera, but, he recalled, "it wasn't attractive: *The Girl of the Golden West*. And they wanted to use the old sets and the approach to it was kind of shabby. But this was interesting. I met the people and the singers—it was a whole different world than actors. The management regarded them the same way a lion tamer does his charges: They didn't know which way they were going to jump, so they didn't want to turn their backs for too long. They were, in turn, terrified of the conductor. Because if the conductor didn't like them he could practically ruin a reputation. And the set designer let them know who *he* was: a well-known artist, as very often they were. Cagli was one.

"The conductor was maestro. As was the set designer. I wasn't maestro. They didn't know quite what to call me. The fourth day of rehearsal I told one of the singers what to do about an entrance and he did just the opposite. He said, 'Show me.' So I showed him. And he said, 'Yes, maestro.'"

When the others also began calling him maestro, he thought of his Aunt Margaret, the most cultured member of his family. "My God," he marveled, "if Aunt Margaret could hear them."

John took Anjelica and Ava Gardner to the premiere of *The Mines of Sulfur* on March 1, 1966. The boos and cheers it received were a new experience for him. "The first night, half the audience was modern and

looked to the future," he said, "and the other half was there for the
operas of Verdi and Puccini. The reviews were more or less good for the
whole thing. It was avant-garde but not John Cage. However, I couldn't
sing a single bar of the opera. There was no melody whatever."

Anjelica, who was fifteen, was radiant in her dress and jewelry and
John was rightly proud of her, although he didn't approve of her
wearing makeup. "I didn't feel particularly pretty at the time and clung
to my makeup with some persistence," she said. "I was very, very
skinny—the second tallest girl in my class. I had knobby knees and this
nose, which gave me some tribulation. I was prone to wearing a lot of
black eye makeup and Max Factor Pan Stick. My father would say,
'Wash your face! Why are you covering that lovely skin?' There was a
streak of the Victorian in him. Remember, this was a father with
a daughter who was away from him a lot of the time. He knew her as a
little child and all of a sudden she was a young woman."

"Anjelica wanted to be trendy," said writer Peter Menegas, who had
become a close friend of Ricki's in 1966. "She was in mini-skirts up to
her eyebrows. And Ricki encouraged theatricality in Anjelica."
    Menegas first met Ricki in Norway. She and John Julius were on the
London board of the English Theatre Company of Norway, established
by Richard Svare, an actor. When Svare went to the States to raise
money for the company, he met Menegas and invited him to Norway to
be the writer-in-residence.
    Menegas was planning to write a musical about Gertrude Stein.
When Ricki told him that she had ambitions of her own to be a writer,
he asked her if she would like to work with him, doing research at the
London library. "She jumped on it," Menegas recalled. He was twenty-
four at the time, Ricki thirty-seven. Three months later he went to
London and found that Ricki had compiled notebooks about Stein.
"From there," he said, "we went to collaborating on the book of the
play. She was a stickler for detail." When Menegas wrote the songs, he
recorded Ricki singing them.
    Menegas was thoroughly taken with Ricki and her bohemian style.
Although still married to a famous man, Ricki was extremely thrifty,
he noticed. She saved the foil butter was wrapped in to rub on the
bottom of pans. "And one of the strongest memories I have is Ricki
with her bills. The greengrocer, the butcher, she was very efficient.

She wasn't in London spending John's money. She was there raising John's family."

Her house was furnished in such an eccentric fashion that there were times when workmen delivered things COD and wouldn't collect the money because they thought that "absolutely impoverished people lived there." Menegas laughed. "Other people would come into the house and think it would be terrific. In the sitting room there would be no carpeting on the floor and no overstuffed furniture. In an antique shop she found some nineteenth-century Indian silk curtains that were in shreds. They were bright yellow, blue, red—like a circus print. She sent them out to be dry-cleaned, then got someone to mend them by hand, and hung these ragged circus curtains. The ceilings were fourteen feet high and these curtains would reach from ceiling to floor."

Dirk Bogarde considered Ricki "a very successful woman in her friends, in her life, in her children. But not altogether happy. She was avid for new ideas, new writers and painters, and the young people adored her. Her ability to mix the young and the old, the successful and the rising-successful, was amazing. And she supervised, with Anjelica at her side, the salads and steaks and whatever she was cooking, from pasta to Chateaubriand, with elegance and a complete lack of 'fuss.' "

Bogarde thought Ricki "adored her children and they adored her. There seemed to be no age difference at all. Tony had a bedroom swamped with falcons on their perches; Anjelica drew and wrote and painted quite marvelously. It was not an 'amateur' talent."

Menegas considered Ricki "a good Italian earth mother." He thought she, Tony, and Anjelica were all "terrific" with Allegra, a precocious child who learned to walk at eighteen months and to read soon after. Nurse Kathleen looked after Allegra and called Ricki "madam." John Julius, whom Ricki called J.J., would often come by in the afternoon and "keep everyone entertained at the table," Menegas said. "He was very attentive to Ricki—they would have their little private jokes—but not particularly to Allegra. He would pick Allegra up, but no more than anybody else would. She didn't call him daddy or father, she called him John Julius."

Ricki helped John Julius correct the proofs of his book, which he dedicated to his wife. For her collaboration with Menegas, she used Jules Buck's office to Xerox pages. Ricki empathized with Buck's wounded feelings over John, and they remained close friends. Ricki stayed in touch with John mostly through Gladys or Betty O'Kelly. "They were like emissaries from a court," Menegas observed, "coming to visit the banished princess. Ricki also had her court, but hers was much, much younger."

On the few occasions when Ricki saw John in London, she found it difficult to retain her composure. To Tony it was perfectly clear that "Mum still loved Dad. No matter what had happened between them. He made her quite nervous. I remember when she came to see him. She was trembling." Peter Menegas said that when she got tense she emitted a certain "drawing-room laugh," which he called her "Harrod's laugh. It wasn't a giggle and it wasn't shrill, but a slightly posh laugh."

While John had done nothing to encourage Ricki as an actress, he had given Zoe a moment in the spotlight with *The Bible.* She even went to the States to help promote the film, but the desire wasn't there.

"Instead," she said, "Danny became my life. John never took part in any of the upbringing, but we saw him on holidays and in the summer. He always kept in touch and made sure that we were okay and he would see us whenever he could. It was very close and civilized. He didn't have much communication with Danny when he was developing because John wasn't very good at early stages. But he was a father figure, and whenever he met him it was wonderful for Danny. If you have one parent who is doing it all right, it's better than two parents who are doing it badly. If John had been there it may not have turned out so good, who knows?"

But John could never have been there. He was always too busy. And even when he wasn't he'd manage to find a project to occupy him. The *Waterloo* project fell through when the Russians agreed to finance it on the condition that a Russian direct. De Laurentiis came to see Huston and said, "I asked you to do the film and if you don't approve we'll just forget about it." John was disappointed, but he appreciated De Laurentiis's decency. "I approve, for chrissake," he said, "go through with it."

Then along came an offer that seemed like a perfect interlude for him: directing and acting in the first of a five-segment spoof of the James Bond films. *Casino Royale* was Ian Fleming's first Bond novel, and when producer Charles Feldman bought it, he had hoped to lure Sean Connery to continue the series of Bond thrillers. When that failed Feldman opted for satire and convinced Orson Welles, Woody Allen, Peter Sellers, David Niven, William Holden, Charles Boyer, Jean-Paul Belmondo, Deborah Kerr, Ursula Andress, and Jacqueline Bisset to appear in what would turn out to be a $10 million picture that nobody would be proud of but would become a commercial success. Feldman

also talked Huston into playing Bond's boss, M, for the opening sequence in which he manages to bring Bond (David Niven) out of
retirement after Bond's house is blown up, and M is killed.

It's a silly movie that has little to do with Fleming's original story.
Robert Parrish, one of the five directors involved in the picture, called
it a "bastardized, episodic parody . . . in which each episode had a
different James Bond." John admitted that "It turned out to be not
worth a damn, but I liked playing M. It was great fun." Part of his fun,
Orson Welles noted, was that "John *immediately* moved everybody to
Ireland because he wanted to go fox hunting." Huston knew it was
nothing more than a lark and told one reporter, "It's just as well that
my father can't see me now." Walter, of course, would have understood.
He, too, made quite a few pictures he would have liked to forget.

In June 1966, John received Chapman Mortimer's final draft of
Reflections in a Golden Eye. It was much closer to McCullers's vision,
but Mortimer was a novelist not a screenwriter, and John decided to
rewrite it with Gladys before sending it on to McCullers. The picture
was set to begin in August. As a measure of Huston's unpredictability
he agreed to use Montgomery Clift as the repressed homosexual Major
Penderton. Elizabeth Taylor was to play his boisterous, buxom wife;
Brian Keith the lieutenant colonel with whom she carried on an affair;
and Julie Harris Keith's mousy, neurotic wife. It was Taylor who had
insisted to Ray Stark that Clift be given the lead role. They had always
been close, and she wanted to help Clift, who had deteriorated considerably since *Freud.* When Taylor was told that Clift was uninsurable,
she put up the bond herself.

But how desperate was Clift to accept another film directed by
Huston, who he had thought was trying to destroy him during *Freud?*
Doc Erickson, who had been disturbed over Huston's behavior at that
time, asked Clift, "Jesus, Monty, what are you doing? You've got to be
out of your mind." "Oh, no," Clift assured him. "I talked to John. It's
going to be great." All Erickson could think was, "Oh, God, what are
we getting into?"

John figured that if he could tap Clift's subconscious, he might be
able to pull out the revealing performance the part of Major Penderton
required. It was a difficult, sensitive theme: a respected married man,
living in the macho world of a postwar Southern army post, obsessed
with his sexual feelings for another soldier. It was a subject Huston had
been uncomfortable with for most of his own life, and it took courage

for both Huston and Clift to take it on. "He would have been good in it," John said. "It wasn't the same sort of thing as *Freud* at all."

But Clift never got the chance to prove that he wasn't finished as an actor. On July 22, 1966, he died in his New York brownstone. They called it occlusive coronary artery disease. *Reflections* would have to be postponed until another actor could be found to replace him.

John knew it would take an actor of extraordinary brilliance and sensitivity to get into the grotesque head of Major Penderton, whose every gesture had to show the inner conflicts that were tearing at him. From arguing with his wife, who strips before him and defiantly throws her brassiere in his face, to saving the discarded candy wrapper of the soldier he has fallen in love with, the role demanded a full spectrum of subtleties and savageries. There was only one actor with the range to pull it off, Huston felt. The only actor, with the exception of his father, whom he considered to be an artist: Marlon Brando.

McCullers's book was sent to Brando as John flew to New York to finish casting with Ray Stark. Before leaving New York, John traveled to Nyack to visit Carson McCullers, who was paralyzed from the waist down from a stroke. Although her words were slurred, her observations, Huston noted, "were acute and pointed." She was excited by the prospect of his doing a movie of her novel and jumped at John's invitation to visit him in Ireland after the movie was done. Her acceptance surprised him; the offer was made out of politeness and John never expected someone in her condition to travel across the Atlantic.

When Huston returned to Ireland Brando was ready to see him. The timing was finally right. Brando was coming off a terrible experience working under the direction of Charlie Chaplin in *The Countess from Hong Kong*. In fact, Brando was, like Huston, experiencing a decline. Since 1960 he had made eight films, and none of them was commercially or critically successful. But he and Huston seemed to share some common ground: Both had carved out their reputations with their early work, both men respected the written word, both had scandalous reputations with women, and both had worked with the best producers.

Brando was the epitome of the "method" actor, who worked best when left alone, and there was no better director to leave him alone than John. But getting Brando to agree to take over a role that was to have been Montgomery Clift's, the only actor Brando ever considered a rival, took some maneuvering.

"I was delighted that he wanted to come and talk about making the picture," John said. "He was there for a couple of days before we had a conversation where he talked uninterruptedly for several hours, telling me his thoughts about the book. As he talked, Gladys was typing the last draft of *Reflections*. When he was through I thanked him for his observations, none of which coincided with what had been written, and I suggested that before I answered any of his statements he read the new script."

Brando read the script but did not respond immediately. Instead he took a long walk in the pouring rain. "It was a terribly stormy night," Tony Huston remembered. "Gladys said, 'He'll never do it.' I said, 'He wouldn't be making this amount of fuss if he wasn't going to do it,' which was pretty perceptive for a sixteen-year-old." By midnight Brando hadn't returned and there was some concern that he had gotten lost. Tony and Anjelica got in the car with Gladys and they went out into the night in search of Marlon. "We found him two miles away," Tony said. "He looked kind of like an old woman, in a mishmash of various raincoats. There were lots of little side roads, but he knew exactly where he was and he wouldn't get in the car. He was having a wonderful time. Where else could he walk through the rain and have nobody give a damn?"

When he returned, rain-soaked from his walk, he had decided to play the part of Major Penderton as written, one of the most challenging and difficult roles of his career. "I have nothing to say," he told John. They were just the words Huston wanted to hear.

"It was a very brave picture for Marlon to do," Ray Stark said, "because it was the first picture that dealt with homosexuality in an intelligent way. It wasn't a subject matter that Warner Bros. really wanted. It was provocative, but it wasn't just a straight commercial picture, so they were always on my tail about the budget. Because of tax problems at the time, we had to shoot a film taking place in the American South of the 1940s in southern Italy using an Italian crew and Italian extras."

The Italian cinematographer who began the film didn't work out for Huston. The man brought in to replace him was Ossie Morris, whom Huston had wanted all along but couldn't have because of the unions in Italy. It took Ray Stark's threats never to shoot any more films there to get Morris approved, although Morris refused a credit for the film.

John wanted to experiment with color once again. Only this time he was going for a more desaturated golden effect. "It was a psychological story," he said, "and I didn't want to have the distraction of too many colors. The Italian lab worked on this for weeks, and it was through their invention and determination that we were able to achieve success. The significance of 'reflections in a golden eye' was found in the soldier who watches the behavior of the characters, and it's rather the eye of Pan, the eye of nature that beholds all this. Then the little Filipino makes a drawing of an imaginary bird. The bird has a golden eye."

To find the Filipino boy who plays a companion to Julie Harris, Huston asked William Hamilton, a young man he had hired as his assistant, to scout New York, where the early scenes of the film were shot. Hamilton had written to Huston the year before from Alaska, where he had been stationed in the army. He had ambitions to be a writer, a cartoonist, and a director, so he did what any brash potential filmmaker would do while stationed in one of the world's more isolated regions, he wrote letters to directors he admired—Fellini, Hitchcock, and Huston—and heard from one. John liked his drawings, which would soon be appearing regularly in *The New Yorker,* and his boldness. He also welcomed Hamilton into his home, even though he appeared uninvited.

"I called him from Shannon airport," Hamilton related. "A fellow answered and said John was out riding and asked where I was and whether they should send a car. 'No, no, don't send a car,' I said and I hung up, elated! I had fourteen dollars and I took a bus for an hour and a half. At the last stop there was a fellow leaning against the depot and he asked me if I was William Hamilton. We got into a little black car and tore off at a huge rate of speed, way out in the middle of nowhere. Eventually we pulled up in front of this great mansion in the moonlight with a cow out in front. We go up the steps into a hallway and there were people speaking Italian in this very dramatic mansion. There were some very beautiful women and then a man stood up. 'Well, Bill, so good to see you.' It couldn't have been a better adventure."

When Hamilton later visited Huston while he was shooting some of the outdoor scenes on the Long Island campus of Nassau Community College, where they still had army barracks, John invited him to join the crew. His first assignment was: "Find us a Filipino fag." Hamilton went to a dinner party "and a grand old dowager told me 'There's this most darling little one at Saks.' So I went over there and he was hired to be in the movie." When he went before the cameras he did his best to act as normal and unaffected as possible, exactly what Huston *didn't* want. But, said Hamilton, "John couldn't bring himself to tell him what he wanted. It gives you an idea how old-fashioned, Hemingway-macho Huston was being as a director. Finally, the Filipino figured it out and said, 'Am I supposed to be gay?' And he came back and acted in an effeminate way."

When they moved to Rome, Stark said that John's diversion was "visiting all the churches, looking at all the art." William Hamilton thought the principals saw the film as "a sort of holiday, they were all indulging themselves enormously." Ossie Morris said, "They made the film in an atmosphere of total bewilderment. It was a very tricky story to do. They were all powerful individuals—Brian Keith, Julie Harris, Brando, Taylor—and they didn't quite know what was going on. And John wasn't very good, as usual, at communicating. But they respected him. The name of Huston meant something to all of them."

Hamilton, who was only twenty-five and had no film experience, observed that "the only thing John did in that picture was place the camera and get everybody there, which wasn't easy to do." Stark agreed that "John really let actors direct themselves, and he edited them, more than anything else." But production manager Doc Erickson was able to appreciate Huston's meticulous eye.

The scene that Erickson most appreciated in *Reflections* was the one where Elizabeth Taylor and Brian Keith return to the car after a tryst in the woods. "It was the way he set it up, the geography of it all, that was outstanding," Erickson said. "Keith got into the front seat and he's wiping off the lipstick, and she put the seat down and got in the backseat, where she adjusted the mirror to put on her lipstick. Why did Huston do it that way? Because normally, two people would get in and sit side by side. But he chose to put her in the backseat so we've got that separation. And Brian played his dialogue straightforward while she's back there talking over his shoulder. It was a touch that impressed the hell out of me."

Although he had given up cigarettes John was smoking, and inhaling, at least five cigars a day, and his health wasn't very good. "Part of it was his emphysema," said Ernie Anderson, "and it was also his back. Every once in a while he'd have to lie down on the floor. Stephen Grimes, the second-unit director, helped him out enormously. He did the scene with Brando galloping through the woods."

Grimes was amused by John's insistence that the stallion, which was called Firebird and was red in the novel, be a white Lippizaner. They got two of them from Austria, along with a groom who was very strict about their workouts. But as Grimes discovered, "they couldn't run worth toffee. So I got the Italian grooms together and said, 'Get me a white horse to rehearse with.' So they brought an elderly gray mare. John came out one day and saw this little thing and said, 'You're not going to shoot on *that,* are you?' 'It's just a stand-in,' I said. In fact, we shot the whole sequence with that little gray mare. She'd just go on running all day."

A stand-in was also used for Elizabeth Taylor's nude scene, where, flinging off her bra, she walks up the stairs. Taylor wouldn't take her clothes off. "Elizabeth's a bit heavily endowed, I'm afraid," Ossie Morris said. "We got another girl to do the long shot. There was a hassle about that because Taylor didn't approve of the girl's figure. Originally she was supposed to strip off, bare waist, full front, but she wouldn't do that and John was not about to press the point. Ray Stark would have loved it. So it all had to be done in very subdued lighting." "You didn't see her breasts," John said. "She threw the bra, certainly. But the whole picture was a make-believe, you know."

Ernie Anderson noted that there was a lot of commotion on the picture "because Elizabeth Taylor used to come on the set like a battleship surrounded by a flotilla." Costume designer Dorothy Jeakins found Taylor to be "very difficult. She's very spoiled. She'd break appointments with the bootmaker, who would say, 'I'll never make boots for this woman. I've made boots for kings and they didn't keep me waiting two hours.' Then you'd try everything in the book to get a few minutes of her time. John wasn't interested in these problems. And she'd say, 'Let me know twenty minutes before you want me, then ten minutes, five, one . . . and then I'll do the shot. But don't keep *me* waiting.' "

Her lateness also exasperated Ray Stark. "I used to pick up Taylor every morning," he said, "she'd always be late. Then when she got to the set she'd be with her hair . . . and we'd lose about two hours. I finally said to John, 'I'm not going to take it anymore.' John said, 'Why don't you just cool it for a day and see what happens at the end of the day?' So I had my secretary take note of all the times that Elizabeth was behind the camera or in front of the camera, and at the end of the day I found it was all evened out. Because she is such a remarkable per-former, she only had to be told once how John wanted the performance."

Having some experience as an actor under his belt, John was able to empathize with Taylor. "When I'm an actor," he said, "I like to not go on the set and sit half a day waiting for someone to finish a scene. And this can happen very easily unless you have assistants who are on the ball and who know you want your actor there in time and not before time. Elizabeth comes to the set beautifully prepared. If she does a scene six times, there'll be six renditions that are almost exactly alike. That sort of attention and concentration deserves some attention itself."

In contrast, Huston found that when Brando repeated a scene it was *never* the same, which commanded even more attention and respect. "He's an extraordinary, amazing actor. He reaches down to some recess, at the end of some cavern in his spirit, and comes up with a revelation that's unexpected and shocking. You feel something smoldering, explosive, like a furnace door opening, with the heat coming off the screen. If you remember the scene where he talks about the army, standing at the mantelpiece, it's a long speech and he fiddles with a candle. Well, after the first time I could have said, 'That's it,' as I often do; but knowing Marlon and the way he works, I said, 'Let's do it again.' We did it three times, and each time was different; any of them could have been used.

"In another scene he gives a lecture on leadership to a class as his wife is in the background, on horseback, with the man she was having an affair with. He did that completely different two or three times. I've never seen any other actor do that."

Huston never had problems with Brando being late, and according to Ossie Morris, "Marlon totally accepted anything John said or did." Of course, part of Brando's acceptance might have been because he couldn't *hear* anything John, or anyone else, said since he wore earplugs throughout the film. "He developed a Southern accent," Morris said. "Brando was quite isolated and detached on the set. I put it down to the fact that he couldn't hear half the time what was going on. I don't think the others got on with him very well either. And you had to be very careful the way you handled him. You mustn't go in the last minute and give him an instruction or you'd have your head torn off."

The biggest complaint about Brando was that he spoke too softly and swallowed his words, so the other actors could hardly hear him. "The whole thing with Marlon was a game," Angela Allen said. "It was quite deliberate with him. He was play-acting. There was a scene where Elizabeth and Brian and Julie Harris were sitting at a table and he was in the corner. Elizabeth was speaking and then Marlon spoke and then she had to speak again. Well, Elizabeth spoke and then carried on ad-libbing because nothing was coming out of his mouth. And John said, 'Cut. Elizabeth flopped.' And I said, 'No, she didn't. She ad-libbed as long as she possibly could.' And Elizabeth said to him, 'Yes.

When Mr. Mumbles can open his mouth so any of us can even hear what he says, it would be wonderful.' "

Bill Hamilton got some insight into Brando when he once drove him to the studio. "He began to talk about how he hated acting and the theater, and how sick it was that there was a need for acting. I was astonished. There was a big truck next to us and we stopped at a light. The truck driver leaned down and said, 'Hey, Marlon Brando. Marlon Brando!' And Marlon changed. He puffed himself up. He was really enjoying it. Too much!"

John thought Brando's disdain for acting was real, "though he takes his acting very seriously. He is not a dilettante in that sense. I can't imagine him being bad in anything."

He certainly wasn't bad with women. Even though he had brought Tarita, the Tahitian mother of his baby son, with him, "he was trying to screw everyone else around," said Hamilton. "Brian Keith told me he had an English nanny who was taking care of his kids in California, and she had begged him to get an autographed picture of Brando. And Marlon was like a male nymphomaniac, propositioning everybody. Keith said, 'If I'd known he was like this, I would have brought her over here and just stood her up next to the set, picked up her skirt, and got him to service her. Much better than an autographed picture.' "

As *Reflections* began to finish up John was liking it as much as anything he'd ever done. But then Ray Stark began to pressure him about not going over schedule, and Elizabeth Taylor refused to work additional days beyond her contract without being handsomely rewarded. Ossie Morris thought Ray was trying to pull something over on Huston by forcing him to finish the picture on schedule. "Ray was driving him to get the crew signed off by Christmas Eve because it was going to cost him money if it went later than that. It was obvious we couldn't get the picture done properly by that time, and in the end John just shot it, didn't care. It was the climax of the picture and he just blew the whole thing. Ray thought he was getting his way but John was just screwing him right into the ground."

While John found "very little to fault in *Reflections*," and Stark considered it "the most beautiful color picture I had ever seen," the critics found plenty to fault, and the color was destroyed by executive decision at Warner's. "John spent months getting the correct color," Stark said. "It wasn't sepia, it wasn't amber. Then the head of distribution said, 'What's all the arty-farty stuff? To hell with it, it costs too much.' And he sent it out in regular color, which really hurt the picture critically."

The picture was actually released in the desaturated color John had wanted, but the prints were made in regular color. Some critics who saw it as it was intended to be seen still found it "abhorrent," as John Simon complained: "The film emerges in one color, a kind of burnished gold, but with one other color allowed to peep through: red, which comes out as a sickly rose. . . . This envelops a painfully artless film in a painfully arty shell." Simon would find the movie "distasteful . . . pedestrian, crass, and uninvolving to the point of repellence." The *New York Times* would call it "banal"; the *Village Voice*, overdirected. The picture would fail miserably at the box office, and Ray Stark blamed it on the fact that "People weren't willing to understand or accept homosexuality at the time." Stark considered it "one of Brando's most brilliant performances," and thought that "the picture was ahead of its time, like everything John had pretty much done. It's a picture I'm very proud of."

25

NO LOVE, AND DEATH

ON MONDAY, NOVEMBER 28, 1966, WHILE JOHN WAS IN
Rome, Truman Capote threw the "party of the century" at the Plaza in
New York. It was a celebration of his hugely successful book *In Cold
Blood*, and his five hundred guests were asked to wear a mask and dress
in black or white. The guest list was published in the *New York Times*.
And Ricki Huston was upset that she hadn't been on it.

Ricki was beginning to feel as if the only people who paid her any
serious attention were the construction workers who whistled when she
walked by. But then Sunday would come and the actors, artists, and
writers would start showing up at her house around four in the afternoon, and she would forget about Capote's snub and the crass whistlers
and become the perfect hostess.

Playwright Adrienne Kennedy, who had won an Obie in 1964 for her
play *Funnyhouse of a Negro*, came to London at the end of November
1966 on Rockefeller and Guggenheim grants and was given Ricki's
name by actress Diana Sands. Sands had starred in *The Owl and the
Pussycat* in London and knew Ricki then. She told Kennedy, "The one
person I want you to call as soon as you get off the plane is Ricki
Huston. She has a child the same age as your son Adam, she lives in

this wonderful house, and *she's* so wonderful, maybe she'll invite you over."

So Kennedy made the call and Ricki invited her to tea that Sunday and from that day on they became friends. "Ricki had a deep sense of people who were slightly on the outside," Kennedy said. "I was a black woman, a writer, who lived sort of vicariously, divorced, with a small child. I just hit it off with her and I went there almost every Sunday." At those Sunday gatherings she saw John Julius, James Fox, Peter Menegas, and an artist named Gina Metcalf who was Ricki's best friend. Allegra was always running around, dressed in Victorian dresses, Tony was "always watching television in the laundry room," and Anjelica "seemed always to be in and out." When Kennedy commented on Anjelica and Tony, Ricki proudly said, "They are part of a dynasty."

Kennedy had the feeling that Ricki was "very proud of still being Mrs. Huston," and that she really wanted her children to be Hustons. When Kennedy said, almost in awe, "You're really married to John Huston?" Ricki told her, "I was really in love with John, and he used to have all these women fall in love with him, and I never knew they were his girlfriends."

On one of her visits Kennedy, curious about all the chests of drawers in Ricki's living room, asked what was in them. Ricki showed her the objects that were carefully arranged inside: polished figures, paperweights, and jewelry that John had given her over the years. Then Ricki showed her a picture of her and John on their wedding day. "You look so in love," Kennedy said. "I was," Ricki answered.

"She struck me as being truly, deeply, deeply bitter," Adrienne Kennedy observed.

When Kennedy asked her about her early days in Hollywood, Ricki said she didn't like living there. "I was bored," she said. "I had to go to a lot of parties with all those old guys."

"Who were those old guys?" Kennedy asked.

"Oh, Spencer Tracy, Humphrey Bogart."

Kennedy didn't know what to say. Ricki was beautiful, talented, intelligent, dedicated to her children, and yet "there was this tragic thing about her. That she was married to John Huston and was so unhappy, that made a very big impression on me. But after I knew Ricki I really understood what greatness was in a woman. She knew a lot about literature, history, fashion, furniture, society. And the way she could cook and arrange food was dazzling. I never knew a woman who knew so much about all these different things.

"And she had this incredible vision about what she wanted for her children. She wanted Tony to be a writer, and would have him come in on Sundays to read his poems. Anjelica was more arrogant than Tony, who was more removed. I always found Anjelica very hard to talk to, and I told Ricki that once, and she said that was because she was always daydreaming. She never seemed to worry about Allegra, but she was very concerned about Anjelica's appearance. She bought all of Anjelica's clothes, and she worried that Anjelica would get mixed up with movie people. She would also, from time to time, reveal that she was making too many sacrifices for them."

Because the food at Westminster was so horrendous, Tony looked forward to the holidays when he could go to St. Clerans and enjoy the feast. But his behavior often appalled John. "At Westminster the food was made at nine A.M. for lunch," Tony said. "It was the most ghastly, indescribably awful food. If anything appeared on the table that *was* edible, it was fifteen pubescent boys making a grab, and the tables looked like battlefields at the end of a meal. And then I would come back to St. Clerans, where everybody had perfect manners, and Dad would take a look at this savage."

When Tony made a lunge for some food John took it as a personal attack. "If you did something wrong," Tony said, "he assumed that you were doing it because you were evil. It was almost Victorian. And he would take you to bits. Not only me, but my sister. He drove Anjelica out of the room crying on any number of occasions."

What didn't help matters any was that John would often drink himself into anger. "Dad would get drunk," Tony said. "Every single night he had eight vodka martinis. It was sheer hell. And he was erratic." The conflict between them came to a head one evening when Tony, then sixteen, appeared for dinner in a suit and found the men at the table all wearing dinner jackets.

"Tony," John said, "go and change."

"Dad, I have changed."

"You have not. Go and change!"

"Dad, I've just been to the loft. I've had a bath and I've changed."

"*Go and change!*"

Tony left the room and walked out the back stairs to a passage that led to a back wall. When Tony reached the wall he heard footsteps coming after him. He turned, and there was John, furious, his fists clenched, about to strike him.

"Don't you *dare* touch me!" Tony shouted, mustering all the defiance he had stored within him. It was the first time Tony had ever challenged him so directly and the closest thing to a Zen moment he had ever experienced. "I knew that I would kill him," Tony said. "The injustice had got to that point." John's clenched hands began to quiver. Tony looked into his father's red eyes, trying to stare him down. It was an unnerving moment for both of them.

"This was a scary man," Tony said. "He was absolutely terrifying. He was the only person I knew whose eyes went completely red when he was angry."

The incident convinced John that what he had suspected was true: Ricki had turned Tony against him. "The fall in our relationship lay entirely with Tony," John said. "Relationships between fathers and sons are usually not one-sided, but Tony . . . it was almost as though he had been primed against me. There was a tendency to be suspicious, as though he were being, in some way, taken advantage of. As though he thought I was his enemy. It led him to do foolish things. And I would try to snap him out of it. At the same time, while he was behaving in this almost boorish manner, I still recognized there was a decent, wonderful heart there. But it was as though the well had been poisoned."

It was a belief he could never shake, even though both kids strongly denied it. "I was aware of Dad thinking that in some way Mum had turned me against him," Tony said. "This was absolutely untrue. My greatest feeling around Dad that whole period was of great injustice. Because I knew that I was decent. My mother had given me a great sense of decency. But for some perverse reason Dad was sure you were resisting him, and he would never talk to you about it."

"He wasn't there to watch our progress," added Anjelica. "In Ireland, nothing changes all that much. All of a sudden, his children were living in London, listening to the Beatles and Bob Dylan, interrelating with a lot of other kids, picking up a lot of idiosyncrasies that maybe he didn't approve of. We were teenagers and there were a lot of changes going on. We weren't babies anymore, happily tucked away in the country. It was a whole other life. I think he regretted the passing of our innocence."

Dorothy Soma supported John's suspicions, saying that "Ricki would make snide remarks about John in front of the children. Kind of making fun of him as a father and as a husband." But Peter Menegas defended

Ricki: "She showed respect for John. She would never say awful things about him, but she did slightly send him up on his pretensions. Like how he would buy antiques. She said his idea of getting a good bargain was to pull up in front of a store with his car and driver and retinue. Naturally, she said, people were going to add on prices."

Tony was able to elaborate, recalling how his father had "a Cassius Clay complex. From the time I was growing up," he said, "everybody was 'the greatest.' We never had anybody working for us, or became involved with anybody, who was not first rate. Everything was the greatest: the greatest gardener, the greatest bricklayer, the greatest horse, the greatest dog. It was all superlatives. Today I was going to be the prime minister of Ireland, tomorrow the greatest lawyer who had ever been. With Dad, instead of trying to become who you were, you were given these phantoms."

As he got older Tony was able to realize that people often didn't measure up to John's expectations. When a chosen "greatest" disappointed, "we'd have nothing more to do with him." Tony laughed. "Ironically, very few of Dad's real friends were of his stature. The people who tended to be his friends were slightly sycophantic. And when a Marlon Brando, or even Burgess Meredith, came over, it would be almost like two fighting bulls. You'd get this feeling of egos avoiding one another. I mean, Dad absolutely had to be *the* master."

Once, when an English television crew came to shoot a documentary on John's life in Ireland, John insisted on putting on a great show even if it meant staging most of the scenes. "The director encouraged Dad to portray himself," Tony said, "and Dad was in this continual process of invention, so Dad cooked up this image of himself. There was an element of it being amusing. For instance, Dad insisted that our butler serve him champagne while he was in the Japanese bath. Well, the butler had never seen Dad in the nude and indeed had never served Dad champagne. Dad liked the documentary, but there were things which shocked some of the people he hunted with. Dad was talking about the pleasures of fox hunting and there was a cutaway to a hound with a fox's head in its mouth."

John wished the boy could lighten up a bit and accept life for the game it obviously was. "Tony has conceptions of integrity that are a little old-fashioned," he commented. "The idea of integrity with a capital *I*. Life does not come easy for Tony. Whereas Anjelica runs through life as though it were a BMW."

When another TV crew came to St. Clerans, journalist Alexander Walker "gained a disturbing impression of the splendid isolation" John had created around himself. "He treated us all with impeccable yet distancing courtesy: the Great White Father trading beads of courtly geniality with us respectful Indians. He 'performed' for the cameras as if to the manor born—and what a manner it was . . . Huston had filled it with *objets d'art* that recalled the movies he had shot around the world. Beyond the moat, the fountain, and the huge stone lions were rooms that held his collection of Impressionists, original posters by Lautrec, a medieval wooden Christ astride a donkey, Indian jade deities, African sculptures, heads from New Guinea, six-foot-high candles and silk screens from Japan, Spanish Colonial chairs, a bed that belonged to Napoleon, myriad pieces of Inca and Aztec handiwork, and everywhere so much gleam of gold that it looked as if it wasn't the Galway Blazers that the host followed, but the Royal Hunt of the Sun. The effect was of a well-ordered treasure house into which the living Pharaoh would ultimately retire himself. . . .

"The feeling I took away with me was one of awe and disenchantment—of a man who has used his films to construct his life-style. His passions have attached themselves to *things*—rare, beautiful and precious things, but things that are impedimenta to the creative willpower. The temptation of playing roles—to which he has unwisely yielded in well-rewarded but sub-standard films directed by other people— had found its apotheosis in playing The Role. The saddest thing in the world is seeing an erstwhile iconoclast set himself up in his own temple."

If John had set himself up to reign he made sure that his subjects and his guests would never want when they entered his kingdom. When any of his staff took sick he made sure they had the best medical attention and paid all the bills. When Carson McCullers took him up on his invitation to visit St. Clerans in April 1967, he had a special reclining seat installed in the airplane, an ambulance to transport her to his house, and a doctor who was in contact with McCullers's in case of any emergency. When McCullers arrived, John had her carried on a stretcher from room to room so she could see his treasures, then put her in an upstairs bedroom where she remained for the rest of her stay. He arranged for an interview with the *Irish Times,* joined her for conversation and drinks, and laughed with her when the fourteenth-century wooden crucifix above her bed slipped on the wall and hung sideways just as she said that "Writing, for me, is a search for God." When she became ill she flew home to New York, where she died on September 29.

Like his Aunt Margaret, whose life may have been shortened by the trip to Connecticut, Huston had no regrets about Carson McCullers's visit and considered it a fulfillment and a liberation for her.

The same could be said of John's next visitor, whom he had run into at the Beverly Hills Hotel while he was editing *Reflections in a Golden Eye.* "Come to Ireland, Olivia," he said to his old paramour. And since she was separated from her spouse, she took him up on the invitation.

"But before I went," de Havilland said, "I did something very daring. I had sensed when I saw him that he was sick. So I called his doctor and he said, 'I think it's all right to say now, he does have emphysema.'

"In Ireland he took me on a tour of his estate and he kept treating me as if I was visiting royalty. He was very courtly with me. And I was fascinated by lots of things about the house. The bedroom was done in rose and gray, which was the way mine was done many years ago. And he had a Japanese screen and I was born in Japan. I thought, 'It's so strange that all these things were in his unconscious which were also part of my consciousness.' "

After all those years apart, Olivia still couldn't help imagining what it might have been like had John returned to her after the war. "Then he took me to a room in which he painted and showed me his various canvases. There was a painting of his housekeeper, Betty, who had just greeted me, and she was stark naked, eating an apple and lying on the floor. 'Oh,' he said, 'and this is something else.' And I said, 'Indeed it is!'

"Then I realized the affront of his asking me to come stay at St. Clerans. I understood Betty O'Kelly and I understood Gladys—they symbolized parts of his mother, in a way. What he needed from a mother. One was his Madonna mother, the part that every fellow has to have as an image, and the other was his governess mother. So I couldn't wait to leave. I cut my visit short by two days.

"It turned out that he wanted to go on the same plane with me. He was leaving his houseguests. He had been working on a script with two writers and he was going off to paint with a French countess, who was another adjunct to his life. And he wanted to go to Paris with me. I thought, 'Oh, my God, this is going to stop right now!' I said, 'I am going to give you one last gift. I will tell you what I did in Los Angeles. I called your doctor and he told me that Ireland is very, very bad for you. You need a hot, dry climate. I am trying to save your life by telling you this. You'd better do something about it. And that's the last gift I am going to give you.'

"He looked at me with absolute rage. I thought he was going to do something violent, but he didn't. It was the last time I saw him. And when we got off the plane he wanted me to go on with him. I said, 'You're in transit, but *I* have arrived!' "

The script John was working on during de Havilland's visit was *Sinful Davey*, by James Webb. John saw it as a "lighthearted romp" about a young deserter who follows in his outlaw father's footsteps. "Davey expects to end up on the gallows as his father did," John summed up, "but not before rivaling his father's record for sinfulness." A young actor named John Hurt was cast as Davey and Anjelica, who appeared as one of the riders in the film, developed a crush on him. "God!" John's old friend Cherokee exclaimed. "I watched Anjelica go through that horrible little John Hurt, who was half her size and everything else. Her father was furious about it." Cherokee had come to Ireland on a visit and John hired her to work as a publicist for the picture.

During this time John began suggesting to the Irish government that they consider establishing a film board to provide funds for films to be produced in Ireland. He invited the prime minister, Jack Lynch, and his cabinet to join him for a luncheon. Ernie Anderson made the arrangements at an old prison outside of Dublin, where a scene from *Davey* was being shot, and the prime minister and a dozen government officials joined the film crew for a catered lunch. Then John delivered a speech, written for him by Anderson, extolling the virtues of an Irish film industry, and the next day the *Irish Times* printed it as their main editorial.

"As a result of that," John said, "the prime minister had me be chairman of an Irish Film Board, which was never formed. Just a lot of publicity."

Writer J. P. Donleavy credits John for being "one of the background reasons for the present tax-free status of artists in Ireland. His living presence for many years added an international cultural importance to Ireland, which in turn was an influence attracting the present legislation."

"In pursuing the motion picture thing," Huston said, "I asked that artists should be tax free. They brought credit to the country and their early efforts went unrewarded. It would bring the sort of people to Ireland that Ireland wanted. Well, I'll be darned if they didn't enact the

592 Lawrence Grobel

legislation for artists, painters, sculptors, writers." Unfortunately for John, however, "motion pictures weren't included."

After *Sinful Davey* was cut and scored, line producer William Graf delivered the picture to Walter Mirisch and United Artists. And then, what happened to *The Barbarian and the Geisha* happened again. The picture was altered considerably, which infuriated Huston. "It was a very good picture until it came under the artistic domination of the producer, Walter Mirisch," John said. "He had promised not to inter-fere. He had proposed certain things and I had been against them and finally he gave me his word that the film would be as I wanted it. He betrayed his word and really ruined it. He changed the sequence of events. He put a narration over it—dreadful, dreadful! What was rather blithe and unserious became clotted and cluttered and distasteful. I was away when it was released, otherwise I'd have taken my name off the picture."

"John was off somewhere when we previewed the picture," Walter Mirisch said in his defense. "It was the worst preview I have ever experienced. People just left their seats in droves." Mirisch called Paul Kohner, who attended the next screening, and again, Mirisch said, "It was just bloody awful. United Artists was terribly upset. Paul talked with John, who thought it was just fine and was very angry with me. I said to Paul, 'The amount of pressure I'm under from the financiers and the distributors is unbearable.' " "Do whatever you have to do," Kohner said. "So," Mirisch explained, "we started to do things that would make it more accessible and less confusing. And while the picture may not have gotten better, people weren't walking out of the theaters anymore. I've always felt that it was John's responsibility to come to those previews and see what the problem was. But in John's eyes I turned out to be the heavy. We obviously never released his picture. I'm terribly sorry he felt that way."

After *Sinful Davey* John agreed to play a small role as a lecherous hospital administrator in *Candy*, in which he, Marlon Brando, Richard Burton, and Walter Matthau combined couldn't justify such a film being made. He also agreed to direct Katharine Hepburn in Jean Giraudoux's *The Madwoman of Chaillot* once an acceptable script was written. But mostly he spent his time at St. Clerans, painting. While Ricki went to New York to try to drum up support for the play she wrote with Peter Menegas, John worked on a painting of Anjelica.

Peter Menegas remembered a dinner he and Ricki attended at a restaurant called Toque Blanche on the East Side of Manhattan with

George Plimpton, Kevin McCarthy, Jean and Stephen Smith, and Jackie
Kennedy. "We didn't know Jackie was going to be there," Menegas
said. "She was a widow then and would say, 'When I was married and
living in Washington.' She said that she had seen pictures of Ricki in a
magazine in Ireland and was intrigued by her. She wondered what Ricki
did with all her time. Ricki was very amused that she was someone
whom people wondered about. But she wasn't taken aback by Jackie.
Because Ricki had a touch of the theatrical in her."

Ricki saw her father in New York and began to ask him questions
about his life. She had an idea to write a musical about him called
Speakeasy. "She was proud of his zaniness," Menegas said. "She babied
him like a child. It was a fabulous relationship on that level."

Nothing came of their play, but Menegas's first novel, *Jacklove*, was
published and he dedicated it to "ESH": the pen name Ricki made of
her initials. With the advance he received for his second novel he
invited Ricki to join him on a trip to Italy, where they rented a car and
met Gore Vidal, who was taken with her. Adrienne Kennedy always
thought that Ricki should have married Menegas, and when she asked
her about it Ricki would say, "I don't know if he'd want to." But Ricki
was crazy about Peter, Kennedy said. "She went everyplace with him.
John Julius came to the Sundays, but she went to movies with Peter, art
galleries with Peter, made dinner for Peter."

It was Menegas, too, who brought a seventeen-year-old art student
named Jeremy Railton to one of Ricki's parties, and he became Anjelica's
best friend. Railton had grown up on a game reserve in Rhodesia and
had come to London at sixteen to study. "As I walked in the door," he
said of his first visit to 31 Maida Avenue, "Anjelica turned and looked
at me and it was like, 'Oh, God, it's you!' From the moment that I laid
eyes on her I was madly in love with her. I had never seen anything more
graceful and more beautiful *ever*. And it became the best friendship I've
ever had, because we don't need anything from each other." What they
both shared was a confidence that they were destined to be *known*. "We
always thought we'd be rich and famous immediately," Railton said.

For Railton, Anjelica and Ricki and their Sunday gatherings were
"like a finishing school. And being around Ricki and Anjelica was the
center of everything. I was meeting movie people, artists, writers,
dancers, hooking up for the first time with a professional world of people
who were doing things. Until then it had all been theory and art school."

To Railton, Ricki was "beautiful, graceful, exquisite. Her taste was
the most important thing. Anjelica was a little wilder than her mother.
Ricki would buy cashmere, Anjelica was a bit more flash."

Allegra, who was three, was the smartest child he had ever seen. Often Railton would spend hours sitting and drawing with her. But he never quite understood why John Julius "wasn't taking care of Allegra more. It goes back to that English thing, that no matter how wonderful the child is, in their mind she's illegitimate. Especially when you're dealing with a family that's well connected and has long bloodlines. He was reserved and would always seem to be on the run."

Ricki had never told Adrienne Kennedy that John Julius was Allegra's father, and it never occurred to Kennedy until someone else told her. "She just referred to him as her neighbor." Lady Diana Cooper, Allegra's unacknowledged grandmother, had a backyard that overlooked Ricki's, and Ricki would often see her peeking out a window when Allegra was playing in the garden.

After Anjelica turned sixteen, Ricki began to worry about her. "She worried that she was with people Ricki didn't know," Adrienne Kennedy said. "She worried about who Anjelica might be sleeping with. She felt that Anjelica was doing secretive things. She found out that Anjelica was at a party with some people she didn't approve of. 'I think they all take drugs.'" Ricki's concerns had some basis. "Ricki was not at all a drug person," Jeremy Railton said. "Anjelica and I would have pretensions in that area."

Kennedy thought Anjelica felt that "Ricki was trying to hold her back." But Railton thought that "If anything, Ricki was the one who was pulling away: looking for a career, looking for love, looking for things without wanting to be Mom, Mom, Mom. Her kids were sort of grown up now. They could have kept her enslaved forever. She was the one feeling kind of restless. She wanted to pick up her career again, that's why she started writing."

"There definitely was jealousy between Ricki and Anjelica," Adrienne Kennedy said. "There seemed to be a competition between them, like in the way they dressed."

Ricki's concerns with Anjelica were of a social nature, but Tony, too, caused her anguish. One day Adrienne visited Ricki, who was in the kitchen, scrubbing the sink, looking very sad. "I'm so worried about Tony," she said. "He didn't get into Oxford."

Ricki had decided that Tony would go on to Oxford after he graduated from Westminster in 1968. The tutor she hired to prep Tony for the entrance exam singled out Balliol as the college he should apply to. "I was very badly informed," Tony said after he failed to get in. "To get into Balliol, which is, perhaps, the most intellectual college in Oxford, either you're a genius or, as frequently happens, you use some form of influence. My education had been a complete mess. It really wasn't looked after. Dad had never shown any great interest in my education. I can't remember ever having a conversation with him about it."

It wasn't so much that John didn't care as that he had entrusted the children's education to Ricki. "His mother was taking care of all this," John said. "She had great friends in the literary circle in London— Stephen Spender and that group. She assured me that everything was being done about Tony's going to Oxford. I suppose I could have done a lot better than I did about Tony when he was in Westminster. I wasn't sufficiently aware of his day-by-day life to know about this. But in three years going to Westminster he didn't have a friend. Not one single friend. That's extraordinary. When I was in school, and I quit halfway through high school, my God, I had a lot of companions!

"Now, when he got out of Westminster, Ricki had him apply to college. The one application was made to Balliol, not to any other place. This was unheard of. You put down for at least a half dozen colleges. Balliol is one of the most difficult to get into."

It was too late for any strings to be pulled to get Tony into either of England's most prestigious universities, but there was still an outside chance that Stephen Spender could get him into London University, "which was a big, big drop from either Oxford or Cambridge," John said. And while those efforts were being made, John flew to France to prepare for *The Madwoman of Chaillot.*

William Hamilton was vacationing in Paris when he ran into Gladys Hill, who told him that John was at the Lancaster and would love to see him. Ely Landau and Henry Weinstein, the producers of *Madwoman*, were in Huston's suite when Hamilton arrived. "John was in an absolute *state!*" Hamilton recalled. "He gave me the script, shut me in the bedroom, and told me to read it. When I came out, John said, 'What'd you think, kid?' I said, 'It's really awful.' He just chuckled and five hours later I was hired to rewrite the thing. But I think my being hired was part of a lark; he wanted to get out of it. We all went to Nice and had villas and visited the Picasso Museum in Antibes. John felt that he was a master manipulator but also the dupe of a huge apparatus, and he seemed to have an almost envy for Picasso, who had lived the perfect old man's life: gotten all the nookie there was in the world, and even more than that, was able to live without other people. Not only the flunkies but also producers and movie deals. All he needed was paint and the world came to his door. But I noticed that grand old men, of which John was certainly one, tend to size themselves up against other grand old men. They're competitive sons of bitches, or they wouldn't be grand old men!"

After Hamilton finished his script John met with Landau, whom he disliked. "They sent me out to walk around," Hamilton said. "I was such an egotist, I expected that I'd soon have a Ferrari and be living in Hollywood. Then I walked back to the house and there was this cigar smoke hanging over it because they both smoked cigars. And John said to me, 'Okay, we've all been fired.' And he left to go off on a trip."

"He dropped it," said Katharine Hepburn, who was disappointed since she had agreed to do the film because Huston was directing. "I felt it was unfair to Ely Landau. But those things happen, so, too bad."

"Hepburn was involved first," Huston said, "and then they approached me. The producer had an idea that the young people of the world were going to hell—this is the one point he wanted to make, why he was doing the picture. But it was the faceless money that was the message of the play. I assumed that they would do it my way but that wasn't what they wanted. So I withdrew."

Bill Hamilton didn't know what to think. His vacation had turned into a job, his hopes had been raised so that he was dreaming of fame and Ferraris. "You're sort of brought up so high with Huston," he reflected, "and then you realize you're just kind of an amusement for him. It wasn't like a mentor who was going to help you. And after all those intense discussions, when you think you've really got a fantastic friend and a great life ahead, you realize you don't mean anything. And it's a big shock. There's something greedy about that. He didn't seem so human to me. He seemed more like a production."

What John needed, after his problems with producers like Walter Mirisch and Ely Landau, was a producer he could control, someone younger, eager to establish himself in the business, who would look up to him with respect and admiration. He found such a man in Carter De Haven, who had come to see him at St. Clerans. The thirty-six-year-old producer brought with him a script by Dale Wasserman, the man who wrote *The Man of La Mancha.* Wasserman had found an obscure novel of young, fated love set in 1358, at the beginning of the Hundred Years War in France. It was *A Walk with Love and Death* by Hans Koningsberger, a story of a peasant rebellion against the knights and landed gentry in medieval France. In the midst of the violence and madness a nineteen-year-old student named Heron crosses the countryside to study in England. Stopping at a nobleman's house, he falls in love with his host's sixteen-year-old daughter, Claudia. Later, when he learns that the nobleman has been killed and his home destroyed, he returns to rescue her. Together they travel to her uncle, Robert the Elder, but when Claudia demands revenge she learns that her uncle has joined the peasants. Mercenary knights come to slay Robert and his sons, as Claudia and Heron seek refuge in an abbey. The monks refuse to marry them, so instead they marry each other under the eyes of God, and join in love as they await certain death.

John liked the script and agreed to do it. Then De Haven noticed a picture of Anjelica and Ricki and asked who they were. When Huston told him, De Haven asked if Anjelica could act. "I would think so," John answered. "I'd like to talk to her," De Haven said, believing he had found the girl to play Claudia. John suggested he go to London to meet her. "If you think she isn't right for the part, let's not let that stand in our way. But," he added, "if we're going to do this picture for a price and want to bring something fresh and new to it, why not?"

De Haven found Anjelica "absolutely charming. She was like a water nymph, a filly full of energy, long-legged, beautiful hair. There was a naturalness about her." But he also found Ricki less than enthusiastic about Anjelica dropping out of school to make a movie.

"She was very candid about it," De Haven said. "She said all her life had been around the arts, and she thought to do this to a young person before she finished school . . . then chances are if it got under Anjelica's skin she wouldn't go back." Although this was only his second picture as a producer, De Haven had also grown up around show business. "I explained the timing," he said, that "if you put something on the back burner the likelihood of its ever reappearing was rather slim."

Although Anjelica wanted very much to be in the movies, her heart was set on landing the lead in Franco Zeffirelli's *Romeo and Juliet.* She had tried out for the part and had been called back by the casting director three times when De Haven appeared with *A Walk with Love and Death.* "I really didn't see myself in that part," she said, "and I wasn't all that receptive to what I felt were handouts from people who knew me or were close to my family. I wanted to do things *my* way. Maybe it sounds a little spoiled, but it's not an unusual feeling among children of people who are famous. I didn't want to hurt my father. It was a very generous gesture on his part. I know it was helping me and furthering a career that I had definitely given the impression that I was interested in.

"It was a strange time for me because I wanted to play Juliet. That was a part any young girl who wants to be an actress would kill to play. But it coincided with *A Walk with Love and Death,* and it was ultimately decided that I would do that."

Dorothy Soma said that "Ricki was a little bit afraid of Anjelica doing it. She didn't think that she could pull it off. But it was something that John wanted to *do* for her. It was a gift in a way." John agreed: "The reason I did it was for Anjelica. No other reason."

Landing Huston as director made De Haven feel he had a chance at something memorable. "If you strike the lightning with John," he said, "you may get a classic movie, which also could be commercial." Darryl Zanuck's son, Richard, was in charge of production at 20th Century-Fox at the time and De Haven said that Huston "let me run with the ball. All the contact with Fox during this period was ninety-five percent mine. He left the business end of it to me."

Before the rest of the picture was cast in London, Dale Wasserman, who, besides being the screenwriter, owned the rights to the novel, flew to St. Clerans to work on the script with Huston. Carter De Haven was also at these meetings, but Wasserman felt that "he just didn't have the clout to exert his opinions very strongly." Wasserman, on the other hand, was extremely opinionated, especially when it came to Huston and his life-style.

"The reason I couldn't really get along with John, and didn't really like him," Wasserman said, "is perhaps the same thing that Lillian Ross expressed in her book about him. Everything about John was artificially composed. The exquisite composition of St. Clerans did not strike me as the natural expression of a person at all, but the expression of a conceptualist. I always felt as though St. Clerans was some kind of archeological museum. Though very beautiful, it seemed to belong on the pages of a magazine rather than as a place to live. There was no spontaneity to it. Deep in the building John had his pre-Columbian museum, naturally lighted, an eerie effect, as though you were walking into a mausoleum. And the rituals: drinks at a certain time, knockout martinis. And even the giant dog, Seamus—his paw weighed forty pounds! I loved that dog; it's just that he was a little preposterous, too. Someone had cast him."

Wasserman wasn't pleased when De Haven told him that to get Huston they would have to take Anjelica to play Claudia. When he met her in London he found her, "gawky, awkward, not pretty. And she had a curiously intense interest in drugs then. She questioned me at great length about drugs and had I ever tried them. I had a definite apprehension about her. Number one, I had a strong impression that she was afraid of her father."

The actor chosen to play Anjelica's young lover was Assaf Dayan, son of Israel's defense minister, Moshe Dayan. John said he settled on

Dayan without knowing who he was. "He was a very cocky, charming fellow," Dale Wasserman noted, "but not precisely a great actor. His heart and passion were not in it."

Anjelica had gone to Paris to be outfitted for the movie when the student riots of 1968 erupted, putting Paris in chaos. She had flown into the city for just one day and got stuck in her hotel for three days. The issues the students were fighting for were of less concern to her than the fact that she hadn't brought any toiletries with her. "I didn't have so much as a hairbrush," she complained. "I finally left Paris with unbrushed hair. I looked a fright. I was not happy."

As the uprising continued, John told Wasserman, "I was here when De Gaulle came in and I'd like to be here when he falls." But Wasserman had other concerns. "I just want to make this damn movie," he responded, "so I'm going to get out of Paris!" Wasserman drove to Brussels and began to call people he knew who might help him find another location. A friend had a production company in Vienna, and A Walk with Love and Death was shut down for more than a month so preproduction could relocate to Austria.

It was impossible to ignore the student unrest and ferment that was occurring not only in France but also in the United States. Wasserman attempted to make Love and Death "as contemporary in feeling as I could." But, he said, "John felt it was strictly a period picture and should adhere to period mores."

John contended that keeping it a period piece would demonstrate that history repeated itself, thus making the film universal. "The setting seems to be Europe," he said, "but actually it's anyplace and every-place. The time seems to be in the middle of the fourteenth century, but it's just as much now, today, this moment. Young people of today think that their problems are unique, but the facts are that there has always been a generation gap. Moreover, young people in the throes of first love have always felt and will always feel that they are sharing an experience that can never be understood by any other than themselves. The book seems to express a philosophy peculiar to the young people of today. But actually what is expressed is timeless. My great wish was to make a film that would be faithful to that idea."

As new locations were being scouted, John returned to St. Clerans to paint. James Real, a writer, visited him at this time and reported John slamming down the phone on an assistant producer who was asking him to come to England for a casting meeting. "My God!" John shouted,

"France is in catastrophe, and you're mewling about a damn movie!" Real found Huston unwilling to talk about movies. "Horses, yes. Artists and all their doings, yes. Irish lore, yes. But not movies." And he was duly impressed with John's ten-hour days spent painting in his studio.

While John was wrestling with perspective, Tony was out in the bogs flying his hawks. One day a friend of his brought his cousin, who was an art student visiting from London, to watch. Her name was Margot and Tony found her to be "somebody quite unlike anybody I'd ever met. She had a very mysterious air about her." Her parents were the Marquis and Marchioness of Cholmondeley of Cheshire. It was one of her father's duties to lead the Queen into Parliament for its opening session. Her grandparents lived in a forty-four-room palace in Norfolk, her parents in a castle, and she and her sisters were taught at home by governesses. Her initial impression of Tony was that "he was very weird, very strange." But she also thought herself "pretty strange." Tony only remembers that she had a headache and returned to the Big House to look through John's art books. "We didn't become involved then," Tony said.

In London Ricki was visited by her brother, Philip, and his wife, Avril. Before they arrived Ricki had sent them pictures of the children and wrote a note saying, "Wait till you see them in person!" But her cheerfulness was a facade, according to Adrienne Kennedy, who remembered that Ricki was very depressed at the time. "She was in analysis then," Kennedy said, "and she was just totally down. It was, 'No one cares about me'—that sort of feeling. She was a cauldron of unfulfilled desires."

Her analysis was Jungian and Jeremy Railton remembered Ricki once coming back from a session "and being freaked out because he would analyze her dreams and then she couldn't dream. The worst thing was to be in a Jungian analysis and not have a dream to tell." Peter Menegas said that Ricki often spent a lot of time crying in her room.

To her brother, Ricki was what she wanted to be, which was "the center of a group of illuminators. But I got the idea that she would have been a lot happier being John Huston's only wife, and having John be her only husband. She didn't like just being the mother of his children." At the time of their visit Ricki didn't have a car and they went everywhere by cab. "We met Peter O'Toole, that was a thrill. Ricki was well known and established in London society."

Through Adrienne Kennedy, Ricki got to meet James Earl Jones and James Baldwin. "Ricki could be like a little girl," Kennedy said. "When I gave this party she was so excited. 'Oh, I'm going to talk to James Baldwin!' she said. She had an affinity for black people. I remember one time she said to me, 'How are you getting along? You must get lonely sometimes. There aren't many black people in London.' Ricki sensed that there was a lot of me that was lonely. I was convincing myself that I was having a good time."

Through Adrienne, Ricki met a handsome Jamaican musician in his mid-twenties. They had gone to the Round House to see a play by John Arden. During intermission they saw Brian Anderson Thomas, and when the play resumed Ricki excused herself to go to the ladies room. She later told Kennedy that she had gone back to give Brian her address and a month later she said that she'd been seeing a lot of him.

So, between her bouts with depression and her inability to dream for her analyst, Ricki found solace in the youth and vitality of men like Thomas and Peter Menegas. But friends like Dirk Bogarde could see how troubled she really was. "Beneath the gaiety, the laughter, and the beauty," commented Bogarde, "she was often sad."

Bogarde was at a party Ricki threw for Jack Clayton in honor of his latest movie, *A Mother's House*. Clayton remembered it mostly because Anjelica cried throughout the screening and "was seriously disturbed" by it. "It's a story about children with no father," Clayton said, "and so religious that when their mother dies they decide to bury her in the garden. They succeed in existing for six months until the father, who was no good anyway, appears and one of the girls kills him with a poker. It sounds macabre but it's a lovely story." Clayton speculated that "maybe with all the damage done by both John and Ricki to Anjelica, she might have been affected by it."

As she was living in fear of her father's directing her in *A Walk with Love and Death*, Clayton's small movie might have caused her more anxieties than he could have imagined. "It must be terribly oppressive to have your father direct you in something," Clayton said upon reflection. "The director should be a father figure to the actors but not a real father."

Just before she left for Austria to star in her first picture Anjelica cut her hair short, which deeply troubled John. "We hadn't seen Anjelica in a while," Carter De Haven said. "When she showed up for wardrobe, here was the haircut. John was disappointed. And angry. He asked me why she did it. John had about as much idea as a yo-yo. Remember, she was a young girl. It could have been subconscious, or it might have been totally intentional to let him know that she was a woman and wanted to be independent." Peter Menegas considered her action a display of her rebellious spirit. Anjelica, though, downplayed the symbolic significance. "It wasn't a big thing for me," she said. "It wasn't a reactionary gesture. I felt like cutting my hair and I cut my hair."

But since the part called for a girl with long hair, John brought in a hairdresser to make hairpieces, and Anjelica perhaps began to wish she had left her hair alone, because the wigs and pieces made her uncomfortable. "I had a lot of hair," she said, "and I felt that I looked unattractive."

To overcome this feeling she hoped to cover her face with the makeup she loved to put on. But, again, John opposed her. His concern was that a girl in war-torn France in the fourteenth century wouldn't wear black eyeliner. John also wouldn't allow her to pluck her eyebrows. "Suddenly," remarked Joan Buck, "there she was with nothing on her eyes and the big eyebrows and this ridiculous cape with hair on her head and she didn't look good and she didn't feel good."

Uncomfortable with her looks, disliking her role, unsure about her talent, afraid of her father, and not very fond of Austria because "the people were somewhat imperialistic," her problems were further compounded when she tried to move from the hotel where John was staying to the one where the other actors lived. "I wanted to be with kids my age," she recalled. Lola Finkelstein, a friend of Carter De Haven's who was visiting the set with her husband, said that Anjelica didn't seem very "daughterly," and that "she had a crush on a musician who was around, and there was a lot of wondering if she was going to bed on time and if she was going to be overtired." "I wouldn't permit her to live somewhere else," John said, adding, "She would cry mysteriously during the film. I didn't know what her tears were about."

Dale Wasserman thought he knew: "She was just scared shitless and felt that if she could remove herself from this concentrated group of people, which included her dominant father, she might save her spirit a little." And Jeremy Railton, who exchanged daily letters with her, also knew: "She'd always wanted to be an actress, but she had done no studying, and she was scared of doing it with her father. Suddenly she was whipped off to be directed in a movie. No wonder she spent the time crying. She was miserably unhappy."

"She wasn't *prepared*," said Lupita Kohner, who had gone to Vienna with her husband. "She was too young, and scared to death." Paul Kohner agreed: "John practically forced her to be an actress. She was in no way qualified."

Anjelica tried to pretend to friends like Lizzie Spender, who visited the set, that real acting was just an extension of what they used to do over the holidays at St. Clerans. "She only painted it as a portrait of something that was great fun to do," Lizzie recalled. Joan Buck, though, thought she had been miscast. "Anjelica is one of the funniest people I know, if not *the* funniest," Buck said. "She does caricature, pastiche, parody, and she's very, very quick. For her to play a fucking princess was not Anjel. She doesn't have those looks, she is not a simperer, she's not an ingenue."

When Ricki briefly visited her daughter she told Stephen Grimes, "This is a bad part for Anjel. The girl's a comedienne, why'd he put her in a role like this?"

But Anjelica didn't dare complain to John. "I didn't talk about it. I felt that I had to do the movie to please him, which is certainly not the way to go into any project. That was my primary mistake. And not being verbal with him, I'm sure he felt somewhat thwarted and uncomfortable with me. I didn't go to him for a lot of advice. I kept to myself, which has been my way in times of distress. It was not a pleasant experience for him either. He probably felt very rejected by me. I wasn't exactly bouncing into work every morning with a smile plastered on. Quite the contrary. The fact that I was ungrateful and petulant about it was hardly something he could have expected. After all, Katharine Hepburn didn't criticize his direction. Why should I? I got through it, but it wasn't an easy time for me."

To a reporter John praised Anjelica. "What really counts in film acting is that rare moment," he said, "just a flickering, when through the eyes you get a glimpse of the real meaning of the character. It is not technique or professionalism—just truth. Garbo had it. Monroe had it. I can see it in Anjelica."

But during rehearsals in Vienna Dale Wasserman noticed that the naturalness he had seen in Anjelica as a person was not there. "She was just rigid, an icicle, frozen stiff. There was no performance happening there. There was a terror of her father. And curiously, John was not allaying her fear. In a drunken moment one night I said, 'Are you repaying a debt by putting Anjelica in this picture?' He said, 'What debt?' I said, 'The fact that you have ignored her all these years . . . is this your beau geste to make up for all that?' I didn't get much of an answer."

Wasserman came to believe that "there was a very definite sadistic quality in John. My business as a writer is to understand what people are like rather than how they wish to appear. In John I sensed this cruelty, which particularly manifested itself with people who couldn't effectively strike back. I resented that very much. I saw him take it out on small people—flunkies, hangers-on, the coterie around him. There was a little God complex there. And cruelty often for the sake of experimentation."

Wasserman also didn't feel that John was being truthful with him. Wasserman had an ironclad contract which said that he couldn't be rewritten, and he resented that Huston was "tampering with my script." He thought that "Gladys did most of John's writing for him, most of his *thinking* for him. She really ran things." And he was angered when John brought in Hans Koningsberger, "which my contract forbade," Wasserman said. "But Huston did it regardless."

"I wasn't satisfied with the script," John said. "And Dale Wasserman was a sonofabitch. A very strange man. He was quite gifted at staging, and not a bad writer, but a black character. And he had in the contract, which I didn't know about until after, that the writer of the book was to have no say whatsoever in the picture. He was threatening lawsuits—not against me but against the company."

"If he was dissatisfied with the script," Wasserman said, "he never said so to me. And if I appeared to him as a black-natured person and a sonofabitch, I feel rather *good* about that! Because it meant that I took no shit from him. And I watched other people taking it in ways that made me cringe."

Carter De Haven, though, recalled an occasion when some shit *was* taken. "We were sitting in John's suite and Dale was describing why he had written this scene. But John said, 'It just doesn't progress right.' Dale tried to defend what he had done and John looked at him. 'I want to tell you something,' he said, 'if an albatross flew through that window with a good idea in his mouth, I would grab it and it would be in the picture in a second. So let's not have this fear of change and this priority of rightness and possession. If you can't help me make it work, I'm going to make it work.' Dale understood, rewrote the scene, and it was wonderful."

Off the set a flow of visitors came to Austria. After Ricki left Zoe arrived, then Valeria. There were the usual members of the press, many of John's friends, the Kohners and other of his business people. Both of Anjelica's step-grandmothers, Dorothy Soma and Nan Huston, also appeared. Anjel liked Dorothy, whom she called "Nana," because she was "jolly and had soft skin." But Nan she found "not terribly magnetic to children. And she wasn't terribly well. She was always ailing from something."

John, too, had health problems in Vienna. Driving to a small town in the hills he had trouble breathing. A doctor was summoned and he was put on oxygen for two days. "But nothing got him down," said De Haven. "He was the most resilient man I've ever met."

The visitors kept coming and the circuslike atmosphere that existed on a Huston picture finally got to Dale Wasserman. "As I watched the press, the extraneous people, and the beautiful women coming in and out, I kept thinking, 'What *is* this bullshit? We are here to knock ourselves out making the most wonderful movie we can make, and there is all this superfluous activity going on.' It was destroying my concentration. As the writer I was used to being very respected and listened to, but there's this attitude on movies that once the thing's written, get rid of the writer. I didn't buy any of that. And because of the Huston/Anjelica situation, I didn't see any way I could win. And disagreeing with John, I saw that one of two things would happen: Either we would have a major blow-up and somebody would get killed, or I'd better get myself out of there because John was in charge. So I just arranged to walk from it."

When Wasserman left Koningsberger arrived, although Wasserman would fight his attempt at getting a screenplay credit. Koningsberger, unlike Wasserman, was fascinated to be on a movie set and eager to please. He found Huston to be gentle, with "boundless patience" and a "bitter aversion to shortcuts, clichés, mixed metaphors." In an article he wrote about his experience he said, "It was my good fortune as a writer that Huston is a man who believes in books. . . . He wanted to film a *novel*: not the movements of the people in a story but the idea of the book."

When he wasn't working on *Love and Death* Huston spent his time with Gladys Hill adapting another novel he had decided to make as his next picture. It was a complex spy thriller dealing with the duplicity of both Russian and American spies, called *The Kremlin Letter*, by Noel Behn. John had gotten Fox to option the book and told Richard Zanuck he wanted Carter De Haven to produce it. De Haven worried that it was too complicated, but John told him, "I think I can lick that." It was a completely different genre than the film he was working on, but "the exercise in morality" that it presented, plus the $400,000 he would receive to write and direct, convinced him of the validity of the project.

* * *

Because of his conflicts with Wasserman, his difficulties with Anjelica, the abrupt change in locations, the limited (under $1.5 million) budget, his poor health, and weekends spent working on another script, John never felt he was in control of *A Walk with Love and Death*. "There were so many loose ends," he said, "that it didn't get the power of concentration that I should have given it. That's in the way of an explanation, not an excuse. There's no such thing as an excuse."

As the picture progressed the acting of Anjelica and Assaf Dayan seemed to improve. John had cast himself as Robert the Elder, and there was understandable tension on the set when he played his scenes with Anjelica, but De Haven felt that she "got better and better. She got along well with young Dayan, and, of course, instantly fell into being the star of the movie, and she loved it."

Anjelica liked Dayan but felt that his part, like hers, "was so stilted, it would be hard to know how his performance was. He was getting through it the same way I was." As for herself, contrary to what De Haven perceived, she recognized that she was "untrained" and felt "more like I was to be carried along on this wave. There was no joy in it for me."

After Austria the production moved to northern Italy, and then to Ireland for some horse riding shots. Cherokee was again in Ireland, angrily watching John directing Anjelica. "I could have killed John because he rode her right to the wall," she said. "It would be getting twilight, with the mist and cold in Ireland, and she'd have to get on that horse and ride in hair-raising situations. I said, 'John, she's going to die on that horse.' He said, 'She wants to be an actress.' He'd practically try to do her in in order to get her out of the business. He was very brutal to her."

The frustrations of the film had finally gotten to Huston, and he took it out on those who loved him. Cherokee was no exception. "He asked who could drive the car and I said I would. It was late and dark and we were at each other's throats and I put the car in the wrong gear and went up against a tree. And this monster sitting next to me turned and said, 'What the fuck! You always say you can do something, you can't do *anything*! Go back to the farm! You're ignorant, you're dumb, you're stupid! You've never done anything with your life and you never will.' It was like he was possessed by devils—and he was. The reason you forgave him was because he was as tender as he was violent, as good as he was evil. And I think that was the biggest fight in John's life."

Joan Buck thought that the way John juxtaposed tender and brutal images at the end of *A Walk with Love and Death* made it his most "horrifying" movie. "It was astounding," she said. "It was when the heroine and the hero seek refuge in a fortress made of very thick stones, and they spend the night together, naked under a rough wool blanket. The angry peasants are marching up to kill them, and you hear the clacking, you have close-ups of the hatchets and the primitive, sharp instruments, and there's such a foretaste of that metal touching that flesh. I don't know why he did it."

Dale Wasserman, too, found the ending "oddly frustrating and baffling," because there was no buildup to it. "There has to be a rising line of emotion that is replete with anguish up to that moment where they accept it. But the crescendo isn't there." Wasserman found the movie "an interesting, but definite dramatic failure. I regret the picture couldn't have been made with people with a real passion for making it. It was a very unhappy experience for me. I did not enjoy knowing John Huston."

Wasserman also blamed the destruction of the movie on Anjelica's "ineptitude as an actress. She remains completely wooden and unbelievable throughout." Such comment would be echoed by the critics when the film was released. John Simon cruelly wrote, "There is a perfectly blank, supremely inept performance . . . by Huston's daughter, Anjelica, who has the face of an exhausted gnu, the voice of an unstrung tennis racket, and a figure of no describable shape." Charles Champlin knocked both Anjelica and Dayan, who "have the embarrassed stiffness of high schoolers performing before an audience for the very first time." But in the late 1980s the film was reassessed. *A Walk with Love and Death* would be called Huston's "most neglected movie," and its eclipse "undeserved." John would be praised for managing "to hold up a clear, sensible mirror to the turbulent, late sixties." And Anjelica would be called a "beautiful actress," the film "prophesies well the maturity of her later work in *Prizzi's Honor*."

In retrospect, Anjelica could appreciate the romantic idea of the film but found that even "knowing what I know now as opposed to my ignorance then, I don't know how differently I could have played the part." The only positive that came out of that movie was that she didn't become a successful teenage actress. "There's an advantage in not being successful as a child actor," she said. "Although one doesn't necessarily *invite* the whips and arrows, at the same time, I see very young people who become larger-than-life and whose careers literally last five years, and then it's 'Whatever happened to so-and-so?' I'm glad that pitfall was avoided . . . if there was ever any danger of that."

John realized that Anjelica wasn't ready to be an actress and wound up with mixed feelings about the project. "I feel I was very much at fault in making it," he conceded. "I made it under circumstances that I wouldn't repeat." But Anjelica wasn't completely disillusioned. "It didn't turn me away from acting," she said. "I wanted to act, I just wanted to do it *my* way. To do things because I wanted to do them."

What she found to do, after *Love and Death* was completed in October, was to understudy Marianne Faithful as Ophelia in Tony Richardson's stage production of *Hamlet.* "I very much wanted to play Ophelia," she said, "but didn't get it. Marianne wasn't very well, so I got to go on quite a bit, and I really loved playing that part."

While Anjelica was auditioning for Ophelia, Tony was accepted at London University. Ricki was relieved that Tony was going to continue his education, and she came around to accept that Anjelica was not and that she wanted to be an actress. "To prove that she wasn't jealous of her," Peter Menegas said, "Ricki organized Richard Avedon to photograph Anjelica. 'Being as Anjelica's involved with this anyway,' she said, 'we might as well really make her into a star and get her eight or ten pages in *Vogue.*' " Ricki had been touched by the Cartier watch Anjelica had bought her from some of the money she earned from the movie, and Menegas said there was a great rapport between them at the time. To her brother, Philip, Ricki had sent pictures and "glowing letters" after her return from visiting Anjelica in Vienna. "She was so proud of that child," Philip said, "and how beautiful she was, and she was so happy that John was finally coming through for her."

But then she went back to dwelling on her own life. Tony and Anjelica were almost grown; they could fend for themselves. John was out of her life, John Julius wasn't going to leave his wife and children, Peter Menegas was just a good friend. The house needed painting and she didn't have the money for it. She was thirty-nine years old with a four-year-old child and she had no direction for the second half of her life.

When her thoughts turned sour she began to think of the painter Morris Graves, who always seemed to bring her out of such funks. He was living in the woods in northern California and she decided to meet Dorothy Jeakins and drive up the coast to visit him.

She left Allegra with Nurse in October and flew directly to Los Angeles. "We packed up the car," remembered Jeakins, who was sixteen years older than Ricki, "and drove up to visit Morris Graves for a few days. I was almost old enough to be Ricki's mother, yet it wasn't a factor in our friendship. We could have been sisters." Ricki told Dorothy about her therapy and Jeakins felt that Ricki was going through a "heavy, depressing time. She was suicidal at times and I tried to talk her out of it. She just wanted to see her stable friends, Morris and me, before she went back." Ricki also stopped in New York to see her father and stepmother. She stayed with Joan Buck, who was then twenty and living in her uncle's large apartment.

Ricki's unhappiness turned to despair after she returned to London and received an anonymous letter from Italy saying that a photograph of a topless Anjelica was going to appear in a magazine. A friend who visited her at the time said Ricki burst into tears about it and was so distraught she couldn't stop weeping.

In November, John was in Berlin making a brief appearance as yet another lecherous old man, the Abbé de Sade, in an American-International production of *De Sade*. He returned to Ireland in December to prepare for the holidays and to continue working with Gladys on *The Kremlin Letter*. But the usually congenial holiday season lost its luster and turned tragic. On December 19, 1968, John lost a dear friend when John Steinbeck died. He was sixty-six, the same age as Walter when he died. Then, from Los Angeles, came the shocking news of the abduction and brutal murder of Cherokee's daughter Marina.

Marina had returned for the holidays from her first semester at the University of Hawaii. A few days after Christmas she went out with a friend. After midnight Cherokee heard Marina's car come screeching into her West Hollywood driveway. She got out of bed and looked through the window just as another car appeared. A man jumped out and forced Marina into his car. Panic-stricken, Cherokee called the police, who tried to calm her down, but her instincts made her howl like an animal. A few days later Marina's battered and sexually abused body was found in a ditch off Mulholland Drive.

"I was walking a very thin line trying to hold on to my sanity," Cherokee said. Unable to cope with her grief in California, she went to London to work like a robot among strangers in a public relations office.

*   *   *

A few days before Marina's death Ricki had thrown a huge Christmas party in London. She had spent a lot of time doing different things with her children, was proud of seeing Anjelica in *Hamlet,* and was very happy with a present John Julius had given her. "It was the best Christmas I've ever had!" she told Adrienne Kennedy.

Ricki also saw John at the Connaught Hotel in London. He was there with Gladys, getting ready to go to Helsinki and Rome for final preparations for *The Kremlin Letter.* She was nervous around John and they kept their conversation centered around the children. She didn't tell him about the sporty red four-door MG Jules and Joyce Buck had given her because she knew John would disapprove. Nor did she tell him of her plans to drive with Brian Anderson Thomas through France and into Italy, where she hoped to do some work on her father's villa near Milan and visit a mystical Hungarian artist in Venice named Monina who made amulets of semiprecious stones and bits of wood.

After Ricki left John spent an uncomfortable evening at the hotel. At three that morning Gladys Hill was awakened by a moaning she heard coming from Huston's room. She rushed down the hall and when she entered his suite she found him on the floor, gasping for air. She summoned a doctor, who said Huston's lung had collapsed. His need for oxygen in Vienna had been a warning. Now it was more serious. The doctor felt it was too risky to move him, so an oxygen tent and respiratory equipment were brought to the hotel. For the next few days Gladys took care of business as John swiftly improved. His ability to recover was nothing short of miraculous, and since the doctor had prohibited flying, he soon left for Rome by train and boat.

By the end of January Ricki, too, was ready for her trip. She phoned Adrienne Kennedy and told her, "I'm off to Italy and I'll be gone for ten days." She sounded happy, Kennedy thought.

Ricki and Brian took the same Channel ferry to the Continent that John and Gladys had taken earlier. She was in good spirits as they enjoyed the drive through France, playing some of the cassettes that Anjelica had prepared for them. But on January 29, at three P.M., just outside the town of Gray, twenty-five miles from Dijon, their car hit a pothole and swerved across the lane, crushing into an oncoming van. Thomas, who was driving, suffered facial lacerations and cracked ribs. Ricki took the full force of the collision and was instantly killed.

PART EIGHT

26

HARD TIMES

NEWS OF RICKI'S SUDDEN DEATH SPREAD QUICKLY. JOHN was in Rome, staying with Valeria and working with Carter De Haven on *The Kremlin Letter*. De Haven received a call from a London newspaper reporter who was trying to locate John for a comment. Then someone from 20th Century-Fox, who had heard it over the news, called as well. John was out driving with Valeria when De Haven found him. He pulled his car alongside Huston's and signaled to him. John smiled and said, "Oh, great, we'll have lunch."

"I've got to speak to you outside the car," De Haven said. The two men walked a few feet and De Haven told him that Ricki had been killed.

"Anybody else?" John asked.

"She seemed to be the only one. I'm really sorry."

"I am, too, kid," John said, showing no emotion as he got back into the car. As soon as they reached Valeria's house John made some calls, including one to his lawyer, who would make sure the accident didn't become a scandal, then packed his bags and caught a train to London. He still couldn't fly because of his lungs.

"John was quite upset," Valeria said, "and couldn't understand the mechanics of the accident."

Tony was in Ireland when he got the call, and though it was, by far, the most crushing blow of his life, his reaction was similar to John's. "It took me months to have any reaction whatsoever," he said. "It took the form of a great sort of coldness. I didn't weep or cry, it was almost too much for that."

Anjelica was awakened by Leslie Waddington from a dream she was having where her spine was being pulled out. "Ricki's dead," he said. She thought she was losing her mind.

"How did it hit me?" Anjelica said. "It *hit* me. My whole world collapsed. It changed my life. It changed my entire consciousness. I don't believe that I can ever really be shocked again. Barring the loss of a child, to be told that your very young parent is overnight dead almost takes you beyond the realms of sanity. It almost makes you crazy.

"I'd always considered the idea of my father dying—he had emphysema, he'd go riding and have falls, he drank—but my mother . . . I used to sit around with her and look in her jewel box and ask if she'd leave me things in her will. The idea of her dying never occurred to me. Only the idea that she would grow old and gray and be a grandmother."

Anjelica called Jeremy Railton, who had gone to California three months before to design costumes for a show called *Black Girl in Search of God.* "She was quietly crying," Railton remembered. Jeremy was at Western Costume Company in Hollywood when Anjelica reached him. Dorothy Jeakins was there also. She had been working on Mike Nichols's *Catch-22* and was there to costume Orson Welles. She said Gladys Hill had called to tell her. Railton and Jeakins hugged each other and cried. "Then Dorothy brought me a photograph," Jeremy said, "just of her eyes. Ricki's eyes were her. You looked at her eyes and you could float on forever."

Anjelica also called Cherokee, who was still suffering from her daughter's death the month before. "I couldn't believe what I was hearing," Cherokee remembered. "She said that Ricki had burned up in a car and she was with a black man. Anjel was sobbing and sobbing. I couldn't get through my own pain to answer. It was like I was in some kind of nightmare that was never ending."

Leslie Waddington told Joyce Buck, who called Jules, who was at a fat farm. "Christ," Joyce said, "Ricki has been killed." Joyce then called Joan in New York, reaching her at her desk in the fashion department of *Glamour* magazine. "I knew it was something terrible because of the tone of her voice," Joan recalled, "and I said, 'Is it Dad?' 'No, it's Ricki.' It was the most horrible thing I had heard in my life. I let out a huge scream. Then the phone on the next desk rang and it was Ricki's stepmother, Dorothy. Her first words were, 'Have you heard?' I said yes. She said, 'Who is Brian Anderson Thomas?' "

Joan didn't know, but Dorothy was determined to find out, because John had called her from Rome asking the same question. "The implication," Dorothy said, "was that he wanted to find him and shoot him. I'm sure he felt Ricki's death very keenly. Probably some feelings of guilt there." Both Dorothy and Tony Soma were in shock. "He just wilted," Dorothy said of Tony. They went for a long walk along Lexington Avenue and found themselves disoriented. "I didn't know where I was," Dorothy recalled. "I felt that I'd lost my best friend."

Tony Soma called Philip at three A.M. and Avril said it was the first time she had ever heard her husband cry. Philip, Tony, and Dorothy made plans to meet with Henry Hyde, who handled Ricki's estate, and then fly to London.

Dorothy said that when the police had come to Ricki's house after the accident, Nurse Kathleen Shine insisted that they were mistaken because, as far as Nurse knew, Ricki always flew to Italy. "Poor Nurse was just knocked off her pins," Dorothy said. "Ricki did not tell her she was driving, which was real naughty of her. After all, Nurse was in charge of the children. I think, in the end, Ricki just gave up. She didn't know what the hell to do with her life. I'm not saying she had a death wish, but she got *awfully* careless."

Peter Menegas was in the gym, holding a twenty-five-pound weight in each hand, when someone he knew said, "Did you hear, Ricki was killed?" Menegas stopped for a moment, then continued his workout in a state of shock. When he entered the sauna room he heard men talking about how John Huston's wife had been killed and felt he had to get out of there. He had completed the manuscript of his next book the previous night and remembered how he had felt "a strong physical presence" in his room, as if his flat was haunted. After he left the gym he went to deliver his book to his publisher, but he didn't stay. Instead, he got on the underground and headed for Maida Avenue. Then he wondered why he hadn't taken a taxi, so he got off the train, bought a French pastry, and caught a taxi. The pastry was sour and he threw it away. When he reached Ricki's house, Leslie Waddington answered the door. There were other people already there, and Peter began to cry.

Gina Metcalf was there and told Menegas that the night before she was at a dinner party and had to get up from the table to go out and vomit, for no particular reason. Adrienne Kennedy, who had heard about it from an actress who had been in one of her plays, asked, "Are they going to bring her body back?"

"There's nothing much to bring back," Metcalf answered. In fact, the French authorities hadn't found any identification on Ricki, and even though Thomas told them who she was, they didn't release her body for six days because of the French Cartier watch on her wrist. The watch Anjelica had given her.

Dirk Bogarde was making a movie in Spoleto, Italy, when a friend called at four A.M. to tell him what had happened. "It was a wretched time by any standards for terrible news," Bogarde said. "Ricki was dead. I'd never see those humorous eyes, the sadness beneath them almost concealed; I'd never see the idiotic daisy-chains, hear the laughter, discuss the latest book, play, ballet, or opera; never see her come in from a walk, muddy, wet, with the dogs. Life would go on, but never quite in the same way ever again."

On the plane to London Joan Buck kept thinking about how, the night before Ricki was killed, she was reading Ricki's favorite book, Jung's *Dreams, Memories and Reflections,* and in a dream that night she heard Jung's voice saying, "I'm going to tell you something and you're not going to like it." "No, no, no," Buck resisted. And when she awoke she found her clock had stopped. On her way to work that morning she bought a yogurt, but it was sweet and she threw it away. She thought of how, whenever Ricki walked into a restaurant, everybody stopped eating; and of the time she and Ricki had attended the premiere of a play her father had produced and how, on their way backstage, Ricki was saying, "One, two, three, *marvelous!* One, two, three, *fabulous!*" When they reached the actors' dressing rooms, they gushed "marvelous," "fabulous" without the "one, two, three," but Joan remembered how Ricki was "ironic about fawning, show business, heavy money premieres."

When she got to Ricki's house Anjelica was upstairs and Joan just moved in. "I slept at the foot of Anjel's bed and started cooking chickens and catered food, because that's all you can really do. It hurt me, in a strange way, because there was an avalanche of telegrams and letters for Anjelica and Tony and not for me. I'd open all this stuff and take the phone calls and I hated and despised the people who didn't know her well and who were suddenly getting in on this death with their telegrams."

Joan couldn't remember seeing John Julius at the house that week, but she would never forget how Gladys Hill arrived "and whipped the jewelry, the way you raid a safety-deposit box when somebody dies." Ricki had left no will, and Gladys was taking care of business, making sure Ricki's jewelry stayed in the family.

Tony and Anjelica went to Victoria Station to meet John's train. "He was devastated," Anjelica recalled. "I thought he was going to die. I don't remember sitting down and having any long talks. It seemed unnecessary. It's like if an atom bomb goes off, there's not a whole lot to talk about, and that's how it felt."

Two days before the Quaker service, which Gladys organized, Adrienne Kennedy and Gina Metcalf were sitting in Ricki's bedroom. Gina told Adrienne that Leslie Waddington was going to adopt Allegra. Ricki had once asked Waddington if he would be willing to take care of Allegra if anything ever happened to her. "She's not going to go with John Julius?" Kennedy asked. "John Julius doesn't want her," Metcalf replied.

Waddington said that he paid for Ricki's funeral expenses assuming he would be reimbursed by John, but it was a long time coming. "I was unable to recover this money and other expenses we incurred from

John's lawyers," Waddington said. "Eventually I got this money," but it was difficult for him to straighten matters out with John because "he was surrounded by a whole lot of acolytes."

It was only after Ricki's death that John first saw Allegra. Waddington said that "he was obviously enamored with the little plaything. I said to John that we would take over Allegra and this was all agreed." Peter Menegas said that Ricki wanted Allegra with Leslie because he had a house and a family. But other people were also interested in adopting her. Philip and Avril Soma thought that Allegra would be best served if she was brought up in their household. "She is six months younger than our second son and three years older than our daughter," Avril said, "she would have fit into our family perfectly." But just as Tony Soma wouldn't allow Ricki and Philip's aunt to raise them after their mother, Angelica, died, now it was Dorothy Soma who told Philip that Tony, Anjelica, and Allegra belonged together, even though Allegra was going to the Waddingtons'. "She was perfectly happy to have her adopted by someone in an art gallery," Philip Soma said bitterly.

Adrienne Kennedy remembered meeting John for the first time at Ricki's memorial service. "I had a good impression of him," she said. "He was standing near a card table, and when I walked in Anjelica came and hugged me. And she said, 'She's not gone, she's standing behind me.' She had never been that warm to me. Then John came up and said, 'I don't believe I've met you.' I couldn't believe it. I couldn't believe he'd be nice enough to do that."

Kennedy noticed that John, who seemed "awfully sad," sat near John Julius in the small room. "It was very good that John Julius was there," Joan Buck said. "It was also *dreadful* that he was there." Anne Selepegno had flown from Paris to attend the service, which John took as extremely thoughtful. Sam Spiegel and Jules Buck were also there. "Jules went up to extend his sympathies," Selepegno said, "and John just walked away from him." It was the first time John had seen Buck in three years. Another person said that they actually shook hands, but then John wiped his with a handkerchief.

The Somas never made it for the service. They were delayed by a combination of a severe snowstorm in New York and an airline strike that grounded all planes. Dorothy Soma said that Tony didn't want to go at first. "I thought maybe it would kill him," she said. "But he fought it, and he was always very proud of himself, that he did not crumble." Philip said that his father "wanted to see what had to be done with Allegra. He wanted to see Anjelica and Tony, but since he arrived after the service Tony wasn't there, and Anjelica was in a play." What Tony Soma also wanted, and got, were Ricki's ashes, to put on the mantel beside her mother's urn and to be buried with him when he died.

Peter Menegas was at the house when Dorothy Soma arrived. "She walked into the sitting room," he remembered, "and looked around and her eyebrows went up and you could see she was thinking, 'Ummm, there's lots of things in here I'd like to put my mark on.' "

"Ricki had furnished that house with a little bit of everything," Dorothy recalled. "When she was alive it was just fine. Without her presence to give those things meaning, it was absolute crap! I was surprised by my reaction." It was an observation Peter Menegas didn't find at all surprising. "The house looked like a junk shop," he concurred.

"It was as if everything had died," Anjelica said. "The entire house was lost, gone, finished. It is hard to describe what it is like when actual objects lose their lives. I went into her closet . . . all her beautiful Balenciagas I used to crave, it was as if they had gone limp. They didn't even smell like her anymore."

"January 29, 1969, was the cutoff date for happiness," Joan Buck said. When she returned to New York she phoned Richard Avedon, "because he was the only person I knew in New York who had been close to her. He had sort of a passion for her. He wanted to know about the memorial service and I went over to see him. He had a pile of these contact sheets with multiple photographs of Ricki in the house, and Anjelica, Tony, Nurse, and Allegra. He said to me, 'I want to give you one of these prints that I'm giving to the people who really loved her.' And he took one and said, 'Oh, no, this is a *good* one.' Then he found another and said, 'This is an early print. It's not as good as the others.' And it was written, 'To Tony, with love from Dick.' And he changed the 'Tony' to 'Joan.' I was appalled. And then he put it in an unlined envelope and sent me away. Of course, the first bit of wind that came along cracked the picture in two. I've never forgiven Richard Avedon for that."

After Ricki's death her friends seemed to scatter. "Ricki was kind of like a housemother . . . she liked being an umbrella for a certain kind," said Peter Menegas, who rented a house in Italy with Gina

Metcalf soon after Ricki died. Jeremy Railton joined Menegas in Rome. Adrienne Kennedy, before returning to New York, ran into Brian Anderson Thomas at a London theater. "He came up to me and put his arm around me and kissed me. I was baffled by that. I still didn't know that he was with Ricki when she was killed." Kennedy said that Anjelica became close to Thomas after Ricki's death, although Anjelica didn't remain in London long. *Hamlet* was going to tour the States and she decided to stay with it. Also, the publicity campaign for *A Walk with Love and Death* was cranking up and she had agreed to do what she could to promote it. "My instinct was to run as far as I could, as fast as I could," Anjelica said. "It actually saved my sanity after my mother was killed. I was very glad that I didn't have to stay in London. I was pretty vulnerable at the time."

Tony also packed his bags and took off, only his was a longer, more solitary journey. "I went to Australia," he said. "I had a friend there. I hitchhiked and took buses across the country. Then I went up through Indonesia, across to India, and got as far as Delhi. I was very low on money and had to get back because I was going to go to London University. I flew back from Delhi via Moscow, the cheapest way home."

In May, Joan Buck had another dream. She was in an antique shop with Ricki, who gave her a small heart and said, "This is mine, but I'd like you to keep it for a while." When she woke up that morning the phone rang. Anjelica was coming to New York and wanted to know if she could stay with her. Joan didn't tell her the dream but prepared a room for Ricki's little heart.

During the time *Hamlet* ran in New York, Anjelica would often go to Tony Soma's restaurant, where he would feed her steaks and spinach and tell her, "You think you're beautiful. Your mother was beautiful. You're very strong, very interesting, but not beautiful."

"My grandfather was like that," Anjelica said. "He was mad about us all, but he was outspoken and extremely voluble. He would say things like, 'There's no intelligence without a tongue.' Where that came from I never knew."

Anjelica's own ideas at the time were not as definite. Understudying Ophelia was a temporary job. Promoting a movie she wasn't happy about only underscored the difficulties of acting as a profession. So when *Harper's Bazaar* called and wanted to photograph her, she began to consider modeling as a career. She was seventeen, and Joan Buck had the perfect photographer.

"His name was Bob Richardson. I thought he was brilliant," Joan said. "He was about forty and was the spirit of the times. He once gave me a piece of brain coral and said, 'This is what you don't use enough.' All that symbolic sixties stuff. He was tall and slightly stooped; he didn't have any money and he had bad teeth. But he was the one photographer who should have been a movie director. His things were always mise-en-scène, always dramatic and weird and dark and change-able. I was thinking, 'I know who this guy has to meet. It's perfect!' So when the *Harper's Bazaar* thing came up, I said, 'Well, it has to be Bob Richardson or Anjelica won't do it.' So they met and, of course, they fell in love. And she lived with him from 1969 until 1973."

Anjelica described Richardson as "very tall, very brilliant. I worked with him a lot and we had a very good working relationship." They lived together for a month at the Chelsea Hotel, then moved to an apartment on Gramercy Park. As she got jobs as a photographer's model, they'd travel to Europe together, to Paris, London, Germany.

Joan Buck thought that Anjelica "went into the Richardson thing numb. After the shock of Ricki you don't even have to bother to rebel. The big criterion for me and Anjelica for years was: Would Ricki have liked him? And Bob was somebody who would have been in Ricki's living room." But the relationship wasn't an easy one. Richardson displayed certain dark qualities that Buck thought were similar to John's, "but he wasn't of John's calibre."

"It could be great," Anjelica said of their relationship, "just terrific, and then. . . . All would be well, then he would wake up in the morning and all would be hell."

Richardson wasn't liked by friends who knew Anjelica before Ricki died and she became, as Adrienne Kennedy described, "a different person." Peter Menegas had dinner with Anjelica and Richardson and found him being "snappish to her." Lizzie Spender remembered a lunch where Anjelica looked "quite frightening. Very black and thin and red lipstick, sort of sixties starved." And Jeremy Railton, Anjelica's closest confidant, kept asking her, "Who *is* this guy?" the first time they saw each other after Ricki's death.

"I was on my way to Italy," Railton said, "and I stopped in New York to see her. It was very tense. She just wanted to forget about what happened, and I kept bringing it up. Anjelica broke away from everybody from that era completely. Tony, too. They didn't want to have any-thing that reminded them of that time. It got so awful between us that Joan stepped in. I felt like I was being rejected and she thought that she was rejecting me but she couldn't help herself." Railton saw Richardson as "just another dominating male." When he saw them together in Paris he remembered that Richardson was "glowering" and Anjelica "got weird and ran off. He was real possessive and really kept her under."

With Anjelica in America (but before her involvement with Richardson), Tony in Australia, Allegra with Leslie Waddington in London, and Danny and Zoe in Rome, John prepared to begin *The Kremlin Letter* in Helsinki the last week of February. For a while he thought his next picture would be John Cheever's *Bullet Park*. After meeting with a not-too-sober Cheever in New York, it was optioned by Fox. Huston and Gladys wrote a screenplay, but Fox didn't think it good enough, so they dropped it and returned to *The Kremlin Letter*.

"It was a complicated picture logistically," De Haven recalled. "We built seventy sets—a monster to do. It required a big cast." Originally, De Haven had suggested Warren Beatty to play the American spy Rone, but Beatty turned it down and De Haven suggested Robert Redford. This time it was Richard Zanuck at Fox who said no. Redford had just completed a film that they didn't think was going to do much box office and he didn't want to have two Redford movies in the same year. (The film was *Butch Cassidy and the Sundance Kid.*) After losing Beatty and Redford, John told De Haven to hire an old friend of his, Patrick O'Neal. Once that was settled, John started filling in the other parts. "John always had a bevy of ideas for casting," De Haven said. Richard Boone was hired. George Sanders. Max von Sydow. Orson Welles. Bibi Andersson. Nigel Green. Michael MacLiammoir. And Huston agreed to play an admiral, the only character in the film who takes a stand against spying.

"When I read *The Kremlin Letter*," he said, "I was shocked at the cynicism we have all come to take for granted in everyday life today. The depravity and immorality expressed in the story hold up a reducing mirror to some of the more reprehensible aspects of the world we live in. The senseless violence and tasteless amorality that this story reveals stunned me." John thought *The Kremlin Letter*, coming soon after the assassinations of Martin Luther King and Robert Kennedy and the election of Richard Nixon as President of the United States, might just shake up a thinking audience. And as a mystery-spy drama, he also felt that it had the potential to be a popular, commercial success. "It was an amusing idea," he said, "of the old-fashioned spy brought back into service, who didn't hold with the computer approach to international intelligence, and whose motive was purely revenge."

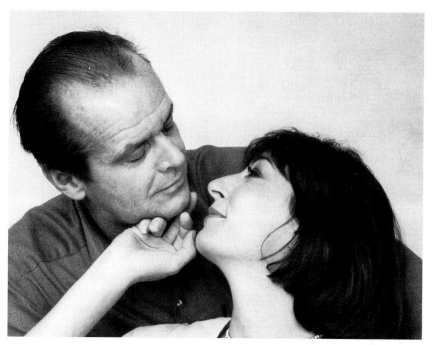

Jack Nicholson and Anjelica, 1985. (Photo © Harry Benson 1985)

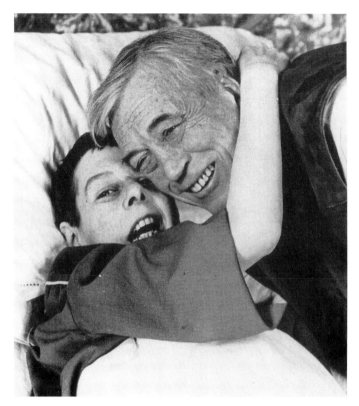

Carson McCullers and John, St. Clerans, Ireland, 1967. (Photo by
Irish Times. Courtesy of The Academy of Motion Picture Arts and
Sciences)

Nan Sunderland Huston and Montgomery Clift. Mid-1960s.
(Courtesy of Nan Sunderland estate)

From left: Gladys Hill, John, Valeria Alberti, mid-1960s. (Photo by Sam Shaw. Courtesy of The Academy of Motion Picture Arts and Sciences)

John with Billy Pearson on the set of *The Life and Times of Judge Roy Bean*, 1972. (Courtesy of The Academy of Motion Picture Arts and Sciences)

Cici. (Courtesy of Celeste Huston)

Las Caletas, Mexico. John's last home. (Photo by Stephanie Zimbalist)

John and Maricela Hernandez,
1973. (Courtesy of Celeste
Huston)

From left: Anjelica, Tony, John, Danny,
Allegra at Tony's wedding, 1978.

Tony (left) and Danny, 1987.
(Photo by Neil Jacobs)

Lawrence Grobel, John, 1986. (Photo by Larry Logan. Playboy Enterprises)

Pablo Huston Albarran, 1988. (Photo by Lawrence Grobel)

JH in wheelchair on the set of *The Dead*, 1987.

From left: Zoe, Allegra, Danny, John, Anjelica. John's last (eighty-first) birthday, August 5, 1987. In Rhode Island, during the filming of *Mr. North*. (Photo © 1987 by A. K. Roberts)

Anjelica and Jack Nicholson arriving at Hollywood Memorial Park for John's funeral, August 31, 1987. (Photo by Bob Halvorsen/*Los Angeles Daily News*)

(Photo by Maureen Lambray)

What fascinated De Haven about the story was that "it showed a side of both Russia and America that I'd never really focused in on. The secrecy, the brutality, the cooperation and all the things that probably have gone on between major powers forever but are never publicized. It was one of the few pictures that I've ever been involved with where I wanted to make a statement and be critical of the way the world is."

They shot for a month in Helsinki, then moved to Rome, where John saw a great deal of Valeria. "She was the closest person in his life," De Haven observed. "She was very Roman, with a great smile and an extraordinary heart." Orson Welles also came to Rome, after some tough negotiations, to earn his $50,000 fee as Bresnavitch, a high-ranking Soviet official whose smuggling activities lead to his being blackmailed into helping the American spies get out of Russia.

De Haven was impressed with what a quick study Welles was. A completely new scene had been given to him the night before it was to be shot, and by morning Welles had it down pat. "It was a long soliloquy," De Haven said. "He went straight to the set and didn't blow a line . . . unbelievable."

While Welles was on the set he told John about a movie he wanted to make called *The Other Side of the Wind*. It was about a director making a pornographic movie and would be Welles's comment on the movie industry. He hadn't yet written the script, but he wanted Huston to play the director. John said of course, and then didn't hear anything more about it for another year.

In Rome, De Haven heard twice from Richard Zanuck about *A Walk with Love and Death*. First came a telex, saying the film was not only beautiful, but a masterpiece. Then, after it was booed at a preview, he became worried and began suggesting changes. De Haven discussed it with John, who was beginning to tire of preview audiences altering his version of a movie, and the changes were made. It didn't help.

In June, Huston went to New York to complete *The Kremlin Letter* and see Anjelica. Lillian Ross described in a "Talk of the Town" piece for *The New Yorker* how delighted John was to be back in New York. A mini-skirted Anjelica joined them in a limousine ride through Central Park on their way to a location shot at the Museum of the Hispanic

Society of America. Ross reported "considerable rapport" between John and Anjelica.

John's friendship with Lillian Ross led to his often being featured in "Talk of the Town," in the front of the magazine. Unfortunately, toward the back, where movies were reviewed, Pauline Kael had the last word. The advertising for *The Kremlin Letter* warned viewers to be on time, "For, if you miss the first five minutes, you miss one suicide, two executions, one seduction, and the key to the plot." When Pauline Kael reviewed it, she added, "If you don't go at all, you can miss that and a lot more." William S. Pechter in *Commentary* used the picture to analyze Huston's fall from grace. "American directors are usually in and out of decline," he wrote, "but there are declines and declines, and Huston's is a prodigy: in the strict, classical purity of its prolonged downward movement, perhaps unrivaled even in the decline-crammed annals of the cinema."

Carter De Haven looked upon Huston as "the greatest teacher I've ever seen. He was never dull, always inquisitive, never stopped asking questions." De Haven was with him when John lunched with Ingmar Bergman, a director they both respected. But it was Bergman who kept asking the questions. He wanted to know about directing American actors. And he wanted to know about *Moby Dick* and how John was able to achieve certain shots. De Haven also remembered another occasion, just about the time *The Kremlin Letter* was completed, when he and John were in Italy. "It was one of the most extraordinary evenings I've ever spent," De Haven recalled, a dinner attended by Buckminster Fuller, Stephen Spender, Isamu Noguchi, and William de Kooning.

De Haven was in awe of Fuller's vision of the future and how he kept the table spellbound. And he was equally impressed with how everyone there wanted to hear from Huston. "I've never seen such art and power and intellect in one room, and yet they were always fascinated by John, always interested in what he was doing. Now, you don't have that mix of friends unless you make a contribution. And John kept up a constant correspondence with most of them."

While John was finishing *The Kremlin Letter* he received a letter from Leslie Waddington telling him about problems he was having concerning Allegra. It seemed that Nurse "could not accept that my wife was in charge of the house," Waddington said, "and so two households seemed to be developing in one." Waddington was also concerned that under English law, since neither he nor his wife was related to Allegra, "if anything happened to her medically, we would have been unable to instruct the doctor to operate."

After Tony returned from his travels he went to visit Nurse and Allegra and found them both "clearly unhappy. Leslie had very strange ideas about how to deal with children. He was a disciplinarian."

John didn't immediately respond to Waddington's letter, but after he returned to England he called and told Mrs. Waddington that he was going to take Allegra back. Waddington was out of the country on business and returned immediately, "but Nurse and Allegra left the next morning." Waddington never saw Allegra or spoke to John again and said that his memories of John's behavior "on this and many other matters are not good."

With the child now at St. Clerans, John began to think of who might best take care of her. He thought of Cherokee, and the tragedy she had gone through, and called her. "I've got Ricki's baby here," he said, "why don't you come stay here and help with the baby?"

Cherokee was appalled at his "one-upmanship—he'll take the baby," and screamed at him, "Never! You're so insensitive! You don't know anything!" It all seemed so wrong to her. "I just rejected that kind of incestuous life that went on at St. Clerans," she said.

Tony was with John at St. Clerans when Neil Armstrong walked on the moon in July 1969. Anjelica was also in Ireland, modeling for Richard Avedon for a thirty-page *Vogue* layout. "We were in Connemara when the astronauts landed," Anjelica recalled. "That was a very beautiful trip." When Ricki was alive Avedon had told her that he didn't think Anjelica could be a model because her shoulders were too big. But Diana Vreeland liked the way she looked, and off she went to Ireland.

That job led to others, and Anjelica was soon having to come to grips with her looks. "I had a big nose," she said. "I was still growing into my body. The idea of beauty for me was Jean Shrimpton—big blue eyes and little noses, wide bee-stung mouths. It was an odd dichotomy— and this happens to many girls who find themselves in front of the camera a lot, who truly don't like their looks. It's almost as though they can forget their looks in front of the camera. And I used to love working for the camera. But when faced with the reality of my pictures, I was generally deeply depressed.

"On the other hand, people talked about the way I looked. There was something about me that people wanted to see, but I wondered what it was." Avedon used her as a high-fashion model, but when she returned to the States she found that the other photographers didn't know what to do with her. "I was still considered very unusual for America," she said, "where Cheryl Tiegs and girls with big wide smiles were more the thing. I was not all that successful at getting advertising, where the money lies. So it was tough. Then I went to Europe and worked a lot there and returned with a real good book, having worked with Helmut Newton and a lot of very good European photographers."

She became a runway model when she was in England, when a few designers, like Halston, Giorgio di Sant'Angelo, and some of the Japanese fashion leaders, began using photographic models for their shows. "I loved doing shows, it was freeing. And you weren't working for the camera. They were often innovative, and it was fun being with the girls, driving in limos, drinking champagne. Great time. It wasn't hideously hard work at all."

While Anjelica was drinking champagne and walking down runways, John was appearing in three films while unsuccessfully trying to develop Joyce's *Portrait of the Artist as a Young Man*. The first was a brief role in Paramount's *The Deserter*. Then a more substantial but patently ridiculous part as the outrageous Hollywood cowboy and acting school owner Buck Loner in the campy movie send-up *Myra Breckinridge*, based on Gore Vidal's novel. Raquel Welch and critic Rex Reed also appeared in it, but what got the headlines was the return of Mae West, her first film in twenty-seven years. Huston saw it as "a well-paid lark." But the twenty-nine-year-old director, Michael Sarne, complained that Huston was an "old hack"; after that John dutifully completed his contractual obligations but offered the novice director no assistance.

Huston brought in the new decade by starring in *The Bridge in the Jungle*. The novel, by B. Traven, picked up where *The Treasure of the Sierra Madre* left off, following Walter's character Howard, the old prospector, as he lived among the Indians in Mexico. Paul Kohner's twenty-nine-year-old son, Pancho, somehow managed to convince Traven that he wouldn't bring in a screenwriter but would just film the book. He offered Traven $50,000 and obtained the rights.

Pancho then bought a book on screenwriting, and began working on the script himself. He convinced David Picker at United Artists that he could make the movie with Huston starring in it, and suggested himself as the director. To his surprise he was given a go-ahead. UA agreed to put up half the money. His budget for the entire project was $283,000, which included the money that went to Traven.

John had agreed to star in the picture free because of his long association with Paul Kohner. And because it would give him a chance to spend a few months in Mexico. But John didn't like Pancho's script and told him so.

Pancho tried to change the script, but when he couldn't get past the censors he went to John and offered to excuse him from the film. "No," John said, "I'll do it your way."

Before Pancho began *The Bridge in the Jungle* he asked Ingmar Bergman and Mel Frank if they had any advice for him as a first-time director. Bergman said, "Don't commit suicide after the second day; just later on reshoot those first two days." And Mel Frank said, "I've only three things to tell you: Don't screw your leading lady, don't screw your leading lady, and don't screw your leading lady." Pancho didn't remember asking John for advice, but John said he gave him some anyway: "not to do it."

On Pancho's first day on the set, before Huston got there, he announced to the crew that it was his first directorial job and he didn't know what he was doing and would they please bear with him. Five days later John arrived. Pancho had worried that John wouldn't want to play his role the same way Walter had played the old man. "I made an effort to make it different," he said, "but when he got on the set John turned into his father, doing the same rapid clipped speech, the same mannerisms, he even danced a little jig!"

Paul Kohner, who had helped secure new financing when the other half of the money had fallen through, flew down to watch his son direct. "I had asked John to do me a favor and help Pancho," Kohner said. "John said, 'Paul, I'm an actor in this film. If he asks me, I'll help him.' "

As Kohner watched Pancho trying to do everything, he encouraged him to seek John's advice, but Pancho told him, "If I ask John to help me, everybody will know and I will lose all my authority and their respect. I cannot do that. He's got to act the way I tell him to."

The Bridge in the Jungle would never be released and Pancho would end up showing it at festivals and on special occasions honoring Huston, but John didn't seem to mind. It was an enjoyable two months in the jungles of Mexico. He saw old friends, including Billy Pearson, who flew down for a weekend, hired every marimba band in the nearby town, transported them on flatbed trucks to John's hotel, and had them play one song all night long. For a while it was Paris in the fifties all over again, with John and Billy entertaining each other with stories that brought tears to their eyes.

The tears in Tony's eyes over in England were of a more melancholic kind. With Ricki dead, Anjelica living with her boyfriend in New York, and John off acting in pictures, Tony felt an even greater isolation at London University than he did at Westminster. When John returned from Mexico and heard about Tony's unhappiness, he thought that perhaps college wasn't where he belonged. For years he had considered making a film based on some of Buckminster Fuller's ideas, and it occurred to him that Tony might be better off working for Fuller than continuing at the university. Fuller was a university unto himself, and Tony would benefit from being around such a mind. He suggested to Fuller that Tony act as liaison between them and Fuller agreed. Tony's formal education was over.

"Bucky had this different viewpoint of world history," Tony recalled. "We have always considered it from the point of view of men on the land, but his interpretation was of men from the sea. Bucky's version of the Garden of Eden was completely different from the conventional one, and it made a great deal more sense.

"I originally went with Bucky to see if there was a film in his ideas. I did a lot of research on that and most of what I worked on came out subsequently in Bucky's books, but it never became a picture."

Tony was grateful to John for bringing him together with Fuller. Of all the people he met through his father, Fuller was the most remarkable. "Without a doubt. The only truly great man I've ever met, in all respects. Bucky had an absence of vanity. If you said something provoking, he would look at you and you would feel shame. It would almost be like if you hit a child."

Tony spent six months on the American college circuit with Fuller, listening to his ideas, reading his works, transcribing his tapes, and when he left, it was to join John on his next picture, *The Last Run*. The script, written by Alan Sharp, was a chase story about an escaped convict, driven across Spain by a retired gangster who is one of the most wanted men in Spain, pursued by both the mob and the police. George C. Scott, coming off his dynamic portrayal of Patton, had agreed to make this his next movie. Carter De Haven saw it as a Bogart kind of picture. "It was very Hemingway in its approach—about a man's last point of redemption. It was the right age for George, and he was suited for it physically."

Scott chose John to direct. Remembering how he had acted like a cad with Ava Gardner during the filming of *The Bible*, Scott had appreciated John's understanding and told De Haven, "John practically saved my life. I'd do anything for him."

Robert Littman, the thirty-two-year-old managing director of European production for MGM, was excited when Huston's name was suggested. "I thought *The Last Run* could have been the sort of Huston of *Treasure of the Sierra Madre*," he said. Carter De Haven brought Sharp's script to Huston at the Connaught Hotel in London where he was staying and he read it that night. "It's a natural," he told De Haven the next day. "I don't want to change a word, I love it. There may be a couple of areas we should discuss when we get into it." He thought Scott was perfect casting and everyone seemed delighted to have the hottest actor in the world and the director who they all hoped would return to his early, legendary form.

The picture was set to begin on January 4, 1971, and Littman began to worry on New Year's Eve, when Huston had still not turned up in Alhambra, Spain. "John arrived the night before principal photography began," Littman said. "He'd never seen the sets, which was disconcerting. But I thought, 'What do I know?' Was I going to argue with the great master?"

John had come down with Gladys, and Tony soon joined them. Stephen Grimes was the set designer. Ingmar Bergman's cinematographer, Sven Nykvist, was the cameraman. As soon as he was settled John set to work revising the script with Gladys. Tony was also asked for his ideas once he voiced the opinion that the original script wasn't very good. "The influence of *Easy Rider* was around," he said, "and there was an idea that you could make a kind of loose, drifty picture. Now this wasn't Dad at all."

Robert Littman said Sharp's script was an "explicit, sexually violent film," and was under the impression that "Tony was rewriting the script every night, so that the film John was shooting had absolutely nothing to do with the film we intended to make." Carter De Haven thought that John and Gladys were doing the nightly rewrites, although he, too, suspected Tony was involved. "I think that John wanted to give Tony a chance." But Tony said that he didn't write very much. "In actual fact, it was Dad and Gladys, ninety-nine percent." According to Gladys Hill's diary, Robert Littman thought the first seventy-four pages that she and John had rewritten were "simply marvelous."

By the second week of shooting Scott got sick and production came to a halt for a few days. John approached Scott and asked if there was anything troubling him. Scott said he was completely happy with the way things were going. The following week, however, Scott got drunk and began complaining about certain scenes, but his complaints didn't reach John on the set. Scott told him, "You're the boss and anything you say goes." And to his driver, Scott said, "Huston's the greatest man who ever lived."

But that certainly wasn't what Scott was feeling or thinking. He was upset with Tina Aumont, the actress who played his love interest, and wanted her replaced because, he told De Haven, her eyes weren't working. He was even more upset with the rewritten script, which, he said, was not the script he had agreed to play.

Tony Huston, who said that Scott had his uniforms from *Patton* sent over and would parade around in them during the evening, thought that the real problem was between Scott and John. "I'd seen Scott and Dad over the years . . . there was some sort of strange chemistry there. I don't think it was the script; there was something else cooking between them. Dad said that he thought George C. Scott was a coward. To Dad, this was like seeing a flaw going right through the spirit of a man. And for this reason, Scott drinks. Whenever Scott was around Dad on a picture, you would end up with Scott drinking and trouble."

John would later write to Paul Kohner that Scott's agent "had tears in her eyes and apologized for his holding up production and she assured me that we would lose no time because of him. Scott's second flyer came three days later. He missed another day's work on this occasion."

Scott's third alcoholic binge was the one that De Haven most remembered. At two-thirty one morning Scott woke De Haven and started to rant. "I just want to tell you that I've had it, I can't do this fucking script! I've chartered a plane to take me to Madrid and I'm going home." De Haven rubbed the sleep from his eyes and attempted to calm Scott down. "It looked to me like he'd been crying," De Haven said.

"George," said De Haven, "don't be a quitter. Are you willing to talk about it?"

"Of course," Scott said. "But it's not going to do any good. He's more stubborn than I am."

De Haven called Huston and woke him up. John came right over. "John was in total control of himself," De Haven remembered, "and he was absolutely convinced that what he was doing was right. I said,

'Look, John, you agreed to do this script, as George and I did. Why can't we just make the picture that we have in the six weeks left to go?' "

"I want to make it a better picture," John said.

"A better picture!" Scott bellowed. "Jesus Christ, we're going to be ruined."

And then Scott did something that shocked De Haven. John had been sitting in a wingback chair and Scott had been pacing the room like a panther when he suddenly dropped to his knees beside Huston and grabbed him. "John, you can't do this. Not to yourself, not to me!"

"Scott was *pleading* with him," De Haven said. "I'd never seen that before."

"George," John said, "the pages that I've written, and what I want to do, I think are right. But I will discuss all these scenes with you much more than we have before, which will help everybody understand what I'm trying to get. And where there are areas of real opposite poles, I'm afraid I am going to have to make the picture that I believe is right."

"That's a *wonderful* way to approach each day's work," said De Haven, hoping the crisis was solved. It was five in the morning and Scott agreed to be on the set for his eight A.M. call. He appeared and when De Haven asked him how he was, he answered, "I've had better mornings, but I'm ready."

That afternoon, though, Scott told De Haven, "It's not going to work. I'm not doing this movie."

De Haven went to see Huston at his hotel. "We can't all be wrong, John," De Haven said. "George can't be one hundred percent wrong, I can't be one hundred percent wrong, the studio can't be one hundred percent wrong. We need a little bit of a compromise." John answered, "I can't. You'd better trust me here and it will be just fine."

"De Haven was caught in the middle," Tony observed. "Everybody except Dad detested him. Carter was always trying to pull fast ones. Over the years you got used to seeing these eager young men who kind of snowballed Dad, and for five minutes they were the greatest thing around. And then, like Carter, something goes seriously wrong and we don't talk to them again. There was an opportunity to stand by Dad and say, 'If John goes, I go, too.' But that didn't happen."

De Haven said that he had "many, many hours of personal debate as to whether I should leave or stay with the picture. I decided that the right thing was not to be a quitter, because I disagreed with what John was doing one hundred percent.

"John was intractable. Scott wanted to quit, and MGM had two and a half million bucks in it. You had to take that seriously." De Haven felt he had no choice but to summon Robert Littman from London. De Haven showed him the dailies and Littman saw that "the three weeks of shooting had very, very little to do with the screenplay that we'd approved and developed. There were scenes that were already anachronistic from the sixties." Littman went to see Scott, who "was considerably inebriated."

"You don't have to worry about the way I'm drinking brandy," Scott had told him just before filming started. "If you see me with a glass of vodka in my hand, you can get excited." Scott was now drinking vodka. It had boiled down to him or John.

When Littman returned to De Haven's room after talking to the home office he said that if John didn't agree to return to the original script, he'd have to be fired. De Haven offered to go with Littman to see John, but Littman felt "cocky and full of himself" and said he'd go alone.

By this time John had had a phone conversation with Paul Kohner, who told him it would be costly if he quit. "Don't you ever say you are going to quit," Kohner said. "Just say you're sorry you cannot do it."

John told him not to worry. But then Littman, with his youth, his arrogance, his walrus mustache, came into John's room and started talking about Scott's anger, about how John had to make the film they had all agreed upon. "I'll tell you what I'll do," John finally said. "You come to the set every morning and tell me where to put the camera, what lines the actors should read, tell them how to do it, and I'll be very happy to direct under your direction."

"That's ludicrous," Littman protested.

"Is it now?"

"You're the director. It's your job to do all that. You just have to do the script *we* want to make."

"What if I refuse?" John said.

"Then you've put me in a very embarrassing position," Littman stammered, "of having to fire a living legend."

"In that case," John smiled, "I withdraw."

"Cost him $150,000!" Paul Kohner said in dismay. "I had warned him to keep his mouth shut and they'd have had to pay him off." But John just couldn't let a guy like Littman have the last word.

"Littman came back with his tail between his legs," De Haven remembered.

On January 27 at 12:30 A.M., Carter De Haven and George C. Scott called the cast and crew together to inform them that production would be shut down for a few days until a new director was hired to replace Huston. Scott said that he had worked with Huston before and that there was no director he respected more. "God help me, I had to make a decision. I dumped John Huston."

As Scott's words were translated into Spanish, the crew seemed stunned. To Stephen Grimes, Scott said he resented having to do a script that was being rewritten by "a maiden lady and an adolescent boy." Grimes decided to quit, but John didn't want a mass defection and the next day he met with everyone connected with the picture at the Palace Hotel.

"In this vast room, with a huge walk-in fireplace and all these Castillian flags along the walls, John sat in a hand-carved wooden throne, wearing a black cape," Littman recalled. "One by one, with their caps in their hands, the Spanish crew walked through the hallway into the throne room. It was almost as though they were kissing the pope's hand and receiving benediction. He said good-bye to each one of them. He behaved like a God."

"It was incredibly emotional," Tony Huston said. "There were these great scenes with people weeping. This was the first picture that he'd been fired off during filming."

"I remember the whole very painful, ugly occasion," John said, "and I have no use for Scott as a result. Carter is an uninformed person. His judgment was of no particular value. Nor was Scott's, for that matter. The things that I advised doing were excellent. I don't know whether they'd have saved the picture, but they would have made a hell of a lot better picture out of it than it was."

Huston, Gladys, Tony, and Stephen Grimes traveled by car to Malaga. After Grimes left, Valeria Alberti joined them for a week's cooling-off in Morocco. "Our march through Morocco was at full tilt," Tony said. "We went a few days to Tangiers, then to Fez. It was a lightning tour."

Throughout Morocco John was thinking about how he had been exploited and began to feel bitter about his situation. For the first time in his career he was having doubts about his life and whether he would be able to continue to support not only himself but all those who depended upon him. Tony left after they returned to Madrid and Valeria tried to raise his spirits. But just as he was feeling it was all over for him, he was asked to act in a movie to be shot in Spain called *Man in the Wilderness.* It was a story of survival and revenge, about a trapper mauled by a grizzly bear and left to die by the captain of his expedition. Richard Harris was cast as the long-suffering man. John was offered $40,000 to play the part of the eccentric, sadistic captain. After he read the script he met with the forty-year-old director, Richard Sarafian.

"I was scared to death, intimidated being around him at first," Sarafian said. "He was my hero." John told him he liked the script and the part. "He had a marvelous understanding of the character," Sarafian said, "saw him a lot more clearly than I did." Sarafian saw the story of a trapper left behind to suffer and die as allegorical. "It was about Job," he said.

John liked Sarafian and over a game of backgammon he began to give him some advice. "On all the films I've ever done," he said, "I've always done my best. However, there have been times when my reason for doing a film hasn't been absolutely pure. And in those instances I could see the whole thing crumble before my very eyes. My advice is to get your family set up and get that out of the way and then get on with the job."

One day, Sarafian remembered, Sam Spiegel appeared to talk with John. Since they had dissolved their partnership after *The African Queen,* John had only seen Spiegel once, at Ricki's memorial service, and they hadn't really talked. Spiegel had become a rich man and he thought that perhaps the time was right for them to bury the past and work together again. Sarafian recalled how Spiegel attempted to seduce Huston over dinner. "Spiegel wanted to know when he would be available again." But John was far too proud to go back into business with him.

Instead, John immersed himself in the role of the demented Captain Henry, making suggestions to Sarafian when he thought it appropriate. Richard Harris refused to do the last shot of the movie the way Sarafian designed it and John came to his aid. "Why don't you just end up on the shot of the boat?" he offered. "Think of the purity."

Sarafian used the shot and was thankful that John had held up throughout the grueling filming, remembering how he often heard John coughing at night, and how Valeria was there for him. "She seemed to be a bit matronly, but she projected a tremendous warmth," he said. "And she cared for him."

While their friendship would continue, the intimate relationship between John and Valeria ended in 1971. She was with him when his friendship with Jules Buck came to a dramatic end, when his health began to fail, when he heard of Ricki's death. She had spent a lot of time with him in Rome, and also at St. Clerans; she experienced his cruelty and his generosity, and she came away believing that he was a magician. "John was the number one in the tarot cards," she said, "the *bagatto* card, which can be interpreted as the magician or the player. And all magicians are players. He was the master of magicians."

27

TAKING THE FIFTH

MAN IN THE WILDERNESS HAD GIVEN JOHN SOME TIME TO recharge. "It was a chance for him to get back inside of himself," Richard Sarafian believed, "to rebuild and get his strength back." Huston had been developing a project with Ray Stark about two down-and-out small-time boxers, one hoping to come up, the other to come back. *Fat City*, a novel written by Leonard Gardner, captured the gritty, low-down world of boxing. "It's about people who are beaten before they start but who never stop dreaming," John said. When Stark first approached him about it, Huston saw it, once again, as a perfect vehicle for Marlon Brando. The two men went to see Brando, who was in London, but Brando was involved in causes then and wouldn't commit.

"Then," John said, "in Spain, they were shooting a picture about Doc Holliday and Wyatt Earp with a young actor, Stacy Keach. I went over to see him and was shown some film on him. I was very impressed."

Keach, who was twenty-nine when John showed up on the set in Madrid, was aware of John's sliding reputation, but it didn't tarnish his legend. "I just felt he was going through a period that every artist goes through sometime or another," Keach said. "He came with an offer in hand and was very excited about *Fat City.* Particularly because he had experiences himself as a boxer."

Keach was signed to play Billy Tully, the older fighter. Huston heard about an actor Burgess Meredith had recently directed in *The Yin and Yang of Mr. Go.* Jeff Bridges had also appeared in *The Last Picture Show,* and Huston thought he might be right for the younger fighter, Ernie Munger. "It was one of the most unusual interviews I ever had in my life," Bridges recalled. "My agent called and said Huston wanted to see me and I said great and he said the interview was in Madrid. So I went over there, and that night, while I'm pulling into this hotel, I met this girl in the lobby who proceeded to take me out on the town. We had a *great* night. Drank too much, ate too much. I woke up the next morning feeling strange. I had been food poisoned. Didn't even get laid!

"Coming on with this sickness, I had this interview, which was to be at the Prado. I met John there and he gave me a tour, showed me all his favorite paintings, and never once spoke about the movie. I never even had the sense that he was checking me out. And all the time I was praying to God that I wouldn't puke on him.

"The next morning I got a call from my agent saying, 'Congratulations, you got the job.' And I was saying, 'Great. If I live.' "

John saw *Fat City* as a picture "about hope and failure, great misery alongside great wealth." It was his first American film since *The Misfits* eleven years before. What John wanted was the look, the smell, the feel of those dank, depressed towns to which fighters traveled in order to beat their brains out in front of drunken, boisterous crowds. He found exactly what he was looking for in California, on Stockton's skid row.

"I always had the feeling that there was the hand of somebody very special on the pulse of that film," said Stacy Keach, who considered it the best work he ever did. "I learned so much about not only acting but also directing. He was used to being an actor, so he knew actors and let them find their way. Then he would point the camera."

John "never intellectualized about motivation," according to Keach, "or about objectives. He worked with actors the way a conductor works with a great orchestra. There was nobody like him."

For the fight scenes between Keach and the Mexican fighter Lucero, played by Sixto Rodriguez, a one-time light-heavyweight contender, Keach worked with José Torres carefully staging the bout, but when it came time to film it, Huston said, "All right boys, now we're just going to have two minutes of boxing. Just go out there and fight!"

The direction surprised Keach, and he wondered if this was one of those practical jokes he had heard Huston loved to play, or perhaps it was "that quasi-sadistic element that people told about John." Huston said that he wanted Keach to fight, but that he fully expected Rodriguez to hold back.

But tell that to Keach. "Every time I would hit this guy," he remembered, "he couldn't help it, his left hand would come out and he really got me good. That shot is in the film. There's nothing fake about it, when I go down to the mat, it's real!"

The singer Judy Collins was Keach's girlfriend at the time, and as she watched her man being pounded, Huston patted her on the shoulder and said, "It's only a movie, my dear."

Jeff Bridges also had to fight in the movie and shuddered whenever John would tease him: "We're going to put you in a fight with some *real* guys and see how you do." And when his fight scene was filmed, he, too, got nailed. "I got cut," Bridges said, "real blood was coming out."

Knowing Huston's need for a diversion when not filming, Ray Stark worried that John would get bored in Stockton. "The only entertainment was women's roller derby every Friday night," Stark recalled. But John managed. Stacy Keach said that Stark would often run movies after dinner, and one night he showed *The Battle of San Pietro* and *Let There Be Light*. Afterward John talked for hours about them.

When they weren't watching movies or going to the roller derby, John would play pool or backgammon with Keach. "He taught me how to play backgammon," Keach said, "and he'd beat me badly, too. We used to play it all the time between takes until Ray Stark grew upset because we were way behind schedule. He took it away from us, like two kids. And when we played pool, he was very good. He was an incredible competitor."

Keach remembered one time when John was asked to be a judge at one of the boxing matches at the Stockton Civic Center. "It involved one of the club fighters who was in our film," Keach said. "They were three-round matches. I'll never forget, this one kid got up and he clearly, absolutely, no question lost—hands down. And John cast the deciding vote, so he won. There was a series of boos. But John was very partial to his own." Said John: "I always wanted to be a crooked judge."

As she had on many of his other films, Nan Huston came to Stockton to watch John work. John was always kind and polite to his stepmother, although by this time she was deeply involved in her Christian Science beliefs; no matter how sick she was she refused any medical attention. "Poor woman," John said, "her mind was gone. Her behavior became worse and worse until she really went off the deep end. Yet I felt responsible about her. My father had invested a hell of a lot in her."

John also wasn't well during *Fat City*, and often had to use an oxygen tank to help him breathe. Yet he continued to smoke his cigars each day and cough himself to sleep at night. Jeff Bridges remembered how Ray Stark would sometimes pamper John. But Stark also was worried about the look of the film. He thought it was too grainy and washed out. John and Conrad Hall, the cinematographer, wanted that gritty look, the kind that hits you like sunlight after coming out of a dim bar. "The picture was supposed to look poor," John said, "but not seedy. There's a big difference between photographing a hovel so it looks to be a hovel and doing it so it looks like bad photography."

Jeff Bridges thought that Hall "shot his ass off for that movie. The look was just incredible! John Huston had his stamp on it." Dorothy Jeakins, who designed the costumes, also had a hand in the look of the picture. "I tried to use very bright, sort of Filipino colors on the men," she said, "the fighters and the little bar that they went to." Jeakins thought John was making a small classic and observed his attention to details.

For John, making *Fat City* was like a return in his mind to the days when he wasn't hampered by a nagging cough and didn't need oxygen in order to breathe deeply. It wasn't a depressing film about life's losers but rather a swan song to his own glorious youth, to the days when all that mattered was getting into the ring to show what you had, of being, for however short a time, the very best that you could be.

At the end of the picture there was a scene with Jeff Bridges and Stacy Keach in a cafe, when Keach turns and sees men playing cards. For both Keach and Bridges it became a Huston moment to treasure. "It was one of those calls, report to the set at two A.M.," Bridges said. "It was an actual location. John was there with his oxygen tank—he looked like he was asleep or dead. Nobody had the balls to go to him and say, 'We're ready, Mr. Huston.' All of a sudden his eyes bolted open and he said, 'I've got it. Have you ever been at a party when for no reason everybody just stops? When all of a sudden it's all a tableau;

you're alone in eternity for a moment? When Stacy turns around, I want everybody to just stop what they're doing.' "

"Why, John?" Keach asked.

"I have no idea," Huston answered. "Sometimes the devil just gets into me."

"We can just freeze frame," Russ Saunders, the assistant director, suggested.

"No, no, no," John said. "I want the cigarette smoke to continue going. I don't want it to look like a stock frame. I just want everybody to stop."

Keach saw it as "brilliant. Time stops for a moment." And Bridges said, "Everybody thought he was in a trance, receiving messages from God knows where. Seeing him in such a feeble way, and then having him spring to life like that with a great idea. It was memorable."

In that scene John did what he often did, he turned away from the actors, so he could concentrate on what they were saying. "I was standing behind them where I couldn't see the close-ups," John said. "I could tell by their voices if it was right."

"That was the only argument I ever had with John in my life," Stark recalled. "Stacy Keach was talking to an old Chinese guy and John wasn't looking at them. I noticed about four takes, which was more than John usually made. Then I finally said, 'C'mon John, let's get off our ass. Will you turn around and let's get this thing done.' And he just blew up at me. He was listening to what they said, which was more important than watching them, which I didn't understand."

After the film was cut Stacy Keach was disappointed that two key scenes were missing. "What's been cut was when Billy was at the top, when he was the champ. It was a flashback. And there's a whole twenty minutes of film of the downward spiral of Tully after he wins the fight and doesn't get the money that's missing. He goes back to the boardinghouse, they throw him out, he almost gets knifed in the rain by a guy in the city; he ends up having to sleep in an incinerator, where he's kicked out by this old Chinese guy. You see him just go down, down, down. I was devastated when all that was taken out. That was a decision that Ray Stark and editor Maggie Booth made. Ray said, 'It's a downer picture as it is, if it goes any farther down, it's going to make it worse.' " Keach didn't agree. "The movie would have *really* been a great film if you had a chance to see him hit the real bottom. But John thought it was a decision that was made for the best."

"Ray and I saw a cut of the picture in Phoenix," John said. "Dr. and Mrs. Loyal Davis came to see it. I was so aware of the words *shit* and *piss* that were in the picture that I was embarrassed. So we both decided that a number of cuts were required."

While *Fat City* was being cut, John began preparations for his next film, an outrageous western about Judge Roy Bean, which was written by a gifted young screenwriter named John Milius, who had also written *Dirty Harry* and *Jeremiah Johnson*. The script of *The Life and Times of Judge Roy Bean* attracted Huston because it reminded him of the stories his grandmother used to tell him about John Gore during his wild years when he was a drunken judge and a sober saloon owner in the Oklahoma Territories.

In Los Angeles, John visited Cherokee and her new husband, Paul MacNamara, who was in public relations. John joined them at a wedding of some older friends and when she looked at John and her husband, "I saw that these two Irish bastards were crying. When we got John home he was drunk and Mac was sympathizing with him: 'Yes, that's the way to get married, to somebody you really know.' And John said, 'I want to get married, I want this same kind of situation.' I said, 'Okay, John, if you want to get married, I'm going to pass these dames through here.' "

One of those "dames" came to a dinner party at the MacNamaras'. Her name was Celeste Shane. Everyone called her Cici. She was thirty-one and had recently been divorced from an eight-year marriage to her childhood sweetheart, screenwriter Wally Green. Her father had made his fortune in the car leasing business, and she and her three brothers had a privileged childhood. She lived in the Pacific Palisades and had a passion for horses, which she raised. "I was on my way out when in walked this man," she remembered. "I just saw an aura around him, I swear. And I said to myself, I'm going to marry him. I didn't even know who he was.

"I came back to the party and sat next to him. We yapped all evening about wolves, because I had raised one and he was very excited about it. Anyone who can discuss horses and wolves with me, that was just it. It was the first time I forgot my ex-husband for more than twenty minutes. So, we kind of flirted. But I didn't hear from him. A friend said, 'You have to pursue him.' So I called him and he came over."

John was attracted to her youth, her love of horses, her unconventional manner, and her sensuality.

"My friend had dressed me in these really tight chaps and this hot top," Cici remembered about John's first visit. "I was down by the stalls working with the horses. I had a saddle thrown over the door and he picked the saddle up and said, 'Is there anything I can do for you, Ma'am?' Again, there was this aura. So then we walked through the jungle near my house and he said, 'How would you like to come to Arizona?' 'Would I!' I said."

John Milius had hoped to direct *Judge Roy Bean*, but Paul Newman and producer John Foreman wanted Huston. Milius didn't object to Huston as a director. Indeed, he thought that Huston tried hard to make his films "unusual. He wasn't a mainstream filmmaker. He was always exploring areas that were interesting. He lived this great wild life. It's that old thing that Oscar Wilde said: 'My talent for my work, but my genius for my life.' That's what happened to Huston. His genius was really for his life. He would sort of entertain himself with work. But his life had a shape and style, and there is something to be said for that. People's lives have no shape anymore."

Milius considered *Roy Bean* the best script he'd ever written, but felt that Huston "ruined it, because I don't think he was terribly interested in making the movie." He blamed Newman and Foreman for wanting to make the picture another *Butch Cassidy and the Sundance Kid.* "They wanted a Beverly Hills western," he said. "It should have been a very gritty kind of Sergio Leone–looking film. Instead it became a caricature. My script had a much tougher, harder tone to it. The judge was like Patton. In this, the judge is cute."

Huston didn't disagree with some of Milius's criticisms, but he told Victoria Principal, who was cast in her first picture as the judge's young Mexican common-law wife, that he wanted to make "a turd smell sweet."

"He thought my script was a turd?" Milius exploded when he heard the remark. "Jesus! The script he started with was absolutely terrific."

Judge Roy Bean was an outrageous figure who was obsessed with a love for Lillie Langtry, a performer he had never met. Huston never saw him as seriously as Milius wrote him, and when Huston asked for rewrites, Milius often balked. "He would threaten to get Miss Hill to write it if I didn't," Milius recalled. "So I was blackmailed. I hated what was happening to the film, but I stayed and it was a very good thing for me. When Huston realized I was going to stick around no matter what, he stopped arguing with me so much. He'd just say, 'I'm going to do it this way.' But he started telling me about directing, because he knew that I wanted to be a director."

"Milius's macho never disturbed me," Huston said. "I liked him. I always felt like indulging him, going along into his fantasies."

Milius, who would go on to direct films like *The Wind and the Lion, Conan the Barbarian, Red Dawn,* and *Farewell to the King,* conceded that Huston taught him a lot about directing. One of the things he emphasized was that "people are basically characters. What you want to do is try to get that up there on the screen. There really is no more to it." Huston also told him, "Never raise your voice, never get excited on the set. First, it looks really bad for the crew; second, the actors can see that you can get angry; and third, it takes a lot of energy. Always sit down when there's a scene. Remember that you are trying to conserve energy, because you've got to have more than anyone else."

Milius listened, and rewrote, and brought John his "water" when they got back to his trailer. "I took a sip of it and it was straight vodka. He'd drink it and then say, 'Now bring me my vodka.' He really taught me the *spirit* of directing!" One time Huston expounded on what being a director was really all about.

"You will confer with generals," he said, "you will dine at the table with kings, and you will sleep with titled women. All of this you will do while being dead broke. *That's* what being a director is."

When Milius asked him what was the best part of being a director, John answered with one word: "Sadism." He recommended that Milius read the Marquis de Sade at night and Jim Corbett during the day. "If you read Corbett at night," he warned, "it will scare the holy shit out of you. De Sade you can read anytime."

"He became one of the great influences on my life," Milius said. "I had a father/son thing with him." When Milius asked John about women, John's advice was, "Be anything they want. Mold to their caresses. Tell them anything. Just fuck 'em! Fuck 'em all!"

When Milius met Cici he thought she was formidable. "I was kind of scared of her," he said. "She was outrageous—bawdy and wild. Had I met her under different circumstances I would have attacked her. I walked into John's trailer and she was in a robe and began talking about her sexual prowess with John. Here was this very attractive woman, almost naked, telling me about how good she was. And the feeling I had was that there was some sort of terrible thing going on there, like there was going to be a murder or something."

Billy Pearson, who had been cast in a small part so he and John could finally work together, first met Cici at John's motel in Tucson. "I opened the door and Jesus! There were about two hundred candles lit in this room, and incense and grass, you could smell it right away. I'd never seen a couple who were, mentally, total opposites. What Cici knew about art you could put in your eye. The only thing that they agreed upon was that they both loved horses. I said to John, 'I've never seen anyone more incompatible in my life than you two. She must be the greatest fuck in the Western world.' And Huston said, 'Yes, that's right.' "

Paul Newman isn't the kind of man who likes to speculate on other people's relationships, but he couldn't keep from saying of Cici, "She appeared to me to be a functioning voluptuary." Victoria Principal's first reaction when she saw Cici and John together was that it was a "very physical relationship," and not one "that was going to make it."

John and Cici celebrated Thanksgiving together in his trailer, where they had moved to eliminate the time spent commuting to and from the location . . . and to be alone. "It was one of the most romantic moments for me," said Cici: "to be in the Arizona desert in a house trailer drinking champagne and eating popcorn with John Huston reading Kipling. That was the beginning of our relationship."

John Milius thought Huston was lucky to have a woman like Cici to share his trailer and assumed that she was the reason he didn't go after Victoria Principal. "He had his hands full with Cici."

Principal, who lived in Mexico and would go on to become a household name in the television series "Dallas," had only been in the country eight months and had no movie credits when she was first interviewed by Huston. She managed to read the script beforehand, dyed her hair jet black the night before, cut up a burlap flour sack for a shawl, and walked into John's office barefoot. "Buenos días, Señor Huston," she said. John laughed. "He was impressed with my desire," she said, "and he brought me back to read with Paul. You can imagine how nervous I was. The idea of working with John Huston and Paul Newman seemed pretty awesome."

After she was cast, Principal felt alienated and intimidated at first. "John really didn't seek to draw me out," she said. "I began to worry that I was going to be fired. Then, as time went by, I would quietly sit by his seat and not say anything. One day he put his hand on my head and it became a habit. I would sit barefoot like a little Mexican girl at his feet and he would put his hand on my head. And I loved it. It was very fatherly. And he began telling me bawdy, raucous jokes. There was sexual innuendo, but I didn't take it seriously. I always felt that he treated me as an innocent, and that was the relationship that we had: that of a child and a revered older man.

"I remember the first time he actually directed me. Often he would say, 'Do what feels right.' I was so young and inexperienced I didn't realize that he was trusting my instincts. I didn't know enough to trust my own. But one day there was a scene that wasn't going right. He took me aside and asked, 'Have you ever seen baby fawns when they are frightened? You know how they become very stiff-legged and they tremble, and you see the whites of their eyes? I want you to do that in this scene.' And it worked wonderfully. That day broke the ice for me."

As was usual on a Huston picture, various people came to visit. This time, besides the publicists and producers and old friends, Principal remembered seeing Clint Eastwood in the dining room and Marlon Brando at the dailies. Brando stayed for three days and was interested in Principal. "I was requested to come to a screening one night because I was his type," she said. "I was petrified. But Brando hadn't realized how tall I was. He didn't like tall women."

John Milius said that "everybody wanted to fuck her. But she was aloof and was supposedly going off on the weekends with Frank Sinatra. She was very ambitious."

Principal didn't find Milius's chauvinistic nature very attractive. "I preferred someone I could have an ongoing conversation with," she said. Someone like Paul Newman, whom she found "out of this world." She used to baby-sit for his children so he and his wife, Joanne Woodward, could have time together.

"One day when Huston said something, I said, 'But Paul said. . . .' And Paul took me aside and said, 'Don't you *ever* turn to me in front of John Huston and do that again. John Huston is the director and don't forget it!' "

Newman was in awe of Huston. "I always considered him such an artist," he said. "I always felt very bourgeois around him. One always feels a certain sense of uneasiness around a man of genius. I was intimidated. When John was at his peak, he was royalty. The last of a breed."

Newman's admiration went beyond John as a filmmaker. "John was unusual in that he didn't have a lot of regrets in his life. He was an adventurer and he was also extraordinarily well rounded. He was really such a graceful man. And in so many arenas: literature, horsemanship . . . living. He had that wonderful gift that is the mark of a good director: to speak when necessary and let his actors fly, if they were flying. He had a great ability to liberate people."

As Newman watched John work, he came to the conclusion that "the seat of his invention was in his cigar. He would watch a rehearsal and seem to be slightly puzzled. Then he'd smoke a cigar and ruminate. I always felt that the solution was in the cigar."

Contrary to what John Milius thought, Newman felt that if *Roy Bean* "had been the way that Milius had wanted it, then it would have been pretty boring. Huston gave it class, really. He made people interested in that character. The philosophy is outrageous, the structure is outrageous, the progression of the story is outrageous, and that's the fun of it."

The structure of the movie was different from any of Huston's other films in that he used what he called a "fragmented" technique, "in which all sorts of things can be happening without necessarily justifying them logically; things appear, things happen. It seemed to reflect the old American spirit that was capable of doing so many unlikely things. There was a breadth and a generosity and a carelessness about it that I fostered in the picture. It was an allegory, and the vengeance of the past was interesting to me. My grandfather would have been quite capable of coming back and destroying a place the way the judge did. I loved the audacity of the film."

One of the most audacious moments in the movie comes in the scene between the judge and Bad Bob, an albino wild man whom Newman shoots in the back. The hole he blasts is so large that one sees daylight through his body. Stacy Keach came to Tucson for one day to play Bad Bob. John wanted him to play it like a crazed rabbit and it was Keach's idea to make him an albino. It took five hours for Keach to get made up and he wore red contact lenses to color his eyes.

From what John had told him, Keach had envisioned a very surreal western. "But apparently only my sequences were surreal," he said. "When I look down and see this hole in my chest—that's a thing Huston decided on the spot. That was one of the best days of shooting I ever had."

Huston's audacity off the set reached its apex when he befriended a lion. In the movie, the judge had a pet bear and the bear's trainer just happened to have a pet lion, which he would bring to John's trailer. John would invite people in for lunch, Paul Newman said, "and then he'd spring the lion. He certainly did separate the men from the boys. One guy tried to crawl up the drapes. Another guy jumped on the desk." Milius recalled that the lion drove Jackie Bisset from the trailer and caused a visiting writer to freeze in terror, as the lion relieved himself all over him. "Don't be afraid," Huston would always caution, "it'll know and go for you."

Huston also loved the bear. "We couldn't get the bear to do what was written," John said, "but he was a wonderful, gentle creature who'd sell his soul for a Tootsie Roll. I wanted to go on a holiday up in the mountains with the bear. Just the bear and me." Newman also fell for the bear. "I had to hit him once," he remembered, "which startled both him and me."

"The bear loved Paul," Victoria Principal said. When someone joked that the bear was stealing all the scenes, she said, "I didn't care if he upstaged us, I was worried that he was going to *eat* me. It was unnatural for a wild animal to be given so much freedom around human beings."

If the bear didn't impress her, Ava Gardner did. "We had a small dinner for her and she was over two hours late," Principal recalled. "She arrived in white jeans and a white shirt that fit her magnificently. And she didn't walk into the room, she came in like a cat. I had never seen a woman move like that or have that kind of presence, before or since. I've never seen a woman electrify a room sexually like she did. You were aware that she was on the prowl."

If Ava *was* on the prowl, John Milius was not interested. "She got drunk," Milius said, "and got angry at everybody, broke some glasses and stormed off into the desert. I was to go get her and bring her back, but I didn't want to deal with this predatory woman. Looking back, I wish I had. But she was old. There is something about people when they age and look like they have been rebuilt. It was very unappealing."

George C. Scott was also shooting a film near Tucson while Ava was there and when Huston found out about it, he decided to protect her. "I found out later that Scott was working in the same little town," she said, "and John had a guard at my door twenty-four hours a day and never mentioned it to me. Now, that's pretty sweet. He was a fine man."

Billy Pearson's big scene was to greet Ava Gardner when she arrived on the train at the end of the picture. "John wanted a shot where the train would come in and out of the corner of the lens," Pearson said. "This was all a buildup for the great Lillie Langtry, who arrived in Langtry, Texas, to see this town that had been built for her. This other guy and me were the two old idiots who were to greet her. I wanted to fuck it up. I knew I was the only guy in the living world who could have done it, because everybody else there was serious in the motion picture business and I just did it as a joke. So when John called 'Action' and they take ten minutes to get the train coming in just as the sun was going down, I knew it would be impossible to get this antique train to stop on cue a second time. And Ava Gardner didn't know me from Adam. So when she got off the train, I said, 'Well, Miss Langtry, you don't know how nice it is to see you. All I can think about is eatin' your pussy!' And she said, 'Oh, really?' So I said, 'Hector and me been out here so long, all we do is jack off dreamin' about ya.' And she just goes right ahead saying her lines exactly as if what I had said was what I was supposed to have said. She was such a professional, I could not shock her. When we came to the end of the thing where we're starting down the stairs, people were rolling. John was wiping tears from his eyes. John Foreman was a basket case, because if they had to keep Ava another day he had to buy her a Mercedes as a penalty. And of course it all had to be shot again. It would have been the end of me if John and I hadn't been buddies."

Paul Newman said that making *Roy Bean* was "one of the best experiences I've had as an actor." He thought the film did well critically, even if it bombed at the box office, and blamed the ending—Lillie Langtry's visit twenty years after the judge's wild escapades—as being a problem "we never did lick. Maybe it had no ending. But if we had found one, then the picture might have been a serious classic."

Victoria Principal said that the movie "continues to be one of the most wonderful working experiences I've ever had in my entire life."

The New Yorker's Pauline Kael would take exception, only because "the ugly right-wing fantasy" might have been better "if Huston and Newman hadn't softened the viciousness; then they'd have to face the disgrace of what they were working on." She considered it a "logy, thick-skinned movie that seems to spend most of its time trying to tone down the moral ugliness of its premises."

John disagreed. "I thought it was a quite well-done film," he said. "I think we put the judge into the legendary class. It was in the fine old American tradition of the Tall Tale, the Whopper, the yarn. At the same time, it said something important about frontier life and the loss of America's innocence."

With *Judge Roy Bean* in the can, John returned to the Pacific Palisades to stay with Cici and her five-year-old son, Collin. "He was a sick boy," Cici said. "Atraxic cerebral palsy, where the muscles don't control mobility. He had three braces. It's kind of hard for me to talk about it. John was wonderful to him. He bought him a bicycle."

Having been away from St. Clerans for most of the year John was anxious to get back to Ireland, and invited Cici to come with him. "I told him I couldn't," she said, "because I come from this rigid family and I didn't want to start having hassles with my mother and father. I was thirty-one years old but I still had this loyalty to my family."

"Do not let this man take you to Europe," her mother told her. "You were not raised to be anyone's mistress. I don't care if he is John Huston; he will destroy you if he doesn't respect you. No mistress, only Mrs."

So John left by himself, stopping off in New York to catch Stacy Keach and Victoria Principal in *Hamlet* in Central Park. For a year that began with his feeling it was "all over" for him, 1971 had turned into one of his most active years, acting in *Man in the Wilderness* in Spain, directing *Fat City* and *Judge Roy Bean* in the States, easing out of his relationship with Valeria, and entering into a new one with Cici, who was "pissed because I didn't want him to leave."

The person with a privileged view of the relationship between John and Cici was Cici's young Mexican maid, Maricela Hernandez, who had come to work for her when Collin was a year old. Maricela was amused and astonished by Cici, and they became close friends. Cici trusted her to take care of the sick boy. Maricela considered herself lucky to have a comfortable job, although it was never her desire to work as a maid.

"I had aspirations to become a biologist," Maricela said, reflecting on how her life changed after she sneaked across the border when she was fifteen. "The time came when my mother couldn't afford to send me to school. My father died when I was five years old." To earn money so she could continue her schooling, Maricela decided to run away from home and pay a "coyote" to help get her into California. "I crossed the border illegally. It was very dangerous. I witnessed a couple of guys who were shot in the back by immigration officers on the American side.

"I don't recall being afraid. Although everybody was trembling and a lot of people were crying. You have to run and it's the most horrendous experience. Somehow I made it over."

For a week she stayed with a friend in San Diego, but then there was an immigration raid and she fled to Los Angeles. Traumatized in a city where she knew no one, speaking only Spanish, she survived by drinking Coca-Cola and sleeping in trucks and parks. When she began to look for work, she was asked for her papers, which she didn't have. She found herself, at times, reduced to begging in the streets.

"A woman found me and offered me work in a store downtown. She sold clothes. I had the opportunity to make a little money and to have something to eat. She let me sleep in her garage. One day she had somebody who was going to do her furniture and this man said, 'My God, are you happy?' I said, 'No, but what else can I do?' And he said, 'Would you be interested in a job taking care of a kid?' "

The woman was Cici; the kid, Collin. Cici, who spoke broken Spanish, was living in her parents' house because her own had recently burned down. Maricela got to know Collin. "There was something about this little boy that was terribly wrong. I tried to play games with him, then I was told he had a problem with his legs and I had to watch him all the time. I immediately fell in love with the little boy."

On her second day Cici's mother asked her to help clear the table. Collin was upstairs with Cici, so Maricela obliged. When Mrs. Shane went to rinse some dishes, a broken faucet sent a force of water into her face, ruining her hair and makeup. "I looked at the poor woman and she looked at me furious," Maricela recalled, "and it's like you want to laugh and you can't. I used to laugh a lot, it was like a circus. Being completely out of your country and environment, everything became terribly funny to me."

There were times when she was convinced Cici was slightly mad, like when Cici once said the flowers were trying to bite her. Maricela looked at the flowers and nothing happened. She reached for a hose to water them and she heard the *sssssss* of a rattlesnake. "Oh, I tell you, we used to laugh," Maricela said. "John, too—that was one of the reasons they were together—John loved to laugh. And she certainly knew how to make him laugh."

If Cici made John laugh, she also brought out his cruel side. Before he left for Ireland he had told her, "Oh, honey, you could end up like a John O'Hara heroine who, after she's gone down on all the guys in town, turns into a lesbian." But in his calls to her he was more intimate and tender. His longing was real. He told her about his preparations for his next movie, another spy film to be shot in London, Ireland, and Malta called *The Mackintosh Man*, which Paul Newman had brought to him. And he described a special screening of *Fat City* he had for Mohammed Ali in Dublin before his fight with Blue Lewis and how Ali had shouted at the screen, "That's the way it is!"

At Ray Stark's house in Los Angeles, at another screening of *Fat City* before it was released, Jack Clayton almost came to blows with director

Peter Bogdanovich and actor Ryan O'Neal because of their lack of respect for the film. Clayton, who was preparing to direct *The Great Gatsby*, sat between them as they "sat and joked throughout the film. At the end," recalled Clayton, "one of them said, 'I wish that old fart would give up directing.' I have an enormous temper and I said, 'If you two children had in your tiny fingernail the genius of that man, I would be proud to speak to you. I'm disgusted with you both.' And I had to be parted from Ryan."

As John prepared to go to New York in July 1972 to attend the premiere of *Fat City* at the Museum of Modern Art, he found himself thinking more and more about Cici. But she was still angry with him for the things he had said about her when she refused to join him in Ireland a few months earlier. When he called to invite her to the premiere, she wouldn't talk to him.

"I told Maricela to say she couldn't reach me because I had a horrible accident at a horse show," Cici said. "I didn't even ride—I fell off a bar stool in Laguna. He totally freaked out. Called my parents. They called the horse show grounds. Finally he got me and he said he couldn't stand it without me and I said I couldn't stand it without him. I said, 'Let's just get married.' He said, 'Fly to New York, we'll get married there.' "

Like Evelyn Keyes, Cici proposed marriage. And once again John couldn't say no. "So I flew to New York," Cici recalled, "and was just about to go into his hotel room when I heard his voice. 'Oh, no,' he was saying, 'I'll get her over that. Hell no, I'm not getting married.'

"I went in and said, 'You *what?*' I was just so pissed off."

In another of her "Talk of the Town" pieces in *The New Yorker*, Lillian Ross wrote about John's New York visit for the opening of *Fat City*, but missed the behind-the-scenes drama between Huston and Cici. She described Tony Huston as being two inches taller than John and wrote of them both sporting beards—John's gray and scraggly, Tony's spare and black—and wearing "crisp seersucker jackets, the father with a white shirt and a rakish black bow tie, the son with a brick-red shirt and a multicolored Art Nouveau tie." She also wrote about Anjelica, who was dressed in a "white chiffon shimmery gown and pearls," but she made no mention of little Allegra, almost eight, whom John brought with him to live with Nurse at Tony and Dorothy Soma's house on Long Island.

When Cici saw Allegra she "fell in love with her sadness. Allegra came to the hotel and danced for the entourage. I felt she needed someone. I didn't see her again until a year later. Neither did John."

Philip and Avril Soma also felt Allegra needed a secure home, and they were still hoping that they could adopt her. When they visited Tony and Dorothy during the summer Allegra arrived, Avril noticed that "she was already starting to pull back and be too careful. I'm sure that she felt that she really couldn't trust anybody but Nurse." Avril saw how Allegra attempted to please Tony by being the first one to finish her food and removing her plate from the table. "She was just being manipulative, trying to get attention or to get love. She was too old for her age."

On the night of the museum opening of *Fat City*, John stood behind a four-foot-high ribbon and goaded Ray Stark to jump over it. When Stark hesitated, Huston commanded, "Jump!" and Ray did. "Huston received him with a hug," reported Lillian Ross. During a television interview Huston was asked what "fat city" meant. "It's a jazz musician's term," he explained. "A dreamer's term, meaning no boundaries to the possibilities. It's the pot of gold at the end of the rainbow."

Just before John and Cici left for the Museum of Modern Art, Cici received a phone call from Jill St. John, who told her that their childhood friend, Lance Reventlow, Barbara Hutton's son, had been killed in a plane crash. "I was still recovering from this trickery John had pulled about not being serious about our getting married when I got this call and I was just torn apart," she said. "Then, during the movie, came this Kristofferson song, 'Put a ribbon around your hair . . . help me make it through the night.' And I just fled out of the theater and went back to the hotel. Jill called again and I said, 'What do I do?' She said, 'Just get the fuck out of there, you don't need him. He's not going to marry you.' I left him a message: 'Leaving in the morning.' "

But on the plane back to Los Angeles Cici couldn't get John out of her mind. "I kept thinking, 'I can't handle it, what am I going to do? I really care about him.' I got back to L.A. and John called and said, 'I can't stand it without you, let's get married.' "

Cici agreed, and John's lawyer drew up papers for her to sign. "He had this horrible lawyer, Henry Hyde," Cici said. "He hated my guts.

He had me sign all sorts of prenuptials, which I made John rescind. Money! My parents could buy and sell half of California."

As *Fat City* was being hailed as a masterpiece and Huston's best film in years, John continued to have his doubts about getting married for the fifth time. When he joined Cici in Los Angeles they visited Sam and Betty Jaffe. Betty thought John was gracious and Cici charming, and a few nights later, they all met again at Edward G. Robinson's house. Cici approached Betty and said, "It's because of you and Sam that we are going to get married." When Betty asked what she meant, Cici said it was the fact that despite the differences in their ages, they were so happy together. Betty's impression of Cici was "very favorable. And she was crazy about John."

Billy Pearson took a more sarcastic view of their relationship. "He didn't completely dominate her," Pearson remarked. "He dominated all his wives. And all his wives put up with any kind of shit because they loved John. Cici was so full of her own shit. I mean, they were *both* full of shit!"

After committing to the marriage John said, "I knew I was making a mistake. One does that sort of thing—you know damn well it's self-destructive." They were invited to a dinner party at Jennifer Jones's house. Jones was now married to Norton Simon, one of the wealthiest men in Los Angeles, whose art collection filled his own museum.

"That was the night we decided to get married," John said. "Or rather, that I was convinced by her that we *should* get married. I would hardly have been convinced without the benefit of alcohol.

"I arrived at Norton Simon's place on the beach more than half drunk. It was an absolutely dreadful evening. And I announced that Cici and I were going to get married. Brought in on a cold platter, why, there's little to recommend her. You have to be infatuated with Cici even to like her. And she contributed nothing, of course. The whole evening was a social blunder which I look back at with utter shame."

Talli Wyler was asked about that night and filled in some details that John had forgotten. "When he came down to dinner," she said, "he was so drunk that he fell forward and his face landed in his soup. They lifted him up and he said, 'I'm engaged to be married.' He already knew it was a terrible idea. And he was sorry ever afterward."

On August 8, 1972, three days after Huston turned sixty-six, he and Cici were married. "I arranged the wedding for two hundred people, at my mother's, so that everyone wouldn't think that he was marrying some scag," Cici said. "My parents have this enormous estate in Beverly Hills. And John cried when we got married. I liked that. Zsa Zsa Gabor came up to my mother and said, 'Your daughter is in such trouble with John, who is the only person in the whole world that I walk into a room, my heart leaps up in my throat. He ruined my marriage to George Sanders, you know. He made me such a very famous woman. When I was only thirteen I was in *Moulin Rouge.*' Only thirteen! Cute."

Neither Tony nor Anjelica was invited to the wedding, although John did tell Anjelica about it. "I didn't know he was getting married until very shortly before the wedding," Anjelica said. "I thought Cici was fun. I don't dislike her. We all have to live our lives and we do it the best we can. Unless somebody injures me personally, I'm not about to pass judgment."

But others did. Paul Kohner was in Cuernavaca and flew in for the wedding. When he returned he told Lupita, "Oh, boy, he didn't have to do *that!*" And Peter Viertel told Evelyn Keyes that John had made "a big mistake." When Keyes said that John had made mistakes before, Viertel said, "No, no, he didn't make a mistake like this before."

"Cici was as out of place at St. Clerans as anyone could possibly be," John said. "This was a little half-Jewish princess from Hollywood in one of the oldest settings in Christendom. I'm not being anti-Semitic with this remark at all. She wanted to establish her authority as the mistress of St. Clerans and didn't know how to do that."

"I arrived in Ireland with my five-year-old son and my nineteen-year-old maid, who was like a daughter, and I absolutely couldn't believe it," Cici recalled. "Here I am, a reasonably sophisticated, Beverly Hills brat. However, I wasn't prepared for the eleven servants, the mistresses, Betty O'Kelly, Gladys. I loved Gladys and I hated her at the same time. She had too many people inside of her. One day she'd get drunk and tell me everything and the next day she'd be awful. But Betty O'Kelly was a terrible woman. She looked like an old leather shoe, a prune face, hard, nasty piece of work. But she was very loyal to John; she was in love with him. She had set the groundwork before I came, saying I beat my servants. And these people were simpleminded. They were terrified of me at first. Except the cook, she sympathized with me."

The cook, Mrs. Creagh, was also kind to Maricela, who felt most comfortable in the kitchen, where Mrs. Creagh made her delicious bread and asked her if she went to church. "I hate to go to church," Maricela said. A shocked Mrs. Creagh would then lecture Maricela. "I used to laugh," Maricela recalled. "I laughed at everything."

But Maricela didn't find it at all funny when she and Collin were put in the Little House, away from John and Cici, who stayed in the Big House. "I was told that we were going to be like a family," Maricela said, "but when we got there Collin and I were far away, around the stables. I was scared shitless. All I could think of was, I want to go home."

Cici hadn't realized that they had been separated on the very first night and when she saw them the next morning, Maricela told her, "If you leave me here, I'll do something to you that you'll never, ever forget."

Cici felt sorry for her, but her attention was diverted when she discovered that they weren't alone on her honeymoon. "I didn't realize there was this bitch mistress living there named Zoe. Good-looking but a real cunt. I didn't know who this woman was. Finally, when I realized that she was his mistress, I got furious. John loved the fact that I didn't know who she was." When she saw that Zoe was having breakfast served to her in her room, Cici told one of the servants, "You tell Princess Pooh-Pooey to get off her back and get her ass down into the breakfast room. If I'm going down there, she can go down there."

Her anger grew as John attempted to placate her. "John said, 'You have to understand, she's coming here to find out if she should marry a Jew. And if she marries, will I keep paying her support?' I said, 'She's coming here to ask you if she can marry a Jew? What is this shit?' Oooh, did I hate her!"

The feeling was mutual. "We were there when he brought her home to St. Clerans," Zoe remembered. "It was a summer holiday, nobody knew he was getting married. I was there every summer with Danny. I wouldn't have gone if I knew that was the scene. I was perfectly nice to her, but I could understand that she didn't want all those people hanging on. But she was paranoid, neurotic. These things have to be dealt with with a certain amount of intelligence, not through hysteria."

Danny was too young to form an opinion, but said, "I just hate her because everybody else hates her. I didn't even know her that well." But Zoe concluded that "Cici's the only person who had anything to do with John that I don't like. I had no reason to hate her, because if that's what John wanted it was okay by me. When I first met her I just thought he was happy with her and I had no animosity toward her. My animosity came from the fact that I saw him being treated so badly."

The jealousy between the two women created all sorts of amusing dilemmas for John. When Cici noticed Zoe "wearing these dribblings of gems around her neck," she asked her where she got them and Zoe told her from John. When John heard that he went upstairs and came down with a little bag of *two* necklaces and gave them to Cici. "You miserable sonofabitch," Cici thanked him.

"I was always jealous," Cici frankly admitted. "But so was Zoe. She was furious that I married him. When she said, 'You married John, what is your key to success?' I answered, 'Don't forget the day, the month, and the year you were born. Time flies.' I'm supposed to give this scag, this two-thousand-dollar-a-month hanger-on, advice? Who had this illegitimate child when poor Ricki was stressed out over in England raising his family?"

Zoe said that the most John ever paid her was $1,400 a month, not $2,000, and resented Cici's interference in her affairs. "John always supported us," she said. "But when you're paying nine hundred a month for rent, that fourteen hundred made it tough. I felt very hurt about it for a long time, but I refused to ask for more. I never worked; I was totally involved with Danny. I remember one Christmas we had thirty pounds for the whole of the holidays to eat. But I didn't spend. We don't drink; we don't eat meat. It started getting grim when we had to move from our apartment in Rome. And then when things started getting tight, Cici took away one-fifty each month because she felt the fourteen hundred dollars was too much. She told John's business manager to cut it back. So it got worse and worse."

Zoe and Danny didn't stay the entire month of August as they usually did, but saw enough of John and Cici's "honeymoon" to consider it "very weird. She pressured him into marrying her in a devious, manipulating way. She must have said, 'Either we get married or else I'm not going to be with you.' And he probably thought he was going to lose her and he didn't want to.

"I didn't see any great tenderness or great love, devotion, respect. There was passion and rows and sex. Violent emotion can't last. There was little sharing."

Maricela thought that "everything was sort of crazy in Ireland." One time John came and asked her, "What kind of a person is Cici?" And Maricela answered, "She's the most noble and wonderful woman I've ever encountered." When Joan Buck, who was then a features editor for British *Vogue*, came to visit, she found John to be very sweet when he introduced her to Cici, who, Joan felt, "looked like Jane Fonda, wearing this hippy dress and carrying a flower." But soon, Maricela said, "things got very tense."

"Gladys, from the word *go*, disliked Cici," John said. "She was outraged at my marrying her or anyone *like* her. And I know that the staff was uptight." Betty O'Kelly decided to quit after Cici started going through the account books and accused her of stealing from John by spending a fortune on liquor.

Cici defended her actions because John had told her that running St. Clerans had become so expensive, he didn't know if he could continue to live there. "After I saw the way things were run," Cici said, "I wanted to re-do the books. I wanted to figure out where all the money was going. As I went through them I uncovered each and every criminal. And his employees really freaked out. I took Betty in another room and I just laid her out. I said, 'Why is there so much alcohol drunk when Master John is not here? You're costing us more in alcohol when he's not here than when he is here.' She hated that. And then the groom. I caught him with quadruple charges for horseshoeing. I know about horses. He couldn't screw me around."

Cici wanted to fire everyone except for the cook and hire a completely new staff. "John, of course, wouldn't do that, because he is that sort of loyal person. So we had these kinds of confrontations every night."

"Generally speaking," John said, "a new wife wants to cut her man off from everything that's preceded her and Cici was no exception. You can imagine, she came in under critical eyes."

When Betty O'Kelly announced that she was leaving, John bought her a new car and gave her a bonus, which burned Cici. When O'Kelly mentioned that she was having mechanical problems with her new car, Cici snapped, "Well, Betty, I think what you need is a Ferrari." Maricela had to excuse herself to run into the kitchen, where she burst into laughter. "That's what I mean about being in a circus," she said. "Those things happened all the time."

Soon after they came to Ireland John took Cici to the Edinburgh Film Festival in Scotland, leaving Collin and Maricela behind. Maricela felt even more isolated and trapped when Cici left. She had no money, no one to talk to. "I went crazy with all these people who were total strangers to me," she said. "I thought, 'How could she do this to me?'" Cici said she called them twice a day and Maricela told her, "I'm gonna get you for this."

"One of the Irishmen had a crush on Maricela and followed her around," said Cici. "He'd never seen a dark-skinned woman before—

they're all pure white over there. She said he tried to rape her and so she took that venomous hatred out on me."

The "funny-looking" Irishman who followed Maricela around was usually drunk. "I remember one time I walked in when the servants were having their meal," Maricela said, "and I said to this guy, 'Hello, handsome.' And he said, 'Well, hello, hello, will you marry me?' And I said, 'Any time, any day. Right here? Right now?' A joke. And when Cici went away, one night I was asleep. I heard noises and I smelled this terrible smell and I opened my eyes and there he was totally naked. And I thought, oh, shit. He said, 'We're going to get married.' I said, 'I cannot marry you. You ought to take a shower.' He came back and said, 'Now that I took a shower, will you marry me?' And I said, 'Certainly not. You're drunk.' And he said, 'Well, whether you want to or not, we're going to get married.' By that time I managed to ring a bell and Gladys came in her nightgown. I said, 'I'm leaving. This guy who came was totally naked. And I didn't do anything to provoke him. I didn't come here to fool around.' "

When Cici returned Maricela shouted at her, "You just take off and all hell breaks loose. I'm not sure he's not going to come another night and spook the bejesus out of me. I miss my gun."

Cici tried to calm her. "You should put your complaints to John." So Maricela told John, who just laughed and said, "I promise you that he will never bother you again."

Cici empathized with Maricela's state of mind, since they basically felt the same way about their Irish adventure. "Maricela was the only friend I had over there," she said. "My mail all came opened. And my mail didn't go out. I think Gladys tore it up or put it in her secret file. I was virtually a prisoner there. The only time I could get any freedom was to ride and they would give me these shitbag horses. I'm used to great horses and wonderful rides and there I rode on a fucking cement road. John thought I was having a great time."

By October Maricela had had enough. She said to Cici, "Listen, we've been here for two months. Every time I need something I come to you like you were my mom. You said we were coming here for a month. I want to hear the Rolling Stones, the Beatles . . . for chrissake, *do* something, I'm scratching the walls. I'm perfectly capable of going to the Mexican commission and telling them under what conditions I am here."

"If I ever hear this 'I want to go home' again," Cici warned, "I'll pull your teeth, one by one, make a necklace like those they sell in Tijuana, and send it to your sister."

*   *   *

"But the time came when I just had it," Maricela related. She went to John and told him, "I need airfare. Just to go from Dublin straight to L.A." She went down on her knees and pleaded, "Boss, chief, please."

"It's quite impossible," John inhaled. "Do you realize the commotion that you will cause?"

"I was so exasperated," said Maricela. "So what I did was I took my camera and my twenty Irish pounds and began to walk out of the castle. I didn't care if I had to swim, canoe, I was going to make it back to America.

"So I took off. I began to walk. And, oh, God, those Irish roads never end. I ended up in a little town and I was so thirsty. There was no bus station, only a train station. In the meantime everybody at St. Clerans was looking for me. Somehow I ended up in Dublin. It became a nightmare, really a nightmare. I spent five of my twenty pounds.

"I decided to call them. That was a mistake. Cici told me, 'You have twenty-four hours to come back . . . or else you are a dead dog.' I don't know how I managed to get there, but I got back."

Maricela's attempted escape only served to further Cici's stress. She didn't want to be there any more than Maricela, but if she was going to give her marriage a shot, she knew she needed Maricela to be there for both Collin and her.

"They thought my son was a freak," Cici said. "The kids threw rocks at him. And he almost committed suicide by jumping out of the second-floor window once. John ran out and got him."

Cici felt that "John loved Collin. He thought he was very like himself when he was young. John used to say, 'Forget all this. Throw those braces away and take him to the waves and let him fight the ocean.' "

Collin's childhood memory of John was that of a rather awesome man with a deep voice. Once, when Collin was abusing a dog, John approached him. "He told me why I shouldn't do that," Collin said, "and how everything was connected and I hung on every word. He seemed like God to me."

John recalled once putting his arm around Collin. "I felt gratitude. He came closer to me. It was a natural expression on my part, but I didn't want to overdo it."

Tony Huston, then twenty-two, found Cici "fairly strange" and "rather attractive." At the time he was trying to write a novel and feeling competitive, sexually and in many other ways, with his father.

John never discussed sex with him as a young man. "That competitive-
ness hit me in my early twenties," he said, "particularly growing up in
the shadow of a legendary Don Juan figure. One is tempted to emulate
some of that just for the sake of being able to prove that some of the
genes are there." Tony found Cici "exciting," and said he did things
with her that he hadn't done before, "nothing reprehensible, but I
don't really want to talk about them."

"Tony befriended me," Cici said, also indicating that nothing "reprehensible" went on between them, "but then he turned on me so he
could have John to himself. Once Tony and I were down by the stream,
talking. I was really down and said, 'I don't think I can survive here.
No one helps me.' I looked up the hill and said, 'Tony, who's that?' It
was some gorgeous guy. 'My God,' I said, 'it's Wally.' My ex-husband.
And I went running up the hill and he came running down, like one of
those commercials with flowers in the Irish countryside. I gave him this
big hug and I looked up at the house. There was John, watching from
his room."

Wally Green had come to Ireland to see his son, Collin. "As my
girlfriend Jill St. John said," Cici observed, "he wouldn't come to the
Palisades but he came to Ireland." Nonetheless, she was so glad to see
him she "fell madly in love" with Wally again.

Before she went to tell John of Green's arrival, Tony gave her a
warning: "Cici, I'm going to tell you something. Beware of the red devil."
Cici didn't know what he meant and he said, "When the red devil comes,
don't turn your back on him. Someone did once and the red devil
almost killed him." Cici looked at him strangely and ran upstairs to John.

"Guess who arrived?" she said. "I can't imagine," he said, not
looking up from his book.

"That night at dinner," remembered Cici, "it was Wally, John, Paul
Newman, and John Foreman, who were there because of *The Mackintosh Man*. John was directing the course of conversation. Everything
was directed by him. And John said, 'I hear you know about African
art?' Gamesmanship. So Wally said, 'Oh, I know lots about it.' So John
took us all down for a tour of the house, which normally was relegated
to Gladys. This evening he just wanted to do Wally-world, you see.

"So we went down to the African Room and he took us to the two
worst pieces there. 'These are wonderful, aren't they?' he said, 'Oh,
God, yes, just superb,' Wally said. And then he showed his two best
pieces and said, 'These are awful, just horrible, aren't they?' I'm going,
Holy Christ, how do I warn Wally that he's being manipulated? I was
furious with John. Why did he do this? He was jealous.

"Finally we went up to the main room. So John said to Tony, 'Go get Joyce.' Tony rumbled off and came back with a black velvet pillow with the death mask of James Joyce on it. John asked, 'What do you think?' Wally said, 'Well, the old boy at least died with a smile on his face, didn't he, John?' I thought, touché.

"The next morning Wally said, 'I'm leaving. I'm going to Michael Butler's with Collin and Maricela." He was working with Michael on the musical *1776*. Michael, who produced the play *Hair*, was an old love of mine I stopped seeing when I met John. So they took off for London and suddenly I was in love with my ex-husband again, which was stupid."

"Wally was a very nice guy, I had tremendous respect," said Maricela, who asked him if he could help her get out of the country. She told Cici that she just didn't want to stay any longer. "Everything was getting so tense, everybody spying on everybody. And Cici was very very unhappy. John would say to her, 'Tomorrow we're going to pick out locations,' for *The Mackintosh Man*. And she would say to me, 'I'm not going on the fucking location with John.' And John would not be far away from us."

But Cici did go with John and the others as they looked for locations in Connemara after Wally and Collin and Maricela left. "I was with people who weren't friendly to me," she said. "And Tony said, 'Oh, you're going to their honeymoon cottage,' meaning Betty O'Kelly and John. And there I was in his fucking honeymoon cottage, which was the most awful, dank, disastrous-looking place that I've ever seen. The caravan went on and he started drinking, because he was pissed at me.

"By the time we got back to the house he was toasted. He went upstairs. Tony and I were talking downstairs when he shouted, 'Send Cici up here.' Tony said, 'You'd better go.' I said, 'Fuck him, I'm upset. My kid is gone to my ex-boyfriend's house with my ex-husband, Maricela is gone, I'm all alone, and nobody likes me.' Ring, ring again. 'God-damnit, send her up!' 'You'd better go,' Tony said. 'And don't forget what I told you about the red devil.'

"So I went upstairs and he locked the door. He said, 'Now tell me what the hell is bothering you?' I said, 'Never mind.' He said, 'I insist!' pacing around. So finally I told him, 'I'm upset about Collin.' 'Fuck Collin,' he said.

" 'What do you mean, "fuck Collin"? I'm upset that he's gone off. And Maricela . . .'

" 'Fuck 'em all!'

" 'You sonofabitch,' I said and raced to the door. But he came up behind me. He had these massive hands and his hand went *whap!* And I saw his hand and it was red. I turned around and there was this red fucking devil! His hair kind of tufted up and it looked like there was smoke around him. Holy shit. I just made a fist and went *wham!* I socked him as hard as I could. I'd never done that before because he always said, 'I'm a boxer and I can really get you.' So I just knocked the red devil and he turned back into John.

" 'Oh, my God,' he said and he got on his hands and knees and begged forgiveness. Of course, we made love that night. He loved that. Lots of that. I loved having sex with John—he was the best of my whole life. Honest to God. John was an incredible lover.

"Anyway, at four in the morning the phone rang. It was little Miss Maricela. 'Oh, Cici, I lost my passport.' They hadn't even gotten out of Ireland. Four A.M.! I said, 'Look, have a good trip. Everything is fine.' The next day I went down to the Little House with Tony and I got a call from Wally in London. Tony said, 'Have him call you on this secret number. My mother had this number.' So they called me back and Maricela said, 'We've lost the passport.' I said, 'Are you trying to get me out of here?' Wally got on the phone and said, 'Yeah, we're trying to save you from that miserable sonofabitch.' I said, 'I'm afraid that I'm just newly married, Wally. Newly buried, maybe, but I can't walk. I care about him.' "

It was Maricela's idea to say she lost her passport and that she needed Cici to help her. "I figured she'd be able to get out for a few days, figure things out, and then decide," Maricela said. "But she was meant to be stuck there. And me with her. This was a tremendously ironic thing: I went to America to be free and there I was, in Green country, where all I heard was lambs."

"It was very sweet of them, their little plot," Cici said. "But Wally wasn't going to get me and torture me again. So I stayed." But Maricela and Collin didn't stay with her for long. Collin's needs couldn't be provided for in Ireland.

"So I had to send Collin back with Maricela," Cici said. It was this, as much as the rising cost of living like a lord at St. Clerans that caused Huston to give up the only place he ever really felt at home. "My leaving St. Clerans, Cici was somewhat responsible for," John said. "Collin required treatment and we went to Dublin to see about putting him in some kind of school. It was conceded that there was no way of treating him in Ireland. They could do nothing to help him. That's when I gave up St. Clerans. I was determined to save this goddamned marriage. And I couldn't have supported two places—in Los Angeles and Ireland. And the thought of her separated from Collin, I just couldn't perceive such a situation."

But Cici was separated from Collin for only a few weeks, when she herself got sick. "I broke out in all these rashes," she said. "The doctor called it the Huston disease. I was sent to England. John never got sick. Doctor Tequila was his best doctor. He was a medical miracle, bless his heart."

Cici's parents flew to London to see her and then they all returned to Ireland. Mrs. Creagh told Cici, "I felt so sorry for you. This place is full of ghosts, you should get out of here and take Mr. Huston away from all this."

Less than four months after Cici first arrived, John agreed that it would be best for her to leave Ireland to be with Collin and to take care of herself. He would stay behind to make *The Mackintosh Man* and sell St. Clerans. Before she and her parents departed Cici said her mother "snooped through everything. She told me that I should make John buy me a fur coat, because Ricki had all these clothes, Balenciagas. So I did. I made him buy me a fur coat."

28

ENJOINING HEARTS

WALTER HILL IS A SUCCESSFUL MOVIE DIRECTOR WHO, between 1975 and 1989, directed twelve films, including *The Warriors, The Long Riders, 48 Hours,* and *Johnny Handsome.* But in 1972 he was a fledgling screenwriter with one credit to his name, and he just could not believe that anyone, let alone Paul Newman and John Huston, wanted to make a movie of *The Mackintosh Man* based on the script he wrote from Desmond Bagley's novel *The Freedom Trap.* Hill had written it to get out of a contract with Warner Bros., who, he felt, had cheated him when they sold to United Artists an earlier script he had written and received a lot more money for it than they had paid him. Hill was only thirty, but he was already experiencing what it was like to be a writer in Hollywood. No matter *what* studios paid the writers, the writers always wound up feeling screwed.

Hill's contract stipulated that he write another original script for Warner's, which he refused to do. Warner's was willing to compromise. They showed him five books they owned; he could choose to adapt any one of them. Still angry about the way he was treated, Hill picked the book that seemed least likely to become a film and adapted Bagley's novel in five days. "I was vaguely ashamed of the whole thing," he said, but his shame turned to surprise when he heard about Newman and Huston's interest. "I thought these guys were going crazy, because the story didn't make sense."

The story was about an Australian government agent named Joseph Reardon who agrees to be thrown into prison so he can make a connection with a Soviet spy named Slade. The hope is that Slade will lead to exposing a British M.P., Sir George Wheeler, as his leader. Reardon and Slade make their escape and wind up in Ireland. But Reardon's boss, Mackintosh, betrays him and puts his life in danger. Mackintosh is then killed and Reardon manages to escape. He teams up with Mackintosh's daughter and pursues Slade and Wheeler to Malta, where Mackintosh's daughter kills Slade and Wheeler in revenge for her father's death.

Paul Newman had enjoyed working with Huston and Foreman on *Judge Roy Bean* and thought they could repeat the magic on this one. "Huston agreed to do it as a friend," Newman said. "He turned it down at first, then his conscience got to him and he decided to do it. But I don't think he ever thought very much of it."

"I didn't," said Huston. "It was only done because it relieved Paul of a commitment. None of us had any illusions as to its worth."

John had pneumonia when Walter Hill met with him at St. Clerans. They discovered they had "fundamental differences" in how they saw the story. "He felt it could work as a serious story," Hill said, "about espionage and the Cold War. I thought the only thing you could do was to try to make it a thriller, in the Hitchcockian *North-by-Northwest* vein. We got along amiably, but we were on divergent paths. But who the hell was I? Huston was a great film director and I was a beginning screenwriter with one minor credit."

Hill saw Huston as "a wry, benevolent, jolly old fellow. I think Huston was one of those guys who believed that serious artists were novelists and playwrights and painters, and motion pictures were a second-rate trashy profession. And his films have a lot of that kind of cynicism in them. His career ran downhill from the middle fifties until the middle seventies, and maybe *The Mackintosh Man* was the bottom out."

After the first week of shooting, when he realized that John wasn't going to follow his suggestions, Hill left. Other writers were brought in, but Hill believes that the film was mostly written by Huston and Gladys. "I wrote about sixty percent of the first half," he said, "after that, there was nothing there that was mine."

Ossie Morris was once again behind the camera. When Foreman and others began to worry that Huston's health might delay the picture, Ossie assured them, "Don't worry, everything will be quite all right with the shooting." Hill said the implication was that Ossie would take care of everything.

"John only did *The Mackintosh Man* for the money," Morris said. "You could tell if he was bored by how late he arrived. It might be ten o'clock and Paul would be there and he'd say, 'What are we going to shoot today, Ossie?' And I'd say, 'Well, we're doing this scene, Paul.' He'd say, 'John's not in yet?' 'No, not yet, no.' He'd say, 'Why don't we work something out?'"

What surprised Morris was how docile Paul Newman was around Huston, how unlike a big star he behaved. "John was always the top dog. Paul would never do anything to cross John. Paul was a bit of a boy scout."

Cici wrote John from California and called occasionally. She told him how much she missed him, and of her frustrations over Collin, who had been diagnosed as having a form of epilepsy. "One day I'm ready to take a tub of strychnine and then, when he says, 'Mommy, I love you more than anyone,' I feel life's beautiful." But her anxieties focused on their separation. "Where are you?" she asked. "I cannot live this way, I am not happy! . . . Goddamnit, where are you! Then, when you return—what the hell does that mean? It never ceases to amaze me, my feeling of not being a part of you. . . . In your life you have had them all but only one me! In my life I've seen them all and had only you."

"Bear up," John would respond. "One of these days all the difficulties will dissolve and we'll have clear, lovely sailing." He told her not to get so upset over the doctors' "nomenclature. . . . We laymen endow certain medical designations with meanings they don't possess for the really informed. There are kinds and degrees of 'epilepsy.' Collin's most surely is one of the minor forms. . . . How I wish I were with you so we could cope with these developments together."

John fed on Cici's letters. "You have such a free, open way," he wrote to her. "I hear your voice as I read them. But those echoes aren't enough. I long, long for your *presence*—and to feel your touch. I tried to imagine feeling you last night. It didn't work." He kept her informed of the filming, counting down the weeks until they would be together, and told her that "although I swore I wouldn't, I'm working on the script at nights." But it was Cici, not *The Mackintosh Man*, who occupied his thoughts.

"My bed gets emptier & emptier. I hardly realized how much a habit you'd become. Never a night passes I don't wake up groping around for your lovely ass."

When Cici received one of John's long, handwritten letters—"a very rare item indeed," he told her—she responded in kind. "I do so love and need you—only you!" she wrote. "No matter how much we try to rationalize our being separated, it isn't good, John. . . . I am mad for you—desperately anxious and frightfully empty." Often her emptiness led her to want him more to herself. "Have you not finally cooled your 'ardor-ego' enough *not* to need your entourage of jesters, mistresses from year one, and court à la JH?? I think you are through with that part of your life. . . . I'm not attacking you or what you have done—*but*—I must tell you from the very depths of my heart—I am never going to be able to become another character in your interwoven cast of many!"

Of course, that is exactly what Cici had become. Anyone involved with John became a character in the cast of his life's movie. She would write him three letters to every one he wrote, and he would read her letters in the evening, while soaking in a hot bath. Once, he wrote to her, the phone rang while he was reading her letters and he ran to pick it up. "Ass dripping, I took a call from Tony in London and heard about the play he's writing (it sounds quite good) then went back to the bath and your letters. But I splattered them getting out of the tub. Red & green inks had run together so that whole paragraphs were sunsets or meadows & utterly indecipherable. . . . But I got the gist: the house is in chaos, you love your new car, Maricela is away & most important, you miss me."

Missing each other was the subject of many of their letters. "Miss me more every day," Cici wrote, "and especially when your darlings from the past begin looming around you, having been promptly informed of the *new* Mrs. Huston's not being by his majesty's side. And, if any new twats come around—be my guest, darling, but, I pity you if I hear a whisper! I hope you are above tramping now—title or no—they are all alike *cunts*!"

"Your letters are coming almost every day," John would respond. "I adore them and you. They're ever so upsetting: not only do they turn me upside down but also inside out." Then he would tell her, "All I know is I want to be with you forever and ever." And, "Christ, I wish you were here. The Irish days have been magical: downpours of rain in flooding sunshine with three & four rainbows showing at once."

Huston, knowing that he would have to give up St. Clerans, still harbored hopes of keeping a place in Ireland. In one letter to Cici he told of an English couple who were interested in buying the Big House "to run as a kind of hostel for visiting fox hunters. . . . That would leave us with the stable complex—Little House . . . the expenses would be cut way, way down and we'd still have a place in Ireland."

When the production moved to a distant location in Connemara, where there were no telephones to connect them, he wrote: "No talk here of impinging souls, enjoining hearts or entwining psyches: I mean that instant when our limbs & our very assholes tangle.

"But I must compose myself.

"I can't!

"I long for your embrace darling.

"There won't be any talking to you on the telephone for three days. Where I am is just that much too remote so I'm trying ESP—do you hear what I'm thinking? I love you—love you."

When Anjelica visited Cici in the Palisades, John was pleased to hear how well she and Anjelica were getting along. "She is so amusing and fun to be with," Cici wrote. "We really do laugh and enjoy just having a good time being girls." Anjelica was still living in New York, and she would sometimes call Tony and Dorothy Soma to find out about Allegra, then eight, and that became a subject of concern for John.

In one letter to Cici John wrote, "got a call from Anjelica re Allegra. I had Gladys telephone Dorothy Soma who averred that things couldn't be happier so far as Allegra was concerned: that old Tony adored the child with an unbounded Italian grandpere's passion, etc. etc. Now on the heels of that Anjel tells me she got a second call from the demented old dago this morning demanding money for the child's support. Of course I'll give him whatever he wants—until I come through N.Y. before Christmas & take her away from him. Meanwhile I'm only concerned about the atmosphere of her environment."

In another letter he wrote, "Gladys spoke again to Dorothy Soma— after old Tony had again called Anjel. It seems he's gone senile & has an obsession about money. Dorothy herself is utterly ashamed. She wept in her embarrassment having to admit to this old asshole's behavior. In any case she swears that Allegra is completely unaware & a thoroughly happy child. Still & all . . ."

Allegra's memories of that time were that it was "lovely living there," although she found her grandfather "around the twist." She recalled how "he stood on his head most of the day, on the roof, singing either 'O Solo Mio' or 'Oh What a Beautiful Morning!' He used to wear a sarong that looked like a carpet. It didn't meet in the middle, so that when he stood on his head it had the opposite of the desired effect. When I brought friends home, it was, 'There's my grandfather standing on his head on the roof with no clothes on singing 'Oh What a Beautiful Morning!' It didn't embarrass me but I was always terribly embarrassed for them."

With Tony Soma demanding money to care for Allegra, Collin having epileptic seizures, Cici being six thousand miles away, his own health questionable, and St. Clerans on the market, it was no wonder that John complained about the movie being tiring. As with *Beat the Devil,* he was writing at night for the next day's shoot. And all along he knew "it can't really be any good. I wish I could put another name than my own to it," he wrote Cici. "But I guess what I'm doing is better than robbing a bank—well not better maybe—only safer, less dangerous."

When *The Mackintosh Man* was completed John put Gladys in charge of determining what parts of his extensive collections at St. Clerans to sell and what to keep. It was all too painful for him. And the sale of St. Clerans was also a cause of anger and anguish for Anjelica and Tony. Tony, especially, was outraged. "He resented it," John said, "as though I had done him out of a birthright. But it couldn't possibly have been otherwise. St. Clerans could only have been supported by someone who could put quite a large sum of money into it each year."

Tony blamed the loss on the "tremendous mismanagement." He acknowledged that it was "impossible to own a place like that and not be there. Dad only came back for one month a year. While he wasn't there he had a staff of twelve who most of the time sat around doing nothing. In a comparable house in England you would have had a couple looking after the house inside and someone else on the outside. Also, salaries quadrupled while we were there."

Still, Tony felt that with proper management St. Clerans could have been saved. He agreed with Cici that too many people took advantage of John. "I was often there for months on end," he said, "so I saw everything that was going on. I saw people stealing petrol, stealing hay out of the barn, people not turning up for work until eleven A.M. And I also had gone to an English school that teaches you how to manage an estate—that's what those public schools are for."

But John just couldn't see how Tony could manage. "There was no way of making it pay. If it had been turned over to him, why he couldn't have kept it for a year. He might have run it cheaper than I ran it, cut the costs in half, but he couldn't have paid that half, or a quarter or an eighth or a *tenth* of that himself!"

Of course it wasn't about money or management or acreage, it was about roots. The selling of St. Clerans made both Tony and Anjelica nomads like their father.

It would take another half year to sell the estate, but Ireland was now in John's past (although he did keep the small cottage in Connemara). As he prepared to fly to California to be with Cici, he had other fantasies on his mind. "My own precious darling," he wrote to her, "a request: do not meet me at the airport! Be home & in bed. Send everyone off so we can be alone. Don't answer the door when my car drives up. I'll undress in the other room & come into you. . . .

"Let's not say *anything* at all but just hold each other until we can't bear it any longer & then make love & then perhaps exchange a few remarks before making love again.

"I've taken sleeping tablets now thinking what I'm thinking—imagining what it will be like, having my cock hard against your belly isn't inducive to slumber. So I'd better stop. No—I can't possibly! Fantasy has taken over. My groin is throbbing. I close my eyes & memories, ever so sweet, take over.

"I love you with all my body and blood and soul. I count the hours now."

Although Cici claimed that sex with John was "fantastic," she left a different impression with people like Cherokee, who believed Cici was "disappointed in their sexual relationship, judging from the way she complained about it night and day. I mean, God, what woman comes to you and says, 'Jesus Christ, I married an old fart! He needs all kinds of excitement.' And I thought, 'Cici, you wanted to get married and settle down, you didn't want to go have a sideshow every night. What are you doing, trying to kill him off?' I don't think he ever cared about sex. It may have been his mother who took that manhood away from him.

"Sex is a private affair and he was a very sensitive man, but what would come out would be an ugly kind of sex. He always made women impossible. John hated the person who married him or loved him."

Cherokee may have been mistaken in thinking that John didn't care that much about sex, if his letters to Cici are any indication. Cici recalled how, during the holidays when he returned, she had to have a hemorrhoidectomy—"one of John's favorite places. When I went into the hospital John stayed with me. It was New Year's Eve. John got the nurses drunk. I was in bed screaming in pain from this headache and he came in and fucked me. I'll never forget the look in his eyes."

Once John was gone from St. Clerans he lived with Cici in the Pacific Palisades, but since he was no longer an American citizen—and didn't want to jeopardize his tax status by obtaining a visa as the husband of an American citizen—he could only remain for a certain length of time and then had to go to Mexico for a while. Cici recalled those trips, where they "discovered ruins, slept at night under dried fish in these little boats, swam with sea turtles, went up in balloons. Once we went on a shark expedition in the Yucatán. We were looking for the cave of a sleeping shark. We were twenty-one guys and three girls. I had a horrible case of constipation and finally, when I decided it was time, I went out to sea as far as I could. Suddenly, this needlefish bit me on the ass and nearly scared me to death. I ran screaming to the camp where they were making a campfire. John was drunk and said, 'My, my, my, how times have changed. The last great campfire I sat before was with a Maharaja of Jaipur and we were hunting the great white tiger.'

"He got so mad at me on that trip. He made me walk in these tongs to take my picture, with snakes crawling around my ankles. Then, in a ruin, there was some kind of thing that I almost touched. They said don't touch that or it's instant death. The next day, John said, 'Why don't you grab it?' "

Cici said that while John enjoyed living in Mexico, she didn't, and she described how she and Maricela would often have to smuggle him across the Tijuana border. She would tell John to hide under blankets on the floor of her Toyota pickup and he would say, "Goddamnit, honey. They're not looking for me. They're looking for beaners." "I was shaking," Cici said, "because I was driving with my beaner maid, for chrissake."

But John never worried about borders. "If anything happened," Cici said with a laugh, "he would just go into one of his coughing fits. We were smuggling silver through customs once and he went into his coughing fit just when they were going to open it. They had to take him out on a stretcher. They pushed the silver on through."

Cici thought John was very good in dealing with Collin. And with his own children she felt "he wasn't a bad or cruel father. He was just this fancy character. Tony and Anjelica were terrified of him. Anjelica was full of hatred because of what happened with her mother. And Tony was full of lots of hatred."

Tony's letters to John during this period reveal a tormented young man desperately reaching out for John's love and approval. Selling St. Clerans had created a rift, and Tony was the first to try and break the silence between them. "I love you very deeply," he wrote, "and as far as I am concerned, nothing can sever our friendship." He mentioned that he was thinking of coming to the States with a friend who wanted to start a band, with Tony as lead singer. And he told John that he was ready to learn about writing if John was willing to teach him. To Gladys Hill, Tony wrote that "I've got to start making my own life and face the difficulties which come from living under a shadow which one loves nonetheless." After John commanded Tony to come see him in Mexico, Tony became defiant, reprimanding John for his tone of voice and saying that he felt John loved him only as his firstborn in a biblical sense and not for any other reason.

Neither Cici nor John thought much of Anjelica's boyfriend, Bob Richardson, and Cici bragged that she helped break up their "bad news" relationship by inviting them to join John and her on a deep-sea fishing trip along the Baja peninsula. "He was mean to her, treated her like shit," Cici said. "I told him to go fuck himself."

Anjelica admitted that Richardson "was inclined to very dark moods. Ultimately the relationship was untenable." It was her first trip with John and Cici, and while they appeared to be having a good time, she wasn't, "because I was breaking up with Bob. Frankly, I was more concerned with what I was going through than I was observing Cici's and my father's relationship."

The trip was a disaster. When it ended, Anjelica recalled, "we said good-bye at the airport in California and I never saw him again."

Anjelica moved into her friend Jeremy Railton's apartment for a while, then stayed with John and Cici in the Palisades, putting her modeling career on hold. "I didn't want to do anything for a while," she said. "I was not in New York, so it wasn't possible to model in the same way, because I'm not a California girl and I wasn't cut out for TV commercials. I couldn't imagine going back to New York—a city that I didn't particularly like to live in anyway. I just wanted to be left alone for a while." With Jeremy Railton she found a house on Beachwood Drive, where she could be left alone without being alone.

•　　•　　•

Not long after their breakup Bob Richardson wrote a long, rambling letter to John, where he detailed how, on their first date, Anjelica turned him on to marijuana (although later in the letter he admitted to a much more serious drug problem) and introduced him to the world of the London teeny-bopper. He mentioned how Jules Buck tried to help his budding film career and how Buck said bad things about John. He bragged that he was the greatest fashion photographer in the world but was giving it up to become a painter. He apologized for his bad behavior in Mexico, said he wasn't the kind of man Huston was, mentioned that he had found a new love and hoped to be a father soon. He talked of his other two children and wondered how prevalent cocaine was among the young in Beverly Hills, made a twisted remark about Jews, said he was going to repay Anjelica the $10,000 she had loaned him, and closed telling John how much he loved and would never forget him. An altogether bizarre letter that made John wonder how Anjelica could have ever been involved with him for as long as she had.

While Anjelica recovered from her failed relationship, John and Cici continued to develop their own. "We have passed the father-figure stage, John," Cici wrote when they were apart. "We are operating as two adults and unless we give openly from the heart and soul—we are on a timed cycle." Yet when they were together they shared a fondness for parties and being cruel to each other in ways that were most certainly damaging.

"We loved to play practical jokes," said Cici. "One of my favorites was when Paul Kohner came to lunch. I couldn't stand the man; I don't like agents. John and I couldn't believe his food fetishes, so we put some rubber peanuts with the regular peanuts and he kept pushing them over to Paul. Kohner would eat them and every now and then he'd put one in his pocket."

At a party at Cherokee and Paul MacNamara's, Cici decided to dress as a nun. "I went down to Western Costume with a couple of my gay friends and said that I was going to be playing the part of a nun in a film"—she laughed—"because you can't just rent nuns' costumes. On the way to the party I was driving and John started getting grouchy. There were weights in the skirt of my outfit to make it hang properly, and because my skirt was hanging out they would hit the side of the car. 'What's that noise, goddamnit?' John asked. I said, 'That's the voice from Him up above.' He had this religious kind of fear and he didn't speak for the rest of the trip. John had a very naive side through all his worldliness. When we got to the party, every old codger was chasing me, of course, and he didn't like it at all."

At a party at Cici's house John got drunk and stood up to make a toast: "To all the bitches . . . and to you, too, Cici darling." Then he collapsed. "I bent over him," said Cici, "and whispered in his ear, 'I'm Audie Murphy, General. The troops are coming, do you hear them?' He lifted his head and listened and said yes, he heard them. I then told him I had to get him out of there before the enemy troops arrived and I dragged him into the bedroom and got him on the bed. I stood there looking at him passed out and said out loud, 'Is this what my life has come to?' Then, as I walked out, I heard him say, 'Goodnight, my dear.' "

As Maricela watched their antics she began to feel sorry for John. "Several times she made him drink more than he should, intentionally," Maricela said. "Instead of taking the vodka away, she'd say, 'You want another drink?' I began to realize that this woman, who had been beautiful, wonderful, funny, was going through changes. Her relationship with John went from good to bad and from bad to worse. And I was watching."

Cici denied that she intentionally got John drunk. "It was the drinking that I couldn't handle," she said. "We once went to a restaurant and he threw the table to the floor. On the way home he called me a nameless creature. He loathed me. If I'd be silent, he'd ask, 'What's wrong?' I'd tell him, 'I'm a very complicated person.' He said, 'Take your complications to a cancer ward where they're more interested in complications than I am.' "

When he couldn't get a straight answer from Cici, John would go to Maricela. "Couldn't you please tell me what happens in this house when I'm away?" he once asked her.

"I don't know," Maricela would demur. "My job is to take care of the kid."

"It's impossible that you don't know what's going on," he said.

"Well, ask your wife," she said.

"I will. Because a lot of things are getting out of hand. I happen to like you. I see that whenever I need a shirt pressed, it's you who's pressing it; and whenever I want a good Mexican breakfast, it's you who are doing it. But every time I turn around there is something wrong. This is no way to live. I go away for a certain period of time; I come back and instead of finding a wife with open arms I find a crocodile, snapping at me *all* the time." That was the first time that Maricela heard him call Cici a crocodile.

"Sure, I saw a lot of things," said Maricela. "I couldn't explain others. There were times when Cici would do terrible things. For instance, she would invite a group of friends over. John hadn't been in the house for two or three months. These friends came and had a party, and John wanted to be just with her. Then there were times when she'd express herself about John as 'nothing but an old fart.'

"He liked to watch boxing matches, football games. And she would come into the living room and tell him something about the house and when John went to check, she would disconnect the cable. Then she'd say, 'Something's wrong with the TV, you can't watch it.' Then John would say, 'I can always go to Paul Kohner's.' Little by little I began to lose respect for her. I told her, 'You don't love him anymore, tell him.' "

One day when John was feeling down, an Irish wolfhound appeared in front of her house and John ran out, thinking it was his. "Oh, Seamus, you've come for me, lad," he said. "He thought he'd died and the dog had come to take him away," said Cici.

"He was always afraid that he was going to die," Cici said. "Sometimes he'd have a nightmare and he'd shoot up in bed and say, 'Grandma, I didn't mean to kill them.' I was never able to find out what that was about."

John's fear of death deepened when a floating cancerous tumor was discovered in his bladder, "but they caught it in time," Cici said. "He went in the hospital to have it removed and there were these tubes up him. When I visited him he said, 'Look at me.' He had this enormous hard-on. I said, 'You're the only person I know who would have one of those with tubes up your nose.' "

Six months after Anjelica broke up with Richardson she would become indebted to Cici for taking her into her house and then introducing her to Jack Nicholson. Nicholson had invited Cici to a party, and she brought along Anjelica. When Cici asked if she saw anyone there she was interested in, Anjelica nodded toward Jack. Somehow, she said, she recognized his essence and felt she had known him a long time. When Jack caught sight of Anjelica, "I saw cla-a-a-ss," he later told a reporter. Anjelica said she was attracted to his eyes. "They were kind, and his whole face lit up when he smiled." And when he looked at her he was doing a lot of smiling.

•   •   •

Nicholson had appeared in eighteen films before he broke into the national consciousness in 1969 as a crazed lawyer who stole each scene he was in from Dennis Hopper and Peter Fonda in *Easy Rider*. That film made him a star, and he followed it with memorable appearances in *Five Easy Pieces, Carnal Knowledge, The King of Marvin Gardens,* and *The Last Detail*. He was an established, bona fide antihero, an actor who could speak for a generation of protesters and dopers, who did more with a raised eyebrow than most actors could do with their entire body. And, like John Huston, he appreciated the finer things in life: good art, good sports, good women, good times. He hung out with Warren Beatty, told reporters he liked to smoke dope at least four times a week, had a nine-year-old daughter named Jennifer from his marriage to Sandra Knight, which ended after six years in 1968. He then had two long relationships, one with model Mimi Machu, the other with singer Michelle Phillips, before he spotted Anjelica at his party in 1973 and called her, literally, "Mine." Anjelica was twenty-two, Nicholson thirty-six. If she gave him "class," he opened her up like a flower.

They began dating immediately. Jeremy Railton remembered how Anjelica would come to their house on Beachwood and do all the dishes, "hang out during the day, and then go back to Jack's in the evening. She was Jack's finishing school. She brought culture and art and beauty into his life, just the way Ricki did to me." An old friend of Nicholson's, Sue Barton, recalled when Jack first told her about Anjelica: "Not only did he think she was superb, but what excited him most of all was that she was John's daughter. He was so thrilled that he, from Neptune, New Jersey, could have captured this princess whose father was John Huston." When Nicholson went to Italy to make *The Passenger* for Michelangelo Antonioni, Anjelica accepted a few modeling assignments in Europe so she could continue seeing him. When they returned to Los Angeles Anjelica moved into his house on Mulholland Drive.

When asked what she liked about Jack, Anjelica told *Interview* magazine, "He makes me laugh. When I was working in New York it was very difficult to meet real men. It's so easy to become a fag hag if you're a successful model. Jack is very definitely a real man, one who gets your blood going."

When Nicholson interrupted her interview to say that she called him "The Hot Pole," Anjelica squealed, "That's a total lie!" But then she laughed and one had the impression that things were just fine with their early relationship.

Comparisons to her father seemed inevitable and Anjelica said she saw "an element of my father in Jack. I've never been attracted to weak men. They're both very generous, they're both honorable. The most attractive thing about Jack is his humor. And the fact that he's never boring. My father has never been boring either."

But with all the talk of Irish Jack and Irish John, Anjelica also saw a lot of Ricki in Nicholson. "There's a certain kind of square-earthed presence about Jack that reminds me of my mother," she said. "He's a Taurus. She was a Taurus. He's very bright and very solid. I'm waftier. I'm apt to blow in the breeze a little. He's good blood, Jack. He's true blue."

It was her own admitted waftiness that kept her out of the limelight and in Jack's shadow when they first came together. When Jack's hip friends would come by, Anjelica found herself terrified. "I'd stand in the corner like a schlump. I'd spend a lot of time hiding in the bathroom, usually throwing up from nerves." Some of Jack's friends, however, didn't see Anjelica as a "schlump," but rather as aloof and somewhat pretentious, carrying herself as if she was already a star, rather than the girlfriend of one.

Jack's stardom was of a different kind from her father's. A director's face is not the same wattage as a movie star's. "It's hard to be around someone who's extremely famous, who gets an enormous amount of attention, and still put your own energies into your work," Anjelica said. "When I met Jack I was tired. I wanted to rest. I took a rest for a year, and that, insidiously, turned into two or three. And I'm quite lazy." To her friend Joan Buck, she described herself then as being "a lady of leisure."

One description that never fit John Huston was "gentleman of leisure." He always had an urgent need to make money. While filming *The Mackintosh Man*, John Foreman came upon John's files for *The Man Who Would Be King* and convinced Huston that he could finally raise the money to make it. But John wasn't sure *anyone* could make it happen. He had wanted it for his father a quarter of a century ago, then for Bogart and Gable. He had considered Peter O'Toole and Richard Burton. When Foreman entered into the project he thought of Paul Newman and Robert Redford. But Newman didn't think they were right, and suggested Michael Caine and Sean Connery. Huston agreed, and so did Caine and Connery. When shooting was delayed for a year, John took acting jobs to pick up his gambling money. One was *Battle for the Planet of the Apes*, where he put on a simian face and played an animal he had once hunted during the making of *The African Queen*.

A more important part was that of the aging, repressed homosexual director trying to make a comeback in *The Other Side of the Wind*, Orson Welles's epic about the business. Welles summoned John to Arizona and Huston discovered that he'd be playing scenes without the other actors present.

"I had enormous regard for Orson," John said. "As a director, he was the best audience you could imagine. He just thought you, the actor, were superb and he applauded. And sometimes you were so funny that he couldn't contain himself and he laughed and broke up the scene, ruining the take as an expression of his delight." John was full of admiration for the way Welles took total control over his pictures. "More than any other director I have ever seen," he said, "he arranged the words, wrote the scenes overnight, did the lighting and the set decorations, took a camera and shot the scene himself—it was awesome."

Huston also learned something from his old friend. "He would write a scene the night before we shot and I would try to memorize it. And he would say, 'John, don't worry about it, I'll have it on boards behind the camera, or just say something *like* it.' " John had habitually opposed the use of "idiot cards." "I would damn well want my people to know their lines," Huston said. "But when I discovered how easy it was to do it that way, I didn't want to do it any other way!"

John brought Cici with him to Carefree, Arizona. Although he would later swear that he couldn't remember her presence there, Cici didn't forget. "One of the few times that I've been around John when I had a good time with other people was when he went to Carefree to work with Orson Welles on *The Other Side of the Wind*," she said. "Those men loved each other. And they respected each other. I remember when John and Orson were in this house and Orson had no permission to use it for filming, so they covered the house with a tent. Suddenly we heard this coyote and Orson said, 'Keep it rolling.' Then we heard this voice, this horrible old critter who lived next door said, 'I don't care who you are, get out of Carefree, Arizona!' And Orson said, 'Keep 'em rolling.' It's in the film. John loved doing it."

One night after they had finished shooting, Huston and Welles were each sitting under a beam of light when John said, "Let me ask you something, Orson. What is *The Other Side of the Wind*?"

"Well, John," Orson said, "it's a film about a bastard director who's full of himself, who catches people and creates and then destroys them. It's about us, John. It's a film about us."

To the *New York Times* Welles gave Huston high praise, calling his performance "one of the best I've ever seen on the screen. When I get to the Heavenly Gates, if I'm allowed in, it will be because I cast the best part I ever could have played myself with John Huston. He's better than I would have been—and I would have been great!"

"That was a good time," Cici said about the making of that never-completed picture. "Normally, the hangers-on were always very jealous of the fact that John cared about me, so they did everything to fuck it up. I always went with him to the parties, but I couldn't handle the alcohol and the people who created problems. The worst times were when he was in between projects, when he was doing 'waities.' That's drunkies, flirties, screw-aroundies. Just anything to keep him going."

While John went through his "waities" for word that *The Man Who Would Be King* was finally ready to shoot, he accepted a part as Secretary of State John Hay in John Milius's attempt at a larger-than-life picture, *The Wind and the Lion*, to be shot in Spain. It was about the United States's bravado attempt to rescue an American woman and her children kidnapped by a Berber chieftain in Morocco in 1904. Milius said he cast Huston because he wanted him to play himself. "You sort of visualize John Hay as being John Huston."

In Spain, Milius recalled how John once conned a gambling friend of Milius's into betting against him in a live pigeon shoot. "John pretended he was so infirm that he couldn't see, and he sucked this friend of mine in on the bet. It took him all afternoon, and I saw it coming. He hustled him, and then shot brilliantly and beat the hell out of him."

With John away Cici would pick up her pen and let her feelings be known. "I married you because I thought you were a great man who loved me and my son and that though you were operated and maneuvered by a handful of people, that I meant more to you than anyone & we'd work through the shit. I'm so saddened that we are the strangers we seem to be. . . . You have a very low opinion of women, which I understand completely as your business, film, is one of body exchanges, whoring, pimping, etc. and what kind of female wishes this life but a basic slut? . . . You have shown distrust and hatred toward me . . . I have asked for absolutely nothing except that you love me and live for me! You do love me I feel certain, but because of your love you hate me at the same time. I am unable to accept your ambivalent attitude!"

* * *

When John returned from Spain their stormy relationship continued as his "waities" did. He appeared as Charles Bronson's grandfather in a thriller called *Breakout.* Then came what would be recognized as his most chilling performance (at least until *The Other Side of the Wind* gets released) when he played Noah Cross, the Machiavellian magnate who had a child with his daughter, in Roman Polanski's *Chinatown.*

Chinatown harked back to the *film noir* pictures of the forties. Its star was Nicholson, as private investigator J. J. Gittes, who uncovers the plot that kept the water system in 1937 Los Angeles under the control of Noah Cross. Nicholson was living with Anjelica at the time, which provided a different kind of pressure for the actor.

"One of the secrets of *Chinatown,*" Nicholson told writer Ron Rosenbaum, "is that there was a kind of triangular offstage situation. I had just started going with John Huston's daughter, which the *world* might not have been aware of, but it actually fed the moment-to-moment reality of my scene with John."

Roman Polanski thought their situation was funny and remembered the scene well. "Anjelica was with Jack and John knew it, but it wasn't yet so cemented, their relationship. The only time that Anjelica came to visit us on the set was that scene with Jack Nicholson, when John asked him, 'Mr. Gittes . . . do you sleep with my daughter? Come, come, you don't have to think about it to remember.' And Anjelica was watching the scene and she turned and walked away. She laughed later and told me that she was a bit embarrassed."

Polanski said that "Jack loved John, really. He admired him." Huston also felt fondness and admiration for the arrogant and at times cocky Polanski, calling him "an outstanding director. There was no question, after three days seeing him operate, that here was a really top talent."

Although the stars of the picture were Nicholson and Faye Dunaway, whenever Huston appeared his presence filled the screen. He even went so far as to acknowledge liking his performance. Polanski said he wanted Huston from the moment he read the script. "He was *exactly* the character," Polanski said. "I know those people. And I always would associate them with him. Somebody who's rich, who lives sort of western style, close to horses, who's got this Mexico culture, who likes the pussy." Or, as Pauline Kael put it, "Huston was used for his rotting charm and the associations he carries with him. Like Orson Welles, Huston drags his legend right into a role, and that is why directors want him."

．　　　．　　　．

Directors also, by then, wanted Jack Nicholson, who had become one of the most sought-after actors in the film business. The next picture he chose was a poorly received comedy called *The Fortune* with his buddy, Warren Beatty, and Stockard Channing. It was during this time that Nicholson found out what he had never known before, secrets about his family that overwhelmed him. He was so stunned he warned the director, Mike Nichols, that his acting might be affected. Nicholson had grown up believing his grandmother was his mother and now found out, from a reporter no less, that his older sister, June, who had just died of cancer, was his real mother. June was seventeen when she had him illegitimately. He never knew who his father was.

If the news made him cynical about the nature of mother-son relationships, he could at least appreciate that Anjelica would be sympathetic because of the nature of her relationship with her father. "I think John Huston was just hoping to get his children to the point where they could see that all father-child roles were off, that he was just a man dealing with events," Nicholson said. "One of the difficulties of being an artist is that you don't want to exclude your family from your life, but you don't want your family and your circumstances to intervene with your art." He was referring to John's relationship with Anjelica and Tony, but Anjelica was smart enough to see that it also applied to her and Jack.

Nicholson had hoped that Anjelica would test for the female lead in *The Fortune,* but she wasn't ready to return to acting. Also, she didn't want to be in a "situation where people would say you got the part only because you're with someone who's got power." And Nicholson certainly had the power. People were constantly trying to get to him through her, but she kept them at bay. "I don't want to be the one to belabor him with more work than he has already. Or to bring other people's work to him. That's his agent's job."

Sometimes, however, a project seemed strong enough for her to get involved. "Michael Douglas talked to me early on about *One Flew Over the Cuckoo's Nest,*" she said. "I don't know if I was the instrumental factor in that, but I mentioned to Jack that Michael wanted to see him about it."

By the time Nicholson got involved with *Cuckoo's Nest,* Huston was deeply into *The Man Who Would Be King.* Working on that picture brought back memories of Walter, and even more so when, on November 23, 1973, Nan Sunderland Huston died in New York.

"When Walter died, she died with him, although it took her nearly twenty-five more years," said Dorothy Soma, who often visited with her. Dorothy could never understand why Nan never talked about Walter. "It seems to me that if I were the widow of some really wonderful man like that, that my heart would *sing* if I saw him on the screen or heard him sing 'September Song.' But she apparently shut all that out."

Someone else who had the ability to shut out the past was Allegra, who had been shuffled from place to place and from family to family with such regularity during her childhood that it all began to seem normal to her. "I've just got one of those temperaments that takes everything for granted," she said.

When John brought her from the Somas in the summer of 1974 he took her to California, where she stayed with Cici's parents. Then she and Nurse moved into a house in Santa Monica with Gladys Hill. On her tenth birthday in August she went to stay with John and Cici at Paul Kohner's house in Cuernavaca, where Huston and Gladys were writing the final draft of *The Man Who Would Be King*. Then, on their return, she moved into Cici's house for the next three years. Although she came to think of Collin as a brother, she never called Cici mother. "She was the person who looked after me," Allegra said. "She was my stepmother. I called her Cici and got along with her very well. I never called anybody my mother."

Cici claimed to be fond of Allegra from the moment she met her, but Tony Huston believed that "Cici wasn't interested in Allegra until she discovered that Allegra had an IQ in the 150s. Then she suddenly decided that she wanted her. Then Cici got rid of Nurse, who had been with Allegra since she'd been born and had been devoted to her. Cici just packed her off."

"Nurse just disappeared," recalled Allegra. "I missed her, but it wasn't my nature to cry and lie awake at night."

Since Maricela was already there Cici felt Nurse was no longer needed. And she wanted as much privacy as possible. "When John and I were alone it was nice," she said. "We spent hours in the Jacuzzi discussing *The Man Who Would Be King*. But then the spirits would come—strange, dark things. I think I reminded him of his mother. Loyal Davis told me that I looked a little like her. He said that John didn't deserve me and that Walter would have been more my type. 'Walter was nice.' He didn't like John very much. He thought he was a shit."

With John getting ready to go to Morocco, Cici grew anxious. She promised to visit, but knowing of his behavior and infidelities, she once again began to get testy. When Billy Pearson came to visit, she overheard a conversation.

"I was sitting outside the door and he and Billy were drunk," she said. "Billy was saying, 'Oh, John, leave all this shit. Let's got to Bora Bora and get our cocks sucked.' I started crying. Eventually it was one big rage."

While Cici boiled John made creative use out of the turmoil in his life. His attention turned to *The Man Who Would Be King.* John thought it had "everything a good story should have: excitement, color, spectacle, humor, high drama, tragedy, good conversation. There is truth, honesty, and irony. The story echoes some dream that is in all our hearts, even as we grow older. That continual longing for the great adventure."

His lifelong love of Kipling was finally going to be realized. He believed that Kipling ranked as "one of the major writers and influences of the century." He felt that the script was as good as any he had ever written. The leading roles would be played by Michael Caine and Sean Connery, with Christopher Plummer as Rudyard Kipling.

It was a simple tale of two former British army sergeants, Peachy Carnehan and Daniel Dravot, living in India who decide to seek the treasure of Alexander believed to be hidden in the primitive country of Kafiristan. After successfully fighting off robbers and successfully leading one tribe to victory over another in battle, they reach their goal and are declared heroes. After an arrow that has been shot into him does no harm, Dravot is welcomed as both a God and a king. But the power goes to his head and when he takes a local beauty as his wife, she draws his blood at the ceremony, proving he isn't immortal. Exposed, Dravot is forced to cross a rope bridge, from which he plunges to his death. Peachy returns a mangled man and tells their story to a young journalist named Rudyard Kipling.

Stephen Grimes, who had suggested Morocco as a location, also took credit for rewriting *The Man Who Would Be King.* "The thing about the arrow, a lot of the dialogue, were all my inventions," he said. "But John didn't admit it. He just said what I wrote wasn't any good. But Gladys said, 'You'll find quite a lot of your work still there.' "

By the time the picture was ready to shoot in January 1975, Grimes was committed to another project and had to be replaced by Alex Trauner as art director. Tommy Shaw was also busy, but Huston found an admirable replacement as his assistant director in Bert Batt. Edith Head agreed to be the costume designer, Angela Allen was back as his script supervisor, and Ossie Morris signed on as cinematographer. It would be the last film Ossie and John would make together.

Morris was feeling disillusioned after working with John on *The Mackintosh Man*. He wasn't pleased with how Huston often left certain scenes to be directed by his assistant. But he knew John really cared about the Kipling project, and he wasn't disappointed with the outcome.

Before John left, Cici convinced him to give Tony a shot at doing the music for the film. Tony had been studying in London and had the idea that the score should reflect Danny and Peachy's journey: the sitar in India, tribal music in the mountains, Tibetan music at Kafiristan.

"Tony wanted to be heard so badly," said Cici. "John didn't want to hear from him, so he shut himself in the bathroom and turned the water on. The whole bathroom was so full of steam, it was leaking through the door. Tony came with his clarinet and his stand and he went into the bathroom and started playing. John screamed, 'Get out of the fucking bathroom!' I was laughing, but I felt terribly sorry for Tony. Finally John said to John Foreman, 'I think Tony and Maurice Jarre should work together.' Later Maurice told me how Tony drove him crazy. But he had to put one of his songs in in the end."

"Some of my music was used in the finished score," Tony said, "but not very much. The theme tune was an idea I came up with. It was an old Irish tune that adapted to Kipling's work, which Jarre then orchestrated."

The financing for *The Man Who Would Be King* was complicated, with money coming from Columbia Pictures, Allied Artists, and from Canada. The people who put up the money, John came to believe, "were dismal assholes who wanted their way about certain things." His dealings with these people made him long for the Hollywood of old, where the moguls may have given him a hard time, but at least they knew something about filmmaking. "They were people who wanted to make pictures, and they knew how to make them," he lamented. "They weren't accountants and bookkeepers, tax consultants and efficiency experts who don't know how to make pictures."

But once he reached Morocco the money problems were left to John Foreman, who found that bribery and corruption were rampant in that country. "It was cheaper to pay the bribe than try to arbitrate," Huston said.

Morris remembers that John was alone during the Christmas holidays, "and it was very sad, really." On New Year's Eve, before the picture started, there was a party at their hotel. "John didn't want to come down," said Morris, "because he didn't like parties much. He had emphysema and he had a good book to read." Around midnight Ossie and his wife went up to John's room. "And there he was, the great John Huston, New Year's Eve, Marrakech, on his own, reading a book."

John wasn't completely alone for the holidays. Zoe and Danny came to visit him. Ossie Morris saw that John "worshiped young Danny," who was twelve and a half, but had "no time for Zoe. She was only there to look after Danny. And John took Danny everywhere with him in the Land Rover. Zoe was left back at the Hotel La Mamounia." Danny's memories of his visit are of seeing an older woman among "the blue people" they visited showing her breasts to John, and of riding Arabian horses by himself into the Atlas mountains. John wrote Cici about their visit, which may have prompted her to decide to go to Morocco a few weeks later.

For insurance purposes John had to pass a physical, which was administered by Len Petrie, the English doctor who had been hired for the film. "He was as tough as an old ox," Petrie recalled when he examined and passed Huston.

One near-accident that still made Petrie wince when he recalled it came during a scene in which an Arab was to attack Sean Connery on horseback. A wire was strung between Connery's legs to get him to fall off his horse, but it wasn't set properly, and when it was pulled Connery "nearly lost his balls," said Petrie. "He fell off his horse, walked off the set, and went back to the hotel. It was so close, and he knew it."

"Physically," said Michael Caine, "it was one of the hardest movies I ever had to make. But because of Sean Connery and John Huston, who were wonderful to work with, the whole thing was a very happy time. Sean and I were sort of born to play those two fellas." Caine got diarrhea soon after he arrived in Morocco, then had sinus trouble, and a mild dose of typhoid. Still, he said, "I can't remember laughing like that on a movie even though the conditions were really dreadful."

Petrie remembered how one time Caine and Connery were going "up toward the snow mountains and they couldn't get their lines right and they started giggling. Their giggles got worse and worse and Huston actually lost his temper and said, 'Christ, enough is enough, I'm going back to the hotel.' Talk about a thirty-thousand-dollar day!"

Caine was delighted to be working with Huston. When he was a teenager he saw *The Treasure of the Sierra Madre* six times in six nights. "John had one theme," Caine said, "and it was attaining the impossible dream. If you look at his movies there's always the improbable chasing the impossible, and rarely getting it." Caine, whose father died when he was twenty-four, looked on Huston as a father figure. "He was a very important man in my life," he said. "You always felt you could go to John with your troubles, and he was the first man I'd ever met who I felt like that about."

For John, working with Connery and Caine "was like watching a polished vaudeville act—everything on cue and with perfect timing." More often than not, the two worked out their routines together. The only direction John gave to Caine, whom he called Peachy on and off the set, was, "You can speak faster, Peachy—he's an honest man."

At night John would read Cici's letters. There was her loneliness and her diatribes against joining "the Huston circus," and he would respond. "You say you're lonely," he wrote. "Truly? Are you not disconsolate rather? Troubled and anxious about our life—together & apart. You: When we're apart I love you completely. When we're together I love you half the time & hate you half.

"I am not so sure I wouldn't prefer it the other way around. At least it would make for a happier time when we're able to share the odd weeks now & then. But that wouldn't work in the long run. Hating me in my absence would lead to unfaithfulness & then there's no hope whatsoever." Still, with all his fears, he would end his letters with, "I love you dear & long for you."

When Cici arrived after the holidays she brought a friend named Perra Maloof. Angela Allen was put off by Cici immediately. "I found it slightly amazing that the woman who'd only been married to John for two years had come all the way to Morocco and had to bring her girlfriend with her." Allen was curious enough to make sure that John introduced her. "I was absolutely stunned," she said. "I assessed her as being a scheming cow. I didn't even find her attractive."

Ossie Morris recalled that after Cici arrived "it got awful. There were all sorts of strange noises that came from their room. She was quite loud, abrasive, very aggressive. Had a gruff sort of voice. A bit crude. I couldn't believe that John could have married somebody who didn't have a bit of good taste. We all thought she was just awful."

"Marrying Cici was one of the most foolhardy things he ever did," Angela Allen said. "She didn't seem to me to have a mind. All she could talk about was sex."

Sex was something Dr. Petrie very much had on his mind when he was introduced to Cici's friend. "Perra and I connected," Petrie said. "We spent ten days at a ranch fifty miles outside Marrakech, along with John and Cici, Caine, Connery—it was a small, intimate crowd, about ten of us. The rest of the crew had to travel those fifty miles every day to get to work." Petrie found Cici to be "an intelligent woman with a wonderful voice," recalling spending a night listening to her and Perra singing.

Cici only stayed a few weeks, but during that time she made sure that John didn't cast Zoe in the part of the young virgin Sean Connery chooses to be his bride. "They wanted me to play the part," Zoe Sallis said, "which would have been absolutely fabulous. Cici said, 'If she gets it, I'll never speak to you again.' Maricela later told me this. Maricela said I didn't get the part because Cici threatened John with practically everything in the book. I wasn't taking anything away from her and it would have helped me a lot."

"So there we were in the middle of nowhere," recalled Michael Caine, "and everyone was saying, 'Now where are we going to get an Indian princess?' " Caine's beautiful young wife, Shakira, a former model, onetime Miss Guyana, and a Miss World contestant, happened to be there with him. "My wife was eating her dinner one night," Caine said, "when she looked up and everyone was staring at her. It took me three days to talk her into playing it. Considering she had never acted before and had no interest in it, I think Huston got a wonderful performance out of her."

John also got a professional performance out of another amateur, the 103-year-old man who played Kafu-Selim, the high priest. It was Ossie Morris who first spotted him. "He was apparently a watchman looking after this derelict house we were thinking of using. I said to the production people, 'When we bring Huston here, don't let him see this

man or he'll want him in the film.' So we took Huston to the location
and this bugger appeared and John was immediately off the location and
onto this man. 'What a marvelous face! He's Kafu-Selim.' I said, 'John,
he can't speak English.' 'He doesn't have to. We'll give him some
gestures.' When he told John Foreman, Foreman went ashen. Because
they can't insure these people. If he'd collapsed and died halfway
through, it would have been a mass of retakes. But John didn't care.
He's the only director I know who would have done that. And it
worked! John would mime the thing to the old boy, and the old boy
would do it!"

When Cici returned to Los Angeles she continued to write to John. She
urged him to let his lawyer and business manager sell much of the art he
had stored in warehouses, pointing out, "It is truly silly to have *things*
when you are trying to establish a program for an easier life after this
film." And she mentioned that she spoke to Nancy Reagan's mother,
Edith, who said "you are succeeding for the first time at being happy
and it's because you love me & I'm so good for you." She reflected on
seeing him in Morocco: "It's quite sad and lonely for you to be so feared
and yet treated with such a reverence." But she was still so jealous that
she asked him to either tear up her letters or conceal them. "I'd rather
our lives now were not discussed over a bottle of vodka and drunken
women!"

She boasted that Allegra had received ten A's at school and that she
was "going to go to be with Anjelica up in Oregon for a week as J.
Nicholson's daughter is there." And she heard that "John Julius is
leaving Allegra a small inheritance. Joan Buck bumped into him in
Venice and he informed her that if Allegra were ever really in any
serious position, he would come to her aid. How bloody *big* of him."

At the time, Allegra, who was eleven, still believed Huston was her
father. Anjelica and Joan Buck discussed whether they should tell
Allegra the truth, but thought it best to put it off.

After Cici returned from Morocco, things began to get strange between
Maricela and her. Once, when Cici left her alone in the house for a few
days, Maricela asked permission to use the Jacuzzi. "Oh, absolutely, the
house is yours," Cici said. But on the day Maricela went to use it, "out
of nowhere came all these naked women who jumped in the Jacuzzi
with me," Maricela said. "I got out, took a shower, and they all

laughed. When Cici came back, she said, 'How were the girls?' I said, 'I don't know what you're talking about.' Oh, she used to laugh hysterically."

Cici's behavior began to confuse Maricela. "There were times when she would grab me by the pants," recalled Maricela, "and she would throw ice cubes at me. It wasn't funny anymore. At one point she said to me, 'Well, what do you like, boys or girls?' I said, 'I like to be left alone.'

"She used to say, 'It's time for you to go out with boys.' "

Maricela finally gave notice when she was cleaning Cici's bedroom "and I found these terrible photographs of her. She was all by herself, but in a way that . . . well, certain things in life shock you, and this was one. Jesus, I'd never seen anything like it in my life. I said, 'Cici, I want you to find someone else to take care of the kid.'

" 'What is the reason?'

"I took out the pictures and said, 'This is one of them.'

" 'Where did you find them?'

" 'Believe me, I didn't search for them. You know where you left them. I think you should put them in a safe place.' I walked out of her house and went to Baja."

"The new couple are adorable," Cici wrote John. "He and she love kids and horses. They are so far really wonderful. Maricela is in TJ but is staying in the studio till she comes to visit you." It had been arranged that Maricela would go to Morocco to look after John for a few weeks when Cici returned. In another letter Cici informed him that Maricela "like an ass" was thrown from the black mare and broke her nose. "Do you think she wants to deliberately hurt herself so she doesn't have to leave??" And in a third letter: "Collin is becoming upset about Maricela's leaving. It is a big break for both of them. I am a bit concerned for her as she is so withdrawn."

Once, when Maricela was with John in Marrakech, he wrote to Cici that she was "in splendid spirits. . . . She has dinners with me quite often & seems to be entirely recovered from her depression." He estimated they were more than two-thirds through with the film and looked forward to being with her soon. "My time sense is all twisted where you're concerned. I guess it's because I miss you so much."

When Ossie Morris met Maricela he said her command of English was still quite poor. "She had no conversation. And John liked conversation. I couldn't imagine what those two would talk about when they were alone together."

"When the Mexican maid came," Dr. Petrie said somewhat enigmatically, "that's when the fun started." By then Petrie was strongly disliked by Angela Allen who, he said, "tried to get me off the film because I was socializing with everybody."

John must not have completely trusted Petrie, because when a growth started to appear on his elbow, he allowed what Anjelica later called "some Moroccan butcher behind an oilcloth curtain" to cut his arm open as he drank a bottle of whiskey. The result gave him a permanent knob on his elbow. He was later told that such an operation hadn't been performed in England in over forty years.

When the time came to shoot the scene where Connery falls off the bridge, Michael Caine said, "It was the first time I saw John really concerned. We were both pretty nervous." It was one of the most difficult stunts ever put on film and Connery's double, stuntman Joe Powell, was paid $10,000 to do it. Dr. Petrie saw that Powell "was supremely confident." Connery had to walk out onto the bridge first, before the shot of Powell falling off. After Connery returned, Ossie Morris steadied his cameras as Powell walked out onto the bridge. "Okay . . . Action!" John said. They cut the ropes, and Powell went down. Ossie Morris thought the shot was remarkable. Caine said, "John looked up with tears in his eyes and said, 'That's the goddamnedest stunt I ever did see. What a man, what a man!'" The entire crew of 150 people, plus the hundreds of Moroccan extras, all broke out in cheers and applause. And Ossie Morris breathed a sigh of relief that the camera had caught it perfectly.

It was a fitting cap to a remarkable picture, one that Michael Caine would call "a classic of its kind" and rate as the "only film I've done that will last after I'm gone." Comparing Huston with other directors, he said, "Most directors today don't know what they want—so they shoot everything they can think of. They use the camera like a machine gun. John used it like a sniper." Critic John Simon called it Huston's "best film in 23 years, or since *The African Queen.*"

While John was in London working on the score for *The Man Who Would Be King,* Cici's younger brother committed suicide. John left immediately to be with Cici. Her brother's death came as a terrific shock to her. "He hated John," she said. "He said, 'You've got to get away from this man, he's destroying you.'"

But John and Cici seemed bent on destroying each other. While at the house in the Pacific Palisades, he came upon a scene between Cici and another woman that truly disgusted him. "I had a girlfriend who is gay, who was wild about me," Cici said. "John was being a beast one night and I was real upset. She was rubbing my back and then took a beer and poured it down my back and started licking my back, the dyke! He walked in and thought she was doing things to me. That was his big lesbian story about me."

When John was asked about this incident it was the only time in over a hundred hours of conversation that he replied, abruptly and succinctly, "No comment."

If John was understandably embittered by the event, so was Cici about another. "It was Tony who told me about John fucking the maid," she said. "He said, 'I was in London and I think there's something you should know about. I walked in on Maricela and Dad, naked, wrapped around each other like two pretzels.' "

Cici was almost as angry with Tony for telling her as she was with John and Maricela. "Tony pretended to be my great friend and he really worked against me," Cici said. "He saw me taking his dead mother's place, so he loved me and absolutely hated me. I think Tony has a female sadistic part.

"John wanted him to be something and not just John Huston's son. Tony sat and studied his father and wrote about him and fucked his women. Tony was trying to satisfy the poor image his father had of him. We're so complicated, aren't we?"

What Maricela did, Cici felt sure, was for revenge. "She did it because I left her in Ireland. She did it to get back at me. With all the beauty and glory of living with him, John was a very sadistic man. He knew I loved her, so he figured he'd fuck her. Maricela is a very smart little girl, and a very complicated girl. She's got to be one of the most unhappy people on God's earth because of what she's done to people who love her—my son, myself. I helped her get her papers. Maricela had even confided to my friend that she thought John had gotten her pregnant."

"My God," said Maricela when she heard this, "she certainly has an imagination!"

The give-and-take between John and Cici became more savage. Cici wrote John one of her "missles" calling Gladys Hill "an alcoholic to be pitied," and condemning his involvement with Maricela as "completely disgusting, *vile* and loathsome! . . . Perhaps your massive ego needed to sacrifice the seven-year relationship of a young girl who was part of my life and heart. I do not wish to dignify the disgrace you put upon her by violating everything the poor kid had tried to stand up to and for."

She burned the painting John had done of her in Ireland, which John himself described as unflattering. "He got all my worst qualities and exaggerated them," Cici said. "It looked like I had blood dripping from my fingernails. I had a stern, awful face. . . . I'll be damned if it didn't have a heart, skeleton, and parts in it. Hydra woman. Anjelica and I burned it together. Every woman I've heard to whom he gave the work he did of them has turned it to the wall."

She recalled how John Foreman "once really did a terrible thing to me. He got me to confide in him over the phone, and he had John on the other phone, which I thought was one of the lowest things that I've ever had done to me, because what I was saying was pretty heavy stuff—that I didn't love him anymore, that I couldn't live with somebody who was drinking and smoking and destroying himself."

She dismissed John's disgust at seeing another woman licking beer off her back because "after that, he fucked my brains out. He was hooked on me," she said, "but I dumped him. I just couldn't forgive what he'd done with Maricela."

She found her own revenge with a young Mexican who stayed with her in the Palisades for a week and made her laugh and feel young. "I never cheated on John until the very end," she said.

"Cici blew it with John," said Zoe Sallis when she heard of the difficulties they were having. "He did all these wonderful things for her, gave up Ireland, which was devastating for him. But she treated him very badly. She spoke humiliating, disgusting stuff about him behind his back."

After one brutal argument John's clothes were thrown into the driveway, and he moved into the Miramar Hotel in Santa Monica. Their relationship was finished. He called Maricela, who was then in Baja, and asked her to come to him. "I was trying to figure out if I should stay down there or look for another job," Maricela recalled. "What is the point of being in a country if you are illegal and you are afraid of everything and everybody? To my astonishment, a phone call came in from John. He said that he needed help. 'Where's Gladys?' I said. 'No, I need you, I need you to come and give an old man some help.'

"So I went and talked with John," Maricela said. "He said he had made a terrible discovery. He woke up in the middle of the night and found his wife with another woman. 'It's the most shocking thing I ever witnessed in my entire life,' he said to me. 'At this point I realized that I'd been with spoiled meat.'

"Things were worse than I ever suspected. But I said, 'What do you want me to do?' "

"Drive me to my doctor's," John said. "And take care of my clothes, my medication. Gladys's mother is dying, I have no one here."

"What about Anjelica?" Maricela asked.

"Anjelica won't come."

"I don't believe that."

"I promise you. That's why I sent for you from Baja. Please help me." By then, Maricela said, John was "drinking like a fish, rivers of vodka. He looked terrible. Depressed, crying."

During the time John stayed at the Miramar, Maricela lived with her mother and went to see him every day. "Sometimes we would talk into the late hours," she said, as she joined him drinking vodka and smoking cigars. "It was always what went wrong with his marriage. I was trying to tell John that he didn't do anything wrong and asked him what he was planning to do."

"They want me to do a picture," John said, "but I don't know. Tell me something, honey. If you had the chance to choose the place that *you* would like to live, where in the world would that be?"

"Puerto Vallarta," Maricela automatically said.

"Well, tell me why."

"Because one of my brothers is down there. I love the place. I'm a flower of the tropics."

"Wouldn't you like Europe?" he asked.

"I'm Mexican. I would love to go to Europe, but I wouldn't dream of living there."

John had agreed to act in a film called *Angela* with Sophia Loren, which was to be shot in Canada, and he asked Maricela if she would come with him. Maricela said no, but indicated that she'd be there for him when he returned.

A month later John came back from Canada and arranged to rent a beautiful house in Puerto Vallarta. Then he was commissioned to do the screenplay of Hemingway's *Across the River and into the Trees* and said to Maricela, "We're going to Puerto."

"What do you mean *we*, kimosabe?"

"Please come with me, live with me, and love me," he said.

And so in early 1976 they went to Puerto Vallarta. "Cici suspected that I had arranged all this," Maricela said. "She said that I was the cause for her marriage being broken. But in reality it was she who destroyed whatever was built there. She created it and she destroyed it."

Until Cici, said Maricela, "I never had a burned bridge in my life. She was my dear, dear friend, someone I admired tremendously and she sort of crumbled in front of me with her bad behavior. She hurt John in a manner that I think it would have been better if she had grabbed a gun and shot him. But she did what you call soft-killing, slowly, slowly, slowly. She knows what she did to John particularly and to a lot of people that were her friends but she began to behave in a rotten way and lost them. You cannot do that in life.

"Also, she's probably the biggest coward the United States ever produced. I always expected her to come up with a gun and shoot me. I would have done it. And I was quite prepared, although I hadn't done anything wrong, I knew that going with John would infuriate her to the point where it would lead to a confrontation. But it never did. Just yap yap yap yap yap. No real person-to-person talk. Nothing. She sent a silly letter. And then she began to brainwash Allegra and Collin about me."

Advised by John's lawyers to refrain from any further contact with Collin, Maricela never saw him again. Allegra had also turned against her. As she got older she would periodically visit John, and when she would see Maricela with him she "would look at me in a way that, oh Jesus, there was so much hatred," said Maricela. "To her, I was a whore, bad for John. This was another of the terrible things that Cici did."

Zoe also had a hard time accepting Maricela as the next woman in John's life, but she recognized her importance. "She looked after him. She was a very good friend to him. I respect her for what she did. And she loves Danny. She told me, 'The most important things to John are you and Danny.' I melted."

Cherokee, who had introduced John and Cici, was more cynical about Maricela. "He needed someone when he married Cici," she said, "and she wouldn't let him lean on her, so he leaned on Maricela. It was her one shot at any kind of glamour or excitement and she took it and she did well with it."

In the end, Maricela never cared what anyone said about her either to her or behind her back. And she kept to herself what John had told her. That it was *she* who gave him life . . . and hope.

* * *

On July 14, 1975, John and Cici's separation had become official and divorce papers were filed in August, three years after they had married. "All I wanted when we divorced was a hundred thousand dollars," Cici said. "He got everything else back—the silverware, the wine, everything. And I have the lists to prove it." The lists of John's possessions ran fourteen legal-sized pages and included Etruscan vases, Chinese porcelain frogs, Egyptian ceramics, Guerrero stone sculptures; Manzu, Epstein, and Noguchi bronzes; Graves, Tomayo, and Turcato paintings; a silver fox, a Navajo blanket, kachina dolls, Georgian candlesticks, and silver service, including six pistol-handled dessert knives and forks; and a three-volume signed first edition of the works of Rudyard Kipling.

Maricela was at the hotel with John when the divorce papers were served. "Cici wrote a stupid note, 'Congratulations to you both,' and said something about Moby Dick, which we didn't understand. And then her demands came little by little. She wanted this, she wanted that. And the last thing she wanted was the wine. I said, 'John, you've been very generous with her, so why not give her the wine?' And John said he hated to do that."

John's reluctance stemmed from a time in Ireland when he was away and Cici and some friends drank up a case of Bordeaux that was a gift from Baron Philippe de Rothschild's personal cellar.

Maricela continued, "So I said he should put in a condition: 'Give her the wine, but she must drink it in front of you. At least you'll have the satisfaction that she herself is consuming it and not her stupid friends.' He did that and she didn't want it."

"John was destroyed about Cici," Zoe acknowledged. "She says she got 'only' a hundred thousand from him. Well, that's not bad. I didn't get that. But I got Danny."

The last time Cici saw Tony she asked him to leave her house. He had told her that "Dad really hates you. He says the most horrible things about you."

"Whatever bitterness John had for me," Cici believed, "was seventy-five percent false. Maricela knew everything, every secret for eight, nine years. If he really felt adamantly against me, he wouldn't have allowed little Allegra to stay with me or in my parents' house and he wouldn't have kept in touch."

John kept in touch with Cici mainly because of Allegra. "Allegra was wooed by Cici and stayed on with her after I left," he said. "I was afraid that since I had no legal claim over Allegra, Cici would use her to compel me to do certain things. But she was very good to Allegra. So good to her that I contemplated trouble getting her away, because I didn't want her raised by Cici."

Cici only wanted John to do the right thing by Allegra. After Anjelica visited her and said that John was thinking of taking Allegra from her and Collin, Cici wrote to him. "She loves us and we love her . . . I must inform you that I will *not* offer any resistance as the child is a creature of love and purity—this must be protected at all costs. Please look into your soul (if there be a tad of righteousness there) and make the best decision, for Allegra's sake."

But much to John's "pleasure and delight" Cici suddenly decided that she no longer wanted Allegra. "I was away," John said, "and got a peremptory call from Cici, who wanted to wash her hands of Allegra. Her parents had become very attached to Allegra and they took her for two years and they were marvelous, they couldn't have been kinder or better to her."

Allegra never thought Cici was a "crocodile" in her relationship with John. "Everybody said he married her because she was good in bed," Allegra said. "But she's very funny, she's incredibly good company. She's beautiful. And she's not stupid by any means. They were just two personalities who should never, ever have been so close. They brought out all of each other's worst qualities."

"Evelyn Keyes's book, *Scarlett O'Hara's Younger Sister*, was tacky," Cici said, "because she said nasty things about him. You don't get me anywhere saying nasty things. John tortured women, but I think he really was in love with me. It's too bad that it didn't work out, because we had so much fun together."

PART NINE

29

BLOOD TIES

"YOU KNOW, KID," JOHN SAID TO STEPHEN GRIMES, TRYING to explain his marriage to Cici, "when I think of the terrible things I've done to the female sex in my life, she just made up for it in one fell blow. So I feel better about it."

Grimes and Huston were together again, in Philadelphia, working on a half-hour film for the National Park Service to honor America's Bicentennial. Lloyd Ritter, the producer and co-writer of *Independence*, wanted John to direct Eli Wallach as Benjamin Franklin, Patrick O'Neal as George Washington, Ken Howard as Thomas Jefferson, and a whole roster of actors as the other Founding Fathers in a short film that could be shown thirty-two times a day, seven days a week in two specially built cinemas in Independence Hall National Park. John liked the idea and thought it "an excellent way to mark the Bicentennial and as a way to make my obeisance to the progenitors of Uncle Sam."

John realized "there haven't been many films made about 1776 and the events leading up to it." The idea for the film stemmed from something Benjamin Franklin supposedly wished for on his deathbed: to observe America two centuries later. "So we bring him back," Huston said, "with the other Founding Fathers, to give them a look at us today."

E. G. Marshall narrated the story, which took less than two weeks to film. Stephen Grimes was the art director and thought it was "a nice little picture." He said that John "really didn't have time to get bored because it was so short."

"Huston condescends to neither his subject nor his audience," wrote Scott Hammen about the film. "The spirit of patriotism is genuine and appealing; the wayward international filmmaker paid sincere tribute to the democratic traditions of his native land."

With *Independence* finished, John left with Gladys and Maricela for Puerto Vallarta. Gladys was still the person closest to John. She had suffered through Cici and she wasn't at all pleased with Maricela as the latest woman in John's life. "Gladys was like iron," Maricela said, "except that she drank and turned ugly." When Maricela once asked her what she didn't like, Gladys answered curtly, "Your presence."

When John was gone and the two women were left alone matters grew worse. Maricela would invite her friends to play tennis and go for a swim and Gladys would glare at them. Tony came to visit and he told Maricela that he had heard that Glades, as the children called her, was a lesbian. Maricela avoided Gladys until she confronted her. Maricela told her what Tony had said and that she was scared Gladys might jump her. "I have been called many things," Gladys said, breaking into tears, "but I am *not* a lesbian!"

Work seemed to bring a sense of normalcy to John's life, as he and Gladys began their adaptation of *Across the River and into the Trees* for producer Robert Haggiag. John was still fascinated by Hemingway and thought the challenge of the story was "to define what a soldier is." Haggiag liked the finished script but no star was interested. Eventually Richard Burton said he wanted to do it, but by then John was busy with other films, and Burton died before they could get together.

One of the projects that interested John was a script based on Richard Condon's *Winter Kills*, a thinly disguised story about the Kennedy assassination. William Richert, a young writer who had never directed before, was offered $75,000 to write and direct it. Paul Kohner was against John's playing the part of the patriarch, based on Joe Kennedy, who wound up being the person who ordered his son's assassination. But, Richert said, "another agent snuck John the script and he read it and liked it."

After their initial meeting Richert went to Puerto Vallarta and stayed with John in the house that Richard Burton and Elizabeth Taylor had built. He met Gladys, who was like "the chief wife. He was with this Mexican girl, Maricela. Huston's belly was hanging over this red bikini, which is how I got the idea of having him do that in the movie. And I was thinking, man, a man of his age and still getting it on with this girl, that's exactly the way to be!"

Raising the money to make the film was difficult. "The money was coming out of paper bags from the Bahamas," Richert said. "Mafia guys were on the set, looking around. I had never directed an actor; I had never been on a soundstage. I just started to imitate everything and act like a director with total authority and everybody believed me. Including John."

Jeff Bridges played Huston's son, the president, and Richard Boone and Elizabeth Taylor also had parts. There was a gunfight scene between Boone and Bridges that Richert couldn't figure out how to stage. "Suddenly," Richert recalled, "John was saying, 'Look, if you do this and you do that and you come over here, then it's done.' He spun around the room like a dervish, showed me all these different things, went back and got quiet again. It was amazing!"

John also gave Richert advice. "He told me, you don't cut to the guy you've just seen in the same way you've just seen him. If you're on his face, you go to his back. It was such a simple piece of information. I thought, 'Wow! now I know how to make a movie.' "

But the money ran out. *Winter Kills* was shut down for two years. The film was finally released in 1978 and disappeared as quickly as the fur coat given to Elizabeth Taylor, which was repossessed. The movie has since developed a cult following.

During the summer that officially ended John and Cici's marriage, Anjelica and Allegra were in Montana with Jack, who was starring with Marlon Brando in *The Missouri Breaks*. Joan Buck visited them and remembered how Anjelica "was always cooking chickens." They wondered again if the time had come to tell Allegra who all the people were in her life. "But then we thought that maybe we shouldn't tell her," Buck said, "because even though he had asked about her, who knew how John Julius was going to react? And so we couldn't do it."

•   •   •

In the fall of 1975 Anjelica suffered through her first breakup with Nicholson. She had come out of her "retirement" to take a small role in *The Last Tycoon,* her first film since *A Walk with Love and Death.* It was directed by Elia Kazan, featured Robert De Niro as Irving Thalberg, and was produced, ironically, by John's former partner and nemesis, Sam Spiegel. She was thrilled to be working for Kazan, whom she found to be a "very brilliant director, wonderful for actors."

While she was working on the film Nicholson was in New York promoting *One Flew Over the Cuckoo's Nest.* The Oscar push was on, and Jack and *Cuckoo's Nest* were definitely front-runners. *People* magazine predicted, "*Cuckoo's Nest* should bring Nicholson his long-overdue Oscar and public acceptance as the first American actor since Marlon Brando and James Dean with the elemental energy to wildcat new wells of awareness in the national unconscious."

Nicholson's "elemental energy" wasn't confined to the screen, as reports started to reach Anjelica that he was dating various women she knew. "I think I may have started a few brushfires in New York that could burn all the way to the coast," he told a friend. And sure enough, when he got back Anjelica was gone. She had moved into an apartment in Beverly Hills and began dating Ryan O'Neal. O'Neal, also a notorious womanizer, was currently starring in Stanley Kubrick's *Barry Lyndon,* which was in Oscar competition with *Cuckoo's Nest.* "Perfect *National Enquirer* fare," said Anjelica.

But Nicholson was able to defuse Anjelica's anger and on March 29, 1976, she accompanied Jack and his twelve-year-old daughter to the Academy Awards ceremony at the Dorothy Chandler Pavilion in Los Angeles. *Cuckoo's Nest* won awards for Best Picture, Screenplay, Best Director, Best Actor, and Best Actress. By all appearances it seemed that Anjelica had backed a winner.

In July, Jack bought Anjelica a Mercedes for her twenty-fifth birthday. He also started calling her "Anjelica the Moan," because she was "filled with such debilitating self-judgments." He encouraged her to take acting classes, which she did, with Peggy Feury, whom she found to be "a great, wonderful teacher, very intelligent. I went every day for a couple of years and I stayed all day. I was full of doubts and inhibitions about acting again."

She appeared in a nonspeaking part as "the woman of dark visage" in a movie called *Swashbuckler*. "It was agonizing to watch myself in rushes—it was like watching Theda Bara. You have to be careful when you're not armed with dialogue that you don't get into silent acting."

John thought that Anjelica should seriously consider marrying Nicholson, but all was not well between them, and by the end of the year Ryan O'Neal was back in the picture. "We split up for a couple of years," Anjelica said. She moved in with Ryan, and once again her life became "fodder for gossip. I took a trip to England and it was hard to escape photographers on every corner." As for her affair with O'Neal, "it had its times," she said.

Anjelica described Nicholson during this period as "possessive more than jealous. Jealousy involves insecurity." Nicholson agreed with her. To reporter Nancy Collins, he said, "I didn't like it, but I think being my girlfriend has so many things even I couldn't deal with that I can honestly say I don't blame her, although I was hurt."

He told David Lewin, "While I went out with other women, I put my emotions in neutral and my pride was never so wounded that I said I would never take her back. So when the reconciliation came, we never had to recriminate over who said what while we were apart. . . . All the time she was away I made it clear that I still wanted to see her. But I did it in a sort of negative way. There was none of that 'Hey, are you ready yet?' bull."

One ill-fated day in March 1977, Anjelica went to Nicholson's house on Mulholland Drive to pick up some clothes to take back to Ryan O'Neal's house. Jack was away, but Roman Polanski was using the house to take pictures of a thirteen-year-old girl named Sandra. By the time Anjelica arrived, Polanski had finished taking his pictures, shared some Crystal champagne with the girl, taken a swim while she enjoyed the Jacuzzi, and made love to her in Nicholson's TV room on the ground floor. Anjelica didn't know they were there when she went into the living room to use the phone, but Sandra was embarrassed, dressed quickly, and ran out to wait in Polanski's car. "When Anjelica had finished her phone call," Polanski described in his autobiography, "I explained that we'd been taking pictures and swimming. I didn't mention making love, although that must have been pretty obvious."

The next day, after Sandra's mother found out what had happened, a warrant was issued for Polanski's arrest for raping a minor. "I was incredulous," Polanski said. "I couldn't equate what had happened the day before with rape in any form." Polanski was no stranger to trouble;

his wife, actress Sharon Tate, had been brutally murdered by members of Charles Manson's "family" in Los Angeles in 1969. Now, eight years later, he was the victim of a rising scandal.

A search warrant had been issued for Jack's house and Polanski agreed to accompany the police to the compound, which Nicholson shared with Marlon Brando. On the street level, a large, imposing gate had been installed to keep the various crazies away from these stars. There was no response when they rang. But instead of leaving the compound Polanski "scaled the fence and opened the gate manually from the inside. It was an old late-night trick of mine," he wrote. "Many times, when staying at Jack's, I'd gotten in that way to avoid disturbing anyone."

Outside Nicholson's house Polanski saw Anjelica leaning out a first-floor window. He didn't know then that she and Jack had broken up and that she wasn't supposed to be in the house—"that's why she hadn't answered the bell to let us in," Polanski said. He explained he was with the police, who had a search warrant, but didn't tell her what it was for. When one of the cops went upstairs with her, Polanski tried to reassure her by saying, "It's okay, it's not about drugs or anything." But when they searched her purse, she knew she was in trouble.

When they came downstairs Anjelica whispered to Polanski, "They've got it."

"What?" Polanski asked.

They had found a small amount of cocaine in her purse. "I didn't know what she was talking about," Polanski said. "She didn't seem particularly upset. Certainly not afraid. It was rather an exclamation that equals a '*damn it!*' "

Anjelica and Polanski were taken in separate cars to the West Los Angeles police precinct, where they were kept apart. "We were not allowed to talk to each other," Polanski said. "They had no right to search her bag." When he saw her, he shrugged and said, "Sorry about this."

"I was victimized in the situation," Anjelica said, her voice still angry ten years later. "And so was Roman. It was absolutely absurd that I should have been arrested. I still try to figure where the justification for any of it came in. I think that it just hurt a lot of people. Period."

"How did I feel?" Polanski asked rhetorically when questioned about involving Anjelica. "I felt like shit!" He also felt angry when he heard, after the grand jury had indicted him on six counts, "that Anjelica had been granted immunity on all charges of drug possession in return for undertaking to give evidence for the prosecution. I couldn't really blame her for accepting the deal, though it left me feeling slightly bitter." The six counts were: furnishing a controlled substance to a minor, committing a lewd or lascivious act, having unlawful sexual intercourse, perversion, sodomy, and rape by use of drugs. Polanski said that his lawyer explained that "the DA's case would be weak without some supporting testimony from Anjelica Huston, who could place me in the house and the room where Sandra and I had made love."

But with Anjelica trying to save herself, Polanski felt his luck had run out. He spent forty-two days under psychiatric observation in Chino prison and was then released to be further sentenced. He didn't want to spend any more time in jail for what he never considered a crime in the first place, and so he fled the country, knowing that he could never return to the United States again.

"From her point of view," Polanski said from his apartment in Paris, "she didn't do anything wrong. At this time I don't think she did. But I did then."

"I was completely innocent," Anjelica told Roderick Mann of the *Los Angeles Times*, "so it was one of the most hurtful things that has ever happened to me. I felt maligned and ill done. And the fact that it was printed in newspapers that I was prepared to testify against Roman was the worst part of the whole episode. You don't testify for or against anyone. When you testify you tell the truth, which is what I'd have done. The fact that it was printed in that way made me look not only unattractive but also a sneak."

When John heard of Anjelica's troubles he did what he could to get her the best legal advice and to keep it from damaging her by being blown out of proportion. Scandal was not something the Hustons encouraged. Walter did whatever he could to keep John from serious damage when he ran over Tosca Roulien in 1933; John did what he had to do to keep the circumstances surrounding Ricki's death out of the news; now it was Anjelica who needed protection. As for Polanski's behavior, John had little to say about what happened with the girl, but he frowned upon his leaving the country. "He did something against the law and he skipped bail," John said. "I wish that he hadn't done that." Even if it meant jail? he was asked. "If necessary, sure. Why not?"

As for Anjelica, it's a topic she wanted buried. "I've done my best to forget it."

Anjelica continued to live with Ryan O'Neal in Malibu and Beverly Hills. Allegra, who had turned thirteen, came to stay with them for six months. "I was living half with them and half with the Shanes," Allegra recalled. Allegra found Anjelica to be very vulnerable when she was with O'Neal and felt that "Ryan didn't treat her so well."

O'Neal had a reputation for having a short fuse, and the kind of life Anjelica was living with him was more often detailed in the syndicated gossip column of Liz Smith than in either of the Hollywood trade papers. "Out in Beverly Hills," wrote Smith, "the sound of falling bodies was punctuated only by the hopes of some onlookers that the guy doing the felling—Ryan O'Neal—might be riding for a fall himself if he doesn't get his act together."

Cici was concerned about how Anjelica's life-style might affect Allegra. She called John to see what he thought, but John wouldn't listen to her. "Allegra was being used between Ryan and Jack," Cici said. "When Anjelica was with Ryan he would pick up Allegra at Marymount High School. Then Anjelica would break up with him and Jack would pick up Allegra. Anjelica and I had a big beef because I accused her of involving Allegra in her sexual life between these guys. I said that I'd take her outside and punch her fucking teeth down her throat if she didn't stop."

Allegra decided it was best for her to move back to the Shanes'. "For three days," she said, "Ryan would be the nicest person you'd ever want to meet, and then for three days you'd just avoid him." She needed a more stable family situation while she was going to school. "The Shanes always treated me like I was family. They still do. They've got two grandchildren: me and Collin."

Cici further angered John when she decided that it was time Allegra found out who her real father was. "I was working with this shrinker who said, 'You must tell Allegra the truth.' So I sat her down and told her. She started weeping and I said, 'Have I done the wrong thing?' And she said, 'No, now I understand so much.' Then I made John Julius come over here and he wept and finally they got close."

"She didn't tell him to come," Allegra said about her one-day visit with John Julius. "He happened to be in L.A. It's extremely unlikely he'd take an eleven-hour plane ride because Cici told him to." When she was introduced to him, "I took it for granted, like everything else. It didn't faze me at all. After my mother died, nothing has ever fazed me since."

Between August and October 1977, John Julius corresponded with Cici regarding Allegra. He was thankful for Cici's taking Ricki's place in Allegra's upbringing and shared her concern about Anjelica's not being a proper guardian. He explained how his wife had suffered after she learned of his infidelity and Allegra's existence, and that it would be awkward for him to take full responsibility for Allegra, because his wife didn't want to raise another child. Matters were further complicated when John Julius wrote that he was going to leave his wife and move in with his lover of the past ten years (indicating that he was involved with someone other than Ricki two years before her death). She had four children of her own and he didn't feel he could bring Allegra into that situation. He wondered if Cici might consider legally adopting her. He expressed love for Allegra, but wasn't willing to alter his own life to accommodate her. If Cici refused he would understand, and hoped to find someone else who might act as her guardian or adoptive parent.

Once she was aware of who her real father was, Allegra made a conscious decision to continue calling herself a Huston, since she considered John her father more than John Julius. This pleased Huston, who thought of her as a daughter. But when it came to observing the behavior of his real daughter, Cherokee noticed that John had mellowed. "When Anjelica started going through her affairs and smoking pot," Cherokee said, "John was preening over the whole thing. Once when she was going with Ryan O'Neal I said to John, 'If my daughter was sleeping with this man, I couldn't accept that.' He looked at me like I was crazy. The sensitive younger man I first knew would no more have approved of that than fly to the moon."

But John had other things on his mind besides Anjelica's love life. After *Across the River and into the Trees* fell through, John got involved with an enthusiastic young man named Michael Fitzgerald, who wanted to produce a movie based on Flannery O'Connor's *Wise Blood*, an offbeat look at Southern religious fanatics. John invited him down to Puerto Vallarta, where he said he was interested in making the picture but thought that the chances of ever getting it done were remote. Fitzgerald was encouraged and set off to raise the money.

John also agreed to direct a Charles Bronson movie for Pancho Kohner, who was now a producer. Called *Love and Bullets*, "it was pretty terrible, one of those cops and robbers, shoot-'em-out things," said Stephen Grimes. John wanted Tony to be his assistant on the picture and Pancho Kohner agreed. Then, in the fall of 1977, John went into the hospital for a routine insurance examination. While his lungs were being X-rayed "they saw this aneurysm," John said, "of the abdominal aorta, exactly the same as what killed my father." Huston called Loyal Davis, who made some inquiries and told John he should have the operation in California, and that it was a standard procedure now.

When John entered the hospital at the end of September he underwent a number of tests before surgery. "It was quite elaborate, the breathing tests, my God!" John recalled. "The reports came through, and all of a sudden I didn't need to go into surgery the same afternoon or the next morning. Maybe it could be put off for a while. Finally I was under the impression that it was practically an *asset* to have an aneurysm. It gave flavor to your life!

"It was apparent that my lungs wouldn't be able to take over when they tried to shift me back from the machine to the lungs. Here was something that forty-eight hours before was life-or-death. Now they wanted to build up my breathing capacity."

When his cardiologist, Dr. Gary Sugarman, asked him how many cigars he smoked in a day, John answered, "All I had."

"How much do you inhale?" Sugarman asked.

"All I can."

Sugarman told John he had smoked his last cigar.

The operation for an aneurysm was "very, very serious in a man with mammoth emphysema, because it's a big abdominal incision," Dr. Sugarman said. "All too often the operation is a great success and the patient dies of respiratory insufficiency."

Ten days after he went into the hospital, on October 6, they operated. But, John said, "something went wrong and they had to go in again. The first surgery took eleven hours, and the next one took nine hours, which was three days later. And then there was a third operation that took seven hours. How I survived all this was really extraordinary."

Sugarman said that John's serious complication was an obstruction and he had to have his gallbladder removed, "which was also a difficult operation because of the respiratory problem."

Stephen Grimes was in Rio when he heard that John was seriously ill and wouldn't be able to direct *Love and Bullets*. "God," Grimes thought, "he's finally read the script!" The film had been cast, the sets mostly built, but once John was gone, so was Grimes. "Pancho never forgave me, but Paul Kohner did."

When Paul and Lupita Kohner visited John at Cedars-Sinai, Paul said to her, "This is the last time we'll see John alive." Lupita saw that John didn't have the strength to hold Paul's hand, and when she came out of his room she began to cry.

When Michael Caine and Sean Connery went to see him, the nurse gave them only two minutes. "He's going fast, you know," she whispered. John opened his eyes and mumbled, "Danny, Peachy," when he saw them. Then he started to tell them a story about his early boxing days. Connery and Caine were crying as he talked, convinced that John was dying.

"That was a horrible time," said Anjelica, who, with Allegra, kept a vigil in John's room, spending hours doing jigsaw puzzles. "He was in pretty dire straits."

But John's will to live was so strong that within a week he had recovered from the three operations and not long after that he was released. He remained in Los Angeles "for a hell of a long time," he groused, but was eventually permitted to return to Puerto Vallarta to work on a book about his life while he recuperated.

Pancho Kohner kept Tony on *Love and Bullets*, although not as an assistant director. "There wasn't a specific job," Pancho said, "so Tony worked with the publicist, Ernie Anderson." And there was a resolution to Tony's on-again, off-again relationship with Lady Margot Cholmondeley. He married her in 1978.

They were both twenty-eight and Tony felt the time had finally come for him to settle into some kind of life of his own. He had fallen in love with Margot years before. Then their relationship cooled as each traveled—he to follow John on various projects, she to South America for a year. But at some point, Tony said, "your resistance is worn down and you decide to get married. It was pretty mutual." Tony may have lost St. Clerans, but he couldn't have married into a more established English family. Margot's father, the Lord Great Chamberlain, "is very, very much involved with the Queen," said Tony.

Although Margot would have preferred a small wedding, their marriage was "a *big* occasion," she recalled. "For Tony it was the first time he got all his family together in one place." John sufficiently recovered from his operations to make it to Norfolk, along with Anjelica, Allegra, Danny, Zoe, Lesley Black, Baron Philippe de Rothschild, and Buckminster Fuller. "Tony enjoyed it immensely," said Margot. "He was the center of the whole thing." Allegra thought Margot "very beautiful, like a Vermeer painting." But with all of her extensive relations under one roof, Margot said she was "a nervous wreck, what with the family arguments and all."

Margot's grandmother gave them a house at Houghton Hall in Norfolk and ten months after their wedding Margot gave birth to their first child, a boy they named Matthew. "We wanted to have children," Tony said. "There's no other good reason to get married now, is there?"

Anjelica, who had finally left Ryan O'Neal and was back with Nicholson, was pleased that Tony had decided to get married, but when the question was put to her about herself she said, "I find marriage outmoded. I was not brought up very traditionally in terms of marriage. I see married people having this terrible struggle *against* being married. It doesn't seem to be the joyous release one would like to believe."

It wasn't as if she hadn't given the subject a lot of thought. Ever since she was a little girl she had fantasized about wearing veils and getting married. But that was before she saw what marriage did to people, especially her parents. "To get married because people think you should or because people think it's a good idea seems to me the wrong reasons. If you're asked over and over again, 'Are you going to jump into the pool?' the pool doesn't become all that interesting. It's more interesting to stay out of the pool.

"People talk about marriage being hard work. I'd like to see the hard work taken out of it. I find I am where I am and I'm with who I'm with because that's where my heart is, not because I'm forced to be there or feel that it's my duty to be there, as commitment would imply. Quite frankly, I think that it's for money, mostly, that people get married in America. And for security. And I don't really feel that it's of tantamount importance that I be married right now."

Anjelica felt their relationship was "good and very solid. So far we don't have children so it's not a question of giving them a name." Still, she never quite closed the door on the subject. "If the idea appealed to both of us at the same time, then possibly we'd go ahead and get married."

And how did Jack feel about all this? He told one reporter that he was "iconoclastic about marriage," believing that "children are the primary reason" for it. "I got married one time not thinking one way or the other about it," he said. "I loved the girl, but it wasn't a big-time act to me. Just like not being married now isn't. A lot of people have been married two or three times in the period that I've had this allegedly impossible-to-maintain relationship, which, quite frankly, I've been very happy with, for the most part." Nicholson admitted that he was angry when Anjelica went off with Ryan and "fucked one of my best friends." The "pop" chronicler Andy Warhol noted in his diaries that "the gossip from Saturday night [April 15, 1978] was that Jack Nicholson came in and Ryan O'Neal was there . . . and everyone was trying to keep Jack and Ryan apart so they wouldn't see each other . . . because of the situation with Anjelica." But Nicholson calmed considerably to the point where he could finally say he didn't "give a shit."

"Ryan was probably one of the weakest men in the world," Cherokee MacNamara observed, "but Jack is strong; he's Irish and has this same evil in him that John had, so she understands all that. She's sleeping with her father, her lover, her brother, everyone. Plus, she knows exactly how to live with him. There's a real fit with the two of them. But it's also, 'I don't care if you leave me or not, I can live without you and I'm never going to commit.' They're transient. Their love's a different kind of love."

"Anjelica and I had a lot of clarifications and adjustments we had to make," Nicholson admitted. "It was hard to work out the living arrangements, how to be in tandem and still have your freedom." When he went to England for ten months to make *The Shining* with Stanley Kubrick, Anjelica joined him. Enough time—almost ten years—had passed since Ricki's death for her to be able to enjoy London again. It also gave her a chance to renew old friendships.

"That's when we came back into each other's lives," said Lizzie Spender, who was then seeing the Iranian ambassador in London. "She had a house down in Chelsea and I had a very grand boyfriend who used to give extremely grand parties. Anjelica used to enjoy that." Spender said that the first thing Nicholson asked her when they were introduced was, "Why won't Anjelica marry me?" Lizzie felt she knew why. "Anjelica *is* Hollywood aristocracy," she believed. "She doesn't want to be anybody's satellite."

Before Tony's wedding but after John had recovered from his operations he returned to Mexico, where he and Maricela scoured the coast by boat looking for a place to settle. When his teenaged son Danny visited, they went to see a plot of land that the local Indians were willing to lease. "It was a little hillside with a stream running through," Danny remembered. Called Las Caletas, it was fifteen miles south of Puerto Vallarta and over thirty minutes by small boat from Boca de

Tomatlán. John was allowed to lease it for ten years, with an option for another ten. The land, which bordered the sea, was nothing but jungle. The place appealed to the romantic in him. It was as simple as St. Clerans was elaborate, and, now in his seventies, he could relinquish the role of lord of the manor to become the old man by the sea.

When Cherokee and Paul MacNamara came to visit John, he told them how he was going to clear the jungle and Paul said, "Yeah, yeah, yeah, and you're going to carve it out of rock?"

"And he did it!" Cherokee said. "It took about two years to build Las Caletas," said Maricela. "And every single worker was drunk, that's why all the walls are crooked."

"Maricela runs everything, including me," John said. "There would be no Las Caletas without her."

While they were in Puerto Vallarta John gave Cherokee a draft of his book to read. "That's a lovely story, John; I wonder who that is?" she chided him. "Well, I'm writing this for the public," John replied. "I'm not going to expose my personal life."

It was John's personal life, of course, that Cherokee came to know so intimately over the years. The Huston she knew was not the man whose book she had just read. "John's just an actor who plays roles all of his life," she said. "His mother brought him up that way, he expected the rest of the world to keep fawning over him. He never had a come-home-and-wash-the-kids-and-change-the-diaper experience. He couldn't stand living through that, there wouldn't be enough time to worship him.

"I don't think John had ever been in love in his life. He'd been in love with love many times, but his ego killed him off. He was willing to roll over for, 'Just say you love me and worship and idolize me,' so he sacrificed other things. But there was a godly man in there. He wanted me to believe that he did have a good soul."

She saw John as "a giant because he had the guts to be whatever color he was, and to be that color big and bold and bright. He was as evil as he was good, as dumb as he was brilliant. Dumb in his human relationships and in the way he allowed a man of such great potential as himself to become a petty womanizer, an object so desperate for love that he let himself get so tawdry around the edges.

"John lived from within. He fed himself. If he didn't paint, he'd write; if he didn't write, he'd direct. He was totally self-sufficient. And the core of the man was a loner."

•   •   •

At Las Caletas John found comfort in the wildlife that surrounded them. When Maricela rescued a baby boa constrictor from an Indian boy's machete, John "picked it up and it was on his fingers like a worm," she said. "He went to the San Diego Zoo to find out the way to feed it. I had a glass case made for the snake and John got so angry at me, he said it had to be in the open. So I had a cage built and it became his pet. He used to put it by his ear and around his neck, and it became very tame. It began sleeping in our bedroom. Sometimes it would be in the bed in the middle of the night! We became very close to the snake.

"There was a time when we were attacked by ants, and the snake was loose. I remember the snake hissing and John went running toward it—he got stung by the ants but he managed to rescue the snake and put it in his pocket."

While John attempted to tame his snake, news of Tony Soma's death in March of 1979 reached him. Soma was on the second floor of his house when a fire broke out between the floors. He rushed to the bathroom to escape from the heat and smoke but the fire spread too quickly and the smoke fried his lungs. Dorothy Soma was also in the house but managed to escape. They had been married for forty-five years when Tony died at eighty-nine.

"I used to talk to my kids when the old man was just so unreasonable with them," she recalled. "I said, 'Look, it doesn't matter what you think of your father. But I will tell you this: When he dies, you will know you've *had* a father.' And they did. They sure as hell did."

Also in 1979, Michael Fitzgerald surprised John by coming up with a million dollars to make *Wise Blood*, provided he accept the low fee of $125,000, that they use a mostly nonunion crew of twenty-five, no stars, and a Macon, Georgia, location. John was impressed with Fitzgerald's mettle and, against the advice of Paul Kohner, agreed to make one of his most striking films.

Huston always disclaimed the notion that he had a particular style. One could usually identify a Bergman, Fellini, or Hitchcock movie after watching a few frames of film, but John was proud that his pictures were as diverse as they were, and often chose a film because it was unlike any other he had done. That certainly was the case with *Wise Blood*. True, he had dealt with the nature of obsession with Captain Ahab in *Moby Dick*, had covered the bizarre Southern writer mentality with Carson

McCullers's *Reflections in a Golden Eye,* and made a noble film of a cast of losers in *Fat City,* but in each of those films, one was, however obliquely, able to relate to, or at least understand, the nature of the characters and their problems. *Wise Blood* was so strange, so offbeat, so insular, that John had his own hard time figuring out what it was about. "It's the story of a young religious fanatic's brief rebellion against Christ," he said. "He's been scared pissless by the figure of Christ and God Almighty. By rebelling, he's punished. And to atone, he puts his eyes out and wraps himself in barbed wire. From page one you don't know whether to laugh or to be appalled."

When John first went to Macon, Georgia, to begin the film, most of the cast had already been selected. Fitzgerald had suggested Brad Dourif for Hazel Motes, the main character. John had seen Dourif as one of the asylum patients in *One Flew Over the Cuckoo's Nest,* and agreed that he seemed right for the part. Harry Dean Stanton was cast as Asa Hawks, a "blind" evangelist who preached the gospel, led around town by his daughter, Sabbath Lily. Amy Wright was chosen to play the young girl who handed out "Jesus Saves" pamphlets and wound up with Hazel Motes after he proved her father was a fraud and a hypocrite. Ned Beatty played Hoover Shoates, a con man who attempts to exploit Motes by competing with his radical ideas. Dan Shor was given the role of Enoch Emory, a crazy young man who becomes a disciple of Motes, breaking into a museum to steal a mummy and dressing in a gorilla outfit. These are not the kind of people one would like to meet, but Huston stayed true to Flannery O'Connor's vision to produce a riveting and fascinating film.

"Hazel Motes," wrote Gavin Miller in *Sight and Sound,* "is the ultimate Huston protagonist. He manages to do what Ahab was trying to do in *Moby Dick*—beat the devil. . . . Hazel is a self-driven derelict with no insight whatsoever into his motives or his aims. . . . But for the first time in his work the Huston misfit drives himself, comically, or tragicomically, not toward survival, but to extinction."

Once John knew that they would make the film, he had Fitzgerald hire Tom Shaw to oversee production matters. As it was Fitzgerald's first film, Shaw told him, "It's gonna seem to you that I'm doing it all, but I'm really not." Angela Allen was brought in to supervise the script. It was the last picture on which she worked for John in that capacity and she was impressed that he "worked harder on *Wise Blood* than I'd seen him work in a long time."

Michael Fitzgerald's wife co-produced the movie and worked on the sets and costumes, his mother was also involved, and his brother, Benedict, wrote the script. John got Tony on the film as the second assistant director, but Angela Allen said that "Tony wasn't madly happy. The boys used to give him a bit of a rough ride. And John and Tony were going through a rather difficult period. Very argumentative."

Tony brought Margot, then pregnant with their first child, with him, which was "the biggest mistake that I made," he said. "My wife comes from a family that doesn't work and I realized that one shouldn't have anybody close to you on a set, unless they're incredibly self-sufficient."

Although it was mostly a nonunion film there were still union problems, Fitzgerald said, and one of them was that in order to hire Tony, a union member had to be hired and paid "a considerable amount of money," even though that person wasn't even on the set. Tony got $250 per week and "complained bitterly to John that he was underpaid." John became incensed and felt that Tony should be grateful to have been given a job at all. "There was an enormous row between John and Tony," Fitzgerald said, "when John tried to explain that the world didn't owe him anything just because he was John Huston's son. Tony was a complainer, and John couldn't bear it."

Angela Allen thought that Michael Fitzgerald "was the sort of son John wished he had." Tony also saw that "Michael was a sort of spiritual son of Dad's. Mike is a very classy guy. He was also able to sit at Dad's knee the way one can only do with an adopted father." According to Fitzgerald, "that's all I ever did on that picture, all day long, was just sit next to John at his knee, and say, 'Now why are you doing this?' "

What Fitzgerald learned about filmmaking would give him the confidence to continue producing films, including another of John's, *Under the Volcano*. "He had a unique view of how to tell a story," Fitzgerald believed. "It's the most barren type of moviemaking. All his pictures were shot the same way. Every scene starts in A and always winds up in Z. It never goes back and forth. What he tried to do was to have an entire dramatic play in each scene. He made each scene seem inevitable. His camera was always bringing you into the scene, never out.

"He saw what nobody else saw. We had a crowd scene in *Wise Blood* of a bunch of black guys listening to this asshole talk. Some idiot said they ought to be nodding their heads. And John said, 'Have you ever seen a crowd listen to someone? They just stare.' "

When it came to cutting, Fitzgerald learned that you don't have to shoot a lot of film, and you don't have to sit in the editing room night after night. "John would leave at the end of a picture and see it after it's been cut. He chose his collaborators and then trusted them. I've copied from him. I won't sit in an editing room all day long and get confused."

What astounded Brad Dourif was that "John was the fastest thinker on his feet about how to shoot something than anybody I've ever seen. Neither Milos Foreman, who is great, nor David Lynch, also great, knew shots as well as he did."

Dourif had problems with Huston's attitude toward the story. Dourif felt John was making a different picture than the one the Fitzgeralds thought they were making. "He felt it was about how ridiculous Christianity was. But the Fitzgeralds felt it was a film about redemption. The Fitzgeralds turned out to be right. And John gave them what they wanted in some kind of backhanded way."

When they began to rehearse the ending Dourif wasn't clear about John's vision. "If I don't revert to Christianity, what does happen?" he asked. "Oh," John told him, "I think that's just some kind of existential rebellion." "But what about the line where it says, 'My Christ' and I kneel down?" Dourif challenged, noticing that Huston "went white" and started to flip through the script. "Oh, that's a mistake," John said. But Dourif felt that the whole movie was leading up to that point. Huston went off to confer with the Fitzgeralds and when he returned he sat down, looked at Dourif, and said, "The end of the film, Jesus wins."

Michael Fitzgerald agreed that he and Huston approached the movie "from different points of view" and that "John's understanding of certain elements was just not there. But what he wanted and what I wanted was the same. And that can be summed up in one of the few remarks John made during the filming. At one point he just broke out laughing uncontrollably, then shook his head and said, 'Christ, he's quite a guy!' And that's what I felt about Hazel Motes. It was the scene when he walked up to the door of a boardinghouse and the landlady asks if he's in the ministry and he says he has a church without Christ, and she says, 'Is it Protestant or something foreign?' and he says, 'Oh, no, it's Protestant.' Which is just so funny. It was a terribly funny movie."

Both Huston and Fitzgerald saw from the beginning that Dourif had an instinctual grasp of his character, which was why they left him alone. "Brad's instinct of what he had to do was right on the button," Fitzgerald said. "Then Brad thought, 'Oh, my God, it's too monotonal, I've got to shape it.' And he started to *act*. John didn't want any part of that. Hazel Motes is not a shaded character. He's got blinders on and he's striving forward, with that wonderful walk. And there was a major conflict between Brad and John about that. John went with Brad's first instinct. When an actor gives him something right, he grabbed it. John operated by reaction rather than action. Once you've given him something, he'd come up with something ten times better. Brad was just like so many actors, just totally insecure. I think it's the best performance of his life."

"I thought what he was doing was superb," John said of Dourif's performance. "There was nothing conscious about not talking to him, he just didn't need to be talked to." That wasn't the way Dourif felt, but it was just his anger and insecurity that gave his acting the deranged edge the part called for.

When Dan Shor threw a tantrum during the scene where he hid a stolen mummy under his raincoat, "John really fucking took him apart, really wrung his ass out," Tom Shaw recalled. Brad Dourif thought that John was right. "Danny got out of hand, which is very common because you're under a lot of pressure, and John was real quick, he hit hard, and he did it in a way that let Danny know that he was mad but that it wasn't permanent. 'You don't be a prima donna, you don't do that, kid,' he said."

One of the things Brad Dourif wished he didn't do was take Harry Dean Stanton's character, Asa Hawks, seriously instead of laughing at him. "It would have given the film a lot less flatness," Dourif believes. But nobody agreed with him. Dourif's position was that the film could have been more poetic, but Michael Fitzgerald thought "there was nothing poetic about Flannery. It is as black and brutal as you can get."

While John was working in Macon he began receiving strange telegrams. Then, one day, a package arrived for him. Inside was a golden hunting horn wrapped in black velvet and a nineteenth-century poem, "The Hound of Heaven." There was no return address and no indication who had sent it. A week later a well-dressed young woman arrived at John's hotel, inquiring whether he had received her package. Intrigued, John met with her. She apologized for being so mysterious but thought it would get his attention. She said, "About two years ago I had a dream, and in the dream you were dying. Then God spoke to me and said, 'I am going to spare him, because he has got something important to do before he dies. You find him and tell him that.' That's what I came to tell you. I'm embarrassed, but I had to do this."

John looked at this woman, trying to figure out what she wanted. All he could say, finally, was, "Well, honey, I just don't believe in this. I'm sorry." The woman left and John never heard from her again. That evening he played poker and everyone joked about God's message, but when he finally went to bed, he couldn't sleep. At midnight, he rang Michael Fitzgerald. "Remember the girl?" he asked. "If I'd had an ounce of class I would have said to her, 'Honey, you can go and tell your God that I understand.' And I didn't have it."

When John's doctor, Gary Sugarman, visited him during the sound editing, he sat in during the scene where Hazel Motes visits a "big fat ugly prostitute sitting on her bed, clipping her toenails." What convinced Sugarman of Huston's genius was his asking the technicians to raise the sound of the clipping. "When he edited it," Sugarman said, "it was, 'What do you want?' CLIP! God, here's a man who says, 'Bring up her toenails!' "

Huston was also involved in the music, suggesting to Alex North, who had scored *The Misfits,* that he use some variation of "The Tennessee Waltz." "I don't like using a theme that is that common," North said. "So I treated it in a nonpopular fashion and took the curse off of it. But John was thinking more of locale and the folk quality he thought it had."

When Charles Champlin wrote an appreciation of North for the *Los Angeles Times,* he said of his *Wise Blood* score, "this was the South of plucked strings and earthy ballads and hellfire piety, but equally the music conveyed the wry wit and the sorrow of Flannery O'Connor's bizarre chronicle."

Wise Blood gave Michael Fitzgerald instant credibility as a movie producer, gave John the best reviews he'd received in years, and made no one any money. "I couldn't sell it to anybody," Fitzgerald said. "Everyone was terrified of the story and felt that it was the least commercial movie ever made." Brad Dourif read all the positive reviews of his work and was convinced the critics "were all crazy."

Newsweek called it "virulently comic, grotesquely unforgettable . . . as strange and original a movie as Huston has ever made." *Time* thought it was "the most eccentric American movie in years." John Simon wrote, "It is all horrible and funny. . . . And it is so outrageous you have to believe it; something so crazy, tormented, pitiful has to be beyond anyone's ability to invent." Even the *Village Voice*'s Andrew Sarris, who was no great admirer of Huston's, admitted to enormous respect for the film, although he qualified his praise by adding that he didn't think he'd like to sit through it a second time.

Huston was stunned when he received a standing ovation after *Wise Blood* was screened at the Cannes Film Festival. Along with the overwhelmingly favorable reviews, he told Michael Fitzgerald, "Enjoy it, kid, it's never going to happen to you again."

Huston's next film, a psychological thriller called *Phobia*, proved that no matter how good your last picture might be, there was no guarantee for the next one. *Phobia* was "a little like *Ten Little Indians*," said John, recalling *And Then There Were None*, one of Walter's films. "Everybody gets killed except the killer, of course." The killer was the psychiatrist who treated his patients—sufferers from agoraphobia, claustrophobia, acrophobia, a fear of snakes, and a fear of man—with a radical therapy in which they confronted their fears by watching them on a large screen. The result was that each patient was driven to commit violent acts, and each died by what he most feared.

The film was shot in Toronto from October through December 1979. "I just took the film because I needed money fast," Huston admitted. "I wouldn't dream of looking at it. I told the producers all along that it was awful." Paramount agreed with Huston's assessment and never released the movie theatrically. Instead it was sold to television, where it has had a short life on cable channels and, in an edited version, on network TV.

While John continued to make films, Anjelica was enjoying herself traveling around Europe and North Africa. After spending Christmas in Mexico, John, too, prepared to venture abroad for his next film, a prison escape war adventure called *Victory*. After the commercial failures of his last two films John knew that with his advancing age it was necessary to do what theater wizard Jed Harris did and "pull rabbits out of hats." If he couldn't find a small, artistic film to do he might just as well get involved in a big-budget ($15 million), big-name, UA-Lorimar production with Freddie Fields as the producer. The story itself seemed foolproof: A group of POWs challenge their German captors to a soccer match to be played in Paris. Their intention is to make a daring escape during halftime, but when the game itself becomes a parable for the war they decide to play the second half. When they win the fans pour onto the field, providing them with an unexpected escape route amid the confusion and excitement. "I suppose the picture says something about the sporting instinct of mankind," Huston said. "We're at our best when it's exercised to its fullest. It had some of the moral themes of *The Bridge on the River Kwai*, with a great deal more action."

Sylvester Stallone, Michael Caine, Max von Sydow, and soccer superstar Pélé were hired to ensure star attraction. John brought in Tommy Shaw as production manager and assistant director and sent him off to Hungary to prepare locations that would be shot between May and July of 1980.

While Shaw was preparing the way, Huston finished proofing the galleys of his book and brought them to his publisher, Knopf, in New York, where he was also to be honored for his film career at a gala tribute at Lincoln Center. He also agreed to speak at a memorial service for Jed Harris.

Harris had died on November 15, 1979, while Huston was making *Phobia.* John had only become friendly with Harris after his fall from eminence and was surprised when Harris's son, Jones, called and asked him to be part of the memorial service. Because of the film, Huston didn't think he could attend, but Jones wanted him to be there and said he would postpone the memorial until Huston could make it.

Harris's death came as a surprise to John, who had recently helped him out financially. "No big sum, but I knew he really needed it." There was a young woman named Pat Burroughs, John said, who was looking after Jed, and when Harris came to John's hotel for breakfast he brought her along.

The delayed service took place on May 4, 1980, at the Booth Theatre on W. 45th Street. Huston was saddened to see how few theater people showed up. "Before the war, my God, Jed Harris was the biggest thing on Broadway," John said. "Nobody compared to him. Margaret Sullavan had been in love with him. Ruth Gordon had been the mother of his son. And when he was at the end of his tether, he had to turn to me.

"There were thirty or forty theater types at the service. I didn't call them to task. They asked me to speak and I said that the person who distinguished herself as being truly his friend should be mentioned along with the days of his great celebration. And I said thank heavens this girl was around, otherwise he'd have been alone. And it turned out to mean a lot to her. She wrote to me afterward." John, who had Maricela, understood the importance of the girl's companionship to Jed Harris.

Maricela was never comfortable sharing John's limelight, and at the Lincoln Center tribute for Huston at Avery Fisher Hall the following night it was Gladys Hill who laughed with him at the reminiscences of

Richard Burton, Lauren Bacall, and Bill Mauldin. Guests received a stagebill with an introduction written by *The New Yorker*'s Brendan Gill. "One can imagine John Huston as a superlatively persuasive nineteenth-century confidence man," Gill wrote, "striking up an acquaintance with some suggestible innocent on the dock of a Mississippi River steamboat and at once proposing to sell him a hundred acres of land on the very riverbank past which the boat is gliding. . . . The energy that emanates from him is charged with melodrama; though silent, the message is unmistakable: *Take care! Something is about to happen!*"

Gill went on to describe Huston's world as one of "male virtues . . . a world in which women often turn out to be hazardous distractions." He praised Huston's "forty-year-long career" and his "zest for life. There he stands, his shaggy white beard held high above the crowd, and we do well to salute him."

Critic Andrew Sarris agreed with Gill in a piece he wrote for the *Village Voice*. "The honor to Huston was long overdue," he wrote, "and I write this quite candidly as one of his erstwhile nonadmirers. . . . I could not help wondering whether he was the god of light or the god of darkness. Probably, he was a tantalizing mixture of both, capable of both tenderness and cruelty in equal measure."

He then proceeded to revise his opinions of Huston's more neglected films: *Heaven Knows, Mr. Allison; The Unforgiven* ("with the racist intensity of *The Searchers*, and a fiery performance by Audrey Hepburn"); *The Kremlin Letter* ("with its remarkable sophisticated awareness of evil in every facet of life"); *The Life and Times of Judge Roy Bean*; and *The Mackintosh Man* ("a work of pitiless nihilism").

The salute, shown on public television, consisted of a photomontage of John's life plus excerpts from nineteen of his films, along with six in which he appeared as an actor. There was a party on the stage at the end of the tribute and Joan Buck, who had been invited by Lauren Bacall, stood next to John and began to feel somewhat odd. "People came up to me and started calling me Ricki," she said. "Others were calling me Anjelica. Some thought I was Cici. There was this legendary thing about John where time stopped and things were just floating around."

Anjelica heard from Buck about the party and wished she could have been there. But she was in Santa Barbara working on a small part as a lion tamer in Nicholson's next film, *The Postman Always Rings Twice*, and could only watch it on TV.

A week later, on a Monday evening, Anjelica pushed a cassette into her Mercedes's tape deck and had a flash of recognition, remembering that she had given her mother some tapes to listen to before Ricki left on her fatal trip. The recollection of Ricki's death made her think about fastening her seat belt, but she didn't bother as she drove down Coldwater Canyon on her way to go roller skating in the valley. Speeding in the other direction was a BMW, driven by a sixteen-year-old boy. He had been drinking and lost control of the car, which crashed into the back of the car in front of Anjelica's. The BMW then ricocheted and smashed head-on into her car. Because she wasn't wearing her seat belt her body flew forward and her face slammed into the windshield, breaking her nose in four places. Her eyes were blackened and her teeth felt loose in her head and she thought that she had lost her sight as well as her looks.

"I remember being ejected and then coming back into my seat and seeing nothing. Blackout. And feeling my face to see if my eyes were there. Then my hands traveled down my face and I knew that my nose was no longer where it once had been. There was a lot of blood. I ran out of the car. That's when the police came. I kept asking, 'Do I have lacerations?' You become very pinpointed in those moments."

The paramedics showed her what she looked like in a mirror. "I saw it was mostly my nose," Anjelica said. They wanted to take her to the nearest hospital, but she knew she needed plastic surgery and insisted that they call Jack Nicholson's secretary, Annie Marshall, who came immediately and took her to Cedars-Sinai.

The surgery gave her a nose she thought looked straighter from the front and slightly bumpier on the ridge, and she joked that people suspected she had the accident on purpose to get a better nose. After three days of recovery Anjelica returned to Jack's house and wrote a long letter to John explaining the accident and how it wasn't her fault. Huston had left for Budapest right after the Lincoln Center tribute to begin work on *Victory* and Anjelica gave the letter to Allegra, who was going over there to work with him for the first time.

The accident had a profound effect on Anjelica. "It made me aware that life is fleeting and tenuous," she said. "And that I really wanted to work."

The most immediate change was her decision to move out of Nicholson's house and into her own. "I had a good life with Jack," she said, "but it was necessary to remove myself from the entourage a career like his engenders. I needed to get back to myself and find out what exactly it was I wanted to do. Not just in acting. I had never lived alone. I didn't even know what color I liked my coffee in the morning. I didn't know what *I* was like. I needed to draw away. To know that when the phone rang it rang for me."

"It was the smartest thing she ever did," Jeremy Railton said when Anjelica told him of the canyon house she found on Beverly Glen above Sunset. "She got out of the shadow of all those older actors. She started to do little jobs around town, just to get her feet wet, and got some independence."

Allegra was also feeling pretty independent when she arrived in Budapest in June to join John. After filling him in on Anjelica's recovery she began to observe the way he worked. "He didn't talk to his actors very much," she noticed. "He'd say something, then go off, they'd do it, he'd come back. He adored Michael Caine. Had no time for Stallone. And he and Pélé got along brilliantly. Pélé was just the nicest person, so sweet." A person Allegra found even sweeter was one of the soccer players who was the captain of the Cosmos and played a mean German. "I spent a lot of time with him," she said. "I was only fifteen, so don't read things into this that aren't there. It lasted as long as he was there, for half the picture."

John, too, enjoyed a brief romantic interlude when Marietta Tree flew in for a few days. When he wasn't working they would go for picnics on mountaintops or eat apricot ice cream in the village square. She was enthralled watching John direct scenes in the dead of night and then seeing the rushes, which she likened to a "film within a film."

"Dad was thrilled that she was there," said Allegra, "and she was thrilled to be there. They clearly adored each other."

Sylvester Stallone, who wasn't off on mountaintops eating apricot ice cream with Huston, didn't adore John at all. Especially when he struggled through action scenes having to take his cues from Tommy Shaw. "Action is not my strongest suit," John admitted, saying he left most of those sequences in Shaw's hands. Because the weather in Hungary was cold, John often directed, or watched Shaw direct, from inside a car.

For one scene Stallone had to crawl under a barbed wire fence and he saw Huston far away from the action, by his trailer. He thought John was watching from a distance and after he struggled through it, he looked up toward the trailer and Huston wasn't even there. He walked over to talk to John, knocked at his trailer door, and found it locked. He was angry and later, after the film was completed, told John Milius about it. "John didn't give a shit," Milius said. "He just didn't want to be bothered with Sylvester Stallone."

To the press, though, Huston was polite and full of praise about Stallone. "I'd heard Sly's reputation for throwing his weight around," John said. "But his behavior here has been as modest as one could hope for. He couldn't be more disciplined." But the difference between the men was as clear as that between *Fat City* and *Rocky*. John appreciated the first *Rocky*; he saw it as "mythological and legendary. But it wasn't the true world of boxing." And that, perhaps, was how he saw Stallone as well—as not quite real.

"I knew he had problems with Stallone," said Pélé, "but with me there were none." It was working for Huston that made the picture "an important experience in my personal and professional life," Pélé said. Professionally it came at a time when he was "just beginning to gain confidence as an actor on an international level. It convinced me to make movies my new career. Huston taught me a lot about life. I have met popes, presidents, kings, and queens, but I have never been so impressed with a man's charisma as with John Huston."

The shot John wanted from Pélé was the game-winning goal, where he flipped upside down and kicked the ball into the net from an impossible position. Pélé was known around the world for his acrobatic play and worked to exhaustion getting that shot. "I don't remember exactly how many times we did it," he said, "but Huston wanted the play to be perfect, so we did it until perfection. It was very gratifying for me to do it the way he expected it to be done."

Newsweek called John "a sly old pro" when it reviewed *Victory*, predicting a commercial hit. *Time* praised Pélé's "wondrous tricks on the field" and concluded, "Anyone who does not find himself yelling along with the extras should probably have stayed home with his Proust and bitters." There must have been a lot more readers than *Time* imagined. *Victory* was forgotten soon after its release.

After *Victory* was completed Allegra went to London, where she stayed with Tony and visited with Danny. She told them how she had worked part-time as a secretary for Jack Nicholson's friend, Helena Kallianiotes, who ran a fashionable roller skating rink, but Tony wasn't impressed. "What are you going to do when you go back to L.A.?" he challenged her. "Vegetate?" It occurred to her that Tony was right, and she decided to stay in England, find a flat of her own, and apply to Oxford.

Allegra's education was very much on Huston's mind when he wrote a carefully worded letter to John Julius, which a lawyer went over before it was sent. Huston wanted to arrange a meeting with Norwich in London, "at which time I would be most grateful to hear what material provision you have made—or will make—for Allegra's future." He noted it wasn't a subject he would normally broach, "but the circumstances are unusual—and I'm not getting any younger." He worried that, at sixteen, Allegra might be too young to aim for Oxford. John Julius agreed to provide her with a French tutor and an interview with a close friend of his, who was also the English literature tutor at Oxford's New College. Satisfied that John Julius would begin to take some responsibility for Allegra, John returned to the States, where he prepared to make the obligatory author's tour to promote the release of his autobiography.

On August 24, 1980, the *Chicago Tribune* ran a story about Cici, who was described as wearing "an enormous diamond ring on her right hand," which, she explained, she got when she traded in a Maserati a friend had given to her as a Christmas gift. Described as a "world-wide traveler" and an "eminent horsewoman" who was "always attractive to men," Cici announced that she was about to marry composer Maurice Jarre (who did the music for *The Man Who Would Be King*). "Huston left taking the silver, my Mexican maid, and the wine," she told the *Tribune*, "but if John hadn't left, I wouldn't have had Maurice, so I can't complain." The marriage would never take place, but Cici was holding up nicely as a woman of independent and iconoclastic means.

Maricela would get upset whenever she read things Cici said about her. "Who is Cici?" John would then say to her. "She's nothing but a cobra. As long as you listen to me you don't have to care about what anybody says."

Cici, on the other hand, cared a great deal about the notoriety she received when John dubbed her "a crocodile" in his autobiography. Ironically titled *An Open Book*, it gave an elegant account of Huston as a public figure and received praise from the critics, but those who knew him were disappointed. Anjelica thought "he left out as much as he put in." Tony read it as "cheery chat," and thought it was too much "on the surface." Danny liked the stories but didn't think the title was accurate. Billy Pearson thought that what was "lousy" in John's book, as in most autobiographies, "is that you never come out a really good guy and you never come out an asshole." Evelyn Keyes, whose tell-all *Scarlett O'Hara's Younger Sister* appeared in 1977, felt "nobody was home, including him. I loved the part of the book where I left him flat broke," she said with a laugh. Jules Buck considered it "dreadful. He had an opportunity to really write a wonderful book. But it was just shit." John never mentioned Buck in his book, just as he refused to name Cici. The only thing he had to say about his fifth marriage was that it "was tantamount to putting my finger in the seasnake's mouth." He ended his book by answering what he would or would not do if he had it all to do over again: "I would spend more time with my children. I would make my money before spending it. I would learn the joys of wine instead of hard liquor. I would not smoke cigarettes when I had pneumonia. I would not marry the fifth time." Cici's opinion of John's book: "I never read it."

"Your letter was waiting for me when I got back from hustling my book," Huston wrote to John Julius on November 1. Norwich had written Huston about having helped Allegra find a flat at 113 Sloane Street and her upcoming written and oral exams for Oxford. "Maybe she's that much better off, having two fathers," Huston wrote back. He also indicated that "whenever the financial end of it becomes burden-some, don't hesitate to let me know. I like the feeling of being responsible for her—either more or less."

During the first two months of 1981 Huston and John Julius ex-changed a series of letters regarding Allegra, who had failed in her first attempt to get into Oxford. She had done well in her written papers but wasn't prepared for the detailed intensity of the orals. Norwich began to investigate which girl's school might be best for her to attend until she was ready to repeat the Oxford entrance exams. He agreed to put £3,000 into an account he set up for her and asked Huston to contrib-ute £5,000. While John Julius described Allegra as having cried over the phone about her rejection, Huston wrote that "she showed no signs of shock whatever. . . . In any case, I think it's time for such an incident in her life. She had every reason to believe that she was vastly superior in matters of intellect. This experience . . . will prepare her for similar disappointments when (God forbid) they come to her."

Huston wasn't worried about Allegra as a student and knew that she would get accepted by Oxford when she was a year older and more prepared. Her education was important to him; he had always thought of himself as a perennial student, and was forever interested in the passing parade of current affairs. During the publicity tour for his book he became concerned with the conservative direction the United States had taken with the election of Ronald Reagan as president. Ever since Reagan was president of the Screen Actors Guild during the HUAC inquisition and the anti-Communist hysteria that led to the blacklist, Huston "had very little use for him politically." He considered Reagan both "a bore" and "a bad actor." He also thought "he has a low order of intelligence. With a certain cunning. He's one of those people who thinks he is right. And he's not right about anything."

John felt differently about Bill Moyers, and agreed to be interviewed by him for his PBS series on "Creativity." Moyers sent Janet Roach down to Las Caletas to pre-interview Huston. Roach was an experienced journalist, having graduated from Barnard and the Columbia School of Journalism before she joined CBS in 1967. When Moyers left the network to join Public Broadcasting, he hired her away to come with him.

"You know how sometimes you meet somebody and you know that there is something there?" Janet Roach said. "It was like that with John." Roach was concerned that Bill Moyers wasn't well-enough versed in Huston's films to pull off an in-depth interview with him, but she knew that Moyers had read An Open Book and that he prepared many of his own questions.

On the night before their interview Moyers wrote Huston a two-page letter outlining the topics he wanted to cover. He wasn't interested in Hollywood gossip, Moyers said, but rather in the influences during the first third of Huston's life, where he believed one's creative urges are formed. He hoped to get into Henry Blanke's advice to him about directing each scene as if it was the most important, and about the relationship between writing and directing and the "grammar" of film. He mentioned his own favorite scenes in some of Huston's movies (which should have eased Janet Roach's concerns) that inspired him to include John in the series. Those scenes were Walter's dance upon the discovery of gold in Treasure, the creation of Adam and Eve in The Bible, and when the tribal armies genuflected to the holy men who passed between them before their battle began in The Man Who Would Be King.

"We filmed all morning long," Janet Roach remembered. "They talked about Michelangelo and all kinds of things. When we broke for lunch, Moyers told Huston stories about Lyndon Johnson that I had never heard him tell. I went away not quite sure what we had, but it worked out just fine."

While she was there Roach was struck by a small, radiant girl who was always around. She soon found out that the child already had quite a history: Apparently, Lillian Ross had mentioned to John that she wanted to adopt another child. The opportunity arose when a child was born to a prostitute who was willing to give her up. "She was just a town charge," John said. "A newborn of a lady of the evening. I want to give her that high a grade." Gladys made the necessary arrangements, but when she told Ross that all she had to do was come down and bring her back across the border Ross backed out. "Lillian was afraid of the legalities," said her friend, Lola Finkelstein. "Gladys kept telling Lillian you just take her in your arms onto the plane and go home. Lillian said that's not real, that's not the way it works." By then Gladys had fallen for the child and decided to adopt her herself.

The presence of a little girl around the compound was fitting, for John was then preparing to make a film unlike anything he had ever attempted. Ray Stark had brought him one of the biggest musicals ever to appear on Broadway, based on a popular cartoon character named Little Orphan Annie, about a little girl who made it out of the orphanage to find happiness with her Daddy Warbucks. *Annie* won seven Tonys, including Best Musical, when it appeared on Broadway in 1976 and it cost Columbia $9.5 million to secure the film rights—the highest price ever paid for a Broadway show. Frank Price was head of Columbia's film and television operations and he put Ray Stark in charge of producing *Annie*, which, at close to $40 million, would become their most expensive film since *Close Encounters of the Third Kind.*

"I really disliked the play," Ray Stark said. "I thought it was a kid's play, a caricature, good for a New York audience who had three martinis, or for kids who sit on telephone books, or for people in wheelchairs. The only thing I thought I could do with the play, which maybe was a mistake, was to try to make it better. I thought it certainly would be classy with John, because John *was* Daddy Warbucks!"

But with John's hacking cough, acting *and* singing would be impossible. Stark knew that John needed money, and he thought that directing *Annie* could make him some big bucks. John would eventually earn about $1 million on the project, but he would never consider it a John Huston film. "It was a Ray Stark picture," he would say. "I had little or nothing to do with it."

Albert Finney, cast as Daddy Warbucks, found his inspiration, as Ray

Stark had hoped, in John. Carol Burnett was cast as Miss Hannigan, the mean head of the orphanage; Bernadette Peters and Tim Curry as Lily and Rooster, the impostors who claim to be Annie's parents so they can receive the $50,000 offered by Warbucks; and Aileen Quinn was to play Annie. "We had auditioned thousands of little girls and it wasn't simply a publicity job to find the right one," said Huston. "Very early I had made my choice, but I wanted to let the auditions take their course. It turned out my choice was the same as all the others. Aileen could have served as the model for the original cartoon." Her smile, he felt, was like a light brightening a room.

"Then we got a very good writer," said Ray Stark, "Carol Sobieski, who wrote much tougher than the play was, but wonderful kid stuff." While preparations were under way to turn Annie into a film, John enjoyed himself planting bamboo trees and relaxing at Las Caletas.

In April 1981, John, Gladys, and Maricela went to New York to begin Annie. They were staying at the Essex House, visiting with old friends, making plans to go to the theater and to museums. Allegra had also joined them and she, Gladys, Lola Finkelstein, Lillian Ross, and her son Eric went to see a musical adaptation of a Dickens play. Earlier that afternoon Michael Fitzgerald and his wife visited John and Gladys to show them their new baby. Fitzgerald was always impressed with Gladys, whom he saw as John's "alter ego." "She was the operational side of John," he said. "She functioned as his memory. She was remarkable in her constancy." When the Fitzgeralds left, Gladys met Elaine Steinbeck for dinner.

The following night Gladys and John were invited to join Bill Moyers and his executive producer for a dinner at Janet Roach's apartment. Moyers was still putting the finishing touches on his interview with Huston and John had taken a liking to Roach, whom he had invited to dinner at "21" with Gladys earlier that week. In the afternoon John and Gladys went to a movie and then returned to their hotel to get ready for dinner. Gladys told John she wanted to go to her room to lie down for a while. When the time came for them to meet downstairs Gladys wasn't there; knowing her punctuality John became concerned. He called her suite but no one answered. He had the housekeeper send up a security man who unlocked her door. "And there she was on the bed," John said, "still in her street clothes. She was dead—her hands and face were cold. Apparently she had had a heart attack."

Her death, at sixty-one, was so unexpected, so shocking, that John felt as if a part of him had died. He called his lawyer, Henry Hyde, who told John to let him handle it. Hyde went immediately to the Essex House, where he identified Gladys to the police and escorted her body to a funeral home.

The funeral was held at a small Unitarian church on Madison Avenue a few days later. Thirty people came to pay their respects, including Ray Stark, John Foreman, the Hydes, the Finkelsteins, Elaine Steinbeck, Eve Arnold, Lillian Ross, Janet Roach, and Anjelica, who had flown in from Aspen. "John was deeply grieved," recalled Lola Finkelstein. "He sobbed during the funeral. It was very moving."

Maricela didn't attend the funeral, but when it was over John returned to the hotel to take her on a horse-drawn carriage ride through Central Park. "He was very quiet," Maricela said. He was trying to come to grips with what life would be like without Gladys. She made his appointments, kept his correspondence, looked after his business, wrote with him, typed their scripts, purchased and sold his art, remembered birthdays, bought gifts, took his abuse. As their carriage passed a black street musician playing a saxophone, John asked the driver to stop. He listened a while and then began to cry. He took some money from his pocket, gave it to Maricela, and told her to give it to the musician. "Tell him he's very good," John said.

Maricela had seen John give his money to beggars, street people, to anyone he thought might be suffering. "In New York he would have sums of cash in his pocket and he would take everybody to lunch all the time. It was John always inviting the world to dine."

As their carriage clip-clopped through the park, Maricela brought up his largesse as a way to break his silence. "Poppy, I crossed the border and have to work for my money, it doesn't grow on trees. Why do you sort of throw it away?"

"I don't throw my money away," he said. "I'm making people happy. If somebody smiles, it gives me pleasure. It's like a chain. If my kids are ever in trouble, someone might be able to help them. So what's the point of keeping the money? Money doesn't keep you warm, but a smile warms you up."

He needed to feel warm. He was chilled by the sudden loss of Gladys. She had put up with so much of his foolishness, with his disastrous last marriage, his dalliances, his faults and weaknesses that only she knew. She had meant more to him than any of his wives.

30

MEPHISTOPHELES TO HIS OWN FAUST

"I THOUGHT IT WOULD BE THE END OF HIM," SAID TOM Shaw about Gladys's death. "He said it was worse than losing all of his wives *together*," Betty Jaffe recalled. "That's exactly the way he expressed it." Years later when John talked of her he admitted to still being at "something of a loss without her. Gladys really ran my life."

Most people who knew him believed that Huston would never fully recover, but they soon began to see a different John. "He started initiating telephone calls and conversations in the way that Gladys did," said Lola Finkelstein. "It was amazing, John functioned very well."

Janet Roach wrote to him offering to adopt Gladys's adopted child, but John had decided it would be best for Maricela to do that. Maricela wasn't sure she would be able to divide her time fairly between the child and John's needs, but she agreed to go through the legalities of the adoption.

John didn't have much time to dwell on Gladys's passing. Even if he didn't care for *Annie,* he still had to make the film, and he was able to enjoy the performances of his cast, especially Aileen Quinn. "I know some directors say that you should never direct children or animals," he told writer Gregg Kilday. "Well, that comes from somebody who doesn't understand animals. I think little girls are animals, and if you understand animals, they are the easiest things in the world to direct."

Huston invited Bill Moyers and Janet Roach on the New Jersey set on the day Quinn sang "Tomorrow." "John insisted that we be allowed to film this particular scene for our profile," said Roach. "It was *the* scene, *the* song, *the* moment of the whole shebang. That was typical of John's generosity. Who else gets a documentary of that?"

As Roach observed Huston working she realized that, in the hands of a master, it all seemed so effortless. "John never looked like he was working. Because most of the work went on inside his head. And what does thinking *look* like? It looks like somebody sitting still and doing nothing. There are an awful lot of people who don't have the courage to do that."

When Huston agreed to meet with Wieland Schulz-Keil, a young producer who had just purchased the rights to *Under the Volcano*, Malcolm Lowry's classic novel of drunkenness and despair, he put his crafty casting eye on the bearded German who had a wild look in his eye, and asked if he'd like to play the part of the bomb-throwing anarchist in *Annie*. Schulz-Keil figured if he did the scene then perhaps John would get behind his project. "I wasn't just to throw a bomb," he said, "but Annie's dog was supposed to prevent me from throwing it. And this was a mutt, absolutely incapable of attacking anybody. The trainer gave me a big stick and asked me to hit the dog so that it would hate me and attack me. But I wasn't going to hit the dog. The scene was dreadful. I would throw the bomb and the dog stood there, wagging its tail. What was supposed to be an afternoon became two weeks."

Being there so long gave Schulz-Keil the opportunity to discuss *Under the Volcano* with Huston, who had been interested in the book for years and had read dozens of script adaptations, including one by Gabriel García Marquez. But none solved the problems the book presented. As Schulz-Keil watched Finney (whose Daddy Warbucks delighted Ray Stark because he "used to copy John all the time"), it became clear to him that Finney would make a terrific Consul, the main character in *Under the Volcano*.

It also became clear to Schulz-Keil that *Annie* was not the kind of picture Huston felt comfortable making. "John did not relate very well to the choreographer and the dancers and what they were doing there.

It was alien territory for him. Then, also, Ray Stark considered this his own chef d'oeuvre. He was all over the place. He kept insisting on John's shooting scenes that John just didn't want to shoot. Some cutesy little cutaways that didn't end up in the movie; the dog peeing on one of the pillows in the house, that sort of thing." What Schulz-Keil could appreciate, though, was how John kept cutting off many of the production numbers in the middle. "I can't stand it when they go on and on dancing and singing," Schulz-Keil said.

The film's editor, Margaret Booth, felt that "John did the best he could with it, although he should never have done it—never, never, never. But he was hard up."

Annie wasn't a film John liked to talk about, wasn't proud of, and totally disowned. "It wasn't Huston's kind of movie," said Ray Stark, "but he did a fabulous job with it. And he wasn't in the best health at the time." Stark blamed the disappointing box office on the critics, who "really dumped down on it because of the cost of the picture." But, Stark said, if you took away the nearly $10 million paid for the rights, the film cost about $28 million, "which is nothing for a huge period picture to be shot in New York and New Jersey where the Teamsters alone can break you."

As soon as *Annie* was done John went to work drawing the label for the 1982 Château Mouton Rothschild, which would turn out to be one of the most exceptional Bordeaux vintages of the century ("which goes to prove that great destinies are planned for some of us," John would joke). The tradition of having well-known artists contribute their talents began in 1944 and Huston's design of a dancing ram and purple grapes was put in the company of Braque, Chagall, Cocteau, Dali, Kandinsky, Miró, Moore, Motherwell, Picasso, and Warhol. He was also invited to guest edit the December 1981/January 1982 issue of French *Vogue*, where he wrote short character sketches of some of his favorite people for "the gallery of portraits of people who make up my life," ranging from Billy Pearson and Arthur Miller, to Suzanne Flon and Marietta Tree. Of Marietta he wondered, "Can I still think about this woman as the girl with whom I was in love sometime back? . . . When I have doubts I go to see her, and naturally, it is the same charming young girl and I fall in love all over again." And of Suzanne he wrote: "Although no official ties had united us, I view Suzanne as my wife and our relationship as the best of my marriages. The most precious qualities that a woman can possess are found integrated in her being: tenderness, fidelity, gaiety, depth of emotion."

When Suzanne read John's words she was deeply moved and wrote to him that it was good to know she was still in his heart, as he was in hers, after so many years. "It means more to me than any official tie."

Soon after the death of Gladys, Tony and Margot had another child, a girl, making John a grandfather for the second time. Tony's birth had come shortly after Walter's death in 1950; Tony's daughter made John again conscious of the cycle of life.

After John read A. E. Ellis's *The Rack,* which was written in the mid-fifties, he gave it to Michael Fitzgerald and suggested that "it would make a hell of a movie." The story was about a young man's tortured treatment for tuberculosis in a Swiss sanatorium. "Dire stuff," Huston said, "but it includes a deeply moving love story."

Fitzgerald liked it. John thought the novelist Edna O'Brien, an old friend of his, might be right for the job. By this time Ray Stark and Columbia Pictures were involved and Fitzgerald paid O'Brien $80,000 to write the script, fully expecting to be reimbursed by Stark.

While O'Brien wrote in Ireland, Fitzgerald sent Tom Shaw and Stephen Grimes to Switzerland to scout locations. Five miles from the French-Swiss border they found what used to be a tuberculosis sanatorium, but both men had their doubts about the picture. "I told Fitzgerald you've got to invent a new disease," Shaw said. "It was old hat." Paul Kohner had warned Grimes that he didn't think the picture would ever happen and advised him to tell John he needed a minimum guarantee. "John got very cross," Grimes remembered. "He said, 'I made that boy what he is.' But I was going to get stuck if it folded."

John and Fitzgerald didn't want to be told the picture was too grim and proceeded to cast the stars. Nastassia Kinski said she was interested and so did Mark Lee, who had appeared in the Australian film *Gallipoli,* which Huston thought was one of the finest contemporary films he had seen. "I saw it twice," he wrote to Lee, "the second time to try and fault it—I couldn't."

When Edna O'Brien had completed her first draft she flew to New York to meet with John and to accompany him to the premiere of *Annie.* "He was great that night," O'Brien recalled. "They had streamers, balloons, cars, traffic stopped. And he had a great dignity. We went to a party and he was sitting next to Nancy Reagan and I was at another table next to Albert Finney and we met about eleven P.M. out in the street, where people were calling his name. He loved praise and admiration, but he didn't want to let on he loved it." After the premiere they got down to work and O'Brien agreed to fly to Puerto Vallarta to write the second draft.

"John," she said, "before we start I have one favor to ask. Please don't ever shout at me."

"Such a thing would never enter my head," Huston said, placing his hand to his heart.

O'Brien knew Huston well and had found him "an extraordinary and complex character." She had been his guest at St. Clerans in the early sixties and admitted to once being "stuck on him. I was thrilled by his energy. And that voice—which was totally seductive."

"I liked Edna very much," John said. "And I like what she does about Ireland. She had these children—I don't know the details of her past, but I think it was something less than romantic. It strangulated her in some way."

So in the summer of 1982 she left her children to work with John on what would become one of the most grueling and humiliating experiences of her life. "I had heard before I went about what happened with other writers and I think he always liked it to be remembered that he was originally a writer. But he was really a cowboy who wished he was an intellectual."

One day Huston would tell her, "Oh, my God, only written by a spirit." The next day he'd say, "What *is* this half-baked scene, honey? You'd better read some good scripts. Have you *ever* read a script?"

"He could be so fucking condescending," O'Brien declared. "I had read scripts. I had written some as well. But he totally flummoxed me. My character and my talent just collapses under that kind of psychological pressure."

"I thought for five minutes that she was doing good work," reflected Huston. "Then I had to face up to the fact that it was no good. I told her this and apparently I said something cynical that got to her and she broke down and wept. I consoled her—or tried to—but it was a failure, and I think she recognized it."

To Huston's credit O'Brien found that "he was absolutely never malicious about people behind their backs. His cruelty was frontline." She had given Huston some pages and when she went to see him "he just tore me apart. Said that the kind of stuff I wrote would have been laughable even in the thirties. For two hours he just totally slaughtered me in a way that is unforgivable."

Emotionally unraveled by what she called John's "brain torture," she told him he was being too destructive, mixing up personal cruelty with the work. Believing that he had a "murderous feeling toward women," she said, "What you're doing to me is awful. You're just trying to kill me." He realized he had gone too far and asked her if she wanted a drink. She refused and went back to her house.

The next morning she called John and said she wanted to see him. "Edna's quitting," Huston told Maricela, who drove him to her house and waited for him outside. For a half hour John talked with her. He told her the biggest unhappinesses in his life had been caused by women. And she told him, "That's true for women about men." But she began to sense something else: that she reminded him of his journalist mother. "My theory is that a lot of his cruelty to me was also made worse by self-hatred and guilt. If you said the word *guilt* to John, he'd say, 'Oh, honey, you've got it so wrong.' But I don't think so. I honestly think his frustrations had to do with his mother, with an anger about women."

Although he was "a much-married man and a man whom women had been in love with all his life, he had a distance from women. Not sexually, but emotionally and psychologically. He had more tenderness for a hummingbird, a dog, or a monkey than a woman. Combine that with his anxiety and his sadism and it was a losing situation before you even started."

She began to wonder about the women who were closest to him, about Gladys and Maricela. "Gladys was in love with him all her life. She endured things. Gladys was like a nun: She devoted her life to him and died young. Maricela was harder for me to know. She's a more elusive person. But she has enormous instinctive self-protection, so she could not be hurt by John the way Gladys was."

O'Brien continued working on the script, but the atmosphere was filled with tension. After three tortured months she was finally ready to leave. Huston was impressed that she had stayed as long as she had and when he came to visit her, he saw three withering roses that a maid had given to her. "He looked at the roses," she said, "he looked at me, and he said, 'Which of these do you think you are, honey?' I pointed to the most collapsing rose. 'No, you do yourself an injustice. I think you're that one,' pointing to the next. He thought it was funny, but it wasn't funny at all."

O'Brien left thinking what a monster Huston truly was. "If he was just a straight monster nobody would have bothered with him. It was his unpredictability that was so fascinating. He once told me that he hated physical cowardice. Well, he went into the physical terror zones, but not the psychological ones. In many ways, for all the bravura, he was a lost man. Alone, coughing, in that white shirt, looking at television at four A.M., you wondered what went on in there."

*   *   *

Michael Fitzgerald was in Puerto Vallarta part of the time Edna O'Brien was there. But Fitzgerald had less regard for her as a writer than John had. "I think she's considerably less than secondary," Fitzgerald said. "Her reputation is founded on a kind of kinkiness that appeared at a certain moment in Irish literature without having the talent to support it."

Fitzgerald was there when John got angry with her work and defended John. "He didn't say, 'You can't write, Edna.' He would say, 'Maybe we could make this better.' Or, 'This line is no good.' My God, I heard that from John a thousand times, but that would be sufficient for Edna to become hysterical."

As far as Fitzgerald was concerned, "*The Rack* was a monumental fucking catastrophe." Aside from the difficulties in getting a workable script, he also had to deal with Ray Stark's unwillingness to pay for O'Brien's work. "Ray resented me because John was making pictures with me and refusing to make Ray's pictures. Ray somehow needed John in his life. It was a question of need; it wasn't a friendship or a professional relationship or a sense of admiration or affection or love or anything which had a certain amount of detachment to it. It was a *need.*

"When *The Rack* came along and Ray agreed to do it, I never had any illusions about his reasons. He wanted to do something for John. Now came the time to deliver and Ray didn't. And I was out a lot of money, which I was very angry about. I wrote him a letter in which I described exactly what happened and what I thought he owed. And I sent a copy to John. Because of that Ray felt obliged to pay me, otherwise he was going to look like shit. John, who was staying at Ray's apartment in Los Angeles, moved out. He took a dim view of what Ray was doing at the time."

During that summer John was also developing *Under the Volcano.* The script, written by a young graduate student named Guy Gallo, seemed to solve some of the problems of the novel. Fitzgerald had discovered the script when he was looking for a writer to work on *The Rack* before O'Brien had gotten involved.

On June 12, 1982, John wrote a letter to Gallo, which he gave to Fitzgerald to deliver. Knowing that Wieland Schulz-Keil owned the rights to the book, John also told him about Gallo's script and suggested they meet. John liked how Gallo had combined two characters—the

Consul's half-brother, Hugh, and the film director, Laruelle, both of whom have had affairs with the Consul's wife. Gallo had eliminated Hugh, but John preferred to eliminate the director. "The relationship would be that much more complicated," he wrote. "I think the Consul would find much more difficulty in dealing with his cuckoldry if the lover were his beloved brother."

Soon after he received John's letter Gallo heard from Schulz-Keil and they worked together revising the script. Schulz-Keil liked how Gallo had turned Lowry's convoluted story into one that began in the evening and ended the next evening with the Consul's death. "He did precisely what had interested me from the outset," Schulz-Keil said. "He tried to look at things from the outside. The book was overwritten and turned inside out and didn't lend itself to being adapted. I felt if one could show from the outside what the book described from the inside, it might work as a film."

By October, after Gallo had written four new drafts, John invited him down to Puerto Vallarta. Joan Blake, who had worked for Gladys and was now Huston's secretary, met him at the airport and brought him to Boca de Tomatlán, where he got on the *panga* to Las Caletas. Gallo was nervous, and when he arrived he met Maka Czernichew, John's ex-lover and confidante since they first met during the making of *The Unforgiven*.

The previous week John had given Maka four scripts to read. The only one she thought had potential was Gallo's *Volcano*; when she told John he began to argue with her. "We went on a terrible riot for four days and four nights," she recalled. "Fight and fight and fight. Finally he told me, 'I sent for that Guy Gallo.' "

Maka had been glad that John was back in a fighting mood. The inability to solve *The Rack* had disturbed him, and *Under the Volcano* was an even greater challenge. When Gallo arrived John refused to see him at first. "Will I like him?" John asked Maka.

"No," Maka said. "Do you want to see him?"

"No, show him his room."

So Maka showed Gallo to his room at the top of the hill. "What type of man is he?" Gallo asked her. "Will he like me?"

"I don't think so, but don't be afraid. He's going to be very rude. He is that way with everyone, just don't pay attention."

Maka suggested that he and John play backgammon before they discussed the script and Gallo's ability saved him. "Guy was like a professional, very quick," she noted. "John was very slow. John said, 'We are playing for money,' and I could see Guy had none. John was doubling and doubling, and Guy kept winning. They played for hours."

During their first discussion of the script it struck Gallo that the film John was interested in had little to do with the version he and Schulz-Keil had been working on for months. "A lot of the political stuff was not interesting to John," Gallo said. "What interested him almost exclusively was the Consul. We talked about character analysis and story. At the end he said, 'Okay, go fix it, and don't bother with the first nineteen pages because we're going to use someone else's beginning.' " Gallo went to his room and stewed. He wasn't clear about what John wanted him to change and he went back down to talk it out.

"You want specifics?" Huston said, going through the script page by page. "Forget this," he'd say, "forget this. Re-do it as an adventure story. Do it as *Casablanca* in the tropics and forget about the rest."

Gallo squirmed as John brutally went through his script. "And then he left to play poker in Vallarta for two days, leaving me there with Maka," Gallo said. "I immediately rewrote the first pages and talked with Maka long into the night. She told me about John and how he controlled people and got what he wanted. When John got back she said to him, 'You really ought to be careful because he's about to leave and his is the only script you've got.' I went in to meet with him and he was a completely different person. We worked specifically, vigorously."

Some days later Gallo noticed Maka's luggage in John's living room and asked if she was leaving. "Yes," she said, "I'm fed up with Malcolm Lowry and with you and with John."

"I'm leaving, too," Gallo said. When John appeared he just looked at them. Gallo told him he would rewrite the script in New York and send it to him.

Gallo finished his revisions and John liked them enough to commit to the project. Then John instructed Paul Kohner to send Gallo Edna O'Brien's script of *The Rack* to see if he had any ideas. Gallo found O'Brien's script sentimental and precious. He talked with Huston and agreed to rewrite the script by March, when Huston would be in Los Angeles to receive the American Film Institute's Life Achievement Award.

In December 1982, John was in San Diego appearing as a priest in a film called *A Minor Miracle*, which also featured Pélé, when he received the news that Tony and Margot had their third child, a boy they named Jack. Huston then flew to Toronto to narrate a film about MacArthur called *American Caesar*. He was back at Las Caletas for the holidays, then prepared to act as Dudley Moore's analyst in *Lovesick* before the AFI tribute.

*   *   *

Two days before he was celebrated in Hollywood Huston and Michael Fitzgerald met with Guy Gallo to discuss his draft of *The Rack*. "I was filled with all kinds of hubris," remembered Gallo, "because here I had two scripts that John Huston was even vaguely thinking about. I was feeling capable and powerful." He had no idea how much Huston had disliked what he had done. "It was an incredible meeting in which John just racked him off the map," Fitzgerald recalled.

At the AFI dinner Fitzgerald sat at Huston's table and John suggested that with *The Rack* a dead project he should get together with Wieland Schulz-Keil and his partner, Moritz Borman, to executive produce *Under the Volcano*. "Well," Fitzgerald said, "now that the *The Rack* has gone to hell, why not?"

Fitzgerald had come from Italy to be with John and thought it was a "wonderful tribute." An edited version was shown on television, but Fitzgerald thought that the best-told anecdotes were those that couldn't possibly be repeated on TV. What the public saw was as much a coronation as a celebration. There Huston sat, Ava Gardner on his left, Anjelica and Nicholson on his right, in formal evening wear, his white beard perfectly barbered, smiling and blowing kisses to an adoring audience. Lauren Bacall hosted the affair and told stories about John and his friendship with Bogie. Clips from his movies were shown, then Orson Welles appeared. Welles disliked such ceremonies, but he came to honor John. "We've been friends since the world was young," he said, "and we have heard the chimes at midnight. We've turned the moon to blood. I come before you as an expert witness." Comparing John to a Renaissance prince, a regency rake, and a gentleman cardsharp, Welles hinted at something deeper and more Freudian when he said, "John is also Mephistopheles to his own Faust." He spoke of Huston having played "Svengali to the likes of Humphrey Bogart and Marilyn Monroe." And made note of his hypnotic voice and his ability to be a great listener. "This carries with it a faint whiff of the confessional, a priestly touch of incense with just that tang of sulfur which befits an outrageously seductive, unfrocked Cardinal. You all know what I mean. That air of high benevolence amounting to a benediction." He mentioned John's various talents and interests and called him "an epicurean, an amiable Count Dracula."

He touched on how "the ladies . . . sigh most swoonishly . . . for Don John." And he spoke with admiration of John's ability to handle producers, "the grand panjandrums of the industry, from Stark to Spiegel, there is not one specimen of that ferocious breed whom John, when need arises, cannot most sweetly cause to lie down, roll over . . . and purr."

Then ninety-two-year-old Sam Jaffe stood and reminded seventy-six-year-old John of the horse he pushed up the stairs for John's birthday when they lived in New York. Ava Gardner, making a rare public appearance, said that the only joy and fun she ever had as an actress was working with Huston. Max von Sydow would later echo her sentiments, thanking John "for your great confidence in your actors; thank you for letting us loose." Robert Mitchum spoke about *Heaven Knows, Mr. Allison*, Bill Mauldin about *San Pietro*, Pélé about the miracle Huston performed: "He made me a movie star."

When Sam Spiegel, who was seventy-nine, appeared, there were those who wondered what the renowned producer who took all the profits from *The African Queen* would say. As it turned out it wasn't much. He spoke of Huston's "insatiable curiosity" and touched upon a subject many considered gauche. "He is so curious that he even permitted himself a glimpse of the hereafter before he returned to our midsts. You remember, John, how we all hoped that you would rejoin us?"

Ray Stark was more in tune with the evening when he spoke of John's friendship. "When I recall the happiest and most adventurous times of my career, I think of John. John has been a teacher, my buddy, my alter ego, my trouble-shooter, and my trouble-maker. I once thought that if there was such a thing as reincarnation, I'd like to come back as one of my Labradors. Then I thought, on further consideration, that perhaps I'd like to come back as John Huston. To be a tall, handsome WASP; highly intelligent; with a great wit; and downright funny besides."

Jack Nicholson seemed to stumble, as if he hadn't expected to say a few words. "You've inspired me to go to work and you've inspired me to try and keep doing it well without fooling around too much," he said. "Obviously I'm grateful to you . . . for the love of your wonderful daughter. But tonight I think you really did something great for me. I got to check Ava Gardner's white fox fur."

When Anjelica came center stage she introduced Jeff Bridges, James Mason, Richard Brooks, Zsa Zsa Gabor, Stacy Keach, Max von Sydow, Aileen Quinn, Robert Blake, and Dudley Moore, who all had kind words to say. (Moore was most exact when he joked, "I always thought that a man who could persuade Elizabeth Taylor to throw an undergarment at Marlon Brando *should* direct.") And before blowing her own kiss at him Anjelica referred to the past and looked to the future. "Dad,

I know I gave you a lot more trouble than Walter ever did when we were working together. But I'm here tonight to tell you that I'm willing to try again."

For television, Anjelica had appeared as a fashion model who wore the Eiffel Tower on her head in an episode of the sit-com "Laverne & Shirley"; as one of the mean sisters in "Beauty and the Beast" for "Faerie Tale Theatre"; as Emily in *A Rose for Emily*, an independent film based on a William Faulkner short story. In movies, she made brief appearances in *This Is Spinal Tap*, a satirical look at the decline of a rock band; and as a lunatic in *Frances*, based on the life of the decline of actress Frances Farmer, from movie star to an institutionalized lobotomy patient. She was about to be a master swordswoman in producer John Foreman's *The Ice Pirates*, a shameless, unimaginative *Star Wars/Road Warrior* imitation. So her gentle hint to her old man was really a reaching out. If she was ever going to become an actress of any recognizable ability, it certainly wasn't through the kind of work she had been doing.

After more clips from Huston's movies were shown, John was presented with his Life Achievement Award and rose to the occasion by crediting his longevity to "surgery." He compared himself to a salmon, who, after covering some forty spawnings, was beginning to disintegrate, "fin by fin, gill by gill."

About his movies he said he felt a certain detachment. "I rarely stay with them on TV and I cannot be dragged to a Huston retrospective. But things that happened during the making of the films I relive over and over. . . . What other pursuit, what other occupation, could offer such a rich, wild, rushing variety of incident?" he asked. He then confessed that he often felt guilty taking money for doing something he so loved. "Maybe that's why I always got rid of it so quickly. It was like money you win at the races, not the rewards of honest toil."

It was a sentimental evening that ended well past midnight and when the two-hour program was aired, one was aware that Huston truly was the last of a breed. But to those who knew John well and watched the show, the evening lacked any hint of who Huston really was.

To Ossie Morris it was a "nostalgic" show. As the camera kept coming back to Huston he noticed that "John's face didn't reveal anything, but I knew he knew that half of what was said was a bit over the top." Edna O'Brien was "sickened" by the tribute. "Bilge from start to finish," she said. "And Anjelica blowing a kiss, 'I'm proud of you, Dad.' *Fuck* that! Anjelica is certainly not mindless of her father's complex character and his cruelty."

The way Cherokee saw it the AFI tribute "was the beginning of Anjelica's putting in a public appearance for John. Tony wasn't there because he was very much involved with his wife and kids and making babies. He thought that was going to be his whole life. He wasn't vying for the Hollywood life at all when he was in England." As for Danny, he wasn't there either because he was in India, where he spent six months after graduating from the London International Film School, discovering a side of himself that had previously gone unexplored.

Danny was twenty-one years old when his mother married for the first time in 1983. The man was a German-French banker, not at all like John, and Danny didn't much care for him. But Zoe was alone and hoped the marriage would work out. It lasted three years.

"My marriage was a total disaster," Zoe said. "I had been in seclusion for a year and a half, didn't go out at all, and at the first thing I went to I met him. Danny didn't approve of him because of his Fascist tendencies. He was sweet but very German. He was going toward the material and I was going more toward the spiritual."

"I don't think he could quite understand my mother's way of thought," Danny said. "She believes very strongly in the life she's leading—vegetarian, meditating—she's got very strong views."

Danny, also a vegetarian but not into concentrating on his third eye, had many similarities to John when he was young, Zoe felt. He had a talent for painting and loved girls. Where John liked to drink, Danny experimented with mind-altering substances. "Lots of drugs growing up," he said. "I had my first joint when I was fifteen, but it never had a grip on me."

"Like John, his happiest moments were when he was painting, which I encouraged," Zoe said. "But you can't make money painting. So he went to film school for two years."

"When kids used to say, 'I want to be a fireman,' I used to say I wanted to be a film director," said Danny, "until I was about seventeen and realized what actually went into making a film as far as the people, the money, the total chaos, and then decided not to do it. I'd much rather paint. But I wasn't really that good and I certainly couldn't make a living from it. Filmmaking is a craft; painting is a dream."

At the London Film School he learned how to make documentaries, and when John invited him to Mexico to work with him on *Under the Volcano,* he was able to put what he knew about cameras and equipment to good use. John had someone else shoot the opening title sequence of skulls and skeletons, but he wasn't pleased with how it turned out and asked Danny to try it. Danny used a special snorkel camera he learned about in film school. Mounted on an arm, it enabled the user to look through and around things. He then set up the skeletons in a hotel lobby against a black backdrop and shot it in two days. John was very impressed.

"The big relationship with Danny started with *Under the Volcano,*" Zoe recalled. "He was there for the whole film. John didn't have much to do with Danny's upbringing, so he got the end result. He said that Danny was his best friend. Danny and Anjelica are very close and he gets on perfectly well with Allegra. With Tony there's always an ego problem. He's a very aggressive person and rubs people the wrong way. John would try to correct Tony and that was what they argued about. Danny doesn't have that arrogance. He underplays everything. He listened to John and respected him."

Michael Fitzgerald, who had to deal with Tony's complaints during *Wise Blood,* found Danny to be completely different during *Volcano.* "He was helpful beyond belief," Fitzgerald said. "Whatever we wanted Danny was running. And he would not accept a cent. I couldn't pay him the price of a Coca-Cola. He was learning; he was delighted to be down there, happy to be with his old man. Now that's the way to behave, as far as John was concerned."

"The whole making of *Volcano* was very strange," Danny remembered. "There was a lot of drinking, the crew was all mad, and Mexico is so surreal. Dad's idea of God during the film was a man riding a black bat drunk with disillusionment, on tequila, circulating around the world."

Before John began shooting *Volcano* in August 1983, he composed a letter to director Jack Clayton, his former production manager for *Moulin Rouge* and *Beat the Devil.* "You probably never have had and never will have another letter quite like this one with its unique request," John wrote. "It is the only one of its kind I suppose I shall ever write." He went on to explain how he had finally found a script for *Under the Volcano* that showed real promise and was getting ready to shoot it. He said he was in "as good health as anyone 76 years old who has fallen on his head as often as I have and has smoked as many cigars and cigarettes can possibly be." But then he came to the purpose of his letter: "There is an outside chance that I might not make it to the end of the picture, in which case the person I would prefer to see take over would be yourself. No one knows I'm writing you this letter and for obvious reasons I'm keeping it confidential."

Then John had second thoughts and decided that he wasn't ready to die just yet and filed the letter away. Jack Clayton never knew about it.

To get a satisfactory script Guy Gallo returned to Puerto Vallarta along with Wieland Schulz-Keil, where they worked with John for six weeks. "I absolutely refused to play backgammon," recalled Schulz-Keil. "We just worked."

After a few weeks it was apparent that their collaboration was working and Schulz-Keil felt he learned "a hell of a lot about screenplays from John." There were a few scenes, he said, that were all Huston's. One was in a bar when a drunk American began confusing Moses with Mozart. "That's in the book," Guy Gallo said. "John adapted it and wrote it in the voice he wanted it in. Very definitely John's. The procedure was usually a group discussion, then I'd go away and write. There was nothing proprietary about these discussions, it didn't really matter who had the idea."

Michael Fitzgerald said that Gallo and Schulz-Keil were both quite literate, but they would get on John's nerves. "Gallo was just full of big words," Fitzgerald said. "Every once in a while the word *subtext* would come out and John would just recoil. It was a constant struggle when these people would talk about literary meanings and subtexts and John would say it's complete horseshit."

"What he meant," Guy Gallo said, "was, 'Don't talk to me about subtext. Talk to me about visceral effect.' "

When Tom Shaw saw how different the finished script was from the earlier drafts he told Gallo, "You ought to kiss his ass until the day he dies." Both Shaw and Fitzgerald felt it was really John who wrote the script. Wieland Schulz-Keil, who didn't like Fitzgerald, disagreed. "Guy did practically all of the writing, so it's perfectly correct that he should be credited with the screenplay."

Fitzgerald and Moritz Borman made the necessary arrangements to film the picture in Yautepec, thirty miles outside Cuernavaca. Albert Finney was all set to play the Consul and Jacqueline Bisset had agreed to fly to Puerto Vallarta to talk with John about playing Yvonne. "I felt like I had three or four Ping-Pong balls in my mouth," Bisset said of her meeting with Huston. She was relieved to find how gentle and mellow John seemed, and signed on after hearing how his changes in the script coincided with how she felt about Yvonne. She saw it as "a story about wasted love."

Fitzgerald suggested Anthony Andrews to play Hugh and showed John his performance in the television mini-series *Brideshead Revisited.* Once the three main characters were chosen, John went to Cuernavaca to cast the bandits, soldiers, whores, bartenders, old ladies, and dwarf who populate the story. He found the Consul's killer while watching a television program in his hotel. For the others, John sat on his terrace and interviewed actors. "They would come in," recalled Schulz-Keil, "and have conversations with John about bullfights, about Mexico City twenty years ago . . . I was surprised how many topics he could come up with to get through these tedious meetings."

"There were Mexican actors who are cheese in Mexico," said Maricela, who would be in the kitchen "laughing hysterically" while they came for their interviews. "They were sweating. Jesus. Trembling. And these poor souls asked me what kind of a person he was and I said, 'He's very demanding, you better say your lines right.' "

John refused to settle for actresses to play the whores. He told Moritz Borman, "No decent lady can play a prostitute as well as a real one." So Wieland Schulz-Keil went to Mexico City where he made the acquaintance of "two dubious people who helped me by running behind me with their guns in their pockets and I went from one brothel to another and recruited sixty candidates and brought them in buses to Cuernavaca." John selected the twenty he wanted to use and they were very sweet to him. "It was like he was sort of their grandfather," Schulz-Keil remembered.

In Cuernavaca, Schulz-Keil was amazed with how John acted as if he didn't know anything about the book or the script on which they had labored so diligently. "There came that moment," John said, "when I had to make a picture without any further reference to the book." John's ability to dismiss the script fascinated Schulz-Keil. "He acted like he needed other people to tell him what was in the screenplay. Of course he knew it better than anybody."

John's method was to have his actors *show* him what they had come up with. Guy Gallo observed similarities between Huston's directing and his writing, how he edited in the camera, didn't do master shots, used only two setups instead of five. "The kernel that he was trying to locate in the film style was the same as what he was trying to locate in the writing of the script," Gallo said. "Which is, what piece of the scene is going to be real. Not symbolism, not metaphor, not subtext, not something that you're going to get fifteen minutes from now—what are you going to get *now?*" Gallo recalled how the novel began in the rain and ended in the rain, but the day before the first day of shooting Tom Shaw complained that the rain was "a real pain in the ass." John turned to Gallo and asked, "What does the rain mean?"

"Well, John," Gallo stammered, knowing he might as well not bother, "it resonates there, it has a rhythm at the end, it has to do with darkness, there's a circularity to it."

"Yeah," John said, "but what does it *mean?*"

"You're right," Gallo sighed, "cut the rain."

Schulz-Keil thought John had a "peculiar way of working, a kind of unsystematic efficiency which was amazing. There was a scene of fifty people and it was total chaos on the set. Nobody was ever told what to do, they were kind of milling around; it made no sense whatsoever. Then there were two or three surprisingly strategic interventions of John's and before you knew it, it was all wonderful. I hadn't seen that before. I'd seen other directors work but nobody ever worked like that."

Anthony Andrews, who had never seen a bullfight, had to learn how to fight a young bull for one scene. Wieland Schulz-Keil took him to some bullfights in Mexico City, then hired a matador to work with him, and Andrews became confident. Came the day to shoot the scene, everyone forgot how quickly a bull understands his situation. Because so much time was spent getting ready for the scene, the bull had become more dangerous than expected. In the center of the ring there was a construction that housed the camera and the first thing the bull did was attack it. "The matador and everybody else was running around trying to get the bull's attention," Schulz-Keil said. "He turned around and threw the matador. Then he knocked the matador's father over and broke his foot. The matador's uncle got into the ring and was knocked over. Then the bull calmed down and the scene was orchestrated in such a way that Anthony was supposed to jump into the arena and change places with the matador. So Anthony jumped in with his muleta and confronted the bull. He did three decent passes before being knocked over the fourth time."

Michael Fitzgerald said he had never seen John "so completely pissed off" as he was with Andrews during this scene. "The dumb sonofabitch just ran out and started doing passes," Fitzgerald recalled, "and almost got killed. He had to crawl back with the bull behind him at the wrong angle. We had bullfighters in the ring immediately, but it was almost a tragedy. Just fucking insanity. Andrews barely got out of there with his life. John was absolutely raving with anger that someone would do something that stupid."

Huston also, at times, became exasperated with Bisset. "Sometimes I've been tempted to tell her *not* to think so much," John said. And when he tried she would nod in agreement and then "proceeded to analyze the next scene in infinite detail."

But it was Finney's performance that made the picture. "Finney is giving one of the finest performances I've ever seen," John said. "He was never drunk during shooting, only after hours. His understanding of drunkenness is a very profound one, based on his own experience."

Finney thought the part allowed him to do what he did best: to record feeling. He prepared for his part by downing a shot of tequila before a take. "I like immersing myself in the Consul's world. I like to have the taste of tequila, which I've never tasted before, in my mouth, just as I like smoking Mexican cigarettes and eating Mexican food."

Because of Finney's ability to consistently surprise John, Huston rarely felt the need to discuss scenes with him. "We spoke in a kind of coded communication," he said. "I would nod and he would look at me and smile and that's all there was to it. There was little or no directing required."

Finney explained their method of work to writer Pete Hamill. John would tell Finney to show him what he had in mind. Once Finney showed him, John would say, "Well, maybe." Then, Finney said, "he will cajole it, nudge it, bully it, or just say, 'A little less oil and vinegar . . . a little more lemon.' When you get to know him a bit you know that when he doesn't say anything, he's happy."

During filming Anjelica and Jack Nicholson came down to visit, and while John and Nicholson got along well, Wieland Schulz-Keil noticed that Anjelica and John "didn't have much to say to each other." Anjelica thought John's latest film was apt, for she often thought that he lived his life on the dark side of a volcano. She had completed her work in *Ice Pirates* and had just read an interesting novel by *Winter Kills* author Richard Condon. Huston had also read the book and given it to John Foreman as their next project. It was called *Prizzi's Honor*.

But John had *Volanco* and didn't have time to spend discussing what attracted him to *Prizzi's*. Both Gallo and Fitzgerald agreed that John was willing to sacrifice large portions of Lowry's book to concentrate on what most interested him: the character of the Consul, who meets his end at a hellish whore's bar called the Farolito.

"The Consul is the most complicated character I've ever had in a film," John said. "He's like a Churchill gone bad, a great man with a flaw. Or is it? Is drunkenness a flaw or is it—as the primitives thought of epilepsy—a manifestation of divinity?" True, he was a victim, "but he is also a giant, a kind of hero, an adventurer. The Consul's adventures were of the mind, of the soul. The grandeur of his nature was that he wants to love these people who have wronged him; he wants to love the world, to love life, and yet it offends him, outrages him. At the end he takes on the enemies of life and it's they who destroy him."

"John was most interested in getting to the Farolito," said Gallo, "where we have this nightmare vision of this man on the edge of his personal boundaries, which is what interested him in the book itself— that edge."

John couldn't have selected a more appropriate proprietor of the Farolito than his wild old friend Emilio Fernandez, now seventy-nine, who had been his assistant director on *The Night of the Iguana* and *The Unforgiven*. Huston's painter's eye also perfectly composed the Goya-esque scene where the Consul enters a world of grotesques, of vicious soldiers, worn-out prostitutes, and an evil dwarf. It becomes, significantly, the end of his world, and his death will cause the accidental death of Yvonne, who is run down by a white horse who bolted into the woods when the Consul was shot.

This bitter, disillusioning ending, which Malcolm Lowry conceived, was not how John saw Mexico when he worked on *Volcano*. Ironically, however, it was how he would come to feel when, sometime after the film's completion near the end of 1983, he and Maricela learned of the terrible abuse Gladys's, and then Maricela's, adopted child suffered at the hands of one of the people with whom Maricela had entrusted the child while she and John were gone. "Maricela had to make a decision who to care for when my father would go away to make movies," Danny Huston said. "She stayed with John. So the girl grew up with these servants. And then they discovered that these servants had abused the child. My father was shocked. Maricela became hysterical. They took it to court and got the servant who did what he did to the girl thrown into jail. This was a big scandal. The servant had ten brothers and they threatened Maricela. They had guns and would shoot into her house in Puerto Vallarta.

"The little girl became a problem child," Danny continued. "She was put in school with nuns. Anjelica said that she represents Mexico: The white man comes to help the Indian and the Indian, out of pride, doesn't accept the extended hand, and then all this chaos happens because of that. When Anjelica told this to John, he said, 'That's a good way of thinking about this.' But it made him almost ill when it happened. My father knew the president of Mexico, he helped Mexico a lot, and then this happened. It made him very bitter about Mexico."

In October 1983, before these troubles erupted, John saw a rough cut of *Volcano* and wrote letters to cinematographer Gabriel Figueroa and set designer Gunther Gerzso. "It's been years since I enjoyed making a film as much as *Volcano,*" he wrote Figueroa. "It is surely one of the handsomest pictures ever made. The connoisseurs of fine photography will surely observe this. The play of light and shade, its color that is never simply self-serving, but enhances the spirit of every scene . . . Pictures like *Days of Heaven, Gandhi, Barry Lyndon* are beautiful tableaus to be sure and one stands back and admires them as from a distance. But *Volcano* gathers one in. Your photography makes it a living experience."

To Gerzso, who, according to Schulz-Keil, didn't get along with Huston, John wrote: "Physically, the picture is a triumph. Time after time in the projection room I wanted to applaud, but refrained because others might think I was applauding myself rather than the performances, Gaby's work, or yours. What an extraordinary look you and Gaby have given *Volcano.* Unlike any picture I know of, it has its own very special beauty."

John had been paid $250,000 up front for *Volcano* and another $250,000 was deferred, which may have been incentive enough to give as many interviews to promote the movie as he did. He even went to the Cannes Film Festival in May 1984, where he was given a special award "for his extraordinary contribution to the cinema." He was treated like an international treasure and was overwhelmed at the standing ovations and standing-room-only crowds he attracted at his press conference. French critic Serge Danet said, "He's the last of the biggies, our last link with the Hemingway age, the last monument there is."

A New York writer called John a bold visionary, to which he replied with a statement that applied to all of the literature he adapted to the screen throughout his career: "I'm a bold visionary with other people's work. It's the work of Malcolm Lowry, simplified, given shape, so that it now has a dramatic form."

*   *   *

Michael Fitzgerald recalled how he and Danny spent the whole night drinking at the bar of their hotel in Cannes where they anxiously awaited the reviews of *Volcano.* By five A.M., still in their tuxedos, they walked two miles to a newspaper stand. The papers were there, but they were still wrapped. "We were pissed out of our minds," Fitzgerald said, "and we stole a few. Most of the reviews were wonderful. We desperately wanted to go and tell John, but we waited a half hour because we thought he'd still be asleep. He'd been up thinking about it as well, and when he saw Danny he was reminded of the time when he went to see his father after the reviews of *Othello* came out. It was a very important moment in John's life, seeing his father laughing hysterically, the tears rolling at the sheer absurdity of it."

When the film opened in the States the reviews were mixed. Considering the subject matter and the complexities of the novel, John was not surprised. What *was* revealing, however, was how stridently divided certain critics were. Both Janet Maslin and Vincent Canby of the *New York Times* liked it. Canby was mesmerized and ranked it "with the best work Mr. Huston has ever done." Maslin viewed it as "a serious work rather than an entertainment of universal appeal," and thought it "especially impressive for the courage, intelligence and restraint with which it tackles an impossible task." Guy Flatley in *Cosmopolitan* called it "an astonishing, viscerally gripping tour de force." And both *Time* and *Newsweek* praised it ("My God, a movie for grown-ups!" exclaimed *Newsweek*'s Jack Kroll).

Pauline Kael, though, didn't care for it. Neither did Rex Reed ("a turgid, pretentious, and ultimately pointless mess") or the *New Republic*'s Stanley Kaufman. David Denby in *New York* called it a "failure." Jack Mathews in *USA Today* said, "Finding . . . *Under the Volcano* in the summer movie marketplace is like finding a Greek classic among a stack of *Archie* comic books." David Sterritt, writing in the *Christian Science Monitor,* called it "a model of literary adaptation—intensely dramatic, sharply cinematic, and full of passionate performances." Judith Crist recommended it. And Ron Rosenbaum in *Mademoiselle* found it "incredibly depressing . . . Bleaker than the black view of human nature in *Treasure of the Sierra Madre,* grimmer than the grotesque and twisted religious pessimism of . . . *Wise Blood,* steeped in a conception of the corruption of human character more corrosive than that embodied in the hideously corrupt man Huston plays in *Chinatown, Under the Volcano* establishes Huston as the true Prince of Darkness of American films."

* * *

As soon as *Volcano* was completed Danny Huston was asked to work on a documentary in Peru. "That was very rough," he said. "I did the camerawork. The director lost his finger the first day of filming when he closed a door on it. After we finished I spent three months in Peru. Met one beautiful green-eyed, high-cheekboned Indian woman. Then she came to London a year later. She was wearing high-heeled shoes, plucked her eyebrows, lipstick—it was incredible." Like John, Danny never seemed to have problems falling for women. "I'm a romantic. I fall in love all the time," he said and laughed, "and crash back down on my ass, get up, and start all over again. I've had self-destructive relationships as well, that's why I could understand Dad with Cici. I'm happy I have *his* experience plus mine at such an early age."

While Danny was off having adventures John was back at Las Caletas, where he invited Janet Roach to come for the holidays. On the same day Roach arrived, John received Richard Condon's first draft of the script for *Prizzi's Honor* and wasn't pleased with it. He gave it to Roach to read and when her opinion confirmed his own, he asked her, "How'd you like to try your hand at rewriting this?" (Condon was undergoing heart bypass surgery and wasn't available to work on it.)

"I gulped and said, 'Sure, John,' " she recalled, "thinking, 'Oh, God, I'm going to make a terrible fool out of myself in front of this man that I adore.' " Joan Blake got her a typewriter and Roach looked upon the assignment not as a breakthrough into the movies but "as earning my keep as a houseguest."

Prizzi's was a black comedy, a satire about a Brooklyn Mafia family whose chief hitman, Charley Partanna, falls in love with an outsider named Irene, who happens to be a free-lance hitlady. Their romance is complicated because Irene has taken $720,000 that was the Prizzis' and is under suspicion by the family. When Charley marries Irene it allows his old girlfriend, Maerose, granddaughter of the Don, to return to her father's good graces. Maerose plays the Prizzis like a master puppeteer as she cunningly manipulates events so that Charley winds up having to kill Irene in order to become head of the family . . . and return to Maerose.

When John Foreman read the book and suggested that Anjelica would make a good Maerose, John agreed. And with the character of Maerose, Anjelica felt an immediate affinity. "There's nothing about her that I *don't* understand," she said. "She comes from a recent ostracization, she's been in a certain amount of pain. She's on her way back; she's not a victim. Women who were raised with very strong parental influences generally carry some of that into their own lives. If

Maerose was a man, she would definitely wind up head of the family. She wants to prove her existence. And she carries a certain amount of dignity and power."

It seemed the perfect part, and the perfect time. Anjelica was waiting for a role like this. And who better to play Charley Partanna, she felt, than Jack? John concurred, but when Nicholson read it he wasn't sure. Joan Buck remembered seeing Anjelica and Jack for dinner in January 1984, when Jack took two and a half hours to describe the plot, and all the time Buck kept saying, "This is a movie?" Which was what Nicholson was thinking as well. He liked the idea of working with John, of acting with Anjelica, but he was coming off an Oscar-winning performance as a retired astronaut in *Terms of Endearment,* and he just couldn't get a grasp on the character of Charley Partanna.

As Janet Roach began to rewrite Condon's script, she, too, began to identify with the character of Maerose, "the outsider clamoring to get in. I would work by myself in the morning, then I'd bring the pages that I'd done and John would take them to his studio. Around six o'clock I'd hear that voice calling up the hill. If something had been done to his liking: 'Very good, darling, very good.' And if it hadn't, it would be sifted to the bottom of the pile of pages and we'd go over it again. No bullying, no fear. I've worked for Mike Wallace, so I know what browbeating is. Although sometimes we would have heated discussions. There was a line in the script when Charley says to his father, 'I didn't get married so my wife could keep working.' It isn't in the book. And John didn't understand why that was funny. Late twentieth-century feminist thinking was not in John's camp. Every time he would cross it out, I'd put it back in. Finally John lost his cool and said, 'Fuck you!' 'You should be so lucky!' I said. And he said, 'Shall we continue?' The line stayed in."

In February, after Janet had departed, John invited Marietta Tree and her daughter, Frances FitzGerald, whose *The Fire in the Lake* had won a Pulitzer Prize, to Las Caletas. Because he didn't think they would like the local food, he hired a French chef for their visit. "We started in the morning with scrambled eggs and caviar," FitzGerald recalled, "and meals would go on like that." She remembered how John spoke "in enormous detail, very lovingly" about his children, "but he still didn't understand them very well." She found John's hideaway both charming and "very black." Marietta, though, saw only Eden: the black-eyed children, the white cat with blue and green eyes, the birds, shells, books, the water. "What a marvelous life you have made!" she wrote John in thanks. "I have loved you for a long time and expected great things of you, but I never thought you would turn out so well." To which John responded, "There are two big holes in the environment at Las Caletas that you and Frankie left behind."

Lizzie Spender, another visitor from the past, also saw the light and dark of Las Caletas when she went there with Anjelica. "I had expected to see something from the past," she said, "and there was nothing." Lizzie noticed that John seemed "completely different. Quieter. More affectionate." He looked at Anjelica in "absolute amazement that this was his daughter." But then, as soon as they left Las Caletas to go into Puerto Vallarta, "he started being the old John. He was always a great one for telling you absolutely irrefutable nonsense. And there was no point in arguing once he got the bit between his teeth."

John's insistence was a trait that Margot noticed in Tony, who she began to see was "sort of obsessive. Whatever he is doing he is doing it ninety-nine percent. Tony would say, 'But this is how it is.' You can't romanticize around Tony," she found, "and that was jarring." Their country life in Norfolk was wonderful for the children—they learned to ride and swim—but Margot found it confining. "Neither of us was used to children, so it's been sort of hard. Tony can be marvelous with them, but he can also be quite impatient. They've learned how to handle it and know when not to be around him. Patience is not his great virtue. And Tony demands a lot of attention."

"One of the reasons I stayed at home for my three children," Tony said, "was because I came to the conclusion that it was very, very important that the bonds are formed early. If you don't have that innate trust in one another, it's very hard to develop it. Hopefully I will never face the sort of problems Anjelica and I faced with Dad. I'm fortunate that my children have grown up in a conventional, happy home."

Tony was very conscious of the patterns that seemed to occur in his family and was fascinated "how families repeat similar patterns. In the Huston family we are attracted to mates who come from backgrounds similar to our own—so if you lost a parent at an early age, the chances are your spouse will have gone through something similar. In our family there is a thing about a father leaving home at an early age. Dad and

Zoe and Danny—that's identical to what went on with Dad and his father. Indeed, we know enough about Jack Nicholson's background to see that there, again, is that unsettled childhood." At the time, Tony saw himself as the exception to this pattern, but within a few years, he, too, would fit into his theory.

When Tony, thirty-four, took his son Matthew to the zoo he was amazed when they came to a tiny monkey's cage and Matthew said, "That looks like my grandfather." Matthew had not seen John for six months, "but he was dead right," Tony said. "Dad had that simian thing about his face—which was incredibly appealing and also was very strongly animal. It staggered me, for a five-year-old to spot this. The monkey was a foot high and it was a dead ringer for him."

If John looked like a monkey to Tony, he behaved more like a horse. In a book about Chinese horoscopes Tony discovered that 1906, the year John was born, "was what they called a Fire Horse year, which only happens once every sixty years. It was remarkable; it gave a description of a Fire Horse personality that was Dad to a T: proud, independent-minded, lofty. It was the only time I've ever read a horoscope that sounded remotely correct."

Another aspect of John, the Fire Horse, was his unbridled siding with animals. Had he not been involved with the arts he would have liked to be a thoroughbred horse trainer. When his pet snake bit his finger he blamed himself for disturbing it. When the monkey peed in the bowl of nuts they were still good enough for Sam Spiegel to eat. When the chimp wrecked Evelyn Keyes's apartment it was she who left, not the animal. And when Diego, his pet Rottweiler, leaped at a close friend of John's at Las Caletas and tore off her upper lip, it was *her* fault for not understanding the animal's nature.

Whenever anyone leaned over Diego the dog would growl and bare his teeth. He behaved that way with John and Maricela as well, only John took it as a challenge and would pet Diego anyway. Eventually, said John, "his growl became an expression of pleasure when either I or Maricela would pet him." But when a visitor tried it she quickly learned that Diego was growling at *her* in earnest. "It was terrifying," John said. "We had to get her to Los Angeles to a plastic surgeon." When the woman insisted that Diego be destroyed, John told Maricela that it wasn't really the dog's fault. That being the case, Maricela told John, if he shot Diego, she would shoot herself.

"John had a taste for half-wild creatures all his life," said Janet Roach, who often had to work under the menacing glare and intimidating growl of the large black dog. "That was why he had a fascination with Maricela. Diego represented the physical power Maricela didn't have and felt she needed. He was a tough, monster dog."

In a letter to Suzanne Flon, John attempted to describe Diego. "He's a big dog whose misdeeds have at moments threatened to bring down the house of Huston. He guards the shore of Las Caletas against all encroachments. The fact that all Mexican beaches are open to the public doesn't deflect him from his born purpose. He's attacked politicians, policemen, and their children. I've gone into hiding with him on occasion. I spirited him across frontiers at midnight. His very existence is an invitation to my ruin, but there is nothing I can do about it. We've been joined in heaven, Maricela, Diego, and me, required to protect each other, each in his own way."

By mid-March 1984, John wrote to Janet Roach in exasperation over the way the studios had received *Prizzi's Honor*. "The script has had the craziest reception I have ever known," he said. "There is immediate enthusiasm and it would seem that only the price had to be negotiated. Foreman thought he was in a position to play the studios off against one another. But then they suddenly retract. This has happened now four times. Not even Jack Nicholson, say they, could make lovable a man who would kill his wife for money. All of which serves to demonstrate to what low depths the intelligentsia of the present masters of our great industry have fallen. They all miss the point, of course, that the picture is a comedy, a fact very hard to get over. Have you ever tried explaining a joke to someone?"

But Huston was confident that the script was "just too good not to come off," and a month later Foreman closed a deal with ABC Motion Pictures. John called Roach immediately and asked her to meet him in Los Angeles so they could work some more on the script.

Roach gave full credit to Foreman's perseverance for making it happen. "Foreman got *Prizzi's Honor* on the boards against all odds," she said. "He did it not just out of belief in the project but out of real belief in John Huston and wanting to see him do one more great picture." Yet even with a development deal Jack Nicholson was still not fully committed. Nicholson told writer Ron Rosenbaum that the first thing Huston said to him about playing Charley Partanna was that he had to be dumb. "It seems to me, Jack," Huston said, "everything you've done is informed by intelligence. And you can't have that with this film. It's got to be dumb, very dumb."

Later, John wrote to Nicholson. "I know, Jack, that you want handles by which to get hold of the character. Making the audience understand at the earliest possible moment that you are playing an entirely different role than the high-flying, liberated one it's used to is extremely important. I'm sure, however, that during rehearsal we will discover a number of ways to bring this about. I'm still of the opinion that Charley's having a wig is a good idea. One of its virtues, by the way, is that it doesn't require dialogue.

"You said during our conversation the other day that P's H is essentially a story about greed. It's greed all right, but marching under the banner of honor: whatever is good for the family materially speaking is morally justifiable according to the Prizzis. This is a trait that might well describe society at large at the present moment.

"I understand that you have some connections in the Cosa Nostra. Someone, maybe Anjelica, said something about your going to one of their haunts catering to the netherworld. If that is a fact, I wish you'd be my guide and take me there when we get to New York."

John concluded his letter by suggesting that Nicholson brush up on his Brooklyn accent, which "should be of some help too with your characterization."

Jack wasn't comfortable with John's idea of wearing a bad wig to give Charley Partanna a dumb look, but while hanging out in Brooklyn bars he started noticing the way Italian men often didn't move their upper lip when they talked. Nicholson decided to stuff some tissue paper into his mouth, as his neighbor, Marlon Brando, had done with his role in *The Godfather*, "to immobilize that part of my face." He also ate a lot of pasta to give him a squat, fireplug look, and tried for "a two-ton Tony Galento walk, with my palms facing backward. Charley's eyes I took from the eyes of my dog when he killed another dog."

But Nicholson *still* hadn't signed a contract committing himself to the role when Huston met with Kathleen Turner, his choice for Irene, at the St. Moritz Hotel in New York. "Supposedly," recalled Turner, whose sizzling performance in *Body Heat* convinced John she could play the always-in-control hitlady, "we were going to start rehearsal in ten days, but I didn't even know if I had the role and it was still up in the air whether or not Jack was going to commit to it. And if we didn't have Jack, that meant the whole project had to be rethought."

She listened as John praised the work of hers that he had seen and she told him that she was thrilled to be considered for *Prizzi's* but, as far as she knew, no offer had been made. "This is outrageous!" Huston said. "By the time I got home," Turner related, "my agent called saying there was an offer. I said, 'Well, the man works fast.' "

Turner recognized that the supporting role of Maerose was more intriguing than the part she was being asked to play, which was "the only white person in the film; the only one outside of the family." But it wasn't the role as much as the opportunity to work with Huston that convinced Turner to do it. "I figured I'd be working with Jack again at some point," she said, "so the priority was to work with Huston."

Turner finally pushed Nicholson into a commitment when she called him directly to let him know that she had turned down another film to do *Prizzi's* and she wanted some hint whether or not he was going to be her leading man. The following week Nicholson was at the table for the first reading and the mystery of his reluctance was at last revealed. He thought they were attempting another *Godfather*. Nobody had told him that this movie was a send-up. "Jack took the first reading," Turner said, "and as soon as I read my line, 'What kind of creep wouldn't catch a baby?' we're all laughing and Jack goes, 'This is funny.' And we go, 'Yeah.' John said, 'It's a very funny story, what's wrong with you?' And Jack said, 'It's a comedy?' He never thought that until he heard it out loud!"

At the first rehearsal Turner asked John for some advice on how to play Irene. "Oh, no, my dear," John answered, "you already have her." After she and Jack were left to work things out on their own, he would return and make subtle suggestions. "Which was such a respectful attitude from a director," she felt, "because the way I work, and the way Jack works, is the whole thing's mapped out in your mind anyway. And then to be given that space. So I found that immensely encouraging."

She found John intimidating but also reassuring. "John had a very proper manner of speaking," Turner said. "I rarely heard him use contractions . . . or inexact words. He was very specific. He didn't say 'I will,' but rather, 'I shall.' I was brought up in schools in England and South America and the reason the language is so exact was half the time English wasn't people's first language. So I found myself relaxing into my usual way of speaking. And he said to me once, 'If I were fifty . . . never mind fifty, if I were twenty years younger, my dear, you'd have to slap my face.' And I said, 'I should be charmed.' "

Language was very much on Huston's mind when he realized that neither Nicholson nor Anjelica had quite gotten the Brooklyn accent he wanted to hear. He hired Julie Bovasso, the actress who played John Travolta's mother in *Saturday Night Fever,* as dialogue coach. "She had a gift for dialects," John said, "so she could do different parts of Brooklyn: from Brooklyn Heights, a Jewish Brooklynese, an Irish Brooklynese, she was marvelous. Gave me a whole line of country to explore."

On the fifth day of rehearsals he telephoned Jack and Anjelica and told them to expect a visit. "Kids," he said when he arrived, "I've found the voice of our movie." He brought Bovasso up and she read two pages of the script. "Isn't it wonderful?" John exclaimed. "The Voice of the Movie." He stood up, noticed the view from the window, and left the two of them thinking, "Oh, shit . . . *these* are our words of wisdom?"

"It was up to us to get our accents down," Anjelica said, "so Jack went to the Brooklyn betting shops and I went to a Brooklyn church." During preproduction she was in the costume department trying on a black designer dress from the fifties with a frilly taffeta piece that came over the shoulder. She told the designer it would be interesting to take off the ruffle and drape it in Schiaparelli pink. "Just then my father entered the room," Anjelica recalled, "and said, 'Well, what do you think about making the ruffle in Schiaparelli pink?' That was the moment I knew there was no separation in how we saw the character."

They had come a long way from the time she arrived in Vienna to begin *A Walk with Love and Death* with her hair chopped defiantly short. Now she was confident that "my father would do his best to make me look good." And also "Jack wouldn't belittle me." She was ready to give the performance of her life.

31

THE COLLECTOR
OF SOULS

KATHLEEN TURNER CONSIDERED JACK NICHOLSON THE FIN-
est actor she'd ever worked with, a man who took care of himself
and allowed her to concentrate on acting. But she couldn't get over the
fact that John Huston was her director. "The man was a legendary
figure. Why was he there, working with *us*?"

She was also pleased that John didn't put distance between himself
and his actors, although at the beginning she had to straighten him
out. "I heard him actually say, 'Where's the girl?' And I said, 'The *girl* is
here.' It became a joke. '*Nobody* calls me The Girl, Mr. Huston.' "

John liked Turner, thought she was a born actress. "The good ones
don't remind you of anybody else," he said. To play the Don's two sons,
Huston and Foreman selected Robert Loggia and Lee Richardson. John
Rudolph was set to play Nicholson's "Pop," Angelo. Huston's former
secretary and family friend, Anne Selepegno, was given the role of the
Don's wife. And William Hickey, who appeared in *Wise Blood*, was cast
as Don Corrado Prizzi, the devilish octogenarian head of the family.

John also assembled some key people who had worked with him in
the forties. Meta Wilde, who had been his first script girl on *The Maltese
Falcon*, was made script supervisor. Rudi Fehr, who had edited *Key*

Largo, came out of retirement to edit *Prizzi's*. Both Tom Shaw and Stephen Grimes were previously committed, but John found a good cinematographer in Andre Bartkowiak and hired Dennis Washington, who had done *Victory*, as the production designer.

"Although we weren't doing a period film," Washington noted, "John wanted to give it a sense the family was living in an atmosphere of thirty years ago, which was tough. The only way to work it was that they sort of lived in their own world."

Though he had confidence in his cast and crew, John was especially attentive to Anjelica. In his last years Huston had his family very much on his mind. He wanted to do what he could to ensure them a foothold so they could find their way in the world without his assistance. "He desperately wanted her to be marvelous," Kathleen Turner noticed. "Which she was."

"When John said he was going to have Anjelica in *Prizzi's Honor*, I was a little worried," said Paul Kohner, who never wanted to represent her. But he visited the set and saw how she had "grown immeasurably. The years with Jack Nicholson had a great deal to do with it. She'd become a woman."

Jack and Anjelica's relationship during the making of *Prizzi's* was good. "They have an understanding between them and you can't miss it," Kathleen Turner said. "They have a common language." Turner had no scenes with Anjelica. "We were opposite women in the film, totally antagonistic to each other through our characters, so she didn't want to risk a friendship with me. But I would love to know her better. God, she intrigues the hell out of me."

While on location in Brooklyn, Anjelica and Jack stayed at separate hotels, preferring not to mix their private lives with their characters. "I don't endorse the idea that actors should live their parts," Anjelica said, "but in spite of oneself, it sometimes does follow you home. There were elements of the hitman in Jack at the time and I didn't want to be around him too much. Jack said that he generally dropped Charley Partanna toward dinnertime. I said that I often carried Maerose through to dessert."

"We ran down the motivations of the people in different scenes," Nicholson said. "She's like Lady Macbeth. She's going to be the queen of this realm, and I'm going to be the king. Anjelica has a part in this picture similar to mine in *Easy Rider*—her character is contra to the rest of the cast, and that's a good spot to be in a film."

Anjelica first appears on the screen during the opening wedding shot. The elaborate, ambitious shot inside the Church of St. Ann and the

Holy Trinity sets the pace and tone for the rest of the movie. Alex North's clever operatic score establishes the mood; the Don's sleeping during the ceremony lends a comical reality to the proceedings; Nicholson's turning his head and noticing Kathleen Turner up in the balcony informs the audience that the two of them are going to be somehow bound together; and the dead-on full-face shot of Anjelica, her seriousness shadowed by her wide-brimmed hat, leaves no doubt that she was not just a woman of substance, but a woman with a history.

Anjelica said she felt like "a good instrument" for her first scene with Nicholson, when he tells her she should get married and practice her meatballs. "I was seeking a particular frame of mind," she said, "and as I looked around at some latticework, I saw two perfect ovals. Jack was behind one and my father was behind the other. I could look from one to the other and use it for Maerose. It raised the hair on my arms."

She also sensed what it meant to be a Huston when she overheard an old man say, "Oh, there's Walter's son." It made her realize that Americans, "who don't have all that much history, are very pleased to have whatever history they have. And I think my family's name is strong in the theater and strong in movie history, and I think people like that. It makes me feel good. I feel very much backed by my ancestors."

As the wedding scene sequence was being set up, a crowd of school kids stood outside St. Ann's, looking for a glimpse of Nicholson. It wasn't difficult for one slim fourteen-year-old boy to slip unnoticed into the church. He watched from the balcony and then went down for a closer look. There was Nicholson. And there was the old man in tan fatigues and a white beard, whose hacking cough didn't detract from the fact that he was in charge. "Are you John Huston?" the boy asked.

"I am. And who might you be?"

"Justin Miller. My friends call me Jud."

"Well, Jud." He motioned to the boy to come sit by him, and for the next few hours, as they waited between shots, they found out things about each other.

"Have you ever been married?" the boy asked.

"Many times," Huston said.

"What did your father do?"

"I'll tell you," John said. And did.

"Do you think a lot about him?"

"Just about every day. I hope you're as close to your father as I was to mine."

"I was very close to my grandfather," Justin said. He told John how, when he was a small boy, he would always watch his grandfather wake up in the morning, and how they did special things. One day he went to play with him and his grandfather didn't get up. He was dead. Justin was four years old and needed a psychiatrist to help him through his grief.

John put his hand on Justin's head. "I'll be your surrogate grandpa," he said quietly.

"It was like spending time with someone that I'd known a long time," Justin said. Over the next six weeks, while they shot in Brooklyn, Justin would sit next to Huston, talking with him for hours, joining him each day for lunch.

He became the object of some considerable dislike among the cast and crew who were all vying for John's attention. "Everybody else was jealous," recalled Janet Roach, "because here was this pimple-faced boy in a ridiculous tweed overcoat when it was eighty degrees outside, getting John's attention. It created sibling rivalry. It was extraordinary."

Meta Wilde, who was always by John's *other* side, became exasperated by Justin. "Honestly," she said, "that young man did not have the sensitivity that he should have had to understand and realize that it was an intrusion. And John was so nice and courteous and kind and sweet I couldn't believe it. He was told every day not to get too close to John when the scene was being made. He just imposed. I resented it very much at times."

Justin learned a great deal about filmmaking during his time on the set, but he learned even more about art. "I knew nothing about art before I met him," Justin said. "I was preoccupied with myself. But the time I was with him, I never felt like I was wasting a second." Huston told him to read Vasari's *Lives of the Painters*, to study Michelangelo and da Vinci, and then to read about the Tuscan primitives.

"I didn't really ever see him give outward direction," Justin recalled. But John did use a video monitor for the first time during *Prizzi's*. "He always had a headset on," Justin said. "He'd be in his own world then."

Justin would sometimes accompany John to see the dailies. "Anjelica went there often," Justin said. "Kathleen Turner never went. She was anxious to get home and see her new husband. She was like the odd one who never really associated the same way with anyone else. It was almost a family movie."

Although John was constantly coughing and had oxygen available to him in his trailer, Justin had no idea of just how sick Huston was. Before the movie started Huston had told an interviewer that he was in such bad shape that a flight of steps was like a short climb up Mt. Everest for him.

When William Hamilton visited the set he thought that perhaps John was too infirm to tackle something as clever and darkly humorous as *Prizzi's*. "I had lunch with him," said Hamilton, who had become a regular *New Yorker* cartoonist and had styled two characters in his 1981 novel, *The Love of Rich Women*, on John and Gladys Hill. "I thought, Jesus, he was just ga-ga. He was talking about what sounded like old New Deal talk. The guy was just riding on the past. Then I saw the picture and I thought it was *terrific*! And I realized, back to those years when I was involved with him, what he really needed was a perverse subject. Then he was in business!"

For Jack Nicholson, watching John in action was like being on the sidelines as Magic Johnson steered the Lakers downcourt. "He's one of those people in life whose approval I seek," Nicholson said. During the first courtship scene between Nicholson and Turner, Jack was set to shoot it again when he heard John say, "Another scene now, Jack." Nicholson looked at John as if he hadn't heard correctly. "The scene is done now, Jack," Huston said. Nicholson just shook his head and whispered, "I've worked with everybody and his mother and I've never made a picture like this, and if it works I'm never going to make one any other way." He just couldn't get over how confident John was as a director.

"I'm glad that I saw John Huston commanding," Nicholson said. "It's always the director that gets me going. My whole craft is developed to be able to do what that guy wants."

John Foreman thought that playing Charley Partanna "really put Jack through the wringer. It forced him to give up everything the public has loved about him—his smile, his charm, his wit, his way of letting you in on the character's naughty secrets. It took great courage to do what Jack did."

What most struck Kathleen Turner was the way Huston paced each scene. "I was amazed by the rhythm of the film and how deliberate it was," she said. But she didn't always agree with John's interpretation of her character. Turner felt that Irene never really loved Charley, but used him to protect herself from the family. She wanted to show Irene's contempt for Charley, but John, she said, "felt it more important that she really, against her will, be drawn and attracted by this man."

John was convinced that audiences would appreciate *Prizzi's* original-
ity even though it didn't abide by "the usual set of rules. One liked,
even loved, the principals despite their complete amorality. But *Prizzi's*
Honor is also funny, and the addition of humor makes it unique in my
experience. Charley, Irene, and Maerose are all three vicious as sin, yet
they have a certain purity—they're not depraved. This holds true for all
the other characters in the picture and, for that matter, for the picture
itself."

For Anjelica, being directed by her father was an entirely different
experience from the first time years earlier. "He pulled gently on the
reins," she said. "And before I knew it I was performing dressage."

She also found how generous Nicholson could be as an actor. "Whenever you work with someone good, you sure do know it," she said,
"because it makes life so much easier for you. It's a feeling of, 'Ah, I'm
getting so much, so many ideas.' Good actors make you feel good."

Nicholson returned the compliment. "The main thing to know about
Anjelica," he said, "is that there's a certain level of sophistication
among modern young women in acting where, frankly, she simply owns
the category. And she just gets better, continues to grow."

Nicholson would also say of Anjelica's performance that "acting
doesn't come any better than that"—a remark that Meta Wilde would
echo about John's directing. "He knew what the camera was seeing and
he had very definite ideas."

Wilde enjoyed herself on what she described as a very "loose set.
Everybody was so happy." Wilde was the only one on the set other than
John who could compare the acting of Nicholson and Humphrey
Bogart. "If Bogie had a long scene to do, he sometimes would flub it.
And he had a problem with his front teeth, he had that lisp. I don't
think Jack flubs at all. His timing is impeccable."

Kathleen Turner said Huston gave her "the greatest compliment I'd
ever had. We were doing a scene in the trailer. After one take he said,
'It's not right. I need you to out-Sicilian a Sicilian.' We did a second
take and he said, 'You can really think, can't you?' I said, 'I can live off
that for about six months, thank you.' "

Turner could appreciate John's praise, but she remained unsatisfied
with the way he shot her death scene. "It was in slow motion, when
she goes to shoot Charley and he throws the knife. She was such an
excellent marksman, it was impossible that she could miss. By using
slow motion he took away the clarity that she was *choosing* to be killed
rather than to kill him. I wanted it to be in real time, so that it would
be clear it had to be *her* choice."

That scene, with the shot of the dagger pinning Turner's throat to the wall, brought full circle Huston's heroes' treatment of women who have lied to their men. In *The Maltese Falcon* Bogart smacks Mary Astor and tells her she's got to take the fall; in *Prizzi's* Nicholson ducks a bullet and gruesomely kills his wife. For the women in John's life, from Doris Lilly to Edna O'Brien, who believed that John was capable of destroying women who loved him, Huston couldn't have made a more personal statement.

John had approved so many first takes that a week after the $15 million picture was finished, Rudi Fehr and his daughter, Kaja, had a two-and-a-half-hour rough cut assembled. The first time *Prizzi's* was screened, Huston invited Billy Pearson and Michael Fitzgerald to join him, Fehr, and John Foreman. When the picture ended John turned to Pearson and Fitzgerald for their opinions and ignored Foreman. Fehr was quick to notice this and said that Foreman was "so furious. He had made notes and notes." A few days later Fehr mentioned to Huston that Foreman had taken notes, but John said, "You'll never see them." And neither Fehr nor Huston ever did.

ABC thought the movie ran too long and wanted twenty minutes cut, which John found particularly hard to do. "I was cutting very close to the bone," he said, "although I don't think the picture was damaged by it."

The music added to the picture enormously. John had enlisted his favorite composer, Alex North. "When we were ready to spot the music," North recalled, "we ran the picture, just Huston, Foreman, and me. I said, 'Before you say anything, I'd like to tell you what I think. My feeling is to do it opera-wise.' Huston tapped me on my knee and said, 'Okay, Alex, you can go home.' And he yelled, 'Puccini! Puccini!' Which I used, of course, with Donizetti and Verdi."

North's music was hailed by serious music critics. Michael Walsh in *Film Comment* wrote, "In opera, the orchestra acts as an unseen protagonist, commenting on the action and sometimes dictating it. It does the same thing in Huston's stylish film."

Richard Condon saw the movie with Janet Roach. He was so thrilled that he gave her a big kiss on the cheek and said, "Thank God, it's still funny." To John he wrote, "The movie is as contiguous as a stream of gravity-pulled water—a clear mountain stream." Then he went on to express his one big problem with the picture: "And it is not an easy one—I have fallen in love with your daughter."

When Ricki's brother Philip Soma saw it he was startled at how much Anjelica had grown to resemble Ricki. "She's damn near her double," Soma said. Joan Buck credited Anjelica's "four years of being alone, going to those crummy little classes, doing the badly written plays. Also John's failing health, his age, the idea that she had to help him instead of him helping her."

"I was bowled over by it," Frances FitzGerald wrote John, calling *Prizzi's* "miraculous" and "extraordinary. . . . It was very funny; it was scary and gruesome and terrible; and it was—in its way—quite moving. . . . You could have lost all of us at any given moment—but it was perfect to the very last shot."

Kathleen Turner agreed with those critics who hailed *Prizzi's* as a classic. ("If John Huston's name were not on *Prizzi's Honor*," Pauline Kael began her review, "I'd have thought a fresh, new talent had burst on the scene, and he'd certainly be the hottest new director in Hollywood.") "I've done nine films," Turner said, "and definitely two of them were classics: *Body Heat* and *Prizzi's Honor*. That's fantastic!"

Besides Anjelica, perhaps the person whose life was most affected by *Prizzi's* was young Justin Miller, who began a correspondence with Huston and a mutual exchange of expensive art books. "After he left," Justin said, "I felt different, as though I really met someone who kind of shaped my life. If you take life in different stages, that stage really brought my confidence up a level. I don't know what my life would have been like if I'd never met him."

In March 1985, John decided it was time for an adventure. He had always been fascinated by the east coast of Baja and he thought he and Danny might be able to join forces to make a documentary based on John Steinbeck's *Sea of Cortez*. Danny had previously directed a documentary on the making of the movie *Santa Claus* starring Dudley Moore and thought it would be educational working with John on one. They found a marine biologist to work with them, and together with Maricela and Huston's old friend Burgess Meredith they made a scouting cruise of the coast.

When they returned to Las Caletas at the end of the month, John took time out to catch up on his correspondence and to do some painting. One of the letters he owed was to John Julius. He asked to be filled in about Allegra, who had gotten into Oxford now and was in her third and final year. "Allegra, for all I know, might be residing in the Antarctic," he wrote. "It's been months since I've heard from her. . . . She ought to be ashamed, and you can quote me."

Danny returned to England, and soon afterward John's lungs got congested and he had to fly to Los Angeles for treatment. He was released after a few weeks, but by the summer he had had a relapse and was back in Cedars-Sinai in intensive care.

While he was there, on July 8, Jack and Anjelica appeared on the cover of *People* magazine. Inside Anjelica was praised for having created "a grand grotesque" as Maerose: "Lucrezia Borgia with a Brooklyn accent, Iago in high heels." Their love affair was touted in the same glowing terms. Producer Robert Evans was quoted as saying that Nicholson would never leave Anjelica. "He was a glittering vagrant, and she gave him the solid core he needed. Her breeding and culture have refined his life. The man is a diamond, and she's given him a beautiful setting." And Huston added his own comment on the relationship. "There is a rare devotion between them," he said. "You see it in life and you feel it in their scenes together. Twelve years! That's longer than any of my five marriages lasted."

Anjelica cunningly couched her comments within the framework of the part that brought her such acclaim. "Maerose is a woman scorned," she said, "but she has the womanly wisdom to know that the only way to keep something forever is to let it go. And when she does that he becomes hers forever. I learned from Maerose that you have to allow the things you love to be free."

The article, and the publicity surrounding *Prizzi's*, pleased John. His illness had also brought Danny back from London, along with Allegra, who had finished her studies at Oxford and had gotten a job at a publishing house. By the end of July, when Allegra returned to her job, Tony also came to be with his father. Jack Nicholson offered John his house in Ventura, and that's where he stayed with Maricela, Tony, and Danny. "I had a wonderful time with Danny," Tony said, recalling how John's illness put them in a situation where they finally had a chance to get to know each other. "We spent quite some time looking after Dad together."

"It was very shaky," Danny said. "Dad couldn't sleep and we couldn't give him anything to sleep because that slowed down his breathing. He was given stimulants, so he was basically speeding."

"I hope death approaches me very quietly," John told a reporter around this time, "touches me with a sleeve, says lie down, puts its fingers over my eyes." But when he was asked if he had come to terms with religion or an afterlife, he said, simply, "I'm not religious. It would be great solace in believing in Jesus H. Christ. I envy those who are capable of taking such superstition seriously."

John described his condition in a letter to Suzanne Flon. "Either I or someone else has to carry a little tank of oxygen around with me wherever I go, which is rather humiliating. . . . Danny and Allegra came running when they heard I was in trouble. Anjelica is here, of course. Tony [is] on his way. So my offspring are satisfactorily dutiful."

He then proceeded to talk about the children. "Danny, age 23, is everything one could hope for from a son. He is intelligent, imaginative, inclined to be brave, and gentle, and besides, or rather on top of all that, he's physically quite beautiful, 6 ft. 2 in., and an athlete.

"Allegra . . . just finished three years at Oxford. She's been an exceptional student, and will probably graduate with honors. . . . She already has her future cut out—a job at a prestigious publishing house that will lead to an editorship. Not bad for a 20-year-old.

"As you have heard, Anjelica had a great personal success in the picture. Review after review had her down as stealing it. . . . You would love Anjelica; she's tall, slender, very beautiful, and ever so amusing—a joy to be with. She and Jack Nicholson have been together some twelve years. He wants to get married, but Anjel wants to put marriage off until she has made her reputation as an actress. I don't understand the theory behind this, but her decisions regarding herself have been quite correct ever since she was a little girl. I'm very fond of Jack. He's an extremely interesting individual, and oddly enough shares my interest in a number of things, painting, boxing, etc. He refers to himself as my son-in-law.

"Tony has been living in Norfolk in a house Margot's parents gave them. He rears children and hawks—three of the former who are fire-engines of energy. He shoots and fishes. He is curator of the Flyfishers Club of London, which I'm told is a distinction. He's writing—about falcons. He seems to be happy.

"You know about Maricela. She was the only thing I could salvage from that lunatic marriage I contracted with the rhinoceros. . . . Most probably, I couldn't have survived without her. She dishes out the medication, cooks, puts my contact lens in, cuts my hair, manicures me, puts me to bed, and sometimes when I'm done in, she gives me a massage."

John also mentioned that he might be in London in November to appear in a cameo role in an hour-long film Danny wanted to make called Mr. *Corbett's Ghost.* The project came to Danny from two of his film school friends, Barry Navidi, who wanted to produce it, and Gerry Wilson, who wrote it. The Dickensian story, about a man willing to sell his soul to the devil in return for having his boss dead, needed some star power to get it off the ground, and John was only too happy to do for Danny what his father had done for him. He had to be in Italy toward the end of the year to appear in a film called *Momo,* and he told Danny that if he raised the money for Mr. *Corbett's Ghost* by then, he would be available to play the collector of souls. He also suggested that Danny send the script to Paul Scofield and to Burgess Meredith, and when both actors heard that John was involved, they, too, signed on. Excited, Danny returned to London where he and Navidi began their attempt to raise the £600,000 needed to make their movie.

In the spring, before John got sick, he had gone to see Anjelica in a play she was doing at the Il Vittoriale in Hollywood. It was an unusual and successful production called *Tamara,* which takes place in January 1927 in the house of the Italian writer Gabriele D'Annunzio and is described as a "living movie." "It's a mystery," Anjelica said, "sort of operatic. The audience separates and follows the character of their choice around a large house, from room to room. Some nights, forty people will follow you. Very clever idea. My father described it quite well as an arabesque."

Lizzie Spender flew out to Los Angeles to write an article about Anjelica and was taken aback when she went to the play. "Fifteen minutes into the action in walks Greta Garbo . . . at least this was my momentary first impression. It shocks me—as I realize that from the earliest days of my friendship with the Huston family I have known that Anjelica was destined to be the Greta Garbo of her time. . . . Certainly, there is a Garbo-esque quality in the deep strong voice with an exotic accent, that dark, mysterious, slightly amused, mockingly restrained demeanor. I realize that the ragged edges of energy which I have observed over the years are now focused into a dramatic performance. Anjelica *is* an actress."

Spender saw Jack Nicholson in the audience, following Anjelica, wearing dark glasses and grinning wickedly. " 'Isn't Toots good?' Jack whispers to me. Toots is one of several nicknames he has for her. Apparently Jack comes to almost every performance."

When Spender returned to Anjelica's small house she noticed Ricki's eclectic influence in the way it was decorated "entirely in a muted, dusty pink, giving the impression of the texture of old silk. Not only the walls but the sofas, the curtains, and the bedcover. She likes to quote Maerose, 'Everybody sees shapes differently, but colors are forever.' . . . There are tea chests inlaid with mother-of-pearl, an Art Deco silver airplane, a bedstead with curled swans heads at either end, and a white china human head on which are marked the areas of the brain—an ancient teaching device. In the bathroom is a tray with hundreds of glass bottles of perfume. In the bedroom, fitted wardrobes with doors made from old mirror contain an enormous collection of clothes."

Anjelica stayed with *Tamara* for just over three months, then left to work in the summer of 1985 with Francis Coppola and George Lucas in a seventeen-minute, $20 million, 3-D Disney film called *Captain EO*, starring Michael Jackson. The film was to be shown only at Disneyland and Walt Disney World Epcot Center. Jackson, as Captain EO, played a space commander who crash-lands on a hostile planet ruled by a grotesque, evil queen played by Anjelica. After seven minutes of song and dance, EO defeats the power of evil and turns the place into a peace-loving planet.

Anjelica's role called for her to be suspended in midair by harnesses. "I wasn't wild about the makeup and being strapped upside down suspended from a ceiling for eight hours at a time," she confessed. "But it actually worked well for being a witch because I was quite unhappy up there. Meanness was natural."

She found Michael Jackson—whose much-operated-on face and reclusive behavior has turned him into a mystery man—to be shy and quiet, surrounded by an entourage who often maliciously teased him about his big feet. She said that he always had an eleven-year-old boy with him who carried his cape and gloves and sat on Jackson's lap; they whispered and giggled together. Anjelica found Jackson's face unreal up close, but dazzlingly beautiful from six feet away. To Anjelica, Jackson was two people: a Peter Pan–like angel who transformed himself into a dynamo when he performed. "When he'd start to sing," she said, "my heart began to beat fast, I felt a flush coming to my cheeks. I've never seen such a transformation—on the instant!"

While Anjelica was swinging from the rafters the London *Times* published a list of Oxford's graduating class, with Allegra's name among those who received a double first in English Language and Literature. She sent the list with her name underlined to John and wrote him birthday greetings on her Chatto & Windus stationery. They both celebrated their birthdays in August—John turned seventy-nine, Allegra twenty-one.

Tony took credit for pointing Allegra in the direction of publishing. He had once asked her to comment on something he was writing and her advice was so good that he suggested she write to a number of publishers seeking a summer job. Chatto & Windus hired her and after her first year there she received three promotions.

John was on oxygen full time when he arrived in England in the fall, but didn't want his grandchildren to see him breathing through a plastic tube. "He didn't want them to think of him as being old," Tony said. "So he put on this marvelous performance. I had to keep them in the next room for five minutes and then he came in without the machine. It struck me as being funny, because that's not at all the way kids think. They love the oxygen machine and the bubbles."

The bad news in London was that Danny had been unsuccessful in raising the money for his film. When John saw how disappointed Danny was, he thought of Sir John Woolf and Roberto Haggiag, two producers who might be of help. But neither liked the script and turned John down, leaving him feeling depressed. "There's nothing like having friends when you need something," he joked to Danny.

John then went to Italy with Maricela, Zoe, and Danny to act in *Momo*. "We were getting panic-stricken," Zoe said. "Because when John finished *Momo* he would have to return to the States. He couldn't hang around endlessly in London. And once he left it would be difficult to get him back because of his health."

Barry Navidi had a family contact with a Swiss cigar company and they agreed to put up half the money, but efforts to raise the other half fell through. "We kept on failing," Danny remembered. "In the end, Dad was staring at the blank wall and not eating. I was in a state of total depression."

"The whole thing collapsed," Zoe said. "So I had this brain wave. I said, 'Let's just knock on *any* door.' It was eight at night and everybody was committing suicide, the atmosphere was just so deathly. John was staying in Tony's flat, which was tiny and terribly uncomfortable, boxes everywhere, oxygen bottles. He didn't want to go to a hotel unless we were going to make the film."

The door Zoe thought of knocking on belonged to J. Paul Getty, the eccentric multimillionaire with whom she had once been friends. "I didn't even have Getty's number because I hadn't called him for so long," she said. "So we just went to his door in Chelsea in the pouring rain and knocked. This voice said he wasn't there and I asked if he was in the London Clinic, because I knew he went there. The voice said yes. So I called him and he was just adorable and said to come tomorrow. I thought, 'You don't see somebody for ages and you go to him and ask for three hundred thousand pounds.' I was so embarrassed. But you have to do it.

"So I went to Paul the next day and he said absolutely, he'd do anything for John. So Danny rehired everybody and got the whole thing moving . . . and then the Swiss backed out!"

Zoe thought of asking Getty for the other half of the money, but she was afraid that he'd think she had been conning him. Four hours before they'd have to start letting the crew go, however, she decided to see Getty and just tell him the truth. "The fact that somebody pulled out made it look like a shifty deal. So I thought the best thing was to be totally, utterly straight. So I said, 'If you want to take your money out, I'm not holding you to anything. Just because you've given half doesn't mean you have to give the rest.' "

"I wouldn't disappoint you," Getty said. "How much do you need?"

"Six," Zoe said.

"Six million?"

"No, six hundred thousand."

"Yes, that would be fine," he said and called his lawyers.

An elated Zoe returned to Tony's flat. "It's okay," she said, "he's going to do it!" John couldn't believe it. Then Zoe rang Danny and told him. "I could hear three guys just *screaming* on the other end," she said. "Hugging each other and shouting. I was like the saint of the day!"

It took just four weeks to make *Mr. Corbett's Ghost* and Danny had help from some of John's favorite people: Angela Allen worked as his script supervisor, Stephen Grimes made some preliminary sketches and had his assistant scout locations, Eva Monley "backstopped" the production manager. Both Allen and Monley thought that John was trying *too* hard to make a director of Danny, and that Danny relied too much on his support. "John was *willing* him to be a brilliant young director," Monley said.

During the making of the film, Tony told John that he had run out of money and John came up with something for them to do together. "Because he felt he should love Tony more than he did," Eva Monley said.

"I had gone broke," Tony admitted. "Dad was asked by Ray Stark if he would help sort out a project called *The Springs*, written by Robert Towne's brother, Roger. Dad asked me to work with him because he always collaborated with somebody. I'm pretty good at all the organizational things. So while he was acting in Danny's picture, we analyzed the existing script, wrote a critique on it, and then embarked on a treatment, which showed how it could be made into a reasonable picture. This went extremely well. It was the first time that I'd ever gotten on so well with Dad."

John left soon after for Los Angeles to attend the Academy Awards ceremony at the Dorothy Chandler Pavilion on March 24, 1986. *Prizzi's Honor* had received eight nominations, including Best Picture, Best Actor (Nicholson's eighth), Best Director, Best Supporting Actor (Hickey) and Actress, Screenplay, Editing, and Costume. John's inclusion made him the oldest director ever to be nominated; Anjelica's put her in contention to follow Walter and John and be the first third-generation Oscar winner. The New York Film Critics had made *Prizzi's* an early front-runner when they named it best picture and also awarded John best director, Nicholson best actor, and Anjelica best supporting actress. *Prizzi's* also won the British Academy Award and the Writers Guild Award.

Ten minutes before a nervous Janet Roach took her seat at the Pavilion, she ran into Brandon Stoddard, who was in charge of ABC Motion Pictures. But instead of congratulating her he said, "Frankly, I am amazed that it got so many nominations."

"What a tactless, stupid thing to say," Roach thought. "I was standing there in my dress-up dress, trying not to sweat for an hour and a half, and this short twerp said that to me. I wanted to pound the little bastard right into the floor."

Prizzi's Honor was destined to win only one award that evening, but it was the one Nicholson and Huston most wanted, the one that would make history for the Huston family and give Anjelica the confidence she needed. "That's all we wanted out of the night," said Nicholson. "Just wanted one for Toots." Nicholson was only too aware of what the Oscar meant to her. "*Prizzi's Honor* dropped a lot of dead weight off

Anjelica's psyche," he said. When Anjelica's name was read by Marsha Mason and Richard Dryfuss, "I never had a greater moment."

"This means a lot to me," Anjelica said, holding her Oscar, "since it comes from a role in which I was directed by my father. And I know it means a lot to him." She returned to the audience to hug Jack before she went backstage to face the press.

The award made her feel "justified in thinking that I was any good to begin with. Thinking that I had a place at all in movies or acting." And then she thought, "God, I've got to win another, because then it will be *really* real, really serious."

There was great disappointment when Sydney Pollack was named Best Director for *Out of Africa*, because the press was hoping to re-create the father/child picture of 1949, when Walter and John stood before them with their Oscars in hand. "Everyone was a bit pissed off that he didn't get it," Anjelica said, "but I wasn't going to allow that to spoil my parade. I knew he and Jack would've preferred I win, rather than the flip." Also, "there couldn't have been a clearer statement from the Academy: You won it on your own."

Tony, who watched the awards show in England, considered Anjelica's Oscar a long-awaited crowning. "The most noticeable thing about Anjel is the way becoming a star has affected her," he said. "She is absolutely magnificent now. She is a queen. Or the closest thing to a queen you'll get in Los Angeles."

But even queens have their trials. Three days after she won the Oscar, Anjelica read for a part as one of the three witches in Nichol-son's next film, *The Witches of Eastwick*. She thought she was "very right" for the role, which eventually went to Cher, "but I was foolish to test right after I got the Academy Award because it made me very nervous. I wasn't pleased with my reading."

A week after the Oscar ceremonies John entered the hospital for a cataract operation. He complained to a friend, "I have given up on the delights of the flesh—Havana cigars, maidens, vodka martinis, and the midnight hours. I must face up to the shameful confession that all these depravations are endured simply to go on living. . . . Not only does my body not furnish up delights, it is becoming an outright enemy."

To earn some easy money Paul Kohner got John some voiceover com-mercial television and radio work for Dodge and Calistoga water. The ten

Calistoga spots were worth $25,000. The futuristic Dodge commercial brought his recognizable voice into millions of homes. Perhaps the only person who *didn't* recognize his voice was John himself! "One day I was watching TV and the ads came on," he recalled. "I said to Maricela, 'Whoever's speaking has listened to my father, that's the way he would phrase things.' Then I heard a familiar phrase. It was me!"

Even with the money from the commercials and the fees he earned from acting and directing, Huston *still* couldn't afford the price of a Beverly Hills house. "I was marveling at the price of those houses," he said. "The big Breeder's Cup Race was for three million dollars. Well, Christ, the byways of Beverly Hills are nothing but three-million-dollar houses. I don't understand the relative values of things. I've never been truly comfortable. The last year or two is the only time in my life when I haven't *had* to work." Although there was anticipated money from films on which he had deferred payments, he still estimated his worth at under $2 million.

He had never received the money owed him from *The Man Who Would Be King.* And any anticipated money from *Prizzi's Honor* was blown by the way ABC handled the deal. "The worst deal I've ever made," John said. "It would have been very lucrative, but ABC did the silliest thing in the world. They sold it to video *before* it came out. So the video only paid something like five million dollars."

Another source of aggravation was the colorization of black-and-white films, done mostly by Ted Turner, who had bought the MGM library and the early Warner Bros. films. To John, adding computerized color to some of the classic early films was like tinting a Cartier-Bresson or Ansel Adams photograph. "Will you then go on to color da Vinci, Michelangelo, Bellini?" he asked.

In a letter to Gil Cates, the president of the Directors Guild, John wrote that colorization was "as great an impertinence as for someone to wash flesh tones on a da Vinci drawing. I am only astounded as to the vulgarity of the whole idea and hope that discrimination and respect for the arts will triumph over the unchecked employment of the process." But when the process continued, and even *The Maltese Falcon* was colorized, Huston, at a press conference at the Directors Guild and later on a nationally syndicated radio talk show, made headlines when he lashed out against those who would destroy an art form.

"A couple of generations back," he spoke from a prepared statement, "screenwriters used to tell a story about two producers lost in the desert and dying of thirst. About to give up the ghost, they crawl into view of a miraculous spring of pure effervescent water and they go joyously to drink, when one says, 'no, *wait,* don't drink, *wait* till I piss in it.'

"To bring the story up to date, I have only to add that in my opinion both producers are members of the Turner organization.

"Last night I looked for as long as I could bear at a colorized print of *The Maltese Falcon*. I asked myself if such an example of mindless insipidity is worthy of notice in a threatened world—a world beset by terrorists. The answer of course is 'yes,' for mindlessness alone is what allows for the assaults of crazed zealots, mad rulers and falsifying politicians.

"The black-and-white film has been defended on a number of counts: aesthetic, historical, philosophical, material . . . but there is one flank in deepest peril: the poor f——ing audience. Witness, in my opinion, the gathering together of clowns by the Turner organization to express their admiration of colorization: simple, yea innocent souls as open to corruption as the original South Sea Islanders were to the clap."

On a KABC talk radio program in Los Angeles John compared what Ted Turner was doing to being the father of children who have been sold into white slavery, "beaten by brutes, their teeth knocked out, noses broken, poor little whores. Now, on top of everything else, the pimps want to rinse their hair in peroxide. That's what it amounts to."

Unfortunately it was a losing battle. John was disgusted but put it out of his mind when his emphysema got so bad he was forced to give up his hopes for directing *Haunted Summer* in Europe. Instead he agreed to work with Tony on two projects: *The Dead* and *Revenge*. Tony set to work immediately, without a contract, attempting a first draft of the Joyce story. Because of John's failing health Tony decided to leave his family and make yet another attempt at finding a profession.

After meeting in New York with Wieland Schulz-Keil, who had acquired the rights to *The Dead*, Tony went to stay with John at Burgess Meredith's house in Malibu. Together they worked on both *The Dead* and *Revenge*. "On *Revenge* I regarded myself as very much the junior partner," Tony said. "With *The Dead*, what I had was Dad's advice. But in *Revenge* I was steering very much according to Dad's perception of the way the story ought to go. I was his amanuensis."

John disliked the act of writing but found that with Tony he was able to "slip into a flow of dialogue. I'm only thinking of the line as I say it," he said, "not of what went before or what comes after. I can do this with Tony. If I start to *write*, I start going back and criticizing and editing. I write a line and cross half of it out."

As they worked on these projects it struck Tony that John reminded him of the nineteenth-century Spanish painter Francisco Goya in his later years. *Wise Blood, Under the Volcano, Prizzi's Honor, The Dead* were comparable to Goya's black paintings. Tony saw an artistic unanimity to John's films (with the exception of *Annie*) of the last decade. Even *Revenge*, which ended on a positive note, was full of "hell and damnation."

John felt that Tony had finally turned around in his attitude toward him, but for Tony, working under John's laser-beam intelligence was, at times, a trial by fire. Cherokee recalled how Tony would sometimes come to dinner at their house and complain about the difficulties he was having with John. "One Sunday," she said, "he had had a very bad conference over a script and he was pacing and he said, 'He'll never hurt me again. I thank God I've reached the point in my life that he cannot hurt me.' And I said, 'Tony, don't say that, because you know some bitterness will take place and that's one thing you don't want.' "

During dinner Tony began talking to her guests about falcon training. "Everybody thought, 'Who is this dude putting on this show?' " remembered Cherokee. "But in the end he won them. He reminded me of the first days I used to see John at the head of the table and I used to sit spellbound when he talked about things."

After Tony left Cherokee called John to tell him how proud she was of Tony. "I said, 'John, you can go now, because Tony's got it all.' Well, the next day we were at Buzz Meredith's with John and he was tearing Tony apart something awful! And Tony said, 'You had to go open your big mouth and pay me a compliment in front of my father. I've had it all day!' "

Cherokee came to believe that John, once her "knight in shining armor," was embarrassed by the truth. "He really didn't care. God shone His grace on him beyond all belief and John shit on it." John thought that he and Anjelica were alike, but Cherokee felt it was Tony, more than Anjelica or Danny, who had "John's original soul."

"Of all the people who traipsed through John's life," she said, "Tony got the biggest hurt. The scars are millions all over his body. And Tony is so talented, so gentle and sweet. Anytime that he's rude to people it's because he's inherited John's streak of impatience with mediocrity. But Tony doesn't have any love from anyplace.

"I had prayed that he would stay away from this world. That's what broke me up, when he finally made the decision to come here, because he had a niche there."

Part of the price Tony paid for working with John was Margot and his children. Tony had returned to Norfolk in September 1986 "expecting my wife and children to greet me with the slippers—and my wife had decided that she no longer wanted to be married to me. It was the greatest surprise I ever had in my life. I had no idea, whatsoever, that this was cooking. I was absolutely staggered."

It didn't happen the moment he walked through the door. It was when he decided to go hawking in Scotland after being home just three weeks that Margot went to see her solicitor. "I really wanted to go with my hawks and be in a wild place and be free," Tony said. "Falcons, spiritually, have represented freedom for me. I had built up a certain tension with Dad being sick and working on the scripts and I wanted to get away, I didn't want to be involved in washing the dishes." When he returned Margot went down to London and the solicitor's letter arrived, telling him that the house was in her name and she didn't want him around anymore.

"I felt like I had my teeth knocked out," he said when trying to make sense of what had happened. "Margot's got money and her family's extremely wealthy. I think she saw me as possibly becoming a liability. And I saw it, too, that's why I said I've got to get out and work."

At the end of Joyce's "The Dead," Gabriel looks out the window at the snowflakes falling and knows that "the time had come for him to set out on his journey westward." Tony, whose life had become intertwined with the fiction he was involved with, left England and returned to Los Angeles to continue work on the Joyce story. Like Gabriel, he couldn't help wondering that "perhaps she had not told him all the story." Nevertheless, he had the great satisfaction of being able to send Margot $50,000. Money he had earned by himself.

John was saddened by the breakup of Tony's marriage, but he was also philosophical about it. Marriage was one arena where the Hustons didn't have much success. Perhaps Anjelica had understood this best of all. Although her relationship with Jack was often rocky, they were still together in their independent way.

At thirty-five, Anjelica had talked about wanting to have a baby when she turned thirty-six, and Jack had also expressed his desire for children. Nicholson had told a friend that he had wanted Anjelica to be tested to see if she *could* have a baby but she had refused. Anjelica told a family friend that their relationship had gone on too long and he didn't really excite her. But to writer James Kaplan for a profile in the *New York Times Magazine* she said, "The relationship is a fact of my life. Whatever it is Jack wants to do, and whatever it is I want to do, we seem to accommodate each other. He's a soulmate. It goes beyond commitment. It's not as if one has any choice in the matter. . . . I hate to think of a world without Jack."

When Anjelica took a part opposite James Caan in Francis Ford Coppola's *Gardens of Stone*, Nicholson decided to follow *The Witches of Eastwick* with *Ironweed*. "A lot of that has to do with Anjelica's working again," he told a reporter. "I might not have taken that much on, but I don't want to sit around while she's working."

In *Gardens of Stone* Anjelica played a *Washington Post* reporter who falls in love with a career soldier (Caan). The main relationship, however, is one between Caan and a young gung-ho soldier eager to go off to fight in Vietnam. *Gardens of Stone* is an elegy for the soldiers who went to fight there. Anjelica saw it as "the flip side" of *Apocalypse Now*. "It may have shown the soldier in a somewhat glorified light," she said, "but it also showed the absurdity of the whole process." What attracted her to the part was that it "expressed a woman's feeling about men and war."

She was also attracted to working again for Coppola, who, like her father, surrounded himself with familiar faces. But a family tragedy struck Coppola on Memorial Day, a week after the movie started, when his son Gio was killed in a boating accident.

"It was a very hard movie for Francis to complete," said Anjelica. "We stopped for three days, but he wanted to go right on. Everyone was very sad. We all wanted to make it easier if we possibly could for Francis. But that was impossible; he suffered an absolutely irretrievable loss."

Anjelica's performance was strong and skillful, but as more than one critic opined, she didn't get enough to do. "The sinewy Anjelica Huston," wrote *New York*'s David Denby, "is wasted in an unwritten part."

In spite of all the offers that came to her after she won the Oscar, Anjelica still looked to her father to find a part that was right for her. "I didn't know that he was working on *The Dead*," she said, "until he was having an eye operation. I found myself reading the screenplay to him because he couldn't see at that time. It moved me to tears. A while later he asked me if I'd play Gretta."

Anjelica knew how much Joyce meant to her father and how much he wanted to do "The Dead." "It says what he felt about life and love and marriage and death," she said, "and where we're from and where we're going and passing the goose. The story is full of little epiphanies."

*   *   *

With the possibility of *The Dead* actually making it to the screen, Tony was able to put the sorrow of his personal life aside and concentrate on making the script as perfect as he could. He also decided to keep a journal once the movie got under way, and he began to harbor ideas of forgetting about his ego to impartially observe John so that he himself might learn how to direct one day.

John knew his weak condition meant he would have to rely on others to help get the job done and was pleased that Stephen Grimes, Tom Shaw, Dorothy Jeakins, Alex North, and Roberto Silvi would all be available to give him the support he needed. The film, to be shot in early 1987, was something to look forward to, but before they got started John wanted to spend the Christmas holidays in Puerto Vallarta and Las Caletas. He had been away from Mexico too long. He felt unsettled staying in borrowed houses in Malibu, West Hollywood, and the canyons of Beverly Hills between visits to Cedars-Sinai Hospital. He was sick of feeling tired and tired of being sick and thought that the holidays would be the perfect time to bring family and friends together. Anjelica would go off to Aspen with Jack, but Danny, Zoe, and Allegra would appreciate getting away from the cold English winter. Tony could use a vacation. Maricela had her family down there. So what if his doctors advised against it; he had never lived his life according to what others thought and he wasn't about to begin now. He had another movie to make, it would be a family affair, after he rejuvenated himself floating like a baby in the warm Pacific currents along the western coast of Mexico.

EPILOGUE

JOHN DIED IN BED AS HE HOPED HE WOULD. BUT DEATH didn't come gently tapping. His body fought for over twenty years before succumbing on August 28, 1987. He lived twenty-four years longer than his mother and fifteen years longer than Walter, and had packed his life so full, it seemed hard to believe he was *only* eighty-one. While his death was not unexpected, it was still difficult for his friends and family. Suddenly there was a large gap in their lives. One impossible to fill . . . or forget.

Danny Huston couldn't get over how John's will was such a thought-out message from the grave. "Dad obviously didn't have a great mathematical brain, and you can tell the painstaking time that it took him to come up with a will. He put so much thought into it. It all adapted completely into our life-styles, our ages, and to what we are doing; whether we have children or not; whether we've had a good career or are at the beginning, like I am."

Danny had flown up from Mexico to attend a family meeting with John's lawyer, Henry Hyde, and business manager, Jess Morgan. Before the meeting Danny called Maricela to ask if there was anything he could do to help her, and Maricela told him she wasn't going to the meeting because Tony had asked her not to. Danny insisted that she was expected to be there. "If I've got anything to fight about, I've got my own lawyers," Maricela said. "And if you are trying to keep the family together or create some kind of happiness between all of us, forget it."

At the meeting Danny wondered whether he should confront Tony. "I didn't want to speak to him about anything that required a certain amount of delicacy," he said. While Danny understood that it was difficult for Allegra to fly over from London, he felt that they could all protect her interests. But Maricela was another story. "Why on earth did you tell Maricela not to come?" he finally asked Tony. Tony denied ever having said anything of the kind to her, and "for the first time," said Danny, "I believed Tony completely."

Danny didn't know what to make of Maricela. Did she really destroy John's papers and drawings at *his* request? "I don't see him saying burn all the papers," Danny said. Tony, too, had a hard time believing it. He also thought it a bit "surreal" when Maricela told him that John had sent her a "mysterious poem, delivered in a kind of broken English," when she visited his grave soon after the funeral. "It was kind of a spiritual poem about being good to others. It didn't sound like Dad's writing to me."

"If you start to look at the horrors that might have occurred during the last week of my father's life," Danny said, "and dissect Maricela's behavior, you begin to perceive differently the past two years of Dad's life. A little friction or conflict between my father and Maricela a year ago I thought was kind of cute. Here he was having a relationship and it was keeping him alive. But if you look at Maricela as somebody who's slightly evil, then it takes on a whole new light. And it's hard to deal with the horror of that. Maybe I didn't want to see it."

Danny, who was admittedly biased because of his mother's conflicts with Maricela, remembered how John always seemed uncomfortable with himself at the end, how windows were either opened too wide or not enough, and how his fears were fed by Maricela. "It was as if she was helping him remove himself from everything. I didn't see her challenging him or making him deny his thoughts. It was a very strange, almost perverse thing that went on between them."

Maricela didn't feel comfortable around John's family and business associates. Henry Hyde, she felt, was domineering; Tony had upset John in the end and she couldn't forgive him for that. "John used to say that Tony speaks with the conviction of the ignorant," she said. "Now Tony is saying, 'I am the captain of the Huston family.' And I laugh. I can't help it. John said that time and Tony's three children will show him.

"John was very proud of Danny. But he said that he had a long way to go. He certainly has a lot of things to learn and a lot of books to read. John used to say to him, 'It's not with your charm or with your smile that you'll get what you're supposed to get; it's with hard work. And you have to have character.' Not that Danny doesn't have it, but he's in the process of learning."

John was often disappointed with Allegra, Maricela said, because she didn't keep in touch with him as much as he would have liked. As for Anjelica, "John said that she was a goddamn fool," Maricela said, "because Jack had proposed many, many times and she just didn't want to get married. Anjelica had her way with John, in a very special place."

When John's will was broken down, Danny said, Maricela received some money immediately "so that she didn't have to wait for any bureaucratic outcome or red tape. Maricela and my mother got the largest percentage, except Maricela has the houses and this figure off the top. Anjel has the interest of what she will get when she's something like fifty-seven; a little dribble now, but when she really needs it is when she's lost her looks and she might not find work as easily, then she'll get her full figure. Tony has the interest of what he has only until his children are of age, then his children get the full amount. Dad never wanted the Cholmondeley family to look after Tony or his kids, so he's given Tony the opportunity to reap the benefits from the interest for his needs now to get his career going, with everything going to his children in the end. With me, he's done the total opposite. My mother reaps the interest off the figure he's left us until I am a certain age, which is a long time from now when my mother will be in her seventies and close to dying and I will be in my middle age with a family, and I'll be able to have the full amount. But he hasn't given me anything until then, apart from a gold watch, his art books, and a few other objects. It's giving me no chance to feel comfortable now, where I should be at full force in my career. It's the most wonderful equation."

After John died Danny felt as if John's spirit had somehow entered him to enable him to complete *Mr. North*. "There was a moment when I was hesitant," he admitted. "I didn't want to go back to Newport to finish it. But then I felt that a part of Dad was in me, that he was speaking to me, like I never felt when he was alive. I think I freaked the fellows at Heritage Entertainment when they began to fuck me around in the cutting room. I said, 'You can't do this.' One of the producers said to another. 'This kid is having some problems, he's hearing his father speak to him.' But it wasn't only for myself that I was fighting."

When *Mr. North* was released it was compared with the upbeat Frank Capra films of the forties. The *New York Post* gave it four stars and said, "If you have just one film to see this summer, make it this one." And Bruce Williamson in *Playboy* wrote that the picture was "reassuring evidence that the Huston dynasty lives." Danny Huston, he said, "manages his first feature stint with the kind of relish for human frailty that shows him to be a chip off the old block." The reviews weren't all raves, but following *Mr. Corbett's Ghost*, Danny's career as a director was solidly established.

Tony Huston's screenwriting career was also given a boost when he was nominated for an Oscar for his adaptation of *The Dead.* He didn't win, but the nomination was enough of a confidence builder. So, too, was the reception the film received when it was released. "The story's majesty is so thoroughly mated to the genius of its prose that only a madman, a fool or an inspired amateur would try to put it on film," wrote one reviewer. "Happily, the late John Huston was a bit of all three." *People* called it "a movie masterwork." The *New York Times*'s Vincent Canby observed that "no other American filmmaker has ended a comparatively long career on such a note of triumph. *The Dead* and *Prizzi's Honor* . . . comprise a one-two punch quite unlike anything I can remember in movies. Who would have thought the old man had so much passion in him?"

Canby thought *The Dead* was "so fine, in unexpected ways, that it almost demands a reevaluation of Huston's entire body of work. . . . That Huston should have dared search for the story's cinema life is astonishing. That he should have found it with such seeming ease is the mark of a master."

Anjelica's performance as Gretta was rich and subtle. Canby called her "splendid, a figure of such self-contained sorrow that it's difficult to believe she was ever Maerose Prizzi."

The National Society of Film Critics chose *The Dead* as the best film of 1987 and Huston was the sentimental favorite to get a posthumous Oscar nomination. There was considerable disappointment when he was passed over. But John would have been pleased to see that he had helped Tony, at long last, get some recognition of his own.

Tony took Maricela to the Academy Awards on April 11, 1988, and remembers mostly how "extremely nervous" he was that night. "My pants didn't fit," he said, "they kept falling down. And I was loaded with rabbits feet, the Huston watch. I had my speech all worked out, how I owed Dad my resurgence." Tony never got to deliver his speech because Bernardo Bertolucci and Mark Peploe were awarded the Oscar for Best Screenplay Adaptation for *The Last Emperor.* Tony rationalized that it was just as well he didn't win, "because the biggest danger in this town is getting jumped up too quickly. And, in a way, it makes more of a difference to be a nominee than to get the Oscar, because the nomination is by one's peers."

Maricela was moved by John's dedicating *The Dead* to her, the first film he had ever dedicated. Jack Nicholson was even more moved. "Do you realize what he did when he dedicated that to you?" he asked Maricela. "I would never fucking do that with *anyone.* That tells you what he thought about you."

Maricela had come to change her opinion of Nicholson at John's funeral, when "he wept and wept and wept like a little boy. I used to be afraid of him. I thought he was just another goddamn actor. How wrong I was. He's the most sensible, intelligent man."

Maricela's respect for Nicholson increased even more when she called him and asked if she could buy a painting he owned of John as an Indian. "I cannot sell it to you," Nicholson told her, "and I cannot lend it to you, but you must come and pick it up." His generosity astonished her.

Nicholson's relationship with Anjelica remained on a seesaw after John's death. There were rumors that he had fallen for his *Ironweed* co-star, Meryl Streep, but such rumors passed as Streep remained with her husband and family. Anjelica, though, was upset by seeing Nicholson in that film. "I think of Jack as being there when the world crumbles," she told Roderick Mann of the *Los Angeles Times.* "To see him in a role in which he's on his way to ruin upset me very much."

Anjelica also found it hard "to come to terms with my father's death." To a reporter she spoke of how she missed "being able to report to him. He kept us straight. And his humor and his great joy in life and his interests and his plans. I miss that. I feel strangely abandoned . . . because I realized that a lot of what I did was for him and to him."

Following her small part in *Mr. North,* Anjelica appeared in another cameo role as a pilot in *A Handful of Dust,* based on Evelyn Waugh's novel. She was then in the last two episodes of the highly rated television mini-series *Lonesome Dove.* In defense of such minor parts she jokingly quoted Tony Curtis, saying that "it's better to play small roles when you're doing well because then you don't notice them getting smaller later on." It was her hope to play Maria Callas in a movie based on the life of the opera diva. While that was in development Anjelica played the evil Miss Ernst in an adaptation of Roald Dahl's *The Witches*, directed by Nicolas Roeg. She also had a wish fulfilled when she got a chance to work with Woody Allen, who cast her as an obsessed airline stewardess in his 1989 movie. And she acted opposite Ron Silver under Paul Mazursky's direction in *Enemies: A Love Story*, from the novel by Issac Bashevis Singer.

Anjelica also felt "destined to do other things. Such as writing. Costume design. Art direction. Directing. Dancing. Painting. Jewelry design." With Jeremy Railton she bought some property in the foothills of the Sierras. "I've got fifteen acres, she's got five," Railton said. "We're just keeping it as a secret hideaway. Jack doesn't know about it. We go up there and work like slaves. The day after Anjelica's picture was on the cover of the *Los Angeles Times Magazine* she was up in the country, carrying duck food through a mud pond. What guy cannot possibly fall wildly in love with that? She's the most glamorous, beautiful, delicate thing in the world—yet you can take her out in the country and she knows all the trees, leaves, bushes, and grasses. I've never, ever met a girl who vaguely comes anywhere near her."

Anjelica appeared on the cover of *American Film* in September 1987, just a week after John died. The cover blurb was "The Hustons Do Joyce by Tony Huston." The story inside was taken from his journal. Tony followed *The Dead* with a script he wrote for HBO about the lives of Alexander Hamilton and Aaron Burr and their famous duel. *Revenge*, the script he and John wrote for Ray Stark, was finally put into production with Kevin Costner *and* Anthony Quinn. (Other writers later worked on it, and the Hustons' work went uncredited.) And before he returned to England to see his children, Tony managed to raise $3,500 to produce and direct a seven-minute short film about a horny emu owned by a friend of his in Houston. He wrote a letter to potential investors, describing the emu's problem and his idea for the film. His friend, he wrote, told him that "her imprinted male emu is suffering the pangs of Spring. Unfortunately female emus are somewhat scarce in the Houston suburbs and he has been compelled to find other substitutes for his procreative energies. He is a horny big devil (ostrich-sized) and, in the absence of animate outlets, has had carnal knowledge of his food dish and a gaggle of chairs. . . ."

"My immediate family contributed a total of $2.45," Tony laughed. Burgess Meredith sent him a telegram, "Bless you and the emu too," but no money. But two total strangers sent him $1,250, and he eventually was able to make his comic film. "Directing was really strange," he said. "Because for all my life Dad was the director. But by the second day I loved it, it felt marvelous."

Tony saw Margot when he went to England during the Writers Guild strike in 1988. "I'm kind of slow to get the message sometimes, but I know one thing," he said of his former marriage, "this bird has flown." He received a letter from Margot's mother asking him if he might know where Margot's lost earrings were. "It was a very strange letter," Tony said. "She also asked me if I sell my flat in London, which I'm intending to do, would I please help Margot to buy a larger house? That flat is my sole piece of property and here is the wife of the Lord Great Chamberlain, owners of vast industrial estates, asking me to help Margot when, of course, Margot is much wealthier than I am. That was hysterically funny to me."

In January 1989, Tony returned to California, bought a small house in Santa Monica, and resumed his writing career. Danny was living in a house off Laurel Canyon with Virginia Madsen, who had acted in *Mr. North*. He was developing a James M. Cain novel, *The Magician's Wife*, his next picture, for a Scandinavian film company. Allegra had moved to a new flat on St. Lukes Mews in London and become a senior editor at Weidenfeld & Nicolson, one of England's most established publishing houses. Among the writers assigned to her was Edna O'Brien, who found her a "splendid" and diligent editor, "dedicated to Literature, a surprising thing perhaps in one so young." And Anjelica had flown to England to bring in the new year with Nicholson, who was there completing his role as The Joker in *Batman*.

One thing Anjelica, Tony, Danny, and Allegra shared was their love for and involvement with stories, just as John, Walter, Margaret, Rhea, Adelia, and John Gore had before them.

One of Rhea Gore's earliest memories was of her mother, Adelia, setting letters into blocks to be transformed into stories for the newspaper John Gore published. And in the years between her first and second marriage, while John was a young boy, she often went off on her own in pursuit of some story that touched her heart. Her reporting, and later her fiction, had as much an effect on her son as did Walter's playacting. Walter spent years on the vaudeville circuit entertaining audiences with skits and stories he wrote himself, until he made the leap to the legitimate stage, with the help of his sister Margaret, and the stories of O'Neill, Lardner, and Shakespeare. Toward the end of his life he asked only one thing of his son: to find him a good story. John not only found it but adapted it himself, and his father won his only Oscar after he removed his bridge and danced his memorable jig.

Stories, good stories—the stories of Kipling and Joyce; of Melville and Tennessee Williams; of W. R. Burnett and B. Traven; Dashiell Hammett and Stephen Crane; C. S. Forester, Truman Capote, Christopher Fry, and Carson McCullers; Ernest Hemingway, Arthur Miller, Flannery O'Connor, and Malcolm Lowry—were John's inspiration. He wrapped himself in the blanket of literature and shaped these writers' visions to a different, broader medium. The sharing, the passing on of good stories, by newsprint, magazine, book, play, opera, or film was part of the Huston tradition. And after John's death the tradition continues. Tony, Anjelica, Danny, Allegra all share his love of books well written, ideas neatly expressed. Of good stories.

But a story that combined many of the elements of John's films was the real life adventure Maricela lived to tell a few months after John's funeral. In October she went down to Las Caletas. But this time it was different. A boatload of local Indians came and started to push her around. "We heard the gringo has died, this place belongs to the community. Unless you pay . . ." Maricela just looked at them; they were strong, they wanted her gone. But the little wild animal in her that John so enjoyed came out. She told them she wasn't leaving.

One of the Indians kicked her in the stomach, she said. "I fell down. I threw up. I pissed in my pants." She asked to fight them, if that was what they wanted. The leader drew out his machete and she picked up another one. She also took out her pistol and shot twice, wounding two of them. Then they struck at her, slashed her arms, back, legs. She fought wildly, but she knew she was losing. Then something strange and wondrous happened. A huge manta ray jumped from the sea. As it leaped in the air John's face appeared on the ray's broad flat body. She could swear she heard his voice, "Give 'em hell!" She fought more ferociously, but it was just too much. One Indian took off his belt and started to whip her back.

"Okay," she said, "you win." It was Monday and she said she would sign over papers and give everything back to them on Wednesday. She had said she came back to Caletas "to plant a flower." But the flower had turned into asafetida. It was ugly and rotten now.

The Indians agreed to return then. Maricela went into town, to a lawyer. He didn't believe her story until she took off her top and showed the cuts, welts, bruises. He was shocked and took her to a police captain who said he'd have to go through channels. Then she was taken to an army captain who said he could help but it was getting close to Christmas and that was an expensive time. "I'll pay," she said, and he agreed to send men to Caletas.

On Wednesday thirty soldiers with machine guns came by boat and hid in the bushes. They told Maricela to wear a red scarf around her neck. If she felt she was in trouble, she was to untie the scarf and let it fall. That would be the signal for the soldiers to come out.

Fifteen Indians came. Their leader approached her. She had packed two bags and put them in the *panga*. But when he said, "Are you ready to leave?" something inside her rebelled. No, she was not ready. This was *her* place. She said, "I want to talk."

"We can't talk to you, you're a woman."

Then he made an obscene gesture. He rubbed his groin in a mastur-bating motion. She was afraid they would try to rape her. The leader told another Indian to take care of her. He grabbed her by the collar and pulled. Maricela let the scarf drop and she could hear the sound of machine guns being cocked in the bushes. Then the soldiers appeared.

The Indians were taken by surprise. They had come to intimidate a girl, now they were facing soldiers and bullets. The soldiers started to beat up the Indians, threatening to come back if they ever bothered her again. Maricela wanted revenge against the Indian who whipped her. She chose the biggest and most fearsome of the soldiers and told him to take off his belt and whip the Indian the way he had whipped her.

When it was over the captain told her that there was still the matter of the two men she shot. Her lawyer arranged to pay them off, pay their doctor's bills. It would cost two million pesos—$10,000—but it would be hushed up and there would be no more trouble. The captain also told her that as far as he was concerned, nothing had happened at all. She understood. It was Mexico, and she was Mexican.

After the two wounded men had been taken care of, Maricela was told it would be best if she left the country. Worried that she wouldn't be allowed back into the States if she looked all beaten up, she bought leeches to suck up her wounds so her bruises wouldn't be so obvious. She was escorted by two soldiers, taken to the airport, put on a plane. She was told to let things quiet down before attempting to return.

Some family members and certain friends and associates of John's had difficulty believing Maricela's story. They felt she had a wild imagina-tion. There were remarkable similarities with John's death scene: the thirty armed men, the ammunition, the give-'em-hell coda. And there were similarities from some of John's best-known films—the Mexican bandits in *Treasure*, the leeches from *The African Queen*, the gunplay from *Key Largo* to *Prizzi's*, the righteousness and stubborn defiance of Ahab and the Consul.

Irene Heyman, Paul Kohner's assistant, who continued at her job after Kohner's death at eighty-five on March 16, 1988, was highly skeptical. "Maricela's stories are smoke dreams. Everyone else is going ahead with their lives, but she's stuck remembering John. She believes what she says, but I don't believe any of it." Tony didn't know what to make of it, and Danny wondered, "Did she shoot two guys in the legs or didn't she? How will we ever know?"

But Maricela stuck to her story. John had warned her that people would turn against her, she'd have to be strong. She didn't care if the family didn't believe her when she said John's Oscars and awards were accidentally placed in a garbage bag and thrown away, or were put in a box and given to one of the film academies, which lost them.

What Maricela remembered was how John told her to believe in herself. "The moment I began to close my ears and just listen to him, everything was okay," she said. "Every now and then there would be shitty articles written, things said, who cares? That's why we were able to live and love, because we didn't care what anybody said.

"I never believed that I was going to be able to be with him for so long, because he was so demanding. And he said to me, 'I've been with you for more time than any wife, than any girlfriend.' I suppose I became some sort of a rare thing for him. I know in some very special way he loved me very dearly.

"John was someone who was big, big, big," Maricela continued. "He might have made a mistake or two, but he wasn't a bad guy. He was able to find a little happiness with me, and I was able to be happy around him. We had one hell of a time until the very, very end."

So it didn't matter if no one believed her when she said she had been attacked at Las Caletas. It didn't matter if no one believed that John's face had appeared on the body of the manta ray, or that he had whispered a poem to her at his grave. Nor did it matter that the gray marble slab the children wanted at his grave site took eighteen months to install. His spirit was far beyond the slightly run-down graveyard where his ashes lay beneath the ground. His life force was out there, in the movies he made, in the hearts of those who benefited by his generosity and thoughtfulness, in the spirit of his family and friends, who continued to tell the stories that enriched an audience. He liked to say that he lived where there was always an element of danger or change, because it quickened his life and kept his heart beating. He'd be a tough act to follow, his children knew. But that had been John Gore's challenge. And Walter's. The Hustons usually find a way to rise to the top.

NOTES

All interviews with LG were conducted between 1986 and 1989. The conversations with John Huston began in May 1984 until one month before his death in August 1987. Primary-source quotes are not attributed in these notes.

Chapter 1: "Just Give 'em Hell!"

1   "the worst case of emphysema": Dr. Gary Sugarman to LG
4   "quest for adventure": JH interview with Joe Persico, 8/81
12 "I am not bemooned . . .": "What IS IT About Anjelica Huston?," Richard Condon, *Esquire,* 9/87
13 "The biggest piece of action . . .": *Time,* 3/16/87
     "faintly illuminated . . .": "The Dead," James Joyce
14 Huston . . . looking for O'Neill: "Eugene O'Neill, Playwright," JH, 1926, published in *Action,* May/June 1970
15 "his own identity . . .": "The Dead," James Joyce
19 "Freddy's on hooch . . .": "The Hustons Do Joyce," Tony Huston, *American Film,* 9/87
     "like the Zen teacher": *L.A. Weekly,* 12/25–31/87
     "What is success anyway?": "The Master Huston," Paul Rosenfield, *Los Angeles Times Calendar,* 2/22/87
     "how much of it . . . was fortuitous?": "Meditations on Life & Family," Lynn Darling, *Newsday,* 12/23/87
20 "man being revealed to himself": *John Huston & the Dubliners,* Lilyan Sievernich, documentary, 1987
     "The night before I left . . .": "The Dead," James Joyce
21 "I was growing up": "Patient: John Huston. Rx: Film," Aljean Harmetz, *New York Times,* 3/8/87
26 "his eyes were no good": Janet Roach, Santa Fe Film Festival seminar, 9/17/87
27 bill for $13,000: Stephanie Zimbalist, Maricela Hernandez to LG
28 "You suckered me": Robert Mitchum, DGA Memorial, 9/12/87
     "like a bull elephant": "Movie Legend John Huston Is Dead at 81," Leslie Gevirtz and Steven Silverman, *New York Post,* 8/29/87
29 Nancy Reagan tried to telephone: Zoe Sallis to LG
32 "You're too grumpy . . .": Maricela Hernandez to LG
34 Maricela started to scream: Zoe Sallis to LG
     "I take full responsibility": Maricela Hernandez to LG
35 *Daily Variety* covered: "Huston, 81, Dies In His Sleep," Todd McCarthy, *Daily Variety,* 8/31/87
     "a born storyteller": "John Huston, A Born Storyteller," Joseph Gelmis, *Newsday,* 8/29/87
     Roger Ebert's salute: "Salute to a Legend," Roger Ebert, *New York Post,* 8/29/87

36 "writer's passionate admiration . . .": Charles Champlin, *Los Angeles Times*, 8/31/87
    Vincent Canby: Vincent Canby, *New York Times*, 9/6/87
    "drive a stake": Liz Smith, *Daily News*, 9/1/87
37 "can't talk back to me": Stephanie Zimbalist to LG
    "his mind expanded": Joan Buck, *Interview*, 12/87
    "greatest joy of my adult life . . .": Carole Mazur, *Albuquerque Journal*, 9/19/87
    loaned Maricela $15,000: Stephanie Zimbalist to LG
38 Mitchum told the story: Robert Mitchum, DGA Memorial, 9/12/87

Chapter 2: Ma, Where's Pa?

47 "We came to a white house . . .": OB
    In the blood of my father . . .: from the unpublished writings of John Huston's mother, Rhea Gore Huston Stevens. All quotes from this source in Chapters 2–8 are italicized in the text and not noted further here.

Chapter 3: To Be or Not to Be

60 "it had the devil in it": JH to LG
61 "I'll put you to the stranger!": from the unpublished manuscript *September Song*, Walter Huston's autobiography, ghostwritten by John Weld. In the special collection of JH at the Academy of Motion Picture Arts and Sciences Library in Beverly Hills. The manuscript covers Mr. Huston's early life up until his 1937 Broadway appearance in *Othello*. I am indebted to this work for many of the facts about Walter Huston's life. I also spent a pleasant afternoon with John Weld and his wife, Katy, in their home in Laguna Niguel talking about both Walter and John.
    "When I was a boy . . .": "The Actor No Picturegoer Really Knows," Faith Service, *Picturegoer Weekly*, 1/14/33
63 Margaret Huston Benefit Recital: OB
    "I'm Going to Be a Millionaire": John Weld to LG
    "From that moment . . .": OB
64 Shaw School of Acting: "Hometown Stories of the Stars," Hal Miller, *New Movie*, 6/31, quoting Walter's brother, Alec
    "weak, thieving, shiftless . . .": SS
    "More of my illusions . . .": SS
65 "Arabia . . .": SS
67 "My mother never tried . . .": SS
    "He had a voice . . .": SS
68 "Faces seemed to swim . . .": SS
    "There has never been . . .": SS
69 "He was the first man . . .": SS

Chapter 4: Getting Married

73 "I had grown . . .": "My Philosophy of Life," Walter Huston, *Picturegoer Weekly*, 8/19/33
75 "a resourceful, capable woman": SS
79 "Being twenty-one . . .": SS
80 "rare combination . . .": SS
81 "something told me": SS
82 Union Electric Power: from a condolence letter to JH written by H. A. Woodworth, who worked with Walter Huston in St. Louis, 4/7/50
    "ecstatic mates": SS

Chapter 5: The Heart of a Trouper

85 "rep, tent and tab": OB
    "To be trouping . . .": SS
86 big feet, skinny legs: "The Hopadeen," an unpublished story by JH, 3/1/62
    "self-disgust": SS
87 "loved trains": OB
88 "Circulating . . .": SS
90 "friend of people like": OB
    "fucking a girl": *Groucho*, Hector Arce (Putnam, 1979)
93 "Shadow of Death": OB
94 "an audience of one": OB
95 "There was funny dialogue . . .": *The Vaudevillians*, Bill Smith (Macmillan, 1976)
96 "The Palace": SS
    "Don't worry about Wally . . .": SS
    Margaret's voice as "majestic": *Damned in Paradise, The Life of John Barrymore*, John Kobler (Atheneum, 1977)
97 "to free the speaking voice": *Damned in Paradise*
98 "a sorcerer's apprentice": OB
    Dear Mother . . .: JH correspondence, pre-1943, Special Collections, Academy of Motion Picture Arts and Sciences Library, Beverly Hills
99 "the new stagecraft": "Legacy," Lee Simonson, in *The Theatre of Robert Edmund Jones*, ed. Ralph Pendleton (Wesleyan Univ. Press, 1958)
100 "We use light . . .": *The Dramatic Imagination*, Robert Edmund Jones (Theatre Arts Books, 1941)

100 "Costuming is not dressmaking": "Practical Dreams," Jo Mielziner, in *The Theatre of Robert Edmund Jones*
      "jack-of-all-trades": *The Dramatic Imagination*
      Stark Young: *Damned in Paradise*
101 Mr. Lott: OB
      "so damned skinny": CJH
102 "Life at Denby . . .": OB
      Eddie Darling: *American Vaudeville*, Douglas Gilbert (Whittlesey, 1940)
103 "the longest of long shots": SS
105 "gift for drawing": OB
      Stanton MacDonald-Wright: OB
      "exposed to music": CJH
106 became an American: SS
107 "the pangs of loneliness": SS
108 "one common interest—work": SS
      "Jack Dempsey and Estelle Taylor": from an undated manuscript by Dorothy Haas, in JH's personal papers
      at the Academy of Motion Picture Arts and Sciences Library
      in a dream: *Eugene O'Neill*, Frederic J. Carpenter (Twayne Publishers, 1979)
109 O'Neill wasn't sure: *O'Neill, Son and Artist*, Louis Shaeffer (Little, Brown, 1973)
      "Your Hamlet . . .": *O'Neill, Son and Artist*
      he summarized the plot: *The Plays of Eugene O'Neill*, Virginia Floyd (Frederick Ungar Publishing, 1985)
110 "one of the greatest": OB
      "great sense of power": OB
      "the rhythm and cadence . . .": OB
      "cantankerous cancerous . . .": *O'Neill, Son and Artist*
111 Stark Young: Stark Young, *New York Times*, 11/12/24
      "Hain't the sun strong . . .": *Desire Under the Elms*, Eugene O'Neill
112 "Only those three . . .": *O'Neill, Son and Artist*

Chapter 6: Rising Stars

113 "the star part": CJH
      "If he wants to write . . .": JH to LG
114 "not to be an actor": CJH
      "gin as a payoff": OB
      "best birthday present": *Picture*, Lillian Ross (Proscenium Publishers); originally appeared as a series of
      articles in *The New Yorker*, 1952
      "Not inspiring": *O'Neill, Son and Artist*
115 "dull": Stark Young, *New Republic*, 12/30/25
      "Young picked my work . . .": "My Philosophy of Life," *Picturegoer Weekly*, 8/33
      "the hard lessons . . .": SS
      "squarish German woman": OB
116 "heart-shaped face": OB
117 "cheap piece of melodrama": SS
118 "You a college man?": SS
119 "a thousand a week": *George M. Cohan: Prince of the American Theatre*, Ward Morehouse (J. P. Lippincott,
      1943)
      "complete surrender": OB
120 "depressing reception": OB
      "hadn't worried": SOYS
121 "happier than we'd ever been": OB
      "greatest stage director": SS
122 "a great actor": *George M. Cohan*
      other members included . . .: SS
124 "the worst possible . . .": CJH
      "John was not . . .": Haas manuscript in JH papers
127 "so many levels": CJH
128 Lou Paley gave George: *Gershwin*, Edward Jablonski (Doubleday, 1987)
      "sweeping eyebrows . . .": OB
129 "the most important formative . . .": OB
      Frankie and Johnny: *Frankie and Johnny*, John Huston (Albert & Charles Boni, 1930)
      "The avant-garde . . .": *Hello, Hollywood!*, Allen Rivkin and Laura Kerr (Doubleday, 1962)
      "The damned thing went over . . .": OB
131 "began rolling naturals": OB
132 angry with himself: SS
133 "tour de force": OB
      struck the rattler dead: SS
134 Victor Fleming marveled: "He Won't Argue," Sara Hamilton, *Photoplay*, 3/32
      "the intelligent acting of . . .": Mordaunt Hall, *New York Times*, 12/23/29
135 "homesick for Broadway": SS
      "play Grover Cleveland": SS
136 "nightmare of the mind": *The Film Encyclopedia*, Ephraim Katz (Crowell, 1979)
      "creation of something immortal": SS
138 "For God's sake, Huston . . .": "He Won't Argue"
139 "He knows much more . . .": "The Peerless Huston!," Harriet Parsons, *Photoplay*, 12/30

Chapter 7: Dreadful Melodramas

141 "doting parent brag": *Young Man in Paris*, John Weld (Academy Chicago Publishers, 1985)
"to be seen by millions": SS
"complete disentanglement": SS
"Nan Sunderland was . . .": *Young Man in Paris*
143 "Although I recommended him . . .": "Walter & John," Jack Austin, *Picture Play*, 9/32
144 "This plot," wrote John: OB
"pictures where the speech . . .": *The New Yorker*, 1/16/32
145 "everything about it was wrong": *Backstory: Interviews with Screenwriters of Hollywood's Golden Age*, Pat McGilligan (Univ. of California Press, 1986)
"I tried to bring Poe's prose . . .": OB
147 "a new spirit in the air": OB
150 Morgan Russell paintings: letter from Barbara Evans-Decker to JH, 2/2/72
"I've never had a home": "The Actor No Picturegoer Really Knows"
151 "fed up with the kind of parts . . .": "How I Shall Play Rhodes," Walter Huston to T. T. Fleming, *Film Weekly*, 8/23/35
"vainglorious": "Is Walter Huston a Genius?," Peter Day, *Film Weekly*, 7/1/32
"moronic old roué": Jerry Vermilye, *Films in Review*, 2/60
"poor, besotted weakling": *Picturegoer Weekly*, 1/14/33
152 "It all was very silly": SS
"simply a bad picture": SS
his own self-image: *Picturegoer Weekly*, 1/14/33
"dreadful melodrama": SS
153 "worked like a truck-horse": SS
"hypocritical, thoroughly . . .": *Picturegoer Weekly*, 1/14/33
"such a box-office star as . . .": SS
"star-studded box-office . . . go to hell!": SS
154 "didn't develop dramatically": SS
155 "a voice several decibels": OB
156 "didn't hold a candle": OB
"My professional life was in bondage": SS
157 "I am perfectly and completely . . .": *Picturegoer Weekly*, 1/14/33
158 "winning one's spurs": "Why Hollywood Doesn't Appeal to Me," *Picturegoer Weekly*, 10/26/35
159 "my whole miserable existence": OB
161 "She didn't look well": OB
163 "She was shaking convulsively": OB
164 "It was a bad time": Roderick Mann, *Sunday Express*, 11/17/68
"I don't believe in God": Roderick Mann, *Sunday Express*, 11/17/68
166 "as a sort of ransom": OB
"on pages of magazines": CJH

Chapter 8: Father and Son: Center Stage

168 Max Gordon had pawned . . .: SS
169 "I admit I was worried": "They Swim in a Bowl for All to See," *Buffalo Sunday Times* (n.d.)
"crawl back into . . .": SS
"Everybody knows Sam . . .": William Stiegler, *Cincinnati Times Star*, 3/31/36
171 "I think Shakespeare . . .": "A Lamb in Lion's Clothing," Frederick Russell, *Film Pictorial*, 6/21/34
"I had contracted a disease": SS
174 missing the letters: *Film Weekly*, 6/2/34
"more a legend . . .": "How I Shall Play Rhodes"
"easy to show him": William Stiegler, *Cincinnati Times Star*, 3/31/36
175 "What a thrill . . .": Nan Huston's letters to her mother, 2/12–14/35
177 Walter had it written: "Walter Huston Shuns Pictures," Walter D. Shackleton, *Photoplay*, 8/34
178 "played Fran like . . .": *William Wyler*, Axel Madsen (Crowell, 1973)
179 "Sam showed the kind of class . . .": *Goldwyn*, Arthur Marx (Norton, 1976)
"completely rattleproof": *A Life on Film*, Mary Astor (W. H. Allen, 1973)
"Her future in films . . .": "Dodsworth Stirs Curiosity," Kate Cameron, *Cincinnati Post*, 9/20/36
"glimpse into her private": *Cincinnati Post*, 10/1/36
"*Dodsworth* is all . . .": *Cincinnati Post*, 10/3/36
"You can't sell a middle-age . . .": *Hollywood*, Garson Kanin (Viking, 1974)
181 "no discordant notes": SS
"swashbuckling villain": SS
"uneasy by what I saw": OB
182 "in the palms of": SS
"Did they not know . . .": SS
"I knew this meant . . .": OB
183 "Not since *The Easy Mark* . . .": SS
"10–20–30 melodrama": SS
184 "Best Lincoln . . .": Walter Huston to Dorothy Haas
185 "You alone existed . . .": *As Time Goes By*, Howard Koch (Harcourt Brace Jovanovich, 1979)
"the Arthurian legends": OB
"no more business": OB
191 Wallis wrote to Henry: *Inside Warner Bros. (1935–51)*, ed. Rudy Behlmer (Viking, 1985)
"the level of taste": CJH

192 "Just a drunken boy": "Undirectable Director," James Agee, *Life*, 9/18/50
193 "One can't help notice . . .": *The Films of John Huston*, John McCarty (Citadel Press, 1987)
194 "Wolfgang had a scholar's . . .": OB
     "His changes did . . .": OB
     Dieterle's wife . . .: *Actor: The Life & Times of Paul Muni*, Jerome Lawrence (Putnam, 1974)
197 "At first her answers . . .": OB
     "old fat Dutch burghers": *Josh*, Josh Logan (Delacorte Press, 1976)
199 "Mother, they know . . .": OB

Chapter 9: "The Stuff That Dreams Are Made Of "

202 "crawling with Secret Service": *Josh*
203 cloth sling and wooden braces: E. B. Radcliff, *Cincinnati Enquirer*, 1939 (n.d.)
204 "Margaret at her best": OB
205 "it's a lucky place": *As Time Goes By*
206 "venereal diseases": letter from Hal Wallis to Will Hays, 8/24/39, *Inside Warner Bros.*
207 "one of the most distinguished . . .": *Edward G. Robinson: An Autobiography: All My Yesterdays*, Edward G. Robinson with Leonard Spigelgass (Hawthorn Books, 1973)
208 "The question propounded . . .": OB
209 "finished *High Sierra*": letter from JH to Hal Wallis, 3/21/40, *Inside Warner Bros.*
211 "I never had so much fun . . .": interview with W. R. Burnett, *Backstory*
     "reverse the billing": letter from Hal Wallis to Jack Warner, 9/18/40, *Inside Warner Bros.*
212 "Bogart must have . . .": *City of Nets*, Otto Friedrich (Harper & Row, 1986)
213 "stop his sketching": *As Time Goes By*
214 "seven acres at the foot": OB
216 "uncomfortable and ridiculous": *My Path and My Detours*, Jane Russell (Franklin Watts, 1985)
217 68⅓-week contract: Warner Bros. collection, USC Doheny Library
     "not an important picture": *Inside Warner Bros.*
     "He fancied himself an actor . . .": CJH
     "I thanked God": CJH
218 "finest and most subtle": OB
219 "dramatization of myself": JH interview with Joe Persico, 8/81
     "highly individual style": JH letter, as quoted in "The Monitor Image," Alan S. Downer, in *Men and the Movies*, ed. W. R. Robinson (Viking Penguin, 1969); also quoted in CJH
     "The studio wanted that": JH interview with Joe Persico, 8/81
     Friedrich noted: *City of Nets*
220 "jigsaw puzzle": *A Life on Film*, Mary Astor (W. H. Allen, 1973)
     "Mary dear, hold . . .": *A Life on Film*
     "incredible camera setup": *A Loving Gentleman*, Meta Wilde and Orin Borsten (Simon & Schuster, 1976)
221 "Didn't expect to have . . .": *A Life on Film*
223 "The best private-eye . . .": "Undirectable Director"
     "high-style thriller": *I Lost It at the Movies*, Pauline Kael (Little, Brown, 1965)
     "Bryan Foy . . .": CJH
224 "comedy relief": CJH
     the congenial way: "New Love for Livvie," John Burton, *Photoplay*, 7/43
     Dotson Rader: "Rewards and Regrets," Dotson Rader, *Daily News Parade*, 9/7/86
225 "as troubled as . . .": *As Time Goes By*
226 "My God, John . . .": CJH
228 "Won't give Hammett . . .": *Inside Warner Bros.*
229 "My mother told me . . .": "Joan Fontaine," Gregory Speck, *Interview*, 2/87
230 "my Oscar for Brigid": *A Life on Film*
231 "remarkable reproduction": *A Life on Film*
233 "make things as difficult . . .": OB

Chapter 10: Women and War

235 "for 1,500 miles": OB
236 "my one-man army": *Film: Book 2*, ed. Robert Hughes (Grove Press, 1962)
     " 'Nerves of steel' ": OB
     "belly gunner": OB
237 hire the Biltmore: "Skolsky's Hollywood," Sidney Skolsky, syndicated newspaper column, 10/14/42
     "the most beautiful and desirable": OB
239 "The brass was acutely . . .": OB
241 "very fine material": CJH
244 Major Joseph McKeon: *Sisters*, Charles Higham (Putnam, 1984)
245 "doesn't look like me": *As Time Goes By*
246 "most disgraceful appointments": "In the Days of Mr. Roosevelt," Saul Bellow, *Esquire*, 12/83
     "When the film was released . . .": *As Time Goes By*
247 "getting to know Joe Davies": "A Star Comes Back to B'Way," Seymour Peck, *PM*, 2/5/46
     read a statement: *Inside Warner Bros.*
248 "sentimental, badly directed": *An Unfinished Woman*, Lillian Hellman (Little, Brown, 1969)
     "knew *nothing* about Russia": *Lillian Hellman, The Image, The Woman*, William Wright (Simon & Schuster, 1986)
250 "fiercely contested": OB

251   "The Germans thought . . .": *Film: Book 2*
      "filthy little shit": *Here Lies Eric Ambler*, Eric Ambler (Weidenfeld & Nicolson, 1985)
252   dirty Jew: Jules Buck to LG, telephone, 10/26/88
      letter to Colonel Frank: *Here Lies Eric Ambler*
      "the rubble gave . . .": OB
255   "anxiety neurosis": OB

Chapter 11: Psychic Landscapes

262   "anti-war": CJH
263   "my possible mortality": "The Real Thing," Herbert Gold, in *Film: Book 2*
      "As good a war film . . .": James Agee, *The Nation*, 5/26/45
      "masterpieces": *The Liveliest Art*, Arthur Knight (Macmillan, 1957)
268   "The atom bomb . . .": JH to Richard Leacock on his war films
269   ten weeks at $4,000: *Selznick*, Bob Thomas (Doubleday, 1970)
272   "Some had tics . . .": OB
273   "the 'warrior' myth": OB
274   "the reality of human behavior": JH interview with Joe Persico, 8/81
      "a light little comedy": "A Star Comes Back to B'Way" (quoting Walter Huston)
      "to live on a farm": *The Baltimore Sun*, 1/14/46
275   "easier for me, the stage": "A Star Comes Back to B'Way"
      "I lived from one call . . .": OB

Chapter 12: Keyes to a Treasure

278   "more beautiful than ever": SOYS
279   "I missed my darling . . .": SOYS
282   "for the tax": "Show Mirror," E. B. Radcliffe, *Cincinnati Enquirer*, 2/47
283   "to be a legend": SOYS
285   "delighted over your script": B. Traven to JH, 9/2/46, *Inside Warner Bros.*
286   "Howard, not Dobbs": B. Traven to JH, 1/4/47, *Inside Warner Bros.*
      "Croves had a slight accent": OB
287   signed up a bargaining agent: JH to Philip K. Scheuer, 6/29/47
288   According to Reagan: letter from Anne Higgins, special assistant to the president, 7/21/87
      "saw my part as an old man": "Hustons, Senior and Junior, Work Amicably," Harold Heffernan, *Dallas Morning News*, 5/5/47
      "couple of kids together": *By Myself*, Lauren Bacall (Knopf, 1979)
289   "to balance things out": SOYS
      "Dos Equis": SOYS
      "pilot tried to land": Humphrey Bogart to Lowell E. Redelings
      "Viennese chef": Humphrey Bogart to Lowell E. Redelings
      "fish with bulging eyes": *By Myself*
291   "Conrad and Dreiser": JH to Philip K. Scheuer, 6/29/47
293   "crazy idea": Lauren Bacall to LG
      "fuckin' masterpiece": SOYS
294   "My heart sank . . .": SOYS

Chapter 13: Wheel of Fortune

296   "a sad and revealing remark": *By Myself*
297   "GREATEST MOTION PICTURE": *Inside Warner Bros.*
      "best goddamn party": SOYS
300   "the witch-hunters": OB
      "cry for help": *By Myself*
301   "We timed our flight . . .": *Take Two*, Philip Dunne (McGraw-Hill, 1980)
302   "The strategy would underline . . .": *Take Two*
303   "stony silence": OB
      "they were knocked down": OB
304   "Huston is the brains": OB
      "discharge or suspend": *The Inquisition in Hollywood*, Larry Ceplair and Steven Englund (Univ. of California Press, 1979)
      "a sorry time": SOYS
305   "was hysterically funny": *By Myself*
306   "The number of lost dollars . . .": SOYS
308   "unzipped his fly": SOYS
      "up the Amazon!": SOYS
309   monkey peed: SOYS
310   *Time* called it . . .: James Agee, *Time*, 2/2/48
      "next only to Chaplin": James Agee, *The Nation*, 1/31/48
      "seethe with schemes": *James Agee: A Life*, Laurence Bergreen (Dutton, 1984)
312   $33 million: *Los Angeles Times*, Business, 12/23/87
313   "I didn't even argue": *Edward G. Robinson: An Autobiography: All My Yesterdays*
      "If a guy points a gun . . .": *Bogart and Bacall*, Joe Hyams (Warner Books, 1975)
314   "as feisty, individual": *All My Yesterdays*
315   "greatest news I'd ever": OB

315 "You bitch!": OB
316 "most entertaining persons": OB
319 "such a good job so far": letter from Walter Huston to Paul Kohner, received 3/22/48
"ruined my sex appeal": letter from Walter Huston to Jack Fife, 2/20/48
"any worthwhile proposal": letter from Paul Kohner to Walter Huston, 2/19/48
"putting up photos": letter from Walter Huston to Paul Kohner, 2/19/48
"go out for Henry Wallace": letter from Walter Huston to Paul Kohner, received 3/22/48
"stay away from all politics": letter from Paul Kohner to Walter Huston, 3/23/48
"my objections to the Wallace . . .": Take Two
320 "father-son relationship": OB
321 "like chastised children": SOYS
"such persistence and determination": OB
322 "You crazy . . . lunatic!": SOYS
"it's over between us": SOYS
"good for polar bears": letter from Walter Huston to Paul Kohner, received 6/2/48
"accept this part": letter from Paul Kohner to Walter Huston, 7/24/48
"the question of our salary": letter from Paul Kohner to Walter Huston, 8/30/48
323 film historian, Scott: John Huston, Scott Hammen (Twayne Publishers, 1985)
324 "often gave people credit": OB
"hunting lodge nestled": SOYS
325 "best part of our life": SOYS
"Talk to them": Things I Did . . . and Things I Think I Did, Jean Negulesco (Simon & Schuster, 1984)
326 "she is fine now": Nan Huston to Paul Kohner, 9/48
327 "he had a gun": Doris Lilly to LG

Chapter 14: "There'll Never Be Another Like Me"

329 "a fuckable age": SOYS
330 "I'm proud and delighted . . .": The Fifty Year Decline and Fall of Hollywood, Ezra Goodman (Simon & Schuster, 1951)
331 "Nero really plumbed": CJH
"had built his reputation": The Asphalt Jungle, Afterword by W. R. Burnett (Southern Illinois Press, 1980)
334 "moment John sees you": Wanderer, Sterling Hayden (Knopf, 1963)
"first kind man I ever met": Hollywood
336 "best films of its genre": The Asphalt Jungle, Afterword
"He not only watched . . .": The Unabridged Marilyn, R. Riese and N. Hitchens (Congdon & Weed, 1987)
"In a part practically . . .": Timebends, Arthur Miller (Grove Press, 1987)
"The story of the good doctor . . .": CJH
337 "sure it's yours, John?": SOYS
339 "lived with such an intensity": letter from Ellie Frohnmaier Schmidt to LG, 8/22/87
341 "perfection in every sense": letter from Barbara Stanwyck to LG, 8/21/86
"Barbara has guts . . .": Darr Smith, Daily News, 12/2/49
"never saw anybody . . .": "Walter Huston Would Cherish Life of Ease," Philip K. Scheuer, Los Angeles Times, 12/4/49
"One picture a year . . .": "Walter Huston Would Cherish Life of Ease"
342 "When they sent me the play . . .": "Walter Huston Would Cherish Life of Ease"
343 "too good a thing": letter from Paul Kohner to Walter Huston, 2/18/50
"I ought to have a checkup": Jacqueline de Wit to LG, telephone, 6/19/88
half-hour documentary: Helen Parkhurst condolence letter (n.d.)
349 "half-muffled sob": By Myself
ashes on a shelf": Cici Huston to LG
ashes to Fresno: Lynn Lemoyne to LG
circumcised: Philip Soma to LG

Chapter 15: Red Badge and the Queen

353 they were "cowards": Heyday, Dore Schary (Little, Brown, 1979)
"complete shit": Heyday
354 Kay Proctor: Kay Proctor, Los Angeles Examiner, 8/11/50
355 "cut any number of 'famous' ": OB
356 "As a journalist . . .": CJH
357 "I tried to reproduce . . .": CJH
359 "a solid mass of medals": Billy Pearson, French Vogue, 12/81–1/82
360 "You tell me what's wrong . . .": Gottfried Reinhardt, DGA Memorial, 9/12/87
362 "no word from John or Ricki": letter from Nan Huston to Paul Kohner, 11/30/50
"a rumor that Ricki": letter from Paul Kohner to Nan Huston, 12/6/50
363 "intelligence and instinct": James Agee: A Life
"same ringing affirmation": James Agee: A Life
364 "Disastrous": Heyday
"a call from London": Heyday
"The Red Badge was safe": JH interview with Joe Persico, 8/81
366 "total frenzy": The Making of The African Queen, Katharine Hepburn (Knopf, 1987)
368 "utterly piggish": The Making of The African Queen
"stay downwind": By Myself

368 "We got into a pirogue . . .": Kevin McClory to Frank Martin, John Huston documentary "The Man, the Movies, the Maverick," 1988
369 "fury, insecurity and indecision": *The Making of The African Queen*
"two over-male men": *The Making of The African Queen*
"Queen's Throne": Kevin McClory to Frank Martin
"goddamnedest best": *The Making of The African Queen*
370 Mamsahib Mbila: David Lewin, *Daily Express* (n.d.)
"I can't believe my ears . . .": *By Myself*
371 "fight the jungle": David Lewin, *Daily Express* (n.d.)
374 "knock-down-drag-out": *By Myself*
375 "So bloody stupid": *The Making of The African Queen*
378 "movie hoodwinking": Bosley Crowther, *New York Times*, 2/21/52
"seen to better advantage": *Variety*, 12/26/51
"a misfire": BFI *Monthly Bulletin*, 1/52
"positively lyrical": JH letter to Katharine Hepburn, 1/8/52

Chapter 16: Wild in Paris

381 "alimony and other indebtedness": OB
383 "The only suggestion . . .": letter from JH to Morgan Maree, 3/13/52
"sufficient scope for Jennifer's . . .": letter from JH to David Selznick, 2/8/52
384 "horse-crazy": *Never Look Back*, Billy Pearson and Stephen Longstreet (Simon & Schuster, 1958)
385 "Billy committed every foul . . .": OB
392 "Honey, I've always thought . . .": SOYS
394 "just a little better person": OB
"dour, listening man": *Zsa Zsa Gabor*, Gerald Frank (World, 1960)
396 "Dear Fly in the Ointment": letter from Humphrey Bogart to JH, 10/8/52
"would its sale . . . to television": letter from JH to Humphrey Bogart, 11/19/52
398 "pretentious . . . slick": BFI *Monthly Film Bulletin*, 4/53
"great films": *Cue*, 2/14/53
"flawlessly directed": *Hollywood Reporter*, 12/24/52
"class by himself": Louella Parsons, *Los Angeles Examiner*, 12/24/52

Chapter 17: The Devil and the Deep-Blue Sea

400 "My first night in Ireland": letter from JH to George Sullivan, 11/11/81
401 "mother of my children": OB
402 "the freshest and most original": *Memoir from David O. Selznick*, ed. Rudy Behlmer (Viking, 1971)
"He was probably hoping . . .": "Movie Making Beats the Devil," Humphrey Bogart to Joe Hyams, *Cue*, 11/28/53
403 "cast was completely bewildered": *Paris Review No. 16*, Pati Hill interview with Truman Capote, 1957
404 a "classic seducer": *Observations*, Truman Capote with Richard Avedon (Simon & Schuster, 1957)
408 Pablo "must return . . .": letter from Mark Cohen to JH, 1/20/53
409 "more beautiful in color": memo from David Selznick to JH, 2/15/53
410 "Veiller and Viertel conceived . . .": letter from JH to Morgan Maree, 6/10/53
412 "felt confused": cable from Humphrey Bogart to JH, 9/53
415 "unadulterated joy": *News of the World*, 11/29/53
"Huston's worst film": *Sunday Graphic*, 11/29/53
"shaggy-dog story": *Time*, 3/8/54
"hugely entertaining": *The New Yorker*, 3/20/54
"parody within a parody": *Films & Filming*, Eugene Archer monograph of JH, Pt. 1, 9/59
"rather quirky way": Charles Champlin, DGA Memorial, 9/12/87
Letters from irate . . .: in Special Collections, Academy of Motion Picture Arts and Sciences Library
416 "a minor disaster": CJH
"the most American character": "The Illustrated Man: An Interview with Ray Bradbury," Thomas R. Atkins, *Sight and Sound*, Spring 1974
417 "Are you a Freudian?": Ray Bradbury to LG, 1975
"the same confusion": "The Illustrated Man: An Interview with Ray Bradbury"
418 "The ghost of Melville . . .": "The Illustrated Man: An Interview with Ray Bradbury"
419 "deeply grateful to him": Ray Bradbury to LG, 1975
radio interviewer: Ciji Ware, KABC radio, 10/30/88
422 traditional Irish song: *Living Like a Lord*, John Godley, Lord Kilbracken (Houghton Mifflin, 1956)
425 "he needed me to finance": *Films in Review*, Jeanne Stein, 3/67
"Huston was more Ahab . . .": *Warner Bros. Directors*, William R. Meyer (Arlington House, 1978)
"not that great an actor's director": "Gregory Peck: He's the Man," Ron Haver, *American Film*, 3/89
"Feel the camera on your face": *Films in Review*, 3/67
427 "strode like a Colossus": Kevin McClory to Frank Martin, JH documentary, 1988
"became chaotic": *Living Like a Lord*
"an impossible picture to make": *Newsweek*, 1/9/56
428 "They tied me on": *Newsweek*, 1/9/56
"the contraption might get stuck": OB

Chapter 18: Up to Their Heads

431 "yellow-and-black flashes": OB
434 "Billy covets the Cimabue *Christus*": *Never Look Back*, JH introduction
435 "obvious sexual implications": OB
     "itchy cunt": interview with John Lee Mahin, *Backstory*
436 "God, it was awful": interview with John Lee Mahin, *Backstory*
     "queer, clumsy piece of behavior": OB
439 "It was horrible": BBC interview with Deborah Kerr
446 "less than candid": memo from David Selznick to JH, 3/19/57
448 "his massive frame": OB
449 "unable to establish": *John Wayne: My Life with the Duke*, Pilar Wayne with Alex Thorleifson (McGraw-Hill, 1987)
454 "a hard safari": CJH

Chapter 19: Shooting in Mexico

464 "nothing I can say about him": Burt Lancaster to LG, telephone, 1987
466 "secretary-mistress": *Parade*, 11/23/80 copyright Walter Scott
     "Olmec jaguar's mouth": letter from JH to Maka, 1977
471 "It was a triumph": OB
     "Even during tense moments . . .": "Trailing *The Unforgiven* below the Border," Paul P. Kennedy, *New York Times*, 2/1/59
474 "appearance this was a burial": "Pre-Columbian Works Could Be Fakes," Douglas McGill, *New York Times*, 5/20/87

Chapter 20: The Philosopher, the King, and the Goddess

476 "a great Romantic": *Lettres au Castor et à quelques autres*, vol. 2, Jean-Paul Sartre (Gallimard, 1983)
477 "One tooth more or less . . .": OB
     "concerns two cowboys": letter from Arthur Miller to JH, 7/14/58
     "Not since . . . *Salesman* . . .": letter from Arthur Miller to JH, 10/5/58
478 "an Eastern western": *Timebends*
483 Joyce Buck's first reaction: Joan Buck to LG
486 "Ireland is the reverse . . .": *Conversations with Marilyn*, W. J. Weatherby (Mason/Charter, 1976)
487 "like being at your own funeral": *Marilyn Monroe, An Appreciation*, Eve Arnold (Knopf, 1987)
488 "A hodgepodge": *A World on Film*, Stanley Kaufman (Harper, 1966)
     "profound phoniness": *Dwight Macdonald on Movies*, Dwight Macdonald (Prentice-Hall, 1969)
489 "By the start of *The Misfits*": *Timebends*
     "dunce cap of old": *Marilyn Monroe, An Appreciation*
490 "standing up all night": *Timebends*
     "Paula had finally won . . .": *Timebends*
491 "psychic twins": *Montgomery Clift*, Patricia Bosworth (Harcourt Brace Jovanovich, 1978)
492 "Everything continues swimmingly . . .": letter from JH to Marietta Tree, 8/22/60
     "scattering the crowd": OB
493 "Eli," John said: *The Story of The Misfits*, James Goode (Bobbs-Merrill, 1963)
     "a virility complex": *Long Live the King*, Lyn Tornabene (Putnam, 1976)
494 "dragged on a rope": *Gable's Women*, Jane Ellen Wayne (Prentice-Hall, 1987)
     "Monty did his own thing . . .": *Gable's Women*
495 "do it over and over": *Gable's Women*
     "away from the television": *The Story of The Misfits*
     "the aesthetic slant": *Marilyn—A Bio*, Norman Mailer (Grosset & Dunlap, 1973)
     "worse then useless": *Timebends*
     "John has meant . . .": *The Story of The Misfits*
496 "Don't think, honey": *The Story of The Misfits*
     "some wish-fulfillment": *Conversations with Marilyn*
498 "an idea of what Gable": *Marilyn—A Bio*
499 "wasn't the physical exertion": *Gable's Women*
     "guilty when he died": *Conversations with Marilyn*
     "Clark was one of the few . . .": *The Story of The Misfits*

Chapter 21: Civilization and Its Discontents

502 "The fault is partly mine": *Tynan Right & Left*, Kenneth Tynan (Atheneum, 1967)
506 "incident seemed trashy": *Montgomery Clift*
510 "You're paranoid, boy": *Montgomery Clift*
512 "laughing sadist": *Montgomery Clift*
     "Unthinkable nonsense": OB
514 "uninformed arrogance of youth": OB
516 "take the plunge! ": *Never Before Noon*, Afdera Fonda (Weidenfeld & Nicolson, 1987)
     "Have dreamt of you . . .": letter from Marietta Tree to JH, 12/29/61

Chapter 22: "I Have a New Brother"

521 "I know you are very busy": letter from Pablo Huston Albarran to JH, 5/2/62
522 "When I heard 'Tony Veiller' ": letter from Ricki Huston to JH, 7/29/62
523 "the usual overdose": letter from Angela Allen to JH, 8/20/62
525 "guts spread on my face": "Life With Father," Mark Morrison, *Los Angeles Times Magazine*, 6/2/87
526 "small joke of a film": "John Huston and the Figure in the Carpet," John Russell Taylor, *Sight and Sound*, Winter 68/69
529 "soft as pussywillows": letter from Dorothy Soma to JH (n.d.)
     "from bonhomie": OB
530 "full of despair": letter from JH to Ray Stark, 1/7/63
533 Lillian Ross: Lillian Ross, *The New Yorker*, 9/25/65
534 "only one who wasn't having an affair": Deborah Kerr, BBC-TV interview (n.d.)
540 letter from Ricki: 11/15/63

Chapter 23: "And the Children Struggled Together"

546 "This is my gift to you": letter from Dirk Bogarde to LG, 8/22/86
547 "unable to channel her energies": letter from Leslie Waddington to LG, 2/8/88
548 "ask him in advance": "The Bible in Dinocitta," Lillian Ross, *The New Yorker*, 9/25/65
     "I'm not an orthodoxly . . .": CJH
549 "what do angels look like": OB
551 "all their 'fads' ": letter from Dirk Bogarde to LG, 8/22/86
554 "She didn't have to do it to me!": Jules Buck to LG, telephone, 10/26/88
555 "Everything for a hundred yards . . .": CJH
     "I had bridles made . . .": CJH
     writer Scott Hammen: *John Huston*
556 "triumph of ingenuity": CJH
     "Stones were flying . . .": OB
559 "a fairy-tale love": letter from Valeria Alberti to LG, 7/4/87
560 "I think often of Daly . . .": *Steinbeck: A Life in Letters*, ed. Elaine Steinbeck and Robert Wallsten (Viking, 1975)
562 "007⅛": *Steinbeck: A Life in Letters*
563 "Huston has made my dream come true": Lillian Ross, *The New Yorker*, 9/25/65
     "Huston's triumph": *Kiss Kiss Bang Bang*, Pauline Kael (Little, Brown, 1968)
     "Christians, Jews . . .": *Big Screen Little Screen*, Rex Reed (Macmillan, 1971)
564 "write your own ticket": Eugene Frenke to JH, 8/65, Production Files, Special Collections, Academy of Motion Picture Arts and Sciences Library
566 "terrified of John": The Hemphills to Frank Martin, JH documentary, 1988

Chapter 24: Reflections

568 "My head is bloody . . .": cable from Joe Levine to JH, 9/16/65
569 "white-haired gentleman": SOYS
570 "save you the postage": Jules Buck to LG, telephone, 10/26/88
     "an unmitigated shit": Jules Buck to LG, telephone, 6/16/86
572 "Max Factor Pan Stick": "Life With Father," Mark Morrison, *Los Angeles Times Magazine*, 6/21/87
573 "from pasta to Chateaubriand": letter from Dirk Bogarde to LG, 8/22/86
575 "bastardized, episodic": *Hollywood Doesn't Live Here Anymore*, Robert Parrish (Little, Brown, 1988)
     "John *immediately* moved": *Orson Welles*, Barbara Leaming (Viking, 1985)
583 "abhorrent": *Movies into Film*, John Simon (Dial, 1971)

Chapter 25: No Love, and Death

588 Alexander Walker: *Double Takes*, Alexander Walker (Elm Tree Books, 1977)
591 "tax-free status": letter from J. P. Donleavy to LG, 5/16/86
592 "the artistic domination": CJH
599 "now, today, this moment": CJH
603 To a reporter John . . .: "*Love and Death* Film Debut for Miss Huston," Sally K. Brass, *Los Angeles Times Calendar*, 11/24/68
605 In an article he wrote . . .: "From Book to Film vis John Huston," Hans Koningsberger, *Film Quarterly*, Spring 1969
607 "exhausted gnu": *Movies into Film*
     "stiffness of high schoolers": Charles Champlin, *Los Angeles Times*, 4/24/70
     "most neglected movie": F. X. Feeney, *Z Channel Cable Guide*, July 1986

Chapter 26: Hard Times

617 "her beautiful Balenciagas": "Cool Angel," Marie Brenner, *Vanity Fair*, 9/85
622 "considerable rapport": Lillian Ross, *The New Yorker*, 6/14/69
     "If you don't go at all . . .": Pauline Kael, *The New Yorker*, 2/7/70
     "declines and declines": William S. Pechter, *Commentary*, 11/70
     "my wife was in charge": letter from Leslie Waddington to LG, 9/29/88
628 Scott's agent "had tears": letter from JH to Paul Kohner, 2/6/71
631 "I dumped John Huston": Gladys Hill diary entry, 1/28/71, Academy of Motion Picture Arts and Sciences Library
633 "the tarot cards": letter from Valeria Alberti to LG, 7/4/87

Chapter 27: Taking the Fifth

634   "people who are beaten": OB
644   "fragmented" technique: CJH
646   "the Tall Tale": OB
649   "crisp seersucker jackets": Lillian Ross, The New Yorker, 8/5/72
650   "received him with a hug": The New Yorker, 8/5/72

Chapter 28: Enjoining Hearts

664   "tub of strychnine": this and subsequent letters between JH and Cici were written between 11/72
         and 1/76
673   "cla-a-a-ss": "Jack Finds His Queen of Hearts," Brad Darrach, People, 7/8/85
674   "fag hag": Rosemary Kent, Interview, 4/74
675   "my father in Jack": "Anjelica," Joseph Gelmis, Newsday, 5/8/87
         "He's a Taurus": Los Angeles Herald-Examiner, 3/24/86
         "stand in the corner": "Nicholson," Leo Janus, Cosmopolitan, 12/76
         "When I met Jack . . .": "Cool Angel"
         "I'm quite lazy": "Anjelica," Joseph Gelmis, Newsday, 5/8/87
677   "the Heavenly Gates": Celebrity Circus, Charles Higham (Delacorte Press, 1979)
678   "secrets of Chinatown": "Acting," Ron Rosenbaum, New York Times Magazine, 7/13/86
         "drags his legend": Reeling, Pauline Kael (Warner Books, 1976)
679   "father-child roles": "Cool Angel"
681   "excitement, color, spectacle": CJH
683   "Physically," said Michael Caine: Michael Caine to Frank Martin, JH documentary, 1988
684   "polished vaudeville act": OB
685   "My wife was eating . . .": Take 22, Judith Crist (Viking, 1984)
688   "a classic of its kind": Michael Caine to Frank Martin
         "like a sniper": "Saints & Stinkers," Rolling Stone, 2/19/81
         "best film in 23 years": Reverse Angle, John Simon (Potter, 1981)

Chapter 29: Blood Ties

695   "progenitors of Uncle Sam": CJH
696   "Huston condescends . . .": John Huston
698   "a few brushfires": Leo Janos, Cosmopolitan, 12/76
         "Anjelica the Moan": "Cool Angel"
699   "I don't blame her": Rolling Stone interview, Nancy Collins, 3/29/84
         "emotions in neutral": David Lewin, US, 3/16/82
         "Anjelica had finished her phone call": Roman, Roman Polanski (William Morrow, 1984)
700   "granted immunity": Roman
701   "I was completely innocent": Roderick Mann, Los Angeles Times, 4/14/83
706   "iconoclastic about marriage": Rolling Stone interview, Nancy Collins, 3/29/84
707   "the gossip from Saturday": Andy Warhol, The Andy Warhol Diaries (Warner Books, 1989)
         "clarifications and adjustments": "Cool Angel"
708   "Maricela runs everything . . .": OB
710   "brief rebellion against Christ": OB
         "self-driven derelict": Gavin Miller, Sight and Sound, 1981
714   "the South of plucked strings": "Alex North: A Score for Reticence," Charles Champlin, Los Angeles
         Times, 8/23/84
         "horrible and funny": Reverse Angle
715   "the sporting instinct": "Stallone Abandons the Rocky Road," Bart Mills, Los Angeles Times, 7/4/80
717   "erstwhile nonadmirers": "Johnny, We Finally Knew Ye," Andrew Sarris, Village Voice, 5/19/80
718   "a good life with Jack": Anjelica to LG, to Aljean Harmetz (New York Times, 6/27/85), to Cynthia
         Gorney (Washington Post, 3/12/86)
719   "film within a film": letter from Marietta Tree to JH, 8/3/80
         "Action is not my strongest suit": "Stallone Abandons the Rocky Road"
720   "Sly's reputation": "Stallone Abandons the Rocky Road"
         "problems with Stallone": letter from Pélé to LG, 2/27/87
721   "material provision": letter from JH to John Julius, 8/21/80
         "dreadful": Jules Buck to LG, telephone, 1/5/89
722   "no signs of shock": letter from JH to John Julius, 2/5/81
723   "a certain cunning": "Saints & Stinkers"

Chapter 30: Mephistopheles to His Own Faust

728   "children or animals": "How Huston Beats the Hollywood Odds," Gregg Kilday, Saturday Review, 9/81
730   "Dire stuff": letter from JH to Angela Allen, 5/28/82
741   "four Ping-Pong": "Huston Filming Under the Volcano," Aljean Harmetz, New York Times, 8/23/83
742   "No decent lady . . .": "Huston Filming Under the Volcano"
744   "not to think so much": "The Volcanic Splendor of Jackie Bisset," Guy Flatley, Cosmopolitan, 7/84
         "taste of tequila": "Fun Under the Volcano," Marjorie Rosen, Sunday News Magazine, 6/17/84
         "coded communication": "A Portrayal of Alcoholism," E. J. Dionne, New York Times, 6/10/84
745   "Churchill gone bad": "Huston Filming Under the Volcano"
746   "last of the biggies": "Newsmakers," Eileen Keerdoja, Newsweek, 6/4/84
747   "best work Mr. Huston": "Huston's Volcano," Vincent Canby, New York Times, 6/24/84

747 "a serious work": Janet Maslin, *New York Times*, 6/13/84
     "tour de force": Guy Flatley, *Cosmopolitan*, 8/84
     "turgid, pretentious": Rex Reed, *New York Post*, 6/13/84
     "*Archie* comic": Jack Mathews, *USA Today*, 6/13/84
     "a model of literary": David Sterritt, *Christian Science Monitor*, 7/5/84
     "incredibly depressing": Ron Rosenbaum, *Mademoiselle*, 9/84
748 "recent ostracization": interview with Anjelica, Showtime/The Movie Channel, 12/10/85
750 "marvelous life": letter from Marietta Tree to JH, 3/1/84
     "two big holes": letter from JH to Marietta Tree, 4/3/84
752 "the house of Huston": letter from JH to Suzanne Flon, 7/23/85
     "the craziest reception": letter from JH to Janet Roach, 3/19/84
753 "It's got to be dumb": "Acting," *New York Times Magazine*, 7/13/86
     "a two-ton Tony Galento": "Jack Finds His Queen of Hearts"
755 "words of wisdom": "Love & Death," Brian Case, *Time Out* (London), 11/11/87
     "Schiaparelli pink": "Anjelica," Beverly Walker, *Film Comment*, 10/87
     "Jack wouldn't belittle me": "Anjelica of the Hustons," Aljean Harmetz, *New York Times*, 6/27/85

Chapter 31: The Collector of Souls

757 "elements of the hitman": "Jack Finds His Queen of Hearts"
     "Maerose through to dessert": "Do Angels Always Have Happy Holidays?" W. H. Bowart, *Palm Springs Life*, 12/85
758 "two perfect ovals": "Anjelica"
     "Walter's son": "Anjelica Rising," James Kaplan, *New York Times Magazine*, 2/12/89
760 "John Huston commanding": *Rolling Stone* interview, Fred Schruers, 8/14/86
     "through the wringer": *People*, 7/8/85
761 "performing dressage": *People*, 7/8/85
     "owns the category": *New York Times Magazine*, 2/12/89
762 "In opera, the orchestra": "Prizzi's Opera," Michael Walsh, *Film Comment*, 9–10/85
     "The movie is as contiguous . . .": letter from Richard Condon to JH, 6/2/85
763 "I was bowled over by it": letter from Frances FitzGerald to JH, 6/1/85
     "hottest new director": Pauline Kael, *The New Yorker*, 7/1/85
764 "residing in the Antarctic": letter from JH to John Julius, 3/21/85
     "I hope death approaches . . .": LG, *Playboy* interview, 9/85
765 "rather humiliating": letter from JH to Suzanne Flon, 7/23/85
766 "in walks Greta Garbo": Lizzie Spender, unpublished manuscript
767 "When he'd start to sing": Richard Natale, *Los Angeles Herald-Examiner*, 3/24/86
770 "one for Toots": "Wild in the Seats," Rick Reilly, *Sports Illustrated*, 11/3/86
     "dead weight off Anjelica's psyche": "Cool Angel"
771 "I never had a greater moment": *Rolling Stone* interview, 8/14/86
     "a bit pissed off": *Film Comment*, 10/87
     "on your own": "Living With Runaway Fame," Aljean Harmetz, *New York Times*, 5/18/86
     "delights of the flesh": letter from JH to "Laudy," 1/2/85
772 "to wash flesh tones": letter from JH to Gil Cates, 4/6/86
773 "beaten by brutes": Michael Jackson Talk Radio, KABC-LA, 11/14/86
776 "a world without Jack": *New York Times Magazine*, 2/12/89
     "Anjelica's working again": *Rolling Stone* interview, 8/14/86
     "somewhat glorified light": *Film Comment*, 10/87
     "The sinewy Anjelica Huston": David Denby, *New York*, 5/18/87
     "he couldn't see": "Love & Death"

Epilogue

781 "The story's majesty . . .": "Let There Be Light," F. X. Feeney, *L.A. Weekly*, 12/18–24/87
     "one-two punch": Vincent Canby, *New York Times*, 12/17/87
782 "when the world crumbles": "Anjelica Takes Center Stage," Roderick Mann, *Los Angeles Times*, 12/26/87
     "to report to him": "Meditations," Lynn Darling, *Newsday*, 12/23/87
783 "to play small roles": Roderick Mann, *Los Angeles Times*, 12/26/87
784 "dedicated to Literature": letter from Edna O'Brien to LG, 2/8/89
787 "stories are smoke dreams": Irene Heyman to LG, telephone, 12/21/88

FILMS AND PLAYS

Walter Huston (1884–1950)

Rain (United Artists, 1932)
Hell Below (MGM, 1933)
Gabriel Over the White House (Cosmopolitan-MGM, 1933)
Storm at Daybreak (MGM, 1933)
Ann Vickers (RKO, 1933)
The Prizefighter and the Lady (MGM, 1933)
Keep 'em Rolling (RKO, 1934)
Trans-Atlantic Tunnel (Gaumont-British, 1935)
Rhodes of Africa (Gaumont-British, 1936)
Dodsworth (Goldwyn-United Artists, 1936)
Of Human Hearts (MGM, 1938)
The Light That Failed (Paramount, 1940)
The Devil and Daniel Webster (RKO, 1941)
Swamp Water (20th Century-Fox, 1941)
The Maltese Falcon (Warner Bros., 1941)
The Shanghai Gesture (United Artists, 1941)
In This Our Life (Warner Bros., 1942)
Yankee Doodle Dandy (Warner Bros., 1942)
Always in My Heart (Warner Bros., 1942)
The Outlaw (RKO, 1943)
Edge of Darkness (Warner Bros., 1943)
The North Star (Goldwyn-RKO, 1943)
Mission to Moscow (Warner Bros., 1943)
Dragon Seed (MGM, 1944)
And Then There Were None (20th Century-Fox, 1945)
Dragonwyck (20th Century-Fox, 1946)
Duel in the Sun (SRO, 1946)
Summer Holiday (MGM, 1948)
The Treasure of the Sierra Madre (Warner Bros., 1948)
The Great Sinner (MGM, 1949)
The Furies (Paramount, 1950)

John Huston (1906–87)

A S   W R I T E R   O N L Y :

Frankie and Johnny (play, pub. Albert & Charles Boni, 1930)
A House Divided (Universal, 1932, with John Clymer, Dale Van Every)
Law and Order (Universal, 1932, with Tom Reed)
Murders in the Rue Morgue (Universal, 1932, with Tom Reed, Dale Van Every)
Death Drives Through (Gaumont-British, 1935)
Rhodes of Africa (Gaumont-British, 1936; polish)
Jezebel (Warner Bros., 1938, with Clements Ripley, Abem Finkel)
The Amazing Dr. Clitterhouse (Warner Bros, 1938, with John Wexley)
Juarez (Warner Bros., 1939, with Aeneas MacKenzie, Wolfgang Reinhardt)
Wuthering Heights (Goldwyn–United Artists, 1939, with Ben Hecht, Charles MacArthur)
Dr. Erhlich's Magic Bullet (Warner Bros., 1940, with Norman Burnside, Heinz Herald)
High Sierra (Warner Bros., 1941, with W. R. Burnett)
Sergeant York (Warner Bros., 1941, with Harry Chandler, Abem Finkel, Howard Koch)
In Time to Come (play, 1941–42, with Howard Koch)
The Killers (Universal, 1946, with Anthony Veiller)
The Stranger (RKO, 1946, with Anthony Veiller, Orson Welles)
Three Strangers (Warner Bros., 1946, with Howard Koch)
An Open Book (autobiography; Alfred Knopf, 1980)
Revenge (1989, with Tony Huston, uncredited)

A S   D I R E C T O R :

A Passenger to Bali (play, 1940)
The Maltese Falcon (Warner Bros., 1941, + screenplay)
In This Our Life (Warner Bros., 1942)
Across the Pacific (Warner Bros., 1942)
Report from the Aleutians (WWII documentary, 1943)
The Battle of San Pietro (WWII documentary, 1945)
Let There Be Light (WWII documentary, 1946)
No Exit (play, 1946)
The Treasure of the Sierra Madre (Warner Bros., 1948, + screenplay and acting)
Key Largo (Warner Bros., 1948, + screenplay with Richard Brooks)
We Were Strangers (Horizon, 1949, + screenplay with Peter Viertel, and acting)
The Asphalt Jungle (MGM, 1950, + screenplay with Ben Maddow)
The Red Badge of Courage (MGM, 1951, + screenplay)
The African Queen (Horizon-Romulus/United Artists, 1952, + screenplay with James Agee)
Moulin Rouge (Romulus/United Artists, 1953, + screenplay with Anthony Veiller)
Beat the Devil (Romulus–Santana/United Artists, 1954, + screenplay with Truman Capote)

Moby Dick (Moulin/Warner Bros., 1956, + screenplay with Ray Bradbury)
Heaven Knows, Mr. Allison (20th Century-Fox, 1957, + screenplay with John Lee Mahin)
The Barbarian and the Geisha (20th Century-Fox, 1958)
The Roots of Heaven (20th Century-Fox, 1958)
The Unforgiven (Hecht-Hill-Lancaster/United Artists, 1960)
The Misfits (Seven Arts/United Artists, 1961)
Freud (Universal, 1962)
The List of Adrian Messenger (Universal, 1963, + acting)
The Night of the Iguana (Seven Arts/MGM, 1964, + screenplay with Anthony Veiller)
The Bible (Dino De Laurentiis/20th Century-Fox, 1966, + acting)
The Mines of Sulfur (opera, La Scala, 1966)
Casino Royale (Columbia, 1967, with directors Ken Hughes, Val Guest, Robert Parrish, Joseph McGrath, +
    acting)
Reflections in a Golden Eye (Warner Bros./Seven Arts, 1967)
Sinful Davey (Mirisch/United Artists, 1969)
A Walk with Love and Death (20th Century-Fox, 1969, + acting)
The Kremlin Letter (20th Century-Fox, 1970, + screenplay with Gladys Hill, + acting)
Fat City (Columbia, 1972)
The Life and Times of Judge Roy Bean (National General, 1972, + acting)
The Mackintosh Man (Warner Bros., 1973)
The Man Who Would Be King (Allied Artists, 1975, + screenplay with Gladys Hill)
Independence (short, 1976)
Wise Blood (Ithaca–Anthea/New Line Cinema, 1980, + acting)
Phobia (Paramount, 1980)
Victory (Paramount, 1981)
Annie (Columbia, 1982)
Under the Volcano (Universal, 1984)
Prizzi's Honor (ABC/20th Century-Fox, 1985)
The Dead (Vestron, 1987)

AS ACTOR ONLY:

The Easy Mark (play, 1924)
The Triumph of the Egg (play, Sherwood Anderson, 1924)
Ruint (play, Hatcher Hughes, 1924)
Two Americans (Paramount, 1929)
The Lonely Man (play, Howard Koch, 1937)
The Cardinal (Columbia, 1963)
Candy (Cinerama, 1968)
De Sade (American-International, 1969)
Myra Breckinridge (20th Century-Fox, 1970)
The Bridge in the Jungle (Independent, 1971)
The Other Side of the Wind (Independent, 1971–75, unfinished)
The Deserter (Paramount, 1971)
Man in the Wilderness (Warner Bros., 1971)
Battle for the Planet of the Apes (20th Century-Fox, 1971)
Chinatown (Paramount, 1974)
Breakout (Columbia, 1975)
The Wind and the Lion (MGM/United Artists, 1975)
Sherlock Holmes in New York (TV, 1976)
Circasia (Independent, 1976)
Tentacles (American-International, 1977)
The Rhinemann Exchange (TV, 1977)
The Hobbit (TV, voice, 1977)
The Word (TV, 1978)
The Bermuda Triangle (Independent, 1978)
Angela (Independent, 1978)
Jaguar Lives! (American-International, 1979)
Winter Kills (Avco-Embassy, 1979)
The Greatest Battle (Independent, 1979)
Head On (Independent, 1979)
The Visitor (Independent, 1980)
The Return of the King (TV, 1980)
Cannery Row (narrator, MGM/UA, 1982)
Lovesick (Warner Bros., 1983)
A Minor Miracle (Independent, 1983)
"Alfred Hitchcock Presents": "Man from the South" (TV, 1985)
Momo (Independent, 1986)
Mr. Corbett's Ghost (Independent, 1986)

Tony Huston (1950–   )

A S   S C R E E N W R I T E R :

The Dead (Vestron, 1987)
Revenge (Columbia, 1989, with John Huston, uncredited)
Hamilton & Burr (HBO-TV, unproduced)

Anjelica Huston (1951–   )

P L A Y S

Hamlet (1969, William Shakespeare)
Tamara (1985, John Kriezank)

F I L M S

A Walk with Love and Death (20th Century-Fox, 1969)
The Last Tycoon (Paramount, 1976)
Swashbuckler (Universal, 1976)
The Postman Always Rings Twice (Paramount, 1981)
Frances (Universal/AFD, 1982)
A Rose for Emily (PBS-TV, 1983)
The Nightingale (Faerie Tale Theatre, TV, 1983)
This Is Spinal Tap (Embassy, 1984)
The Ice Pirates (MGM/United Artists, 1984)
Prizzi's Honor (ABC, 1985)
Captain EO (Disney short, 1986)
The Dead (Vestron, 1987)
Gardens of Stone (Tri-Star, 1987)
Mr. North (Heritage Entertainment, 1988)
A Handful of Dust (New Line Cinema, 1988)
Lonesome Dove (TV mini-series, 1989)
The Witches (Warner Bros., 1989)
Woody Allen's 1989 movie (Orion, 1989)
Enemies: A Love Story (20th Century-Fox, 1989–90)

Danny Huston (1962–   )

Alpaca: The Fiber of the Gods (documentary, cameraman, 1984)

A S   D I R E C T O R :

The Making of Santa Claus (documentary, 1984)
Mr. Corbett's Ghost (Independent, 1986)
Bigfoot (Disney-TV, 1987)
Mr. North (Heritage Entertainment, 1988)
The Magician's Wife (Sfensz Films, 1990)

INDEX